The Blackwell Companion to Consciousness

THE BLACKWELL COMPANION TO CONSCIOUSNESS

Max Velmans
Science Editor

Susan Schneider
Philosophy Editor

Advisory Editors

Science of Consciousness: Jeffrey Gray, John Kihlstrom, Phil Merikle, Stevan Harnad

Philosophy of Consciousness: Ned Block, David Chalmers, José Bermúdez, Brian McLaughlin, George Graham

Blackwell Publishing

BLACKWELL PUBLISHING
350 Main Street, Malden, MA 02148–5020, USA
9600 Garsington Road, Oxford OX4 2DQ, UK
550 Swanston Street, Carlton, Victoria 3053, Australia

First published 2007 by Blackwell Publishing Ltd

1   2007

Library of Congress Cataloging-in-Publication Data

The Blackwell companion to consciousness / edited by Max Velmans, science editor and
Susan Schneider, philosophy editor
p.   cm.
Includes bibliographical references and index
ISBN-13: 978–1–4051–2019–7 (hardback)
ISBN-13: 978–1–4051–6000–1 (pbk.)
1. Consciousness. I. Velmans, Max, 1942– II. Schneider, Susan, 1968– III.
Companion to consciousness.
BF311.B5348 2006
153—dc22   2006026291

A catalogue record for this title is available from the British Library.

Set in 10/12.5 pt Minion Pro
by The Running Head Limited, Cambridge, www.therunninghead.com
Printed and bound in Great Britain
by TJ International Ltd, Padstow, Cornwall

The publisher's policy is to use permanent paper from mills that operate a sustainable
forestry policy, and which has been manufactured from pulp processed using acid-free and
elementary chlorine-free practices. Furthermore, the publisher ensures that the text
paper and cover board used have met acceptable environmental accreditation standards.

For further information on
Blackwell Publishing, visit our website:
www.blackwellpublishing.com

Contents

List of Figures and Tables

Tables

Notes on Contributors

Igor Aleksander is Emeritus Professor of Neural Systems Engineering at Imperial College, London. Winner of the year 2000 Lifetime Achievement Medal for Informatics by the Institution of Electrical Engineers, his publications include *The World in My Mind, My Mind in the World* (2005) among 13 books and over 200 papers.

Colin Allen is Professor in the Department of History and Philosophy of Science and Professor of Cognitive Science at Indiana University, Bloomington, and he is also a core faculty member of IU's Center for the Integrative Study of Animal Behavior. He is Associate Editor of the *Stanford Encyclopedia of Philosophy*, and author of its entry on animal consciousness, on which the present chapter is based. As well as working to understand the scientific disputes about animal mind and cognition, he has published on other topics in the philosophy of mind, philosophy of biology, and artificial intelligence.

Torin Alter is Associate Professor of Philosophy at The University of Alabama. He specializes in philosophy of mind and language, with a special interest in consciousness, intentionality, and the mind–body problem. He has also written on free will and personal identity.

Bernard J. Baars PhD is an affiliate research Fellow of the Neurosciences Institute in San Diego, California (www.nsi.edu). He is the author of *A Cognitive Theory of Consciousness* (1988), *In the Theater of Consciousness: The Workspace of the Mind* (1997), and editor of *Essential Sources in the Scientific Study of Consciousness* (2003, with William P. Banks and James R. Newman). Baars was founding co-editor of the Elsevier/Academic Press journal *Consciousness and Cognition* with William P. Banks. Recent journal articles have appeared in *Trends in Cognitive Sciences* and *Trends in Neurosciences*.

William P. Banks is Professor of Psychology at Pomona College, Claremont, California. He is editor-in-chief of the Elsevier journal *Consciousness and Cognition*. His most recent publication is "Does consciousness cause misbehavior?" in *Does Consciousness Cause Behavior?* edited by Sue Pockett, William Banks, and Shaun Gallagher (2006). Professional publications have appeared in *Psychological Science*, *The Journal of Experimental Psychology*, *Perception and Psychophysics*, and *Psychological Review*.

Marc Bekoff is Professor of Biology at the University of Colorado, Boulder, and co-founder with Jane Goodall of Ethologists for the Ethical Treatment of Animals: Citizens for Responsible Animal Behavior Studies. He is a prolific writer with more than 200 articles as well as two encyclopedias to his credit. The author or editor of numerous books, including the *Encyclopedia of Animal Rights and Animal Welfare*, *The Cognitive Animal* (co-edited with C. Allen and G. M. Burghardt), *The Ten Trusts: What We Must Do to Care for the Animals We Love* (with Jane Goodall), and *The Encyclopedia of Animal Behavior*. His most recent books include *The Smile of a Dolphin*, *Minding Animals*, and *Animal Passions and Beastly Virtues: Reflections on Redecorating Nature*. In 2005, Bekoff was presented with The Bank One Faculty Community Service Award for the work he has done with children, senior citizens, and prisoners. His homepage is http://literati.net/Bekoff.

Richard P. Bentall is Professor of Experimental Clinical Psychology in the School of Psychological Sciences at the University of Manchester. He has published *Sensory Deceptions* (with Peter Slade, 1988); *Reconstructing Schizophrenia* (edited, 1990), *Madness Explained: Psychosis and Human Nature* (2003), *Models of Madness* (edited with John Read and Loren Mosher, 2004), and *The Psychology of Bipolar Disorder* (edited with Steven Jones, 2006).

José Luis Bermúdez is a professor of philosophy and the director of the Philosophy-Neuroscience-Psychology program at Washington University in St Louis. He is the author of *The Paradox of Self-Consciousness* (1998), *Thinking without Words* (2003), and *Philosophy of Psychology: A Contemporary Introduction* (2005).

David Bourget is completing his PhD at the University of Toronto and is currently on exchange to the Australian National University. His work centers around the topics of consciousness and representation, although he has recently published an article on quantum mechanics and consciousness in the *Journal of Consciousness Studies*.

Peter Carruthers is Professor and Chair of the Philosophy Department at the University of Maryland (College Park). He works primarily on issues in the philosophy of psychology: on consciousness, on modularity, on innateness, on the nature of intentional content, and on the place of natural language in human cognition.

David Chalmers is a Professor of Philosophy and Director of the Centre for Consciousness at the Australian National University, and an ARC Federation Fellow. He works especially in the philosophy of mind, and in related areas of philosophy and cognitive science. He is especially interested in consciousness, but also in philosophical issues about meaning and possibility, and in the foundations of cognitive science.

Austen Clark studied philosophy at Wesleyan University, Middletown, Connecticut. He received a DPhil from Oxford, supervised by Brian Farrell of Corpus Christi College. He teaches at the University of Connecticut in Storrs.

Mary K. "Molly" Colvin is a post-doctoral research fellow in the Department of Psychological and Brain Sciences at Dartmouth College. In July 2006, she will become a Clinical Fellow in Psychology at Harvard Medical School.

Randall Cork is Professor and Chair of Anesthesiology at Louisiana State University. His publications include chapters in *Medical Devices and Instrumentation* (2006), *Advances in Clinical Neurosciences* (2003), and *Essence of Anesthesia Practice* (2002), as well as publications in the *Journal of Education in Perioperative Medicine* (2006) and the *Journal of Clinical Anesthesia* (2004).

Francis Harris Compton Crick was instrumental in the discovery of the structure of the DNA molecule, for which he was awarded the 1962 Nobel Prize for Physiology (with James D. Watson and Maurice Wilkins) and in the deciphering of the genetic code. His interest later in life turned to theoretical neuroscience, and he promoted dialogs across disciplines to increase our understanding of consciousness. His books include *Of Molecules and Men* (1967), *Life Itself* (1981), *What Mad Pursuit: A Personal View of Scientific Discovery* (1988), and *The Astonishing Hypothesis: The Scientific Search for the Soul* (1994).

Barry Dainton is Professor of Philosophy at the University of Liverpool, and author of *Stream of Consciousness* (2000) and *Time and Space* (2001).

Jennifer Dorfman has held postdoctoral fellowships at University of Arizona, University of Memphis, and Northwestern University. She has contributed chapters on implicit and explicit cognition to *The Other Side of the Error Term: Aging and Development as Model Systems in Cognitive Neuroscience* (ed. N. Raz, 1998), and *Implicit Cognition* (ed. G. Underwood, 1996).

David Fontana, a Fellow of the British Psychological Society, is currently Visiting Professor in the Applied Psychology Department at Liverpool John Moores University. He is the author of over 150 published papers and articles on psychology, and of 28 books that have been translated into 26 languages. Among his most recent books are *Psychology, Religion and Spirituality*, published by Blackwell, and *Is There an Afterlife?* published by John Hunt. Meditation and Eastern psychospiritual traditions are among his research interests; he has written a number of books on the subject, including *The Meditator's Handbook*, published by HarperCollins/Thorsons and *Learn to Meditate*, published by Duncan Baird.

Chris D. Frith is Professor in Neuropsychology at University College London. His publications include *The Cognitive Neuropsychology of Schizophrenia* (1992), *The Neuroscience of Social Interaction* (with Daniel Wolpert, 2004), and *Making up the Mind: How the Brain Creates Our Mental World* (2006).

Shaun Gallagher is Professor and Chair of the Philosophy Department and Director of the Cognitive Sciences Program at the University of Central Florida. His most recent books are *How the Body Shapes the Mind* (2005) and *The Inordinance of Time* (1998). He edits the interdisciplinary journal *Phenomenology and the Cognitive Sciences*.

Michael S. Gazzaniga is a Professor of Psychology and the Director of the Sage Center for the Study of the Mind at the University of California, Santa Barbara.

Melvyn A. Goodale holds the Canada Research Chair in Visual Neuroscience at the University of Western Ontario. He is best known for his work on the functional organization of the visual pathways in the cerebral cortex, and was a pioneer in the study of visuomotor control in neurological patients. His recent book with David Milner, *Sight Unseen: An Exploration of Conscious and Unconscious Vision*, provides compelling arguments that the brain mechanisms underlying our conscious visual experience of the world are quite separate from those involved in the visual control of skilled actions.

George Graham is A. C. Reid Professor of Philosophy at Wake Forest University. He writes on topics in the philosophy of mind, metaphysics of consciousness, and philosophical psychopathology. His most recent book is *Oxford Textbook in Philosophy and Psychiatry* (with K. W. M. Fulford and T. Thornton, 2006).

Dr J. Allan Hobson is Professor of Psychiatry at Harvard Medical School. His publications include *Thirteen Dreams Freud Never Had* (2004), *Consciousness* (1994), and *Dreaming as Delirium* (1999).

Terence Horgan is Professor of Philosophy at the University of Arizona. He is author of *Connectionism and the Philosophy of Psychology* (with J. Tienson, 1996), and is a contributor to the following collections: *Philosophy of Mind: Classical and Contemporary Readings* (2002), *Physicalism and Mental Causation: The Metaphysics of Mind* (2003), and *The Externalist Challenge* (2004).

Susan Hurley hails from Santa Barbara, California, and was educated at Princeton, Harvard, and Oxford. Prior to taking up a chair in Philosophy at the University of Bristol, she held teaching positions at Oxford and Warwick, and visiting appointments at Berkeley, Princeton, Harvard, and RSSS, Australian National University. She is a Fellow of All Souls College, Oxford. She is the author of *Natural Reasons* (1989), *Consciousness in Action* (1998), *Justice, Luck and Knowledge* (2003), and numerous articles, and editor of *Foundations of Decision Theory* (1991), *Perspectives on Imitation* (2005), and *Rational Animals?* (2006).

Marc Jeannerod is Emeritus Professor at the Claude Bernard University, Lyon, France. He is the author of *The Brain Machine* (1985), *The Neural and Behavioral Organization of Goal-Directed Movements* (1988), *The Neuroscience of Action* (1997), *Ways of Seeing: The Scope and Limits of Visual Cognition* (with P. Jacob, 2003), and *Motor Cognition: What Actions Tell the Self* (2006).

John Kihlstrom is Professor in the Department of Psychology, University of California, Berkeley. His 1987 *Science* article on "The cognitive unconscious" is widely recognized as stimulating interest in non-Freudian approaches to unconscious mental life.

Jaegwon Kim is William Perry Faunce Professor of Philosophy at Brown University. His books include *Mind in a Physical World* (1998), *Supervenience and Mind* (1993), *Physicalism, or Something Near Enough* (2005), and *Philosophy of Mind* (second edition, 2006).

Christof Koch is Professor of Biology and Engineering and Applied Science at the California Institute of Technology. His publications include *The Quest for Consciousness: A Neurobiological Approach* (2004). His research and more than 200 publications can be found at www.klab.caltech.edu.

Nilli Lavie is a Professor of Psychology and Brain Sciences at University College London. She has been published in, among others, *Trends in Cognitive Sciences*, the *Journal of Experimental Psychology: General*, *Science*, *Nature Neuroscience*, and *Science*.

Joe Levine is a professor of philosophy at Ohio State University. He is the author of numerous articles as well as the book, *Purple Haze: The Puzzle of Consciousness* (2001).

Brian P. McLaughlin is Professor of Philosophy at Rutgers University. He is the author of numerous articles on the philosophy of mind.

Pete Mandik is Cognitive Science Laboratory Coordinator, Associate Professor, and Chairman of the Philosophy Department of William Paterson University, New Jersey, USA. He is a junior member and co-director of the McDonnell Project in Philosophy and the Neurosciences, Simon Fraser University, Canada. He is co-editor of *Philosophy and the Neurosciences: A Reader* (2001).

Bruce Mangan teaches psychology at the University of California, Berkeley. His work has appeared in *Consciousness and Cognition*, *Behavioral and Brain Sciences*, *Journal of Consciousness Studies*, and *Psyche*.

Phil Merikle is Professor of Psychology at the University of Waterloo. Recent publications have appeared in *Cognition, Perception and Psychophysics, Visual Cognition, Nature*, and *Psychological Science*.

Alva Noë is a Professor of Philosophy at the University of California, Berkeley. He works primarily in philosophy of mind and cognitive science, with special interest in the theory of perception. He is the author of *Action in Perception* (2004).

Edward F. Pace-Schott MS MA LMHC PhD is Instructor in Psychiatry at Harvard Medical School in the Center for Sleep and Cognition, Department of Psychiatry, Beth Israel Deaconess Medical Center. He is also a psychotherapist. He has contributed to *Principles and Practise of Sleep Medicine* (fourth edition, 2005), *Sleep and Dreaming* (ed., with M. Solms, M. Blagrove, and S. Harnad, 2005), *Nature Reviews: Neuroscience* (with J. A. Hobson, 2002), and *Behavioral and Brain Sciences* (with R. Stickgold, 2000).

Jaak Panksepp is Professor and Endowed Chair of Animal Well-Being Science at the College of Veterinary Medicine at Washington State University. His publications can be found at http://www.vetmed.wsu.edu/depts-vcapp/Panksepp-endowed.asp. He wrote *Affective Neuroscience: The Foundation of Human and Animal Emotions* (1998), contributed to *Physiology and Behavior* (2003), *Consciousness and Cognition* (2005), and the *Journal of Consciousness Studies* (2005), and edited the *Textbook of Biological Psychiatry* (2004).

Lillian Park is a postdoctoral fellow at the Rotman Research Institute at Baycrest in Toronto, Ontario. She has published in *Psychological Science* and co-authored an overview of cognitive psychology for *Encyclopedia of the Human Brain* (ed. V. S. Ramachandran, 2002).

Susan Pockett is a neuroscientist working in the Department of Physics at the University of Auckland, New Zealand, and the Department of Vision Science at the University of California Berkeley. Her publications include *The Nature of Consciousness: A Hypothesis* (2000) and *Does Consciousness Cause Behavior? An Investigation of the Nature of Volition* (2006).

Thomas Polger is Assistant Professor of Philosophy at the University of Cincinnati. His work is organized around the project of exploring how to understand conscious experience as a natural feature of biological organisms, working from the perspectives of philosophy of mind, philosophy of science, and metaphysics. He is the author of numerous articles and the book, *Natural Minds* (2003).

Jesse Prinz is Associate Professor of Philosophy at the University of North Carolina, Chapel Hill. His books include *Furnishing the Mind: Concepts and Their Perceptual Basis*, *Gut Reactions: A Perceptual Theory of Emotion*, *The Emotional Construction of Morals*, and *The Conscious Brain* (forthcoming).

Vasudevi Reddy is Reader in Developmental and Cultural Psychology at the University of Portsmouth, UK. She has appeared in publication in *Theory and Psychology* (2004), *Trends in Cognitive Science* (2003), *Developmental Science* (2000), and *First Language* (1995).

Geraint Rees is a cognitive neurologist and Wellcome Senior Clinical Fellow at University College London. His publications include *Neurobiology of Attention* (with Laurent Itti and John Tsotsos, 2005) and numerous journal articles and book chapters on the neural basis of human consciousness.

Mark Rowlands is Professor of Mental and Moral Philosophy at the University of Hertfordshire. His publications include *The Body in Mind: Understanding Cognitive Processes* (1999), *The Nature of Consciousness* (2001), and *Body Language: Representation in Action* (2006).

Nicholas D. Schiff is Associate Professor of Neurology and Neuroscience at the Weill Medical College of Cornell University and Associate Attending Neurologist at the New York Presbyterian Hospital. His publications include original articles in the journals *Brain*, *Journal of Clinical Investigation*, *Journal of Cognitive Neuroscience*, *Journal of Neurophysiology*, and *Neurology*.

Susan Schneider is an Assistant Professor of Philosophy at the University of Pennsylvania. She works in philosophy of cognitive science (including philosophy of mind), metaphysics, and philosophy of science. Her current work centers on computational theories of mind, domain general reasoning, and the format of thought. Her pieces have appeared in journals such as *Psyche*, *Australasian Journal of Philosophy*, and *Mind and Language*. Her books include the present volume and *Science Fiction and Philosophy* (forthcoming, Blackwell).

William Seager is Professor of Philosophy at the University of Toronto at Scarborough. He has published many articles on the philosophy of mind and two books on consciousness, *The Metaphysics of Consciousness* (1991) and *Theories of Consciousness* (1999).

John Searle is Mills Professor of the Philosophy of Mind and Language at the University of California, Berkeley. He is the author of numerous articles and over a dozen books on the philosophy of mind, including *Speech Acts: An Essay in the Philosophy of Language* (1969), *Intentionality: An Essay in the Philosophy of Mind* (1983), *The Rediscovery of the Mind* (1992), *The Construction of Social Reality* (1995) and *Mind: A Brief Introduction* (2004).

Jonathan Shear is Affiliated Associate Professor of Philosophy at Virginia Commonwealth University in Richmond, Virginia. His publications include *The View from Within: First-Person Approaches to the Study of Consciousness* (co-editor, 1999), *Models of the Self* (co-editor, 1999), and *The Experience of Meditation: Experts Introduce the Major Systems* (ed., 2006).

Wolf Singer is Director at the Max Planck Institute for Brain Research and Founding Director at the Frankfurt Institute for Advanced Studies (FIAS). His publications include "Control of thalamic transmission by cortico-fugal and ascending reticular pathways in the visual system" in the *Physiological Reviews* (1977), "Oscillatory responses in cat visual cortex exhibit inter-columnar synchronization which reflects global stimulus properties" in *Nature* (with C. M. Gray, P. König, and A. K. Engel, 1989), "Development and plasticity of cortical processing architectures" in *Science* (1995), "Dynamic predictions: oscillations and synchrony in top-down processing" in *Nature Reviews: Neuroscience* (with A. K. Engel and P. Fries, 2001), and *Der Beobachter im Gehirn: Essays zur Hirnforschung* (2002).

Henry Stapp is a theoretical physicist with a long-term special interest in mathematical and conceptual problems in the foundations of quantum theory. He worked with Wolfgang Pauli and with Werner Heisenberg and has published extensively on the subjects of axiomatic S-matrix theory, quantum non-locality, philosophy of quantum theory, and the mind–brain interaction.

G. Lynn Stephens is Professor of Philosophy at the University of Alabama at Birmingham. He has published in philosophy of mind and philosophical psychopathology. He is the co-author of *When Self-Consciousness Breaks* (with George Graham, 2000).

John Tienson is Professor of Philosophy at The University of Memphis. He publishes on metaphysics, the philosophy of mind, and the foundations of cognitive science. He is author of *Connectionism and the Philosophy of Psychology* (with Terence Horgan, 1996).

Giulio Tononi is Professor of Psychiatry at the University of Wisconsin-Madison, where he is studying consciousness and its disorders as well as the mechanisms and functions of sleep. He is the author of over 100 scientific publications, co-editor of the volume *Selectionism and the Brain* (with Olaf Sporns, 1994), and author of two recent books on the neural basis of consciousness: *A Universe of Consciousness* (with Gerald M. Edelman, 2000) and *Galileo and the Photodiode* (2003).

Colwyn Trevarthen is Professor (Emeritus) of Child Psychology and Psychobiology at the University of Edinburgh. He has published widely on the neuropsychology of consciousness, infant intersubjectivity, and companionship in learning, including *Children with Autism: Diagnosis and Interventions to Meet Their Needs* (with J. K. Aitken, D. Papoudi, and

J. Z. Roberts, second edition, 1998). He has also contributed to *Intersubjective Communication and Emotion in Early Ontogeny* (1998), *Annual Research Review: The Journal of Child Psychology and Psychiatry and Allied Disciplines* (2001), *Handbook on Brain and Behavior in Human Development* (2001), the *Oxford Companion to the Mind* (second edition, 2001), and *Emotional Development* (2005).

Michael Tye is Professor of Philosophy at the University of Texas at Austin. He has published extensively on phenomenal consciousness and is a leading advocate of the representationalist approach.

Robert Van Gulick is Professor of Philosophy and Director of the Cognitive Science Program at Syracuse University. He is the co-author of *John Searle and His Critics*, and has published on mind and consciousness in a variety of journals and volumes including the *Philosophical Review*, *Philosophical Studies*, *Philosophical Topics*, and the *Journal of Consciousness Studies*.

Max Velmans has a Personal Chair in Psychology at the University of London and is Emeritus Professor of Psychology at Goldsmiths College. He has around 80 publications on consciousness including *Understanding Consciousness* (2000), which was shortlisted for the British Psychological Society book of the year award in 2001 and 2002. Other publications include *The Science of Consciousness: Psychological, Neuropsychological and Clinical Reviews* (1996), *Investigating Phenomenal Consciousness: New Methodologies and Maps* (2000), and *How Could Conscious Experiences Affect Brains?* (2003). He was a co-founder and, from 2004 to 2006, Chair of the Consciousness and Experiential Psychology Section of the British Psychological Society.

Lawrence Weiskrantz was Professor of Psychology at the University of Oxford from 1967 to 1993. He is the author of *Blindsight* (1986), and *Consciousness Lost and Found* (1997).

Semir Zeki is Professor of Neurobiology at University College London. His publications include three books: *A Vision of the Brain* (1993), *Inner Vision: An Exploration of Art and the Brain* (1999), and *La Quête de l'Essentiel* (with Balthus, 1995).

Introduction

SUSAN SCHNEIDER AND MAX VELMANS

Listen to the sound of Beethoven's Ninth Symphony, taste the flavor of a strong espresso, or feel the heat of a summer day. There is something that it's like to have these experiences; something that it's like to be conscious. Indeed, anything that we are aware of at a given moment forms part of our consciousness, making conscious experience at once the most familiar and most mysterious aspect of our lives.

One distinctive thing about consciousness is that it can be studied both from "the inside," that is, from the perspective of the conscious subject, and from the "outside," that is, by any of the academic fields that study the mind. Indeed, over the last 15 years or so, many scholars have developed an intense interest in consciousness. Some of its features are beginning to be understood in detail, and some amazing and surprising discoveries have been made. This interest has given rise to a new discipline which has consciousness as its primary focus – "consciousness studies." "Consciousness studies" is an umbrella term for the multidisciplinary study of consciousness in fields such as neuroscience, psychology, philosophy, artificial intelligence, and linguistics. Over the brief period of its existence, this field has become extensive. For example, as we write this introduction, a Google Scholar search yields over 600,000 books and articles with "consciousness" in the title!

This *Companion* contains chapters that both introduce and refine ideas that are at the heart of the new discipline. We hope that those new to consciousness studies will use this book to learn the main trends and issues in the field, and thereby be better able to navigate through its extensive publications. Over and above this function, we hope that this book makes it possible for academics in one subdiscipline to have better access to what might be highly relevant work in other disciplines. In addition, the book is designed to serve students by both introducing issues key to their own primary areas of study, and forging connections to work in other areas of consciousness studies. It is our view that if students fail to take an interdisciplinary approach to consciousness, they risk being unaware of work outside of their own discipline that has a direct bearing on the questions they wish to address.

Given that our readers will include both students and seasoned members of the consciousness studies community, we have encouraged our authors to offer new information or a fresh perspective, while at the same time providing comprehensive, accessible surveys of the terrain. For example, where authors were invited to present their own, well-known views, they were also encouraged to deal with any major objections to those views, especially new ones. Many of the chapters also detail new areas of work.

Unusually, for a book of this kind, a wide range of contemporary experts, including an extensive editorial advisory board, have been involved in the selection of chapter topics and authors. In addition, nearly all chapters, including those of the editors and advisory editors, have been anonymously refereed, following procedures more common to academic journals than to edited books. We have been fortunate in that many of the 55 chapters in this volume have been written by some of the best writers, researchers, and thinkers in the field. Inevitably, even with 55 chapters, there were many fine authors who we could not include. In some cases, these authors were kind enough to act as advisors or referees. In other cases, competing commitments, illness, or even death, sadly intervened. Given the wide range of the chapters and the extensive bibliography, we nevertheless hope that most authors who have made a major empirical or theoretical contribution to contemporary consciousness studies will find some reference in the *Companion* to sources of their work, and we offer our sincere apologies to those that we have missed.

The Scope of the Volume

As will be clear from the Table of Contents, the book largely focuses on consciousness studies as it has developed in the West over the last 100 or so years, particularly in psychology, philosophy, neuroscience, and related disciplines. While this has mainly been a development within conventional third-person science, it has also tacitly and, at times explicitly, drawn on and developed a form of first-person science, and in this regard, along with recent work, we are pleased to be able to include some overviews of more ancient traditions of consciousness studies that have developed in the East.

As will be apparent from the Table of Contents, Part I aims to provide some background to current research and controversies in the field – how empirical studies of consciousness originally developed in psychology and related sciences, and what the unique, enduring philosophical problems surrounding consciousness seem to be.

Part II charts many of the forms of consciousness that have been the subject of investigation and speculation, ranging from consciousness in young infants and nonhuman animals to machine consciousness. The varieties of conscious experience that are most easily studied are those in human adults, and here we deal both with the states of the brain that condition its *presence* or *absence* in waking, sleeping, dreaming, and coma, and with some of the *forms* (both normal and abnormal) that consciousness takes within those states. For example, in this section, we focus on some aspects of cognition and emotion that might have a particular bearing on an understanding of consciousness, and then deal with a wide range of altered states of consciousness, such as drug-induced altered states of consciousness, clinical pathologies of consciousness, meditation, and mystical states. We then introduce some of the major dissociations of consciousness that have emerged from neurological syndromes, as well as an initial discussion of their philosophical implications. Given the major neuroscientific contributions to recent studies of visual perception and the startling dissociations of consciousness that result from brain damage or neurosurgery, we return to a more detailed treatment of these topics in the section of the book that focuses specifically on neuroscience (Part V).

In Part III, we turn to contemporary philosophical and scientific theories about the nature of consciousness that address the following fundamental questions: What is consciousness? Where is it? What does consciousness do? How does the phenomenology of consciousness relate to the workings of the brain? Are the problems of consciousness ones that can be resolved by empirical research, or are there aspects of consciousness that cannot be understood without major changes in the way that we conceptualize those problems? And what are the implications of the major positions on the nature of consciousness for our understanding of mind, human nature, and the physical world? Finding answers to such questions is widely thought to present a major challenge to contemporary science, and in this section we deliberately sample from a wide range of approaches and theories that reflect the controversy and ferment in this field. To some extent, these wide differences in theory reflect fundamental philosophical differences, for example, between those who believe that everything of interest about consciousness can be explained in physical terms or the functionalist terms used by cognitive science, and those who believe that what it's like to be conscious (from a first-person perspective) requires something more. While some readers may initially find such controversies confusing, their resolution is likely to have far-reaching implications for the ways that we think about ourselves and the world in which we live.

Part IV deals with some of the topics that currently attract special interest among professional philosophers. In many cases, work has been included because it is extremely interdisciplinary, bringing together key issues in both the philosophy and science of consciousness, and having an important bearing on both. Indeed, philosophers have increasingly become engaged with scientific research. The chapters on sensory and perceptual consciousness, the neurophilosophy of consciousness, and self-consciousness are excellent examples of this tendency. In addition to including philosophical work that draws from science, the remainder of the section concerns topics which are largely philosophical in nature, being state-of-the-art reviews or opinion pieces on topics of central import to philosophical thinking on the nature of consciousness. Many of these chapters take as their point of departure the simple observation that there is something that it's like to be conscious; that is, there is a felt quality to our experience. At least prima facie, it is difficult to grasp how an underlying scientific account of neural processes captures the essence of such experience. Philosophers are very concerned with the relationship that our first-person conscious experience has to the world that science investigates. Questions addressed include: Is conscious experience entirely determined by the underlying states of the brain? Is conscious experience capable of causing events in our brains and the larger world? What is the relationship between the felt quality of experience, on the one hand, and the representational aspect of certain conscious states, on the other? Philosophical work on such questions is key to understanding foundational problems concerning the nature of consciousness; an issue which, as Part III emphasizes, also concerns many scientists.

Part V focuses on further, leading edge, empirical studies of consciousness. The bulk of contemporary consciousness studies is empirical, so this section is the largest in the book. For convenience, the chapters are roughly grouped according to investigative approach, that is, according to whether they adopt cognitive psychological, neuroscientific, or first-person investigative methods. It will become apparent, however, that no clear separation can be made between these. Depending on the problem, one might use one or two of these investigative approaches simultaneously, or all three.

Cognitive studies of consciousness try to locate conscious experience within the human information processing system, for example by specifying what kind of processing takes place before consciousness arises, the conditions that determine whether and when consciousness arises, and the function of consciousness (if any) once it does arise. Following classical traditions in this area, the cognitive chapters begin with studies of attention, long thought to be one of the gateways to consciousness in human beings. The chapters then turn to contrasts between mental processing that is unconscious, preconscious, or conscious in perception, learning, and memory, as well as preconscious vs. conscious processing in motor control. Such studies follow the traditional "method of contrasts" (see also Baars, chapter 18). In contrasting conscious with nonconscious processing, researchers hope to discover what might be special about conscious processing – although there are various ways of interpreting such contrasts (for example, there is an enduring debate, dating back to the time of Descartes, about what role consciousness experience might play in the mental processing that it accompanies – see Velmans 1991, 2000, chs. 2 to 5).

Neuroscientific studies of the mind focus on the brain hardware (sometimes described as "wetware") that embodies mental processes of the kind studied by cognitive psychologists, and neuroscientific studies of consciousness traditionally focus on finding its neural causal antecedents and correlates. Consequently this section begins with a broad review of the neuroscientific methods used to study the neural causes and correlates of consciousness along with some overall conclusions that one might draw from them. In recent years, studies of the visual system have been particularly productive, so this is followed by two alternative analyses of the neural underpinnings of consciousness based on investigations of normal and disordered functioning in the visual system, and (later in the section) by a review of surprising evidence that conscious visual experience may be at least partly dissociated from the visual feedback required for motor control. The section goes on to review broad insights that have been gained into conditions required for human consciousness arising from studies of its global disorders, a review of evidence for what is currently one of the most popular theories about what makes an integrated experience possible – the large-scale temporal coordination of activity in the brain – and a review of the conditions that determine presence or absence of consciousness in anesthesia. The section then concludes with reviews of two areas of neuroscientific research that have some particularly interesting philosophical, as well as scientific implications: the extent to which the qualia of consciousness are determined by the functional relations of particular brain areas to activities in the external world, and the neuroscience of free will (are voluntary actions determined by conscious choices, by preconscious processes in the brain, or by both – and what are the implications for ethics and legal responsibility?). Readers will note that scientific controversies about the neural causes and correlates of consciousness and about the implications of such empirical findings are as common as they are about some of the global philosophical issues discussed in Part III. While all these chapters review extensive evidence in support of their theoretical positions, and while their conclusions are convergent in some respects, they also have some major differences. As elsewhere in the book, our aim in the *Companion* is simply to present a representative sample of current research and opinion in this field.

In the final section of Part V, "First-Person Contributions to the Science of Consciousness," we return to the question of how one can investigate conscious experience as such (as opposed to its functionally or physically specified causes and correlates). This raises issues that have concerned researchers from the dawn of psychological science, which, at its inception, was thought of as the study of conscious experience. Although for much of the twentieth century, psychology ostensibly tried to rid itself of the problems associated with such a first-person science, it never did so consistently. For example, in studies of perception, cognition, emotion, etc., researchers commonly relied to some extent on subjective reports of experience, whether in the form of verbal reports, or some other overt response, for example, pressing one button if subjects could see a difference between two stimuli and another button if not, placing a mark on a rating scale, filling out a questionnaire (about their feelings, thoughts, and behavior), and so on. Once consciousness itself becomes the topic of study, such methods become particularly important. For example, although the neuroscientific investigations introduced in the previous section are a very clear example of how consciousness studies has become part of normal third-person science, nearly all these investigations rely to some extent on subjects being able to report (at least in a minimal way) on what they currently experience – for the reason that without such reports it is impossible to know how observed activity in the brain *relates* to what subjects experience. In other areas of psychological and social research there has been a renewed interest in investigating how subjects experience what it's like to be in different social situations with the use of "qualitative methods" as well as "quantitative methods" and there has also been a revisiting of European and Eastern phenomenological traditions, which suggest that by refocusing and training attention it is possible to investigate the finer detail of one's own conscious experience. Given his major contributions to the early study of consciousness and to the development of psychological science, it is appropriate that this section begins with a review of the contemporary relevance of the work of William James. We then introduce some of the contributions of European and Eastern traditions (see also Fontana, chapters 11 and 12). The section, and the book, then closes with a re-examination of the status of the different first- and third-person ways in which one can examine consciousness and suggests how this might produce some subtle changes in the ways that we normally think about the nature of science.

Acknowledgements and Caveats

We would like to thank our many authors for their inspiring contributions and also give special thanks to our advisory editors for their guidance at many points in the planning of this book. All of these editors have been enormously helpful in advising us about which pieces to include, and many have anonymously reviewed one or more chapters, as have many of our authors. In particular, Ned Block, David Chalmers, George Graham, John Kihlstrom, Brian McLaughlin, and Phil Merikle have been involved with this project from the beginning, and have been key advisors. We would also like to thank our editor, Jeff Dean, and our assistant editor, Danielle Descoteaux, for their very thoughtful editing. Susan Schneider would like to thank her research assistant, Johanna Robinson, and Moravian College for a grant to support work on this volume. We also want to thank the following external referees for their valuable comments including (in alphabetical order) Michael Arbib, Mark Bickhard, Andy Bremmner, Jonathan Cohen, Michael Corballis, Antonio Damasio, Stan Dehaene, Ralph Ellis, Lisa Geraci, Mark Haggard, Charles Heywood, Michael Huemer, Glyn Humphreys, Karl Jansen, Jason Mattingly, Colin McGinn, Thomas Metzinger, Mike Morgan, Dominic Murphy, Erik Myin, James Pagel, Chris Richards, Alan Richardson-Klavehn, Mark Solms, Sean Spence, Adam Wager, Alan Wallace, Doug Watt, and Eran Zaidel. Sadly, we lost two contributors before the completion of the book. Jeffrey Gray, one of our valued advisory editors, passed away before he could complete his own chapter for the book – but his final thoughts on consciousness can be found in his 2004 book. Francis Crick, one of the founders of the modern neuroscience of consciousness studies, also died; his chapter in the *Companion*, co-authored with Christof Koch, is one of his last writings on this subject.

We hope that we have kept errors and omissions to a minimum, and we take full responsibility for those that have crept in. Although it was impossible to include work by all of the leading scholars in this field, we have drawn from a wide spectrum and endeavored to present a balanced sample. The aim of the *Companion* is to present a fair account of the field as it is – intriguing, full of controversy, and constantly extending the boundaries of our knowledge.

Susan Schneider and Max Velmans

References

Velmans, M. (1991) Is human information processing conscious? *Behavioral and Brain Sciences* 14: 4, 651–726.

Velmans, M. (2000) *Understanding Consciousness*. London: Routledge, Psychology Press.

Part I

PROBLEMS OF CONSCIOUSNESS

1

A Brief History of the Scientific Approach to the Study of Consciousness

CHRIS FRITH AND GERAINT REES

The Origin of Consciousness Studies: René Descartes

The attempt to develop a systematic approach to the study of consciousness begins with René Descartes (1596–1650) and his ideas still have a major influence today. He is best known for the sharp distinction he made between the physical and the mental (Cartesian dualism). According to Descartes, the body is one sort of substance and the mind another because each can be conceived in terms of totally distinct attributes. The body (matter) is characterized by spatial extension and motion, while the mind is characterized by thought. This characterization of the mind also renders it private, a precursor of the distinction between the first-person and the third-person perspectives. Today, most scientists do not accept dualism, believing that mind somehow emerges from the physical properties of the brain. However, the distinction between mind and matter is still perceived as being so clear cut that explaining how mind can emerge from matter, and reconciling the first-person and third-person perspectives, remain the hardest problems facing the student of consciousness.

Some consider that Descartes has impeded the scientific study of consciousness, since his development of dualism placed consciousness outside the domain of science. However, Descartes was an interactive dualist and, as such, was the first to think seriously about the neural correlates of consciousness. He recognized that the brain has a key role for sensory input and motor output, but this did not make it the basis of mind. He considered that non-human animals did not have minds, but were unthinking automata for which a brain was sufficient. There is an interesting parallel here with current distinctions between conscious and unconscious processes. For Descartes, consciousness was a state of mind, with the brain having a role restricted to nonconscious processes. Nevertheless the brain had a key role in linking matter and mind. Physical bodies in the world have an impact on the sense organs. This impact creates motion in the body's nervous system that is somehow translated into the mind's experience of color, sound, and other sensations. These motions are transmitted to the pineal gland where they act as cues to the rational soul, enabling this to have specific types of conscious experience or ideas. We now know that Descartes was wrong about the importance of the pineal gland. But his account is not that different from recent proposals that, for example, neural activity in the fusiform region of the brain somehow leads to the conscious experience of a face.

Descartes also made a distinction between what would now be called "bottom-up" and "top-down" processes. The passions, such as joy and anger, agitate and disturb the mind. Conflicts between the passions and the will occur when the body (bottom-up) and the soul (top-down) cause opposing movements in the pineal gland, that unique structure in the brain where mind and body interact. The interplay between top-down and bottom-up processes in determining the outcome of cognitive processes remains a common motif in contemporary cognitive neuroscience.

After Descartes

Since Descartes much effort was devoted in trying to put the physical and the mental back together again. Baruch Spinoza (1632–77) proposed that the mental and the physical are different aspects of the same substance (*dual aspect theory*), while Gottfried Leibniz (1646–1716) proposed that the mind and the body were separate substances, but constructed from the outset to run together in perfect harmony (*psychophysical parallelism*). George Berkeley (1685–1753) denied the possibility of mindless material substances (*immaterialism*). He proposed that things could only exist through being a mind or through being perceived by a mind. In contrast *materialism* holds that matter is fundamental and is the cause of mental events. This is an ancient idea championed by, among others, Julien Offray de la Mettrie (1709–51) in his book *L'homme machine*. La Mettrie extended to man Descartes's idea of animals as automata. In particular, he proposed that conscious and voluntary processes result simply from more complex mechanisms than involuntary and instinctive processes. This is in essence the belief held by many of us who are searching for the neural correlates of consciousness in the twenty-first century.

John Locke (1632–1704) and the empiricist philosophers who followed him were less concerned with the mind–body distinction and more concerned with the problem of knowledge: how the mind learns about the world. Locke contrasted *outer sense*, the mind's experience of things, with *inner sense*, the mind's reflective experience of its own experience of things. He also recognized the importance of the *association of ideas*, a concept taken further by David Hartley (1705–57) and the direct precursor of *associationism* in psychology. Hartley also proposed that sensations were paralleled by vibrations . . . or "elemental" particles in the nerves and brain providing the basis for physiological psychology. Thomas Reid (1710–96) developed Locke's idea of *inner sense* to postulate that the mind contained a number of innate faculties. It was from these faculties that Franz Joseph Gall (1758–1828) derived his list of "powers of the mind" that he attempted to localize in the brain.

However, while the British empiricists were laying the foundation for a science of psychology, Immanuel Kant (1724–1804) was denying that such a science was possible. Kant pointed out that the scientific method requires the use of mathematics and experimentation. He considered that mathematics could not be applied to the description of mental phenomena because these phenomena vary in only one dimension – time. Likewise, experimentation could not be applied to psychology because mental phenomena are private and therefore inaccessible to experimental manipulation. If we accept Kant's ideas, then physiology (the study of the brain) is a scientific discipline, while psychology (the study of the mind) is not. As a result of this distinction psychology was long considered not to be a proper subject for scientific enquiry, especially when restricted to the study of subjective experience. Even today, many traces of this unfortunate notion remain. For example, one of the many websites we consulted in the course of writing this chapter names people who have had an important role in the study of consciousness. The names are presented in three lists headed: Philosophers, Psychologists, and Scientists. Furthermore, a very eminent academic colleague of the authors recently informed us that he welcomed the advent of brain imaging since this technique would permit an objective (i.e., physiological) measure of happiness.

The Scientific Study of the Mental in the Nineteenth Century

The development of the methods of psychophysics in the nineteenth century can be seen as a reaction against the idea that mental phenomena are not amenable to experimental study and mathematical modeling. The key figure in the development of psychophysics was Gustav Fechner (1801–87). Fechner believed, against Descartes, that mind and body were two aspects of a single entity. He also believed, against Kant, that mental processes could be measured. His method of psychophysics (Fechner 1860) built on the demonstration by Herbart (1824) that mental experiences (sensations) vary in intensity and that there is a threshold (or *limen*) such that below a certain stimulus intensity there is *no* sensation. Fechner also built upon Weber's concept of the *just noticeable difference* (JND) (Weber 1834). The JND is the smallest increase in stimulus intensity that is required to produce a *change* in sensation. Fechner used the JND as the unit of measurement and showed that there was a systematic relationship between JNDs (a subjective measure of sensation) and intensity of the physical signal. Across many modalities he found that the relationship between physical stimulus intensity and subjective sensation was logarithmic (the Weber-Fechner law). He speculated that the relationship between intensity of sensation and nervous activity would also be logarithmic, but had no way of measuring nervous activity. Fechner succeeded in showing that the mental could be measured and was closely linked to the physical. He also developed some of the basic methods of experimental psychology that we still use today.

Helmholtz's unconscious inferences

In parallel with the emergence of experimental psychology great advances were made in the understanding of the nervous system. A key figure in this development was Hermann Helmholtz (1821–94, enobled to von Helmholtz in 1882). Helmholtz began his studies of physiology with Johannes Müller. Like most biologists of his day, Müller was a vitalist who believed that living processes could never be reduced to the mechanical laws of physics and chemistry. Life depended on a vital force that was not susceptible to experimental investigation. In particular, he believed that the nerve impulse was a vital function that could never be measured experimentally since it was not extended in time. With proper disdain for the beliefs of his PhD supervisor, Helmholtz developed the myograph and measured the speed of travel of nerve impulses. He found that this was rather slow (~27 meters per second). The slow speed of travel of nerve impulses raised the possibility that mental processes might also be slow enough to measure, a possibility that led Donders to develop the reaction time task (see below).

Helmholtz made a particular study of the neural basis of perception (Helmholtz 1866). Müller had made the important observation (which he called *the law of specific nerve energies*) that sense organs cause the same subjective experience however they are stimulated. A mechanical blow to my eye, a stimulation that has nothing to do with light, nevertheless causes me to "see stars." Müller proposed that there were specific kinds of nerves associated with each sense organ that created the subjective quality associated with each modality. Helmholtz took this idea a step further and proposed that there might be different kinds of nerves supporting perception even within modalities. Since the experience of all hues can be created by mixing three primary colors, Helmholtz followed Young (1802) in proposing that there were three different kinds of nerve fiber in the human eye concerned with color. He calculated curves for the wavelength sensitivity of these three kinds of receptor. These speculations were subsequently confirmed experimentally.

Helmholtz recognized that the law of specific nervous energies implied that sensations do not provide direct access to objects, but are signs of reality that have to be interpreted. He demonstrated this clearly in relation to the perception of depth in 3-D space. There are many visual cues to the distance of objects from us. One is the disparity between the views received by the two eyes. Another is motion parallax: the observation that, when we are moving, nearby objects move across our eye much faster than objects that are far away. Helmholtz realized that, in order to create a percept from these sensory cues, the brain must make inferences based on prior knowledge. He concluded that perception depends upon *unconscious inferences*; unconscious because our experience of perception is that it is immediate. We are not aware of the inferences being made. Through his concept of unconscious inferences Helmholtz was anticipating the idea of the cognitive unconscious that became a key feature of cognitive psychology 100 years later. He was also anticipating the recent idea of perception as Bayesian inference (Kersten, Mamassian, & Yuille 2004). The idea that inferences can be made unconsciously was controversial and Helmholtz subsequently regretted using this term. "Recently I have refrained from using the phrase *unconscious inference in* order to avoid confusion with what seems to me a completely obscure and unjustified idea which Schopenhauer and his followers have designated by the same name." (Helmholtz 1878). He presumably had in mind Schopenhauer's claim that the will is largely unconscious and manifests itself in sexual desire. But there were additional reasons for the controversy. Making inferences is an example of the rational decision-making that Descartes proposed was the preserve of the soul. By taking decisions away from the soul and assigning them to the brain, Helmholtz seemed to be undermining the idea of personal responsibility, which many people continue to believe is the basis of moral behavior. Similar arguments continue today in relation to free will and the brain (e.g., Wegner 2002; Banks & Pockett, chapter 51).

Early progress in physiology and psychology

By the end of the nineteenth century much had been learned about the brain. Nerve fibers had been identified as extensions of nerve cells. This paved the way for Ramon y Cajal to propose the neuron doctrine, the idea that the nerve cell is the basic unit of the nervous system (Jones 1994). Helmholtz's fellow student, du Bois-Reymond, had demonstrated the electrical basis of nerve impulses, leading to the idea that it was energy rather than motion that was transmitted through neurons (Du Bois-Reymond 1848). Ferrier and others had located motor and sensory regions in the brain and Korbinian Brodmann had begun to identify the discrete brain regions that still bear his name (Brodmann 1909).

At the same time psychology had been established as a scientific discipline and Wilhelm Wundt had founded the first psychology laboratory in Leipzig in 1879. Reaction Time had been established by Frans Donders (1818–89) as an important technique for measuring the duration of mental events. Donders found that simple reaction times (one stimulus and one possible response) were always faster than choice reaction times (two stimuli and two possible responses). He proposed that this difference reflected the purely mental process of making a choice (Donders 1868). This "subtraction" method for isolating correlates of mental processes later became the standard procedure in functional brain imaging (Posner et al. 1988).

Wundt and other early psychologists used the reaction time method extensively, but very differently from the way it is used today. Their emphasis was very much on the first-person perspective. They wanted to measure pure apperception time (the time it takes to perceive something for what it is) by subtracting away the motor response time. Subjects were instructed to move in response to a stimulus and their reaction times were measured. In one condition subjects were instructed to attend to the movement to be executed. This condition gave a measure of the motor response time (or muscular reaction time). In the other condition subjects were asked to attend to the sense impression received from the stimulus (sensorial reaction time). The sensorial reaction time was supposed to be longer than muscular reaction time because the apperception time was added onto the motor time. In practice, the results were very variable and many subjects simply could not do the task (Cattell 1893). Great introspective skill is required to decide when a stimulus has been fully perceived.

The dominant figure in psychology at the end of the nineteenth century was William James (1842–1910), whose two-volume textbook, *Principles of Psychology*, is still well worth reading today. James identified consciousness with the stream of thought. He recognized the power of attention to give a focus and a margin to consciousness (see Mangan, chapter 52). He also recognized the importance of unconscious processes.

Psycho-physical processes in attention

Given all these advances, everything was in place for renewed attempts to speculate about the neural correlates of consciousness. One such speculation comes from an article in *Brain* (1890), in which James Sully of University College London considers "Psycho-physical processes in attention." Three commentaries on this article appeared in a later issue of the journal. The paper is about the neural correlates of selective attention. The discussion makes an interesting comparison with discussions on the same topic over 100 years later.

In most cases of selective visual attention there is an obvious motor factor in that we move our eyes to fixate the attended object. However, Sully recognized the importance of covert attention. Once again it was Helmholtz who had pointed out this phenomenon. "It is a curious fact . . . that the observer may be gazing steadily . . . yet at the same time he can concentrate his attention on any part of the dark field he likes." In the case of covert attention, Sully asks "where is the motor factor?" In his commentary, Alfred Fouillée concludes that the answer "lies in the liberation of cerebral energy upon the sensory centers of vision, not upon the ocular muscles. Certain parts of cerebral cortex are excited, others are inhibited." Today the same ideas would be expressed with phrases such as "top-down modulation of early visual areas" and "biased competition." Attempts to discuss the neural correlates of selective attention in 1890 suffered from two major disadvantages. First, nervous activity could be described only in terms of energy. The idea that neurons could transmit and store *information* had yet to be developed (see below). Second, experimental studies of attention emphasized subjective experience rather than behavior. Researchers were concerned to explore the experience of the act of attending and its consequences. "We are conscious of the *starting* of the centrifugal (i.e., top-down) current at the instant it is liberated by the brain" (the effort of will). "The effect of this current is to make the attended object appear more vivid" (Sully 1890).

The behaviorist school arose in part because of the difficulty and unreliability of this experimental study of subjective experience. Through their emphasis on the study of animals, the behaviorists identified markers of mental processes that did not depend upon verbal reports. The unintended legacy of behaviorism is that we now have many experimental techniques that provide robust, objective markers of conscious and unconscious processes.

Developments in the Early Twentieth Century

This period is sometimes represented as a desert as far as consciousness studies are concerned, but this is an exaggeration. It is true that John B. Watson tried to eliminate both reference to consciousness and use of introspective methods from psychology, but he did not succeed even in the United States. Woodworth's introductory textbook of psychology, which remained in print from 1921 to 1947 was subtitled *a study of mental life*. Stanley S. Stevens, while avoiding mentalistic language, continued the psychophysical programme of research started by Fechner (Stevens 1936). Of course, psychophysics depends fundamentally upon introspection. Edward C. Tolman criticized the idea that behavior could be fully explained by chains of stimulus-response associations and proposed that both humans and rats used internal perceptual representations (cognitive maps) to guide their behavior (Tolman 1948).

In Europe, Piaget studied the development of mental processes. Bartlett studied mental processes in long-term memory. The Gestalt psychologists studied the mental processes that underlie perception. The slogan of the Gestalt psychologists, "The whole is more than the sum of its parts" implied that complex dynamic interactions in the nervous system were fundamental to conscious experience. Of particular interest for later studies of the neural correlates of consciousness are the various perceptual illusions in which subjective experience is decoupled from physical stimulation. Many such illusions, including binocular rivalry, had already been described in the nineteenth century. However, the Gestalt psychologists emphasized the importance of these phenomena for understanding the mechanisms of perception.

However, the key development in the early twentieth century was the introduction of information theory by Hartley (1928) and Shannon and Weaver (1949). This is a mathematical technique that allows the amount of information in a signal, the rate of transmission of information through a communication channel, and the capacity of a communication channel to be quantified. The development of information theory was the first step in a mathematical account of cognition. If we consider information to lie in the realm of the mental rather than the physical, then information theory is also the first step in solving the difficult problem of bridging the mental and the physical domains. It is important to note, however, that the information in a signal is not the same as the meaning of a signal. Computers can transmit information but whether that information is meaningful depends on whether the receiver can interpret it.

It was immediately recognized that the brain could be treated as a communications system that processes and transmits information, rather than motion or energy. Conceiving of the brain in this way allowed the realization that it was now possible to develop intelligent machines. McCulloch and Pitts (1943) updated the neuron doctrine to state that the neuron was not simply the basic anatomical unit of the central nervous system (as Cajal had proposed) but the basic *information processing* unit. McCulloch and Pitts also proposed that the brain could be modeled by artificial neural nets constructed from very simple information processing units.

The Last 50 Years: The Triumph of Cognitive Psychology

Information theory had an immediate impact on psychology. Hick (1952) applied information theory to choice reaction time and showed that response time was directly proportional to the amount of information in the signal (i.e., log of the number of choices). Miller (1956) applied information theory to psychophysical judgments and showed that there was an upper limit (~2.6 bits, i.e., seven, plus or minus two items) to the number of categories that could be handled. He also showed that there was an upper limit for the capacity of immediate memory, but that this limit was determined by the number of items (or chunks), not by information. This approach rapidly led to the development of cognitive psychology in which psychological processes are described in engineering terms (Kenneth Craik's *The Nature of Explanation* also had a key role in this development) taken from communication theory (e.g., channel capacity), control systems theory (e.g., feedback) and computing (e.g., central processor, response buffer) (e.g., Broadbent 1958). Psychologists began to use "box and arrow" diagrams, flow charts of systems in terms of processes and information transmission.

While cognitive psychologists tended not to use the word "consciousness," this was nevertheless frequently the object of their study. Following James, the contents of "working" or "active" memory as studied by Alan Baddeley and colleagues (Baddeley 1986), can be equated (roughly) with the contents of consciousness. Deploying selective attention, as in Broadbent's dichotic listening task and Posner's covert spatial attention task (Posner 1978), requires a voluntary effort. However, cognitive psychologists tended not to use introspection as a direct source of data. Intuitions derived from introspection had to be confirmed by behavioral data. For example, introspection suggests that, after reading a telephone number, we maintain our consciousness of that number in working memory by saying it to ourselves. This implies that the visual material has been converted to an auditory representation. This intuition was confirmed when Conrad showed that confusion errors were better predicted by auditory rather than visual similarity even though the numbers had been presented visually (Conrad 1962).

The cognitive unconscious

Perhaps the major development for consciousness research during the past 50 years has been the demonstration of unconscious, automatic psychological processes in perception, memory, and action, named the *cognitive unconscious* by John Kihlstrom (1987). The term subliminal perception, for example, describes the situation where the presentation of a stimulus affects subsequent behavior of the observer even though the stimulus never enters the consciousness of the observer (see Merikle, chapter 40). In the 1960s, claims about subliminal perception were dismissed by experimental psychologists on the basis of methodological inadequacy, but the development of more sophisticated experimental techniques, such as priming (Marcel 1983) and analytic techniques such as signal detection theory (Swets, Tanner, & Birdsall 1961) provided convincing evidence. Such unconscious psychological processes were observed in more exaggerated form in patients with brain damage. Some patients with lesions in visual cortex can make correct "guesses" about the properties of visual stimuli that they cannot "see" (Weiskrantz & Warrington 1975; Weiskrantz, chapter 13). Patients with dense amnesia can retain knowledge about stimuli they have no memory of having seen before (Warrington & Weiskrantz 1968). Patient DF, with damage to inferior temporal cortex, can use visual information of which she is unaware to guide her movements (Goodale et al. 1991; see Goodale, chapter 48). More recently, social psychologists have demonstrated that a whole range of unconscious processes influence social behavior (Bargh & Chartrand 1999).

The problem for psychological studies of unconscious processes is that we need a marker that such processing has taken place, but at the same time we do not want to draw the subject's attention to the stimulus that they are unconsciously processing (Mack & Rock 1998). The subject can tell us that they did not see a stimulus, but to know that they have nevertheless processed it we need additional markers, for example facilitation or interference with the processing of subsequent stimuli of which they are aware. The development of brain imaging techniques has provided additional markers of such unconscious processing. Using these techniques, we can ask if unconscious processing is associated with a specific pattern of brain activity. For example, Beck et al. (2001) showed that undetected faces in a change blindness paradigm elicited activity in fusiform cortex (see Rees & Frith, chapter 43).

Many now believe that most of the processing undertaken by the brain occurs without our awareness (Velmans 1991), but many have found the term "cognitive unconscious" confusing. This confusion results from a shift in the meaning of the word "cognitive." Previously the term cognitive (as in the term cognitive therapy) referred to knowledge, beliefs, and attitudes, all key components of consciousness. Furthermore, following Kant, sharp distinctions were made between cognition (to do with knowledge), emotion (to do with feelings) and conation (to do with will). Today, following Neisser's 1967 book *Cognitive Psychology*, many use *cognitive* (as in the terms cognitive psychology and cognitive neuroscience) to replace the older term "information processing" and to refer to what the brain does. An account of a psychological or a neural system that included a box and arrow diagram involving representations, transformations, and information flow would be called a cognitive account. From this point of view cognitive processes exist in the computational domain that lies between neural activity on the one hand and behavior and conscious experience on the other hand. Such cognitive processes need not lead to consciousness and can be evoked to explain feeling and will as well as knowledge.

The demonstration of unconscious processes raises a new problem for the study of consciousness. Just because subjects can detect or discriminate a stimulus, does not mean that they are conscious of it. Their success may be the result of unconscious processes. From their first person perspective they are just guessing.

Introspection, Protocol Analysis, and Meta-cognition

While introspection was the method of choice for nineteenth-century psychologists, this method was used far less in the twentieth century. It was not abandoned completely, however. In particular it was used in the study of problem solving. In order to gain access to the conscious processes used to solve a problem subjects were asked to "think aloud." Indeed, the arch-behaviorist John B. Watson was a pioneer in the use of this method. "The present writer has often felt that a good deal more can be learned about the psychology of thinking by making subjects think aloud about definite problems, than by trusting to the unscientific method of introspection" (Watson 1920). For Watson thinking aloud was not introspection, but verbal behavior. However, it is not clear to us what someone "thinking aloud" is doing, if not introspecting. The method was used extensively by Duncker (1945), one of the Gestalt psychologists, and refined as "protocol analysis" by Ericsson and Simon (1984). Nevertheless, methodologies for harnessing introspection as a source of data have lagged behind those developed for behavioral tasks. In recent years there has been increasing interest in developing such methods (Jack & Roepstorff 2004).

Thinking aloud is a form of meta-cognition since subjects must reflect upon and report their thoughts. Meta-cognition has been used in a clever way to provide behavioral measures that reflect consciousness and hence a first-person perspective. For example, to make the confidence ratings used in psychophysics experiments, subjects must think about their perceptions. If the degree of confidence correlates with the accuracy of the judgments then we can conclude that the subjects were conscious of the stimuli rather than just guessing (Kunimoto, Miller, & Pashler 2001). This approach has been used in the study of animal consciousness. Monkeys can be trained to make confidence judgments and these behavioral responses can be used as evidence of whether or not they are conscious of stimuli (Cowey & Stoerig 1997; Hampton 2001).

The same idea underlies the process dissociation technique developed by Jacoby (1992). Subjects are asked to decide whether a word was previously presented in list A rather than list B. The assumption is that subjects can reject a familiar word from list A only if they can consciously recollect that it was in list B. Here again a behavioral response is being driven by introspection.

The Current State of Consciousness Research

Despite much progress consciousness remains as elusive as ever. Some difficulties have been resolved, but new ones have emerged. At the beginning of the nineteenth century, there was little distinction between consciousness and life itself, with both depending upon vital essences that were not amenable to experimental study. The monster created by Frankenstein in Mary Shelley's novel has not only life, but also an exquisite sensitivity to human experience and suffering. Science gradually dispelled the need for vital essences to explain life, but consciousness remained unexplained. By the early twentieth century, in James Whale's version, the monster lives, but is only dimly conscious. By the end of the century the monster has evolved into a plague of zombies who behave like humans (Horne 1992), while having no consciousness.

Zombies retain a surprisingly strong influence on contemporary philosophers of consciousness. They (that is the philosophers) are interested in the existence of a particular kind of zombie, which is physically and behaviorally identical to us, but is not conscious. Neuroscientists and psychologists, in contrast, are interested in a form of Haitian zombie that is not conscious, but in which the cognitive unconscious (the zombie within) is intact (Koch & Crick 2001). In what way would such a creature be distinguishable from us?

At the beginning of the twenty-first century, we know that life does not depend upon a vital essence, but we are still not sure about consciousness. Perhaps there is a vital essence that turns a zombie into a human. There are various proposals as to the nature of this vital essence. Eliminative materialists (e.g., Paul and Patricia Churchland) have concluded that consciousness is itself a vital essence and therefore does not really exist (see Mandik, chapter 33). For *functionalists*, following in the footsteps of La Mettrie, the vital essence is a computational algorithm of sufficient complexity. This can be instantiated in silicon just as well as in neurons. If a machine has the right kind of complexity it will be conscious. No new physical principles will be required to understand how it works (see Aleksander, chapter 6). Others claim that some as yet undiscovered scientific process, such as quantum entanglement at a macroscopic level, is needed to explain consciousness (e.g., Stuart Hameroff, see Stapp, chapter 23). And finally *mysterians* think that the problem of consciousness is so complex that the human brain can never explain it (e.g., Colin McGinn, see Rowlands, chapter 26).

Meanwhile the scientific study of mental processes has revealed that consciousness is not necessary for rational thought. Inferences can be drawn and decisions made without awareness. This raises a new problem for our understanding of consciousness. Descartes and his contemporaries took it for granted that consciousness was necessary for rational thought and willed, as opposed to automatic, behavior. If not the basis of rational thought, what is the function of consciousness? Again extreme positions have been taken up. On the one hand, consciousness is considered to have no function. It is just an epiphenomenon, which can have no impact on the physical world (see Kim, chapter 32; and Banks & Pockett, chapter 51). On the other hand, the followers of Darwin claim that consciousness has evolved and must therefore give some advantage to those of us who have it (see Polger, chapter 5). From this perspective the sophisticated forms of consciousness found in humans may be associated with language and the creation of culture. Perhaps consciousness is necessary for communicating mental states and sharing experiences? This is not a new idea. Nietzsche made the conjecture "that consciousness in general developed itself only under the pressure of the need to communicate."

Consciousness studies are frequently criticized for failing to define precisely what consciousness is. In this respect there has been little change over the past few centuries. In part the problem arises because consciousness remains a common-sense term rather than a scientific one. Different people use the term to mean different things (see Tye, chapter 2). Studies purporting to define the neural correlates of consciousness often address only one aspect of consciousness (e.g., access consciousness) while leaving other aspects (e.g., phenomenal consciousness) untouched. A likely consequence of the intellectual endeavors promoted in this book is that this fractionation of consciousness will become more explicit and the different components associated with specific operational definitions. In the final section of this introduction we describe some specific problems in the study of consciousness, which, when answered, will aid the development of such fractionations and definitions.

Scientific Questions

The historical developments that we have charted in this chapter have profoundly shaped current thinking about the outstanding major scientific questions concerning consciousness. Many of these questions, particularly those concerning the cognitive and neural basis of consciousness, could not have been asked even 20 years ago. These are not questions about the really hard problems of consciousness (see Chalmers, chapter 17). Rather they are questions for which satisfactory answers will soon be found. When they are answered the hard problems may seem easier.

A. Are there different kinds of consciousness?

A major section of this book is devoted to varieties of consciousness, so the answer to this question must be affirmative (see the section on *Some Varieties of Conscious Experience*; also Tye, chapter 2). However, we neither know the precise fractionation of consciousness, nor yet know in what way these different kinds of consciousness will vary. Are the differences simply quantitative, with dreaming, fringe consciousness and core consciousness being just simplified versions of waking, focal and self-consciousness? Or are there qualitative differences between these different kinds of consciousness? These questions about the varieties of consciousness can be answered through studying the cognitive and neural correlates of the different varieties of consciousness (as well as introspective reports). Are certain representations and computations only possible for certain kinds of consciousness? Are different patterns of neural activity associated with different kinds of consciousness? The questions can also be addressed by contrasting the consciousness of animals and humans (Allen & Bekoff, chapter 4), or the consciousness of infants and adults (Trevarthen & Reddy, chapter 3).

B. Are there biological markers of consciousness?

This question has been dramatically sharpened by the demonstration of multiple unconscious processes. We can now ask about the differences between those processes that are associated with consciousness and those that are not (see the section on *Cognitive Psychology of Consciousness* and chapters by Crick & Koch (44), Baars (18), Merikle (40), Kihlstrom, Dorfman, & Park (41) and Rees & Frith (43)). Do the processes associated with consciousness involve specific kinds of computations and representations? Are they associated with specific kinds of neural activity, and do they involve particular regions of the brain? By contrasting conscious and unconscious processes we already know, for example, that activity in a region of human fusiform cortex is necessary, but not sufficient for the conscious experience of a face.

C. How do we determine the presence of consciousness?

This is an intensely practical question that confronts clinicians in the intensive therapy unit and the operating theater (see Kihlstrom & Cork, chapter 49). Is this brain-damaged patient in a coma (i.e., unconscious) or are they instead in a locked-in state: conscious of everything that is being said, but unable to move any part of their body? Evidence of consciousness is currently inferred behaviorally, but does the resulting classification of patients into coma, minimally conscious, persistent vegetative state or locked-in syndrome accurately reflect the underlying degree of consciousness of such patients?

Precisely the same problem confronts anesthetists daily. The patient on the operating table cannot move because they have been injected with a muscle relaxant, but if they become conscious in the middle of the operation they will sue the hospital. How can the anesthetist tell if their patient is awake? The solution is to find reliable neural correlates of consciousness, or to find some way of communicating with the patient. But how do we determine consciousness when high-level communication is not available, as with animals, infants, or machines? Neural markers of consciousness may be relevant for determining consciousness in animals and infants with brains, but is not relevant for most machines. Is there some cognitive process that is a marker of consciousness?

D. What is consciousness for?
The demonstration of unconscious processes has also sharpened our thinking on this question. We can ask whether there is some kind of problem that can be solved by conscious processes, but not by unconscious ones. In other words, although Hollywood zombies can go shopping (Romero 1978), are there other tasks that they find more difficult, or cannot perform? Various candidates have been proposed, for example, the analysis of complex or novel input, the operation of working memory, learning of novel material, thinking and planning, speech production and reading, and the performance of any task that is novel, or that requires flexibility and feedback.

The reader will have noticed that all these questions are closely inter-related. Determining if someone is conscious will depend upon finding markers of consciousness. Finding cognitive markers of consciousness may give clues about what consciousness is for. Alternatively if we knew what consciousness was for, then it might be easier to find markers of consciousness, and so on. More importantly, by the end of this book, the reader should be convinced that these are questions we are now in a better position to answer.

See also 2 Philosophical problems of consciousness; 43 Methodologies for identifying the neural correlates of consciousness; 52 Cognition, fringe consciousness, and the legacy of William James.

Further Readings

Hilgard, E. R. (1980) Consciousness in contemporary psychology. *Annual Review of Psychology* 31, 1–26.
Velmans, M. (2000) *Understanding Consciousness*. London: Routledge/Psychology Press, chs. 1 to 5.

References

Baddeley, A. (1986) *Working Memory*. Oxford: Oxford University Press.
Bargh, J. A. and Chartrand, T. L. (1999) The unbearable automaticity of being. *American Psychologist* 54: 7, 462–79.
Beck, D. M., Rees, G., Frith, C. D., and Lavie, N. (2001) Neural correlates of change detection and change blindness. *Nature Neuroscience* 4: 6, 645–50.
Broadbent, D. E. (1958) *Perception and Communication*. London and New York: Pergamon Press.

Brodmann, K. (1909) *Vergleichende Lokalisationslehre der Grosshirnrinde in ihren Principien, dargestellt auf grund des Zellenbaues*. Leipzig: Johann Ambrosius Barth.

Cattell, J. M. (1893) Aufmerksamkeit und Reaction. *Philosophische Studien* 8, 403–6.

Conrad, R. (1962) An association between memory errors and errors due to acoustic masking of speech. *Nature* 193, 1314–15.

Cowey, A. and Stoerig, P. (1997) Visual detection in monkeys with blindsight. *Neuropsychologia* 35: 7, 929–39.

Donders, F. C. (1868) On the speed of mental processes. Translated by W. G. Koster 1969. *Acta Psychologica* 30, 412–31.

Du Bois-Reymond, E. (1848) *Untersuchungen über thierische Elektricität*. Berlin: Georg Reimer.

Duncker, K. (1945) *On Problem Solving*. Washington, DC: American Psychological Association.

Ericsson, K. A. and Simon, H. (1984) *Protocol Analysis: Verbal Reports as Data*, Cambridge, MA: MIT Press.

Fechner, G. T. (1860) *Elemente der Psychophysik*. Leipzig: Breitkopf und Härtel.

Goodale, M. A., Milner, A. D., Jakobson, L. S. and Carey, D. P. (1991) A neurological dissociation between perceiving objects and grasping them. *Nature* 349: 6305, 154–6.

Hampton, R. R. (2001) Rhesus monkeys know when they remember. *Proceedings of the National Academy of Sciences of the United States of America* 98: 9, 5359–62.

Hartley, R. V. L. (1928) Transmission of information. *Bell Systems Technical Journal* 7, 535.

Helmholtz, H. v. (1866) *Handbuch der Physiologischen Optik*. Leipzig: Voss.

Helmholtz, H. v. (1878) The facts of perception. *Selected Writings of Hermann Helmholtz*. Middletown, CT: Wesleyan University Press.

Herbart, J. F. (1824) *Psychologie als Wissenschaft, neu gegründet auf Erfahrung, Metaphysik und Mathematik*. Königsberg: A. W. Unzer.

Hick, W. E. (1952) On the rate of gain of information. *Quarterly Journal of Experimental Psychology* 4, 11–26.

Horne, P. (1992) I shopped with a zombie: consumer culture, fiction and cinema. *Critical Quarterly* 34: 4, 97–110.

Jack, A. I. and Roepstorff, A. (2004) *Trusting the Subject?* Exeter, UK: Imprint Academic.

Jacoby, L. L. (1992) A process dissociation framework: separating automatic from intentional uses of memory. *Journal of Memory and Language* 30, 513–41.

Jones, E. G. (1994) The neuron doctrine. *Journal of History of Neuroscience* 3, 3–20.

Kersten, D., Mamassian, P., and Yuille, A. (2004) Object perception as Bayesian inference. *Annual Review of Psychology* 55, 271–304.

Kihlstrom, J. F. (1987) The cognitive unconscious. *Science* 237: 4821, 1445–52.

Koch, C. and Crick, F. (2001) The zombie within. *Nature* 411: 6840, 893.

Kunimoto, C., Miller, J., and Pashler, H. (2001) Confidence and accuracy of near-threshold discrimination responses. *Consciousness and Cognition* 10: 3, 294–340.

Mack, A. and Rock, I. (1998) *Inattentional Blindness*. Cambridge, MA: MIT Press.

Marcel, A. J. (1983) Conscious and unconscious perception: experiments on visual masking and word recognition. *Cognitive Psychology* 15: 2, 197–237.

McCulloch, W. S. and Pitts, W. H. (1943) A logical calculus of the ideas immanent in nervous activity. *Bulletin of Mathematical Biophysics* 5, 115–33.

Miller, G. A. (1956) The magical number seven, plus or minus two. *The Psychological Review* 63, 81–97.

Posner, M. I. (1978) *Chronometric Explorations of Mind*. Oxford: Lawrence Erlbaum.

Posner, M. I., Petersen, S. E., Fox, P. T., and Raichle, M. E. (1988) Localization of cognitive operations in the human brain. *Science* 240: 4859, 1627–31.

Romero, G. A. (1978) *Dawn of the Dead* (Italy/USA, United Film Distribution Company).

Shannon, C. E. and Weaver, W. (1949) *The Mathematical Theory of Communication*. Urbana: University of Illinois Press.

Stevens, S. S. (1936) A scale for the measurement of a psychological magnitude: loudness. *Psychological Review* 43, 405–16.

Sully, J. (1890) The psychophysical process in attention. *Brain* 13: 2, 145–64.

Swets, J. A., Tanner, W. P. J., and Birdsall, T. G. (1961) Decision processes in perception. *Psychological Review* 68, 301–40.

Tolman, E. C. (1948) Cognitive maps in rats and men. *Psychological Review* 55: 4, 189–208.

Velmans, M. (1991) Is human information processing conscious? *Behavioural and Brain Sciences* 14: 4, 651–68.

Warrington, E. K. and Weiskrantz, L. (1968) New method of testing long-term retention with special reference to amnesic patients. *Nature* 217: 132, 972–4.

Watson, J. B. (1920) Is thinking merely the action of language mechanisms? *British Journal of Psychology* 11: 8, 7–104.

Weber, E. H. (1834) *De pulsu, resorptione, auditu et tactu. Annotationes anatomicae et physiologicae.* Leipzig: Koehler.

Wegner, D. (2002) *The Illusion of Conscious Will.* Cambridge, MA: Bradford Books, MIT Press.

Weiskrantz, L. and Warrington, E. K. (1975) Blindsight – residual vision following occipital lesions in man and monkey. *Brain Research* 85: 1, 184–5.

Young, T. (1802) On the theory of light and colours. *Philosophical Transactions of the Royal Society of London* 92, 12–48.

2

Philosophical Problems of Consciousness

MICHAEL TYE

Of our conscious mental states, some are inherently conscious. That is to say, some of our mental states cannot *fail* to be conscious. For each such mental state, there is a *subjective* perspective that goes along with it. This perspective is conferred upon the subject simply by his or her undergoing the mental state. It is captured in everyday language by talk of "what it's like." There is something it's like subjectively to feel an itch, to smell rotten eggs, to taste a lemon, to feel elated. Furthermore, what it's like to undergo one inherently conscious mental state can be compared with what it's like to undergo another. For example, what it's like to experience bright red is subjectively more similar to what it's like to experience bright orange than to what it's like to experience dark green.

Mental states that are inherently conscious are said to be "phenomenally conscious" by philosophers. But just which mental states are these? One not very informative answer is that they are experiences. More helpfully, we can classify the relevant states into at least the following categories:

1 Perceptual experiences, for example, experiences of the sort involved in seeing green, hearing loud trumpets, tasting chocolate, smelling the sea air, running one's fingers over sandpaper.
2 Bodily sensations, for example, feeling a twinge of pain, feeling an itch, feeling hungry, having a stomach ache, feeling hot, feeling dizzy. Think here also of experiences such as those present during orgasm or while running flat-out.
3 Felt reactions or passions or emotions, for example, feeling anger, lust, fear, love, grief, jealousy, regret.
4 Felt moods, for example, feeling happy, depressed, calm, bored, tense, miserable.

Some philosophers claim that there are also such experiences as, for example, the experience of suddenly remembering something or the experience of understanding a story. Others insist that insofar as there are experiences in these cases, they are simply various perceptual and/or bodily experiences that accompany memory and understanding.

Phenomenal consciousness attaches to mental states. What it's like subjectively to undergo a given phenomenally conscious mental state is known as the *phenomenal character* of the state. Phenomenally conscious states vary in what it's like subjectively to undergo them, and in so doing they vary in phenomenal character. Possession of a phenomenal character by a mental state endows it with the property of being phenomenally conscious.

In everyday life, we often attribute consciousness to persons (and other sentient creatures) in addition to mental states. We think of *ourselves* as being conscious of things (for example, a rock, a tree, a car) and also of facts (for example, the fact that there is an apple on the table). This kind of consciousness is standardly called "creature consciousness." Some philosophers also claim that there is a kind of consciousness that attaches to some mental states simply by virtue of their being available for certain sorts of information processing. This kind of consciousness is sometimes called "access consciousness." Exactly how creature consciousness, access consciousness, and phenomenal consciousness are related is a matter on which there is as yet no clear agreement in philosophy (Block 1995). But this does not matter for present purposes, for there is broad agreement that phenomenal consciousness is what makes consciousness so deeply puzzling. The problems presented below (with the exception of the last one) all pertain directly to one or other aspect of phenomenal consciousness.

The Problem of Ownership

This problem is one which must be faced by any philosopher who wants to hold that phenomenally conscious states are physical. The problem is that of explaining how the mental objects of experience and feeling – such as particular pains, after-images, tickles, itches – *could* be physical, given that they are necessarily owned and necessarily private to their owners. Unless these objects are themselves physical, the phenomenal states involving them, states like having a yellow after-image or feeling a tickle, cannot themselves be physical either.

Let us take a concrete example to illustrate the problem. Suppose that you are lying in the sun with your eyes closed. You have not a care in the world. Life is good. Suddenly you feel intense pain in your right leg – a hornet, trapped beneath your leg on the grass, has stung you. There is something it's like for you at this decidedly unlucky moment.

This is an objective fact about you, not dependent for its existence on anyone else seeing or thinking about your situation. But the pain you are feeling – that particular pain – is private to you. It is yours alone, and necessarily so. No one else could have that particular pain. Of course, conceivably somebody else could have a pain that felt just like your pain, but only you could have that very pain. What is true for this one pain is true for pains generally. Indeed, it is true for all mental objects of experience. None of these items of experience can be shared. I cannot have your visual images or feel your tickles, for example. Your images and tickles necessarily belong to you.

The problem, in part, is that ordinary physical things do not seem to be owned in this way. For example, my house is something you could own. Likewise, my tie or my car. But the problem runs deeper. For any pain or itch or image is always *some creature's* pain or itch or image. Each mental object of experience necessarily has *an* owner. So, pains in this respect are not like dogs or tables or even legs. Legs can exist amputated, and dogs and tables can belong to no one at all. Pains, however, *must* have owners.

The challenge for the philosopher, who wants to hold that experiences and feelings are wholly physical, is to explain how it is that pains and other mental objects of experience can have the above features, if they really are just ordinary physical things. This is the problem of ownership.

The Problem of Perspectival Subjectivity

Consider the experience of pain again. It seems highly plausible to suppose that *fully* comprehending this experience requires knowing what it's like to undergo it. And knowing what it's like to undergo an experience requires a certain experiential point of view or perspective. This is why a child born without the capacity to feel pain and kept alive in a very carefully controlled environment could never come to know what it's like to experience pain. Such a child could never herself adopt the relevant perspective. And lacking that perspective, she could never comprehend fully what that type of feeling was, no matter how much information was supplied about the firing patterns in your brain, the biochemical processes, and the chemical changes.

Phenomenally conscious states are perspectival in that fully comprehending them requires adopting a certain experiential point of view. But physical states are not perspectival in this way. Understanding fully what lightning is, or gold, does not require any particular experiential point of view. For example, there is no requirement that one undergo the experiences normal human beings undergo as they watch the sky in a storm or examine a gold ring. A man who is blind and deaf cannot experience lightning by sight or hearing at all, but he can understand fully just what it is, namely a certain sort of electrical discharge between clouds. Similarly, if gold presents a very different appearance to Martians, say, this does not automatically preclude them from fully grasping what gold is, namely the element with atomic number 79. Physical items, then, are not perspectival (Nagel 1979). They are, in the relevant way, objective.

These points allow us to appreciate why some philosophers claim that an android who is incapable of any feeling or experience lacks the resources to grasp the concept of phenomenal consciousness. Lacking any phenomenal consciousness herself, she would not know what it's like to be phenomenally conscious. And not knowing that, she could not occupy *any* experiential perspective. So, she could not fully understand the nature of phenomenal consciousness; nor could she properly grasp the meaning of the term "phenomenal consciousness."

The problem of perspectival subjectivity can be illustrated in other ways. Consider a brilliant scientist of the future, Mary, who has lived in a black and white room since birth and who acquires information about the world via banks of computers and black and white television screens depicting the outside world (Jackson 1982; Alter, chapter 31). Suppose that Mary has at her disposal in the room all the objective, physical information there is about what goes on when humans see roses, trees, sunsets, rainbows, and other phenomena. She knows everything there is to know about the surfaces of the objects, the ways in which they reflect light, the changes on the retina and in the optic nerve, the firing patterns in the visual cortex, and so on. Still, there is something she does not know. She does not know what it's like to see red or green or the other colors. This is shown by the fact that when she finally steps outside her room and looks at a rose, say, she will certainly learn something. Only then will she appreciate what it's like to see red. So, physicalism is incomplete.

Alternatively, suppose that we make contact with some extraterrestrials, and that scientists from Earth eventually come to have exhaustive knowledge of their physical states. It turns out that their physiology is very different from that of any Earth creatures. Surely our scientists can wonder what it feels like to be an extraterrestrial; whether their feelings and experiences are the same as ours. But if they can wonder this, then they are not yet in a position to know everything by means of their objective, scientific investigations. For there is something they do not yet know, namely, what it's like for the extraterrestrials. This is something subjective, something not contained in the information about the objective facts already available to them.

The problem, then, can be put this way: What accounts for the fact that fully comprehending the nature of pain, the feeling of depression, or the visual experience of red requires having the appropriate experiential perspective?

The Problem of Mechanism

Somehow, physical changes in the soggy gray and white matter composing our brains produce feeling, experience, "technicolor phenomenology" (McGinn 1991). How is this possible? What is it about the brain that is responsible for the production of states with phenomenal character? These questions ask for a specification of the *mechanism* which underlies the generation of phenomenally conscious states by physical states, and which closes the explanatory gap we feel intuitively between the two (Levine 1983; Levine, chapter 29). This explanatory gap was the one puzzling T. H. Huxley when he commented in 1866, "How it is that anything so remarkable as a state of consciousness comes about as a result of irritating nervous tissue, is just as unaccountable as the appearance of Djin when Aladdin rubbed his lamp."

Here is a thought experiment which brings out the explanatory gap very clearly. Suppose that scientists develop a device that can be attached to the head and that permits the recipient to view physical changes in his own brain. This device, which is sometimes called "an autocerebroscope," can be thought of as being something like the virtual reality headgear that is beginning to be marketed today except that what the recipient sees in this case, via probes which pass painlessly through the skull, is the inside of his own brain. Suppose that you put the device on your head, and lo and behold, firing patterns appear projected on to a screen before your eyes! As you move a hand control, further firing patterns from other regions of the cortex appear before you. Imagine now that whenever you are tickled with a feather, you see that a certain fixed set of neurons in the somato-sensory cortex is firing. At other times, when you are not being tickled, these neurons are dormant. Is it not going to seem amazing to you that *that* electrical activity generates the subjective tickle feeling? *How*, on earth, does that particular neural activity produce a *feeling* at all? And why does it feel like *that* rather than some other way?

The need for a mechanism can also be appreciated once when we reflect upon some real life examples from science. Consider the production of brittleness in a thin glass sheet or liquidity in water or digestion in a human being. In each of these cases there is a mechanism which explains how the higher-level property or process is generated from the lower level one.

In the case of liquidity, for example, once we appreciate that liquidity is a disposition, namely the disposition to pour easily, and we are told that in liquid water the H_2O molecules are free to slide past one another instead of being trapped in fixed locations (as they are in ice), we have no difficulty in seeing how liquidity is generated from the underlying molecular properties. There is no explanatory gap.

A similar account is available in the case of brittleness. Like liquidity, brittleness is a disposition. Brittle objects are disposed to shatter easily. This disposition is produced in a thin glass sheet via the irregular alignment of crystals. Such an alignment results in there being weak forces between crystals holding them together. So, when a force is applied, the glass shatters. The generation of brittleness is now explained.

Digestion is a matter of undergoing a process whose function is to change food into energy. So digestion is a functionally characterized process. It follows that digestion takes place in a given organism via any set of internal changes which performs the relevant function for that organism. In this way, digestion is realized in the organism. In human beings, for example, digestion is realized chiefly by the action of certain enzymes secreted into the alimentary canal. These enzymes cause the food to become absorbable and hence available as energy by dissolving it and breaking it down into simpler chemical compounds. Once one grasps these facts, there is no deep mystery about how digestion is generated.

What the above examples strongly suggest is that, in the natural world, the generation of higher-level states or processes or properties by what is going on at lower neurophysiological or chemical or microphysical levels is grounded in mechanisms which *explain* the generation of the higher-level items. So, if phenomenal consciousness is a natural phenomenon, a part of the physical world, there should be a mechanism which provides an explanatory link between the subjective and the objective. Given that there is such a mechanism, the place of phenomenally conscious states in the natural, physical domain is not threatened. But what could this mechanism be? We currently have no idea. Nor is it easy to see what scientific discoveries in biology, neurophysiology, chemistry, or physics could help us. For these sciences are sciences of the objective. And no fully objective mechanism could close the explanatory gap between the objective and the subjective. No matter how deeply we probe into the physical structure of neurons and the chemical transactions which occur when they fire, no matter how much objective information we acquire, we still seem to be left with something that cries out for a further explanation, namely, why and how *this* collection of neural and/or chemical changes produces *that* subjective feeling, or any subjective feeling at all.

The problem of mechanism, then, can be put as follows: How do objective, physical changes in the brain generate subjective feelings and experiences? What is the mechanism which is responsible for the production of the "what it's like" aspects of our mental lives?

The Problem of Duplicates

Hollywood zombies are not difficult to spot. They inhabit the world of films, wandering around in a trance-like state, typically unable to control their behavior in a voluntary manner. They are usually very pale, preferring the night to the day for their carnivorous activities, and their clothes are normally disheveled and old. Hollywood zombies, then, are significantly different from the rest of us at a functional level. Moreover, they need not be wholly without phenomenal consciousness. Philosophical zombies are a very different kettle of fish.

A philosophical zombie is a molecule-by-molecule duplicate of a sentient creature, a normal human being, for example, but who differs from that creature in lacking *any* phenomenal consciousness. For me, as I lie on the beach, happily drinking some wine and watching the waves, I undergo a variety of visual, olfactory, and gustatory experiences. But my zombie twin experiences nothing at all. He has no phenomenal consciousness. Since my twin is an exact physical duplicate of me, his inner psychological states will be *functionally* isomorphic with my own (assuming he is located in an identical environment). Whatever physical stimulus is applied, he will process the stimulus in the same way as I do, and produce *exactly* the same behavioral responses. Indeed, on the assumption that non-phenomenal psychological states are functional states (that is, states definable in terms of their role or function in mediating between stimuli and behavior), my zombie twin has just the same beliefs, thoughts, and desires as I do. He differs from me only with respect to experience. For him, there is nothing it's like to stare at the waves or to sip wine.

The hypothesis that there can be philosophical zombies is not normally the hypothesis that such zombies are *nomically* possible, that their existence is consistent with the actual laws of nature. Rather the suggestion is that the hypothesis is coherent, that zombie replicas of this sort are at least *imaginable* and hence logically or metaphysically possible.

Philosophical zombies pose a serious threat to any sort of physicalist view of phenomenal consciousness. To begin with, if zombie replicas are possible, then phenomenal states are not identical with internal, objective, physical states, as the following simple argument shows. Suppose objective, physical state P can occur without phenomenal state S in some appropriate zombie replica (in the logical sense of "can" noted above). But, intuitively, S cannot occur without S. Pain, for example, cannot be felt without pain. So, P has a modal property S lacks, namely the property of *possibly* occurring without S. So, by Leibniz' Law (the law that for anything x and for anything y, if x is identical with y then x and y share *all* the same properties), S is not identical with P.

Second, if a person microphysically identical with me, located in an identical environment, can lack *any* phenomenal experiences, then facts pertaining to experience and feeling, facts about what it's like, are not necessarily fixed or determined by the objective microphysical facts. And this the physicalist cannot allow, even if she concedes that phenomenally conscious states are not strictly identical with internal, objective, physical states. For the physicalist, whatever her stripe, must at least believe that the microphysical facts determine all the facts; that any world that was exactly like ours in *all* microphysical respects (down to the smallest detail) would have to be like our world in all respects (having identical mountains, lakes, glaciers, trees, rocks, sentient creatures, cities, and so on).

So, the physicalist again has a serious problem. Phenomenal states, it seems, are not identical with internal, objective physical states, nor are they determined by physical states. This is the problem of microphysical duplicates.

Philosophical zombies are microphysical duplicates that lack phenomenal consciousness. Other duplicates lacking consciousness have also concerned philosophers. In particular, there has been considerable debate about possible functional duplicates that are not philosophical zombies. So, for example, one writer (Block 1980) asks us to imagine that a billion Chinese people are each given a two-way radio with which to communicate with one another and with an artificial (brainless) body. The movements of the body are controlled by the radio signals, and the signals themselves are made in accordance with instructions that the Chinese people receive from a vast display in the sky, which is visible to all of them. The instructions are such that the participating Chinese people function like individual neurons, and the radio links like synapses, so that together the Chinese people duplicate the causal organization of a human brain down to a very fine-grained level. Block claims that intuitively, this system does not undergo any experiences or feelings. Since the system is possible and it is functionally equivalent to a normal human being, it supposedly presents an illustration of the absent qualia hypothesis. Block concludes that functional organization is not what determines or fixes phenomenal consciousness.

It is important to understand what is being claimed about the China-Body system to appreciate the full force of the example. The claim is not that the individual Chinese people do not undergo experiences and feelings as they participate in the game. That obviously is false. The claim is rather that we have a strong intuition that the system *as a whole*, of which the individual Chinese people are parts, does not feel or experience anything – that it is the wrong sort of thing to undergo experiences and feelings.

The problem of duplicates, then, amounts to the following questions: Are zombie replicas possible? Are total functional duplicates without any phenomenal consciousness possible? If so, what does this tell us about phenomenal consciousness?

The Problem of the Inverted Spectrum

The classic inverted spectrum argument goes as follows. Suppose that Tom has a very peculiar visual system. His color experiences are systematically inverted with respect to those of his fellows. When Tom looks at red objects, for example, what it's like for him is the same as what it's like for other people when they look at green objects and vice versa. This peculiarity is one of which neither he nor others are aware. Tom has learned the meanings of color words in the usual way and he applies these words correctly. Moreover, his non-linguistic behavior is standard in every way.

Now when Tom views a ripe tomato, say, in good light, his experience is phenomenally, subjectively, different from the experiences you and I undergo. But his experience is *functionally* just like ours. For his experience is of the sort that is usually produced in him by viewing red objects (in the same sort of way that our experiences of red are produced) and that usually leads him (again in parallel fashion) to believe that a red object is present. In short, his experience functions in just the same way as ours. So the phenomenal quality of Tom's experience is not a matter of its functional role. This conclusion cannot be accepted by any philosopher who wants to analyze, or understand, phenomenal consciousness functionally. But what, if anything, is wrong with the above reasoning? This is the problem of the inverted spectrum (Lycan 1973; Shoemaker 1982).

One way to fix the puzzle clearly in your mind is to imagine that you are operated upon by microsurgeons who alter some of the connections between neurons in your visual system. These alterations have the effect of making neurons that used to fire as a result of retinal cell activity produced by viewing red objects now fire in response to such cell activity produced by seeing green objects and vice versa. Upon awakening from the operation, you find the world very weird indeed. Your lawn now looks red to you, the trees are varying shades of red and purple, the flamingo statues that decorated your garden look light green instead of pink. These changes in your experiences will be reflected in your behavior, for example, in your verbal reports. So, there will be straightforward evidence that an inversion has occurred.

Now suppose that the microsurgeons operated upon you at birth, so that you learn to apply color vocabulary to things with anomalous looks. For you, these looks are not anomalous, of course. So, you use color terms in precisely the same circumstances as everyone else. Is this not imaginable? If we agree it is, however difficult it might be in practice to produce such an inversion, then functionally identical inverted experiences are metaphysically possible. So functionalism cannot be the truth about phenomenal consciousness.

The problem of the inverted spectrum is sometimes presented with respect to a single individual who, after the operation described two paragraphs ago, adapts to it through time and eventually forgets that things ever looked any different to him. In this case, it is suggested (Putnam 1981; Block 1990), the later person is subject to visual experiences which are functionally isomorphic to the earlier ones but which are subjectively different.

So, the problem of the inverted spectrum amounts to the following questions: Can two people who are functionally identical undergo experiences that are phenomenally inverted? Can one person, at different times, undergo experiences that are phenomenally inverted but functionally identical? Can there be phenomenal inversion in the case of microphysical duplication? What should we conclude about phenomenal consciousness from reflection upon inverted experiences?

The Problem of Transparency

Suppose that you are standing before a tapestry in an art gallery. As you take in the rich and varied colors of the cloth, you are told to pay close attention to your visual experience and its phenomenology. What do you do? Many philosophers claim that you attend closely to the *tapestry* and the details in it. You are aware of something outside you – the tapestry – and of various qualities that you experience as being qualities of parts of the tapestry, and by being aware of these things, you are aware of what it's like for you subjectively or phenomenally. But your awareness of what it's like, of the phenomenology of your experience, is not awareness *of* the experience or its qualities. It is awareness *that* you have an experience with a certain phenomenal character or "feel."

Here is another example to illustrate these preliminary points. Suppose that you have just entered a friend's country house for the first time and you are standing in the living room, looking out at a courtyard filled with flowers. It seems to you that the room is open, that you can walk straight out into the courtyard. You try to do so and, alas, you bang hard into a sheet of glass, which extends from ceiling to floor and separates the courtyard from the room. You bang into the glass because you do not see it. You are not aware of it, nor are you aware of any of its qualities. No matter how hard you peer, you cannot discern the glass. It is transparent to you. You see right through it to the flowers beyond. You are aware of the flowers, not by being aware of the glass, but by being aware of the facing surfaces of the flowers. And in being aware of these surfaces, you are also aware of a myriad of qualities that seem to you to belong to these surfaces. You may not be able to name or describe these qualities but they look to you to qualify the surfaces. You experience them as being qualities of the surfaces. None of the qualities of which you are directly aware in seeing the various surfaces look to you to be qualities of your experience. You do not experience any of these qualities as qualities of your experience. For example, if redness is one of the qualities and roundness another, you do not experience your experience as red or round.

If your friend tells you that there are several ceiling-to-floor sheets of glass in the house and that they all produce a subtle change in the light passing through them so that things seen from the other side appear more vividly colored than is usually the case, as you walk gingerly into the next room, you may become aware that there is another partitioning sheet of glass before you by being aware of the qualities that appear to belong to non-glass surfaces before your eyes. You are not aware of the second sheet of glass any more than you were aware of the first; but you are now aware that there is a sheet of glass in the room by being aware of qualities apparently possessed by non-glass surfaces before you.

Visual experiences, according to many philosophers, are like such sheets of glass. Peer as hard as you like via introspection, focus your attention in any way you please, and you will only come across surfaces, volumes, films, and their apparent qualities. Visual experiences thus are transparent to their subjects (Moore 1922). We are not introspectively aware of our visual experiences any more than we are perceptually aware of transparent sheets of glass. If we try to focus on our experiences, we see right through them to the world outside. By being aware of the qualities apparently possessed by surfaces, volumes, etc., we become aware that we are undergoing visual experiences. But we are not aware of the experiences themselves. This is true, even if we are hallucinating. It is just that in this case the qualities apparently possessed by surfaces, volumes, etc. before our eyes are not so possessed. The surfaces, volumes, etc. do not exist.

Introspection, on the view just presented, is importantly like displaced perception or secondary seeing-that. When I see that the gas tank is nearly empty by seeing the gas gauge or when I see that the door has been forced by seeing the marks on the door, I do not see the gas tank or the forcing of the door. My seeing-that is secondary or displaced. I am not aware – I am not conscious – of either the gas tank or the forcing of the door. I am aware of something else – the gas gauge or the marks on the door – and by being aware of this other thing, I am aware that so-and-so is the case.

Similarly, in the case of introspection of a visual experience, I am not aware or conscious of the experience itself. I am aware that I am having a certain sort of experience by being aware of something other than the experience of the surfaces apparently outside and their apparent qualities (Tye 2000).

What is true for vision is true for the other senses. Attending to the phenomenology of a perceptual experience, to its felt character, is a matter of attending to the ways things look, smell, taste, sound, or feel by touch. In the case of bodily sensations, the object of your attention is the way a certain part of your body feels. With emotions and moods, the attentional focus is often on things outside – things perceived as dangerous, foul, or pleasing – but there is also attention to the ways in which one's body is changing (pounding heart, shaky legs, higher blood pressure). More generally, attention to phenomenal character is a matter of attention to the ways things other than the experience seem, that is, to qualities that are not qualities of experiences.

Not all philosophers accept that experiences are transparent in the way described above. But if the transparency thesis is correct, an explanation is needed for how experiences can be transparent and yet also have phenomenal character. What is it about phenomenal consciousness that is responsible for its diaphanous character?

The Problem of Unity

There is no one problem of unity for experiences, and there is no one kind of unity either. One important focus of recent investigation in cognitive psychology and neurophysiology has been how the visual system brings together information about shape and color. If I view a green, circular object, the greenness and roundness I experience are represented in different parts of my visual system. In my experience, however, the color and shape are unified. I experience a *single* green, circular object. I notice and report on only one such object. How can this be? How are the color and shape unified as belonging to a single object in my consciousness? This is often called "the binding problem" and the kind of unity it concerns is *object unity*.

One putative solution to the binding problem at the neurological level is that there is a common neuronal oscillation (40 Hz) that binds together the relevant neural events. This is known as the 40 Hz hypothesis (Crick & Koch 1990). The main philosophical problem of unity for experiences does not concern object unity, however. It concerns phenomenal unity (see Dainton, chapter 16). One version of it may be brought out in the following way. Suppose that at midday a wine taster is tasting a Cabernet Sauvignon. He sees the red wine in the wine glass beneath his nose, as he brings the wine to his lips. He smells the rich bouquet of the wine, as he tastes its fruity flavor in his mouth; and in tasting it, he experiences the liquid touching his tongue and the back of his mouth. Perhaps, as he does this, he flicks a finger against the glass, thereby producing a high-pitched sound. One way to describe the wine taster's phenomenal state is to say that he has an experience of a certain colored shape, *and* further, he has an experience of a certain smell, *and,* in addition, he has an experience of a taste *and* . . . etc. But intuitively, this is unsatisfactory. It misses something out: the unity of these experiences. There is something it's like for the wine taster *overall* at midday, as he brings the wine to his lips and smells and tastes it. There is a unified phenomenology. How can this be? After all, it is natural to suppose that the wine taster here is subject to five separate experiences, each one produced by the operation of a single sense. If this is the case – if the wine taster is undergoing five different simultaneous perceptual experiences – how can it be, phenomenologically, as if he were undergoing one? How is it that the five experiences are phenomenologically unified? Of course, for each of these experiences, there is something it's like to undergo the experience. But there is also something it's like to have these experiences together. And that remains to be accounted for.

Here is another example. Holding a ripe apple in my hand, I experience a red surface and I experience a cold surface. These experiences are not experienced in isolation, however. They are experienced together. This is part of the phenomenology of my experience overall. There is a unity in my experience. Of what does this unity consist, given that I am subject to two different particular experiences, one visual and one tactual?

The above version of the philosophical problem of unity for experiences pertains to unity at a time. But there is also a problem of unity through time too. As I rub my forefinger with my thumb and I feel the smoothness of the skin, my experience of smoothness is not merely a succession of independent momentary experiences of smoothness. It is a continuous sensation. This continuing of the sensation is not just an objective fact about it. It is something I experience, or so it is standardly supposed. The streamlike quality of the sensation is itself a phenomenal feature. This is true for experiences generally. My experience of a dull pain that lasts several minutes has a continuous character to it that is itself experienced. Change is experienced too. If my pain suddenly changes from being dull and constant to throbbing, I experience this change in it. Thinking through something, I undergo a sequence of successive thoughts. It is sometimes held that the continuity in my thoughts, their succession one after another, is something I experience. What accounts for the phenomenal unity of our experiences through time? As William James (1952) put it:

A succession of feelings, in and of itself, is not a feeling of succession. And since, to our successive feelings, a feeling of their own succession is added, that must be treated as an additional
fact requiring its own special elucidation . . .

This is the philosophical problem of unity *through* time.

The Problem of Divided Consciousness

The human brain is divided into two more or less symmetrical hemispheres. The surgical
removal of one of these hemispheres does not eliminate consciousness and neither does
cutting the many connections of the corpus callosum between hemispheres. The latter
operation, originally performed by Roger Sperry in the 1960s on some epileptic patients,
with the aim of controlling epileptic seizures, has a remarkable consequence. In addition
to reducing greatly the number and intensity of the seizures themselves, it also produces a
kind of mental bifurcation in the epileptic patients (Sperry 1968).

Here is an illustration. A subject, S, is told to stare fixedly at the center of a translucent
screen which fills his visual field. Two words are flashed onto the screen by means of a projec-
tor located behind, one to the left of the fixation point and one to the right. Let us suppose the
words used are "pen" and "knife." The words are flashed very quickly (for just 1/10 of a second)
so that eye movements from one word to the other are not possible. This arrangement is one
that ensures that the word on the left (i.e., "pen") provides input only to the right hemisphere
of the brain and the word on the right (i.e., "knife") provides input only to the left.

S is then asked what he saw. S shows no awareness, in his verbal responses, of "pen."
However, if S is asked to retrieve the object corresponding to the word he saw from a group
of objects concealed from sight, using his left hand alone, he will pick out a pen while rejecting knives. Alternatively, if S is asked to point with his left hand to the object corresponding
to the word he saw, he will point to a pen. Moreover, if S is asked to sort through the group
of objects using both hands, he will pick out a pen with his left and a knife with his right. In
this case, the two hands work independently with the left rejecting the knives in the group
and the right rejecting the pens. (For further detail, see Colvin and Gazzaniga, chapter 14.)

What are we to make of this phenomenon? Evidently, there is a kind of disunity in the
mental life of split-brain subjects. But just where psychologically is the unity best located?
Is it at the level of phenomenal consciousness? And what, if anything, does the behavior of
split-brain subjects tell us about the nature of persons and the relationship of personal identity to a unified consciousness? This is the problem of divided consciousness.

Philosophers who have discussed split-brain subjects have variously suggested that:

1   split-brain subjects are really two persons having two separate minds (Pucetti 1972);
2   that the responses produced by the right hemisphere are those of an unconscious autom-
    aton (Parfit 1987);
3   that it is indeterminate how many persons split-brain subjects are and that the concept
    of a person is thrown into jeopardy by the experimental results (Nagel 1971);
4   that split-brain subjects have a unified phenomenal consciousness but a disunified access
    consciousness (Bayne & Chalmers 2003);
5   that split-brain subjects are single persons who undergo two separate streams of con-
    sciousness that remain two from the time of the commissurotomy (Parfit 1987);

6 that split-brain subjects are single persons whose phenomenal consciousness is briefly split into two under certain special experimental conditions, but whose consciousness at other times is unified (Marks 1980).

On some of these proposals, there is really no division in the consciousness of a single person; on others, there is such a division but only at the level of access; on others, there is a genuine split in the phenomenal consciousness of the subject.

These are not the only philosophical problems of consciousness, but they are some of the most puzzling ones (see also Chalmers, chapter 17). Together they form perhaps the hardest nut to crack in all of philosophy – so hard that some philosophers of mind, not generally opposed to substantive philosophical theorizing, see little or no hope of coming to a satisfactory understanding of phenomenal consciousness.

See also 14 Split-brain cases; 15 Philosophical psychopathology and self-consciousness; 16 Coming together: the unity of conscious experience; 17 The hard problem of consciousness; 29 Anti-materialist arguments and influential replies; 30 Functionalism and qualia; 31 The knowledge argument; 35 Sensory and perceptual consciousness.

Further Readings

Chalmers, D. (1996) *The Conscious Mind*. Oxford: Oxford University Press.
Dretske, F. (1995) *Naturalizing the Mind*. Cambridge, MA: MIT Press, Bradford Books.
Tye, M. (1995) *Ten Problems of Consciousness: A Representational Theory of the Phenomenal Mind*. Cambridge, MA: MIT Press, Bradford Books.
Tye, M. (2003) *Consciousness and Persons: Unity and Identity*. Cambridge: MA: MIT Press, Bradford Books.

References

Bayne, T. and Chalmers, D. (2003) What is the unity of consciousness? In A. Cleeremans (ed.), *The Unity of Consciousness: Binding, Integration, Dissociation*, 23–58. Oxford: Oxford University Press.
Block, N. (1980) Troubles with functionalism. In Ned Block (ed.), *Readings in the Philosophy of Psychology*, vol. 1, 268–305. Cambridge, MA: Harvard University Press.
Block, N. (1990) Inverted earth. In J. Tomberlin (ed.), *Philosophical Perspectives* 4, 53–79. Atascadero, CA: Ridgeview.
Block, N. (1995) On a confusion about a function of consciousness. *Behavioral and Brain Science* 18, 227–47.
Crick, F. and Koch, C. (1990) Towards a neurobiological theory of consciousness. *Seminars in the Neurosciences* 2, 263–75.
Huxley, T. (1866) *Lessons on Elementary Physiology*. London: Macmillan.
Jackson, F. (1982) Epiphenomenal qualia. *Philosophical Quarterly* 32, 127–36.
James, W. (1952) *The Principles of Psychology*. Chicago: Encyclopedia Britannica.
Levine, J. (1983) Materialism and qualia: the explanatory gap. *Pacific Philosophical Quarterly* 64, 354–61.
Lycan, W. (1973) Inverted spectrum. *Ratio* 15, 315–19.
McGinn, C. (1991) *The Problem of Consciousness*. Oxford: Blackwell.

Marks, C. (1980) *Commissurotomy, Consciousness and the Unity of Mind*. Cambridge, MA: MIT Press, Bradford Books.

Moore, G. E. (1922) The refutation of idealism. In *Philosophical Studies*. London: Routledge and Kegan Paul.

Nagel, T. (1979) *Mortal Questions*. Cambridge: Cambridge University Press.

Nagel, T. (1971) Brain bisection and the unity of consciousness. *Synthese* 22, 396–413.

Parfit, D. (1987) Divided minds and the nature of persons. In C. Blakemore and S. Greenfield (eds.), *Mindwaves*, 19–26. Oxford: Blackwell.

Pucetti, R. (1972) Multiple identity. *The Personalist* 54, 203–15.

Putnam, H. (1981) *Reason, Truth, and History*. Cambridge: Cambridge University Press.

Shoemaker, S. (1982) The inverted spectrum. *Journal of Philosophy* 79, 357–81.

Sperry, R. (1968) Hemisphere deconnection and unity in conscious awareness. *American Psychologist* 23, 723–33.

Tye, M. (2000) *Consciousness, Color, and Content*. Cambridge, MA: MIT Press, Bradford Books.

Part II

THE DOMAIN OF CONSCIOUSNESS

ORIGINS AND EXTENT OF CONSCIOUSNESS

3

Consciousness in Infants

COLWYN TREVARTHEN AND VASUDEVI REDDY

Primary Human Consciousness: Its Natural Origins and Growth in Human Company

In this chapter, we review evidence that infants, although they cannot speak to us about it, are conscious, not just "preconscious." We believe that it is important for an understanding of adult consciousness that an infant is perceived to engage actively and emotionally with the consciousness of other persons.

In the first two years, infants develop rational skills and gain a richer awareness by exercising a range of innate capacities of body and brain that are specifically adapted to learn from the inter-mental human world (Trevarthen 2004a). They acquire a cultural "human sense" of things by communicating in humorous ways with other persons (Reddy 2003). Their uniquely human awareness has conspicuous biological foundations. Organs of perception and action for communicating consciousness with other people form in the body and brain of a fetus, and there are signs that foetal expressions and senses are active and responsive before birth (Trevarthen 2004b; Trevarthen et al. 2006).

We focus on *intention* in the earliest movements. Conscious awareness is adapted to detect the prospects for actions that have definite purposes in the outside world. Infants apparently sense that their bodies are separate from that world. We look for signs that infants perceive that objects and persons are different and have different uses. We trace evidence for grades of conscious agency that depend on innate emotions of sympathy for other persons' rhythmic, "musical," patterns of intention, and that lead to understanding of what older persons' more elaborately conscious minds are knowing and intending (Trevarthen 1998). Finally, we will consider what infant consciousness contributes to language learning – how narrative-making talk becomes a tool for a child's conventional, socially adapted self-consciousness and personality (Trevarthen 2004c).

We define *primary consciousness* as manifested in how the body of any animal is coordinated in its movements as a single agent, or "self," engaged with the world, and how the body-related anticipations of these movements in the brain project feelings onto the perceived world's properties, determining what will and will not be learned. Consciousness, as herein conceived, is the integrated neural activity in body-representing systems that coordinates perception-in-action-in-the-environment, enabling an animal to move in its world as it intends, safely, and with benefit to felt needs (Merker 2005).

Primary human consciousness, much evolved from humbler ways of life, has unique powers, especially in the social or interpersonal realm (Donaldson 1992). Many highly developed social animals respond with insight to the impulses and feelings of individuals of their own and other species, showing intersubjective consciousness (Smuts 2001). Human infants, however, show evidence of a richer sociability – a *cultural intersubjectivity*. Transmission of intelligence from generation to generation in many artificial forms, including language, depends on inherent capacities for acting in intimate mutual awareness of the intentions, feelings, and beliefs of other individuals in ways that no other species of animal can do.

How Can Infant Consciousness Be Proved?

Philosophers, psychologists, and now brain scientists, frequently examine conscious awareness by a combination of introspection and verbal report. Most investigations are carried out with fabricated visual stimuli, and with the subject doing little with their bodies but respond to experimental questions. Research on the control of movements and the learning of new skills in moving is more relevant to investigation of infant consciousness (Lacerda, von Hofsten, & Heimann 2001), and ecological perception theory broadens the enquiry, proposing that what is perceived in all modalities are "affordances" for moving – information the subject takes up to guide actions with appropriate prospective control (Lee 2004).

Infants, by definition, can give no verbal report, and they are not often cooperative subjects in controlled experiments where they are expected to attend to what the experimenter decides is the question. It is more productive to study the infant's preferences. Evidence of the limits and sensitivity of their awareness has been obtained by stimulus-response methods and "classical conditioning," but the richest data have been gained by recording preferential looking at pairs of stimuli, by examining the recovery from habituation when a repeating stimulus changes, and by "operant conditioning," in which the infant actively generates stimuli and learns from what they cause to happen. In his classical investigations of the development of object concepts Piaget (1954) used a "clinical method" of testing, matching problems to be solved to the infant's own actions of orientation and manipulation. Variations of this experimental method have been employed to greatly enrich understanding of the growth of cognitive abilities before language.

Infant psychology has been an intensely active field for several decades (see Donaldson 1992; Lacerda, von Hofsten, & Heimann 2001; Trevarthen & Aitken 2003). The movements infants make to track the motions, appearances and disappearances, and transformations of objects prove that they are capable, even in early months, of predicting paths of motion to intercept objects. Their awareness of the location, three-dimensional form and substance of things can be revealed by recording how they control their actions – sucking, looking, touching, tracking, reaching, and grasping. This research has found that the *timing* of movements is crucial to their prospective control, voluntary movements being rhythmic and guided to their goals with a periodicity and a modulation of acceleration imposed from the brain (Lee 2004). But, all these ways of experimenting with infants' sentience and discriminations have an important limitation – they consider infants as individuals, and fail to investigate their precocious talents for communicating with people.

A quite different view of the infant mind has come from microanalysis of film and video records of the expressive movements the infant makes in communication, while they are engaged in immediate response to the expressive movements of another person (Newson 1977; Bullowa 1979). This has led to recognition of emotional life specific to intersubjective relationships (Trevarthen 1998). Research on early social consciousness meets that concerned with infant mental health, and the dependence of a child's future well-being on intimate affectionate regulation within parental care (Bowlby 1988; Trevarthen 2005b; Trevarthen et al. 2006). Evidence of infants' consciousness of persons as companions in learning has also become of central importance for guiding early education (Rogoff 2003).

Infant Consciousness Is Active, Emotional, and Communicative

An infant shows consciousness by moving in interested, selectively attentive, and well-coordinated volitional ways, showing emotions about what happens. This is demonstrated, for example, when a 3-month-old "works" in an "operant" apparatus in which the baby can control the presentation and timing of audible or visible stimuli by head or limb movements (e.g., Papousek 1967). The baby repeats actions to control the contingent events, and learns to make predictions. If these predictions are correct and bring the expected result, the infant shows joy; if they fail, for whatever reason, the infant shows annoyance or disappointment and becomes avoidant. As Papousek says, the infant reacts "in human ways" to the events – with expressions that invite sharing of feelings about what they do, and about what happens.

The same kind of emotional responses to interruptions in "the game" are seen when the mother of a 2-month-old presents an artificially impassive and unresponsive "still" or "blank" face after communicating cheerfully, or when, in a double video communication set-up, in which mother and baby are in different rooms and communicating with one another's televised image, the recording of the mothers normal chatting behavior is replayed so the infant's expectations of contingent communicative response are violated (Murray & Trevarthen 1985; Trevarthen 2005a; Tronick 2005). Close observation of young infants communicating demonstrates that an "expectation" of well-timed and harmoniously modulated responses from a partner in communication is innate, and that it is regulated by dynamic emotional, rhythmic, expressions of sympathetic "attunement" (Papousek et al. 1990; Malloch 1999; Trevarthen 1999, 2005a; Stern 2000, 2004; Jaffe et al. 2001; Tronick 2005).

Infants' emotions compare in general features with the emotions generated by inherent "affective neural systems" in other mammals that regulate vital functions of the individual, engagements with the environment and social contacts and relationships (Panksepp 2000; see also Panksepp, chapter 8; Trevarthen 2005a, 2005b). They communicate with voice, face, and hands both curiosity about the world and their felt needs for comfort and security. Movements of eyes, pupils, lids, and brows, show the aim and intensity of interest and changes in how the infant feels about the success of expectations. The lower face expresses joy and sadness, wonder and anger, and liking or loathing, all important to other persons (Darwin 1872). There is disagreement about how to classify facial expressions of emotion, whether of infants or adults, but they are of rich variety in infants and have immediate emotive effects on parents (Oster 2005). The search for simple basic emotion "action units" has limited success, and there is evidence that complex dynamic social emotions, including moral ones of "pride," "shame," "jealousy," "shyness," and "showing off" that make interpersonal evaluations, are felt and expressed by infants with powerful effect on others (Reddy 2003, 2005; Trevarthen 2005b).

Innate Rhythms of the Infant Mind, and Their Importance in Communication and the Development of Consciousness

Infants are born exhibiting the rhythmic pulse of action that coordinates several limbs and many senses in regulated ways (Trevarthen 1999). This pulse divides what the self sees, hears, and feels, inside and outside its body, into "moments of contact" in phenomenal awareness (Stern 2004). For sure, conscious experience is enormously enriched in child-hood by learning the features, categories, and qualities of things that can be known and communicated about in language, out of time and out of place – but these semantic ele-ments that guide more intelligent actions and thoughts, and elaborate their sequential coordination or syntax, are first learned by means of carefully chosen experiences shared nonverbally (Trevarthen 2004c). The first real-world experience is driven wordlessly by inherent motives that determine the timing of object-directed, emotionally regulated and ordered actions (Trevarthen 2005a).

The rhythms and expressive qualities of infants' actions are immediately appreciated by the awareness of human partners who share the thinking implied in them (Hobson 2002). Recent research has proved that, from birth, infants have flexible parameters of timing and regulation of expression or dynamic control in movement that match those demonstrated as basic in adult actions and communicative expressions (Trevarthen 1999; Jaffe et al. 2001). However, although the fundamental rhythms of adults and infants appear to be the same, one difficulty for a researcher seeking to fathom the consciousness of infants is that infants "think," or track events, slowly. When an experimenter wants to test responses to change with an infant who is already showing attention to the proffered lure or target, it is necessary to moderate the rate of change or displacement. For example, under the age of 4 months, an infant cannot match the velocity of an object in motion with a smooth trajectory of eye movements – tracking is a "saccadic" series of steps (Trevarthen & Aitken 2003).

Our adult capacity for "multi-tasking" in thought appears to be dependent on multiple recollections of action in the world, including the social world where many distinct protag-onists, with their own intentions, may be represented. A young infant appears to act in the present, in one-on-one encounters, later gaining capacities to predict changes and to make quick shifts of purpose, and gaining adroit sociability. Margaret Donaldson (1992) judges that infants are conscious in the "point mode" of "here and now." But, experiments show that a baby a few months old can connect experiences lived at different times or consider several factors that could affect the outcome of his or her actions, especially when those factors are other persons.

Experimental research on infants' "knowing" seeks evidence about how the infant "constructs" schemas to know objects and physical events by acting to test and learn their properties. These schemas are retained to represent the "permanence" of object identi-ties (Piaget 1954; Lacerda, von Hofsten, & Heimann 2001). "Object relations" with other humans are, likewise, described as persistent internal working models of life events with the attachment figure, their construction being directed by innate responses of a mammalian kind that seek proximity to a protective mother and that feel comfort from her touch, breast milk, loving eyes, and affectionate voice, attracting her as an "external regulator" of physiological states (Bowlby 1988).

Processing information and regulating emotions in attachment relationships are indeed vital activities, but an infant seeks more from emotional experiences in human company (Hobson 2002; Trevarthen 2004a, 2005b). To understand the development of consciousness of meaning in the world, we must observe, without preconceptions, how the infant *chooses* to engage with the perceived world in its natural richness, and with others (Stern 2004; Tronick 2005). Expressions of infants' feelings as they attempt to perform tasks give information about what they *want* the world to be like (Papousek 1967; Trevarthen 2005a). By tracing age-related events, it is possible to give an account of how the biological endowment for being a conscious and communicative human being is elaborated and enriched through infancy by learning from experience (Trevarthen & Aitken 2003).

Newborn Consciousness (Figure 3.1)

Evidence that a premature newborn can be conscious comes from observing how an "aroused" baby can move in coordinated ways and with selective orientation to events outside the body (Lecanuet et al. 1995). The power and "grace" of these movements appear to signal regulation of the risks and benefits of moving as these are detected by the newborn's "affective consciousness" (Panksepp 2000). They are important clinical signs of neurological health (Lecanuet et al. 1995; Trevarthen & Aitken 2003). A full-term newborn turns to track and may point or vocalize to a moving object nearby, or to the sound of a mother's voice. A touch on the cheek attracts the mouth for suckling. The heart slows with intent looking or listening. Blinking and conjugate saccades above a few degrees are well developed and newborns can look to a gentle voice in the dark. Vision has low resolution at first, but acuity develops rapidly in the first two months (Trevarthen & Aitken 2003).

Cognitive psychologists propose that infants are born with "core concepts" or strategies for learning that are adapted to perceive natural phenomena (Lacerda, von Hofsten, & Heimann 2001). But a newborn is not just conceiving solid continuous objects, concave spaces, physical motions or pattern changes. He or she is particularly sensitive to stimuli from people and is ready to identify a caregiver (Trevarthen 1998; Stern 2000; Hobson 2002). Inborn skills assisting maternal care include grasping hold of the mother, orienting to and feeding from her breast, recognizing her odor and voice, and seeking to look at and know her face (Lecanuet et al. 1995; Trevarthen et al. 2006). Complex suckling movements are guided prospectively by patterns of neuron activity so the baby can interrupt breathing to draw in then swallow milk without choking (Lee 2004).

A baby looks longer at the mother's face than a stranger's a few hours after birth, even when all other sensory cues are excluded. Knowing the mother's voice and odor from prenatal experience helps this rapid visual learning. The baby reacts to facial expressions of emotion and can imitate "artificially marked" expressions of another person, for example, emphatic eye closing, tongue protrusion or finger extensions (Meltzoff & Moore 1999). Imitations of face, voice, and hand gestures within minutes of birth prove to be intentional acts, multimodally regulated, that are adapted to engage with other sympathetic or "respectful" persons, as Giannis Kugiumutzakis has demonstrated (see Hobson 2002), and these responses show up individual differences (Heimann 2002). A baby is born motivated to

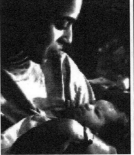

Figure 3.1 Primary human consciousness of objects and persons.

Left: A newborn baby, 20-minutes old, is evidently interested in an object outside his body and orients his eyes, mouth, ears, hands, and one foot to track it. *Right:* A baby girl, 30-minutes old, takes an active part in imitating the expressions of an adult. (photos Kevan Bundell)

know human beings and their emotions in a personal, self-related way, and to communicate this knowing in other-awareness.

A newborn infant can also "invite" or "provoke" an imitation, taking the *initiative* (Nagy & Molnár 2004). The exchange then becomes a dialog, animated by the adult's anticipation and pleasure and by the infant's emotions: the pulse of the baby's heart accelerates just before the baby imitates a movement, but slows when the baby is about to "provocate." Occasionally, the imitated infant may smile. The infant and adult have feelings of a subtle sympathy promoting co-consciousness (Hobson 2002; Tronick 2005), not just "external regulation" of one another's physiological state. From the start, the dynamic generation of sympathetic rhythms is a bridge of "attunement" between the vitality of minds (Stern 2000). They take turns in "asserting" or "showing" and "apprehending" or "receiving" human will and interest.

The "Musicality" of Protoconversation at 2 Months

By 6 weeks, the infant responds to contingent human signals with smiles, hand gestures, and cooing in the first "protoconversations" (Bullowa 1979; Trevarthen 1998). The infant shares rhythms of address and reply (Newson 1977; Jaffe et al. 2001), and the affectionate talk of a parent that pleases a young baby has the formal structure of music or poetry (Trevarthen 1999; Dissanayake 2000).

A mother "chatting" with a 2-month-old responds intuitively to the expectant gaze and expressions of hands, face, and voice. Cycles of excitement, with expressions of affectionate pleasure, display "socio-dramatic episodes," or "emotional narrative envelopes" extending beyond the few seconds of the "psychological present" (Stern 2004). As described above, when the "dance" between infant and mother is ruptured by experimental procedures, the infant expresses withdrawal and distress, and a depressed mother who cannot sympathize with her infant's efforts to communicate is also confronted with discomfort and withdrawal (Murray & Cooper 1997).

The mechanism for regulating a flexible rhythmic "improvisation" of moving with another person is innate (Trevarthen 1999). A 2-month-premature infant (32 weeks gestational age) has been videoed in an intimate vocal exchange with the father while resting under his shirt against his chest in "kangarooing." Spectrographic microanalysis of the short "coo" sounds, in which the father imitated the infant, shows that both infant and adult were "imagining" the same intervals of time, for syllables (0.7 seconds) and phrases (4.0 seconds), to pace the alternation of sounds (Malloch 1999). When the father paused, the infant sustained expectation over several seconds, and regulated the intersubjective contingency of events with that time base. She had an "internal guide" or action clock (Lee 2004) that estimated when the father should "coo" to be "in time" with her.

From 6 Weeks to 6 Months: Tightening up Movements and Sharpening Awareness; Exploring and Using Things

As the infant's body grows, head and limb action become stronger, and the baby spends more hours awake and alert. The world away from the body is sensed more clearly and examined more deeply. Reaching out and fingering with the hands under visual guidance increases after 3 months. Turning the head and arms tracks objects smoothly, and resting postures are more coherent. Evidently the "feel" of the body is "tighter." Locating hidden sounds also becomes more accurate, especially in light. Anticipatory heart-rate change when attention is narrowed to one modality, to look or listen or to feel with the hands, develops over 2 to 6 months, and the infant becomes skilled at shifting attention quickly between lateral and central parts of the visual field (Trevarthen & Aitken 2003).

Infants over 3 months are curious, learning categories of objects and animals and noting spatial relations between manipulated objects. Sensitivity to contingent motion helps learning of live movements and animate displays (Markova & Legerstee 2006). Cognitive achievements (what is being perceived and learned) are part of the infant's powers of intention, and they grow as intentions grow. Infants are more playful and socially "self–other conscious" from this time on, attracted to have "fun" with willing playmates, which escapes the attention of studies that are directed to elucidating the infants' mastery of physical phenomena, or their reactions to events as "little scientists." They expect to have particular "games" with individuals they know well, and are receptive to others' feelings about them. But by 3 months, infants look about more, are less attentive to the mother for herself, and are gaining interest for sharing games with objects they want to look at and grasp in the hands (Trevarthen 2004a, 2005a). A simple disruption of communication is not so distressing for a baby as it was at 2 months. The infant can now shift interest to somewhere else to escape an unresponsive person; indeed the older infant can take the lead in "disrupting" communication playfully, to "tease" or make a "joke" (Reddy 2003, 2005).

After 4 months, infants are cooperative subjects in tests of what they can see and hear. They watch displays and listen attentively, track motions, and orient quickly, and they soon become bored or "habituated" with repeated stimuli, alerting when a new event occurs. Their choices between stimuli in tests prove that they develop stereoscopic vision to detect small differences in the 3-D image of nearby objects, which aids precise manipulation, and they have a rich color vision that detects people, earth, and sky, and the substance of objects. In the past 50 years, much has been discovered about what a baby can be conscious of, and the results have surprised philosophers and psychologists. Age-related advances reflect changes in investigative motives for handling, seeing, and hearing things, as well as motives to communicate and play with other people – they are not just manifestations of the influence of mere exposure to stimuli from physical configurations and events (Lacerda, von Hofsten, & Heimann 2001; Trevarthen & Aitken 2003).

Tests of what infants notice about what other people do have been especially rewarding. Vocal pattern recognition is proficient at 6 months, rhythms of syllabic sounds are quickly learned and native language contrasts in speech begin to affect the baby's vocalizations. Words for objects that interest the infant are noticed first – both frequency and social value of utterances clearly influence learning (Locke 1993; Lacerda, von Hofsten, & Heimann 2001; Trevarthen 2004c). The detection of speech depends on sight as well as hearing. Infants expect mouth movements of speakers facing them to match and synchronize with the sounds produced in the speech. But the greatest sensitivity and interest of infants at this age is, as it was earlier, in the affective tone of utterances. Babies are sensing the qualities of human experiences in the very complex sound world of the home (Lacerda, von Hofsten, & Heimann 2001).

Sharing Routines and Rituals: Performing "Musically," and Showing Off a Personality (Figure 3.2)

Four- or 6-month-olds exhibit growing talents of "communicative musicality" (Malloch 1999). They are attracted to rhythmic melodies and dance to simple songs, responding to changes of pulse, loudness, pitch, and "voice quality" or vocal timbre of the singer, and are especially alert to rhyming vowels that mark the climaxes and conclusions of principle phrases (Papousek et al. 1990; Trevarthen 1999). Parents use baby songs and nonsense "chants," crooning, humming, etc., to entertain the baby, to regulate activity or "arousal," or to distract and calm one who is tired, angry, or in pain. An alert and cheerful infant anticipates the climax and resolution in a song game, moving in rhythm and synchronizing pleasure vocalizations with the closing cadence. Long before the infant can stand, the innate pulses of walking, from *presto* to *largo*, form the time base of their expressive actions, as in the diverse cultural traditions of music. The beat of experience on the move is born in us and used to communicate, even while the brain is acquiring mastery of emergent biomechanical problems presented by a growing body, and attempting new ways of using the environment (Clark 1999; Lee 2004).

A baby who has learned to display hand rhythms for a clapping song may respond to a prompt by showing clapping, with an intent regard and a broad smile of pride (Trevarthen 2005a, 2005b; Figure 3.2). The showing is a "declaration" referring to a past event charged with emotion, offered for sharing with known others. The fact that the behavior so presented is marked as something valued or "special" makes it a work of art (Dissanayake 2000). We conclude that sharing meaning with prideful artistry is a primary human motive for cultural learning. It attracts "teaching" by "intent participation" – a kind of teaching/learning where a more experienced person works with a novice in construction and completion of a well-intended or "meaningful" task, scaffolding what the learner does and sharing inventions, purposes, and evaluations (Rogoff 2003). Without the kind of satisfaction of shared learning that comes with the interest and admiration of others to whom the child is attached, the child's life with *all* others can lose its energy and pleasure.

Around the middle of the first year, infants become adventurous, playful, and emotionally demonstrative, and they watch the emotions others display to events and objects,

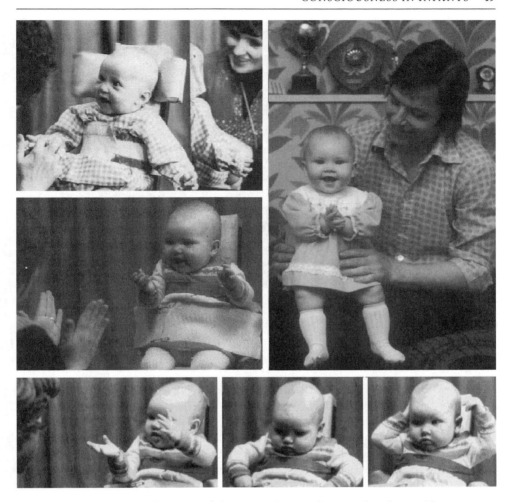

Figure 3.2 Sharing songs and games, and showing pride in performance, but shame with a stranger.

Six-month-olds enjoy sharing games with songs, such as "Round-and-round-the-garden" and "Clappa-clappa-handies," with their parents. Emma, who is shown practicing with her mother on the lower left, smiles with pride in knowing the ritual when, sitting on her father's knee, she responds to her mother's request to show "clap handies." Emma is not confident (below) when she tries to show a stranger, who does not understand. (photos Colwyn Trevarthen, and John and Penelope Hubley)

learning what is good and safe, and what to fear and avoid by "emotional referencing." They exclaim with surprise, show off, respond to playful teasing with laughter, and may act silly or "naughty" (Reddy 2003, 2005). All these signs of social "self-awareness" and play with signs and skills disappear if a child is severely frightened, neglected, or abused. Recovery from such neglect can be supported by careful incitement to play, reactivating shared joy (Trevarthen 2005b; Trevarthen et al. 2006).

At the same time as babies "show off" with those they know well, unfamiliar persons are regarded with a new suspicion as "strangers," and an awkwardness is expressed by the infant

Figure 3.3 Confidence in sharing a task and consciousness of meaning.

A one-year-old girl eagerly cooperates with her mother in a shared task and shows satisfaction when praised. (photos Colwyn Trevarthen)

In a literate world she is happy at home studying a book while her mother reads. (photo John and Penelope Hubley)

that may take on an appearance of "embarrassment" or "shame" (Figure 3.2). Even much younger babies display awareness of the regard of unfamiliar others by watchful caution, or by "coy" withdrawal with a smile (Reddy 2003). Infants show constitutional "individual differences" in timidity or self-confidence (Kagan 1994).

The baby's growing curiosity and demonstrative sociability stimulates adults to offer objects for play, and infants attend more to a toy someone is presenting, looking less at other toys. A parent holds the infant's attention by talking and acting playfully while sharing the interest, inviting the infant to look at and touch toys or other interesting objects. When an infant of 7–10 months encounters a problem in attempting to reach over a barrier the infant may look up at the experimenter for guidance, then successfully reach to and pick up the object. The infant is developing a lively sharing of purposes, attentions, and feelings or evaluations, and this is the natural process of development that opens the way to the world of cultural meanings (Trevarthen 2004a, 2005a).

From 9 to 18 Months: Making Sense of a Human-Made World (Figures 3.4 and 3.5)

In the last months of the first year, infants pass through five stages of mastery of negotiating barriers or remove covers in the object retrieval task, at the same time as they master the A-not-B "object permanence" task (Piaget 1954; Lacerda, von Hofsten, & Heimann 2001).

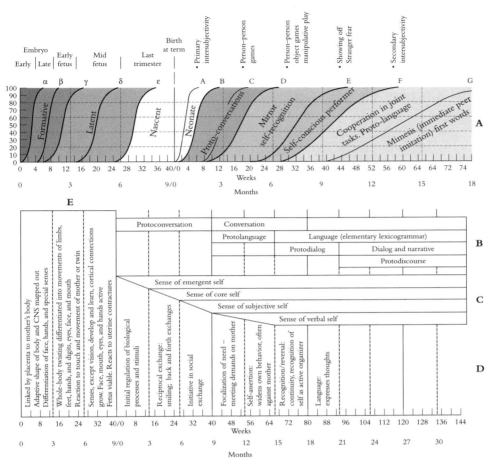

Figure 3.4 The first 30 months of human life. Phases of human sociable consciousness that have been charted in the period before language.

A: Developments from conception to 18 months after birth at full term – formative, latent and nascent consciousness *in utero*, and the first elaborations of emergent consciousness in infancy. Every stage depends on interaction with the accessible human world, and the processes are transformed by the developing motives of the child, first inside the mother's body, then in communication with her and other persons (Trevarthen & Aitken 2003; Trevarthen et al. 2006).

B: Stages in the acquisition of communication and language, or "learning how to mean" (Halliday 1975).

C: Emerging senses of the self, according to Stern (2000).

D: Developments in and infant's communication with the mother (Sander 1964).

E: Actions and awareness in the three months of gestation (Piontelli 2002; Trevarthen et al. 2006).

That is, when the infant is watching an object they want to get hold of, they can keep track of steps another person takes to hide the object under one of two containers and shift their positions. There is variation between infants, but performances of the two tasks by a given infant change at the same rate. Both tasks are interpreted as requiring the "information-maintenance component" of "working memory." Alternatively, they can be explained as reflecting developments in "seeking" motivation, which change a child's ability to attend to how to get to the "reward."

One-year-olds can watch what other people are doing, taking increasing interest in new uses for objects, sensing the expressive kinematics in human movements. They are dismayed by robots that move "mechanically" on their own, apparently sensing that machines do not move in a humanly aware way. Infants of this age are proficient at "delayed imitation" of an action they saw some time before, which shows their recognition and retention of ideas about what other persons intend. This is also the time when speech awareness begins – the detecting and learning of rhythmic and prosodic contrasts that define the speaker's intentions and "name" important things. One-year-olds are starting to remember common words designating objects and actions of common interest, and beginning to use speech for denotation, social sharing, and recall (Halliday 1975; Locke 1993).

Between 18 months and 2 years, there is a "vocabulary burst," two- and three-word sentences appearing followed by inflection and function words (Trevarthen 2004c). Thinking in words, the child can "decenter" and master navigational maps or orienteering descriptions. Language is about shared "sense," not just perceived entities (Donaldson 1992; Locke 1993; Hobson 2002). At 2 years, a toddler is actively comparing words and their referents, learning meaning in "intent participation" (Rogoff 2003). There is great variation in the paths followed by individual children (Locke 1993), and the child's talk reflects the sharing of imaginative mimetic play with friends of all ages.

Consciousness Before Birth?

If we accept that the newborn is already conscious and ready for enrichment of experience by communicating with other persons' consciousness, what happens before birth in body and brain to make this possible? Study of the embryos of birds and mammals have revealed that there are elaborate anatomical preparations for a future mobile and intelligent life (Lecanuet et al. 1995). Brain systems and sensory and motor structures of the body are complex before they become active and responsive to the environment, and, in fact, every animal embryo makes integrated movements before it senses anything.

Human motor nerves move muscles to make the body bend in the embryo, at 7 weeks, before the sensory nerves connect to the central nervous system. The first nerve tracts are those that will activate movements to express different orientations and emotional states. In the fetus, after 8 weeks, the networks of the neocortex are shaped by the same intrinsic core neurochemical systems of the subcortical brain that will select and evaluate experiences throughout life. The developmental rule is that intentions are mapped out inside the embryo brain and body, and then elaborated in sought-for engagement with the environment (Trevarthen 2004b; Trevarthen et al. 2006).

The human brain and body are shaped for an intimate social life long before birth. In the fetus, organs of expressive communication – eyes and retina, facial muscles, vocal system, ears and auditory receptors, and hands – gain their special adaptive forms, and they are

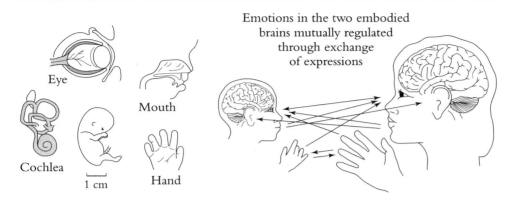

Figure 3.5 *Left:* How the sensory-motor organs of the 8-week human fetus are formed in readiness for communication. *Right:* The rhythm of behaviors in protoconversation with a 2-month-old child.

functional before term, such that a premature baby can use them to communicate (Figure 3.5). The affective motor capacities of mammals, that produce the expressions of seeking, fear, anger, social love and so forth (Panksepp 2000), are built within the central nervous system of the embryo and fetus.

During gestation, sensory inputs are incorporated to guide movement, first by *proprioception*, monitoring displacement of body parts relative to one another or in the gravitational field, then by touch *exteroception* and *ex-proprioception*, sensing immediate surroundings outside the body and changes with body displacement. Human fetuses tentatively touch the placenta, umbilicus, and the uterine wall with their hands at 11 weeks. They make jaw movements and swallow amniotic fluid, expressing pleasure or disapproval at tastes injected into it by sucking and smiling or grimacing with disgust. Complex movements of trunk, arms, and legs position the body, and may react to the mother's body movements and the contractions of the muscles of her uterus (Lecanuet et al. 1995; Piontelli 2002; Trevarthen et al. 2006).

After 20 weeks, hand movements explore the fetus's own body and surroundings and eyes turn in coordination with head movements. Twins touch one another and adjust positions in the confined space. "Temperamental" differences between twins in activity and reactivity recorded in ultra-sound movies around mid gestation persist through to several years after birth (Piontelli 2002). Fetuses hear from 20 weeks, and tests of babies' recognition of their mother's voice immediately after birth prove that a baby can distinguish her speech or singing from that of another woman. A pregnant woman feels the life of her fetus from mid gestation, and this prompts her to imagine the baby she will meet at birth, and sometimes she talks to the expected one.

By 24 weeks, heart rate changes of a fetus are coupled to episodes of movement – the autonomic system is starting to make prospective regulations to supply the energy and nourishment for vital activities that provide the energy for behavior. The last trimester of gestation, after 27 weeks, completes preparation for a more independent self-regulated life, free of the placental link with the mother's body. In protective care, the infant can now live by its own breathing and sleeping. At term, 40 weeks after conception, the actions and responses of the newborn baby show that body and brain are prepared for consciousness of a larger space inhabited by persons whose communications are perceived by touch, sound, and sight (Lecanuet et al. 1995; Trevarthen et al. 2006).

The methods of functional brain imaging to identify activity in conscious subjects have recently identified systems that represent the intentions and emotions of other individuals, coupled with expressive states to communicate with them, and these are present in a young infant, laying the foundations for mutual awareness and cultural learning (Tzourio-Mazoyer et al. 2002; Gallese, Keysers, & Rizzolatti 2004; Trevarthen et al. 2006).

Summarizing Our Case

We can summarize our review of evidence on early human consciousness by presenting the following developmental scheme (Figure 3.4).

1   In the embryo and early fetus, the biological potential for acting with consciousness is *in formation*, laid out in anatomical and physiological preparations of body and brain that are adapted to serve future conscious action.
2   In a late fetus, conscious life is *latent*, beginning to act toward and engage with what may be sensed of surroundings, and getting equipped for dealing with a bigger world, showing special sensitivity for messages from the mother's body and for her voice, and beginning to be in an attachment relation to her (Figure 3.5).
3   In a newborn, consciousness is *nascent*, coming to active life in real exploration of things that may be sensed to come from outside the body, and finding its complement in the conscious attentions and emotions of other human beings (Figure 3.1).
4   In an infant, a child, and an adult human, consciousness is developing or *emergent*, as knowledge and skills build their scope and power within the making and breaking of collaborative relationships (Figures 3.2 and 3.3).
5   With the internalization of language and through education in this and other conventional and symbolic arts of culture, consciousness is increasingly *reflective and transcendent*.

Coda: If Consciousness Is a Naturally Developing Function of Animal Life, Why Then Do Philosophers and Psychologists Have Problems with It?

The nature of consciousness defined in subtle ways has frustrated the understanding of philosophers, and acceptance of a form of consciousness in non-verbal creatures, including infants, has eluded natural scientists. Why has it been so difficult? What stands in the way? Two related habits of thought, deeply embedded in our language and in our meta-theoretical assumptions, appear to have contributed: first, thinking of *organisms* as fundamentally separated from their *environments*, and second, assuming a categorical division between the *intentional or mental* and the *physical or behavioral*. These divisions – or dualisms – grant the scientist analytic ease and fluency. However, there are problems inherent in them, which have been pointed out frequently enough: by William James, Lev Smeonivitch Vygotsky, John Dewey, and many others. The assumption of an organism/

environment separation has been strongly criticized many times, and has been identified as a problem in applied cognitive science and robotics (e.g., Clark 1999).

The traditional dualistic assumptions lead us to believe that consciousness can live as thoughts, locked away inside the brain of each animal rather than in its relations with its physical and social world, and that it is only indirectly inferable from the animal's actions. Consciousness in human infants, who do not have language to confirm our inferences, becomes unchartable territory.

The research reported in this chapter on infants' behaviors with other people supports an approach to consciousness that is both less disembodied and less individualist. It suggests that infants are conscious of the world (and indeed of themselves) in a different way when they are in normal relation with other people.

We conclude with the words of Evan Thompson, with whom we are in full agreement, excepting one "semantic" quibble. The word "empathy" derives from the Greek *empatheia,* which means an egocentric, one-sided, "projection" of feeling. We, with Adam Smith (1759), would call the motive for human encounters "sympathy" – meaning equal sharing of purposes, experiences, and feelings of all kinds. Unfortunately "empathy" has become favored in English. We believe this misrepresents the natural relating between persons.

(1) Individual human consciousness is formed in the dynamic interrelation of self and other, and therefore is inherently intersubjective. (2) The concrete encounter of self and other fundamentally involves empathy, understood as a unique and irreducible kind of intentionality. (3) Empathy is the precondition (the condition of possibility) of the science of consciousness. (4) Human empathy is inherently developmental: open to it are pathways to non-egocentric or self-transcendent modes of intersubjectivity. (Thompson 2001, p. 1)

See also 8 Affective consciousness.

References

Bowlby, J. (1988) *A Secure Base: Parent–Child Attachment and Healthy Human Development.* New York: Basic Books.

Bullowa, M. (ed.) (1979) *Before Speech: The Beginning of Human Communication.* London: Cambridge University Press.

Clark, A. (1999) An embodied cognitive science? *Trends in Cognitive Sciences* 3: 9, 345–51.

Darwin, C. (1872/1998) *The Expression of the Emotions in Man and Animals,* 3rd edn. New York: Oxford University Press.

Dissanayake, E. (2000) *Art and Intimacy: How the Arts Began.* Seattle: University of Washington Press.

Donaldson, M. (1992) *Human Minds: An Exploration.* London: Allen Lane/Penguin Books.

Gallese, V., Keysers, C., and Rizzolatti, G. (2004) A unifying view of the basis of social cognition. *TRENDS in Cognitive Sciences* 8: 9, 396–403.

Halliday, M. A. K. (1975) *Learning How to Mean: Explorations in the Development of Language.* London: Edward Arnold.

Heimann, M. (2002) Notes on individual differences and the assumed elusiveness of neonatal imitation. In A. N. Meltzoff and W. Prinz (eds.), *The Imitative Mind: Development, Evolution and Brain Bases,* 74–84. Cambridge: Cambridge University Press.

Hobson, P. (2002) *The Cradle of Thought: Exploring the Origins of Thinking.* London: Macmillan.

Jaffe, J., Beebe, B., Felstein, S., Crown, C., and Jasnow, M. D. (2001) Rhythms of dialogue in infancy: coordinated timing and social development. *Society of Child Development Monographs*, 66, 2, Serial No. 264. Oxford: Blackwell.

Kagan, J. (1994) *Galen's Prophecy: Temperament in Human Nature*. London: Free Association Books.

Lacerda, F., von Hofsten, C., and Heimann, M. (2001) *Emerging Cognitive Abilities in Early Infancy*. Mahwah, NJ: Erlbaum.

Lecanuet, J.-P., Fifer, W. P., Krasnegor, N. A., and Smotherman, W. P. (eds.) (1995) *Fetal Development: A Psychobiological Perspective*. Hillsdale, NJ: Erlbaum.

Lee, D. N. (2004) Tau in action in development. In J. J. Rieser, J. J. Lockman and C. A. Nelson (eds.), *Action, Perception and Cognition in Learning and Development*. Hillsdale, NJ: Erlbaum.

Locke, J. L. (1993) *The Child's Path to Spoken Language*. Cambridge, MA: Harvard University Press.

Malloch, S. (1999) Mother and infants and communicative musicality. In I. Deliège (ed.), *Rhythms, Musical Narrative, and the Origins of Human Communication. Musicae Scientiae*, Special Issue, 1999–2000, 29–57. Liège: European Society for the Cognitive Sciences of Music.

Markova, G. and Legerstee, M. (2006) Contingency, imitation and affect sharing: foundations of infants' social awareness. *Developmental Psychology* 42: 1, 132–41.

Meltzoff, A. N. and Moore, M. H. (1999) Persons and representation: why infant imitation is important for theories of human development. In J. Nadel and G. Butterworth (eds.), *Imitation in Infancy*, 9–35. Cambridge: Cambridge University Press.

Merker, B. (2005) The liabilities of mobility: a selection pressure for the transition to consciousness in animal evolution. *Consciousness and Cognition* 14: 1, 89–114.

Murray, L. and Cooper, P. J. (eds.) (1997) *Postpartum Depression and Child Development*. New York: Guilford Press.

Murray, L. and Trevarthen, C. (1985) Emotional regulation of interactions between two-month-olds and their mothers. In T. M. Field and N. A. Fox (eds.), *Social Perception in Infants*, 177–97. Norwood, NJ: Ablex.

Nagy, E. and Molnár, P. (2004) Homo imitans or Homo provocans? Human imprinting model of neonatal imitation. *Infant Behaviour and Development* 27: 1, 54–63.

Newson, J. (1977) An intersubjective approach to the systematic description of mother–infant interaction. In H. R. Schaffer (ed.), *Studies in Mother–Infant Interaction: The Loch Lomond Symposium*, 47–61. London: Academic Press.

Oster, H. (2005) The repertoire of infant facial expressions: an ontogenetic perspective. In J. Nadel and D. Muir (eds.), *Emotional Development*, 261–92. Oxford: Oxford University Press.

Panksepp, J. (2000) Affective consciousness and the instinctual motor system: the neural sources of sadness and joy. In R. Ellis and N. Newton (eds.), *The Caldron of Consciousness, Motivation, Affect and Self-Organization*, vol. 16, 27–54. *Advances in Consciousness Research*. Amsterdam: John Benjamins.

Papousek, H. (1967) Experimental studies of appetitional behaviour in human newborns and infants. In H. W. Stevenson, E. H. Hess, and H. L. Rheingold (eds.), *Early Behaviour: Comparative and Developmental Approaches*, 249–77. New York: John Wiley.

Papousek, M., Bornstein, M. H., Nuzzo, C., Papousek, H., and Symmes, D. (1990) Infant responses to prototypical melodic contours in parental speech. *Infant Behavior and Development* 13, 539–45.

Piaget, J. (1954) *The Construction of Reality in the Child*. New York: Basic Books.

Piontelli, A. (2002) *Twins: From Fetus to Child*. London: Routledge.

Reddy, V. (2003) On being the object of attention: implications for self–other consciousness. *Trends in Cognitive Sciences* 7, 397–402.

Reddy, V. (2005) Feeling shy and showing-off: self-conscious emotions must regulate self-awareness. In J. Nadel and D. Muir (eds.), *Emotional Development*, 183–204. Oxford: Oxford University Press.

Rogoff, B. (2003) *The Cultural Nature of Human Development*. Oxford: Oxford University Press.

Smith, A. (1759) *Theory of Moral Sentiments*. Edinburgh (modern edn.: D. D. Raphael and A. L. Macfie (eds.), (Glasgow edn.). Oxford: Clarendon, 1976; also Indianapolis: Liberty Fund, 1984.

Smuts, B. (2001) Encounters with animal minds. In E. Thompson (ed.), *Between Ourselves: Second-Person Issues in the Study of Consciousness*, 293–309. Charlottesville, VA/Thorverton, UK: Imprint Academic (also *Journal of Consciousness Studies* 8: 5–7, 293–309).

Stern, D. N. (2000) *The Interpersonal World of the Infant: A View from Psychoanalysis and Development Psychology*, 2nd edn. New York: Basic Books.

Stern, D. N. (2004) *The Present Moment in Psychotherapy and Everyday Life*. New York: Norton.

Thompson, E. (2001) Empathy and consciousness. In E. Thompson (ed.), *Between Ourselves: Second-Person Issues in the Study of Consciousness*, 1–32. Charlottesville, VA/Thorverton, UK: Imprint Academic (also *Journal of Consciousness Studies* 8: 5–7, 1–32).

Trevarthen, C. (1998) The concept and foundations of infant intersubjectivity. In S. Bråten (ed.), *Intersubjective Communication and Emotion in Early Ontogeny*, 15–46. Cambridge: Cambridge University Press.

Trevarthen, C. (1999) Musicality and the intrinsic motive pulse: evidence from human psychobiology and infant communication. In *Rhythms, Musical Narrative, and the Origins of Human Communication. Musicae Scientiae*, Special Issue, 1999–2000, 157–213. Liège: European Society for the Cognitive Sciences of Music.

Trevarthen, C. (2004a) Infancy, mind in. In R. L. Gregory (ed.), *Oxford Companion to the Mind*, 2nd edn., 455–64. Oxford: Oxford University Press.

Trevarthen, C. (2004b) Brain development. In R. L. Gregory (ed.), *Oxford Companion to the Mind*, 2nd edn., 116–27. Oxford: Oxford University Press.

Trevarthen, C. (2004c) Language development: mechanisms in the brain. In G. Adelman and B. H. Smith (eds.), *Encyclopedia of Neuroscience*, 2nd edn., with CD-ROM. Amsterdam: Elsevier Science.

Trevarthen, C. (2005a) Action and emotion in development of the human self, its sociability and cultural intelligence: why infants have feelings like ours. In J. Nadel and D. Muir (eds.), *Emotional Development*, 61–91. Oxford: Oxford University Press.

Trevarthen, C. (2005b) Stepping away from the mirror: pride and shame in adventures of companionship. Reflections on the nature and emotional needs of infant intersubjectivity. In C. S. Carter, L. Ahnert et al. (eds.), *Attachment and Bonding: A New Synthesis*. Dahlem Workshop Report 92. Cambridge, MA: MIT Press.

Trevarthen, C. and Aitken, K. J. (2003) Regulation of brain development and age-related changes in infants' motives: the developmental function of regressive periods. In M. Heimann (ed.), *Regression Periods in Human Infancy*, 107–84. Mahwah, NJ: Erlbaum.

Trevarthen, C., Aitken, K. J., Vandekerckhove, M., Delafield-Butt, J., and Nagy, E. (2006) Collaborative regulations of vitality in early childhood: stress in intimate relationships and postnatal psychopathology. In D. Cicchetti and D. J. Cohen (eds.), *Developmental Psychopathology*, 2nd edn. Hoboken, NJ: Wiley.

Tronick, E. Z. (2005) Why is connection with others so critical? The formation of dyadic states of consciousness: coherence governed selection and the co-creation of meaning out of messy meaning making. In J. Nadel and D. Muir (eds.), *Emotional Development*, 293–315. Oxford: Oxford University Press.

Tzourio-Mazoyer, N., De Schonen, S., Crivello, F., Reutter, B., Aujard, Y., and Mazoyer, B. (2002) Neural correlates of woman face processing by 2-month-old infants. *NeuroImage* 15, 454–61.

4

Animal Consciousness[1]

COLIN ALLEN AND MARC BEKOFF

There are many reasons besides sheer fascination with animals to be interested in animal consciousness. First, one way in which we, as humans, may seek to understand ourselves is to compare and contrast ourselves with whatever in nature is most similar to us, i.e., other animals. Second, the problem of determining the nature of animal consciousness raises challenging questions about the limits of knowledge and scientific methodology. Third, animal consciousness is of considerable moral significance given the dependence of modern societies on mass farming and the use of animals for biomedical research, education, and entertainment. Fourth, while general theories of consciousness are frequently developed without special regard to questions about animal consciousness, the plausibility of such theories can be tested against the results of their application to animals.

Questions about animal consciousness are just one corner of a more general set of questions about animal cognition and mind. The so-called "cognitive revolution" that took place during the latter half of the twentieth century has led to many innovative experiments by comparative psychologists and ethologists probing the cognitive capacities of animals. Despite all this work, the topic of consciousness per se in animals has remained controversial, even taboo, among many scientists, even while it remains a matter of common sense to most people that many other animals do have conscious experiences.

Concepts of Consciousness

In discussions of animal consciousness there is no clearly agreed upon sense in which the term "consciousness" is used. Having origins in folk psychology, "consciousness" has a multitude of uses that may not be resolvable into a single, coherent concept (Wilkes 1984). Nevertheless, several useful distinctions among different notions of consciousness have been made, and with the help of these distinctions it is possible to gain some clarity on the important questions that remain about animal consciousness.

Two ordinary senses of consciousness that are not in dispute when applied to animals are the sense of consciousness involved when a creature is awake rather than asleep or in a coma, and the sense of consciousness implicated in the basic ability of organisms to perceive and thereby respond to selected features of their environments, thus making them conscious or aware of those features. Consciousness in both these senses is identifiable in organisms belonging to a wide variety of taxonomic groups.

A third, more technical notion of consciousness, *access consciousness*, has been introduced by Block (1995) to capture the sense in which mental representations may be poised for use in rational control of action or speech. Block himself believes that many animals possess access consciousness (he does not make speech a requirement), but clearly an author such as Descartes, who, we will see, denied speech and language to animals, would also deny access consciousness to them. Those who follow Davidson (1975) in denying intentional states to animals would likely concur.

Two additional senses of consciousness that cause controversy when applied to animals are *phenomenal consciousness* and *self-consciousness*.

Phenomenal consciousness refers to the qualitative, subjective, experiential, or phenomenological aspects of conscious experience, sometimes identified with qualia. (In this chapter we also use the term "sentience" to refer to phenomenal consciousness.) To contemplate animal consciousness in this sense is to consider the possibility that, in Nagel's (1974) phrase, there might be "something it's like" to be a member of another species. Nagel disputes our capacity to know, imagine, or describe in scientific (objective) terms what it's like to be a bat, but he assumes that there is something it's like. There are those, however, who would challenge this assumption directly. Others would less directly challenge the possibility of scientifically investigating its truth. Nevertheless, there is broad common-sense agreement that phenomenal consciousness is more likely in mammals and birds than it is in invertebrates, such as insects, crustaceans, or molluscs (with the possible exception of some cephalopods), while reptiles, amphibians, and fish constitute an enormous gray area.

Self-consciousness usually refers to an organism's capacity for second-order representation of the organism's own mental states. Because of its second-order character ("thought about thought") the capacity for self-consciousness is closely related to questions about "theory of mind" in nonhuman animals – whether any animals are capable of attributing mental states to others. Questions about self-consciousness and theory of mind in animals are a matter of active scientific controversy, with the most attention focused on chimpanzees and to a more limited extent on the other great apes. As attested by this controversy (and unlike questions about animal sentience) questions about self-consciousness in animals are commonly regarded as tractable by empirical means.

The bulk of this chapter deals primarily with the attribution of consciousness in its phenomenal sense to animals. However, because one of the most sustained attacks on the notion of phenomenal consciousness (Carruthers 1998a, 1998b, 2000) invokes the absence of "theory of mind" capacities that have been linked to self-consciousness, the next section provides some background on this topic.

Self-Consciousness

The systematic study of self-consciousness and theory of mind in nonhuman animals has its roots in an approach to the study of self-consciousness pioneered by Gallup (1970). It was long known that chimpanzees would use mirrors to inspect their images, but Gallup developed a protocol that appears to allow a scientific determination of whether it is merely the mirror image per se that is the object of interest to the animal inspecting it, or whether it is the mirror image qua proxy for the animal itself that is the object of interest. Gallup's protocol has been repeated with other great apes and some monkey species, but chimpanzees and orangutans are the only primate species who consistently "pass" the test. Reiss and Marino (2001) have recently provided positive evidence of mirror self-recognition in two bottlenose dolphins.

According to Gallup et al. (2002) "Mirror self-recognition is an indicator of self-awareness." Furthermore, he claims that "the ability to infer the existence of mental states in others (known as theory of mind, or mental state attribution) is a byproduct of being self-aware." He describes the connection between self-awareness and theory of mind thus: "If you are self-aware then you are in a position to use your experience to model the existence of comparable processes in others." A full assessment of Gallup's reasoning cannot be provided here, but the chapters in Parker et al. (1994) and Heyes (1998) cover much of the debate (see also Shumaker & Schwartz 2002).

The theory of mind debate has its origins in the hypothesis that primate intelligence in general, and human intelligence in particular, is specially adapted for social cognition (see Byrne & Whiten 1988, especially the first two chapters, by Jolly and Humphrey). Consequently, it has been argued that evidence for the ability to attribute mental states in a wide range of species might be better sought in natural activities such as social play, rather than in laboratory designed experiments that place the animals in artificial situations (Allen & Bekoff 1997; see esp. ch. 6; see also Hare et al. 2000; Hare et al. 2001; and Hare & Wrangham 2002). Furthermore, it is possible that the mirror test is not an appropriate test for theory of mind in most species because of its specific dependence on the ability to match motor to visual information, a skill that may not have needed to evolve in a majority of species, for example those species that depend more on chemical or auditory cues.

Along similar lines, Bekoff and Sherman (2004) develop three categories (or degrees) of "self-cognizance" – a phrase they introduce to standardize terminology and to cover a continuum from "self-referencing" (a non-cognitive capacity for perceptual discrimination of self and other) to self-consciousness. They suggest a broader perspective on self-consciousness should include "body consciousness" and a sense of possession – "mine-ness" ("my body," "my territory"). These are features that could lead to empirical studies that are more relevant to species's evolved capacities. Alternative approaches that have attempted to provide strong evidence of theory of mind in nonhuman animals under natural conditions have generally failed to produce such evidence (e.g., the conclusions of Cheney & Seyfarth 1990), although anecdotal evidence tantalizingly suggests that researchers still have not managed to devise the right experiments.

Phenomenal Consciousness: Basic Questions – Epistemological and Ontological

Among philosophers of mind, the topic of consciousness in nonhuman animals has been primarily of epistemological interest. Two central questions are:

1 Can we know which animals beside humans are conscious? (The Distribution Question)
2 Can we know what, if anything, the experiences of animals are like? (The Phenomenological Question)

In his seminal paper "What is it like to be a bat?" Thomas Nagel (1974) simply assumes that there is something that it's like to be a bat, and focuses his attention on what he argues is the scientifically intractable problem of knowing what it's like. Nagel's confidence in the existence of conscious bat experiences would generally be held to be the common-sense view, but there are those who would argue that the Distribution Question is just as intractable as the Phenomenological Question.

The two questions might be seen as special cases of the general skeptical "problem of other minds," which, even if intractable, is nevertheless generally ignored to good effect by psychologists. However, it is often thought that knowledge of animal minds – what Allen & Bekoff (1997) refer to as "the other species of mind problem" – presents special methodological problems because animals cannot be interrogated directly about their experiences (see Sober 2000 for an alternative approach to tractability within an evolutionary framework). Although there have been attempts to teach human-like languages to members of other species, none has reached a level of conversational ability that would solve this problem directly. Furthermore, except for some language-related work with parrots and dolphins, such approaches are generally limited to those animals most like ourselves, particularly the great apes. But there is great interest in possible forms of consciousness in a much wider variety of species than are suitable for such research, both in connection with questions about the ethical treatment of animals (e.g., Singer 1975/1990; Regan 1983; Rollin 1989; Varner 1999), and in connection with questions about the natural history of consciousness (Griffin 1976, 1984, 1992; Bekoff 2002; Bekoff et al. 2002; Griffin & Speck 2004).

Griffin's agenda for the discipline he labeled "cognitive ethology" features the topic of animal consciousness and advocates a methodology, inherited from classical ethology, that is based in naturalistic observations of animal behavior (Allen 2004a). This agenda has been strongly criticized, with his methodological suggestions often dismissed as anthropomorphic (see Bekoff & Allen 1997 for a survey). But such criticisms may have overestimated the dangers of anthropomorphism (Fisher 1990; Keeley 2004) and many of the critics themselves rely on claims for which there are scant scientific data (e.g., Kennedy 1992, who claims that the "sin" of anthropomorphism may be programmed into humans genetically).

While epistemological and related methodological issues have been at the forefront of discussions about animal consciousness, the main wave of more general recent philosophical attention to consciousness has been focused on ontological questions about the nature of phenomenal consciousness. One might reasonably think that the question of what consciousness is should be settled prior to tackling the Distribution Question – that ontology should drive the epistemology. In an ideal world this order of proceeding might be the preferred one, but as we shall see in the next section, the current state of disarray among the ontological theories makes such an approach untenable.

Applying Ontological Theories

Nonreductive accounts

Whether because they are traditional dualists, or because they think that (phenomenal) consciousness is an as-yet-undescribed fundamental constituent of the physical Universe, some theorists maintain that consciousness is not explainable in familiar scientific terms. Such nonreductive accounts of consciousness (with the possible exception of those based in anthropocentric theology) provide no principled ontological reasons, however, for doubting that animals are conscious. Cartesian dualism is, of course, traditionally associated with the view that animals lack minds. But Descartes's argument for this view was not based on any ontological principles, but upon what he took to be the failure of animals to use language conversationally, or to reason generally. On this basis he claimed that nothing in animal behavior requires a non-mechanical (mental) explanation; hence he saw no reason to attribute possession of mind to animals.

There is, however, no ontological reason why animal bodies are any less suitable vehicles for embodying a Cartesian mind than are human bodies. Hence dualism itself does not preclude animal minds. Similarly, more recent nonreductive accounts of consciousness in terms of fundamental properties are compatible with the idea of animal consciousness. None of these accounts provides any constitutional reason why those fundamental properties should not be located in animals. Furthermore, given that none of these theories specify empirical means for detecting the right stuff for consciousness, and indeed dualist theories cannot do so, they seem forced to rely upon behavioral criteria rather than ontological criteria for deciding the Distribution Question.

Reductive accounts

Other theorists have tried to give reductive accounts of (phenomenal) consciousness in terms either of the physical, biochemical, or neurological properties of nervous systems (physicalist accounts) or in terms of other cognitive processes (functionalist-reductive accounts).

Physicalist accounts of (phenomenal) consciousness, which identify it with physical or physiological properties of neurons, do not provide any particular obstacles to attributing consciousness to animals, given that animals and humans share the same basic biology. Of course there is no consensus about which physical or neurological properties are to be identified with consciousness. But if it could be determined that phenomenal consciousness was identical to a property such as quantum coherence in the microtubules of neurons, or brain waves of a specific frequency, then settling the Distribution Question would be a straightforward empirical matter of establishing whether or not members of other species possess the specified properties.

Functionalist-reductive accounts have sought to explain consciousness in terms of other cognitive processes. Some of these accounts identify phenomenal consciousness with the (first-order) representational properties of mental states. Such accounts are generally quite friendly to attributions of consciousness to animals, for it is relatively uncontroversial that animals have internal states that have the requisite representational properties; for example, consider Dretske's (1995) claim that phenomenal consciousness is inseparable from a creature's capacity to perceive and respond to features of its environment. Likewise, Tye (2000) argues, based upon his first-order representational account of phenomenal consciousness, that it extends even to honeybees.

Functionalist theories of phenomenal consciousness that rely on more elaborately structured cognitive capacities can be less accommodating to the belief that animals do have conscious mental states. For example, some twentieth-century philosophers, while rejecting Cartesian dualism, have turned his epistemological reliance upon language as an indicator of consciousness into an ontological point about the essential involvement of linguistic processing in human consciousness. Such insistence on the importance of language for consciousness underwrites the tendency of philosophers such as Dennett (1969, 1995, 1997) to deny that animals are conscious in anything like the same sense that humans are (see also Carruthers 1996).

For Carruthers (1998a, 1998b, 2000) the issue is not language but the capacity for higher-order thought (thoughts about thoughts), sometimes called "theory of mind." According to Carruthers, a mental state is phenomenally conscious for a subject just in case it is available to be thought about directly by that subject. Furthermore, according to Carruthers, such higher-order thoughts are not possible unless a creature has a "theory of mind" to provide it with the concepts necessary for thought about mental states. But, Carruthers argues, there is little, if any, scientific support for theory of mind in nonhuman animals, even among the great apes (with the possible exception of chimpanzees), so he concludes that there is little support either for the view that any animals possess phenomenological consciousness.

In contrast to Carruthers's higher-order thought account of sentience, other theorists, such as Armstrong (1980), and Lycan (1996), have preferred a higher-order experience account, where consciousness is explained in terms of inner perception of mental states, a view that can be traced back to Aristotle, and also to John Locke. Because such models do not require the ability to conceptualize mental states, proponents of higher-order experience theories have been slightly more inclined than higher-order theorists to allow that such abilities may be found in other animals.

Limits of Ontology

It is beyond the scope of this chapter to survey the strong attacks that have been mounted against the various accounts of consciousness, but it is safe to say that none of them seems secure enough to hang a decisive endorsement or denial of animal consciousness upon it. Accounts of consciousness in terms of basic neurophysiological properties, the quantum-mechanical properties of neurons, or *sui generis* properties of the Universe are just as insecure as the various functionalist accounts. And even those ontological accounts that are, in general outline, compatible with animal sentience are not specific enough to permit ready answers to the Distribution Question. Hence no firm conclusions about the distribution of consciousness can be drawn on the basis of the work to date by philosophers on the ontology of consciousness.

Where does this leave the epistemological questions about animal consciousness? While it may seem natural to think that we must have a theory of what consciousness is before we try to determine whether other animals have it, this may in fact be putting the conceptual cart before the empirical horse. In the early stages of the scientific investigation of any phenomenon, putative samples must be identified by rough rules of thumb (or working definitions) rather than complete theories. Early scientists identified gold by contingent characteristics rather than its atomic essence, knowledge of which had to await thorough investigation of many putative examples – some of which turned out to be gold and some not. Likewise, at this stage of the game, perhaps the study of animal consciousness would benefit from the identification of animal traits worthy of further investigation, with no firm commitment to the idea that all these examples will involve conscious experience.

Of course, as a part of this process some reasons must be given for identifying specific animal traits as "interesting" for the study of consciousness, and in a weak sense such reasons will constitute an argument for attributing consciousness to the animals possessing those traits. These reasons can be evaluated even in the absence of an accepted ontology for consciousness. Furthermore, those who would bring animal consciousness into the scientific fold in this way must also explain how scientific methodology is adequate to the task in the face of various arguments that it is inadequate. These arguments, and the response to them, can also be evaluated in the absence of ontological certitude. Thus there is plenty to cover in the rest of this chapter.

Evaluation of Arguments Against Animal Consciousness

Similarity arguments

One kind of strategy that has been used to deny animal consciousness is to focus on certain similarities between animal behaviors and behaviors that may be conducted unconsciously by humans. Thus, for example, Carruthers (1989, 1992) argued that all animal behavior can be assimilated to the nonconscious activities of humans, such as driving while distracted ("on autopilot"), or to the capacities of "blindsight" patients whose damage to visual cortex leaves them phenomenologically blind in a portion of their visual fields (a "scotoma") but nonetheless able to identify things presented to the scotoma. (He refers to both of these as examples of "unconscious experiences.")

This comparison of animal behavior to the unconscious capacities of humans can be criticized on the grounds that, like Descartes's pronouncements on parrots, it is based only on unsystematic observation of animal behavior. There are grounds for thinking that careful investigation would reveal that there is not a very close analogy between animal behavior and human behaviors associated with these putative cases of unconscious experience. For instance, it is notable that the unconscious experiences of automatic driving are not remembered by their subjects, whereas there is no evidence that animals are similarly unable to recall their allegedly unconscious experiences. Likewise, blindsight subjects do not spontaneously respond to things presented to their scotomas, but must be trained to make responses using a forced-response paradigm (Stoerig & Cowey 1997). There is no evidence that such limitations are normal for animals, or that animals behave like blindsight victims with respect to their visual experiences (Jamieson & Bekoff 1992).

Dissimilarity arguments

The Cartesian argument against animal consciousness, which is based on the alleged failure of animals to display certain intellectual capacities, is illustrative of a general pattern of using certain specific dissimilarities between animals and humans to argue that animals lack consciousness. Descartes dismissed parrots vocalizing human words because he thought it was merely meaningless repetition. This judgment may have been appropriate for the few parrots he encountered, but it was not based on a systematic, scientific investigation of the capacities of parrots. Nowadays many would argue that Pepperberg's studies of the African Grey parrot "Alex" (Pepperberg 1999, 2002) should lay the Cartesian prejudice to rest. These studies, along with several on the acquisition of a certain amount of linguistic competence by chimpanzees and bonobos (e.g., Gardner et al. 1989; Savage-Rumbaugh 1996; Fouts et al. 2002) would seem to undermine Descartes's assertions, even if it remains true that other animals have not fully mastered the recursive phrase structure grammar of natural human languages (Hauser et al. 2002).

Convinced by evidence of sophisticated cognitive abilities, most theorists these days agree with Block that something like access consciousness is properly attributed to many animals. Nevertheless, when it comes to phenomenal consciousness, dissimilarity arguments may give pause to defenders of animal sentience, for surely most would agree that, at some point, the neurological, anatomical, and behavioral dissimilarities between normal adult humans and members of other species (the common earthworm *Lumbricus terrestris*, for example) are so great that it is unlikely that such creatures are sentient. A gray area arises because few can say how much dissimilarity is enough to trigger the judgment that sentience is absent.

Methodological arguments

Many scientists remain convinced that even if questions about self-consciousness are empirically tractable, no amount of experimentation can provide access to phenomenal consciousness in nonhuman animals. This remains true even among those scientists who are willing to invoke cognitive explanations of animal behavior that advert to mental representations or cognitive states. Opposition to dealing with consciousness can be partly understood as a legacy of behavioristic psychology, first because of the behaviorists' rejection of terms for unobservables unless they could be formally defined in terms of observables, and second because of the strong association in many behaviorists' minds between the use of mentalistic terms and the twin bugaboos of Cartesian dualism and introspectionist psychology (Bekoff & Allen 1997). In some cases these scientists are even dualists themselves, but they are strongly committed to denying the possibility of scientifically investigating consciousness, and remain skeptical of all attempts to bring it into the scientific mainstream.

Because consciousness is assumed to be private or subjective, it is often taken to be beyond the reach of objective scientific methods (Nagel 1974). This claim might be taken in either of two ways. On the one hand it might be taken to bear on the possibility of answering the Distribution Question, that is, to reject the possibility of knowledge that a member of another taxonomic group (e.g., a bat) has conscious states. On the other hand it might be taken to bear on the possibility of answering the Phenomenological Question, that is, to reject the possibility of knowledge of the phenomenological details of the mental states of a member of another taxonomic group. The difference between believing with justification that a bat is conscious and knowing what it's like to be a bat is important because, at best, the privacy of conscious experience supports a negative conclusion only about the latter. To support a negative conclusion about the former one must also assume that consciousness has absolutely no measurable effects on behavior, that is, one must accept epiphenomenalism. But if one rejects epiphenomenalism and maintains that consciousness does have effects on behavior then a strategy of inference to the best explanation may be used to support its attribution.

Evaluation of Arguments for Animal Consciousness

Similarity arguments

Most people, if asked why they think familiar animals such as their pets are conscious, would point to similarities between the behavior of those animals and human behavior. Similarity arguments for animal consciousness thus have roots in common-sense observations. But they may also be bolstered by scientific investigations of behavior and neurology as well as considerations of evolutionary continuity (homology) between species. Many judgments of the similarity between human and animal behavior are readily made by ordinary observers. The reactions of many animals, particularly other mammals, to bodily events that humans would report as painful are easily and automatically recognized by most people as pain responses. High-pitched vocalizations, fear responses, nursing of injuries, and learned avoidance are among the responses to noxious stimuli that are all part of the common mammalian heritage. Similar responses are also visible to some degree or other in organisms from other taxonomic groups. Less accessible to casual observation, but still in the realm of behavioral evidence are scientific demonstrations that members of other species, even of other phyla, are susceptible to the same visual illusions as we are (e.g., Fujita et al. 1991) suggesting that their visual experiences are similar.

Neurological similarities between humans and other animals have also been taken to suggest commonality of conscious experience. All mammals share the same basic brain anatomy, and much is shared with vertebrates more generally. A large amount of scientific research that is of direct relevance to the treatment of conscious human pain, including on the efficacy of analgesics and anesthetics, is conducted on rats and other animals. The validity of this research depends on the similar mechanisms involved and to many it seems arbitrary to deny that injured rats, who respond well to opiates for example, feel pain. Likewise, much of the basic research that is of direct relevance to understanding human visual consciousness has been conducted on the very similar visual systems of monkeys.

Such similarity arguments are, of course, inherently weak for it is always open to critics to exploit some disanalogy between animals and humans to argue that the similarities don't entail the conclusion that both are sentient (Allen 1998). Even when bolstered by evolutionary considerations of continuity between the species, the arguments are vulnerable, for the mere fact that humans have a trait does not entail that our closest relatives must have that trait too. There is no inconsistency with evolutionary continuity to maintain that only humans have the capacity to learn to play chess. Likewise for consciousness. Perhaps a combination of behavioral, physiological, and morphological similarities with evolutionary theory amounts to a stronger overall case. But in the absence of more specific theoretical grounds for attributing consciousness to animals, this composite argument – which might be called "the argument from homology" – despite its comportment with common sense, is unlikely to change the minds of those who are skeptical.

Inference to the Best Explanation

One way to get beyond the weaknesses in the similarity arguments is to try to articulate a theoretical basis for connecting the observable characteristics of animals (behavioral or neurological) to consciousness. Inferences of this kind would be strengthened by a good understanding of the biological function or functions of consciousness. If one knew what phenomenal conscious is for then one could exploit that knowledge to infer its presence in cases where that function is fulfilled, so long as other kinds of explanations can be shown less satisfactory – an inference to the best explanation.

If phenomenal consciousness is completely epiphenomenal, as some philosophers believe, then a search for the functions of consciousness is doomed to futility. In fact, if consciousness is completely epiphenomenal then it cannot have evolved by natural selection. On the assumption that phenomenal consciousness is an evolved characteristic of human minds, at least, and therefore that epiphenomenalism is false, then an attempt to understand the biological functions of consciousness may provide the best chance of identifying its occurrence in different species.

Such an approach is nascent in Griffin's attempts to force ethologists to pay attention to questions about animal consciousness. (For the purposes of this discussion we assume that Griffin's proposals are intended to relate to phenomenal consciousness, as well, perhaps, as to consciousness in its other senses.) In a series of books, Griffin (who made his scientific reputation by carefully detailing the physical and physiological characteristics of echolocation by bats) provides examples of communicative and problem-solving behavior by animals, particularly under natural conditions, and argues that these are prime places for ethologists to begin their investigations of animal consciousness (Griffin 1976, 1984, 1992). Although he thinks that the intelligence displayed by these examples suggests conscious thought, many critics have been disappointed by the lack of systematic connection between Griffin's examples and the attribution of consciousness (see Alcock 1992; Bekoff & Allen 1997; Allen & Bekoff 1997). Griffin's main positive proposal in this respect has been the rather implausible suggestion that consciousness might have the function of compensating for limited neural machinery. Thus Griffin is motivated to suggest that consciousness may be more important to honeybees than to humans.

If compensating for small sets of neurons is not a plausible function for consciousness, what might be? The commonsensical answer would be that consciousness "tells" the organism about events in the environment, or, in the case of pain and other proprioceptive sensations, about the state of the body. But this answer begs the question against higher-order accounts of consciousness for it fails to respect the distinction between phenomenal consciousness and mere awareness (in the uncontroversial sense of detection) of environmental or bodily events.

Perhaps more sophisticated attempts to spell out the functions of consciousness are similarly doomed. But Allen & Bekoff (1997, ch. 8) suggest that progress might be made by investigating the capacities of animals to adjust to their own perceptual errors. Not all adjustments to error provide grounds for suspecting that consciousness is involved, but in cases where an organism can adjust to a perceptual error while retaining the capacity to exploit the content of the erroneous perception, then there may be a robust sense in which the animal internally distinguishes its own appearance states from other judgments about the world. (Humans, for instance, have conscious visual experiences that they know are misleading – i.e., visual illusions – yet they can exploit the erroneous content of these experiences for various purposes, such as deceiving others or answering questions about how things appear to them.) Given that there are theoretical grounds for identifying conscious experiences with "appearance states," attempts to discover whether animals have such capacities might be a good place to start looking for animal consciousness. It is important, however, to emphasize that such capacities are not themselves intended to be definitive or in any way criterial for consciousness.

Carruthers (2000) makes a similar suggestion about the function of consciousness, relating it to the general capacity for making an appearance-reality distinction; of course he continues to maintain that this capacity depends upon having higher-order concepts that are beyond the grasp of nonhuman animals.

Broader Implications

Many of the issues raised above are couched abstractly, but questions about animal consciousness, especially sentience, are also enormously important for practical matters of applied animal welfare (Bekoff 2002; Mendl & Paul 2004). The authors of animal welfare laws struggle to define sentience in a way that makes objective legal enforcement possible (Allen 2004b). The topic of animal consciousness connects to theoretical issues in ethics because of wide, although by no means universal, acceptance of the biconditional statement [A]: animals deserve moral consideration if and only if they are sentient (especially possessing the capacity to feel pain). Many are inclined to take it for granted that animals are conscious, regarding any theory of consciousness that denies this as defective, and concluding from [A] that animals deserve moral protection. In this connection it is also sometimes argued that if there is uncertainty about whether other animals really are conscious, the morally safe position is to give them the benefit of the doubt. Others, however, are inclined to use [A] in the other direction, denying that animals are sentient and concluding that animals do not deserve moral consideration. Indeed Carruthers (1989) even argued that given their lack of sentience, it would be immoral not to use animals for research and other experimentation if doing so would improve the lot of sentient creatures such as ourselves. He has more recently backed off this view (1998b), denying [A] by claiming that sentience is not the sole basis for moral consideration, and claiming that animals qualify for consideration on the basis of frustration of their unconscious desires. Varner (1999) disagrees with Carruthers by arguing for conscious desires throughout mammals and birds, but like Carruthers he also rejects [A], arguing for an even more inclusive criterion of moral considerability in terms of the biological "interests" that all living things have.

Neuroscientists regularly use animal models for empirical investigation of conscious phenomena. For most philosophers, however, the topic of animal consciousness is of peripheral interest to their main project of understanding the ontology of consciousness. Because of their focus on ontological rather than epistemological issues, there is often a disconnection between philosophers and scientists on these issues. Nevertheless, there are encouraging signs that interdisciplinary work between philosophers and behavioral scientists is beginning to lay the groundwork for addressing some questions about animal consciousness in a philosophically sophisticated yet empirically tractable way (Allen et al. 2005; Aydede 2005). In some ways, perhaps, we are not much further along than the cave artists of Lascaux, painting animals on the walls of their cave 17,000 years ago. These ancient hunters were no doubt careful observers of the wild behavior of the animals they depended on for survival. We shall never know, but we might reasonably guess that, not being very different from ourselves, these early naturalists would have wondered what it was like to be the aurochs, horses, and deer they depicted. A modern, integrated science of animal consciousness must combine functional understanding derived from naturalistic observation with the latest techniques from the lab. Philosophers, in particular, have much to gain and to contribute by getting out of the armchair and into the field. The stakes are high – answers inform where humans fall in the evolutionary scheme of things and influence how animals are treated – and more detailed interdisciplinary studies are needed.

See also 3 Consciousness in infants; 8 Affective consciousness; 21 Higher-order theories of consciousness.

Note

1   This chapter is adapted from Allen, C. (2003) Animal consciousness. In Edward N. Zalta (ed.), *Stanford Encyclopedia of Philosophy* (Summer 2003 edn.), http://plato.stanford.edu/archives/sum2003/entries/consciousness-animal/.

Further Readings

Griffin, D. R. and Speck, G. B. (2004) New evidence of animal consciousness. *Animal Cognition* 7, 5–18.

Hare, B., Call, J., Agnetta, B., and Tomasello, M. (2000) Chimpanzees know what conspecifics do and do not see. *Animal Behavior* 59, 771–85.

Hare, B., Call, J., and Tomasello, M. (2001) Do chimpanzees know what conspecifics know? *Animal Behaviour* 63, 139–51.

Pepperberg, I. M. (2002) Cognitive and communicative abilities of grey parrots (*Psittacus erithacus*). In M. Bekoff, C. Allen, and G. M. Burghardt (eds.), *The Cognitive Animal*, 247–255. Cambridge, MA: MIT Press.

Stoerig, P. and Cowey, A. (1997) Blindsight in man and monkey. *Brain* 120, 535–59.

References

Alcock, J. (1992) Review of Griffin 1992. *Natural History* September, 62–5.

Allen, C. (1997) Animal cognition and animal minds. In P. Machamer and M. Carrier (eds.), *Philosophy and the Sciences of the Mind: Pittsburgh-Konstanz Series in the Philosophy and History of Science*, vol. 4, 227–43. Pittsburgh and Konstanz: Pittsburgh University Press and the Universitätsverlag Konstanz.

Allen, C. (1998) The discovery of animal consciousness: an optimistic assessment. *Journal of Agricultural and Environmental Ethics* 10: 217–25.

Allen, C. (2004a) Is anyone a cognitive ethologist? *Biology and Philosophy* 19, 589–607.

Allen, C. (2004b) Animal pain. *Noûs* 38, 617–43.

Allen, C. and Bekoff, M. (1997) *Species of Mind*. Cambridge, MA: MIT Press. See especially ch. 8.

Allen, C., Fuchs, P. N., Shriver, A., and Wilson, H. D. (2005) Deciphering animal pain. In M. Aydede (ed.), *Pain: New Essays on the Nature of Pain and the Methodology of its Study*, 352–66. Cambridge, MA: MIT Press.

Armstrong, D. A. (1980) *The Nature of Mind and Other Essays*. Ithaca, NY: Cornell University Press.

Aydede, M. (ed.) (2005) *Pain: New Essays on the Nature of Pain and the Methodology of its Study*. Cambridge, MA: MIT Press.

Bekoff, M. (2002) *Minding Animals: Awareness, Emotions, and Heart*. New York: Oxford University Press.

Bekoff, M. and Allen, C. (1997) Cognitive ethology: slayers, skeptics, and proponents. In R. Mitchell et al. (eds.), *Anthropomorphism, Anecdote, and Animals*. New York: SUNY Press.

Bekoff, M. and Sherman, P. (2004) Reflections on animal selves. *Trends in Ecology and Evolution* 19, 176–80.

Bekoff, M., Allen, C., and Burghardt, G. M. (eds.) (2002) *The Cognitive Animal*. Cambridge, MA: MIT Press.

Block, N. (1995) On a confusion about a function of consciousness. *Behavioral and Brain Sciences* 18, 227–47.

Byrne, R. W. and Whiten, A. (1988) *Machiavellian Intelligence: Social Expertise and the Evolution of Intellect in Monkeys, Apes and Humans*. Oxford: Oxford University Press.

Carruthers, P. (1989) Brute experience. *Journal of Philosophy* 86, 258–69.

Carruthers, P. (1992) *The Animals Issue*. Cambridge: Cambridge University Press.

Carruthers, P. (1996) *Language, Thought and Consciousness*. Cambridge: Cambridge University Press.

Carruthers, P. (1998a) Natural theories of consciousness. *European Journal of Philosophy* 6, 203–22.

Carruthers, P. (1998b) Animal subjectivity. *Psyche* 4, 3 (April 1998) <http://psyche.cs.monash.edu.au/v4/psyche-4-03-carruthers.html>.

Carruthers, P. (2000) *Phenomenal Consciousness: A Naturalistic Theory*. Cambridge: Cambridge University Press.

Cheney, D. L. and Seyfarth, R. M. (1990) *How Monkeys See the World: Inside the Mind of Another Species*. Chicago: University of Chicago Press.

Davidson, D. (1975) Thought and talk. In S. Guttenplan (ed.), *Mind and Language*. Oxford: Oxford University Press.

Dennett, D. C. (1969) *Content and Consciousness*. London: Routledge and Kegan Paul.

Dennett, D. C. (1995) Animal consciousness and why it matters. *Social Research* 62, 691–710.

Dennett, D. C. (1997) *Kinds of Minds: Towards an Understanding of Consciousness*. New York: Basic Books (Science Masters Series).

Dretske, F. (1995) *Naturalizing the Mind*. Cambridge, MA: MIT Press.

Fisher, J. A. (1990) The myth of anthropomorphism. Originally published in M. Bekoff and D. Jamieson (eds.), *Interpretation and Explanation in the Study of Animal Behavior: Vol. 1, Interpretation, Intentionality, and Communication*. Boulder, CO: Westview Press. Reprinted in M. Bekoff and D. Jamieson (eds.) (1996) *Readings in Animal Cognition*. Cambridge, MA: MIT Press.

Fouts, R. S., Jensvold, M. L. A., and Fouts, D. H. (2002) Chimpanzee signing: Darwinian realities and Cartesian delusions. In M. Bekoff, C. Allen, and G. M. Burghardt (eds.), *The Cognitive Animal* 285–293. Cambridge, MA: MIT Press.

Fujita, K., Blough, D. S., and Blough, P. M. (1991) Pigeons see the Ponzo illusion. *Animal Learning and Behavior* 19, 283–93.

Gallup, G. G., Jr. (1970) Chimpanzees: self-recognition. *Science* 167, 86–7.

Gallup, G. G., Jr., Anderson, J. R., and Shillito, D. J. (2002) The mirror test. In M. Bekoff, C. Allen, and G. M. Burghardt (eds.), *The Cognitive Animal*, 325–34. Cambridge, MA: MIT Press.

Gardner, R. A., Gardner, B. T., and Van Cantfort, T. E. (1989) *Teaching Sign Language to Chimpanzees*. Albany, NY: SUNY Press.

Griffin, D. R. (1976) *The Question of Animal Awareness: Evolutionary Continuity of Mental Experience*. New York: Rockefeller University Press (2nd edn. 1981).

Griffin, D. R. (1984) *Animal Thinking*. Cambridge, MA: Harvard University Press.

Griffin, D. R. (1992) *Animal Minds*. Chicago: University of Chicago Press.

Griffin, D. R. and Speck, G. B. (2004) New evidence of animal consciousness. *Animal Cognition* 7, 5–18.

Hare, B. and Wrangham, R. (2002) Integrating two evolutionary models for the study of social cognition. In M. Bekoff, C. Allen, and G. M. Burghardt (eds.), *The Cognitive Animal* 363–69. Cambridge, MA: MIT Press.

Hare, B., Call, J., Agnetta, B., and Tomasello, M. (2000) Chimpanzees know what conspecifics do and do not see. *Animal Behavior* 59, 771–85.

Hare, B., Call, J., and Tomasello, M. (2001) Do chimpanzees know what conspecifics know? *Animal Behaviour* 63, 139–51.

Hauser, M., Chomsky, N., and Fitch, W. Tecumseh (2002) The faculty of language: what is it, who has it, and how did it evolve? *Science* 298, 1569–79.

Heyes, C. (1998) Theory of mind in nonhuman primates. *Behavioral and Brain Sciences* 21, 101–48.

Jamieson, D. and Bekoff, M. (1992) Carruthers on nonconscious experience. *Analysis* 52, 23–8.

Keeley, B. (2004) Anthropomorphism, primatomorphism, mammalomorphism: understanding cross-species comparisons. *Biology and Philosophy* 19, 521–40.

Kennedy, J. S. (1992) *The New Anthropomorphism*. New York: Cambridge University Press.

Lycan, W. (1996) *Consciousness and Experience*. Cambridge, MA: MIT Press.

Mendl, M. and Paul, E. S. (2004) Consciousness, emotion and animal welfare: insights from cognitive science. *Animal Welfare* 13, S17–25.

Nagel, T. (1974) What is it like to be a bat? *Philosophical Review* 83, 435–50.

Parker, S. T., Mitchell, R. W., and Boccia, M. L. (eds.) (1994) *Self-Awareness in Animals and Humans: Developmental Perspectives*. New York: Cambridge University Press.

Pepperberg, I. M. (1999) *The Alex Studies: Cognitive and Communicative Abilities of Grey Parrots*. Cambridge, MA: Harvard University Press.

Pepperberg, I. M. (2002) Cognitive and communicative abilities of grey parrots (*Psittacus erithacus*). In M. Bekoff, C. Allen, and G. M. Burghardt (eds.), *The Cognitive Animal*, 247–255. Cambridge, MA: MIT Press.

Regan, T. (1983) *The Case for Animal Rights*. Berkeley: University of California Press (see especially chs. 1 and 2).

Reiss, D. and Marino, L. (2001) Mirror self-recognition in the bottlenose dolphin: a case of cognitive convergence. *Proceedings of the National Academy of Science* 98, 5937–942.

Rollin, B. E. (1989) *The Unheeded Cry: Animal Consciousness, Animal Pain and Science*. New York: Oxford University Press.

Savage-Rumbaugh, S. (1996) *Kanzi: The Ape at the Brink of the Human Mind*. New York: John Wiley and Sons.

Shumaker, R. W. and Schwartz, K. B. (2002) When traditional methodologies fail: cognitive studies of great apes. In M. Bekoff, C. Allen, and G. M. Burghardt (eds.), *The Cognitive Animal*, 335–44. Cambridge, MA: MIT Press.

Singer, P. (1975/1990) *Animal Liberation*, rev. edn. 1990. New York: Avon Books.

Sober, E. (2000) Evolution and the problem of other minds. *Journal of Philosophy* 97, 365–86.

Stoerig, P. and Cowey, A. (1997) Blindsight in man and monkey. *Brain* 120, 535–59.

Tye, M. (2000) *Consciousness, Color, and Content*. Cambridge, MA: MIT Press.

Varner, G. (1999) *In Nature's Interests?* New York: Oxford University Press.

Wilkes, K. (1984) Is consciousness important? *British Journal for the Philosophy of Science* 35, 223–43.

5

Rethinking the Evolution of Consciousness

THOMAS POLGER

Introduction

Suppose that consciousness is a natural feature of biological organisms, and that it is a capacity or property or process that resides in a single organ. In that case there is a straightforward question about the consciousness organ, namely: How did the consciousness organ come to be formed and why is its presence maintained in those organisms that have it? Of course answering this question might be rather difficult, particularly if the consciousness organ is made of soft tissue that leaves at best indirect fossil records, or if it has been fixed in the populations for such a long time that there are few available examples of organisms that lack the consciousness organ on which to conduct comparative experiments. No doubt there are other confounding practical obstacles as well. But these are just the complications that face biologists and natural historians on a regular basis, and they do not reflect any special problems about the study of consciousness. This is just to say that if consciousness is a natural feature of biological organisms then its origins and history can be studied in the same manner as other features of the biological world. It is a hard business, but biologists are pretty good at it.

The situation that I have asked you to imagine is a caricature that lies somewhere between simplification and sheer fantasy. In all likelihood there is no consciousness organ. But then again, there is no single circulatory organ, or respiratory organ, or digestive organ. Nevertheless, it is a respectable pursuit to inquire about the natural histories of circulation, respiration, and digestion; and to inquire about the organs and systems that enable those capacities and activities. The idea that hearts by themselves circulate blood is fine for grade school. But full understanding of the metabolic interdependence of the totality of systems that compose an organism surely reveals the idea of an isolable circulatory system as a gross simplification. This, of course, is no obstacle to studying the natural history of circulatory systems. (For qualifications see Allen 2002.) Indeed, although complexity makes the task hard it also provides some of the most compelling evidence.

What, then, of the imaginary consciousness organ? Is this idea a useful simplification or a misleading fantasy? My own view is that the imaginary consciousness organ is more like a simplification than a fable, just like the grade school stories about hearts, lungs, and stomachs. Conscious experiences are natural features or processes that occur in biological organisms. I doubt that there is a single consciousness organ that is localized and modular. This does not mean that the goals of discovering the mechanisms and natural history of conscious experiences are hopeless. It does suggest that the task will be difficult. Later, I will return to consider what such projects might look like, and what progress may have been made.

But most discussion of the origins and maintenance of consciousness is not about the relative merits of one or another natural history explanation of consciousness. Instead, the focus tends to be on various lines of reasoning that purport to show that *if* some particular explanation (or general class of explanations) of the history of consciousness were correct, then this would reveal something about the fundamental nature of consciousness. In contrast to the relatively straightforward "natural history" reasoning about consciousness, this second kind of consideration concerns theoretical connections between the etiology of consciousness and philosophical theories of its nature. These lines of reasoning are speculative or philosophical; they focus on what some evidence might show rather than on what evidence we actually have. In this way, discussions concerning the origins of consciousness are different from those about the origins of hearts, lungs, and stomachs. And it is these lines of reasoning that concern me in this chapter.

There is a third line of reasoning about the etiology of consciousness that I will mention only to set aside. These are the so-called teleological or teleofunctional theories of consciousness. Roughly speaking, these are theories according to which conscious mental states are a special kind of representational or functional state of brains or nervous systems, and according to which representational or functional states must be understood in terms of biological function. The most explicit applications of such theories to consciousness come from William Lycan (1987), Fred Dretske (1995), and Robert Van Gulick (1980). Likewise, Jerry Fodor (1968), Daniel Dennett (1991), and Owen Flanagan (1992) have hinted at such a theory for some mental states, if not conscious mental states specifically. Although the teleofunctional view of mind is perhaps most often associated with Ruth Millikan (1984, 1993), she does not seem to offer it as a theory of consciousness. I will now set these theories aside because they are best thought of as representational theories of consciousness which also take a teleological or etiological approach to explaining representation. This is not to suggest that they have nothing to say concerning the natural history of consciousness – see especially Dretske (1995). But my focus here is on the second kind of reasoning about consciousness.

Natural History, Adaptation, and Just-So Stories

Excepting the title of this chapter, I have not yet used the term "evolution" or any of its related terms. Instead I have spoken only about the origins and natural histories of biological organisms, and their features, capacities, or organs. Now I will begin to use the terminology of evolutionary theory, the theory of the origins and natural histories of organisms and their traits.

If conscious experience is a natural trait of biological organisms then there is an evolutionary explanation for its presence in those organisms. But we must be cautious. Not every property of an organism is a trait – Stephen J. Gould famously argued that the panda's "thumb" and the shape of human chins are not traits. And not all evolutionary explanations of traits are adaptation explanations, for not all traits are formed or maintained by a process of adaptation through natural selection. Some traits could be formed or sustained by chance – mutation or drift – or by self-organization. Nevertheless, adaptation explanations are the default explanations for complex traits. (Needless to say, deciding what is a complex trait directs our attention back to my first caution, concerning which features of organisms are genuine traits.) Traits formed by natural selection are adaptations, and they are sometimes said to have evolutionary, etiological, or "proper" functions.

Many people who have only a casual familiarity with evolutionary theory think that all evolutionary explanations are adaptation explanations – that every evolved trait is an adaptation. But this is not correct. There is an important difference between evolution and selection. The panda's "thumb" evolved, but if Gould (1980) is right it was not selected for by natural selection, so it is not an adaptation. Additionally, we have already noted that not all properties exhibited by organisms are traits at all – so it is with the shape of the human chin, and probably the ability to do calculus as well. (Though both the shape of the chin and the ability to do calculus are good candidates for features that are made possible by the adaptation of other traits – of the developmental path and shape of our jaw bones, and the structure of the brain, respectively.) Also, some features of organisms that originally appear by chance may later prove to be useful and subsequently be favored in the process of natural selection. The length of the bone that forms the panda's "thumb" may be one such case of *exaptation* (Gould & Vrba 1982). Finally, some people identify evolution with gradualist theories of change over time, according to which descent with modification occurs slowly and continuously. My discussion of evolution will be entirely neutral about whether evolutionary change is gradual, or "punctuated," or sometimes both. These disputes concern not whether adaptation is the primary mechanism that shapes organisms on our planet, but how dominant it is, just how it works, and what other biological processes also play a role in evolution. Such disagreements are, as they say, in-house.

Now we have the resources we need to restate our questions about consciousness. If consciousness is a natural biological trait, or is a system of such traits, then we should expect that there is an evolutionary explanation for its presence in those organisms that have it. If it is complex or is part of a complex system, then we should expect that there will be an adaptation explanation for it, or for some of its features, or for the organization of the complex system. I claimed that there will be evolutionary explanations for conscious experiences. Moreover, I expect that some of these will be adaptation explanations – that some sorts of consciousness, at least, were selected for by natural selection. Just what these explanations might be is a topic that we will return to later. But as I indicated above, most discussion of the evolution of consciousness does not concern how such evolutionary explanations ought to go. They concern, instead, whether consciousness is a natural phenomenon at all, if so whether it is a trait in the special sense relevant to evolutionary theory, and if not, whether anything can be inferred about its origins. These lines of reasoning concern whether there are general considerations about consciousness or about evolution that can help settle the questions of whether consciousness is a trait, or an adaptation, or a natural phenomenon at all. Such are the most prominent questions about the evolution of consciousness.

Before we examine some arguments concerning the evolution of consciousness, we need to understand what a good explanation of the adaptation of consciousness would look like. Such an explanation would ideally include (i) evidence that selection has occurred, (ii) an ecological explanation of adaptive advantage, (iii) evidence that the trait is heritable, (iv) information about the population structure, and (v) phylogenetic information about trait polarity (Brandon 1990, pp. 165–74). Of course, most actual adaptation explanations are not ideally complete, but that does not undermine the regulative ideal. In this framework we can make some general observations about the evolutionary explanations of consciousness that have been offered. Most theories of the evolution of consciousness simply take for granted that trait polarity (v) favors consciousness – that conscious creatures evolved from nonconscious creatures. Practically no theorist says anything at all about the population structures in the proposed adaptive environment of consciousness (iv). But almost every theorist assumes that consciousness or the capacity for consciousness is (or is dependent on) a biological trait (or set of traits) that can be passed from parent to offspring (iii). And almost every so-called evolutionary explanation of consciousness is in fact an ecological story about the purported adaptive advantage of consciousness (ii). Often it is argued that such a story, given the presence of consciousness in some creatures, shows that consciousness could have evolved; but practically no theorist bothers to give evidence that consciousness did in fact evolve (i).

My purpose in making these observations is not to offer a blanket critique of evolutionary theories of consciousness, but only to draw attention to their incompleteness. It is important to notice that most stories of the "evolution" of consciousness are stories about what adaptive advantage consciousness might have had in some hypothetical environment. These are ecological stories of the sort that are sometimes ridiculed as "just-so" or "how-possibly" stories. One reason that just-so stories are derided is that typically no evidence is offered that supports any claims about the adaptive environment for the evolution of consciousness – for example, no evidence is given regarding the other organisms that were competing in the environment. Lacking that information, we have no evidence that creatures with consciousness were more fit than their nonconscious peers, no evidence that consciousness conferred any advantages at all. Such omissions are what separates these works of historical fiction from genuine explanations. Converting "how possibly" stories into adaptation explanations requires filling in the other parts of the explanation to show that adaptation not only could have occurred but did in fact occur.

The above complaint would be devastating to any theory that mistook a "just-so" story for an explanation. But most philosophical and psychological theorists writing about consciousness are not aspiring to give ideally complete adaptation explanations, or even to approximate them. So while we should keep the ideal of complete adaptation explanations in mind, we should also look at the other uses for how-possibly stories. It seems that many theorists, rather than aiming to establish the facts of natural history, are arguing that the availability (or lack thereof) of some evolutionary or ecological story helps (or would help) to favor some theories of the nature of consciousness over others. As we shall see, there are problems with this methodology that are more serious than the mere failure to satisfy an explanatory ideal.

Questions About the Natural History of Consciousness

Later I will outline a few explanations of the etiology of consciousness that attempt to go beyond just-so stories. Only time and evidence will tell us whether any of those particular explanations is on the right track. What we can presently evaluate is the role that evolutionary explanations are claimed to play in broader theorizing about consciousness. In this section I will consider some of the most prominent questions that arise in evolutionary reasoning about consciousness. There are four basic questions and each comes in two versions.

Q1a. *If consciousness can be shown to have evolved, does that establish that it is a natural phenomenon?* This is an odd question, admittedly – for how could we know ahead of time that consciousness has evolved? But it is just another way of asking whether consciousness could evolve if it were not a natural phenomenon. Without further constraint, the answer is clearly that nonnatural consciousness could have evolved. Versions of dualism are easy to think of, and it is not hard to concoct an epiphenomenalist version according to which consciousness is a free-rider that manifests itself in certain animals. Perhaps Thomas Huxley held such a view. Perhaps David Chalmers (chapter 17 and 1996) holds this view; and, if Chalmers is right, then all nonreductive physicalists are stuck with this view. If we want to know what such a view would look like, just imagine a dualist panpsychism according to which the nonnatural properties need to be organized in a certain way in order to constitute consciousness, and then let evolution of animals happen to sometimes form that arrangement. Consciousness, on this picture, is a nonnatural feature that supervenes on the natural features.

At this point it is useful to say something about the distinction between natural and nonnatural phenomena. I have been assuming that any philosophical theory of consciousness that is broadly dualist will also be one that counts consciousness as nonnatural. This is not an unusual assumption. Nevertheless, it should be noted that some theorists adopt an expanded conception of the "natural" which allows for at least certain kinds of dualistic properties to count as "natural" (e.g., Chalmers, chapter 17 and 1996; Velmans, chapter 27 and 2000). These do not count as versions of naturalism for me. But this may be a merely terminological stipulation. The crucial point, as will become clear, is not the distinction between natural and nonnatural but between causal and noncausal. I hold that these distinctions go together: natural with causal, nonnatural with noncausal. But for present purposes this can be regarded as a terminological stipulation. In this chapter I am not concerned to establish the truth of any particular theory. Rather, I am concerned about the relationships between claims of naturalism or epiphenomenalism on the one hand, and claims about the evolution of consciousness on the other.

Because consciousness could evolve even if it were nonnatural or noncausal (epiphenomenal), the mere claim that it evolved will not tell us whether or not it is natural or causally potent. So the negative answer to Q1a has little to do with evolution, and much to do with creative freedom of theorizing about nonnatural phenomena.

Q1b. If consciousness can be shown to have been selected for by natural selection, does that establish that it is a natural phenomenon? While it is easy to imagine the evolution of nonnatural or noncausal consciousness, it is harder to see how such consciousness could be selected for. That is because selection requires causal interaction; it requires that consciousness make a difference in the world by making a difference for the creature that has it. If immaterial or otherwise nonnatural consciousness can causally interact with the world, then I suppose that it could be selected for. In that case, the fact that consciousness was selected for (that it is an adaptation) does not show that it is a natural phenomenon. But if, as I suppose, only natural phenomena can causally interact, then consciousness could not have been selected for unless it is a natural phenomenon. I conclude that if consciousness is an adaptation then it is a natural phenomenon. (Although Descartes would disagree, the position that consciousness is both nonnatural and causally efficacious is not prominent among contemporary theorists.)

Q2a. If consciousness can be shown to have evolved, does that show that it is causally potent? For the same reasons mentioned in answering Q1a, consciousness need not be causally efficacious in order for it to have evolved. Consciousness can be an impotent immaterial or nonnatural free-rider, a side effect of the evolution of natural organisms. But, also following Q1a, this conclusion is too weak to be of much interest. The mere claim that consciousness evolved does not tell us much about the nature of consciousness at all. For the evolution of consciousness is compatible with any (noneliminativist) account of its nature.

Q2b. If consciousness can be shown to have been selected for by natural selection, does that establish that it is causally potent? Consciousness would have to be causally potent in order to be selected for. If consciousness makes no difference in the world, then there would be no ecological advantage for the things that have it over the things that do not, which could be the basis for selection. There might, of course, be other differences between the conscious and nonconscious creatures, such that the ones that are conscious happen to have some selection advantage. But that is precisely the Q1a/Q2a scenarios, in which consciousness evolves without having been selected for. Per Q1b, if consciousness was selected for – if it is an adaptation – then it is causally efficacious.

Given my terminological stipulation concerning naturalism and causal powers, Q2a and Q2b only repeat Q1a and Q1b, respectively. But if causal efficacy and naturalness come apart, the Q1 and Q2 questions will be distinct in the ways noted.

Q3a. If consciousness is necessary for some capacity φ in creature C, does that show that it is causally potent with respect to the φ-ing of C? Some theories of consciousness hold that it is causally impotent, that it is not capable of bringing about causal effects. Against this kind of epiphenomenalism, some have argued that consciousness must have causal effects because it is necessary for some capacity that conscious creatures actually have. This line of response appears to be valid. If some creature C can do φ and if only consciousness enables one to φ, then it seems clear that consciousness is causally responsible for the φ-ing of C. So, yes, if consciousness is necessary for some capacity φ in creature C (and creature C can φ), then consciousness is causally potent with respect to C's φ-ing. But is there any such φ?

Many theories of consciousness attempt to identify a feature or ability φ that cannot occur nonconsciously. Among the most popular options are flexible behavior (William James), creativity (Selmer Bringsjord), communication or mental rehearsal (Peter Carruthers), self-knowledge (Nicolas Humphreys), mentalistic language (Todd Moody) and self-awareness of a special sort (Daniel Dennett). Of course different theorists have different ideas about the nature of consciousness, and so these proposals may seem more or less radical. What concerns me, however, is the general form of the claims: that there is some φ that cannot be performed (by creature C) without having trait T – where T is consciousness, in the case at hand. If this is true, then consciousness is a very unique trait, indeed. Is there any other biological trait for which an analogous claim would be true? You might think that, say, birds cannot fly without wings. Since birds do fly, and they do have wings, then it looks as though we have a valid argument that wings are causally efficacious in bird flight. And since the conclusion is true, the reasoning looks good. But is it really true that birds could not fly without wings? Birds, being as they are, cannot fly when their wings are damaged in certain ways. But with a bit of ingenuity we can imagine that the ancestors of birds could have come to fly without evolving wings – by evolving sails, or parachutes, or balloons, or rockets or some such. These alternatives are fantastic, but fantasy is all that it takes if our only task is to undermine the incredible and overly strong claim that wings are necessary for flight – that there is no way to fly without wings.

Less fancifully, the purported example assumes that "winged" is a trait. But birds and insects and bats each have a specific kind of wing, as does each kind of bird. Once we notice this variation, is it particularly plausible that it would be impossible for sparrows to fly if they didn't have the exact wings that they do? After all, they could have wings of a different sort – perhaps even wings more like those of bats or insects than those of other birds. Of course if "wing" is just a stand-in for whatever produces lift to allow birds to fly, then the argument looks sound. But then we have only the empirically empty claim that birds cannot fly without some flight-enabling structure.

Question Q3a arises in the context of trying to establish some theory of the nature of consciousness. If on theory T consciousness is necessary for the capacity to φ and we are φ-ers then we are entitled to conclude that consciousness$_T$ (consciousness as explained by theory T) is what enables us to φ, and thereby entitled to conclude that T is the correct theory of consciousness. (This line of reasoning is usually paired with the negative argument discussed in Q3b, below, to the effect that no other theory of consciousness can explain why consciousness is necessary.) But I do not see that we have reason to suppose that there is any φ that is necessary for any capacity of biological organisms in the strong sense that would be required to infer the presence of φ from the presence of the capacity.

Q3b. If consciousness is not necessary for some capacity φ in creature C, does that show that it is not causally potent with respect to the φ-ing of C? One reason that many theorists seem to think that consciousness must be necessary for some capacity φ or other is the fear that consciousness will otherwise prove to be epiphenomenal (Polger & Flanagan 2002). If there is no φ for which consciousness is necessary, then we do not know what consciousness does (or why nature would contrive to provide us with consciousness – see Q4b, below), and we should conclude that consciousness is epiphenomenal after all. But this line of reasoning is fallacious. Carburetors are not necessary for mixing air and fuel in combustion engines (the job can be done by fuel injectors, among other devices), but it does not follow that carburetors do not mix air and fuel in those vehicles that have them. Bird wings are not necessary for flight (rockets, helicopters, and insects can all fly), but it does not follow that bird wings are causally impotent with respect to flight. Four chambered hearts are not necessary for circulation, but it does not follow that some of the chambers of human hearts are epiphenomenal. The argument form that moves from inessentialism to epiphenomenalism is clearly invalid (Flanagan 1992; Polger & Flanagan 2002). It is hard to understand why it seems to be so attractive to so many thinkers, yet it appears over and over.

It may be useful to notice that reasoning from conscious inessentialism to epiphenomenalism is not mistaken only in the difficult case of consciousness. In general, from the fact that *x* is not necessarily *P* it does not follow that *x* is not *P*. The argument is not even tempting in its simple forms. Consider: Sally's car is not necessarily silver, therefore Sally's car is not silver. But for some reason this argument form has proven unusually alluring for those thinking about the evolution of consciousness. If some theory T asserts that consciousness gives us some capacity φ, then the opponent objects by telling a just-so story (T*) about how φ can be had without consciousness or without consciousness being implemented in the way that theory T supposes. The availability of the just-so story is taken to show that consciousness does not do φ, for a creature without consciousness$_T$ – a zombie – could do φ. Since T says that consciousness *does* φ, we are urged to conclude that T is false. But the line of reasoning from "does not necessarily" to "does not" is invalid.

Notice that the emphasis in the inessentialist reasoning suggested by Q3b is on positing an alternative theory, T*, to explain φ. Offering an alternative explanation is quite different from showing that T is false by experimentally showing that mechanism M invoked by T can be interfered with without disrupting φ – experimentally dissociating M (hypothesized by T) from φ. The former aims to show that M is not necessary for φ, that it is inessential. The latter aims to show that M is insufficient for φ. This illustrates the difference between merely possible dissociations and actual deficit studies. Seen in this light, what is posing as an "evolutionary" argument against a theory of consciousness is revealed to be simply a skeptical argument: Because it is possible that theory T is not correct, it is concluded that T is false.

Q4a. If consciousness is necessary for some capacity φ in creature C, does that show that it has the evolutionary function of φ-ing in C? If consciousness is necessary for capacity φ in creature C, and C is a φ-er, then consciousness *is causally effective* in the φ-ing of C. This was the answer to Q3a, though I expressed my doubt that there is any such φ. Now we are asking whether, if consciousness is necessary for φ in C, and C is a φ-er, then we can conclude that consciousness *was selected by natural selection* for (i.e., given the evolutionary function of) φ-ing in C. This stronger claim is too strong. But there is a related claim that is quite reasonable: Suppose that there are some features of creatures that are in fact necessary for some activities of those creatures. Again, I doubt this occurs, but let us pretend that bird wings are in some sense necessary for flight in birds. If so, then this is strong evidence that the trait in question was selected for by natural selection. However, the evidence is defeasible, and it could turn out that the trait was not selected for the capacity to φ, and so does not have the function of φ-ing. A trivial example is having mass, which is necessary for many terrestrial activities but was not selected for by natural selection. In fact, in such cases of trivial and universal features like having mass, their necessity even suggests that they were not selected for. After all, mass is had by all creatures. Science fiction aside, there were no massless creatures relative to which the massed creatures could have selective advantage. There was no opportunity for selection for "having mass." (It is doubtful that having mass is a biological trait at all. That is another reason for doubting that having mass has a biological function.)

A less trivial but still silly example is the ability to do calculus. Whereas we may suppose that various brain structures are necessary (in some sense) for our ability to do calculus, it does not follow that those structures have the evolutionary function of permitting us to do calculus. It may be that those structures came about for other reasons, and were co-opted for doing calculus. The point here is that not every ability φ is one that is selectively relevant for a particular creature in a particular environment. If consciousness is necessary for some ability that did not make a fitness difference in its selective environment, then it will not have the function of φ-ing.

Evolution and natural selection produce contingent features in the world. We do not need evolution to explain necessary features of organisms. We need evolution precisely to explain those features that are not necessary, for example particular size, or the presence of eyes.

Q4b. If consciousness is not necessary for some capacity φ in creature C, does that show that it does not have the evolutionary function of φ-ing in C? The fact that a trait is necessary for some φ does not entail that it was selected for φ. But if it is not necessary for φ-ing, then does that show that it was not selected for that ability? Of course not. As I have emphasized above, evolution is an engine of contingency. It takes in contingencies and spits out contingencies. Human beings have opposable thumbs, which come in handy. We are able to do many things with our opposable thumbs. Opposable thumbs are not necessary. They are a contingent feature, but one which evidently put some of our ancestors at a selective advantage over their peers. I do not know exactly how to explain what opposable thumbs have the function of doing; that is, I do not know exactly for which capacity of the capacities that they enable they were selected by natural selection. But there is good reason to think that they do have some such function or functions; that opposable thumbs are adaptations (Gould 1980).

Unfortunately, like the bad reasoning explained in Q3b, the line of reasoning in Q4b has tempted many theorists to despair that an adaptation explanation for consciousness can be found if consciousness is not necessary for some capacity or other. These theorists are generally resistant to my claim that there is no capacity φ for which consciousness or wings are strictly necessary. Sometimes that is because they are taken in by the Q3b reasoning, and then wonder whether a causally impotent trait could be an adaptation. (They correctly conclude that it cannot.) Others succumb directly to the fallacious argument from conscious inessentialism to adaptive irrelevance. Carruthers (2000), who is usually cautious, argues that higher-order perception (he says "experience") theories of consciousness are implausible on these grounds. Carruthers reasons that evolving higher-order perceptions require that we already have higher-order thoughts. But once we have higher-order thoughts we do not need higher-order perceptions; they are inessential. So we ought to reject the higher-order perception theory. That is, since higher-order perceptions are not necessary, the implication is that evolution is unlikely to have provided us with them. (There is an alternative reading of this argument, which claims not that higher-order perception is inessential but that it is redundant. I maintain that redundancy arguments presuppose inessentialist reasoning. See Polger 2004, ch. 6.)

Now it is true that Carruthers stops at the claim that evolving unnecessary traits is unlikely, and does not go so far as to claim that it is impossible. But even the likelihood conclusion is unwarranted. From the fact that we can tell a just-so story about how a creature could do without some trait, nothing at all follows about what the trait actually does (its efficacy, per Q3b), about its history (whether it has an evolutionary function, per Q4b), or about the likelihood of its occurrence.

Consciousness and the Complexity Argument

The problematic lines of reasoning discussed in the previous section run into trouble for two general reasons. One is that some mistakenly try to draw conclusions about the actual state of affairs based solely on considerations about what states of affairs are or are not necessary. Another is that they try to make reasoning about the natural world into a deductive enterprise. They ask whether some facts about consciousness or evolution entail others, rather than asking what kinds of evidence we have for claims about consciousness. This is why even the positive results are not very interesting, for example, that if bird wings are (in some sense) necessary for flight in birds, then bird wings are causally efficacious in actual bird flight.

There is at least one line of evolutionary reasoning that avoids these pitfalls. As noted in passing above, evolution by natural selection is the most likely source of complex traits in living creatures. When we find a complex trait in a living thing we can reasonably expect that the trait was formed by natural selection. The connection is defeasible, of course. Complexity may sometimes come about and be maintained by chance alone. But as a line of reasoning about empirical contingencies, the complexity argument is a good one. Grantham and Nichols (1999) have done the most to defend the application of complexity considerations to the evolution of consciousness.

Grantham and Nichols begin with the general principle of evolutionary reasoning and apply it to the case of consciousness: "According to contemporary evolutionary biology, it is reasonable to assume that complex biological structures are adaptations – even if we do not know precisely how the organ functions or how it evolved. The complexity of phenomenal consciousness thus provides an argument that phenomenal consciousness is an adaptation" (2000, p. 649). The burden, then, is to argue that consciousness is complex in the appropriate way. Grantham and Nichols proceed cautiously because they are concerned to keep at bay the critic who adopts a skeptical or epiphenomenalist critique. Working under these constraints, they outline evidence for thinking that some systems implicated in conscious perception are anatomically complex. (They are unwilling to accept evidence of merely functional complexity because it is more vulnerable to epiphenomenalist concerns.) Their conclusion is that "if given an abstract characterization of the structure of phenomenal consciousness, biologists wouldn't even entertain the hypothesis that the system is functionless" (2000, p. 664). Thus anatomical complexity is evidence of adaptation.

I do not think that Grantham and Nichols's gambit of relying on structural complexity works out, but it is not one that they ought to require anyhow. They recognize that their success must be qualified:

> For those with an abiding metaphysical conviction that phenomenal consciousness can't be causally relevant, [the] complexity argument is unlikely to carry much weight. However, if we view phenomenal consciousness from the perspective of biology rather than metaphysics, we have good reason to think that phenomenal consciousness is an evolutionary adaptation and hence causally relevant. (Grantham & Nichols 2000, p. 664)

The troubles are twofold. First, the epiphenomenalist skeptic will not be satisfied by restricting one's concerns to only the anatomical complexity of consciousness, even if that is successful. For such a critic will be willing to be skeptical about those systems as well. Second, it is unclear how the anatomy of consciousness can be located without any appeal to evidence of functional organization. (Nor do Grantham and Nichols suppose that it can, entirely.) The mapping of the functional and phenomenal structures of experience onto anatomical structures in the nervous system is part of the argument for identifying those neural structures as the locus of consciousness (Polger & Flanagan 1999; Polger & Sufka 2006). Without that mapping we cannot be sure that we are considering the right anatomical features.

The lesson is that one should not try to fend off the skeptical epiphenomenalist and provide a positive theory of the evolution of consciousness at the same time. And if I am right, there is no need to pursue these goals simultaneously. For the main arguments appealed to by skeptical epiphenomenalists are those considered above, which reason from the fact that consciousness is not causally or evolutionarily necessary for some or any φ to the conclusion that consciousness does not do φ. We have seen that these arguments are invalid, so we can safely set aside these kinds of epiphenomenalist worries when it comes to giving an account of the natural history of consciousness.

It is important that what we are setting aside are the inessentialist-based epiphenomenal concerns, epitomized by the reasoning discussed with respect to Q3b and Q4b. If there are other reasons to consider epiphenomenalism about consciousness, then those will have to be settled. Some will think that the timing studies discussed by Libet (1993), Wegner (2002), or Gray (2004) give such reasons. (For an alternative interpretation of these experiments, see Nahmias 2002.) If we are independently convinced that consciousness is epiphenomenal then the complexity argument will cut no ice, for epiphenomenalists will be prepared to think of consciousness as a mere byproduct of that complexity. Of course, as epiphenomenalists, they will also eschew any adaptationist explanation for the features of consciousness, per Q1b and Q2b, and our interest in the evolution of consciousness will be rather limited, per Q1a and Q2a. At best one would be able to say that an epiphenomenalist theory of consciousness is not incompatible with the evolution of the systems with which consciousness is associated. And, of course, epiphenomenalists will not be able to explain the complexity of conscious experience in terms of the complexity of the systems on which (they may agree) consciousness depends.

If we are not worried about epiphenomenalism, the evidence of the complexity of conscious experience is obvious and abundant. My own favorite example is the rich phenomenal and functional structure of color vision. Human color experience varies along the dimensions of hue, saturation, and brightness; these factors interact to yield a distinctive asymmetric color space that appears to be different from the perceptual spaces of other species, that is well explained by the anatomical organization of the visual system (and by differences between our anatomy and, say, pigeon anatomy), and that is well-tuned for guiding activity within the constraints of our spectral environmental (Hardin 1988; Thompson 1995; Purves et al. 2003). Once we understand that evolution produces contingencies and that consciousness is part of nature, then visual consciousness evolved if eyes and brains did. The complexity argument gives us reason to think that eyes and visual systems evolved even if we had no other evidence that they did and even if we did not know what they are good for. Of course, in the case of conscious visual perception we have a pretty good idea what it does for us, so the complexity argument is not our only source of information.

Just-So Stories and Beyond

A general pitfall in evolutionary reasoning about consciousness, and about evolutionary psychology broadly, is the use of just-so stories to postulate the existence of neural or psychological mechanisms that could have, should have, or must have evolved. Since evolution is an engine of contingency, this kind of reasoning is likely to go awry. It is simply not the case that evolutionary forces should have, or must have, produced anything at all. So it is foolhardy to try to reason from evolutionary stories to the existence of physiological structures (Grantham & Nichols 1999).

A better methodology is to instead think about the evolutionary history of features that are known and understood. But this is hard work – this is evolutionary biology. Good theorizing requires a tremendous amount of historical and comparative study, much of which is hard to do with soft tissue systems such as the neural mechanisms that presumably mediate conscious experience. But there is, for example, some elegant comparative work on color vision across animal species (see Thompson 1995 and Clark 1993 for discussion) that can be used in reasoning about the etiology and functions of color vision.

Once one adopts the view that consciousness is a natural process that occurs in some kind of creatures, then there is no philosophical puzzle about how consciousness evolved, just the hard work of evolutionary biology. Eyes have always been central to the discussion of human evolution. No scientist now doubts that our eyes and brains are products of evolution by natural selection. None doubt that brain areas V1–V5 are implicated in visual processing, and that their structures are products of natural selection. Activation in visual cortex is also associated with conscious visual sensations. Understanding exactly how sensations are manifested by brains is a difficult problem indeed, and the object of much scientific and philosophical theorizing. The naturalist holds that whatever the evolutionary explanation of how the visual system came to be how it is, that will be the story of how visual consciousness came to be how it is. It is utterly irrelevant whether the same information-gathering capabilities could be achieved by some system that has different conscious experiences or none at all, or whether our visual system could be replaced with a silicon prosthetic. In us, those capabilities are performed by conscious mechanisms.

Consider the case of blindsight (Weiskrantz, chapter 13 and 1986). Philosophers and cognitive scientists have tended to focus on what you might think of as the silver lining for blindsight patients, which is that they seem to demonstrate that some perceptual information can be processed in the absence of visual sensation. After all, this is the surprising part of the phenomenon. But let us not forget that blindsight is a deficit, and that visual consciousness is lacking because there is damage to the visual system. It is true that blind-sighters perform better than chance at certain tasks. But normally sighted persons perform almost perfectly in the same tasks. So at the same time that blindsight suggests that visual sensation is (in some sense) not necessary for visual information gathering, it also provides evidence that conscious mechanisms – as a matter of contingent fact – play an important role in normal human perception. Of course the evidence is subject to further investigation. If we had actual evidence of double-dissociation between conscious visual experience and visual competence – for example, actual evidence of "super-blindsight" patients who show no performance deficit while reporting lack of visual sensation, rather than the mere philosophical possibility of such (Block 1995) – we would have experimental reason to doubt that consciousness itself is doing some work. But the mere possibility of super-blindsight at best shows that consciousness is inessential, not that it is inefficacious, per Q3b. It gives us no reason to doubt that consciousness is implicated in (rather than merely correlated with) our visual processing.

There are also some deflationary evolutionary explanations, which take what we know about existing brain systems as evidence that some manifestations of conscious experience are not adaptations. Flanagan (1995, 2000) argues that dream consciousness is not an adaptation, but a spandrel. His reasoning does not depend on the claim that brains could do what they do without consciousness, though that might be true. Instead, he argues that the best current theories of dreaming and brain activity during sleep do not invoke a role for conscious visual experience. The best candidates for the function of brain activity during sleep are memory consolidation and memory purging. But experiments show that dream experiences do not have the content that they would be predicted to have if the conscious content of dreams were to play a role. We do not dream about things that our brains are trying to remember, nor about things that we are trying to forget. Instead, the stimulation of conscious experience during sleep appears to be a side effect of those other brain activities.

Similarly, Sufka (2000) argues that chronic pain sensation does not serve an adaptive function. Sufka assumes that the acute pain system is an adaptation. But, he argues, the neuronal changes that seem to explain chronic pain are part of the basic cellular mechanisms in neurons, not special to the pain sensory system. The cellular changes involved in chronic pain are nearly identical to those thought to be involved in the cellular basis of learning and memory. Sufka speculates that these basic cellular mechanisms are adaptations for learning and memory and that they are universal in neurons. Chronic pain, then, is the byproduct of two systems that are adaptations, the pain sensory system and the cellular learning mechanisms. The result is that the pain sensory system can, in effect, learn to be in pain. Something like this account may apply to some mood disorders such as depression and anxiety.

These evolutionary explanations of the experiences of dreaming and chronic pain are deflationary in that they deny that some kind of consciousness is an adaptation. And in each case it should be conceded that little evidence is provided to support the claim that consciousness is a spandrel of some other trait that is an adaptation. Still, these accounts are at least off on the right foot because they begin with empirical consideration of known neural mechanisms. These deflationary theories may not be borne out in the long run. But, if so, it will be because they do not stand up to the evidence, not because someone has an account according to which consciousness is necessary for any familiar or heretofore unnoticed capacity of human beings. Though there are many potential flaws in these accounts, they are the typical flaws of empirical theories. They are subject to experimental disconfirmation. But they avoid the pitfall of relying on claims of evolutionary necessity.

Conclusion

Clinical cases like blindsight lend credibility to philosophical intuitions that consciousness is not (in a sense) necessary for vision. But the empirical cases also suggest that consciousness is crucial to the ordinary operation of human cognitive and perceptual systems. The lesson, I have urged, is that it is a mistake to think about consciousness – and especially about the evolution of consciousness – in terms of necessity or lack thereof.

If birds were aware that their wings are what enables them to fly away from predators, they would be right to think that having wings was awfully important. One might even say that having wings is essential to birds being the kinds of creatures that they are. But that does not show that wings had to evolve to "solve" some evolutionary challenge in the ancestors of birds. Evolution might have pushed the bird ancestors in a different direction, making them fast runners or whatever. This does not show that wings are not for flight; it just shows that wings never had to come into existence at all.

We humans are conscious creatures. We are aware of, and appreciate that, we are conscious creatures. We value our consciousness, for among other reasons we think that we could not be the kinds of creatures we are without being conscious. In this sense we regard consciousness as necessary for, and essential to, our form of life. All this is true, but it does not show that consciousness is necessary for any particular capacity that we have. Consciousness may, of course, be necessary for our way of doing things. But that will not show that consciousness had to occur unless it is also necessary that we evolved to be as we are – which surely it is not. The sense in which consciousness is necessary for us is quite a contingent sort of necessity, but that is the only kind that evolution provides.

None of these considerations undermines the claims that we are conscious beings, that consciousness plays a role in our psychology, or that consciousness has evolved. But saying more about the nature of consciousness, what it does, and where it came from, will require hard empirical work, not more "just-so" stories.

See also 8 Affective consciousness; 13 The case of blindsight; 17 The hard problem of consciousness; 21 Higher-order theories of consciousness; 32 The causal efficacy of consciousness.

Acknowledgements

This chapter is a development of earlier ideas that were published with Owen Flanagan. I benefited from discussion of this chapter with the Cognition, Action, Perception, and Performance group in the Psychology Department of the University of Cincinnati. Colin Allen, Eddy Nahmias, Shaun Nichols, Michael Riley, Susan Schneider, Robert Skipper, and Max Velmans commented on versions of the manuscript. Of course any errors are my own.

Further Readings

Brandon, R. (1990) *Adaptation and Environment*. Princeton, NJ: Princeton University Press.

Flanagan, O. (2000) *Dreaming Souls*. New York: Oxford University Press.

Nichols, S. and Grantham, T. (2000) Adaptive complexity and phenomenal consciousness. *Philosophy of Science* 67, 648–70.

Polger, T. and Flanagan, O. (2002) Consciousness, adaptation and epiphenomenalism. In James Fetzer (ed.), *Consciousness Evolving*, 21–41. Amsterdam: John Benjamins.

References

Allen, C. (2002) Real traits, real functions? In A. Ariew, R. Cummins, and M. Perlman (eds.), *Functions: New Readings in the Philosophy of Psychology and Biology*, 373–89. New York: Oxford University Press.

Block, N. (1995) On a confusion about a function of consciousness. *Behavioral and Brain Sciences* 18, 2, 227–87.

Brandon, R. (1990) *Adaptation and Environment*. Princeton, NJ: Princeton University Press.

Bringsjord, S. and Noel, R. (2002) Why did evolution engineer consciousness? In James Fetzer (ed.), *Consciousness Evolving*, 111–138. Amsterdam: John Benjamins.

Carruthers, P. (2000) *Phenomenal Consciousness: A Naturalistic Theory*. New York: Cambridge University Press.

Chalmers, D. J. (1996) *The Conscious Mind: In Search of a Fundamental Theory*. Oxford: Oxford University Press.

Clark, Austen (1993) *Sensory Qualities*. Oxford: Clarendon/Oxford University Press.

Dennett, D. (1991) *Consciousness Explained*. Boston: Little, Brown, and Co.

Dretske, F. (1995) *Naturalizing the Mind*. Cambridge, MA: MIT Press.

Flanagan, O. (1992) *Consciousness Reconsidered*. Cambridge, MA: MIT Press.

Flanagan, O. (1995) Deconstructing dreams: the spandrels of sleep. *Journal of Philosophy* XCII, 5–27.

Flanagan, O. (2000) *Dreaming Souls*. New York: Oxford University Press.

Fodor, J. (1968) *Psychological Explanation*. New York: Random House.

Gould, S. J. (1980) *The Panda's Thumb: More Reflections in Natural History*. New York: Norton.

Gould, S. J. and Vrba, E. S. (1982) Exaptation: a missing term in the science of form. *Paleobiology* 8, 4–15.

Grantham, T. and Nichols, S. (1999) Evolutionary psychology: ultimate explanations and Panglossian predictions. In Valerie Hardcastle (ed.), *Where Biology Meets Psychology: Philosophical Essays*, 47–88. Cambridge, MA: MIT Press.

Gray, J. (2004) *Consciousness: Creeping up on the Hard Problem*. Oxford: Oxford University Press.

Hardin, C. (1988) *Color for Philosophers*. Indianapolis: Hackett.

Humphreys, N. (2002) *The Mind Made Flesh: Essays from the Frontiers of Evolution and Psychology*. Oxford: Oxford University Press.

Libet, B. (1993) *Neurophysiology of Consciousness: Selected Papers and New Essays*. Boston, MA: Birkhäuser.

Lycan, W. (1987) *Consciousness*. Cambridge, MA: MIT Press.

Millikan, R. (1984) *Language, Thought, and Other Biological Categories*. Cambridge, MA: MIT Press.

Millikan, R. (1993) *White Queen Psychology and Other Essays for Alice*. Cambridge, MA: MIT Press.

Moody, T. (1994) Conversations with zombies. *Journal of Consciousness Studies* 1, 2, 196–200.

Nahmias, E. (2002) When consciousness matters: a critical review of Daniel Wegner's *The Illusion of Conscious Will*. *Philosophical Psychology* 15, 4, 527–41.

Nichols, S. and Grantham, T. (2000) Adaptive complexity and phenomenal consciousness. *Philosophy of Science* 67, 648–70.

Polger, T. (2004) *Natural Minds*. Cambridge, MA: MIT Press.

Polger, T. and Sufka, K. (2006) Closing the gap on pain: mechanism, theory, and fit. In M. Aydede (ed.), *New Essays on the Nature of Pain and the Methodology of Its Study*, 325–350. Cambridge, MA: MIT Press.

Polger, T. and Flanagan, O. (1999) Natural answers to natural questions. In Valerie Hardcastle (ed.), *Where Biology Meets Psychology: Philosophical Essays*, 221–247. Cambridge, MA: MIT Press.

Polger, T. and Flanagan, O. (2002) Consciousness, adaptation and epiphenomenalism. In James Fetzer (ed.), *Consciousness Evolving*, 21–41. Amsterdam: John Benjamins.

Purves, D. and Lotto, R. B. (2003) *Why We See What We Do*. Sunderland, MA: Sinauer.

Sufka, K. (2000) Chronic pain explained. *Brain and Mind* 1, 155–79.

Thompson, E. (1995) *Colour: A Study in Cognitive Science and the Philosophy of Perception*. Boston, MA: Blackwell Publishers.

Van Gulick, R. (1980) Functionalism, information, and content. *Nature and System* 2, 139–62.

Velmans, M. (2000) *Understanding Consciousness*. London: Routledge.

Wegner, D. M. (2002) *The Illusion of Conscious Will*. Cambridge, MA: MIT Press.

Weiskrantz, L. (1986) *Blindsight: A Case Study and Implications*. New York: Oxford University Press.

6

Machine Consciousness

IGOR ALEKSANDER

Introduction

Increasingly, scientists are trying to understand consciousness as the product of the most complex machine on Earth: the living brain. Machine modeling of consciousness (MMC) is the name given to the work of those who use not only their analytic skills but also their ability to design machines to understand better what "being conscious" might mean as the property of a machine.

While science progresses through a process of analysis of complex matter, engineering advances through a process of synthesis based on knowledge gleaned from analysis. A complex example of such synthesis is the control system for a jet airplane. This can only be created by bringing together aerodynamics, jet engine behavior equations, fuel science, mathematical control theory, computing, electronics, and much else. From all of this emerges the comfort, safety, and convenience of airline passengers. Similarly, designing machine models of consciousness is an exceedingly multidisciplinary process that not only involves computing, mathematics, control theory, chaos theory, and automata theory but also all that can be gathered from the contributions of psychologists, neuroscientists, and philosophers.

This approach to the understanding of consciousness is a relatively new enterprise. Although suggestions for the constructive method were fielded in the 1990s (e.g., Aleksander 1996, and Taylor 1999), May 2001 was a seminal date for establishing a machine consciousness paradigm. Philosopher David Chalmers of Arizona State University, neurologist Christof Koch and computer engineer Rod Goodman of the California Institute of Technology, organized a small meeting of computer scientists, neuroscientists, and philosophers at Cold Spring Harbor Laboratories (CHSL) in New York. To keep the proceedings informal, no written record of this meeting was kept. Its task was to discuss the extent to which attempting to design a conscious machine could contribute to an understanding of consciousness in general. The seminal nature of this meeting, coming as it did after more than fifty years of claims that intelligent machines have been constructed, needs some explaining. The machine modeling of consciousness sets out by distinguishing the activity from classical AI and Neural networks. As we shall see below, the modeling fits the "consciousness" appellative if and only if it addresses the mental state of a machine either as an explicit, symbolic model of the world with the machine computation explicitly represented within it (the functional stance) or if it addresses mechanisms that materially are capable of such representations in a cellular non-symbolic way (the material stance). Only the latter addresses some of the phenomenological issues associated with consciousness, but this does not cut out the former, where one looks for behavioral clues for the presence of consciousness. At the CHSL meeting there was a surprising degree of agreement that the concept was beneficial for the following reasons. To define a conscious machine one has to be clear, with the precision of designing a jet airplane, about the difference between a machine that is said to be conscious and one that is not. Of course this is not a current achievement although we shall see that in the functional work of Sloman and Chrisley and the material work of Aleksander that a start has been made with the creation of frameworks that attempt to achieve this precision. Such schemas not only allow the mechanisms of consciousness to be discussed with precision, but also lead to methods for confirming formally whether a seemingly conscious object conforms with a well stated set of rules for being conscious. This helps to address the third-person problem of discerning consciousness in organisms whether human, animal or, indeed, machines.

In this chapter, I pursue some of the arguments initiated at the CHSL meeting and others that have taken place since (a symposium at the 2003 meeting of the Association for the Scientific Study of Consciousness in Memphis, Tennessee; workshops by the European Science Foundation in Birmingham, UK in 2003 and by the European Community complexity community in Turin in 2003, and Antwerp in 2004). I review various typical contributions to MMC, recognizing that there are also many others.

Criteria for a Conscious Machine

Because the paradigm is still evolving, different designers justify different criteria to distinguish work on conscious machines from more conventional AI. Anticipating the details of some designs, some emerging criteria are listed below. These are stated in different engineering frameworks ranging from the functional to the materially neurological.

1   *There needs to be a demonstrable representation of a multi-featured world with the organism within it.* This is evident in the work of Holland and Goodman (2003) as a dynamic system, Aleksander (2005) as a "depictive" cellular system and Haikonen (2003) as a cellular scheme of features of world and self.
2   *The machine must show a sufficient understanding of its human interlocutors to be judged to be potentially conscious.* This is a strong feature of the work of Franklin (2003).
3   *Reactive, contemplative and supervisory levels of reasoning must be discernible in the architecture that links perception to internal processing to action.* This is the "schema" for conscious machines devised by Sloman and Chrisley (2003).
4   *The machine could be characterized by low-level mechanisms that are equivalent to those known to be crucial to consciousness in the neurology of living organisms.* This is the approach taken by Taylor (2002) and Cotterill (2003).
5   *The machine must have means of demonstrably depicting and using the out-thereness of the perceived world and be able to use such depictions to imagine worlds and the effect of its actions.* This is the stance taken by Aleksander (2005) in his depictive scheme.
6   *Having adhered to some of the criteria above, the design must qualify what is meant by an emotional evaluation of the content of consciousness.* Most of the authors below have included this criterion in their work.

Clearly, these criteria are currently more useful in defining what it is to contribute to the MMC paradigm than in defining what it is for a machine to be conscious. At least *some* of the criteria need to be embraced to argue that consciousness is under scrutiny. Some might argue that most AI programs fit some of these criteria. But I demur from this as, for example, were I to be working on a classical chess-playing algorithm, I would not satisfy criterion (1) due to the narrow nature of the representation of board states. I would fail (2) as the only understanding of the human opponent would be lodged in an assumption that he adheres to a move optimization algorithm which does not easily lead the non-naive human player to treat the machine as being conscious. While the chess machine could satisfy (3) in its architecture, it need not do so and usually does not do so. I would not be able to benefit from (4) as this is stated at too physical a level to incorporate into a symbolic algorithm. Equally inappropriate would be to insist on the depictive attitude of (5). Some emotional evaluation (6) could be introduced but this would be without the context of any of the other criteria, which does not satisfy the emotion criterion as stated.

Why Build Conscious Machines?

The key intention of the MMC paradigm is to clarify through synthesis the notion of what it is to be conscious. Of course, whatever is synthesized can also be built, and if the resulting artifact captures consciousness in some way, then it can, *in some sense*, be said to be conscious. At the end of this chapter I return to this point. But whichever way a machine can be said to be conscious, there might be a performance payoff brought by the influence that attempting to capture consciousness in a machine has on its design. It is likely that a "conscious" machine will produce an advance in ability with respect to the artificial intelligence and neural network machines produced to date. This is to be found in better autonomy, freedom from pre-programming, and an ability to represent the machine's own role in its environment. This would improve the capacity for action based on an inner "contemplative" activity rather than reactive action largely based on table-lookup of pre-stored contingency-action couplings. Whether this is beneficial or not, conscious machine designers argue that having consciousness rather than intelligence as a target, focuses design on the excellence of internal representations and their acquisition as indicated in the above criteria. This provides a machine with a significant opportunity for dealing with circumstances unforeseen by the programmer.

A Spectrum and a Paradigm

Not all designers approach MMC in the same way. While what unites them is the desire to clarify, what often distinguishes between them is whether the isomorphism with brain mechanisms is important or not. In fact, the differences reflect the functionalist/physicalist spectrum in theories of consciousness. That is, at the functionalist end of the spectrum, the main concern with the mental state is the way it serves the purposes of the organism. Consciousness is said to be in evidence in what the organism does, where the details of the mechanism responsible for the mental state are not important. Among physicalists, however, the concern is largely with the material nature of mechanisms and what it is about these that can be said to capture a conscious state. This inevitably examines living neurological machinery for appropriate design clues.

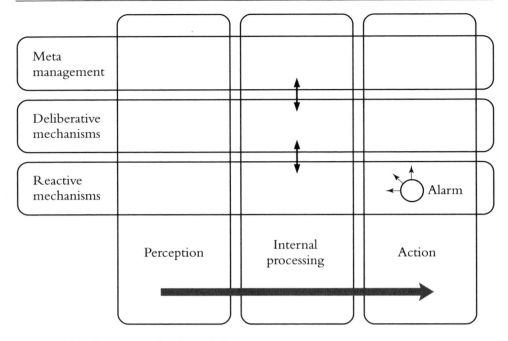

Figure 6.1 The Sloman-Chrisley CogAff schema.

Technologically, the functional work relates more closely to conventional computation and "artificial intelligence" styles of programming where achieving a certain behavior is paramount. The physicalist end is closer to neural network ideas where network dynamics and their emergent properties are important elements of conscious machine model design. Obviously, some models fall between the two extremes drawing on the useful aspects of each method.

At the time of writing, MMC workers have shown considerable determination to accept the work anywhere on this spectrum as contributing to the MMC paradigm, hoping to learn from one another and work toward a unified understanding. There is also considerable shared hope that the improved machinery mentioned earlier will arise from this effort as dictated by the need for achieving as yet unattained performance. For example, using systems that follow an appropriate group of criteria mentioned earlier it might be possible to design exploratory robots that understand the mission, are aware of their environment and their own self in it, where currently they rely heavily on pre-programmed control or human intervention from the control base. It needs to be stressed that while AI systems may be written that are so well endowed with contingency rules and analyses of their environment, it is not their performance that is under discussion here. The point is that conscious machine designers feel that they have an alternative principled way for creating inner representations. This is in its infancy and future maturity is thought to provide opportunities for the design of machines that overcome some of the limitations of AI of needing solution algorithms. Machine modeling of consciousness is seen as a way of getting closer to the methods of a conscious organism. Other applications are systems that go beyond intelligence, requiring understanding and sensitivity of the behavior of their environment or their users as seen in the next example.

Franklin's IDA System

A good example of a machine that requires understanding and sensitivity is the intelligent distribution agent designed by Stan Franklin of Memphis University (Franklin 2003). Based on Bernard Baars's global workspace theory of consciousness (see chapter 18), Franklin's IDA was designed to replace human operators in a seaman billeting task. The focus of this model is a competitive arrangement where many partial thoughts that come from a variety of memory mechanisms (short-term, episodic, etc.) compete, and for the winner to enter a consciousness area. The content of this is broadcast to address the memories afresh, generating a new set of "thoughtlets" for competition. The sequence of the states of the consciousness area represents a developing thought.

In IDA, the communication link between a seaman seeking a new billet and the machine is e-mail. The intelligent distribution agent receives information about the current postings, the seaman's skills, and desires for a new location. It then attempts to match this to the current state of available billets, perhaps having several cycles of interaction in order to achieve a result. The key feature is that the seaman using the system should not feel that there has been a change from human billeters to a machine in terms of the sensitivity and concern with which their case is handled. This could be mistaken for passing some kind of Turing test. But this is a little too superficial. The IDA generates an important and useful emotion in the user: it makes the user feel that the machine is interested in him. A Turing test is passed if the human user mistakenly thinks that the machine is *intelligent* enough to be human. The test can be passed even if the machine engenders no emotions in the user whatsoever except perhaps for a shallow "oh it's human." The IDA is more like the classical Eliza psychotherapy program but without the bluff. The global workspace machinery develops the output from a model of the user rather than playing set linguistic games with the interlocutor that have no internal model whatsoever. The system contains processing modules that implement, in traditional computing formats, various forms of memory (working, autobiographical, associative, and episodic). These are addressed from external stimuli ("I, sailor, need to work in a warm climate") as well as internal stimuli ("I, IDA might suggest Florida"). Memories produce cues and associations that compete to enter the area of "consciousness." In IDA, this takes the form of a coalition manager, an attention mechanism and a broadcast mechanism. Communication is based on "codelets," that are structured programs also called "mini agents" in computing. So the content of the consciousness area starts as a partially formed thought that broadcasts information back to address memory areas. This results in new cues and the process repeats until the "thought" is sufficiently well formed to activate an action selection mechanism that communicates with the sailor and initiates a new set of internal and external inputs for further consideration. In recent versions of IDA, "emotional" information (such as "guilt" for, say, not achieving all of a sailor's requests) enters the operation of a large number of modules.

Franklin makes no claim that there is any phenomenological consciousness in this system and is content with the functional stance that is sufficiently effective to leave users satisfied that they are interacting with a system that is "conscious" of their needs.

Consciousness in Virtual Machines

In the United Kingdom, Aaron Sloman of the University of Birmingham and Ron Chrisley of the University of Sussex have set out to discuss functional, computational ideas as a way of clarifying seemingly arbitrary opinions that enter discussions about consciousness (Sloman & Chrisley 2003). For example, some think that dreams are in consciousness, others do not, some think that consciousness is a matter of degree, others think it is either-or, and so on. They argue that a computational model has the power of making these issues explicit.

The authors evoke the concept of a *virtual machine* that can possess a mixture of states that are important in clarifying consciousness. Virtuality permits one to distinguish the properties of an emulated machine that models aspects of consciousness from those of the underlying host mechanism, that is, a general-purpose computer. This "virtual machine functionalism" is illustrated by an architectural "schema" (a discussion framework for architectures of consciousness) called CogAff (cognition and affect) and a specific architecture called H-CogAff (human-like architecture for cognition and affect). The CogAff scheme provides a framework for discussing specific aspects of consciousness that will be mentioned later (see Figure 6.1).

With information processes rather than physical processes being the elements of the schema, these can be structured to represent *perception*, *internal processing*, and *action* as well as the relationships between them. This "three-tower" vertical division is further divided into three horizontal layers. The first is for *reactive mechanisms* that link perception to action in a direct way (e.g., reflexes). The second represents *deliberative mechanisms* which are capable of "what-if" computations for planning ("I use a stick to knock the banana off the tree"). The third is a *meta-management* layer that senses the lower planning process and is capable of modifying it ("Using sticks is unfriendly, I should try something else."). Nestling among the reactive mechanisms is an "alarm" process that has rapid access to all the other parts of the architecture should an emergency be discovered.

Sloman and Chrisley's virtual-machine functionalism (VMF) is distinguished from a more general (atomic) form of functionalism where the latter treats a mental state as just one overall internal state of a machine from which stems the organism's behavior. However, VMF permits models of interacting architectural features that give rise to many, concurrently acting, interacting mental states. There are several characteristics of VMF that permit the modeling of phenomena that, at the outset, appear puzzling. For example, Chrisley and Sloman see emotion is an ill-defined concept which, in their scheme, becomes separated out as being of at least three types that relate closely to the horizontal layers. These are reactive emotions such as anger, deliberative ones such as frustration, and meta-management disruptions such as grief or jealousy. Another example where modeling is helpful is in vision where there are multiple "what" and "where" paths that are explicit in the CogAff structure, clarifying their parallel functions and interactions. Further, localized disruptions due to lesions can be modeled, explaining how some functions are disadvantaged, while others are left intact. The model makes clear how resources that control learning must be distributed. The authors also use the model to approach explanations of perceptual failures such as inattention blindness (we think we see everything, but we only see that to which we attend). Abstract thinking, as when doing mathematics, becomes a task for the meta-management layer. Finally, "qualia" are explained as the observation exercised by the meta-layer on the activity of lower layers and its ability to monitor and interpret these lower-level processes.

Cognitive Neural Architectures

Pentti Haikonen of the Nokia Company in Helsinki, Finland, has created architectural models that capture consciousness by having a comprehensive set of cognitive competences (Haikonen 2003). This relies heavily on the ability of recursive or re-entrant neural networks to store and retrieve states. Based very roughly on the operation of a brain cell, an artificial neuron is a device that receives input signals and "learns" to output an appropriate response. Recursive networks have stable states by virtue of the fact that neurons not only receive signals from external sources such as vision or audition, but also from the signals generated by other neurons in the same network. Of course, timing issues arise in this type of model: how does the internal state follow a changing input, and so on. The reader is advised to read Haikonen's work to get a full understanding of his mechanisms. So, say that a network has learned to represent the image of a cat, this image can be sustained as each neuron will output its feature of the cat image in response to other neurons outputting cat features. This means that such a network can store several images as stable states and, if the net is given only a fragment of an image "it knows" it will reconstruct the whole image as more and more neurons will be recruited to output the same image. The mechanism works not only for single unchanging inputs, but also it can track a time-varying input. This kind of re-entrant, dynamic mechanism is thought to be important in living brains and it is for this reason that Haikonen's models are sited closer to the physicalist end of the functional/physicalist spectrum than the earlier examples in this article.

Haikonen's cognitive architecture is based on a collection of similar modules. Each module consists of sensory input and a preprocess that extracts important features from the input. This is followed by a *perception generator* that feeds "a distributed representation of a percept" (say a set of features of a cat) to a neural network called the *inner process*. But the network also feeds back to the perception generator. The resulting feedback loop causes the system to be able to represent both sensory inputs and inner reconstructions of meaningful states in the absence of input.

There is one such module for each sensory modality. Some modalities, primarily vision, are divided into more detailed submodules that specialize in features such as shape, color, and motion, which reflect some divisions that are known to exist in the brain. The key feature of this architecture is that there is feedback at an even higher level: each inner process of a module receives input from the perception generators of other modules. That is, a module is influenced by what other modules are representing, leading to overall states in the system that are capable of associating, for example, the features of a cat represented in a visual module with the word "cat" represented in another module. This collection of modules is the cognitive part of the architecture. Haikonen also envisages a "motor" part that processes the state of the cognitive part, leading to actions such as the generation of speech or motion.

Another feature of the architecture is that one of the modules is positioned to act at a level higher than the sensory processing of the others. What it does is to monitor the patterns of activity of the lower level modules. This can assign word meaning to this overall state which can then make use of the word "I" in a meaningful way. Emotions too are not neglected. They are the product of central sensing of the *reactions* to certain sensory input (e.g., forward-going for pleasure and retracting for fear). Haikonen sees "conscious" as being an accurate term to describe the normal modes and styles of operation of his architecture. He distinguishes between conscious and unconscious modes through the degree of engagement that the inner mechanisms have with a task. For example, he quotes "the bedtime story effect" where a parent reads automatically to a child while thinking of something else. The reading does not reach consciousness as it goes directly from sensor to actuator without entering the representational loops. In summary, in common with other physicalist approaches, Haikonen suggests that consciousness is a product of the firing of neurons, which sometimes can be due to sensory information and importantly, at other times, to the sustained states of several levels of feedback in the machinery of the artificial or the living brain. In terms of our criteria, the claim for consciousness is based mainly on (1) and (6). One notes that Haikonen's system respects the CogAff structure while making use of the emergent properties of his components: CogAff does not concern itself with that level of functional detail.

Attention and Consciousness

Close to the physicalist end of the spectrum is the work of John Taylor, a mathematician and theoretical physicist at King's College London. The key to his model (CODAM: COrollary Discharge of Attention Movement) is based on the principle that without attention to an input there can be no awareness of it (Taylor 2002). Consequently, he investigates a specific brain mechanism called the "corollary discharge" that is responsible for changes in attention. He expresses this within a framework of control engineering. The control model involves an *object map* within which objects are selected for "coming into consciousness" by a competitive process involving working memory and the corollary discharge mechanism. Taylor identifies a "pre-reflective self," that is, the feeling of ownership of the content of being conscious, with the corollary discharge, and distinguishes it from "pure consciousness experience." He reasons that there exists a buffer in the model, the neural activity of which is the correlate of the consciousness of the organism. The corollary discharge signal appears in this buffer briefly, to be immediately followed by the sensory signal of that which has been attended as selected by the discharge. Therefore, the pure content state is a temporal extension of the contentless pre-reflective self state.

The CODAM model allows Taylor and his colleagues to arrive at several important conclusions. For example, they explain the meditational processes aimed at achieving a state of "pure consciousness" found in several Eastern religions. They argue that advanced forms of meditation force the attentional corollary discharge to block sensory input and turn attention to attending only to itself. Another application is the explanation of the attentional blink which occurs when someone is asked to attend to several objects presented in succession to one another. Schizophrenia, inattention blindness and blindsight are also approached through the CODAM model.

At the Physicalist End of the Spectrum

Rodney Cotterill, a British scientist working at the Danish Technical University in Copenhagen, contributes to MMC by searching for consciousness in a young developing child (Cotterill 2003). Called "Cyberchild," this simulation is a comprehensive model not only of the cortical regions that may be present and necessary in a very young child, but also of the endocrine system (blood control system), the thalamic regions, and the autonomic nervous system. The model makes it possible to study a biochemical state that could be described as hunger. It can then be given "milk" to increase its simulated glucose levels. Should these fall to zero, the system stops functioning and the child dies. However, the child has a vocal output that enables it to cry and alert an observer that action is needed either to provide milk or change the nappies as the model is capable of urinating and sensing a wet nappy. The crying reaction is built into the system. The model has only two sensory modalities, hearing and touch, these being dominant in the very young child and sufficient to model the effect of sensory input.

Cotterill raises important questions as to whether even a perfectly executed model of a young child is likely to be conscious in some way. He remains skeptical of this, claiming only that his work provides a deep understanding of the complex neural mechanisms of a living child: a step that has to be taken if one is to understand its consciousness. With respect to the criteria set out in this article, Cotterill firmly operates on the basis of criterion 4 and identifies the inner mechanisms of the outward signs that a baby can emit. It would be wrong, however, to interpret this as a sign of consciousness in every mammal that cries. Cotterill's philosophy is just the opposite: crying is an element of a vast and intricate electrochemical machine, the simulation of which gives us a grip on its complexity.

A Depictive Model

Also close to the physicalist end of the spectrum, the author's own approach has sought to identify mechanisms which, through the action of neurons (real or simulated), are capable of representing the world with the "depictive" accuracy that is felt introspectively in reporting a sensation (Aleksander & Dunmall 2003; Aleksander 2005). The model of being conscious stems from five features of consciousness that appear important through introspection. Dubbed "axioms" (as they are intuited but not proven) they are:

1 perception of oneself in an "out-there" world;
2 imagination of past events and fiction;
3 inner and outer attention;
4 volition and planning;
5 emotion.

This is not an exhaustive list, but is felt to be necessary for a modeling study. In the belief that consciousness is the name given to a composition of the above sensations, the methodology seeks a variety of mechanistic models each of which can support a depiction of at least one of the above basic sensations.

Perception requires a neural network that is capable of registering accurately (i.e., depicting) the content of a current perceptual sensation. "Out-thereness," particularly in vision, is ensured through the mediation of muscles: eye movement, convergence, head movement, and body movement all create signals that integrate with sensory signals to produce depictions of being an entity in an out-there world. *Imagination* requires classical mechanisms of recursion in neural networks. That is, memory of an experienced state creates a re-entrant set of states in a neural net or set of neural modules with feedback (as explained for Haikonen's work, above). That this is experienced as a less accurate version of the original stems from the known characteristic of recursive networks that their depictive power

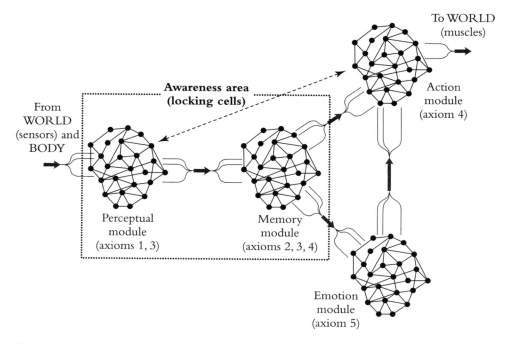

Figure 6.2 A minimal architecture with axiomatic/depictive properties.

weakens as the network learns a significant number of states. The experience of being able to create a memory of environments (technically very much like the memory of experienced environments) uses a mechanism where memory states are created and entered as controlled from natural language sensory input, a property that has been demonstrated in simulations. *Outer attention* (such as foveal movement) is due to a completion of the loop of objects being depicted and triggering further need for muscular movement to complete the depiction. *Inner attention* requires a "vetoed" movement signal (that is the initiation of a movement which is not actually carried out) to imagine, say, looking around a remembered scene. Mechanisms that lead to sensations of *volition, planning,* and *emotions* have been shown to emerge from the interaction of neural modules that are involved in imagination (in which state sequences constitute "what if" plans) and particular modules that non-depictively (unconsciously) evaluate emotions associated with predicted outcomes of planned events. This methodology has led to an integrative physical, cellular structure shown in Figure 6.2.

This indicates that two major areas (perception and imagination) contribute to consciousness and cohere through muscle-controlled depiction, while unconscious areas of emotion and action interact with them.

The scheme has been used in a variety of applications ranging from the assessment of distortions of visual consciousness in Parkinson's sufferers to identifying the possibility of a brain-wide spread of the neural correlates of "self." It has also resulted in models of visual awareness that explain inattention and change blindness.

The Emerging Paradigm

So is there evidence to show that MMC serves to clarify concepts of consciousness? This chapter has described a spectrum of methods that attempt to achieve an understanding of consciousness through *synthesis* based on notions gleaned from psychology, neurology, and introspection. While the differences between approaches have been highlighted, important common ground has also been found that contributes to an emerging explanatory paradigm. First, most designers see the role of the brain as a control mechanism which ensures that the organism deals appropriately with its environment and its internal parameters. But consciousness is not present in all control mechanisms. Room thermostats are not conscious. Ricardo Sanz, a control engineer at Madrid University points out that only control systems with non-trivial representational powers qualify as "being conscious of something." This has been refined by Owen Holland of the University of Essex and Rod Goodman (2003), who argue that the internal representation required for consciousness can be engineered through a structure that contains both a world model and an agent model. These are control systems where the two models are interconnected and improve their mutual performance.

It was said at the outset that the MMC paradigm helps to assess the presence of consciousness in an organism. This mainly relies on the discovery of the presence of the above control mechanisms with the ability to model the world and themselves. It cuts out thermostats but includes bees and properly designed planetary exploration robots. So the "sense" in which a robot could be said to be conscious is that it passes the structural and architectural assessments that satisfy the conditions of world and self modeling.

Another point of agreement is that consciousness should be seen as having different degrees. A robot conscious of the needs of an exploratory mission on Mars may not have the complex consciousness of a human immersed in daily life, but may have a higher level of consciousness than a bee on a pollen-finding mission. These differences are due to mechanisms that are similar at some level of abstraction and so constitute a model that explains what is needed by an organism to be conscious. It does not trivialize the difference between the content of the consciousness of a bee and that of a human: it teaches us to respect it. At least, this is the promise of the emergent paradigm of machine models of consciousness.

See also 17 The hard problem of consciousness; 29 Anti-materialist arguments and influential replies; 30 Functionalism and qualia.

Further Readings

Holland, Owen (ed.) (2003) *Machine Consciousness*. Exeter: Imprint Academic.
Harnad, S. (1991) Other bodies, Other minds: a machine incarnation of an old philosophical problem. *Minds and Machines* 1, 43–54. http://cogprints.org/1578/
On-line resource: The Turing Test Page, http://cogsci.ucsd.edu/%7Easaygin/tt/ttest.html#onlineref

References

Aleksander, I. (1996) *Impossible Minds, My Neurons My Consciousness*. London: IC Press.

Aleksander, I. (2005) *The World in My Mind: Five Steps to Consciousness*. Exeter: Imprint Academic.

Aleksander, I. and Dunmall, B. (2003) Axioms and tests for the presence of minimal consciousness in agents. *Journal of Consciousness Studies* 10, 7–18.

Cotterill, R. M. J. (2003) Cyberchild. *Journal of Consciousness Studies* 10: 4–5 (April/May), 31–45.

Franklin, S. (2003) IDA: a conscious artifact? *Journal of Consciousness Studies* 10: 4–5 (April/May), 47–66.

Haikonen, P. O. (2003) *The Cognitive Approach to Machine Consciousness*. Exeter: Imprint Academic.

Holland, O. and Goodman, R. (2003), Robots with internal models – a route to machine consciousness? *Journal of Consciousness Studies* 10: 4–5, 77–109.

Sloman, A. and Chrisley, R. (2003) Virtual machines and consciousness. *Journal of Consciousness Studies* 10: 4–5 (April/May), 133–72.

Taylor, J. G. (1999) *The Race for Consciousness*. Cambridge, MA: MIT Press.

Taylor, J. G. (2002) Theories of consciousness. In M. Arbib (ed.), *Handbook of Brain Theory and Neural Networks*. Cambridge, MA: MIT Press.

SOME VARIETIES OF CONSCIOUS EXPERIENCE

7

Normal and Abnormal States of Consciousness

J. ALLAN HOBSON

The changes in brain state that result in normal and abnormal changes in the state of the mind all share a common process: an alteration in the influence of lower centers, principally located in the brain stem, upon the thalamus and cortex located in the upper brain. This means that consciousness is state dependent and that understanding the mechanisms of brain state control contributes indirectly to a solution of the mind–brain problem.

The normal and abnormal variations in conscious state operate through three physiological processes: activation (A), input–output gating (I), and modulation (M).

The goal of this chapter is to give an account of the phenomenology of the variations in conscious state and to show how the three mediating brain processes interact so as to account for those variations in a unified way. A four-dimensional model called AIM, which pictorializes both normal and abnormal changes in brain state, will be presented.

In chapter 10, drug effects on consciousness will be described in terms of the concepts and model presented here.

Definition and Components of Consciousness

Consciousness may be defined as our awareness of our environment, our bodies, and ourselves. Awareness of ourselves implies an awareness of awareness, that is, the conscious recognition that we are conscious beings.

The approach taken here is based upon the author's discoveries concerning cellular and molecular mediation of the brain states underlying waking and sleeping. The current position of the reciprocal interaction model of sleep cycle control is present in full and its assertions are debated by peers in Hobson et al. (2000). The associated activation-synthesis theory of dreaming and other conscious states focuses on differences between wake-state cognition and that of dreaming by objectively mapping formal aspects of mentation from and to the brain states with which they are associated. The current theory, called AIM because it describes and accounts for activation (A), input–output gating (I), and modulation (M) is also presented in full and discussed in detail by peers (Hobson et al. 2000). Both the physiological and psychophysiological models are complex and controversial. The account that follows is admittedly oversimplified in the interests of brevity and clarity.

Formal Capacities of Mind

To develop an experimental, scientific approach to the study of consciousness, it is convenient to subdivide the mental elements that constitute consciousness. We may discern at least nine distinct capacities of mind defined in Table 7.1. These are the faculties of the mind which have been investigated by scientific psychologists since their formation by William James in 1890. From an examination of this table, it can be appreciated that consciousness is componential. That is to say, consciousness is made up of the many faculties of mind which are seamlessly integrated in our conscious experience.

Only human beings fulfill all of the demands of the definition given in the text and the components listed in the table. And humans are only fully conscious when they are awake. It is evident that higher mammals have many of the components of consciousness and may thus be considered partially conscious. Consciousness is thus graded in both the presence and intensity of its components.

In Edelman's terms, animals possess primary consciousness (composed of sensory awareness, attention, perception, memory (or learning), emotion and action) (Edelman 1992). This point is of more than theoretical interest since so much that we know about the brain physiology upon which consciousness depends comes from experimental work in animals. In making inferences about how our own conscious experience is mediated by the brain, the attribution of primary consciousness to animals is not only naturalistic but strategic.

What differentiates man from his fellow mammals, and gives man what Edelman calls secondary consciousness, depends upon language and the associated enrichment of cognition that allows humans to develop and to use verbal and numeric abstractions. These mental capacities contribute to our sense of self as agents and as creative beings. It also determines the awareness of awareness that we assume our animal collaborators do not possess.

Since the most uniquely human cognitive faculties are likely to be functions of our massive cerebral cortex, it is unlikely that the study of animal brains will ever tell us what we would like to know about these aspects of consciousness. Nonetheless, animals can and do tell us a great deal about how other components of consciousness change with changes in brain physiology. The reader who wishes to learn more about the brain basis of consciousness may wish to consult Hobson (1998).

Conscious state paradigm

It is obvious that when we go to sleep we lose sensation and the ability to act upon the world. In varying degree, all the components of consciousness listed in Table 7.1 are changed as the brain changes state. According to the conscious state paradigm, consciousness changes state in a repetitive and stereotyped way over the sleep–wake cycle. These changes are so dramatic that we can expect to make strong inferences about the major physiological underpinnings of consciousness.

Two conclusions stem from this recognition: The first is that consciousness is graded within and across individuals and species. The second is that consciousness is more radically altered by diurnal changes in brain state than it has been by millions of years of evolution. We take advantage of these two facts by studying normal sleep in man and in those subhuman species with secondary consciousness.

Table 7.1 Definition of the components of consciousness

Perception	Representation of input data
Attention	Selection of input data
Memory	Retrieval of stored representations
Orientation	Representation of time, place, and person
Thought	Reflection upon representations
Narrative	Linguistic symbolization of representations
Instinct	Innate propensities to act
Intention	Representations of goals
Volition	Decisions to act

The Sleep–Waking Cycle

When humans go to sleep, they rapidly become less conscious. The initial loss of awareness of the external world that may occur when we are reading in bed is associated with the slowing of the EEG that is called Stage I (see Figures 7.1 and 7.2). Frank sleep onset is defined by the appearance of a characteristic EEG wave, the sleep spindle (see again Figure 7.1) that reflects independent oscillation of the thalamocortical system.

Consciousness is altered in a regular way at sleep onset. While awareness of the outside world is lost, subjects may continue to have visual imagery and associated reflective consciousness. Sleep onset dreams are short-lived and their content departs progressively from the contents of previous waking consciousness. They are associated with Stage I EEG, rapidly decreasing muscle tone, and slow rolling eye movements. As the brain activation level falls further, consciousness is further altered and may be obliterated as the EEG spindles of Stage II NREM sleep block the thalamocortical transmission of both external and internal signals within the brain (see Figure 7.2). When the spindles of Stage II are joined by high voltage slow waves in over half the record, the sleep is called NREM Stage III and NREM Stage IV when the whole record comes to be dominated by them.

Arousal from Stage NREM IV is difficult, often requiring strong and repeated stimulation. On arousal, subjects evince confusion and disorientation that may take minutes to subside. When asked about their mental activity after sleep lab awakenings, they often give long, elaborate reports, which judges score as dreams even though they may continue to evince slow waves in their EEG as they give the reports, raising questions about their validity. The tendency to return to sleep is strong. This process, which is called sleep inertia, is enhanced in recovery sleep following deprivation (Dinges et al. 1997).

As the activation level is falling resulting in the sequence of sleep Stages I to IV, muscle tone continues to abate passively and the rolling eye movements cease. In Stage IV, the brain is maximally deactivated and responsiveness to external stimuli is at its lowest point. Consciousness, if it is present at all, is limited to low-level, non-progressive thought (see Figure 7.2). It is important to note three points about these facts. The first is that since consciousness rides on the crest of the brain activation process, even slight dips in activation level lead to lapses in waking vigilance. The second is that even in the depths of Stage IV NREM sleep when consciousness is largely obliterated, the brain remains highly active and is still capable of processing its own information. From PET and single

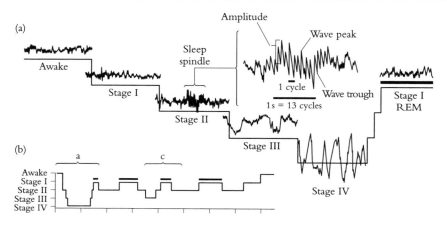

Figure 7.1 Sleep cycle basics.

NREM sleep is divided into four stages, corresponding to increasing depth of sleep as indicated by progressive dominance of the EEG by high-voltage, low-frequency ("synchronized") wave activity. Such low-frequency waves dominate the deepest stages of NREM (stages III and IV, also termed "slow-wave" sleep). Stage II NREM is characterized by distinctive sleep spindle and K-complex waveforms as well as a slow (<1Hz) oscillation which influences their timing. Panel *a* shows the characteristic wave forms of the different sleep stages.

NREM and REM sleep alternate in each of the four or five cycles that occur in each night of adult human sleep. Early in the night, NREM sleep is deeper and occupies a disproportionately large time, especially in cycle I when the REM epoch may be short or aborted. Later in the night, NREM sleep is shallow and more of each cycle is devoted to REM. Panel *b* illustrates these changes over the course of a night's sleep. Panel *a* depicts, in detail, features of an early-night sleep cycle in which NREM reaches its greatest depth at stage III and IV (delta) sleep.

neurone studies, it can safely be concluded that the brain remains about 80 percent active in the depths of sleep.

These conclusions not only emphasize the graded and state dependent nature of consciousness. They also indicate how small a fraction of brain activation is devoted to consciousness and that most brain activity is *not* associated with consciousness. From this it follows that consciousness, being evanescent, is a very poor judge of its own causation and of information processing by the brain. It is evident that consciousness requires a very specific set of neurophysiological conditions for its occurrence.

REM sleep

In 1953, Aserinsky and Kleitman reported that the sleep EEG was periodically activated to near waking levels and that rapid eye movements (the REMs) could then be recorded. When aroused from this REM sleep state, subjects frequently reported hallucinoid dreaming (Dement & Kleitman 1957). It was later discovered by Jouvet and Michel (1959) that the EMG of the cat was actively inhibited as the brain was sleep activated and the same inhibition of motor output occurs in man during REM (Hodes & Dement 1964).

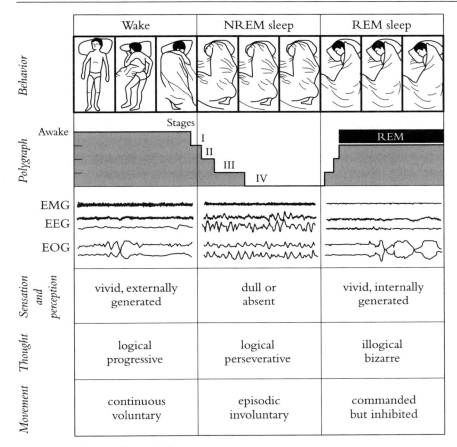

Figure 7.2 Behavioral states in humans.

Body position changes during waking and at the time of phase changes in the sleep cycle. Removal of facilitation (during stages I–IV of NREM sleep) and addition of inhibition (during REM sleep) account for immobility during sleep. In dreams, we imagine that we move, but no movement occurs. Tracings of electrical activity are shown in ~20-s sample records. The amplitude of the electromyogram (EMG) is highest in waking, intermediate in NREM sleep, and lowest in REM sleep. The electroencephalogram (EEG) and electroculogram (EOG) are activated in waking and REM sleep and inactivated in NREM sleep.

As can be seen in Figure 7.1b, the overnight tendency is for the periods of Stage I–IV brain deactivation to become shorter and less deep while the REM periods become longer and more intense. As the brain is more and more activated, the differentiation in consciousness is similarly less marked with reports from early morning Stage II coming more and more to resemble those of Stage I. Dreaming, it can thus be reasonably concluded, is our conscious experience of brain activation in sleep. Since brain activation is most intense in REM sleep, dreaming is most highly correlated with that brain state (see Figure 7.2). The fact that reports of dreaming can be elicited in other states (such as sleep onset, Stage I, and late night Stage II) can be explained by AIM as manifestations of REM-like brain conditions (Nielsen 2000). The possibly artefactual quality of Stage IV "dream" reports needs to be further investigated.

Table 7.2 Contrasts in the phenomenology of waking and dreaming consciousness

Function	Nature of difference	Causal hypothesis
Sensory input	Blocked	Pre-synaptic inhibition
Perception (external)	Diminished	Blockade of sensory input
Perception (internal)	Enhanced	Disinhibition of networks storing sensory representations
Attention	Lost	Decreased aminergic modulation causes a (decrease in) signal to noise ratio
Memory (recent)	Diminished	Because of aminergic demodulation activated representations are not restored in memory
Memory (remote)	Enhanced	Disinhibition of networks storing mnemonic representations increases access to consciousness
Orientation	Unstable	Internally inconsistent orienting signals are generated by cholinergic system
Thought	Reasoning ad hoc Logical rigor weak Processing hyper-associative	Loss of attention memory and volition leads to failure of sequencing and rule inconstancy Analogy replaces analysis
Insight	Self-reflection lost (failure to recognize state as dreaming)	Failure of attention, logic, and memory weaken second (and third) order representations
Language (internal)	Confabulatory	Aminergic demodulation frees narrative synthesis from logical restraints
Emotion	Episodically strong	Cholinergic hyperstimulation of amygdala and related temporal lobe structures triggers emotional storms, which are unmodulated by aminergic restraint
Instinct	Episodically strong	Cholinergic hyperstimulation of hypothalamus and limbic forebrain triggers fixed action motor programs, which are experienced fictively but not enacted
Volition	Weak	Top down motor control and frontal executive power cannot compete with disinhibited sub-cortical network activation
Output	Blocked	Post-synaptic inhibition

Table 7.2 contrasts waking and dreaming consciousness along many of the dimensions shown in Table 7.1. It can be seen that while dreaming constitutes a remarkable perceptual and emotional simulacrum of waking it has equally remarkable cognitive differences. The internally generated visual percepts of dreaming are so rich and vivid that they regularly lead to the delusion that we are awake. When they are associated with strong emotions

(principally joy-elation, fear-anxiety, and anger), they can even be surreal: as Leonardo da Vinci pointed out, dream consciousness may be even more intense than that of normal waking: "Why does the eye see a thing more clearly in dreaming than when we are awake?" Such phenomenology suggests that perception and emotion centers of the brain are activated (or even hyperactivated) in REM sleep and this is indeed the case.

At the same time that the perceptual and emotional components of consciousness are enhanced in dreams, such cognitive functions as memory, orientation, and insight are altered. It is not only difficult upon awakening to remember one's dreams, but it is also difficult to remember previous scenes as the dream unfolds (Fosse et al. 2002). It has recently been shown that even well-remembered dreams do not faithfully reproduce waking experience (Fosse et al. 2002), although dream characters and events may be dredged up from the distant past. Perhaps related to the memory defect is the microscopic disorientation called dream bizarreness which results in extreme inconstancy of the unities of time, place, person, and action (Fosse, Stickgold, & Hobson 2001). It is these unities that constitute the anchors of waking consciousness.

Reports of thinking are rare on arousal from REM sleep and the thinking that is reported, while logical within the fanciful assumptions of the dream (Kahn & Hobson 2005), is almost wholly lacking in insight as to the true state of the mind (Fosse, Stickgold, & Hobson 2001). Thus, in dreams, we typically assume we are awake when we are in fact asleep. The converse almost never occurs, weakening the thesis of such skeptical philosophers as Malcolm (1956), who hold that we never know certainly what state we are in and that reports of dreaming are fabricated upon awakening.

The Neurophysiology of Sleep with Special Reference to Consciousness

The deactivation of the brain at sleep onset is seen as the characteristic EEG changes and is experienced as an impairment of consciousness. It is related to decreases in activity of the neurones that constitute the brain stem core. This finding is in concordance with the classical experiments of Moruzzi and Magoun (1949), who showed that arousal and EEG activation were a function of the electrical impulse traffic in the reticular formation of the brain stem.

Since 1949, the reticular activating system has been shown to be anything but non-specific (Hobson & Brazier 1980). Instead, it consists of highly specific interneurones that project mainly locally but also reach upward to the thalamus and downward to the spinal cord. By means of these connections, reticular formation neurones regulate muscle tone, eye movements, and other sensorimotor functions necessary to waking consciousness. The fact that these changes in neuromodulation are progressive in NREM sleep means that that state is neurophysiologically as well as temporally intermediate between waking and REM. No wonder subjects often confound waking and sleep and no wonder they sometimes report dreaming as NREM sleep.

The reticular formation also contains chemically specific neuronal systems whose axons project widely throughout the brain where they secrete the so-called neuromodulators, dopamine, norepinephrine, and serotonin (on the aminergic side) and acetylcholine (on the cholinergic side). The state of the brain and consciousness is thus determined not only by its activation level but also by its mix of neuromodulators.

Single cell recording studies

In cats, single cell recording studies have revealed that in REM sleep, when global brain activation levels are as high as in waking, the firing of two aminergic groups is shut off (Hobson, McCarley, & Wyzinski 1975; McCarley & Hobson 1975). Thus the activated brain of REM sleep is aminergically demodulated with respect to norepinephrine and serotonin. Since norepinephrine is known to be necessary for attention (Foote, Bloom, & Aston-Jones 1983) and serotonin is necessary for memory (Martin et al. 1997), we can begin to understand the cognitive deficiencies of dreaming consciousness in physiological terms.

What about the enhancement of internal perception and emotion that characterizes dream consciousness? Could it be related to the persistence of the secretion of dopamine and the increase in output of the cholinergic neurones of the brainstem? It turns out that the cholinergic neurones of the reticular formation are indeed hyperexcitable in REM; in fact, they fire in bursts that are tightly linked in a directionally specific way to the eye movements that give REM sleep its name. The result is that such forebrain structures as the amygdala (in the limbic, emotion mediating brain) and the posterolateral cortex (in the multimodal sensory brain) are bombarded with cholinergically mediated internal activation waves during REM.

In the transition from waking to REM, consciousness has shifted from exteroceptive perception to interoceptive and from moderated to unmoderated emotion. To explain this shift, cholinergic hypermodulation together with persistent dopaminergic modulation is a candidate mechanism. The mind has simultaneously shifted from oriented to disoriented and from mnemonic to amnesic cognition. To explain this shift, aminergic demodulation is the best current candidate mechanism.

Input–output gating

If the brain is activated in sleep, why don't we wake up? One reason is the aminergic demodulation. Another powerful reason is that in REM sensory input and motor output are actively blocked. This closing of the input and output gates is an active inhibitory process in the spinal- and the motorneurones which convey movement commands to the muscles. Sensorimotor reticular formation neurones inhibit the sensory afferent sensory fibers coming from the periphery.

The net result is that in dreams we are not only perceptually and emotionally hyperconscious but cognitively deficient and off-line to sensory inputs and motor outputs. That is to say, we are anesthetized and paralyzed in addition to being hallucinated, emotional, disoriented, and amnesic. This is the activation-synthesis theory of dreaming (Hobson & McCarley 1977). What other evidence can be brought to test these hypotheses?

A Four-Dimensional Model of Conscious State

Three factors, activation level (A), input–output gating (I), and neuromodulation ratio (M) determine the normal changes in the state of the brain that give rise to changes in the state of consciousness that differentiate waking, sleeping, and dreaming. Because these three variables can be measured in animals, it is appropriate and heuristically valuable to model them. In so doing, we replace the traditional two-dimensional model (shown in Figures 7.1 and 7.2) with the four-dimensional model shown in Figures 7.3 and 7.4 below.

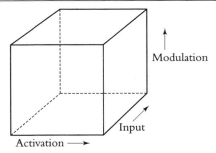

Figure 7.3 The Activation-Input Source-Neuromodulation model (AIM). Illustration of three-dimensional state space.

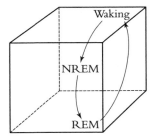

Figure 7.4 Normal transitioning within the AIM state space from waking to NREM and then to REM.

In the AIM model, time is the fourth dimension because the instantaneous values of A, I, and M are points that move in the three-dimensional state space forming an elliptical trajectory that represents the sleep–wake sequence as a cyclical function rather than as the stairway that is represented in the traditional two-dimensional model where activation is plotted against time.

To understand the AIM model, it is helpful to grasp the fact that the waking domain is in the upper right corner of the state space. It is there, and only there, that activation (A) level is high, input–output gates (I) are wide open, and the modulatory mix (M) measured as the aminergic/cholinergic ratio is also high. Since all three measures change from moment to moment, the AIM points form a cloud in the waking domain of the state space.

When sleep supervenes, all three AIM variables fall. The net result is that the NREM (N) sleep domain is the center of the state space. With the advent of REM, the activation level rises again to waking levels but the input–output gates are actively closed and aminergic neurones shut off. Factors I and M therefore fall to their lowest possible levels. The REM sleep domain (R) is thus in the right anterior lower corner of the state space.

The AIM model clearly differentiates REM from wake. It also affords a valuable picture of how and why the conscious states of waking and dreaming differ in the way that they do.

As shown by the arrowed lines forming an elliptical trajectory through the state space, the sleep–wake cycle is represented as a recurrent cycle. Actually the sequential cycles of sleep move to the right (as activation level increases overnight) and downward as the brain comes to occupy the REM domain for longer and longer periods.

Lucid dreaming

Lucid dreaming is a normal variation in conscious state which serves to illustrate and emphasize the value of the AIM model. When subjects learn to recognize that they are dreaming while they are dreaming, they obviously have elements of both REM and waking consciousness. They can continue to hallucinate but they are no longer deluded about the provenance of the imagery. Lucid dreamers typically report that while they may learn to watch and consciously influence the course of their dreams and even to voluntarily awaken to enhance recall, lucidity is difficult to maintain and they often are either pulled back down into non-lucid dreaming or wake up involuntarily. The lucid dreaming domain lies between REM and wake in the middle near the right side wall of the state space. Subjects normally cross the REM–wake transition zone rapidly suggesting that lucid dreaming is a forbidden zone of the state space. Such unwelcome processes as sleep paralysis and hypno-pompic hallucinations occur when subjects wake up but one or another REM process persists.

Brain Imaging and Lesion Studies in Humans

Over the past decade, two parallel lines of scientific inquiry have contributed striking insights to the brain basis of conscious experience via the conscious state paradigm.

Brain imaging

Taking advantage of PET technology, three separate independent groups have imaged the human brain in normal waking and sleep (Braun et al. 1997; Nofzinger et al. 1997; Maquet et al. 2000). At sleep onset, the blood flow to all regions of the brain declines. When REM sleep supervenes, most brain regions resume the wake state brain perfusion levels (from which we infer a restored activation level compared to waking). But several brain regions are selectively hyperactivated in REM. They include the pontine reticular formation (which previous animal studies have shown to regulate REM sleep), the amygdala and the deep basal forebrain (which are thought to mediate emotion), the parietal operculum (which is known to be involved in visuospatial integration), and the paralimbic cortices (which integrate emotion with other modalities of conscious experience).

It is important to stress again the important advantages of MRI over PET and to explain why it has been difficult to use MRI in sleep studies.

With PET imaging, the investigator gets one and only one look at the regional activation pattern. And the subject must be exposed to a radioactive isotope to yield that single image. This means that all of the marvelous studies of sleep using PET are "snapshots," not movies or even time-lapse photographs.

While PET and MRI both have limited degrees of spatial resolution, the temporal resolution of MRI far exceeds PET. With MRI, a continuous succession of images can be collected across the entire night of sleep. This allows second-to-second comparison of activation to be made. That is the good news. The bad news is that MRI depends upon the frequent induction of magnetic field changes. To achieve these changes, the magnet literally clanks and the noise is as disrupting of sleep as the fields are disruptive of the electrographic recordings we use to objectify the brain states.

Spontaneous brain damage

Patients who have suffered brain damage due to stroke, report a complete cessation of dreaming when their lesion impairs either the parietal operculum or the deep frontal white matter (Solms 1997). This suggests that those structures mediate connections that are essential to dream consciousness. When damage is restricted to the visual brain, subjects continue to dream; they lack visual imagery but otherwise dream vividly.

Intentional lobotomy

Solms (1997) has also reported that the clinical histories of patients with mental illness who had undergone frontal lobotomy in the 1950s revealed an effect on dreaming. This surgical procedure was designed to cut the fibers connecting the frontal lobes to other parts of the limbic lobe on the assumption that the emotion which was thought to be driving the patient's psychosis was mediated by these fibers. Some patients did indeed benefit from the surgery, but many reported a loss of dreaming, again suggesting that fronto-limbic connections were as essential to that normal hallucinatory process as they were to psychosis.

Other abnormal conditions

When traumatic brain damage or stroke affects the brain stem, the resulting injury to neurones mediating activation, input–output gating, and modulation can render subjects comatose for long periods of time. Such subjects may be unable to wake or to sleep normally in which case they are said to be in a chronic vegetative state. They have been permanently moved to the left half of the AIM state space. As they move further and further, to the left, they may lose the capacity to activate their thalamocortical system even to the NREM sleep level. A flat EEG indicates a complete absence of activation and intrinsic oscillation.

Locked-in syndrome

Patients with amytrophic lateral sclerosis (popularly known as Lou Gehrig's disease) remain conscious during waking but are unable to signal out because of motor-neuronal death. Recent research suggests that they can be taught to signal out and say "yes" or "no" by raising or lowering their cortical DC potentials (Wolpaw et al. 2002). It is not known whether these subjects have normal sleep cycles but the assumptions of the AIM model predict that they should.

Temporal lobe epilepsy and "dreamy states"

When neuronal excitability is locally altered (as in temporal lobe epilepsy), the patients sometimes experience the intrusion of dream-like states into waking consciousness. This phenomenon serves to illustrate both the value and the limitations of the AIM model.

If the abnormal discharge of the epileptic focus in the temporal lobe is strong enough, it can come to dominate the rest of the brain and cause it to enter an altered state of waking consciousness akin to dreaming. This shift, which is caused by an increase in internal stimulus strength, causes a change in the I dimension of AIM in the direction of REM. Such a formulation is compatible with the PET finding of selective temporal lobe activation in normal REM sleep. It is reasonable to propose that the kinship of temporal lobe epilepsy "dreamy" states and normal dreaming is due to a shared selective activation of limbic structures.

But this local excitability change cannot be easily modeled by AIM because the activation measure is global and, as PET studies indicate, the activation of REM (and TLE) is regionally selective, there being some brain areas (such as the limbic lobe) that are turned on and others (such as the dorsolateral prefrontal cortex) that are turned off.

The only way to deal with this reality is to add brain regions as a fifth dimension to the AIM model. Because it is impossible to represent brain regions within the state space of AIM, the easiest way to represent and visualize this modification is to see the brain as a regionally diverse set of AIM models. Thus the value of the AIM may be locally altered with profound effects upon consciousness.

Conclusions

By studying the way in which consciousness is normally altered when we fall asleep and when we dream, it is possible to obtain insights about how the brain mediates consciousness. So stereotyped and so robust are the corresponding changes in brain and conscious state as to assure the following conclusions:

1 Consciousness is componential. It is composed of many diverse mental functions which, in waking, operate in a remarkably unified fashion to mediate our experience of the world, our bodies, and ourselves.
2 Consciousness is graded. Within and across species, animals are continually more or less conscious depending upon the componential complexity and the state of their brains.
3 Consciousness is state dependent. During normal sleep, consciousness undergoes both global and selective componential differentiation as the brain regions mediating the components of consciousness are globally or selectively activated and deactivated.
4 Conscious state is a function of brain state. Experimental studies of sleep have identified three factors which determine brain state. They are activation level (A), input–output gating (I), and modulation (M). With time as a fourth dimension, the resulting AIM model represents the sleep cycle as an ellipse and more clearly differentiates waking and REM as the substrate of the conscious states of waking and dreaming.
5 Recent brain imaging and brain lesion studies in humans indicate that activation (A) is not only global, but also regional and that selective activations and inactivations of specific brain subregions contribute to differences in conscious experience. A fifth dimension must therefore be added to AIM.
6 Armed with the 5-D AIM model, it is possible to obtain a unified view of the genesis of a wide variety of normal and abnormal changes in conscious experience.

Further Readings

Solms, M. (2002) The neurochemistry of dreaming: cholinergic and dopaminergic hypotheses. In E. Perry, H. Ashton, and A. Young (eds.), *The Neurochemistry of Consciousness. Advances in Consciousness Research series* (M. Stamenov, series ed.), 123–31. Amsterdam: John Benjamins.

References

Aserinsky, E. and Kleitman, N. (1953) Regularly occurring periods of eye motility and concomitant phenomena during sleep. *Science* 118, 273–4.

Braun, A. R., Balkin, T. J., Wesenten, N. J., Carson, R. E., Varga, M., Baldwin, P. et al. (1997) Regional cerebral blood flow throughout the sleep-wake cycle. An H2(15)O PET study. *Brain* 120: 7, 1173–97.

Dement, W. C. and Kleitman, N. (1957) The relation of eye movements during sleep to dream activity: an objective method for the study of dreaming. *Journal of Experimental Psychology* 53: 3, 339–46.

Dinges, D. F., Pack, F., Williams, K., Gillen, K. A., Powell, J. W., Ott, G. E. et al. (1997) Cumulative sleepiness, mood disturbance, and psychomotor vigilance performance decrements during a week of sleep restricted to 4–5 hours per night. *Sleep* 20: 4, 267–77.

Edelman, Gerald M. (1992) *Bright Air, Brilliant Fire: On the Matter of the Mind.* New York: Basic Books.

Foote, S. L., Bloom, F. E., and Aston-Jones, G. (1983) Nucleus locus coeruleus: new evidence of anatomical physiological specificity. *Physiological Review* 63, 844–914.

Fosse, R., Stickgold, R., and Hobson, J. A. (2001) Brain-mind states: reciprocal variation in thoughts and hallucinations. *Psychological Science* 12: 1, 30–6.

Fosse, M. J., Fosse, R., Hobson, J. A., and Stickgold, R. (2002) Dreaming and episodic memory: a functional dissociation? *Journal of Cognitive Neuroscience* 15: 1, 1–9.

Hobson, J. A. (1998) *Consciousness.* Scientific American Library. New York: W. H. Freeman.

Hobson, J. A. and Brazier, M. A. B. (eds.) (1980) *The Reticular Formation Revisited: Specifying Function for a Nonspecific System.* New York: Raven Press.

Hobson, J. A. and McCarley, R. W. (1977) The brain as a dream state generator: an activation synthesis hypothesis of the dream process. *American Journal of Psychiatry* 134: 12, 1335–48.

Hobson, J. A., McCarley, R. W., and Wyzinski, P. W. (1975) Sleep cycle oscillation: reciprocal discharge by two brain stem neuronal groups. *Science* 189, 55–8.

Hobson, J. A., Pace-Schott, E. F., and Stickgold, R. (2000) Dreaming and the brain: Toward a cognitive neuroscience of conscious states. *Behavioral and Brain Sciences* 23: 793–842.

Hodes, R. and Dement, W. C. (1964) Depression of electrically induced reflexes ("H-reflexes") in man during low voltage EEG sleep. *Electroencephalography and Clinical Neurophysiology* 17, 617–29.

Jouvet, M. and Michel, F. (1959) Correlation electromyographiques du sommeil chez le chat decortique mesencephalique chronique. *Comptes Rendues des Séances de la Societé de Biologie et de Ses Filiales* 153, 422–5.

Kahn, D. and Hobson, J. A. (2005) State-dependent thinking: a comparison of waking and dreaming thought. *Consciousness and Cognition* 14: 3, 429–38.

McCarley, R. W. and Hobson, J. A. (1975) Neuronal excitability modulation over the sleep cycle: a structural and mathematical model. *Science* 189, 58–60.

Malcolm, N. (1956) Dreaming and skepticism. *Philosophical Review* 65, 14–37.

Maquet, P. (2000) Functional neuroimaging of sleep by positron emission tomography. *Journal of Sleep Research* 9, 207–31.

Martin, K. C., Casadio, A., Zhu, H., Yaping, E., Rose, J. C., Chen, M. et al. (1997) Synapse-specific, long-term facilitation of aplysia sensory to motor synapses: a function for local protein synthesis in memory storage. *Cell* 91: 7, 927–38.

Moruzzi, G. and Magoun, H. W. (1949) Brainstem reticular formation and activation of the EEG. *Electroencephalography and Clinical Neurophysiology* 1, 455–73.

Nielsen, T. A. (2000) A review of mentation in REM and NREM sleep: "covert" REM sleep as a possible reconciliation of two opposing models. *Behavioral Brain Sciences* 23, 851–66.

Nofzinger, E. A., Mintun, M. A., Wiseman, M., Kupfer, D. J., and Moore, R. Y. (1997) Forebrain activation in REM sleep: an FDG PET study. *Brain Research* Oct. 3; 770: 1–2, 192–201.

Solms, M. (1997) *The Neuropsychology of Dreams.* Mahwah, NJ: Lawrence Erlbaum Associates.

Wolpaw, J. R., Birbaumer, N., McFarland, D. J., Pfurtscheller, G., and Vaughan, T. M. (2002) Brain–computer interfaces for communication and control. *Journal of Clinical Neurophysiology* June; 113: 6, 767–91.

8

Affective Consciousness

JAAK PANKSEPP

Evolution of Affective and Cognitive Processes

A most difficult problem in neuroscience is how conscious mind emerges from brain activities. To make headway on this, we may need to focus more on the vast neuronal *contexts* that unconditionally enable phenomenal experience rather than on the specific *contents* of consciousness. From this perspective, consciousness was initially built on fundamental survival concerns of organisms. Psychologically, such concerns may have been first instantiated in the glimmers of affective feelings – basic, internally felt neurodynamics reflecting intrinsic survival values that are experienced but not necessarily reflected upon. Unfortunately, affective experience has been profoundly neglected in consciousness studies.

It is commonly assumed that consciousness cannot be scientifically studied without linguistic reports of subjective experiences. That premise arbitrarily limits consciousness studies to humans. A neuro-evolutionary view suggests that primary-process consciousness emerged long before organisms had enough brain matter to speak or to cognitively reflect on their experiences. In any event, current knowledge supports the conjecture that primary-process affective experience emerged in brain evolution much earlier than the cognitive processes that allow us to think and talk about our internal experiences (i.e., secondary and tertiary forms of consciousness). As we begin to accept that various emotional behaviors in other animals may be excellent indicators of primal affective states (Panksepp 2005a), it may be wise to consider that the neural substrates of such experiences are sufficiently distinct from those that are essential for cognitive variants of consciousness – those sensorially-based "information-processing" functions of the brain that parse the many differences in the external world to generate the highly variable contents of consciousness.

Most of the neural systems that are essential for unconditioned emotional behaviors in animals and affective states in humans are situated in medial and ventral regions of the brain. Those cognitive processes that detect changes in the external world are situated more laterally and dorsally in the brain (neural areas that blossomed more recently in brain evolution). In general, the former functions of the brain are more ancient than the latter. It seems that affect preceded cognitions in brain evolution, providing a useful heuristic for animals to anticipate life challenging situations. It is better to anticipate survival needs (e.g., to feel hunger with modest energy depletion) than to respond to them when in dire need (e.g., when one's internal energy resources are severely compromised). Similarly, emotional feelings provide animals with "simple" anticipatory codes of value. The only reason such neural codes have been long ignored is because no "mindscopes" exist for skeptical neuroscientists to achieve agreement.

To adequately understand the cognitive experiences that arise from more recent brain–mind developments, we may first need to understand the pre-propositional nature of affective experience. It is possible that cognitive variants of consciousness remain critically linked to the integrity of those earlier stages of brain–mind evolution. For instance, we may never understand why we mentally dwell on a lost love, with all the torments of broken-hearted feelings, until we understand the ache of physical pain (Panksepp 2005b). All forms of consciousness may remain tethered to that solid neural platform that constitutes primary-process emotional actions and affective experience.

Cognitive forms of consciousness are bound to vary more across mammalian species than the more ancient affective foundations. For instance, much of the neocortex of the platypus is devoted to analyzing the inputs from an electro-sensory detector in their bills that guide such creatures through murky waters in search of food (Pettigrew, Manger, & Fine 1998). However, their felt urge to seek resources may be a primitive psycho-behavioral function shared with other mammals. Similarly, much of the neocortex of the star-nosed mole, with the 22 fleshy tentacles surrounding the nose, may be devoted to the construction of a tactile world that is as hard for us to imagine as the sound-based world of bats (Catania & Kaas 1997). But such creatures may also forage with the same primal emotional behaviors and affective "energies" that remain conserved across all mammals. Such basic emotional action urges, sustained by brain dopamine facilitated *seeking* circuitry, may be evolutionarily homologous across all mammals. There are many other emotional operating systems, each with their apparent quota of feelings, which constitute the ancestral, genetically provided tools for living (Panksepp 1998a).

Arousal of such complex survival systems help constitute affective feelings. Such primordial states, as difficult to describe linguistically as pain, may be the bedrock for subjective experience. With cerebral encephalization, pre-existing raw feelings may have set the stage for the emergence of various cognitive-perceptual experiences, with ever increasing species variability as different organisms adapted to vastly different environments. In any event, this chapter is premised on the assumption that cognitive consciousness, which helps parse environmental events, was built upon a solidly embodied platform of complex instinctual emotional action tendencies. The resulting affective feeling states may have constituted the first glimmers of consciousness in brain evolution since they were each organism's major compasses for survival.

Presumably organisms as cerebrally complex as mammals possess many affective abilities as genetic birthrights, although all are refined in the caldron of environmental experiences. At minimum, affective consciousness can be parsed into at least three general varieties: (i) the exteroceptively driven *sensory-affects* that reflect the pleasures and aversions of worldly objects and events; (ii) the interoceptively driven *homeostatic-affects*, such as hunger and thirst, that reflect the states of the peripheral body along the continuum of survival, and (iii) the *emotional-affects* that reflect the arousal of brain instinctual action systems that are built into sub-neocortical regions of the brain as basic tools for living – to respond to major life challenges such as various life-threatening stimuli (leading to fear, anger, and separation-distress) and the search for various life-supporting stimuli and interactions (reflected in species-typical seeking and playfulness, as well as socio-sexual eagerness and maternal care).

Table 8.1 Distinct attributes of types of cognitive and affective consciousness (see Panksepp 2003)

Affective	*Cognitive*
State functions	Channel functions
Less computational	More computational
More analog	More digital
Intentions-in-action	Intentions-to-act
Action-to-perception	Perceptions-to-action
Neuromodulator codes (e.g., neuropeptides)	No apparent neurotransmitter codes (e.g., heavily general purpose glutamatergic)
More sub-neocortical	More neocortical

Ever since Wilhelm Wundt's initial analysis, affective feelings have been parsed along three dimensions – (i) feelings of goodness or badness (positive and negative affective *valence*), (ii) with various degrees of *arousal*, and (iii) penetrance into all mental experience (i.e., their *power* or *surgency*). How such pre-propositional affective features of mental life interact with the capacity of organisms to be aware of the objects and events of the external world – raw sensory-perceptual phenomenology – remains empirically uncultivated territory. However, conjoint interactions of such primary process variants of affective and cognitive consciousness, within extended representational spaces permitted by cortical encephalization, may be essential substrates for the brain to generate thoughts (*secondary consciousness*) and eventually thoughts about thoughts and feelings (a *tertiary* form of consciousness which may be unique to species that have linguistic abilities).

The failure to distinguish between the evolutionary layers of consciousness can lead to many conceptual conundrums and communicative confusions. For instance, the tendency of some emotion researchers to envision that affective feelings arise from the highest neocortical reaches of the human brain (e.g., LeDoux 1996) may not advance our understanding of the fundamental sources of raw feelings. The implicit species-dualism of such views retards our understanding of emotional feelings. A focus on cortico-cognitive processes will inform us of the emergence of emotional awareness and how ideational consciousness is buffeted by emotional storms, but not how raw affects first emerged within brains (Panksepp 1998a, 1998b; Damasio 1999; Parvizi & Damasio 2001).

My initial aim here is conceptually to distinguish affective and cognitive forms of consciousness, and to highlight how *emotional* affects might be best understood empirically through the detailed study of instinctual brain action systems all mammals share as evolutionary birthrights. The overriding general principle is that primary-process affective consciousness is critically related to the instinctual-emotional action tendencies that are genetically constructed within para-median, sub-neocortical circuits of the brain. Affective consciousness may be more dependent on motor-action urges than in the sensory-cognitive parsing of world events. Then I will highlight seven core emotional systems that could elaborate distinct affective feelings. Finally, I will consider the implications of a cross-species affective consciousness for novel scientific predictions in humans as well as other animals. For instance, all emotional systems have neuropeptidergic codes that concurrently regulate behav-

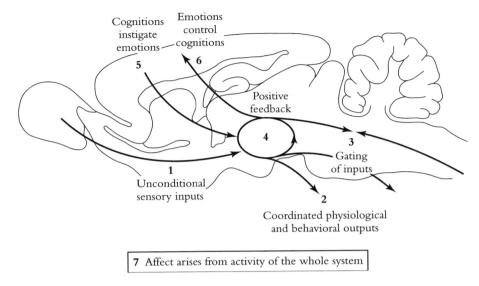

Figure 8.1 Neural definition of an emotional system.

The various neural interactions that are characteristics of all major emotional systems of the brain: (1) various sensory stimuli can unconditionally access emotional systems; (2) emotional systems can generate instinctual motor outputs, as well as (3) modulate sensory inputs; (4) emotional systems have positive-feedback components that can sustain emotional arousal after precipitating events have passed; also (5) these systems can be modulated by cognitive inputs, and (6) can modify and channel cognitive activities. In addition (7), the important criterion that emotional systems create affective states is not included, but it is assumed that arousal of the executive circuit for each emotion is essential for elaborating emotional feelings within the brain, perhaps by interacting with other brain circuits for self-representation such as those that exist in extended centromedial mid-brain circuits (e.g. PAG) that interact with anterior cingulate, insular, and frontal cortical systems (adapted from Figure 3.3 in *Affective Neuroscience* (Panksepp 1998a), with permission of Oxford University Press).

ioral output and the corresponding affective feeling states, all of which are candidates for the development of novel and affectively precise psychiatric drugs (Panksepp & Harro 2004).

Neuro-conceptual Distinctions between Affective and Cognitive Variants of Consciousness

Can meaningful neurobiological distinctions be made between cognitive and affective forms of consciousness, or are they comprised essentially of the same type of neural cloth? There are various ways to distinguish between these two general types of consciousness, with considerable overlap among the attributes (Table 8.1). My thesis is that valenced biological values (affects) are ultimately linked to the neural infrastructure of ancient emotional operating systems, rather than the overarching cognitive apparatus devoted to exteroceptive information-processing. However, our ability to reflect on feelings, and to become aware of their role in our existence, requires many higher processes.

There are presently two very distinct ways to envision how affect emerges from brain activities. The traditional "geocentric" view is that primitive unconscious emotional information has to interact with higher cognitive circuits in order to emerge into a neocortically based consciousness. (I use the term "geocentric" because such theories are based on a very anthropocentric cognitive view of how the mental world is organized.) How this read-out from "implicit" to "explicit" processes is accomplished remains totally mysterious, and has a neuro-dualistic flavor that helps distinguish us from the rest of the animal estate. The alternative, a *dual-aspect monism* perspective advanced here, is that the sub-neocortical emotional action apparatus is sufficiently complex to generate not only emotional behaviors but the corresponding affective feelings. For a resonant discussion of dual aspect monism see Velmans (2000). The present physicalist perspective is that the sub-neocortical emotional action apparatus generates brain processes that have two coordinated aspects: (a) instinctual emotional behaviors and (b) raw experiential states. In this, affect emerges largely from the primordial viscero-somatic self-representation circuitries that exist within those core brain systems that generate instinctual emotional actions (Panksepp 1998b). With cortical encephalization such "energies" come to be parsed and regulated by higher cognitive processes.

The traditional cognocentric view of mind envisions affect to be an information-processing function of the brain. The affect-centered perspective advanced here is that raw emotional feelings largely reflect the operations of large-scale neurodynamics (Figure 8.1) whose basic character is closer to those energetic metaphors that were discarded in psychology at the beginning of the computer-driven cognitive revolution. Affective consciousness (Panksepp 2003) may be more closely linked to the contextual-background activities of the brain that consume more cerebral energy than the cognitive activities that generate the perceptual-foreground contents of consciousness (Shulman & Rothman 2004).

State functions vs. channel functions

Some aspects of the brain operate via discrete information channels linked to stimuli in the external world (e.g., sensory-perceptual processes), while others operate more endogenously and globally to control wide swaths of more endogenously sustained brain activities. Examples of the latter are the biogenic amine transmitters, such as norepinephrine and serotonin, which regulate neuronal arousability through most of the brain. They do not control specific emotional or cognitive states, even though they elaborate and modulate all of them. Neuropeptide systems operate in similar, albeit in functionally more discrete ways, and appear to regulate specific affective tendencies (Panksepp & Harro 2004). Others, for instance gaseous transmitters such as nitric oxide, operate on no neuronal receptors, but directly on neuronal metabolic controls. They also act in global ways, but quite rapidly. The channel–state distinction appears essential to understand processes that produce highly resolved perceptual cognitive-type qualia vs. those affective aspects of consciousness that are more holistic, reflecting evolutionary qualia (i.e., ancestral "memories" which arise from genetically prescribed emotional and motivational circuits concentrated in medial strata of the brain).

Computational vs. non-computational forms of consciousness

Brain *state processes* may be so integrally linked to organic processes, at such deep sub-cortical network levels, that they are not as susceptible to computational solutions as the more highly resolved cognitive *channel functions*, which are neural systems devoted to discrete information processing that are essential for perceptual and linguistic processing. The traditional computational view of mind claims that cognitive channel functions, since they are dependent on the coding of neuronal firing patterns in anatomically delimited channels, can be instantiated on any computational platform that can simulate the correct symbolic infrastructures of mind. However, affective consciousness may be so deeply dependent on certain kinds of organic state processes, that it may not be instantiated on inorganic man-made information-processing devices. If certain types of organic platforms are essential for affective state functions, it may be a category error to believe that one can compute anything more than pale and affectively superficial shadows of real emotional feelings. From this perspective, it is inconceivable that anyone will ever compute an orgasm that had a real phenomenological feel to it.

Analog vs. digital distinctions

Affective systems depend on extensive networks in which the patterns of firings of individual neurons do not convey discrete information; rather, ensembles of neurons create certain types of holistic action tendencies that, according to the *dual-aspect monism* perspective advanced here, may objectively reflect how emotional feelings emerge from large-scale brain dynamics. Emotional affect may be a fundamental property of broad-scale analog networks for the generation of emotional-instinctual action tendencies (Figure 8.1).

Intentions-in-action vs. intentions-to-act

During mind–brain evolution, the instinctive state-control systems of the brain were critical for creating fundamental forms of intentionality – intrinsic-action readiness – that are integral features of different emotional states (Panksepp 1998a, 1998b). Obviously, soon after birth, organisms must have various forms of intrinsically organized (instinctual) action tendencies at their disposal for confronting the archetypal survival challenges of the world. Core emotional feelings may be fundamentally based on these genetically ingrained forms of intentionality, providing value-laden infrastructures that allow young organisms to learn about the life-supporting and life-detracting features of the world, gradually molding cognitive structures from which more elaborate, learned forms of intentionality can emerge. This distinction between affectively rich *intention-in-action* and perceptually-cognitively rich *intentions-to-act*, as conceptualized by John Searle, allows us to envision how intrinsic emotional abilities and the associated core affects are related to inherited genetic processes (emotional motor-action apparatus) on the one hand and to epigenetically derived cognitive mechanisms (sensory-perceptual functions) on the other.

Emotional action-to-perception processes vs. cognitive perception-to-action processes

This distinction, similar to the previous one, is that affective/emotional state-control systems promote action processes that help focus perceptual fields. For instance, when organisms are angry, they zero in on the potential source of irritation; when sexually aroused, they focus on various intrinsic sexual cues. However, cognitive information-parsing processes generate perceptions that can lead to actions. With learning and conditioning, namely when the two modes of processing become intermixed, adaptive responses are extended into the world in ever more subtle ways.

Differential neurochemical controls

There exist meaningful neurochemical distinctions between affective and cognitive variants of consciousness. Neuroscientists have long recognized that a distinction needs to be made between the rapidly acting neurotransmitters that directly generate action potentials in discrete information *channels* (with glutamate being the prime example of an excitatory transmitter, and GABA the main inhibitory transmitter), and those neuromodulatory *state influences* that more broadly bias how effectively the rapidly acting transmitters operate. Neuropeptides are prime examples of neuromodulators that may regulate emotionally and motivationally specific state variables in widely ramifying neural networks. These peptides are also enriched in the visceral-enteric nervous systems, helping explain why strong emotions are typically accompanied by gut feelings, much of which may depend on visceral homunculi in the brain. This is not to suggest that the affective and cognitive controls are not highly interpenetrated in the mind. They simply have different evolutionary histories and many distinct characteristics.

Sub-neocortical vs. neocortical locus of control

Anatomically, the neural system characteristics of affective-limbic regions are sufficiently distinct from those of the exteroceptive-cognitive apparatus. The neural principles that apply to one are not as evident in the other (Panksepp 2003). While many neocortical areas are uniquely devoted to perceiving and parsing the many differences in the external world (and the extension of the affective "self" into world events), the core affective brain systems devoted to elaborating the internal world of the self are more medially situated, concentrated in viscerally based circuitry extending from the mesencephalic central gray regions to cingulate and orbitomedial frontal cortices. The cognitively enriched neocortical areas devoted to sensory-perceptual analyzers toward the back of the brain and the working memory regions toward the front (e.g., dorsolateral prefrontal regions) are also in intimate contact with basal ganglia (e.g., dorsal striatum) and thalamic sensory relay nuclei. The more ancient, affectively rich limbic circuits are intimately related to midline mesencephalic and diencephalic systems and closely associated frontal and cingulate cortices. The activities of those midline brain regions, devoted to elaborating the basic emotions and motivations, are often aroused in reciprocal relation to the more cognitive brain zones (Goel & Dolan 2003; Liotti & Panksepp 2004; Northoff et al. 2004).

In sum, affective states may need to be understood in terms other than those that have become second nature in our traditional information-processing views of the brain. A better recognition of such distinctions may loosen the grip of information-processing computer metaphors that remain *au courant* in most cognitively oriented approaches to mind science. The rest of this essay will focus on the paramedian limbic emotional circuits that are critical for the phenomenal feel of affective states.

Sub-neocortical Systems for Affective Consciousness

Because of the critical importance of sub-neocortical sources of affective consciousness for mental life, let us dwell briefly on relevant empirical issues. The weight of evidence indicates that basic affective states can be elaborated in the absence of most, perhaps all, of neocortex.

Evidence from neo-decortication studies

If one surgically eliminates neocortical influences in very young mammals, especially "primitive" mammals such as laboratory rats, one consistently obtains adult animals that are outwardly indistinguishable from normal (Panksepp et al. 1994). After neo-decortication most instinctual operating systems remain intact, even disinhibited. For instance, once I prepared a set of neonatal decorticated rats and presented fully grown pairs (one decorticate, and one normal) to each of 16 students in a neuroscience practicum. During a lab session devoted to the observation of behavior, the students' task was to identify which animal of each pair was missing approximately a third of their brain. The result was that 12 of 16 students selected the decorticated animals as being normal. This statistically significant mistake apparently emerged because the decorticates readily exhibited their subcortical "instinctual energies." They were more active, explored and investigated their environments more vigorously, while the normals were comparatively inactive, and seemingly more timid.

Of course, comparable brain damage in mature animals yields more obvious behavioral deficits. Once behavior comes to be controlled by higher brain functions, neocortical ablations produce more evident behavioral impairments. Such patterns have also been observed in humans. Massive deficits in higher cerebral functions that would, in adults, lead to the unconsciousness of persistent vegetative states (Watt & Pincus 2004), do not have comparable effects in children. Infants born with very extensive higher cortical deficits exhibit evident wakefulness and clear emotional/affective responsivity throughout development, especially clearly if they have been reared in socially supportive and loving environments (Shewmon, Holmes, & Byrne 1999).

The retention of an affective/instinctual life following neonatal neo-decortication affirms that lower regions of the brain suffice to sustain organismic emotional-affective coherence. The fact that such animals exhibit normal patterns of the most complex instinctual tendencies, including those that require complex interaction with other animals, such as rough-and-tumble play (Panksepp et al. 1994), affirms that the higher cognitive regions of the brain are not essential for the generation of emotionality. Frontal neocortical areas inhibit and regulate emotionality. One could argue that such animals are unfeeling "zombies" but that is an unlikely inference. Indeed, one cannot impose comparatively modest damage subcortically and expect consciousness to continue (Watt & Pincus 2004). Many other lines of evidence suggest that basic emotional systems have a mind of their own.

Evidence from localized electrical stimulation of the brain

In animals, localized electrical stimulation of the brain (ESB) can evoke a series of core instinctual behaviors, and to the best of our ability to evaluate such issues animals are experiencing the stimulation as either desirable or aversive (Panksepp 1998a, 2005a). Animals work vigorously to sustain such affective states (i.e., they self-stimulate for the ESB) and they escape and/or avoid stimulation that evokes aversive behavior patterns. They also exhibit conditioned place preference and aversions for environments paired with such stimulation, and exhibit conditioned positive and negative vocalizations when confined in those environments where they experience such ESB (Knutson, Burgdorf, & Panksepp 2002).

Such effects are concentrated in sub-neocortical paramedian limbic regions, and a few frontal cortical areas where such systems project. Human studies yield the same patterns. One can provoke feelings of anxiety, anger, desire, and many of the social feelings such as sadness, sexual arousal, and mirth by stimulating the same brain regions where comparable effects are obtained in other animals (Heath 1996). It is noteworthy that with our ability to non-invasively stimulate and inhibit neocortical regions with transcranial magnetic stimulation (TMS), no clear evidence has emerged that one can arouse emotional states via localized neocortical activations. Although mood can be mildly modified by TMS to frontal cortical regions, those effects may reflect indirect sub-neocortical arousal rather than direct neocortical processing of affect (Nahas et al. 2004).

Evidence from chemical stimulation of the brain

There is abundant evidence that pharmacological modulation of the same brain systems that lead to positive reward effects in animals can lead to various positive feelings in humans. Especially striking examples come from addictive drugs. Opiates and psychostimulants, that lead to persistent affect-mediated addictive behaviors in humans lead to vigorous self-administration patterns in animals. Although the major loci of control have not been worked out in humans, brain self-injection studies in animals indicate that such effects are readily obtained from sub-neocortical sites (Panksepp 2005a).

There are abundant predictions about human feelings that can already be made from our understanding of the neurochemical controls of animal emotional tendencies, especially among the many visceral neuropeptides that can regulate emotional behaviors (Panksepp & Harro 2004). For instance, oxytocin in the mammalian brain reduces separation distress and facilitates social attachments and positive engagements. It could be predicted, from existing animal data and a few straightforward psychological extensions, that intra-nasal administration of oxytocin (the only path presently available for getting exogenous oxytocin into the human brain) will reduce various negative emotional feelings, especially those related to sadness and social loss, and strengthen feeling of being more strongly connected to social networks. It should reduce shyness and increase confidence, and facilitate one's capacity for giving and sharing, and perhaps the capacity for forgiveness. Considering that this system is almost exclusively sub-neocortical, it will be most interesting to see how cognitions change when the affective fabric of experience is modified with this and many other neuropeptide manipulations.

Evidence from human brain imaging

Modern brain imaging only provides correlative evidence for the locus of control for brain–mind functions. It says little about causal issues. Also, such indirect measures (e.g., blood flow changes) are highly biased in that they neglect most of the background (contextual) activity of the brain, which consumes over ten times the energetic requirements of the brain than the small changes typically monitored in modern brain imaging (Schulman & Rothman 2004). We should not construct our understanding of mind on methods that only envision a narrow slice of the pie. Transient blood flow changes more clearly reflect rapidly firing networks of fairly large neocortical regions which integrate cognitive information processing than identifying the locations of slowly firing, highly concentrated subcortical neural systems for basic emotions and motivations that overlap extensively, often in opponent-process ways. Investigators who seek to understand brain emotional processes by presenting cognitive-type emotional information to subjects rarely monitor either global affective changes (valence, arousal and surgency) nor the more specific emotional feelings (see part IV). They have been more interested in the perceptions and cognitions associated with brief exposures to emotional stimuli. Thus, most fMRI brain-imaging studies of emotions have highlighted the perceptual-cognitive processes that instigate and/or accompany emotional-affective arousal – brain state changes that are hard to bring under temporal control and hence are often "smeared" across experimental conditions as background error variance.

The best estimates of hot spots for affective change in human brains, as achieved with metabolic PET studies (e.g., Damasio et al. 2000), highlight paramedian limbic cortical and sub-neocortical loci-of-control for the processing of affect (Liotti & Panksepp 2004; Northoff et al. 2004). Thus, internally generated emotional affects are accompanied by increased arousal of sub-neocortical brain areas that have been implicated in the generation of instinctual emotional action tendencies in animals, and decreased arousal of neocortical areas devoted to cognitive processes. Certain areas are bound to be more important than others in the genesis of affective states. It is natural to try to reserve that role for the higher regions, such as the anterior cingulate cortex and insula, but I think the whole network is essential (Figure 8.1), and developmentally some of the lowest integrative reaches, such as the periaqueductal gray (PAG), may be more essential for developmentally bootstrapping the whole system with affect.

Summary of Emotional Systems

The underlying *dual-aspect monism* premise of affective neuroscience is that core emotional feelings arise from basic emotional systems that govern the respective instinctual urges. Seven emotional systems – *lust, care, panic, play, fear, rage*, and *seeking* – appear to be necessary brain substrates for the affective feelings of nurturance, anxiety, eroticism, joyfulness, sadness, anger, and desire, respectively. These systems are in italics to highlight that specific neural circuits are being discussed, each with characteristics that constitute a neural definition of emotional systems (Figure 8.1). The italicization of vernacular terms is also intended to highlight that animal brain research can reveal the command structure of these affect-relevant, brain-emotional operating systems of humans, while acknowledging that the interactions with the human cognitive apparatus need to be clarified largely through human research. The animal data may tell us comparatively little about the cognitive side of the affective equation – the second-order awareness and metacognitions – that are associated with each of the emotions, and about which much has been written in the human literature (e.g., Manstead, Frijda, & Fischer 2004). The following short introduction to the main *emotional* systems is designed to whet appetites for a more detailed coverage (see Panksepp 1998a, 2005a).

1   *Lust*: How would mammals propagate if they did not have brain systems to feel *erotic desire*? The neural seeds of male and female sexual systems are laid down early in development, while babies are still gestating, but they do not fully germinate until puberty, when the maturing gonadal hormones begin to fertilize male and female sexual arousals (heavily centered on vasopressinergic and oxytocinergic brain systems respectively). However, because of the way the brain and body get organized, female-type desires can also exist in male brains, and male-typical desires in female brains. Of course, learning and culture persistently add layers of control and complexity to each emotional system that cannot be disentangled through animal brain research.

2   *Care*: How would we mammals survive if we did not have brain systems to *nurture* each other? The maternal instinct, so rich in every species of mammal (and bird too), allows us to propagate effectively. To have left this to chance, or just the vagaries of individual learning, would have assured the end of social species. These hormonally primed urges, still present in humans, condition the way we respond to newborn babies. The changing tides of peripheral estrogen, progesterone, prolactin, and brain oxytocin figure heavily in the transformation of a first-time mother into a fully maternal state, through actions on extensive sub-neocortical systems. Because males have intrinsically weaker care systems, they require more emotional education to become fully engaged caretakers. Care chemistries may also be one cornerstone of love.

3   *Panic*: When young children get lost, they exhibit intense *separation distress*. They cry out for care, and their feelings of sudden aloneness, verging on panic, may reflect the ancestral pain codes upon which adult sadness and grief are built. Brain systems yielding separation distress calls (crying) in mammals and birds have been identified using ESB techniques. They resemble each other so closely as to suggest a shared ancestral heritage. Brain chemistries that exacerbate feelings of distress (e.g., corticotrophin releasing factor) and those that can powerfully alleviate distress (e.g., brain opioids, oxytocin, and prolactin) figure heavily in the genesis of social attachments (as well as sexuality and nurturance) and may ameliorate depression. These chemistries help create those inter-subjective spaces with others that allow organisms to learn the emotional ways of our kind, paving the way for empathy and love. An understanding of such social chemistries may eventually yield new psychiatric medicines to help those whose social emotional "energies" are more or less than they desire. This knowledge may also link up with a better understanding of childhood disorders such as autism. A subset of such children may be socially aloof because they are addicted to their own self-released social-reward chemistries as opposed to activation by significant others.

4   *Play*: Young animals frolic with each other in order to navigate social possibilities in joyous ways. The urge to play was also not left to chance by evolution, but is built into the instinctual action apparatus of the mammalian brain. Indeed, such systems can even promote a joyous "laughter" in other species (Panksepp & Burgdorf 2003). These are "experience expectant" systems that bring young animals to the perimeter of their social knowledge, to psychic places where they must pause to cognitively consider what they can or cannot do to others. Such social activities help program brain circuits essential for well-modulated social abilities, perhaps partly by activating genes that promote neuronal growth and emotional homeostasis. Children who are not allowed sufficient time to play may express such ancient urges in situations where they should not, thereby exhibiting symptoms of attention deficit hyperactivity disorders. Psychostimulants, which can

help everyone to better attend to cognitive demands, are also strong anti-play drugs. Perhaps many of these kids would benefit from enhanced daily rations of rough-and-tumble activities.

5 *Fear*: The world has abundant dangers some of which can arouse the major fear system of the brain. Although stimuli that intrinsically provoke fearfulness may differ among species, the evolved core structure of aroused fear is similar across all mammalian species. Many other external stimuli gain access to this circuitry through learning – via cognitive-perceptual "high-roads" and more rapid, unconscious thalamic "low-roads" (LeDoux 1996). However, it is the evolutionarily provided "royal road" – the unconditional fear circuitry that courses between the central amygdala to the PAG of the midbrain – that concurrently controls the instinctual action apparatus and those deeply aversive feelings that intrinsically help animals avoid dangers. It is more adaptive to feel anticipatory fear than to be bitten.

6 *Rage*: Anger can be evoked by any of a variety of situations where there is stiff competition for resources. The rage system can be aroused by restraint, frustration, and various other irritations. Anger is provoked when organisms do not get what they want. Just like every sub-neocortical emotional system, higher cortico-cognitive systems are able to provide inhibition, guidance, and other forms of emotional regulation. Adults can modulate their anger in ways that children and animals cannot. Individuals with frontal lobe damage exhibit more anger than those with intact brains (Berlin et al. 2003). We presently have no psychotropic medications that can specifically control pathological anger, but the neuroscientific analysis of rage circuitry has revealed neuropeptide controls, such as opioids and substance P, which may eventually yield new pharmacological tools to facilitate such emotional self-regulation.

7 *Seeking*: This remarkable system mediates all appetitive desire to find and harvest the fruits of the world. This dopamine-facilitated seeking system energizes all our goal-directed urges and positive expectancies about the world. Animals vigorously self-stimulate this system in addictive ways, and the neural substrates are critical for humans and other animals to obsessively self-administer all varieties of addictive drugs and to crave more and more. The underlying system is the one that mediates our intense appetitive motivation to obtain the fruits of the environment, and highlights how a basic state control system that mediates the primary process phenomenology of appetitive actions can readily link up with cognitive systems that mediate thoughtful awareness and appraisals (Ikemoto & Panksepp 1999).

There may be other core emotional systems, such as those for social dominance, but it is currently easy to envision how such processes, and many other higher-order emotions (shame, jealousy, greed, disgust, etc.), could be created epigenetically from the basic emotional circuits interacting with cognitive systems. Thus, even though there may exist additional core emotional systems, as well as many poorly understood interdependencies among the various networks, only the above list can be well defended on the basis of essential neural criteria (Figure 8.1) and the weight of evidence based on the neuro-psycho-behavioral triangulation strategy that is the hallmark of affective neuroscience (Panksepp 1998a). Of course, there are other affects (e.g., many sensory and homeostatic ones), but the above systems are ones that belong properly in the *emotion* category (Figure 8.1). Each allows organisms to "move out" dynamically to engage and feel their environment in characteristically emotional ways.

Pervasive Cognition–Emotion Interactions

The identification of the primary loci of control for affective processing is critical for how we develop hard scientific strategies to decode the neural nature of affect. The evidence is strong for a paramedian brain localization running from frontal to mesencephalic central gray (PAG) regions. My own advocacy of a primary sub-neocortical locus of control for emotional affects is premised on the likelihood that this will allow us to utilize animal neuro-ethological models, where "spontaneous" emotionality can be studied directly, to clarify the neural nature of raw affective processes that contribute so heavily to psychiatric disorders (Panksepp & Harro 2004).

The *dual-aspect monism* strategy advanced here is that the weight of evidence indicates that raw emotional affects are part and parcel of the extended genetically inbuilt and epigenetically refined emotional action systems of ancient medial regions of the mammalian brain extending from centromedial midbrain structures such as the PAG to medial frontal cortical regions. A striking recent example of this principle is evident in the PET imaging of human orgasms, where brain arousal corresponds well to what we know about brain circuits that control animal sexuality (Holstege et al. 2003). Likewise, the passions of REM dreams appear to be elaborated by widespread limbic arousal that is disconnected from the more deliberative and rational-cognitive regions of our brains (Braun et al. 1997). During waking, projection of such limbic processes into the more lateral neocortical working-memory spaces may allow us to dwell on our feelings, but there is no evidence that those higher brain regions can create raw affective experience on their own or even through some yet undemonstrated type of "read-out" of lower brain processes. The subcortical affective systems may directly provide the experiential background "context" for all of the rest of conscious mental activity.

If one believes that affective feelings are a neocortical function, a critical test would be to inhibit attribute #6 in Figure 8.1 to see if affective feelings disappear. Such tests are currently empirically feasible in animals using conditioned place preference and aversion paradigms with localized neurochemical and ESB manipulations in conjunction with inhibition of those ascending pathways. In this context, it should be re-emphasized that the more thoughtful dorsolateral regions of the cortex that mediate working memories tend to be inhibited when the more medial affective regions are aroused (Goel & Dolan 2003; Northoff et al. 2004). At the same time, there is abundant evidence that emotional arousal can dictate and guide thinking, suggesting that affective neuroscience approaches to cognitions need as much attention as the cognitive neuroscience approaches to emotions.

Since emotional states are so effective in channeling perceptual and cognitive processes, an increasing number of investigators have been eager to conflate cognitive and affective processes during the current "emotion revolution" that has captivated cognitive science. Although it is essential eventually to understand how emotional and cognitive processes interact so massively at both neuronal and psychological levels, only modest progress can be made in grasping such interactions until the details of the individual emotional systems are better understood. That simply cannot be achieved without animal brain research, which makes it so important to resolve whether other animals do have emotional experiences.

Obviously the existence of subjectivity in other animals cannot be "proved" with mathematical-syllogistic rigor. Such issues must be adjudicated on the basis of the weight of relevant evidence, and the fruitfulness of new predictions that can be generated. If other mammals do share homologous foundations of affective consciousness, then we can use animal models to predict general principles by which affective states are constructed in the human mind (Panksepp 2005a). Neurochemical evidence for specific emotional and motivational controls derived from animal studies can be validated in humans who can provide propositional feedback about their internal subjective experiences. Animals cannot, even though their emotional actions speak loudly about their affective states, just as with babies before they talk. So far, it is clear that our understanding of addictions, appetite control, and new ideas for psychiatric medicines to control emotional affective energies, are emerging most clearly from the animal work (Panksepp & Harro 2004).

Within cognitive realms, species differences are bound to be so vast that the general principles to be derived from animal learning will be more modest than those from a study of their basic emotions and motivations. Although the animal data may tell us little about how we can reflect on our affective states with higher-order, thoughtful aspects of human consciousness, it is equally important to consider how cold non-emotional cognition becomes so easily drenched with affectively "hot" animalian appraisals. Part of this emerges simply from classical conditioning principles (LeDoux 1996), but that is only a fraction of the story. It is possible that cognitions become hot because they easily become embedded in the global *state* processes of emotional dynamics. In any event, the cognitive–emotional interactions, so important for all artistic and humanistic endeavors are best resolved through the study of human minds.

Although there is still a persistent desire in cognitive neuroscience to envision consciousness as a unitary process, critically dependent on cortico-cognitive structures, the wider recognition of an affective-emotional-motivational consciousness may help solve many foundational problems that a cognition-only view may never overcome. For instance, since emotional instinctual behaviors reflect intrinsic evolved action plans of organisms, we can now envision that all forms of consciousness are firmly grounded on the brain's capacity to encode biological values in action readiness. Such contextual issues, which consume a great deal of brain activity, not usually differentiated in human brain imaging studies (Shulman & Rothman 2004), may be essential for understanding the evolutionary bedrock of consciousness.

My premise here is that this bedrock is not just "permissive" but is differentiated in terms of various affective qualities. Although this mental background of affective consciousness may become peri-conscious in the "glare" of intense cognitive processing (like stars fading in the glare of Times Square), it is likely that those higher mental abilities remain critically dependent on the intrinsic, neurobiologically instantiated brain values of our various affective states – brain processes that are grounded in ancient neurosymbolic viscero-somatomotor virtual body representations (Panksepp 1998b; Damasio 1999).

Affective pre-adaptations may have provided a solid platform for the emergence of the more sensorial-perceptual forms of consciousness that characterize cognitive life, where rational discourse was eventually possible. An understanding of pre-propositional affective consciousness may also afford new inroads for bridging the seemingly uncrossable explanatory gaps that characterize consciousness studies. It is easier to envision why certain affective experiences have the phenomenological feel that they do than rational cognitive processes. The dynamics of emotional feelings may have more than a passing resemblance to the psychodynamics of instinctual emotional actions. It is possible that such large-scale neurodynamics provide self-referential envelopes that are able to ensnare perceptual cognitive states into various attractor basins. In sum, affective consciousness – a primary process kind of phenomenology – may have been an essential, and highly conserved, evolutionary platform for the emergence of more cognitively resolved forms of awareness, where much vaster species differences have emerged in the neuro-evolutionary emergence of mind.

See also 4 Animal consciousness; 5 Rethinking the evolution of consciousness.

Further Readings

McMillan, F. D. (ed.) (2005) *Animal Mental Health and Well-Being.* Iowa City: Blackwell Publishing.
Panksepp, J. (2005) On the embodied neural nature of core emotional affects. *Journal of Consciousness Studies* 12, 158–84.
Watt, D. F. and Pincus, D. I. (2004) Neural substrates of consciousness: implications for clinical psychiatry. In J. Panksepp (ed.), *Textbook of Biological Psychiatry*, 75–110. Hoboken, NJ: Wiley.

References

Braun, A. R., Balkin, T. J., Wesensten, N. J., Carson, R. E., Varga, M., Baldwin, P. et al. (1997) Regional cerebral blood flow throughout the sleep-wake cycle. A $H_2^{15}O$ PET study. *Brain* 120, 1173–97.
Catania, K. C. and Kaas, J. H. (1997) Somatosensory fovea in the star-nosed mole: behavioral use of the star in relation to innervation patterns and cortical representation. *Journal of Comparative Neurology* 387, 215–33.
Damasio, A. R. (1999) *The Feeling of What Happens.* New York: Harcourt Brace.
Damasio, A. R., Grabowski, T. J., Bechara, A., Damasio, H., Ponto, L. L. B., Parvizi, J. et al. (2000) Subcortical and cortical brain activity during the feeling of self-generated emotions. *Nature Neuroscience* 3, 1049–56.
Goel, V. and Dolan, R. J. (2003) Reciprocal neural response within lateral and ventral medial prefrontal cortex during hot and cold reasoning. *Neuroimage* 20, 2314–21.
Heath, R. G. (1996) *Exploring the Mind–Body Relationship.* Baton Rouge, LA: Moran Printing.
Holstege, G., Georgiadis, J. R., Paans, A. M., Meiners, L. C., van der Graaf, F. H., and Reinders, A. A. (2003) Brain activation during human male ejaculation. *Journal of Neuroscience* 23, 9185–93.
Ikemoto, S. and Panksepp, J. (1999) The role of nucleus accumbens DA in motivated behavior, a unifying interpretation with special reference to reward-seeking. *Brain Research Reviews* 25, 261–74.
Knutson, B., Burgdorf, J., and Panksepp, J. (2002) Ultrasonic vocalizations as indices of affective states in rats. *Psychological Bulletin* 128, 961–77.
LeDoux, J. E. (1996) *The Emotional Brain.* New York: Simon and Schuster.
Liotti, M. and Panksepp, J. (2004) Imaging human emotions and affective feelings: implications for biological psychiatry. In J. Panksepp (ed.), *Textbook of Biological Psychiatry*, 33–74. Hoboken, NJ: Wiley.
Manstead, A. S. R., Frijda, N., and Fischer, A. (eds.) (2004) *Feelings and Emotions: The Amsterdam Symposium.* Cambridge: Cambridge University Press.
Nahas, Z., Loberbaum, J. P., Kozel, F. A., and George, M. S. (2004) *Somatic Treatments in Psychiatry.* In J. Panksepp (ed.), *Textbook of Biological Psychiatry*, 521–48. Hoboken, NJ: Wiley.
Northoff, G., Heinzel, A., Bermpohl, F., Niese, R., Pfennig, A., Pascual-Leone, A. et al. (2004) Reciprocal modulation and attenuation in the prefrontal cortex: an fMRI study on emotional-cognitive interaction. *Human Brain Mapping* 21, 202–12.
Panksepp, J. (1982) Toward a general psychobiological theory of emotions. *The Behavioral and Brain Sciences* 5, 407–467.

Panksepp, J. (1992). A critical role for "affective neuroscience" in resolving what is basic about basic emotions. *Psychological Review* 99, 554–560.

Panksepp, J. (1998a) *Affective Neuroscience: The Foundations of Human and Animal Emotions*. New York: Oxford University Press.

Panksepp, J. (1998b) The periconscious substrates of consciousness: affective states and the evolutionary origins of the SELF. *Journal of Consciousness Studies* 5, 566–82.

Panksepp, J. (2003) At the interface of affective, behavioral and cognitive neurosciences. Decoding the emotional feelings of the brain. *Brain and Cognition* 52, 4–14.

Panksepp, J. (2005a) Affective consciousness: Core emotional feelings in animals and humans. *Cognition and Consciousness*. 14, 30–80.

Panksepp, J. (2005b) Why does separation-distress hurt? A comment on MacDonald and Leary. *Psychological Bulletin* 131, 224–30.

Panksepp, J. and Burgdorf, J. (2003) "Laughing" rats and the evolutionary antecedents of human joy? *Physiology and Behavior* 79, 533–547.

Panksepp, J. and Harro, J. (2004) The future of neuropeptides in biological psychiatry and emotional psychopharmacology: goals and strategies. In J. Panksepp (ed.), *Textbook of Biological Psychiatry*, 627–60. New York: Wiley.

Panksepp, J., Normansell, L. A., Cox, J. F., and Siviy, S. (1994) Effects of neonatal decortication on the social play of juvenile rats. *Physiology and Behavior* 56, 429–43.

Parvizi, J. and Damasio, A. (2001) Consciousness and the brainstem. *Cognition* 79 (1–2), 135–60.

Pettigrew, J. D., Manger, P. R., and Fine, S. L. B. (1998) The sensory world of the platypus. *Philosophical Transactions of the Royal Society of London: Biological Science* 353: 1199–210.

Schulman, R. G. and Rothman, D. L. (eds.) (2004) *Brain Energetics and Neuronal Activity: Applications to fMRI and Medicine*. London: Wiley.

Shewmon, D. A., Holmes, D. A., and Byrne, P. A. (1999) Consciousness in congenitally decorticate children: developmental vegetative state as self-fulfilling prophecy. *Developmental Medicine and Child Neurology* 41, 364–74.

Velmans, M. (2000) *Understanding Consciousness*. London: Routledge.

Watt, D. F. and Pincus, D. I. (2004) Neural substrates of consciousness: implications for clinical psychiatry. In J. Panksepp (ed.), *Textbook of Biological Psychiatry*, 75–110. Hoboken, NJ: Wiley.

9

Clinical Pathologies and Unusual Experiences

RICHARD P. BENTALL

Defining Psychopathological States

It is true, although only in a relatively trivial sense, that most if not all commonly recognized forms of psychopathology involve some kind of abnormality of conscious awareness. For example, depressed patients are usually excessively aware of negative aspects of themselves, and are often tormented by memories of enterprises that have ended in failure. Anxious patients, however, are typically extremely vigilant for potential threats in their environment. On first sight, therefore, the task of delineating the relationship between clinical pathologies and abnormal consciousness involves simply generating a list describing how consciousness is altered in each condition. In reality, however, the task is much more complex for at least two reasons.

First, and most obviously, a simple descriptive account of the relationship between abnormal consciousness and psychopathology is unlikely to be entirely satisfactory. Ideally, we would like to know *why* experience is abnormal in different psychiatric conditions, and this will require reference to the relevant psychological processes and etiological factors.

Second, in order to generate such a list it would first be necessary to define the various types of psychopathology. In fact, arguments about how many different kinds of psychopathology there are, whether or not they are qualitatively different from normal functioning, and whether or not they should be considered analogous to physical diseases, have raged since the first systematic attempts to construct a science of psychopathology. Modern diagnostic systems used by psychiatrists and clinical psychologists (e.g., the American Psychiatric Association's *Diagnostic and Statistical Manual for Mental Disorders*, currently in its fourth edition (American Psychiatric Association 1994) and the World Health Organization's *International Classification of Disease*, currently in its tenth edition (World Health Organization 1992) are based on several assumptions about mental illness made by psychiatrists in the late nineteenth century, namely that there is a clear difference between "abnormal" and "normal" mental states, that there are a number (in principle, a countable number) of qualitatively different types of psychopathology (leading to a categorical approach to classification), and that these different disorders are best regarded as "diseases" or medical conditions (see Bentall 2003 for a historical account).

It is easy to see the limitations of this approach by considering the diagnosis of schizophrenia. Examination of the criteria for schizophrenia as listed in DSM-IV reveals that they consist of several symptoms that apparently involve alterations in consciousness, including hallucinations, abnormal beliefs, and problems of attention. However, none of these symptoms is either necessary or sufficient to determine that someone is schizophrenic, as the diagnosis is a disjunctive category and it is possible for two patients to qualify as "schizophrenic" without having any symptoms in common. This kind of problem should not seem surprising when it is recalled that current approaches to psychiatric diagnosis have been developed largely on the basis of clinical intuition and folklore, rather than as a consequence of scientific research. The designers of widely used diagnostic manuals such as DSM-IV and ICD-10 simply determined their diagnostic criteria by seeking consensuses among their fellow clinicians. In as much as research played any role in this process, it tended to focus on the reliability of psychiatric diagnoses (whether or not different clinicians can apply the diagnostic guidelines consistently) rather than on their validity (whether different diagnoses single out patients with common difficulties resulting from common etiological factors, and whether they are useful in predicting either long-term outcome or response to particular kinds of treatment).

In fact, when research into the validity of psychiatric disorders has been carried out, it has consistently revealed that the standard diagnostic systems fail to "cleave nature at its joints." Although details of these kinds of research studies are too complex to consider here (see Bentall (2003) for details), a few examples will suffice to illustrate the point. In general, studies have shown that, when traditional diagnoses are used, "comorbidity" – the tendency for people to meet the criteria for more than one diagnosis – is the norm, implying that they are failing to divide patients into groups with qualitatively distinct conditions. Whereas less serious psychiatric conditions are usually divided into depression and anxiety disorders, research has consistently shown that depression and anxiety are highly correlated in both clinical and non-clinical samples (Goldberg & Huxley 1992), so that the assignment of patients to either one category or the other is often arbitrary. In the case of the more severe "psychotic" disorders (see below), patients also fail to fall clearly into the two major categories of schizophrenia and the affective psychoses (psychotic depression and bipolar disorder) as supposed by the major diagnostic systems, and many patients present with a mixture of "schizoaffective" symptoms (Bentall 2003).

As a consequence of these difficulties, most standard accounts of mental illness contain something of a theoretical chasm. Whereas a rich literature on descriptive psychopathology that dates back to before the nineteenth century contains many detailed accounts of abnormal mental states, modern theories that attempt to explain psychiatric disorders in terms of neurobiological or etiological processes make few, if any, references to the patient's subjective experiences, which are seen more as pointers to diagnoses than phenomena of interest in their own right.

In recent years, this chasm has begun to be bridged by researchers employing the tools of cognitive psychology. For the most part, research in this area has tended to avoid the problems of psychiatric classification by focusing on particular psychological complaints (what psychiatrists describe as "symptoms") rather than broad diagnostic categories.

Common Psychological Conditions

Depression and anxiety are the most common reasons why people seek psychiatric or psychological treatment and, as we have already seen, these emotions are usually highly correlated (Goldberg & Huxley 1992). In the standard diagnostic systems, distinctions are often made between different kinds of anxiety disorders, for example generalized anxiety disorder (in which the patient feels anxious for no obvious reason) and panic disorder (in which panic attacks occur, usually triggered by particular stimuli), but the high levels of comorbidity that are often observed between these different types suggest that these distinctions may not be particularly important.

Although the common psychiatric disorders are not typically thought of as involving abnormal consciousness, an impressive body of evidence accumulated over the past three decades suggests that they are associated with systematic biases in the extent to which different kinds of stimuli become available to awareness. For example, numerous studies have shown that depressed patients preferentially recall negative information compared to positive information, whereas a similarly impressive body of evidence has shown that feelings of anxiety are associated with excessive attention to threat-related stimuli. Whether these processes are diagnostically specific seems doubtful (see Harvey et al. (2004) for a review of this issue).

Research with patients with obsessional problems has raised the interesting possibility that dysfunctional attempts to control the contents of consciousness may help to maintain some common psychological disorders. Unwanted, intrusive thoughts (e.g., about embarrassing past experiences) seem to be an almost universal phenomenon and obsessional patients appear to differ from ordinary people in their catastrophizing response to these kinds of experiences (Salkovskis 1998). Consistent with this idea, obsessional patients often harbor dysfunctional metacognitive beliefs (beliefs about their own cognitive processes), for example by having excessive expectations about their mental efficiency, catastrophic fears about losing control of their thoughts, and superstitious beliefs about the consequences of this happening ("If I did not control a worrying thought, and then what I worried about really happened, it would be my fault") (Wells & Papageorgiou 1998).

The Psychoses

It is the psychotic disorders, rather than the more common depressive and anxiety disorders, that are usually associated with unusual experiences, and hence distortions of normal conscious awareness. Although the use of the term "psychosis" has changed somewhat during the history of psychiatry, in current usage it refers to the broad class of psychiatric disorders in which patients experience hallucinations and delusions (abnormal beliefs) and appear to "lose contact with reality." In practice, "schizophrenia," "bipolar disorder," and "delusional disorder" are the most common diagnoses given to psychotic patients, depending on the exact combination of symptoms experienced. Because these disorders have been seen as consequences of neuropathology, psychological researchers have usually focused on gross cognitive deficits when trying to explain them.

This approach can be traced back to the work of Emil Kraepelin (1899–1990), who first proposed the concept of schizophrenia, and who argued that problems of attention were central features of the disorder:

> The slightest degree of increased distractibility can be observed as a temporary phenomenon in the state of distraction as it occurs in progressive fatigue. In spite of all efforts we are no longer

able methodologically to follow a series of coherent sensory impressions, but realize again and again that we are diverted by other impressions or ideas and that we can only grapple with the task in a fragmentary way. This disorder is developed to a higher degree in chronic nervous exhaustion, in the period of convalescence following severe mental or physical diseases, to an even higher degree in acute exhaustion psychoses strictly speaking moreover in mania, often also in paralysis and dementia praecox. Here in many cases, an exclamation, a single word, even the exhibition of an object suffices for immediately diverting the direction of attention and suggesting quite complex conceptions.

More than sixty years later, interest in the attentional difficulties of psychotic patients was renewed following the publication of a study by McGhie and Chapman (1961), who interviewed a small group of schizophrenia patients about their subjective experiences. The majority reported subjective cognitive difficulties such as increased distractability, heightened sensory impressions, and awareness of processes that would normally be automatic. For example, one patient reported that:

> My concentration is very poor. I jump from one thing to another. If I am talking to someone they only need to cross their legs or scratch their heads and I am distracted and forget what I am saying.

And another said that:

> I have to do everything step by step, nothing is automatic now. Everything has to be considered.

In the four decades since McGhie and Chapman reported their findings, numerous studies have demonstrated that schizophrenia patients perform poorly on objective measures of attention. For example, in an influential series of studies conducted in the 1970s, Oltmanns and Neale (1978) reported that schizophrenia patients perform poorly when asked to repeat back a series of digits while a voice reads out irrelevant distraction digits in the background; as a similar deficit was not observed when participants were asked to repeat digits without the distracting stimuli present, the findings seemed to imply a specific difficulty in screening out irrelevant information, rather than a general performance deficit. In other studies using the continuous performance test (CPT), participants were asked to watch a computer screen and press a button whenever they saw a particular target, but not when other stimuli were presented; numerous studies have shown that schizophrenia patients have difficulty maintaining vigilance when performing this kind of task (Nuechterlein & Subotnik 1998).

Despite the consistency of the available research findings, it is questionable whether cognitive deficits can provide a satisfactory explanation for psychotic illnesses as normally conceived. One problem is that, although the lion's share of research on cognitive performance and psychosis has been carried out on patients diagnosed as suffering from schizophrenia, and appears to support Kraepelin's original formulation of the disorder, in fact similar cognitive deficits have been found in association with a range of diagnoses. A related difficulty is that the cognitive deficits of schizophrenia patients do not correlate with the severity of those symptoms – hallucinations and delusions – which most obviously reflect distortions of conscious awareness (Green 1998).

Hallucinations

Hallucinations are often reported by psychotic patients, and are most often experienced in the auditory modality, although visual, tactile, and olfactory hallucinations are sometimes also experienced (Slade & Bentall 1988). The rules embodied in modern diagnostic systems ensure that many patients with experiences of this kind are diagnosed as suffering from schizophrenia, but patients diagnosed as suffering from bipolar disorder and psychotic depression may also have this kind of experience. Recent epidemiological studies have challenged the idea that hallucinations are necessarily associated with psychopathology by revealing that a surprising proportion of the population experience them at some point in their lives. For example, Tien (1991) estimated that the proportion of the 18,000 participants in the US Epidemiological Catchment Area Study who had experienced hallucinations at some time in their lives was between 11 and 13 percent. In a similar study of 7,000 Dutch citizens, it was found that 1.7 percent of those interviewed had experienced "true" hallucinations that could not be attributed to drug-taking or physical illness, but a further 6.2 percent had experienced hallucinations that were judged not clinically relevant because they were not associated with distress (van Os et al. 2000).

A distinction has sometimes been made between true hallucinations experienced as originating outside the body and "pseudohallucinations" which are experienced as being alien but nonetheless originating inside the head. However, this distinction has never been meaningfully related to any other variable, and is not currently believed to be of scientific or clinical importance. Patients may experience one or more hallucinated voices, which may comment on the patient's actions, or talk directly to the patient, sometimes issuing commands. Clinicians seeing distressed voice hearers often gain the impression that auditory-verbal hallucinations are typically highly negative in content, often deriding the patient or issuing commands to carry out acts that are inconsistent with the individual's values of self-concept (e.g., goading the patient to assault other people or even to commit suicide). However, even in patients seeking treatment, many voices are experienced as being friendly and supportive, to the point that some patients would rather that they not be removed. Perhaps not surprisingly, the voices of individuals who do not seek treatment tend to be more positive than those of people who become psychiatric patients. Another important distinction between psychiatric hallucinators and non-psychiatric hallucinators concerns the individual's attitude toward the voices; in the former group, the self is often experienced as weaker than the voices whereas, in the latter group, the opposite is often the case (Honig et al. 1998). Indeed, psychiatric patients' beliefs that their voices are omniscient and omnipotent have been identified as an important cause of distress, and therefore a potential target for psychotherapeutic intervention (Chadwick & Birchwood 1994). Interestingly, hallucinating patients appear to have dysfunctional metacognitive beliefs that are quite similar to those reported by patients with obsessional thoughts (Morrison & Wells 2003).

When patients have been questioned about their life histories, evidence has emerged of a relationship between the experience of trauma and hallucinations. For example, in a study conducted in New Zealand, where psychiatric patients are routinely questioned about unwanted sexual experiences, Read et al. (2003) found a specific association between reports of childhood sexual abuse and hallucinations. In another recent study of patients with a primary diagnosis of bipolar disorder who were receiving psychological treatment, it was found that patients who had disclosed experiences of childhood sexual abuse to their therapists were especially likely to have suffered from auditory hallucinations (Hammersley et al. 2003).

The normal phenomenon of "inner speech" provides a clue to the psychological mechanisms involved in auditory hallucinations. The ability to regulate one's behavior by means of self-directed speech develops in early childhood, when children first talk out aloud to themselves before learning to internalize this process, culminating in adulthood in the capacity for mature, verbal thought (Vygotsky 1962). Even in adulthood, this kind of thought is accompanied by "subvocalization" – covert activations of the speech muscles that can be detected by electromyography. It has been known for many years that auditory hallucinations are also accompanied by subvocalization (e.g., Gould 1948). This observation has inevitably suggested to many researchers that auditory hallucinations occur when inner speech is misattributed to an external source.

Evidence for this hypothesis has become available from a number of studies which have attempted to directly measure the capacity to distinguish between self-generated thoughts and externally presented stimuli. For example, using signal detection paradigms, some investigators have shown that people who hallucinate, or whose questionnaire responses suggest that they are vulnerable to hallucinations, have an abnormal response bias, leading to "false positive" responses, when asked to detect an externally presented voice against a background of "white noise" (Bentall & Slade 1985). In another series of studies, Johns et al. (2001) found that hallucinating patients were especially likely to mistake their own voice, after it had been electronically distorted, for speech by someone else. The new neuroimaging technologies have provided a further source of evidence for the inner speech hypothesis, as a number of studies have reported that hallucinations are associated with activations in language-related brain regions (Woodruff 2004).

This account of hallucinations might help to explain the observed relationship between hallucinations and trauma, as it is known that traumatic experiences often lead to a flood of intrusive thoughts, which may be unusually vivid and hence difficult to source-monitor. However, the causes of the hallucinator's source monitoring errors are only beginning to be understood. It has been suggested that they may reflect a general failure to monitor one's own intentional states. Blakemore et al. (2000) showed that psychotic patients who experienced hallucinations were more able to tickle themselves than healthy individuals (whose unresponsiveness under these circumstances presumably reflected their awareness of their own intentions during the tickling process). An important series of electrophysiological studies recently conducted by Ford and Mathalon (2004) found more direct evidence consistent with this account; they observed that talking and inner speech resulted in a dampening of responsivity of the auditory perception areas in the temporal lobes (a process that they identified as indicating a corollary discharge from the frontal cortex which prevents one's own speech from being attributed externally) but not in hallucinating patients.

However, several studies (e.g., Haddock, Slade, & Bentall 1995), have also shown that hallucinatory experiences can be influenced by suggestions indicating that voice-hearers' beliefs and expectations may influence the extent to which they make source monitoring errors. This kind of effect could help explain the well-documented cross-cultural differences in the prevalence of hallucinations (Al-Issa 1995), which are experienced more often in non-industrialized countries (where expectations of confrontations with supernatural agencies may be widespread) than in the developed world.

Delusional beliefs

Like hallucinations, beliefs that are considered delusional by psychiatrists are often found in people who do not seek psychiatric treatment; the findings from a recent study, for example, suggested a hierarchical ordering of paranoid beliefs, with feelings of threat and suspicion being quite common, but with the most bizarre forms of these beliefs being held only by a small minority (Freeman et al. 2005).

Jaspers (1913/1963) argued that true delusions, unlike overvalued beliefs, are "ununder-standable," by which he meant that they are not amenable to empathy, and therefore cannot be understood in the light of the patient's personality and life experiences. This idea that delusions are not true beliefs, but rather meaningless spasms of a damaged nervous system, still enjoys some support today. However, recent research suggests that they may be amenable to psychological analysis.

Current definitions of delusions suggest that, in contrast to ordinary beliefs and attitudes, they are "firmly sustained in spite of what almost everyone else believes and in spite of what usually constitutes incontrovertible and obvious proof or evidence to the contrary" (American Psychiatric Association 1994), but the same might be said to be true of minority political and religious belief systems. In fact, the patient's conviction in their delusions may wax and wane over time and conviction may correlate poorly with other important aspects of experience, such as preoccupation with the belief or the distress experienced as a consequence (Kendler, Glazer, & Morgenstern 1983). When the unusual beliefs of psychiatric patients have been compared with those of members of religious sects, it is distress rather than any other characteristic that seems to distinguish between the groups (Peters et al. 1999).

The psychiatrist Kurt Schneider (1949/1974) long ago noted that, in the deluded patient, "Abnormal significance tends mostly toward self-reference and is almost always of a special kind: it is momentous, urgent, somehow filled with personal significance." It is certainly true that most, if not all of the commonly reported delusional systems reflect that individual's concern with their position in the social universe. The most frequently observed system is paranoid or persecutory. It has recently been argued that these kinds of delusions fall into two distinct types: "poor-me" paranoia, in which the individual feels unjustly victimized, and "bad-me" paranoia, in which the individual feels that persecution is deserved because of some terrible character defect or sin (Trower & Chadwick 1995). However, in a recent study it was found that patients' beliefs about whether their persecution is deserved fluctuate across time, so that they sometimes shift from the "poor-me" to the "bad-me" belief systems (Melo, Taylor, & Bentall 2006).

Grandiose delusions in which individuals believe that they have special status, talents, or wealth, are also fairly common, especially in patients suffering from mania. Other delusional systems commonly encountered in the psychiatric clinic are delusions of reference, in which innocuous events are held to have some special significance for the patient, and erotomania, in which the patient believes that he or she is secretly loved by someone who is in fact indifferent (usually a person who is famous or holds a position of authority), and delusional jealousy, in which the individual believes against all evidence to the contrary that his or her partner is being unfaithful.

Three main kinds of theories have been proposed to account for delusions. Maher (1988) has argued that they arise as a consequence of rational efforts to explain anomalous experiences, and that cognitive or thinking errors are therefore not required for their occurrence.

Some types of delusion appear to be explicable in this fashion. Perhaps the best known is the quite rarely encountered Capgras delusion (named after the French psychiatrist who first described the condition) in which the individual believes that a loved one has been replaced by an impostor or doppelganger. As the majority of patients experiencing this kind of delusion have demonstrable brain damage, and as the delusion only occurs in the visual modality (patients do not accuse their loved ones of being impostors when talking to them on the telephone), it has been suggested that this kind of belief arises following disruption of the cerebral processes that generate the feeling of familiarity when recognizing faces. Consistent with this account, Capgras patients, in contrast to healthy individuals, do not show a change in skin conductance (indicative of brief emotional arousal) when viewing familiar faces (Ellis et al. 2000).

Other delusional systems are perhaps better accounted for by cognitive biases or errors of reasoning. For example, Garety, Hemsley, and Wessely (1991) found that deluded patients tend to "jump to conclusions" (JTC) on probabilistic reasoning tasks in which they were given the choice of making a guess or seeking more information to test their hypotheses, and this finding has subsequently been widely replicated. More-over, the JTC bias appears to be more marked when patients reason about personally salient material (Dudley et al. 1997). Freeman et al. (2004) have also reported evidence that deluded patients have difficulty when attempting to generate alternative hypothe-ses to account for experiences which they have explained in a delusional way. However, whether this deficit is sufficient to account for the JTC bias seems doubtful. In a version of Garety's task in which participants are first presented with evidence favoring one hypothesis before being presented with evidence favoring another, Garety, Hemsley, and Wessely (1991) reported that deluded patients changed their minds more readily than healthy controls, a finding that seems paradoxical, given the apparent incorrigibility of delusional beliefs.

Other researchers have explored motivational factors that might be responsible for delusions, a possibility that is suggested by the social nature of most delusional beliefs. Researchers inspired by psychoanalysis have suggested that paranoid beliefs might arise from attempts by the individual to maintain self-esteem following failure experiences, or that paranoia is a form of camouflaged depression (Zigler & Glick 1988). Following the observation that paranoid patients tend to assume that negative events in their lives are caused by external, stable (unchangeable), and global (likely to affect all aspects of life) causes (e.g., Kaney & Bentall 1989), Bentall, Kinderman, and Kaney (1994) argued that beliefs about persecution arise from patients' attempts to avoid explanations that are self-blaming, and that would therefore have a negative effect on self-esteem. One objection to this kind of account is that paranoid patients often have low self-esteem.

Trower and Chadwick's (1995) distinction between "poor-me" and "bad-me" paranoia may help to clarify these findings. It will be recalled that actively deluded patients some-times seem to switch between these two kinds of delusional systems. Melo, Taylor, and Bentall (2006) observed that "poor-me" paranoia is associated with excessively external attributions for negative events, whereas "bad-me" paranoia is not. Not surprisingly, in the same study it was observed that "bad-me" paranoia is associated with higher levels of depression than "poor-me" paranoia. These findings point to a complex, dynamic rel-ationship between self-esteem and paranoid thinking, in which paranoid thoughts are initially provoked by negative attitudes toward the self, until defensive processes are activated.

Conclusions and Clinical Implications

This brief review has highlighted some of the ways in which psychiatric conditions are manifest in abnormal conscious experiences. Important advances in our understanding of the cognitive processes underlying these experiences have been made in the past few decades. These advances have been possible because researchers have focused on particular kinds of experiences (e.g., obsessional thoughts, hallucinations, delusional beliefs) rather than the broad diagnostic categories described in the standard diagnostic systems. Importantly, studies have consistently found that these experiences are reported by ordinary people as well as by psychiatric patients, raising the crucial question of why some people become patients and others do not.

These advances have been accompanied by the development of clinical techniques to manipulate the relevant cognitive processes, under the general banner of cognitive behavior therapy. Most cognitive behavioral interventions involve challenging the dysfunctional belief systems of patients, and these approaches have shown considerable promise in the treatment of both the common psychiatric disorders and also the psychoses (Rector & Beck 2001). However, there has been recent interest in the development of strategies to help patients change their attitude toward their thoughts and feelings, rather than the thoughts and feelings themselves. These approaches, which have borrowed from the mindfulness meditation techniques developed within the Buddhist tradition, have shown especial promise in the treatment of patients with chronic, recurring conditions (Segal, Williams, & Teasdale 2002).

See also 7 Normal and abnormal states of consciousness; 15 Philosophical psychopathology and self-consciousness.

Further Readings

Bentall, R. P. (2003) *Madness Explained: Psychosis and Human Nature*. London: Penguin.
Frith, C. and Johnstone, E. C. (2003) *Schizophrenia: A Very Short Introduction*. Oxford: Oxford University Press.
Spence, S. A. and David, A. S. (2004) *Voices in the Brain: The Cognitive Neuropsychiatry of Auditory Verbal Hallucinations*. Hove: Psychology Press.

References

Al-Issa, I. (1995) The illusion of reality or the reality of an illusion: hallucinations and culture. *British Journal of Psychiatry* 166, 368–73.
American Psychiatric Association (1994) *Diagnostic and Statistical Manual for Mental Disorders*, 4th edn. Washington, DC: American Psychiatric Association.
Bentall, R. P. (2003) *Madness Explained: Psychosis and Human Nature*. London: Penguin.
Bentall, R. P. and Slade, P. D. (1985) Reality testing and auditory hallucinations: a signal-detection analysis. *British Journal of Clinical Psychology* 24, 159–69.
Bentall, R. P., Kinderman, P., and Kaney, S. (1994) The self, attributional processes and abnormal beliefs: towards a model of persecutory delusions. *Behaviour Research and Therapy* 32, 331–41.

Blakemore, S. J., Smith, J., Steel, R., Johnstone, E. C., and Frith, C. D. (2000) The perception of self-produced sensory stimuli in patients with auditory hallucinations and passivity experiences: evidence for a breakdown in self-monitoring. *Psychological Medicine* 30, 1131–39.

Chadwick, P. and Birchwood, M. (1994) The omnipotence of voices: a cognitive approach to auditory hallucinations. *British Journal of Psychiatry* 164, 190–201.

Dudley, R. E. J., John, C. H., Young, A. W., and Over, D. E. (1997) The effect of self-referent material on the reasoning of people with delusions. *British Journal of Clinical Psychology* 36, 575–84.

Ellis, H. D., Lewis, M. B., Moselhy, H. F., and Young, A. W. (2000) Automatic without autonomic responses to familiar faces: differential components of covert face recognition in a case of Capgras delusion. *Cognitive Neuropsychiatry* 5, 255–69.

Ford, J. M. and Mathalon, D. H. (2004) Electrophysiological evidence of corollary discharge dysfunction in schizophrenia during talking and thinking. *Journal of Psychiatric Research* 38, 37–46.

Freeman, D., Garety, P. A., Fowler, D., Kuipers, E., Bebbington, P. E., and Dunn, G. (2004) Why do people with delusions fail to choose more realistic explanations for their experiences? An empirical investigation. *Journal of Consulting and Clinical Psychology* 72, 671–80.

Freeman, D., Garety, P. A., Bebbington, P. E., Smith, B., Rollinson, R., Fowler, D. et al. (2005) Psychological investigation of the structure of paranoia in a non-clinical population. *British Journal of Psychiatry* 186, 427–35.

Garety, P. A., Hemsley, D. R., and Wessely, S. (1991) Reasoning in deluded schizophrenic and paranoid patients. *Journal of Nervous and Mental Disease* 179: 4, 194–201.

Goldberg, D. and Huxley, P. (1992) *Common Mental Disorders: A Bio-social Model*. London: Routledge.

Gould, L. N. (1948) Verbal hallucinations and activity of vocal musculature. *American Journal of Psychiatry* 105, 367–72.

Green, M. F. (1998) *Schizophrenia from a Neurocognitive Perspective: Probing the Impenetrable Darkness*. Boston, MA: Allyn and Bacon.

Haddock, G., Slade, P. D., and Bentall, R. P. (1995) Auditory hallucinations and the verbal transformation effect: the role of suggestions. *Personality and Individual Differences* 19, 301–6.

Hammersley, P., Dias, A., Todd, G., Bowen-Jones, K., Reilly, B., and Bentall, R. P. (2003) Childhood trauma and hallucinations in bipolar affective disorder: a preliminary investigation. *British Journal of Psychiatry* 182, 543–47.

Harvey, A., Watkins, E. R., Mansell, W., and Shafran, R. (2004) *Cognitive Behavioural Processes across Psychological Disorders: A Transdiagnostic Approach to Research and Treatment*. Oxford: Oxford University Press.

Honig, A., Romme, M. A. J., Ensink, B. J., Escher, S. D. M. A. C., Pennings, M. H. A., and DeVries, M. W. (1998) Auditory hallucinations: a comparison between patients and nonpatients. *Journal of Nervous and Mental Disease* 186, 646–51.

Jaspers, K. (1913/1963) *General Psychopathology* (J. Hoenig and M. W. Hamilton, trans.). Manchester: Manchester University Press.

Johns, L. C., Rossell, S., Frith, C., Ahmad, F., Hemsley, D., Kuipers, E. et al. (2001) Verbal self-monitoring and auditory hallucinations in people with schizophrenia. *Psychological Medicine* 31, 705–15.

Kaney, S. and Bentall, R. P. (1989) Persecutory delusions and attributional style. *British Journal of Medical Psychology* 62, 191–8.

Kendler, K. S., Glazer, W., and Morgenstern, H. (1983) Dimensions of delusional experience. *American Journal of Psychiatry*, 140, 466–9.

Kraepelin, E. (1899/1990) *Psychiatry: A Textbook for Students and Physicians. Volume 1: General Psychiatry*. Canton, MA: Watson Publishing International.

McGhie, A. and Chapman, J. (1961) Disorders of attention and perception in early schizophrenia. *British Journal of Medical Psychology* 34, 103–16.

Maher, B. A. (1988) Anomalous experience and delusional thinking: the logic of explanations. In T. F. Oltmanns and B. A. Maher (eds.), *Delusional Beliefs*, 15–33. New York: Wiley.

Melo, S., Taylor, J., and Bentall, R. P. (2006) "Poor me" versus "bad me": paranoia and the instability of persecutory ideation. *Psychology and Psychotherapy: Theory, Research, Practice* 79: 271–87.

Morrison, A. P. and Wells, A. (2003) Metacognition across disorders: a comparison of patients with hallucinations, delusions, and panic disorder with non-patients. *Behaviour Research and Therapy* 41, 251–56.

Nuechterlein, K. H. and Subotnik, K. L. (1998) The cognitive origins of schizophrenia and prospects for intervention. In T. Wykes, N. Tarrier, and S. Lewis (eds.), *Outcome and Innovation in Psychological Treatment of Schizophrenia*, 17–42. Chichester: Wiley.

Oltmanns, T. F. and Neale, J. M. (1978) Distractability in relation to other aspects of schizophrenic disorder. In S. Schwartz (ed.), *Language and Cognition in Schizophrenia*, 117–43. Hillsdale, NJ: Erlbaum.

Peters, E., Day, S., McKenna, J., and Orbach, G. (1999) Delusional ideation in religious and psychotic populations. *British Journal of Clinical Psychology* 38, 83–96.

Read, J., Agar, K., Argyle, N., and Aderhold, V. (2003) Sexual and physical abuse during childhood and adulthood as predictors of hallucinations, delusions and thought disorder. *Psychology and Psychotherapy: Theory, Research and Practice* 76, 1–22.

Rector, N. A. and Beck, A. T. (2001) Cognitive behavioural therapy for schizophrenia: an empirical review. *Journal of Nervous and Mental Disease* 189, 278–87.

Salkovskis, P. M. (1998) Psychological approaches to the understanding of obsessional problems. In R. Swinton (ed.), *Obsessive Compulsive Disorder: Theory, Research and Treatment*. New York: Guilford.

Schneider, K. (1949/1974) The concept of delusion (H. Marshall, trans.). In S. R. Hirsch and M. Shepherd (eds.), *Themes and Variations in European Psychiatry*, 33–9. Bristol: John Wright and Sons.

Segal, Z. V., Williams, J. M. G., and Teasdale, J. D. (2002) *Mindfulness-Based Cognitive Therapy for Depression*. London: Guilford.

Slade, P. D. and Bentall, R. P. (1988) *Sensory Deception: A Scientific Analysis of Hallucination*. London: Croom Helm.

Tien, A. Y. (1991) Distribution of hallucinations in the population. *Social Psychiatry and Psychiatric Epidemiology* 26, 287–92.

Trower, P. and Chadwick, P. (1995) Pathways to defense of the self: a theory of two types of paranoia. *Clinical Psychology: Science and Practice* 2, 263–78.

van Os, J., Hanssen, M., Bijl, R. V., and Ravelli, A. (2000) Strauss (1969) revisited: a psychosis continuum in the normal population? *Schizophrenia Research* 45, 11–20.

Vygotsky, L. S. V. (1962) *Thought and Language*. Cambridge, MA: MIT Press.

Wells, A. and Papageorgiou, C. (1998) Relationships between worry, obsessive-compulsive symptoms and meta-cognitive beliefs. *Behaviour Research and Therapy* 36, 899–913.

Woodruff, P. W. R. (2004) Auditory hallucinations: insights and questions from neuroimaging. *Cognitive Neuropsychiatry* 9, 73–91.

World Health Organization (1992) *ICD-10: International Statistical Classification of Diseases and Related Health Problems*, 10th revised edn. Geneva: World Health Organization.

Zigler, E. and Glick, M. (1988) Is paranoid schizophrenia really camouflaged depression? *American Psychologist* 43, 284–90.

10

Altered States of Consciousness: Drug Induced States

EDWARD F. PACE-SCHOTT AND J. ALLAN HOBSON

The brain is the organ of consciousness. Since the brain is chemically composed and because the brain uses specific chemical molecules both to permit communication between neurons and to engineer major changes in its state, exogenous chemicals can exert a wide variety of effects on consciousness via their interaction with endogenous chemical systems. We will use a clinical framework for discussing drug effects on consciousness discussing first anesthetics, then psychoactive prescription drugs and finally recreational drugs. An organizing theme within each section is that psychoactive drugs exert their effects by mimicking (agonism) or blocking (antagonism) endogenous substances with which groups of neurons normally communicate with one another. The understanding of these chemically induced changes is of enormous practical and theoretical interest (Snyder 1986; Hobson 2001).

The ubiquity of medical modifications of consciousness in modern everyday life underscores the intimate linkage between psychopharmacology and the physiological basis of consciousness. Recently, much scientific and popular attention has focused on the nebulous distinction between treatment of true mental disorders, pharmacological normalization of socioculturally based behavioral standards, and "cosmetic psychopharmacology" to enhance career or interpersonal achievement (Kramer 1993).

However, the pharmacological alteration of consciousness has been ubiquitous in societies throughout the world. This includes dramatic changes in consciousness such as hallucinogen-induced alterations of consciousness during religious practices or the profound narrowing and debilitation of consciousness in addiction. But it also includes culturally normative manipulations of consciousness undertaken by large segments of any given society. These include enhancement of alertness via mild psychostimulants like caffeine and nicotine or, in some cultures, chewed coca leaves (cocaine) or betel nut (arecholine). Similarly, ethanol is a ubiquitous mood enhancer, anxiety reducer, and facilitator of sociability used throughout the world while, in certain cultures, other mild intoxicants such as cannabis are similarly used.

Surgical Anesthesia

The fact that anesthetic agents can be used to suspend consciousness in a controlled way makes modern surgery possible. A systematic discussion of the pharmacology of anesthesia is beyond the scope of this chapter (but see chapter 49).

Most general and local anesthetics act by interfering with neural function at the level of the cell membrane. They block normal conduction of electrical impulses. It is the disablement of neuronal function that renders anesthetic agents so potent and so useful. However, even certain anesthetics act according to the general theme we have introduced via stimulation of inhibitory or blockade of excitatory brain neurotransmitter systems as we will illustrate below when we consider the barbiturates.

Most surgical procedures go smoothly. Patients lose consciousness completely during the procedure and have no recollection of it afterward. There is, however, a small but significant incidence of retained conscious awareness and later recall of conscious experience that is troubling to both patient and physician (Sigalovsky 2003).

This is easily understood when the co-administration of a neuromuscular blocking agent makes it impossible for the subject to communicate distress. Such patients are introgenically locked-in, a terrifying experience that can cause a syndrome similar to post-traumatic stress disorder (Sigalovsky 2003), and their misfortune is actionable. Most of the cases of recall of surgical pain do not fit into this category and remain unexplained.

A recent PET study by Finset et al. (1999) suggests a similarity between anesthesia and sleep. During the progressive loss of consciousness with increasing levels of the anesthetic propofol, there is seen a proportional decrease in blood flow to the thalamus and midbrain (and, less proportionately, to much of the cortex). This finding suggests a similarity between anesthesia and the progressive deactivation of the reticulothalamic system seen in descending non-REM sleep (Finset et al. 1999).

The main message of anesthesia during surgery is that interference with neuronal transmission can wholly and reversibly obliterate consciousness.

Prescription Drugs

Many sedatives and other psychoactive drugs that are prescribed by physicians interact with the neurotransmitter and neuromodulatory systems of the brain in robust and informative ways. The phenomena and proposed physiological mechanisms involved are further described in the discussion of waking, sleeping, and dreaming states in chapter 7.

Manipulation of the dimensions of normal consciousness (e.g., mood, arousal, attention, aggression, extraversion) has become commonplace in our society. In this category we include not only psychoactive prescription medicines (e.g., antidepressants, psychostimulants, and atypical antipsychotics), but also over the counter medications (ephedra, St. John's Wort), social beverages (e.g., coffee, alcohol), "nutriceuticals" (e.g omega-3 fatty acids) or the milder intoxicants (e.g., cannabis, alcohol). This section will deal with the medical uses of psychoactive drugs but we will revisit several of these classes of drugs when considering drugs of abuse.

Sedatives, Anxiolytics and Hypnotics

In keeping with our organizing theme of interaction of psychoactive drugs with endogenous systems, we note that the sedatives, minor tranquilizers, and hypnotics all enhance the effect of gamma-aminobutyric acid (GABA) on neurons. They are therefore termed GABAergic drugs. Release of GABA is the most common way in which neurons inhibit the activity of other neurons in the brain. Sedatives, minor tranquilizers and hypnotics all render GABA more effective at suppressing activity of neurons. These agents do so by binding to GABA receptors on the surface of neurons, but different agents do this in different ways by binding to different parts of the receptor (Malcolm 2003). The sedating, tranquilizing, and, in different forms or doses, the sleep-inducing (hypnotic) effect of these drugs all result from their GABAergic properties. Indeed, normal falling asleep involves extensive activation of GABA receptors at many sites in the subcortical brain (Pace-Schott & Hobson 2002).

Before 1975, most sedatives were simply low doses of anesthetic agents. The barbiturates (e.g., phenobarbital) are a good example of GABAergic anesthetics that were subsequently used as sedatives. Barbiturates reliably attenuated consciousness thereby reducing anxiety and facilitating sleep but they had relatively low margins of safety and were powerfully addicting. Inadvertent and intentional overdoses caused coma and sometimes death by radically suppressing neuronal activation especially in the reticular formation, which includes the respiratory center. Even at prescribed dose levels, the barbiturates suppress normal sleep often eliminating both Stage IV and REM. Barbiturates specifically influence the thalamocortical oscillator producing a spindle-like EEG waveform that is faster and longer than the physiological spindles of Stage II sleep. The main point here is that the suppression of consciousness that is necessary for sleep can be chemically induced but the physiology of the "sleep" that is induced may be quite unlike that of normal sleep.

More recently, the benzodiazepines (e.g., Valium), another class of GABAergic drugs, were introduced as selective suppressors of anxiety (anxiolytics), an unpleasant emotional component of consciousness. When it was found that they were also effective sedatives and hypnotics, they came to replace the barbiturates because they had a much wider margin of safety and they did not suppress REM sleep (although they *did* suppress Stage IV). A specific benzodiazepine-binding site on the GABA receptor was identified in the brain and shown to facilitate inhibitory neurotransmission leading to a generalized suppression of brain activation. The suppression of Stage IV sleep by these agents is as yet unexplained but their reduction of conscious awareness via generalized neuronal inhibition makes sense in terms of the global activation model described in chapter 7. Benzodiazepines may cause confusional states, especially in the elderly, and some cause amnesia in the waking periods that follow their administration as sedatives. Moreover, like the barbiturates, they can be abused and can result in a withdrawal syndrome when discontinued. New hypnotics such as zolpidem (Ambien) were therefore developed. These drugs, like barbiturates and benzodiazepines, exert their hypnotic effects by acting on the GABA receptor. However, they do not produce euphoria at high doses and are less likely to be abused. But patients can become habituated to these drugs, which, as a result, lose their hypnotic benefit. For this reason, behavioral techniques have become the preferred method of treating long-term insomnia (Morin 1993).

Antipsychotics

Psychosis is defined by the presence of hallucinations and delusions that, in healthy individuals, are usually only experienced during dream consciousness. They are experienced in waking in three major classes of mental illness: schizophrenia, affective disorder, and delirium.

The emptying of the mental hospitals after 1955 is widely attributed to the antipsychotic effect, primarily in chronically schizophrenic patients, of a now very large number of agents that include phenothiazines such as Thorazine. Thorazine was discovered by accident in Paris when patients who were being tested for the effects on cold symptoms of anti-histamines (of which Thorazine is one), described an unexpected lessening of their anxiety. In larger doses, which produced relatively little sedation, they were effective in reducing hallucinations and delusions.

The antipsychotic efficacy of the phenothiazines as well as the newer ("atypical") anti-psychotics such as clozapine (Clozaril), olanzapine (Zyprexa) and risperidone (Risperdal) has proved to be proportional to their ability to block the dopamine D2 receptors of the brain, even though the atypical antipsychotics have powerful effects on other neuro-modulatory systems (Andersson et al. 1998). Dopamine is an aminergic neuromodulator, which, together with acetylcholine, may mediate dream consciousness because unlike norepinephrine and serotonin, its liberation is not suppressed in REM (Gottesman 2002; Pace-Schott & Hobson 2002).

The take home message is that antidopaminergic drugs like the phenothiazines can exert relatively selective effects upon the emotional, hallucinatory, and delusional components of consciousness via their blockade of dopamine.

Antidepressants

Depression is a painful suppression of interest in and energy for life. Consciousness in depression assumes a bleak and even a black coloration as positive emotion fades and is replaced by sadness, guilt, retardation of thought, obsessive rumination, anxiety, and even suicidal ideation.

Most antidepressant drugs act by enhancing the effects of the endogenous biogenic amines, serotonin, and norepinephrine. These neuromodulators mediate the mnemonic, attentional, and emotional aspects of waking consciousness. The primary and most sought after of these effects is an increase in energy and positive emotions, especially a sense of interest in the social world and optimism about social transactions.

Some antidepressants enhance the effects of serotonin and norepinephrine by pre-venting its re-uptake by the (pre-synaptic) neuron from which it was secreted, thereby leaving more serotonin and norepinephrine in the tiny fluid-filled space between neurons (synapse) where they can more greatly affect their target (post-synaptic) neurons. Selective serotonin reuptake inhibitors (SSRIs such as Prozac) prevent reuptake of only serotonin, others (SNRIs) selectively block norepinephrine reuptake (e.g., Strattera) while some block reuptake of both (most of the older tricyclic antidepressants such as Elavil). The effects of serotonin and norepinephrine can also be enhanced by blocking their enzymatic degra-dation by monoamine oxidase inhibitors (MAOIs) such as Nardil or by a variety of other mechanisms in newer, "novel" antidepressants (e.g., Wellbutrin, Serzone).

Psychostimulants

Like all psychoactive drugs, therapeutic psychostimulants such as methylphenidate (Ritalin) and the amphetamines (e.g., Adderall) act upon endogenous neurochemical systems in the brain. In this case, they act by increasing levels of dopamine available to stimulate post-synaptic neurons by preventing its re-uptake by the cells from which it was secreted (the presynaptic cell). This is exactly like the above action of the antidepressants on serotonin and norepinephrine re-uptake, and indeed, most psychostimulants also prevent serotonin and norepinephrine re-uptake but, in addition, the amphetamines cause the neurons to release more of these neuromodulators. These psychostimulants, along with a new, non-amphetamine stimulant modafinil (Provigil) are used to prevent excessive sleepiness and sleep attacks in the sleep disorder narcolepsy. However, the most well-known and controversial use of therapeutic psychostimulants is in the treatment of attention deficit disorder (ADD) in both children and adults (Stubbe 2000). It is believed that the attention promoting effect of psychostimulants results from enhanced functioning of the prefrontal cortex, an "executive" region of the brain involved in attention as well as self-control, which often is also deficient in ADD.

Another class of aminergic drugs which mimic the effects of norepinephrine (agonists), have psychostimulant side effects such as pseudoephedrine (Sudafed), which is used to treat respiratory congestion. Pseudoephedrine's naturally occurring cousin, ephedrine, a component of plants of the genus *Ephedra*, has been sold as a "herbal" stimulant until its recent ban in the US due to its dangerous cardiovascular effects. Given the stimulating effects of norepinephrine agonists, it is not surprising that norepinephrine antagonists such as the anti-hypertensive beta blockers sometimes produce depression.

A ubiquitous social psychostimulant is caffeine. It is believed that caffeine promotes waking and alertness by blocking the adenosine receptors. Adenosine is believed to be the endogenous substance whose buildup over continued waking produces a homeostatic drive to sleep which, in combination with circadian rhythms, determines when we fall asleep (Strecker et al. 2000). Other similar stimulating substances are found in asthma medications (theophylline) and chocolate (theobromides).

Cholinergic Agents

Like other psychoactive drugs, cholinergic agents act upon endogenous neuromodulatory systems, in this case, the acetylcholine system. Acetylcholine is a neuromodulator which enhances attention and memory by activating two classes of acetylcholine receptors. Nicotinic receptors are activated by nicotine (a cholinergic agonist), which explains why cigarettes containing nicotine have such potent effects. Muscarinic receptors are activated by another cholinergic agonist, muscarine, found in the toxic mushroom *Amanita muscarica*. The activity of the cholinergic system can also be enhanced by preventing the breakdown of acetylcholine by the enzyme acetylcholinesterase as is done by the anti-Alzheimer's disease drug donepizil (Aricept).

Both peripheral (cardiovascular and muscular) and central effects are mediated by acetylcholine. Of great interest to students of consciousness is that REM sleep can be markedly potentiated by muscarinic acetylcholine-like drugs when microinjected into the pontine brain stem. Acetylcholine is released by two groups of neurons in the brainstem (Mesulam 2004, chs. 5 and 6) and by four nuclei in the basal forebrain (Mesulam 2004, chs. 1–4). Basal forebrain cholinergic neurons project to the cerebral cortex where the release of acetylcholine is equally high in waking and REM sleep. Acetylcholine may thus mediate aspects of both waking and dreaming consciousness.

When acetylcholine effects upon the brain are countered by cholinergic antagonists (or anticholinergics) such as the mixed muscarinic and nicotinic blocking agent atropine, subjects are often rendered delirious (as well as visually impaired, hyperthermic, and dehydrated). The medical students mnemonic for atropine intoxication is: blind as a bat, dry as a bone, hot as a fire, and – mad as a hatter. It is not surprising, therefore, that a cholinergic *agonist*, pilocarpine, is used to treat excessively dry eyes and mouth in Sjogren's syndrome. Other anticholinergics, such as cogentin, are used to treat the side effects of other drugs like the phenothiazine antipsychotics.

It may seem paradoxical that both blockade and enhancement of acetylcholine lead to changes in consciousness but the reader should remember that it is the balance (or ratio) of neuromodulators that determine the mode of action of cortical circuits. Too much acetylcholine (in the presence of dopamine but in the absence of serotonin and norepinephrine) may contribute to dream delirium, while too little (in the presence of all the aminergic modulators) may mediate waking delirium.

The point is that consciousness is the product of a very delicate balance of neuromodulation as well as of generalized activation. Both processes are mediated by subcortical neuronal systems.

"Nutriceuticals"

It can even be argued that food itself alters consciousness. This may take place in reference to food constituents or lack thereof such as occurs in malnutrition, voluntary fasting, certain forms of vegetarianism, or in psychological reaction to religious prescription or proscription. The general characteristics of food itself (e.g., caloric) may affect aspects of consciousness via interactions of appetite and satiation with alertness (Stahl, Orr, & Bollinger 1983). Similarly, appetite and satiation interact with mood via the mediation of culturally conditioned personality dimensions (e.g., body image stereotypes) or psychopathology (e.g., eating disorders). Specific neurophysiological bases of nutrition-consciousness interactions are also well documented. These include, for example, effects on arousal states by neural modulators of hunger and satiety such as leptins and orexins (Sakurai 2003; Gale, Castracane, & Montzoros 2004) and protein constituents such as tryptophan (e.g., Thorleifsdottir et al. 1989) as well as mood effects of omega-3 fatty acids (Freeman 2000) or reward effects of desirable foods such as chocolate (Small et al. 2001) – see below.

Many such putative effects of these "nutriceuticals," however, remain confounded by the intervening variables of cognitions, beliefs, and biases, which are, more often than not, manipulated by advertising, "fads," or other cultural influences. Recently, however, a brain basis for even such psychosomatic or "placebo effect" phenomena has been documented (Wager et al. 2004).

Recreational Drugs

Some prescription drugs are sold on the street for recreational purposes so the classification of them is arbitrary. Recreational users of prescription drugs have made their own decisions about use of the substances whether or not they have consulted physicians or co-opted them to obtain the drugs.

Some recreational drugs, like prescription and over-the-counter drugs discussed above, are used to adjust commonplace dimensions of consciousness such as mood states (e.g., alcohol, prescription sedatives, cannabis). Some investigators suggest such drug abuse constitutes "self-medication" of pathological states of consciousness such as depression, anxiety disorders or even psychosis (Khantzian 1997), a theory that remains controversial (Mueser, Drake, & Wallach 1998). Indeed, substance abuse is significantly more common among the psychiatrically ill than in the population as a whole (Greenfield, Weiss, & Tohen 1995).

However, extreme human states of consciousness that only rarely occur spontaneously, can result from more powerful, abused, recreational substances, most notably the hallucinogens. For example, religious epiphany is reported by users of indolamine and tryptamine hallucinogens (e.g., LSD, DMT), "peak" experiences are reported by users of "entactogens" (e.g., MDMA, MDE), paranoid schizophreniform states can occur in stimulant abusers (e.g., cocaine, methamphetamine), dissociative or fugue-like states occur with NMDA-blocking hallucinogens (e.g., ketamine, PCP) which, along with general anesthetics, have been reported to produce "near-death experiences" (Ring 1996; Jansen 2000).

Therefore, almost the entire spectrum of conscious experience can be affected by prescription and/or recreational drugs. This should not be surprising given the fact that psychoactive drugs act upon endogenous neurochemical systems which are the basis of neuronal communication in the brain. We will first discuss the recreational use of common mood altering substances such as alcohol, sedatives, cannabis, and stimulants then we will discuss the more extreme forms of consciousness produced by the hallucinogens.

Recreational Sedatives: Alcohol, Tranquilizers, and Opiates

Many people, even those with normal mood, enjoy feeling "high." That is why alcohol is so popular. There is a lightening of mood, and a lessening of social anxiety that occurs before the CNS depressant effects set in. Like alcohol, these mood enhancing (euphoriogenic) and anxiety reducing (anxiolytic) effects are sought by those recreationally using prescription sedatives such as benzodiazepines, gamma-amino-hydroxybutyrate (GHB) and barbiturates. As noted above, these sedating drugs enhance the action of GABA, our main endogenous inhibitor of nerve activity, and at high doses can lead to sleep, unconsciousness, and respiratory depression.

Like GABAergic sedatives, the opiates (opium and its derivatives morphine and heroin as well as their numerous synthetic analogs such as fentanyl and oxycodone) exert their effects by binding to receptors for substances that occur endogenously in the brain, the endorphins and enkephalins or "endogenous opiates" (Cooper, Bloom, & Roth 1996). The opiate drugs bind specifically to the mu opiate receptor at several subcortical sites including the ventral tegmental area (VTA) of the midbrain and the nucleus accumbens (NAc). These two structures, the "mesoaccumbens reward system," are believed to be involved to varying degrees in pleasurable (euphorigenic or reward) effects of all recreational drugs including even alcohol, nicotine, the GABAergic sedatives and cannabis as well as natural rewards such as food or sex (Koob 2003). In general, euphorigenic drugs act by increasing the release of the neurotransmitter dopamine, manufactured by cells of the VTA, at their termini in the NAc. The NAc, in turn, sends GABAergic messages on to other subcortical sites eventually reaching the prefrontal cortex where the drug effects are consciously perceived. Although far from the whole story, this mechanism appears an important component of all drug reward.

In addition to the therapeutic uses of certain psychostimulants (see above), others such as cocaine and methamphetamine, are major drugs of abuse worldwide. As noted above, psychostimulants act by directly increasing levels of dopamine by re-uptake blockade as well as its enhanced release. They, therefore, directly affect the mesoaccumbens reward system described above and in doing so are highly addictive. Their subjective effects include extreme but short-lived euphoria (especially injected or smoked "crack" cocaine) and a sense of alertness and energy without need for sleep that can be maintained for extended periods of time during psychostimulant "binges." Inevitably, however, a "crash" occurs when stimulant effects wear off. The subject may then find his consciousness to be clouded by an even blacker mood than before the drug was taken. Worse yet, extended use of psychostimulants may result in transient psychotic states, indistinguishable from paranoid schizophrenia (Rosse et al. 1994). This again should not be surprising given the *anti*-dopamine basis of the antipsychotic drugs (see above).

Marijuana

By far the most popular and commonly used consciousness altering drugs are the cannabinoids (e.g., delta-9-tetrahydrocannabinol or delta-9-THC) found in the plant *Cannabis sativa*, also known as cannabis, marijuana, grass, or weed. The biological basis of marijuana's effects has only recently been discovered and, like other psychoactive substances, marijuana cannabinoids mimic endogenous substances, the endogenous cannabinoids anandamide and 2-arachidonoylglycerol, which act upon endogenous cannabinoid receptors. Animal models suggest an important role for endogenous cannabinoids in facilitating the extinction of memory traces in the hippocampus, an important process if we are not to have our important memories overwhelmed by the myriad daily input of our senses (Marsicano et al. 2002). The well-known amnesic effects of cannabis may mirror this important function of the endogenous cannabinoids.

People who smoke marijuana cigarettes claim that their consciousness is altered such that they are less anxious and are better able to concentrate their attention on themselves and issues that they consider to be important. They also claim that the drug makes them euphoric or "high" which is not surprising given that THC, like other recreational drugs, increases dopamine release in the nucleus accumbens (Gardner 2000). Some individuals also experience cannabis intoxication as sedating and sleep-promoting and, interestingly, substances closely related to anandamide such as oleamide possess powerful hypnotic properties which can be blocked by cannabinoid receptor antagonists (Mendelson & Basile 1999). Because it is easily grown, it is widely available and because its effects are mild, many experts feel that its use should be legalized. Marijuana is, arguably, less dangerous than alcohol whose prohibition failed even after a constitutional amendment was passed. The side effects are minimal and some may be advantageous and desirable: susceptibility to pain from disease processes such as cancer may decrease; so may the nausea associated with gastrointestinal diseases or with chemotherapy.

Drug Craving

Drug craving is a drug-induced state of mind that accompanies addiction to many drugs, particularly stimulants, opiates, and alcohol. Craving is a state of consciousness pathologically focused on the rewarding properties of the abused substance and is the most proximal cause of addictive relapse. Craving may reflect a state of "allostasis," whereby normal mood states and hedonic capacity are persistently altered by neuronal adaptations of the meso-accumbens reward system (Koob 2003).

Psychedelic Drugs

The hallucinogens are substances that produce hallucinations, alterations of thinking, emotional changes, and dissociated states with some features of dreaming in waking. Psychedelic drugs produce their hallucinatory effects by tipping the balance in sensory systems in favor of endogenous stimulation. In the case of the visual system, the hallucinations arise in activated cortical networks that usually process external data. Since the access of external data is impeded by the drug's blockade of modulators such as serotonin, the system responds – as it does in dreaming – to endogenous stimuli.

One striking fact about hallucinogens is the diversity of endogenous neuromodulatory systems by which they exert their effects. The most well known hallucinogenic substances, the indolamines such as LSD and psilocybin, produce hallucinations and other effects by interfering with the brain's serotonin (or 5-HT) system. This is also true of the tryptamine derivatives such as N,N-dimethyltryptamine (DMT) and the phenylethylamines such as mescaline. The main site of action of these drugs are believed to be presynaptic 5-HT2A receptors located on excitatory inputs to large neurons in a deep layer (layer V) of the cerebral cortex where they abnormally prolong excitation (Aghajanian & Marek 1999).

Serotonergic hallucinogens are often used in the religious ceremonies of traditional cultures such as the Navajo, who believe that peyote cactus (mescaline) experiences provide religious insight and treatment for alcoholism (de Rios, Grob, & Baker 2002). Similar religious insight was attributed to serotonergic hallucinogen experiences (e.g., LSD) by Western psychedelic users in the 1960s, a lucid account of which can be found in Ram Dass (1971). A particularly interesting serotonergic intoxicant is the psychoactive drink Ayahuasca used in religious ceremonies by indigenous people of the Amazon and Orinoco rainforest as well as by more Westernized religious groups (Riba et al. 2001). This natural source of DMT contains a mixture of herbally derived substances, which include the beta-carbolines harmine and harmoline, natural MAOIs which prevent the breakdown of DMT by monoamine oxidase allowing intoxication following oral intake (Riba et al. 2001).

Although the serotonergic hallucinogens are best known, other equally powerful psychedelic effects are produced by substances acting upon entirely different neurochemical systems. Substances that block the action of the brain's most common excitatory neurotransmitter, glutamate, on its NMDA receptor, produce profound dissociative experiences with illusions of physical power (Rosse et al. 1994). These compounds include phencyclidine (PCP), ketamine, MK-801 and high doses of the cough suppressant dextromethorphan.

Another powerful hallucinogen, salvinorin A, is a diterpene substance that acts as an agonist of the kappa opioid receptor, an opioid receptor differing from the mu receptor mediating the euphoriant and anesthetic actions of opiate drugs (Roth et al. 2002). This substance is derived from the mint *Salvia divinorum* and is used in the religious ceremonies of the Mazatek native population of Mexico. Plant derived hallucinogens which act upon cholinergic systems include both anticholinergics such as atropine from *Datura stramonium* (Greene, Patterson, & Warner 1996) and the cholinergic agonist muscarine from the mushroom *Amanita muscarica* (Stephens 1999). Even cannabis products, gaseous neuroactive substances such as nitrous oxide, and solvents contained in commercial chemicals ("inhalants") can result in hallucinogen-like effects.

Entactogens

There is debate how the methylenedioxyamphetamines such as MDMA, MDE, and MDA, all usually sold as "ecstasy," should be classified as their effects combine aspects of both stimulants and hallucinogens. These drugs have been classified as "entactogens" because in addition to stimulant and mild hallucinogenic effects, they show the unique properties of evoking feelings of happiness, emotional excitation, safety, and closeness to others (Gouzoulis-Mayfrank et al. 1999). It is primarily these emotional effects that made such "designer drugs," staples of the "rave" culture of the 1990s. These drugs are taken up by the presynaptic serotonin transporter and promote release of serotonin stores from the presynaptic nerve terminal while also, like the stimulants, enhancing dopamine neurotransmission (Liechti et al. 2000). Although the entactogens have ongoing popularity, they represent a major public health hazard because of their destructive effects on serotonin neurons with resulting cognitive and emotional dysfunction (Montoya et al. 2002).

In addition to potential addiction, the problem with the use of recreational drugs in unsupervised settings is that dosage is uncontrolled and often unknown and drugs may contain toxic adulterants. Also, because individual reactions to the drug can be idiosyncratic, adverse effects such as poor risk judgment and potentially self-damaging behaviors may be the cost of altering consciousness in an artificial way. Again, behaviorally induced and harmless means of altering conscious state, such as meditation, exercise, and artistic expression, are better advocated.

Drugs and Dreaming

Interestingly, from the point of view of the conscious state theory expounded in chapter 7, the stimulants, alcohol, and barbiturates all suppress REM sleep during use. The rebound that occurs during subsequent abstinence may be so intense as to create delirium. Toxic delirium is characterized by visual hallucinations, disorientation, memory loss and confabulation. It is, therefore, a pathological state of consciousness which shares many formal features with dreaming.

Susceptible subjects need to realize that natural dreaming affords them with the same sort of altered consciousness that they seek in drug use. The advantages of a natural psychedelic is obvious: it is free (i.e., costs nothing), and it is harmless (i.e., it has no side effects and no withdrawal syndrome). Toward the end of increasing awareness and positive emotion in dreams, lucidity training is quite useful (LaBerge 1990).

Conclusions

1 Consciousness is altered when drugs affect state control and other endogenous neuromodulatory systems of the brain by acting as their mimics (agonists) or blockers (antagonists).
2 Consciousness can be ablated by anesthetics permitting surgery. Anesthetic agents act by suppressing brain activity sometimes via the brain's own inhibitory systems.

3 Consciousness can be altered by chemically changing one or another of its component systems. Drugs that disrupt consciousness change the delicate chemical balance mediated by the sleep state control systems of the brainstem and subcortex as well as neuronal systems controlling alertness, mood, thought, and perception.

4 Benzodiazepines and other hypnotic sedatives enhance sleep by enhancing GABAergic inhibition of neurons throughout the brain.

5 Antipsychotics quell hallucinations and delusions by blocking dopamine neuromodulation.

6 Stimulants enhance energy and mood by enhancing synaptic levels of the neuromodulator, dopamine.

7 The antidepressants enhance alertness, energy, and mood by increasing the synaptic efficacy of serotonin and norepinephrine.

8 Abused euphorigenic substances all affect, to a greater or lesser extent, the brain's endogenous mesoaccumbens reward system and drug craving may result from deregulation of this natural reward system.

9 Abused substances are often prescription drugs taken in above-therapeutic doses and acting upon the same systems as with their legitimate use.

10 Serotonergic psychedelics produce hallucinations by interfering with serotonergic neurotransmission in sensory and multimodal areas of the cerebral cortex while entactogens also change serotonergic modulation of emotional systems. Disruption of many different neuronal systems can result in hallucinations.

11 Many of the effects of drugs upon consciousness can now be understood in terms of the neurophysiological mechanisms of normal conscious state control.

See also 7 Normal and abnormal states of consciousness.

Further Readings

Cooper, J. R., Bloom, F. E., and Roth, R. H. (eds.) (2002) *The Biochemical Basis of Neuropharmacology*, 8th edn. New York: Oxford University Press.

Hobson, J. A. (2001) *The Dream Drug Store*. Cambridge, MA: MIT Press.

Julien, R. M. (2004) *A Primer of Drug Action: A Concise, Non-technical Guide to the Actions, Uses, and Side Effects of Psychoactive Drugs*, 10th edn. New York: W. H. Freeman.

References

Aghajanian, G. K. and Marek, G. J. (1999) Serotonin and hallucinogens. *Neuropsychopharmacology* 21, Suppl. 1: S16–S23.

Andersson, C., Chakos, M., Mailman, R., and Lieberman, J. (1998) Emerging roles for novel antipsychotic medications in the treatment of schizophrenia. *Clinics of North America* 21, 151–79.

Cooper, J. R., Bloom, F. E., and Roth, R. H. (eds.) (2002) *The Biochemical Basis of Neuropharmacology*, 8th edn. New York: Oxford University Press.

de Rios, M. D., Grob, C. S., and Baker, J. R. (2002) Hallucinogens and redemption. *Journal of Psychoactive Drugs* 34, 239–48.

Finset, P., Paus, T., Daloze, T., Plourde, G., Meuret, P., Bonhomme, V. et al. (1999) Brain mechanisms of propofol-induced loss of consciousness in humans: a positron emission tomographic study. *The Journal of Neuroscience* 19, 5506–13.

Freeman, M. P. (2000) Omega-3 fatty acids in psychiatry: a review. *Annals of Clinical Psychiatry* 12, 159–65.

Gale, S. M., Castracane, V. D., and Mantzoros, C. S. (2004) Energy homeostasis, obesity and eating disorders: recent advances in endocrinology. *Journal of Nutrition* 134, 295–8.

Gardner E. L. (2000) What we have learned about addiction from animal models of drug self-administration. *American Journal on Addictions* 9: 4, 285–313.

Gouzoulis-Mayfrank, E., Thelen, B., Habermeyer, E., Kunert, H. J., Kovar, K. A., Lindenblatt, H. et al. (1999) Psychopathological, neuroendocrine and autonomic effects of 3,4-methylenedioxyethyl-amphetamine (MDE), psilocybin and d-methamphetamine in healthy volunteers. Results of an experimental double-blind placebo-controlled study. *Psychopharmacology* 142, 41–50.

Gottesmann, C. (2002) The neurochemistry of waking and sleeping mental activity: the disinhibition-dopamine hypothesis. *Psychiatry and Clinical Neurosciences* 56, 345–54.

Greene, G. S., Patterson, S. G., and Warner, E. (1996) Ingestion of angel's trumpet: an increasingly common source of toxicity. *Southern Medical Journal* 89, 365–9.

Greenfield, S. F., Weiss, R. D., and Tohen, M. (1995) Substance abuse and the chronically mentally ill: a description of dual diagnosis treatment services in a psychiatric hospital. *Community Mental Health Journal* 31, 265–77.

Hobson, J. A. (2001) *The Dream Drugstore.* Cambridge, MA: MIT Press.

Hobson, J. A., Pace-Schott, E. F., and Stickgold, R. (2000) Dreaming and the brain: toward a cognitive neuroscience of conscious states. *Behavioral and Brain Sciences* 23, 793–842.

Jansen, K. L. (2000) A review of the nonmedical use of ketamine: use, users and consequences. *Journal of Psychoactive Drugs* 32, 419–33.

Khantzian, E. J. (1997) The self-medication hypothesis of substance use disorders: a reconsideration and recent applications. *Harvard Review of Psychiatry* 4: 5, 231–44.

Koob, G. F. (2003) Drug reward and addiction. In L. E. Squire et al. (eds.), *Fundamental Neuroscience*, 2nd edn. Amsterdam: Academic Press.

Kramer, P. D. (1993) *Listening to Prozac.* New York: Viking.

LaBerge, Stephen (1990) Lucid dreaming: psychophysiological studies of consciousness during REM sleep. In R. R. Bootzin, J. F. Kihlstrom et al. (eds.), *Sleep and Cognition*, 109–26. Washington, DC: American Psychological Association.

Liechti, M. E., Baumann, C., Gamma, A., and Vollenweider, F. X. (2000) Acute psychological effects of 3,4-methylenedioxymethamphetamine (MDMA, "Ecstasy") are attenuated by the serotonin uptake inhibitor citalopram. *Neuropsychopharmacology* 22, 513–21.

Malcolm, R. J. (2003) GABA systems, benzodiazepines, and substance dependence. *Journal of Clinical Psychiatry* 64 Suppl 3, 36–40.

Marsicano, G., Wotjak, C. T., Azad, S. C., Bisogno, T., Rammes, G., Cascio, M. G. et al. (2002) The endogenous cannabinoid system controls extinction of aversive memories. *Nature* 418, 6897: 530.

Mendelson, W. B., and Basile, A. S. (1999) The hypnotic actions of oleamide are blocked by a cannabinoid receptor antagonist. *NeuroReport* 10, 3237–9.

Mesulam, M. M. (2004) The cholinergic innervation of the human cerebral cortex. *Progress in Brain Research* 145, 67–78.

Montoya, A. G., Sorrentino, R., Lukas, S. E., and Price, B. H. (2002) Long-term neuropsychiatric consequences of "ecstasy" (MDMA): a review. *Harvard Review of Psychiatry* 10, 212–20.

Morin C. M. (1993) *Insomnia, Psychological Assessment and Management.* New York: The Guilford Press.

Mueser, K. T., Drake, R. E., Wallach, M. A. (1998) Dual diagnosis: a review of etiological theories. *Addictive Behaviors* 23, 717–34.

Pace-Schott, E. F. and Hobson, J. A. (2002) The neurobiology of sleep: genetics, cellular physiology and subcortical networks. *Nature Reviews: Neuroscience* 3: 8, 591–605.

Ram Dass (1971) *Be Here Now.* San Christobal, NM: Lama Foundation.

Riba, J., Rodriguez-Fornells, A., Urbano, G., Morte, A., Antonijoan, R., Montero, M. et al. (2001) Subjective effects and tolerability of the South American psychoactive beverage Ayahuasca in healthy volunteers. *Psychopharmacology* 154, 85–95.

Ring, K. (1996) A note on anesthetically-induced frightening "near-death experiences." *Journal of Near-Death Studies* 15, 17–23.

Rosse, R. B., Collins, J. P. Jr., Fay-McCarthy, M., Alim, T. N., Wyatt, R. J., and Deutsch, S. I. (1994) Phenomenologic comparison of the idiopathic psychosis of schizophrenia and drug-induced cocaine and phencyclidine psychoses: a retrospective study. *Clinical Neuropharmacology* 17, 359–69.

Roth, B. L., Baner, K., Westkaemper, R., Siebert, D., Rice, K. C., Steinberg, S. et al. (2002) Salvinorin A: a potent naturally occurring nonnitrogenous kappa opioid selective agonist. *Proceedings of the National Academy of Sciences of the United States of America* 99, 11,934–9.

Sakurai, T. (2003) Orexin: a link between energy homeostasis and adaptive behaviour. *Current Opinion in Clinical Nutrition and Metabolic Care* 6, 353–60.

Sigalovsky, N. (2003) Awareness under general anesthesia. *American Association of Nurse Anesthetists Journal* 71, 373–9.

Small, D. M., Zatorre, R. J., Dagher, A., Evans, A. C., and Jones-Gotman, M. (2001) Changes in brain activity related to eating chocolate: from pleasure to aversion. *Brain* 124, 1720–33.

Snyder, Solomon H. (1986) *Drugs and the Brain*. New York: Scientific American Books.

Stahl, M. L., Orr, W. C., and Bollinger, C. (1983) Postprandial sleepiness: objective documentation via polysomnography *Sleep* 6, 29–35.

Stephens, R. S. (1999) Cannabis and hallucinogens. In B. S. McCrady and E. E. Epstein (eds.), *Addictions: A Comprehensive Guidebook*, 121–40. New York: Oxford University Press.

Strecker, R. E., Morairty, S., Thakkar, M. M., Porkka-Heiskanen, T., Basheer, R., Dauphin, L. J. et al. (2000) Adenosinergic modulation of basal forebrain and preoptic/anterior hypothalamic neuronal activity in the control of behavioral state. *Behavioural Brain Research* 115, 183–204.

Stubbe, D. E. (2000) Attention-deficit/hyperactivity disorder overview. Historical perspective, current controversies, and future directions. *Child and Adolescent Psychiatric Clinics of North America* 9: 3, 469–79.

Thorleifsdottir, B., Bjornsson, J. K., Kjeld, M., and Kristbjarnarson, H. (1989) Effects of L-tryptophan on daytime arousal. *Neuropsychobiology* 21, 170–6.

Wager, T. D., Rilling, J. K., Smith, E. E., Sokolik, A., Casey, K. L., Davidson, R. J. et al. (2004) Placebo-induced changes in FMRI in the anticipation and experience of pain. *Science* 303, 1162–7.

11

Meditation

DAVID FONTANA

There is no agreed definition for meditation, and accordingly I shall attempt to clarify matters somewhat by first discussing the most common features of the practice. I shall also touch on attempts to explain what may be happening during the meditation experience. The chapter will conclude with a discussion of the relationship between meditation and what many authorities consider to be a related area, namely mysticism (covered more fully in chapter 12).

Common Features in Meditation

There are many forms of meditation, and not infrequently practitioners of one form tend to dismiss other forms by failing to recognize that what is common between them all may outweigh any differences. This commonality reduces to three things, namely *concentration*, *tranquillity*, and *insight*, and I shall return to these in due course. But first, without doing too much violence to the rich variety of practices that exist in both the Eastern and the Western psycho-spiritual traditions (Fontana 1992; Walsh 1999), it is fair to say that the differences between them reduce to two major strands with considerable overlap between them, namely meditation with ideation, and meditation without ideation, the first sometimes referred to in the East as meditation with seed and the second as meditation without seed.

Ideational meditation

The Western Christian tradition, as Naranjo and Ornstein (1972) point out, has traditionally focused upon meditation with ideation, which means in effect that the meditator holds an idea or a group of ideas in the forefront of awareness, and uses them to stimulate a directed course of intellectual activity. The best example of such meditation in this tradition is the series of *Spiritual Exercises* developed in the sixteenth century by St. Ignatius Loyola, and used ever since as an essential part of training within the Jesuit order which he founded (see e.g., Corbishley (1963) for an accessible English translation). In these exercises, sometimes referred to as contemplations, the meditator is progressively given scenes by his spiritual director from the life of Christ which he learns to visualize with great clarity before "putting" himself imaginatively into each of them, and experiencing in consequence the emotions of spiritual love and reverence that he would have experienced had he actually been present. The *Exercises* appear remarkably effective in arousing in the meditator not only emotions whose strength and profundity he may never otherwise have experienced, but also in developing in him the spiritual qualities with which these emotions are connected. It is claimed in fact that anyone who has worked through the *Exercises* under the guidance of an appropriate spiritual director is permanently changed by the experience. The history of the Jesuits, a highly intellectual order well versed in psychological theory and practice as well as in spiritual development, would suggest that this claim is not without justification.

Ideational meditation also features in Hindu and Buddhist traditions, for example those traditions that follow the Vajrayana tantric practices of Tibetan Buddhism, and Theravadin meditations such as the Four Divine Abidings (i.e., *loving-kindness, compassion, empathetic joy* and *equanimity*). These practices are far too detailed and complex to be discussed in the available space, but visualization is again central to many of them (see, for example, Norbu 1986). An example from Tibetan Buddhism, referred to as an aspect of the *guru yoga* practice, involves the meditator in constructing a meticulously detailed visual image of one of the Buddhas as if the latter is sitting in front of him, which is then held at the center of awareness for the whole of the meditation session while the meditator sees each aspect of the vision as symbolizing one or other of the Buddha's qualities (compassion, determination, courage, clarity, love, etc.). At the end of the meditation, the visual image is then "seen" to rise into the air, move above the crown of the meditator's head, then sink down through his body and come to rest in the heart. Dependent upon how one wishes to interpret these things, this practice awakens the same potential qualities within the meditator, or actually transmits these qualities to him through an act of divine, all-seeing benevolence.

Nonideational meditation

By contrast, in meditation without ideation, the meditator seeks to divert attention from the processes of cognition, and experience in their place what is referred to as the content-less awareness of the mind, an awareness that is said by some traditions to be the mind's natural condition. The argument is that the mind is typically so dominated by internal cognitive activity that it is never in control of itself. The truth of this is readily demonstrated by the simple experiment of asking any group of people (except experienced meditators) to stop thinking for one minute. In my experience, very few succeed. In the light of this it is hardly surprising that one of the symbols of the mind used by the Eastern psycho-spiritual traditions is the monkey, with the constant activity of the mind likened to a monkey's meaningless chatter. However, until one arrives at an advanced stage of practice, even in ideational meditation the mind is, except for brief interludes, still likely to find that thoughts persist in arising.

When learning to practice meditation without ideation, the student is taught in some traditions progressively to withdraw attention from these thoughts, dismissing them as temporary mental events that arise within the mind but that do not represent the essence of mind itself. By contrast, other traditions teach that one should attend vigilantly to whatever arises, though without identifying with it or being distracted by it. As the training progresses, a point is reached where thoughts arise less and less frequently, and the mind becomes increasingly "still." In this state of increasing stillness, even when thoughts do arise the meditator's awareness remains still in that it views the thoughts objectively and dispassionately, as things that happen to the mind but that do not constitute the mind. The meditator is fully psychologically present on these occasions and certainly not in trance, but his field of awareness has become free from perturbations. His mind is clear and alert, which enables him to experience what is said to be its true nature (Buddhism claims, for example, that the whole purpose of Buddhist psychology is to enable you to see what is going on in your own mind and in its relationship to the rest of the world).

Overlap between the two forms of meditation

As indicated, there is some overlap between these two strands of meditation practice. In the Rinzai school of Buddhism (and to some extent also in the Soto school), use is made of the *koan*, which is an enigmatic or paradoxical statement or question to which there is no logical answer. The best-known koan is "What is the sound of one hand clapping?," and there are major collections of them such as the *Mumonkan* (the "Gateless Gate" – a title that is a koan in itself; what is a gateless gate?) and the *Hekiganroku* (the "Blue Cliff Record") which the meditator works through progressively (see Sekida 1977). Among other things, the koan takes the mind beyond its habitual linear thinking, and leads to moments of special clarity, to which I return later. Meditating with koans is both ideational and non-ideational (or neither ideational nor nonideational, as the Zen master might well insist). The meditator "enquires" into the meaning of the koan, and this can be done either by examining it as one would any question (the ideational or conceptual method), or simply holding it in the mind until a resolution appears of itself (the nonideational or non-conceptual method). It can even be a combination of the two, with the meditator experimenting with both approaches. It is said that one does not "solve" a koan, for such a thing is logically impossible, but that one "resolves" it by achieving with its help the clarity provided by an insight into some deep aspect of reality. When a resolution presents itself, which may only be after many months or even years of practice, the meditator then confides it to the Zen master, who identifies whether or not it is a genuine insight (not by what the meditator says but by recognizing how the resolution has or has not changed him). If it is not, the meditator is given no clues but simply told to go back to the koan.

Another example of overlap is mantra meditation (the repetition of a sacred word or phrase as the point of focus). One of the forms of mantra meditation best known in the West is transcendental meditation (TM), a practice grounded in the Hindu tradition that uses a single Sanskrit word given personally to the student by the teacher that is then held in the mind by internal repetition. In this version of mantra meditation the sound of the mantra itself is said to help bring about internal transformations (Sanskrit is claimed to be a language composed of sacred syllables), but in other versions the meditator may be taught to reflect also upon the meaning of the words he is using. One of the best-known instances in Christianity of this latter form of mantra meditation is the *Jesus Prayer*, used particularly in the Eastern Orthodox traditions, "Lord Jesus Christ have mercy on me," in which the meditator reflects upon sin, mercy, and the spirit of divine compassion that produces forgiveness (see Kadloubovsky & Palmer 1951; French 1954a, 1954b; Hester 2001). These instances of overlap between the two major strands of meditation practice illustrate not only the dangers attendant upon an over-rigid attempt at classification of meditation methods but the importance for the meditator of working with an experienced teacher who can give guidance as to the fine details of the technique that is to be used. It is claimed that confusing these details can seriously hinder or even prevent progress.

Concentration

As already indicated, both these strands of meditation practice – together with those methods that may include a degree of overlap – typically involve the three stages of concentration, tranquillity, and insight (a full discussion of these three stages from the perspective of *vipassana*, the oldest form of Buddhist meditation, is given by Solé-Leris (1986)), three stages that are cumulative and not sequential. The meditator starts by receiving guidance from the teacher on a particular point of focus on which attention has to be concentrated. In meditation with ideation, as we have seen, this point of focus can be a visual image with certain associated concepts, while in meditation without ideation it can be, for example, his own breathing, or the point between the eyes, or a symbolic diagram. In both cases, the meditator works upon refining his powers of concentration so that the mind does not wander away from this point of focus. When distracting thoughts or emotions arise they are released, and if the attention wanders it is brought gently back, time and time again. Although some effort is involved, concentration of this type is not a fierce, intensive process that paradoxically would actually interfere with the meditation. Instead, the attention is allowed to rest gently upon the point of focus, as if accepting that the latter is all that there is (classic works on this form of concentration are Sadhu (1959) and Wood (1981)).

Many traditions emphasize the importance of teaching *right conduct* as an essential accompaniment to any meditation practice, and this teaching usually begins in concert with the work on concentration. Some authorities even teach that meditation without the simultaneous development of right conduct can actually be harmful, in that it may develop acute mental powers yet without conveying the realization that these are to be used in the service of others rather than of oneself, thus actively strengthening not only selfishness but the deluded ego that in reality should be progressively discarded as the meditator comes increasingly to recognize the mind's natural state. The reference made earlier in the chapter to the Four Divine Abidings (i.e., loving-kindness, compassion, empathetic joy and equanimity) is a good example both of the nature of right conduct and of the way in which its development can actually be an integral part of meditation practice itself. The meditator is taught to use the Four Abidings as a focus in his or her ideational practice and, as the practice develops, the right conduct associated with the Abidings arises naturally from within oneself. *Guru Yoga*, also mentioned earlier, in which the meditator focuses on the divine qualities of the Buddha or of another spiritual teacher and then takes them into the heart, is another example of the way right conduct develops through the practice itself; so too is the *Jesus Prayer*, which assists the meditator to identify with the infinite love and divine mercy of Christ.

Tranquillity

Once this form of concentration becomes established even for short periods – which may take many months or even years of daily practice – the experience of tranquillity arises as a natural psychological consequence. Stress and tension typically occur as a consequence of identifying with and/or grasping thoughts or emotions, but now that the mind has released identification and grasping, the root cause of suffering is said to be removed. Consciousness is at this moment no longer consciousness of mental or physical disturbances, but is said to be consciousness *of itself*. Phenomenologists such as Husserl and Bretano would object that such a form of consciousness is impossible, while positivist philosophers would ally themselves with Hume, who argued that he could not catch himself devoid of perceptions. However, as Forman (1998) points out, such objections tell us nothing about the inner experience of a Hindu sadhu, a Buddhist monk, a Jesuit priest, or a practitioner of the Jesus Prayer who has been engaged in long and intensive meditation training for many years. Meditation is above all else a practical discipline. One can only truly know what meditation is and the state of consciousness associated with it when one is familiar with it at first-hand. Rather than commenting on this state of consciousness, the role of the scientific researcher is ideally to assemble an extensive data bank of self-reports by experienced meditators together with data on the neurophysiological and behavioral correlates of meditation, and then to seek similarities and differences between what is said in these reports and between what is reported in the neurophysiological and behavioral data. Attempts to do this have so far revealed an impressive body of agreement that supports the hypothesis that meditation does indeed appear to produce an altered state of consciousness that conforms to the claims made on its behalf (Wilber 1998; see also chapter 54).

Insight

Writing from within the Japanese Zen Buddhist tradition, Dainin Katagiri (Katagiri 1988) uses the term "silence" to represent tranquillity (and indeed all aspects of meditation), and puts it that "Buddhist teaching is, very naturally [that] you come back to silence. Even though you don't want to, you return to an area of no-sound. It cannot be explained, but in this silence you can realize, even if only dimly, what the real point is you want to know." This brings us to the next stage of meditation, the experience of insight. In both ideational and nonideational practices, this insight is said to arise sometimes spontaneously and to provide clues as to one's own self-nature, but it also provides the ground within which the meditator can commence active inquiry into self-nature by identifying those areas of mental life that, habitually thought to be permanent, are in fact transient and therefore empty of this nature. The Christian would say such insight into oneself comes ultimately as an act of grace from God, while the Buddhist would say it arises from the active contemplative cultivation of insight, the insight that led to Gautama becoming the Buddha. Such descriptions may be less mutually contradictory than they at first sight appear, since they apply to states for which there is no agreed common vocabulary, but clearly very much more work needs to be done into the similarities and differences between traditions on these crucial issues. Tsongkapa, the fourteenth–fifteenth-century founder of Tibet's three greatest monasteries and said to be the single most important commentator on Buddhism in its 2,500-year history, favored a form of analytical meditation (Tsongkapa 1988) in which the meditator holds in the center of his mind a particular teaching or viewpoint which he then tries to prove or disprove using statements from accepted authorities and various lines of reasoning as a path to insight, and clearly such a method lends itself to use in any tradition.

Decisions about the origin of the insights that arise during meditation are likely to be partly a matter of prior belief, though it is said that one should then look in turn at the nature and origins of these beliefs and the decisions to which they give rise. And so the meditative process can go on until doubts and differences are progressively resolved. Insight is not therefore seen as necessarily a once and for all revelation. Rather, there are many insights, each of which takes one closer to an understanding of one's own being.

Within the West, many of the best-known writings on the insight stage of meditation (and indeed on meditation in general) come from the Buddhist tradition (e.g., Achaan Chah 1985; Lamrimpa 1995; Cooper 1996; Bucknell & Kang 1997; Wallace 1998) and for those who are familiar with the literature and who have practiced in the traditions concerned, there can be little doubt that if Western psychology wishes to develop a science of consciousness it would be well advised to draw guidance and inspiration from the insights gained by this tradition and from those arising from the equally detailed explorations of the mind conducted over the centuries by the various schools of Hindu thought (e.g., Radhakrishnan 1923; Aurobindo 1957; Radhakrishnan & Moore 1957; Renou 1962; Vivekananda 1963; Krishnananda 1969; Osborne 1971; de Riencourt 1980; Godman 1985; Goodall 1996). The point is fully acknowledged by some of the contributors to Velmans (2000).

Other methods for investigating meditation exist. We can research the physiological correlates of different forms of meditation experience, study the behavioral changes associated with progress in meditation practice, and of course study the self-reports of meditators. The extensive research into these variables is well summarized and discussed by West (1987), Murphy (1992), Murphy and Donovan (1997), and Newberg and d'Aquili (2000). Such research shows significant changes in brainwave patterns in advanced meditators during practice (e.g., the presence of high amplitude theta and delta rhythms and hemispheric synchronization), but as Wilber (2000) points out, none of these changes tell us anything about the experience itself or its value to the experiencer. As Wallace (1998) puts it, "Physical events modify and condition mental events without transforming into them; and, conversely, mental events modify and condition physical events without transforming into them" (although there seems no doubt of the ability of the mind to modify physical conditions to an extraordinary extent by intensive meditative practices – see, e.g., Evans-Wentz (1958)). Thus we cannot truly know either of these sets of events simply by studying the other, a point stressed also at several points by Wilber (e.g., 1993). First-hand accounts by meditators of the phenomenology of meditation are in my view of greater value than physiological studies, particularly as such accounts can be studied for similarities and differences, much as we study reports of other areas of psychological experience.

Relationship Between Meditation and Mysticism

Does meditation lead to mystical experience, and is the insight said to be experienced in the third stage of meditation related in any way to this experience? The answer to both questions would appear to be yes, although in Hindu and Buddhist meditative traditions it is stressed that one does not meditate with the intention of achieving any predetermined or exalted states (Dogen, the founder of the Soto Zen school, insisted that one does not meditate in order to become enlightened, one meditates because that is what enlightened people do). Certainly, it is stressed in Buddhism that one meditates in order to obtain liberation from suffering, and that the motivation to achieve such liberation should be strong, but the subtle point here as I understand it is that one does not decide in advance what liberation is "like." One accepts that it exists and that one wishes to achieve it, but puts aside any fixed preconceptions as to its nature. Meditation essentially involves remaining in the present moment and aware of the point of focus – for example, the inhalation and exhalation of each breath, the successive syllables of the mantra, the visual experience of mandala, the processes of self-enquiry. Even in Buddhist practices that take meditation on imperma-nence and death as their point of focus (see, e.g., the Dalai Lama 1995), one remains, as I understand it, aware of oneself as "presence," that is as present in the here and now, rather than as identified with imagined future states whose nature, at the level of deep conscious-ness, is dependent not upon the future but upon the quality of present actions. Speculations, vain imaginings, fragments of memory – in short much of the stuff of normal conscious-ness – are all recognized as transitory rather than as manifestations of the true nature of mind. Thus meditation is simply meditation. Until they have been realized, the medita-tor recognizes that, although his studies may have given him some idea as to what they are about, he does not know the exact nature of concentration, tranquillity, or insight. Such states are sometimes described as "things in themselves," that is as things that can only be fully known through direct experience (the same can be said of many other human experi-ences which second-hand knowledge deludes us into supposing we fully understand). If he already "knows" what concentration, tranquillity, and insight are, he has no need to seek them and no need of meditation. This is one reason why the Zen master does not assess whether or not the pupil has resolved – had insight into – the koan merely by anything he says. His speech may simply represent book learning. The master does not assume that insight can only be – or perhaps can even be – expressed in words. He recognizes insight in others because he has experienced insight himself. In addition, as evidenced by the fact that collections of koans such as the *Mumonkan* and the *Hekiganroku* are graded in order of dif-ficulty, it is accepted, at least in Zen Buddhism, that although true insight is one, there are various levels in the approach to it, and the pupil depends upon the master for confirmation that he has reached various of them.

The master will also teach the pupil that he should not become satisfied or complacent or boastful when he receives such confirmation. Right at the outset, when he first experiences the reality of concentration, he will be taught that when concentration arises, the realization "I am concentrating" can too easily lead to degenerating into thoughts *about* concentration. It is further taught that the next time he sits on his cushion he should set aside any thoughts of what happened last time, and instead focus once more simply upon the coming and going of his breathing, or upon whatever other practice he has been instructed to follow. And in Zen Buddhism, even though the reason for meditating may be recognized as lib-eration, the end of suffering, or even happiness, this in itself is not sufficient. When Zen Master Dogen was studying in China, he answered his teacher's question as to the purpose of his meditation by saying that he "would like to be free from suffering." The Master replied with another question "What for?" Dogen answered that this would enable him to help all other beings who suffer, to which the master once again replied "What for?" And so the interrogation went on, with each attempt by Dogen to answer the teacher's questions met with a further "What for?" Finally Dogen fell silent, realizing the teacher was touching the very core of life and so-called death (Katagiri 1988, and see also Masunaga 1972, and Yokoi 1976). This is typical of the Zen method of attaining insight, which depends upon forcing the mind to recognize the empty (we might say baseless) nature of conceptual thought. The method uses thought to take us beyond thought.

We could say that it is at this point beyond thought that meditation and mystical experi-ence may become one. This would be an oversimplification of course, but at an advanced stage of meditation it is said that a state, variously referred to as enlightenment, samadhi, or satori (although each of these terms may, strictly speaking, apply to subtly different conditions) can arise which is considered essentially to represent an insight into the true nature of reality. Such a state can arise outside meditation, but it would appear that meditation, by helping to still the constant mental activity that is a feature of waking consciousness, can facilitate its occurrence or, perhaps more accurately, its emergence from unconscious levels that are normally inaccessible while awareness is directed exclusively to this activity. For this state may be, as Wilber (e.g., 1993) insists, the state that underlies all states, and that enables the mind to recognize its mystic identity with the rest of creation.

See also 12 Mystical experience; 54 Eastern methods for investigating mind and consciousness.

Further Readings

Fontana, D. (1992) *The Meditator's Handbook*. Rockport, MA: Element Books.
Thich Nhat Hanh (1990) *Breathe! You Are Alive*. London: Rider.
Wood, E. (1981) *Concentration: An Approach to Meditation*. Wheaton, IL: Quest Books (original edn. 1949).

References

Achaan Chah (1985) *A Still Forest Pool*. Wheaton, IL: Quest Books.
Aurobindo, Sri (1957) *The Synthesis of Yoga*. Pondicherry: Sri Aurobindo Ashram.
Bucknell, R. and Kang, C. (1997). *The Meditative Way: Readings in the Theory and Practice of Buddhist Meditation*. Richmond, Surrey: Curzon Press.
Cooper, R. (1996) *The Evolving Mind: Buddhism, Biology and Consciousness*. Birmingham: Windhorse Publications.
Corbishley, T. (trans.) (1963) *The Spiritual Exercises of St. Ignatius Loyola*. Wheathampstead: Anthony Clarke.
Dalai Lama (1995) *The Path to Enlightenment* (G. H. Mullin, trans.). Ithaca, NY: Snow Lion.
de Riencourt, A. (1980) *The Eye of Shiva*. London: Souvenir Press.
Evans-Wentz, W. Y. (1958) *Tibetan Yoga and Secret Doctrines*, 2nd edn. Oxford: Oxford University Press.
Fontana, D. (1992) *The Meditator's Handbook*. Rockport, MA: Element Books.
Forman, R. K. C. (1998) Mystical consciousness, the innate capacity, and the perennial wisdom. In R. K. C. Forman (ed.), *The Innate Philosophy*. New York: Oxford University Press.
French, R. M. (trans.) (1954a) *The Way of a Pilgrim*. London: SPCK.
French, R. M. (trans.) (1954b) *The Pilgrim Continues His Way*. London: SPCK.
Godman, D. (ed.) (1985) *Be As You Are*. Boston, MA: Arkana.
Goodall, D. (ed.) (1996) *Hindu Scriptures*. London: Dent.
Hester, D. (2001) *The Jesus Prayer*. Ben Lomond, CA: Concilliar Press.
Kadloubovsky, E. and Palmer, G. E. H. (trans.) (1951) *Writings from the Philokalia, the Prayer of the Heart*. London: Faber and Faber.
Katagiri, D. (1988) *Returning to Silence: Zen Practice in Daily Life*. Boston, MA: Shambhala.
Krishnananda, Swami (1969) *The Philosophy of Life*. Tehri-Garhwal, India: Divine Life Society.
Lamrimpa Gen (1995) *Calming the Mind: Tibetan Buddhist Teachings on Cultivating Meditative Quiescence* (B. Alan Wallace, trans.). Ithaca, NY: Snow Lion.

Masunaga, R. (1972) *A Primer of Soto Zen: A Translation of Dogen's "Shobogenso Zuimonki."* London: Routledge and Kegan Paul.

Murphy, M. (1992) *The Future of the Body: Explorations into the Future Evolution of Human Nature.* New York: Tarcher/Putnam.

Murphy, M. and Donovan, S. (1997) *The Physical and Psychological Effects of Meditation: A Review of Contemporary Research*, 2nd edn. San Francisco: Institute of Noetic Sciences.

Naranjo, C. and Ornstein, R. E. (1972) *On the Psychology of Meditation.* New York: George Allen and Unwin.

Newberg, A. B. and d'Aquili, E. G. (2000) The neuropsychology of religious and spiritual experience. *Journal of Consciousness Studies* 7: 11–12, 251–66.

Norbu, N. (1986) *The Crystal and the Way of Light: Sutra, Tantra and Dzogchen.* New York and London: Routledge and Kegan Paul.

Osborne, A. (ed.) (1971) *The Teachings of Bhagavan Sri Ramana Maharishi in His Own Words.* Tiruvannamalai: Venkataraman.

Radhakrishnan, S. (1923) *Indian Philosophy.* New York: Macmillan.

Radhakrishnan, S. and Moore, C. (1957) *A Sourcebook in Indian Philosophy.* Princeton, NJ: Princeton University Press.

Renou, L. (ed.) (1962) *Hinduism.* New York: Braziller.

Sadhu, M. (1959) *Concentration.* London: George Allen and Unwin.

Sekida, K. (1977) *Two Zen Classics.* New York: Wetherhill.

Solé-Leris, A. (1986) *Tranquillity and Insight.* London: Century Hutchinson.

Tsongkapa, Je Rinpoche (1988). *The Principal Teachings of Buddhism.* Howell, NJ: Mahayana Sutra and Tantra Press (Tsongkapa's *Three Principal Paths* with commentary by Pabongka Rinpoche).

Velmans, M. (2000) (ed.). *Investigating Phenomenal Consciousness: New Methodologies and Maps.* Amsterdam: John Benjamins.

Vivekananda, Swami (1963) *Inspired Talks.* Madras: Sri Ramakrishna Math.

Wallace, B. A. (1998) *The Bridge of Quiescence: Experiencing Tibetan Buddhist Meditation.* Chicago: Open Court.

Walsh, R. (1999) *Essential Spirituality.* New York: Wiley.

West, M. (1987) (ed.). *The Psychology of Meditation.* Oxford: Clarendon Press.

Wilber, K. (1993) *The Spectrum of Consciousness*, 2nd edn. Wheaton, IL: Quest.

Wilber, K. (1998) *The Marriage of Sense and Soul.* Dublin: Newleaf.

Wilber, K. (2000) *Integral Psychology.* Boston, MA: Shambhala.

Wood, E. (1981) *Concentration: An Approach to Meditation.* Wheaton, IL: Quest Books (original edn. 1949).

Yokoi, Y. (1976) *Zen Master Dogen: An Introduction and Selected Writings.* New York: Weatherhill.

12

Mystical Experience

DAVID FONTANA

The Nature of Mystical Experience

Mystical states are said to arise spontaneously rather than through an act of will, and to represent a state of altered consciousness almost impossible to convey to others through the medium of language. A good example of the various attempts to do so is provided by the nineteenth-century Canadian psychiatrist Richard Bucke (most recent edition 1991) who used the term "cosmic consciousness" for his experience. Speaking of himself in the third person, Bucke puts it that:

> All at once, without warning . . . he found himself wrapped around . . . by a flame-coloured cloud . . . Directly afterwards came upon him a sense of exultation, of immense joyousness, accompanied or immediately followed by an intellectual illumination quite impossible to describe . . . one momentary lightening-flash of Brahmic Splendour which has ever lightened his life . . . leaving thenceforward for always an after-taste of heaven.

However, despite Bucke's references to "Brahmic" and to "heaven," mysticism is by no means confined to those with prior religious belief, although it is undoubtedly the essence of religious experience, and both for those who are prior believers and for those who are not, the experience – if as profound as that detailed by Bucke – is typically life-changing. In fact in many cases it is reported as leading to the conviction that there is a dimension to existence unimagined and unimaginable in normal states of consciousness and that extends beyond the narrow limits of the space/time world. Despite the difficulty of describing a state so far outside the conceptual framework of normal existence, there does appear to be a wide measure of agreement among the various accounts available to us. Stace (1960) identifies across traditions repeated references to such things as the experience of unity, the sense of being outside time and space, a sense of the sacred, feelings of joy and bliss, a unity that is both empty yet full and complete, and an awareness of an ultimate eternal reality.

These accounts suggest in addition that, as with meditation, mystical states can be divided into two distinct categories, namely *transcendent* and *immanent* (e.g., Hardy 1979; Hood 1995).

Transcendent mysticism

Put at its simplest, transcendent mysticism is said, particularly in the theistic traditions, to be the overwhelming awareness of some benevolent power outside of and greater than oneself that transcends the material world and is identified as divine and the source of all that exists. Cox (1983) describes this as the direct experience of God and as "the unitive acquisition of knowledge that is inaccessible to human understanding." The Hindu tradition describes this state as *Savikalpa Samadhi*, a state in which the consciousness of self remains, but in which this consciousness is directed entirely toward the blissful awareness of the divine (sometimes described as "tasting the sweetness"). This is the mysticism of Hindu scriptures such as the *Upanishads* and of the Hebrew *Torah*, of the holy *Koran* and of the Christian Bible. Research reveals that in the United Kingdom at least, this is the most frequently experienced form of mysticism (Hardy 1979), and it seems probable from comparative studies of mysticism such as those of Spencer (1963), Smart (1968), and Staal (1975) that this holds good for all the Western theistic religions and for much of Hinduism and for some experiences reported by followers of the Shin (Pure Land) tradition in Buddhism. What is *being transcended* is the belief that we are nothing more than material beings, and what *is transcendent* is the Divine, the creator of the material world yet who transcends it as Pure Spirit. In theistic religions transcendence refers to the reliance upon an "Other Power," a power outside and greater than oneself, to bring about an essential spiritual transformation within one's inner being that could not be realized alone (Smart 1968; Cox 1983). The relationship of the individual to this "Other Power" is expressed in Hinduism by the practice of *Bhakti Yoga*, the yoga of devotion, in which all one's thoughts and energies are directed toward worship of the Divine, and the supreme examples of it in Islam are the profound mystical experience of Mohammed when taken up to Heaven by the Angel Gabriel, and his receipt of the holy Koran direct from Allah.

However, in Buddhism generally and in the Advaita tradition of Hinduism the term "transcendence" is used to describe a rather different experience: an insight into the deepest nature of one's own being rather than an experience of something outside oneself. In effect, it is described in these traditions as an experience that "transcends" everything imaginable in one's normal state of consciousness, and as being empty of sense-perceptions, images, thoughts, feelings, or even of the phenomenological space in which such things could occur. Such a description is an example of what in Hinduism would be called *netti*, that is, an attempt to describe something – in this case a state of emptiness (a state of pure consciousness or pure being) – by saying what it is not. One problem with such a description is that it does not tell us what the experience actually *is*, and a second problem is that if this experience does indeed exclude so much of normal consciousness then it can hardly be said to be all-encompassing or all-embracing, two terms that are often used for mystical states. This is not in any sense to negate it as an experience, simply to illustrate the psychological and philosophical difficulties of talking about states that are in themselves indescribable.

In view of these difficulties of description, a problem that arises is whether these two forms of transcendence are indeed different states, or whether they are simply expressed differently due to cultural factors and to the limitations of language and meaning. A further problem is whether these forms of transcendent mysticism are really distinct from immanent mysticism (discussed below), or whether once more cultural and linguistic factors distort meaning. Transcendent and immanent mysticism certainly appear different (although there are obvious similarities between them, as discussed below), and in some traditions it is claimed that transcendent mysticism is simply a stage on the path to immanence. However, the great Bengali saint Ramakrishna taught from his own direct experiences that although both states should be experienced neither should be thought of as "superior" to the other (Ramakrishna 1975; Gupta 1978). Allied to this problem is the very real question about the true nature of the "self" that undergoes mystical experience, whether transcendent or immanent. So complex are the issues raised by this question that they would require a chapter to themselves if we are even to begin to do them justice. In fact it could be argued that we cannot usefully address them unless we have experienced deep mystical or insightful states for ourselves. However, most traditions would probably agree – as would modern psychology – that the "self" with which we usually identify is not our true nature. Simple exploration of one's own mind reveals the transient nature of thoughts, memories, ideas, and even of self-concepts. Simple exploration also reveals that the struggle to hold onto this transient self, to defend it, to empower it, to abide in it, are doomed to failure. It thus seems reasonable to try to look beyond this "self" in order to find what if anything lies behind (or beneath) it. Theistic religions speak, at least at their more esoteric levels, of losing oneself in order to find oneself, of surrendering the self to God, of becoming as nothing, of God within, even of becoming one with the Father. Hindu traditions also speak of Brahman (the divine absolute) and Atman (the indwelling divine) as being in essence one. Buddhism teaches the *anatta* doctrine of no-self, the absence of any permanent self. Many aspects of these descriptions reduce to the ultimate question "Who am I?," sometimes used as an explicit exercise during the active enquiry into self-nature mentioned in chapter 11, and whether explicit or not, always at the root of this enquiry. For present purposes, all that can be said is that we cannot know the boundaries of self – if indeed it has boundaries – or anything of its nature unless we begin a personal enquiry into the matter, and for many centuries and many traditions it has been taught that this enquiry must begin by self exploration, and that meditation is the best context in which to conduct it.

Immanent mysticism

Be this as it may, Buddhist traditions together with the Advaita tradition in Hinduism and Western commentators such as Wilber (1993, 2000) insist that immanent mysticism marks a stage of spiritual development beyond that of transcendent mysticism (some authorities consider in fact that it develops out of the emptiness referred to above in the context of Advaita and Buddhist descriptions of transcendence). In immanent mysticism, all sense of a personal self disappears and one comes to recognize the essential unity of all existence. In theistic language, instead of contemplating the divine as in transcendent mysticism, the distinction between oneself and the Divine disappears. In fact all distinctions disappear, and the mystic experiences oneness with all that exists and ever has existed. Referred to as *Nirvikalpa Samadhi* in the Hindu tradition, the mystic is said not just to "taste the sweetness" but to "*become* the sweetness" in that the indwelling spirit, the *Atman*, is actually *realized* as being one with *Brahman*, the Absolute. Vedantic traditions within Hinduism (Isherwood 1963), and certain of the schools of Far-Eastern Buddhism, describe this not as the annihilation of the individual self but as its infinite expansion – the dewdrop of the individual self does not just slip into the shining sea of the Absolute during mystical experience as is some-times said but, as one Zen master explained to me, realizes that it *is* the shining sea.

Immanent mysticism is much less common in Theistic religions such as Christianity than is transcendent mysticism, possibly because in the past the assertion that the indi-vidual was one with the Divine rendered the speaker liable to persecution as a heretic. The best-known example of a Christian mystic who had personal experience of immanence is Meister Ekhart, who in his teachings insisted that "God must be very I and I very God, so consummately one that he and this I are one 'is'" (see, e.g., Forman 1991). In an extensive comparison between Ekhart's mystical experiences and those reported in Zen Buddhism, D. T. Suzuki, one of the best-known interpreters of Zen for the West, concludes that "Ekhart is in perfect accord with the Buddhist doctrine of *sunyata*, when he advances the notion of Godhead as 'pure nothingness'" (Suzuki 1979).

Similarities between transcendent and immanent mysticism

As with the two strands of meditation discussed in chapter 11, the two forms of mysti-cism have things in common (and may even contain elements of each other, as in Bucke's experience quoted earlier). Not only are both states said to be indescribably blissful and life-changing, they impart a sense of obtaining access to knowledge inaccessible by other means, in particular to the recognition that love – spiritual love – is the root of all exist-ence, and that existence is eternal and not limited to the material form. It is even possible in fact that the experiences are sometimes one and the same, and that it is the cultural accretions which the mystic attaches to them, particularly when he or she struggles to put them into words, that give them their supposed differences. Suzuki (1979, 1998) takes an example from Shin Buddhism to show how they are in fact reconciled within the Shin Buddhist tradition. A central meditative practice in Shin Buddhism, which lays empha-sis not only upon Shakyamuni Buddha, the historical Buddha, but also on the so-called Cosmic Buddha *Amida* (the synthesis of *Amitabha* Buddha, the Buddha of Boundless Light, and *Amitayus* Buddha, the Buddha of Boundless Life) consists of repetition of the *Nembutsu*, the mantra *Namu Amida Butsu* which is usually translated as "Adoration to the Buddha Amida." However, Suzuki explains that although the mantra symbolizes the uni-fication of the devotee with Amida, the presence of the word *Namu* symbolizes the fact that this does not mean that he is "lost or absorbed in Amida so that his individuality is no longer tenable." The devotee is there "as if [he] were not there. This ambivalence is the mystery of the *Nembutsu*." The devotee is thus both adoring Amida (transcendence) and becoming one with Amida (immanence). This ambivalence is perfectly acceptable to the Eastern mind (Shin Buddhism is the most widely practiced form of Buddhism in Japan), yet inconsistent with Western logic that adheres to the "either-or" principle rather than to that of "both-and." Yet there is little that is logical about mysticism, and we are told that the attempt to comprehend it logically not only robs us of any chance of understanding it but is also a major hindrance to experiencing the mystical state for ourselves, although in the initial stages of the insight practices (referred to earlier) logic can be used to help one realize that true insight transcends both logic and reason. Mysticism is a state of mind like no other state, and although it cannot be induced simply by an act of will, it seems that it can certainly be inhibited by such an act, in particular if this act involves a refusal to accept even the possibility that such a state can exist.

Levels or Stages in Mystical Experience

Studying the accounts of mystical experience from the various traditions it would seem that the existence of "levels" is generally recognized. There are many stages on the path toward what might be termed peak mystical experience (whether transcendent or immanent), and in the case of Christian mysticism these were charted by Underhill nearly a century ago after studying the carefully documented first-hand accounts written by many of the best-known mystics within the Christian tradition (Underhill, most recent edition 1995). In her submission they reduce to five, each of which is associated with an intense personal revelation or insight, namely *awakening* (the realization that there is a divine reality), *purgation* (the recognition that one has distanced oneself from this reality and must follow a path of purification and self-discipline), *illumination* (the blissful assurance of the proximity of the divine), *the dark night* (the sense that nevertheless a gulf still remains by reason of the ego and its belief that the mystical experience is something given to or earned by oneself), and finally *union* (the self is surrendered to the divine and realizes that it is one with it).

It might be insisted that stage three, *illumination*, is the level of transcendent mysticism, while the final stage is the level of immanence. This is perhaps so. Only in the final stage is dualism, the distinction between the mystic and the divine, replaced by unification, in which the distinction disappears. This does not mean that stage five replaces the first four stages. If indeed stage five is the stage of unity, then the first four stages cannot be separate from it, just as the adult cannot be separate from (or indeed valued above) the child he once was. Thus it might be more correct to say that stage five subsumes stages one to four.

Underhill's work is still regarded as a classic within Christian mysticism, based as it is upon the direct experience of men and women writing at a time when the Christian mystical tradition, although never fully accepted by the Church of the day, was at its height. To dismiss her work on the basis that it was first written a century ago is to subscribe to the myth of eternal progress, the myth that we always inevitably know more and understand more than did the men and women of the past. One of the first lessons learned by the student of mysticism is the timeless quality of the experience. The majority of the great psycho-spiritual traditions – Christianity, Islam, Judaism, Taoism, and the many schools of Buddhism and Hinduism – had their origins in the mystical experiences of those we regard as their founders and of their immediate followers, and these experiences and our understanding of them cannot be said to have been superseded by subsequent practitioners or by modern scholarship.

Classics similar to that of Underhill exist in other traditions, and it is interesting to note that the stages or levels identified by the writers concerned show some differences from those identified by her. These differences may again be due to the problems of language and meaning that we face when discussing states so far outside those of normal consciousness. However, they may also point to the influence of cultural differences and belief systems, and/or to differences in the way in which practices such as meditation, prayer, ritual, study, and physical privations such as self-denial have prepared the way for mystical experience. In the Buddhist tradition Luk (1971, 1974, 1976, 1984) gives several case histories of the path to enlightenment, drawn both from the experiences of noted teachers from the past and from contemporary sources. Unlike the experiences of the Christian mystics surveyed by Underhill, which suggest that the devotee might remain at any one level for a considerable period, Luk's case histories indicate these levels or stages might be either spread over time or encountered during the course of a single intensive meditation retreat. The essence of these stages is, first, a "dropping of the ego," which is experienced as a feeling of weightlessness in body and mind accompanied by a "burst of light" in which the whole cosmos seems to dissolve amid a sense of "incredible bliss." This is followed by an experience of the unity of each atom of existence with the consciousness that experiences them, and at this point the individual consciousness appears to dissolve into Oneness. After these initial experiences, there comes a return to a sense of consciousness of oneself as a being, but this sense is no longer located in the body. Instead, it is as if the whole world is a conscious living body of energy and the individual mind is empty of thought and simply aware of the environment without judgment or attachment. The whole world is then experienced as radiant, and the mind that experiences the world also becomes the thing that is experienced. Henceforth there is no feeling of duality, and only content-less consciousness.

Without pressing the point too much, there are similarities here with Underhill's levels. The level of purgation is comparable to the intense initial desire to be free of suffering that drives the Buddhist to practice, while Underhill's levels of illumination and unity correspond respectively to the dropping of the ego and to the realization of non-duality. This is not to suggest all differences between the various mystical traditions can be resolved, or that the problem is only one of the varying usage of words. Nevertheless, as Smart (1996) suggests, we in the West are more used to theism, perhaps because of the monarchical system that evolved with the papacy and with the patriarchal system that is a feature of orthodox traditions; by contrast, in Eastern traditions such as Hinduism, Buddhism, and Confucianism authority was vested more in senior monks and commentators whose eminence was due to their personal spiritual experience and philosophical expertise. This is not to argue against theism, but perhaps to illuminate the various culture-bound ways in which an experience of the divine essence encountered in mystical experience is expressed.

These differences between East and West apart, it is clear there are stages in mystical experience, and that although such experience is not the prerogative of any one group of people or any one way of being, it does appear to favor a mind prepared by intensive motivation and by meditation practice. It seems that when the meditator reaches the stage of insight he enters the mystical state in that he recognizes that the self, the ego with which he has always identified, does not represent his true being but a device that, albeit unwittingly, has divided him from the rest of a creation of which he is an inseparable part. In Zen Buddhism, one of the Buddhist traditions that has focused most upon probing the psychology of the self, it is said that all meditation is an approach to the question "Who am I?" On the face of it the simplest of questions, yet as one looks into it and strips away the various labels that express personal identity it emerges as one of the most puzzling.

The importance of this stripping away is well illustrated by the story of Han Shan, an early Chinese Zen (known in China as Ch'an) master, who initially practiced the Shin form of Buddhism mentioned earlier and which focuses on the repetition of the *Nembutsu*. The result of this prolonged practice led Han Shan to have a mystical vision of Amida Buddha, and to receive the assurance that after death he would be reborn not on Earth, but as every Shin practitioner hopes, in Amida's "Pure Land" where the stages to final enlightenment are easier. This transcendent experience must have greatly heartened Han Shan, but it also determined him to try even harder to obtain final enlightenment during this lifetime instead of waiting for the Pure Land. After much further effort he met an advanced practitioner who advised him that instead of the *Nembutsu* he should now use the koan "Who is it meditating on the Buddha's name?" (i.e., who is it who is repeating the *Nembutsu*?). After a further eight years of meditating upon this koan Han Shan experienced the state of imma-nence. In Luk's translation of Han Shan's description of this state (1971), Han Shan uses the third person to refer to himself:

> his body and mind disappeared and were replaced by a great brightness, spheric and full, clear and still, like a huge round mirror containing all the mountains, rivers and great earth. There-after he noticed a still serenity inside and outside his body, and met no more hindrance from sounds and forms.

We do not know whether Han Shan used his koan in the conceptual or in the non-conceptual way, but it seems that it was through meditating upon it that he attained this state of imma-nence. It seems that by stilling (or at least quietening) the activity of the conscious mind through meditation, the mind becomes increasingly open to subtle inner states of aware-ness that normally never intrude into consciousness. The potential for experiencing these states may be universal, but it is when the mind is in a certain condition that we become aware of them. However, meditation is not the only way of putting the mind into this con-dition. Hardy's research (Hardy 1979) revealed that although in his sample meditation and prayer were one of the main triggers for mystical experiences, depression and despair were referred to even more often. This may surprise us, although it is acknowledged in the Eastern traditions that intense need for the Divine – which can arise from despair at one's present condition – can be a powerful stimulus. The Hindu saint Ramakrishna put it that when one needs the Divine like a drowning man needs air, then the Divine will be found (Gupta 1978). A possible reason is that depression and despair may serve to reduce self-pride and other aspects of the ego, and as noted when discussing the stages in mystical development identi-fied by Underhill, the individual ego may serve as a hindrance to such development. Other triggers for mystical experience referred to by Hardy's sample included nature, music, the creative arts and acts of worship. Maslow (1970) also found that what he called *peak experi-ences*, experiences which touch on the mystical in that the individual enters a state seemingly outside time and space in which the overriding emotions are those of awe, wonder, and ecstasy, could sometimes be triggered by one or other of these things. In addition, Murphy and White (1995) have published accounts that suggest certain forms of sporting activity, in particular long distance running, can produce elements of mystical experience.

However, an important distinction is necessary here between what in personality research are referred to as "states" and "traits," the former a transitory condition and the latter a more enduring aspect of oneself. One may have a seemingly mystical experience, but the effects upon mood and behavior may be short-lived. In some cases, one may even look back upon the experience and feel one was deluded by it. However, a true mystical experience, as mentioned earlier, typically leads to profound changes in thought and behav-ior, in fact to what is sometimes called a "turning around" at the deepest level of being. The former more superficial experience leads only to a temporary state-based change, whereas the latter produces something that is trait-based and enduring. This is not to dismiss the state-based experience as being of no value. It may indeed have contained some elements of mystical awareness, yet, rather in the way that a book or a poem or a picture may have an impact upon us that fades quite quickly with time, its impact may not have touched us deeply enough, or this impact may have been too rapidly overtaken by other events (as can happen when one leaves a meditation retreat and returns to daily life) or we ourselves may not have been able to integrate it fully into our being.

Clearly more research is needed into the various triggers of mystical experience, into the reasons for the effectiveness of this experience, and into the variables within the individuals that may influence this effectiveness. In particular we need to know more about the apparent link between depression/despair and mystical experiences, including the prior belief systems of the depressives concerned. For example does a belief in the existence of a transcendent power render mystical experiences more likely in such cases? Do the precipitating causes of depression play some part in determining whether or not the mystical experiences occur?

Mysticism and the Brain

Despite the fact that research into meditation and mysticism has not attracted the attention within psychology and brain science that it should, several findings have been published that identify certain of their neurophysiological correlates. Of recent interest is the demonstration by Ramachandran and Blakeslee (1998), following on from earlier work by Persinger (1987), that when individuals are exposed to evocatively religious or spiritual words or ideas, the electrical activity in the frontal lobes of the cerebral cortex increases to a level comparable to that experienced during epileptic seizures. Epileptic seizures are known on occasions to be associated with subsequent reports of experiences comparable to mystical states – for example, bright lights, visions, apparent divine insights and unitary feelings. Ramachandran has also shown that stimulation of certain areas of the temporal lobes with magnetic field activity appears to induce mystical-type experiences even in non-epileptics. These results have prompted Persinger, Ramachandran, and their colleagues to label the most active area of the temporal lobes the "God Spot" or the "God Module." Results of this kind raise the possibility that mystical states are simply the consequence of cortical aberrations. Brain states appear also to be linked to experiences in meditation, with alpha rhythms, theta and even delta rhythms apparent in advanced meditators, although to date there is no evidence that progressive stimulation of the temporal lobes can produce the deep levels of tranquillity and the subsequent insights into self-nature developed through intensive meditation practice (or the resolution of a koan!).

Results such as these raise several issues. Do the mystical-type experiences sometimes reported by epileptics and those receiving temporal lobe stimulation lead to the lasting changes in behavior and belief apparent in those who have spontaneous mystical experiences? The same question can be asked of those who report mystical-type experiences after ingesting psychedelics. And if the frontal lobes are responsible for mystical experience, what is the purpose of these experiences and why should the brain have evolved the capacity to have them? Zohar and Marshall (2000) suggest that the "God Spot" is linked to "spiritual intelligence," defined as the ability to go beyond the boundaries of current thought and to contemplate infinite possibilities and higher meaning in life. Since some of these abilities do not appear linked to species survival, Zohar and Marshall suggest they have a psychological function linked to what is loosely called a spiritual dimension. Be this as it may, there is no hard evidence that all mystical experiences are actually generated by the frontal lobes. Stimulation of these lobes might allow access to experiences that are normally filtered out by brain mechanisms. A further objection to equating artificially induced experiences with true mystical states is that the latter occur spontaneously (no mystic to my knowledge walked around equipped with devices for providing temporal lobe stimulation), and we have no direct knowledge of the state of their temporal lobes at such a time. Nevertheless, attempts to induce mystical experiences by artificial stimulation are of obvious importance. Perhaps the best use that could be made of such stimulation would be administer it to a sample of subjects who have already reported spontaneous experiences in order to establish similarities and differences between these experiences and those artificially induced.

However, a major problem for the scientist when researching mystical experience is that, as with meditation, no method for assessing the inner nature of the experience has so far been developed, and indeed it is difficult to see what form such assessment could take, given the fact that mystical experiences are not objective events. Does this mean that despite what has been said in this chapter, the reality of the mystical experience must always be open to challenge? As Mangan (1994) argues, even the "language-focused approach to mysticism" does not take us into the heart of the matter. Nevertheless language is our most objective tool when discussing experiences that are, in themselves, ineffable (I am not here considering the special sense of *presence* that we may feel on sitting with certain men and women who have had abiding mystical experiences, and which the Hindus call *darshan*), and Lancaster (2000) is surely correct in maintaining that we have no reason to contradict the evidence for mystical experiences conveyed to us by mystics through language.

It is appropriate to conclude by stressing that scientists researching into meditation and mystical states should themselves seek some prior experience of serious meditation training. Without such training they are unlikely to be in a position to make pronouncements on the nature and meaning of these experiences or of the insights to which they may lead.

See also 11 Meditation; 54 Eastern methods for investigating mind and consciousness.

Further Readings

Chang, C.-C. (1978) *The Practice of Zen*, Westport, CT: Greenwood Press.

Cox, M. (1983) *Mysticism: The Direct Experience of God*. Wellingborough: Aquarian Press.

Fontana, D. (2003) *Psychology, Religion and Spirituality*. Oxford: BPS Books/Blackwell.

Forman, R. K. C. (1998) Mystical consciousness, the innate capacity, and the perennial wisdom. In R. K. C. Forman (ed.), *The Innate Philosophy*. New York: Oxford University Press.

References

Bucke, R. M. (1991) *Cosmic Consciousness:* Harmondsworth: Penguin Arkana (originally published 1901).

Cox, M. (1983) *Mysticism: The Direct Experience of God*. Wellingborough: Aquarian Press.

Forman, R. K. C. (1991) *Meister Eckhart*. Rockport, MA: Element Books.

Gupta, M. N. (1978) *The Condensed Gospel of Sri Ramakrishna*. Madras: Sri Ramakrishna Math.

Hardy, Sir A. (1979) *The Spiritual Nature of Man*. Oxford: Oxford University Press.

Hood, R. W. (1995) The facilitation of religious experience. In R. W. Hood (ed.), *Handbook of Religious Experience*. Birmingham, AL: Religious Education Press.

Isherwood, C. (ed.) (1963) *Vedanta for the Western World*. London: Unwin Books.

Kadloubovsky, E. and Palmer, G. E. H. (trans.) (1951) *Writings from the Philokalia, the Prayer of the Heart*. London: Faber and Faber.

Lancaster, B. L. (2000) Cognitive models and spiritual maps. *Journal of Consciousness Studies* 7: 11–12, 231–50.

Luk, C. (Lu K'uan Yu) (1971) *Practical Buddhism*. London: Rider.

Luk, C. (Lu K'uan Yu) (1974) *The Transmission of the Mind outside the Teachings*. New York: Grove Press.

Luk, C. (Lu K'uan Yu) (1976) *Ch'an and Zen Teachings*. London: Rider (new edn.).

Luk, C. (Lu K'uan Yu) (1984) *The Secrets of Chinese Meditation*. London: Rider (revised edn.).

Mangan, B. (1994) Language and experience in the cognitive study of mysticism. *Journal of Consciousness Studies* 1: 2, 250–52.

Maslow, A. H. (1970) *Religion, Values and Peak Experiences*. New York: Viking.

Murphy, M. and White, R. (1995) *In the Zone: Transcendent Experience in Sport*. Harmondsworth: Penguin.

Persinger, M. A. (1987) *Neuropsychological Bases of God Beliefs*. New York: Praeger.

Ramachandran, V. S. and Blakeslee, S. (1998) *Phantoms in the Brain*. London: Fourth Estate.

Ramakrishna, Sri (1975) *Teachings of Sri Ramakrishna*. Bourne End: Ramakrishna Vedanta Centre.

Smart, N. (1968) *The Yogi and the Devotee*. London: George Allen and Unwin.

Smart, N. (1996) *Dimensions of the Sacred: An Anatomy of the World's Beliefs*. London: Harper-Collins.

Spencer, S. (1963) *Mysticism in World Religions*. Harmondsworth: Penguin.

Staal, F. (1975) *Exploring Mysticism*. Harmondsworth: Penguin.

Stace, W. T. (1960) *The Teachings of the Mystics*. New York: New American Library.

Suzuki, D. T. (1979) *Mysticism Christian and Buddhist*. Boston, MA: Mandala Books.

Suzuki, D. T. (1998) *Bubbha of Infinite Light*. Boston, MA: Shambhala.

Underhill, E. (1995) *Mysticism: The Development of Humankind Spiritual Consciousness*. 14th edn. London: Bracken Books.

Wilber, K. (1993) *The Spectrum of Consciousness*, 2nd edn. Wheaton, IL: Quest Books.

Wilber, K. (2000) *Integral Psychology*. Boston, MA: Shambhala.

Zohar, D. and Marshall, I. (2000) *Spiritual Intelligence: The Ultimate Intelligence*. London: Bloomsbury.

BREAKDOWNS AND THE UNITY OF CONSCIOUSNESS

13

The Case of Blindsight

LAWRENCE WEISKRANTZ

Chambers Dictionary, among others, provides a concise definition: Blindsight – a condition caused by brain damage in which a person is able to respond to visual stimuli without consciously perceiving them. It is associated with damage to human primary visual cortex (otherwise known as striate cortex or area V1, which causes blindness in parts of the affected visual fields, with a size and shape to be expected from the classical retino-cortical maps (Holmes 1918). If, however, subjects are required to guess about stimuli presented to their blind fields, they may be able to locate them in space or to discriminate them from each other, despite saying that they do not see them and have no awareness of them (Pöppel, Held, & Frost 1973; Weiskrantz et al. 1974; Weiskrantz 1998). (It is worth nothing that in clinical cases damage to V1 is rarely complete. Typically it is confined to one cerebral hemisphere and therefore the region of blindness in most patients is restricted to one half of the visual field [hemianopia] or less, located contralateral to the damaged hemisphere. In everyday life the normal half-field is sufficient for most visual negotiations, and a hemianopic human or monkey would appear to be quite normal to the casual observer.)

The historical origin of the oxymoron "blindsight" stems from animal research. The primate retina, including that of humans, sends its major nerve tract (after a relay in the lateral geniculate of the thalamus) to the visual cortex (striate cortex, V1). When this cortex is blocked or removed (with histological confirmation of the completeness of the V1 removal) in monkeys, the animals can still carry out visual discriminations, albeit with certain changes. Such a residual capacity is, in itself, not surprising because the optic nerve leaving the retina also traverses a number of routes, reaching other targets in the brain located mainly in the midbrain and thalamus (Cowey & Stoerig 1991). These targets, in turn, provide relays that project widely to a number of other regions in the brain (Cowey & Stoerig 1991). These routes remain intact even if V1 is removed or damaged. The extra-striate tracts from the eye contain fewer nerve fibers than those in the pathway that normally reaches V1, only about one sixth as many, but this smaller number is not trivial. For example, the pathway from the retina to the superior colliculus in the midbrain contains about five times as many fibers as there are in the whole auditory nerve. Animal research also demonstrates that residual capacity can be improved by repeated practice with stimuli in specific regions of the blind field. And so there is no mystery in the fact that animals can make some visual discriminations in the absence of V1: the mystery is that human subjects are blind.

Blindsight first emerged when human subjects were tested in the manner with which one is forced to study visual capacity in animals (Pöppel, Held, & Frost 1973; Weiskrantz et al. 1974), leading to the realization that the methodology is typically deeply different in humans than in other animals. Humans are usually asked to give verbal descriptions or to comment on visual appearances and differences, whereas animals are trained to reach for the location of visual events or to make alternative choices for which they are differentially rewarded, necessarily devoid of any commentary. When a human subject is asked to make a discrimination between, say, two colors, there is typically an explicit verbal instruction about the color as such, and more importantly there is an important implicit assumption that the subject will be aware of that attribute and make a report about it accordingly. But an alternative is to test a human subject in a manner that is closer to animal methodology, for example, to be instructed simply to reach toward the stimulus or to make a forced-choice "guess" about the visual stimuli. Forced-choice guessing entails asking whether a visual event is, say, located at position A or B, whether its color is X or Y, whether it falls in the first or second of two temporal intervals, or whether its shape or brightness is different in the first or second interval. When tested in such a forced-choice discriminative way, independently of verbal responses or commentaries, human subjects can sometimes match the performance of monkeys with visual cortex damage even though they may lack any acknowledged awareness of visual stimuli that they nevertheless can tell apart. Hence, the term "blindsight."

Blindsight is but one example of a number of dissociations in brain-damaged patients between an intact capacity and absence or altered awareness (Weiskrantz 1991, 1997). For example, good storage can be demonstrated in amnesic patients with medial temporal lobe damage for events that they say they do not "remember," visual responsiveness can be demonstrated in a "neglected" field by patients with unilateral visual neglect, good differential sensitivity can be found to unfamiliar faces vs. familiar faces by prosopagnosic patients who have no recognition of the faces as such, and "blind touch" or "numbsense" can be demonstrated in parietal lobe patients with loss of touch sensitivity, which appears to be a homolog of blindsight in the tactile mode.

The visual parameters that blindsight subjects have been reported to be able to discriminate include color, orientation of lines or gratings, simple shapes, motion, onset and offset of visual events (for reviews, see Stoerig & Cowey 1997; Weiskrantz 1998; Weiskrantz 2003). Attention can also be controlled by unseen cues in the blind field controlling the responses to loci of unseen targets (Kentridge, Heywood, & Weiskrantz 1999). Recent research also has found that the emotional expression of unseen faces in the blind field can be guessed at better than chance levels (deGelder et al. 1999). In connection with possible extra-striate routes in the absence of V1, it is of interest that fearful and fear-conditioned faces generate differential amygdala responses in blindsight subject GY, and that the amygdala responses covary with neural activity in the posterior thalamus and superior colliculus (Morris et al. 2001).

Blindsight, however, is altered compared to the capacity of normal vision. By varying the spatial frequency of a sine-wave grating until it can no longer be discriminated from a homogenous patch, it is possible to measure the subject's acuity. It is reduced by about two octaves in spatial frequency, relative to the normal seeing hemifield, but is still creditable (Weiskrantz 1998). Contrast sensitivity is also reduced. There is good motion sensitivity for the detection of simple displacement of bars or solid spots, and there can be sensitive judgments about the direction of movement of a bar or a spot (Weiskrantz, Barbur, & Sahraie

1995). More complex patterns of motion, however ("third order motion"), seem to be seriously affected (Azzopardi & Cowey 2001). Color discrimination remains (Barbur et al. 1994), again in the absence of any experience of color per se, although there is a relative shift in sensitivity toward the long wavelengths (red) and a decrease in sensitivity to middle wavelengths (green). Otherwise the shape of the spectral sensitivity curve is qualitatively normal, although with reduced sensitivity. Also, the change in spectral sensitivity under dark adaptation is preserved (Stoerig & Cowey 1992).

Damage absolutely restricted to the visual cortex occurs relatively rarely in clinical patients. Animal work with monkeys has made it clear that if the damage extends outside the striate cortex, the residual visual capacity is reduced (Pasik & Pasik 1982). Therefore, most human blindsight research has concentrated on a small number of well-chosen subjects (e.g., DB, GY, FS, CS), with appropriately restricted pathology (and who are willing to endure the long testing sessions). This self-imposed restriction, however, may be too conservative. Current research suggests that residual visual function occurs in the majority of cases of visual cortical damage if additional brain damage is only moderate and if a common metrical range of spatio-temporal parameters (Sahraie et al. 2002) is used in each case.

Given the counter-intuitive nature of blindsight, early skepticism naturally led to questions about its validity (just as was true for earlier examples of implicit processing in neuropsychology, e.g., intact memory in the absence of "remembering" in amnesia). It has been suggested by Campion, Latto, and Smith (1983), for example, that there may be stray light falling in the intact visual field, or that the cortical lesion in particular cases may be incomplete and patchy (Wessinger, Fendrich, & Gazzaniga 1997) or that subjects really see but deny this, perhaps because of a very conservative criterion, or that their vision is really essentially qualitatively normal but the percepts are rendered very faint because of the brain damage. All of these alternatives are important, but have been directly addressed in various focused reviews, experimental analyses, and by MRI and ERP analyses of the lesions of blindsight patients (cf. Weiskrantz 1998, 2001, 2003; Azzopardi & Cowey 1997; Kentridge, Heywood, & Weiskrantz 1997). In particular, stray light has been stringently controlled, especially by the use of stimuli equiluminant with the background, and the use of the optic disc (blind spot) as a control region. Regarding incomplete lesions, subjects such as GY have been extensively and repeatedly mapped in MRI and the lesion is found to be complete except for the most posterior region, corresponding to the small area of macular sparing in the visual field (which, of course, is not used for testing blindsight), and islands of intact vision are not found in him (Kentridge, Heywood, & Weiskrantz 1997). Of course, in the monkey (in whom there is "blindsight"; see below) the completeness of the V1 lesion can be confirmed histologically. Regarding criteria in signal detection terms, the use of criterion-independent two-alternative forced-choice psychophysical methods still reveal blindsight. Blindsight as studied in subjects such as DB cannot be simulated by weak normal vision (Azzopardi & Cowey 1997), and in any event there are aspects of the subject's commentaries that are not touched by signal detection theory (Weiskrantz 2001). This subject continues to provoke lively discussion not only among neuroscientists but also among philosophers and others interested in the nature of conscious awareness and its putative neural basis.

Under certain conditions, blindsight subjects may say that they are aware that something is happening, they may feel it. This is especially the case when a stimulus contains rapid transient onsets and offsets, or moves very rapidly. This has been labeled "Blindsight Type 2" in contrast to "Blindsight Type 1," when discriminations occur in the total absence of any acknowledged awareness (Weiskrantz 1998). The distinction between Blindsight Type 1 and Type 2 has allowed one to carry out functional brain imaging contrasting states *with* awareness and *without* awareness, in both conditions using simple movement discriminations, which can be carried out with a high level of success – 90 percent or better (Weiskrantz, Barbur, & Sahraie 1995). In the unaware condition, but not the aware condition, activity is seen in the superior colliculus of the midbrain (Sahraie et al. 1997). This structure also was active in a blindsight subject in response to red stimuli but not to equiluminant green (Barbur et al. 1998), in line with the greater sensitivity of blindsight subjects toward the red end of the spectrum. In contrast, in the aware Type 2 state, dorsal cortical areas, especially foci in the right prefrontal cortex, are active. Such research reflects one of the strong interests of neuroscientists in blindsight and related phenomena in seeking routes to unravelling the neural mechanisms that underlie conscious awareness. The distinction between Type 1 and Type 2 is not assumed to be absolute and binary – it is possible, in principle, that there may be gradations; the distinction between its two extreme states has heuristic value.

The range of stimuli that can be discriminated by blindsight subjects – from simple form to facial expression to color to location of spatial locus by reaching or saccading – is such as to discount any simplistic relationship between them and the differential capacities of the ventral and dorsal cortical streams (Milner & Goodale 1995). Also, fMRI evidence exists that robust activation in either the dorsal and ventral streams occurs given the appropriate visual stimuli (e.g., movement vs. colored objects), leading to the conclusion that neither dorsal nor ventral cortical activity is sufficient in blindsight to generate conscious vision, nor that there is an imbalance between the two streams in blindsight (Goebel et al. 2001).

To be asked to discriminate stimuli that they cannot see is a patently strange request, and some subjects balk at it (as, indeed, do some experimenters in issuing the instruction). Therefore, other counter-intuitive methods of assessing residual function commend themselves, especially for screening of brain-damaged subjects for possible rehabilitation (with repeated practice of stimuli in the blind field). Some of these methods depend upon asking the subjects to discriminate stimuli lying entirely in their intact, seeing hemifields, but with the experimental demonstration that their performance can be altered by the presentation of stimuli in their blind fields, which can enhance or interfere with intact perception (see review by Weiskrantz 1990). Visual reflexes can be used: the most quantitatively sensitive method depends upon changes in the diameter of the pupil, which constricts not only to increase in light energy, but to a wide variety of stimuli without any energy change, including color, movement, and spatial frequency of sine-wave gratings. By varying spatial frequency of sine-wave gratings, the contrast sensitivity and acuity of the blind field can be accurately measured by pupillometry (Barbur & Thomson 1987), with results that mirror the psychophysical capacity as measured by forced-choice guessing. From these one can identify a narrowly-tuned spatiotemporal visual channel that remains in the absence of V1, a peak sensitivity in the region of 1–3 cycles per degree (Barbur, Harlow, & Weiskrantz 1994). Also, sensitivity to color and complementary color after-images can be detected (Barbur, Weiskrantz, & Harlow 1999). The pupil can also be used to measure similar capacities in animals, where verbal report of course is impossible (Weiskrantz, Cowey, & Le Mare 1998).

Finally, given that the existence of residual visual capacity was first definitively demonstrated in animals with visual cortex lesions, the question arises as to whether they too show blindsight for the discriminations they can perform. Recent experiments yield a positive answer (Cowey & Stoerig 1997; Stoerig & Cowey 1997). Monkeys with unilateral removal of V1 can detect and locate light stimuli with impressive sensitivity in their affected hemifield. They can also readily be trained, of course, to make differential responses in their normal visual hemifields for lights vs. non-lights (blanks). But when the same lights are projected into their affected field, the monkeys reliably treat them as blanks. That is, the very stimuli that they can detect with impressive sensitivity are classified by them as being blanks, as non-lights – just as a human blindsight subject does. Thus, the contribution made by the primary visual cortex to visual awareness appears to be similar in humans and other primates, and brings into common perspective and framework both the historical animal research and the more recent human blindsight research. Blindsight has made us aware that there is more to vision than seeing, and more to seeing than vision.

See also 14 Split-brain cases; 16 Coming together: the unity of conscious experience; 40 Preconscious processing; 42 Consciousness of action; 48 Duplex vision: separate cortical pathways for conscious perception and the control of action.

Further Readings

Weiskrantz, L. (1997) *Consciousness Lost and Found: A Neuropsychological Exploration.* Oxford: Oxford University Press.

Weiskrantz, L. (1998) paperback edn. (with additional material) of 1986 edn. of *Blindsight: A Case Study and Implications.* Oxford: Oxford University Press.

References

Azzopardi, P. and Cowey, A. (1997) Is blindsight like normal, near-threshold vision? *Proceedings of National Academy of Sciences, USA* 14, 190–4.

Azzopardi, P. and Cowey, A. (2001) Motion discrimination in cortically blind patients. *Brain* 124, 30–46.

Barbur, J. L. and Thomson, W. D. (1987) Pupil response as an objective measure of visual acuity. *Ophthalmic and Physiological Optics* 7, 425–9.

Barbur, J. L., Harlow, A., and Weiskrantz, L. (1994) Spatial and temporal response properties of residual vision in a case of hemianopia. *Philosophical Transactions of the Royal Society B* 343, 157–66.

Barbur, J. L., Harlow, A., Sahraie, A., Stoerig, P., and Weiskrantz, L. (1994) Responses to chromatic stimuli in the absence of V1: pupillometric and psychophysical studies. In: Vision science and its applications. *Optical Society of America Technical Digest* 2, 312–15.

Barbur, J. L., Sahraie, A., Simmons, A., Weiskrantz, L., and Williams, S. C. R. (1998) Residual processing of chromatic signals in the absence of a geniculostriate projection. *Vision Research* 38, 3447–53.

Barbur, J. L., Weiskrantz, L., and Harlow, J. A. (1999) The unseen color after-effect of an unseen stimulus: insight from blindsight into mechanisms of colour afterimages. *Proceedings of the National Academy of Sciences* 96, 11,637–41.

Campion, J., Latto, J. R., and Smith, Y. M. (1983) Is blindsight an effect of scattered light, spared cortex, and near-threshold vision? *Behavioral and Brain Sciences* 6, 423–48.

Cowey, A. and Stoerig, P. (1991) The neurobiology of blindsight. *Trends in Neurosciences* 29, 65–80.

Cowey, A. and Stoerig, P. (1997) Visual detection in monkeys with blindsight. *Neuropsychology* 35, 929–37.

deGelder, B., Vroomen, J., Pourtois, G., and Weiskrantz, L. (1999) Non-conscious recognition of affect in the absence of striate cortex. *NeuroReport* 10, 3759–63.

Goebel, R., Muckli, L., Friedhelm, E., Singer, W., and Stoerig, P. (2001) Sustained extrastriate cortical activation without visual awareness revealed by fMRI studies of hemianopic patients. *Vision Research* 41, 1459–74.

Holmes, G. (1918) Disturbances of vision by cerebral lesions. *British Journal of Ophthalmology* 2, 353–84.

Kentridge, R. W., Heywood, C. A., and Weiskrantz, L. (1997) Residual vision in multiple retinal locations within a scotoma: Implications for blindsight. *Journal of Cognitive Neuroscience* 9, 191–202.

Kentridge, R. W., Heywood, C. A., and Weiskrantz, L. (1999) Attention without awareness in blindsight. *Proceedings of the Royal Society B* 266, 1805.

Milner, A. D. and Goodale, M. A. (1995) *The Visual Brain in Action*. Oxford: Oxford University Press.

Morris, J. S., DeGelder, B., Weiskrantz, L., and Dolan, R. J. (2001) Differential extrangeniculate and amygdala responses to presentation of emotional faces in a cortically blind field. *Brain* 124, 1241–52.

Pasik, P. and Pasik, T. (1982) Visual functions in monkeys after total removal of visual cerebral cortex. *Contributions to sensory physiology* 7, 147–200.

Pöppel, E., Held, R., and Frost, E. (1973) Residual visual function after brain wounds involving the central visual pathways in man. *Nature* 243, 295–96.

Sahraie, A., Weiskrantz, L., Barbur, J. L., Simmons, A., Williams, S. C. R., and Brammer, M. L. (1997) Pattern of neuronal activity associated with conscious and unconscious processing of visual signals. *Proceedings of the National Academy of Sciences* 94, 9406–11.

Sahraie, A., Weiskrantz, L., Trevethan, C. T., Cruce, R., and Murray, A. D. (2002) Psychophysical and pupillometric study of spatial channels of visual processing on blindsight. *Experimental Brain Research* 143, 249–56.

Stoerig, P. and Cowey, A. (1992) Wavelength sensitivity in blindsight. *Brain* 115, 425–44.

Stoerig, P. and Cowey, A. (1997) Blindsight in man and monkey. *Brain* 120, 535–59.

Weiskrantz, L. (1990) Outlooks for blindsight: explicit methodologies for implicit processes. The Ferrier Lecture. *Proceedings of the Royal Society B* 239, 247.

Weiskrantz, L. (1991) Disconnected awareness in detecting, processing, and remembering in neurological patients. The Hughlings Jackson Lecture. *Journal of the Royal Society of Medicine* 84: 466–70.

Weiskrantz, L. (1997) *Consciousness Lost and Found: A Neuropsychological Exploration*. Oxford: Oxford University Press.

Weiskrantz, L. (1998) paperback edn. (with additional material) of 1986 edn. of *Blindsight: A Case Study and Implications*. Oxford: Oxford University Press.

Weiskrantz, L. (2001) Putting beta β on the back burner. In B. deGelder, E. DeHaan, and C. A. Heywood (eds.), *Out of Mind*, 20–31. Oxford: Oxford University Press.

Weiskrantz, L. (2003) Unconscious perception: blindsight. In M. Fahle and M. Greenlee (eds.), *The Neuropsychology of Vision*, 283–306. Oxford: Oxford University Press.

Weiskrantz, L., Barbur, J. L., and Sahraie, A. (1995) Parameters affecting conscious versus unconscious visual discrimination without V1. *Proceedings of the National Academy of Sciences* 92, 6122–6.

Weiskrantz, L., Cowey, A., and Le Mare, C. (1998) Learning from the pupil: a spatial visual channel in the absence of V1 in monkey and human. *Brain* 121, 1065–72.

Weiskrantz, L., Warrington, E. K., Sanders, M. D., and Marshall, J. (1974) Visual capacity in the hemianopic field following a restricted occipital ablation. *Brain* 97, 709–28.

Wessinger, C. M., Fendrich, R., and Gazzaniga, M. S. (1997) Islands of residual vision in hemianopic patients. *Journal of Cognitive Neuroscience* 9, 203–21.

14

Split-Brain Cases

MARY K. COLVIN AND MICHAEL S. GAZZANIGA

After the first callosotomy surgeries were performed, the general consensus among the medical community was that severing the corpus callosum had relatively little, if any, effect on an individual's behavior (Akelaitis 1941). Nearly twenty years later, it was quite a shock to discover that under experimental conditions, the two hemispheres could simultaneously maintain very different interpretations of the same stimulus. These findings immediately called into question the unity of subjective experience, a fundamental characteristic of human consciousness. How could the split-brain patient not experience any disruption in their experience as a unified self when the two hemispheres are physically and functionally disconnected? In this chapter, we review the research that has led to a conceptualization of the split brain as two minds within one body and the implications of this research for the scientific study of consciousness. We argue that consciousness is a neural function that emerges from the integration of information across available functional modules.

Characterizing Consciousness in the Split-Brain Patient

Since the first reports of hemispheric differences in information processing and impaired interhemispheric transfer in split-brain patients, there has been a great deal of interest in the subjective experiences of these patients. Despite the substantial literature documenting split-brain patients' reports of no alterations in senses of self following callosotomy surgery, the common interpretation of the split-brain condition is that disconnection of the two hemispheres results in a "splitting of the self." Given the prevalence of such misconceptions, we would like to take this opportunity to review what is known about the subjective experiences of split-brain patients and how this information shapes our understanding of neural bases of consciousness.

Bilateral representation of fundamental sensory information

Both hemispheres of the split-brain patient receive ascending projections from a common brainstem, enabling duplicate representation of a great deal of basic sensory information. Both hemispheres receive proprioceptive information, automatically coding the body's position in space (Sperry 1984). Both hemispheres can perceive painful stimuli or light and deep touch presented to either side of the body, although the stimulus intensity may be diminished on the ipsilateral side and the ipsilateral representation may be extinguished under conditions of bilateral stimulation. Both hemispheres can initiate eye saccades and it seems as though both hemispheres can monitor the amplitude of a saccade generated by the ipsilateral hemisphere, even in the absence of visual feedback (for review, see Gazzaniga 2000). Similarly, brainstem mechanisms support similar arousal levels within each hemisphere so that both hemispheres fall asleep and wake at the same time (Sperry 1984).

In contrast, higher-order sensory information processed at the cortical level tends to be unilaterally represented. Although both hemispheres can guide facial and proximal muscles, including the upper arms and legs, control of distal muscles, including the hands, is lateralized. The majority of auditory information is relayed to the contralateral hemisphere, although there are significant ipsilateral projections (Langers, van Dijk, & Backes 2005). The projection of visual information to the two hemispheres is strictly lateralized. Information presented to the right visual field, most likely including information presented to the right half of the fovea, projects solely to the left hemisphere and information presented to the left visual field, most likely including information presented to the left half of the fovea, projects solely to the right hemisphere (Lavidor & Walsh 2004). Thus, visual information, and to a lesser extent, auditory information, is represented by the single contralateral hemisphere (for review, see Gazzaniga 2000). However, despite this anatomical organization, split-brain patients do not experience two halves of visual or auditory space. Similar to normal individuals, the visual and auditory midlines are virtual distinctions; split-brain patients' subjective experiences of their sensory worlds are unified.

Limited access to the knowledge of the opposite hemisphere

Although there are subcortical routes of interhemispheric communication, the corpus callosum vastly augments these primitive mechanisms, providing a more sophisticated mechanism for bihemispheric representation. In the absence of a corpus callosum, only simple information can be transferred between hemispheres, such as crude spatial information or the binary value of "present" or "not present." Interhemispheric communication of the majority of information, particularly higher-order information, is dependent upon the integrity of the corpus callosum (for review, see Gazzaniga 2000). Thus, in the absence of the corpus callosum, what is known by one hemisphere is isolated from the other hemisphere.

To compensate for the loss of the callosal pathways, the split-brain patient may engage in subtle cross-cueing behavior so that both hemispheres have access to information presented on both sides of the midline. These behaviors include moving his/her head, talking aloud, or making symbolic hand movements. Under experimental conditions, such cross-cueing behavior is eliminated. The resulting absence of interhemispheric transfer clearly demonstrates that in the intact brain, the corpus callosum is the primary conduit between the hemispheres, seamlessly and automatically integrating information across the two halves of the brain. Without the corpus callosum, most mental representations are computed intra-hemispherically and the two hemispheres may develop separate stores of knowledge, reflecting individualized learning and experiences.

States of co-consciousness

One question arising from early studies of split-brain primates was whether the two disconnected hemispheres could operate in parallel. In a seminal study addressing this issue, Trevarthen (1962) trained each hemisphere of a split-brain primate to make different responses to a particular visual stimulus. Both hemispheres could perform their respective tasks concurrently, indicating that in the split-brain, both hemispheres can independently and simultaneously execute conflicting visuomotor responses. In contrast, a monkey with an intact corpus callosum was unable to decide between the two competing responses and "showed signs of extreme frustration" (Trevarthen 1962).

Later studies of split-brain humans confirmed and extended this early work. In one experiment, split-brain patients were better than normal controls in performing a bimanual task requiring each hand to simultaneously draw simple stimuli that differed in their spatial orientations (Franz, Ivry, & Gazzaniga 1996). Subsequent research identified the posterior third of the corpus callosum as critical for bimanual spatial coordination (Eliassen, Baynes, & Gazzaniga 1999, 2000). In another task involving the simultaneous and bilateral presentation of streams of stimuli, split-brain patients more readily identified whether a stimulus had been presented than normal controls, presumably because stimuli were combined across the visual fields in the normal controls, thereby increasing the task difficulty (Holtzman & Gazzaniga 1985). Similarly, Luck and colleagues (1989) demonstrated that relative to normal controls, when split-brain participants search a visual array that spans both visual fields, there is a significant reduction in response delay as the array size increases (Luck et al. 1989). This research demonstrated that like split-brain animals, the two hemispheres of a split-brain human are free to independently operate in parallel, while the corpus callosum automatically attempts to integrate across the hemispheres of normal controls, confounding the performance of both hemispheres.

Thus, under conditions when each hemisphere is simultaneously processing and generating conflicting representations and responses, cortical disconnection of the two hemispheres can result in a processing advantage. However, it is important to point out that severing the corpus callosum does not result in a gain of processing resources. Holtzman and Gazzaniga (1982) demonstrated that when one hemisphere of a split-brain patient performed a difficult task, the other hemisphere performed worse on a simultaneous task (Holtzman & Gazzaniga 1982), indicating that while the two disconnected hemispheres are free to independently allocate attention, they share a limited pool of central attentional resources. Similarly, Reuter-Lorenz and Fendrich demonstrated that the two disconnected hemispheres could independently allocate spatial attention, but were unable to concurrently allocate spatial attention to two different locations, also suggesting shared central resources (Reuter-Lorenz & Fendrich 1990). These central attentional resources are almost certainly allocated subcortically, most likely at the level of the brainstem, and limit the two hemispheres' functional independence.

The research reviewed above clearly demonstrates that in both the intact and split brain, the two hemispheres are able to simultaneously process and organize responses to different, if not conflicting, representations. The question that naturally follows is whether the two hemispheres are simultaneously *conscious* of different representations. Evidence that the split-brain patient is able to simultaneously execute conflicting responses, certainly creates the impression that the two hemispheres are, as Sperry described, "co-conscious in parallel" (Sperry 1990). However, it is possible that the consciousness rapidly alternates between the two hemispheres in both the split and intact brain, enabling the execution or resolution of conflicting responses. Regardless of whether this state of co-consciousness is sequential or simultaneous in nature, the split-brain condition represents an exaggeration of the normal state, where the contents of consciousness reflect the domain-specific neural processes that are currently active and drawing upon central processing resources. The two hemispheres can be conscious of different representations of the same stimuli. Throughout this chapter, we will use the term "co-conscious" to refer to the ability of the two hemispheres to simultaneously generate independent representational states of the world, allowing for either rapid sequential shifting or simultaneous conscious awareness of those representations.

Differing interpretations: the impact of hemispheric asymmetries

If the two hemispheres can be independently co-conscious, then is their conscious experience of the world equivalent? Above, we reviewed evidence demonstrating that the two hemispheres of a split-brain patient can simultaneously maintain and act upon conflicting representations. In this section, we explore whether this situation arises naturally in the intact and split brain as a result of hemispheric asymmetries in the processing of external stimuli. We propose that the conscious experiences of the two hemispheres may reflect the activity of specialized and lateralized processes. Thus, conflicting interpretations of the outside world may simultaneously emerge from one brain.

Heavily influenced by the long neuropsychological tradition of studying loss of function following unilateral brain lesions, studies of split-brain patients have revealed specialized functions of the left and right hemispheres. To date, a large number of hemispheric asymmetries have been reported and this literature is thoroughly reviewed elsewhere (Gazzaniga 2000). For the purposes of this chapter, we will briefly address the most prevalent conception of the differences between the two hemispheres – that the left hemisphere is specialized for verbal processes, while the right hemisphere is specialized for visuospatial processes. This conceptualization is not entirely accurate and is somewhat oversimplified. For example, in some cases, the right hemisphere may possess a lexicon that is roughly equivalent to that of the left hemisphere. However, even in these cases, the left hemisphere retains the specialized ability to manipulate the rules of syntax and phonology to generate expressive output. In other words, the basic processes of language may be present in both hemispheres, but only the left hemisphere has the specialized neural processes required to carry out the complex linguistic functions of daily life. Similarly, both hemispheres are equally able to perform simple perceptual processes, but only the right hemisphere is able to perform sophisticated higher-order visual processes. For example, both hemispheres are able to determine whether two sequentially presented stimuli were identical, but the right hemisphere is better than the left in determining whether two sequentially presented stimuli were in the same spatial location. Thus, while the differences between the left and right hemispheres' functions can be broadly captured by a verbal/visuospatial dichotomy, this distinction is most accurate when referencing higher-order cognitive processes within these domains (Gazzaniga 2000).

In considering the influence of hemispheric asymmetries on the two hemispheres' conscious representations of the external environment, the confounding impact of individual differences on the strength of functional lateralization should be taken into account. Right-handed individuals are more likely to have the "typical" pattern of hemispheric asymmetries; left-handed individuals may be less lateralized, particularly with respect to language function. Sex differences in functional lateralization have also been described, although these findings are controversial. In general, sex differences research emphasizes language function, with men being more lateralized than women. Recent preliminary work from our laboratory suggests that the extent of functional lateralization more directly reflects callosal organization. Interestingly, callosal organization, particularly the extent of myelination, changes across the lifespan and may differ between the sexes (Aboitiz et al. 1996). Indeed, there is a growing body of work suggesting that the strength of hemispheric asymmetries shifts across the lifespan (for review, see Cabeza 2002), possibly reflecting the extent of callosal myelination. Thus, in studying patterns of hemispheric asymmetries, it is important to weigh the relative influence of individual difference variables such as age, sex, and callosal organization. These variables may determine whether the differences between the two hemispheres' interpretations of external stimuli are subtle or dramatic. More importantly, individual differences in callosal organization and functional lateralization may make significant contributions toward the creation of our own unique, subjective experiences of the world.

With this general pattern of hemispheric asymmetries and the potential influence of individual differences on functional lateralization in mind, we turn to the question of whether hemispheric asymmetries in cognitive processing give rise to different conscious interpretations of the same stimulus between the two hemispheres. Simple observations of split-brain patients performing experimental tests tapping hemispheric asymmetries clearly reveal that the two halves of the brain can simultaneously maintain different interpretations of the same stimulus. Further, this state does not affect the patient's sense of a unified self. The patient will calmly respond to a stimulus with the appropriate hand, even when the responses to the same stimulus differ between the two hands. Different conscious representations of the external environment, created by lateralized functional modules can peacefully coexist within the same brain.

Accessing and understanding the conscious experiences of the two hemispheres

From the very first studies of split-brain patients in Roger Sperry's laboratory, it was clear that the right hemisphere had limited linguistic skills. One of us (M.S.G.) came to realize this when he flashed a stimulus to split-brain patient W. J.'s right hemisphere. W. J. verbally reported that he did not see anything even though his left hand made the appropriate manual response (Gazzaniga 1995). Only the left hemisphere could verbally report its conscious experience. These findings have been corroborated by Wada testing of normal individuals. In most cases, when amobarbitol is used to put the left hemisphere to sleep, the participant cannot speak. However, when the right hemisphere is put to sleep, the participant can comment on his conscious experience (Wada 1949). Exceptions to this pattern have been found in cases of atypical cerebral dominance, usually found within a small proportion of left-handed individuals. In addition, there have been reports that right hemisphere speech may emerge many years after callosotomy surgery (Gazzaniga 2000). However, these cases of right hemisphere speech represent variation in a limited sample of the normal population and/or years of neural plasticity. In the vast majority of intact brains, only the left hemisphere retains the ability to speak, enabling verbal report of conscious experience.

In the intact brain, the left hemisphere produces verbal explanations for actions executed by both hemispheres. The right hemisphere's mental representations are accessible through the corpus callosum. In the split brain, the left hemisphere continues to generate verbal explanations for the patient's behavior, even though the representation causing the right hemisphere's action is inaccessible. This specialized ability of the left hemisphere to generate verbal explanations even in the absence of relevant information has become known as the interpreter. In a now classic study demonstrating the left hemisphere interpreter, a picture was first presented to each visual field of split-brain patient P. S., who was then asked to choose two related pictures, one with each hand, from an array of eight choices. When a chicken claw was presented in the right visual field (left hemisphere) and a snow scene was presented in the left visual field (right hemisphere), P. S. correctly chose a chicken with his right hand (left hemisphere) and a snow shovel with his left hand (right hemisphere). But when asked why he chose those two pictures, the left hemisphere spun a story to integrate the actions of the two hemispheres. P. S. said, "Oh that's simple. The chicken claw goes with the chicken, and you need a shovel to clean out the chicken shed" (Gazzaniga 2000). The left hemisphere is unaware that the right hemisphere's selection of the shovel followed seeing a snow scene picture, but nonetheless integrated the shovel into its explanation of the relationship between the chicken claw and the chicken.

Thus, the left hemisphere maintains a unique ability to generate a linguistic explanation for observable behavior that can be communicated to the outside world. The left hemisphere's conscious state is directly accessible, while the right hemisphere's conscious state must be indirectly interpreted by observing corresponding actions. Although some have argued that this inequality of accessibility must mean that the right hemisphere is not fully conscious, the right hemisphere does maintain distinct interpretations of the external environment, often reflecting its superior visuospatial processes. Both hemispheres are co-conscious, but only the left hemisphere's conscious awareness can be directly accessed by verbal query.

Examining the Corpus Callosum's Contribution to Unified Subjective Experience

A central question is whether the corpus callosum gives rise to the unity of subjective conscious experience. The easiest route to examine this question is to observe the experiences of split-brain and callosal agenesis patients. In callosal agenesis patients, the corpus callosum failed to develop. Compared to split-brain patients, callosal agenesis patients may have different patterns of hemispheric asymmetries and interhemispheric communication, reflecting years of neural plasticity during critical developmental periods. For this reason, we have chosen to limit our discussion to split-brain patients. However, it is worth noting that the subjective experiences of these acallosal patients are remarkably similar. No split-brain patient has ever woken up following callosotomy surgery and felt as though his/her experience of self had fundamentally changed or that two selves now inhabited the same body. Split-brain patients do not report any disruption in their unified experiences of themselves. Likewise, callosal agenesis patients report a fully integrated sense of one's self. In both cases, the two hemispheres may be independently co-conscious, but the subjective experience of a unified self is preserved, suggesting that this state does not require the development or preservation of the corpus callosum.

In the intact brain, hemispheric asymmetries may still be elicited when normal controls are subjected to the same experimental situations as split-brain patients. For example, normal individuals are often more accurate in deciding whether a word is real or not when it is presented to the right visual field (left hemisphere) than when the same word is presented to the left visual field (right hemisphere), reflecting the left hemisphere's specialization for linguistic processing. Such left or right visual field advantages in normal individuals are often less exaggerated than those observed in split-brain patients, but nonetheless reflect that the two hemispheres retain some degree of independent processing capacity in the presence of a fully functioning corpus callosum.

The co-existence of hemispheric differences in cognitive processing and unified subjective experience in both the split and the intact brain suggests that callosally mediated resolution of different co-conscious representations is not required for the experience of a unified self. However, the corpus callosum does make significant contributions toward the neural construction of a unified self. Anterior callosal lesions may result in intermanual conflict, which can be a component of alien hand syndrome. Patients with this disorder may report that the action of one hand (usually the left) "undoes" the action of the other hand (Feinberg et al. 1992). In these moments, the patients do not report being consciously aware of the actions of the competing hand and often report that the alien hand "has a mind of its own." Immediately after their surgeries, split-brain patients may also experience intermanual conflict (Akelaitis 1945). Although this state usually resolves, an inability to verbally explain the actions of the left hand, as well as a sense that the left hand "has a mind of its own" often persists indefinitely. These cases demonstrate that the corpus callosum does contribute to the integration of information across the entire body. However, even in those moments when the left hand's actions are unknowable to the verbal left hemisphere, the patient's subjective experience of a unified self is preserved. The corpus callosum enables the integration of experience across both hemispheres, but it is neither necessary nor sufficient to give rise to the unification of subjective experience.

Explaining Unified Conscious Experience in the Split Brain

The evidence for the independent function of two hemispheres, even in the presence of massive interhemispheric connections fundamentally challenges the conceptualization of a one-to-one correspondence between brain and mind. Many have found this quite unsettling, resorting to dualistic explanations of the origin of the mind. However, the vast majority of alternative explanations have preserved the materialistic connection between mind and brain. Nagel (1971) classified each of these alternative arguments into five major positions. Three of these positions arise from varying the relative contribution of the two hemispheres to the split-brain patient's unified conscious experience (left is solely responsible, left is primarily responsible, left and right make equal contributions but only the left can talk). The other two positions maintain that split-brain patients have one mind. One of these positions argues that both hemispheres contribute to that mind, while the other position argues that the mind divides under special experimental conditions eliciting the independent activity of the two hemispheres. Nagel does an excellent job reviewing the evidence for and against each of these positions and refutes each one systematically (Nagel 1971). Thus, we will confine our discussion to recent work that qualifies and extends

Nagel's discussion of a few of these positions. In particular, we will discuss the hypothesis that split-brain patients have two minds and briefly discuss an alternative hypothesis that split-brain consciousness arises solely or primarily from the activity of the verbal left hemisphere.

The bicameral mind argument

The argument that the two hemispheres each maintain an independent mind, regardless of the presence of the corpus callosum, stems from early anatomical observations of the separation of two hemispheres. Some early anatomists referred to the two hemispheres as half brains or as individual brains. Given the marked anatomical separation of the two hemispheres, it seemed to naturally follow that the hemispheres were also functionally independent (Puccetti 1981). The first description of split-brain patients' abilities to simultaneously execute conflicting actions independently directed by each hemisphere led to the strong version of the bicameral mind argument, most notably advanced by Puccetti (1981).

Throughout this chapter, we have proposed that the two hemispheres are co-conscious and that the functional independence of the two hemispheres in the split-brain condition represents an exaggeration of the normal state. At first glance, this position can be interpreted as support for the bicameral mind argument. However, the critical test of the strong version of the bicameral mind argument is one's answer to the following question: Is anything gained by functional independence of the two hemispheres? Puccetti's position is that there is nothing gained, that in the normal individual, the two hemispheres operate in parallel and "the function of the corpus callosum is to duplicate conscious experience on both sides of the brain, without subsequent fusion" (Puccetti 1981).

Our own position on this conceptualization of mental duality is similar to that of others who have argued against this strong version of the bicameral mind argument (e.g., Bogen 1981). First, although the two hemispheres may be co-conscious in parallel, hemispheric asymmetries in cognitive processing result in an inequality between the two hemispheres' conscious representations, even in the intact brain. The conscious experiences of the two hemispheres are not identical. Second, it is clear that the corpus callosum does much more than shuttle copies of mental representations between the two hemispheres. As seen in studies requiring the two hemispheres of an intact brain to perform conflicting tasks, the resulting actions are some fusion of the appropriate responses. Similarly, the corpus callosum enables interhemispheric excitation (Innocenti 1986) and possibly interhemispheric inhibition (Doty & Negrao 1973; Toyama, Matsunami et al. 1974; Toyama, Tokashiki, & Matsunami 1969) that allow one hemisphere to influence the processing of the other hemisphere. Finally, the corpus callosum does appear to make significant contributions to unified subjective experience, as evidenced by intermanual conflict following anterior callosal lesions. In such cases, the intentions of the right hand are unknowable to the left hemisphere and the patient reports that the alien hand "has a mind of its own." Although the corpus callosum is neither necessary nor sufficient to create a unified subjective experience, it does enable important integrative functions between the two hemispheres that contribute to the normal conscious state. Thus, the co-localization of the two hemispheres to the same head, joined by the corpus callosum, contributes something fundamental to the human condition that is not captured by the bicameral mind argument.

The left hemisphere argument

Facing mounting evidence that the two hemispheres of the brain could simultaneously operate in parallel, some resolved to preserve a one-to-one correspondence between brain and mind by arguing that only the left hemisphere was conscious. Because the right hemisphere could not speak and elaborate upon its actions, those actions were assumed to be automatic responses to the environment (e.g., Penfield 1966; Eccles 1973). As additional experiments revealed that the right hemisphere was able to generate complex responses and had specialized visuospatial skills, this strong position of left hemisphere consciousness was revised to allow for limited and inferior right hemisphere consciousness (Sperry 1990).

As with the bicameral mind argument, the arguments against assigning consciousness only to the left hemisphere have been thoroughly treated elsewhere so we only summarize them here. The central issue is whether the right hemisphere's inability to verbally report its experiences renders it nonconscious. On this question, we agree with Sperry, Nagel, and others that there is no reason to deny consciousness to the right hemisphere simply because it cannot speak (Nagel 1971; Sperry 1990). The nature of the right hemisphere's conscious state may be fundamentally different from that of the left hemisphere, reflecting its tendency to report experiences without elaboration and its own specialized skills, but it is clearly conscious. The right hemisphere of a split-brain patient can learn new skills, execute volitional acts, and may outperform the verbal left hemisphere on certain tasks (Sperry 1990). The interpretive capacity of the left hemisphere clearly distinguishes its conscious experience and we allow for the possibility that left hemisphere consciousness may be considered superior to that of the right hemisphere. However, the right hemisphere has some conscious experience accessible through nonverbal means.

Toward an Understanding of the Neural Bases of Consciousness

The preserved unification of self within the split-brain patient is a daunting puzzle. No explanation seems to fit, unless one abandons the notion that there is only one neural source of conscious unification. As Dennett (1991) first discussed, the idea that there is a single neural structure that knits together representations emerging from cognitive processes throughout the brainstems from Descartes's hypothesis that the pineal gland was the interface between the material brain and the immaterial mind. Information from all parts of the brain was funneled to the pineal gland and then integrated into a unified concept of self. Although modern neuroscience has rejected this functional role of the pineal gland, as well as the conceptualization of an immaterial mind, the notion persists that there is a "center of gravity" in the brain from which conscious experience arises (Dennett 1991). When this concept was applied to conceptualize consciousness in the split brain, it led to the bicameral mind and left hemisphere arguments discussed in the previous section. Respectively, these hypotheses state that each hemisphere maintains an independent "center of gravity" or that a single center resides in the verbal left hemisphere. However, if the concept of a single source of unification is discarded, then explaining the split-brain patient's unified sense of self becomes a tractable problem.

Our own view is that consciousness emerges from the integration of information across accessible neural processing modules. This information is not first transported to a single place in the brain, rather it is automatically integrated across time and neural space into conscious experience. Before we delve into the details of how this explains the split-brain condition as well as a host of other neurological and psychiatric conditions, it is worth addressing what we mean by neural processing modules. Fodor first conceptualized discrete functional units in the brain each having a particular function (Fodor 1983). Neuropsychological research demonstrating the loss of specific functions following focal lesions and neuroimaging research demonstrating distinctive patterns of activity associated with particular cognitive processes has provided great support for a modular organization of the brain. One of the earliest neural modules to be identified was Broca's area, located in the left inferior frontal cortex. Selective damage to this region results in an inability to generate fluent and grammatical speech in the absence of language comprehension deficits. Similarly, multiple neuroimaging studies have shown that a particular region of the inferotemporal cortex, now known as the fusiform face area, is active during the perception of faces. Selective damage to this area can result in a condition known as prosopagnosia, or an inability to identify even familiar faces. The culmination of neuropsychological and more recently, neuroimaging research has demonstrated that it is reasonable to view the brain as a system of interconnected collections of processing modules.

Studies of split-brain patients have revealed that some of these processing modules are bilaterally represented while others are lateralized to one hemisphere. For example, both hemispheres are able to make simple quantity judgments about groups of dots, suggesting that the neural processing module(s) underlying this cognitive ability are present in both hemispheres (Colvin, Funnell, & Gazzaniga 2005). In contrast, only the left hemisphere is able to engage in semantic processing, in keeping with a specialized neural processing module for this function localized in Broca's area. The right hemisphere is unable to engage in semantic processing because it is cut off from the lateralized processing module specialized for this cognitive function. Thus, when the left or right hemisphere of a split-brain patient generates a conscious response to external stimuli, each hemisphere is only able to integrate across modules located within that hemisphere. Some of these modules are identical to that of the disconnected hemisphere and some modules are unique. As a result, the conscious experiences of the two hemispheres may differ depending upon whether the task taps lateralized processing modules. The observed differences between the conscious experiences of the left and right hemispheres clearly illustrate Dennett's point that there is no single "center of gravity" for subjective experience. The neural activity available for integration into conscious experience depends upon where one is in the brain. When the left hemisphere of a split-brain patient is asked to respond, it integrates all available information, excluding the inaccessible information of the right hemisphere. When the right hemisphere of a split-brain patient is asked to respond, it integrates all available information, excluding the inaccessible information of the left hemisphere. Both hemispheres create conscious experience from accessible processing modules. When a specialized processing module is tapped or is unavailable, differences in the states of co-consciousness are observed.

The idea that consciousness emerges from the automatic integration of information across available processing modules has the potential to explain a number of disorders of consciousness associated with neurological and psychiatric conditions (Gazzaniga 2000; Cooney & Gazzaniga 2003). For example, patients with visuospatial neglect fail to spontaneously attend to the left side of space. This condition typically results from damage to the right inferior parietal lobe, a cortical module that directs attention to both sides of space. The homologous region in the left hemisphere, a cortical module that only directs attention to the right hemispace, remains intact (Heilman & van den Abell 1980). Thus, when conscious experience emerges from integration across available processing modules, the input of the right inferior parietal lobe is absent and is not included. Disorders of consciousness arise when modules that normally contribute to conscious experience are inaccessible or damaged.

As in the split-brain patient, when disorders of consciousness arise due to localized cortical damage, there is typically little disruption in a unified sense of self. The visuospatial neglect patient does not report feeling as though one half of his or her world is inaccessible. The anosognostic patient provides an even more dramatic illustration of this point. In these cases, right parietal damage results in an inability to incorporate the left body space into one's conscious awareness. However, the patient is not disturbed by this great loss. Further, when presented with his or her arm and asked whether it is his or her own, the anosognostic patient will deny that it is. The left hemisphere's specialized interpretative ability constructs an explanation for the patient's distorted conscious experience. Such patients clearly demonstrate that a unified conscious experience arises from the integration of information across available processing modules and is not dependent upon the function of a single brain region.

Conclusions

The great puzzle of split-brain patients has been their preserved unity of conscious experience following callosal section. Despite the functional isolation of the two hemispheres, the split-brain patient does not report feeling as two divided selves inhabiting the same body. These cases fundamentally challenge traditional conceptualizations of the one-to-one correspondence between mind and body, illustrating that two disconnected hemispheres can independently utilize a shared pool of processing resources within the same head. However, the split-brain condition should not be taken as evidence for a bicameral mind. Rather, the split-brain condition illustrates that consciousness emerges from the automatic integration of modular neural processes across time and brain space. When the corpus callosum is severed, the information available for integration into conscious experience is restricted to a single hemisphere; in the intact brain, the information available for integration into conscious experience includes both hemispheres. Thus, in the split-brain patient, the unification of subjective experience is preserved by a lack of awareness that any information from the other hemisphere is missing in the construction of conscious experience.

See also 13 The case of blindsight; 15 Philosophical psychopathology and self-consciousness; 16 Coming together: the unity of conscious experience.

Further Readings

Nagel, T. (1971) Brain bisection and the unity of consciousness. *Synthese* 22, 396–413.

Sperry, R. (1984) Consciousness, personal identity and the divided brain. *Neuropsychologia* 22: 6, 661–73.

Sperry, R. (1990) Forebrain commissurotomy and conscious awareness. In C. B. Trevarthen (ed.), *Brain Circuits and Functions of the Mind: Essays in Honor of Roger W. Sperry*, 371–88. Cambridge: Cambridge University Press.

Zaidel, E., Iacoboni, M., Zaidel, D. W., and Bogen, J. (2003) The callosal syndromes. In K. M. Heilman and E. Valenstein (eds.), *Clinical Neuropsychology*, 347–403, 4th edn. New York: Oxford University Press.

References

Aboitiz, F., Rodriguez, E., Olivares, R., and Zaidel, E. (1996) Age-related changes in fibre composition of the human corpus callosum: sex differences. *NeuroReport* 7: 11, 1761–4.

Akelaitis, A. J. (1941) Studies on the corpus callosum: higher visual functions in each homonymous visual field following complete section of corpus callosum. *Archives of Neurology and Psychiatry* 45, 788.

Akelaitis, A. J. (1945) Studies on the corpus callosum. IV. Diagnostic dyspraxia in epileptics following partial and complete section of the corpus callosum. *American Journal of Psychiatry* 101, 594–9.

Bogen, J. E. (1981) Mental numerosity: Is one head better than two? *Behavioral and Brain Sciences* 4: 1, 100–1.

Cabeza, R. (2002) Hemispheric asymmetry reduction in older adults: the HAROLD model. *Psychology of Aging* 17: 1, 85–100.

Colvin, M. K., Funnell, M. G., and Gazzaniga, M. S. (2005) Numerical processing in the two hemispheres: studies of a split-brain patient. *Brain and Cognition* 57: 1, 43–52.

Cooney, J. W. and Gazzaniga, M. S. (2003) Neurological disorders and the structure of human consciousness. *Trends in Cognitive Sciences* 7: 4, 161–5.

Dennett, D. C. (1991) *Consciousness Explained*. Boston, MA: Little, Brown, and Company.

Doty, R. W. and Negrao, N. (1973) Forebrain commissures and vision. In R. Jung (ed.), *Handbook of Sensory Physiology* 7: 3, 543–82. Berlin: Springer Verlag.

Eccles, J. C. (1973) *The Understanding of the Brain*. New York: McGraw-Hill.

Eliassen, J. C., Baynes, K., and Gazzaniga, M. S. (1999) Direction information coordinated via the posterior third of the corpus callosum during bimanual movements. *Experimental Brain Research* 128, 573–7.

Eliassen, J. C., Baynes, K., and Gazzaniga, M. S. (2000) Anterior and posterior callosal contributions to simultaneous bimanual movements of the hands and fingers. *Brain* 123: 12, 2501–11.

Feinberg, T. E., Schindler, R. J., Flanagan, N. G., and Haber, L. D. (1992) Two alien hand syndromes. *Neurology* 42: 1, 19–24.

Fodor, J. (1983) *The Modularity of Mind*. Cambridge, MA: MIT Press.

Franz, E., Ivry, R., and Gazzaniga, M. S. (1996) Dissociation of spatial and temporal coupling in the bimanual movements of callosotomy patients. *Psychological Science* 7, 306–10.

Gazzaniga, M. S. (1995) Consciousness and the cerebral hemispheres. In M. S. Gazzaniga (ed.), *The Cognitive Neurosciences*, 1391–400. Cambridge, MA: MIT Press.

Gazzaniga, M. S. (2000) Cerebral specialization and interhemispheric communication: Does the corpus callosum enable the human condition. *Brain* 123, 1293–1326.

Heilman, K. M. and van den Abell, T. (1980) Right hemisphere dominance for attention: the mechanism underlying hemispheric asymmetries of inattention (neglect). *Neurology* 30, 327–30.

Holtzman, J. D. and Gazzaniga, M. S. (1982) Dual task interactions due exclusively to limits in processing resources. *Science* 218: 4579, 1325–7.

Holtzman, J. D. and Gazzaniga, M. S. (1985) Enhanced dual task performance following corpus commissurotomy in humans. *Neuropsychologia* 23: 3, 315–21.

Innocenti, G. M. (1986) General organization of callosal connections in the cerebral cortex. In A. Peters and E. G. Jones (eds.), *Cerebral Cortex* 5, 291–353. New York: Plenum Press.

Langers, D. R. M., van Dijk, P., and Backes, W. H. (2005) Lateralization, connectivity and plasticity in the human central auditory system. *NeuroImage* 28: 2, 490–9.

Lavidor, M. and Walsh, V. (2004) The nature of foveal representation. *Nature Reviews: Neuroscience* 5, 729–35.

Luck, S. J., Hillyard, S. A., Mangun, G. R., and Gazzaniga, M. S. (1989) Independent hemispheric attentional systems mediate visual search in split-brain patients. *Nature* 342: 6249, 543–55.

Nagel, T. (1971) Brain bisection and the unity of consciousness. *Synthese* 22, 396–413.

Penfield, W. (1966) Speech, perception and the cortex. In J. C. Eccles (ed.), *Brain and Conscious Experience*. New York: Springer-Verlag.

Puccetti, R. (1981) The case for mental duality: evidence from split-brain data and other considerations. *Behavioral and Brain Sciences* 4: 1, 93–123.

Reuter-Lorenz, P. A. and Fendrich, R. (1990) Orienting attention across the vertical meridian: evidence from callosotomy patients. *Journal of Cognitive Neuroscience* 2, 232–7.

Sperry, R. (1984) Consciousness, personal identity and the divided brain. *Neuropsychologia* 22: 6, 661–73.

Sperry, R. (1990) Forebrain commissurotomy and conscious awareness. In C. B. Trevarthen (ed.), *Brain Circuits and Functions of the Mind: Essays in Honor of Roger W. Sperry*. Cambridge: Cambridge University Press.

Toyama, K., Matsunami, K., Ono, T., and Tokashiki, S. (1974) An intracellular study of neuronal organization in the visual cortex. *Experimental Brain Research* 21, 45–66.

Toyama, K., Tokashiki, S., and Matsunami, K. (1969) Synaptic action of commissural impulses upon association efferent cells in cat visual cortex. *Brain Research* 14: 2, 518–20.

Trevarthen, C. (1962) Double visual learning in split-brain monkeys. *Science* 136, 258–9.

Wada, J. (1949) A new method for determination of the side of cerebral speech dominance: a preliminary report on the intracarotid injection of sodium amytal in man. *Iqakaa te Seibutzuqaki* 14, 221–2.

15

Philosophical Psychopathology and Self-Consciousness

G. LYNN STEPHENS AND GEORGE GRAHAM

Introduction

Much that goes seriously awry or inescapably amiss in consciousness and behavior – in action, memory, emotion, reason, and perception – is the focus of a field at the intersection of philosophy and psychiatry that is known as philosophical psychopathology (cf. Graham & Stephens 1994; Graham 2002; Fulford, Thornton, & Graham 2006). One of the most compelling features of this field consists in its recognition that while our capacities for self-consciousness and self-identification help to distinguish us as persons and agents from animals of lesser orders of psychological sophistication, these capacities are fragile. They are vulnerable to breakdown and disorder, and therein are the source of much that is puzzling and difficult in various psychopathologies and symptoms of mental disorder or illness (cf. Stephens & Graham 2000; Graham 2004). So, no companion to consciousness studies is complete without attention to the philosophical psychopathology of self-consciousness.

Perhaps the most obvious topic to which to attend is the fact that, to echo a remark of Harry Frankfurt appropriated from another context, the capacity for self-consciousness that is "characteristic of human beings makes us susceptible to an inner division in which we separate from . . . ourselves" (2004, p. 18). Our vulnerability to division or self separation is not restricted to psychopathologies, of course, as Frankfurt's discussions of identification and externality in human non-pathological mental life make clear, but such divisions are most vivid and difficult to comprehend in cases of mental illness or disorder. This chapter is about susceptibility to one type of division within our selves that can occur within self-conscious experience and is present in certain mental disorders. This is the separation between experiencing oneself as subject and as agent. In the following pages we consider some disorders of self-consciousness and examine the role that this particular division may play in those disorders.

We begin in "My Body, My Mind" by noting that conscious identification of one's thoughts as one's own seems to enjoy epistemic privilege. The self-possession of thought appears somehow to be given in self-consciousness or self-awareness and is not inferred. I don't have to note the presence of a thought in my stream of consciousness and then infer or decide that it is mine (cf. Shoemaker 1986 and Kriegel 2004). The next three sections then discuss various mental disorders or symptoms of disorder that raise the possibility of misattribution of one's thoughts and of division in one's sense of self between being subject and agent. The closing sections of the chapter describe the division in question and discuss some of its implications for understanding the unity of self-consciousness and the phenomenal experience of being oneself.

My Body, My Mind

We are all familiar with the distinction between seeing something and seeing it as something. Once, one of us looked for himself in a photograph of several dozen people at a professional society meeting. The photo had been taken more than two dozen years ago. He couldn't find himself. As it turned out, he was, several times, looking right at himself, but this was not the person whom he identified as himself. He didn't recognize himself in the photo. He saw himself but did not see himself as himself.

Though we persons, in such and related manners, are sometimes unable to identify or apprehend ourselves as ourselves, such failures of self-identification or self-recognition seem not to be part of the episodes of thinking and feeling that occur in our stream of consciousness. It is hard to imagine having trouble recognizing or identifying one's thoughts or feelings as one's own. In *The Principles of Psychology* (1918), William James writes: "The elementary psychic fact is not *thought* or *this thought*, but *my thought*." "The universal conscious fact is not, 'Feelings and thoughts exist,' but 'I think' and 'I feel'" (vol 1, p. 226).

James, it seems, is right. I do not first come across a thought or feeling and then attempt to decide whether it is my thought or feeling, in the way, for example, I might come across a photographic image of myself in a crowd of people and then try to identify which person in the photo I am.

Notoriously, however, mental disorder unravels what experience seems to weave seamlessly together. It prizes apart otherwise inseparable elements of our psychic lives. Korsakoff's syndrome, for instance, leaves recollection of temporally distant events intact while disrupting recall of more recent events, thereby revealing a distinction between long-term and short-term memory that may not be apparent to casual introspection (cf. Kopelman 1996, pp. 428–36). Prosopagnosia, a form of visual agnosia, demonstrates that face recognition is not simply the application of a general ability to visually identify familiar objects (cf. Young 1996, pp. 341–5). It is a perceptual skill distinct and isolable in itself. Similarly unexpected divisions may take place in the experience of being self-conscious. Self-consciousness may contain isolable or divisible elements that may not be apparent in normal introspective experience.

Freud inspected the unapparent. Freud (1962, p. 13) remarked that "pathology has made us acquainted with a great number of states in which the boundary line between the ego and the external world becomes uncertain or in which they are actually drawn incorrectly." To which he adds: "There are cases in which parts of a person's own body, even portions of his mental life – his perceptions, thoughts, and feelings – appear alien to him and as not belonging to his own ego." Freud suggests that psychopathological phenomena sometimes blur the line between self and non-self. In a disordered or disorientated condition I might perceive some feature of myself without recognizing it as my own. Indeed, the feature may seem "alien" to me and as belonging to another person.

With respect to identifying one's body, Freud's suggestion surely is correct. People do sometimes perceive their own bodies or parts of their bodies as alien or belonging to another. A case in tragic point is reported in the *British Journal of Psychiatry* (Ames 1984), in which a patient insisted that a head, belonging to his wife's gynecologist, was attached between the patient's shoulders. The head, he said, spoke to him with the doctor's voice. In attempting to silence it, the patient shot himself through the palate. The neurologist V. S. Ramachandran describes a woman, rendered hemiplegic by a stroke, who claimed to have full use of her now paralyzed left arm. When the doctor called her attention to the arm lying immobile at her side, she denied that it was her arm and described it as belonging to her brother (Ramachandran & Blakeslee 1998, p. 2).

Yet thoughts and feelings seem to relate very differently epistemically to the human capacity for self-identification than do bodies or body parts. Is misattribution possible regarding episodes of one's own conscious mental life? I see bodies other than my own. So, it makes perfectly good sense to suppose that I must have some means of telling whether a body that I see belongs to me or to someone else. So perhaps it's not surprising that I might, under certain circumstances, perceive my own body but mistake it for someone else's body. Introspection, however, unlike a photographic image, gives me direct access only to one person viz., me. Any thoughts or feelings with which I am directly presented on introspection or of which I am immediately aware must be my own. So, how could there be conceptual room for error or misidentification here?

Searching for Real Cases of Misidentification

The question is not entirely speculative either, for remember Freud's comment about pathology. Consider the following remarks about hallucinations. Here is one from Slade and Bentall (1988): "There is a fundamental assumption about the nature of hallucinations that all theories have in common, that hallucinators mistake their own internal, mental, or private events for external or publicly observable events" (p. 205). Here is another from McGuire et al. (1996): "Auditory verbal hallucinations are related to the psychotic patient's own verbal thoughts. They arise when verbal thoughts are misrecognized as being of alien [non-self] origin and are perceived as external voices" (p. 148).

Or consider the following observation about delusions of thought insertion, made by Sims (1995): "In thought insertion [the patient] experiences thoughts that do not have the feeling of being his own, but he feels that they have been put into his mind without his own volition, from the outside. There is clearly a disturbance of self-image, and especially in the boundary between what is self and what is not" (p. 152).

Also worth mentioning is the experience of "alters" or "alternate personalities" in Multiple Personality Disorder (Dissociative Identity Disorder). These experiences provide particularly striking examples of seemingly alienated awareness of one's own thoughts. Patients attribute their thoughts and feelings, even their dreams, to another person with whom the patient shares her body. Bliss (1986) records one such case: "Joy is happy and playful, so sometimes when I'm down she becomes me. Sometimes it cheers me up, but sometimes it is only Joy who is happy and I'm still upset" (p. 231).

Let us label the sort of misidentification of episodes of mind of interest to us here by saying the following: A person who is introspectively or directly aware of some episode in her conscious mental life or psychological history, but fails to recognize this episode as her own and attributes it to another person or agent, experiences *alienated self-consciousness*. In alienated self-consciousness, people experience their own conscious episodes as those of another person or agent and therein fail to identify their own thoughts or feelings as their own. Or so it seems from the quotes cited above and other examples that could be mentioned. However, before we conclude that such cases constitute existence proofs for alienated self-consciousness, we need to examine them. Should we take them at face value? Is self-consciousness truly alienated in such cases? What more is involved in my recognition that I think a certain thought other than my introspective awareness of its occurrence? In answering these and related questions, let us first examine the case of Multiple Personality Disorder.

Multiple Personality Disorder and Self-Consciousness

The *Diagnostic and Statistical Manual* of the American Psychiatric Association (APA 1994) defines Multiple Personality Disorder (now officially designated as Dissociative Identity Disorder) as: "The presence of two or more distinct identities or personality states, each with its own relatively enduring pattern of perceiving, relating to, and thinking about the environment and the self. At least two of these personality states recurrently take control of the person's behavior" (p. 487).

Typically the "presenting" personality – the one who seeks medical assistance – professes to be unaware of any other personalities ("alters") and is amnesic concerning events that happened when other alters were "out"; in other words in control of the person's body. (Generally, it is concern about such "blackouts" that leads the presenting personality to seek medical advice.) However, the patient usually harbors other personalities that are much more in the purported know. For example, suppose that the patient's presenting personality is called "Wilma," a timid, fastidious, abstemious young woman. Wilma visits the doctor complaining of headaches and blackouts. On examination (perhaps under hypnosis) the patient exhibits another personality, Fred. Fred is an assertive slob who smokes, drinks, and abuses amphetamines. Though Wilma seems unaware of Fred's existence, Fred claims to know all about Wilma. He knows what she does, what she thinks and feels – even the contents of her dreams. However despite this intimate acquaintance, Fred denies that he is Wilma. Wilma, he says, is afraid of her father, but he, Fred, regards the old man only with contempt. Fred enjoys cigarettes, but reports that smoking gives Wilma a headache.

The excerpt below, recorded in Confer and Ables (1983, p. 131) from a patient's conversation with her therapist, illustrates one alter's comment on another.

Therapist:	"What are the feelings she has trouble with?"
Patient:	"Getting mad. She can't get mad."
Therapist:	"She can't get mad, but you can?"
Patient:	"Oh, yes, I get furious. But she can't get mad."

On the assumption, common among mental health professionals, that alters are not in fact distinct persons sharing a single body, but one person in different modes or guises, when the patient, as Fred, comments on Wilma's fears and headaches, the patient is describing her own fears and pains. In her "Fred-mode," however, the patient does not regard these psychological states as her own. She denies that she is the subject in whom these fears and pains occur. They are, she insists, Wilma's pains, not her own.

Accepting the above (one person, different modes) as an accurate representation of the experience of alters in MPD, it certainly suggests something interesting about one's sense of self – at least one's retrospective sense of self. It shows that I can remember episodes in my own psychological history without remembering that these episodes happened to me and, in fact, attributing them to another person or agent. That is, for example, I can be aware of my headache at time T and remember that very same headache at a later time T + 1, but sincerely believe that at T it was someone else whose head hurt.

Such cases of retrospective "misidentification" are interesting in their own right, but they are not yet examples of alienated self-consciousness (as defined above). For that, it must also be the case that I'm aware of my headache at T and, at T, I believe that it's someone else's headache. The patient never plays Fred and Wilma at one and the same time, and when she comments, as Fred or Wilma, on the other's mental life, she's commenting from her current perspective on what Fred or Wilma felt at some previous time.

Some students of the MPD phenomenon, it may be noted, believe that one alter's awareness of another is not always retrospective. Alters sometimes claim that they were conscious of another alter's thoughts at the time when the other was thinking those thoughts (cf. Zemach 1986, p. 126). Thus, suppose Fred insists that, even though Wilma was "out," in control of the body, he was still in there looking in on her mental activities. Patient reports of such a phenomenon, sometimes called reports of "intraconsciousness" or "co-consciousness," are taken seriously by some investigators. Wilkes (1988, p. 125) describes a classic case as follows:

> We should observe that Miss Beauchamp's plurality was not only diachronic – Sally, B1, and B4 by turns – but also synchronic. For whenever B1, B2, and B4 were in control, Sally co-existed as a second consciousness, aware of all their actions, and the thoughts of at least B1 and B2, while keeping her own counsel. Her consciousness was substantially independent of that of the personality in charge of the body at the time. Sally observed, as an amused spectator, B1's dreams, even being able to give a fuller account of then than B1.

So Miss Beauchamp, speaking as Sally, claims to have been aware of the episodes in a dream as they unfolded, and to have experienced this event, not as her own dream, but as someone else's dream. Wilkes treats this as an instance of (what we are calling) alienated self-consciousness. She maintains that, despite their high degree of functional independence, Sally and B1 are states of the same person: Miss Beauchamp. Though Miss Beauchamp enjoys a multiplex mental life, she thinks both Sally's thoughts and B1's thoughts. When Sally looks in on B1's thoughts or dreams, Miss Beauchamp undergoes an alienated experience of her own mental life.

One might resist this conclusion, of course. Zemach (1986) argues that Sally, B1, and Miss Beauchamp are so distinct that they must be regarded as separate persons. In such a case, Sally's awareness of B1's thoughts does not count as an instance of self-consciousness. Sally correctly rejects the suggestion that these are her thoughts. As Zemach interprets it, Sally's awareness of B1's thoughts represents a case in which one person has direct (presumably introspective) access to another's thoughts, not an instance of alienated self-consciousness. Introspection, then, for Zemach, is not necessarily a capacity to look within one's own mind; in rare cases one can have direct access to episodes in the mind of another person.

Or, in an alternative interpretation of MPD that still resists description as a case of alienated self-consciousness, one might take a skeptical attitude toward the reality of co-consciousness period. Experiences of co-consciousness get reported after the fact. Sally claims that, although she wasn't "out" when B1 was dreaming, she was concurrently aware of B1's dream. Does this represent an accurate report of a previous experience of co-

consciousness, or an *ex post facto* reconstruction or confabulation of what Sally ought to have experienced had she been co-conscious with B1? It is difficult to rule out the possibility of confabulation or clinically induced fabrication (or worse deception) here – possibilities which threaten, more generally, to undermine the reality as the illness of MPD itself (cf. Spanos 1996). It would be theoretically prudent, therefore, not to let the argument for the reality of alienated self-consciousness hinge just on evidence drawn from the study of MPD. MPD is too interpretatively contestable in its own right to bear the weight of being an existence proof for alienated self-consciousness.

Can human beings have an experience of alienated self-consciousness that does not rest on some controversial interpretation of MPD?

A Case of Alienated Self-Consciousness

Let us examine, next, the case of verbal auditory hallucinations. Investigators often say that hallucinations involve "loss of ego boundaries" or "internal/external confusion." Snyder (1974) describes verbal auditory hallucinations or (as they often are called) "voices" as follows: "The voices are strictly the patient's own verbal thoughts, which he has chosen, presumably without conscious awareness, to project onto the external world" (p. 121).

Slade and Bentall (1988) maintain that hallucinators, in general, regardless of the form of hallucination, verbal or otherwise, "mistake their own internal, mental events, for external" events (p. 205). Taken literally, this view supposes that the hallucinator is in fact aware of an episode in his mental life, but mistakenly believes this very episode to be occurring outside his own mind. However, Slade and Bentall's reading surely is an uncharitable interpretation of the hallucinator's error. No doubt, the hallucinator has the impression that something occurs in the external world when it really "exists" only in his imagination (e.g., a giant rabbit or some person speaking to him). But one can explain his misimpression without supposing that he believes of one of his mental events that it itself is occurring outside his psychological history. Rather, he mistakes one sort of mental event, an imagined experience, for another, a veridical sensory perception. He believes that he sees a giant rabbit – and, hence that a giant rabbit exists in his external environment – but he doesn't believe that his perception of the rabbit occurs outside his ego boundary. Indeed, speaking more carefully in the language of source or origin and not episode, Slade and Bentall (1988) say that the hallucinatory subject "misattributes his or her self-generated private events to a source external to him- or herself" (p. 214). In other words, the error of hallucination concerns the source or cause of the hallucinatory experience: not its location or the hallucinator's external environment. The victim of hallucination takes his experience to have been caused by physical interaction with a giant rabbit when, in reality, its causes are exclusively internal.

We shall have more to say about hallucinations later in the chapter, but for the present, we wish to note that they do not represent cases in which someone experiences his own mental episodes as external or alien. The hallucinatory experience is thought by the hallucinator to be his experience. The episode is in him and he recognizes this even though he is in error about the intentional content of the hallucination (e.g., a giant rabbit). So, now in continuing to search for a case of alienated self-consciousness, let us examine, third, the phenomenon of thought insertion.

Fish (1962) writes: "Thinking, like all conscious activities, is experienced as an activity which is being carried on by the subject. There is a quality of 'my-ness' connected with thought. In schizophrenia this sense of the possession of one's own thoughts may be impaired and the patient may suffer from alienation of thought. [The patient] is certain that alien thoughts have been inserted into his mind" (p. 48). Frith (1992) quotes one patient's account: "Thoughts are put into my mind like 'kill God.' It is just like my mind working, but it isn't. They come from this chap, Chris. They are his thoughts" (p. 66). Finally Mellor (1970) recounts a particularly vivid description of one of his patients: "I look out the window and I think that the garden looks nice and the grass looks cool, but the thoughts of Eamonn Andrews come into my mind. There are no other thoughts there, only his. He treats my mind like a screen and flashes thoughts onto it like you flash a picture" (p. 17).

Such assertions, of course, are bizarre, but, alas, delusions of thought insertion are not particularly rare. One extensive survey reported that 52 percent of schizophrenic patients reported them (Sartorius et al. 1977). They are, after verbal hallucinations, probably the "positive" symptom of schizophrenia that is most widely discussed in the psychiatric literature. Investigators do not suspect patients of confabulating stories about thought insertion to please their therapists. So it seems they count as genuine instances of alienated self-consciousness, if anything does.

One might wonder, however, whether reports of thought insertion really do describe experiences of alienated self-consciousness. Perhaps they represent the patient's attempt to express, metaphorically, her feeling or belief that another person influences or controls her thinking. People do suffer delusions of thought control, but these consist in believing that someone else causes me to think certain thoughts, not the conviction that the thoughts themselves are not my own. Clinicians are well aware of this possibility, and so maintain that each thought insertion and thought control are distinct delusions. Fulford (1989, p. 221), for example, writes:

> The normal experience of one's own thoughts being influenced is like thought insertion to the extent that it is something that is 'done to or happens' to one. But the similarity is only superficial. [I]n the normal case, that which is being done or is happening to one is simply the *influencing* of one's thoughts, whereas in the case of thought insertion it is (bizarrely) the thinking itself.

Wing (1978) likewise remarks that "the symptom is not that [the patient] has been caused to have unusual thoughts, but that the thoughts *themselves* are not his own" (p. 105).

According to the standard or traditional account of thought insertion, the patient is aware of her own thoughts, but denies that they are hers and attributes them to someone else. So, thought insertion certainly seems to constitute alienated awareness of one's own thoughts. It seems to be a case of alienated self-consciousness. Is it?

Thought Insertion

In order to be clear about whether thought insertion counts as a genuine case of alienated self-consciousness, we need to be clear about an interpretative puzzle raised by patient reports of the phenomenon. The patient's attitude toward her alien thoughts is not merely bizarre. It appears conceptually inconsistent. Notice that, while the patient denies that the alien thoughts are her own, she admits that they occur in her mind. Contrast this with what is supposed to happen in MPD. Sally does not say that B1's thoughts occur in Sally's mind: she says that she is aware of thoughts occurring in B1's mind. Assuming that only one person or subject is involved in the experience of co-consciousness, this person could be truly said to have lost track of her ego boundaries. She is conscious of a thought, which she takes to be happening in another's mind, when in fact that thought is an event in her own psychological history. She misidentifies this thought relative to her self/non-self boundary. She thinks it lies outside her, but in fact it lies inside.

This is not the error made by victims of thought insertion. Patients undergoing thought insertion do not mistake the location of their thoughts. They know in which subject the alien thought occurs: it is in their mind. "Thoughts are put into my mind." They have not lost sight of their ego boundaries. Rather, they feel or believe that another person or agent has penetrated or transgressed those boundaries and inserted an alien thought inside their mind. As Fish (1962) notes, this sense that the other invades one's own mind forms an essential part of the experience. As he puts it, "in thought alienation [i.e., thought insertion] the patient has the experience that others are participating in his thinking." "He feels that thoughts are being inserted into his mind and he recognizes them as foreign and coming from without" (p. 49). The patient does not suppose that she has special access to someone else's mind. She believes that Mr. Andrews (a TV personality) has access to her mind.

It is helpful here to draw a distinction in order to clearly describe just what is *not* going on in the self-conscious experience of a victim of thought insertion. Let us distinguish a person's introspective awareness of her own thoughts from her sense that these thoughts occur in her mind, that is to say, that she is the subject in whose psychological history these thoughts occur. Call this latter form of awareness one's sense of *subjectivity* or sense of oneself as subject of experience. Describing thought insertion in terms of "loss of ego boundaries" or "internal/external confusion" suggests that the breakdown in normal self-consciousness responsible for delusions of thought insertion involves dissociation between introspective awareness and the sense of subjectivity. So understood, the patient remains introspectively aware of her thoughts, but loses the sense that these episodes occur in her mind. People, however, who suffer from delusions of thought insertion do not undergo such a breakdown. Their sense of subjectivity of their alien thought is intact. But, then, here is a puzzle that threatens conceptual incoherence in patient reports. The patient insists that the thoughts are not her thoughts – that is, they are Mr. Andrews's thoughts – all the while acknowledging that they occur in her mind (and are accessible on introspection). However, as noted earlier, isn't any thought occurring in my mind, as a matter of logical or conceptual necessity, therein mine? I should recognize that a thought is my thought just because it occurs in me.

So, one might suspect that, whatever may occasion claims of thought insertion, reports of thought insertion do not offer an intelligible or conceptually coherent description of a possible experience. Victims do not really *believe* that the thoughts that occur to them are not their own and belong to someone else. But, then, doesn't this mean that inserted thoughts fail to constitute instances of alienated self-consciousness? Before we can accept that experiences of thought insertion are instances of alienated self-consciousness, we still have yet to provide a coherent interpretation of what these patients are telling us.

There is, in addition to the interpretative question, a closely related explanatory puzzle raised by thought insertion. Frith (1992, p. 80) remarks that "thought insertion, in particular, is an experience that is difficult to understand." He notes that the fact that people have such experiences suggests that "we have some way of recognizing our own thoughts." "It is as if each thought had a label on it saying 'mine.' If the labeling process goes wrong, then the thought would be perceived as alien" (pp. 80–1). But however sincere a report of thought insertion might be, there is "no possibility of having thoughts other than our own." So, puzzles Frith, what could be the point of having a "monitoring system" that decides whether a thought presented to my introspective awareness is my thought or someone else's thought? (Frith & Done 1988, p. 438) True, postulating the existence of such a monitoring system might allow us to explain thought insertion by invoking some sort of breakdown in the system. But, what useful task would this hypothetical system do for us when it is working properly?

The question being asked is not why we as persons have a capacity for introspection. In introspection the mind monitors its own contents. The question being asked is why we might have an ownership monitoring system that might somehow underpin nearly every mental operation – not just introspection – aligning some thoughts with a sense of being mine or self possession and others not.

Consider, by way of a contrasting case, the proposal that verbal auditory hallucinations result from the breakdown of a monitoring system that determines whether an experience of verbal imagery represents auditory perception of one's own inner speech. I am aware both of what others say to me and of what I say to myself. If I am to preserve a sense of the coherence of my own thinking and to respond appropriately to others, I need somehow to keep track of or monitor which episodes of awareness are auditory perceptual and which introspective. But what comparable story could we tell about a system that monitors whether a thought is mine or someone else's thought? Isn't it obvious that I don't have to figure out the source or ownership of thoughts which present themselves to me?

Frith tries to answer this explanatory question by proposing that the monitoring system whose breakdown results in delusions of thought insertion is not in the business of distinguishing one's own from other people's thoughts. Rather, it is in the business of monitoring whether I intended to think a given thought. Some thoughts occur in me as a result of my intention to (for example) solve a certain problem or attend to or carry out a certain cognitive task. Other thoughts come to me unbidden due to causes independent of my current goals and ongoing projects. Frequently such unintended thoughts are, in Frith's terminology, "stimulus driven," that is, more or less automatic responses to environmental events. Pathological impairment of this monitoring system might lead me to experience my intended thoughts as stimulus-driven responses to external events and thus as not mine.

Frith is clearly motivated by the notion that thoughts are very often parts of purposive mental activities or mental actions and somehow owe their occurrence to conditions of their intentional generation (cf. Campbell 1999 and Gallagher 2000). Recognizing the prominence of delusions of thought insertion in schizophrenia, Frith (1992) comments as follows:

> How could failure of central monitoring give rise to schizophrenia symptoms? I suggest that a failure to monitor intentions to act would result in delusions of control and other passivity experiences. Thinking, like all of our actions, is normally accompanied by a sense of effort and deliberate choice as we move from one thought to the next. If we found ourselves thinking without any awareness of the sense of effort that reflects central monitoring, we might well experience these thoughts as alien and, thus, being inserted into our minds. (p. 81)

In other words, for Frith, failure of central monitoring might cause me to experience a thought as unintended by me, and that particular feature of experience might somehow also lead me to infer or believe that the thought is alien, i.e., not my own but someone else's.

Frith's specific strategy for resolving the explanatory puzzle about thought insertion by appeal to monitoring invites further exploration for several reasons. Only two can be mentioned here (see also Stephens & Graham 2000 and Graham 2004). First, it resembles a proposal, independently developed by Ralph Hoffman (1986), for explaining the occurrence of verbal auditory hallucinations. (We promised to return to the topic of hallucinations and so we will, momentarily.) Second, it suggests a strategy for resolving the conceptual or interpretative puzzle about thought insertion mentioned above.

Trying to Resolve the Interpretative Puzzle

Remember, here is the puzzle. If reports of thought insertion are intelligible or coherent, it seems that they cannot be reports of dissociation between introspection of one's thoughts, on the one hand, and one's sense of subjectivity with respect to them, on the other. That specific sort of dissociation appears precluded by the fact that victims of thought insertion report inserted thoughts as occurring in them. Their sense of subjectivity or ego boundary is not lost. So, then, what else could they be reports of? When we are aware of thoughts occurring in us as subjects, how can these thoughts be experienced as those of another person or agent?

As we noted earlier, verbal hallucinations, as traditionally described, are not instances of alienated self-consciousness. The patient mistakes his awareness of the "voice" for the perception of something external, but does not suppose that the episode of "perception" itself is external. However, there is an element of alienation in verbal hallucinations. It is just that it does not occur in the patient's sense of subjectivity. It occurs in a different sense of oneself entirely. The patient produces the speech uttered by the voice, but supposes that the speech is produced or generated by someone else. He is talking (silently) to himself, but believes that another is doing the talking and that he is only listening.

According to a traditional account, the patient takes himself to be hearing another person speak rather than himself speaking because, in verbal hallucinations, his experience of his own inner speech bears a strong qualitative or phenomenological resemblance to what he typically feels when he hears another speak. Hoffman (1986) argues, however, that the weight of clinical evidence does not support this traditional hypothesis. Hallucinators generally do not describe voices as qualitatively or phenomenally similar to ordinary audition or speech perception. Quite often they remark that their experience of the voice is not unlike their normal experience of their own inner speech (cf. Hoffman 1986, pp. 503–5). So what leads them to judge that their experience of voices is a perception of another's speech?

Hoffman's proposal is that the "verbal imagery," or inner speech, seems alien because the patient experiences it as personally unintended. That is, the patient does not have the sense that he intended to say to himself what the voice tells him. By contrast in normal speech perception, awareness of unintended verbal imagery derives from perception of another person's speech. As Hoffman (1986) describes it, perceiving one's own speech as the hearing of another's speech "is plausible because the great abundance of images experienced as unintended during the day are sensory impressions derived from the outside world" (p. 509). Such voices do not appear to belong, to the patient, in what might be called his "field of intentional speech act activity" but rather belong in the category of the intentional speech acts of another person or agent.

Hoffman's tale about the alien character of voices, like Frith's story about thought insertion, involves more than the hypothesis that patients experience their alien mental activities as unintended (or unbidden). In both stories, however, it is the patient's impression that he did not intend or actively produce a given episode in his mental life that first arouses his suspicion that the episode is somehow alien – not his but another's.

So, again, suppose as a victim of thought insertion I admit that a thought occurred in my mind. How can I deny, intelligibly, it as my thought? To help to answer this question, and with ideas of both Frith and Hoffman fresh in our mind, let us go back briefly to Frankfurt, a philosophical author mentioned at the very beginning of the chapter.

Frankfurt (1988, p. 59) insists that "it is not incoherent, despite the air of paradox, to say that a thought occurring in my mind may or may not be something that *I think*." The air of paradox vanishes, Frankfurt claims, if we consider a similar point concerning bodily behavior. I may admit that my arm moved, but deny that I moved my arm. My arm might move due to causes that have nothing to do with what I want or intend: in response, e.g., to an epileptic seizure or electric shock. In such cases, I recognize that I am the person whose arm moved, but I deny, correctly, that I moved the arm or that I am the agent of the movement. That is, I deny that moving my arm was my action: something that I did (cf. Frankfurt 1988, p. 61).

Frankfurt argues that the same applies to "movements" of or episodes in my mind. I may have the sense of actively directing and controlling my thoughts. Thinking can itself seem like a species of action. It may be not like ideas just passing unbidden through the mind, but as (to co-opt some words of D. M. Armstrong [1999, p. 118]) "doing something purposive inside the head." True, thoughts can, of course, also arise in me unbidden and seem to occur independent of my intentions. This happens, for example, when an irritating advertising slogan keeps running through my head. But as Frankfurt notes (1988, p. 59):

> the thoughts that beset us in those ways do not occur by our own active doing . . . It is tempting, indeed, to suggest that they are not thoughts that *we think* at all, but rather thoughts that we *find* occurring within us. This would express our sense that, although these thoughts are events in the histories of our minds, we do not actively participate in their occurrence. A thought that occurs in my mind may or may not be something that *I think*.

Frankfurt's remarks suggest that I may experience a thought as mine in two quite different senses or ways. One consists in experiencing my self as subject of the thought. I am conscious of a thought as mine *subjectively* insofar as it presents itself to me. Precisely just what this involves is worth independent and detailed discussion that cannot be undertaken here (compare Kriegel 2004 with Kennedy and Graham in press). But the other, the second way, consists of experiencing my self as actively involved in the thought – as thinker or agent behind it. Let us say that this experience of being the agent exhibits my sense (not of subjectivity) but of *agency* regarding the thought. I am conscious of the thought as mine, in this second or agentic sense, insofar as I represent thinking it as my deed.

No doubt the distinction between the senses of subjectivity and agency with respect to thought requires analysis or unpacking. We have tried to do that elsewhere (Stephens & Graham 2000 and Graham 2004). But even pending further analysis, the distinction seems, at least initially, to clarify something about what victims of thought insertion report when they report inserted thoughts. It also offers a solution to the interpretative or conceptual puzzle about thought insertion.

Interpretation and Explanation

The solution to the interpretative puzzle goes like this: When the patient denies that the "alien" thought is hers, all the while insisting that it occurs in her mind, she is not saying something that is incoherent, unintelligible, or inconsistent. Rather, she is denying that she is the *thinker* (mental agent) of the thought. She is saying that *thinking* it is not something she is doing. But she also is acknowledging that she is the subject of the thought; it occurs in her mind. So, her beliefs about this thought may be false, or even delusional, but they are not unintelligible or incoherent. She is saying that the thought is hers insofar as it occurs in her, but not hers in the sense that she is not its author or agent. "It's in me but not mine."

The distinction between the sense of self as subject and as agent also recommends itself as part of the psychological explanation for why I might attribute thoughts that occur to me to another person or agent. Consider, again, an instance of overt behavior. Just as I may admit that my arm moved while denying that I moved my arm, I may also believe that someone else moved my arm. I might feel that another caused my arm to move, e.g., by grasping and lifting my arm, or by electrically stimulating my deltoid muscles. In such a case, moving my arm is another person's deed, not my own. Interestingly, there is a class of delusions that involves precisely the supposition that someone else is moving my body. Mellor (1970, p. 18) quotes a patient's description of an experience of possession as follows: "When I reach for the comb it is my hand and arm which move, [but] I don't control them. I sit watching them and they are quite independent, what they do is nothing to do with me. I am just a puppet manipulated by cosmic strings." Bliss (1986, p. 140) describes a patient who "despondent and guilty on the anniversary of her mother's death, watched another personality put her arm in a fire. The patient had no control over the movement and felt the pain as she watched the skin char."

Our proposal is that thought insertion consists of an analogous experience of mental activity. That is, the patient believes that another person is the agent or thinker of thoughts occurring in her mind. So, although she recognizes that the relevant thoughts occur in her, she believes that Mr. Andrews is the agent who thinks them. Her sense of self as subject is decoupled from her sense of self as agent. It is as if her stream of consciousness has become occupied by another person or agent.

The hypothesis outlined above of distinguishing between the senses of subjectivity and agency in order to resolve the interpretative puzzle, and therein also to suggest an account of the alien character of thought insertion, dovetails nicely with Firth's and Hoffman's independent proposals. Remember, each attempts to connect experience of alienation with experience of unintendedness. The patient's sense that she didn't intend to think a certain thought or to say something to herself might well lead her to believe that she was not the agent of the relevant episode of thinking or inner speech. But should she believe or feel, in addition, that intentions from a source other than her self gave rise to these episodes, she may attribute the relevant thought or speech to another person or agent.

Indeed, recognizing the role of the sense of agency in the experience of verbal hallucination helps to resolve a problem about voices overlooked by Hoffman. In Hoffman's account, the patient's belief that she really *hears* the voice explains her inference that she is not producing the voice herself. But, investigators have often observed that, even patients who are firmly convinced that their voices represent communications from another person may be well aware that they are not really *hearing* anything when the voice speaks to them. Allen, Halpern, and Friend (1985, p. 603) describe one patient's experience as follows: "The voices are not received as auditory events coming from without through the ears. They feel distant and diffuse, 'like thoughts,' she adds ironically. 'Ironically' because she cannot accept them as her thoughts, but as messages sent to her by a being external to herself." Investigators have marked the difference between auditory and non-auditory verbal hallucinations by introducing distinctive terminology such as "psychosensory hallucinations" vs. "psychic hallucinations" or "outer voices" vs. "inner voices" (cf. Stephens & Graham 2000).

Perhaps surprisingly, patients who recognize that the voice occurs only in their minds are just as prone to regard them as genuine communications from another person, as patients who describe their voices as robustly auditory. Such alien but non-auditory voices, raise interpretative problems similar to those posed by alien (inserted) thoughts. If a person recognizes that she is not listening to someone else's external speech, that the voice is in her mind, how can she intelligibly or consistently insist that it is another's speech? The hypothesis that she regards another as the agent of a speech act occurring in her mind provides a plausible interpretation of the alien character of nonauditory voices. To the patient, the voice may seem to betray an agency, intelligence, or intentionality, which accounts for its salience, coherence, and communicative directedness (cf. Stephens & Graham 2000).

Conclusion

We have learned something. James's "elementary psychic fact" – *my thought* rather than *this thought*, not "thoughts exist" but "I think" – is interpretatively complex. "My thought" may mean that I experience myself as the subject in whom the thought occurs as well as the agent responsible for its occurrence. But the phenomenon of thought insertion shows that the senses of subjectivity and agency are functionally separable as well as conceptually distinct. Patients suffering from delusions of thought insertion – on our proposed picture – retain the sense of subjectivity of their thoughts, but, in such delusions, lose the sense of self as agent. Whether one may retain one's introspective consciousness of one's thoughts, but lose one's sense of subjectivity, one's sense that thoughts occur in one, remains, in our judgment, unclear. Perhaps such an ego-boundary deficit can only occur with respect to memory of a past introspected state of mind (as may occur in MPD).

Our goal in this chapter has been to examine the relevance of certain disorders or pathologies of self-conscious experience for understanding a capacity within self-consciousness that may not be as vivid or salient in ordinary conscious activity. This is the capacity for a decoupling of the sense of subjectivity from the sense of agency. Philosophers have given a great deal of attention to what it seems or feels like to be the conscious beings that we are. "There is something that it feels like to be oneself," writes Barry Dainton (2000), and this something is part of the "atmosphere of the conscious mind" (p. 32). As this chapter has tried to make plain, the sense of self as mental agent, not just as subject, needs to be given its proper due in any understanding of self-consciousness.

See also 9 Clinical pathologies and unusual experiences; 10 Altered states of consciousness; 13 The case of blindsight; 16 Coming together: The unity of conscious experience; 36 Self-consciousness; 53 Phenomenological approaches to consciousness.

Further Readings

Fulford, K., Thornton, T., and Graham, G. (2005) *Oxford Textbook in Philosophy and Psychiatry.* Oxford: Oxford University Press.

Graham, G. and Stephens, G. L. (eds.) (1994) *Philosophical Psychopathology.* Cambridge, MA: MIT Press.

Graham, G. (2002) Recent work in philosophical psychopathology. *American Philosophical Quarterly* 39, 109–33.

Graham, G. (2004) Self-ascription: thought insertion. In J. Radden (ed.), *The Philosophy of Psychiatry: A Companion*, 89–105. Oxford: Oxford University Press.

References

Allen, J., Halpern, J., and Friend, R. (1985) Removal and diversion tactics and the control of auditory hallucinations. *Behavior Research and Therapy* 23, 601–5.

American Psychiatric Association (1994) *Diagnostic and Statistical Manual of Mental Disorders*, 4th edn. [DSM-IV]. Washington, DC: American Psychiatric Association.

Ames, D. (1984) Self-shooting of a phantom head. *British Journal of Psychiatry* 145, 193–4.

Armstrong, D. (1999) *The Mind–Body Problem: An Opinionated Introduction*. Boulder, CO: Westview Press.

Bliss, E. (1986) *Multiple Personality, Allied Disorders, and Hypnosis*. Oxford: Oxford University Press.

Campbell, J. (1999) Schizophrenia, the space of reasons and thinking as a motor process. *The Monist* 82, 609–25.

Confer, W. and Ables, B. (1983) *Multiple Personality: Etiology, Diagnosis, and Treatment*. New York: Human Sciences Press.

Dainton, B. (2000) *Stream of Consciousness: Unity and Continuity in Conscious Experience*. London: Routledge.

Fish, F. J. (1962) *Fish's Schizophrenia*, 3rd edn., M. Hamilton (ed.). Bristol: Wright.

Frankfurt, H. (1988) *The Importance of What We Care About*. Cambridge: Cambridge University Press.

Frankfurt, H. (2004) *The Reasons of Love*. Princeton, NJ: Princeton University Press.

Freud, S. (1962) *Civilization and Its Discontents*. J. Strachey, trans. Boston, MA: Norton.

Frith, C. (1992) *The Cognitive Neuropsychology of Schizophrenia*. Hillsdale, NJ: Lawrence Erlbaum.

Frith, C. and Done, D. (1988) Towards a neuropsychology of schizophrenia. *British Journal of Psychiatry* 153, 437–43.

Fulford, K. (1989) *Moral Theory and Medical Practice*. Cambridge: Cambridge University Press.

Fulford, K., Thornton, T., and Graham, G. (2006) *Oxford Textbook of Philosophy and Psychiatry*. Oxford: Oxford University Press.

Gallagher, S. (2000) Self-reference and schizophrenia: a cognitive model of immunity to error through misidentification. In D. Zahavi (ed.), *Exploring the Self*, 203–39. Amsterdam: John Benjamins.

Graham, G. (2002) Recent work in philosophical psychopathology. *American Philosophical Quarterly* 39, 109–33.

Graham, G. (2004) Self-ascription: thought insertion. In J. Radden (ed.), *The Philosophy of Psychiatry: A Companion*, 89–105. Oxford: Oxford University Press.

Graham, G. and Stephens, G. L. (eds.) (1994) *Philosophical Psychopathology*. Cambridge: MA: MIT Press.

Hoffman, R. (1986) Verbal hallucinations and language production processes in schizophrenia. *Behavioral and Brain Sciences* 9, 503–17.

James, W. (1918) *The Principles of Psychology*, vol. 1. New York: Dover.

Kennedy, R. and Graham, G. (in press) Extreme self-denial. In M. De Caro, F. Ferretti, and M. Maraffa (eds.), *A Cartography of Mind*. Dordrecht: Kluwer.

Kopleman, M. (1996) Korsakoff's syndrome. In J. Beaumont, P. Kenealy, and M. Rogers (eds.), *Blackwell Dictionary of Neuropsychology*, 428–36. Malden, MA: Blackwell.

Kriegel, U. (2004) Consciousness and self-consciousness. *The Monist* 87, 185–207.

McGuire, P., Silberweig, D., Wright, I., Murray, R., Frackowiak, R., and Frith, C. (1996) The neural correlates of inner speech and auditory verbal imagery in schizophrenia: relationship to auditory verbal hallucinations. *British Journal of Psychiatry* 109, 148–59.

Mellor, C. (1970) First rank symptoms of schizophrenia. *British Journal of Psychiatry* 117, 15–23.

Ramachandran, V. S. and Blakeslee, S. (1994) *Phantoms in the Brain*. New York: William Morrow.

Sartorius, N., Jablensky, R., and Shapiro, R. (1977) Two year follow up of patients included in WHO international pilot study of schizophrenia. *Psychological Medicine* 7, 529–41.

Shoemaker, S. (1986) Introspection and the self. In P. French, T. Uehling, and W. Wettstein (eds.), *Studies in the Philosophy of Mind. Midwest Studies in Philosophy* 10, 101–20. Minneapolis: University of Minnesota.

Sims, W. (1995) *Symptoms in the Mind: An Introduction to Descriptive Phenomenology*, 2nd edn. Philadelphia, PA: Saunders.

Slade, P. and Bentall, R. (1988) *Sensory Deception: A Scientific Analysis of Hallucinations*. Baltimore, MD.: Johns Hopkins University Press.

Snyder, S. (1974) *Madness and the Brain*. New York: McGraw-Hill.

Spanos, N. (1996) *Multiple Identities and False Memories: A Sociocognitive Perspective*. Washington, DC: American Psychological Association.

Stephens, G. L. and Graham, G. (2000) *When Self-Consciousness Breaks: Alien Voices and Inserted Thoughts*. Cambridge, MA: MIT Press.

Wilkes, K. (1988) *Real People: Personal Identity without Thought Experiments*. Oxford: Clarendon.

Wing, J. (1978) *Reasoning about Madness*. Oxford: Oxford University Press.

Young, A. (1996) Face recognition. In J. Beaumont, P. Kennealy, and M. Rogers (eds.), *Blackwell Dictionary of Neuropsychology*, 341–5. Malden, MA: Blackwell.

Zemach, E. (1986) Unconscious mind or conscious minds. In P. French, T. Uehling, and W. Wettstein (eds.), *Studies in the Philosophy of Mind. Midwest Studies in Philosophy* 10, 101–20. Minneapolis: University of Minnosota.

16

Coming Together: The Unity of Conscious Experience

BARRY DAINTON

An Elusive Query

You are, let us suppose, studying a landscape painting hung on a museum wall; while so doing you are absentmindedly playing with a pen, exploring its shape with your fingers, and over to your right you can hear a murmured conversation. The painting, as it features in your consciousness, is a complex of many parts all of which are unified in a distinctive way: you see the depicted tree-covered mountains, the bubbling brook, the frame and surrounding wall. The same applies to your experiences of the pen and the conversation: these too are unified complexes – albeit in different sensory modalities.

As is obvious, our ordinary experience is replete with objects of this kind, and each such object is a unified phenomenal whole – each exemplifies *thematic* or *objectual* unity. But as is equally obvious, our typical streams of consciousness exhibit a more far-reaching kind of unity. Your experiences of the painting, the pen and the conversation are not entirely separate, rather they are themselves unified within your consciousness: they are experienced together, they are *co-conscious*. This mode of unity – *phenomenal unity* – typically extends to the farthest reaches of our consciousness at a given time. Your experience of the painting is experienced along with your tactile explorations of the pen, but also with the remainder of your bodily experience, your conscious thoughts, mental images, and your current emotional feelings. As a first approximation it seems reasonable to suppose that at any one time, all our experiences (all our conscious states) are mutually co-conscious.

Although the character and reach of phenomenal unity is obvious enough when pointed out, it is also easy to overlook. Ask someone to try and describe in as much detail as possible the contents of their consciousness at a given time and they could easily come up with a lengthy list of particular experiences but neglect to mention the fact that these items are all experienced together. Phenomenal unity is such a basic and ubiquitous feature of our consciousness that for the most part we take it for granted. But the fact that it is easy to overlook does not mean it is insignificant, or absent.

This too is easy to appreciate. Suppose it were possible to eradicate all trace of phenomenal unity from one's consciousness at the press of a button. Naturally curious you press the button. What would it be like? What would be *left*? Do entities such as individual conscious thoughts, smells, or sounds possess parts which could become separated? It is not easy to say. One might be inclined to think "We can at least predict what would happen to the visual field: it would surely disintegrate into a constellation of pixel-like points of color."

But this underestimates the depth of the envisaged disintegration. The points in such a constellation – think of how the stars in a night-sky look – are all phenomenally unified, since each point appears at a certain distance from the others. If we remove *all* trace of phenomenal unity each momentary point-color would be experienced all by itself, in total isolation. This simple thought-experiment suggests that experience in the absence of phenomenal unity might be possible, but only experience of the most primitive conceivable kind. Unity is thus a key ingredient in the phenomenological character of the sorts of experience we typically enjoy. (It would be wrong to regard our tendency to overlook phenomenal unity as an instance of *habituation*. An example of the latter is the sound of the ticking clock, which after a while ceases to be experienced at all. Phenomenal unity goes unnoticed, but it remains very much a feature of our ordinary experience – all the time.)

Bringing phenomenal unity into the light of day is one thing, but to understand it fully we would need satisfactory answers to a range of questions, among the most important of which are the following:

1   On the assumption that our unified conscious states are generated by neural activity in our brains, how do our brains do it?

The short answer is we don't yet know. Since it remains a mystery how the brain manages to generate even the simplest forms of consciousness, this is scarcely, surprising, but the unified character of consciousness has proved peculiarly problematic: the more we learn about the brain, the more difficult the problem seems to get. What is now called the "binding problem" (see chapter 47) arose from the discovery that the neural processes associated with seeing shape, color, and location occur in different parts of the brain's visual centers. How do these spatially separated neural systems cooperate to produce unified visual experience of the sort which results from watching a red ball rolling across a green lawn? And what of inter-modal unity, where processes in the auditory and tactile centers of the brain somehow combine to generate phenomenally unified experiences? So intractable is this problem that some have declared it insoluble, and urge us instead to recognize that consciousness is much less unified than we are inclined to believe, much less unified than it seems (Opie & O'Brian 1998). But since – as everyone concedes – there is a lot about the brain that we do not yet understand, this drastic step seems premature. Moving on:

2   How is the unity of consciousness related to other forms of mental unity?

In addition to unified conscious states there are also psychological states and capacities, and these possess a unity of their own, characterizable in part at least in causal or functional terms. How are these related? Are phenomenal unity and psychofunctional unity necessarily correlated, or is some degree of dissociation possible? In extremis, could a single psychological system inform more than one stream of consciousness, or a single stream of consciousness be informed by more than one psychological system? Conceptual and empirical considerations are equally relevant here, but whatever one's philosophical predilections there are findings from psychology and neurology that cannot be ignored, findings which suggest mental disunity can come in many strange shapes and forms. On one interpretation, for example, Multiple Personality (or Associative Identity) Disorder shows that a unified stream of consciousness can be associated with multiple psychological systems (see chapter 15; Radden 1996). Hence, and in a more general vein, our third question:

3 What can be learned from the range of abnormal conditions which appear to impact upon mental unity in general, and the unity of consciousness in particular?

Of particular interest are the consequences of cerebral commissurotomy operations. This procedure involves cutting the main neural pathways linking the cerebral hemispheres. Although under most ordinary circumstances "split-brain" patients behave in a seemingly ordinary way, tests show that under certain circumstances information possessed by the right hemisphere is not passed on to the left hemisphere, and vice versa. Exactly what this result shows remains a matter of controversy (see chapter 14). Whereas some hold that the consciousness of such patients is divided into two distinct streams – perhaps only temporarily, perhaps permanently – the odd behavioral patterns could also be due solely to a fragmentation at the purely cognitive level. As things stand, only one thing is clear: Descartes's confident assertion of the necessary indivisibility of the mind has been cast into serious doubt.

These results also have implications for the possible forms the unity of consciousness can take. Each part of a *fully* unified conscious state is co-conscious with every other part of the same state; in a *partially* unified state, by contrast, although each part is co-conscious with at least one other part, there are also parts that are not co-conscious with each other. It is very natural to suppose that consciousness is always and necessarily fully unified – just try to imagine a conscious state that includes three simultaneous experiences where the first experience is co-conscious with the second, and the second is co-conscious with the third, but the first and the third are not co-conscious. Nonetheless, some have argued (e.g., Lockwood 1989, 1994) that precisely this situation may be realized in the consciousness of split-brain patients, some or all of the time; see Dainton (2005, ch. 4) for further discussion.

Taking a different tack, we can ask:

4 How should the unity of consciousness be understood on the purely phenomenal level? Precisely what sort of unity are we concerned with? What feature or structure of consciousness underpins phenomenal unity?

Since the other issues are well-covered elsewhere in this volume, this is the question I will be focusing on here. It may seem comparatively unglamorous, but the question of how we should make sense of phenomenal unity in experiential terms is by no means a trivial one. The various proposals we shall be considering have very different implications for the structure of consciousness as well as its distinctive mode of unity. The issue also has wider ramifications. We will only be in a position to appreciate fully what is lost if and when the unity of consciousness breaks down if we know what that unity actually involves in the normal run of things; knowing this is also a precondition of properly understanding how phenomenal unity relates to other forms of mental unity, or to the brain. I will start by looking in some detail at synchronic (at-a-time) unity and conclude by taking a brief look at diachronic (over time) unity.

Ownership and awareness

You are a subject of experience, and so am I. At the present time your experiences are phenomenally unified, and so are mine. Such facts suggest a simple and obvious answer to the synchronic unity question:

The Consubjectivity Thesis: a collection of experiences at a given time *t* are phenomenally unified in virtue of belonging to the same subject.

It is certainly difficult to see how experiences could be parts of a unified state of consciousness unless they all belonged to the same subject, but can we confidently rule out the possibility of a single subject having a disunified consciousness? Although on some views of what subjects are – the Cartesian Ego comes to mind – this is impossible, other views have no such implication. More importantly, even if we learned that the Consubjectivity Thesis were true, would we be any more enlightened as to the *nature* of phenomenal unity? Would we have learned much about the character of the connection which binds the constituents of unified conscious states together? It is not obvious that we would. Hence even if true, the Consubjectivity Thesis does not tell us a great deal. The same goes for the following:

The Co-instantiation Thesis: a collection of experiences at a given time *t* are phenomenally unified in virtue of being co-instantiated.

Since properties other than phenomenal properties find themselves co-instantiated – for example, the mass and charge of an electron – the co-instantiation relationship and the phenomenal unity relationship are distinct. Consequently, to learn that unified phenomenal states are always related by the co-instantiation relationship would tell us nothing about the distinctive nature of the phenomenal unity relationship.

If we want a more informative answer to our question we must look elsewhere. Might it be that what unifies a collection of conscious states is another conscious state or process? Might phenomenal unity be a product of a *higher-order* state of consciousness?

One obvious candidate is introspection. If I focus my attention on what I am currently seeing and hearing, then the auditory and visual contents I detect are experienced together. Could phenomenal unity be a product of introspection, thus construed? It seems unlikely. The fact that our consciousness seems unified all the time, despite the fact that we are not introspecting all the time, can be accommodated by holding that experiences are co-conscious in virtue of the fact that they *could* be introspected. The trouble is, intuitively it seems far more plausible to suppose that our experiences are introspectible *because they are phenomenally unified*, rather than the other way about. Even if unity and introspectibility always go hand in hand, the notion that phenomenal unity depends on introspectibility lacks plausibility.

There are other possibilities. Some take the view that all conscious states are necessarily apprehended by a higher-order state, and are so due to the essential internal architecture of consciousness itself. If this were the case, the higher-order state would be an obvious candidate for the unifying agency we are seeking to elucidate. The two principal versions of the so-called "higher-order" conceptions of consciousness both start from the plausible-sounding premise that what differentiates states that are conscious from those that are not is that we are *aware* of the former but not the latter. They diverge over what the relevant form of awareness consists in.

According to the "higher-order thought" (HOT) doctrine, for a conscious state M, the consciousness-conferring awareness takes the form of a thought whose content is (roughly) "I am currently in M." There is a natural way of extending this doctrine to provide an account of the conditions under which a multiplicity of experiences are conscious together:

if M and N are phenomenally unified, their subject must have a higher-order thought with content "I am currently in M and N," and similarly for larger numbers (see Rosenthal 2003). More formally:

> **The HOT Unity Thesis:** a collection of experiences at a given time *t* are phenomenally unified if and only if they are all the objects of a higher-order thought.

According to the alternative "higher-order sense" (HOS) view, a state M is conscious only if it falls under the gaze of "inner sense," a quasi-perceptual form of awareness (Lycan 1997). This doctrine also lends itself, in a very natural way, to an account of the unity of consciousness:

> **The HOS Unity Thesis:** a collection of experiences at a given time *t* are phenomenally unified if and only if they are all apprehended together by the same act of inner sensing.

Since these theses are offering different and competing accounts of one and the same thing – phenomenal unity – they cannot both be correct. And although each view has its proponents (see Carruthers, chapter 21), from a neutral standpoint each also looks to be problematic.

From an intuitive standpoint, the HOS theory provides an attractive picture of phenomenal unity. Everything I can see at a given time is unified in my consciousness, and the same applies to everything I can hear. If there were an *additional* sensory modality, one capable of apprehending the diverse phenomena presented by all of our first-order senses (sight, hearing, touch, etc.), along with all the other forms of consciousness we enjoy, then it would not be surprising that our consciousness is unified in the way it is. But with further scrutiny the appeal of this position diminishes. Is there any reason for supposing that the higher-order sensory faculty exists? It is hard to see that there is. The deliverances of our ordinary first-order senses each have a distinctive phenomenal character (auditory, visual, etc.). Since the higher-order sense faculty evidently lacks a range of distinctive sensory qualities to call its own, if it exists at all it must be nothing more than a locus of featureless apprehension. Even assuming we can make sense of such a thing, it appears entirely redundant. Since a featureless apprehension adds nothing to the character of ordinary phenomenal contents, why suppose these contents – or our experience as a whole – would be in any way different if it were absent?

The HOT Unity Thesis is confronted with difficulties of a different kind. On the face of it, there is no reason whatsoever for supposing that we have to be thinking about an experience in order for that experience to be conscious. If I am consciously thinking about my supper tonight I am not consciously thinking about my toothache, and yet the latter is both conscious and phenomenally unified with the rest of my experience at the time in question. To circumvent this objection HOT theorists hold that consciousness-conferring higher-order thoughts need not themselves be conscious. On Rosenthal's view, if I have a conscious state M that I am not consciously thinking about I must have an actual but nonconscious thought about M. On Carruthers's view (2000), I need not have an actual nonconscious thought, but I must at least have the *capacity* to have a thought about M – it is the capacity which renders M conscious. Whatever one makes of either of these positions, it is difficult to see how either version of the HOT theory can hope to shed light on the nature of phenomenal unity viewed as a real and occurrent feature of consciousness. It is equally difficult to see how the existence of nonconscious or merely dispositional higher-order thoughts could actually *constitute* phenomenal unity, assuming again that the latter is an occurrent phenomenal feature. (For further discussion see Carruthers, chapter 21; Seager & Bourget, chapter 20.)

Phenomenal space

Generally speaking, all our bodily sensations and perceptual experiences are experienced as spatially related to one another. (Recall our initial example: you are aware of the conversation you hear as being to the right of the painting you see.) Since the items thus related are phenomenal, so too is the space they inhabit, but it is nonetheless *spatial* for that. This suggests a further proposal concerning the source of phenomenal unity:

> **The Spatial Unity Thesis:** a collection of experiences at a given time *t* are phenomenally unified by virtue of being located within a common phenomenal space.

If this were true, space in the phenomenal realm would perform the same unifying role as it does in the physical realm. This appealing notion has been taken up by Searle, who has recently advocated a "unified field" conception of consciousness:

> Instead of thinking of my current state of consciousness as made up of the various bits – the perception of the computer screen, the sound of the brook outside, the shadows cast by the evening sun falling on the wall – we should think of all of these as modifications, forms that the underlying basal conscious field takes after my peripheral nerve endings have been assaulted by the various external stimuli. (Searle 2000, p. 575)

If there were a "basal conscious field" of this sort, the Spatial Unity Thesis would stand a good chance of being true. But is there? It is by no means evident that there is any phenomenological evidence for supposing such a thing exists. I am aware of various auditory, visual, and tactile objects existing in various spatial relationships with one another, but I am not aware of any *spatial medium* that exists in addition to these objects. It may be that phenomenal objects of all kinds are in fact modifications of a single field of some kind, but if it is, the field in question lacks any discernible phenomenal features.

Even if we reject a basal phenomenal field, and construe "phenomenal space" in a relational way, as involving no more than the existence of phenomenal distance relations between phenomenal objects, there is room for doubt. Is it really the case that *all* forms of experience must *necessarily* seem to be spatially related in order to be phenomenally unified? The sensory elements of our experience may be spatial in nature, but what of conscious thoughts, or moods? A stream of consciousness consisting of nothing but conscious thoughts (of a non-imagistic kind) and various emotional feelings (e.g., a vague feeling of apprehension) would have multiple elements, elements that are experienced together, but it is not at all clear that these elements would be experienced as being spatially related to one another. Being experienced as spatially related is certainly sufficient for co-consciousness. However, it seems not to be necessary.

In a more speculative vein, we have no reason to suppose all conscious beings have sensory organs on the surfaces of a single spatially localized body. Consider a creature (a sentient plant, perhaps) whose sensory organs are dotted about over an area of several square miles. If the perceptual experiences of such a being *were* spatially integrated, its perceptual system would be less accurate than if they were not. Do we have any grounds for ruling out the possibility of a being whose experience takes the form of several spatially unconnected but phenomenally unified perceptual fields? For more on this theme see Dainton (2005, pp. 65–83, 2004) and Bayne (2004).

Primitive connections

In the light of the preceding, phenomenal unity may seem more elusive than ever, but in fact we are some way closer to pinning our quarry down, for at the very least it is now clear that several seemingly promising ways forward are less than adequate. As for what we should make of this, there are two options: we either explicate phenomenal unity in a way not yet considered, or give up the search for a single overarching or underlying mode of unity, and hold instead that there are several different modes of unity, each of which is sufficient for consciousness to be unified in *some* way, but none of which is privileged.

The latter conclusion is reached by Hill, after a survey not dissimilar to the one just conducted (1991, ch. 10). Hill suggests that *belonging to the same subject* is a distinctive mode of unity, but so too are *being jointly introspectible, two sensations being proper parts of a third sensation, being counterfactually related* and *being phenomeno-spatially related* – these all involve different unifying relations, and none is significantly more important than the rest. As for whether there is a mode of unity additional to these, Hill tells us that on occasion he was tempted to think that it was possible to detect such a mode in his experience – a pure form of co-consciousness possessing no distinguishing features apart from its ability to unify experiences – but he finally came round to the view that there is no such thing: "I now feel that this view is wrong. It isn't possible to find this ghostly form of co-consciousness within one's experience. Hence, there is no reason to believe it exists" (1991, p. 239).

Is Hill's case for a pluralistic view of phenomenal unity compelling? Arguably not; a case for recognizing a basic and *sui generis* relationship of phenomenal unity – let us simply call it *co-consciousness** to distinguish it from other forms – can certainly be made.

As we have seen, the phenomenal unity relationship is distinct from the co-instantiation relation, and there are grounds for supposing that experiences can be phenomenally unified in the absence of any higher-order conscious state, and in the absence of any spatial relations of a phenomenal kind. If this is right, if experiences can be phenomenally unified without being unified in any *other* discernible way, are we not forced to recognize the existence of a "pure" relationship of co-consciousness*? As for Hill's failure to find this relationship in his experience, it may be that he was looking for the wrong sort of thing. Suppose you are outside on a dark night when you hear two persistent sounds, the howling of a dog and the droning of a distant car. These sounds are *experienced together*, and they are related in this way irrespective of whether you divert your attention onto them (which you may do intermittently), and irrespective of whether they are experienced as spatially related (this may vary too). This relationship of "experienced togetherness" can plausibly be taken to be a basic and unmediated phenomenal relationship; it does not consist of a separate ingredient in experience, it does not have intrinsic phenomenal features to call its own. Nonetheless, this relationship is perfectly real. If we identify this relationship with co-consciousness*, we should not expect to be able to detect the latter as a separate feature or object within our consciousness. It does not follow that co-consciousness* is in any way spectral or mysterious: we all know *exactly what it's like* for two or more experiences to be related in this way.

Once our attention is drawn to the distinctive character of co-consciousness* it soon becomes obvious that the relationship is pervasive: it is to be found *everywhere* we look in our experience. It unifies collections of sounds, but it also holds between collections of bodily sensations, and the various regions of our visual field; it holds across modalities, between all these and our conscious thoughts and mental images, between those parts of our overall consciousness we introspect and those parts that we do not introspect. Experiences that are not unified in any other way can be co-conscious*, but experiences that are unified in one or more other ways can also be co-conscious*. Irrespective of how we decide to carve our overall consciousness into parts, each and every part is co-conscious* with every other part. The pervasive character of co-consciousness* is a reason for supposing that it is the central and most fundamental form of phenomenal unity. Hence we have:

> **The Co-consciousness* Thesis:** A state of consciousness is fully phenomenally unified at a given time by virtue of the fact that its constituent experiences are all mutually co-conscious*.

This general line is taken in Dainton (2000). If it is possible for conscious states to be less than fully unified, this possibility is easily accommodated within this framework.

Subsumption and singularity

There is an alternative way in which phenomenal unity can be construed as a primitive feature of experience. Rather than starting off from the perspective of particular experiences and looking for what binds them into more complex states, we can start with the more complex states, and regard simpler token experiences as unified by virtue of being parts of such states. The primitive unifying relationship is no longer a direct connection between phenomenal states – co-consciousness* has vanished from the scene – but rather something along the lines of *being experienced as part of a phenomenal state*. This relationship shares with co-consciousness* the advantage of not being in the least mysterious. We all know what it's like for various lesser visual experiences (of a tree, of a dog) to be experienced as parts or elements of a more encompassing visual scene; similarly, we all know what it's like for auditory and visual experiences to be parts of a more encompassing state, and the same holds true for all the experiences that feature in our consciousness at a given time: they are all parts of a single all-encompassing state.

This line, developed in a restricted way by Hill (1991, pp. 235–6), has recently been extended and elaborated by Bayne and Chalmers. They prefer to talk of more encompassing states *subsuming* lesser states: "a set of states is phenomenally unified when there is something it's like to be in all those states at once. When this is the case, the subject will have a phenomenal state . . . that *subsumes* each of the states in the original set" (2003, §6). The notion that all of a subject's simultaneous experiences are phenomenally unified can then be formulated thus:

> **The Subsumptive Unity Thesis:** For any set of phenomenal states of a subject at a time, the subject has a phenomenal state that subsumes each of the states in that set.

Although the maximal subsuming state is a conscious state in its own right, it does not exist as separate or independent from its elements; it is more akin to a fusion of the latter. As for the subsumption relationship itself, although far from hostile to the view that it is primitive, they suggest that it can be explicated, and perhaps even defined, in terms of the "what it's like" concept: a phenomenal state A subsumes phenomenal state B when what it's like to have A and B simultaneously is the same as what it's like to have A.

The "top-down" approach advocated by Bayne and Chalmers is in some ways a very natural one – it accords with the phenomenological fact that our experience at any one time usually takes the form of an already-unified ensemble – and it is certainly a fruitful one from the point of formalization, as they go on to demonstrate. But it is not obviously inconsistent with the "bottom-up" approach: after all, any collection of states jointly related by co-consciousness* will constitute a whole which subsumes its parts. Nor does recognizing the fact of subsumption render the co-consciousness* relationship redundant.

To appreciate this it suffices to pose the question "If a state S subsumes states $s_1, s_2 \ldots s_n$, just what is S itself *like*?" In spelling out the answer we will mention the qualitative character of the various constituents subsumed in S; if some of these constituents are spatially related or introspected we will mention this too. Is this enough? Arguably not, for we have not yet made explicit the particular *manner* in which the states subsumed in S are unified. The Pacific Ocean subsumes many watery parts, the moon subsumes many rocky parts, but neither are phenomenally unified, neither is unified in the distinctive way conscious states are unified. For our description to be phenomenologically adequate – for it to capture *what it's like* to have S – it will also need to mention that each part of S is connected to every other part by the relationship of experienced togetherness. Hence not only does co-consciousness* remain very much present (albeit tacitly) in the subsumption approach, it is (arguably) responsible for conscious states having the distinctive form of unity that they do.

The top-down approach is given an intriguing additional twist in Tye (2003). Tye argues that the traditional approach to the unity of consciousness is fundamentally misconceived. The mistake comes in supposing that a subject's state of consciousness at a given time is composed of various different experiences that need to be unified in some way. Tye urges us to reject this picture, and recognize instead that we each have *just one experience* at a given time. If we do accept this – not surprisingly Tye calls it the "one experience view" – the traditional problem of unity evaporates. We can call off the search for a phenomenal unity relationship: if the one experience view is correct, there is nothing for such a relationship to relate. As Tye goes on to point out, the one experience view has a striking consequence: there are "no such entities as purely visual experiences or purely auditory experiences or purely olfactory experiences in normal, everyday consciousness. Where there is phenomenological unity across sense-modalities, sense-specific experiences do not exist" (2003, p. 28).

Although Tye shows that the one experience view is by no means as bizarre as it may initially seem, it is by no means clear that the traditional problem of unity can be simply sidestepped in this way. Suppose we accept that our ordinary (total) states of consciousness do not have experiences as parts. It remains the case that they possess *parts* or *regions*, and even if the latter are not "experiences" they are nonetheless unified in a distinctive way, and an account of this unity is called for. The phenomenal unity relationship can as easily be viewed as a relationship between experiential parts, as it can experiential wholes.

"Just more content"?

Despite their differences, all the approaches discussed so far agree on one thing: that phe-nomenal unity consists of structures or relationships that are internal to consciousness. In recent writings Susan Hurley has argued that all such internalist approaches are flawed: "making sense of the unity of consciousness requires . . . something outside of the contents of consciousness" (1994, p. 49). As for which external factors are required, Hurley proposes a "two-level interdependence" account: viewed from the "sub-personal" perspective, phe-nomenal unity requires a distinctive kind of dynamic causal flow between an organism and its environment, viewed from the "personal perspective," phenomenal unity requires nor-mative coherence (1998, pp. 216–17). Since Hurley's intriguing positive proposals defy easy summary – for a sympathetic but critical assessment see Kobes (2000) – I will confine myself here to a brief remark on the negative part of her case. (For further discussion, from a different angle, see Bayne and Chalmers (2003: §6.3)).

Hurley suggests that any attempt to explicate phenomenal unity in purely subjective terms is vulnerable to the "just more contents" objection (JMC): "the unity or separateness of consciousness cannot be accounted for in terms of the subjective contents of conscious-ness because the same question of unity or separateness arises again for any such contents" (1998, p. 5). There is no denying that JMC is effective against certain forms of internal-ism. Suppose, for example, that someone were to propose this: "A collection of experiences constitutes a unified conscious state by virtue of being linked by experiences of a certain particular kind: *connecting experiences*, that is, phenomenal contents which hold complex phenomenal states together." This proposal falls to JMC: since the hypothetical connecting experiences are themselves experiences, the question arises as to what binds experiences of this sort to the experiences they connect. If the answer is "nothing does," then the proposed account is incomplete, if the answer is "connecting experiences," then we are faced with a definitely problematic infinite regress.

But not all internalist accounts of phenomenal unity are of this kind. It is not at all obvious, for example, that the HOS theory is vulnerable to JMC, since the hypotheti-cal higher-order sense is certainly not "just another experience, or content" – and in the case of HOT accounts, the unifying higher-order thought is not itself conscious. Similarly, although co-consciousness* is a relationship between phenomenal contents, it is not itself a phenomenal content: it has no discernible phenomenal features of its own, it is a way experiences are experienced as related, but not itself an experience. As for the subsumption approach, since no appeal is made to anything resembling connecting experiences (or uni-fying contents), there is no obvious way for JMC to get a grip here either. Hurley's objection may be effective against some forms of internalism, but other forms – the more plausible forms – appear to be immune to it.

Diachronic unity

The conundrums posed by the unity of consciousness-at-a-time can easily seem straight-forward in comparison to those posed by its across-time counterpart. Indeed, whether synchronic phenomenal unity even has a diachronic counterpart is a contested issue. Those who believe it does face the challenge of explaining just how consciousness manages to knit itself together over time; those who do not face the challenge of explaining why conscious-ness can seem to extend through time if it does not in fact do so. It is not possible here to enter these matters in any detail here, but no survey of the issues pertaining to the unity of consciousness would be complete without some mention of them.

Why suppose there is a diachronic counterpart to synchronic phenomenal unity? For those inclined to think there is such a counterpart, the answer lies in the character of ordinary experience: we are directly aware of motion, change, and persistence in our experience. (If this isn't obvious, just wave your hand in front of your face, or whistle a tune.) If we are *directly* aware of change and persistence, then since both change and persistence occur over an interval of time, our direct awareness must extend over an interval of time. If when listening to a scale played on a piano I hear middle *C* being followed by *D* – if the latter note is directly experienced as following-on from the former – then both notes must be present together within my consciousness, in the form of an experienced succession, even though *C* occurs earlier than *D*.

Phenomenological considerations may suggest that our immediate awareness extends through time, but they also suggest that it does not extend very far. If I hear *C*-being-followed-by-*D*, and *D*-being-followed-by-*E*, then unless the tones are of very short duration, I will no longer be directly experiencing *C* by the time *E* occurs. The brief temporal window within which we seem able to directly apprehend change and persistence is the so-called *specious present*. Estimates of the apparent extent of the specious present do vary – from less than a second to several seconds (Pöppel 1985) – but by all measures and criteria it does not last long.

A Branching of the Ways

The idea that the experienced present is temporally extended may find support in the phenomenological data, but some are understandably wary of supposing that we really can be directly aware both of what is happening now and what happened in the recent past. Are we really to suppose that we all have the sort of powers usually only ascribed to clairvoyants and crystal-gazers? This consideration aside, some have taken the view that to apprehend a succession of contents as a succession, the relevant contents must be present in our awareness *simultaneously*, in a momentary act of awareness – see James (1890, ch. 15) and Miller (1984). Hence the project of trying to explicate the temporal appearances without attributing genuine temporal depth to consciousness.

The obvious (and perhaps only) way to do this is by holding that a specious present consists of two simultaneously apprehended aspects: (i) the presently occurring contents, (ii) a *representation* of non-present contents. Although in reality durationless (or very brief) the represented contents are such that they seem to extend a short way through time. The most common implementation of this "representationalist" proposal is illustrated below:

t_1:   **C**
t_2:   **D** [*C]
t_3:   **E** [*D **C]
t_4:   **F** [*E **D ***C]
t_5:   **G** [*F **E ***D]

Here the bold-faced letters stand for tones experienced at a succession of closely neighboring times. First C is heard, all by itself and preceded by silence; then D is heard simultaneously with [*C], where the latter is a representation of C as just having occurred;

then E is heard together with a representation of a very recently experienced D, and a not quite so recently experienced C – the greater the number of "*" the "more past" a represented content seems. Hence from t_2 to t_4 C appears to be gradually sliding into the past. But by the time t_5 is reached, C has slipped out of the specious present, and from now on can be apprehended only by means of ordinary memory. Although individual specious presents are momentary (or very brief), they *appear* to have temporal depth. As for the nature of the representations involved, different theorists adopt very different positions. Some opt for short-term memories. Broad (1938) talks of different degrees of a primitive property he calls "presentedness." In a more complex analysis (or series of such), Husserl (1991) posits "retentions," which are related to "primal impressions" by a distinctive form of intentionality. Husserl also holds that specious presents contain anticipatory representations of what is about to occur, which he calls "protentions."

Despite the degree of sophistication they can achieve, the viability of such theories is questionable. Representationalism faces two challenges: the proposed representations must be of such a kind as to provide a compelling illusion of temporal depth, but in addition, the relationships between neighboring specious presents must be of such a kind as to make it possible for experience to seem continuous in the way it does. Even if the depth problem could be solved in a satisfactory manner, and this is by no means clear, the continuity problem remains a serious hurdle.

If I hear the succession C-D-E-F-G I experience each tone flowing smoothly into its successor. More generally, all the brief phases of our streams of consciousness flow seamlessly into their successors. Yet according to representationalism, neighboring specious presents – such as those occurring at t_4 and t_5 above – are completely distinct experiences. There are of course similarities between neighboring specious presents, and there may also be (depending on the form of representationalism) causal or intentional relations, but by hypothesis there are no *direct experiential* connections. So far as phenomenal relationships are concerned, each specious present is an entirely self-contained entity. So far as critics of representationalism are concerned, since phenomenology reveals the existence of direct experiential connections between adjoining stream-phases, representationalism is a doomed strategy. We saw right at the start that our conscious states at any one time would be fragmented beyond recognition if their constituent parts were not connected by relationships of synchronic phenomenal unity. Is the same not true of the diachronic case also?

To succeed where representationalism fails an account of diachronic phenomenal unity must be non-discriminatory: it must be possible for contents in different (but neighboring) specious presents to be phenomenally connected in just the same way, or to just the same degree, as contents within a single specious present. The easiest (and perhaps only) way in which this is possible is if the following are true: (i) specious presents extend through time, just as they seem to, (ii) the contents within a specious present are diachronically co-conscious, and (iii) neighboring specious presents overlap by possessing parts in common. To see how this works in practice, consider again the series of tones C-D-E-F-G, and suppose this stream of auditory consciousness consists of just the following succession of specious presents: $S_1 = [C\text{-}D]$, $S_2 = [D\text{-}E]$, $S_3 = [E\text{-}F]$, $S_4 = [F\text{-}G]$. Here contents connected by a hyphen are diachronically co-conscious, and D in S_1 is numerically identical with D in S_2, E in S_2 is numerically identical with E in S_3 and so forth. By holding that a diachronic phenomenal unity relation connects *all* successive phases of the same stream of consciousness we accommodate phenomenal continuity; by holding that this same relation only extends a brief way through time we account for the fact that only closely neighboring parts of a stream of consciousness are experienced together.

An account along these lines was outlined by Russell (1915), and in several places subsequently by Foster (e.g., 1991, pp. 246–50). For further discussion see Lockwood (1989, ch. 15), Dainton (2003) and Gallagher (2003).

Tye advocates a seemingly more radical approach. He extends the "one experience view" of synchronic unity to the diachronic case: he holds that even a stream of consciousness lasting many hours, with highly varied contents, is but a single experience (2003, p. 97). But as with the synchronic case, it is far from evident that trying to sidestep the unity issue in this way is successful. As Tye recognizes, we are not aware of the entire contents of day-long streams of consciousness all at once. Accordingly, he is obliged to distinguish between "direct phenomenal unity" and "indirect phenomenal unity." In the case of successions such as C-D-E, assuming the same spacing as before, C-D and D-E are directly phenomenally continuous, in Tye's sense, but C and E are only indirectly phenomenally continuous. A diachronic phenomenal unity relation thus remains alive and well in Tye's scheme.

See also 2 Philosophical problems of consciousness; 13 The case of blindsight; 14 Split-brain cases; 15 Philosophical psychopathology and self-consciousness; 20 Representationalism about consciousness; 21 Higher-order theories of consciousness; 53 Phenomenological approaches to consciousness.

Further Readings

Bayne, T. and Chalmers, D. (2003) What is the unity of consciousness? In A. Cleeremans (ed.), *The Unity of Consciousness: Binding, Integration, Dissociation*. Oxford: Oxford University Press.

Dainton, B. (2005), *Stream of Consciousness*, 2nd edn. London: Routledge.

Hurley, S. (1998) *Consciousness in Action*. Cambridge, MA: Harvard University Press.

Peacocke, C. (ed.) (1994) *Objectivity, Simulation and the Unity of Consciousness*. Oxford: Oxford University Press.

Tye, M. (2003) *Consciousness and Persons*. Cambridge, MA: MIT Press.

References

Bayne, T. and Chalmers, D. (2003) What is the unity of consciousness? In A. Cleeremans (ed.), *The Unity of Consciousness: Binding, Integration, Dissociation*. Oxford: Oxford University Press.

Bayne, T. (2004) Self-consciousness and the unity of consciousness. *The Monist* 87, 2, 224–31.

Broad, C. D. (1938) *An Examination of McTaggart's Philosophy* (3 vols.). Cambridge: Cambridge University Press.

Carruthers, P. (2000) *Phenomenal Consciousness: A Naturalistic Theory*. Cambridge: Cambridge University Press.

Dainton, B. (2003) Time in experience: reply to Gallagher. *Psyche* 9, 12. http://psyche.cs.monash.edu.au/symposia/dainton/index.html

Dainton, B. (2004) Higher-order consciousness and phenomenal space: reply to Meehan. *Psyche* 10: 1. http://psyche.cs.monash.edu.au/symposia/dainton/index.html

Dainton, B. (2005) *Stream of Consciousness*, 2nd edn. London: Routledge.

Foster, J. (1991) *The Immaterial Self*. London: Routledge.

Gallagher, S. (2003) Sync-ing in the stream of experience: time-consciousness in Husserl, Broad and Dainton. *Psyche* 9, 10. http://psyche.cs.monash.edu.au/symposia/dainton/gallagher.html

Hill, C. (1991) *Sensations: A Defence of Type Materialism*. Cambridge: Cambridge University Press.

Hurley, S. (1994) Unity and Objectivity. In C. Peacocke (ed.), *Objectivity, Simulation and the Unity of Consciousness*. Oxford: Oxford University Press.

Hurley, S. (1998) *Consciousness in Action*. Cambridge, MA: Harvard University Press.

Husserl, E. (1991) *On the Phenomenology of the Consciousness of Internal Time (1893–1917)*. Edited and translated by J. B. Brough. Dordrecht: Kluwer.

James, W. (1890) *The Principles of Psychology*. New York: Dover (1950).

Kobes, B. (2000) Unity of consciousness and bi-level externalism. *Mind and Language* 15, 5, 528–44.

Lockwood, M. (1989) *Mind, Brain and the Quantum*. Oxford: Blackwell.

Lockwood, M. (1994) Issues of Unity and Objectivity. In C. Peacocke (ed.), *Objectivity, Simulation and the Unity of Consciousness*. Oxford: Oxford University Press.

Lycan, W. (1997) Consciousness as internal monitoring. In N. Block, O. Flanagan, and G. Güzeldere (eds), *The Nature of Consciousness*. Cambridge, MA: MIT Press.

Miller, I. (1984) *Husserl, Perception, and Temporal Awareness*. Cambridge, MA: MIT Press.

Opie, J. and O'Brian, G. (1998) The Disunity of Consciousness. *Australasian Journal of Philosophy* 76, 3, 378–95.

Pöppel, E. (1985) *Mindworks: Time and Conscious Experience*. New York: Harcourt, Brace Jovanovich.

Radden, J. (1996) *Divided Minds and Successive Selves*. Cambridge, MA: MIT Press.

Rosenthal, D. (2003) Unity of consciousness and the self. *Proceedings of the Aristotelian Society* 103: 3, 325–352.

Russell, B. (1915) On the experience of time. *Monist* 25, 212–33.

Searle, J. (2000) Consciousness. *Annual Review of Neuroscience* 23, 55ed.

Tye, M. (2003) *Consciousness and Persons*. Cambridge, MA: MIT Press.

Part III

SOME CONTEMPORARY THEORIES OF CONSCIOUSNESS

17

The Hard Problem of Consciousness

DAVID CHALMERS

The Easy Problems and the Hard Problem

There is not just one problem of consciousness. "Consciousness" is an ambiguous term, referring to many different phenomena. Each of these phenomena needs to be explained, but some are easier to explain than others. At the start, it is useful to divide the associated problems of consciousness into "hard" and "easy" problems. The easy problems of consciousness are those that seem directly susceptible to the standard methods of cognitive science, whereby a phenomenon is explained in terms of computational or neural mechanisms. The hard problems are those that seem to resist those methods.

The easy problems of consciousness include those of explaining the following phenomena:

1 the ability to discriminate, categorize, and react to environmental stimuli;
2 the integration of information by a cognitive system;
3 the reportability of mental states;
4 the ability of a system to access its own internal states;
5 the focus of attention;
6 the deliberate control of behavior;
7 the difference between wakefulness and sleep.

All of these phenomena are associated with the notion of consciousness. For example, one sometimes says that a mental state is conscious when it is verbally reportable, or when it is internally accessible. Sometimes a system is said to be conscious of some information when it has the ability to react on the basis of that information, or, more strongly, when it attends to that information, or when it can integrate that information and exploit it in the sophisticated control of behavior. We sometimes say that an action is conscious precisely when it is deliberate. Often, we say that an organism is conscious as another way of saying that it is awake.

There is no real issue about whether *these* phenomena can be explained scientifically. All of them are straightforwardly vulnerable to explanation in terms of computational or neural mechanisms. To explain access and reportability, for example, we need only specify the mechanism by which information about internal states is retrieved and made available for verbal report. To explain the integration of information, we need only exhibit mechanisms by which information is brought together and exploited by later processes. For an account of sleep and wakefulness, an appropriate neurophysiological account of the processes responsible for organisms' contrasting behavior in those states will suffice. In each case, an appropriate cognitive or neurophysiological model can clearly do the explanatory work.

If these phenomena were all there was to consciousness, then consciousness would not be a significant problem. Although we do not yet have anything close to a complete explanation of these phenomena, we have a clear idea of how we might go about explaining them. This is why I call these problems the easy problems. Of course, "easy" is a relative term. Getting the details right will probably take a century or two of difficult empirical work. Still, there is every reason to believe that the methods of cognitive science and neuroscience will succeed.

The hard problem of consciousness is the problem of *experience*. When we think and perceive, there is a whir of information-processing, but there is also a subjective aspect. As Nagel (1974) has put it, there is *something it's like* to be a conscious organism. This subjective aspect is experience. When we see, for example, we *experience* visual sensations: the felt quality of redness, the experience of dark and light, the quality of depth in a visual field. Other experiences go along with perception in different modalities: the sound of a clarinet, the smell of mothballs. Then there are bodily sensations, from pains to orgasms; mental images that are conjured up internally; the felt quality of emotion, and the experience of a stream of conscious thought. What unites all of these states is that there is something it's like to be in them. All of them are states of experience.

It is undeniable that some organisms are subjects of experience. But the question of how it is that these systems are subjects of experience is perplexing. Why is it that when our cognitive systems engage in visual and auditory information-processing, we have visual or auditory experience: the quality of deep blue, the sensation of middle C? How can we explain why there is something it's like to entertain a mental image, or to experience an emotion? It is widely agreed that experience arises from a physical basis, but we have no good explanation of why and how it so arises. Why should physical processing give rise to a rich inner life at all? It seems objectively unreasonable that it should, and yet it does.

If any problem qualifies as *the* problem of consciousness, it is this one. In this central sense of "consciousness," an organism is conscious if there is something it's like to be that organism, and a mental state is conscious if there is something it's like to be in that state. Sometimes terms such as "phenomenal consciousness" and "qualia" are also used here, but I find it more natural to speak of "conscious experience" or simply "experience." Another useful way to avoid confusion (used by, e.g., Newell 1990; Chalmers 1996) is to reserve the term "consciousness" for the phenomena of experience, using the less loaded term "awareness" for the more straightforward phenomena described earlier. If such a convention were widely adopted, communication would be much easier; as things stand, those who talk about "consciousness" are frequently talking past each other.

The ambiguity of the term "consciousness" is often exploited by both philosophers and scientists writing on the subject. It is common to see a paper on consciousness begin with an invocation of the mystery of consciousness, noting the strange intangibility and ineffability of subjectivity, and worrying that so far we have no theory of the phenomenon. Here, the topic is clearly the hard problem – the problem of experience. In the second half of the paper, the tone becomes more optimistic, and the author's own theory of consciousness is outlined. Upon examination, this theory turns out to be a theory of one of the more straightforward phenomena – of reportability, of introspective access, or whatever. At the close, the author declares that consciousness has turned out to be tractable after all, but the reader is left feeling like the victim of a bait-and-switch. The hard problem remains untouched.

Functional Explanation

Why are the easy problems easy, and why is the hard problem hard? The easy problems are easy precisely because they concern the explanation of cognitive *abilities* and *functions*. To explain a cognitive function, we need only specify a mechanism that can perform the function. The methods of cognitive science are well-suited for this sort of explanation, and so are well-suited to the easy problems of consciousness. By contrast, the hard problem is hard precisely because it is not a problem about the performance of functions. The problem persists even when the performance of all the relevant functions is explained. (Here "function" is not used in the narrow teleological sense of something that a system is designed to do, but in the broader sense of any causal role in the production of behavior that a system might perform.)

To explain reportability, for instance, is just to explain how a system could perform the function of producing reports on internal states. To explain internal access, we need to explain how a system could be appropriately affected by its internal states and use information about those states in directing later processes. To explain integration and control, we need to explain how a system's central processes can bring information contents together and use them in the facilitation of various behaviors. These are all problems about the explanation of functions.

How do we explain the performance of a function? By specifying a *mechanism* that performs the function. Here, neurophysiological and cognitive modeling are perfect for the task. If we want a detailed low-level explanation, we can specify the neural mechanism that is responsible for the function. If we want a more abstract explanation, we can specify a mechanism in computational terms. Either way, a full and satisfying explanation will result. Once we have specified the neural or computational mechanism that performs the function of verbal report, for example, the bulk of our work in explaining reportability is over.

In a way, the point is trivial. It is a *conceptual* fact about these phenomena that their explanation only involves the explanation of various functions, as the phenomena are *functionally definable*. All it *means* for reportability to be instantiated in a system is that the system has the capacity for verbal reports of internal information. All it means for a system to be awake is for it to be appropriately receptive to information from the environment and for it to be able to use this information in directing behavior in an appropriate way. To see that this sort of thing is a conceptual fact, note that someone who says "you have explained the performance of the verbal report function, but you have not explained reportability" is making a trivial conceptual mistake about reportability. All it could *possibly* take to explain reportability is an explanation of how the relevant function is performed; the same goes for the other phenomena in question.

Throughout the higher-level sciences, reductive explanation works in just this way. To explain the gene, for instance, we needed to specify the mechanism that stores and transmits hereditary information from one generation to the next. It turns out that DNA performs this function; once we explain how the function is performed, we have explained the gene. To explain life, we ultimately need to explain how a system can reproduce, adapt to its environment, metabolize, and so on. All of these are questions about the perform-ance of functions, and so are well-suited to reductive explanation. The same holds for most problems in cognitive science. To explain learning, we need to explain the way in which a system's behavioral capacities are modified in light of environmental information, and the way in which new information can be brought to bear in adapting a system's actions to its environment. If we show how a neural or computational mechanism does the job, we have explained learning. We can say the same for other cognitive phenomena, such as percep-tion, memory, and language. Sometimes the relevant functions need to be characterized quite subtly, but it is clear that insofar as cognitive science explains these phenomena at all, it does so by explaining the performance of functions.

When it comes to conscious experience, this sort of explanation fails. What makes the hard problem hard and almost unique is that it goes *beyond* problems about the perform-ance of functions. To see this, note that even when we have explained the performance of all the cognitive and behavioral functions in the vicinity of experience – perceptual dis-crimination, categorization, internal access, verbal report – there may still remain a further unanswered question: *Why is the performance of these functions accompanied by experience?* A simple explanation of the functions leaves this question open (the same point is made from the perspective of cognitive science by Velmans 1991).

There is no analogous further question in the explanation of genes, or of life, or of learn-ing. If someone says "I can see that you have explained how DNA stores and transmits hereditary information from one generation to the next, but you have not explained how it is a *gene*," then they are making a conceptual mistake. All it means to be a gene is to be an entity that performs the relevant storage and transmission function. But if someone says "I can see that you have explained how information is discriminated, integrated, and reported, but you have not explained how it is *experienced*," they are not making a concep-tual mistake. This is a nontrivial further question.

This further question is the key question in the problem of consciousness. Why doesn't all this information-processing go on "in the dark," free of any inner feel? Why is it that when electromagnetic waveforms impinge on a retina and are discriminated and catego-rized by a visual system, this discrimination and categorization is experienced as a sensation of vivid red? We know that conscious experience *does* arise when these functions are per-formed, but the very fact that it arises is the central mystery. There is an *explanatory gap* (a term due to Levine 1983) between the functions and experience, and we need an explana-tory bridge to cross it. A mere account of the functions stays on one side of the gap, so the materials for the bridge must be found elsewhere.

This is not to say that experience *has* no function. Perhaps it will turn out to play an important cognitive role. But for any role it might play, there will be more to the explana-tion of experience than a simple explanation of the function. Perhaps it will even turn out that in the course of explaining a function, we will be led to the key insight that allows an explanation of experience. If this happens, though, the discovery will be an *extra* explana-tory reward. There is no cognitive function such that we can say in advance that explanation of that function will *automatically* explain experience.

To explain experience, we need a new approach. The usual explanatory methods of cognitive science and neuroscience do not suffice. These methods have been developed precisely to explain the performance of cognitive functions, and they do a good job. But as these methods stand, they are *only* equipped to explain the performance of functions. When it comes to the hard problem, the standard approach has nothing to say.

Some Case Studies

In the last few years, a number of works have addressed the problems of consciousness within the framework of cognitive science and neuroscience. This might suggest that the analysis above is faulty, but in fact a close examination of the relevant work only lends the analysis further support. When we investigate just which aspects of consciousness these studies are aimed at, and which aspects they end up explaining, we find that the ultimate target of explanation is always one of the easy problems. I will illustrate this with two representative examples.

The first is the "neurobiological theory of consciousness" outlined by Crick and Koch (1990; see also Crick 1994). This theory centers on certain 35–75 Hz neural oscillations in the cerebral cortex; Crick and Koch hypothesize that these oscillations are the basis of consciousness. This is partly because the oscillations seem to be correlated with awareness in a number of different modalities – within the visual and olfactory systems, for example – and also because they suggest a mechanism by which the *binding* of information contents might be achieved. Binding is the process whereby separately represented pieces of information about a single entity are brought together to be used by later processing, as when information about the color and shape of a perceived object is integrated from separate visual pathways. Following others (e.g., Eckhorn et al. 1988), Crick and Koch hypothesize that binding may be achieved by the synchronized oscillations of neuronal groups representing the relevant contents. When two pieces of information are to be bound together, the relevant neural groups will oscillate with the same frequency and phase.

The details of how this binding might be achieved are still poorly understood, but suppose that they can be worked out. What might the resulting theory explain? Clearly it might explain the binding of information contents, and perhaps it might yield a more general account of the integration of information in the brain. Crick and Koch also suggest that these oscillations activate the mechanisms of working memory, so that there may be an account of this and perhaps other forms of memory in the distance. The theory might eventually lead to a general account of how perceived information is bound and stored in memory, for use by later processing.

Such a theory would be valuable, but it would tell us nothing about why the relevant contents are experienced. Crick and Koch suggest that these oscillations are the neural *correlates* of experience. (See Crick & Koch, chapter 44.) This claim is arguable – does not binding also take place in the processing of unconscious information? – but even if it is accepted, the *explanatory* question remains: Why do the oscillations give rise to experience? The only basis for an explanatory connection is the role they play in binding and storage, but the question of why binding and storage should themselves be accompanied by experience is never addressed. If we do not know why binding and storage should give rise to experience, telling a story about the oscillations cannot help us. Conversely, if we *knew* why binding and storage gave rise to experience, the neurophysiological details would be just the icing on the cake. Crick and Koch's theory gains its purchase by *assuming* a connection between binding and experience, and so can do nothing to explain that link.

I do not think that Crick and Koch are ultimately claiming to address the hard problem, although some have interpreted them otherwise. A published interview with Koch gives a clear statement of the limitations on the theory's ambitions.

> Well, let's first forget about the really difficult aspects, like subjective feelings, for they may not
> have a scientific solution. The subjective state of play, of pain, of pleasure, of seeing blue, of

smelling a rose – there seems to be a huge jump between the materialistic level, of explaining molecules and neurons, and the subjective level. Let's focus on things that are easier to study – like visual awareness. You're now talking to me, but you're not looking at me, you're looking at the cappuccino, and so you are aware of it. You can say, "It's a cup and there's some liquid in it." If I give it to you, you'll move your arm and you'll take it – you'll respond in a meaningful manner. That's what I call awareness. (Koch 1992, p. 96)

The second example is an approach at the level of cognitive psychology. This is Bernard Baars's global workspace theory of consciousness, presented in his book *A Cognitive Theory of Consciousness* (Baars 1998). According to this theory, the contents of consciousness are contained in a *global workspace*, a central processor used to mediate communication between a host of specialized nonconscious processors. When these specialized processors need to broadcast information to the rest of the system, they do so by sending this information to the workspace, which acts as a kind of communal blackboard for the rest of the system, accessible to all the other processors. (For further detail see Baars, chapter 18.)

Baars uses this model to address many aspects of human cognition, and to explain a number of contrasts between conscious and unconscious cognitive functioning. Ultimately, however, it is a theory of *cognitive accessibility*, explaining how it is that certain information contents are widely accessible within a system, as well as a theory of informational integration and reportability. The theory shows promise as a theory of awareness, the functional *correlate* of conscious experience, but an explanation of experience itself is not on offer.

One might suppose that according to this theory, the contents of experience are precisely the contents of the workspace. But even if this is so, nothing internal to the theory *explains* why the information within the global workspace is experienced. The best the theory can do is to say that the information is experienced because it is *globally accessible*. But now the question arises in a different form: why should global accessibility give rise to conscious experience? As always, this bridging question is unanswered.

Almost all work taking a cognitive or neuroscientific approach to consciousness in recent years could be subjected to a similar critique. The "Neural Darwinism" model of Edelman (1989), for instance, addresses questions about perceptual awareness and the self-concept, but says nothing about why there should also be experience. The "multiple drafts" model of Dennett (1991) is largely directed at explaining the reportability of certain mental contents (see Schneider, chapter 24). The "intermediate level" theory of Jackendoff (1987) provides an account of some computational processes that underlie consciousness, but Jackendoff stresses that the question of how these "project" into conscious experience remains mysterious (see Prinz, chapter 19).

Researchers using these methods are often inexplicit about their attitudes to the problem of conscious experience, although sometimes they take a clear stand. Even among those who are clear about it, attitudes differ widely. In placing this sort of work with respect to the problem of experience, a number of different strategies are available. It would be useful if these strategic choices were more often made explicit.

The first strategy is simply to *explain something else*. Some researchers are explicit that the problem of experience is too difficult for now, and perhaps even outside the domain of science altogether. These researchers instead choose to address one of the more tractable problems such as reportability or the self-concept. Although I have called these problems the "easy" problems, they are among the most interesting unsolved problems in cognitive science, so this work is certainly worthwhile. The worst that can be said of this choice is that in the context of research on consciousness it is relatively unambitious, and the work can sometimes be misinterpreted.

The second choice is to take a harder line and *deny the phenomenon*. (Variations on this approach are taken by Allport 1988; Wilkes 1988; Dennett 1991.) According to this line, once we have explained the functions such as accessibility, reportability, and the like, there is no further phenomenon called "experience" to explain. Some explicitly deny the phenomenon, holding for example that what is not externally verifiable cannot be real. Others achieve the same effect by allowing that experience exists, but only if we equate "experience" with something like the capacity to discriminate and report. These approaches lead to a simpler theory, but are ultimately unsatisfactory. Experience is the most central and manifest aspect of our mental lives, and indeed is perhaps the key explanandum in the science of the mind. Because of this status as an explanandum, experience cannot be discarded like the vital spirit when a new theory comes along. Rather, it is the central fact that any theory of consciousness must explain. A theory that denies the phenomenon "solves" the problem by ducking the question.

In a third option, some researchers *claim to be explaining experience* in the full sense. These researchers (unlike those above) wish to take experience very seriously; they lay out their functional model or theory, and claim that it explains the full subjective quality of experience (e.g., Flohr 1992; Humphrey 1992). The relevant step in the explanation is usually passed over quickly, however, and ends up looking something like magic. After some details about information processing are given, experience suddenly enters the picture, but it is left obscure *how* these processes should suddenly give rise to experience. Perhaps it is simply taken for granted that it does, but then we have an incomplete explanation and a version of the fifth strategy below.

A fourth, more promising approach appeals to these methods to *explain the structure of experience*. For example, it is arguable that an account of the discriminations made by the visual system can account for the structural relations between different color experiences, as well as for the geometric structure of the visual field (see e.g., Clark 1992; Hardin 1992). In general, certain facts about structures found in processing will correspond to and arguably explain facts about the structure of experience. This strategy is plausible but limited. At best, it takes the existence of experience for granted and accounts for some facts about its structure, providing a sort of nonreductive explanation of the structural aspects of experience (I will say more on this in chapter 28). This is useful for many purposes, but it tells us nothing about why there should be experience in the first place.

A fifth and reasonable strategy is to *isolate the substrate of experience*. After all, almost everyone allows that experience *arises* one way or another from brain processes, and it makes sense to identify the sort of process from which it arises. Crick and Koch put their work forward as isolating the neural correlate of consciousness, for example, and Edelman (1989) and Jackendoff (1987) make related claims. Justification of these claims requires a careful theoretical analysis, especially as experience is not directly observable in experimental contexts, but when applied judiciously this strategy can shed indirect light on the problem of experience. Nevertheless, the strategy is clearly incomplete. For a satisfactory theory, we need to know more than *which* processes give rise to experience; we need an account of why and how. A full theory of consciousness must build an explanatory bridge.

The Extra Ingredient

We have seen that there are systematic reasons why the usual methods of cognitive science and neuroscience fail to account for conscious experience. These are simply the wrong sort of methods: nothing that they give to us can yield an explanation. To account for conscious experience, we need an *extra ingredient* in the explanation. This makes for a challenge to those who are serious about the hard problem of consciousness: What is your extra ingredient, and why should *that* account for conscious experience?

There is no shortage of extra ingredients to be had. Some propose an injection of chaos and nonlinear dynamics. Some think that the key lies in nonalgorithmic processing. Some appeal to future discoveries in neurophysiology. Some suppose that the key to the mystery will lie at the level of quantum mechanics. It is easy to see why all these suggestions are put forward. None of the old methods work, so the solution must lie with *something* new. Unfortunately, these suggestions all suffer from the same old problems.

Nonalgorithmic processing, for example, is put forward by Penrose (1989; 1994) because of the role it might play in the process of conscious mathematical insight. The arguments about mathematics are controversial, but even if they succeed and an account of non-algorithmic processing in the human brain is given, it will still only be an account of the *functions* involved in mathematical reasoning and the like. For a nonalgorithmic process as much as an algorithmic process, the question is left unanswered: Why should this process give rise to experience? In answering *this* question, there is no special role for non-algorithmic processing.

The same goes for nonlinear and chaotic dynamics. These might provide a novel account of the dynamics of cognitive functioning, quite different from that given by standard methods in cognitive science. But from dynamics, one only gets more dynamics. The question about experience here is as mysterious as ever. The point is even clearer for new discoveries in neurophysiology. These new discoveries may help us make significant progress in understanding brain function, but for any neural process we isolate, the same question will always arise. It is difficult to imagine what a proponent of new neurophysiology expects to happen, over and above the explanation of further cognitive functions. It is not as if we will suddenly discover a phenomenal glow inside a neuron!

Perhaps the most popular "extra ingredient" of all is quantum mechanics (e.g., Hameroff 1994). The attractiveness of quantum theories of consciousness may stem from a Law of Minimization of Mystery: consciousness is mysterious and quantum mechanics is mysterious, so maybe the two mysteries have a common source. Nevertheless, quantum theories of consciousness suffer from the same difficulties as neural or computational theories. Quantum phenomena have some remarkable functional properties, such as nondeterminism and nonlocality. It is natural to speculate that these properties may play some role in the explanation of cognitive functions, such as random choice and the integration of information, and this hypothesis cannot be ruled out a priori. But when it comes to the explanation of experience, quantum processes are in the same boat as any other. The question of why these processes should give rise to experience is entirely unanswered.

One special attraction of quantum theories is the fact that on some interpretations of quantum mechanics, consciousness plays an active role in "collapsing" the quantum wave function. Such interpretations are controversial, but in any case they offer no hope of *explaining* consciousness in terms of quantum processes. Rather, these theories *assume* the existence of consciousness, and use it in the explanation of quantum processes. At best, these theories tell us something about a physical role that consciousness may play. They tell us nothing about how it arises. For further discussion, see Stapp, chapter 23.

At the end of the day, the same criticism applies to *any* purely physical account of consciousness. For any physical process we specify there will be an unanswered question: Why should this process give rise to experience? Given any such process, it is conceptually coherent that it could be instantiated in the absence of experience. It follows that no mere account of the physical process will tell us why experience arises. The emergence of experience goes beyond what can be derived from physical theory.

Purely physical explanation is well-suited to the explanation of physical *structures*, explaining macroscopic structures in terms of detailed microstructural constituents; and it provides a satisfying explanation of the performance of *functions*, accounting for these functions in terms of the physical mechanisms that perform them. This is because a physical account can *entail* the facts about structures and functions: once the internal details of the physical account are given, the structural and functional properties fall out as an automatic consequence. But the structure and dynamics of physical processes yield only more structure and dynamics, so structures and functions are all we can expect these processes to explain. The facts about experience cannot be an automatic consequence of any physical account, as it is conceptually coherent that any given process could exist without experience. Experience may *arise* from the physical, but it is not *entailed* by the physical.

The moral of all this is that *you cannot explain conscious experience on the cheap*. It is a remarkable fact that reductive methods – methods that explain a high-level phenomenon wholly in terms of more basic physical processes – work well in so many domains. In a sense, one *can* explain most biological and cognitive phenomena on the cheap, in that these phenomena are seen as automatic consequences of more fundamental processes. It would be wonderful if reductive methods could explain experience, too; I hoped for a long time that they might. Unfortunately, there are systematic reasons why these methods must fail. Reductive methods are successful in most domains because what needs explaining in those domains are structures and functions, and these are the kind of thing that a physical account can entail. When it comes to a problem over and above the explanation of structures and functions, these methods are impotent.

This might seem reminiscent of the vitalist claim that no physical account could explain life, but the cases are disanalogous. What drove vitalist skepticism was doubt about whether physical mechanisms could perform the many remarkable functions associated with life, such as complex adaptive behavior and reproduction. The conceptual claim that explanation of functions is what is needed was implicitly accepted, but lacking detailed knowledge of biochemical mechanisms, vitalists doubted whether any physical process could do the job and put forward the hypothesis of the vital spirit as an alternative explanation. Once it turned out that physical processes could perform the relevant functions, vitalist doubts melted away.

With experience, on the other hand, physical explanation of the functions is not in question. The key is instead the *conceptual* point that the explanation of functions does not suffice for the explanation of experience. This basic conceptual point is not something that further neuroscientific investigation will affect. In a similar way, experience is disanalogous to the *élan vital*. The vital spirit was put forward as an explanatory posit, in order to explain the relevant functions, and could therefore be discarded when those functions were explained without it. Experience is not an explanatory posit but an explanandum in its own right, and so is not a candidate for this sort of elimination.

It is tempting to note that all sorts of puzzling phenomena have eventually turned out to be explainable in physical terms. But each of these were problems about the observable behavior of physical objects, coming down to problems in the explanation of structures and functions. Because of this, these phenomena have always been the kind of thing that a physical account *might* explain, even if at some points there have been good reasons to suspect that no such explanation would be forthcoming. The tempting induction from these cases fails in the case of consciousness, which is not a problem about physical structures and functions. The problem of consciousness is puzzling in an entirely different way. An analysis of the problem shows us that conscious experience is just not the kind of thing that a wholly reductive account could succeed in explaining.

The alternative is to build a nonreductive account of consciousness, one that does not attempt to reduce consciousness to something else, but which admits it as an irreducible feature of the world. An account of this sort is discussed in Chalmers, chapter 28.

See also 19 *The intermediate level theory of consciousness;* 23 *Quantum mechanical theories of consciousness;* 24 *Daniel Dennett on the nature of consciousness;* 29 *Anti-materialist arguments and influential replies;* 30 *Functionalism and qualia;* 44 *A neurobiological framework for consciousness.*

Note

This chapter is adapted from a longer essay that appeared in 1995 in *Journal of Consciousness Studies,* 2: 3, 200–19.

Further Readings

Chalmers, D. J. (1996) *The Conscious Mind.* New York: Oxford University Press.
Nagel, T. (1974) What is it like to be a bat? *Philosophical Review* 4, 435–50.

References

Allport, A. (1988) What concept of consciousness? In A. Marcel and E. Bisiach (eds.), *Consciousness in Contemporary Science.* Oxford: Oxford University Press.
Baars, B. J. (1988) *A Cognitive Theory of Consciousness.* Cambridge: Cambridge University Press.
Chalmers, D. J. (1996) *The Conscious Mind.* New York: Oxford University Press.
Clark, A. (1992) *Sensory Qualities.* Oxford: Oxford University Press.
Crick, F. (1994) *The Astonishing Hypothesis: The Scientific Search for the Soul.* New York: Scribners.
Crick, F. and Koch, C. (1990) Toward a neurobiological theory of consciousness. *Seminars in the Neurosciences* 2, 263–75.
Dennett, D. C. (1991) *Consciousness Explained.* Boston, MA: Little, Brown.
Edelman, G. (1989) *The Remembered Present: A Biological Theory of Consciousness.* New York: Basic Books.
Eckhorn, R., Bauer, R., Jordan, W., Brosch, M., Kruse, W., Munk, M. et al. (1988) Coherent oscillations: a mechanism of feature linking in the visual cortex? *Biological Cybernetics* 60, 121–30.
Flohr, H. (1992) Qualia and brain processes. In A. Beckermann, H. Flohr, and J. Kim (eds.), *Emergence or Reduction? Prospects for Nonreductive Physicalism,* 220–40. Berlin: De Gruyter.

Hameroff, S. R. (1994) Quantum coherence in microtubules: a neural basis for emergent consciousness? *Journal of Consciousness Studies* 1, 91–118.

Hardin, C. L. (1992) Physiology, phenomenology, and Spinoza's true colors. In A. Beckermann, H. Flohr, and J. Kim (eds.), *Emergence or Reduction? Prospects for Nonreductive Physicalism*, 201–19. Berlin: De Gruyter.

Hodgson, D. (1988) *The Mind Matters: Consciousness and Choice in a Quantum World*. Oxford: Oxford University Press.

Humphrey, N. (1992) *A History of the Mind*. New York: Simon and Schuster.

Jackendoff, R. (1987) *Consciousness and the Computational Mind*. Cambridge, MA: MIT Press.

Koch, C. (1992) What Is Consciousness? *Discover*, November, 96.

Levine, J. (1983) Materialism and qualia: the explanatory gap. *Pacific Philosophical Quarterly* 64, 354–61.

Nagel, T. (1974) What is it like to be a bat? *Philosophical Review* 4, 435–50.

Newell, A. (1990) *Unified Theories of Cognition*. Cambridge, MA: Harvard University Press.

Penrose, R. (1989) *The Emperor's New Mind*. Oxford: Oxford University Press.

Penrose, R. (1994) *Shadows of the Mind*. Oxford: Oxford University Press.

Velmans, M. (1991) Is human information-processing conscious? *Behavioral and Brain Sciences* 14, 651–69.

Wilkes, K. V. (1988) Yishi, Duh, Um and consciousness. In A. Marcel and E. Bisiach (eds.), *Consciousness in Contemporary Science*, 16–41. Oxford: Oxford University Press.

18

The Global Workspace Theory of Consciousness

BERNARD J. BAARS

Introduction

Scientific studies of consciousness depart from philosophical explorations in one major respect: They must treat consciousness as a testable variable. We therefore study the differences between attended vs. unattended events, masked vs. conscious stimuli, the waking state vs. sleep, and many others. Brain damage shows surprising dissociations between similar conscious and unconscious functions in blindsight, neglect, and even split-brain cases. There is now extensive evidence for unconscious comparison conditions for virtually all known conscious contents. For the past two decades I have called this approach "contrastive analysis" (Baars 1983), but it is of course just the experimental method applied to the study of consciousness. It is quite different from philosophical debates, which always begin with introspective reports without comparison conditions.

For many years the burden of proof was placed on scientists to show that consciousness could be studied empirically (e.g., Dietrich & Hardcastle 2005). It is the only major scientific question in recent history that has been forced to jump that hurdle. However, given the absence of any consensus in mind–body metaphysics, the demand for a philosophical stamp of approval had the effect of blocking any scientific study at all. This special burden parallels the strategy of philosophical vitalism around 1900, which also demanded that scientists must prove that life could be understood empirically. There was a body of evidence for biology in 1900, although not nearly as strong as it is today. For biologists at that time, it was reasonable to sidestep the philosophers' challenge to focus on the evidence. Today, it seems equally sensible to study conscious cognition empirically while leaving mind–body debates to the experts.

Historically, evolving scientific concepts like "heat" do not begin with answers but questions. Adequate definitions come much later. Thermodynamics defined our concept of heat around 1900, but thermometers were discovered centuries before by Galileo, Fahrenheit, and others. Thus science often begins with operational definitions, not conceptual ones. Even behaviorists agreed on an operational definition of consciousness, namely "verbal report." More broadly, "accurate voluntary report" is the most widely used operational index today. By this definition, relevant evidence is plentiful, as shown by William James's magnum opus, *The Principles of Psychology* (1890) (see also Baars et al. 2003). Today, we can see a steady rise in empirical articles that cite consciousness or closely related terms, currently some 5,000 articles per year. That number has been climbing consistently for decades.

A number of scholars raise questions about the causal role of consciousness. However, that debate is entirely dependent on one's definitions. If one treats subjective experience dualistically, as something different from the physical world, a relationship like causality seems paradoxical. But if one views consciousness naturalistically, as an empirical construct like any other, subjective experience simply becomes the viewpoint on the world that is supported by certain brain regions, notably the thalamocortical complex (Edelman & Tononi 2000; Baars et al. 2004). It is certainly private, but by no means a separate division of reality. There is no paradox in speaking of the hippocampus as a region that supports episodic learning, and there should be no difficulty in speaking of the thalamocortical complex as a brain structure that supports conscious functions (in contrast to the cerebellum, for example) (Edelman & Tononi 2000).

A number of philosophers have adopted such a naturalistic approach (Dennett 2001; Churchland 2002). Naturalists maintain, in effect, that there is no reason to doubt the empirical status of consciousness when it is carefully defined as a scientific construct, like memory or language, with a clearly defined role in a nomological network of constructs (Cronbach & Meehl 1955; Hempel 1965).

Here is a straightforward example of "contrastive analysis," treating conscious experience as a variable. We can say a word mentally and let it fade; for about ten seconds afterward it can still be recalled. Our ability to retrieve the word accurately suggests that an unconscious trace must be maintained for a little while. Both the conscious experience of the word and its unconscious memory are believed to involve brain events, many of which can be observed directly via brain recording methods today. This method of contrastive analysis, comparing conscious and unconscious brain events, therefore does not raise the traditional mind–body puzzles. All comparisons are between publicly observable events and constructs inferred from them. Some of these events are reportable and some are not. We therefore have the makings of a controlled experiment on the role of consciousness in immediate memory. We can ask, "What is the effect of being conscious of a word?" With the advent of brain imaging, it has turned out that conscious words show strikingly different brain activity compared to closely comparable unconscious events (e.g., Dehaene et al. 2001; Baars 2002). Thus conscious experience is a difference that makes a difference.

We might avoid the *word* "consciousness" in such studies, and speak only about "reportable" vs. "unreportable" brain events. Behaviorists and operationalists argued for this approach (Stevens 1966). However, radical operationalism loses the advantage of generalization: if we applied it to memory, for example, we would have one kind of memory for button-presses, a different kind for verbal reports, yet a third for confidence ratings, and as many more as we have behavioral measures. We would end up with a swarm of empirical measures. The term "memory" refers to a construct inferred over many observations, just as "gravity" does in physics or "species" in biology.

"Consciousness" refers to a construct that can be inferred from numerous brain and behavioral observations, ranging from verbal reports to waking EEG. We could call it by some arbitrary label C, but fortunately, over a wide range of conditions the concept "conscious cognition" also happens to correspond to our own experience. Researchers in perception and psychophysics have long known this, and have routinely run themselves as subjects in their own experiments. Under the proper conditions, objective and subjective sources of information converge with great precision. Indeed, we cannot have our eyes examined by an optometrist without making use of this fundamental discovery of the early nineteenth century.

While the term "consciousness" extends an everyday word to an empirical construct, this is also historically common. Scientific terms like "force," "matter," "light," "color," and "sleep" began as everyday words that were refined over time. Readers who are used to thinking of consciousness in philosophical terms may need to adjust to its naturalistic use. We will use it like any other psychobiological concept.

Note that contrastive analysis does not evade phenomenology. On the contrary, experiential reports are involved in each contrastive case. In binocular rivalry we compare a conscious stream of optical input to a physically identical unconscious stream. We can directly observe the effect of both streams on the activity of neurons in the visual brain (e.g., Kreiman et al. 2002). This kind of experimental comparison has now been performed in many experiments, using a variety of methods (for reviews, see Baars 2002; Baars et al. 2003; Frackowiak et al. 2004).

Any theory that can account for this evidence deals with some aspect of consciousness. If we ever find a coherent explanation for all the contrastive evidence we will have a complete theory.

The Central Puzzle: Conscious Limits vs. Unconscious Vastness

Conscious cognition is closely associated with "limited capacity" aspects of the brain. Limited capacity phenomena include immediate memory, the selectivity of attention, coherent binding of perceptual features, the limits of voluntary control, and the fact that we cannot do two demanding actions at the same time. If we look only at such evidence, the brain seems to be slow, serial, and error-prone. But when the brain is observed directly, it seems dramatically different: It is a massive collection of neural assemblies, cells, layers, and connections, each specialized in some specific task, such as analyzing visual shape, maintaining body temperature or mapping body space. The great bulk of these functions happen at the same time, in parallel, as one great "society of mind." Together, their processing capacity is enormous, though unconscious. The great puzzle is, why is the conscious aspect of the brain so limited when the unconscious part is so vast?

Brain evidence for vast capacity of unconscious processes

Looking directly at the brain we see great orderly forests of neurons. The cortex, for example, has an estimated 55 billion cells. The interconnectedness of neurons is remarkable; in less than seven steps we can reach any single neuron in the brain from any other. Cortical neurons branch out into vast elegant fiber bundles running between thalamus and cortex; 600 million fibers connect the two hemispheres, and comparable numbers hang in great loops to connect distant points within each hemisphere. It is quite a beautiful and regular arrangement. The brain is massively parallel: many things are happening at the same time. Most of them by far are unconscious.

The brain shows a distributed style of functioning, in which the detailed work is done by millions of specialized neuronal groupings without instructions from some command center. By analogy, the human body works cell by cell; unlike an automobile, it has no central engine that does all the work. Each cell is specialized for a specific function according to its DNA, its developmental history, and chemical influences from other tissues. In its own way the human brain shows the same distributed style of organization as the rest of the body.

It is a remarkable fact that we can create access to almost any part of the brain using consciousness. To gain control over alpha waves in cortex we merely sound a tone when alpha is detected in the EEG, and shortly we will be able to increase alpha at will. To control a single spinal motor neuron we can play back its electrical spikes over headphones; in one half-hour, subjects have been able to play drumrolls on their single motor neurons. Of course we are not conscious of the details of control; rather, conscious feedback seems to mobilize unconscious systems that handle the details. Conscious feedback control over single neurons and even large populations of neurons is well established.

Psychological evidence for vast unconscious capacity

We come to similar conclusions when we look at the mental lexicon, at semantics or grammar. In a fraction of a second after you glance at a word in this chapter, your visual input is converted into a semantic code able to interpret its meaning. Going from words to meanings is believed to require a large, unconscious mental lexicon. The lexicon of educated speakers of English contains about 100,000 words. While we do not use all of them in everyday speech, we can understand each one instantly, as soon as it is presented in a sentence. But words are complicated things. The *Oxford English Dictionary*, for example, devotes 75,000 words to the numerous meanings of the word "set."

Autobiographical memory

The size of long-term memory is unknown, but we know that simply by paying attention to as many as 10,000 distinct pictures over several days, we can learn to recognize each of them without any attempt at memorizing. Stephen Kosslyn writes that

> The capacity of our visual memories is truly staggering; it is so large that it has yet to be estimated . . . Perhaps the most staggering results are reported by Standing (1973) who showed some of his subjects 10,000 arbitrarily selected pictures for 5 seconds each . . . His findings showed that there is no apparent upper bound on human memory for pictures. Moreover, with immediate recall, Standing estimated that if one million vivid pictures were shown, 986,300 would be recognized if one were tested immediately afterward; even after a delay, he estimates that 731,400 would be recalled. (Kosslyn 1980, p. 129)

Remarkable results such as this are common when we just ask people to choose between known and new pictures. Such recognition tests work so well because they re-present the original conscious experience in its entirety. Here the brain does a marvellous job of memory search, with little conscious effort. We can get an everyday sense of this remarkable performance from recognizing a film seen only once, many years ago, with a sudden sense of familiarity. Often we can even predict the following scene. It seems that we create memories of the stream of experience merely by paying attention to something; but human beings are always paying attention to things, suggesting that autobiographical memory must be very large indeed. Once again we have a vast unconscious domain, and we gain access to it using consciousness. Mere consciousness of an event helps to store its memory, and when we experience the same event again that experience also helps us to retrieve it from among millions of other memories.

In sum, it seems that the very limited stream of consciousness gives us access to billions of neurons in the brain and body, to the mental lexicon, and to an inestimably large

Contexts

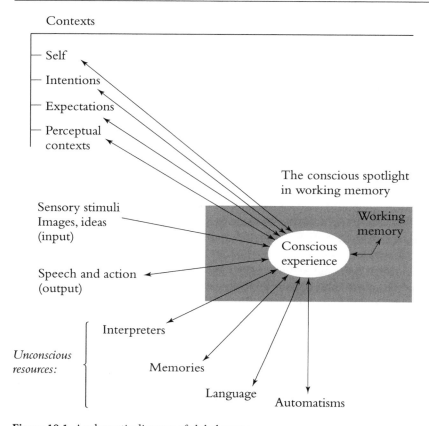

Figure 18.1 A schematic diagram of global access.

source of autobiographical memories. Mere unaided consciousness may be sufficient to create rapid learning and accurate recognition. Consciousness is also needed to trigger a great number of automatic routines that make up specific actions. All these effects of consciousness are unconscious. Consciousness may be considered as the gateway to the brain's unconscious sources of knowledge and control.

Global Access: an Answer to the Puzzle of Limited Capacity?

A theater metaphor gives us a plausible way to think about this evidence. A theater combines very limited events taking place on stage with a vast audience, just as consciousness involves limited information that creates access to a vast number of unconscious sources of knowledge. Consciousness seems to be the publicity organ of the brain, or in Dennett's phrase, it may be "fame in the brain." It is a means for accessing, disseminating, and exchanging information, and for exercising global coordination and control.

The idea that consciousness has an integrative function has a long history. Global workspace theory (GWT) suggests that the brain has a fleeting integrative capacity that enables access between functions that are otherwise separate. This makes sense in a brain that is viewed as a massive parallel set of highly specialized neuronal processors. In such a system

Table 18.1 Theoretical predictions: brain capacities enabled by conscious events (Baars 1988, 2002)

1   Conscious perception enables access to widespread brain sources; unconscious sensory processing is much more limited.

2   Conscious perception, inner speech, and visual imagery enable working memory functions, including executive control.

3   Conscious events enable many kinds of learning: episodic and explicit learning, but also implicit and skill learning.

4   Conscious perceptual feedback enables voluntary control over motor functions, and perhaps over any neuronal population and even single neurons.

5   Conscious contents can evoke selective attention and be reciprocally evoked by it.

6   Consciousness enables access to "self" – executive interpreters, located in frontal and parietal cortex.

coordination and control may take place by way of such a central information exchange, allowing some specialized processors – such as sensory regions in cortex – to distribute information to the system as a whole. This solution also works in large-scale computer architectures, which show typical "limited capacity" behavior when information flows by way of a global workspace. A sizable body of evidence suggests that consciousness is the primary agent of such a global access function in humans and other mammals (Baars 1983, 1988, 1997, 2002).

Figure 18.1 shows a sketch of global access. Table 18.1 shows six general claims made by GWT regarding brain capacities enabled by conscious events (Baars 1988, 1997, 2002; Baars & Franklin 2003; Baars et al. 2004). Several scientists and philosophers now support some version of global access. Their convergence is striking (e.g., Dennett 2001; Dehaene et al. 2001, 2003; Edelman & Tononi 2000; Freeman 2003). While they do not necessarily accept all features of GWT, they tend to agree that consciousness enables widespread access.

Global Workspace Theory and Specific GW Models

The most detailed exposition of GWT developed seven increasingly complex models (Baars 1988), all of which involved competition between global workspace inputs and widespread distribution to a collection of unconscious specialized processors. Because more than a dozen different models have been developed under the umbrella of global workspace theory, it is useful to make a clear distinction between the general features of GWT and specific GW models (GWMs) that apply to experimental data sets, or which make use of specific theoretical mechanisms, such as neural net models or hybrid artificial intelligence architectures.

Table 18.2 shows specific empirical claims made by the seven cumulative GW models of GWT, laid out in depth in *A Cognitive Theory of Consciousness* (Baars 1988). All but one of the major claims, which were highly controversial in 1988, are now supported by substantial bodies of evidence (e.g., Frackowiak et al. 2004). Each of these claims is falsifiable, and has been supported by considerable evidence since publication.

Table 18.3 shows specific global workspace models developed by other authors. These are neural net models tested by standard paradigms like visual backward masking and the attentional blink (studies by Dehaene and co-authors), as well as Franklin's large-scale implementation of GW theory in the context of an inclusive computational model of cognition, called IDA (Franklin 2003). In addition, Shanahan has developed GWT arguments for

Table 18.2 Seven global workspace models: predictions and results (Baars 1988)

Model	Predictions	Evidence
GW Model 1 (p. 73)	1 Conscious representations are internally consistent and globally distributed. 2 Global distribution: Many functional imaging studies.	Internal consistency in visual object recognition appears to be established by area IT.
GW Model 2 (p. 137)	Unconscious contexts shape conscious experiences.	Discovery of unconscious visuospatial maps in parietal cortex, which contextually influence the conscious visual ventral stream.
GW Model 3 (p. 177)	Conscious experience is informative – it always demands a degree of adaptation.	Discovery of loss in cortical activation with redundant practice and automaticity.
GW Model 4 (p. 225)	Conscious contents can establish goal contexts and facilitate spontaneous problem solving.	Model 4 explicitly implemented in large-scale computer model by Franklin (2003). Recent findings unknown.
GW Model 5 (p. 259)	Voluntary control is exercised by global distribution of conscious ideomotor images.	Frackowiak et al. (2005) summarize the relationship of prefrontal voluntary control functions and regions activated by conscious, but not unconscious stimuli.
GW Model 6 (p. 301)	"Attention" involves control of access to consciousness.	Now also proposed by a number of other researchers.
GW Model 7 (p. 325)	"Self" as the dominant context of experience and action.	Baars et al. (2004), frontoparietal hypometabolism in four types of unconscious states. Also overlap of executive regions with cortical areas activated by conscious, but not unconscious events (Frackowiak et al. 2004).

addressing widely debated cognitive science questions like modularity and the frame problem (Shanahan & Baars 2005). Baars and Franklin (2003) have also shown how the IDA model of GWT can account for the role of conscious elements in cognitive working memory (Baddeley 2000).

Gaps and Limits in Current Work

The single biggest "gap in the literature" is between cognitive and brain evidence, but that gap is being bridged with extraordinary rapidity. Functional brain recordings of all kinds, ranging from single-cell studies in epileptic patients to fMRI have all contributed significant new insights. It no longer makes sense to separate brain and cognitive data or theory.

Table 18.3 Dehaene's global workspace models: predictions and results

Model	Predictions	Results
Dehaene and Changeux (2000). Reward-dependent learning in neuronal networks for planning and decision-making.	Dorsolateral prefrontal and anterior cingulate cortex will be mobilized during acquisition of a novel task, effortful execution, and subsequent errors.	Higher fMRI activation during such conditions using the Stroop task.
Dehaene et al. (2001). Cerebral mechanisms of word masking and unconscious repetition priming.	Unconscious visual words will evoke local but not global cortical activity.	Backward-masked words activated left extrastriate, fusiform, and precentral areas, while conscious words activated parietal, prefrontal regions as well.
Dehaene et al. (2003) A neuronal network model linking subjective reports and objective physiological data during conscious perception.	Global neuronal network model predicts sustained activity in primary visual area (V1), amplification of perceptual processing, correlation across distant regions, joint parietal, frontal, and cingulate activation, gamma-band oscillations, and P300 waveform.	All-or-none fMRI activation of frontoparietal regions in attentional blink paradigm, coinciding with subjective report.

Global workspace theory must be a biocognitive theory. Clearly, much more must be done along those lines, to converge with the brain-based globalist theories discussed below.

Some fundamental conceptual questions need to be resolved. For example, the metaphor of global "broadcasting" is not inappropriate for topographically mapped functional systems in the brain (vision, touch, motor control), especially when one level of maps, such as LGN, has a point to point correspondence with a higher level like V1. Such connectivity can support a high-fidelity signal being sent to many topographically mapped brain regions from an input array of sensory receptors. However, as Edelman and Tononi (2000) have argued, the thalamocortical system has more complex re-entrant connectivity than one-directional map-to-map correspondence. In the most complete statement of GWT (Baars 1988), the possibility is explicitly left open that other ways of thinking about global influences must be considered, beyond "broadcasting." Indeed, it is not impossible that there are multiple GW-like systems in the brain, which may operate quite differently from each other. Such functional redundancy (called degeneracy) is typical of all biological systems (Edelman & Gally 2001).

Critiques of globalist approaches

Some critics have wondered whether GWT is a "Cartesian theater," a *reductio ad absurdum* proposed by Daniel Dennett. If it is, that would refute GWT. But Dennett himself has never made such a criticism, and has indeed come out with his own slogan for GWT: "fame in the brain." Those who wonder whether GWT is equivalent to a Cartesian theater should therefore read Dennett (2001). The Cartesian *reductio* involves a point center "where everything comes together," named after Descartes, who proposed that such a point center exists in the pineal gland. But of course there are no such point centers in global workspace models as they were first developed by artificial intelligence researchers (Newell 1994; Franklin 2003). They are "virtual spaces," implemented in a variety of formats. In real theaters many currents of information flow together – including the activities of playwrights, actors, directors, spotlight operators, stage hands, and of course, the attending audience. The brain has many areas of massive convergence and divergence, such as the reticular formation, thalamus, entorhinal cortex, planum temporale, and indeed the entire thalamocortical system. None of these realities involve point centers, so that they are not Cartesian absurdities. The critique of GWT as a Cartesian theater is therefore mistaken.

The same point may be made for other standard philosophical critiques of scientific studies of consciousness. Most scientists and many philosophers reject such "in principle" arguments against empirical work. As we have noted above, GWT is based on comparisons between brain events that support conscious experiences vs. those that do not, such as cortical vs. cerebellar activity. All of GWT is based on comparisons between clearly physical phenomena, though the conscious ones obviously are marked by phenomenological privacy from the perspective of the individual. Thus the standard critiques about qualia, the "hard problem," and so on, simply do not apply.

Given the relative novelty of serious scientific work on this topic, there is a surprising amount of agreement among theorists so far. Most take a system-wide or architectural approach, since conscious experience is so clearly involved in all the major functions of the brain – perception, explicit cognition, learning and memory, imagery, voluntary control, problem-solving, emotional events and the like. A few claim that particular conscious contents involve only local cortical regions. The best known is Semir Zeki's proposal for "micro-conscious" activity in small numbers of cortical neurons (see chapter 45). Thus conscious color perception is proposed to be exclusively dependent on cortical area V4. This hypothesis depends on the finding of differential rise times for different visual regions in some studies (Zeki 2003).

It is not a new observation that different features of a stimulus become available at slightly different exposure times. It was a well-known observation in the nineteenth century. The question is whether such results imply a multitude of different types of consciousness, perhaps one for each kind of cortical feature cell. That would lead to thousands of micro-conscious brain regions.

From a GWT perspective such a very strong localizationist view involves a misunderstanding. Any brain interpretation of GWT must necessarily involve numerous specialized regions with slightly different rise times, because of conduction delays, re-entrant loop thresholds, a changing balance of excitation and inhibition, attentional modulation and numerous other variables. In addition, any interpretation of global distribution must involve thousands of populations of specialized cells, which can obviously be studied locally as well. Finding different operating characteristics of local regions in relation to consciousness is therefore no surprise. It certainly does not falsify GWT.

Indeed, a brain interpretation of GWT requires precisely the kind of convergent visual processing that we know to be happening in the flow from V1 to object representation regions in inferotemporal (IT) cortex. A landmark study by Sheinberg and Logothetis (1997) strongly suggests that for conscious object recognition, integration takes place in human area IT. From a GWT perspective, therefore, divergent broadcasting of visual contents might occur from IT to regions such as hippocampus and Area 46, a visuotopically mapped area of prefrontal cortex. This could occur via cortico-cortical or cortico-thalamo-cortical connections (e.g., Dehaene et al. 2001). Alternatively, widespread distribution could occur via horizontal spreading in the gray matter of cortex (Freeman 2003). In addition, a number of recent studies support the hypothesis that conscious contents involve field potentials in the beta-gamma range, the so-called "40 Hz hypothesis." The predominance of beta-gamma activity in conscious states may reflect resonant interaction between different brain regions. Such resonance may reflect both "binding" of different object features in the case of vision, and widespread distribution and recruitment of additional neuronal populations beyond visual cortex. These different mechanisms for "broadcasting" are by no means mutually exclusive. There may well be multiple brain mechanisms for GW-type functions. As Edelman and Gally (2001) maintain, such functional redundancy is a very general property of biological systems.

Summary and Conclusions

Global workspace theory suggests that conscious cognition involves numerous brain networks that cooperate and compete in solving problems. Consciousness is the gateway to the brain, enabling control even of single neurons and whole neuronal populations. None of these control functions become directly conscious, of course, but conscious feedback seems required to recruit local control by neuronal assemblies. In the metaphor of the theater, it seems as if each specialized audience member can decide locally whether or not to look at the bright spot on stage. Executive functions – the director behind the scenes – are also largely unconscious, often using the actor in the spotlight of consciousness to recruit specific functions.

GW theory does not claim to be exhaustive. Like any theory, it requires a mass of evidence. No doubt our ignorance exceeds what we seem to understand by orders of magnitude. Nevertheless, the convergence of evidence and theory is encouraging so far.

See also 17 The hard problem of consciousness; 22 The information integration theory of consciousness; 24 Daniel Dennett on the nature of consciousness; 30 Functionalism and qualia; 40 Preconscious processing; 41 Implicit and explicit memory and learning 44 A neurobiological framework for consciousness.

Further Reading

Baars, B. J. (2002) The conscious access hypothesis: origins and recent evidence. *Trends in Cognitive Sciences* 6: 1, 47–52.

Baars, B. J. and Franklin, S. (2003) How conscious experience and working memory interact. *Trends in Cognitive Sciences* 7: 4, 166–72.

Baars, B. J., Ramsoy, T. Z., and Laureys, S. (2003) Brain, conscious experience and the observing self. *Trends in Neurosciences* 26: 12, 671–5.

Dehaene, S. and Naccache, L. (2001) Towards a cognitive neuroscience of consciousness: Basic evidence and a workspace framework. *Cognition* 79, 1–37.

Dehaene, S. and Changeux, J.-P. (2005) Ongoing spontaneous activity controls access to consciousness: a neuronal model for inattentional blindness. *PLoS Biology* 3: 5, e141.

References

Baars, B. J. (1983) Conscious contents provide the nervous system with coherent, global information.

In R. J. Davidson, G. E. Schwartz, and D. Shapiro (eds.), *Consciousness and Self-Regulation*, 41. New York: Plenum Press.

Baars, B. J. (1988) *A Cognitive Theory of Consciousness*. New York: Cambridge University Press.

Baars, B. J. (1997) *In the Theater of Consciousness: The Workspace of the Mind*. New York: Oxford University Press.

Baars, B. J. (2002) The conscious access hypothesis: origins and recent evidence. *Trends in Cognitive Sciences* 6, 47–52.

Baars, B. J. (forthcoming) Commentary on Van der Velde and de Kamps, neural blackboard architectures of combinatorial structures in cognition. *Behavioral and Brain Sciences*.

Baars, B. J. and Franklin, S. (2003) How conscious experience and working memory interact. *Trends in Cognitive Sciences* 7, 166–72.

Baars, B. J., Ramsoy, T., and Laureys, S. (2003) Brain, conscious experience and the observing self. *Trends in Neurosciences* 26: 12, 671–5.

Baddeley, A. D. (2000) The episodic buffer: a new component of working memory? *Trends in Cognitive Sciences* 4: 11, 417–23.

Churchland, P. S. (2002) *Brain-Wise: Studies in Neurophilosophy*. Cambridge, MA: MIT Press.

Cronbach, L. and Meehl, P. (1955) Construct validity in psychological tests. *Psychological Bulletin* 52: 4, 281–302.

Dehaene, S., and Changeux, J-P. (1997) A hierarchical neuronal network for planning behaviour. *Proceedings of the National Academy of Sciences USA* 94, 13293–8.

Dehaene, S., Naccache, L., Cohen, L., Le Bihan, D., Mangin, J. F., Poline, J. B. et al. (2001) Cerebral mechanisms of word masking and unconscious repetition priming. *Nature Neuroscience* 4, 752–8.

Dehaene, S., Sergent, C., and Changeux, J-P. (2003) A neuronal network model linking subjective reports and objective physiological data during conscious perception. *Proceedings of the National Academy of Sciences* 100: 14, 8520–5.

Dennett, D. C. (2001) Are we explaining consciousness yet? *Cognition* 79, 221–37.

Dietrich, E. and Hardcastle, V. G. (eds.) (1995) *Sisyphus's Boulder: Consciousness and the limits of the knowable*. Amsterdam: John Benjamins.

Edelman, G. M. (2003) Naturalizing consciousness: a theoretical framework. *Proceedings of the National Academy of Sciences* 100, 5520–34.

Edelman, G. M. and Tononi, G. (2000) *A Universe of Consciousness: How Matter Becomes Imagination*. New York: Basic Books.

Frackowiak, R. S. J., Ashburner, J. T., Penny, W. D., Zeki, S., Friston, K. J., Frith, C. D. et al. (2004) *Human Brain Function*, 2nd edn. London: Elsevier.

Franklin, S. (2000) Deliberation and voluntary action in "conscious" software agents. *Neural Network World* 10, 505–21.

Franklin, S. (2003) IDA: a conscious artifact? *Journal of Consciousness Studies* 10: 4/5, 47–66.

Freeman, W. J. (2003) The wave packet: an action potential for the twenty-first century. *Journal of Integrative Neuroscience* 2: 1, 3–30.

Hempel, C. G. (1965) *Aspects of Scientific Explanation*. New York: Free Press.

Kosslyn, S. M. (1980) *Image and Mind*. Cambridge, MA: Harvard University Press.

Kreiman, G., Fried, I., and Koch, C. (2002) Single-neuron correlates of subjective vision in the human medial temporal lobe. *Proceedings of the National Academy of Sciences* 99: 12, 8378–83.

Newell, A. (1994) *Unified Theories of Cognition: The William James Lectures*. Cambridge, MA: Harvard University Press.

Shanahan, M. and Baars, B. J. (2005) Applying global workspace theory to the frame problem. *Cognition* 98: 2, 157–76.

Sheinberg, D. L. and Logothetis, N. K. (1997) The role of temporal cortical areas in perceptual organization. *Proceedings of the National Academy of Sciences* 94: 7, 3408–13.

Stevens, S. S. (1966) Operations or words? *Psychological Monographs* 80: 19, 33–8.

Zeki, S. (2003) The disunity of consciousness. *Trends in Cognitive Sciences* 7: 5, 214–18.

19

The Intermediate Level Theory of Consciousness

JESSE PRINZ

In 1987, Ray Jackendoff published *Consciousness and the Computational Mind*. In it, he posed an important Where question: Where, in the flow of information, does consciousness arise? Most cognitive scientists agree that the mind is, in some sense, a computer. It is a device that processes information by transforming representations in accordance with rules. Computational devices decompose into various interconnected subsystems, each of which performs some aspect of a complex task. Given such a decompositional analysis, we can ask: in which subsystems does consciousness arise? If we depict the mind as a vast flow chart, and highlight the boxes whose rules and representations are conscious, which boxes should we mark?

Jackendoff's answer is simple and elegant. He noticed that many of our mental capacities, including our senses and our language systems, are organized hierarchically. In each of these hierarchies, it makes sense to talk about low-, intermediate-, and high-level processing systems. We break down tasks into stages. Appealing to prevailing models of these stages, Jackendoff observed that the intermediate level seems to be privileged with respect to consciousness. Consciousness seems to arise in intermediate-level processing systems and not elsewhere. If Jackendoff is right, this is a very important discovery. I have defended the intermediate-level hypothesis (hereafter ILH) in several places (Prinz 2000; 2001; 2005; forthcoming). The hypothesis has also been sympathetically discussed by Christof Koch and his collaborators (Koch & Braun 1996; Crick & Koch, chapter 44 and 2000; Koch 2004). In this chapter, I will review the current evidence. I will not spend a lot of time rehearsing Jackendoff's arguments. When he wrote the book, he relied heavily on current models in linguistics and computational psychology. Those models need to be supplemented by more recent research, especially findings from neuroscience. I think ILH holds up well against this evidence.

Jackendoff does not regard ILH as a fully fledged theory of *how* conscious arises. He expresses some doubts about whether a satisfying materialist theory can ever be given. ILH is presented as a theory of *where* consciousness arises in information processing, not a theory of the physical or functional conditions that are sufficient for conscious experience. I think Jackendoff should not be so modest. Although inadequate on its own, I think ILH is the cornerstone of an adequate theory of consciousness.

Locating Consciousness

Vision

Jackendoff's intermediate-level hypothesis is intended to apply to all sensory experience, including our experience of language. I will focus on vision, because this is the most extensively studied sense. Jackendoff's views on vision were shaped by the seminal work of David Marr (1982). According to Marr, visual object recognition proceeds in three stages. First, the visual system generates a primal sketch of a visual scene. The primal sketch is a mental representation corresponding to local features of the stimulus. Discontinuities in light entering the retina are used to derive a patchwork of oriented edges, bars, ends, and blobs. It is useful to think of the primal sketch as a pixel array. Each pixel indicates, for example, whether there is an edge present at that point in space, but the pixels have not yet been unified with each other to generate a coherent representation of an entire object. Even stereoscopic depth information has not been encoded. At the next state of processes, the visual system generates a 2.5-D sketch. This representation unifies the pixels into a coherent representation of an object's boundaries. It represents surface textures, separates figure from ground, and uses shading and stereoscopic information to capture information about depth. One can think of the resulting representation as an array of bounded, spatially oriented surfaces. Marr thinks the 2.5-D sketch is not ideally suited for object recognition. Unlike the primal sketch, it does represent the bounded contours of objects, but it represents those objects from a specific vantage point. Every time we encounter an object from different vantage points, we end up with a different 2.5-D sketch. The visual system needs a way of determining that these distinct viewpoint-specific representations are images of the same object. To do that, Marr supposes that the visual system generates structural descriptions. It uses information in the 2.5-D sketch to determine what three-dimensional forms comprise the object that is currently being perceived. He calls the resulting representation a 3-D model, to emphasize the fact that it captures the entire three-dimensional structure of an object, rather than merely capturing depth information from a single point of view. 3-D models are built up from volumetric primitives, such as cubes, codes, and three-dimensional cylinders. The exact same 3-D model is derived from different 2.5-D sketches. A cow perceived from different angles will produce the same 3-D model. In fact, 3-D models abstract away from surface textures and information about the specific (i.e., metric) size relationships between parts, so any ordinary cow perceived under decent conditions would generate the same 3-D model. For this reason, 3-D models are ideally suited for object recognition. The visual system stores 3-D models in memory and matches these against the models generated by what we are viewing at any given moment.

With Marr's theory in hand, Jackendoff asks, where in visual processing does consciousness arise? The answer should be obvious. We do not have a visual experience corresponding to the primal sketch. We can see edges and blobs, of course, but, when we look at a scene, adjacent edges blend together, and we experience them as located in depth at some distance from us. The primal sketch is not very different from the 2-D array on the retina. It is a flat disunified jumble. Nor do we have a visual experience corresponding to the 3-D model stage. 3-D models are invariant across viewing positions, and they abstract away from textures and other surface features. In conscious experience, objects are always presented to us from a specific point of view, and we are often vividly aware of surface details.

Of Marr's three levels, only the 2.5-D sketch corresponds to conscious experience. We consciously experience a world of surfaces and shapes oriented in specific ways at various distances from us. If Marr is right about the three levels of vision, then Jackendoff seems to be right about the stage at which visual consciousness arises. Visual conscious arises at a level of processing that is neither too piecemeal, nor too abstract. It arises at an intermediate level, which occurs between discrete pixels and abstract models.

One problem with Jackendoff's proposal is that Marr's theory of vision is out of date. We have learned a lot about vision in the 30 years since Marr originally developed his ideas. Much of that knowledge comes from the neurosciences, and the emerging picture departs from Marr in various respects. One problem is that there are known to be dozens of visual areas, not just three, and these are not strictly hierarchical, because information can flow laterally and backward, rather than just forward. I do not think either of these observations is fatal to Jackendoff's hypothesis, however. First, while there are many visual *areas*, neuroscientists still find it useful to talk about low, intermediate, and high levels of processing; they just point out that each level contains a number of areas. A level can be characterized by whether it detects isolated local features (low level), bound features segmenting perceived objects and distinguishing them from the background (intermediate level), and/or comparatively abstract categorical representations (high level). Second, the fact that information can flow in different directions is compatible with the claim that each level is successively further from the input receptors in the retina, and each level can generate representations by registering features at the prior stage of processing. There is a hierarchy in this sense, even if top-down processing is possible – indeed, the term "top-down" implies a hierarchical ordering.

The real challenge to Marr's theory comes when we look at how each of the levels of visual processing function. We now know that the lowest levels of visual processing in the brain are not quite as simple as a primal sketch. Primary visual cortex (V1) – the first cortical area involved in vision – processes some stereoscopic information (Backus 2000), and can, to some degree, fill in missing contours (Seghier et al. 2000) and distinguish figure from ground (Lamme 1995). High-level visual processing, which has been correlated with activity in portions of inferior temporal cortex, does not make use of 3-D models. There is little evidence for viewpoint invariant volumetric primitives of the kind Marr proposed in object recognition. Instead, high-level vision exploits a repertoire of more idiosyncratic shapes, such as a striped triangle, a circle with a bar protruding from it, or an eight pointed star (Tanaka 1997). The current conception of intermediate-level vision also differs from Marr's. Extrastriate cortex, which is the presumed neural correlate of intermediate-level processing, divides up into a number of functionally distinct subsystems, each of which processes a different aspect of the perceived stimulus (Zeki 1993). Simplifying a little, area V4 responds to color, V3 responds to form, and V5 responds to motion.

Despite these and many other differences in function, the prevailing conception of how vision works is consistent with those aspects of Marr's theory that Jackendoff requires. The prevailing wisdom still aligns with Marr's basic conception of how the visual hierarchy progresses. There is a movement from low-level areas with small receptive fields (V1), to categorical representations in inferotemporal cortex, with intermediate-level object representations in between (extrastriate cortex). More to the point, findings from neuroscience have added support to Jackendoff's conjecture that the intermediate level is the locus of conscious experience. Most of the evidence comes from three sources: cell recordings in nonhuman primates, functional imaging studies of healthy human beings, and neuropsychological studies of people with focal brain injuries.

Single unit recordings in monkey brains can be used to determine what kind of information is encoded in different stages of the visual hierarchy. Such studies cast doubt on the supposition that consciousness is located in low-level or high-level areas. Cells in V1 are not promising candidates, because they do not reliably respond in ways that are consistent with features that we experience consciously. For example, while V1 is responsive to figures containing illusory contours, the cells that respond are ones that normally fire when contours of the opposite orientation are presented; V1 fires as if it were detecting illusory contours at the wrong orientation (Ramsden et al. 2001). In addition, when we are presented with two color patches in rapid succession, we experience one fused color, but V1 cells respond to each color patch separately (Gur & Snodderly 1997). Cells in inferotemporal cortex, the locus of high-level vision are also bad candidates for the correlates of consciousness. They are invariant across a large range of stimulus changes. For example, inferotemporal cells are active across changes in size, position, orientation, luminance inversion, and left/right reversal (Baylis & Driver 2001). This is quite striking. Each of these changes dramatically alters conscious experience, but they do not have a dramatic effect on cells in high-level visual areas. In contrast, cells in intermediate-level visual areas have response profiles that correspond more faithfully to conscious experience. Extrastriate cells respond to illusory contours (von der Heydt et al. 1984), illusory motion (Tootel et al. 1995), and in accordance with color constancy effects (Zeki 1993). They do not respond invariantly across changes in position, size, and left/right reversal. The response profiles of extrastriate cells have not been fully investigated, but current evidence gels well with Jackendoff's formulation of ILH.

Further support for ILH comes from human neuroimaging. For example, Backus et al. (2001) found that stereoscopic depth information correlated well with activity in extrastriate area V3, rather than V1. Humphrey et al. (1999) found that color after-effects correlated with extrastriate response and not V1 response. Lumer and Rees (1999) found that subjects' interpretations of bistable figures correlated with extrastriate activity. ffytche et al. (1998) showed correlations between extrastriate activation and visual hallucinations. Braun et al. (1997) observed extrastriate activation and V1 deactivation during REM sleep. Mendola et al. (1999) found a high degree of responsiveness to illusory contours in extrastriate areas. Most of these studies show that conscious experiences correlate better with extrastriate activation than with activation of other visual areas.

The most compelling evidence for ILH comes from studies of individuals with focal brain injuries. Jackdendoff's hypothesis makes three clear predictions about how conciousness should be affected by brain damage, and those predictions are consistent with existing evidence. The first prediction is that damage to early-level visual areas should ordinarily eliminate visual experience. Early visual areas are the main source of input to intermediate visual areas, so damage to the former should ordinarily eliminate activity in the latter, resulting in a loss of visual experience. This is just what happens. Destruction of V1 usually results in cortical blindness. There are, however, exceptional cases of residual visual awareness after V1 damage. In some cases, individuals with V1 injuries have visual hallucinations (Seguin 1886; Chatterjee & Southwood 1995; Goldenberg, Müllbacher, & Nowak 1995). This is consistent with ILH, because hallucinations are presumably generated by top-down signals into intermediate-level visual areas, which remain intact after V1 injuries. In addition, ILH can explain the fact that high contrast stimuli can generate conscious visual experiences in individuals who are cortically blind. Neuroimaging has confirmed that such stimuli generate V5 activation via a subcortical pathway (Sahraie et al. 1997).

The second prediction generated by ILH is that damage to high-level processing areas should not eliminate conscious visual experiences. The high level is the locus of object recognition, and it is post-experiential. Subjects with high-level damage, should, therefore, have vivid residual experiences, but impaired visual recognition. This is exactly what neuropsychologists report. High-level visual lesions cause associative agnosia (Farah 1990). Individuals with this condition can faithfully copy pictures presented to them in the lab, but they have no idea what they are drawing. We should not presume that their visual experiences are exactly like ours, however. High-level areas have back projections into intermediate-level areas that may help us organize complex visual displays by selectively attending to meaningful parts. But the faithful drawings produced by associative agnosics suggests that they have no difficulty experiencing the same shapes and colors that we experience.

The third prediction provides the most direct test of the theory: if consciousness is located in the intermediate level, then extrastriate lesions should result in blindness. This prediction is complicated by the fact, mentioned above, that extrastriate cortex is not a single structure, but rather a collection of functionally specialized information processing areas. So, properly formulated, the third prediction says that damage to each of these areas should result in blindness for the information they process. This prediction has been confirmed. Damage to extrastriate color areas causes achromatopsia, or cortical color blindness (Bouvier and Engel 2006); damage to the extrastriate motion area causes akinetopsia, or motion blindness (Zeki 1991); and damage to extrastriate form areas causes apperceptive agnosia, or form blindness (Farah 1990). Apperceptive agnosics, unlike associative agnosics, cannot copy pictures accurately. They seem to have a seriously diminished capacity to experience shapes.

In sum, the findings from neuropsychology, electrophysiology, and functional imaging provide a strong case for ILH in vision.

Beyond vision

Jackendoff argues that ILH applied to all sense modalities. Research on the other senses lags woefully behind research on vision. Nevertheless, recent lessons from neuroscience tend to support Jackendoff's conjecture. I review these findings elsewhere (Prinz, forthcoming), and will confine myself to a few brief observation here.

The first thing to note is that all sense modalities are organized hierarchically. Hearing depends on a hierarchy in superior temporal cortex (Kass & Hackett 2000), touch is hierarchically organized in the insular and parietal cortices (Kaas 1993), and both taste and smell are hierarchically organized in frontal areas (Small et al. 1999; Savic et al. 2000). The exact organization of these hierarchies is still being investigated, but there is reason to be optimistic about the applicability of ILH. First, in every case, our sensory experience seems to reside at a level of abstraction that is neither too local, nor too abstract. In listening to music, for example, we experience tones as having a particular time course and as played by instruments with particular pitch, loudness, and timbre. Representations that are both coherent and rich in detail are likely to be located at an intermediate level. All senses progress from local features to representations that are invariant across multiple stimulus conditions, and consciousness seems to reside in between.

The ILH gains further support from neurology. As with vision, brain damage can cause two forms of agnosia in our other senses: associative and apperceptive. In associative agnosias, we have a rich sensory experience, but no access to its significance, and in apperceptive agnosia, experience is disrupted. Associative agnosias suggest that we can have conscious experience in the absence of categorical representations. This implies that experience is not located at the high level. Apperceptive agnosias generally involve focal injuries to subcomponents of intermediate-level sensory systems, suggesting that low-level processing is not sufficient for normal experience. The fact that we find both forms of agnosia in modalities other than vision suggests that the senses are organized in similar ways, and, that in each case, the intermediate level is the best candidate for the locus of consciousness. This conclusion is tentative, given the current state of research, but promising.

Jackendoff argues that ILH also applies to language. We do not have any direct conscious experience of syntactic trees or lexical entries. If we did, linguistics would be much easier. We are conscious only of speech sounds, and the sounds we experience reside at an intermediate level of auditory processing. A raw acoustic signal is a noisy flow of sound waves with no discrete parts. We streamline this signal in experience, filtering out noise, focusing on significant features, and imposing partitions between words. But we do not experience speech sounds at the categorical level. Any given phoneme sounds differ depending on the age, gender, and accent of the speaker. These differences are lost at the level of categorical phoneme perception, but they are all consciously experienced. Speech sounds are experienced at a level that lies above the buzzing confusion of unfiltered sound waves, but below the level of phoneme categories.

Jackendoff also advances a more surprising thesis. He says that we are not directly conscious of our thoughts, because thinking is couched in concepts rather than intermediate-level perceptual states. These concepts are used to produce sentences, however, and sentences can be consciously experienced in the mind's ear through auditory imagery. Consequently, sentences are our primary means of consciously experiencing our thoughts. They are conscious windows into our unconscious minds. In support of this conjecture, Jackendoff notes that we often talk about thinking in a language. Bilingual speakers report thinking in English at home, but thinking in other languages when they travel. There is no such thing as a conscious experience of words in a language of thought. On Jackendoff's view, we do not literally think in English, because thoughts are composed of concepts, but the idiom makes perfect sense, because it is through English that thoughts become consciously experienced. The fact that many of us experience incessant verbal narratives in our native languages as we go through each day makes perfect sense if language is the conscious shadow of thought.

Why the intermediate level?

On the strong version of Jackendoff's view, all consciousness resides at the intermediate level of perceptual systems. I have been arguing that this conjecture is consistent with current evidence. In a moment, I will address some objections, but first there is one pressing question to address: Why should the intermediate level be privileged with respect to consciousness?

This "why" question can be interpreted in two ways: metaphysically and computationally. On the metaphysical interpretation, the "why" question means something like this: Couldn't there be metaphysically possible creatures that had conscious experiences of other levels of processing? This is a close cousin of what Chalmers and others call the hard problem of consciousness (Chalmers, chapter 17 and 1996). It is like asking, "Why is this particular brain state experienced as red rather than green?" I do not think there is a satisfactory answer to questions like that. It's simply a brute fact about the world that certain functional and physical processes are conscious. The best we can do (and all we ever need to do) is explain why this seems so puzzling. Standard solutions to the hard problem emphasize the nature of phenomenal concepts, and the nondeducibility of the material correlates of experience. Any satisfactory account along these lines would fully address the "why" question under the metaphysical interpretation.

Under the computational interpretation, the "why" question means: In what sense are intermediate level representations computationally important or distinctive? This is a tractable question, and it may lead to insights into the function of consciousness. Representations at the intermediate level are ideally suited for real-time deliberative behavioral responses. Low-level representations fail to bind features into coherent wholes. If we are going to interact with our environment, the low level is not a good guide. The high level is a good deal better for action, but also suboptimal. The high level tells us the category of the stimuli we perceive, but from an allocentric point of view. It abstracts away from stimulus features that are crucial for action. If we encounter a predator, the high-level visual representation does not tell us if it is facing toward us or away from us. Without that knowledge, we cannot decide what course of action to take. So, I propose that the intermediate level plays a distinctive role in information processing. It delivers representations that are coherent but viewpoint specific. These representations are useful for determining what to do here and now.

This proposal faces two objections. First, one might point out that high-level representations are also crucial for making real-time decisions (this point has been pressed against me by Tim Bayne and others). When the predator is facing you, your course of action depends on knowing that it is a predator. In response to this objection, I would draw a distinction between two levels at which decisions are made, which might be called allocentric and egocentric planning respectively. In allocentric planning, we decide what type of behavior, characterized at a relatively high level of abstraction, would be appropriate for coping with a situation under consideration. At the egocentric level, we decide how we should move our bodies in response to the stimuli impinging on our senses. If you see a beverage on the counter, allocentric planning might be used to decide if it *is* vodka or water, if it is yours or your dinner companion's, and if drinking is optimal given other ongoing goals. Egocentric planning instructs you to reach for the glass, if you make an allocentric decision to drink. High-level representations are especially well suited for allocentric planning, and intermediate-level representations are especially well suited for egocentric planning.

The second objection to the proposal that intermediate-level representations serve action in a distinctive way comes from recent research on the visual system. Milner and Goodale (1995) have argued that there are actually two anatomically and functionally separate processing streams in vision: a ventral stream that is involved in object recognition, and a dorsal stream that contributes to visually guided action (see Goodale, chapter 48). The dorsal stream is used to determine how, in particular, we should move our bodies when interacting with visually perceived objects. This sounds very much like the function I was proposing for intermediate-level representations. The problem is that the dorsal stream appears to be unconscious. The intermediate-level representations used by the visual system reside in the ventral stream, which, according to Milner and Goodale, does not guide action. They base this claim largely on work with one apperceptively agnosic patient, D. F., who can successfully manipulate objects even though she cannot recognize them, draw them, or describe them.

Does this undermine my proposal that intermediate-level representations are important for egocentric planning? I do not think so. To see why, we need another distinction. Let us define "action guidance" as processes by which we instruct our motor systems to respond to perceived stimuli. These processes tend to be unconscious. We are not aware of the minute changes in muscles necessary for grasping a cup or walking up a flight of stairs. But action guidance differs from egocentric planning. Planning takes place at a different timescale. It is a process by which we decide what course of action to take, not the process by which we control action. My proposal is that intermediate-level visual representations allow us to make plans about how to act. D. F. cannot use vision to decide what course of action to take, because she lacks conscious visual representations of the world around her.

I conclude that the intermediate level plays a distinctive and important computational role. Some researchers find this puzzling. In wondering why the intermediate level is privileged, they note the arbitrariness of the fact that perceptual hierarchies have three levels. Could they not have two? Or a hundred? Do the 50 or so areas that contribute to visual processing really divide neatly into three levels? I think these puzzles depend on a particular understanding of what the word "intermediate" amounts to. One might get caught up in the fact that the intermediate level is the second stage in a sequence. Call this the "serial understanding of the intermediate level." Alternatively, one might think of the intermediate level semantically. On this reading, the intermediate level is one that is not abstract and categorical, but not piecemeal or disunified. These notions are all in need of some refinement, but, as a first approximation, the idea is that intermediate-level representations are neither too specific nor too general.

As it happens, I think that the two ways of being intermediate coincide. The intermediate level in perceptual systems is sequentially nestled between high and low levels, and it is also the level that represents things in a way that is neither too specific nor too general. There are obvious reasons why these come together. To arrive at a representation that is semantically intermediate, the brain must first represent local features and piece them together, and once one has arrived at such a representation, the brain must do a bit more processing to arrive at representations that are better suited for categorization across a range of vantage points. So semantically intermediate representations tend to be sequentially intermediate. This need not be the case. Suppose that the brain could skip the low level or high level under certain circumstances, or suppose that these levels did not exist. This would not undermine ILH. The semantic notion of intermediate is, in my view, what really matters.

Objections

I now turn to arguments that might be marshaled against ILH and the perception hypothesis. My replies are programmatic. Each objection would take much more discussion to address completely, but the replies should establish that ILH is more resilient than it may initially seem.

Objection 1: Feature Consciousness

We can consciously experience local features even when those features are represented at an early stage of perceptual processing.

Consider vision. According to the three-level picture sketched above, low-level vision extracts local edges. But local edges can be experienced. We can focus on a tiny part of a contour and have a conscious experience of it. Does not that show that the low level can be conscious?

This objection rests on a confusion. Of course we can experience an edge, but, when we do so, we are not necessarily experiencing low-level representations. Representations at the intermediate level have edges and, by focusing attention or moving close to an object, we can make a small bit of edge very vivid, while the surrounding bits of edge blur away. The fact that we can experience features that are represented at a low level does not mean that the low level can be experienced. Some of those features are also represented at the intermediate level. If ILH is right, features that are represented *only* at the low level cannot be experienced, and current evidence is consistent with this prediction.

Objection 2: Categorical Awareness

We can be consciously aware of the categories to which perceived stimuli belong, even though such categorical information is represented at the high level.

When you look at a chair, you are aware of its shape from a particular point of view, but you are also aware of its chairness. When you look at a coin from an angle, you experience an ellipse, but you are also experiencing a circle. Such categorical knowledge resides at the high level and, therefore, the high level seems to be conscious in addition to the intermediate level.

I have never quite seen the force of this objection. When I look at a chair, I do not see chairness; I only see a specific chair oriented in a particular way. When I look at a coin, I just experience an ellipse. Why do some people seem to think they are experiencing something more? Here are four possibilities. The first, is that such people may be confusing qualia and intentional content. An experience can represent a circular object even if the qualitative state has an elliptical form (if we can talk of qualia having shapes). Another possibility is that such people are confusing unconscious knowledge with conscious experience. I know that the coin in front of me is circular, of course, and that will affect the inferences I draw about it, and some of these inferences may promote conscious images. A third possibility is that such people are mistaking nonvisual experiences for visual experiences. When I see a coin, I know that it is circular and I know how to grasp it. This knowledge can result in conscious experiences of behavioral affordances and subvocal labeling, "There's a penny!" These experiences are driven by intermediate-level representations in sense modalities other than vision, such as kinesthesia and the auditory system. The fourth possibility is that the issue is merely semantic. The statement "it appears circular" can mean the conscious state is circular in form (if we can talk that way), or it could mean that the object appears the way circles do, when seen from certain angles. The latter reading does not imply that high-level representations are conscious, so it poses no threat to the theory I am defending. The former reading strikes me as obviously false. These options might be used to explain away the impression that we consciously experience categorical representations.

This is not to deny that categorical representations can affect intermediate-level representations. Consider the duck-rabbit. When your unconscious high-level representations shift from duck to rabbit, you focus on the duck's face in your intermediate-level representation, and the rest fades. This is supported by experimental evidence. Chambers and Reisberg (1992) asked subjects to memorize a picture of a duck-rabbit without telling them it was an ambiguous figure. They then asked subjects to identify the picture they had seen from an array of three choices: one was the original, one had been altered in the region of the rabbit's face, and the other had been altered in the region of the duck's face. Subjects who had interpreted the picture as a duck immediately ruled out the image that had been altered in the duck's face, but were at chance in deciding between the other two, and conversely for those who had construed the picture as a rabbit. This suggests that subjects stored an intermediate-level representation that remained sharply focused only on those features of the contour relevant to interpretation.

For people who still insist that we have phenomenal qualities associated with high-level representations, I offer the following intuition pump. Suppose we could anesthetize intermediate-level visual systems while activating the high level. Imagine a viewpoint invariant chair representation is active, but there is no concomitant image of a chair from any specific vantage point. What would that be like? I think it would not be like anything at all – at least not visually. If you are not convinced try to imagine what these high-level visual representations are like. Try to describe one. If that were possible, it would not be so hard for vision scientists to figure out what kinds or representations are used in inferotemporal cortex.

Objection 3: IT as Locus of Visual Consciousness

Neuroscientific research on binocular rivalry proves that visual consciousness is located in the high level.

This objection is based on work by Logothetis and his colleagues (Sheinberg & Logothetis 1997; Leopold & Logothetis 1999). He presented monkeys with two pictures simultaneously, one in each eye. When rivaling stimuli are presented binocularly, monkeys (and humans) experience just one image at a time, but they shift randomly back and forth. Monkeys can be trained to report what image they are seeing, and by measuring cellular activity at different stages of the visual system, Logothetis sought to discover the correlates of conscious experience. He discovered that only 40 percent of the active cells in intermediate-level areas corresponded to what the monkeys reported seeing, whereas 90 percent of the cells in high-level areas corresponded to what the monkeys reported. Logothetis concluded that visual consciousness is located at the high level.

There is a fallacy in this reasoning. Logothetis reports that some of the active intermediate-level cells do not correspond to the percept, and he infers from this that consciousness is not located at the intermediate level. But this inference assumes that, in brain areas that underwrite consciousness, all active cells will contribute to experience. An alternative possibility is that consciousness does not involve mere activity in a privileged brain area but, rather, a specific pattern of activity in that area. In other words, it is possible that the cells corresponding to the percept at the intermediate level are behaving differently than the cells that do not correspond to the percept. For example, they could be firing at a different rate. It could be the case that *this* difference determines which cells contribute to conscious experience and which do not. Logothetis tells us what proportion of active intermediate cells correspond to the percept, but he does not closely investigate how those cells are firing in comparison to the other active cells. There may be a difference. Indeed, *there must be some difference* in how these cells are behaving, because they, and only they, are exerting influence at the next stage of processing. Cells at the intermediate level are in competition, and that competition must be resolved at the intermediate level. Otherwise, it would not be the case that 90 percent of the high-level cells fire in conjunction with the reported percept. We do not know how the competition at the intermediate level works, and we do not know what is distinctive about the behavior of the cells that win the competition, but there must be some difference that tells higher areas to accept afferents from the victors and not the losers. I propose that consciousness arises whenever intermediate-level cells behave in a way that would allow them to propagate activity forward in this system. Without carefully comparing the activity of cells that correspond to the percept and those that do not, Logothetis cannot use his data to refute the proposal that consciousness arises in the intermediate level.

Objection 4: Subliminal Perception

Intermediate-level perceptual representations may be necessary for consciousness, but they cannot be sufficient, because, in cases of subliminal perception, there are unconscious intermediate-level representations.

As Jackendoff formulates ILH, he sometimes implies that activity in intermediate-level perception systems will always be conscious. This is clearly implausible. Subliminal perception, which is easily achieved through masked priming, is a clear counter example. In addition, there are clinical syndromes, such as unilateral neglect, in which subjects perceptually process stimuli in the absence of awareness. Neuroimaging studies of neglect have confirmed that individuals neglect processed visual information all the way through their perceptual pathways, including the intermediate level (Rees et al. 2000; Vuilleumier et al. 2001). Intermediate-level activation can also be observed when healthy individuals are presented with stimuli that never make it into consciousness, as in change blindness paradigms or masked priming (Beck et al. 2001; Davis et al. 2001; Schnyer et al. 2002).

This is the only objection to ILH that I find compelling. I think cases of unconscious perception establish demonstratively that intermediate-level activation is not sufficient for consciousness. Something more is needed. Jackendoff has identified the contents of consciousness, but he has not identified the process by which these contents become conscious. He has told us *what* we are conscious of, but not *how* we become conscious.

I think the missing ingredient is revealed by unilateral neglect. Neglect is an attention disorder. The lesions that cause the syndrome are in inferior parietal cortex, an area associated with attention. Subjects with neglect process perceptual representations in their blind field, but they do not experience those things because they cannot attend to them. This suggests that consciousness requires attention (Bisiach 1992). That assessment has been tested in healthy subjects. Research on inattentional blindness shows that we lose consciousness of foveally present stimuli when we are performing concurrent tasks that demand attention (Mack & Rock 1998). I think that consciousness arises when intermediate-level representations are modulated by attention. But what is attention? I think it is a gateway that links perceptual systems to working memory systems. Working memory systems allow us to temporarily store perceived information, deliberate, and make decisions. When we attend, information in perceptual systems does not necessarily get stored in working memory, but it becomes available to working memory. That is how intermediate-level representations become conscious.

I defend this proposal more fully elsewhere (see Prinz, op cit.). If I am right, Jackendoff's theory is true, but incomplete. It must be supplemented with the thesis that consciousness requires attention. The attended intermediate-level representation theory (or AIR) is driven by empirical findings, and it has more evidence in its favor than many other theories. For example, the hypothesis that consciousness arises only when neurons oscillate in the gamma range has been empirically challenged (Shadlen & Movshon 1999; O'Reilly et al. 2003); the hypothesis that consciousness arises only when information is encoded in a global workspace has not been defined precisely enough to test; the hypothesis that consciousness requires higher-order thoughts has not been empirically investigated in a systematic way. This is not the place to argue against other theories of consciousness; I wish only to point out that, at the current state of play, the ILH theory may enjoy more empirical support than competing theories.

Conclusions

In this chapter, I offered a defense of ILH. When Jackendoff advanced the hypothesis 20 years ago, most of the existing evidence was behavioral. We now have a large body of corroborative evidence from neuroscience. Evidence is still preliminary, but there is reason to be optimistic. I also addressed some objections to ILH, and argued that all can be answered. This does not mean that ILH offers a complete theory of consciousness. In responding to the last objection, I conceded that mere activation of intermediate-level representations is not sufficient for conscious experience. This objection is consistent with the thesis that intermediate activation is necessary, but a full account of conscious experience requires something more. I suggested that the missing ingredient is attention. Conscious states are attentionally modulated intermediate-level representations. If I am right, Jackendoff provides an adequate account of what we are conscious of, and attention provides an account of how those contents become conscious. Together these components deliver a very promising theory of consciousness.

Acknowledgments

I am grateful to Max Velmans and Bernard Baars for giving me immensely helpful feedback on this chapter despite having little sympathy for the position I defend. I am also indebted to Susan Schneider for her patience and for involving me in this *Companion*. My biggest dept is to Ray Jackendoff for inspiration and support.

See also 17 The hard problem of consciousness; 33 The neurophilosophy of consciousness; 44 A neurobiological framework for consciousness; 48 Duplex vision: separate cortical pathways for conscious perception and the control of action.

Further Readings

Jackendoff, R. (1987) *Consciousness and the Computational Mind*. Cambridge, MA: MIT Press.
Prinz, J. J. (2005) A neurofunctional theory of consciousness. In A. Brook and K. Akins (eds.), *Cognition and the Brain: Philosophy and Neuroscience Movement*, 381–96. Cambridge: Cambridge University Press.
Prinz, J. J. (forthcoming) *The Conscious Brain*. New York: Oxford University Press.

References

Backus, B. T. (2000) Stereoscopic vision: what's the first step? *Current Biology* 10: 19, 701–3.
Backus, B., Fleet, D. J., Parker, A. J., and Heeger, D. J. (2001) Human cortical activity correlates with stereoscopic depth perception. *Journal of Neurophysiology* 86, 2054–68.

Baylis, G. C. and Driver, J. (2001) Shape-coding in IT cells generalizes over contrast and mirror reversal, but not figure–ground reversal. *Nature Neuroscience* 4, 937–42.

Beck, D. M., Rees, G., Frith, C. D., and Lavie N. (2001) Neural correlates of change detection and change blindness. *Nature Neuroscience* 4, 645–50.

Bisiach, E. (1992) Understanding consciousness: clues from unilateral neglect and related disorders. In A. D. Milner and M. D. Rugg (eds.), *The Neuropsychology of Consciousness*, 113–39. London: Academic Press.

Bouvier, S. E. and Engel, S. A. (2006) Behavioral deficits and cortical damage loci in cerebral achromatopsia. *Cerebral Cortex* 16, 183–91.

Braun, A. R., Balkin, T. J., Wesensten, N. J., Carson, R. E., Varga, M., Baldwin, P. et al. (1997) Regional cerebral blood flow throughout the sleep-wake cycle: an H250 PET study. *Brain* 120: 7, 1173–1197.

Chalmers, D. J. (1996) *The Conscious Mind: In Search of a Fundamental Theory*. Oxford: Oxford University Press.

Chambers, D. and Reisberg, D. (1992) What an image depicts depends on what an image means. *Cognitive Psychology* 24, 145–74.

Chatterjee, A. and Southwood, M. H. (1995) Cortical blindness and visual imagery. *Neurology* 12, 2189–95.

Crick, F. C. and Koch, C. (2000) The unconscious homunculus. In T. Metzinger (ed.), *The Neuronal Correlate of Consciousness*, 103–10. Cambridge, MA: MIT Press.

Davis, M. H., Henson, R. N. A., Johnsrude, I. S., and Rugg, M. D. (2001) Priming effects in single-word reading: an event-related fMRI study. Society for Neuroscience Abstracts 27, 82.3.

Farah, M. J. (1990) *Visual Agnosia: Disorders of Object Recognition and What They Tell Us about Normal Vision*. Cambridge, MA: MIT Press.

ffytche, D. H., Howard, R. J., Brammer, M. J., David, A., Woodruff, P. W., and Williams, S. (1998) The anatomy of conscious vision: an fMRI study of visual hallucinations. *Nature Neuroscience* 1, 738–42.

Goldenberg, G., Müllbacher, W., and Nowak, A. (1995) Imagery without perception: a case study of anosognosia for cortical blindness. *Neuropsychologia* 33, 1373–82.

Gur, M., and Snodderly, D. M. (1997) A dissociation between brain activity and perception: chromatically opponent cortical neurons signal chromatic flicker that is not perceived. *Vision Research* 37, 377–82.

Humphrey, G. K., James, T. W., Gati, J. S., Menon, R. S., and Goodale, M. A. (1999) Perception of the McCollough effect correlates with activity in extrastriate cortex: a resonance imaging study. *Psychological Science* 10, 444–8.

Jackendoff, R. (1987) *Consciousness and the Computational Mind*. Cambridge, MA: MIT Press.

Kaas, J. H. (1993) The functional organization of the somatosensory cortex in primates. *Annals of Anatomy* 175, 509–18.

Kaas, J. H. and Hackett, T. A. (2000) Subdivisions of auditory cortex and processing streams in primates. *Proceedings of the National Academy of Science* 97, 11,793–9.

Koch, C. (2004) *The Quest for Consciousness: A Neurobiological Approach*. Englewood, CO: Roberts.

Koch, C. and Braun, J. (1996) Towards the neuronal correlate of visual awareness. *Current Opinion in Neurobiology* 4, 158–64.

Lamme, V. A. F. (1995) The neurophysiology of figure–ground segregation in primary visual cortex. *Journal of Neuroscience*, 15, 1605–15.

Leopold, D. A. and Logothetis, N. K. (1999) Multistable phenomena: changing views in perception. *Trends in Cognitive Sciences* 3, 254–64.

Lumer, E. D. and Rees, G. (1999) Covariation of activity in visual and prefrontal cortex associated with subjective visual perception. *Proceedings of the National Academy of Science* 96, 1669–73.

Mack, A. and Rock, I. (1998) *Inattentional Blindness*. Cambridge, MA: MIT Press.

Marr, D. (1982) *Vision*. San Francisco, CA: Freeman.

Mendola, J. D., Dale, A. M., Fischl, B., Liu, A. K., and Tootell, R. B. H. (1999) The representation of illusory and real contours in human cortical visual areas revealed by functional magnetic resonance imaging. *Journal of Neuroscience* 19, 8560–72.

Milner, A. D. and Goodale, M. A. (1995) *The Visual Brain in Action*. Oxford: Oxford University Press.

O'Reilly, R., Busby, R., and Soto, R. (2003) Three forms of binding and their neural substrates: alternatives to temporal synchrony. In A. Cleeremans (ed.), *The Unity of Consciousness: Binding, Integration, and Dissociation*, 168–92. Oxford: Oxford University Press.

Prinz, J. J. (2000) A neurofunctional theory of visual consciousness. *Consciousness and Cognition* 9, 243–59.

Prinz, J. J. (2001) Functionalism, dualism and the neural correlates of consciousness. In W. Bechtel, P. Mandik, J. Mundale, and R. Stufflebeam (eds.), *Philosophy and the Neurosciences: A Reader*. Oxford: Blackwell.

Prinz, J. J. (2005) A neurofunctional theory of consciousness. In A. Brook and K. Akins (eds.), *Cognition and the Brain: Philosophy and Neuroscience Movement*, 381–96. Cambridge: Cambridge University Press.

Prinz, J. J. (forthcoming). *The Conscious Brain*. New York: Oxford University Press.

Ramsden, B. M., Chou, P. H., and Roe, A. W. (2001) Real and illusory contour processing in area V1 of the primate: a cortical balancing act. *Cerebral Cortex*, 11, 648–65, 2001.

Rees, G., Wojciulik, E., Clarke, K., Husain, M., Frith, C., and Driver, J. (2000) Unconscious activation of visual cortex in the damaged right hemisphere of a parietal patient with extinction. *Brain*, 123, 1624–33.

Sahraie, A., Weiskrantz, L., Barbur, J. L., Simmons, A., Williams, S. C. R., and Brammer, M. J. (1997) Pattern of neuronal activity associated with conscious and unconscious processing of visual signals. *Proceedings of the National Academy of Science* 94, 9406–11.

Savic, I., Gulyas, B., Larsson, M., and Roland, P. (2000) Olfactory functions are mediated by parallel and hierarchical processing. *Neuron* 26, 735–45.

Schnyer, D. M., Ryan, L., Trouard, T., and Forster, K. (2002) Masked word repetition results in increased fMRI signal: a framework for understanding signal changes in priming. *NeuroReport* 13, 281–4.

Seghier, M., Dojat, M., Delon-Martin, C., Rubin, C., Warnking, J., Segebarth, C., and Bullier, J. (2000) Moving illusory contours activate primary visual cortex: an fMRI Study. *Cerebral Cortex* 10, 663–70.

Seguin, E. G. (1886) A contribution to the pathology of hemianopsis of central origin (cortex-hemianopsia). *Journal of Nervous and Mental Diseases* 13, 1–38.

Shadlen, M. N. and Movshon, J. A. (1999) Synchrony unbound: a critical evaluation of the temporal binding hypothesis. *Neuron* 24, 67–77.

Sheinberg, D. L. and Logothetis, N. K. (1997) The role of temporal cortical areas in perceptual organization. *Proceedings of the National Academy of Science* 94, 3408–13.

Small, D. M., Zald, D. H., Jones-Gotman, M., Zatorre, R. J., Pardo, J. V., Frey, S. et al. (1999) Human cortical gustatory areas: a review of functional neuroimaging data. *NeuroReport* 10, 7–14.

Tanaka, K. (1997) Mechanisms of visual object recognition: monkey and human studies. *Current Opinion in Neurobiology* 7, 523–29.

von der Heydt, R., Peterhans, E., and Baumgartner, G. (1984) Illusory contours and cortical neuron responses. *Science* 224, 1260–2.

Vuilleumier, P., Sagiv, N., Hazeltine, E., Poldrack, R. A., Swick, D., Rafal, R. D., and Gabrieli, J. (2001) Neural fate of seen and unseen faces in visuospatial neglect: a combined event-related functional MRI and event-related potential study. *Proceedings of the National Academy of Science* 98, 3495–500.

Zeki, S. (1991) Cerebral akinetopsia (visual motion blindness): a review. *Brain* 111, 811–24.

Zeki, S. (1993) *A Vision of the Brain*. Oxford: Blackwell.

20

Representationalism about Consciousness

WILLIAM SEAGER AND DAVID BOURGET

Philosophers have traditionally drawn a sharp distinction between phenomenal and intentional states. Phenomenal states are states with phenomenal or subjective character – something it's like to be in them. The clearest examples of phenomenal states are perceptions, emotions, and sensations, which involve specific qualitative or sensory characters. Intentional states, such as beliefs, are mental states which represent something as being a certain way. It has been commonly held that the intentional aspects of mental states lack phenomenal character and their phenomenal aspects lack intentionality. Modern representationalism about consciousness (MR) challenges this traditional distinction with the claim that phenomenal character is a species of, and exhausted by, representational content.

The Way of Ideas

MR is often conflated with classical representationalism (CR). We will discuss CR first in order to highlight the contrast between old and new representationalism and bring out some of the strengths of the latter.

CR is an answer to a simple question: What are we aware of in perception? Suppose that someone is consciously perceiving a bright red cardinal perched at a bird feeder on a clear winter day. Common sense strongly suggests that this bird and how it looks and moves is what our perceiver is aware of. It is surely the business of anyone trying to understand perception to explain how it is that perceivers become aware of things such as red birds, feeders, the blue sky, and white snow. However, the slightest acquaintance with the history of philosophy reveals that the route from "perceptual experience" to such normal objects of experience is far from clear or straightforward.

Philosophers have often assumed that, necessarily, when one is undergoing a perceptual experience that might be described either as involving or as an awareness of certain qualities (colors, shape, etc.), one must be in the presence of an object with these qualities. C. D. Broad, for example, could not believe we could "see the property of bentness exhibited in a concrete instance, if in fact nothing was present to our minds that possessed that property" (Broad 1952, p. 241). Given the possibility of illusion and hallucination, it was commonly inferred that in perception we are not directly aware of external objects. CR endorses the conclusion that what we directly perceive are mental entities variously called "ideas," "impressions," or "sense-data." This view has been called "representational-ism" because such internal impressions act as pictures or signs of the external world.

While not without insight, CR has several unpalatable consequences. First, it literally cuts us off from the world and each other. No one has ever been directly aware of anything but their own minds, hence no two people have ever been perceptually aware of the same thing. Furthermore, insofar as CR makes it hard to justify beliefs about the external world, general skepticism threatens. CR is also radically revisionist about the phenomenology of perception. Intuitively, we directly perceive things in the external world rather than always and only our own mental states. The phenomenology of experience is *of* the features of the experienced objects themselves and no distinctively mental features intrude into perception (this is the *transparency* of experience, explored below). CR is potentially metaphysically revisionist as well, for the obvious solution to CR's epistemological catastrophe is to reform our conception of the material world itself. This was Berkeley's famous response, but the history of philosophy is rife with other suggestions along the same lines.

Perhaps the main problem with CR's posit of mental entities which possess all the features we are aware of in perception is that it seems to be irreconcilable with a physicalist world view. Consider this simple argument against materialism. Imagine as vividly as you can the Canadian flag, and note the shape and redness of the central maple leaf. Now consider that nothing in your brain is a bright red maple-leaf shaped blob. Nothing in the brain can be identified with the flag you have just mentally generated (and nothing outside the brain is a possible candidate either). So much for materialism!

Representation to the Rescue

MR rejects the assumption that leads to CR: not every perceptual experience requires that there be something perceived with qualities matching its phenomenal character. Instead, perceptual experience is understood in terms of representation, or intentionality. What an intentional state represents is its content, which can be thought of as *accuracy* or *satisfaction conditions*. For example, if someone believes that snow is white, the belief's content will be true just in case snow is really white. It happens that such a belief would be true, but that does not matter to the content; the content of the belief that most mermaids are beautiful is that most mermaids are beautiful, whether or not there are any mermaids and whether or not the majority of them are beautiful. So the idea is that just as one can have a story about mermaids without there being any such objects, one can have a perceptual experience as of a dagger without there being any dagger, or any immaterial stand-in for the dagger. This conception of experience should not be conflated with that of CR; according to MR, perception is representational in the sense that it is intentional, not in the sense that it is mediated by "internal pictures." Early proponents of this reply to CR include Anscombe (1965), Armstrong (1968), and Hintikka (1969). More recently, Harman (1990), Dretske (1995, 2003), and Tye (1995, 2000) have offered representational accounts of perceptual awareness.

Proponents of MR extend the denial of the assumption that leads to CR in two ways. The first is by characterizing the contents of perceptual experience, typically declaring them to be of external objects rather than internal mental entities. CR and its unpalatable implications are thus avoided. When someone perceives a cardinal they are perceiving a bird and not one of their own mental states. While dependent upon there being an active mental representation within the perceiver, proponents of MR deny that perception is indirect, proceeding via an apprehension of this representation. Rather, there is a "presentation" in consciousness of the content of the representation, a content which can be shared by many perceivers. There is no "maple leaf in the head." When one imagines a Canadian flag, one is aware of the content of a flag-representation which encodes shape and color information. This encoding does not have to be flag-shaped and colored red. Whatever the vehicle of this representational content might be, perhaps a neural state, there is no need for there to be any awareness of it. While accepting MR does not refute skepticism, at least it allows for the possibility of "directly veridical" perceptual experiences in its endorsement of the claim that the contents of awareness are *of* a world independent of the perceiver's mind.

The second extension is a core claim we take to define MR (although weaker views have been dubbed "representational"). The claim is that a state's phenomenal character is exhausted by its content. The exact meaning of this *exhaustion thesis* is that for every phenomenal character P there is some content C such that a state with P is nothing more than a phenomenal state with C as content. It does not follow from the exhaustion thesis that the content which specifies the phenomenal character of a phenomenal state suffices to make any state that has it conscious. What follows is that, given that a state is in fact a phenomenal state, its phenomenal character is completely specified by its representational content.

We can now discern three key projects related to MR. The first is that of determining whether its defining claim – the exhaustion thesis – is true. The second is that of explicating the fundamental difference between phenomenal and nonphenomenal states. The third project is that of developing a theory of representation strong and stable enough to support MR. Unfortunately, there is no acknowledged theory of mental representation, so we must assume for the time being that an appropriate account can be developed.

The Exhaustion Thesis

While it perhaps seems rather obvious that experience carries information which is presented in consciousness, the exhaustion thesis is interesting and controversial. The thesis entails that for each phenomenal character, P, there is a content C, such that (1) all phenomenal states with P have C and (2) all phenomenal states that carry C have P.

Experiences of bodily sensations are often brought up against (1). What is the content of an experience of pain, for example (see Searle 1983)? An answer commonly given is that such experiences represent particular types of bodily damage, malfunction, suboptimality, stress, physiological fatigue, or other sorts of misfortune (Armstrong 1968; Tye 1995; Bain 2003). The idea is simply that in pain the body, or a part of it, is represented as being a certain way, including a distinctive evaluative component discussed further below. But do headaches, for example, connote "bodily damage" (see Crane, forthcoming)? Lots of information is provided by the experience of a headache: location, intensity, and duration, in addition to the distinctive evaluative feature that one's head is "not right." This is what is intended under the rubric of bodily damage.

Moods and unfocused feelings are frequently suggested as counterexamples to MR. How could it be that an experience of elation, for example, has representational content? The key to an account of the content of moods and unfocused feelings is to distinguish global vs. local aspects of representation. If someone puts on some rose-colored spectacles, this changes the way everything looks and – apart from one's knowledge of how colored glass works – the world itself appears to have undergone a general change in color. It is no accident that this is the metaphor we use for positive moods such as elation. In terms of representation, elation is a global transformation rather akin to turning up the brightness of a television: as a first approximation we can say that it involves the superimposition of goodness over everything one perceives.

Most opponents of MR grant that all experiences have representational contents but claim, contra to (2), that their phenomenal aspects "outstrip" their contents. Skepticism about (2) has been fueled by the perspectival nature of vision emphasized by Peacocke (1983, ch. 1, 1992). He argues that some perspectival differences in experience cannot be associated with informational differences. To illustrate, suppose you are looking at a tree from a given angle at a given distance and then step away from the tree without changing your viewing angle. It might seem that your experiences of the tree before and after share the same content: both represent a tree of given dimensions at a given position with many other unchanging features. Yet the two experiences are qualitatively different since, as Peacocke puts it, the tree initially occupies more of your visual field. However, informational differences that account for the change in phenomenal character are not hard to find. For example, the resolution with which you are representing the surfaces of the tree changes as you step away from it. Also, the two experiences represent the tree as being at different distances from you (Tye 1996 emphasizes such relational properties).

One might still suspect that there are experiential differences stemming not from position but rather from the representational system itself. Blurry vision is often raised as an aspect of phenomenal consciousness which outstrips representational content (Boghossian & Velleman 1989). But what we *believe* about the world must be separated from the way we experience the world. The satisfaction conditions of the visual content of a shortsighted perceiver without glasses *is* a world in which things have fuzzy edges. To see this, imagine building a strange environment in which the edges of objects are deliberately "fuzzed out." If done right there would be a vantage point from which perceivers could not tell whether they were wearing their glasses in the fuzzy room or were without their glasses in the ordinary room (see also Tye 2002).

Another difficulty for (2) stems from intermodal perception. Block (2003, 1995) offers a case in which vision and hearing seem to both represent an object "as above" in a way contradicting (2). Here the obvious counter is that vision and audition represent distinct properties beyond location. Among other things, it seems that vision must represent some color, or at least brightness and shading, while audition provides information about pitch and timbre. The fact that the total content of a visual experience and an auditory experience can agree on certain represented subfeatures of the environment is harmless so long as additional represented features distinguish the experiences (see Lycan 1996, pp. 135–6).

The classic thought experiment of the "inverted spectrum" (Locke 1690/1990) puts pressure on (1) and (2) simultaneously. A color-invert experiences colors systematically transposed to their spectral opposites: red looks green, blue looks yellow, etc. Suppose there were inverts among us calling ripe tomatoes "red" even as they experience them as green, the sky "blue" even though they see it as yellow, and so on. The question would then arise as to whether their experience of red represents the property we call "green" and their experience of green represents the property we call "red." If this were the case, the qualitative property characteristic of experiences of red would not determine their content, because ours would be representing red while theirs represents green. Conversely, the content of our experiences of red would not determine any particular phenomenal character because inverts would have experiences of green with this content. This would contradict both (1) and (2) above.

However, it does not follow from the fact that inverts use the word "red" to describe ripe tomatoes that their experiences really represent tomatoes as red. MR can maintain that inverts *believe* that ripe tomatoes are red even though their experiences represent them as green. Such perceivers are merely victims of an inversion of semantic belief contents with respect to phenomenal contents, which is harmless to MR.

Wide vs. Narrow Representationalism

Though MR could answer the preceding inverted spectrum argument, things get more complicated when we take into account the commitment of many representational theories to *content externalism.*

Externalism asserts that the content of mental states is determined at least in part by environment or history. For example, one externalist view would be that a representational vehicle represents what causes it in normal conditions. By contrast, internalism is the view that mental content is determined solely by one's intrinsic state. Internalism has tradition-ally been the "default" view of mental content, but recently many theorists have adopted externalism in the wake of Kripke's (1972), Putnam's (1975), and Burge's (1979) influential criticisms of internalism in philosophy of language.

Putnam (1975) famously argued that the term "water" has H_2O as its content because of the causal-historical relation between the introduction and use of "water" and the local prevalence of H_2O. On Putnam's imaginary Twin-Earth, where the lakes, seas, and organ-isms are full of an alternative, but superficially indistinguishable compound XYZ, the Twin-Earth term "water" means XYZ rather than H_2O. It has been argued that thought content similarly depends upon causal-historical relations, so that the natives of Earth and Twin-Earth are thinking *different* thoughts, which they all express by saying "water is wet."

MR naturally bifurcates into externalist and internalist versions, depending upon the favored theory of mental representation. Many proponents of MR endorse the externalist view (e.g., Tye, Lycan, Dretske). The resulting view, *phenomenal externalism* (PE), faces a number of difficulties.

Perhaps the most bizarre consequence of PE is the seeming possibility of "philosophical zombies": creatures physically identical to ourselves but which utterly lack consciousness. Since PE implies that consciousness depends upon content constituting relations, a creature lacking these will not be conscious. An example would be Davidson's (1987) *Swampman*, a spontaneously created physical duplicate of himself lacking causal links with the world or evolutionary history. PE faces the unpleasant choice of denying that Swampman is con-scious (Dretske 1995) or rather unattractively modifying the theory of representation to include Swampman among the conscious (Tye 2000). Internalists, of course, face no such difficulties.

A revamped version of the inverted spectrum also threatens PE. Block (1990, 1996) envisages "Inverted Earth" – a place much like Earth except that the actual colors of things and color terms are – somehow – inverted. Now imagine some people are unknowingly transported to Inverted Earth and, during the trip, are given a secret operation which turns them into color-inverts via the implantation of an Inversion Device (ID). When they arrive, they will notice no difference in the colors of things. Block argues that eventually the trave-lers' color vision states will, via the mechanisms of externalist content fixation, come to veridically represent the colors of Inverted Earth even though there will be no phenomenal change. Such a representational change with no change in experience would refute MR.

A defender of MR can boldly reply that there has after all been an unnoticed phenomenal change with no internal change in the traveler (Lycan 1996). This simply amounts to biting the bullet by accepting the bizarre consequence of PE that two individuals who are in identical intrinsic states can have distinct phenomenal experiences.

This line of reply seems implausible. It asserts that the travelers' color vision gradually de-inverts while they live on Inverted Earth with the ID in place. At first, red things looked green, although the inversion was disguised by the peculiarities of Inverted Earth. In time, however, red things come to look red again but this shift in vision is so "gradual" (or something) that it is not noticed by the travelers. Despite this, it remains clear that removal of the ID will still cause color vision inversion. It follows that for the *acclimatized* travelers, removal of the ID will make it the case that red things look green. So if one of them were suddenly switched to standard Earth immediately after her ID had been removed, she ought to exclaim that ripe tomatoes look green, much to her surprise. But it seems clear that with the ID removed and back on Earth, everything would look perfectly normal.

It seems preferable for the defender of MR to insist, with Block, that there is indeed a constant representational content (and phenomenality) to the travelers' experience just because there is no intrinsic change in the representational systems of either the traveler or her stay-at-home twin. This reply may seem obvious to the reader who has not been exposed to the wonders of PE. By adding epicycles, PE can also embrace this reply, but the point here is simply that an internalist MR has no difficulty with the Inverted Earth thought experiment (see Dretske 1995, ch. 5; Tye 2000, ch. 6; Lycan 1996, ch. 6; Block 1996).

A further issue with wide representationalism stems from the inverted spectrum scenario. All externalist versions of MR are *relational*: they require that a mental state that represents X stands in a given relation to X in the actual world. This represents a requirement that some experiences be veridical, which requires that colors and other such secondary qualities, if they are represented in experience, be objective.

The inverted spectrum thus leads to the problem of the objectivity of color (Byrne & Hilbert 1997). If the phenomenal states of the inverts and the normals disagree about how the world is, which they must according to MR, then at most one group is correct about the colors of things. If the inverts are a minority of the population then it might seem easy to characterize their color vision as systematically in error. But what if the population is split 50–50, or what if, over time, the inverts come to form the majority? There does not seem to be any principled answer to these questions. This suggests that *neither* inverts *nor* normals are correctly perceiving the world, at least not if we take color experiences to be representing an objective continuous surface feature of objects.

Relational and Projectivist Approaches to the Exhaustion Thesis

An alternative to the relational, externalist approach is a *projectivist*, internalist approach. It may be that the experience of colors as intrinsic, continuous features of surfaces misrepresents the nature of color. We might borrow Hume's idea that color vision works by "gilding or staining all natural objects with the colours, borrowed from internal sentiment" (1777/1975, p. 294). Following Hume, we will want to extend the idea beyond the perception of colors, but we will not agree that the colors we see stem from internal sentiment, if that implies that color experience involves directly knowable *mental* qualities which we "project" onto things. Rather, the view is that visual experience represents things as possessing color properties, which in fact they do not possess as represented, although there is an objective ground for our experiences. The term "projectivism" has an unfortunately wide range of uses. The view that we project mental features onto external objects has been called "literal projectivism" by Shoemaker (1990) and defended by Boghossian and Velleman (1989). The view advanced here is more akin to Shoemaker's "figurative projectivism"(see Wright 2003 for a defense of projectivism). This is compatible with MR, exploiting the fact that representations can be more or less inaccurate, or simply false.

This projectivist approach, unlike the relational, leaves it open to what extent the mental representations, which provide the contents of conscious experience, are accurate, but it seems intuitively likely that experience harbors more or less serious errors about the nature of things. Even though we experience material objects as made of continuous substance, as possessing definite locations within a three dimensional space and a one dimensional time in which all events are well ordered, and as possessing surfaces upon which colors are continuously spread out, none of these features seems to be actually instantiated in the world. We should not be surprised if nature, cobbling together cognitive representational mechanisms to aid survival, failed to stumble upon the true nature of things.

It is worth emphasizing that the systematic inaccuracy of perceptual experience does not have disastrous epistemological implications. First, there is still room for perception to be informative and largely veridical. Even though some aspects of the world we experience have no echo in nature, many do. Furthermore, we have the ability to form true beliefs on the basis of perceptions that may be misleading. This ability culminates in the scientific picture of the world, which reveals and explains the erroneous aspects of perceptual experience.

Returning to the exhaustion thesis, there is reason to think that many experiences have nonobjective features as contents. The perceptual experience of possible perceivers, including the whole range of conscious animal life on Earth and any number of alien creatures throughout the Universe, presents a vast panoply of radically diverse modes of perception. MR must handle this by positing an equally vast range of ways of representing things via the cognitive mechanisms of all these more or less different minds. If all that experiences could represent were extant physical properties, this might seem to make it hard to find content that correlates with every possible experience. Furthermore, it is difficult to imagine what some of these experiences are like, that is, to imagine the kind of world that would satisfy their contents (as famously pointed out in Nagel 1974). Arguably, we would not have such difficulties if experiences only represented physical properties, since we can easily form beliefs about the physical properties various creatures might be representing. It thus seems that proponents of MR must posit nonphysical contents, which is compatible with the combination of MR and projectivism, but not with the combination of MR, a relational theory of content, and physicalism.

We noted that pain has an evaluative aspect. The experienced world is suffused with value (positive, negative, or sometimes neutral). This might be the most basic and primitive form of consciousness, in the service of which follow the wide range and fine nuances of perceptual experience and thought. Maybe the first twinges of inchoate sensation were "valuings" of stimuli as good or bad – to be pursued or to be avoided, perhaps in very primitive organisms (Humphreys 1993). This would have been the ultimate origin of pleasure and pain which, roughly speaking, encode what is good and bad at the biological level. Just as in the case of color, we need not accept the naïve pronouncements of experience which presents value as an objective feature of things; value might be something that is projected on the external world.

Projectivism can also help explain the nature of emotional consciousness, including the case of moods briefly discussed above. Emotional response is very complex and the associated states of consciousness are similarly multifaceted, involving perception of the environment and the body as well as possessing rich cognitive dimensions. But arguably the core of emotion is the experience of value (see Edelman 1992; Damasio 1994; LeDoux 1996; Seager 2000, 2002).

Transparent Experience

MR entails an interesting prediction about experience. Since our consciousness is exhausted by the contents of underlying mental representations, there should be nothing apparent to the mind save the way things are represented. It follows that if one should try to attend to the nature of one's own experience, all that one will be able to find are these contents. This has been labeled the *transparency* of experience (an early discussion is in Harman 1990, although the idea can be traced back at least to G. E. Moore (1903); see Kind (2003) and Stoljar (2005) for useful discussions). Specifically, the transparency thesis is the claim that experience and introspection do not make us aware of anything beyond what mental states represent.

We confess that transparency seems so true to our own experience we have difficulty conceiving of consciousness in any other terms. MR does not *follow* from transparency, but MR is the best explanation for this feature of experience (a claim made by Tye 2000; and denied by Stoljar 2005, among others). Transparency can be explicated by considering cases where awareness is nontransparent. The most obvious example is awareness of meaning achieved through linguistic media. Consider how you come to be aware of the meaning of "most mermaids are beautiful." This awareness is indirect and mediated by an awareness of the vehicle of this content. You cannot get to the meaning of "most mermaids are beautiful" except by *perceiving* those lexographical black marks which form the vehicle of this content. The transparency of experience entails that there are no mentalistic "marks" which we must be aware of in order to be aware of the "normal" objects of experience.

Although it is natural to explicate transparency in terms of examples of mediated perception, there is a distinction between mediated awareness and nontransparency. As discussed, many think there are nonrepresentational features of experience that do not contribute to the satisfaction conditions of our states of consciousness but enter into their phenomenal character. Let us call these Qualia (with a capital "Q"). Qualia, if there were such, might be introspectible through a kind of awareness that is not intentional. The traditional view is that Qualia mediate our awareness of the external world, but they need not play this role: we could be directly aware of the external world and simultaneously acquainted with Qualia. However, it is hard to see why there would be such nonmediating Qualia.

Could it be that Qualia are always part of our experience, but that it is "hard" to become aware of them? This flies in the face of characterizations of Qualia as the *most* immediately available and impossible to miss features of experience. Kind (2003) uses an analogy of seeing a landscape through a window where it is possible, if sometimes difficult, to also see the glass itself. Suppose we are looking through a very old and thin window. The landscape beyond looks blurry and wavy. But here the blurriness and waviness are not features of the glass; they are the way the world looks *because* of the nature of the glass. Yet surely it is sometimes possible to see the pane of glass itself. If so, it is because there is some distinctive property of the glass which is visible. The problem in the case of consciousness is that there does not seem to be any such distinctive features of mental states themselves. These states do not intrinsically possess color, shape, sound, smell, or the other "common sensibles" that are experienced as elements of the perceived world. What is this mysterious qualitative feature of conscious experience which normally eludes us but can be appreciated with some "effort"?

An objection to the transparency thesis is that the mere possibility of introspection refutes it. It seems that any discussion of consciousness presupposes that we can take a reflective stance toward our own experiences and regard them as mental, as experiences. Perhaps Wittgenstein had this in mind when he wrote that I can "turn my attention in a particular way on to my own consciousness, and, astonished, say to myself: THIS is supposed to be produced by a process in the brain! – as it were clutching my forehead" (Wittgenstein 1953, I, 412). MR must make room for introspective awareness of our mental states. However, this does not undermine the transparency thesis so long as introspection is thought of as the higher-order representation of mental states, as discussed below. When we become aware of our experiences as such, we form mental representations in addition to, and about, our experiences. Introspective consciousness is of the content of these higher-order representations (Loar 2002).

The Demarcation Problem

The exhaustion thesis tells us little about the relation between consciousness and representation. Most importantly, the exhaustion thesis does not reveal the nature of phenomenal consciousness: what is essential to, and characteristic of it. All it says is that phenomenal states can be specified in terms of their contents. The demarcation problem is to determine what it is about certain representational states which makes them phenomenal (see Kriegel 2002).

The simplest possible solution is to say that what makes a representation phenomenal is just its content. This *radical representationalism* seems preposterous so long as "representation" is construed sufficiently broadly to include anything from markings on paper to mental states, for whatever can be represented in experience can be written about, and markings on paper are not conscious. As far as we know, nobody has ever advocated radical representationalism.

It is therefore important to distinguish radical representationalism from another view we will call *pure representationalism* (our use of the terms "pure" and "impure" maps roughly onto Chalmers's 2004, but not Lycan's 2005). Pure representationalism is the view that phenomenal states are mental representations with contents that explain why they, but not other mental representations, have the phenomenal character they have. What these contents are is left open by pure representationalism, but the most natural account is that mental states which possess the kind of phenomenal character had by perceptual states have qualitative properties as part of their contents. Qualitative properties would be properties of possible perceptible objects as we experience them (such as redness, painfulness, etc.). The idea is that the one and only reason why thoughts about numbers, human rights, and economic systems differ in phenomenal character from perceptual states is that their objects are not qualitative. Thau (2002) defends a kind of pure representationalism. Byrne (2001, 2002) also points toward this view but does not fully endorse it.

A tempting objection to pure representationalism is that it is difficult to spell out what "qualitative" means without explicating it as what is common to the properties sensory states represent, which threatens to make the account circular. This is a complex issue we cannot delve into here. Instead, we focus on three main problems pure representationalism faces apart from this one.

The first is what we might call the "blind man problem." It seems possible to think about the properties represented in experience without experiencing any phenomenal character. For example, those born blind presumably can have beliefs about the properties represented in color vision even though (let us suppose) they cannot experience color (Neander 1998). Similarly, it seems that sighted individuals must be able to think about these properties without experiencing them, otherwise we would spend our time visualizing colors when writing articles like this one. Thau (2002) denies this seemingly obvious fact; he holds that all perceptual experiences represent properties we cannot represent in (nonphenomenal) thoughts. His defense of this conclusion rests on substantial premises in philosophy of language we cannot discuss here, but he appears to be biting a very large bullet.

An alternative approach deploys Frege's sense/reference distinction. Perhaps the properties represented in experience can indeed be represented in thoughts with no, or distinct, phenomenal characters, but only via roundabout descriptions of the form "the content of John's experience" or "the way X tastes." One might then argue that perceptual experiences and states that differ from them in phenomenal character always differ in content at the level of *sense* even though they can have the same content at the level of *reference*.

This Fregean approach gathers support from the intuition that one has to experience red to properly *grasp* the nature of the experience (recall Jackson 1982). Given the exhaustion thesis, this would mean that its content can only be grasped when undergoing it. Intuitively, the difference between sense-level content and reference-level content is that the former is what we can grasp and reason on, while the latter is determined in context by sense but need not be grasped and determined by sense independently of context. From the facts that one can only grasp what is represented in the experience of red by undergoing this experience and sense-level content is content that is grasped, we may conclude that only *experiences* of red have the content they have at the level of sense. (Thau 2002 and Byrne 2002 each makes part of this argument; for a discussion of the sense/reference distinction within the context of MR; see Thompson 2003; Chalmers 2004.)

A second problem for pure representationalism is that subpersonal processes may provide examples of unconscious mental representations that lack phenomenal character. A simple example stems from binocular vision. If you close one eye and note what you see, then open the other and close the first, you will note a difference caused simply by the locations of your eyes. It seems that, under conditions of normal vision, the brain somehow combines or links the contents of these two ocular viewpoints into the 3-D view that informs consciousness. This would mean that we lack consciousness of the individual components even though individual representations remain active within the system (Seager 1999).

A response to this argument questions the assumption that binocular vision combines pre-existing mental contents. It is clear that it combines two sources of information, but we cannot assume that all states or events that carry information are mental representations.

The preceding problem leads naturally to a third issue. Pure representationalism seems to rely on a rather restrictive account of mental representation. Without asking for a full theory, it seems reasonable to ask the pure representationalist to sketch an account of mental representation that excludes subpersonal informational states. A promising approach here is to invoke the distinction between *derived* and *original* intentionality. States with derived intentionality are states that can have content only if other states have the same content. Arguably, natural language expressions have derived intentionality; they are meaningless apart from speakers' intentions. One could argue that mere informational states also have only derived intentionality because they can be construed as signs or indicators only given a certain interpretation of their functions. Searle (1990) and Georgalis (2005) posit the inapplicability of the sense-reference distinction (or something like it) to informational states and argue along similar lines. These suggestions are very controversial.

Such difficulties have led most theorists to reject pure representationalism in favor of "impure" accounts which put less burden on representational content while by and large respecting the exhaustion thesis. Tye (1995, 2000), Dretske (1995), and Jackson (2004) endorse variants of impure representationalism which conform to the exhaustion thesis. Crane (2002), Chalmers (2004), and Lycan (1996) hold impure representationalist views which infringe on it to some extent. What is characteristic of impure representationalism is an appeal to properties of mental representations above and beyond their contents to account for the difference between conscious and unconscious states. Chalmers, Crane, and Jackson describe the relevant features as manners of representation, which are ways of relating to contents comparable to attitudes such as believing and desiring. Dretske, Lycan, and Tye give largely functionalist accounts of the distinction.

All forms of impure representationalism can be classified either as reductive or nonreductive: some hold that the extra ingredient which accounts for consciousness is completely physical or functional, others hold that it is not. Nonreductive impure representationalism takes consciousness as at least relatively fundamental, which dashes the hopes of naturalizing consciousness. It does not forego all the other advantages of representationalism, however. Here we can only offer a cursory discussion of a representative reductive account championed by Tye (1995, 2000).

Tye claims that phenomenal states are *PANIC* states; they have Poised, Abstract, Nonconceptual Intentional Content. Poised content stands at the periphery of and is ready to affect "higher" or "central" cognitive systems, especially those which underlie beliefs. Abstract content does not require the presence of any particular object for its satisfaction. Finally, nonconceptual content, on Tye's definition, is such that the subject need have no matching concept (e.g., we can experience millions of colors yet lack correspondingly specific concepts). This account is partly functional and partly representational: the property of being abstract is an intrinsic property of contents, but the properties of being poised and nonconceptual are causal properties relating contents to cognitive centers and concepts, respectively.

Tye's three conditions are supposed to explain why subpersonal informational processes do not have phenomenal character. On the kind of account of content that comes with the PANIC theory, the states involved in such processes could share nonconceptual, abstract content with experiences, so their lack of phenomenal character must be explained by their not being poised.

But there are plenty of unconscious, subpersonal processes which leak information into and influence cognitive centers. There are many experiments that show how stimuli which are presented for too short a time for conscious awareness nonetheless modify cognition (Murphy & Zajonc 1993). More examples come from dichotic listening, in which two distinct sound streams are played to a subject, one to each ear. In these experiments, only one of the two channels is consciously apprehended, but the other channel can produce cognitive effects (Lackner & Garrett 1972). The phenomenon of blindsight might also be appealed to here (see Siewert 1998 for an extensive philosophical discussion). The existence of such leaks does not immediately refute Tye's theory because we have not shown that their source is located at the fringe or boundary of the higher cognitive system, as required by Tye.

However, consider that perceptual experience appears to depend on multiple stages of processing in the brain. From the receptors of the retina to the structures of the dorsal system that are involved in object-recognition, there are several layers of increasingly abstract representation along pathways spanning a good part of the brain, each of which plays a role in determining what we experience (see Tye's (1995) discussion). If this is correct, it seems that some events relevant to conscious experience are upstream of others. Mother Nature is too parsimonious in her allocation of resources to design a brain where low-level representations are always carried along with the information abstracted from them – this would defeat the very purpose of abstraction. Now conscious representations which are upstream of others cannot sit at the boundary of the cognitive centers, wherever it is. If this is correct, all we are left with of the "poised" condition is that poised states are apt to impinge on cognitive centers. But we saw that unconscious states with nonconceptual, abstract content can do this (for other criticisms of Tye see Block 1995; Seager 1999, 2003; Kriegel 2002; and Byrne 2003).

This objection proceeds on more or less empirical grounds, so it might be hoped that all such objections could be avoided by devising a PANIC-type theory on the basis of more empirical data. Ultimately, however, the real problem is that of locating consciousness in our metaphysical picture of the world. The important lesson to draw from the foregoing discussion is that proponents of reductive impure representationalism have to resort to traditional functionalist and physicalist solutions to this problem. Similarly, proponents of nonreductive impure representationalism have to deal with the difficulties traditionally associated with dualism. Put differently, the main problem faced by impure representationalism is simply the hard problem of consciousness in its traditional form (for more on the general problem, see Nagel 1974; Jackson 1982; Levine 1983; Chalmers 1995).

Introspective Minds

MR is compatible with a range of theories of introspection which we cannot survey here. But there is a view of introspection that seems a natural extension of MR, tying together several strands of the theory into a unified account of the conscious mind. The seeds of this account can be found in Sellars (1956), but it is developed explicitly within MR by Tye (2000) and Dretske (1995). The latter labels it the "displaced perception theory of introspection" (see also Seager 1999).

To begin outlining this account, think about what introspection provides: *knowledge* of our own mental states. Via introspection we come to know what mental states we are in: what we are thinking, feeling, seeing, hearing, wondering, hoping, etc. Thus a necessary condition of being able to introspect is the possession of the concepts of those mental states we can discover we are in or experiencing via introspection.

The family of mental state concepts, with their complex interrelations, forms the "theoretical" core of Folk Psychology, and it would seem that very few animals on Earth (perhaps *only* human beings) have any acquaintance with it. It follows that very few animals can engage in introspection. And yet intuitively it seems that there are many conscious beings on the Earth. Introspection is thus not essential to consciousness.

Introspection requires a special and sophisticated way of thinking about conscious experience. What is needed is the Wittgensteinian attitude discussed above. Consciousness presents, in the first instance, information about the world, the body, and sometimes the mind, but even in the latter case it does not provide this information as being "about the mind." It takes a special reflective stance wherein we apply the concepts of mental states to our ongoing experience to transform consciousness into introspective knowledge of our own mental states.

What exactly is involved in introspection if not some kind of reflexivity intrinsic to consciousness? Dretske (1995) frequently writes as if the transformation needed to generate introspective knowledge is an *inference* from experience. But we need not suppose that inference is essential (a view which faces difficulties – see Bach 1997; Aydede 2003). A better model is that of concept application itself. It seems to be a pervasive feature of experience that the world is presented to us in terms of the concepts we bring with us: we see tables, chairs, cats, and dogs. We do not infer from some primordial visual ur-material to a world of furniture and pets. Similarly, we come to apply mentalistic concepts to our experience with the same kind of effortless spontaneity.

Whether this account of introspection is correct depends in large part upon the acceptability of MR in general. But there is a nice fit between MR's depiction of consciousness as the representation of an external world, and the claim that the mind is not something which is apparent in consciousness unless and until one takes up a reflective stance that permits one to apprehend experience *as* mental.

Conclusion

MR provides a powerful account of the mind which incorporates conscious experience in a way that seems intuitively satisfying, avoids the difficulties associated with such views as CR, opens the door for a variety of naturalistic theories of mind, and integrates introspection without making the implausible requirement that all conscious beings have the conceptual equipment necessary to think about mental states as such.

There is much room for argument and progress within the representationalist framework. Beyond the exhaustion thesis, it seems to us that the two most pressing questions are, first, whether the pure or impure approach is to be favored and, second, whether the internalist (and projectivist) or externalist (and relational) approach is best. These two issues should be investigated jointly in light of more general considerations concerning mental content, including the important project of investigating the specific contents of phenomenal states.

See also 21 Higher-order theories of consciousness; 30 Functionalism and qualia; 37 Consciousness and intentionality.

Further Readings

Chalmers, D. J. (2004) The representational character of experience. In B. Leiter (ed.), *The Future for Philosophy*, 153–82. Oxford: Oxford University Press.
Kim, Jaegwon (2005) *Philosophy of Mind*, 2nd edn., chs. 8 and 9. Boulder, CO: Westview Press.

Lycan, William (2005) Representational theories of consciousness. In the (on-line) *Stanford Encyclopedia of Philosophy*.

Seager, William (1999) *Theories of Consciousness*, chs. 6 and 7. London: Routledge.

References

Anscombe, G. E. (1965) The intentionality of sensation: a grammatical feature. In R. Butler (ed.), *Analytic Philosophy*, second series, 158–80. Oxford: Blackwell.

Armstrong, D. M. (1968) *A Materialist Theory of the Mind*. London: Routledge and Kegan Paul.

Aydede, M. (2003) Is introspection inferential? In B. Gertler (ed.), *Privileged Access*, 55–65. Aldershot: Ashgate.

Bach, K. (1997) Engineering the mind. *Philosophical and Phenomenological Research* 57, 2, 459–68.

Bain, D. (2003) Intentionalism and pain. *Philosophical Quarterly* 53, 502–23.

Block, N. (1990) Inverted earth. *Philosophical Perspectives* 4, 53–79.

Block, N. (1995) On a confusion about the function of consciousness. *Behavioral and Brain Sciences* 18, 227–47.

Block, N. (1996) Mental paint and mental latex. In E. Villanueva (ed.), *Perception*, 19–49. Atascadero, CA: Ridgeview.

Block, N. (2003) Mental paint. In M. Hahn and B. Ramberg (eds.), *Reflections and Replies*. Cambridge, MA: MIT Press.

Boghossian, P. and Velleman, J. D. (1989) Color as a secondary quality. *Mind* 98, 81–103.

Broad, C. D. (1952) *Scientific Thought*. London: Routledge and Kegan Paul.

Burge, T. (1979) Individualism and the mental. *Midwest Studies in Philosophy* 4, 73–122.

Byrne, A. (2001) Intentionalism defended. *Philosophical Review* 110, 199–240.

Byrne, A. (2002) Something about Mary. *Grazer Philosophische Studien* 63, 27–52.

Byrne, A. (2003) Consciousness and nonconceptual content. *Philosophical Studies* 113, 261–74.

Byrne, A. and Hilbert, D. R. (1997) *Readings on Color, vol. 1: The Philosophy of Color*. Cambridge, MA: MIT Press.

Chalmers, D. J. (1995) Facing up to the problem of consciousness. *Journal of Consciousness Studies* 2, 200–19. Also in S. Hameroff, A. Kaszniak, and A. Scott (eds.), *Toward a Science of Consciousness* (1995).

Chalmers, D. J. (2004) The representational character of experience. In B. Leiter (ed.), *The Future for Philosophy*, 153–82. Oxford: Oxford University Press.

Crane, T. (2002) The intentional structure of consciousness. In Q. Smith and A. Jokic (eds.), *Consciousness: New Philosophical Essays*, 33–57. Oxford: Oxford University Press.

Crane, T. (forthcoming) Intentionalism. In Ansgar Beckermann and Brian McLaughlin (eds.), *Oxford Handbook to the Philosophy of Mind*. Oxford: Oxford University Press.

Damasio, A. R. (1994) *Descartes' Error: Emotion, Reason, and the Human Brain*. New York: Putnam.

Davidson, D. (1987) Knowing one's own mind. *Proceedings and Addresses of the American Philosophical Association* 60, 441–58.

Dretske, F. (1995) *Naturalizing the Mind*. Cambridge, MA: MIT Press.

Dretske, F. (2003) Experience as representation. *Philosophical Issues* 13, 67–82.

Edelman, G. (1992) *Bright Air, Brilliant Fire*. New York: Basic Books.

Georgalis, N. (2005) *The Primacy of the Subjective*. Cambridge, MA: MIT Press.

Harman, G. (1990) The intrinsic quality of experience. *Philosophical Perspectives* 4, 31–52. Oxford: Blackwell.

Hintikka, K. J. J. (1969) On the logic of perception. In K. J. J. Hintikka (ed.), *Models for Modalities: Selected Essays*, 161–83. Dordrecht: Reidel.

Hume, D. (1777/1975) An enquiry concerning the principles of morals. In L. Selby-Bigge (ed.),

Enquiries Concerning Human Understanding and Concerning the Principles of Morals, 3rd edn., revised by P. H. Nidditch. Oxford: Clarendon Press.

Humphreys, N. (1993) *A History of the Mind*. New York: HarperPerennial.

Jackson, F. (1982) Epiphenomenal qualia. *Philosophical Quarterly* 32, 127–36.

Jackson, F. (2004) Representation and experience. In H. Clapin, P. Staines, and P. Slezak (eds.), *Representation in Mind*. Oxford: Elsevier Science.

Kind, A. (2003) What's so transparent about transparency? *Philosophical Studies* 115, 2225–44.

Kriegel, U. (2002) Panic theory and the prospects for a representational theory of phenomenal consciousness. *Philosophical Psychology* 15, 55–64.

Kripke, S. A. (1972) *Naming and Necessity*. Cambridge, MA: Harvard University Press.

Lackner, J. and Garrett, M. (1972) Resolving ambiguity: effects of biasing context in the unattended ear. *Cognition* 1, 359–72.

Ledoux, J. (1996) *The Emotional Brain: The Mysterious Underpinnings of Emotional Life*. New York: Simon and Schuster.

Levine, J. (1983) Materialism and qualia: the explanatory gap. *Pacific Philosophical Quarterly* 64, 354–61.

Loar, B. (2002) Transparent experience and the availability of qualia. In Q. Smith and A. Jokic (eds.), *Consciousness: New Philosophical Essays*. Oxford: Oxford University Press.

Locke, J. (1690/1990) *An Essay Concerning Human Understanding*, P. H. Nidditch (ed.). Oxford: Oxford University Press.

Lycan, W. G. (1996) *Consciousness and Experience*. Cambridge, MA: MIT Press.

Lycan, W. G. (2005) Representational theories of consciousness. In Edward N. Zalta (ed.), *Stanford Encyclopedia of Philosophy* (Spring 2005 edn.).

Moore, G. E. (1903) The Refutation of Idealism. *Mind* 12, 433–53.

Murphy, S. and Zajonc, R. (1993) Affect, cognition, and awareness: affective priming with optimal and suboptimal stimulus exposures. *Journal of Personality and Social Psychology* 64, 723–39.

Nagel, T. (1974) What is it like to be a bat? *Philosophical Review* 83, 435–50.

Neander, K. (1998) The division of phenomenal labor: a problem for representationalist theories of consciousness. *Philosophical Perspectives* 12, 411–34.

Peacocke, C. (1983) *Sense and Content: Experience, Thought, and Their Relations*. Oxford: Oxford University Press.

Peacocke, C. (1992) Scenarios, concepts, and perception. In T. Crane (ed.), *The Contents of Experience*, 105–36. Cambridge: Cambridge University Press.

Putnam, H. (1975) The meaning of "meaning," *Minnesota Studies in the Philosophy of Science* 7, 131–93.

Seager, William (1999) *Theories of Consciousness: An Introduction and Assessment*. London: Routledge.

Seager, William (2000) Introspection and the elementary acts of mind. *Dialogue* 39, 53–76.

Seager, William (2002) Emotional introspection. *Consciousness and Cognition* 11: 4, 666–87.

Seager, William (2003) Tye on consciousness: time to panic? *Philosophical Studies* 113, 237–47.

Searle, J. R. (1983) *Intentionality*. Cambridge: Cambridge University Press.

Searle, J. R. (1990) Consciousness, explanatory inversion and cognitive science. *Behavioral and Brain Sciences* 13, 585–642.

Sellars, W. (1956) Empiricism and the philosophy of mind. *Minnesota Studies in the Philosophy of Science* 1, 253–329.

Shoemaker S. (1990) Qualities and qualia: what's in the mind? *Philosophy and Phenomenological Research Supplement* 50, 109–31.

Siewert, C. (1998) *The Significance of Consciousness*. Princeton, NJ: Princeton University Press.

Stoljar, D. (2005) The argument from diaphanousness. In Maite Ezcurdia, Robert Stainton, and Chris Viger (eds.), *Language, Mind and World: Special Issue of the Canadian Journal of Philosophy*, 341–90. Calgary, AB: University of Calgary Press.

Thau, M. (2002) *Consciousness and Cognition*. Oxford: Oxford University Press.

Thompson, B. (2003) The nature of phenomenal content. PhD thesis, University of Arizona.

Tye, M. (1995) *Ten Problems of Consciousness: A Representational Theory of the Phenomenal Mind.* Cambridge, MA: MIT Press.

Tye, M. (1996) Perceptual experience is a many-layered thing. In E. Villaneuva (ed.), *Perception*, 117–26. Atascadero, CA: Ridgeview.

Tye, M. (2000) *Consciousness, Color, and Content*. Cambridge, MA: MIT Press.

Tye, M. (2002) Blurry images, double vision, and other oddities: new problems for representationalism? in Q. Smith and A. Jokic (eds.), *Consciousness: New Philosophical Essays*. Oxford: Oxford University Press.

Wittgenstein, L. (1953) *Philosophical Investigations*. G. E. M. Anscombe, trans. Oxford: Blackwell.

Wright, W. (2003) Projectivist representationalism and color. *Philosophical Psychology* 16, 515–29.

21

Higher-Order Theories of Consciousness

PETER CARRUTHERS

This chapter will focus on three classes of higher-order theory of phenomenal consciousness. Phenomenally conscious states are ones that it's like for something to undergo, which have a distinctive subjective quality or feel. Higher-order theories purport to account for the conscious character of such states in terms of higher-order representations – that is to say, beliefs or percepts *of* the states in question. The first is *inner-sense theory*, represented by Armstrong (1968) and Lycan (1987, 1996). The second is *actualist higher-order thought theory*, represented by Rosenthal (1986, 1997). And the third is *dispositionalist higher-order thought theory* (now referred to by its creator as "*dual-content theory*"), represented by Carruthers (2000, 2005).

All three of these higher-order theories purport to offer reductive explanations of phenomenal consciousness. That is to say, all three claim to give us an understanding, in naturalistically acceptable terms, of what phenomenal consciousness *is*. Hence, each is committed to denying that zombies are metaphysically possible. (Zombies are hypothetical creatures with intentional states, including higher-order intentional states of the sort in question, but supposedly lacking phenomenal consciousness.) But each of the theories can claim to explain how zombies can nevertheless be conceivable, or *conceptually* possible, as we shall see.

Higher-Order Theories Explained and Contrasted with First-Order Ones

Higher-order theories are a subset of a wider class of reductive accounts, generally known as *representational* theories of consciousness. All such theories purport to explain phenomenal consciousness in terms of some combination of intentional/representational content and causal role. All agree that the contents in question should be especially fine-grained (or "analog") in character, and some think further that they should be *non-conceptual*. Either of these options can enable a representationalist to explain the seeming *ineffability* of phenomenally conscious experience, since each postulates a contrast between fine-grained perceptual awareness and the relatively course-grained – or "digital" – character of conceptual thought.

Higher-order representational theories claim that the causal role distinctive of phenomenal consciousness is either that of giving rise to higher-order *percepts* (in the case of inner-sense theory) or that of giving rise to higher-order conceptual *thoughts* (in the case of higher-order thought theory). First-order representational theories of the sorts espoused by Baars (1988, 1997), Dretske (1995), and Tye (1995, 2000), in contrast, claim that the causal role in question is rather that of impacting the subject's (first-order) conceptual belief-forming and decision-making mechanisms. (See also Baars, chapter 18; Seager & Bourget, chapter 20.)

All three of the higher-order theories that we are considering have as one of their main motivations the intuition that conscious mental states are representational states *of which subjects are aware*. First-order theories are committed to denying this intuition, and must explain the connection between consciousness and awareness somewhat differently. Instead of saying, with the higher-order theorist, that conscious states are ones *of which* subjects are aware, they say that conscious states are those *in virtue of which* subjects are *aware of properties of the world* (or of their own bodies).

According to inner-sense theory, the higher-order awareness in question is perceptual. On this account, in addition to our first-order senses (sight, hearing, smell, taste, touch, and proprioception of various sorts), we also have a set of *inner* (higher-order) senses, charged with scanning the outputs of the first-order senses and generating percepts of them. So a conscious experience of red, or of the movement of my own body, will be an analog/non-conceptual representation of a state of the world/body that gives rise to an analog/non-conceptual representation of that very representation. In short, it is by virtue of perceiving our own percepts that the latter become phenomenally conscious. Hence the awareness in question is similar to the sort of awareness that I have of the redness itself – by perceiving the redness, I am aware of it; and by perceiving my percept of redness, I am aware of *it*; and it is the latter awareness that renders the former phenomenally conscious.

According to actualist higher-order thought theory, in contrast, the awareness in question is of a conceptual/propositional sort. It is by coming to *believe* that I am undergoing an experience of red, or of the movement of my own body, that those experiences become phenomenally conscious. So in one sense the awareness in question is similar to the sort of awareness that I have of the date of the battle of Hastings – that is, I believe (in this case, I know) that it was fought in 1066 CE. But in another sense the awareness is different, since the higher-order thought needs to be *occurrent* – actually occurring at the time – in order for the experience that it is about to count as phenomenally conscious; whereas my belief in the date of the battle of Hastings can be *dormant*, and stored in memory. Some theorists say that *mere* higher-order occurrent belief is enough for phenomenal consciousness (Rosenthal 1997); others insist that the belief must also count as *knowledge*, being linked in the right sort of way to the first-order percept that it is about (Gennaro 1996).

In the case of dispositionalist higher-order thought theory the connection between consciousness and awareness is more complicated. The initial move is to say that phenomenally conscious states are ones that are immediately and noninferentially *available to* higher-order thought, rather than actually causing it. Hence the sense of "awareness" in question is similar to the dispositional sense in which someone might be said to be aware (i.e., to know) that zebras in the wild do not wear overcoats – this is something that the subject *would* immediately assent to if asked, even if they have never before explicitly considered it. But by virtue of such availability, and in virtue of the truth of some or other version of consumer semantics (e.g., teleosemantics or inferential-role semantics) the states in question acquire, at the same time, higher-order analog contents that mirror their first-order contents. (For teleosemantics, see Millikan 1984, and Papineau 1987; for inferential-role semantics, see Block 1986, and Peacocke 1992.) So a phenomenally conscious percept of red will be a state with the analog content *red* that also has the higher-order analog content *seeming red* or *experience of red* in virtue of its availability to a faculty of higher-order thought. Hence the appropriateness of the label "dual-content theory": for it is one and the same perceptual state that has both first-order and higher-order analog/non-conceptual contents.

Each of the higher-order theories under consideration will advance similar explanations of the distinction between conscious and unconscious mental states, of the sort that is warranted by the "two visual systems" hypothesis of Milner and Goodale (1995), for example (Goodale, chapter 48). They will claim that the states produced by the ventral/temporal system are ones of which subjects are aware (either perceptually or conceptually), and that this is why those states are phenomenally conscious, whereas the states produced by the movement-controlling dorsal/parietal system are not ones of which subjects are aware, which is why they are not conscious.

Some higher-order theorists have alleged that the ability to explain the conscious/unconscious distinction is a distinctive advantage of higher-order over first-order accounts of phenomenal consciousness (e.g., Carruthers 1998). But it is doubtful whether this charge is warranted, in general. For if a first-order theorist claims, with Tye (1995), that phenomenally conscious percepts are those that are poised to have an impact on conceptual thinking (belief-formation and decision-making), then exactly what should be predicted is that the outputs of the ventral/temporal visual system will be conscious (because they are made available to guide thoughts and planning about the perceived environment), whereas the outputs of the dorsal/parietal visual system will be unconscious (because they are *only* made available for fine-grained on-line control of movement, not for conceptual thought). Hence this instance of the conscious/unconscious distinction, at least, can get explained by the theory, in the sense of being *predicted by* it. Whether this explanation will extend to all other varieties of conscious/unconscious contrast, in addition to the dual visual systems, is moot.

A more successful argument against first-order representational theories is that they are incapable of explaining *why* the states produced by the ventral/temporal system should have the distinctive properties of phenomenal consciousness (subjective dimension, qualitative feel, and the rest) (Carruthers 2005). For it is entirely mysterious why analog intentional states that are available to belief-formation and planning should be *like* anything, or have *feel*, whereas states with exactly similar contents that are not so available should not be. In contrast, some higher-order theories can at least make progress with this issue, as we shall see.

Inner-Sense Theory

We now consider the respective strengths and weaknesses of our three types of higher-order theory of phenomenal consciousness. Inner-sense theory has the longest historical pedigree of the three, going back at least to Locke (1690). One of its most attractive features is the way in which it can explain how phenomenally conscious states come to have a subjective aspect, or "feel." For note that our first-order senses present *the world* (and our own bodies) to us in a manner that is subjective, dependent upon the particular properties and constitution of our sense organs, with their distinctive discrimination profiles, together with the specific manner of their interaction with the environment in local conditions. As a result, *the world* is *like something* to any organism that perceives it (slightly different in each case).

An organ of *inner* sense, similarly then, will present *our own experiences* to us in a subjective manner, and those experiences, too, will be *like something* to us. In which case the "what-it-is-likeness" (Nagel 1974) or subjective feel of our experiences is satisfyingly explained.

Inner-sense theory can also advance a nice explanation of our capacity for *purely recognitional concepts* of experience. The significance of this point will be outlined below. Our first-order senses present the world to us in analog/non-conceptual fashion, and the percepts that they generate can serve to ground recognitional concepts of the secondary qualities perceived (*red, green, smooth*, and so forth). These concepts are not *purely* recognitional, since they are embedded in nascent theories of perception, and of the conditions under which perceptual states can vary. Likewise, then, a faculty of *inner* sense will present our own experiences to us in analog/non-conceptual fashion, and the percepts that inner sense generates will serve to ground recognitional concepts of the qualities perceived (*seeming-red, seeming-green, experienced-smoothness*, and so on). But in this case our higher-order percepts can ground *purely* recognitional concepts of the form, "*This* again." This is because ordinary people lack any sort of theory of the existence or mode of operation of inner sense.

Why does this result matter? It matters because there is an emerging consensus that purely recognitional concepts of experience (sometimes called "phenomenal concepts") are necessary to defuse the "explanatory gap" and "zombie" arguments against the very possibility of providing a reductive explanation of phenomenal consciousness (Tye 1995, 2000; Loar 1997; Carruthers 2000, 2005; Sturgeon 2000; Papineau 2002). So a crucial desideratum of any successful reductive account of phenomenal consciousness has to be the capacity to give a satisfying explanation of the existence of purely-recognitional concepts of experience. Let me elaborate.

Many philosophers believe that there is an explanatory gap between any proposed reductive theory, on the one hand, and the nature of phenomenal consciousness itself, on the other; which means that no reductive explanation of the latter can be successful (Chalmers 1996 and chapter 17; Levine 2001 and chapter 29). And it should be conceded that with respect to any proposed higher-order theory, in particular, it will always remain possible to think, "Well, all *that* might be true, but still *this* [experience] might have been different or absent." But if we can explain the existence of the purely-recognitional concept *this* in naturalistically acceptable terms, then we can simultaneously grant the truth of the gap-inducing thought while maintaining that the property picked out by the recognitional concept (the phenomenally conscious experience) has been fully and naturalistically explained. The "explanatory gap" will then stand revealed as no more than a kind of cognitive illusion (Tye 2000; Carruthers 2005). And zombies, while being conceptually possible, may well be metaphysically *im*possible.

Inner-sense theory has quite a bit to be said for it, then. But it also faces a number of severe problems. One is that if these inner-sense organs exist, then it ought to be possible for them to malfunction, just as our first-order sense organs can (and sometimes do). In which case it ought to be possible to find cases where someone has a first-order experience *as of* red, for example, while undergoing a higher-order experience *as of* seeming yellow. Such a person would be inclined to make the first-order judgment (spontaneously, and without relying on any inferences from the circumstances), "The surface is red," while at the same time judging, "I am experiencing that surface as yellow." Likewise it ought to be possible for someone to be undergoing *no* first-order experience *as of anything* colored, while nevertheless being inclined to judge (on the basis of an "hallucinatory" higher-order experience), "I am experiencing red." Not only do these kinds of things never seem to happen, but they seem barely coherent (Sturgeon 2000).

Another difficulty for inner-sense theory is that it is hard to get oneself to believe in the existence of the relevant sense organs. Our first-order senses are vital to our survival, and are the product of many millions of years of evolution, being roughly homologous in all mammalian species. They are also of staggering internal complexity, since extracting information about distal objects and events from patterns of proximate stimuli proves to be no easy task to accomplish. But it is hard, on the one hand, to discern anything important that an organ of inner sense would be *for*; and yet on the other, it would surely have had to evolve and be subject to significant selection pressure, since extracting information about experiences and their contents from patterns of brain activity is not likely to be a significantly less complex task (Carruthers 1996, 2000).

Actualist Higher-Order Thought Theory

Actualist higher-order thought theory, in contrast, has the advantage that no special organs or mechanisms need to be postulated. Indeed, we are not required to believe in anything that we wouldn't want to believe in anyway. Everyone allows, in particular, that humans have a "mind-reading" or "theory of mind" capacity that enables them to attribute mental states to other people; and there exist sensible accounts of the pressures that would have led to its evolution (Byrne & Whiten 1988, 1998). The faculty of the mind that undertakes this work would, of course, have needed to have access to perceptual input, so that it could set about interpreting the movements, gestures, and utterances of other people. And that faculty would have had embedded within it, moreover, a grasp of the concept *experience*. So all that was then needed was for people to start applying that concept to *themselves*, in response to the relevant kinds of perceptual state. And according to actualist higher-order thought theory, whenever they attribute an experience to themselves they are thereby in a phenomenally conscious mental state.

Likewise the problem of misalignments between first-order and higher-order states is much mitigated, at least, and may well disappear altogether on this approach. For a higher-order thought theorist can claim that the process that generates higher-order awareness of experience is such a simple and immediate one that there is virtually no scope for error or breakdown. Perceptual contents are made available to the conceptual systems, which attempt to classify them and make judgments. Some of these judgments are first-order, as when the system that handles color-classification reaches the intuitive judgment, "That surface is red," on the basis of the input available to it. And some are higher-order, as when the mind-reading faculty generates a description of the experiences that it is receiving as input. Since the mind-reading faculty does not do first-order color recognition, those experiences will either need to be already conceptually tagged, or the mind-reading faculty will need to seek the cooperation of the color-classification system. But either way, all that the higher-order system needs to do is attach the predicate, "I am experiencing . . ." to the front of whatever concept the color-classifying system deems appropriate. So if the latter is inclined to say, "Red," the higher-order faculty generates, "I am experiencing red." There seems little scope for error here.

Although the major problems with inner-sense theory no longer arise, for a higher-order thought theorist, a weaker version of the problem of function recurs – at least, it does if we

allow that our phenomenally conscious experiences can be rich and detailed in their contents, in the way that common-sense intuition dictates. For then there will have to be an
equally rich and detailed higher-order thought. Remember, it requires the *actual* presence
of a higher-order thought to render a given experience phenomenally conscious, on this
account. So there will either have to be a great many discrete higher-order thoughts accompanying each phenomenally conscious experience, or just one, or a few such thoughts
with immensely complex contents. And either way the problem is the same: here, too, we
need to know what all this higher-order cognitive activity is *for*, and why we should have
evolved to engage in so much of it. It is thus no accident that the main proponent of actualist higher-order thought theory has joined Dennett (1991) in declaring that the richness of
phenomenally conscious experience is an illusion (Rosenthal 2004).

Much more seriously, however, it seems that actualist higher-order thought theory lacks
any of the main advantages that inner-sense theory has. In particular, it is far from clear
why an experience that is targeted by a higher-order thought (and only such an experience)
should be *like* anything to undergo. How does targeting by higher-order thought confer on
an experience a subjective aspect, or give it a dimension of "what-it-is-likeness" or *feel*? The
answers are far from transparent, to say the least. An inner-sense theorist can say that our
higher-order experiences present our first-order experiences to us in just the same sort of
subjective, observer-relative, way that our first-order senses present to us the world (and
our own bodies). But an actualist higher-order thought theorist denies the existence of
higher-order experiences. And it is far from clear what can be put in their place.

Neither, it seems, can an actualist higher-order thought theorist give an adequate
account of our purely recognitional concepts of experience of the form, "*This* again." For
there will then be no higher-order experiences to ground the recognitional application of
this, in the sort of way that our first-order experiences ground the recognitional application
of *red*. Granted, we can perhaps imagine ways in which one might acquire higher-order
concepts of experience that are deployed in the face of first-order perceptual contents
alone; where the higher-order character of the concept would derive, not from the manner
in which it is *applied* (in this respect there would be no difference between *this* [experience]
and *red*), but rather in the further inferences and judgments that might be based upon it.
But then it ought to be impossible for someone to think, "*This* [redness] might not have
given rise to *this* [experience *as of* red]." For each of the recognitional concepts in question
(first-order and higher-order) would have the same conditions of application. But it is just
such judgments that we need to be able to explain, if we are to block the explanatory-gap
arguments and zombie-style arguments.

Thus far, then, the moral is that inner-sense theory has important positive virtues, but
faces problems; whereas actualist higher-order thought theory avoids those problems,
but at the cost of losing the positive virtues. Dispositionalist higher-order thought theory
claims to split the difference, providing an account that has all of the advantages of inner-
sense theory with none of the flaws. The dispositionalist approach does face problems of its
own, however, as we shall see.

Dispositionalist Higher-Order Thought Theory

Recall that the dispositionalist's claim is that phenomenally conscious experiences are analog/
non-conceptual states that are immediately and non-inferentially available to a faculty of

higher-order thought; and that by virtue of such availability (together with the truth of some sort of consumer semantics) the states in question possess *dual* analog/non-conceptual contents, both first-order and higher-order. Hence a phenomenally conscious perception of a red surface, for example, will not only have the analog/non-conceptual content *red*, but will also have the analog/non-conceptual content *seems red* or *experience of red*. Thus conscious experiences present *themselves* to us, via their higher-order analog contents, at the same time as presenting properties of the world or of our own bodies.

If some mental states possess dual analog contents of the above sort, then it is clear how this might be used to account for their phenomenally conscious status. For the subjective aspect of a phenomenally conscious experience (its *feel*) can be identified with its higher-order analog content, in virtue of which that experience is presented to us, analog-fashion, in something like the way that its first-order content presents us with fine-grained properties of external objects (or of the body). And just as the world can be said to be *like something* to any perceiver, in virtue of the distinctive fine-grained character of the (first-order) perceptual states of that perceiver; so similarly our own experiences are *like something* to us, in virtue of the distinctive fine-grained character of their higher-order analog contents. And thus the "what-it-is-likeness" of phenomenally conscious experience is explained, it can be claimed.

Likewise, if some mental states possess dual analog contents, then the existence of purely recognitional concepts of experience will be readily explicable. For then we should be capable of forming recognitional concepts for our own experiences, grounded in their higher-order analog contents, in the way that we can form recognitional concepts of secondary qualities of the world (or of our own bodies) grounded in the first-order analog contents of our perceptual states. The concept *this* [experience of red] will be grounded in the higher-order analog/non-conceptual content *experience of red* in the way that the concept *red* is grounded in the analog/non-conceptual content representing redness. But because ordinary folk lack any theory of these higher-order contents or of how they are formed (in contrast with nascent theories of first-order perception, which they *do* have), the concepts in question can be *purely* recognitional, with application-conditions that are unmodulated by theoretical belief.

Dispositionalist higher-order thought theory has all of the advantages of inner-sense theory, then; yet it has none of the associated costs. No "inner scanners" or organs of higher-order perception need be proposed. Rather (in common with the actualist version of higher-order thought theory) all that needs to be postulated is some sort of mind-reading or theory-of-mind faculty, which has available to it concepts of experience, and which can access perceptual input. And here, too, there should be no difficulty in explaining how the mechanisms facilitating phenomenal consciousness might have evolved. For there are ready explanations of the evolution of a mind-reading faculty, and of its need to access perceptual representations in order to do its work. Hence dispositionalist higher-order thought theory has all of the advantages of its actualist cousin, but without losing any of the positive virtues of inner-sense theory, as actualist higher-order thought theory would seem to do.

The success of dispositionalist higher-order thought theory, however, is premised upon the existence of dual analog contents. Can the generation of such contents be explained, adequately and in a naturalistically acceptable manner? How does a perceptual state with the first-order analog/non-conceptual content *red* come to have, at the same time, the higher-order analog/non-conceptual content *experience of red*? The story told by Carruthers (2000) turns on the truth of some or other version of consumer semantics, most plausibly on some sort of inferential-role semantics. It is because a perceptual state with the analog content *red* is made available to a consumer system (the mind-reading faculty) that is apt to infer from it, "I am experiencing red," that the perceptual state in question comes to acquire the higher-order content attributed.

Inferential-role semantics maintains that the content of any mental state will depend, in part, on what the systems that consume that state (using it or drawing inferences from it) are apt to do with it. The point can be illustrated with respect to an example of how first-order perceptual contents can be transformed by changes in consumer-systems; namely, prosthetic vision (Bach-y-Rita 1995). Blind subjects can be fitted with a device that converts the output from a hand-held or head-mounted video-camera into a pattern of electrically-induced tactile stimulation – in the original experiments, via a pad extending across the subject's back; in more recent experiments (and because of its greater sensitivity), via an attachment to the subject's tongue. Initially, of course, the subjects just feel patterns of gentle tickling sensations spreading over the area in question, while the camera scans what is in front of them. But provided that they are allowed to control the movements of the camera themselves, their experiences after a time acquire three-dimensional distal intentional contents, representing the positions and movements of objects in space. It seems that what transforms the contents of these subjects' experiences is that the tactile contents are mapped into the area of the brain that is concerned in building spatial representations (Bach-y-Rita & Kercel 2003). By virtue of the novel use that is made of those states, they thereby acquire new contents.

It is claimed by Carruthers (2000) that essentially the same mechanism is at work in the generation of dual-content perceptual states. Some perceptual experiences (those that are the product of the ventral/temporal visual system, for example) are made available to be consumed by the mind-reading faculty, which makes novel use of them – it uses them to make judgments about those experiences themselves, as opposed to the objects and events that they concern. And by virtue of this novel use, the experiences in question acquire a new, higher-order (but still perceptual) content – higher-order as well as first-order.

One cost of accepting the dual-content account of phenomenal consciousness, then, is that one has to embrace some or other variety of consumer semantics, and dismiss any pure informational/input-side semantics, of the sort espoused by Fodor (1990). Indeed, if inferential-role semantics is the approach of choice, then further costs must be incurred. For it would be highly implausible in the present context to allow that *all* aspects of the inferential-role of a state, no matter how remote, are determinants of its content. Otherwise, besides the contents *red* and *seems red* possessed by an experience in virtue of its availability to color-judging and mind-reading systems, it would also possess the content *Aunt Anne's favorite color*, and many (indefinitely many) others besides. So one had better dismiss so-called "holistic" varieties of inferential-role semantics, claiming instead that only the *immediate* inferences to which a state is subject can be determinants of its content.

So far so good, one might think. But notice that the issue of which judgments and inferences are determinants of the content of a state is closely related to the question of which judgments and inferences are *analytic* (true in virtue of meaning). And there is a long tradition going back at least to Quine (1953) of questioning the naturalistic credentials (and hence the reality of) any sort of analytic/synthetic distinction. Now admittedly the two issues are not quite identical. This is because candidates for analyticity have to be whole propositions, or conditionalizations of inferences involving whole propositions. Whereas in the case of dual-content theory it is an *experience*, not a proposition, that is said to acquire a novel content in virtue of the judgments that subjects are disposed to make on the basis of it. But one still might think that the viability of dual-content theory must stand or fall with the viability of an analytic/synthetic distinction.

What seems to be required if dispositionalist higher-order thought theory is ultimately to be defensible, then, is some way of drawing a principled and naturalistically acceptable distinction between those judgments that are determinants of content and those that are not. Carruthers (2000) has proposed that the relevant judgments are those that are *immediate*, and that do not require the subject to draw on any additional information. But simply postulating that this is so falls a long way short of what is ultimately needed for the account to be viable.

See also 18 The global workspace theory of consciousness; 20 Representationalism about consciousness; 37 Consciousness and intentionality; 48 Duplex vision: separate cortical pathways for conscious perception and the control of action.

Further Readings

Carruthers, P. (2000) *Phenomenal Consciousness: A Naturalistic Theory*. Cambridge: Cambridge University Press.

Carruthers, P. (2005) *Consciousness: Essays from a Higher-Order Perspective*. Oxford: Oxford University Press.

Gennaro, R. (ed.) (2004) *Higher-Order Theories of Consciousness*. Philadelphia, PA: John Benjamins.

Lycan, W. (1996) *Consciousness and Experience*. Cambridge, MA: MIT Press.

Rosenthal, D. (2005) *Consciousness and Mind*. Oxford: Oxford University Press.

References

Armstrong, D. (1968) *A Materialist Theory of the Mind*. London: Routledge.

Baars, B. (1988) *A Cognitive Theory of Consciousness*. Cambridge: Cambridge University Press.

Baars, B. (1997) *In the Theatre of Consciousness*. Oxford: Oxford University Press.

Bach-y-Rita, P. (1995) *Non-synaptic Diffusion Neurotransmission and Late Brain Reorganization*. New York: Demos Press.

Bach-y-Rita, P. and Kercel, S. (2003) Sensory substitution and the human–machine interface. *Trends in Cognitive Sciences* 7, 541–46.

Block, N. (1986) Advertisement for a semantics for psychology. *Midwest Studies in Philosophy* 10, 615–78.

Byrne, R. and Whiten, A. (eds.) (1988) *Machiavellian Intelligence*. Oxford: Oxford University Press.

Byrne, R. and Whiten, A. (eds.) (1998) *Machiavellian Intelligence II: Evaluations and Extensions*. Cambridge: Cambridge University Press.

Carruthers, P. (1996) *Language, Thought and Consciousness*. Cambridge: Cambridge University Press.

Carruthers, P. (1998) Natural theories of consciousness. *European Journal of Philosophy* 6, 203–22.

Carruthers, P. (2000) *Phenomenal Consciousness: A Naturalistic Theory*. Cambridge: Cambridge University Press.

Carruthers, P. (2005) *Consciousness: Essays from a Higher-Order Perspective*. Oxford: Oxford University Press.

Chalmers, D. (1996) *The Conscious Mind*. Oxford: Oxford University Press.

Dennett, D. (1991) *Consciousness Explained*. London: Penguin Press.

Dretske, F. (1995) *Naturalizing the Mind*. Cambridge, MA: MIT Press.

Fodor, J. (1990) *A Theory of Content and Other Essays*. Cambridge, MA: MIT Press.

Gennaro, R. (1996) *Consciousness and Self-Consciousness*. Philadelphia, PA: John Benjamins.

Levine, J. (2001) *Purple Haze*. Oxford: Oxford University Press.

Loar, B. (1990) Phenomenal States. In J. Tomberlin (ed.), *Philosophical Perspectives 4: Action, Theory and Philosophy of Mind* 81–108. Atascadero, CA: Ridgeview.

Locke, J. (1690) *An Essay Concerning Human Understanding*. Many editions now available.

Lycan, W. (1987) *Consciousness*. Cambridge, MA: MIT Press.

Lycan, W. (1996) *Consciousness and Experience*. Cambridge, MA: MIT Press.

Millikan, R. (1984) *Language, Thought, and Other Biological Categories*. Cambridge, MA: MIT Press.

Milner, D. and Goodale, M. (1995) *The Visual Brain in Action*. Oxford: Oxford University Press.

Nagel, T. (1974) What is it like to be a bat? *Philosophical Review* 82, 435–56.

Papineau, D. (1987) *Reality and Representation*. Oxford: Blackwell.

Papineau, D. (2002) *Thinking about Consciousness*. Oxford: Oxford University Press.

Peacocke, C. (1992) *A Study of Concepts*. Cambridge, MA: MIT Press.

Quine, W. (1953) *From a Logical Point of View*. Cambridge, MA: Harvard University Press.

Rosenthal, D. (1986) Two concepts of consciousness. *Philosophical Studies* 49, 329–59.

Rosenthal, D. (1997) A theory of consciousness. In N. Block, O. Flanagan, and G. Güzeldere (eds.), *The Nature of Consciousness*, 729–54. Cambridge, MA: MIT Press.

Rosenthal, D. (2004) Varieties of higher-order theory. In R. Gennaro (ed.), *Higher-Order Theories of Consciousness*, 19–44. Philadelphia, PA: John Benjamins.

Sturgeon, S. (2000) *Matters of Mind*. London: Routledge.

Tye, M. (1995) *Ten Problems of Consciousness*. Cambridge, MA: MIT Press.

Tye, M. (2000) *Consciousness, Color and Content*. Cambridge, MA: MIT Press.

22

The Information Integration Theory of Consciousness

GIULIO TONONI

Hard Problems and Hard Facts: Consciousness and Neuroscience

Consciousness is everything we experience: it can be conceived of, most simply, as what abandons us every night when we fall into dreamless sleep and returns the next morning when we wake up (Tononi & Edelman 1998). Without consciousness, as far as we are concerned, there would be neither an external world nor our own selves: there would be nothing at all.

There are two main problems posed by consciousness, both of which are most profitably considered from a neuroscience perspective (Tononi 2001). The first problem is to understand what features of the brain determine the extent to which consciousness is present. For example, we know that certain thalamocortical circuits are important for conscious experience, whereas cerebellar circuits are not. Why is this so, given that the number of neurons in the two structures is comparable and their neurobiological organization is similarly complicated? Neuroscience poses many other instructive paradoxes related to the first problem of consciousness (Tononi 2004). For example, why is it that the activity of retinal cells, which usually determines what we are going to see, does not contribute directly to conscious experience? Or why is it that many neural processes within cortico-subcortical and even thalamocortical circuits remain largely unconscious, despite contributing to object recognition, depth perception, language parsing, and to the sequencing of action, thought, and speech? Why is consciousness split when the corpus callosum is split, but not if the spinal cord is cut? And why is consciousness strikingly reduced during deep slow-wave sleep or during absence seizures, despite high levels of neuronal firing? Finally, why does the firing of the same cortical neurons correlate with consciousness at certain times, but not at other times?

The second problem of consciousness is to understand what features of the brain determine the specific way consciousness is experienced. For example, what makes the activity of specific cortical areas contribute specific dimensions of conscious experience – auditory cortex to sound, visual cortex to shapes and colors? What aspect of neural organization is responsible for the fact that shapes look the way they do, and different from the way colors appear, or pain feels? Solving the first problem means that we would know to what extent a physical system can generate consciousness – the *quantity* or level of consciousness. Solving the second problem means that we would know what kind of consciousness it generates – the *quality* or content of consciousness.

Neurobiological facts, indicating that different neural structures or modes of functioning

can produce major quantitative and qualitative differences in subjective experience, constitute both challenging paradoxes and precious clues to the enigma of consciousness. This
state of affairs is not unlike the one faced by biologists when, knowing a great deal about
similarities and differences between species, fossil remains, and breeding practices, they
still lacked a theory of how evolution might occur. What was needed, then as now, were not
just more facts, but a theoretical framework that could make sense of them. Here, in order
to offer a tentative but at least unified perspective on the issues that need to be addressed, I
discuss a theoretical approach according to which consciousness corresponds to the brain's
ability to integrate information (Tononi 2001). Closely following the original publications, I
first consider phenomenological thought experiments indicating that subjective experience
has to do with the capacity to integrate information; I then define information integration
and ways to measure it; I next account for basic facts about consciousness and the brain in
terms of information integration; and finally I consider similarities and differences with
related neurobiological approaches. In what follows, I discuss mainly the first problem of
consciousness; the second problem is discussed in Tononi (2003, 2004).

Consciousness as Information Integration:
The Photodiode and the Camera

The information integration theory of consciousness (IITC) claims that a physical system
has subjective experience to the extent that it is capable of integrating information (Tononi
2001, 2003, 2004). This claim may not seem self-evident, perhaps because, being endowed
with consciousness for most of our existence, we take it for granted. To gain some perspective, it is useful to resort to some thought experiments that illustrate key properties of
subjective experience: its informativeness, its unity, and its time course.

Information

Consider the following: You are facing a blank screen that is alternately on and off, and you
have been instructed to say "light" when the screen turns on and "dark" when it turns off.
A photodiode – a very simple light-sensitive device – has also been placed in front of the
screen, and is set up to beep when the screen emits light and to stay silent when the screen
does not. The first problem of consciousness boils down to this. When you differentiate
between the screen being on or off, you have the subjective experience of seeing light or
dark. The photodiode can also differentiate between the screen being on or off, but presumably it does not consciously see light and dark. What is the key difference between you and
the photodiode that makes you see light consciously?

According to the theory, the difference has to do with how much information is generated when that differentiation is made. Information is classically defined as reduction of
uncertainty among a number of alternative outcomes when one of them occurs (Shannon
& Weaver 1963): for example, tossing a fair coin and obtaining heads corresponds to $\log_2(2)$
= 1 bit of information, because there are just two alternatives; throwing a fair die yields
$\log_2(6) = 2.59$ bits of information, because there are six equally likely possibilities. When the
blank screen turns on, the photodiode enters one of its two possible alternative states and
beeps. As with the coin, this corresponds to 1 bit of information. However, when you see

the blank screen turn on, the state you enter, unlike the photodiode, is one out of an extraordinarily large number of possible states. For example, imagine that, instead of turning homogeneously on, the screen were to display at random every frame from every movie that was or could ever be produced. Without any effort, each of these frames would cause you to enter a different state and "see" a different image. This means that when you enter the particular state ("seeing light") you rule out not just "dark," but an extraordinarily large number of alternative possibilities. Whether you think or not of the bewildering number of alternatives, this corresponds to an extraordinary amount of information. Importantly, this information has nothing to do with how complicated the scene is, or how many different objects it appears to contain, but only with the number of alternative outcomes. This point is so simple that its importance has been overlooked.

Integration

While the ability to differentiate among a very large number of states is a major difference between you and the photodiode, by itself it is not enough to account for the presence of subjective experience. To see why, consider an idealized one megapixel digital camera, whose sensor chip is essentially a collection of one million photodiodes. Even if each photodiode in the sensor chip were just binary, the camera could differentiate among $2^{1,000,000}$ states, an immense number, corresponding to 1,000,000 bits of information. Indeed, the camera would easily enter a different state for every frame from every movie that was or could ever be produced. Yet nobody would believe that the camera is conscious. What is the key difference between you and the camera?

According to the theory, the difference has to do with *information integration*. From the perspective of an external observer, the camera chip can certainly enter a very large number of different states. However, the chip could be considered just as well as a collection of 1,000,000 photodiodes with a repertoire of 2 states each, rather than as a single integrated system with a repertoire of $2^{1,000,000}$ states. This is because, due to the absence of interactions among the photodiodes within the sensory chip, the state of each element is causally independent of that of the other elements, and no information can be integrated among them. Indeed, if the sensor chip were literally cut down into its individual photodiodes, the performance of the camera would not change at all.

By contrast, the repertoire of states available to you cannot be subdivided into the repertoire of states available to independent components. Due to the multitude of causal interactions among the elements of your brain that underlie consciousness, the state of each element is causally dependent on that of other elements, which is why information can be integrated among them. Indeed, unlike disconnecting the photodiodes in a camera sensor, disconnecting the elements of your brain that underlie consciousness can have disastrous effects. The integration of information in conscious experience is evident phenomenologically: when you consciously see a certain image, that image is experienced as an integrated whole and cannot be subdivided into component images that are experienced independently: no matter how hard you try, for example, you cannot experience colors independent of shapes, or the left half of the visual field of view independently of the right half. And indeed, the only way to do so is to physically split the brain in two to prevent information integration between the two hemispheres. But then, such split-brain operations yield two separate subjects of conscious experience, each of them having a smaller repertoire of available states and more limited performance (Sperry 1984).

Spatio-temporal characteristics

Finally, conscious experience unfolds at a characteristic spatio-temporal scale. For instance, it flows in time at a characteristic speed and cannot be much faster or much slower. No matter how hard you try, you cannot speed up experience to follow a move accelerated one hundred times, nor can you slow it down if the movie has decelerated. More precisely, as indicated by psychophysical studies, it takes up to 100–200 milliseconds to develop a specific, fully formed sensory experience (Bachmann 2000). On the other hand, a single conscious moment cannot extend beyond 2–3 seconds (Pöppel & Artin 1988). Thus, a phenomenological analysis indicates that consciousness has to do with the ability to integrate a large amount of information and that such integration occurs at a characteristic spatio-temporal scale.

Measuring Information Integration: The Φ of a Complex

If consciousness corresponds to the capacity to integrate information, then a physical system should be able to generate consciousness to the extent that it can enter any of a large number of available states (information), yet it cannot be decomposed into a collection of causally independent subsystems (integration). How can one identify such an integrated system, and how can one measure its repertoire of available states?

As mentioned above, to measure the repertoire of states that are available to a system, one can use the entropy function, but this way of measuring information is completely insensitive to whether the information is integrated. Thus, measuring entropy would not allow us to distinguish between 1,000,000 photodiodes with a repertoire of 2 states each, and a single integrated system with a repertoire of $2^{1,000,000}$ states. To measure information integration, it is essential to know whether a set of elements constitute a causally integrated system, or whether they can be broken down into a number of independent or quasi-independent subsets among which no information can be integrated.

A way to do so has been developed in a series of theoretical publications (Tononi 2001). Briefly, consider an extremely simplified neural system constituted of a set of elements. Each element could represent, for instance, a group of locally interconnected neurons that share inputs and outputs, such as a cortical minicolumn. Assume further that each element can go through discrete activity states, corresponding to different firing levels, each of which lasts for a few hundreds of milliseconds. Finally, imagine that the system is disconnected from external inputs, just as the brain is disconnected from the environment when it is dreaming.

For each subset S of elements taken from such a system, we want to measure the information generated when S enters a particular state out of its repertoire, but only to the extent that such repertoire is integrated, in the sense that it results from causal interactions within S (Figure 22.1). How can one do so? The trick is to divide S into two complementary parts A and B, and evaluate the responses of B that can be caused by all possible inputs originating from A. In neural terms, we try out all possible combinations of firing patterns as outputs from A, and establish how differentiated is the repertoire of firing patterns they produce in B. In information-theoretical terms, this can be done by measuring the *effective information* between A and B as the entropy caused in B when the outputs from A are substituted by independent noise sources (Tononi 2001). Of course, the same can be done for the effective information between B and A.

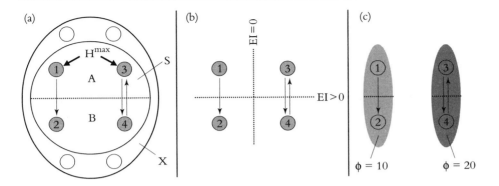

Figure 22.1 Effective information, minimum information bipartition, and complexes

(a) Effective information. Shown is a single subset S of four elements ({1,2,3,4}, gray circle), forming part of a larger system X (black ellipse). This subset is bisected into A and B by a bipartition ({1,3}/{2,4}, indicated by the dotted grey line). Arrows indicate causally effective connections linking A to B and B to A across the bipartition (other connections may link both A and B to the rest of the system X). To measure EI(A→ B), maximum entropy H^{max} is injected into the outgoing connections from A (corresponding to independent noise sources). The entropy of the states of B that is due to the input from A is then measured. Note that A can affect B directly through connections linking the two subsets, as well as indirectly via X. Applying maximum entropy to B allows one to measure EI(B→ A). The effective information for this bipartition is EI(A↔ B) = EI(A→ B) + EI(B→ A).

(b) Minimum information bipartition. For subset S = {1,2,3,4}, the horizontal bipartition {1,3}/{2,4} yields a positive value of EI. However, the bipartition {1,2}/{3,4} yields EI = 0 and is a minimum information bipartition (MIB) for this subset. The other bipartitions of subset S = {1,2,3,4} are {1,4}/{2,3}, {1}/{2,3,4}, {2}/{1,3,4}, {3}/{1,2,4}, {4}/{1,2,3}, all with EI > 0.

(c) Analysis of complexes. By considering all subsets of system X one can identify its complexes and rank them by the respective values of Φ – the value of EI for their minimum information bipartition. Assuming that other elements in X are disconnected, it is easy to see that Φ > 0 for subset {3,4} and {1,2}, but Φ = 0 for subsets {1,3}, {1,4}, {2,3}, {2,4}, {1,2,3}, {1,2,4}, {1,3,4}, {2,3,4}, and {1,2,3,4}. Subsets {3,4} and {1,2} are not part of a larger subset having higher Φ, and therefore they constitute complexes. This is indicated schematically by having them encircled by a gray oval (darker grey indicates higher Φ). In order to identify complexes and their Φ value for systems with many different connection patterns, each system X was implemented as a stationary multidimensional Gaussian process such that values for effective information could be obtained analytically (details in Tononi and Sporns 2003).

By considering the effective information between A and B and between B and A, we can assess how much information can be integrated within a system of elements. To this end, we note that a subset S of elements cannot integrate any information if there is a way to partition S in two parts A and B such that the effective information in both directions is zero. In such a case we would obviously be dealing with at least two causally independent subsets, rather than with a single, integrated subset. This is exactly what would happen with the photodiodes making up the sensor of a digital camera: perturbing the state of some of the photodiodes would make no difference to the state of the others. More generally, to measure the information integration capacity of a subset S, we should search for its *minimum information bipartition*, its informational "weakest link." The effective information for such a bipartition, indicated by Φ, measures to what extent S can *integrate information*. The symbol Φ is meant to indicate that the information (the vertical bar "I") is integrated within a single entity (the circle "O").

We are now in a position to establish which subsets are actually capable of integrating information, and how much of it. To do so, we calculate Φ for every possible subset S of a system, and discard all those subsets that are included in larger subsets having higher Φ (being merely parts of a larger whole). What we are left with are *complexes* – individual entities that can integrate information. For a complex, and only for a complex, it is appropriate to say that, when it enters a particular state out of its repertoire, it generates an amount of integrated information corresponding to its Φ value. Of the complexes that make up a given system, the one with the maximum value of Φ is called the *main complex*.

Some properties of complexes are worth pointing out (Tononi & Sporns 2003). For example, a complex can be causally connected to elements that are not part of it. The elements of a complex that receive inputs from or provide outputs to other elements not part of that complex are called *ports-in* and *ports-out*, respectively. Also, the same element can belong to more than one complex, and complexes can overlap. One should also note that the Φ value of a complex is dependent on both spatial and temporal scales that determine what counts as a state of the underlying system. In general, the relevant spatial and temporal scales are those that jointly maximize Φ. In the case of the brain, the spatial elements and timescales that maximize Φ are likely to be local collections of neurons such as minicolumns and periods of time comprised between tens and hundreds of milliseconds, respectively.

In summary, a system can be analyzed to identify its complexes – those subsets of elements that can integrate information, and each complex will have an associated value of Φ – the amount of information it can integrate. To the extent that consciousness corresponds to the capacity to integrate information, complexes are the "subjects" of experience, being the locus where information can be integrated. Since information can only be integrated *within* a complex and not outside its boundaries, consciousness as information integration is necessarily subjective, private, and related to a single point of view or perspective (Tononi & Edelman 1998; Tononi 2003).

Information Integration and the Brain: Accounting for Neurobiological Facts

Starting from phenomenology and thought experiments, the IITC claims that consciousness corresponds to information integration. It then defines information integration in theoretical terms and suggests ways of measuring it, at least in principle. As a scientific theory, however, the IITC must pass the empirical test. How does it fare when confronted with our main source of empirical evidence, the dependence of our conscious experience on the functioning of our brain? A recent analysis (Tononi 2004) shows that the IITC fits the evidence well, and accounts for many different neurobiological observations in a unified and principled manner. It is worth considering briefly a few examples (Figure 22.2a).

As demonstrated through computer simulations (Figure 22.2b), information integration is optimized (Φ is highest) if the elements of a complex are connected in such a way that they are both functionally specialized (connection patterns are different for different elements) and functionally integrated (all elements can be reached from all other elements of

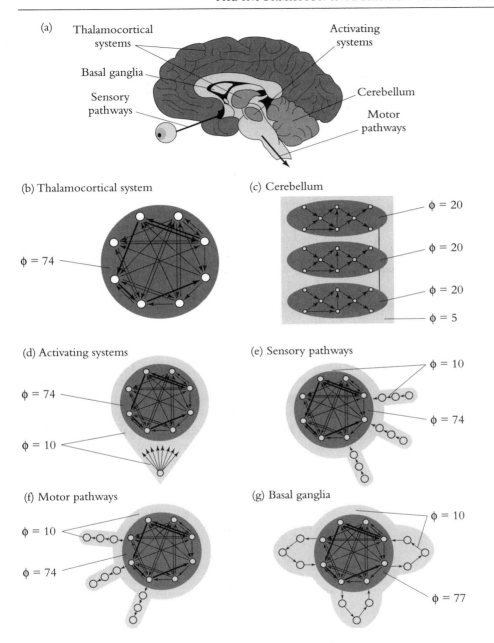

Figure 22.2 Information integration for prototypical neural architectures.

(a) Sagittal section through the human brain showing the approximate location of brain structures whose contribution to consciousness is discussed in the text.

(b–g) Highly schematic diagram of the connectivity of structures in A. The circles indicate elements; the arrows indicate connections among them. The gray areas indicate complexes formed by the elements, and the darker shades of gray indicate a higher capacity to integrate information. Numeric values of information integration (Φ) were obtained through computer simulations (details in Tononi and Sporns 2003).

the network). If functional specialization is lost by replacing the heterogeneous connectivity with a homogeneous one, or if functional integration is lost by rearranging the connections to form small modules, the value of Φ decreases considerably (Tononi 2004).

Based on this analysis, it appears that the thalamocortical system, the part of the brain that is responsible for generating conscious experience (Plum 1991), is organized in a way that is ideally suited to the integration of information. Thus, it comprises a large number of elements that are functionally specialized, becoming activated in different circumstances (Zeki 1993). This is true at multiple spatial scales, from different cortical systems dealing with vision, audition, etc., to different cortical areas dealing with shape, color, motion, etc., to different groups of neurons responding to different directions of motion. However, the specialized elements of the thalamocortical system are integrated through an extended network of intra- and inter-areal connections that permit rapid and effective interactions within and between areas (Engel, Fries, & Singer 2001). In this way, thalamo-cortical neuronal groups are kept ready to respond in a differentiated manner, at multiple spatial and temporal scales, to activity changes in nearby and distant thalamocortical areas. In summary, the thalamocortical system is organized in a way that appears to emphasize at once both functional specialization and functional integration, exactly what is required to support consciousness according to the IITC.

Conversely, simulations show that if neural elements are organized in a strongly modular manner with little interactions among modules, complex size and Φ values are necessarily low (Figure 22.2c; Tononi 2004). In this respect, it is remarkable that the cerebellum, whose direct contribution to conscious experience is minimal, is highly modular and not well suited to information integration. This can be inferred from its anatomical organization, with its characteristic lack of associative connections, and from physiological data indicating that individual patches of cerebellar cortex tend to be activated independently of one another, with little interaction possible between distant patches (Cohen & Yarom 1998; Bower 2002). Thus, although the cerebellum contains more neurons than the cerebral cortex, it likely cannot generate a large complex of high Φ, but rather breaks down into many small complexes each with a low value of Φ. According to the IITC, similar reasons explain why activity in hypothalamic and brainstem circuits that regulate important physiological variables, such as blood pressure, is not associated with conscious experience.

It has been known for a long time that lesions in the reticular formation of the brainstem can produce unconsciousness and coma. Conversely, stimulating the reticular formation can arouse a comatose animal and activate the thalamocortical system, making it ready to respond to stimuli (Moruzzi & Magoun 1949). This is because groups of neurons within the reticular formation are in a unique position to "broadcast" signals diffusely to most of the brain, and to release neuromodulators that have strong effects on both neural excitability and plasticity. However, it would seem that the reticular formation, while necessary for the normal functioning of the thalamocortical system and therefore for the occurrence of conscious experience, may not contribute much in terms of specific dimensions of consciousness – it may work mostly like an external on-switch or as a transient booster of thalamocortical firing. Such a role can be explained readily in terms of information integration. As shown by computer simulations (Figure 22.2d), neural elements that have widespread and effective connections to a main complex of high Φ may nevertheless remain informationally excluded from it. Instead, they are part of a larger complex having a much lower value of Φ.

Further simulations show that afferent pathways to a main complex, while influencing its activity states, do not change its composition, and cause little change in its Φ (Figure 22.2e). Such afferent pathways participate instead in a larger complex, which includes the elements of the main complex, but whose Φ value is very low (Tononi 2004). These simulations provide a principled explanation as to why firing patterns in afferent pathways, while usually influencing conscious experience in a powerful manner, do not contribute directly to consciousness. For example, retinal cells surely can tell light from dark and convey that information to visual cortex. However, they do not contribute directly to visual experience, as indicated by the fact that removal of the retina does not prevent conscious visual experiences (many blind people can dream or imagine visually), and that their rapidly shifting firing patterns do not correspond well with what we perceive. Similar considerations apply to the contribution of efferent pathways (Figure 22.2f; Tononi 2004).

In a similar manner, simulations show that even the addition of parallel loops, while influencing the activity of ports-in and ports-out, generally does not change the composition of the main complex. Instead, the elements of the main complex and of the connected loops form a joint complex that can only integrate the limited amount of information exchanged within each loop (Figure 22.2g; Tononi 2004). According to the theory, this explains why cortical and cortico-subcortical loops (e.g., those including basal ganglia and cerebellum) can implement specialized subroutines that are capable of influencing the states of the main thalamocortical complex without participating in it. Such informationally insulated cortico-subcortical loops could constitute the neural substrates for many processes, such as object recognition, depth perception, language parsing, and the sequencing of action, thought, and speech, which can affect consciousness and be affected by it while remaining themselves unconscious (Baars 1988; Tononi 2004).

As also illustrated by simple computer models (Tononi 2004), a "callosal" cut produces, out of a large complex corresponding to the connected thalamocortical system, two separate complexes. However, because there is redundancy between the two hemispheres, their Φ value is not greatly reduced compared to when they formed a single complex. This prediction is consistent with the data about the splitting of consciousness in split-brain patients (Sperry 1984). Computer simulations also indicate that the size of a complex and its capacity to integrate information can be modified by functional disconnections (Tononi 2004). According to the IITC, functional disconnections between certain parts of the brain and others may underlie the restriction of consciousness in neurological neglect phenomena and in psychiatric conversion and dissociative disorders, may occur during dreaming, may be implicated in conditions such as hypnosis, and may even underlie common attentional phenomena. If the neural substrate of consciousness is not fixed, but can vary to a certain extent, and if the same group of neurons may at times be part of the main complex and at times not, it is appropriate to consider the main thalamocortical complex as a *dynamic complex* or *dynamic core* (Tononi & Edelman 1998; Tononi 2004).

Theoretical considerations, buttressed by computer simulations, further indicate that the extent and Φ value of the thalamocortical main complex can be altered drastically if parameters governing the readiness of neurons to respond or their ability to sustain differentiated responses are modified, even if the anatomical connectivity stays the same. For example, changes in the level of certain neuromodulators occurring at the transition from wakefulness to slow wave sleep, and the resulting changes in intrinsic neuronal currents, lead to a stereotyped bistability of network states and prevent the propagation of differentiated activity patterns (Hill & Tononi 2005). According to the theory, this is why consciousness can be much reduced during certain stages of sleep and during generalized seizures (Tononi 2004).

Finally, the theory predicts that the time requirements for the generation of conscious experience in the brain emerge directly from the time requirements for the build-up of effective interactions among the elements of the main complex. Indeed, the timescale of neurophysiological interactions needed to integrate information among distant cortical regions appears to be consistent with that required by psychophysical observations (Bachmann 2000), by stimulation experiments (Libet 1993), and by recording experiments (Lamme & Spekreijse 2000).

The Information Integration Theory and Other Neurobiological Frameworks

Few neuroscientists have devoted an organized body of work to the neural substrates of consciousness. Crick and Koch were among the first to advocate a research program aimed at identifying in progressively greater detail the neural correlates of consciousness (Crick & Koch 1990). Their proposals are guided primarily by empirical considerations. Over the years, they have made several suggestions, ranging from the role of 40 Hz oscillations in binding different conscious attributes, to suggesting that only a small subset of neurons is associated with consciousness, to the idea that neurons associated with consciousness must project directly to prefrontal cortex, and that neurons in primary visual cortex do not contribute to consciousness (Crick & Koch 1995, 1998). More recently, they have somewhat enlarged their scope and suggested that the substrate of consciousness may be "coalitions" of neurons, both in the front and the back of the cortex, which compete to establish some metastable, strong firing pattern that explicitly represents information and can guide action (Crick & Koch 2003). Related ideas are that higher cortical areas as well as attention can strongly modulate the strength of conscious coalitions, that there is a penumbra of neural activity that gives "meaning" to conscious firing patterns, and that there are "zombie" neural systems that are fast but unconscious.

Dehaene and Changeux (Dehaene & Naccache 2001) have taken as their starting point the global workspace theory, elaborated most extensively in a cognitive context by Baars (1988 and see chapter 18). They have singled out, as experimentally more tractable, the notion of global access – the idea that a "piece of information" encoded in the firing of a group of neurons becomes conscious if it is "broadcast" widely, so that a large part of the brain has access to it. That is, the same information can be conscious or not depending on the size of the audience. This formulation translates in neural terms the "theater" or "TV" metaphor that lies at the heart of the global workspace theory: a message becomes conscious when it becomes accessible to a large audience. Key ideas are that global workspace neurons, characterized by their ability to send and receive projections from many distant areas through long-range excitatory fibers, are especially concentrated in prefrontal, anterior cingulate, and parietal areas, that neurons must be actively firing (broadcasting) to contribute to consciousness, that access to consciousness is an all-or-none phenomenon, requiring the nonlinear ignition of global workspace neurons, and that higher areas play a role in mobilizing lower areas into the global workspace.

There are both similarities and differences between the IITC and neurobiological frameworks such as those just described. Not surprisingly, there is broad convergence on certain key facts: that consciousness is generated by distributed thalamocortical networks, that reentrant interactions among multiple cortical regions are important, that the mechanisms of consciousness and attention overlap but are not the same, and that there are many "unconscious" neural systems. Of course, different approaches may emphasize different aspects. However, at the present stage these differences are not crucial, and fluctuate with the pendulum of experimental evidence.

The important differences lie elsewhere. Unlike other approaches, the IITC addresses head-on the so-called hard problem (Chalmers 1996 and see chapter 17). It takes its start from phenomenology and, by making a critical use of thought experiments, argues that subjective experience *is* integrated information. Therefore, any physical system will have subjective experience to the extent that it is capable of integrating information. In this view, experience – that is, information integration – is a fundamental quantity, just as mass or energy are. Other approaches avoid the hard problem and do not take a theoretical stand concerning the fundamental nature of experience, restricting themselves to the empirical investigation of its neural correlates.

The IITC also addresses, at least in principle, the second problem of consciousness, which is not considered in other approaches. The IITC claims that, as the quantity of consciousness depends on the amount of information that can be integrated within a complex, the quality of consciousness (whether visual, auditory, colored, etc.) depends on the informational relationships among its elements (Tononi 2004). More precisely, it is specified by the matrix of effective information values among all of its subsets. According to the IITC, the "meaning" of each and every quale, such as "red" is provided exclusively by the informational relationships among the elements of the complex. It is therefore private and immanent to each individual complex (it is present, for instance, in dreams), and it can be affected by changes anywhere in the main thalamocortical complex, but not by changes outside it. Of course, the IITC recognizes that the specific informational relationships within the main thalamocortical complex, and thereby many aspects of meaning, have their source in historical events during evolution, development, and experience.

The IITC takes a precise view about information integration, offering a general theoretical definition and a way to measure it as the Φ value of a complex. In other approaches, including the ones inspired by the global workspace metaphor, the notion of information is not well defined. For example, it is often assumed loosely that the firing of specific thalamocortical elements (e.g., those for red) conveys some specific information (e.g., that there is something red), and that such information becomes conscious if it is disseminated widely. However, just like a retinal cell or a photodiode, a given thalamocortical element has no information about whether what made it fire was a particular color rather than a shape, a visual stimulus rather than a sound, a sensory stimulus rather than a thought. All it knows is whether it fired or not, just as each receiving element only knows whether it received an input or not. Thus, the information specifying "red" cannot possibly be in the message conveyed by the firing of any neural element, whether it is broadcasting widely or not. According to the IITC, that information resides instead in the reduction of uncertainty occurring when a whole complex enters one out of a large number of available states. Moreover, within a complex, both active and inactive neurons count, just as the sound of an orchestra is specified both by the instruments that are playing and by those that are silent. In short, what counts is how much integrated information is generated, and not how widely it is disseminated (cf. Figure 22.2d).

By arguing that subjective experience corresponds to a system's capacity to integrate information, and by providing a mathematical definition of information integration, the IITC can go on to show that several observations concerning the neural substrate of consciousness fall naturally into place. Other approaches generally propose a provisional list of neural ingredients that appear to be important, such as synchronization or widespread broadcasting, without providing a principled explanation of why they would be important or whether they would be always necessary. For example, synchronization is usually an indication that the elements of the complex are capable of interacting efficiently, but is neither necessary nor sufficient for consciousness: there can be strong synchronization with little consciousness (absence seizures) as well as consciousness with little synchronization (as indicated by unit recordings in higher-order visual areas). Or there can be extremely widespread "broadcasting," as exemplified most dramatically by the diffuse projections of neuromodulatory systems (cf. Figure 22.2d), yet lesion, stimulation, and recording experiments do not suggest any specific contribution to specific dimensions of consciousness.

Finally, the IITC says that the presence and extent of consciousness can be determined, in principle, also in cases in which we have no verbal report, such as infants or animals, or in neurological conditions such as akinetic mutism, psychomotor seizures, and sleepwalking. In practice, of course, measuring Φ accurately in such systems will not be easy, but approximations and informed guesses are certainly conceivable. The IITC also implies that consciousness is not an all-or-none property, but increases in proportion to a system's ability to integrate information. In fact, any physical system capable of integrating information would have some degree of experience, irrespective of the stuff of which it is made. Concerning such issues, other approaches have little to say, as they have little to say about the ingredients that would be necessary to build a conscious artifact. Do elements need to be neuron-like? Is a body necessary? Would a set of fully connected processors automatically become conscious? According to the IITC, the answer is clear: any artifact would be conscious to the extent that it houses a complex of high Φ.

See also 44 A neurobiological framework for consciousness; 47 Large-scale temporal coordination of cortical activity as a prerequisite for conscious experience.

Further Readings

Edelman, G. M. and Tononi, G. (2000) *A Universe of Consciousness: How Matter Becomes Imagination.* New York: Basic Books.

References

Baars, B. J. (1988) *A Cognitive Theory of Consciousness.* New York: Cambridge University Press.
Bachmann, T. (2000) *Microgenetic Approach to the Conscious Mind.* Amsterdam: John Benjamins.
Bower, J. M. (2002) The organization of cerebellar cortical circuitry revisited: implications for function. *Annals of the New York Academy of Sciences* 978, 135–55.
Chalmers, D. J. (1996) *The Conscious Mind: In Search of a Fundamental Theory. Philosophy of Mind Series.* New York: Oxford University Press.
Cohen, D. and Yarom, Y. (1998) Patches of synchronized activity in the cerebellar cortex evoked by mossy-fiber stimulation: questioning the role of parallel fibers. *Proceedings of the National Academy of Sciences* 95, 15,032–6.
Crick, F. and Koch, C. (1990) Some reflections on visual awareness. *Cold Spring Harbor Symposia on Quantitative Biology* 55, 953–62.

Crick, F. and Koch, C. (1995) Are we aware of neural activity in primary visual cortex? *Nature* 375, 121–3.

Crick, F. and Koch, C. (2003) A framework for consciousness. *Nature Review Neuroscience* 6, 119–26.

Dehaene, S. and Naccache, L. (2001) Towards a cognitive neuroscience of consciousness: basic evidence and a workspace framework. *Cognition* 79, 1–37.

Edelman, G. M. and Tononi, G. (2000) *A Universe of Consciousness: How Matter Becomes Imagination.* New York: Basic Books.

Engel, A. K., Fries, P., and Singer, W. (2001) Dynamic predictions: oscillations and synchrony in top-down processing. *Nature Review Neuroscience* 2, 704–16.

Hill, S. and Tononi, G. (2005) Modeling sleep and wakefulness in the thalamocortical system. *Journal of Neurophysiology* 93, 1671–98.

Lamme, V. A. and Spekreijse, H. (2000) Modulations of primary visual cortex activity representing attentive and conscious scene perception. *Frontiers in Bioscience* 5, D232–43.

Libet, B. (1993) The neural time factor in conscious and unconscious events. *CIBA Foundation Symposium* 174, 123–37.

Moruzzi, G. and Magoun, H. W. (1949) Brain stem reticular formation and activation of the EEG. *Electroencephalography and Clinical Neurophysiology* 1, 455–73.

Plum, F. (1991) Coma and related global disturbances of the human conscious state. In A. Peters and E. G. Jones (eds.), *Normal and Altered States of Function.* New York: Plenum Press.

Pöppel, E. and Artin, T. (1988) *Mindworks: Time and Conscious Experience.* Boston, MA: Harcourt Brace Jovanovich.

Shannon, C. E. and Weaver, W. (1963) *The Mathematical Theory of Communication.* Urbana: University of Illinois Press.

Sperry, R. (1984) Consciousness, personal identity and the divided brain. *Neuropsychologia* 22, 661–73.

Tononi, G. (2001) Information measures for conscious experience. *Archives Italienne de Biologie* 139, 367–71.

Tononi, G. (2003) *Galileo e il fotodiodo.* Bari: Laterza.

Tononi, G. (2004) An information integration theory of consciousness. *BMC Neuroscience* 5, 42.

Tononi, G. and Edelman, G. M. (1998) Consciousness and complexity. *Science* 282, 1846–51.

Tononi, G. and Sporns, O. (2003) Measuring information integration. *BMC Neuroscience* 4, 31.

Zeki, S. (1993) *A Vision of the Brain.* Oxford: Blackwell Scientific Publications.

23

Quantum Mechanical Theories of Consciousness

HENRY STAPP

Introduction

In the seventeenth century, Isaac Newton initiated an approach to understanding nature that, with important contributions from Clerk Maxwell and Albert Einstein, developed into what is called classical mechanics. That theory is now known to be fundamentally incorrect. It was replaced around 1926 by a profoundly different theory called quantum mechanics. A principal conceptual difference between classical mechanics and its quantum successor is that the former is exclusively physical whereas the latter is essentially psychophysical. In particular, classical mechanics is a theory of a material physical world conceived to be completely specified by numbers assigned to points in space and time, and to be, moreover, dynamically complete, in the sense that the behavior of these numbers for all times is completely specified by laws and initial conditions that involve only these numbers themselves. Contrastingly, orthodox quantum mechanics brings into the dynamics certain conscious choices that are not determined by the currently known laws of physics but have important causal effects in the physical world.

The entry of these causally efficacious conscious choices into contemporary physics has led some quantum physicists to believe that an adequate scientific theory of the conscious brain must be quantum mechanical. This view is challenged by some nonphysicists, who argue that quantum theory deals with microscopic atomic-level processes whereas consciousness is associated with macroscopic neuronal processes, and that the concepts of classical physics provide an adequate understanding of such macroscopic systems.

That argument is not valid. Quantum mechanics deals with the observed behaviors of macroscopic systems whenever those behaviors depend sensitively upon the activities of atomic-level entities. Brains are such systems Their behaviors depend strongly upon the effects of, for example, the ions that flow into nerve terminals. Computations show that the quantum uncertainties in the ion-induced release of neurotransmitter molecules at the nerve terminals are large (Stapp 1993, pp. 133, 152). These uncertainties propagate in principle up to the macroscopic level. Thus quantum theory must be used in principle in the treatment of the physical behavior of the brain, in spite of its size.

The entry into quantum dynamics of experiential elements, and in particular of our conscious choices, is rendered possible by the effective elimination from quantum mechanics of the classical concept of material substance. Quantum theory retains the core feature of classical physics, namely a structure of mathematical quantities assigned to points in space and time. But both the behavior and the significance of this structure is greatly altered. The mathematical structure no longer represents a classically conceived material Universe but rather an *informational structure* that represents, in effect, the *knowledge* associated with *psychophysical events* that have already occurred, and also certain *objective tendencies* (propensities) for the occurrence of future psychophysical events This conceptual revision is epitomized by the famous pronouncement of Heisenberg (1958, p. 100):

> The conception of objective reality of the elementary particles has thus evaporated not into the cloud of some obscure new reality concept but into the transparent clarity of a mathematics that represents no longer the behavior of particles but rather our knowledge of this behavior.

The aim of this chapter is to explain briefly, in plain words, how this enormous change came about, how it works, and how this altered conception of the role of consciousness in physics impacts on psychology and neuroscience.

Origin of Quantum Mechanics

Quantum mechanics was initiated by a discovery made by Max Planck in 1900. Planck was studying the distribution over frequencies of the radiant energy emitted from a tiny hole in a hollow container. Classical physics gave clear predictions about the dependence of this energy distribution upon the temperature of the container, but those predictions did not match the empirical facts.

Planck found that the empirical data could be accounted for if one assumed that the radiant energy associated with each given frequency was concentrated in units, or quanta, with the amount of energy in a unit being directly proportional to the frequency of the radiation that carried it. The constant of proportionality was measured by Planck, and is called "Planck's constant."

This discovery was followed by a flood of empirical data that tested various predictions of classical physics that depended sensitively on the classical conceptions of such things as electrons and electromagnetic radiation. The data revealed fascinating mathematical structures, which seemed to involve Planck's constant but, like Planck's data, were essentially incompatible with the classical materialist conception of the world.

Many of the best mathematicians of that generation, men such as Hilbert, Jordan, Weyl, von Neumann, Born, Einstein, Sommerfeld, and Pauli, struggled to unravel this mystery, but it was not until 1925 that the key step was made. Heisenberg found that correct predictions could be obtained if one transformed classical mechanics into a new theory by a certain "quantization" procedure. This procedure replaced the *numbers* that specified the structure of the classically conceived material Universe by *actions*. Actions differ from numbers in that the ordering of numerical factors does not matter – 2 times 3 is the same as 3 times 2 – whereas the order in which two actions are applied can matter.

Problems of Interpretation

This replacement of numbers by actions is the mathematical foundation of quantum mechanics. But an adequate physical theory requires more than just mathematical rules.

It also requires a conceptual framework that allows certain mathematical statements to be tied to human experiences. In classical mechanics the interpretive framework that ties the mathematics to experience does not disturb the mathematics. It *envelops* the mathematical structure *but does not affect it*. The basic idea of the classically conceived connection between the physically and psychologically described aspects of nature is a carry-over from the planetary dynamics that was the origin of classical mechanics: the locations of objects are regarded as being directly knowable, without producing any effects on those objects. But in quantum mechanics, the numbers that in classical mechanics represent, for example, the locations of various material objects, are replaced by actions. These actions are associated with *the process of acquiring information*, or knowledge pertaining to the location of that object, and this action normally affects the state that is being probed: the act of acquiring knowledge about a system becomes entangled in a non-classical way with the information-bearing quantum mechanical state of the system that is being probed.

This elimination of the numbers that were imagined to specify the physical state of the material world, and their replacement by actions associated with the acquisition of knowledge, raises huge technical difficulties. The needed conceptual adjustments were worked out principally by Bohr, Heisenberg, Pauli, and Born. The center of this activity was Bohr's institute in Copenhagen, and the conceptual framework created by these physicists is called "The Copenhagen Interpretation."

The Copenhagen Interpretation

A key feature of the new philosophy is described by Bohr:

> In our description of nature the purpose is not to disclose the real essence of phenomena but only to track down as far as possible relations between the multifold aspects of our experience. (Bohr 1934, p. 18)

> The appropriate physical interpretation of the symbolic quantum mechanical formalism amounts only to prediction of determinate or statistical character, pertaining to individual phenomena appearing under conditions defined by classical physics concepts. (Bohr 1958, p. 64)

The references to "'classical physics concepts'" are explained as follows:

> It is imperative to realize that in every account of physical experience one must describe both experimental conditions and observations by the same means of communication as the one used in classical physics. (Bohr 1958, p. 88)

The decisive point is to recognize that the description of the experimental arrangement and the recording of observations must be given in plain language suitably refined by the usual physical terminology. This is a simple logical demand, since by the word "experiment" we can only mean a procedure regarding which we are able to communicate to others what we have done and what we have learned (Bohr 1958, p. 3).

Bohr is saying that scientists do in fact use, and must use, the concepts of classical physics in communicating to their colleagues the specifications on how the experiment is to be set up, and what will constitute a certain type of outcome. He in no way claims or admits that there is an actual reality out there that conforms to the precepts of classical physics.

But how can one jointly and consistently use these two mutually inconsistent descriptions of nature? That is the problem that the Copenhagen Interpretation solves, at least for all practical purposes.

Quantum dualism

The Copenhagen solution is to divide nature into two parts. One part is the observing system, including the bodies, brains, and minds of the human beings that are setting up the experimental situations and acquiring, via experiential feedbacks, increments in knowledge. This observing part includes also the measuring devices. This observing system is described in ordinary language refined by the concepts of classical physics. Thus the agent can say "I placed the measuring device in the center of the room, and one minute later I saw the pointer swing to the right." The agent's description is a description of what he does – of what probing actions he takes – and of the *experienced* consequences of his actions. The descriptions in terms of the language and concepts of classical physics are regarded as part of this first kind of description.

The other part of nature is the system being probed by the classically conceived and described observing system. This probed system is described in the symbolic language of quantum mathematics.

In classical physics the classical concepts are asserted to be applicable in principle right down to the atomic level. But according to the quantum precepts the quantum mathematical description must be used for any properties of the atomic entities upon which observable features of nature sensitively depend.

This separation between the two parts of nature is called "The Heisenberg Cut." Above the cut one uses experience-based classical descriptions, while below the cut one uses the quantum mathematical description.

The cut can be moved from below a measuring device to above it. This generates two *parallel descriptions* of this device, one classical and the other quantum mechanical. The quantum description is roughly a continuous smear of classical-type states. So, roughly, the postulated theoretical correspondence is that the smeared out mathematical quantum state specifies the *statistical weights* of the various alternative possible classically described experienceable states. The predictions of the theory thereby become, in general, statistical predictions about possible experiences described in the conceptual framework of classical physics.

There is, however, a fly in the ointment. In order to extract statistical predictions about possible experiences, some specific probing question must be physically posed. This probing question must have a *countable* set of experientially distinct alternative possible responses. "Countable" means that the possible responses can be placed in one-to-one correspondence with the whole numbers 1, 2, 3, . . ., or with some finite subset of these numbers. But the number of possible classically describable possibilities is not countable; there is a continuous infinity of such possibilities. So some decision must be made as to which of the possible probing questions will be physically posed.

Conscious choices

The mathematical structure of the theory does not specify what this question is, or even put statistical conditions on the possibilities. Thus the mathematical theory is dynamically incomplete on three counts: it fails to specify *which* probing question will be posed, *when* it will be posed, and *what* response will then appear. The theory does, however, assign a statistical weight (probability) to each of the alternative possible responses to any question that could be posed.

Von Neumann gave the name "Process 1" to the physical posing of a probing question. He specified its general mathematical form, and sharply distinguished it from the very different "Process 2," which is the mathematically specified *evolution* of the quantum state in accordance with the rules specified by the quantization procedure. Process 1 events *intervene* abruptly, from time to time, in the orderly evolution specified by Process 2.

How does orthodox Copenhagen quantum theory resolve this critical problem of the mathematical indeterminateness of the choices of the needed Process 1 probing actions?

Quantum agents

This problem of the indeterminateness of the conscious choices is resolved in orthodox Copenhagen quantum mechanics by adopting a pragmatic stance. The theory is considered to be a set of rules useful to a community of communicating, conscious, observing agents embedded in a physical universe. These agents make conscious decisions about how to probe that universe, in order to observe responses that will augment their knowledge. The difficulty mentioned above, which is that the known laws do not determine which of the possible probing questions will be physically posed, is neatly resolved by saying that this very openness *allows the conscious agents to choose freely* which probing questions they will physically pose. Thus, the causal gap in the mathematically described structure is filled by the free choices made by conscious agents.

Bohr often emphasized the freedom of these agents to make these choices:

> The freedom of experimentation, presupposed in classical physics, is of course retained and corresponds to the free choice of experimental arrangement for which the mathematical structure of the quantum mechanical formalism offers the appropriate latitude. (Bohr 1958, p. 73)

> To my mind there is no other alternative than to admit in this field of experience, we are dealing with individual phenomena and that our possibilities of handling the measuring instruments allow us to make a choice between the different complementary types of phenomena that we want to study. (Bohr 1958, p. 51)

These quotes highlight the key fact that selection of the Process 1 probing events is determined, within the framework of contemporary physics, not by known mathematical or physical laws but rather by free choices made by conscious agents.

Von Neumann's move

John von Neumann formulated Copenhagen quantum mechanics in a mathematically rigorous form, and then, in order to remove ambiguities associated with the placement of the Heisenberg cut, showed that this cut could be pushed all the way up so that the entire physically describable Universe, including the bodies and brains of the agents, are described quantum mechanically. This placement of the cut does not eliminate the need for Process 1. It merely places the physical aspect of the Process 1 psychophysical event in the brain of the conscious agent, while placing the conscious choice of which probing question to pose in his stream of consciousness. That is, the conscious act of choosing the probing question is represented as a psychologically described event in the agent's mind, which is called by von Neumann (1955, p. 421) the "abstract ego." This choice is physically and functionally implemented by a Process 1 action in his brain. The psychologically described and physically described actions are the two aspects of a single psychophysical event, whose physically described aspect intervenes in the orderly Process 2 evolution in a mathematically well defined way.

Bohr emphasized that the laws of quantum theory should continue to be valid in biological systems, but that the latitude introduced by the severe constraints upon observation imposed by the demands of sustaining life could permit concepts such as "teleology" and "volition" to come *consistently* into play (Bohr 1958, pp. 10, 22).

Interactive Dualism

Orthodox quantum theory is a theory of a type called "interactive dualism," which goes back in modern philosophy to Descartes, and before that to the ancient Greeks. Interactive dualism postulates the existence of two entirely different kinds of realities, mental and physical, that interact. Mental realities have the character of *feelings*, broadly construed to include thoughts, ideas, perceptions, pains, joys, sorrows, and all things that enter directly into our streams of conscious experiences, and are described basically in psychological language. Physical realities are elements that are described in our theories of nature in terms of mathematical qualities assigned to space-time points.

Interactive dualism, combined with the precepts of classical physics, gives *classical* interactive dualism. This has been attacked ferociously by philosophers for over 300 years, with an intensity that has been increasing over the past half century. *Quantum* interactive dualism is based, instead, on orthodox (von Neumann) quantum theory.

The first main objection to classical interactive dualism is that it postulates the existence of two entirely different kinds of things, but provides no understanding of how they interact, or even can interact. The second main objection is that the physical description is, by itself, already causally complete, giving a completely deterministic account of the evolution in time of every physically described entity. This means that the mental realities have nothing to do, and no possibility of influencing anything physical. The mental side is a "ghost in the machine" that is imagined to be pulling the levers in order to "work its will" in the physical world, but cannot really be doing so because the behavior of the physically described universe is completely determined independently of the ghostly machinations.

Quantum interactive dualism neatly evades both objections. The answer to the first is that the form of the interaction between the mentally and physically described aspects of nature *is specified* in von Neumann's account of the measurement process. This account is part of a careful mathematical description of the fundamental principles of quantum theory, and of how they are to be employed in practice. The specification of the form of the interaction between the two differently described aspects is an essential part of von Neumann's formulation of quantum theory. It is essential because quantum theory is specifically designed to be a tool that allows physicists to make computations that connect their experiences about setting up probing experiments to their expectations about the observable responses to these probing actions. Such a theory requires an adequate theory of measurement and observation, which von Neumann provides.

As regards the second objection, a huge essential difference between the classical and quantum dualities is that in the quantum case the physically described part is not causally complete. Something else is needed to complete the dynamics. Mental realities function both to complete the causal structure and also to undergird what the theory is basically about, namely the structural relationships between the elements in our streams of conscious experiences.

In my characterization of interactive dualism I spoke of two kinds of *realities*, physical and mental. Mental realities are certainly real: a presently felt pain really does exist. The experiencings of theoretical ideas in the streams of consciousness of physicists are also real happenings. But the existence in nature of real entities that have all the properties ascribed by the precepts of classical physics to, say, "electrons" would be surely denied by most quantum physicists. Quantum philosophy recommends avoiding commitment to the idea that there are realities in nature that accurately conform to our theoretical ideas about the physical Universe. With regard to the physical it is only the *descriptions* themselves, and the way that they are used, that are ascribed significance in orthodox quantum philosophy. Ontological commitments pertaining to the physical are not part of science. In general, the practical meanings of descriptions are defined in the end by how the descriptions are used in practice.

The fact that the form of the interaction between the psychologically and physically described aspects of quantum theory is specified is important: it severely constrains the theory. Arbitrary ad hoc proposals cannot be postulated willy nilly. For example, many proposals are ruled out by the fact that the living brain is large, warm, and wet, and interacts strongly with its environment. The first, and very stringent, demand on any serious proposal is that it works in this hostile-to-quantum-effects setting.

The *only* pertinent quantum effect known to me which survives robustly under these hostile settings is the quantum Zeno effect, so-named because of its rough similarity to the paradox that claims that the hare can never catch the tortoise because, by the time the hare reaches where the tortoise was, the tortoise will have moved on. That claim is obviously false. But there is a vaguely similar claim about quantum mechanics that is unquestionably true (Misra & Sudarshan 1977). If, under appropriate conditions, one repeatedly poses the same probing question at a sufficiently rapid rate, then the sequence of responses will tend to get stuck in place. In the limit of arbitrarily rapid re-posings, the response will become frozen: all the responses will come out to be the same, even though very strong physical forces may be working to make them change. Thus a manipulation of the *timings* of the probing actions, which are under the control of the consciousness of agent, can have, even in a warm, wet brain, a very special kind of physical effect. If, by mental effort, an agent can cause a sufficient increase in *probing rate*, then that agent can cause a state of intention and attention to be held in place much longer than would be the case if no such effort were being made.

The crucial point, here, is that the physically-described laws of quantum mechanics do not fix the *times* at which the physical Process 1 probing actions occur, or *what* these physical probing actions will be. This lacuna is the essential reason why the conscious "free choices" on the part of human agents were brought into quantum mechanics by its founders, and were retained by John von Neumann! These *conscious choices* control the timings of the physical Process 1 events studied by Misra and Sudarshan, and this connection entails, in principle, the capacity of these psychologically described aspects of the streams of consciousness of agents to control, via quantum Zeno holding actions, certain physically described features of the world.

Huge survival benefits could accrue to agents that can exploit this feature of the quantum mechanics, because this intentional stabilizing of attention would also hold in place the corresponding pattern of functional brain activity.

Such a holding effect could, of course, be *postulated*, ad hoc, to occur in a classical-physics-based model. But in that case the holding effect would not be a direct consequence of the same basic psychophysical laws that are used by physicists to explain atomic phenomena. In the quantum case the holding effect is probably the only robust kind of effect of mind on brain that the theory predicts, whereas any desired regularity could be postulated in a theory that simply adds mind ad hoc. As regards classical-physics-based theories, the view of physicists is that classical physics is an *approximation* to quantum physics. All effects of conscious thought upon brain activity that *follow* from quantum theory, such as the quantum Zeno holding effect, are eliminated in the classical physics approximation, because in that approximation, the uncertainty-principle-based latitude within which the causal effects of mind upon the physically described aspects of nature operate shrinks to zero.

Comparison to Psychological Findings

The dynamical effect described above of a volition-induced high rapidity of the Process 1 probing actions is exactly in line with the description of the effects of volition described by William James (1892). In the section entitled *Volitional effort is effort of attention* he writes:

> Thus we find that we reach the heart of our inquiry into volition when we ask by what process is it that the thought of any given action comes to prevail stably in the mind. (p. 417)

> The essential achievement of will, in short, when it is most "voluntary," is to attend to a difficult object and hold it fast before the mind. (p. 417)

> Everywhere, then, the function of effort is the same: to keep affirming and adopting the thought which, if left to itself, would slip away. (p. 421)

James may have foreseen, on the basis of his efforts to understand the mind–brain connection, the eventual downfall of classical mechanics. He closed his book with the prophetic words ". . . and never forget that the natural-science assumptions with which we started are provisional and revisable things" (p. 433).

A lot has happened in psychology since the time of James, but these newer developments support his idea of the holding-attention-in-place action of volition. Much of the recent empirical and theoretical work pertaining to attention is summarized in Harold Pashler's book *The Psychology of Attention* (Pashler 1998). Pashler concluded that the evidence indicates the existence of two distinct kinds of mental processes, one that appears not to involve volition, and that allows several perceptual processes to proceed in parallel without significant interference, and one that does involve volition and that includes planning and memory storage. This latter process seems to involve a linear queuing effect with limited total capacity.

These properties of volition-driven processes appear to be *explainable* in terms of the basic laws of orthodox quantum physics, which entail the existence of Process 1 physical events whose timings are controlled by conscious choices and which can, in principle, by means of the quantum Zeno effect, hold in place a pattern of neural activity that will tend to bring into being an intended effect. But this holding effect drops out in the classical-physics approximation, in which all physically described properties become completely determined by physically described properties alone, with consciousness a causally inert, or causally superfluous, bystander. *Correlations* between physically and psychologically described properties can be described within a classical-physics-based framework, but the psychologically described aspects will remain essentially epiphenomenal byproducts of brain activity.

This evidence from psychology is discussed in detail in Stapp (1999, 2001) and in Schwartz, Stapp, and Beauregard (2003, 2005).

Application in Neuroscience

The most direct evidence pertaining to the effects of conscious choices upon brain processes comes from experiments in which identifiable consciously controllable cognitive processes *seem to be* controlling directly measured physical processes in the brain. An example is the experiment of Ochsner et al. (2001). The subjects are trained how to cognitively re-evaluate emotional scenes by consciously creating and holding in place an alternative fictional story of what is really happening in connection with a scene they are viewing.

> The trial began with a 4 second presentation of a negative or neutral photo, during which participants were instructed simply to view the stimulus on the screen. This interval was intended to provide time for participants to apprehend complex scenes and allow an emotional response to be generated that participants would then be asked to regulate. The word "Attend" (for negative or neutral photos) or "Reappraise" (negative photos only) then appeared beneath the photo and the participants followed this instruction for 4 seconds . . .
>
> To verify whether the participants had, in fact, reappraised in this manner, during the post-scan rating session participants were asked to indicate for each photo whether they had reinterpreted the photo (as instructed) or had used some other type of reappraisal strategy. Compliance was high: On less than 4 percent of trials with highly negative photos did participants report using another type of strategy.

Reports such as these can be taken as evidence that the streams of consciousness of the participants do exist and contain elements identifiable as efforts to reappraise.

Patterns of brain activity accompanying reappraisal were assessed by using functional magnetic imaging resonance (fMRI). The fMRI results were that reappraisal was positively correlated with increased activity in the left lateral prefrontal cortex and the dorsal medial prefrontal cortex (regions thought to be connected to cognitive control) and decreased activity in the (emotion-related) amygdala and medial orbito-frontal cortex.

How can we understand and explain the psychophysical correlations exhibited in this experiment? According to the quantum model, the conscious feelings *cause* the changes in brain activity to occur. This causation is in strict conformity to the known laws of physics, as spelled out in von Neumann's book *Mathematical Foundations of Quantum Mechanics*.

This causal explanation, this whole causal story, falls apart if one tries to explain this psychophysical correlation within the framework of the classical approximation. That approximation entirely eliminates the effects of our conscious choices and efforts upon the physical world, including our brains. But what is the rational motivation for insisting on using this approximation? The applicability of the classical approximation to this phenomenon certainly does not follow from physics considerations; calculations based on the known properties of nerve terminals indicate that quantum theory must in principle be used. Nor does it follow from the fact that classical physics works reasonably well in neuro-anatomy or neurophysiology, for quantum theory explains why the classical approximation works well in those domains. Nor does it follow rationally from the massive analyses and conflicting arguments put forth by philosophers of mind. In view of the turmoil that has engulfed philosophy during the three centuries since Newton cut the bond between mind and matter, the re-bonding achieved by physicists during the first half of the twentieth century must be seen as an enormous development, a lifting of the veil. Ignoring this huge and enormously pertinent development in basic science, and proclaiming the validity of materialism on the basis of inapplicable-in-this-context nineteenth-century science is not a rational judgment.

Of course, one can simply abandon the idea that ideas can actually *cause* anything physical, and view the feeling of effort as not a *cause*, but rather an *effect*, of a prefrontal excitation that causes the suppression of the limbic response, and that is caused entirely by other purely physical activities.

Viewed from a sufficiently narrow perspective, that might seem to be a satisfactory con-clusion, but it leads to the old problem: Why is consciousness present at all, and why does it feel so causally efficacious, if it has no causal efficacy at all? Why this big hoax? Quantum theory answers: There is no a hoax! It was only the premature acceptance of a basically false physical theory, fundamentally inapplicable to the brain, that ever made it seem so!

The only objections I know to applying the basic principles of physics to brain dynamics are, first, the forcefully expressed opinions of some nonphysicists that the classical approx-imation provides an entirely adequate foundation for understanding brain dynamics, in spite of the quantum calculations that indicate the opposite; and, second, the opinions of some physicists that the hugely successful orthodox quantum theory, which is intrinsically dualistic, should, for philosophical reasons, be replaced by some theory that re-converts human consciousness into a causally inert witness to the mindless dance of atoms. Neither of these opinions has any secure scientific basis.

There are several other quantum theories of consciousness, but all of them are based on von Neumann's work. The physics considerations described above rest completely on that work. I shall now describe some proposals that go far beyond von Neumann's secure base, and introduce some very controversial ideas.

The Penrose-Hameroff theory

Roger Penrose and Stuart Hameroff (Hameroff & Penrose 1996) have proposed a quantum theory of consciousness that brings together three exciting but controversial ideas. The first pertains to the still-to-be-worked-out quantum theory of gravity. The second involves the famous incompleteness theorem of Gödel. The third rests upon the fairly recently discov-ered microtubular structure of neurons.

Penrose proposes that the abrupt changes of the quantum state that are associated with conscious experiences are generated by the gravitational effects of particles of the brain upon the structure of space-time in the vicinity of the brain. Ordinarily one would think that the effects of gravity *within the brain* would be too minuscule to have any significant effect on the functioning of the brain. But Penrose and Hameroff come up with an estimate of typical times associated with the gravitational effects that are in the tenth of a second range associated with conscious experiences. This fuels the speculation that the abrupt changes in the quantum state that occur in quantum theory are caused not by the entry of thoughts into brain dynamics, but by quantum effects of gravity.

But then why should thoughts or consciousness be involved at all?

Two reasons are given. Penrose uses Gödel's incompleteness theorem to argue that mental processing cannot be wholly mechanical or algorithmic. The argument takes hundreds of pages (Penrose 1986, 1994) and has been attacked by many seemingly qualified critics (e.g., Putnam 1994). It is fair to say that it has not passed the usual demands made upon mathematical and logical arguments. But the argument claims that both mental processing and the gravitational effects are non-algorithmic, and that the latter could therefore provide in a natural way the non-algorithmic element needed for the former.

The second connection of the proposed gravitational effect with consciousness is that the estimated time associated with the gravitational effect was based on the presumption that the components of the brain critical to consciousness were functioning microtubules. Data pertaining to loss of consciousness under the influence of various anesthetic agents indicate that the proper functioning of microtubules is necessary for consciousness. But many things are *necessary* for consciousness, so this argument that the gravitational effect is connected to consciousness via microtubules is not compelling.

A serious objection to the Penrose-Hameroff theory has been raised by Max Tegmark (2000). The Penrose-Hameroff theory requires that the critical microtubular state be a *coherent* quantum state that extends over a macroscopic region in the brain. Normally one expects any macroscopic coherence of a quantum state in a warm wet brain to be destroyed almost immediately. Tegmark estimates the duration of coherence to be of the order of 10^{-13} seconds, which is far smaller than the one tenth of a second associated with conscious events. Hagen, Hameroff, and Tuszynski (2002) have claimed that Tegmark's assumptions should be amended, so that the decoherence time increases to 10^{-4} seconds, and they suggest that the remaining factors can perhaps be made up by biological factors. In any case, the need to maintain macroscopic quantum cohererence in a warm wet brain is certainly a serious problem for the Penrose-Hameroff model.

It might be mentioned here that in the von Neumann model described in the preceding sections, quantum decoherence is an important *asset*, because it allows the quantum state of the brain to be understood as a smeared out statistical ensemble (i.e., collection) of essentially classically conceived states that, however, can interact with neighboring members of the ensemble in a way that preserves the quantum Zeno effect. This quasi-classical conceptualization of the quantum state of the brain allows nonphysicists to have a relatively simple understanding of the mind–brain system.

The Eccles-Beck approach

An early quantum approach to the mind–brain problem was made by John Eccles (1990) who emphasized the entry of quantum effects into brain dynamics in connection with effects at nerve terminals. However, instead of building directly on the quantum rules and the profound conceptual relationships between quantum and classical mechanics, he introduced a conscious biasing of the quantum statistical rules. This actually contradicts the quantum rules, thereby upsetting the logical coherence of the whole scheme. In a later work with Beck (2003) he retained the quantum rules, while introducing quantum uncertainties at the nerve terminals that can play the same role that they do in the standard approach described earlier. This brings the model into accord with the standard model described above, in regard to this technical point. However, Eccles added a superstructure involving conscious "souls" that can exist apart from physical brains. That suggestion goes beyond the ideas described here.

Other theories

Several other quantum theories of consciousness have been proposed (Bohm 1990; Jibu & Yasue 1995). All are outgrowths of von Neumann's formulation. The differences in these proposals are mainly at the level of technical physics. I have focused here on the overriding general issues of why quantum theory should be relevant to consciousness in the first place, and how the switch to quantum physics impacts upon the question – vital to neuroscience, psychology, and philosophy – of the neural effects of volitional effort.

Acknowledgements

This work was supported by the Director, Office of Science, Office of High Energy and Nuclear Physics, of the US Department of Energy under contract DE-AC02-05CH11231.

Further Readings

Albert, D. (1992) *Quantum Mechanics and Experience*. Cambridge, MA: Harvard University Press.

Atmanspacher, H. (2004) Quantum approaches to consciousness. In Edward N. Zalta (ed.), *Stanford Encyclopedia of Philosophy* (winter 2004 edn.), <http://plato.stanford.edu/archives/win2004/entries/qt-consciousness/>.

Lockwood, M. (1989) *Mind, Brain, and the Quantum: The Compound "I."* Cambridge, MA: Basil Blackwell.

Penrose, R. (1997) *The Large, the Small, and the Human Mind*. Cambridge: Cambridge University Press.

Stapp, H. (2004) *Mind, Matter, and Quantum Mechanics*, 2nd edn. Berlin/Heidelberg: Springer (esp. chapters 3, 6, 12).

References

Beck, F. and Eccles, J. C. (2003) Quantum processes in the brain: a scientific basis of consciousness. In N. Osaka (ed.), *Neural Basis of Consciousness*, 141–66. Amsterdam and Philadelphia, PA: John Benjamins.

Bohm, D. J. (1990) A new theory of the relationship of mind to matter. *Philosophical Psychology* 3, 271–86.

Bohr, N. (1934) *Atomic Theory and the Description of Nature*. Cambridge: Cambridge University Press. (Re-issued in 1961.)

Bohr, N. (1958) *Atomic Physics and Human Knowledge*. New York: Wiley.

Eccles, J. C. (1990) A unitary hypothesis of mind–brain interaction in the cerebral cortex. *Proceedings of the Royal Society of London* B240, 433–51.

Hagen, S., Hameroff, S. R., and Tuszynski, J. A. (2002) Quantum computation in brain microtubules: decoherence and biological feasibility. *Physical Review* E65, 061901-1–061901-11.

Hameroff, S. R. and Penrose, R. (1996) Orchestrated reduction of quantum coherence in brain microtubules: a model for consciousness. *Journal of Consciousness Studies* 3, 36–53.

Heisenberg, W. (1958) The representation of nature in contemporary physics. *Daedalus* 87 (Summer), 95–108.

James, W. (1892) Psychology: the briefer course. In *William James: Writings 1879–1899*. New York: Library of America.

Jibu, M. and Yasue, K. (1995) *Quantum Brain Dynamics and Consciousness*. Amsterdam and Philadelphia, PA: John Benjamins.

Misra, B. and Sudarshan, E. C. G. (1977) The Zeno's paradox in quantum theory. *Journal of Mathematical Physics* 18, 756–63.

Ochsner, K. N., Bunge, S. A., Gross, J. J., and Gabrieli, J. D. E. (2002) Rethinking feelings: an fMRI study of the cognitive regulation of emotion. *Journal of Cognitive Neuroscience* 14: 8, 1215–29.

Pashler, H. (1998) *The Psychology of Attention*. Cambridge, MA: MIT Press.

Penrose, R. (1986) *The Emperor's New Mind*. New York: Oxford University Press.

Penrose, R. (1994) *Shadows of the Mind*. New York: Oxford University Press.

Putnam, H. (1994) Review of Roger Penrose, *Shadows of the Mind*. *New York Times Book Review*, November 20, p. 7. Reprinted in AMS bulletin: www.ams.org/journals/bull/pre-1996data/19950 7/199507015.tex.html

Schwartz, J. M., Stapp, H. P., and Beauregard, M. (2003) The volitional influence of the mind on the brain, with special reference to emotional self regulation. In M. Beauregard (ed.), *Consciousness, Emotional Self-Regulation and the Brain*. [*Advances in Consciousness Research Series, Volume 54*]. Amsterdam and New York: John Benjamins.

Schwartz, J. M., Stapp, H. P., and Beauregard, M. (2005) Quantum theory in neuroscience and psychology: a neurophysical model of the mind–brain interaction. *Philosophical Transactions of the Royal Society (Biological Sciences)* (February). On-line at http://www-physics.lbl.gov/~stapp/ stappfiles.html

Stapp, H. (1993) *Mind, Matter, and Quantum Mechanics*. New York: Springer-Verlag.

Stapp, H. (1999) Attention, intention, and will in quantum physics. *Journal of Consciousness Studies* 6, 143–64.

Stapp, H. (2001) Quantum theory and the role of mind in nature. *Foundations of Physics* 31, 1465–99.

Tegmark, M. (2000) Importance of quantum decoherence in brain process. *Physical Review* E61, 4194–206.

Von Neumann, J. (1955) *Mathematical Foundations of Quantum Mechanics*. Princeton, NJ: Princeton University Press. (Translated by Robert T. Beyer from the 1932 German original, *Mathematische Grundlagen der Quantummechanik*. Berlin: J. Springer).

24

Daniel Dennett on the Nature of Consciousness

SUSAN SCHNEIDER

One of the most influential philosophical voices in the consciousness studies community is that of Daniel Dennett. Outside of consciousness studies, Dennett is well-known for his work on numerous topics, such as intentionality, artificial intelligence, free will, evolutionary theory, and the basis of religious experience (Dennett 1984, 1987, 1995c, 2005). In 1991, just as researchers and philosophers were beginning to turn more attention to the nature of consciousness, Dennett authored his *Consciousness Explained*. *Consciousness Explained* aimed to develop both a theory of consciousness and a powerful critique of the then mainstream view of the nature of consciousness, which Dennett called "The Cartesian Theater View." In this brief discussion, I largely focus on Dennett's influential critique of the Cartesian Theater View, as well as his positive view on the nature of consciousness, called the "Multiple Drafts Model." In keeping with the themes of this section, I also discuss Dennett's views on the hard problem of consciousness (Chalmers, chapter 17). As those familiar with Dennett's views know, his work on consciousness is extensive. The reader is thus encouraged to turn to the suggested readings for further detail.

Dennett's Critique of the Cartesian Theater Model

Suppose that you are sitting in a café studying, right before a big exam or talk. All in one moment, you may taste the espresso you sip, feel a pang of anxiety, consider an idea, and hear the scream of the espresso machine. This is your current stream of consciousness. Conscious streams seem to be very much bound up with who you are. It is not that *this* particular moment is essential to you – although you may feel that certain ones are very important. It is rather that throughout your waking life, you seem to be the subject of a unified stream of experience that presents you as the subject, viewing the stream.

Let us focus on three features of the stream: it may seem to you, put metaphorically, that there is a sort of "screen" or "stage" in which experiences present themselves to you – to your "mind's eye." That is, there appears to be a central *place* where experiences are "screened" before you. Dennett calls this place "the Cartesian Theater." Further, it seems that mental states being screened in the theater are in consciousness and that mental states outside of the theater are not in consciousness. Second, in this central place there seems to be a singular point in *time* which, given a particular sensory input, consciousness of the input happens. For instance, there seems to be one moment in which the scream of the espresso machine begins, pulling you out of your concentration. Finally, there appears to be a *self* – that is, someone who is inside the theater, watching the show. Dennett calls this trifold view "Cartesian Materialism":

> ... the view you arrive at when you discard Descartes' dualism but fail to discard the imagery of a central (but material) Theater where "it all comes together ...". Cartesian Materialism is the view that there is a crucial finish line or boundary somewhere in the brain, marking a place where the order of arrival equals the order of "presentation" in experience because *what happens there* is what you are conscious of. (Dennett 1991, p. 107, original emphasis)

Now, what if you are told that Cartesian Materialism is false? This is the negative or destructive ambition of *Consciousness Explained* – there is a very real sense in which our own first-person experience of consciousness leads us to Cartesian Materialism. Yet Dennett argues that given certain philosophical considerations, together with certain work in the psychology and neuroscience of consciousness, our sense of being in a Cartesian Theater is illusory.

Dennett's critique of Cartesian Materialism can be understood against the backdrop of his own, positive view of consciousness, which he calls the "Multiple Drafts Model." According to the Multiple Drafts Model the brain has many parallel information-processing streams (Dennett 1991, p. 111). At any point in time there are various narrative fragments, or "drafts," which are at different stages of editing. According to Dennett, these drafts are not sent to a single place in the brain for viewing. But some or all of them may come together in the event that they need to determine a behavior for the organism. There is nothing like a Cartesian Theater, or Central Processing Unit (CPU) in the brain, in which all, or even most, commands are executed. Nor is there a viewer of such events, as they flow through the CPU. Furthermore, according to Dennett, asking "which events are conscious?" is to conceive of a Cartesian Theater in which one or more drafts comes before an audience. There is really no audience which has the experiences.

Of course, introspectively, we do have a sense of having sequences of events flowing through consciousness. Dennett does not deny this. But this sense is not due to there being a central place or time in the brain where consciousness comes together, or relatedly, to there being a self as viewer of the events, inside a Cartesian Theater. Instead, the self is a "center of narrative gravity" – a kind of program that has a persistent narrative, and in particular, "a web of words and deeds ... The web protects it, just like the snail's shell, and provides a livelihood, just like the spider's web" (1991, p. 416). The sense in which there is a sequence of events in consciousness occurs when the stream is probed, for example, by asking a question. Consider the earlier example of studying in the café. Dennett would say that your consciousness of the scream of the espresso machine occurred when you probed the stream of multiple drafts at a certain point. This probe fixes the content of consciousness. On Dennett's view, there are no facts about the stream of consciousness aside from particular probes (Dennett 1991, p. 113).

Dennett explains his Multiple Drafts Model through the example of the Phi Phenomenon, and in particular, through the color phi phenomenon. Before reading further, it is best to view the phi phenomenon for yourself by searching for "color phi" on the internet or visiting the following website: http://www.yorku.ca/eye/colorphi.htm. In the colored phi illusion, two differently colored lights, with an angular separation of a few degrees at the eye, are flashed one after the other. Two interesting things happen. First, the first light appears to move across to the position of the second light. And second, the light appears to change color as it moves. For instance, in the webpage cited above, which featured a green light followed by a red one, the green light seems to turn red as it appears to move across to where the red light is.

As Dennett notes, this is quite odd. For one thing, how could the first light seem to change color *before* the second light is observed? Dennett entertains two options, both of which he discards. First, he considers the possibility that the observer makes one conclusion, and then changes her memory when she sees the second light. Dennett calls this option "Orwellian," after George Orwell's *Nineteen Eighty Four*, where history was constantly revised by the Ministry of Truth (Dennett 1991, p. 116). In this scenario, shortly after the second spot goes into consciousness, the brain makes up a narrative about the intervening events, complete with the color change midway through. This new event sequence is encoded into memory, and the original event sequence is not (Dennett 1991, p. 121).

He then suggests a second alternative. According to this scenario, the events are held up in the brain's "editing room" (if you will), before they go into consciousness. More specifically, the first spot arrives in preconsciousness, and then, when the second spot arrives there, some intermediate material is created, and then, the entire, modified sequence is projected in the theater of consciousness. So the sequence which arrives at consciousness has already been edited with the illusory intermediate material (Dennett 1991, p. 120). Dennett calls this second option "Stalinesque," after Stalin's show trials, in which bogus testimonies were staged, and the final verdict was decided in advance (Dennett 1991, p. 117).

Dennett then asks: What reason would we have for choosing one interpretation over the other? He contends that there is no way, even in principle, to select one interpretation over the other, for there is no way to demarcate the place or time in the brain in which material goes into consciousness (Dennett 1991, pp. 126–32). He further claims that since we cannot tell which is the correct interpretation, there really is no difference between the two interpretations; we are left with a "difference that makes no difference" (Dennett 1991, p. 132). He then concludes that the (putative) fact that there is no way of distinguishing between the two interpretations lends plausibility to the Multiple Drafts Model. For according to the model, there is no concrete place or time in which material is, or is not, in consciousness.

There has been much debate over both the plausibility of the above line of reasoning and concerning what Dennett's precise argument is. (See the extensive peer review of Dennett and Kinsbourne 1992 in *Behavioral and Brain Sciences*; Korb 1993; Robinson 1994; Seager 1999). Unfortunately, Dennett's discussion involved heavy use of metaphor, so the underlying argument was unclear. In any case, many critics have resisted Dennett's verificationist suggestion that if there is no way to tell between the interpretations, there is no fact of the matter (Lycan 1992; Van Gulick 1992; Korb 1993; Robinson 1994; McGinn 1995; Seager 1999). Another major source of concern has been whether there is really no difference, even in principle, between the two interpretations. Block has suggested that Dennett's rationale for this hinges on the rejection of phenomenal consciousness (Block 1992). Indeed many have interpreted Dennett as being an eliminativist about phenomenal consciousness (Block 1992; Van Gulick 1992; Seager 1999), a position which Dennett himself has disavowed in a response to critics (Dennett & Kinsbourne 1995b, but see below). In his response to critics, he explains that the reason that the two interpretations cannot be distinguished is *not* because, in general, there is no such thing as phenomenal consciousness, but because such an extremely small timescale is involved.

> Conscious experiences are real events occurring in the real time and space of the brain, and hence they are clockable and locatable within the appropriate limits of precision for real phenomena of their type . . . Certain sorts of questions one might think it appropriate to ask about them, however, have no answers because these questions presuppose inappropriate . . . temporal . . . boundaries that are more fine-grained than the phenomenon admits. (Dennett & Kinsbourne 1995a, p. 235)

Here, the critic would probably object that in this case it is unclear why there would not be a fact of the matter about which interpretation is correct. For according to one version, even at such a small timescale, there would be conscious experience; the conscious events would simply not be remembered. In the other scenario, the conscious experience would not have occurred at all. Indeed, even if the subject herself could not report a difference because, for instance, she could not remember the experience, it seems there would be, at the very least, an in principle way to tell the difference (Korb 1993; Seager 1999). For if one sequence is held up, before entering consciousness, and the other is simply recalled differently, there would be underlying brain states which differ; otherwise, differences in mental processing would fail to supervene on physical states. No physicalist, including Dennett, would be prepared to accept this. In light of this, there should be, at least in principle, a measurable difference between the Orwellian and Stalinesque interpretations, and furthermore, such a difference may even fall in the realm of future, higher resolution, brain imaging techniques. It is only the claim that phenomenal consciousness itself does not exist, at least apart from probes, that would justify the strong conclusion that there is no difference between the two interpretations (Block 1992).

Leaving the phi illusion, let us now ask about the plausibility of the Multiple Drafts Model itself. It has been more than a decade since the Multiple Drafts Model was developed, and there are features of the model which have clearly withstood the test of time. It is widely accepted that processing in the brain is massively parallel and that there is no centrally located homunculus that views all experiences passing before it. However, it is worth mentioning that the idea of massive parallelism was certainly not original to Dennett, and even back in 1991 very few scientists believed that consciousness all came together at one place in the brain. But to fully judge the plausibility of the model, we might ask for the details of the model, because at this point in our discussion at least, we have not really laid out a model of consciousness, but an interesting contrast.

According to Dennett, consciousness is a sort of "virtual machine," a sort of "evolved (and evolving) computer program that shapes the activities of the brain" (Dennett 1991, p. 431). But to have a model of consciousness, there needs to be an answer to the question: What sort of program is the machine running? Dennett has expressed strong sympathy with the *Pandemonium* model of Oliver Selfridge (1959), which was essentially an antecedent to connectionism. *Pandemonium* is a pattern recognition system that consists in four layers (see Figure 24.1). As the diagram illustrates, there are numerous units, called "demons." Each of the members in the lower layers "shout" to be heard by the demons in the layer above. The second layer consists of simple feature detector demons. The "cognitive demons" in the third layer are sensitive to specific weighted features. The final layer consists in a decision-making demon that "hears" the shrieking of the layer immediately below, and decides what pattern was presented to the system (Selfridge 1959).

As Dennett surely knew, Pandemonium is far too simple to be a model of consciousness. But what fascinated Dennett was the parallel nature of Pandemonium, in which there is no central executive. Furthermore, in the case of Pandemonium, as with computational expla-

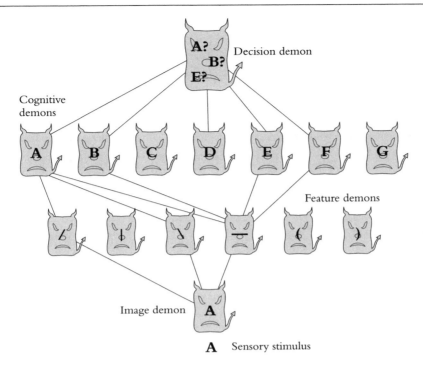

Decision demon

Cognitive demons

Feature demons

Image demon

A Sensory stimulus

Figure 24.1 Pandemonium

nation more generally, a cognitive or perceptual capacity is decomposed into extremely simple and unintelligent components. Indeed, explanation in cognitive science generally proceeds by the method of functional decomposition, a method which, put simply, explains a cognitive capacity by decomposing it into constituent parts, and specifying the causal relationships between the parts, as well as decomposing each part into further constituents, and so on (Cummins 1975). As with many in consciousness studies, Dennett is clearly opposed to functional decompositions that appeal to homuncular theories of the mind, whereby what is meant by "homuncular theories" are theories purporting to explain cognitive capacities by generating a decomposition that ultimately boils down to an internal agent, or homunculus, that has the cognitive capacity which was supposed to be explained by the decomposition in the first place. In the case of Cartesian Materialism, this homunculus is the conscious agent in the theater (Dennett & Kinsbourne 1995a, p. 85). The consciousness of the homunculus would itself need to be explained, so this sort of explanation is circular.

So, trying to further explain the Multiple Drafts Model, it appears that, in addition to appealing to massive parallelism, the model involves a kind of computational functionalism without a homunculus. While this sort of view has been regarded by many as a plausible approach to explaining cognitive capacities, an appeal to non-homuncular computational functionalism does not really make Dennett's view distinctive, for computational functionalism is common throughout cognitive science. Nor would a mere appeal to functionalism do the needed theoretical work of serving to justify Dennett's view that there is no way to differentiate between Orwellian or Stalinesque revisions; for the decompositions of the mental processes underlying Orwellian and Stalinesque accounts of the color phi phenomenon would likely differ (see below). Furthermore, we do not yet have a model of consciousness, for although there is an appeal to the method of functional decomposition, not even the most basic functional decomposition of consciousness has been offered.

But perhaps the following details would yield the needed model, and separate Dennett's model from a generic appeal to functional decomposition. While Dennett shied away from proposing a particular theory of consciousness in *Consciousness Explained*, he expressed sympathy with the Global Workspace (GW) theory of consciousness, and the closely related Global Neuronal Workspace theory of consciousness, and he has recently re-emphasized his alliance with this position (Dennett 1991, 2001). To keep things simple, I will refer to both views as "the GW theory" as they are closely aligned and agree in the dimensions discussed herein. According to the GW theory, the role of consciousness is to facilitate information exchange among multiple parallel specialized unconscious processes in the brain. Consciousness is a state of global activation in a "workspace" in which information in consciousness is "broadcast" back to the rest of the system. At any given moment, there are multiple parallel processes going on in the brain which receive the broadcast. Access to the global workspace is granted by an attentional mechanism and the material in the workspace is then under the "spotlight" of attention. When in the global workspace the material is processed in a serial manner, but this is the result of the contributions of parallel processes which compete for access to the workspace. Introspectively, this seems intuitive, as our conscious, deliberative, thoughts appear to be serial (Baars chapter 18; Baars 1997; Dehaene & Changeux 2004; Dehaene & Naccache 2001; Shanahan & Baars 2005).

At least at first, there are commonalities between the GW theory and the Multiple Drafts Theory. The appeal to massive parallelism is in keeping with the Multiple Drafts Model. And one might find GW theory somewhat reminiscent of Pandemonium: as Dennett describes it, information is sent to the workspace when "demons" competing for access to the workspace "shout" sufficiently loudly to be granted access (Dennett 1991, p. 191). In a recent *Cognition* paper Dennett discusses the GW view, stressing its affinity with the Multiple Drafts Model:

> . . . the specialist demons' accessibility *to each other* (and not to some imagined higher Executive or central Ego) . . . could in principle explain the dramatic increases in cognitive competence that we associate with consciousness: . . . This idea was also central to what I called the Multiple Drafts Model (Dennett 1991), which was offered as an alternative to the traditional, and still popular, Cartesian Theater model, which supposes there is a place in the brain to which all the unconscious modules send their results for ultimate conscious appreciation by the Audience. The Multiple Drafts Model did not provide, however, a sufficiently vivid and imagination-friendly antidote to the Cartesian imagery we have all grown up with, so more recently I have proposed what I consider to be a more useful guiding metaphor: "fame in the brain" or "cerebral celebrity." (Dennett 2001)

Interestingly, in a different place in the *Cognition* paper Dennett goes as far as likening the Global Neuronal Workspace model to "fame in the brain" (Dennett 2001). This does seem to suggest that Dennett thinks of the GW theory as filling in the details of his model, or at least bearing important similarities to it.

So perhaps now we are equipped to return to the question of the plausibility of the Multiple Drafts Model. Many philosophers and scientists find the GW theory to be a promising informational theory of consciousness, although philosophers sympathetic to problems involving qualia may urge that while it might be a promising scientific theory of the information processing involved in consciousness, by itself, it does not answer the hard problem of consciousness (Chalmers 1995). But let us set aside the hard problem for the moment, and pose the question: Would an alliance between Dennett's Multiple Drafts Model and the GW view finally provide the promised model of consciousness? Unfortunately, while the Global Workspace theory might provide the beginnings of an information-processing model of consciousness, there are significant points of tension between it and the Multiple Drafts Model. For one thing, the GW theory has been categorized as a kind of theater model (Blackmore 2004, p. 72). This may seem surprising, for according to the GW theory, consciousness is a highly distributed activity in the cortex, so there is no single spatiotemporal location in the brain where consciousness comes together. But Baars himself makes heavy use of theater metaphors, describing conscious events as happening in "the theatre of consciousness" and in the "screen of consciousness" (Baars 1997, p. 31). Are these metaphors merely misleading descriptions on Baars's part? It appears not, for according to the GW view, there is a definite sense in which certain mental states are *in* consciousness, while others are not: states are conscious when they are in the global workspace (Baars 1997 and chapter 18). This point of contrast is sharpened by reconsidering the color phi case. If one asks the question, "Which account of the color phi illusion is correct, the Orwellian or Stalinesque account?", the Global Workspace theory offers an (at least in principle) route to an answer. The question becomes: Did the subsystem that processed the first light broadcast the state into the GW, before the second light was processed by the subsystem, or was the broadcast held up, until the second light was processed?

There are two further sources of tension as well, the first concerning what the contents of consciousness are, the second concerning the role of a central system. First, the GW view does not seem to require a probe for a state to be broadcast into the workspace; what is conscious is not determined by what is probed. So the contents of consciousness will differ according to each theory. Second, although mental states are not processed in anything like a CPU, the global workspace has been likened to a central system, that is, a nonmodular, "horizontal," system in which material from different sense modalities comes together, and in which deliberation and planning occurs. (Here, it is important to note that a central system is not identical to a CPU. Again, a central system is a subsystem of the brain that integrates material from different modalities; a CPU, on the other hand, is a command center that executes every, or nearly every, command in a computational system.) As Stanislas Dehaene and Jean Pierre Changeux explain:

> The model emphasizes the role of distributed neurons with long-distance connections, particularly dense in prefrontal, cingulate, and parietal regions, which are capable of interconnecting multiple specialized processors and can broadcast signals at the brain scale in a spontaneous and sudden manner. The concept of a "global neuronal workspace" . . . builds upon Fodor's distinction between the vertical "modular faculties" and a distinct "isotropic central and horizontal system" capable of sharing information across modules. (Dehaene & Changeux 2004)

Dahaene and Changeux's claim that the GW view builds upon Fodor's notion of a central system is particularly noteworthy, for it emphasizes that the GW theory has an element of centralization that Dennett has disavowed in the context of his Multiple Drafts Model. Indeed, the appeal to a central system by advocates of the GW theory is not limited to the work of Dehaene and Changeux. For instance, in a 2005 *Cognition* paper, Shanahan and Baars have offered a solution to one version of the frame problem (which arises for systems that involve a central processor) that appeals to the GW theory, presenting details concerning the cognitive architecture of the GW that capture a clear sense in which the workspace operates as a Fodorian "horizontal," or central system (Shanahan & Baars 2005).

But is this sort of centrality really compatible with a view like Dennett's, which vehemently disavowed "central Headquarters" or "Central Meaners"? Indeed, Fodor's central system is the subject of the following attack in *Consciousness Explained*:

> By giving this central facility so much to do, and so much nonmodular power with which to do it, Fodor turns his modules into very implausible agents, agents whose existence only makes sense in the company of a Boss agent of ominous authority . . . Since one of Fodor's main points in describing modules has been to contrast their finite, comprehensible, mindless mechanicity with the unlimited and inexplicable powers of the nonmodular center, theorists who would otherwise be receptive to at least most of his characterization of modules have tended to dismiss his modules as fantasies of a crypto-Cartesian. (1991, p. 261)

In light of the GW appeal to centrality, Dennett's remarks underscore a clear source of tension between GW and the Multiple Drafts Model. It seems fair to say that Dennett's Multiple Drafts Model faces the following dilemma: either, as noted, it lacks sufficient theoretical detail to be a genuine model of consciousness, or it borrows from the GW theory to yield the needed detail. However, given the points of tension, Dennett cannot incorporate GW detail into his theory.

Some Further Features of Dennett's Views on Consciousness

As noted in the introduction, Dennett's contributions to consciousness studies are quite extensive. In addition to offering a critique of Cartesian Materialism and the Multiple Drafts Model, Dennett has attacked certain thought experiments, problems, and arguments that are commonly thought to lend support to the idea that consciousness is an irreducible feature of the world, going beyond the physical realm that science investigates. The hard problem of consciousness is the problem of why, in addition to the information processing that the brain engages in, there must be a feeling of what it's like associated with the neural processing. For how can conscious experience emerge from the gray matter of the brain? (Chalmers 1995 and chapter 17). It is fair to say that the hard problem has been regarded as one of the most central philosophical puzzles about the nature of consciousness. Dennett has been a well-known critic of the hard problem: "Chalmers' (1995) attempt to sort the 'easy' problems of consciousness from the 'really hard' problem is not, I think, a useful contribution to research, but a major misdirector of attention, an illusion-generator" (Dennett 1996).

However, if one finds the hard problem to be a rich and compelling problem, Dennett's Multiple Drafts Model does not yield a satisfying answer. For, as discussed, what Dennett is ultimately defending is a sort of computational functionalism, together with the view that consciousness is a highly distributed activity in the brain. And one could still look to a penultimate functional decomposition of consciousness and ask: But why does experience need to exist, in addition to all this information processing? However, in his 1996 paper, Dennett offers three responses to those who find the hard problem compelling. First, in the context of a comparison between the hard problem and what he called "the hard question for vitalism," he asks us to imagine a vitalist who says:

The easy problems of life include those of explaining the following phenomena: reproduction, development, growth, metabolism, self-repair, immunological self-defense, . . . These are not all that easy, of course, and it may take another century or so to work out the fine points, but they are easy compared to the really hard problem: life itself. We can imagine something that was capable of reproduction, development, growth, metabolism, self-repair and immunological self-defense, but that wasn't, you know, *alive*. (Dennett 1996)

Dennett's vitalist believes that being alive is something above and beyond the other phenomena. Clearly, the vitalist is mistaken. And according to Dennett, those who find the hard problem compelling are making a similar mistake. For their view is that the explanation of functions is not sufficient to explain experience. However, "it is precisely the 'remarkable functions associated with' consciousness that drive them to wonder about how consciousness could possibly reside in a brain" (Dennett 1996).

Dennett further contends that positing something beyond functions is a form of humuncularism. Francis Crick, at the close of his book on consciousness, wrote, "I have said almost nothing about qualia – the redness of red – except to brush it to one side and hope for the best" (1994, p. 256). In light of Crick's remark, Dennett asks us to imagine a neuroscientist, whom he calls "Crock," who substitutes "perception" for "qualia" in the above quotation, saying instead: "I have said almost nothing about perception – the actual analysis and comprehension of the visual input – except to brush it to one side and hope for the best" (Dennett 1996). Dennett points out that Crock is, of course, in error, creating a "hard" problem of perception (Dennett 1996). Analogously, claims Dennett, Crick makes a similar error, because he thinks he can make progress on the easy problems without making progress on the hard problem.

I make the parallel claim about the purported "subjective qualities" or "qualia" of experience: if you don't begin breaking them down into their (functional) components from the outset, and distributing them throughout your model, you create a monster – an imaginary dazzle in the eye of a Cartesian homunculus. (Dennett 1996)

Finally, Dennett charges that Chalmers's claim that consciousness is fundamental is not justified, as the decision to take physical properties as fundamental involves an appeal to independent evidence. However, in the case of consciousness, there is no independent motivation. "It is a belief in a fundamental phenomenon of 'experience'" (Dennett 1996). Dennett charges that this sort of reasoning is circular, comparing Chalmers's proposal to what he calls "cutism": the proposal that

since some things are just plain cute, and other things aren't cute at all – you can just see it, however hard it is to describe or explain – we had better postulate *cuteness* as a fundamental property of physics alongside mass, charge and space-time. (Dennett 1996)

Concerning Dennett's first point, Chalmers has denied that the analogy with vitalism holds. In the case of the problem of life, it is clear that the only thing that needs explaining is structure and function. There is no further property, beyond reproduction, metabolism, adaptation, and so on, that requires explanation. According to Chalmers this is not analogous to the case of consciousness, as what seems to need explanation is experience, and the general view is that experience seems to outrun the functions (Chalmers 1996). Chalmers then asks for a non-question begging argument for the conclusion that function exhausts the nature of consciousness. In light of our discussion of Dennett's third problem above, it appears that both sides believe that their opponent's assertion concerning whether the functions of consciousness are exhaustive is question begging. Dennett, for instance, asks for independent evidence, in his third point above. Chalmers, on the other hand, believes that consciousness is a phenomenon that needs explaining in its own right (Chalmers 1996). "And if it turns out that it cannot be explained in terms of more basic entities, then it must be taken as irreducible"(Chalmers 1996).

Are we thus at a dialectical stalemate? The burden of argument does indeed seem to fall on Dennett, for he is denying the commonplace view that experience seems to outrun function. As Chalmers notes, "Such prima facie intuitions can be overturned, but to do so requires very solid and substantial argument. Otherwise, the problem is being 'resolved' simply by placing one's head in the sand" (Chalmers 1996). Dennett does attempt to make his case in the context of a discussion of the second argument considered above. Here, Dennett appeals to his own phenomenology, claiming that introspectively, only functions need explaining (Dennett 1996). But as Chalmers has observed, the various mental states that Dennett raises, for example, "feelings of foreboding," "fantasies," "delight and dismay," are not at all clearly functional issues (Chalmers 1996). Why would the functions associated with experience be all that needs to be explained? Further argumentation does seem to be required.

In addition to being a vocal critic of the hard problem, Dennett has offered related concerns with philosophical discussions about the possibility of "zombies." Consider a thought experiment in which there is a molecule for molecule duplicate of you. That is, imagine a creature which has your precise neural configuration, having all the same internal brain (and other bodily) states, and which evinces precisely the same behaviors as you do when put in the same situations. And suppose that this duplicate inhabits a world much like ours except, in this case, that the duplicate lacks consciousness. That is, the duplicate has the same type of neural states as you do, including those which are invoked in our best scientific theories of the nature of consciousness, yet the duplicate lacks inner experience, or what philosophers have called "qualia." Some find such a scenario to be conceivable and indeed possible, supporting the dualist position that a state of being conscious is not essentially a physical or neural state (Kirk 1974a, 1974b; Chalmers 1996). That is, it is possible, at least in some broad sense of possibility, that there are duplicates which lack qualia. Such have been called "zombies" by philosophers (where such are understood to be different from Haitian zombies).

Dennett has argued vehemently against this view. "It is an embarrassment to our discipline that what is widely regarded among philosophers as a major theoretical controversy should come down to whether or not zombies (philosophical zombies) are possible/conceivable"(1995d, p. 325). Furthermore, he claims that philosophers discussing this issue frequently assume that there is some physical or behavioral difference between zombies and conscious humans. Zombies are physical and behavioral duplicates (Dennett 1995d; Chalmers 1996). Doing so would indeed be erroneous. Dennett also contends that there has been no plausible argument that zombies differ from humans which employs the correct conception of what zombies are; those who think zombies are possible have not really imagined them correctly. "My conviction is that the philosophical tradition of zombies would die overnight if philosophers ceased to misimagine them, but of course I cannot prove it a priori"(1995d, p. 325).

A further feature of Dennett's extensive views on phenomenal consciousness deserves mention as well. Many have construed Dennett as being an eliminitivist about phenomenal consciousness (Block 1992; Seager 1999; Velmans 2006). Dennett and his coauthor Kinsbourne have denied this charge, as the earlier quoted passage indicates. As it turns out, Dennett and his critics may have been talking past each other, for there is both a sense in which Dennett is an eliminitivist about phenomenal consciousness and a sense in which he is not. The expression "qualia" has commonly been used by philosophers to denote the qualitative features of experience; the feelings of "what it's like" (Nagel 1974) associated with experience, such as the taste of chocolate, the experience of seeing bright red, or the sound of a clarinet. In our discussion of the phi illusion, it was noted that Dennett denied being an eliminitivist about phenomenal consciousness. However, Dennett has in fact argued for eliminitivism about qualia (Dennett 1993) where by "qualia" he has in mind a narrower construal of qualia than the more generic view sketched above. According to this more specific conception of qualia, qualia are the intrinsic, ineffable, private, features of mental states of which we are immediately or directly aware (Dennett 1993). Dennett has argued through the use of extensive thought experiments that there is nothing which satisfies this description; hence, he is an eliminitivist about qualia, where qualia are understood in this more specific sense (Dennett 1993). However, this view is in fact compatible with the reality of qualia, when construed in the more general sense (Tye 2003; Van Gulick, chapter 30).

See also 17 The hard problem of consciousness; 18 The global workspace theory of consciousness; 20 Representationalism about consciousness; 29 Anti-materialist arguments and influential replies; 30 Functionalism and qualia.

Further Readings

Dennett, D. C. (1993) Quining qualia. *Readings in Philosophy and Cognitive Science*, 381–414. Cambridge, MA: MIT Press.

Dennett, D. C. (1991) *Consciousness Explained*. Boston, MA: Little, Brown and Company.

Dennett, D. C. (2005) *Sweet Dreams: Philosophical Obstacles to a Science of Consciousness*. New York: MIT Press.

Seager, William (1999) *Theories of Consciousness: An Introduction and Assessment*, chapters 4 and 5, 85–131. New York: Routledge.

Velmans, Max (2006) Heterophenomenology versus critical phenomenology. *Phenomenology and the Cognitive Sciences* 5: 3/4 (in press).

References

Baars, B. J. (1997) *In the Theater of Consciousness: The Workspace of the Mind*. New York: Oxford University Press.

Blackmore, Susan (2004) *Consciousness: An Introduction*. New York: Oxford University Press.

Block, Ned (1992) Begging the question against phenomenal consciousness. *Behavioral and Brain Sciences* 15, 205–6.

Chalmers, David (1995) Facing up to the problem of consciousness. *Journal of Consciousness Studies* 2, 3, 200–19.

Chalmers, David (1996) Moving forward on the problem of consciousness. *Journal of Consciousness Studies* 4, 1, 3–46.

Cummins, Robert (1975) Functional analysis. *Journal of Philosophy* 72, 741–65.

Dehaene, Stanislas and Changeux, Jean-Pierre (2004) Neural mechanisms for access to consciousness. In Michael Gazzaniga et al., *The Cognitive Neurosciences III*, 3rd edn. 1145–59. Cambridge, MA: MIT Press.

Dehaene, S. and Naccache, L. (2001) Towards a cognitive neuroscience of consciousness: basic evidence and a workspace framework. *Cognition* 2, 79.

Dennett, D. C. (1984) *Elbow Room: Varieties of Free Will Worth Wanting*. Cambridge, MA: MIT Press.

Dennett, D. C. (1987) *The Intentional Stance*. Cambridge, MA: MIT Press.

Dennett, D. C. (1991) *Consciousness Explained*. Boston, MA: Little, Brown and Company.

Dennett, D. C. (1993) Quining qualia. *Readings in Philosophy and Cognitive Science*, 381–414. Cambridge, MA: MIT Press.

Dennett, D. C. and Kinsbourne, M. (1992) Peer review in *Behavioral and Brain Sciences* 15, 183–247.

Dennett, D. C. and Kinsbourne, M. (1995a) Time and the observer: the where and when of consciousness in the brain. *Behavioral and Brain Sciences* 15, 2, 183–247.

Dennett, D. C. and Kinsbourne, M. (1995b) Escape from the Cartesian theater. *Behavioral and Brain Sciences* 15, 234–46.

Dennett, D. C. (1995c) *Darwin's Dangerous Idea: Evolution and the Meanings of Life*. New York: Simon and Schuster.

Dennett, D. C. (1995d) The unimagined preposterousness of zombies. *Journal of Consciousness Studies* 2: 4, 322–6.

Dennett, D. C. (1996) Facing backwards on the problem of consciousness. *Journal of Consciousness Studies* 3, 1, 4–6.

Dennett, D. C. (2001) Are we explaining consciousness yet? *Cognition* 79, 221–37.

Dennett, D. C. (2005) *Sweet Dreams: Philosophical Obstacles to a Science of Consciousness*. New York: MIT Press.

Kirk, R. (1974a) Sentience and behaviour. *Mind* 83, 43–60.

Kirk, R. (1974b) Zombies v. materialists. *Proceedings of the Aristotelian Society,* supplementary vol. 48, 135–52.

Korb, Kevin (1993) Stage effects in the Cartesian theater: review of consciousness explained. *Psyche* 1, 4.

Lycan, William (1992) UnCartesian materialism and Lockean introspection. *Behavioral and Brain Sciences* 15, 216–17.

McGinn, Colin (1995) Consciousness evaded: comments on Dennett, *Philosophical Perspectives* 9: AI, Connectionism and Philosophical Psychology 241–49.

Nagel, T. (1974) What is it like to be a bat? *Philosophical Review* 83, 435–50.

Robinson, W. (1994) Orwell, Stalin, and determinate qualia. *Pacific Philosophical Quarterly* 75, 151–64.

Seager, William (1999) *Theories of Consciousness: An Introduction and Assessment*. New York: Routledge.

Selfridge, Oliver (1959) Pandemonium: a paradigm for learning. In *Symposium on the Mechanization of Thought Processes*. London: HM Stationery Office.

Shanahan, Murray and Baars, Bernie (2005) Applying global workspace theory to the frame problem. *Cognition* 98, 157–76.

Tye, Michael (2003) Qualia. In Edward N. Zalta (ed.), *Stanford Encyclopedia of Philosophy* (Summer 2003 edn.), <http://plato.stanford.edu/archives/sum2003/entries/qualia/>.

Van Gulick, Robert (1992) Time for more alternatives. *Behavioral and Brain Sciences* 15, 228–9.

Velmans, Max (2006) Heterophenomenology versus critical phenomenology. *Phenomenology and the Cognitive Sciences*. 5: 3/4 (in press).

25

Biological Naturalism

JOHN SEARLE

"Biological Naturalism" is a name I have given to an approach to what is traditionally called "the mind–body problem." The way I arrived at it is typical of the way I work: forget about the philosophical history of a problem and remind yourself of what you know for a fact. Any philosophical theory has to be consistent with the facts. Of course, something we think is a fact may turn out not to be, but we have to start with our best information. Biological Naturalism is a theory of mental states in general, but as this book is about consciousness I will develop it as a theory of consciousness.

Biological Naturalism as Scientifically Sophisticated Common Sense

Suppose that you do not know anything about the great history of the philosophical mind–body problem, but suppose also that you have had a normal adult mental life. That is, suppose that you are not a zombie, not suffering from aphasia or blindsight, do not have a split brain, or any other of the philosophers' favorite mental maladies. Suppose also that you have a reasonable scientific education. You understand something about the atomic theory of matter, and the evolutionary theory of biology, and you even understand something about animal biology, including a basic knowledge of the elements of neurobiology. I am, in short, imagining you as you probably are, an educated healthy adult, but I am imagining you without any philosophical history, as you almost certainly are not. Now suppose you asked yourself to describe the nature of consciousness and its relation to the brain. You know the nature of consciousness from your own experience, and not from "introspection" (that term already has a philosophically loaded history); and its general relations to the brain will have to fit what you know about nature in general, as well as what you know about neurobiology. What would you come up with?

Well, here is what I came up with; and if you could just forget about Descartes, dualism, materialism, and other famous disasters, I think you would come up with something very similar. First we need a working definition. Nothing fancy, just enough to identify the target of the investigation. *Consciousness*, I say, *consists in all of one's states of awareness.* Awareness might seem too restricted, so just to be sure to cover all forms of consciousness, I flesh out the definition by adding *awareness or sentience or feeling.* And then to nail it down I give an indexical component to the definition, to bring it down to concrete reality, I say the following: "Conscious states are those states of awareness, sentience, or feeling that begin in the morning when you wake from a dreamless sleep and continue throughout the day until you fall asleep or otherwise become 'unconscious.' (Dreams are also a form of conciousness)."

Having identified the target in general terms I now need to identify its essential features. Here are four of the most important:

1   *Conscious states, so defined, are qualitative, in the sense that there is a qualitative feel to being in any particular conscious state.*

This is the "what-it-feels-like" feature of consciousness. For example, tasting beer is qualitatively different from listening to Beethoven's Third Symphony. Some philosophers use the word "qualia" to mark these qualitative states, but since consciousness and qualia are co-extensive, it is unnecessary to introduce another expression. All qualia are conscious states, all conscious states are qualia. It is important to hammer this point home. There are not two kinds of conscious states, one qualitative, one nonqualitative. All conscious states are qualitative.

2   *Such states are also ontologically subjective in the sense that they only exist as experienced by a human or animal subject.*

In this sense the tree outside my window has an objective ontology, but my conscious visual experience of the tree has a subjective ontology. The objective–subjective distinction is ambiguous and we need to disambiguate it before we go any further. First, there is an epistemic sense of the objective–subjective distinction. The claim that Rembrandt was born in 1606 is a matter of objective fact. The claim that Rembrandt was a better painter than Rubens is a matter of subjective opinion. Objectivity and subjectivity in this epistemic sense are features of claims. But in addition to the epistemic sense there is an ontological sense of the distinction. Most things, such as mountains, molecules, and tectonic plates exist apart from any experiencing subject. They have an objective or third-person ontology. Some things, such as pains and tickles and itches, only exist when experienced by a human or animal subject, and for that reason, they have a subjective or first-person ontology. Consciousness is ontologically subjective in the sense that it only exists when experienced by a human or animal subject. It is important to emphasize that you can have epistemically objective knowledge of a domain that is ontologically subjective. It is for this reason that an epistemically objective science of ontologically subjective consciousness is possible.

3   *Furthermore, it is a striking fact that at any moment in your conscious life all of your conscious states are experienced by you as part of a single unified conscious field.*

Your conscious states at any moment are parts of a single large conscious state. The visual experience of the tree, the tactile experience of the desktop under my hand, and the sight of the moon outside my window are parts of a single total conscious experience. But other entities in the world are not like that. The tree, the desk, and the moon are not in that way parts of a single total large object.

These three features of consciousness – qualitativeness, subjectivity, and unity – are not separate and independent. For a state to be qualitative in this sense implies that it is subjective.

For a state to be qualitative and subjective implies that it is part of a unified field of qualitative subjectivity, even if it is the only thing in the field. If you try to imagine your present conscious field broken into seven parts you will find yourself imagining not one conscious field in seven pieces, but rather seven separate conscious fields.

4 *Most, but not all, conscious states are intentional, in the philosopher's sense that they are about, or refer to, objects and states of affairs.*

I said we were going to forget about the history of the subject and just state facts that we all know. "Intentionality" is a word with a sordid history, so forget about the history if you can. Forget about Brentano's thesis that "intentionality is the mark of the mental" and other famous mistakes. My states of thirst, hunger, and visual perception are all directed at something and so they fit the label of being intentional in this sense. Undirected feelings of well-being or anxiety are not intentional.

So we now have a definition and a description of some of the essential features. What more can you say? Well, if we are going to be careful we want to block some possible misunderstandings. We need to add the following: *Consciousness so defined does not imply self-consciousness.* You can be conscious of something without a higher-order consciousness that you are a self that is conscious of it. For example, you can experience a pain without having an additional experience that you are a self experiencing a pain. *Also, you do not need a general second-order consciousness to have a first-order consciousness.* You can feel a pain, without necessarily reflecting on the fact that you are feeling a pain.

So far we have identified our target, described its essential features and even blocked some misunderstandings. Now we need to say how it fits into the rest of the real world.

1 *The reality and irreducibility of consciousness. Conscious states, so defined, are real parts of the real world and cannot be eliminated or reduced to something else.*

Often when we get a complete causal explanation of something we can show that it can be *eliminated* as an illusion – this happened with sunsets and rainbows, for example – or that it can be *reduced* to some more basic phenomena; it can be shown to be nothing but micro phenomena – this happened to liquidity and solidity, for example. We can't do either of these with consciousness.

We can eliminate something when we show that the epistemic basis for it was an illusion. At dusk it looks like the sun is setting over Mount Tamalpais, and when we see a rainbow it looks like there is an arch in the sky, but in both cases the appearance is an illusion generated by more basic real phenomena – the rotation of the Earth on its axis relative to the sun and the refraction of light rays by water vapor. But we can't do this eliminative reduction with consciousness, because the epistemic basis is the reality itself: if it consciously seems to me that I am conscious, then I am conscious. We can make lots of mistakes about our own consciousness, but where the very existence of consciousness is in question we cannot make the appearance–reality distinction, because the appearance of the existence of consciousness is the reality of its existence.

We cannot do an ontological reduction of consciousness to more fundamental neurobiological processes, for a reason that is implicit in what I have already said: consciousness has a subjective or a first-person ontology; the neurobiological causal basis of consciousness has an objective or a third-person ontology. You cannot show that a first-person ontology is nothing but a third-person ontology. I will say more about this point later. The causal reducibility of consciousness leads to our next point.

2 *The neuronal basis of consciousness. All conscious states are caused by lower level brain processes.*

We do not know all the details of exactly how consciousness is caused by brain processes, but there is no doubt that it is in fact. The thesis that all of our conscious states, from feeling thirsty to experiencing mystical ecstasies, are caused by brain processes is now established by an overwhelming amount of evidence. Indeed the currently most exciting research in the biological sciences is to try to figure out exactly how it works. What are the neuronal correlates of consciousness and how do they function to cause conscious states?

The fact that brain processes cause consciousness does not imply that only brains can be conscious. The brain is a biological machine, and we might build an artificial machine that was conscious; just as the heart is a machine, and we have built artificial hearts. Because we do not know exactly how the brain does it we are not yet in a position to know how to do it artificially.

3 *The neuronal realization of consciousness. All conscious states are realized in the brain as higher-level or system features.*

Everything that has a real existence has it in a single space/time continuum and the real existence of consciousness is in human and animal brains. But conscious experiences do not exist at the level of individual neurons and synapses. Thoughts about your grandmother, for example, are caused by neuron firings and they exist in the brain as a feature of the system at a higher level than that of individual neurons.

4 *The causal efficacy of consciousness. Conscious states, as real parts of the real world, function causally.*

Typically, for example, when I make a conscious decision to raise my arm and my arm goes up, my decision causes my arm to go up. As with all physical systems, the brain admits of different levels of description, all of which are causally real levels of one and the same causal system. Thus we can describe my arm going up at the level of the conscious intention-in-action to raise my arm, and the corresponding bodily movement, or we can describe it at the level of neuron firings and synapses and the secretion of acetylcholine at the axon endplates of my motor neurons, just as we can describe the operation of the car engine at the level of pistons, cylinders, and spark plugs firing, or we can describe it at the level of the oxidization of hydrocarbon molecules and the molecular structure of metal alloys. In both the case of the brain and the case of the car engine, these are not separate causal structures; it is a single causal structure described at different levels. Once you see that the same system can have different levels of description which are not competing or distinct, but rather different levels within a single unified causal system, the fact that the brain has different levels of description is no more mysterious than that any other physical system has different levels of description.

I have now given a definition of consciousness, a brief account of some of its most important structural features, and a general statement of its relations to the brain and other parts of the real world. At one level, this amounts to a proposed solution, or perhaps better, a disso-lution, of the traditional mind–body problem. The views I have advanced are, appropriately understood, matters of scientific common sense in that they are what one would say if one had a modicum of scientific knowledge but was free of the traditional philosophical cat-egories. Notice that in advancing the views I put forward, I made no use of the traditional philosophical vocabulary. None of the famous theories and issues, such a dualism, mat-erialism, epiphenomenalism, Cartesianism, or all the rest of it, were mentioned. If you take seriously the so-called "scientific world view" and forget about the history of philosophy, the views I put forward are, I believe, what you would come up with.

To have a name, I have baptized this view, "Biological Naturalism." "Biological" because it emphasizes that the right level to account for the very existence of consciousness is the biological level. Consciousness is a biological phenomenon common to humans, and higher animals. We do not know how far down the phylogenetic scale it goes but we know that the processes that produce it are neuronal processes in the brain. "Naturalism" because consciousness is part of the natural world along with other biological phenomena such as photosynthesis, digestion, or mitosis, and the explanatory apparatus we need to explain it we need anyway to explain other parts of nature. Sometimes philosophers talk about natu-ralizing consciousness and intentionality, but by "naturalizing" they usually mean denying the first-person or subjective ontology of consciousness. On my view, consciousness does not need naturalizing, for it already is part of nature as the subjective, qualitative biologi-cal part.

Just so I do not sound like I am talking about something abstract and ethereal let me nail the whole discussion down to reality with a real-life example. Right now I am consciously thinking about my desire to drink a cold beer. This conscious thought is *real* in the sense that it cannot be shown to be an illusion or reduced to something else. It is *subjective* in the sense that it has first-person ontology, and the conscious thought is *qualitative* in the sense that it has a certain qualitative feel to it, and it is definitely *intentional* in the sense that it is directed at or about beer drinking. Furthermore, it occurs as part of my *total conscious field* at the moment. My current consciously felt desire is entirely *caused by* brain processes, it is *located in* the brain and it will very soon *cause* me to go to the refrigerator and pour myself a glass of cold beer.

Objections to Biological Naturalism from the Point of View of the Philosophical Tradition

If you find this account of consciousness so obvious as to be hardly worth stating, you are already a healthy Biological Naturalist and can probably stop reading now. However, though I think Biological Naturalism is contemporary scientific common sense, it is rou-tinely challenged by those who accept some or all of the grand philosophical tradition of discussing the mind–body problem, and I now need to address the elements of that tradi-tion that make it difficult to understand Biological Naturalism.

The tradition that blinds us to these facts is vast and deeply embedded in our culture, both our popular culture and our academic philosophy. I cannot expose and answer all of it, but I will try to pick some of the central points. My strategy will be to make a series of objec-tions to Biological Naturalism, and then show how they can be answered once we abandon certain false elements of the tradition.

Objection 1. You cannot have it both ways. You cannot claim that consciousness is an ordinary biological process and thus have a materialist account of consciousness, but at the same time claim that it is irreducibly subjective, which gives you a dualist account of consciousness. You have to be either a materialist or a dualist – you cannot pretend to avoid both or to be both.

Answer to Objection 1. *Objection 1 rests on a mistaken conception of the implications of the real distinction between mental and physical.* The traditional assumption is that mind and body, as ordinarily understood, name mutually exclusive metaphysical categories. If something is mental then it cannot, in that very respect, be physical. If it is physical it cannot, in that very respect, be mental. This is the deepest mistake and it is shared by both materialists and dualists. Dualists think once you respect the reality and irreducibility of consciousness you are forced to dualism; materialists think once you accept a scientific naturalistic conception of the Universe you are forced to deny the reality and irreducibility of consciousness. They are both trying to say something true, but they end up saying something false. There is nothing for it but to expose the falsehood and rescue the truth. If we leave out some special problems about unconscious mental states, we can articulate the traditional picture in Table 25.1. On the traditional conception, if anything is mental it has the left-hand features, if physical, the right-hand features.

Table 25.1 embodies one of the deepest mistakes in our philosophical civilization and once you lay it out in its full nakedness you can see the mistake: the first half of the left-hand column (i.e., items one through four), does not imply the second half (i.e., items five through eight). Consciousness does indeed have features one through four. It is irreducibly subjective and in that sense has a first-person ontology. It is qualitative in the sense that there is a qualitative feel to every conscious state. It is in many cases intrinsically intentional. But consciousness does not have features five through eight. As far as we know anything about how the world works, all such states are spatially located in the brain. (Indeed, with current brain imaging technology we are starting to discover something about their locations and spatial dimensions within the brain.) And they are entirely caused by brain processes. Furthermore, like any other higher-level feature of a physical system, they are capable of functioning causally. The traditional notion of the mental, that distinguishes it from the physical, contains a serious mistake. The mistake is to suppose that the essential features of consciousness prevent it from being an ordinary part of the physical world.

The first and most important step in overcoming this mistake is to recognize that the intrinsic features of consciousness, its subjectivity, first-person ontology and intentionality, do not prevent it from being an ordinary biological feature of the world and thus located spatially in the brain and caused by brain process while itself capable of acting on other brain and bodily processes. Consciousness, though irreducibly mental (features one through four on the left) is in that very respect physical (features five through eight on the right). But because the vocabulary has become so philosophically corrupt I suggest we abandon the traditional terminology of "mental" and "physical" and just say that consciousness is a higher-level biological feature of brain systems. This is the most important objection I am going to make in this chapter to the philosophical tradition. The essential features of consciousness are in no way inconsistent with its biological, and therefore causal, part of three dimensional empirical reality.

Objection 2. Biological Naturalism cannot avoid the charge of epiphenomenalism. That is, the physical Universe is "causally closed," and if consciousness is irreducible to the physical or material Universe, then it can have no causal effects on the physical Universe.

Table 25.1 The traditional conception

	Mental	Physical
1	Subjective	Objective
2	First-person ontology	Third-person ontology
3	Qualitative	Quantitative
4	Intentional	Nonintentional
5	Not spatially located	Spatially located
6	Not extended in space	Spatially extended
7	Not explainable by physical processes	Causally explainable by microphysical processes
8	Incapable of acting causally on the physical	Acts causally and as a system is causally closed

Answer to Objection 2. It is because of the mistake of accepting the dualistic categories that there even seems to be a problem about epiphenomenalism. Typically higher-level features of a system, such as, for example, the solidity of the hammer, function causally even though the higher-level feature is itself entirely caused by and realized in the system of microelements. When the hammer hits the nail, you can tell the causal story, as you would in real life, at the level of weight, solidity, and velocity. Force equals mass times acceleration. But when the macro push comes to the micro shove, the story could also be told at the level of the molecules and energy transfer at the molecular level. These are not two independent stories, they are descriptions, at different levels, of one continuous causal system. No one in her right mind would say that solidity is epiphenomenal on the grounds that it has a microphysical explanation. Exactly analogously, when you decide to raise your arm, you can tell the story at the level of the intention and the bodily movement, but you could also tell the story at the micro level; the level of neuron firings in the motor cortex and the secretion of acetylcholine at the axon end plates of the motor neurons. These are not two independent stories, they are descriptions at different levels of one continuous causal system. No one who was not in the grip of the Cartesian categories would ever think there was a problem about epiphenomenalism.

Indeed, we can turn the epiphenomenalist objection against the objector. We begin with two true assumptions:

1 My conscious intention-in-action causes my arm to go up.
2 Anything that caused my arm to go up, in that way, must have electrochemical properties, such as the secretion of acetylcholine at the axon end plates of the motor neurons.

From these we derive:

3 My conscious intention-in-action has electrochemical properties.

Thus, we can make the causal power of subjective consciousness perfectly consistent with its causal functioning as a natural neurobiological, and therefore electrochemical, set of processes.

Objection 3. Your account seems to be self-contradictory. Is it reductionist or not? On your account, consciousness is clearly causally reducible, because it is entirely caused by neuronal processes, and it has no causal powers beyond those of neuronal processes. But at the same time, though you grant that it is causally reducible, you deny that it is ontologically reducible. You deny that consciousness can be reduced to physical processes and you insist, like old-time dualists, that it is "something over and above" the physical or material processes.

Answer to Objection 3. *Objection 3 rests on a mistake about reduction.* In one crucial respect the analogy with solidity is inaccurate. Solidity can be reduced to molecular behavior and consciousness cannot be reduced to neuronal behavior. To put the point more precisely, in the case of solidity the fact that we can give a complete causal explanation of solidity in terms of microphysical processes leads us to say that solidity is *nothing but* a certain sort of microphysical phenomenon. Causal reduction leads to ontological reduction. But in the case of consciousness we are unwilling to make the ontological reduction. Consciousness is entirely caused by neuronal behavior, but all the same we are unwilling to say that consciousness is nothing but neuronal behavior. Why not?

In the case of solidity we do not regard the surface features – such features as how solid objects feel, that they resist pressure, that they are impenetrable by other solid objects, etc. – as essential to solidity. So we carve them off and set them on one side and redefine solidity in terms of the micro causes of the surface features. Causal reduction leads to ontological reduction by redefinition. This reduction does not show that the surface features do not exist, but it simply excludes them from the essence of solidity. Well, why could we not do that with consciousness – carve off the surface features of what conscious states feel like and redefine them in terms of their micro causes? We could, and if we knew enough, for certain purposes, say medical purposes, we might. We could then say, "This guy is in pain, even though he does not feel it yet. The thalamocortical system definitely shows the presence of pain, though it is unfelt." Just as we can now say, "Glass is really liquid, though on the surface it looks and feels solid." But even if we did this reduction we would still need a vocabulary to name the first-person subjective qualitative features of consciousness, just as we still need a vocabulary to name the surface features of solidity. Because the whole point of having our conceptual apparatus for discussing conscious states is to describe a first-person ontology, we are reluctant to carve off this ontology and redefine the notion in terms of its third-person causal basis. In the case of consciousness the causal reduction does not lead to an ontological reduction by redefinition, because the redefinition would take away the point of having the concept in the first place.

In earlier writings, I said that the irreducibility of consciousness was a trivial consequence of our definitional practices (Searle 1992, ch. 5, especially p. 122). That remark was widely misunderstood, and I think the misunderstanding was probably my fault, so let me clarify it here. Grant me that consciousness exists as a first-person phenomenon in a world composed almost entirely of third-person phenomena and where, indeed, at the micro level the world is entirely constituted by third-person physical particles in fields of force. Then why is consciousness not reducible in the way that, for example, liquidity, solidity, and color are reducible? Well, if you look at the reduction in the case of, let us say color, pre-theoretically, we defined color in terms of how things look. "Red" is defined as what looks red to normal observers under normal circumstances. That looks circular, but it is not really because looking red can be explained ostensively. Once we discover the causal basis of the experience of red, we can redefine the color in terms of the light reflectances that typically produce that experience. We carve off the experience and set it on one side and redefine the concept in terms of its causal base. The causal reduction leads to an ontological reduction by redefinition, by carving off the subjective component. Now, as I argued above, we cannot really do that with consciousness without losing the point of having the concept in the first place, so the asymmetry between consciousness and color is not an asymmetry in the basic structure of the Universe. On the contrary, the two cases are symmetrical. The physics of colored objects, together with our constitution, causes us to have experiences of color, and the physics of our brain, together with its biological constitution, causes us to have the experiences of consciousness in general. But we are willing to make the reduction in the case of color in a way that we are unwilling to make it in the case of consciousness, because we would lose the point of having the concept of consciousness in a way that we do not lose the point of having the concept of color if we make the reduction. That is what I meant when I said that the irreducibility of consciousness is a trivial consequence of our definitional practices. However, this remark produced a lot of misunderstandings so it is better to withdraw it and just describe the facts.

Objection 4. You are still involved in inconsistencies. You say that consciousness is caused by brain processes. But if consciousness is really caused by brain processes, then there must really be two different things there: the brain processes as a cause, and the consciousness as an effect. And that is dualism.

Answer to Objection 4. *Objection 4 rests on a mistake about causation.* We have been taught by Hume that causation is always a relation between discrete events ordered in time and that every singular causal relation is always an instantiation of a universal causal regularity. Lots of causal relations are like that, but not all. Many causal forces are continuous through time. Gravity, for example. The causal explanation of why this table exerts pressure on the floor is the force of gravity, but gravity does not consist in a discrete event. And lots of causal relations are bottom-up and simultaneous with the effect. For example, the causal explanation of why this table supports objects is in terms of the behavior of the micro particles, but the causal explanation of why the table supports objects is not given by first specifying one event, the molecular movements, and then a later event, the support of the object. Rather the two are simultaneous. Similarly the causal explanation of why my brain is in its present state of consciousness is in terms of, let us suppose, massive rates of synchronized neuron firings at synapses. But this does not require that first the brain behaves in a certain way and then later consciousness exists. Rather, the conscious states are realized simultaneously with the neuron firings.

I said that both dualism and materialism are trying to say something true but, because of the philosophical tradition, they end up saying something false. Which part is false and which true? Dualism says truly that consciousness is a real feature of the real world and is not eliminable or reducible to something else. But it says falsely that consciousness is not an ordinary part of the physical world we all live in but inhabits a separate metaphysical realm. Materialism says truly that the Universe consists entirely of physical particles in fields of force (or whatever the ultimately true physical theory says are the basic building blocks of the Universe) but says falsely that consciousness, as an irreducible, subjective, qualitative mental phenomenon does not exist. One way to see Biological Naturalism is as an attempt to preserve what is true in each while discarding what is false. In order to do that, we have to overthrow a set of powerful philosophical presuppositions.

Conclusion

Given a choice between the facts as we know them – consciousness exists, it is caused by neuronal processes, it exists in the brain, and it has causal functions in the life of the organism – and various philosophical theories, I will take the facts any time. Furthermore, I am confident that in the long run, the facts will prevail over the theories that will come to seem more and more obsolete. It is worth pointing out that practicing neurobiologists of my acquaintance, such as the late Francis Crick, Gerald Edelman, and Christof Koch, implicitly or explicitly accept a version of what I have been calling Biological Naturalism. They look to the operations of the brain to find an explanation of consciousness. It will probably take a long time before Biological Naturalism is generally accepted by the academic profession because we follow a long tradition of teaching our students the mistaken view that there is some philosophical problem here of impossible difficulty. But notice that we have to train our students to think there is an impossible mystery as to how neuronal processes could cause conscious states. It is not a view that follows naturally either from reflecting on one's own experiences or on studying brain operations. Once we overcome the mistakes of the tradition, I think the facts will fall naturally in to place.

Further Readings

Searle, John (1983) *Intentionality: An Essay in the Philosophy of Mind.* Cambridge: Cambridge University Press.

Searle, John (1984) *Minds, Brains and Science,* the 1984 Reith Lectures. London: British Broadcasting Corporation (also London: Penguin Books, 1989; Cambridge, MA: Harvard University Press, 1985).

Searle, John (1992) *The Rediscovery of the Mind.* Cambridge, MA, and London: MIT Press, A Bradford Book.

Searle, John (1998) *Mind, Language and Society: Philosophy in the Real World.* New York: Basic Books (also London: Weidenfeld and Nicolson, 1999).

Searle, John (2004) *Mind: A Brief Introduction.* New York and Oxford: Oxford University Press.

References

Searle, John (1983) *Intentionality: An Essay in the Philosophy of Mind.* Cambridge: Cambridge University Press.

Searle, John (1984) *Minds, Brains and Science,* the 1984 Reith Lectures. London: British Broadcasting Corporation (also London: Penguin Books, 1989; Cambridge, MA: Harvard University Press, 1985).

Searle, John (1992) *The Rediscovery of the Mind.* Cambridge, MA, and London: MIT Press, A Bradford Book.

Searle, John (1998) *Mind, Language and Society: Philosophy in the Real World.* New York: Basic Books (also London: Weidenfeld and Nicolson, 1999).

Searle, John (2004) *Mind: A Brief Introduction.* New York and Oxford: Oxford University Press.

26

Mysterianism

MARK ROWLANDS

Mysterianism is a term coined by Owen Flanagan (1992) for a view devised, developed, and largely associated with Colin McGinn. McGinn's position is characterized by two features:

1 *Ontological naturalism*: the view that holds (inter alia) that consciousness is a natural feature of the world;
2 *Epistemic irreducibility*: the view that holds that there is no explanation of consciousness available to us.

McGinn also thinks it likely that a stronger, modal version of the second claim will also turn out to be true:

2* There *can* be no explanation of consciousness available to us.

However, he acknowledges that his arguments do not entirely preclude the possibility of our eventually developing an explanation of consciousness – although they do make this highly unlikely. It is the claim of epistemic irreducibility that constitutes the specifically *mysterian* aspect of McGinn's position.

McGinn's mysterianism can perhaps be best delineated by comparing it to three other, superficially similar, views. All of these views claim to identify serious problems with attempts to incorporate consciousness into the natural order. However, the nature of the problem is, in each case, different. Characteristic of McGinn's view is the idea that the problem with naturalizing consciousness stems from the fact that we are, as we might put it, *faculty-poor*. This is a distinct, and more serious, form of deficiency than simple conceptual poverty. For McGinn, consciousness poses a problem for naturalism not simply because we lack the requisite *concepts* to apply to the natural order – concepts that would allow us to see how the natural order (or simply "nature"?) produces or constitutes consciousness. This is true, but the real problem is that we don't have the appropriate faculties – concept-forming capacities – that would allow us to form the requisite concepts. Thus, McGinn's position differs from views such as Levine (1983), which identify the problem of consciousness as one primarily of conceptual mismatch (see also Levine chapter 29).

McGinn's view is also to be distinguished from that of Chalmers (chapter 17 and 1996). Chalmers, in effect, understands the problem of consciousness as one stemming ultimately from the *ontological poverty* of the sciences of consciousness (although this is reflected in an associated conceptual poverty also). That is, the various sciences of consciousness simply do not posit the right sorts of entities to make consciousness intelligible. It is as if we were to try and understand the nature of physical things without positing the existence of protons, neutrons, or electrons. To rectify this, Chalmers advocates what he calls *Naturalistic Dualism*. He allows that there is an explanation of consciousness we can understand. But to get this explanation we have to be willing to expand our catalog of basic entities (see Chalmers, chapter 17). From McGinn's perspective, such a move is likely to replicate precisely those features of physical explanations that render them inadequate – this would be most obviously true, for example, if the newly posited entities were spatial.

Rowlands (2001) also defends a form of Mysterianism. McGinn's position shares with traditional approaches the idea that consciousness is part of a region of reality. In itself, this region is entirely quotidian – it is not, in itself, a place of mystery. Moreover, it is a region to which we have cognitive access. But the appearance of mystery arises from the fact that this access is, for whatever reason, *idiosyncratic*. It is this idiosyncratic access that, for McGinn, is responsible for consciousness being presented to us nonspatially. While a cat may occupy a certain portion of physical space, and may in turn be located on the mat, an item that also occupies a certain region of space, our experience as of the cat being on the mat does not seem to occupy space in this way at all. Of course, an identity theorist would claim that experiences do in fact occupy space, being identical with some or other configuration in the brain. However, McGinn's point is that they do not *seem* to occupy space in this way. That is, they do not *present themselves* as occupiers of space in the way that physical objects do. This idea of idiosyncratic access would also explain features such as subjectivity that play an important role in the work of Nagel.

Rowlands argues that consciousness is not a region of reality to which our access is idiosyncratic, but rather it exists only in the *accessing* itself. There is no region of reality to which subjective phenomena belong; they simply belong to our accessing of regions of reality that are, in themselves, perfectly objective. For Rowlands, consciousness is essentially *hybrid* – it can be both the *act* and *object* of experience. Consciousness can be both that upon which awareness is *directed* (i.e., inner sense is possible) and the *directing* of awareness (the act of inner sensing is numerically distinct from the states or facts that it reveals to the subject). And what it's like to undergo an experience, Rowlands argues, is something that attaches to consciousness as an *act* not *object*. What it's like to have an experience is not something *of* which we are aware in the having of that experience but, rather, something *in virtue of* which we are aware of distinct, and nonphenomenal, objects.

This view of consciousness has Kantian roots – consciousness is a condition of possibility of objects being presented to a subject under a mode of presentation, and in this sense is a *transcendental* feature of the world. This 'transcendentalist" view of consciousness, when pushed, has a striking consequence: *consciousness is real but nowhere at all*. In this, the position shares McGinn's emphasis on space as the problematic feature that undermines reductive explanations of consciousness. But, unlike McGinn's form of mysterianism, it also entails that there can be no explanation of consciousness at all – even if our conceptual repertoire were Godlike.

In the rest of this chapter I shall focus specifically on McGinn's form of mysterianism.

The Intuition

McGinn's position on consciousness is perhaps best understood as a series of developments, explications, refinements, and defenses of an intuition (henceforth, *The Intuition*):

How is it possible for conscious states to depend on brain states? How can Technicolor phenomenology arise from soggy grey matter? What makes the bodily organ we call the brain so
radically different from other bodily organs, say the kidneys – the body parts without a trace of
consciousness? How could the aggregation of millions of individually insentient neurones generate subjective awareness? We know that brains are the de facto causal basis of consciousness,
but we have, it seems, no understanding whatsoever of how this can be so. It strikes us as mirac-
ulous, eerie, even faintly comic. Somehow, we feel, the water of the brain is turned into the wine
of consciousness, but we draw a total blank on the nature of this conversion. (1991b, p. 1)

The defense McGinn provides of this intuition is not a traditional deductively valid transition from premises to conclusion, and any attempt to evaluate his argument in these terms
will miss the point. So, for example, it would be a mistake to object to McGinn's position on
the grounds that he has not *proved* or demonstrated that consciousness cannot be explained
in neural terms. As he acknowledges, he has attempted no such thing (see especially the
introduction to McGinn 2004).

In understanding how McGinn's argument works, one should take seriously his admo-
nition that,

No one should become a mysterian over night, after a single exposure to the view; it is something
that creeps up on you until, one crepuscular dawn, you find yourself thinking, "Yes, it really *has*
to be so, doesn't it – nothing else works, and it certainly makes sense of it all." (2004, p. 2)

So, the aim of the arguments is not so much to convince an opponent of the mysterian
position of the error of their ways, but to show to someone who has been engaged in prolonged wrestling with this problem why the problem is such a tenacious one and to point
in the direction of a resolution. In this sense, the argument is not deductive but palliative.
To this end, McGinn's arguments are presented with the aim of showing why the suspicion
expressed in the intuition is a good one. The arguments serve to deepen our understanding
of the intuition by explicating and rendering more precise its content.

Can We Solve the Mind–Body Problem?

McGinn's mysterianism was initially propounded in, "Can we solve the mind–body problem?"
– a paper largely responsible for restoring phenomenal consciousness to the forefront of philosophical concern (McGinn 1991b). The argument developed here looks like this:

1 "There exists some property P, instantiated in the brain, in virtue of which the brain is
   the basis of consciousness" (1991b, p. 6).
2 "There seem to be two possible avenues open to us in our aspiration to identify P . . .
   investigating consciousness directly . . . or . . . [through] study of the brain (1991, p. 7).
3 Direct investigation of consciousness cannot identify P.
4 Empirical study of the brain cannot identify P.
5 Therefore, we cannot identify P.

The controversial premises are, of course, 3 and 4. Consider premise 3. 'Direct investigation" of consciousness would proceed by way of introspection. It is fairly obvious, McGinn
argues, that introspection alone cannot enable us to identify P. If it could, we would be able

to solve the problem of consciousness simply by introspecting. Introspection gives us access to only one term of the mind–body problem: it reveals our experience to us, but does not reveal the way in which this experience depends on the brain. Nor does it seem possible, McGinn argues, to extract P from the concepts of consciousness with which introspection does bequeath us by some procedure of conceptual analysis. It seems no more plausible that we could, by conceptual analysis, identify the way in which consciousness depends on the brain than we could discover, by such analysis, how life depends on more basic physical processes. Therefore, P is closed to introspection.

Defense of premise 4 comes in two parts. First, McGinn argues that P is *perceptually* closed to us; P is not an observable feature of the brain. Second, he extends this claim from perceptual to conceptual closure by arguing that no form of inference from what is perceived in the brain can lead us to P. The argument for perceptual closure begins with the thought that, "nothing we can imagine perceiving in the brain would ever convince us that we had located the intelligible nexus we seek" (1991b, p. 11). No matter what property, no matter how complex and abstruse, we could see instantiated in the brain, we would always remain mystified as to how it could give rise to consciousness. The reason is that the senses are geared to representing a spatial world and, as such, essentially represent things as existing in space and with spatially defined properties. It is precisely such properties that are incapable of solving the problem of consciousness.

This claim is then extended to one of conceptual closure by way of the claim that the introduction of theoretical concepts in any given domain of inquiry obeys a principle of *homogeneity*. For example, we arrive at the concept of an atom by taking our perceptual representations of macroscopic objects and conceiving of smaller objects of the same general kind. However, this will not work in the case of P, since analogical extensions of whatever properties it is that we observe in the brain are precisely as useless as the original properties were in explaining how the brain produces consciousness. If observable properties, being spatial, are inappropriate for explaining consciousness then, given the principle of homogeneity, so too will any properties we postulate on the basis of observable properties. The combination of perceptual and conceptual closure yields, in McGinn's terminology, the claim that P is *cognitively closed* to P.

Perhaps the hardest part of this idea to understand is that, for McGinn, P is there, right *under our noses* so to speak. P is not something that can be discovered by poking and slicing our way around a brain (compare Ryle 1949, p. 18). No matter how much we poke around in various colleges, libraries, playing fields, museums, and administrative offices, we will not see the university. To identify P we must not merely *look*, but must look *in the right way*. That is, in looking we must deploy concepts that carve up the brain in a manner suitable for allowing us to see how it produces consciousness. McGinn's argument for cognitive closure, then, is intended to yield the conclusion that such concepts lie outside of our concept-forming capacities. In our investigation of the brain, it is as if we tried to see the university by staring more and more intently at the various buildings that constitute it.

Later Developments

McGinn's later development of the mysterian position consists in articulation, refinement, and defense of the three major strands of the above argument. The *first* strand is concerned with differences in the ways we know about consciousness and the natural world (including the brain). The *second* strand develops the idea that consciousness has a nonspatial character. The *third* strand revolves around inherent limitations to our cognitive capacities: limitations which make the problems of consciousness unavoidable and, in any constructive sense, insoluble.

The strands are connected in the following way. We know about consciousness through *introspection*. In this, consciousness is unique (the first strand). In this way of knowing about consciousness, consciousness presents itself to us as *nonspatial*. And, in this, consciousness is again unique (the second strand). Thus an idiosyncratic mode of access to consciousness yields an idiosyncratic feature of consciousness. Because of this idiosyncratic feature of consciousness, we will encounter major problems trying to incorporate consciousness into the natural order. This is not, however, the disaster many have supposed. To the extent there is a disaster, it is an epistemic, not an ontological one. That is, the disaster is one that pertains to our knowledge of the way things are, but does not extend to the way things in fact are. The problems ultimately stem from natural limitations on our cognitive capacities (the third strand), limitations which make the problem of consciousness insoluble for us, but not for a creature with the appropriate cognitive faculties.

The Role of Introspection

Our access to consciousness is *introspective*, and consciousness is the only thing we access in this way. Our access to the external world (including the body) is perceptual, or inferential-perceptual. These modes of access are very different, and this difference is ultimately responsible for the problem of consciousness. Roughly speaking, we have *the intuition* because the way introspection reveals consciousness to us is radically different from the way perception reveals brain processes to us. This makes it impossible to understand how the former could be produced or constituted by the latter.

In recent work, McGinn has developed the idea that the knowledge of consciousness revealed by introspection is a form of *knowledge by acquaintance*: direct, non-inferential, and not mediated by way of any identifying descriptions (2004, pp. 5–12). Our introspection-based knowledge of consciousness is, therefore, independent of any descriptive or propositionally-expressed truths we might endorse concerning consciousness. This knowledge is a specific type of knowledge in its own right, and, crucially, gives us insight into the *essence* of consciousness. The fact that we know consciousness – and only consciousness – by acquaintance is, McGinn argues, sufficient to ground both our sense that there is a problem of consciousness, and why we feel that our sense of the problem outstrips our ability to articulate it (2004, p. 9).

Consciousness and Space

The importance of introspection consists in the way it reveals consciousness to us as nonspatial. Of course, we typically do not think of conscious experiences as occurring nowhere – their relation to space is not entirely unconstrained. They occur, for example, somewhere in the vicinity of the body. But, McGinn argues, to the extent that we are capable of making locational judgments about consciousness, these judgments are parasitic and causally based. For example, we judge that visual experiences occur somewhere in the vicinity of the eyes. In such judgments, there is no independent way of judging mental location. Moreover, to allow that consciousness can be roughly located is not to allocate to it the full array of spatial properties: shape, size, etc. So the way consciousness is presented to us in introspection is nonspatial in this sense: we may have a derivative and causally-based sense of its rough whereabouts, but apart from this it is nonspatial through and through.

Perception, on the other hand, reveals to us a world extended in space. The Intuition, therefore, ultimately turns on understanding how something essentially nonspatial could be produced or constituted by something essentially spatial. McGinn speculates that the only way this can happen is if space has, in effect, a hidden nature. What we will require, in order to solve the problem of consciousness, is a new conception of space.

> That which we refer to when we use the word 'space' has a nature that is quite different from how we standardly conceive it to be; so different, indeed, that it is capable of "containing" the nonspatial (as we now conceive it) phenomenon of consciousness. (2004, p. 105)

However – and here is the rub – there is no guarantee that we will ever attain this new conception of space. Indeed, there are good reasons for supposing that such a conception lies beyond our intellectual powers.

The Limits of Human Knowledge

The reason for our inability on this score lies in inherent limitations on our knowledge-acquiring faculties. McGinn's position here has a Chomskyan background. Chomsky regards our cognitive system as a set of special purpose modules. These have specific areas of competence and, as a result, other areas of incompetence. The language faculty is one of these. But Chomsky also adopts the same position with regard to what he calls our "science-forming" faculties. These are contingent, cognitive structures, formed by the vicissitudes of biological history. And so there is no reason whatsoever for thinking that they are capable of understanding everything there is to understand about the natural world (Chomsky 1988).

However, is there any positive reason for thinking that consciousness is specifically one of the areas of competence these faculties will fail to target? McGinn argues that there is, and once again, the nonspatial character of consciousness lies at the core of the problem. McGinn develops the Chomskyan speculation in terms of what he calls the CALM conjecture: Combinatorial Atomism with Lawlike Mappings. We can understand a given region of reality only if it is the sort of thing that can be broken down into simpler and simpler elements (or until a basic level is reached). These elements must, in addition, be the sort of things that can combine together so that the properties of complexes in which they occur emerge, in a lawlike way, from the properties of their elements. This conjecture, then, is that we can understand entities that conform to CALM principles but not those that do not. And consciousness, being nonspatial, does not. McGinn's most comprehensive defense of this idea is contained in his *Problems in Philosophy* (1993), where the CALM conjecture is applied not only to the issue of consciousness, but also to the self, meaning, free will, the a priori, and empirical knowledge.

Another important strand in McGinn's defense of the Chomskyan cognitive limitations thesis consists in the development of a line of thought associated with Strawson. McGinn argues that our entire conceptual scheme is thoroughly permeated by spatial concepts. In particular, our ability to identify two particulars as distinct requires us to determine that they are in distinct places. So, without this spatial resource, we would not be able to entertain the concept of multiple instances of the same property. And without this ability, the very notion of a proposition would be unavailable to us.

The result is that when we think about consciousness we are forced to do so through a prism of spatial concepts that are entirely unsuitable vehicles for this purpose. In our attempts to think about consciousness we find ourselves required (by the act of thinking) to impose a framework of concepts that are entirely alien to consciousness's intrinsic nature. Understanding of consciousness as it really is would require us to jettison the spatial skeleton of our thought – leaving us with no propositions and so nothing with which to think (see McGinn 1995 for a detailed development of this idea).

The cognitive limitations thesis plays a crucial role in McGinn's position on the mind–body problem. The nonspatiality of consciousness, he argues, entails that "nothing we can think of has a chance of explaining what needs to be explained" (2004, p. 62). As a result, philosophical attempts to understand consciousness tend to vacillate between four typical positions, offered in response to this lack of understanding – positions that, together, form a DIME shape. "D" stands for "deflationary reductionism"; "I" stands for "irreducibility"; "M" stands for "magical," and "E" stands for "eliminativism." This configuration of conceptual options is, McGinn argues, the hallmark of a philosophical problem (see his *Problems in Philosophy* for a development of this idea).

However, each response is unsatisfactory. And the way to avoid being impaled on the DIME shape is provided by the cognitive limitations thesis and the associated idea that the problem of consciousness is merely an epistemic, but not ontological, one.

Objections to McGinn's Mysterianism

McGinn's position involves two logically distinct claims:

1 An explanation of consciousness must proceed by way of identification of a *mechanism*.

If an explanation of consciousness required only correlations between neural and conscious states, there would be no deep problem of consciousness. Furthermore, if this underlying mechanism is to explain consciousness, it must do so by eliciting in us a certain kind of insight:

2 The neural mechanism that explains consciousness must allow us to see *how* consciousness is produced by the brain.

Accordingly, a genuine explanation of consciousness works only to the extent that it allays, "the feeling of mystery that attends our contemplation of the brain–mind link" (1991b, p. 11). Neither (1) nor (2) are unassailable.

One possible objection to (2) is that it involves a conflation of the concept of *explanatory adequacy* with what we might call *epistemic satisfaction* (see Rowlands 2001, ch. 3, for a development of this line of argument). Some explanations produce in us a feeling of *epistemic satisfaction*: a *Eureka!* feeling of "Now I understand!" or, in a more Wittgensteinian mode, "Now I can go on!" The molecular explanation of the macro-properties of graphite provides a good example of an explanation likely to elicit this sort of feeling. Graphite consists of layers of carbon arranged into hexagonal rings. The atoms in each layer are covalently bonded to three neighboring atoms at an angle of 120 degrees to each other. Within each layer, the covalent forces binding each atom to its neighbor are relatively strong. However, the layers themselves are bound together only by the very weak van der Waals forces. As a result, adjacent layers can slide over each other – resulting in the soft, flaky, nature of graphite, its ability to mark paper, act as a lubricant, etc.

A focus on explanations of this sort might tempt us into thinking that the adequacy of an explanation is to be judged by whether it elicits in us a feeling of epistemic satisfaction. And this assumption is questionable. Consider, for example, the molecular explanation of solidity in terms of a rigid lattice structure of atoms held together by ionic binding. How, one might reasonably ask, can a solid object be made up mostly of empty space? How could such an item, for example, retain its volume? An obvious response is to explain away any lack of epistemic satisfaction in terms of our empirical ignorance – specifically, of relevant atomic or quantum level facts and laws. For example, we might explain the disposition of solids to retain their volume in terms of the characteristics of the specifically ionic bonding that seems to be responsible for this ability. Ionic bonding involves electron transfer of electrons, rather than merely their sharing, and so ionic bonds are very strong. But this merely pushes the problem back a step. Why should bonds that involve transfer of electrons be any stronger than bonds which merely involve their sharing? What reasons are there for supposing that *this* explanation will be any more epistemically satisfying than the original?

We can push the explanation back further, and explain the salient characteristics of ionic bonding in terms of wave interaction, superposition, and so on. Perhaps, once we acquaint ourselves with the relevant laws of wave dynamics, then everything else will fall into place? But, once again, the same question will arise. Why *must* explanations cast at this level be any more epistemically satisfying than the original molecular explanation? Is it *obvious*, for example, why waves should obey the laws of wave dynamics? More generally, why should the world, at a fundamental level, be an epistemically satisfying place?

The dialectic here is tricky because McGinn will, of course, argue precisely that the world is not an epistemically satisfying place, at least not for us; and this is the basis of his mysterianism. The present point, however, is that a lack of epistemic satisfaction need, in itself, be no impediment to recognizing that something is an explanation of a given phenomenon, and an adequate one at that. We can accept that a wave dynamical account of a phenomenon such as solidity is both true *and* an explanation even if it does not produce in us – in *any* of us – the sort of feeling occasioned by the molecular explanation of the macro properties of graphite. If this is correct, then explanatory adequacy is not a function of epistemic satisfaction: explanatory adequacy does not consist in a *specific inner process*.

Some explanations – ones that we recognize as adequate – possess a sort of inchoate proto-version of epistemic satisfaction: *proto-epistemic satisfaction*. At the core of this concept is the notion of *analogy*. Many of our best theories have their origin in provocative initial analogy; one that may be seriously flawed, but subsequently proved to be a fruitful vehicle of understanding (Kuhn 1957; Hesse 1966). Consider, again, the molecular explanation of solidity. While this may not occasion the sort of epistemic satisfaction elicited by other explanations, it does produce a certain form of enlightenment carried, to a considerable extent, by the relations between properties of the reduced domain and those of the reducing. Thus, suppose we accept that a given solid is composed of a lattice structure of atoms tightly bound together, each oscillating around a fixed point. We can then, with relative ease, accept that the addition of energy to this structure might increase the frequency of this oscillation. And then, also, that the addition of sufficient energy might increase the oscillatory frequency to such an extent that the bonds break down. And the addition of further energy might increase this breakdown further. So, *if* we accept that solids are made up of a rigid lattice structure of oscillating atoms, then we can also see that the difference between this sort of structure and one where the bonds are more diffuse is something like, somewhat *analogous* to, the difference between a solid and a liquid. And, in virtue of this sort of rough analogy the molecular explanation of solidity possesses a certain protoepistemic satisfaction.

While it is plausible to suppose that any explanation we recognize as an explanation must elicit some or other psychological states in us, the precise nature of these states may vary considerably from one explanation to another – varying from, at one extreme, the fullblown "Eureka!" feeling to, at the other, a nebulous, imprecise, and analogy-based form of proto-epistemic satisfaction. The latter form of understanding can then be reinforced by the sorts of social pressures characteristic of education (i.e., "that's the way it is and you had better accept it if you want to get on/pass the exam," etc.).

Consider, now, claim (1). This is the claim that mere correlation of neural and conscious states is not sufficient for an explanation of consciousness. That would require identification of a mechanism. The distinction between mechanisms and correlations is, however, a questionable one. Specifically, the sort of enlightenment provided by mechanisms consists in the breaking down of a correlation into a structured series of smaller correlations, where each of the smaller correlations is more readily intelligible than the original one (see Rowlands 2001, ch. 3).

Mechanistic explanation is not something radically different from, or opposed to, the identification of correlations. On the contrary, mechanistic explanation is a specific form of correlation-based explanation. It may be that a correlation between two items can be rendered intelligible by the uncovering of an underlying mechanism. But this is not to replace the correlation with something fundamentally different; it is to break down, and thus explain, the correlation by means of further correlations.

With these points in mind, the best case that can be made for reductive naturalism, and hence against mysterianism, involves three claims:

1 There is no fundamental opposition between mechanistic explanation and the identification of correlations.
2 The explanatory adequacy of correlation-based explanation does not require that it elicit in us epistemic satisfaction in any full-blooded sense.

To these principles, we can add a third:

3 There is not *an* explanation of consciousness. Rather, there are many such explanations – as many as there are features of consciousness that require explanation.

Even in the case of properties such as solidity, there is not necessarily any such thing as *the* explanation of solidity. Rather, there seem to be at least two. There is an explanation of rigidity (i.e., a disposition to resist deformation) and an explanation of the disposition to retain volume. Since not all rigid structures retain volume, an explanation of the former is not, in itself, an explanation of the latter.

We might expect this general point to be reiterated in the case of consciousness. The concept of consciousness almost certainly fragments, upon analysis, into several distinct concepts, including phenomenality, subjectivity, non-relationality, and so on. If this is so, then it is likely that separate explanations will be required for each of them.

With (3)–(5) in mind, consider the much maligned claim of Crick and Koch (1994) to have explained consciousness in terms of 40 Hz oscillations in the sensory cortex. Taken in itself, such a claim is, of course, laughable. However, 40 Hz oscillations might be able to play a role in explaining not consciousness as such, but one of its features: its *gestalt* character or, as we might put it, its *all-at-onceness*. Conscious experience is not presented serially – like, for example, a description of that experience in the form of a sentence. It is presented all at once. Part – though presumably not all – of explaining this feature of consciousness almost certainly involves explaining the brain's capacity for *binding* information together into a unified whole. And this is precisely what the identification of a single oscillatory frequency might enable us to understand. It would do this not in the sense of providing us with full-blooded epistemic satisfaction with regard to the production of consciousness. Rather, it may yield a form of proto-epistemic satisfaction with regard to one aspect of consciousness. That is, we can see that the gestalt character of experience is *something like*, somewhat *analogous to*, disparate information that has been bound together in various ways. Consequently, we can understand, in a somewhat nebulous manner, that changes in the quantity and types of information that are bound together at any given time might systematically vary with changes in the content of the visual gestalt.

In short, the best case that can be made against McGinn's form of mysterianism, I think, involves arguing (a), that McGinn is committed to principles (1) and (2), but that (b), these principles should be rejected in favor of principles (3), (4), and (5), and then arguing that (c), principles (3), (4), and (5) are precisely the sort of principles that drive, in an admittedly non-reflective manner, current scientific research on consciousness.

McGinn is unlikely to be concerned with these objections. One natural response is to undermine the divide and conquer strategy favored by the reductive naturalist. Thus, while McGinn can accept that we might be able to achieve proto-epistemic satisfaction for certain features of consciousness – such as its gestalt character – these are all peripheral aspects of consciousness. The core of consciousness lies in its phenomenality. Then, he can argue that (i), there is not the slightest reason to suppose that we can even get on nodding terms with proto-epistemic satisfaction when we try to explain this property in its unanalyzed form, and (ii), this property cannot be broken down, in under-laborer fashion, into distinct properties which might be plausible candidates for proto-epistemic satisfaction when correlated with neural states. This is not the place to decide these issues – even if I could. But the dispute does at least illustrate the enormous gulf between mysterians and reductive naturalists. The dispute is characterized by the absence of a firm agreement not only on what would constitute an adequate explanation of consciousness – the criteria it would have to satisfy in order to count as an explanation – but even on what constitutes consciousness itself.

See also 17 The hard problem of consciousness; 28 Naturalistic dualism; 29 Anti-materialist arguments and influential replies.

Further Readings

McGinn, C. (1991) Can we solve the mind–body problem? In C. McGinn, *The Problem of Consciousness*. Oxford: Basil Blackwell.

McGinn, C. (2004) *Consciousness and Its Objects*. New York: Oxford University Press.

Rowlands, M. (2001) *The Nature of Consciousness*. Cambridge: Cambridge University Press.

References

Chalmers, D. (1996) *The Conscious Mind: In Search of a Fundamental Theory*. Oxford: Oxford University Press.

Chomsky, N. (1988) *Language and Problems of Knowledge*. Cambridge, MA: MIT Press.

Crick, F. and Koch, C. (1994) *The Astonishing Hypothesis*. New York: Scribner.

Flanagan, O. (1992) *Consciousness Reconsidered*. Cambridge, MA: MIT Press.

Hesse, M. (1966) *Models and Analogies in Science*, Notre Dame, IN: Notre Dame University Press.

Kuhn, T. (1957) *The Copernican Revolution*. Cambridge, MA: Harvard University Press.

Levine, J. (1983) Materialism and qualia: the explanatory gap. *Pacific Philosophical Quarterly* 64, 354–61.

McGinn, C. (1991a) Can we solve the mind–body problem? In C. McGinn, *The Problem of Consciousness*, 1–23. Oxford: Basil Blackwell.

McGinn, C. (1991b) *The Problem of Consciousness*. Oxford: Basil Blackwell.

McGinn, C. (1993) *Problems in Philosophy: The Limits of Enquiry*. Oxford: Basil Blackwell.

McGinn, C. (1995) Consciousness and space. *Journal of Consciousness Studies* 2, 220–30. Reprinted in McGinn (2004), 93–114.

McGinn, C. (2004) *Consciousness and Its Objects*. New York: Oxford University Press.

Rowlands, M. (2001) *The Nature of Consciousness*. Cambridge: Cambridge University Press.

Ryle, G. (1949) *The Concept of Mind*. London: Hutchinson.

27

Dualism, Reductionism, and Reflexive Monism

MAX VELMANS

In essence, dualism, reductionism, and reflexive monism are theories about the nature of phenomenal consciousness and about its relation to what we normally think of as the "physical world."

The Dualist View

The dualist view, which many people intuitively adopt, is shown in schematic form in Figure 27.1.

This assumes perception to involve a simple, linear, causal sequence. Viewed from the perspective of an external observer E, light rays travelling from the physical object (the cat as perceived by E) stimulate the subject's eye, activating her optic nerve, occipital lobes, and associated regions of her brain. Neural representations of the object are formed in the subject's brain, and if the conditions are sufficient to support a conscious experience this will result in a conscious experience (of a cat) in the subject's mind. This model of visual perception is, of course, highly oversimplified, but for now we are not interested in the details. We are interested only in where external physical objects, brains, and experiences are *placed*.

It will be clear that there are two fundamental "splits" in this model. First, the conscious experience (of a cat) is clearly separated from the material world (the conscious, perceptual "stuff" in the upper part of the diagram is separated from the material brain and the physical cat in the lower part of the diagram). This conforms to Descartes's view that consciousness, a state of *res cogitans* (a substance that thinks) is very different to the stuff of which the material world is made (the latter is *res extensa*, a substance that has extension and location in space). Second, the perceiving *subject* is clearly separated from the perceived *object* (the subject and her experiences are on the right of the diagram and the perceived object is on the left of the diagram).

This "substance dualist" model of perception supports the view that the Universe is split into two realms, the material realm and the mental realm (the latter including consciousness, mind, soul, and spirit). In interactionist forms of dualism these two realms interface and causally interact somewhere in the human brain.

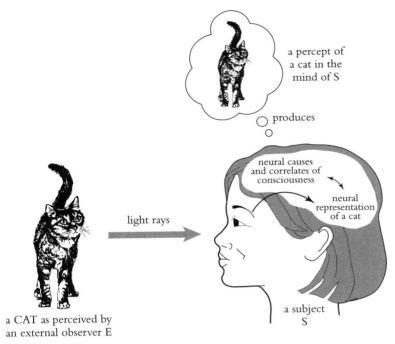

a percept of
a cat in the
mind of S

produces

neural causes
and correlates of
consciousness

neural
representation
of a cat

light rays

a subject
S

a CAT as perceived by
an external observer E

Figure 27.1 A dualist model of perception (adapted from figures drawn by John Wood for Velmans 2000).

The Reductionist View

The problems of assimilating such dualism into a scientific worldview are serious (cf. Velmans 2000, ch. 2). Consequently, it is not surprising that much of twentieth-century philosophy and science tried to naturalize dualism by arguing or attempting to show that conscious experiences are nothing more than states, properties, or functions of the brain. A reductionist model of visual perception is shown in Figure 27.2.

The causal sequence in Figure 27.2 is the same as in Figure 27.1, with two modifications. While reductionists generally accept that the subject's experience of a cat *seems* to be insubstantial and "in the mind," many argue that it is *really* a state, property, or function of the brain. In short, reductionism of the kind shown in Figure 27.2 tries to resolve the conscious experience–physical world split by eliminating conscious experience or reducing it to something physical that E (the external observer) can in principle observe and measure. But this form of reductionism *retains* the split (implicit in dualism) between the observer and the observed. The perceived object (on the left side of the diagram) remains quite separate from the conscious experience *of* the object (on the right side of the diagram). This supports a reductionist view of a universe entirely composed of physical material, of which conscious experiences are a tiny part (they are nothing more than those aspects of human brain that are identified with those experiences).

This division of the conceptual space of theories of consciousness into dualism vs. reductionism is of course oversimplified. For example, some believe conscious experiences to be *non-physical* properties of the brain and are consequently referred to as "property dualists"

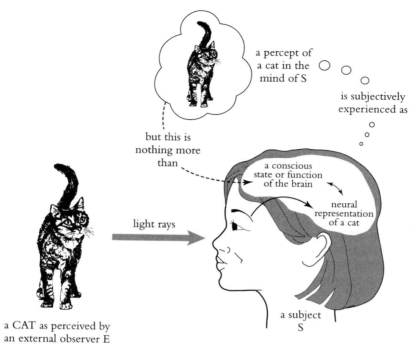

Figure 27.2 A reductionist model of perception (adapted from figures drawn by John Wood for Velmans 2000).

(as opposed to "substance dualists"). Others believe mental properties to be emergent physical properties of the brain and call themselves "nonreductive physicalists." While I do not have space to consider the subtleties of these positions here (but see Velmans 2000, ch. 3), these variants of dualism and physicalism operate within the basic framework of the classical dualist vs. reductionist debate, and are subject to the general critique that I develop below about the *shared presuppositions* that form the basis of this debate.

Note, for example, that despite their disagreement about the *ontology* of conscious experiences, dualists and reductionists agree that conscious experiences have a discoverable causal relationship to the brain and physical world. Descartes, for example, believed that movements in the pineal gland caused consequent changes in conscious experience – and, while no modern dualist would support this 300-year-old theory, they might agree with reductionists that in visual perception, physical input stimuli innervate the optic nerve and visual system, forming preconscious representations of that input in the brain. If that input is attended to, and the necessary and sufficient conditions for consciousness are met, a conscious experience will result along with its neural correlates in the brain.

Given this shared interest in the neural causes and correlates of consciousness, could the discovery of these settle the dualist vs. reductionist dispute? Unfortunately not. Knowing what causes or correlates with something will not tell you *what it is* (causation, correlation, and ontological identity are very different relationships (cf. Velmans 1998a; 2000, ch. 3)). In short, one might discover the neural causes and correlates of consciousness and still have a dispute about whether experiences are *nothing more than* their causes and/or correlates – which makes it clear that the dualist vs. reductionist dispute is as much *conceptual* as it is

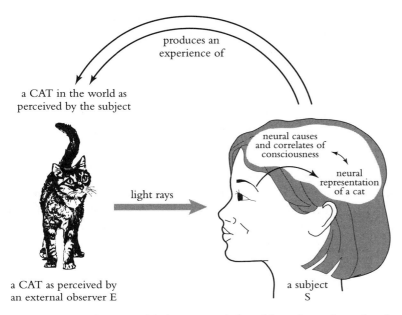

produces an
experience of

a CAT in the world as
perceived by the subject

neural causes
and correlates of
consciousness

neural
representation
of a cat

light rays

a CAT as perceived by
an external observer E

a subject
S

Figure 27.3 A reflexive model of perception (adapted from figures drawn by John Wood for Velmans 2000).

empirical. It has as much to do with *pretheoretical beliefs* about the nature of our everyday experiences (whether they are entirely material, or whether they reside in some separate, spiritual realm) than with anything observable about the brain.

Note too that most dualists and reductionists agree about where the external physical world, the brain, and conscious experiences are *placed*. Despite their dispute about *what* experiences are, they agree (roughly) about *where* they are. Reductionists who take it for granted that experiences are really brain states, properties, or functions, conclude that these must be *in the brain*. Although dualists take experiences to be immaterial (and, strictly speaking, without location or extension) they again commonly take it for granted that these must interface and interact with the physical world somewhere in the brain. In short, the brain is as close to experiences as one can get – and if experiences are in the brain, they cannot be located in, or part of, the external physical world. One could describe this view as *phenomenological internalism*.

Reflexive Monism

According to *reflexive monism*, neither dualist nor reductionist pretheoretical beliefs about the nature of conscious experiences conform to what can be readily observed about those experiences. In fact, both sets of beliefs largely conflict with the first-person evidence. This applies to their shared beliefs about (a) what conscious experiences *seem to be like*, and (b) *where* conscious experiences are placed in relation to the brain and the physical world. If this is true, it is hardly surprising that their dispute is irresolvable, and that the nature of consciousness remains a puzzle for science. An alternative, reflexive model of the nature of conscious experience and how it relates to the brain and physical world is shown in Figure 27.3.

In most respects Figure 27.3 is the same as Figures 27.1 and 27.2. As before, there is a cat in the world (perceived by E) that is the initiating stimulus for what S observes, and the proximal neural causes and correlates of what S experiences are, as before, located in S's brain. The only difference relates to the ontology and location of S's experience. According to substance dualists, S's experience of a cat is a state of "stuff that thinks" that has no location in space; according to most reductionists, S's experience of a cat is a state, property, or function of the brain that is located in her brain; according to the reflexive model, both of the former models are belief driven rather than empirically driven with the consequence that they systematically misdescribe what S actually experiences. If you place a cat in front of S and ask her to describe what she experiences, she should tell you that she experiences a cat in front of her in the world. This phenomenal cat located in a phenomenal world literally *is* what she experiences – and she has no *additional* experience *of* a cat "without location" or "in her brain." According to the reflexive model, this added experience is a myth, and that is why the dualist vs. reductionist argument about the nature of this added experience cannot be resolved. Applying Occam's razor gets rid of both the myth and the argument.

Although this will need a little explaining, the reflexive model also stipulates that, insofar as experiences are anywhere, *they are roughly where they seem to be*. For example, the phenomenal cat in Figure 27.3 both appears to be, and is out in the phenomenal world, a pain in the foot is in the experienced foot, and this perceived print on this visible page really is out here on this page. Nor is a pain in the foot accompanied by some *additional* experience *of* pain in the brain, nor is this perceived print accompanied by some additional experience *of* print in the brain. *In terms of phenomenology*, this perceived print, and my experience *of* this print are *one and the same*.

Technically, this is a form of *phenomenological externalism*. Note, however, that although I will focus on phenomena that have apparent external location and extension for the purposes of my argument, the reflexive model is not externalist (for any doctrinal reason) about all experiences. Whether an experience is located in external phenomenal space, on the experienced body surface, in the experienced head or nowhere, is an empirical matter that is entirely dependent on its phenomenology. For example, the phonemic imagery that accompanies the thought that 2 + 2 = 4 does not have a clear location, or might seem, at best, to be roughly located, "inside the head" (see Velmans 2000, ch. 6).

Given that the reflexive model conforms closely to everyday experience, it should be easy to grasp the essence of the argument so far. Descartes's focus on *thought* as the prime exemplar of conscious experience led him to suggest that experiences are states of "thinking stuff" that have no location and extension is space – and reductionists commonly agree that experiences *seem* to have such ephemeral qualities (that is why they want to give them a more secure ontology in states, properties, or functions of the brain). While I agree that thoughts and some other inner experiences appear to have such qualities, most experiences do not appear to have those qualities. On the contrary, most experienced phenomena seem to have a clear location and extension in phenomenal space.

How Phenomenal Objects Relate to Real Objects

Those accustomed to more traditional dualist or reductionist ways of thinking may find some of the above suggestions confusing. How can experiences *actually* be (roughly) where they seem to be? Physical objects can have a location in the space beyond the brain, but how can phenomenal objects have such an external location? Have I not simply confused phenomenal objects (experienced objects) with physical objects? In any case, what is the ontology of these phenomenal objects, and how do they *relate* to what we normally think of as physical objects? I address these and many other related questions in depth in Velmans (2000, chs 6–12), but will give a brief introduction here.

A first, essential point to keep in mind is that the objects that we actually see around us are in one sense "physical" but in another sense "psychological." This is because they are the objects *as they appear to us* and not the objects as they are in themselves. Although it is natural (and, in a way, correct) to think of these appearances as the appearances of the objects themselves, the fact that they appear to us in the way that they do depends as much on the operation of our own perceptual systems as it does on the nature of the objects themselves. If we did not have color vision they would not appear colored in the way that they do, if we did not have tactile receptors they would not feel solid in the way that they do, and so on. Conversely, modern physics (quantum mechanics, relativity theory, etc.) offers descriptions of the deeper nature of these objects that are very different to their surface appearances.

It follows that once an object appears to us (once it has an appearance) the perceptual processing in our own mind/brain that contributes to that appearance *has already operated.* In short, the world as it appears to us (the phenomenal world) is the end product of our current (and very recent) perceptual processing, and not the cause of that processing. The true initiating cause of our perceptual processing in this situation is the *object (or world) itself.*

Strictly speaking, therefore, the initiating stimulus that provides the surface reflectances for light energy detected by the visual system in Figure 27.3 is the *cat itself.* Why then is it represented in Figure 27.3 as "a cat as perceived by an external observer E"? Because that is how the cat itself appears to E (as a phenomenal cat) just as it does to S. This symmetry between what E and S perceive as they look at the cat itself has far reaching consequences for understanding the relation of subjectivity, intersubjectivity and objectivity, making sense of private vs. public facts in science, and a range of connected issues explored in chapter 55 of this book (and in Velmans 1999, 2000, ch. 8). However, to clarify the way that "the physical cat" relates to the "phenomenal cat" we can simply replace the "cat as perceived by E" with the "cat itself" in Figure 27.3.

Read this way, the reflexive model suggests that a real external object (the cat itself) is the source of the light energy (reflected from its surface) detected by the subject's visual system. Once the information in the light is processed, the subject's mind/brain forms a mental model of the cat itself. Viewed from the perspective of an external observer, this mental model will appear to take the form of a neural representation located in the subject's brain. Viewed from the subject's first-person perspective, this mental model has the appearance of a phenomenal cat in the phenomenal space beyond the subject's brain, located more or less where the cat itself actually is. The *information* about the external object (the cat itself) encoded in the mental model remains the same whichever way it is viewed (see Velmans 1991, 2000, ch. 11).

But in what sense is the *experienced, phenomenal* cat "physical"? Under normal conditions, our mental models provide useful representations of what the world is like, so we are right to treat the phenomenal cat as "physical" not just for the reason that this is how the cat itself looks to us, but also for the reason that the way that it looks usually tells us something useful about how it actually is. But it is also "psychological" for the reason that our own mind/brains have constructed the appearance. As the neutral monists, William James,

Ernst Mach, and Bertrand Russell (in his later work) noted, whether we *choose* to regard such experienced phenomena as "physical" or "psychological" depends entirely on the relationships that are of interest to us at the time. If we are interested in the nature of the cat itself and its relation to other entities and events out in the world we treat its appearance as a "physical appearance" and can investigate the deeper nature of the cat (beyond its surface appearances) with physical instruments. If we are interested in the appearance as such and in how this is influenced by our own perceptual processing we treat the appearance as "psychological" and can investigate its construction with the methodology of psychological science (see also chapter 55). Whether we choose to explore its physical or psychological aspects, *the phenomenology of the cat remains the same.* Such joint physical and psychological investigations can also of course establish that some phenomenal objects are *only* "psychological" – when they do *not* represent autonomously existing things themselves and are just constructions of the mind, as in the case of hallucinations, virtual realities, and so on.

Perceptual projection

The above hopefully clarifies *what* a phenomenal object is (its ontology), but still doesn't settle the question of *where* it is. The phenomenal cat seems to be out there in the world, but the neural causes and correlates of the phenomenal cat are in the brain. Given this, how can we account for this apparent "perceptual projection"?

It is important to be clear about what is meant by "perceptual projection" in order to convey its role in the reflexive model. Crucially, perceptual projection refers to an *empirically observable effect*, for example, to the fact that this print seems to be out here on this page and not in your brain. In short, perceptual projection is an effect that requires explanation; perceptual projection is not itself an explanation. We know that preconscious processes within the brain produce consciously experienced events, which may be subjectively located and extended in the phenomenal space beyond the brain, but we do not really know how this is done. We also know that this effect is subjective, psychological, and viewable only from a first-person perspective. As far as we currently know, nothing *physical*, observable from a third-person perspective, is projected from the brain. Although we do not have a full understanding of how perceptual projection works, there is a large experimental literature about the information that is used by the brain to model distance and location. There are also many ways to demonstrate perceptual projection in action, for example in hallucinations, phantom limbs, stereoscopic pictures, holograms, and virtual realities. I have discussed this literature elsewhere, along with some potentially useful models for understanding it (holography and virtual reality) in Velmans (1990, 1998b, 2000), but for our present purposes we do not need to examine the details. We simply need to note that the evidence for perceptual projection is all around us. In spite of the fact that the proximal neural causes and correlates of conscious experiences are inside our brains, our experienced phenomenal bodies and worlds appear to be outside our brains.

How phenomenal space relates to real space

But are the experiences really where they seem to be? No one doubts that physical bodies can have real extension and location in space. However, dualists and reductionists find it hard to accept that experiences can have a real, as opposed to a "seeming" location and extension.

They do not doubt, for example, that a physical foot has a real location and extension in space, but, for them, a pain in the foot cannot really be in the foot, as they are committed to the view that it is either without location or in the brain. For them, location in phenomenal space is not location in real space.

According to reflexive monism however, this ignores the fact that, in everyday life, we take the phenomenal world to *be* the physical world. It also ignores the pivotal role of phenomenal space in forming our very understanding of space, and with it, our understanding of location and extension in measured or "real" space.

What we normally think of as the "physical foot," for example, is actually the *phenomenal foot* (the foot as seen, felt, and so on). That does not stop us from pointing to it, measuring its location and extension and so on. If so, at least some phenomenal objects can be measured. While a pain in the foot might not be measurable with the same precision, few would doubt that we could specify its rough location and extension (and differentiate it, for example, from a pain in the back).

What we normally think of as "space" also refers, at least in the initial instance, to the phenomenal space that we experience through which we appear to move. Our intuitive understanding of spatial location and extension, for example, derives in the first instance from the way objects and events appear to be arranged relative to each other in phenomenal space (closer, further, behind, in front, left, right, bigger, smaller, and so on). We are also accustomed to making size and distance estimates based on such appearances. This print, for example, appears to be out here in front of my face, and THIS PRINT appears to be bigger than this print. However, we recognize that these ordinal judgments are only rough and ready ones, so when we wish to establish "real" location, distance, size, or some other spatial attribute, we usually resort to some form of *measurement* that quantifies the dimensions of interest using an arbitrary but agreed metric (feet, meters etc.), relative to some agreed frame of reference (e.g., a Cartesian frame of reference with an agreed zero point from which measurement begins). The correspondence, or lack of correspondence, between phenomenal space and measured space is assessed in the same way, by comparing distance judgments with distance measurements in psychology experiments. For example, I can estimate the distance of this phenomenal print from my nose, but I can also place one end of a measuring tape on the tip of my nose (point zero) and the other end on this print to determine its real distance.

Such comparisons allow one to give a broad specification of how well phenomenal space corresponds to or maps onto measured space. There are of course alternative representations of space suggested by physics (four-dimensional space-time, the 11-dimensional space of string theory, etc.) and non-Cartesian geometries (e.g., Riemann geometry). However, a comparison of phenomenal to measured (Cartesian) space is all that we need to decide whether a pain in my foot or this experienced print on this experienced page is, or is not, really in my brain. According to the reflexive model, phenomenal space provides a natural representation, shaped by evolution, of the distance and location of objects viewed from the perspective of the embodied observer, which models real distance and location quite well at close distances, where accuracy is important for effective interaction with the world. My estimate that this page is about 0.5 meters from my nose, for example, is not far off. However, phenomenal appearances and our consequent distance judgments quickly lose accuracy as distances increase. For example, the dome of the night sky provides the outer boundary of the phenomenal world, but gives a completely misleading representation of distances in stellar space.

Note that, although we can use measuring instruments to correct unaided judgments of apparent distance, size, and so on, measuring tapes and related instruments themselves appear to us as phenomenal objects, and *measurement operations appear to us as operations that we are carrying out on phenomenal objects in phenomenal space*. In short, even our understanding of "real" or measured location is underpinned by our experience of phenomenal location. And crucially, whether I make distance judgments about this perceived print and judge it to be around 0.5 meters in front of my face, or measure it to find that it is only 0.42 meters, *does not alter the phenomenon that I am judging or measuring*. The distance of the print that I am judging or measuring is the distance of this perceived print out here on this visible page, and not the distance of some other "experience of print" in my brain.

Why This Matters

These observations about the spatially extended nature of the experienced phenomenal world fit in with common sense and common experience and they will come as no surprise to those versed in European phenomenology. They also have many theoretical antecedents, for example in the work of Berkeley, Kant, and Whitehead, the neutral monism of James, Mach, and Russell, and the scientific writings of Köhler and Pribram. However, entire worldviews hinge on this simple issue. The evidence that some experienced phenomena have a real location and extension outside the brain is threatening for example to most dualists and reductionists, who are committed to the belief that experiences *must* be either without location or in the brain, and therefore *separate* from what we normally think of as the external, "physical" world *no matter how such experiences seem*. Given the deeply rooted nature of their beliefs, some reductionists (e.g., Lehar 2003) claim that even to speak of "perceptual projection" is unscientific (see below).

However, according to reflexive monism, perceptual projection is a readily observable phenomenon that requires explanation, and it is precisely in the confused, unempirical, and doctrinal nature of some philosophical and so-called scientific thinking on this issue that a major source of the hard problem of consciousness is to be found. To understand how conscious experience relates to the brain and physical world, one must first describe the phenomenology of that experience *accurately*. If conscious phenomenology is systematically misdescribed, its relation to the brain and physical world cannot be understood. The empirical fact of the matter appears to be that preconscious processing in the embodied brain interacting with the world results in the three-dimensional, external phenomenal world that we experience. In everyday life, it is precisely this 3-D phenomenal world that we see, hear, touch, taste, and smell around our bodies that we *think of as the physical world*, although we recognize that this *experienced* physical world only models in a rough and ready way the subtler world described by modern physics (in quantum mechanics, relativity theory, etc.). If so, there never was an explanatory gap between what we normally think of as the physical world, and conscious experience. This phenomenal physical world is *part of* conscious experience, not *apart from* it. It should be apparent that this observation, if true, would alter the nature of the "hard problem" of consciousness.

It also forms the basis for a worldview that can be contrasted with both dualism and reductionism. Reflexive monism neither splits consciousness from the "physical" world nor reduces it to something other than it seems. Nor does it (ultimately) separate the observer from the observed. In a reflexive universe, humans are differentiated parts of an embedding wholeness (the Universe itself) that, reflexively, have a conscious view of both that embedding surround and the differentiated parts they think of as themselves. The embedding surround, interacting with brain-based perceptual and cognitive systems provides the supporting *vehicle* for that conscious view, and what we think of as the phenomenal physical world *constitutes* that view.

While a more accurate phenomenology of consciousness provides a more secure departure point for a theory of consciousness, it can be no more than a first step on the way to a theory. There is more than one thing to understand, for example the relation of the phenomenal world and its conscious qualia to the physical causes and correlates of those qualia both in the world and in the brain, the relation of the phenomenal physical world to the world described by modern physics and to the "world itself," the relation of subjective and intersubjective to objective facts in science (see chapter 55), the apparent causal efficacy and function of conscious feelings and thoughts, the relation of such experiences to preconscious and unconscious mental processing, the puzzles surrounding conscious free will and so on.

I do not have space to give a more detailed account of a reflexive monist approach to these issues here, although I have done so elsewhere (see, e.g., Velmans 2000, chs 6–12; further details in Velmans 1990, 1991, 2003, and other papers on-line at http://www.goldsmiths.ac.uk/departments/psychology/staff/velpub.html). I will, however, try to make it clear why the issue of conscious location (the focus of this chapter) is critical for theories of consciousness.

Is the Brain in the World or the World in the Brain?

Readers familiar with the problem of conscious "location" will recognize that the force of my suggestion that some experiences have both a spatial location and extension outside the brain hangs on whether the *appearance-reality* distinction can be applied to conscious phenomenology. Are experiences *really* where they *seem* to be or not?

Although various thinkers have noticed the apparent spatial location and extension of some experiences, and have tried to fit this into a general theory of mind, few workers in modern consciousness studies have noted the potential consequences of this for an understanding of consciousness. Of those that have, some have tried to dismiss the existence of spatially extended phenomenology with the argument that, if the neural causes of experience are in the brain, the experiences themselves must be there too. However, this presupposes the truth of a local model of causation that has long been abandoned by physics, which accepts that electricity inside a wire can cause a magnetic field outside the wire, that planets exert a gravitational pull on each other at great distances, that there are non-local effects in quantum mechanics, and so on. While I am not suggesting that these physical phenomena account for perceptual projection, this opens up the possibility that a natural, nonreductive explanation can be found (see below).

Of more interest are a number of thinkers who take the apparent, spatially extended nature of much of experience very seriously, but nevertheless argue that such experiences are really brain states that are by definition in the brain. As it turns out, their attempt to assimilate 3-D phenomenology into "biological naturalism" (a form of physicalism) is highly instructive.

In the modern era, John Searle was one of the first to address this problem. As he noted,

> Common sense tells us that our pains are located in physical space within our bodies, that for example, a pain in the foot is literally in the physical space of the foot. But we now know that is false. The brain forms a body image, and pains like all bodily sensations, are parts of the body image. The pain in the foot is literally in the physical space in the brain. (Searle 1992, p. 63)

However, Searle does not wish to dismiss conscious phenomenology. Indeed, later in the same book, he concludes that

> consciousness consists in the appearances themselves. Where appearance is concerned we cannot make the appearance-reality distinction because the appearance is the reality. (Searle 1992, p. 121)

This illustrates the acute problem that apparent spatial location poses for biological naturalism: If biological naturalism is true, experiences are states of the brain, which are necessarily in the brain. However, if "the appearance is the reality," and the pain appears to be in the foot, then it really is in the foot. Either biological naturalism is true, or the appearance is the reality. One cannot have both.

Has science discovered that (despite appearances) pains are really in the brain as Searle suggests? It is true of course that science has discovered *representations* of the body in the brain, for example, a tactile mapping of the body surface distributed over the somatosensory cortex (SSC). However, no scientist has observed actual body sensations to be in the brain, and no scientist ever will, for the simple reason that, viewed from an external observer's perspective, the body *as experienced by the subject* cannot be observed (one cannot directly observe another person's experience). Science has nevertheless investigated the *relationship* of the body image (in SSC) to tactile experiences. Penfield and Rassmussen (1950), for example, exposed areas of cortex as they prepared to remove cortical lesions that were responsible for focal epilepsy. To avoid surgical damage to areas essential to normal functioning, they first explored the functions of these areas by lightly stimulating them with a microelectrode and noting the subject's consequent experiences. As expected, stimulation of the somatosensory cortex produced reports of tactile experiences. However, these feelings of numbness, tingling, and so on were subjectively located *in different regions of the body, not in the brain*. In sum, science has discovered that neural excitation of somatosensory cortex *causes* tactile sensations, which are subjectively located in different regions of the body. This effect is precisely the "perceptual projection" that the reflexive model describes.

In recent years the spatially extended nature of visual experience has once more become a topical issue. For example, Karl Pribram (1971, 2004), one of the first scientists to address this problem, has continued to develop his earlier theories of how 3-D phenomenology is a consequence of holographic representation in the brain; Antti Revonsuo (1995) developed the suggestion that the phenomenal world is a form of virtual reality (see also Velmans 1993, 1998b); and Stephen Lehar (2003) in a recent *Behavioural and Brain Sciences* target article has attempted to develop a mathematical model of how objects *appear* as they move in phenomenal space (as opposed to how they really *are* as they move in phenomenal space). Recently, Lynn Robertson (2004) has also reviewed the ways in which the experience of 3-D space can be *destroyed* in Balint's syndrome, unilateral neglect, and integrative agnosia. As these and other scientists such as Jeffrey Gray (2004) have pointed out, the 3-D nature of the phenomenal world is likely to have important consequences for neuroscience, for the obvious reason that the normally functioning brain has to be organized in a way that supports such spatially extended experiences.

However, these theorists remain divided on the issue of whether some experiences really are outside the brain. Pribram (2004) takes the view that they are, and develops a broad theory of perception that he explicitly links to the reflexive monism developed in Velmans (2000). By contrast, Revonsuo, Lehar, and Gray adopt a form of biological naturalism, arguing for example that the entire 3-D phenomenal world, stretching to the horizon and the dome of the sky, is a form of virtual reality that is literally located inside the brain.

Paradigm crunch

Lehar (2003), however, points out that biological naturalism forces one into a surprising conclusion: if the phenomenal world is inside the brain, the real skull must be outside the phenomenal world (the former and the latter are logically equivalent).

Let me be clear: if one accepts that:

1   The phenomenal world appears to have spatial extension to the experienced horizon and dome of the sky.
2   The phenomenal world is literally inside the brain.

It follows that

3   The real skull (as opposed to the phenomenal skull) is beyond the experienced horizon and dome of the sky.

While Lehar, Revonsuo, and Gray accept this conclusion, Lehar admits that this consequence of biological naturalism is "incredible."

Note that the difference between reflexive monism (RM) and biological naturalism (BN) on this issue has major consequences for how one thinks about the nature of the real skull and brain. RM adopts critical realism – the conventional view that, although our experiences do not give us a full representation of how things really are, they normally provide useful approximations. As a first approximation, brains are what one finds inside the skulls that we feel sitting on the top of our necks, that one can find pictures of in neurophysiological textbooks, and that are occasionally to be seen pickled in jars. Although I accept that these "skulls" and "brains" are really phenomenal or experienced skulls and brains, these mental models are roughly accurate. Consequently, the location and extension of the phenomenal and real skull and brain closely correspond.

Lehar also accepts that phenomenal skulls and brains are mental models of real ones, but BN forces him to claim that the real skull is beyond the experienced dome of the sky. If so, our assumption that the real brain is more or less where it seems to be (inside the experienced skull) must be a delusion. The alternative is that biological naturalism is wrong. Not only is the notion of a skull beyond the experienced Universe unfalsifiable (it would always be beyond any phenomena that one could actually experience), but it is also hard to know in what sense something that *surrounds* the experienced Universe could, in any ordinary sense, be a "skull" (it certainly isn't the skull that we can feel on top of our necks). Nor is it easy to grasp in what sense something that *contains* the experienced Universe is a "brain" (it certainly is not the brain that one can perceive inside the skulls on top of our necks).

In my view, this casts an entirely different light on the so-called "scientific" status of biological naturalism and the so-called "unscientific" claims of the reflexive model. Put your hands on your head. Is that the real skull that you feel, located more or less where it seems to be? If that makes sense, the reflexive model makes sense. Or is that just a phenomenal skull inside your brain, with your real skull beyond the dome of the sky? If the latter seems absurd, biological naturalism is absurd. Choose for yourself.

See also 2 Philosophical problems of consciousness; 17 The hard problem of consciousness; 28 Naturalistic dualism; 55 An epistemology for the study of consciousness.

Further Readings

Velmans, M. (1990) Consciousness, brain and the physical world. *Philosophical Psychology* 3, 77–99.
Velmans, M. (2000) *Understanding Consciousness*. London: Routledge/Psychology Press.

References

Gray, J. (2004) *Consciousness: Creeping up on the Hard Problem.* Oxford: Oxford University Press.
Lehar, S. (2003) Gestalt isomorphism and the primacy of subjective conscious experience: a gestalt bubble model. *Behavioral and Brain Sciences* 26: 4, 375–444.
Penfield, W. and Rassmussen, T. B. (1950) *The Cerebral Cortex of Man*, Princeton, NJ: Princeton University Press.
Pribram, K. H. (1971) *Languages of the Brain: Experimental Paradoxes and Principles in Neuropsychology*. New York: Brandon House.
Pribram, K. (2004) Consciousness reassessed. *Mind and Matter* 2: 1, 7–35.
Revonsuo, A. (1995) Consciousness, dreams, and virtual realities. *Philosophical Psychology* 8: 1, 35–58.
Robertson, L. (2004) *Space, Objects, Minds, and Brains.* New York: Psychology Press.
Searle, J. (1992) *The Rediscovery of the Mind*. Cambridge, MA: MIT Press.
Velmans, M. (1990) Consciousness, brain, and the physical world. *Philosophical Psychology* 3, 77–99.
Velmans, M. (1991) Is human information processing conscious? *Behavioral and Brain Sciences* 14: 4, 651–726.
Velmans, M. (1993) A reflexive science of consciousness. In *Experimental and Theoretical Studies of Consciousness. CIBA Foundation Symposium 174*, 81–99. Chichester: Wiley.
Velmans, M. (1998a) Goodbye to reductionism. In S. Hameroff, A. Kaszniak, and A. Scott (eds.), *Towards a Science of Consciousness II: The Second Tucson Discussions and Debates*, 45–52. Cambridge, MA: MIT Press.
Velmans, M. (1998b) Physical, psychological and virtual realities. In J. Wood (ed.), *Virtual and Embodied Realities*, 45–60. London: Routledge.
Velmans, M. (1999) Intersubjective science. *Journal of Consciousness Studies* 6: 2/3, 299–306.
Velmans, M. (2000) *Understanding Consciousness*. London: Routledge/Psychology Press.
Velmans, M. (2003) *How Could Conscious Experiences Affect Brains?* Exeter: Imprint Academic.

28

Naturalistic Dualism

DAVID CHALMERS

Nonreductive Explanation

There are principled reasons to think that no reductive explanation of consciousness, in terms of underlying physical processes, is possible. As I argued in chapter 17, an account of physical processes may solve some of the easy problems of consciousness, concerning the explanation of cognitive functions, but it can never explain the existence of conscious experience. At this point some are tempted to give up, holding that we will never have a theory of conscious experience. McGinn (1989), for example, argues that the problem is too hard for our limited minds; we are "cognitively closed" with respect to the phenomenon. (For further discussion, see Rowlands, chapter 26.) Others have argued that conscious experience lies outside the domain of scientific theory altogether.

I think this pessimism is premature. This is not the place to give up; it is the place where things get interesting. When simple methods of explanation are ruled out, we need to investigate the alternatives. Given that reductive explanation fails, *nonreductive* explanation is the natural choice.

Although a remarkable number of phenomena have turned out to be explicable wholly in terms of entities simpler than themselves, this is not universal. In physics, it occasionally happens that an entity has to be taken as *fundamental*. Fundamental entities are not explained in terms of anything simpler. Instead, one takes them as basic, and gives a theory of how they relate to everything else in the world. For example, in the nineteenth century it turned out that electromagnetic processes could not be explained in terms of the wholly mechanical processes that previous physical theories appealed to, so Maxwell and others introduced electromagnetic charge and electromagnetic forces as new fundamental components of a physical theory. To explain electromagnetism, the ontology of physics had to be expanded. New basic properties and basic laws were needed to give a satisfactory account of the phenomena.

Other features that physical theory takes as fundamental include mass and space-time. No attempt is made to explain these features in terms of anything simpler. But this does not rule out the possibility of a theory of mass or of space-time. There is an intricate theory of how these features interrelate, and of the basic laws they enter into. These basic principles are used to explain many familiar phenomena concerning mass, space, and time at a higher level.

I suggest that a theory of consciousness should take experience as fundamental. We know that a theory of consciousness requires the addition of *something* fundamental to our ontology, as everything in physical theory is compatible with the absence of consciousness. We might add some entirely new nonphysical feature, from which experience can be derived, but it is hard to see what such a feature would be like. More likely, we will take experience itself as a fundamental feature of the world, alongside mass, charge, and space-time. If we take experience as fundamental, then we can go about the business of constructing a theory of experience.

Where there is a fundamental property, there are fundamental laws. A nonreductive theory of experience will add new principles to the furniture of the basic laws of nature. These basic principles will ultimately carry the explanatory burden in a theory of consciousness. Just as we explain familiar high-level phenomena involving mass in terms of more basic principles involving mass and other entities, we might explain familiar phenomena involving experience in terms of more basic principles involving experience and other entities.

In particular, a nonreductive theory of experience will specify basic principles telling us how experience depends on physical features of the world. These *psychophysical* principles will not interfere with physical laws, as it seems that physical laws already form a closed system. Rather, they will be a supplement to a physical theory. A physical theory gives a theory of physical processes, and a psychophysical theory tells us how those processes give rise to experience. We know that experience depends on physical processes, but we also know that this dependence cannot be derived from physical laws alone. The new basic principles postulated by a nonreductive theory give us the extra ingredient that we need to build an explanatory bridge.

Of course, by taking experience as fundamental, there is a sense in which this approach does not tell us why there is experience in the first place. But this is the same for any fundamental theory. Nothing in physics tells us why there is matter in the first place, but we do not count this against theories of matter. Certain features of the world need to be taken as fundamental by any scientific theory. A theory of matter can still explain all sorts of facts about matter, by showing how they are consequences of the basic laws. The same goes for a theory of experience.

This position qualifies as a variety of dualism, as it postulates basic properties over and above the properties invoked by physics. But it is an innocent version of dualism, entirely compatible with the scientific view of the world. Nothing in this approach contradicts anything in physical theory; we simply need to add further *bridging* principles to explain how experience arises from physical processes. There is nothing particularly spiritual or mystical about this theory – its overall shape is like that of a physical theory, with a few fundamental entities connected by fundamental laws. It expands the ontology slightly, to be sure, but Maxwell did the same thing. Indeed, the overall structure of this position is entirely naturalistic, allowing that ultimately the Universe comes down to a network of basic entities obeying simple laws, and allowing that there may ultimately be a theory of consciousness cast in terms of such laws. If the position is to have a name, a good choice might be *naturalistic dualism*.

If this view is right, then in some ways a theory of consciousness will have more in common with a theory in physics than with a theory in biology. Biological theories involve no principles that are fundamental in this way, so biological theory has a certain complexity and messiness to it; but theories in physics, insofar as they deal with fundamental principles, aspire to simplicity and elegance. The fundamental laws of nature are part of the basic furniture of the world, and physical theories are telling us that this basic furniture is remarkably simple. If a theory of consciousness also involves fundamental principles, then we should expect the same. The principles of simplicity, elegance, and even beauty that drive physicists' search for a fundamental theory will also apply to a theory of consciousness.

(A technical note: Some philosophers argue that even though there is a *conceptual* gap between physical processes and experience, there need be no metaphysical gap, so that experience might in a certain sense still be physical (Levine 1983 and chapter 29; Loar 1990; Hill 1991). Usually this line of argument is supported by an appeal to the notion of a posteriori necessity (Kripke 1980). I think that this position rests on a misunderstanding of a posteriori necessity, however, or else requires an entirely new sort of necessity that we have no reason to believe in (see Chalmers 1996; also Jackson 1994 and Lewis 1994 for details). In any case, this position still concedes an *explanatory* gap between physical processes and experience. For example, the principles connecting the physical and the experiential will not be derivable from the laws of physics, so such principles must be taken as *explanatorily* fundamental. So even on this sort of view, the explanatory structure of a theory of consciousness will be much as I have described.

Outline of a Theory of Consciousness

It is not too soon to begin work on a theory. We are already in a position to understand certain key facts about the relationship between physical processes and experience, and about the regularities that connect them. Once reductive explanation is set aside, we can lay those facts on the table so that they can play their proper role as the initial pieces in a non-reductive theory of consciousness, and as constraints on the basic laws that constitute an ultimate theory.

There is an obvious problem that plagues the development of a theory of consciousness, and that is the paucity of objective data. Conscious experience is not directly observable in an experimental context, so we cannot generate data about the relationship between physical processes and experience at will. Nevertheless, we all have access to a rich source of data in our own case. Many important regularities between experience and processing can be inferred from considerations about one's own experience. There are also good indirect sources of data from observable cases, as when one relies on the verbal report of a subject as an indication of experience. These methods have their limitations, but we have more than enough data to get a theory off the ground.

Philosophical analysis is also useful in getting value for money out of the data we have. This sort of analysis can yield a number of principles relating consciousness and cognition, thereby strongly constraining the shape of an ultimate theory. The method of thought-experimentation can also yield significant rewards, as we will see. Finally, the fact that we are searching for a *fundamental* theory means that we can appeal to such nonempirical constraints as simplicity, homogeneity, and the like in developing a theory. We must seek to systematize the information we have, to extend it as far as possible by careful analysis, and then make the inference to the simplest possible theory that explains the data while remaining a plausible candidate to be part of the fundamental furniture of the world.

Such theories will always retain an element of speculation that is not present in other scientific theories, because of the impossibility of conclusive intersubjective experimental tests. Still, we can certainly construct theories that are compatible with the data that we have, and evaluate them in comparison to each other. Even in the absence of intersubjective observation, there are numerous criteria available for the evaluation of such theories: simplicity, internal coherence, coherence with theories in other domains, the ability to reproduce the properties of experience that are familiar from our own case, and even an overall fit with the dictates of common sense. Perhaps there will be significant indeterminacies remaining even when all these constraints are applied, but we can at least develop plausible candidates. Only when candidate theories have been developed will we be able to evaluate them.

A nonreductive theory of consciousness will consist in a number of *psychophysical principles*, principles connecting the properties of physical processes to the properties of experience. We can think of these principles as encapsulating the way in which experience arises from the physical. Ultimately, these principles should tell us what sort of physical systems will have associated experiences, and for the systems that do, they should tell us what sort of physical properties are relevant to the emergence of experience, and just what sort of experience we should expect any given physical system to yield. This is a tall order, but there is no reason why we should not get started.

In what follows, I present my own candidates for the psychophysical principles that might go into a theory of consciousness. The first two of these are *nonbasic principles* – systematic connections between processing and experience at a relatively high level. These principles can play a significant role in developing and constraining a theory of consciousness, but they are not cast at a sufficiently fundamental level to qualify as truly basic laws. The final principle is my candidate for a *basic principle* that might form the cornerstone of a fundamental theory of consciousness. This final principle is particularly speculative, but it is the kind of speculation that is required if we are ever to have a satisfying theory of consciousness. I can present these principles only briefly here; I argue for them at much greater length in Chalmers (1996).

The Principle of Structural Coherence

This is a principle of coherence between the *structure of consciousness* and the *structure of awareness*. Recall that "awareness" was used earlier to refer to the various functional phenomena that are associated with consciousness. I am now using it to refer to a somewhat more specific process in the cognitive underpinnings of experience. In particular, the contents of awareness are to be understood as those information contents that are accessible to central systems, and brought to bear in a widespread way in the control of behavior. Briefly put, we can think of awareness as *direct availability for global control*. To a first approximation, the contents of awareness are the contents that are directly accessible and potentially reportable, at least in a language-using system.

Awareness is a purely functional notion, but it is nevertheless intimately linked to conscious experience. In familiar cases, wherever we find consciousness, we find awareness. Wherever there is conscious experience, there is some corresponding information in the cognitive system that is available in the control of behavior, and available for verbal report. Conversely, it seems that whenever information is available for report and for global control, there is a corresponding conscious experience. Thus, there is a direct correspondence between consciousness and awareness.

The correspondence can be taken further. It is a central fact about experience that it has a complex structure. The visual field has a complex geometry, for instance. There are also relations of similarity and difference between experiences, and relations in such things as relative intensity. Every subject's experience can be at least partly characterized and decomposed in terms of these structural properties: similarity and difference relations, perceived location, relative intensity, geometric structure, and so on. It is also a central fact that to each of these structural features, there is a corresponding feature in the information-processing structure of awareness.

Take color sensations as an example. For every distinction between color experiences, there is a corresponding distinction in processing. The different phenomenal colors that we experience form a complex three-dimensional space, varying in hue, saturation, and intensity. The properties of this space can be recovered from information-processing considerations: examination of the visual systems shows that waveforms of light are discriminated and analyzed along three different axes, and it is this 3-D information that is relevant to later processing. The 3-D structure of phenomenal color space therefore corresponds directly to the 3-D structure of visual awareness. This is precisely what we would expect. After all, every color distinction corresponds to some reportable information, and therefore to a distinction that is represented in the structure of processing.

In a more straightforward way, the geometric structure of the visual field is directly reflected in a structure that can be recovered from visual processing. Every geometric relation corresponds to something that can be reported and is therefore cognitively represented. If we were given only the story about information-processing in an agent's visual and cognitive system, we could not *directly* observe that agent's visual experiences, but we could nevertheless infer those experiences' structural properties.

In general, any information that is consciously experienced will also be cognitively represented. The fine-grained structure of the visual field will correspond to some fine-grained structure in visual processing. The same goes for experiences in other modalities, and even for nonsensory experiences. Internal mental images have geometric properties that are represented in processing. Even emotions have structural properties, such as relative intensity, that correspond directly to a structural property of processing; where there is greater intensity, we find a greater effect on later processes. In general, precisely because the structural properties of experience are accessible and reportable, those properties will be directly represented in the structure of awareness.

It is this isomorphism between the structures of consciousness and awareness that constitutes the principle of structural coherence. This principle reflects the central fact that even though cognitive processes do not conceptually entail facts about conscious experience, consciousness and cognition do not float free of one another but cohere in an intimate way.

This principle has its limits. It allows us to recover structural properties of experience from information-processing properties, but not all properties of experience are structural properties. There are properties of experience, such as the intrinsic nature of a sensation of red, that cannot be fully captured in a structural description. The very intelligibility of inverted spectrum scenarios, where experiences of red and green are inverted but all structural properties remain the same, show that structural properties constrain experience without exhausting it. Nevertheless, the fact that we feel compelled to leave structural properties unaltered when we imagine experiences inverted between functionally identical systems shows how central the principle of structural coherence is to our conception of our mental lives. It is not a *logically* necessary principle, as after all we can imagine all the information processing occurring without any experience at all, but it is nevertheless a strong and familiar constraint on the psychophysical connection.

The principle of structural coherence allows for a very useful kind of indirect explanation of experience in terms of physical processes. For example, we can use facts about neural processing of visual information to indirectly explain the structure of color space. The facts about neural processing can entail and explain the structure of awareness; if we take the coherence principle for granted, the structure of experience will also be explained. Empirical investigation might even lead us to better understand the structure of awareness within a bat, shedding indirect light on Nagel's vexing question of what it's like to be a bat (Nagel 1974). This principle provides a natural interpretation of much existing work on the explanation of consciousness (Clark 1992 and Hardin 1992 on colors, and Akins 1993 on bats), although it is often appealed to inexplicitly. It is so familiar that it is taken for granted by almost everybody, and is a central plank in the cognitive explanation of consciousness.

The coherence between consciousness and awareness also allows a natural interpretation of work in neuroscience directed at isolating the *substrate* (or the *neural correlate*) of consciousness. Various specific hypotheses have been put forward. For example, Crick and Koch (1990) suggest that 40 Hz oscillations may be the neural correlate of consciousness, whereas Libet (1993) suggests that temporally-extended neural activity is central. If we accept the principle of coherence, the most *direct* physical correlate of consciousness is awareness: the process whereby information is made directly available for global control. The different specific hypotheses can be interpreted as empirical suggestions about how awareness might be achieved. For example, Crick and Koch suggest that 40 Hz oscillations are the gateway by which information is integrated into working memory and thereby made available to later processes. Similarly, it is natural to suppose that Libet's temporally extended activity is relevant precisely because only that sort of activity achieves global availability. The same applies to other suggested correlates such as the "global workspace" of Baars (1988), the "high-quality representations" of Farah (1994), and the "selector inputs to action systems" of Shallice (1972). All these can be seen as hypotheses about the *mechanisms of awareness*: the mechanisms that perform the function of making information directly available for global control.

Given the coherence between consciousness and awareness, it follows that a mechanism of awareness will itself be a correlate of conscious experience. The question of just *which* mechanisms in the brain govern global availability is an empirical one; perhaps there are many such mechanisms. But if we accept the coherence principle, we have reason to believe that the processes that *explain* awareness will at the same time be part of the *basis* of consciousness.

The Principle of Organizational Invariance

This principle states that any two systems with the same fine-grained *functional organization* will have qualitatively identical experiences. If the causal patterns of neural organization were duplicated in silicon, for example, with a silicon chip for every neuron and the same patterns of interaction, then the same experiences would arise. According to this principle, what matters for the emergence of experience is not the specific physical makeup of a system, but the abstract pattern of causal interaction between its components. This principle is controversial, of course. Some (e.g., Searle 1980) have thought that consciousness is tied to a specific biology, so that a silicon isomorph of a human need not be conscious. (For further discussion see Searle, chapter 25.) I believe that the principle can be given significant support by the analysis of thought experiments, however.

Very briefly, suppose (for the purposes of a *reductio ad absurdum*) that the principle is false, and that there could be two functionally isomorphic systems with different experiences. Perhaps only one of the systems is conscious, or perhaps both are conscious but they have different experiences. For the purposes of illustration, let us say that one system is made of neurons and the other of silicon, and that one experiences red where the other experiences blue. The two systems have the same organization, so we can imagine gradually transforming one into the other, perhaps replacing neurons one at a time by silicon chips with the same local function. We thus gain a spectrum of intermediate cases, each with the same organization, but with slightly different physical makeup and slightly different experiences. Along this spectrum, there must be two systems A and B between which we replace less than one tenth of the system, but whose experiences differ. These two systems are physically identical, except that a small neural circuit in A has been replaced by a silicon circuit in B.

The key step in the thought-experiment is to take the relevant neural circuit in A, and install alongside it a causally isomorphic silicon circuit, with a switch between the two. What happens when we flip the switch? By hypothesis, the system's conscious experiences will change – from red to blue, say, for the purposes of illustration. This follows from the fact that the system after the change is essentially a version of B, whereas before the change it is just A.

But given the assumptions, there is no way for the system to *notice* the changes! Its causal organization stays constant, so that all of its functional states and behavioral dispositions stay fixed. As far as the system is concerned, nothing unusual has happened. There is no room for the thought, "hmm! Something strange just happened!." In general, the structure of any such thought must be reflected in processing, but the structure of processing remains constant here. If there were to be such a thought it must float entirely free of the system and would be utterly impotent to affect later processing. If it did affect later processing, the systems would be functionally distinct, contrary to hypothesis. We might even flip the switch a number of times, so that experiences of red and blue dance back and forth before the system's "inner eye." According to hypothesis, the system can never notice these "dancing qualia."

This I take to be a *reductio* of the original assumption. It is a central fact about experience, very familiar from our own case, that whenever experiences change significantly and we are paying attention, we can notice the change; if this were not to be the case, we would be led to the skeptical possibility that our experiences are dancing before our eyes all the time. This hypothesis has the same status as the possibility that the world was created five minutes ago: perhaps it is logically coherent, but it is not plausible. Given the extremely plausible assumption that changes in experience correspond to changes in processing, we are led to the conclusion that the original hypothesis is impossible, and that any two functionally isomorphic systems must have the same sort of experiences. To put it in technical terms, the philosophical hypotheses of "absent qualia" and "inverted qualia," while logically possible, are empirically and nomologically impossible. Some may worry that a silicon isomorph of a neural system might be impossible for technical reasons. That question is open. The invariance principle says only that *if* an isomorph is possible, then it will have the same sort of conscious experience.

There is more to be said here, but this gives the basic flavor. Once again, this thought experiment draws on familiar facts about the coherence between consciousness and cognitive processing to yield a strong conclusion about the relation between physical structure and experience. If the argument goes through, we know that the only physical properties directly relevant to the emergence of experience are *organizational* properties. This acts as a further strong constraint on a theory of consciousness.

The Double-Aspect Theory of Information

The two preceding principles have been *nonbasic* principles. They involve high-level notions such as "awareness" and "organization," and therefore lie at the wrong level to constitute the fundamental laws in a theory of consciousness. Nevertheless, they act as strong constraints. What is further needed are *basic* principles that fit these constraints and that might ultimately explain them.

The basic principle that I suggest centrally involves the notion of *information*. I understand information in more or less the sense of Shannon (1948). Where there is information, there are *information states* embedded in an *information space*. An information space has a basic structure of *difference* relations between its elements, characterizing the ways in which different elements in a space are similar or different, possibly in complex ways. An information space is an abstract object, but following Shannon we can see information as *physically embodied* when there is a space of distinct physical states, the differences between which can be transmitted down some causal pathway. The states that are transmitted can be seen as themselves constituting an information space. To borrow a phrase from Bateson (1972), physical information is a "difference that makes a difference."

The double-aspect principle stems from the observation that there is a direct isomorphism between certain physically embodied information spaces and certain *phenomenal* (or experiential) information spaces. From the same sort of observations that went into the principle of structural coherence, we can note that the differences between phenomenal states have a structure that corresponds directly to the differences embedded in physical processes; in particular, to those differences that make a difference down certain causal pathways implicated in global availability and control. That is, we can find the *same* abstract information space embedded in physical processing and in conscious experience.

This leads to a natural hypothesis: that information (or at least some information) has two basic aspects, a physical aspect and a phenomenal aspect. This has the status of a basic principle that might underlie and explain the emergence of experience from the physical. Experience arises by virtue of its status as one aspect of information, when the other aspect is found embodied in physical processing.

This principle is lent support by a number of considerations, which I can only outline briefly here. First, consideration of the sort of physical changes that correspond to changes in conscious experience suggests that such changes are always relevant by virtue of their role in constituting *informational changes* – differences within an abstract space of states that are divided up precisely according to their causal differences along certain causal pathways. Second, if the principle of organizational invariance is to hold, then we need to find some fundamental *organizational* property for experience to be linked to, and information is an organizational property *par excellence*. Third, this principle offers some hope of explaining the principle of structural coherence in terms of the structure present within information spaces. Fourth, analysis of the cognitive explanation of our *judgments* and *claims* about conscious experience – judgments that are functionally explainable but nevertheless deeply tied to experience itself – suggests that explanation centrally involves the information states embedded in cognitive processing. It follows that a theory based on information allows a deep coherence between the explanation of experience and the explanation of our judgments and claims about it.

Wheeler (1990) has suggested that information is fundamental to the physics of the Universe. According to this "it from bit" doctrine, the laws of physics can be cast in terms of information, postulating different states that give rise to different effects without actually saying what those states *are*. It is only their position in an information space that counts. If so, then information is a natural candidate to also play a role in a fundamental theory of consciousness. We are led to a conception of the world on which information is truly fundamental, and on which it has two basic aspects, corresponding to the physical and the phenomenal features of the world.

Of course, the double-aspect principle is extremely speculative and is also underdetermined, leaving a number of key questions unanswered. An obvious question is whether *all* information has a phenomenal aspect. One possibility is that we need a further constraint on the fundamental theory, indicating just what *sort* of information has a phenomenal aspect. The other possibility is that there is no such constraint. If not, then experience is much more widespread than we might have believed, as information is everywhere. This is counter-intuitive at first, but on reflection I think the position gains a certain plausibility and elegance. Where there is simple information processing, there is simple experience, and where there is complex information processing, there is complex experience. A mouse has a simpler information-processing structure than a human, and has correspondingly simpler experience; perhaps a thermostat, a maximally simple information processing structure, might have maximally simple experience? Indeed, if experience is truly a fundamental property, it would be surprising for it to arise only every now and then; most fundamental properties are more evenly spread. In any case, this is very much an open question, but I believe that the position is not as implausible as it is often thought to be.

Once a fundamental link between information and experience is on the table, the door is opened to some grander metaphysical speculation concerning the nature of the world. For example, it is often noted that physics characterizes its basic entities only *extrinsically*, in terms of their relations to other entities, which are themselves characterized extrinsically, and so on. The intrinsic nature of physical entities is left aside. Some argue that no such intrinsic properties exist, but then one is left with a world that is pure causal flux (a pure flow of information) with no properties for the causation to relate. If one allows that intrinsic properties exist, a natural speculation, given the above, is that the intrinsic properties of the physical – the properties that causation ultimately relates – are themselves phenomenal properties. We might say that phenomenal properties are the internal aspect of information. This could answer a concern about the causal relevance of experience – a natural worry, given a picture on which the physical domain is causally closed, and on which experience is supplementary to the physical. The informational view allows us to understand how experience might have a subtle kind of causal relevance in virtue of its status as the intrinsic nature of the physical. This metaphysical speculation is probably best ignored for the purposes of developing a scientific theory, but in addressing some philosophical issues it is quite suggestive.

Conclusion

The theory I have presented is speculative, but it is a candidate theory. I suspect that the principles of structural coherence and organizational invariance will be planks in any satisfactory theory of consciousness; the status of the double-aspect theory of information is less certain. Indeed, right now it is more of an idea than a theory. To have any hope of eventual explanatory success, it will have to be specified more fully and fleshed out into a more powerful form. Still, reflection on just what is plausible and implausible about it, on where it works and where it fails, can only lead to a better theory.

Most existing theories of consciousness either deny the phenomenon, explain something else, or elevate the problem to an eternal mystery. I hope to have shown that it is possible to make progress on the problem even while taking it seriously. To make further progress, we will need further investigation, more refined theories, and more careful analysis. The hard problem is a hard problem, but there is no reason to believe that it will remain permanently unsolved.

See also 17 The hard problem of consciousness; 26 Mysterianism; 29 Anti-materialist arguments and influential replies.

Note

This chapter is adapted from a longer essay that appeared in 1995 in *Journal of Consciousness Studies*, 2: 3, 200–19.

Further Readings

Chalmers, D. J. (1996) *The Conscious Mind*. New York: Oxford University Press.
Wheeler, J. A. (1990) Information, physics, quantum: the search for links. In W. Zurek (ed.), *Complexity, Entropy, and the Physics of Information*. Redwood City, CA: Addison-Wesley.

References

Akins, K. (1993) What is it like to be boring and myopic? In B. Dahlbom (ed.), *Dennett and His Critics*. Oxford: Blackwell.
Baars, B. J. (1988) *A Cognitive Theory of Consciousness*. Cambridge: Cambridge University Press.
Bateson, G. (1972) *Steps to an Ecology of Mind*. New York: Chandler Publishing.
Chalmers, D. J. (1996) *The Conscious Mind*. New York: Oxford University Press.
Clark, A. (1992) *Sensory Qualities*. Oxford: Oxford University Press.
Crick, F. and Koch, C. (1990) Toward a neurobiological theory of consciousness. *Seminars in the Neurosciences* 2, 263–75.
Farah, M. J. (1994) Visual perception and visual awareness after brain damage: a tutorial overview. In C. Umilta and M. Moscovitch (eds.), *Consciousness and Unconscious Information Processing: Attention and Performance 15* Cambridge, MA: MIT Press.
Hardin, C. L. (1992) Physiology, phenomenology, and Spinoza's true colors. In A. Beckermann, H. Flohr, and J. Kim (eds.), *Emergence or Reduction?: Prospects for Nonreductive Physicalism*. Berlin: De Gruyter.
Hill, C. S. (1991) *Sensations: A Defense of Type Materialism*. Cambridge: Cambridge University Press.
Jackson, F. (1994) Finding the mind in the natural world. In R. Casati, B. Smith, and S. White (eds.), *Philosophy and the Cognitive Sciences*. Vienna: Hölder-Pichler-Tempsky.
Kripke, S. (1980) *Naming and Necessity*. Cambridge, MA: Harvard University Press.
Lewis, D. (1994) Reduction of mind. In S. Guttenplan (ed.), *A Companion to the Philosophy of Mind*. Oxford: Blackwell.
Libet, B. (1993) The neural time factor in conscious and unconscious events. In G. R. Block and J. Marsh (eds.), *Experimental and Theoretical Studies of Consciousness* (Ciba Foundation Symposium 174.) Chichester: John Wiley and Sons.
Loar, B. (1990) Phenomenal states. *Philosophical Perspectives* 4, 81–108.
McGinn, C. (1989) Can we solve the mind–body problem? *Mind* 98, 349–66.
Nagel, T. (1974) What is it like to be a bat? *Philosophical Review* 4, 435–50.
Searle, J. R. (1980) Minds, brains and programs. *Behavioral and Brain Sciences* 3, 417–57.
Shallice, T. (1972) Dual functions of consciousness. *Psychological Review* 79, 383–93.
Shannon, C. E. (1948) A mathematical theory of communication. *Bell Systems Technical Journal* 27, 379–423.
Wheeler, J. A. (1990) Information, physics, quantum: the search for links. In W. Zurek (ed.), *Complexity, Entropy, and the Physics of Information*. Redwood City, CA: Addison-Wesley.

Part IV

SOME MAJOR TOPICS IN THE PHILOSOPHY OF CONSCIOUSNESS

Anti-materialist Arguments and Influential Replies

JOE LEVINE

Introduction

Conscious creatures are those for whom there is "something it's like" to be them (Nagel 1974). There are a number of arguments – all connected in one way or another – that purport to show that what it's like to be a conscious subject is either not explicable in physical terms or, even more strongly, is not part of the physical order at all. Before we turn to the arguments, a word is in order about what the thesis is that they attack.

Materialism or physicalism (I use them interchangeably in this chapter) is the doctrine that, ultimately, all phenomena are physical phenomena. That means that every object is physical, in the sense of having certain basic physical properties like mass and spatiotemporal location, and also that all of an object's features derive in some very important way from its physical properties. It's notoriously hard to specify precisely what is meant by "physical," and also just what this important way is, in which all of an object's features derive from its physical properties. To simplify the discussion here we won't try to pin these notions down with any degree of precision. Let me just state the crucial claim, against which the anti-materialist arguments to be discussed here are aimed, as follows: if we understand by "physical" roughly what is talked about in current physical theory, then there are no basic or fundamental laws of nature that deal with anything but physical properties. In particular, mental properties do not introduce any genuinely new, emergent features into the world. The arguments to be discussed below purport to show that conscious phenomena are genuinely new, nonphysical features of reality.

Two Forms of Anti-materialism

Dualism is the view that the mental adds something substantial to nature; it is not somehow constructed out of the non-mental, or physical. There are two forms of dualism: substance dualism and property dualism. Substance dualism is the position that the mind is a nonphysical object – it lacks certain features, such as mass and spatial location, that are definitive of physical objects.

Property dualism is a somewhat weaker doctrine. Property dualists allow that the mind is a physical object – the brain, say – but claim that this physical object, the mind/brain, possesses radically different kinds of properties, mental and physical ones. So while the brain has all the physical properties neuroscience attributes to it, it also has properties like being in pain, or having a certain visual experience. Of course there may be very close relations between the mind/brain's physical and mental properties, but the crucial point – and this is what makes it a form of dualism – is that the latter are not reducible to the former. They are, as stated above, genuinely new, nonphysical features of the mind/brain. Though the most famous dualist, Descartes, was a substance dualist, most contemporary anti-materialist arguments only aim to establish property dualism (see Chalmers, chapter 17).

Objections to the Central State Identity Theory and Functionalism

The most straightforward physicalist theory is the Central State Identity Theory (CSIT). According to this view (Smart 1959) conscious mental states, such as pains or visual sensations, are identical to certain states of the central nervous system. The principal objection to this view is its inherent "chauvinism" (Block 1980). The problem is that if conscious states are identical to neurophysiological states of the sort we enjoy, then it becomes logically impossible for there to be creatures made of different material – say "intelligent life" that evolved on a distant planet – who also enjoy conscious states like pain and visual sensation. Similarly, the very possibility of conscious robots, made out of silicon chips and copper wiring, would be ruled out by CSIT. Most philosophers consider conscious robots and conscious aliens to be live possibilities, at least, so they are reluctant to endorse CSIT.

Functionalism is the doctrine that mental states are identified with "causal roles." The idea is that what human beings, possible conscious robots, and possible conscious aliens all have in common is a system of physical states that relate to each other and to stimuli and behavior in roughly the same way. Minds are functional systems that can be characterized somewhat abstractly and implemented, or realized, in different physical media. To be in pain, for instance, is a matter of being in a state that is typically a response to some type of bodily damage, interferes with normal cognitive functioning in various ways, and causes avoidance behavior. Such states could be realized in the human nervous system, in alien nervous systems, and in the internal electronics of a robot.

There are two major objections to functionalism: the "inverted qualia" argument and the "absent qualia" argument (Block & Fodor 1972; Shoemaker 1984; Van Gulick, chapter 30). The former can be illustrated with the idea of an "inverted spectrum." Imagine someone who makes precisely the same color discriminations that normal humans do, but who, because of differences in how her visual system is "wired up," responds to red objects the way others do to green ones, and to blue ones the way others do to yellow ones. If she lived her entire life this way she would have no reason to think anything was different about her and she would use color terms the way everyone else does. In terms of the causal roles of her internal states, she'd occupy the same functional state as a normal person when viewing a red object. Yet, by hypothesis, her visual experience would be very different. Thus, what it's like to see red, for instance, cannot be identified with a functional state.

The "absent qualia" hypothesis goes even further. A particularly compelling version of it is Block's (1980) thought experiment. He asks us to imagine the entire nation of China connected to each other by phone in such a way that they implement the abstract causal roles definitive of neurological states. So, for instance, if a certain input would cause a neuron to fire and activate ten neurons it's connected to, the person receiving a call would then phone the appropriate ten people on her list. The question is this: If everyone were properly connected in this way, would the entire nation of China now count as a conscious subject – feeling pain and having visual sensations? Block claims that clearly this wouldn't follow. It's at least possible that there is no conscious experience going on here (except within each Chinese individual, but that's not what counts for our purposes). So therefore, being conscious cannot be identical with having a certain functional organization.

The Conceivability Argument

The arguments above specifically target particular materialist doctrines, and clearly contain elements that pertain directly to those doctrines. However, in their use of imagined possibilities – aliens and robots in the one case and inverted spectra and "China"-heads in the other – they are analogous to a more general anti-materialist argument that goes back at least to Descartes, and have a number of contemporary adherents (Kripke 1980; Chalmers 1996), and that is the "conceivability argument."

The conceivability argument sounds much like the absent qualia argument, except that it isn't restricted to functional duplicates. The simplest version involves what's known as a "zombie." A zombie is a creature that shares all its physical features with a normal human being, but nevertheless has no conscious mental states. As we might say, "it's all dark inside." There is nothing it's like to be this creature. The question is, is such a creature conceivable?

Of course, "conceivable" is a term of art here, and it is both much weaker and much stronger in its demands than its colloquial counterpart. It is much weaker in the following sense. If someone were to wonder whether a zombie could really exist, one can imagine all sorts of reasons that would be brought to bear to justify a negative answer. Given what we know already about the dependence of much of our mental life on the brain, that some creature should have a brain like ours and not be conscious seems bizarre. It might also seem so unlikely as not to be taken seriously as a genuine possibility. But all this is consistent with zombies being conceivable in the technical sense at issue, for all that is required is that there be no internal contradiction, no conceptual incoherence in the very idea of a zombie. That the suggestion would seem utterly outlandish is not sufficient to render it inconceivable.

On the other hand, conceivability sets a higher standard than more normal imaginability in this sense: whether or not a scenario, such as the existence of a zombie, is internally consistent, or coherent, is not something that can be ascertained by casual inspection. A situation might seem imaginable or conceivable, and yet conceal within itself contradictory elements. It might take deep reflection and analysis to discover this internal inconsistency. An example of this phenomenon is any difficult theorem of mathematics. Before the proof, it seemed conceivable that the theorem might be false. Yet, once we have the proof, we see that it would be contradictory to assert that it's false. In philosophy, many notions that people have thought quite sound – free will, God, independently existing physical objects, and many more – have been attacked as downright incoherent. So what's really conceivable in the end can be a matter of serious controversy.

With this understanding of conceivability in mind, the anti-materialist claims that zombies are indeed conceivable. There is no contradiction or incoherence lurking within a description of the zombie. Another way to put it is this. From a complete description of a human being's physical state one can't derive, as a matter of conceptual or logical necessity, that the person is conscious. Conjoining this massive physical description with the claim that the person satisfying it isn't conscious does not yield a logical contradiction or conceptual incoherence.

Suppose we accept the premise that zombies are conceivable. To see why this might make trouble for the materialist, we must first consider again what is supposed to distinguish materialism from property dualism. Property dualists are willing to acknowledge that there is a close tie between a person's physical states and her conscious mental states. In fact, the property dualist is apt to claim that there are basic laws of nature connecting the mental and the physical (see Chalmers, chapter 17). The point is that the relation is a causal one, and this means that it preserves a strong sense of ontological, or metaphysical, independence between the two realms, with neither one reducible to the other. But that there might be a strict correlation, as a matter of causal law, between physical states and conscious states is fine by the property dualist.

So what distinguishes the property dualist from the materialist is not the existence of a link between the physical and the mental, but the nature of that link. Where the property dualist sees a causal link between two ontologically independent properties, the materialist sees a constitutive link between properties, one of which is reducible to the other. One common way of articulating this constitutive link is to appeal to the notion of "metaphysical supervenience." One set of properties is said to supervene on another just in case any difference in the former logically, metaphysically, entails a difference in the latter. So, on this view, no two physical duplicates could possibly differ in their mental properties if the mental supervenes on the physical. While the property dualist may allow that, as things stand, there is a causal law that links the two, she also allows that it's possible that the world could be such as to break that link. On the materialist supervenience account, no such possibility exists.

Given this characterization of the difference between the materialist and the property dualist, it becomes clear why the conceivability of a zombie counts against materialism. For the property dualist, zombies are ruled out only as a matter of causal law, not as a matter of logical or metaphysical necessity. But since zombies have to be literally impossible on the materialist view, their conceivability is an embarrassment to the position. How can what's impossible – a situation that is inherently contradictory – be conceivable? It must be that the situation is not really impossible; this is clear support for the dualist view.

At first blush the materialist has an easy response. Just because a description of a situation contains no ascertainable incoherence or logical contradiction – so therefore, the situation is conceivable – doesn't mean that the situation so described is possible. To see why, consider whether there could be a world that has water but no H_2O. That description doesn't sound contradictory or incoherent, yet, if water is in fact H_2O, such a world isn't possible. Identity statements are like that. They express necessary truths but are not formally or conceptually necessary. So if it turns out that conscious mental states are identical to either neurophysiological or functional states, then it will turn out that it's impossible for there to be two physical duplicates, one of which is conscious and the other of which isn't. Conceivability does not guarantee possibility, so the conceivability of a zombie doesn't refute materialism.

However, the anti-materialist has a counter-reply (Kripke 1980; Chalmers 1996). True, identity statements may express necessary truths even though the statements themselves can be coherently doubted, and this shows that what's conceivable may not be possible. But when such situations arise, there is usually a certain kind of story to tell about why they arise. So, for instance, take the claim that water is H_2O. If it indeed is H_2O then, by the logic of identity, it couldn't be anything else. Yet, of course, one could coherently doubt that water is H_2O without committing anything like a logical fallacy or conceptual incoherence.

But what accounts for the slippage between conceivability and possibility here? It seems to be this. This one substance, water/H_2O, has a multitude of properties, such as being liquid at room temperature, falling from the sky occasionally, and having a certain molecular structure. While it is what it is, and couldn't be anything else, it is possible, of course, that something other than H_2O might exhibit some of the superficial properties by which we normally identify water, such as being liquid at room temperature. Now, when we think of water/H_2O by way of the concept we express with "water" we are tacitly thinking of it as that which possesses these standard superficial properties, and when we think of it by way of the concept we express with "H_2O" we are thinking of it as that which has the requisite molecular structure. Since it is really possible that something with these superficial properties might not have this molecular structure, and this captures the conceptual content of our thought that water might not be H_2O, there is no incoherence lurking in the thought that water isn't H_2O, despite the fact that if it is H_2O it's necessary that it is. We have thus explained the gap between conceivability and possibility in this case.

If we try to apply the same procedure to the mental-physical case, however, we run into a serious problem. For instance, suppose that we want to identify pain with a certain neurophysiological state, call it "N." If being in pain is being in state N, then, since everything is what it is and not something else, it isn't possible for a creature to be in pain without being in state N. Yet, of course, it does seem conceivable that one could be in pain without being in state N. So, let's run the procedure described above. We say there are various properties by which we normally identify pain/state N and also its neurophysiological properties. While one couldn't be in pain without being in state N, the various properties could come apart, just as we said that it is indeed possible that something could have the same superficial properties as water, yet not be H_2O. Well, what property of pain is captured by the concept we normally express with the term "pain"? Isn't it just the qualitative character of what it's like to feel pain? What else could it be? But if that's the property by which we normally identify pain, and we're saying that this very property could be possessed by a creature that isn't in state N, then we're admitting that the mental property we're primarily interested in – what it's like to feel pain – isn't in fact identical to, or reducible to, any physical property. Hence, the conceivability argument seems to go through against materialism.

The Knowledge Argument

One of the most influential anti-materialist arguments is the one presented by Frank Jackson (1982). It too relies on a thought-experiment, though this time, instead of a zombie, we have the super-scientist Mary. Jackson starts by assuming that the thesis of physicalism entails that all information is physical information. In other words, once one has been told all of the physical facts (which include, for these purposes, facts about functional states as well) one has been told all there is to know about the world. This is not something that could really be done in practice, but it is intended to be a useful idealization. Now, if this were indeed the case, as the physicalist must assert it is, then the following situation would not occur. Yet, as will be demonstrated, it's plausible that it would occur. Hence physicalism is false.

The situation is this. Imagine Mary is a vision scientist who knows all the physical and functional facts relevant to color vision. Imagine the theory of color vision is complete and Mary has totally mastered the theory. However, suppose that for her entire life she's been locked in a room that contains no color – she lives in a black and white world. She knows others have color vision, and knows all there is to know about how light and the visual system interact in those who see color, but has never seen color herself. Finally, suppose one day Mary is released and shown a red object for the first time. The question is: Would she find what the red color looks like – what it's like for her to see this red object – to be a new piece of information, or not? Could she have predicted from what she knew before what it would be like? Jackson claims that it's immensely plausible to claim that this would be new information for her. She'd have an experience that would prompt her to say something like, "Oh, so that's what it's like to see red!" But, Jackson argues, if materialism were true, and all information was physical information, Mary shouldn't be learning anything new when she emerges from the black-and-white room. Hence, materialism is false (see Alter, chapter 31).

One argument that requires mention in any list of anti-materialist arguments is Nagel's (1974) famous discussion of "what it's like to be a bat." It's included here because it seems closely connected to the Knowledge Argument. Nagel argues that there is a deep divide between phenomena that can be understood, or apprehended from an "objective" standpoint, and phenomena that are essentially subjective. The idea is that the latter can only be understood from a certain "point of view," where the conscious experience of a creature determines a kind of point of view. So, he argues, though we could find out all there is to know concerning the physical and functional features of a bat's echolocation capacity, we would still never know what it's like for the bat to perceive with this system. For that, we'd have to experience it ourselves. Thus, the totality of facts describable from the objective standpoint of science does not exhaust all there is to reality.

The Explanatory Gap

The arguments presented above concern the metaphysical status of conscious states. Physicalism is fundamentally a claim about the structure of the world, and therefore to deny it is also a claim about how the world is put together. But some challenges to materialism are not directly aimed at the metaphysical thesis. Levine (1983, 2001), in particular, argues for the following pair of claims. On the one hand, we have excellent reason for accepting that conscious mental states are indeed constituted by physical states, and so in that sense materialism is probably true. On the other hand, however, we have no idea how we could really explain – in the sense of making intelligible to ourselves – how it is that certain physical or functional configurations have conscious mental features. That is, why is it like this, rather than that, to occupy some neural state, or why is it like anything at all? Levine claims that there is an "explanatory gap" dividing the mental and the physical.

To a large extent, Levine's arguments for the explanatory gap ride piggy-back on the kinds of anti-materialist arguments that we've seen above. Where the advocates of those arguments believe that they establish that conscious mental states are somehow outside the physical natural order, Levine sees their import differently. What they show is that we don't understand how conscious mental states fit into that order, even if they in fact do. For instance, take the case of Mary. Suppose that Mary would indeed learn something new about what it's like to see red when seeing a red object for the first time. Even if one thought that physicalism wasn't committed to the claim that she wouldn't (see below for arguments to that effect), still, if we really did understand what it was about the underlying physical story that explained the qualitative character of seeing red, one would think she could predict what it would be like. Hence, that scenario provides evidence that we don't understand why it's like what it's like in terms of the physical (or functional) story. Similar remarks apply to our ignorance of what it's like to perceive the way a bat does.

Another consideration allegedly supports the existence of an explanatory gap. Remember that functionalists objected to CSIT on the grounds that creatures with different physical constitutions from our own could nevertheless support conscious mental life. The alternative was to adopt the view that whether or not something is conscious, or precisely what its conscious states are like, is a matter of the relatively abstract causal pattern of its internal states. But, as Block's example of the "China-head" shows, not just any implementation of the relevant abstract pattern will do. Furthermore, when we talk about functional organization, it's crucial to note that there are many levels of organization at issue. A creature might obey pretty much the same behavioral and common-sense psychological generalizations that we do, and yet have a very different kind of "depth psychology"; something we might only discover after careful experimental work. So, when deciding whether two creatures are enjoying the same kind of conscious state, or even whether some creature or machine we come across is conscious at all, which level of organization is the one that determines this? The problem is, we can know all about how a creature is put together, and yet still wonder whether it's really conscious – whether there is something it's like to be it – or just what its conscious states are like. How could this be? What sort of fact are we ignorant of here? The answer seems to be this. We don't know what it is about our own physical or functional structure that explains the qualitative character of our conscious mental states. If we did know this, we would know just what to look for in these other creatures.

Replies

Since all of the anti-materialist arguments just presented rely on certain judgments about the outcome of thought-experiments, there are two basic strategies for materialists in response: either dispute the central judgments and intuitions, or show that the anti-materialist conclusion doesn't really follow from them anyway. Let's start with the first strategy.

Consider again the Knowledge Argument. We are asked to endorse the judgment that Mary wouldn't in fact know in advance of leaving the room what it's like to see red, or that we can't know what it's like for a bat to perceive by echolocation. Some philosophers dispute these claims (Churchland 1985; Dennett 1988, 1991; Akins 1993). They argue that our intuition to the effect that the relevant knowledge is lacking derives from our inability to appreciate just how much knowledge of the physical and functional facts is built into the hypothetical situation. Since actual people never know that much, one can't rely on any intuition that demands our imaginatively projecting ourselves into that situation.

Similarly, when it comes to the possibility of zombies, some materialists question whether we really can imagine them. Could we indeed entertain the possibility that the person next to us isn't really conscious? What's more, some argue that there is a buried incoherence in the very idea of a zombie (Shoemaker 1984). The problem is that the possibility of a zombie seems in conflict with the claim that we can know that we ourselves are conscious with certainty. After all, if zombies are functionally identical to us, then wouldn't they have beliefs to the effect that they are conscious? Well, if they can have these beliefs yet be wrong, how do we know for sure that we're not wrong about ourselves? Yet it seems absurd to even entertain doubt concerning our own consciousness. Hence, the argument goes, it must be that zombies aren't really conceivable.

Despite the clearly relevant considerations brought to bear by those who dispute the central judgments and intuitions of the anti-materialist arguments, many materialist philosophers still find these judgments and intuitions compelling. Instead of attacking them, they attempt to render them innocuous. The chief battleground in this debate concerns the relation between conceivability and possibility. The materialists in question here admit that zombies are conceivable, and that in some sense Mary would learn something new when seeing a ripe tomato for the first time, but they insist that these concessions do not entail anything about the metaphysical status of conscious mental states. On the contrary, it is quite consistent to maintain that consciousness is reducible to the physical and also allow that these anti-materialist scenarios are genuinely conceivable.

In presenting the conceivability argument above, it was noted that materialists point to the fact that it is conceivable that water isn't H_2O, yet no one thinks that the identity claim is thereby threatened. So why should the conceivability of a zombie threaten the relevant mental-physical identity statement? Anti-materialists respond by noting that the kind of explanation available for the conceivable falsity of the claim that water is identical to H_2O – that we are thinking of water by way of distinct, contingently connected properties – is not available in the mental-physical case, since it would entail admitting the existence of nonphysical, mental properties.

There are two ways for the materialist to respond to this argument. First, one can just insist that though the kind of explanation for the falsity of the relevant identity claim that is available in the water-H_2O case is not available in the mental-physical case, this doesn't really matter. The very idea that we need an explanation for the conceivable falsity of the identity claim is based on a mistaken view about how our concepts connect to the world.

For the purposes at hand we can think of concepts as stored mental representations – whatever it is in our heads that represents whatever we're thinking about. Thinking, then, is a matter of somehow manipulating these mental representations. So, for instance, when I think that water is a liquid at room temperature, some mental representation that means water, or refers to water, is employed in a particular way in my mind. If one is a materialist, then presumably this will be some particular neural state.

The question then arises, what connects mental representations with what they're about? What makes it the case that this particular mental representation of mine is about water, and not about something else, or even nothing at all? One model has it that the representation has a distinctive "sense" (Frege 1962), or "mode of presentation," which uniquely specifies what it's about. So, for example, my mental representation of water consists of something like a description of water's superficial properties, and it is about whatever substance in the world satisfies that description. This is the model presumed by the anti-materialist argument presented earlier. The point is that if we need such a mode of presentation in order to connect a mental representation with what it's about, then it appears that the only properties available to do the job for mental representations of sensory qualities are sensory qualities themselves, and this seems to entail that they can't be reduced to physical properties.

However, many philosophers question the entire model (Fodor 1990; Levine 2001). They argue that mental representations may contain nothing like a sense, or mode of presentation, but instead pick out their referents by virtue of causal relations between the representation and the referent. If this is so, then one can account for the conceivability of a certain physical state without the corresponding mental state as follows. When we entertain this hypothesis, we are employing two distinct mental representations – one corresponding to the vocabulary of neuroscience, and the other corresponding to the everyday vocabulary in which we talk about our mental states. Though, as a matter of fact, these two representations refer to the same property or state, this is not obvious to us. Merely possessing one way of representing a property does not give us access to the information concerning other ways of representing that same property. Thus, all we need to explain why mental-physical identity statements are conceivably false is to note that distinct concepts, or mental representations, can in fact pick out the same property. That is all there is to the matter.

Of course, anti-materialists have replies to this argument as well (Chalmers 1996). But let's turn to the second kind of materialist response. On this view, the materialist acknowledges the burden to explain why mental-physical identities are conceivably false, not relying merely on the fact that distinct mental representations, or concepts, are involved. However, they think they have an explanation that can do the job without undermining the mental-physical identity thesis itself.

Before presenting this line of response, it's important to note that, even if one accepts the position just outlined above, no explanation of the conceivable falsity of mental-physical identity claims is required, there is still a good reason to seek such an explanation. Remember that aside from the metaphysical arguments based on conceivability, there is also the explanatory gap argument to deal with. Even if one maintains that there is no conflict between the claim that mental properties are physical and yet the relevant identity claims are conceivably false, there is still a problem that remains. When considering the standard theoretical identity claims – for example, that water is H_2O – though they are conceivably false, we do note that once they are accepted we find no explanatory gap associated with them. We see how water could be H_2O, and how its being H_2O explains all of its superficial properties. But discovering that pain or visual experience is a neural state leaves us with a genuine sense of puzzlement about how the relevant qualitative character is explained. The mere fact that different concepts are used to pick out the very same property doesn't help here, because that is the situation with water and H_2O as well.

The materialist response to this problem, which is also another way of addressing the original conceivability argument, is to appeal to the fact that when we entertain concepts of our conscious experiences we are using special forms of representation – they are often called "phenomenal concepts" (Loar 1997; Papineau 2002). The basic idea is this. Most concepts designate the objects and properties they represent by virtue of the same kind of relation, whether it be a causal relation or an associated description specifying conditions that must be satisfied by whatever it is the concept designates. However, when we think about our own experiences – properties and states we come to know "from the inside" – this provides us a unique perspective on them, the "first-person" perspective. When we are then faced with an identity claim that is couched both in terms of these first-person phenomenal concepts and also in terms of standard, third-person theoretical concepts, we find it difficult to integrate the two kinds of concepts. This failure to integrate these different kinds of concepts has two important consequences. First, we find it conceivable that they don't in fact pick out the same properties and states. Second, we find it hard to see how the theoretical concepts can serve to explain the phenomena that we entertain via the first-person, phenomenal concepts. Still, the materialist maintains, the phenomena at issue are thoroughly physical, and therefore, materialism is saved.

Conclusion

Of course, this is not the end of the matter. There are anti-materialist replies to the argument just presented, and many other subtly different formulations of both materialist and anti-materialist arguments. While significant progress has been made, both in refining the arguments on both sides and in relevant empirical investigation concerning the neural basis of mental life, the basic mind–body problem is still with us.

See also 17 The hard problem of consciousness 26 Mysterianism; 30 Functionalism and qualia; 31 The knowledge argument.

Further Readings

Block, N., Flanagan, O., and Güzeldere, G. (eds.) (1997) *The Nature of Consciousness*. Cambridge, MA: MIT Press.

Davies, M. and Humphreys, G. W. (eds.) (1993) *Consciousness: Psychological and Philosophical Essays*. Oxford: Blackwell.

Flanagan, O. (1992) *Consciousness Reconsidered*. Cambridge, MA: Bradford Books/MIT Press.

Lycan, W. G. (1996) *Consciousness and Experience*. Cambridge, MA: Bradford Books/MIT Press.

McGinn, C. (1991) *The Problem of Consciousness*. Oxford: Basil Blackwell.

References

Akins, K. A. (1993) A bat without qualities? In M. Davies and G. W. Humphreys (eds.), *Consciousness: Psychological and Philosophical Essays*, 258–73. Oxford: Blackwell.

Block, N. (1980) Troubles with functionalism. In N. Block (ed.), *Readings in Philosophy of Psychology*, vol. 1, 268–305. Cambridge, MA: Harvard University Press.

Block, N. and Fodor, J. (1972) What psychological states are not. *Philosophical Review* 83, 159–81. Reprinted in N. Block (ed.), *Readings in Philosophy of Psychology*, vol. 1, 237–50. Cambridge, MA: Harvard University Press.

Chalmers, D. (1996) *The Conscious Mind*. Oxford: Oxford University Press.

Churchland, P. (1985) Reduction, qualia, and the direct introspection of brain states. *Journal of Philosophy* 82: 1, 8–28.

Dennett, D. C. (1988) Quining qualia. In A. J. Marcel and E. Bisiach (eds.), *Consciousness in Contemporary Science*, 42–77. Oxford: Oxford University Press.

Dennett, D. C. (1991) *Consciousness Explained*. Boston, MA: Little, Brown, and Co.

Fodor, J. A. (1990) *A Theory of Content and Other Essays*. Cambridge, MA: Bradford Books/MIT Press.

Frege, G. (1962) On sense and reference. In M. Black and P. T. Geach (eds.), *Philosophical Writings*. Oxford: Blackwell.

Jackson, F. (1982) Epiphenomenal qualia. *Philosophical Quarterly* 32, 127–36.

Kripke, S. (1980) *Naming and Necessity*. Cambridge, MA: Harvard University Press.

Levine, J. (1983) Materialism and qualia: the explanatory gap. *Pacific Philosophical Quarterly* 64, 354–61.

Levine, J. (2001) *Purple Haze: The Puzzle of Consciousness*. New York: Oxford University Press.

Loar, B. (1997) Phenomenal states. In N. Block, O. Flanagan, and G. Güzeldere (eds.), *The Nature of Consciousness: Philosophical Debates*. Cambridge, MA: MIT Press.

Nagel, T. (1974) What is it like to be a bat? *The Philosophical Review* 82, 435–50.

Papineau, D. (2002) *Thinking about Consciousness*. Oxford: Oxford University Press.

Shoemaker, S. (1984) *Identity, Cause, and Mind*. Cambridge: Cambridge University Press.

Smart, J. C. C. (1939) Sensations and brain processes. *Philosophical Review* 68, 141–56.

30

Functionalism and Qualia

ROBERT VAN GULICK

Functionalism, in one form or another, is probably at present the most commonly held position concerning the nature of mental states among philosophers. In its most basic form, functionalism is simply the thesis that mental states and processes are defined by the functions or roles they play within a organized network of states mediating the interaction between an organism or system and its world. What makes a particular state a perception, a memory, or a desire of a given type is the role it plays in such a network. A state's underlying substrate, whether material or otherwise, matters to its mental status only insofar as it determines or contributes to its function. Having a mind is simply a matter of being a system organized in the relevant sort of way.

However, many critics have raised doubts about functionalism's ability to explain consciousness, particularly its experiential aspects or qualia (Block 1980a, Searle 1992; Chalmers 1996). The terms "qualia" and "raw feels" are meant to refer to "felt" sensory aspects of experience, such as the red look of a ripe tomato or the particular taste of a fresh pineapple. Functionalism is often faulted for its supposed inability to capture or explain such qualia, which many regard as essential features of our conscious experiential states. If there really are such qualia and functionalism fails to explain them, then it would be at best an incomplete theory of mind.

Many attacks on functionalism involve a priori philosophical arguments meant to show that no functionalist theory or model can ever adequately deal with qualia. Various inverted qualia, absent qualia (Block 1980b), or zombie arguments (Chalmers 1996) have been offered to show the supposed impossibility of functionally explaining qualia. In each case, claims about what we can supposedly conceive or imagine – for example, states without qualia that play the same roles as qualia states – are alleged to show that qualia must inevitably escape the functionalist's explanatory net.

Other critics aim at more modest results, asserting only the inadequacy of particular current functionalist models in dealing with qualia (Levine 1993, 2001). Without excluding the possibility of other different and better future alternatives, they fault current functionalist models of mind for their specific inability to explain qualia, and thus as giving at best a partial account of mind and leaving a problematic explanatory gap.

The defenders of functionalism have responded to both sorts of criticism. They have replied to the first by challenging the a priori thought experiments as being either incoherent or unable to show any inherent limits on functionalism (Shoemaker 1975a, 1981).

In response to attacks of the second sort, defenders of specific models have tried to show either that the models have greater explanatory power than supposed by their critics, or that the incompleteness charge relies upon an unreasonable or mistaken explanatory demand (Flanagan 1990; Van Gulick 1993). Whether pushing from one side or both, the defender's aim is to bring the explanatory power of the functional model in line with the appropriate explanatory standard and thus to show that it does all that it can be reasonably asked to do. A model should not be faulted for failing to meet demands based on misconceptions or illusions.

Like many philosophical controversies, the functionalism–qualia debate is rich with ambiguity. The main issue, "Can functionalism adequately explain qualia?" is not a single well-defined question, but really a family of distinct but related questions, which vary along three main parameters. The specific issue in dispute will depend upon how one spells out three interpretative dimensions:

1   How should one interpret "functionalism"?
2   What real features do qualia have that need to be explained?
3   What counts as the appropriate standard for adequate explanatory success?

Depending on the specific values one plugs in, one gets a diversity of quite different questions. On one hand one might ask, "Is it possible to specify a set of purely computational functions whose implementation is logically sufficient to entail the existence of qualitative experience?" Alternatively one could inquire, "To what degree can our common-sense concept of qualia be explicated in terms of the purposive role that qualia play within our overall mental economy, and the relations they bear to other common-sense mental states such as beliefs, memories, seeings, and intentions?" They are both interesting questions, and just two of the many legitimate parsings one might give to the basic query.

In navigating the functionalism–qualia debate, it is important to remain clear about what specific issue one is addressing; the potential for confusion is all too great. Thus, the next section sorts out the main variants of functionalism, and the following section surveys current views about what real features qualia have that stand in need of explanation. The final two sections then consider arguments meant to show that various forms of functionalism are unable to accommodate or explain some of the real features of qualia, as well as functionalist replies to those arguments.

Varieties of Functionalism

Functionalists all accept the basic thesis that mental kinds are functional kinds, and that what makes a mental item an item of a given mental type is the functional role it plays within a relevantly organized system. What makes a mental state a memory of lunch, an intention to buy a cup of coffee, or a perception of the tree outside the window is the function or role it plays within an organized and interconnected set of states and processes linking a system or organism with its world. Wants and sensations are thus more like hearts and dollars than like water or electrons.

From a functionalist perspective, minds differ from non-minds not so much in terms of their underlying constituents but in how those parts are organized. Most functionalists are also physicalists and regard minds much as we do biological organisms, that is as a special subset of physical systems distinguished by their forms of complex organization. From that perspective, such states and processes are most usefully characterized in terms of their contribution to the effective operation of their containing system.

Thus, to understand the nature of a given type of mental state one needs to have a reasonable grasp of both the specific role that the state plays and the larger network or system within which it functions. One understands what it is to see an approaching storm cloud not only because one understands the specific role such a perceptual experience plays within our mental economy, but also because one understands, in general, what it is to be the sort of mental entity or system within which such experiences occur. One must have a general grasp of what it is to have a conscious mind in order to appreciate the specific roles that conscious visual experiences play within such minds.

Functionalism is thus thoroughly holistic in its orientation. Specific mental states and processes are always to be explained and understood in relation to their larger systemic context. Indeed, it may be impossible in many cases to say anything of much use about the function of a local item except by appeal to more global aspects of the system's overall organization. One would be unlikely to make any sense of the particular role played by a conscious feeling of pain in one's ear if one did not already have a grasp in general of what it is to be a feeling, consciously-minded self that also experiences desires, aversions, and sensations.

Thus, functionalists on the whole agree that mental kinds are holistic and systemic functional kinds. However, as soon as one pushes a bit further, disagreement arises on almost every issue. Which mental states are in the scope of the functionalists' claim? How are their roles to be characterized? What is the force of saying that they "should be understood in term of those roles"? Each question gets answered in a variety of ways, and as a result functionalism splits into a diversity of more specific views and claims, which can be distinguished in large part by their answers to three questions.

The first question is, "Which states are involved in the functionalist claim?" Functionalism is sometimes taken as a claim about ordinary or folk psychological states such as believing, sensing, and remembering, or even as a claim about a restricted subset of such states such as those involving propositional attitudes and rational agency such as belief, desire, and intention (Dennett 1978). Alternatively, the functionalist might be making a claim about the states of some empirical psychological theory, whether current or future, actual or ideal. Such theoretical states might or might not correspond to those of folk psychology, and insofar as they did not, their status as functional would be an independent issue. Following Ned Block (1980a), claims of this second sort are sometime labeled "psychofunctionalist."

Whether the relevant states are folk or theoretical, it is essential that they include experiential states such as seeing a red flag flapping in the wind or smelling a just opened gardenia. Unless such states are included in the scope of the functionalist's claim, the qualia objections do not even come into play.

The second question is, "How are the functional relations to be characterized?" What counts as a *functional* relation in the sense relevant to the functionalist thesis? Various versions of the view interpret "function" in different ways, with the largest division probably coming between those that construe it teleologically and those that do not.

Some theories of the latter sort interpret the word "function" in the strictly mathematical sense simply as a mapping from one set of items to another, perhaps the inputs and outputs of some psychological or information processing module. So called "machine functionalism" is of this sort and restricts the range of functional relations to those that can be spelled out in solely computational or Turing machine terms (Putnam 1960).

Other non-teleological versions of functionalism interpret "function" in terms of simple causal relations, such as dispositions to cause or inhibit the production of other states or outputs either singly or in combinations (Lewis 1972). Folk psychological functionalism is often unpacked in this way. Part of the common-sense causal role associated with having a desire for a cold beer is that it will dispose one to go to the fridge if one believes there are beers in the fridge and one has no countervailing mental states such as an intention to stick to a low-carb diet.

Causal role accounts differ widely in what conceptual resources they allow for specifying the causal roles. Some aim to do so in an austere and mechanistic way, but others allow far richer resources including even rational and intentional concepts. In the latter case, one might, for example, permit the use of intentional boundary conditions such as "no rational grounds to the contrary." In general, there is a tradeoff between the resources one is willing to permit and one's reductive aspirations. The more one construes non-teleological functionalism as a reductive thesis, the more likely one is to restrict the range of concepts one can invoke in specifying functional roles.

The question of which concepts one is allowed to use to characterize the relevant roles has obvious relevance to the qualia question. If, for example, one was able to appeal to distinctively qualitative notions such as "qualitative similarity" in specifying the roles, then it would be much harder to fault the functionalist's conditions as insufficient (Shoemaker 1975b), but also easier to disparage them as not genuinely explanatory.

Teleological versions of functionalism interpret role and functions in terms of goals and purposes (Van Gulick 1980; Lycan 1987, 1996). Like biological functions, such teleological functions focus on the ways in which the relevant mental states contribute to the well being and success of the containing system in ways that reflects its design or intended operation. Just as the function of the heart is to pump the blood and not to make diagnostically relevant sounds, so too the function of the memory is to store information for subsequent retrieval and application. The teleological functionalist requires not only that a given state exhibit the requisite profile of causal links but that it does so because it is *supposed to do so*, because that is its purpose. Thus the challenge to the teleo-functionalist is to explain the real nature of qualia in terms of such purposive roles. Just as with causal roles, there is a further question about the range of concepts one may use in characterizing purposive roles. Again, a great deal is likely to turn on whether or not one is allowed to use rational, mental, or phenomenal concepts in specifying such roles, with a similar tradeoff between sufficiency and explanatory depth.

The third and final question is, "What is the force of saying that mental states *should be understood* in terms of such functional roles?" The claim can be interpreted in a strongly reductive way such that the property of playing such a role essentially constitutes what it is to be a mental state or process of the relevant type. The mental property and the functional role property are one and the same (Block 1980a). The one is reduced to the other as a matter of strict identity, as one might reduce the property of having the value of one dollar to the property of playing a specific role within the American monetary system. A somewhat weaker view takes the functional role as merely specifying a description or condition for picking out the referent of the mental term. The underlying nature or essence of the property that is picked out is not necessarily given by that functional specification. Indeed its essential nature may be more structural. For example, our concept of pain may be defined largely in terms of its role and yet the term "pain" may in fact pick out or refer to a specific type of neural state whose essence is a matter of neurophysiology (Lewis 1972). A third and yet weaker reading of the functionalist claim would interpret "should be understood" as meaning only that it is useful and helpful to study, describe, and model mental states in terms of their functional roles, even if those roles neither define their essence nor provide a means of identifying the states that do define their essence (Chalmers 1996). This third reading of the claim asserts merely that functional roles provide one with a useful way to think about or model mental states.

Thus, insofar as the functionalist aims to explain qualia, the resources on which he can draw will vary with the specific type of functionalism he accepts, and whether it is a version of computational, causal role, or teleological functionalism. Similarly, the criterion for what counts as providing such an explanation will vary with the strength of the claim to which he is committed and the degree to which he interprets functionalism as a reductive thesis.

Views of Qualia

The explanatory target is also a matter of dispute. What is meant by "qualia"? And if there are such things, what real features do they have that the functionalist needs to explain or accommodate within her theory?

In the most basic sense, qualia are simply the sensory qualities associated with our phenomenal experience, the ways in which the world appears to us in experience. Insofar as there is in Thomas Nagel's (1974) phrase "something that it is like" to have or undergo a specific conscious experience, qualia are simply the qualities associated with those distinct experiential aspects. Intuitively, there is something that it's like to smell a gardenia, taste a sip of espresso, hear middle C played on an oboe, or see a bright red ripe tomato. Qualia, in this loose sense, are relatively uncontroversial. Few question that it's like for something to have particular experiences and that we can talk coherently of how a rose smells or how a radish tastes.

However, the term "qualia" is also used in a variety of more theoretical and philosophically more problematic senses. On what might be regarded as the traditional view of qualia, they are intrinsic properties of mental states or objects of which we are introspectively and infallibly aware and with which we are directly acquainted in experience (Dennett 1990). Such qualia are also regarded as essentially private and ineffable. It is impossible for one to observe the qualia associated with anyone else's experience, nor can one describe any such qualia in a way that could make them known to anyone who was not herself already acquainted with them.

Qualia in this traditional sense are special mental properties that are invoked to explain the distinctive what-it-is-likeness of experience. The specific phenomenal character of one's experience, for example of chocolate, is supposed to be a matter of one's acquaintance with private mental properties that are directly present to one in experience. Although there may be regular causal and lawlike links between the external features of the chocolate and the experiential properties it produces, it is those latter subjective properties that constitute the distinctive what-it-is-likeness of one's experience.

The traditional idea of qualia is closely linked with the classic representational theory of perception (see Seager & Bourget, chapter 20). According to that theory, which goes back at least as far as John Locke (1688) in the seventeenth century, we are not directly aware of external objects in perception but only of sensory ideas in the mind which stand for external objects. It is those sensory ideas of which we are directly aware and it is only through them that we are indirectly aware of external objects. On the classic view, qualia are properties of those sensory ideas. In the case of vision, sensory ideas are like pictures present to the mind, and visual qualia, such as the red color of which I am directly aware when I look at a tomato, are properties of those sensory ideas or mental pictures, rather than objective properties of external objects. Thus, Ned Block has talked of qualia in this sense as "mental paint," that is as the mental medium with which such pictures in the mind are painted (Block 1996).

Few current philosophers accept the existence of properties satisfying all the conditions associated with the traditional view. Some, like Dennett (1990, 1991), have taken the fact that nothing satisfies those conditions as a basis for denying the existence of qualia. Others continue to believe in qualia, but take them to be different from the sorts of properties defined by the traditional view (Shoemaker 1990).

These nontraditional models of qualia come in many forms that disavow different aspects of the traditional view. Most drop the requirement that qualia be knowable in an infallible or incorrigible way that involves some mode of direct acquaintance (Churchland 1985). They allow that we can sometimes be mistaken about the phenomenal features of our experience. That, in itself, seems compatible with a continued belief in qualia.

Some nontraditional theories go farther and give up the idea that qualia are essentially objects of awareness at all. They treat qualia as properties of our perceptual states that can occur without our being conscious of them (Nelkin 1989; Rosenthal 1991). The idea of unconscious qualia would be incoherent for those who regard qualia as ways of being conscious, but some notions of qualia consistently allow such an option. For example, some philosophers have interpreted the existence of qualia as requiring nothing more than there be sets of properties that are possessed by our perceptual states, that those properties exhibit similarity relations among themselves, and that those similarities and differences among them give rise to beliefs about objective similarities and differences among perceived external objects (Shoemaker 1975a, 1990).

Qualia of red and yellow and orange need only be properties of our perceptual states that resemble and differ from each other in ways that cause us to perceive a tomato as more like a tangerine in color than like a banana. On such a view we need not be consciously aware of those inner resemblance relations. It is enough that they make us perceptually aware of external similarities and differences. While one's attention is focused elsewhere, one might stop for a red light and go again on green without any need to be aware of the respective qualia of one's perceptual states that underlie one's visual detection first of the one colored light and then of the other.

Some of those who believe in the possibility of unconscious qualia nonetheless allow that they can also sometimes occur consciously. Some (Rosenthal 1991) have held that though we need not be aware of qualia, we sometimes are, and it is only in the latter sort of case that there is anything that it's like to have such an experience. Qualia can be present in unconscious perceptual states and cause appropriate behavioral responses, as when the preoccupied driver stops at the red light. However, according to those like Rosenthal, there is nothing that "it's like" in the Nagel sense to have such a visual perception. Other believers in unconscious qualia deny that we are ever conscious of such qualities. According to Sydney Shoemaker (1990), qualia cause us to become aware of external objects, and we can introspect our experience in terms of how it represents those objects as being. But we cannot be introspectively aware of the inner qualia themselves that give rise to those externally directed perceptions.

Other contemporary views of qualia depart from the traditional view by giving up the requirement that qualia be intrinsic properties of mental states or objects. Defining the distinction between intrinsic and relational properties is notoriously difficult, but the traditional view of qualia was of properties that a mental state might have quite independently of how it was or was not related to things outside itself. The fact that the mental paint on one's inner picture of a tomato was a particular shade of phenomenal red would seem to be a fact about that picture itself rather than about how it was or was not related to things outside itself. Traditional qualia seem intrinsic in that sense and thus more like the property of being square than like relational properties such as being an aunt or being a memory.

Nonetheless, some recent models of qualia treat them as relational rather than intrinsic properties. This is especially so for those who equate a perceptual state's qualia with its representational content (Harman 1990; Tye 1995; Lycan 1996). Proponents of the so-called representational theory of consciousness argue that a perceptual state's mental properties are solely a matter of how it represents the world as being. (For more discussion, see Seager & Bourget, chapter 20.) If such states have no mental properties other than their representational properties, then two perceptual states that have exactly the same content cannot differ in any mental respect. For the representationalist, a perceptual state's intentional content exhausts its mental nature. To put it in a slogan, there can be no mental difference without a difference in representational content.

Some representationalists take their view to refute the existence of qualia (Dennett 1990, 1991). Indeed, representationalism does appear inconsistent with any view of qualia as intrinsic features that can vary among states that share the same content. The representationalist cannot allow for mental differences independent of differences in content.

However, other representationalists draw a different moral. They do not deny the existence of qualia but only the claim that qualia are intrinsic features of perceptual states (Dretske 1995; Tye 1995, 2000). Representationalists of this latter sort identify qualia with representational contents. They do so on the grounds that qualia are supposed to be properties of mental or perceptual states to which we have introspective access and that account for what it's like to be in such experiential states. They argue that it is a perceptual state's representational content that uniquely satisfies those two conditions.

According to the so-called transparency thesis, all we are ever aware of when we introspect our perceptual states is how they represent the world as being (see Tye, chapter 2). We "look right through them" to the world as they represent it to be; we are never introspectively aware of any feature of the representations themselves. When I introspect my visual experience of a tangerine, it is the orange color of the fruit that I encounter, not any orange hued mental paint (Harman 1990). The contemporary representationalist totally rejects the mental picture metaphor and the idea that we are directly aware of images in the mind. Thus, it is only representational contents that can meet the conditions to qualify as qualia. They, and they alone, are mental properties accessible to introspection, and it is they that account for what it's like to have such an experience. It is, for example, like being in a state that represents there being a bright orange tangerine on the brown table before one.

Given the wide diversity of views about the existence and real properties of qualia, the question of whether the functionalist can explain or accommodate qualia within his theory will very much depend on just which notion of qualia one is asking about. The functionalist may well be able to deal with some and not with others. Qualia, in the full blown traditional sense, may well not fit within the functionalist scheme. Other more contemporary notions of qualia may pose less of a conflict, but even some of them may be difficult for the functionalist to accommodate within her scheme.

Anti-functionalist Arguments

The most influential qualia-based anti-functionalist arguments rely on intuitions about certain imaginary cases or thought experiments, especially those involving so-called "inverted qualia" and "absent qualia" (Block 1980a, 1980b; Chalmers 1996).

In inverted qualia cases, one is asked to imagine a person, call him "Flip," whose functional organization is just like that of normal humans but in whom the specific qualia that play the given roles are just the reverse of those that do so in a typical human, call him "Norm." When Flip and Norm look at a ripe tomato, they both describe it as red, and they are both in the state that respectively in each of them tracks the same objective external reflectance property that ripe tomatoes share with radishes. Yet, according to the thought experiment, the inner quale produced in Flip is in fact that which is produced in Norm by looking at limes or lawns, and vice versa. Given that each of them has always been as they are, the inversion of their respective qualia makes no difference to their behavior nor to their functional organization. Yet intuitively there seems to be an important mental difference between them: they are in the same functional state yet one has an experience of phenomenal red while the other has an experience of phenomenal green. Thus the anti-functionalist concludes that the functionalist story is at best an incomplete account of consciousness, one that fails to explain the nature and identity of particular qualia.

Absent qualia arguments go a step farther by asking one to imagine a person, call him Zip, whose functional organization is again just the same as that found in normal humans, but who has no qualia whatsoever. When Zip looks at a ripe tomato, he too is in a state that tracks the relevant external reflectance property and that causes him to call the tomato "red," to sort it with apples and radishes rather than with limes or bananas, and to exhibit the full range of behaviors we associate with perceiving something as red. Yet the states that play these roles in Zip do so without themselves having any qualia. Nor in the Nagel sense is there anything that it's like for Zip to be in such a perceptual state, despite his sharing every aspect of human functional organization. Zip is in effect a zombie (Chalmers 1996). If such absent qualia cases are really possible and the functionalists' requirements could be fully satisfied by zombies, then it would seem that functionalism fails terribly as an account of conscious mentality (Block 1980b). If the functionalist cannot specify conditions that suffice for being conscious in the crucial what-it-is-like sense, then it would seem that functionalism fails to explain the essential core of consciousness.

Functionalists have replied in two main ways. First, they have attacked the coherence of the imagined cases and denied that they describe real possibilities (Dennett 1991). Second, they have disputed the conclusions drawn from such cases about the supposed inadequacies of functionalism as a theory of mind and consciousness (Shoemaker 1990). Each of these two main lines of reply has taken many different forms depending upon the particular version of functionalism being defended and the specific notion of qualia involved.

The coherence of inverted qualia cases has been challenged both on a priori conceptual grounds and also on the basis of empirical evidence about the structure of our sensory color space. On the conceptual side, doubts have been raised about whether any real sense can be attached to the idea of intersubjective differences between essentially private properties (Wittgenstein 1953). How could there ever be any evidence or criterion for verifying that there was or was not such a difference, since by stipulation, normal and inverted individuals are supposed to be the same in all behavioral and functional respects? And if no verification procedure is even possible, the inverted qualia hypothesis may be in danger of becoming a meaningless pseudo-possibility (Dennett 1991).

Indeed, the very notion of one person's qualia being the same or different than those of another has been called into question. Though the idea of resemblance among private properties may make sense in the intrasubjective case where there is a single observer who can anchor such judgments, it is not obvious that it can be extended to intersubjective cases. What could the truth of any such intersubjective resemblance claim consist in, given that there is no possible procedure for comparison or successful reidentification across minds? Each experiential observer is bound in principle to his private mental domain. Even telepathic mind-reading would not be of help since there would always be a residual issue about fidelity of translation and empathic accuracy. The empath would still directly confront only his own qualia, even if they were caused in some nonstandard way by a link to someone else's qualia (Dennett 1991).

In response, some inverted qualia supporters have offered the example of a step-by-step temporally extended intrasubjective inversion to motivate the intersubjective possibility (Shoemaker 1982). In the relevant case an initially normal human, call him "Shifty," undergoes a partial spectrum inversion of his perceptual color space. Most objects look to him as before but some colors are shifted a bit. Thus he would be quite aware of the change, and we could detect that some of his functional and resemblance relations have shifted from what he says and does. Over time, Shifty undergoes a sequence of such partial interchange, each stage of which is both intrasubjectively and externally discernible. However, after several such shifts he ends in a overall arrangement of his color space that is functionally equivalent to that in which he started – for example, all the resemblance relations he perceives between the colors of objects are just like the normal relations with which he began. Yet the particular qualia associated with Shifty's perceptions of a given object are not those with which he began, but rather those associated with such perceptions in Flip. Thus, Shifty at the end of his transformation will differ not only from the way he was at the start; he will also differ from typical humans in just the way Flip is supposed to differ from Norm. Thus, the case of gradual intrasubjective inversion can give a verifiable sense to the contrast that is supposed to obtain in the intrasubjective case.

Other more empirical arguments against inverted spectrum cases rely on evidence about the structured organization of our subjective color space (Hardin 1986). A genuine inversion case requires that all the functional and behavioral equivalencies be retained across the cases. Thus Flip and Norm must agree in all their resemblance judgments; both must judge that a tomato resembles an orange more in color than it does a banana or a lime. Phenomenal colors have inherent relations among themselves that determine those resemblances. For example, some colors are unary or unique hues (pure reds, greens, yellows, and blues), and others are binaries (purples, oranges and aquas) in which we can discern phenomenal components. The blueness or redness of a particular purple hue is part of its phenomenal nature, and thus, the degree to which it resembles pure red or pure blue is not arbitrary but anchored in that nature.

Thus, the possibility of functionally equivalent qualia inverts depends on whether there is any way to map the hues of our subjective color space onto each other that preserves all the resemblance and functional relations among them. There is good evidence to believe that no such mapping is possible in part because of asymmetries in the structure of our color space. Any shift, no matter how local or global, would alter at least some resemblance or functional relations, or so at least it has been claimed (Hardin 1986). If that is so then, as a matter of empirical fact, there can be no cases in which qualia are inverted but all functional relations are retained.

In reply, inverted qualia supporters have conceded that it may in fact be impossible to invert our particular color space without functional consequences (Shoemaker 1990). However, they have claimed that all their argument requires is that there be other possible quality spaces, perhaps ones that are more symmetric, that would allow for such resemblance-preserving inversions. Or alternatively, we can imagine nonhuman creatures, whose qualia are very unlike any we experience, call them "alien qualia," but whose quality space exactly mirrors the resemblance relations in our subjective color space, that is, it has exactly parallel asymmetries. Thus, we and the aliens would be alike in our functional organizations but would still differ in our qualia.

Qualia inversions may thus seem possible for those who regard qualia as intrinsic properties of perceptual states. However, those who equate qualia with representational contents will deny the absent qualia possibility (Harman 1990; Dretske 1995). On such a view, a state's qualitative character or what-it-is-likeness consists in how it represents the world as being. Most representationalists also hold that a state's content depends upon its functional relations to items in the world, for example, on what objective properties it reliably tracks. Thus, if all those relations were preserved, its content would remain unchanged, and so too would its qualitative feel. Thus, given a relational representational view of qualia, functionally identical qualia inversions are impossible.

However, even if the functionalist concedes that inverted qualia cases are possible, it may have few negative consequences for his theory. It all depends on how much the functionalist must be able to explain to count his theory a success. If absent qualia are possible, then the functionalist may not be able to specify conditions that uniquely identify or pick out a specific quale. At most, he may be able to identify an equivalent class of qualia. But if his conditions could be satisfied only by creatures or systems with some qualia, indeed only with sets of qualia exhibiting the required resemblance relations, then that might be enough to count as having explicated phenomenal consciousness and what-it-is-likeness (Shoemaker 1990; Van Gulick 1993). He might leave the identification of particular qualia to the neurophysiologist, as long his functional conditions guarantee that some specific qualia or other must be present.

Thus, the possible absent qualia cases pose a much greater threat to the functionalist. Unsurprisingly, many functionalists have denied their coherence, although they have done so for a variety of reasons. Whether it is possible to specify a set of functional conditions that cannot be realized by non-qualia systems will depend crucially on which notion of qualia and which version of functionalism one is assuming.

If one assumes a computationalist version of functionalism, then the question might be whether there could be robots that shared all our computationally specifiable functional organization but that nonetheless lacked an inner mental life, such that there was nothing that it was like to be them. Alternatively, if one interprets functionalism in terms of causal roles, one might ask whether some system might have a state P that played all the causal roles associated with being in pain but that nonetheless lacked any felt quale of hurtfulness. One might suppose, for instance, that P-states were typically produced by damage or threats of damage to the system, that they in turn caused withdrawal and avoidance behavior, that P-states functioned as negative reenforcers inhibiting the future repetition of behaviors that had lead to past P-states, that P-states produced active desires or motivations to stop being in a state which typically jumped to the top of the system's preference hierarchy, that P-states interfered with the system's ability to focus on other current processes, and that P-states gave rise to memories of having been in a P-state. The absent qualia intuition is that the states of some system might satisfy all those conditions as well as any other causal roles we might add to it and yet not have any qualia in the basic what-it-is-like sense. It might in effect be a pain zombie.

However, that intuition may be challenged, especially by those who take an expansive view of the concepts one can invoke in specifying the required causal roles. For example, pains typically give rise to a belief or awareness that one is in pain, and it is not clear that any state could count as a belief with that content unless it was in fact of a type reliably caused by pain states. Most functionalists hold that the content of a representational state, such as a belief, is at least partly determined by the real features or properties of the world that it tracks or with which it co-varies. If so, it might then not be possible to have beliefs with the content that one is in pain unless those beliefs were in fact typically caused by one's own pain states, which of course could not be the case in an absent qualia system that lacked any real pains (Shoemaker 1975a, 1982). Thus, if the functionalist is allowed to include a tendency to cause beliefs about pain as part of the causal role associated with pain, it would seem that non-qualia systems could not satisfy those conditions.

Anti-functionalist critics might plausibly attack such a move as unfairly circular since it appeals to beliefs that are qualitative in the sense that they depend on qualitative states for their identity. Whether the functionalist would be cheating by appealing to such beliefs will in the end depend upon what resources he is allowed to invoke in specifying causal roles within his theory. However, as noted above, there will likely be a tradeoff between sufficiency and explanatory power. The more the functionalist relies on quasi-qualitative notions in specifying the requisite causal roles, the better her chance of ruling out non-qualia realizations, but also the less her prospects for explaining qualia in non-qualitative terms (Chalmers 1996).

A similar tradeoff arises for those functionalists who aim to explain qualia in terms of their tendency to produce perceptual based beliefs about objective similarities (Rosenthal 1991). Qualia, so construed, are properties of our perceptual states that exhibit a structure of similarity relations among themselves, and in virtue of those similarities produce beliefs about corresponding objective similarities among the objects at which those perceptual states are directed. As noted above, such models are problematic insofar as they may allow for unconscious qualia, an idea that many philosophers resist.

Moreover, they involve a tension between sufficiency and circularity that turns on how the relevant notion of similarity is defined. If one requires that the internal states be *qualitatively* or *phenomenally* similar it may be possible to exclude non-qualia realizations (Shoemaker 1975b). If one did not include such a restriction and interpreted "similarity" more loosely, absent qualia cases would seem to be possible. For example, a computational functionalist might have to allow for robots whose perceptual states generated complex numeric codes for light reflectances and which then compared those codes according to some algorithmically specified similarity measure. The robots might then in turn generate coded representations of external similarities based on those results. Such robots would seem to meet the conditions for having qualia in the relevant functionally defined sense, despite the fact that intuitively it does not seem there would be anything it would be like to be such a robot. Alternatively, if one requires that the relevant internal properties exhibit *qualitative* or *phenomenal similarities*, one could rule out such robots, but only at the price of building qualia-related concepts into one's functional definition from the outset, and thus not fully discharging one's explanatory burden.

The examples of qualitative beliefs and qualitative similarity illustrate a general dilemma that confronts the functionalist concerning which concepts he can use in specifying functional roles. Regardless of whether those functions are thought of computationally, causally, or teleologically, there is the further issue of the degree to which qualitative or phenomenal concepts can be implicitly assumed in specifying the relevant relations and interactions. To the extent that they are not relied on, absent qualia realizations are hard to exclude, but to the degree they are assumed, circularity looms as a danger.

However, the causal status of qualia might give the functionalist a means of attacking absent qualia intuitions as relying on a suspect form of epiphenomenalism, that is, on a view of qualia as not really causal at all. If, as the absent qualia proponent claims, there are possible cases of beings who are just like us in every functional respect but who lack any qualia, it would seem to follow that the qualia that are present in us make no causal differences to the states that have them. The corresponding states in Zip play exactly the same roles as those states do in Norm, and thus share all the same relevant causal powers despite the fact that they lack any qualia (Shoemaker 1975a, Kim 2005).

Thus, the absent qualia hypothesis appears to rely on an implicit assumption that qualia make no difference to a state's causal role and that they are thus epiphenomena, that is mere effects without themselves being causes. Many would find the thesis that qualia are epiphenomenal quite implausible. Could it really be that the cry one utters when one stubs a toe is not due to the hurtful quale of the pain one feels, or more implausibly, that one's answering "red" when asked the color of the tomato in front of one is not due to the quale of one's visual experience? Insofar as absent qualia cases entail such epiphenomenal status for qualia, one might well deny their very possibility.

However, some defenders of absent qualia have denied that entailment. They have argued that in absent qualia cases, some other non-qualia properties, call them "ersatz qualia," would play the causal roles normally played by qualia without themselves being qualia (Block 1980b). So, absent qualia cases do not entail that qualia are epiphenomenal, but only that qualia do not play any unique causal roles that could not be duplicated by non-qualia.

Once again, the issue of how to specify roles arises. Should we say that ersatz red qualia and genuine red qualia play the *same role* but just do so *in different ways*, that is, that they are alternative realizers of one and the same role? Or should we say that the roles they play differ in ways that matter to the functional classification of mental kinds? For example, being in a state with the property of being ersatz red will supposedly cause one to say and believe that one is seeing something red, just as being in a state with a genuine red quale would do. But would the difference in *how* they caused one to say that, or believe that, be a mentally significant difference? The critic of absent qualia would argue that the causal difference would indeed make a mental difference. How could a state without any real qualia affect one's beliefs about one's perceptual experience in the same intimate way that one's genuinely qualitative perceptions do (Van Gulick 1993)? Even if Zip says he is seeing red, the belief he expresses cannot have been produced by the same evidential link to his perceptual states because those states have no red qualia of the sort his beliefs supposedly refer to. Defenders of absent qualia, on the other hand, will dismiss any such differences as insignificant variations in how the same role is realized in Zip and Norm.

Thus, whether or not one believes absent qualia cases are possible is likely to depend on how one specifies functional roles, and whether or not the functionalist can do so in a way that is noncircular but identifies roles that could be filled only by states with genuine qualia. One might argue that no current version of functionalism has as yet offered a detailed specific account of any such roles, and that may or may not be true as a claim about the present status of functionalist theorizing. However, if the anti-functionalist aims to use absent qualia intuitions to prove the stronger thesis that the functionalist *cannot* succeed, then the critic must shoulder a much heavier and more doubtful burden, since it is difficult to say in advance what roles might be captured by future functionalist models. To simply insist that whatever they may be, they will always be open to absent qualia realizations, would seem to beg the question against the functionalist program.

Though inverted and absent qualia arguments have been the most prominent qualia-based challenges to functionalism, others have also been raised of which only a few can be considered here. Two in particular deserve mention: the bizarre realizations objection and the intrinsic property objection.

The bizarre realizations objection has been raised most often against computational versions of functionalism. Given the highly abstract nature of the roles specified in such models, it has been argued that they could be instantiated by systems so bizarre that it would be wildly implausible to suppose that any qualia or what-it-is-likeness could be involved. For example, one could build a system satisfying all the required computational relations out of stones and beer cans with stones being moved algorithmically in and out of the cans (Searle 1992). Or, perhaps even more bizarrely, one might enlist the entire population of China, connected by radio links, to realize all the required formal operations of such a computational model (Block 1980a). The intuition is that no such bizarre system could literally have qualia or consciousness in the what-it-is-like sense.

Computational functionalists have replied either by denying that any such strange components could satisfy the required computational relations, especially if real time constraints were taken into account (Dennett 1991), or by biting the bullet and claiming that if such bizarre realizations were in fact possible they would indeed be conscious in the qualitative sense (Churchland 1985). Other functionalists have taken such examples to demonstrate only the weakness of computational functionalism, not the failure of functionalism in general. Some teleological functionalists, for example, have argued that their theory would not be open to challenge by any such bizarre cases, since whatever causal roles states might play within them would not be grounded in any teleological purpose (Lycan 1987). Only in natural systems akin to biological systems would there be any natural facts that could make it the case that states really had purposes and played their roles in fulfillment of those purposes.

The intrinsic property objection to functionalism might be raised by anyone who accepts the common, though as noted above not universal, view of qualia as intrinsic properties of internal mental states or objects. Given such a view of qualia, there would seem to be a straightforward conflict with functionalism. The functionalist defines mental kinds in terms of the roles they play within a systematic network of interrelated states and processes. Thus, functional kinds would seem to be paradigmatically relational kinds. If so, how could any such mental kinds or properties be identical with qualia, which are supposed to be intrinsic properties of mental states? What is intrinsic is by definition nonrelational, and so any functionalist account of intrinsic qualia would seem to involve a contradiction (Kim 2005).

Two lines of response might be offered. First the functionalist could give up the requirement that qualia be intrinsic properties. Indeed those functionalists who hold a representationalist view of qualia do just that (Tye 1995). According to the representationalist, qualia, insofar as they are real, are identical with the contents of our perceptual states (see

Seager & Bourget, chapter 20). It is only to such contents that we have introspective access, and it is they that determine what is it like to be in such a state. However, since most representationalists regard a state's content to be determined largely, if not wholly, by the causal and informational links it bears to items in the world, it follows that a state's content is one of its relational properties and not an intrinsic property. Thus, for those who interpret qualia in terms of representational content, there need be no intrinsic–extrinsic conflict between qualia and functionalism.

A second line of reply might be to rethink the intrinsic–extrinsic distinction in terms of how it applies to complex, many leveled systems. The aim would be to find a way in which items or states with intrinsic properties might result from, or be realized by, underlying relational networks or structures. If so, the functionalist might be able to retain a belief in qualia as real intrinsic properties of states at one level of organization that were underlain or realized by functionally characterized networks of items at a lower level. The computer-based idea that objects might have intrinsic properties in a virtual reality, as the result of relational links and operations in an underlying base that supports that virtual reality, might offer a possible model or analogy for how the intrinsic–extrinsic distinction might be reapplied to complex systems. There are at present no detailed proposals for doing so, but it remains a possible option for replying to the intrinsic property objection.

Debate continues both about the nature and reality of qualia and about the ability of various versions of functionalism to accommodate whatever real features qualia may have.

See also 20 Representationalism about consciousness; 21 Higher-order theories of consciousness; 24 Daniel Dennett on the nature of consciousness; 29 Anti-materialist arguments and influential replies; 31 The knowledge argument; 34 Type materialism for phenomenal consciousness; 35 Sensory and perceptual consciousness; 37 Consciousness and intentionality.

Further Readings

Block, N. (1980a) Troubles with functionalism. In N. Block (ed.), *Readings in the Philosophy of Psychology*, vol. 1, 268–305. Cambridge, MA: Harvard University Press.

Dennett, D. C. (1990) Quining qualia. In W. Lycan (ed.), *Mind and Cognition*, 519–48. Oxford: Blackwell.

Shoemaker, S. (1975a) Functionalism and qualia. *Philosophical Studies* 27, 291–315.

Tye, M. (2002) Qualia. In *Stanford Encyclopedia of Philosophy*, http://plato.stanford.edu

Van Gulick, R. (2003) Consciousness. In *Stanford Encyclopedia of Philosophy*, http://plato.stanford.edu

References

Block, N. (1980a) Troubles with functionalism. In N. Block (ed.), *Readings in the Philosophy of Psychology*, vol. 1, 268–305. Cambridge, MA: Harvard University Press.

Block, N. (1980b) Are absent qualia impossible? *Philosophical Review* 89, 2, 257–74.

Block, N. (1996) Mental paint and mental latex. In E. Villanueva (ed.), *Perception*. Atascadero, CA: Ridgeview.

Chalmers, D. (1996) *The Conscious Mind*. Oxford: Oxford University Press.

Churchland, P. M. (1985) Reduction, qualia, and direct introspection of brain states. *Journal of Philosophy* 82, 8–28.

Dennett, D. (1978) *Brainstorms*. Cambridge, MA: Bradford Books/MIT Press.

Dennett, D. C. (1990) Quining qualia. In W. Lycan (ed.), *Mind and Cognition*, 519–48. Oxford: Blackwell.

Dennett, D. C. (1991) *Consciousness Explained*. Boston, MA: Little, Brown and Company.

Dretske, F. (1995) *Naturalizing the Mind*. Cambridge, MA: MIT Press/Bradford Books.

Flanagan, O. (1992) *Consciousness Reconsidered*. Cambridge, MA: MIT Press.

Hardin, C. (1986) *Color for Philosophers*. Indianapolis: Hackett.

Harman, G. (1990) The intrinsic quality of experience. In J. Tomberlin (ed.), *Philosophical Perspectives*, vol. 4, 31–52. Atascadero, CA: Ridgeview Publishing.

Hill, C. (1991) *Sensations:A Defense of Type Materialism*. Cambridge: Cambridge University Press.

Kim, Jaegwon (2005) *Physicalism or Something Near Enough*. Princeton, NJ: Princeton University Press.

Levine, J. (1993) On leaving out what it's like. In M. Davies and G. Humphreys (eds.), *Consciousness: Psychological and Philosophical Essays*. Oxford: Blackwell.

Levine, J. (2001) *Purple Haze: The Puzzle of Conscious Experience*. Cambridge, MA: MIT Press.

Lewis, D. (1972) Psychophysical and theoretical identifications. *Australasian Journal of Philosophy* 50, 249–58.

Locke, J. (1688) *An Essay on Human Understanding*.

Lycan, W. (1987) *Consciousness*. Cambridge, MA: MIT Press.

Lycan, W. (1996) *Consciousness and Experience*. Cambridge, MA: MIT Press.

Nagel, T. (1974) What is it like to be a bat? *Philosophical Review* 83, 435–56.

Nelkin, N. 1989. Unconscious sensations. *Philosophical Psychology* 2, 129–41.

Putnam, H. (1960) Minds and machines. In S. Hook (ed.), *Dimensions of Mind*. New York: NYU Press.

Rosenthal, D. (1991) The independence of consciousness and sensory quality. In E. Villanueva (ed.), *Consciousness*, 15–36. Atascadero, CA: Ridgeview.

Searle, J. R. (1992) *The Rediscovery of the Mind*. Cambridge, MA: MIT Press.

Shoemaker, S. (1975a) Functionalism and qualia. *Philosophical Studies* 27, 291–15.

Shoemaker, S. (1975b) Phenomenal similarity. *Critica* 7: 30, 3–24.

Shoemaker, S. (1981) Absent qualia are impossible. *Philosophical Review* 90, 581–99.

Shoemaker, S. (1982) The inverted spectrum. *Journal of Philosophy* 79, 357–81.

Shoemaker, S. (1990) Qualities and qualia: what's in the mind. *Philosophy and Phenomenological Research* 50: Supplement, 109–31.

Shoemaker, S. (1998) Two cheers for representationalism. *Philosophy and Phenomenological Research* 58: 3, 671–8.

Tye, M. (1995) *Ten Problems of Consciousness*. Cambridge, MA: MIT Press.

Tye, M. (2000) *Consciousness, Color, and Content*. Cambridge, MA: MIT Press.

Van Gulick, R. (1980) Functionalism, information and content. *Nature and System* 2, 139–62.

Van Gulick, R. (1993) Understanding the phenomenal mind: are we all just armadillos? In M. Davies and G. Humphreys (eds.), *Consciousness: Psychological and Philosophical Essays,* 137–54. Oxford: Blackwell.

Wittgenstein, L. (1953) *Philosophical Investigation*. New York: Macmillan.

31

The Knowledge Argument

TORIN ALTER

Introduction

The knowledge argument aims to refute physicalism, the doctrine that the world is entirely physical. Physicalism (also known as materialism) is widely accepted in contemporary philosophy. But some doubt that phenomenal consciousness – experience, the subjective aspect of the mind – is physical. The knowledge argument articulates one of the main forms this doubt has taken.

Frank Jackson (1982, 1986) gave the argument its classic statement. He formulates the argument in terms of his famous case of Mary, the super-scientist. Her story takes place in the future, when all physical facts have been discovered. These include "everything in completed physics, chemistry, and neurophysiology, and all there is to know about the causal and relational facts consequent upon all this, including of course functional roles" (Jackson 1982, p. 51). She learns all this by watching lectures on a monochromatic television monitor. But she spends her life in a black-and-white room and has no color experiences. Then she leaves the room and sees colors for the first time. Based on this case, Jackson argues roughly as follows. If physicalism were true, then Mary would know everything about human color vision before leaving the room. But it would seem that she learns something new when she leaves. She learns what it's like to see colors, that is she learns about qualia, the properties that characterize what it's like. Her new *phenomenal knowledge* includes knowledge of truths. Therefore, physicalism is false.

In the late 1990s, Jackson changed his mind: he now defends physicalism and rejects the knowledge argument. But others defend the argument, and even those who reject it often disagree about where it goes awry. The knowledge argument has inspired a sizable literature, which contains insights about consciousness, knowledge, the limits of third-person science, and the nature of the physical. It is also discussed in non-philosophical works, including a book by E. O. Wilson (*Consilience*), a work of fiction by David Lodge (*Thinks . . .*), and a UK television series (*Brainspotting*). Here we will discuss the argument's structure, compare Jackson's version with others, compare the knowledge argument with other anti-physicalist arguments, and summarize the main lines of response.

The Knowledge Intuition and the Inference to Physicalism's Falsity

The knowledge argument has two parts. One says that physical knowledge is not sufficient for phenomenal knowledge. Call this *the knowledge intuition* (Stoljar & Nagasawa 2004). The other says that the knowledge intuition entails the falsity of physicalism.

Thus described, the knowledge argument is not new with Jackson. Locke and other eighteenth-century British empiricists discussed the knowledge intuition. C. D. Broad gave a version of the knowledge argument in 1925. And other versions appear in more recent writings, such as Thomas Nagel's 1974 "What is it like to be a bat?". What is distinctive about Jackson's contribution?

Daniel Stoljar and Yujin Nagasawa (2004) answer this question in their introduction to a volume of essays on the knowledge argument. As they say, Jackson makes at least two distinctive contributions: his Mary example illustrates the knowledge intuition better than previous attempts; and he provides distinctive reasons for inferring physicalism's falsity from the intuition. Let us take these points in order.

The Mary case divides the knowledge intuition into three claims:

1   *The complete-knowledge claim*: before leaving the room, Mary knows everything physical.
2   *The learning claim*: upon leaving, she learns something.
3   *The non-deducibility claim*: if 1 and 2 are true, then what Mary learns when she leaves the room cannot be *a priori* deduced (deduced by reason alone, without empirical investigation) from the complete physical truth.

Physicalists may deny the knowledge intuition. But the Mary case shows that doing so requires rejecting 1, 2, or 3.

The cases discussed by Broad, Nagel, and others do not deliver this result. Consider, for example, Broad's mathematical archangel, a logically omniscient creature who knows all the physical truths about various chemical compounds. Broad calls these truths "mechanistic" instead of "physical," but the point is the same. On his view, the archangel would know all such truths but still lack phenomenal knowledge concerning, for example, "the peculiar smell of ammonia." And Broad infers that physicalism (mechanism) is false. But what if the physicalist denies that the archangel would lack the relevant phenomenal knowledge? We appear to be at an impasse. By contrast, if the physicalist claims that, while in the room, Mary knows what it's like to see colors, he must explain why she seems to acquire this knowledge when she leaves. The Mary case breaks the deadlock in favor of the knowledge intuition. Other illustrations of the intuition that precede Jackson's have further drawbacks. For example, Nagel's claim that humans cannot imagine what it's like to be a bat raises distracting issues about the limits of human imagination, about which physicalism carries no obvious commitments. Mary's fame is just.

The second of Jackson's distinctive contributions concerns his inference from the knowledge intuition to physicalism's falsity. This inference assumes that if physicalism is true then the complete truth about human color vision is *a priori* deducible from the complete physical truth. Why accept this assumption? Consider what Stoljar and Nagasawa call *the psychophysical conditional*: if P then Q, where P is the complete physical truth and Q is the complete psychological truth. As Jackson conceives of physicalism, this theory entails that the psychophysical conditional is *a priori*, in which case all truths about color vision would be deducible from P. Why can't physicalists instead characterize their thesis as a (Kripkean) *a posteriori* necessity, akin to "water is H_2O"? On this characterization, the psychophysical conditional is metaphysically necessary but not *a priori*. (A *metaphysically* necessary truth is a truth that is necessary in the strictest possible sense. Metaphysically necessary truths contrast with truths that owe their necessity to contingent laws of nature, such as the truth that pigs cannot fly like birds.)

In later work, Jackson defends his conception of physicalism in detail. His argument is complex, but the basic idea is simple enough. In his 1995 "Postscript," he reasons as follows. Consider the argument, "H_2O covers most of the planet; therefore, water covers most of the planet." The premise necessitates, but does not a *priori* entail, the conclusion. But suppose we add the premise, "H_2O plays the water role." In that case, the premises do *a priori* entail the conclusion. Moral: "a *rich enough* story about the H_2O way things are does enable the *a priori* deduction of the water way things are" (Jackson 1995, p. 413). Likewise, physicalism entails that "knowing a rich enough story about the physical nature of our world is tantamount to knowing the psychological story about our world" (Jackson 1995, p. 414). But if physicalism is true, then P should provide just that: a rich enough story. Thus, physicalism entails the apriority of the psychophysical conditional after all. Jackson's argument is controversial. But in developing it, he fills an important lacuna in the knowledge argument and thereby improves on earlier versions. Others too have attempted to fill this lacuna. David Chalmers (1996, 2004) has given sophisticated arguments to this end, which are partly inspired by Jackson's argument.

Related Arguments

The knowledge argument is closely related to other anti-physicalist arguments. One of these is the conceivability argument. The conceivability argument descends from Descartes's main argument for mind–body substance dualism. Descartes argues that, since he can clearly and distinctly conceive of his mind without his body and his body without his mind, they can exist without each other and are therefore distinct substances.

Contemporary versions of the conceivability argument usually rely on thought experiments concerning qualia. One such thought experiment involves *inverted qualia*. It seems conceivable that there could be an individual exactly like me, except he and I are red/green inverted. We are physically and functionally identical, but the color experiences he has when viewing a ripe tomato (in normal light, without special contact lenses, etc.) resemble the color experiences I have when viewing a ripe zucchini, and vice versa. Such a person would be my inverted twin. Likewise, it seems conceivable that there could be a world exactly like ours in all physical and functional respects but without phenomenal consciousness. Philosophers call creatures that lack consciousness but are physically and functionally identical to ordinary human beings *zombies*. If it is conceivable that there be creatures such as my inverted twin or my zombie twin then, the conceivability argument runs, this supports the metaphysical possibility of such creatures. Most agree that if such creatures are metaphysically possible, then phenomenal consciousness is neither physical nor functional.

A third anti-physicalist argument is the explanatory argument. This argument begins with the premise that physicalist accounts of consciousness explain only structure (such as spatiotemporal structure) and function (such as causal role). Then it is argued that explaining structure and function does not suffice to explain consciousness, and so physicalist accounts are explanatorily inadequate – and this indicates that physicalism is false.

The knowledge argument, the conceivability argument, and the explanatory argument can be seen as instances of a general argument consisting of two main steps (Chalmers 1996). The first step is to establish an *epistemic gap* between the physical and phenomenal domains. In the case of the knowledge argument, the gap is often put in terms of *a priori* deducibility: there are phenomenal truths that cannot be *a priori* deduced from physical truths. In the case of the conceivability argument, the gap is put in terms of conceivability: it is conceivable that there be inverted qualia or zombies. And in the case of the explanatory argument, the point is put in terms of an explanatory gap. After establishing an epistemic gap, these arguments infer a corresponding *metaphysical gap*: a gap in the world, not just in our epistemic relation to it. The knowledge argument infers a difference in type of fact. The conceivability argument infers the metaphysical possibility of inverted qualia or zombies. And the explanatory argument infers that there are phenomena that are not metaphysically necessitated by the physical. All three results appear to conflict with physicalism. There are important differences among the arguments, and it is not obvious that they stand or fall together. Nevertheless, it is worth noting that they follow a single abstract pattern.

More Physicalist Responses

Most physicalist responses to the knowledge argument fall into three categories: those that reject the inference to physicalism's falsity and thus deny the metaphysical gap; those that reject the knowledge intuition and thus deny the epistemic gap; and those that derive an absurdity from Jackson's reasoning.

We have already noted one way of rejecting the inference from the knowledge intuition to physicalism's falsity: one could defend a version of physicalism on which the psychophysical conditional is necessary but not *a priori*. There are other ways of rejecting the inference. One is to reject the assumption that phenomenal knowledge is propositional knowledge – knowledge of truths or information. That is, one could argue that the type of knowledge Mary gains when she leaves the room is non-propositional. The best known version of this view is based on the ability hypothesis, the claim that to know what it's like is to possess certain abilities, such as the ability to imagine, recognize, and remember experiences (Lewis 1988). On this view, Mary's knowledge gain consists in her acquiring abilities rather than learning truths. As the view is sometimes put, she gains know-how, not knowledge-that. There are other versions, including the view that upon leaving the room Mary acquires only non-propositional acquaintance knowledge (Conee 1994). On this version, her learning consists, not in acquiring information or abilities, but in becoming directly acquainted with the phenomenal character of color experiences, in the way that one can become acquainted with a city by visiting it.

These views allow the physicalist to accept the knowledge intuition without facing objections which Jackson, Chalmers, and others bring against *a posteriori* physicalism. But other problems arise. Regarding the ability hypothesis, some doubt that Mary's learning could consist only in acquiring abilities. Her new knowledge appears to have characteristic marks of propositional knowledge, such as content that can be embedded in conditionals such as "if seeing red is like this, then it is not like that" (Loar 1990/97).

The idea that Mary acquires only acquaintance knowledge has similar difficulties, for it is not clear that all she acquires is acquaintance knowledge or that the requisite distinction between acquaintance knowledge and propositional knowledge is tenable. Also, there is a danger of trading on an ambiguity: sometimes "acquaintance" refers to knowledge, sometimes to experience. On the former, epistemic interpretation, it is unclear that Mary's new acquaintance knowledge includes no factual component. And on the latter, experiential interpretation, the acquaintance hypothesis trivializes the learning claim: no one denies that when Mary leaves the room she has new experiences.

Another way to reject the inference to physicalism's falsity is to argue that Mary's learning consists in acquiring new ways to represent facts she knew before leaving the room (Horgan 1984; McMullen 1985; Loar 1990/97; Tye 2000). This view is often combined with an appeal to *a posteriori* necessity (see "The Knowledge Intuition" section above). But it need not be so: one could argue that while the psychophysical conditional is *a priori* knowable by those who possess the relevant phenomenal concepts, Mary lacks those concepts before leaving the room. The main challenge for this view concerns the status of her new concepts. It is not enough to say that she gains some new concept or other; her conceptual gain must explain her gain in knowledge. The concern is that any concepts adequate to the task – such as the concept *having an experience with phenomenal feel f* – might incorporate a nonphysical component (Chalmers 2006).

Philosophers have also devised ways to reject the knowledge intuition. Some believe that intuitions based on hypothetical cases should be given little or no weight. Also, specific strategies for rejecting the knowledge intuition have been developed. One is to reject the learning claim, arguing that on reflection Mary does not learn anything when she leaves the room. Some defend this position by arguing that the knowledge intuition derives from underestimating the power of complete physical knowledge. Suppose we try to fool Mary by greeting her when she leaves the room with a blue banana (Dennett 1991). Would she be fooled into thinking that seeing yellow is what we would describe as seeing blue? Not necessarily. She could use a brain scanner (perhaps a descendent of a PET device) to examine her own brain processes. She would notice that her brain processes correspond to people having blue experiences, and thereby evade our trap. Maybe our intuition that she learns something fails to take this sort of consideration into account. But many doubt that the intuition derives from any such error.

Another way to reject the knowledge intuition is to challenge the complete-knowledge claim, arguing that not all physical facts about seeing colors can be learned by watching black-and-white lectures. On this view, a fact might be physical but not discursively learnable. How could this be?

Some (e.g., Horgan 1984) use "physical" broadly, so that the physical truths include high-level truths necessitated by the microphysical truths. These physicalists argue that phenomenal truths are themselves high-level physical truths, and that it is question-begging to assume that Mary knows all the physical truths simply because she watches lectures on chemistry, physics, etc. Chalmers (2004) suggests a natural response to this move: use "physical" narrowly, so that the physical truths include only the microphysical truths (or those plus the truths in chemistry or some other specified domains). It is hard to deny that such truths would be accessible to the pre-release Mary. Of course, this entails that high-level biological truths, for example, will count as nonphysical, and thus the existence of nonphysical truths would not defeat physicalism: those truths would still be metaphysically necessitated by the narrowly physical truths. But if Jackson's reasoning is sound, then there are phenomenal truths that are not metaphysically necessitated by the narrowly physical truths, and that result would defeat physicalism.

On another version of the view that the complete-knowledge claim is false, Mary's science lectures allow her to deduce the truths involving structural-dynamical properties of physical phenomena, but not their intrinsic properties. The knowledge argument does not appear to refute this view. If this view is a version of physicalism, then there is one version of physicalism that the knowledge argument appears to leave unchallenged. It is unclear that this is a significant deficiency. Arguably, on the view in question, consciousness (or protoconsciousness) is a fundamental feature of the Universe – or at least no less fundamental than the properties describable in the language of microphysics, chemistry, etc. That sounds like the sort of view the knowledge argument should be used to establish, not refute. (It is a form of neutral monism; see next section.)

Non-physicalist Responses

If we accept the knowledge argument, then how should we understand the relationship between consciousness and the physical world? Jackson (1982) defends epiphenomenalism, on which phenomenal properties are caused by but do not cause physical phenomena. But epiphenomenalism is only one of several nonphysicalist views that the knowledge argument leaves open. Others include interactionist dualism, parallelism, and idealism. These views agree that consciousness is not reducible to the physical, but disagree over how the two interact causally. On interactionist dualism, consciousness affects the physical world and vice versa. On parallelism, physical events and events of consciousness run in parallel but do not affect each other. On idealism, there are only conscious phenomena. The knowledge argument also leaves open neutral monism, the view that phenomenal properties (or protophenomenal properties) are the categorical, intrinsic bases of physical properties, which are at bottom dispositional and relational. This view might or might not be considered a version of physicalism, depending on whether the intrinsic nature of physical properties is considered physical.

All of these views have significant costs and benefits. For example, interactionist dualism is commonsensical but hard to reconcile with the widely held view that the physical world is causally closed, that is, the view that every physical event has a sufficient physical cause. To take another example: epiphenomenalism preserves causal closure but seems to conflict with the widely held naturalistic assumption that consciousness is an integrated part of the natural world. Accepting the knowledge argument forces philosophers to weigh such costs and benefits or develop new, nonphysicalist accounts.

Historically, epiphenomenalism is associated with Huxley, interactionist dualism with Descartes, parallelism with Leibniz, idealism with Berkeley, and neutral monism with Russell. For more recent versions, see Jackson (1982) for epiphenomenalism, Hart (1988) for interactionist dualism, Chalmers (1996, 2004) for neutral monism, and Adams (forthcoming) for idealism (I know of no recent defense of parallelism).

Other Responses

Some claim that Jackson's position is internally inconsistent (Watkins 1989). The argument runs roughly as follows. On the knowledge argument, Mary acquires knowledge when she leaves the room because she has states with new qualia. But this is impossible if, as Jackson (1982) suggests, epiphenomenalism is true. On epiphenomenalism, qualia are causally inefficacious. So, how can qualia produce an increase in knowledge? Thus, Jackson cannot consistently maintain both epiphenomenalism and the learning claim.

However, the sort of epiphenomenalism Jackson defends implies only that phenomenal features have no effects on *physical* phenomena, not that phenomenal features are inefficacious. He might therefore reply that phenomenal knowledge is not a physical phenomenon, and thus qualia may indeed cause Mary to acquire it. Also, he can reasonably reply that the objection assumes a causal theory of knowledge that is not true of phenomenal knowledge.

Despite the availability of such replies, there is a serious problem in the vicinity of the inconsistency objection. We should expect physical or functional explanations of our judgments about qualia. But if the knowledge argument is sound, then qualia would seem to be explanatorily irrelevant to these judgments – including the judgment that qualia cannot be explained in physical or functional terms. This is what Chalmers (1996, ch. 5) calls *the paradox of phenomenal judgment*. It appears to be a real problem, which arises for any nonphysicalist theory of consciousness.

Another important response to the knowledge argument should be noted. The argument seems to assume that "physical" has a clear meaning. But whether this notion can be adequately defined is not obvious. One problem is *Hempel's dilemma*. Arguably, we should not define the physical in terms of current physics, because current physics will be extended and presumably revised in substantial ways. We could define the physical in terms of ideal physics. But who knows what ideal physics will look like? Future physics may invoke novel concepts that we cannot begin to imagine. Thus, how can we judge whether Mary could learn all the physical facts from black-and-white lectures? And how else should we define the physical except by appeal to (current or ideal) physics?

Some take such considerations to show that the debate over whether consciousness is physical is misguided or meaningless (Crane & Mellor 1990). But the difficulty may be surmountable. On one view, ideal physics will not be wholly unrecognizable: like today's physics, it will be concerned entirely with structure and dynamics. And one may be able to argue that any structural/dynamical properties can in principle be imparted by black-and-white lectures.

Summary of Assumptions and Criticisms

As we have seen, the knowledge argument depends on several controversial assumptions. It will be useful to summarize some of these assumptions and criticisms of them. I will include representative sources for the relevant arguments. (For a more comprehensive bibliography, see http://philrsss.anu.edu.au/%7Eyujin/KA.html.)

Assumption 1: *The coherence of the notion of the physical*: physicalism is a substantive doctrine with nontrivial content.

Criticism 1: The notion of the physical is not well defined, and there is no substantive issue of whether physicalism is true (Crane & Mellor 1990). For replies, see Chalmers (1996, 2004).

Assumption 2: *The complete-knowledge claim*: before leaving the room, Mary knows the complete physical truth.

Criticism 2a: Pre-release Mary does not know the complete physical truth, because high-level physical truths cannot in general be *a priori* deduced from low-level physical truths (Horgan 1984, Van Gulick 2004). For replies, see Chalmers (2004).

Criticism 2b: Pre-release Mary does not know all the physical truths, because truths about the intrinsic properties of physical phenomena cannot be discursively learned (Alter 1998). For replies, see Chalmers (1996, 2004).

Assumption 3: *The learning claim*: upon leaving the room, Mary learns something.

Criticism 3a: The learning claim derives from a failure to appreciate the implications of knowing all physical truths (Dennett 1991). For replies, see Chalmers (1996).

Criticism 3b: The learning claim derives from a failure to recognize that phenomenal properties are just representational properties (Jackson 2003). For a reply, see Alter (2006).

Criticism 3c: Mary gains only unjustified beliefs (Beisecker 2000).

Assumption 4: *The propositional-knowledge claim*: the kind of knowledge Mary gains upon leaving the room is propositional or factual, i.e., knowledge of information or truths.

Criticism 4a: Mary gains only abilities (Lewis 1988). For replies, see Jackson (1986), Loar (1990/97), Conee (1994), Alter (1998), and Tye (2000, ch. 1). For counter-replies, see Tye (2000, ch. 1).

Criticism 4b: Mary gains only acquaintance knowledge (Conee 1994). For replies, see Alter (1998), Stoljar & Nagasawa (2004), and Chalmers (2004).

Criticism 4c: Mary gains non-propositional knowledge that does not fit easily into folk categories (Churchland 1985). For a reply, see Jackson (1986).

Assumption 5: *The new-information claim*: the information Mary gains upon leaving the room is genuinely new to her.

Criticism 5: Mary merely comes to know truths she already knew under new, phenomenal representations. This view is sometimes called *the old-fact/new-guise view*. It comes in at least two versions. On one, phenomenal knowledge is assimilated to indexical knowledge: Mary's learning is comparable to the absent-minded US historian's learning that *today* is July 4th, America's Independence Day (McMullen 1985). For replies, see Chalmers (1996, 2004). Another version attaches the old-fact/new-representation view to *a posteriori* physicalism (see criticism 7).

Assumption 6: *The non-deducibility claim*: if Mary learns new phenomenal truths when she leaves the room, then those truths cannot be *a priori* deduced from the complete physical truth.

Criticism 6: Mary cannot deduce certain phenomenal truths from the complete physical truth only because she lacks the relevant concepts, such as the concept of phenomenal redness. Thus, even though Mary cannot deduce Q from P, the psychophysical conditional is *a priori* for those who have the relevant concepts (Tye 2000). For replies, see Chalmers (2004, 2006).

Assumption 7: *The claim that the knowledge intuition entails non-necessitation*: if there are phenomenal truths that cannot be *a priori* deduced from the complete physical truth, then the complete physical truth does not metaphysically necessitate those phenomenal truths.

Criticism 7: Physicalism is an *a posteriori* necessity and is therefore compatible with the claim that the phenomenal truths are not deducible from the complete physical truth (Loar 1990/97). For replies, see Chalmers (1996, 2004).

Assumption 8: *The consistency claim*: the knowledge argument and nonphysicalism are consistent.

Criticism 8: The assumption that Mary gains knowledge is inconsistent with epiphenomenalism (Watkins 1989). For replies, see Nagasawa (n.d.).

The knowledge argument rests on other assumptions. One is that if Mary gains new, nonphysical information, then there are nonphysical properties. Another is that if there are truths that are not metaphysically necessitated by the complete physical truth, then physicalism is false. But criticisms of these assumptions may be terminological variants of the criticisms mentioned above.

William Lycan (2003, p. 384) writes, "Someday there will be no more articles written about the 'Knowledge Argument' . . . That is beyond dispute. What is less certain is, how much sooner that day will come than the heat death of the Universe." At least for now, however, the knowledge argument continues to inspire fruitful reflection on the nature of consciousness and its relation to the natural world.

See also 13 The case of blindsight; 17 The hard problem of consciousness; 29 Anti-materialist arguments and influential replies; 30 Functionalism and qualia; 34 Type materialism for phenomenal consciousness.

Further Readings

Alter, Torin and Walter, Sven (eds.) (2006) *Phenomenal Concepts and Phenomenal Knowledge: New Essays on Consciousness and Physicalism*. New York: Oxford University Press.
Ludlow, Peter, Stoljar, Daniel, and Nagasawa, Yujin (eds.) (2004) *There's Something about Mary: Essays on Phenomenal Consciousness and Frank Jackson's Knowledge Argument*. Cambridge, MA: MIT Press.

References

Adams, Robert (forthcoming) Idealism vindicated. In P. van Inwagen and D. Zimmerman (eds.), *Persons: Human and Divine*. Oxford: Oxford University Press.
Alter, Torin (1998) A limited defense of the knowledge argument. *Philosophical Studies* 90, 35–56.
Alter, Torin (2006) Does representationalism undermine the knowledge argument? In T. Alter and S. Walter (eds.), *Phenomenal Concepts and Phenomenal Knowledge: New Essays on Consciousness and Physicalism*, 65–74. New York: Oxford University Press.
Beisecker, David (2000) There's something about Mary: phenomenal consciousness and its attributions. *Southwest Philosophy Review* 16, 143–52.

Broad, C. D. (1925) *The Mind and Its Place in Nature*. London: Routledge and Kegan Paul.

Chalmers, David J. (1996) *The Conscious Mind: In Search of a Fundamental Theory*. New York: Oxford University Press.

Chalmers, David J. (2004) Phenomenal concepts and the knowledge argument. In P. Ludlow, D. Stoljar, and Y. Nagasawa (eds.), *There's Something about Mary: Essays on Phenomenal Consciousness and Frank Jackson's Knowledge Argument*, 269–98. Cambridge: MIT Press.

Chalmers, David J. (2006) Phenomenal concepts and the explanatory gap. In T. Alter and S. Walter (eds.), *Phenomenal Concepts and Phenomenal Knowledge: New Essays on Consciousness and Physicalism*, 167–94. New York: Oxford University Press.

Churchland, Paul (1985) Reduction, qualia, and the direct introspection of brain states. *Journal of Philosophy* 82, 8–28.

Conee, Earl (1994) Phenomenal knowledge. *Australasian Journal of Philosophy* 72, 136–50.

Crane, Tim and Mellor, Hugh (1990) There is no question of physicalism. *Mind* 99, 185–206.

Dennett, Daniel C. (1991) *Consciousness Explained*, Boston, MA: Little, Brown and Company.

Hart, W. D. (1988) *The Engines of the Soul*. Cambridge: Cambridge University Press.

Horgan, Terence (1984) Jackson on physical information and qualia. *Philosophical Quarterly* 34, 147–52.

Jackson, Frank (1982) Epiphenomenal qualia. *Philosophical Quarterly* 32, 127–36.

Jackson, Frank (1986) What Mary didn't know. *Journal of Philosophy* 83, 291–95.

Jackson, Frank (1995) Postscript. In P. Moser and J. Trout (eds.), *Contemporary Materialism*, 184–9. New York: Routledge.

Jackson, Frank (2003) Mind and illusion. In A. O'Hear (ed.), *Minds and Persons: Royal Institute of Philosophy Supplement* 53, 251–71. Cambridge: Cambridge University Press.

Lewis, David (1988) What experience teaches. *Proceedings of Russellian Society (University of Sydney)*. Reprinted in D. Chalmers (ed.), *The Philosophy of Mind: Classical and Contemporary Readings* (2002), 281–94. New York: Oxford University Press.

Loar, Brian (1990/97) Phenomenal states. Original version in J. Tomberlin (ed.), *Philosophical Perspectives 4: Action Theory and Philosophy of Mind*, 81–108. Atascadero, CA: Ridgeview. Revised version in N. Block, O. Flanagan, and G. Güzeldere (eds.), *The Nature of Consciousness*, 597–616. Cambridge, MA: MIT .

Lycan, William G. (2003) Perspectival representation and the knowledge argument. In Q. Smith and A. Jokic (eds.), *Consciousness: New Philosophical Essays*, 384–95. Oxford: Oxford University Press.

McMullen, Carolyn (1985) "Knowing what it's like" and the essential indexical. *Philosophical Studies* 48, 211–33.

Nagasawa, Yujin. (n.d.) The "most powerful reply" to the knowledge argument. ANU manuscript.

Nagel, Thomas (1974) What is it like to be a bat? *Philosophical Review* 83, 435–50.

Stoljar, Daniel and Nagasawa, Yujin (2004) Introduction to P. Ludlow, D. Stoljar, and Y. Nagasawa (eds.), *There's Something about Mary: Essays on Phenomenal Consciousness and Frank Jackson's Knowledge Argument*, 1–36. Cambridge, MA: MIT Press.

Tye, Michael (2000) *Consciousness, Color, and Content*. Cambridge, MA: MIT Press.

Van Gulick, Robert (2004) So many ways of saying no to Mary. In P. Ludlow, D. Stoljar, and Y. Nagasawa (eds.), *There's Something about Mary: Essays on Phenomenal Consciousness and Frank Jackson's Knowledge Argument*, 365–405. Cambridge, MA: MIT Press.

Watkins, Michael (1989) The knowledge argument against the knowledge argument. *Analysis* 49, 158–60.

32

The Causal Efficacy of Consciousness

JAEGWON KIM

Philosophical concerns about the causal powers of the mental, and specifically about those of consciousness, go back to the ancient Greeks. In Plato's *Phaedo*, there is a well-known exchange between Socrates and Simmias in which Simmias questions, and Socrates defends, the causal efficacy of the soul. If the soul is a mere "harmonia" – that is, a "blending" or "tempering" – of bodily powers and forces, as the tuning of the lyre is to the physical instrument and its workings, how could it exert causal influence on the body, and how could it survive the death and decay of the body (Caston 1997)? It is not clear, however, whether these ancient debates had any influence on the modern philosophy of mind – that is, the philosophy of mind founded by Descartes in the seventeenth century. Contemporary philosophy of mind in the West is essentially continuous with Descartes, and has inherited many of its central problematics from the debates that flourished in his time about the nature and status of the mind. In any case, the problem of mental causation began to loom large with Cartesian interactionist dualism, and since then, it has helped topple more than one doctrine of the mind, Descartes's substance dualism being its first casualty (Watson 1987).

Concerns about the efficacy of consciousness can arise either as part of a broad concern about the efficacy of mentality in general, or as a more specific worry focusing on *conscious* mental states, or the conscious aspects of mental states. It might be that although mental states, including those that are conscious, are causally efficacious, there is a further question of whether the fact that these states are conscious is causally relevant. Thus, consider a conscious thought or belief. Assume it is causally efficacious in generating further thoughts and beliefs and in the production of appropriate bodily behaviors. Even so, its being a *conscious* thought might be causally irrelevant; it might be that what makes a causal difference is only its content. We will discuss in detail why the two issues, the general one concerning the mental, and the more specific issue about consciousness, have come to be distinguished and how they relate to each other. The conceptual distinctions that have lead to the separation of the two issues are relatively new, and the philosophical writings on the issue of causal efficacy of consciousness up to the nineteenth century appear to have addressed the issue in terms of mentality in general, although it is quite clear that consciousness was the focus of attention.

Ever since the Socrates–Simmias debate, the central question about the efficacy of consciousness has always been the same: Is there any reason to think that consciousness has any causal powers at all? Are there convincing arguments to counteract the epiphenomenalist thesis that conscious mental episodes, perhaps along with all other mental events and states, are mere epiphenomena with no powers to affect anything else, whether mental or physical? Aren't the underlying physical/neural processes ultimately doing all the actual pushing and pulling, with no work left for consciousness to do? As these questions indicate, it seems that somehow consciousness has always found itself on the defensive, saddled with a suspect causal status, and under pressure to prove its causal worth again and again.

We will begin with the epiphenomenalist arguments of the nineteenth-century biologist T. H. Huxley.

Huxley's Epiphenomenalism

Huxley was familiar with Descartes's claim that animals are automata whose motions and behaviors are fully explicable mechanically and physiologically, without the intervention of minds – that is, thought or consciousness. Huxley's innovation consists in extending this "automatism" to humans, arguing that mentality and consciousness are no more required to explain human actions and behaviors than for explaining animal behaviors. The experiments and observations that moved Huxley to embrace epiphenomenalism were basically of the following sort: animals for which we have compelling anatomical evidence that they are not conscious can perform activities of the kind that we normally take to require consciousness. He describes frogs whose brain and nervous system are surgically altered (e.g., the anterior part of the brain has been removed) in a way that ensures the absence of conscious perception. But these frogs, Huxley tells us, can perform actions requiring complex coordination such as swimming, leaping to avoid an obstacle, and so on. Since we have every reason to believe that such frogs lack consciousness, Huxley concludes that consciousness cannot be implicated in the production of such behavior as a cause. His overall conclusion is this:

> The consciousness of brutes would appear to be related to the mechanism of their body simply as a collateral product of its working and to be as completely without any power of modifying that working as the steam-whistle which accompanies the work of a locomotive engine is without influence upon its machinery. Their volition, if they have any, is an emotion indicative of physical changes, not a cause of such changes. (Huxley 1874, p. 29)

One might object thus: Granted animals can perform certain complex actions while being unconscious; but this does not mean that when they perform these actions when they are conscious, their consciousness is not part of their cause. There are indications that Huxley's arguments are more complex than they might appear; they are not simply of the form "X can occur when Y is absent; hence, Y is *never* a cause of X." Consider the following statement by Huxley:

> Much ingenious argument has at various times been bestowed upon the question: *How is it possible to imagine that volition, which is a state of consciousness and, as such, has not the slightest community of nature with matter in motion, can act upon the moving matter of which the body is composed, as it is assumed to do in voluntary acts?* But if, as is here suggested, the voluntary acts of brutes . . . are as purely mechanical as the rest of their actions, and are simply accompanied by the state of consciousness called volition, the inquiry, so far as they are concerned, becomes superfluous. *Their volitions do not enter into the chain of causation of their actions at all.* (Huxley 1874, p. 29; emphasis added)

Here Huxley seems to be appealing to what is now called the causal, or explanatory, closure of the physical domain. His reasoning can be roughly fleshed out as follows: "voluntary" actions of animals are mechanical and occur in the physical/material domain, which is causally closed; volitions, however, are conceived as occurrences in the nonphysical mental domain; hence, volitions cannot be implicated in the causal chain leading to animal actions. Understood this way, Huxley's argument is quite general and is apparently independent of examples like the neuroanatomically altered frogs, patients with brain injuries, and the like. We will consider below general arguments of this kind, involving the principle of physical causal closure.

What then of human beings? Huxley describes the case of a French soldier with a serious neurological injury who, in his view, is comparable to the frog with its anterior part of its brain removed in that there is no reason to think the man is conscious. And yet, like the frog, he is able to engage in normal activities like eating, getting dressed and undressed, and going to bed at his usual time – activities that we would normally consider to require consciousness. The conclusion he reaches is unsurprising:

> It is quite true that, to the best of my judgment, the argumentation which applies to brutes holds equally good of men; and, therefore, that all states of consciousness in us, as in them, are immediately caused by molecular changes of the brain-substance. It seems to me that in men, as in brutes, there is no proof that any state of consciousness is the cause of change in the motion of the matter of organism . . . We are conscious automata. (Huxley 1974, p. 30)

We will not further analyze or discuss Huxley's arguments here, but, as we will see, the contemporary considerations that we will take up later echo some of the themes present in Huxley's considerations.

Scientific Considerations: Methodological Epiphenomenalism

One experimental study whose implications for the efficacy of consciousness have been both widely discussed and controversial is a series of experiments performed by Benjamin Libet. In his experiments, Libet found (or so the claim has been made), that the neural event that leads to a voluntary action (e.g., flexing a finger, a wrist) occurs a fraction of a second (roughly 350 milliseconds) *before* the subject becomes consciously aware of deciding to perform the action. Libet and others have claimed that this is an experimental/scientific demonstration of the causal irrelevance/inefficacy of conscious decisions, or acts of will. However, there has been intense controversy about Libet's experimental procedures as well as about the analysis and interpretation of the data obtained. Since this volume includes a chapter that gives a comprehensive survey of Libet's studies and the controversies surrounding their implications (Banks & Pockett, chapter 51), we will not further discuss this issue here. For philosophical discussions of Libet see Dennett (1991, ch. 6), Flanagan (1992, ch. 7), and Mele (2005). See also Velmans (2002) and Wegner (2002).

The causal efficacy of consciousness has an intimate connection with its scientific status, and this is for a simple reason. Suppose conscious events have causal effects in the physical realm. Presumably this could happen only because they have causal effects on the neural processes in the brain (even Descartes located the mind–body interaction in the brain – in the pineal gland). If this is the case, a complete scientific theory of neural phenomena would have to include reference to consciousness as an independent causal agent, for otherwise, there would be neural events, namely those caused by conscious events, that would remain unexplained. If consciousness is thought to lie outside the physical/neural domain, recognizing the causal efficacy of consciousness on neural processes amounts to the admission that the physical/neural domain is not causally, or explanatorily, closed.

Giving up the causal closure of the physical domain is, and should be, recognized as a major move away from the basically physicalist outlook that dominates both philosophy and science. In essence, it amounts to a return to the interactionist dualist framework of Descartes. There are neuroscientists who believe, with some passion, in the causal/explanatory role of consciousness (Marcel 1988); there are others who are highly skeptical about the possibility that consciousness might play a role in neuroscientific theorizing (Bisiach 1988). Suppose that a neuroscientist encounters a neural phenomenon for which she is not able to find an explanation in neural/physical terms, and that she has pretty much exhausted all the possibilities. Would she then begin looking for a nonphysical causal agent, like an act of an immaterial mind, to formulate an explanation? How would she go about executing such a project in concrete terms, and how would she test her hypothesis? What would make one such nonphysical explanation better than another? Isn't the very idea of looking for a nonphysical causal agent or force incoherent?

Sometimes it is pointed out that the supposed objective unobservability of consciousness is not something to worry about, since physics itself posits all sorts of unobservable entities and properties, like magnetic fields, electrons, quarks, charm, spin, and the rest (Marcel 1988). This analogy is a bit too quick and facile. For one thing, theoretical posits of physics do not exhibit the first-person/third-person epistemic asymmetry that characterizes consciousness. It is not the case that consciousness is epistemically inaccessible; it seems accessible *par excellence* to the subject experiencing it (or so it is standardly assumed). We grant the subject special epistemic authority in regard to her own current conscious experience; she need not be thought to be infallible, but what she says goes, at least for the most part. Nothing like this is the case with the unobservable posits of theoretical physics. Moreover, it is usually supposed that these posits do indispensable explanatory work, and that their validity (or that of the theory positing them) can be tested in the usual ways, by deriving further observable predictions. If consciousness – in particular, the phenomenality of phenomenal consciousness – can be shown to be capable of such explanatory and predictive work, combined with an account of the exact mechanism whereby it generates the observable phenomena being explained or predicted, that would go a long way toward vindicating its theoretical role in the sciences. But it is difficult to imagine how all that could come to pass. A position like this, which is fundamentally skeptical about the scientific role of consciousness, can be called *methodological epiphenomenalism*. Science can get by, and must be prepared to get by, without invoking consciousness in its theorizing. A good thing, too – one might add – in view of its in-principle objective inaccessibility and untestability.

Methodological epiphenomenalism differs from consciousness eliminativism (Dennett 1988) in that, unlike the latter, it does not – at least, need not – deny outright that phenomenal consciousness exists. It only denies it a theoretical/explanatory role in the science of human behavior. However, one could question whether there are differences of real significance between the two doctrines. If you find methodological epiphenomenalism compelling, that must be so because you do not believe in the causal efficacy of consciousness. But being real and having causal powers go hand in hand; to deny causal powers to something is, in effect, to deny its reality. If an object, or phenomenon, is totally lacking in causal efficacy, how could its existence even be known?

Philosophical Problems of Mental Causation

Pressures from various sources conspire together to make the possibility of mental causation prima facie problematic. Here we will focus on what is standardly called the "exclusion" problem. Intuitively, the idea is that whenever a mental event is proposed as a cause of another event, whether physical or mental, its status as cause is in danger of being pre-empted by a physical event – that is, a mental cause is liable to be *excluded* by a physical cause.

There are various ways of arguing that mentality is vulnerable to an exclusionary threat of this kind. Ultimately, however, all such arguments can be seen to be based on the idea that the physical domain is causally and explanatorily self-sufficient – that is, to explain a physical event, or to identify its cause, there is no need to look outside the physical domain. It is now standard to call this the "causal closure" of the physical domain (some prefer the term "causal completeness"). This contrasts sharply with the domains of the special sciences – for example, the biological domain is not causally self-sufficient since nonbiological events (e.g., purely physical events such as exposure to strong radiation, natural disasters) can cause biological changes. Nor is the psychological domain causally closed – this for obvious reasons is apparent in daily lives as well as scientific observations. There are various ways of stating the causal closure principle. The following is one of the standard formulations:

> *Physical Causal Closure.* If a physical event has a sufficient cause occurring at t, then it has a physical sufficient cause occurring at t.

The term "physical," in this context, could be understood in two ways. First, it could refer only to the phenomena, properties, and events investigated in theoretical physics; in this sense, the geological, the biological, and the neural will not be part of the physical. Second, the term can be used in a broader sense, to refer to whatever is nonmental or nonpsychological. In the context of the mind–body problem, the latter is usually the sense in which one speaks of "physical." Thus, physical phenomena will include biological and neural phenomena as well as purely physiochemical ones. The causal closure principle is often stated with the narrower sense of "physical" in mind; however, the broader closure principle should be equally plausible, at least for anyone who accepts the narrower closure.

Suppose, then, that a mental event M, occurring at t, causes a physical event P. From the physical causal closure, it follows that there is a physical event, P*, occurring at t, which is a sufficient cause of P. This already is an uncomfortable picture: whenever a mental event has a physical effect, the physical effect has a purely physical cause as well, apparently making it a case of causal overdetermination (and making the supposed mental cause dispensable).

The situation can be seen to be even more dire when we bring onto the scene the following unexceptionable principle:

> *Causal Exclusion.* No event has more than one sufficient cause occurring at t – unless it is a genuine case of causal overdetermination.

Unless one opts for the strange view that every case of mental causation is a case of causal overdetermination, the exclusion principle must be applied to the present case. Since each of M and P* is claimed to be a sufficient cause of P, either M or P* must be excluded as a cause of P. But which one? A moment's reflection shows that M must go. The reason is simple: if we let P go, the causal closure principle kicks in again, requiring us to posit a physical sufficient cause, say P**, for P. (What could P** be if not P*?) And we are off to an unending regress (or, what comes to the same thing, we are forced to keep treading the same water forever).

The foregoing, then, is the exclusion argument, based on the causal closure of the physical domain. It shows that given that the physical world is causally closed, there can be no mental-to-physical causation. But there is more to come. If we bring another plausible thesis into the mix, an argument can be constructed that rules out mental-to-mental causation as well, making mentality causally epiphenomenal *tout court*. This is called the "supervenience" argument, or the argument from "realization." Its basic premise is the widely accepted thesis that mental phenomena "supervene" on, or are "realized" by, physical/biological phenomena. For our purposes, it will be convenient to state this claim in the following form:

Supervenience. Whenever a mental property M is instantiated by a system *x*, it is in virtue of the fact that *x* instantiates some neural/physical base property P at the time, where P is such that any system instantiating it at *t* necessarily instantiates M at *t*.

Given this, consider the following line of reasoning. Suppose that an instantiation of mental property M at *t* causes another mental property M* to be instantiated an instant later, at *t**. Given *Supervenience*, M* has a physical supervenience base P* such that P* is instantiated at *t**, and given this, M* must of necessity be instantiated at *t**. If P* is there, M* must be there no matter what has preceded this instantiation of M*. Moreover, without P*, or an alternative physical base, M* could not be instantiated at *t**. This threatens M's claim to be the cause of M*'s instantiation at *t**; for even if M had not occurred, M* would still have occurred as long as its supervenience base P* was present at *t**. (This argument can be formulated in terms of realization, with "X supervenes on Y" replaced everywhere with "X is (physically) realized by Y.")

The only way to rescue M's causal status vis-à-vis M*'s instantiation at *t** seems to be this: M's instantiation at *t* caused P* to instantiate at *t**, *thereby* bringing about P*'s instantiation at *t**. Given the supervenience of M* on P*, that seems the only thing one could say. But then this involves an instance of mental-to-physical causation. You will remember that this is exactly what the exclusion argument has shown to be impossible. It follows, then, that neither mental-to-mental nor mental-to-physical causation is possible. This is general epiphenomenalism: the mental lacks causal efficacy, period.

Mental Causation and Mind–Body Reduction

It should be clear that the epiphenomenalist conclusions of the two arguments follow only on the assumption that the mental is not reducible to the physical; namely, the assumption that reductionist physicalism has been ruled out. If a mental cause is physically reduced and brought into the physical domain, physical causal closure presents no problem. The mental cause simply is a physical cause. Similarly, if mental property M is reductively identifiable with a physical property, or if any instantiation of M can be identified with an instantiation of some physical property, again there will be no special problem with mental causation, since we would have here only cases of physical-to-physical causation. What physical causal closure excludes is nonphysical-to-physical causation, not necessarily mental-to-physical causation. As long as mind–body reduction remains an option, the epiphenomenalist conclusions of the exclusion and the supervenience arguments can be avoided.

It is, therefore, more accurate to view the two arguments not as foisting epiphenom-enalism on us but rather as urging what may be called "conditional reductionism," the thesis that any causally efficacious property (phenomenon, event, etc.) must be physically reducible. To put it another way, it asks us to make a choice between two stark alternatives – epiphenomenalism and physical reductionism. Neither alternative will seem palatable to most of us. Epiphenomenalism seems to go against everything we believe about ourselves as cognizers and agents in the world. To be an agent means being someone who, in light of his beliefs and desires and intentions, can causally act on the world. If our preferences, beliefs, and intentions have no causal role in moving our limbs and thereby cause things around us to be rearranged, how can we view ourselves as agents, people who can do things like climbing a ladder to retrieve a cat, writing a letter, and buying the morning paper? But physical reductionism doesn't strike most of us as any better: If our consciousness, beliefs, thoughts, and feelings are "nothing but" patterns of electrochemical activity in the brain, plainly visible as bulbous, pulsating globs of red, green, and yellow on a computer display, that might not seem much like saving mentality as something distinctive and special.

In any case, the conclusion of our considerations, to repeat, is that if we want to escape epiphenomenalism, we must embrace physical reductionism. But this is not an argument for reductionism; it only gives us reason for *hoping* that reductionism is true, that mentality will turn out to be physically reducible. There is a general consensus that epiphenomenalism is undesirable, and that we should do what we can to avoid it. That does not mean, however, that epiphenomenalism is false. The causal efficacy of the mental must be vindicated, and our conditional reductionism says that the only way to do so is to show reductionism to be true. So is reductionism true? Can the mental be physically reduced?

As everyone knows, reductionism has had a rough time of it for almost half a century – it has been the *bête noire* of the philosophy of mind, and more generally, of the philosophy of special sciences. Most philosophers abandoned reductionism in the 1970s and 1980s because of what is known as the multiple realization argument. This argument is based on the supposed, and widely accepted, phenomenon of multiple realizability of mental states – the claim that any given mental state has multiple diverse physical realizers (just think of the neural mechanisms implementing pain, or a visual sensory system, or memory, in diverse biological species). Since there is no single neural substrate for a mental state – in fact, there are indefinitely many nomologically possible implementations of any given mental state or function – it is not possible to reductively identify the mental state with a neural state or mechanism. Since pain has multiple neural realizers, N_1, N_2, . . ., it is not possible to pick one of these, say N_i, and claim that pain = N_i.

Psychoneural identities (consciousness = 40 Hz synchronized oscillation, and the like), if available, would succeed in reducing mental properties to physical properties, and that would solve the problem of mental causation. The problem is that there is no reason to think these identities are available (note: these identities go much beyond psychoneural *correlations*). There are no compelling positive arguments for their availability. Simplicity arguments, based on considerations of ontological or theoretical "simplicity," "parsimony," etc. (Smart 1959), fail to convince, and explanatory arguments to the effect that these identities earn their warrant from the supposed explanatory work they can do (Hill 1991; Block & Stalnaker 1999) can be seen to be seriously flawed (Kim 2005, ch. 5). What we have are various nega-tive arguments against their availability, like the multiple realization argument and various epistemological arguments pointing to epistemic asymmetries between the phenomenal and the neural. But identity reduction is not the only kind of reduction; there is also functional reduction which, if it can be carried out for the mental vis-à-vis the physical/neural, could vindicate the causal role of mentality. But what is functional reduction? How does it work?

Functional reduction starts with a functional characterization of the property targeted for reduction. Suppose pain can be functionally defined as follows:

> *Step 1.* Being in pain = $_{def.}$ being in some state S such that S is caused by tissue damage and traumas and S in turn causes aversive behavior.

Thus, on this understanding of what pain is, being in pain simply amounts to being in some state that occupies a certain causal role – pain is the state that, in a given system, causally mediates between tissue damage and traumas (pain input) and certain behavior patterns (pain output). Both input and output could, in principle, include psychological conditions; but we will use a simplified model here. There is nothing more to being in pain than being in a state that makes that kind of causal connections. So, as one says, pain is characterized by its causal role, or a "job description." The definition above speaks of "some state S"; we make the assumption here that this refers only to physical/neural states. This assumption is natural, and necessary, because it is the *physical* reducibility of the mental that is under discussion.

Given that this gives us the concept of pain, the scientist can start looking for the neural mechanisms that in a given organism or population of organisms of interest, play the specified causal role. So the second step in a functional reduction consists in the following:

> *Step 2.* Identify the physical/neural mechanisms, in the population of interest (say, humans, mammals), that fit the causal specification of pain as stated by the functional characterization of pain in Step 1 – that is, identify the physical/neural "realizers" of pain.

Suppose that there is a group of neurons (the nociceptive neurons) in the cortex (or wherever) that gets activated when tissue damage occurs and which, in turn, triggers aversive behavior characteristic of pain. Identifying a neural mechanism of this sort presumably is a central part of pain research in the neural sciences. Obviously, such research must have a specific population of organisms as its target; no pain research would, we may assume, try to uncover the neural mechanisms of pain in all actual and possible species (and perhaps nonbiological pain-capable systems). Even where a specific species has been selected for attention, there may be multiple, diverse, pain realizers; there may well be individual variations among conspecifics and even within an individual over time (and we need not rule out multiple pain mechanisms within a single individual at one time). However, neural research on pain is possible and worthwhile to pursue because conspecifics share largely similar neural mechanisms for pain, and for other psychological capacities and functions.

We may assume that Step 2 will go hand in hand with an explanatory/theoretical project:

> *Step 3.* Build an explanatory theory that explains how the realizers identified in Step 2 actually perform the causal work specified in Step 1.

That is, a neural theory of pain will give us a detailed description of the process whereby tissue damage leads to the activation of the nociceptive neurons and how this latter event triggers a process leading to winces, groans, and avoidance behavior. When all this is in, we may claim that pain, for the population in question, has been physically reduced, and that we now have a reductive understanding of pain phenomena in terms of neural processes (Kim 2005, ch. 4).

Of these three steps, the first is crucial from the philosophical point of view. The reason is that if a mental property can be functionalized – that is, be given a functional characterization – then its reducibility is guaranteed. The actual reduction, Steps 2 and 3, is up to scientific research, which may or may not succeed or may not even be undertaken. If a functionally characterized (functional, for short) property is instantiated, that is so in virtue of the fact that it instantiates a realizer of that property. This is a logical consequence of the concept of a functional property. It is up to science to discover what neural mechanism is the realizer involved in any particular instance. So functionalizability guarantees reducibility, though not actual reduction. Philosophically speaking, it is reducibility that matters; successful reductions are of no concern as far as the metaphysics of the situation is concerned. This means that the question "Is the mental physically reducible?" is transformed into this one "Is the mental functionalizable?" – that is, "Can mental properties be given functional characterizations?"

Functionalization of Mental Properties

One erroneous presumption that is often made is to assume that mentality, taken as an entirety, must be either reducible or irreducible. It may well be that certain subcategories of mental properties are physically reducible, while others are not. It is now customary to divide mental phenomena into two broad, and not necessarily disjoint, categories – intentional phenomena and sensory/qualitative phenomena. The former, also called "propositional attitudes," comprise states with contents, expressed by embedded sentential clauses, like beliefs, desires, and intentions. The latter category consists of states with a qualitative sensory quality – states such that, as the saying goes, there is something "it's like" to be in them. The division is not exclusive since there are content-carrying states that also have a qualitative dimension, for example, emotions and feelings. The question about the causal efficacy of consciousness, then, is a question concerning the phenomena of the second category. But it is also a question about those intentional states with a qualitative aspect. Take your embarrassment at being late for a department meeting. Let us assume that there is a typical qualitative, "what it's like" sort of aspect that characterizes most cases of embarrassment and which distinguishes embarrassment from, say, anger, jealousy, regrets, and the rest. Assuming that your embarrassment has causal effects, does its qualitative aspect make a causal contribution? It might be that all causal effects of a state of embarrassment are exclusively attributable to its status as an intentional state, and that its phenomenal character is causally irrelevant.

We begin with this dichotomous division of mental phenomena because there presumptively is such a dichotomy and because there is reason to think that the two classes of mental phenomena fare differently in regard to their functional reducibility and hence, in regard to the issue of their causal efficacy. But we should keep in mind that there are views that challenge a dichotomous distinction of this kind. According to one such view, qualia representationalism, qualitative conscious states are essentially representational states, and their phenomenality, or qualitative character, is exhausted by their representational contents (Seager & Bourget, chapter 20; Dretske 1995; Tye 1995). So there perhaps is no fundamental difference between phenomenal states of consciousness and sundry representational intentional states like beliefs. Phenomenal consciousness may very well share the fate of intentional states in regard to causal efficacy.

In contrast, it is also possible to hold that every intentional state must have a phenomenal character, and that intentionality is inseparable from phenomenality. (For discussion see Graham, Horgan, & Tienson, chapter 37.) Depending on how this relationship is characterized, a view of this kind is likely to entangle the causal issues about intentional states in the dispute about the causal efficacy of phenomenal consciousness.

Setting these issues aside, let us turn to the functional reducibility of intentional states. Consider creatures that are like us in their behavioral and functional organization. Assume they look like us and behave much the way we do in response to sensory stimuli, and interact with each other much as we do, including in what looks to us like speech behavior. We may also suppose that they are like us in physical/material constitution, but this is not essential. In such a situation, it will be incoherent for us to deny to these creatures beliefs, desires, and other intentional states. The reason is that if they are behaviorally and functionally indistinguishable from us, it will not make sense to deny that they are language-users – they use speech as a tool for social communication and coordinate their actions through interpersonal sharing of information. The primary function of language is to make assertions. If a creature uses sentence S to make an assertion – that is, it asserts that S – it follows that it expresses the belief that S. If it asks the question "Why S?" it expresses a desire to know, or be told, whether S is true. When it issues a command "Shut the door," it expresses the belief that the door is not now shut and a desire that it be shut. And so on. In short, if a group of creatures are behaviorally indistinguishable from us, we cannot withhold from them the capacity for intentional states, like beliefs, desires, and the rest. Intentional states, therefore, supervene on behavior. (If one wanted to bring serious content externalism into discussion at this point, one would have to take the external environment of the subject into the supervenience base. This would somewhat complicate the issue.)

In addition to the supervenience of intentional states on behavior, there are other ways of seeing the point that intentional states are functional states specified by their job descriptions. To believe that it is going to rain later today is to be in a state S such that if you are in S and are asked "What is the weather going to be like today?" S will cause you to answer "It's going to rain"; moreover, if you are in S then, given a desire not to get wet, S will probably cause you to take an umbrella to work, and so on. We can be sure that there will not likely be a full and complete functional definition of believing that it's going to rain, but, given the supervenience of this belief on behavior, there can be no fact about this belief that goes beyond actual and possible behavior. To begin a functional reduction of this belief, we can start looking for a neural mechanism that does the causal work so far specified. In scientific terms, belief may be nothing more than the storage of information, in an accessible and retrievable form, which can be used for inference and the rational guidance of behavior. This is a functional conception, a conception of belief in terms of its work in the cognitive/psychological economy of a psychological subject.

When we turn to phenomenal consciousness, or qualia, the situation looks very different. Qualia do not appear to supervene on behavior. Some argue this (Chalmers 1996) on the basis of the supposed conceivability and hence possibility of "zombies," creatures that are indistinguishable from us in both behavior and material constitution. Such an argument has been controversial (Gendler & Hawthorne 2002). But we do not need the zombie hypothesis. To see the difficulty of functionalizing qualia, all we need is the possibility of qualia inversion. It seems certainly conceivable, and metaphysically possible, that your color spectrum is inverted in relation to the color spectrum of your roommate. When you and your roommate see spinach, you both say "Green"; when the two of you see ripe tomatoes, both of you say "Red." However, the color you visually sense when you look at tomatoes is like the color your roommate sees when she looks at spinach, and similarly the other way around. You and your roommate do equally well in distinguishing red things from green things – in picking out tomatoes from mounds of lettuce, coping with the traffic lights, and so forth. And your verbal behavior with "red" and "green" is indistinguishable from your roommate's. (See also Van Gulick, chapter 30; Levine, chapter 29.)

If such is a possibility, that would show that qualia are not definable in terms of behavior, or any kind of job description. Pain is, of course, caused by certain stimuli and it, in turn, causes a broadly definable set of behaviors. However, many of us do not think that what makes pain pain is the causal work it does. It seems clearly possible – in fact, nomologically possible – that our "pain box" and "itch box" are rewired to afferent and efferent nerve channels so that pain signals are now sent to the itch box and itch signals are sent to the pain box (and the activation of the pain box now triggers scratching behavior, etc.). It would seem that under such a scenario, a sensation of pain is caused not by tissue damage but by mosquito bites. If you are like those who think that what makes pain pain is the fact that it *hurts*, not how the pain mechanism is wired to inputs and outputs, then you will deny that pain, and other qualia, can be given a functional characterization. If this is correct, qualia are not functionalizable and hence, functionally irreducible.

Saving What's Important about Phenomenal Consciousness

All this seems like bad news for phenomenal consciousness: according to conditional reductionism, properties that are not physically reducible are epiphenomenal. There are two presumptive ways of accomplishing reduction: identity reduction and functional reduction. As noted earlier, psychoneural identity reduction seems to have no chance of succeeding, and the considerations of the preceding section show that a functional reduction of qualia is no more promising. So have we lost phenomenal consciousness to epiphenomenalism? Are we forced to accept the epiphenomenalism of qualia?

Not entirely. Because although qualia as absolute intrinsic qualities are irreducible, qualia similarities and differences appear functionally characterizable and hence reducible. Let us begin with an analogy: the traffic lights. Pretty much everywhere in the world, red means "Stop," green means "Go," and yellow means "Slow down." But that is merely a matter of convention, a social arrangement; we could have adopted a system in which red means "Go," green means "Slow down," and yellow means "Stop" (or any other combination), and that would not have affected traffic management one bit. What is important is that drivers discriminate among the three colors and adjust their driving behavior accordingly. We could have used shapes rather than colors for the same purpose: square meaning "Go," etc. The intrinsic qualities discriminated do not matter; it is their observable similarities and differences that matter. The same goes for qualia as qualities of your experiences. You and your color-inverted friend do equally well with tasks involving red and green, for example picking out cherries from mounds of lettuce and spinach, because the two of you can discriminate between red and green equally well. You utter "These cherries are red" when you are presented with ripe cherries. So does your friend. You believe, and know, that cherries are red and that lettuce is green. So does your color-inverted friend. You and your spectrum-inverted friend will do equally well in coping with the world and gaining knowledge of it (of course other things being equal). It does not matter for cognition and action that tomatoes look just *this* way and spinach looks just *that* way. What matters is that they look different; that spinach looks the same color as lettuce, and so do cherries and tomatoes.

Thus, qualia similarities and differences are behaviorally manifest and this opens the door to their functional characterization. This means that what is really important about our perceptual experience – that is, the cognitive role – can be functionally characterizable and hence shown to be causally efficacious. The conclusion, therefore, is that epiphenomenalism cannot claim a total victory over qualia; we can save from the epiphenomenalist threat a crucially important aspect of qualia – that aspect of qualia that makes a difference to our cognition and capacity to cope with the world.

See also 5 Rethinking the evolution of consciousness; 20 Representationalism about consciousness; 29 Anti-materialist arguments and influential replies; 30 Functionalism and qualia; 37 Consciousness and intentionality; 51 Benjamin Libet's work on the neuroscience of free will.

Further Readings

Chalmers, D. J. (1996) *The Conscious Mind*. New York and Oxford: Oxford University Press.
Jackson, F. (1982) Epiphenomenal qualia. *Philosophical Quarterly* 32, 127–36.
Kim, J. (2005) *Physicalism, or Something Near Enough*. Princeton, NJ: Princeton University Press.

References

Bisiach, E. (1988) The (haunted) brain and consciousness. In A. J. Marcel and E. Bisiach (eds.), *Consciousness in Contemporary Science*, 101–20. Oxford: Clarendon Press.
Block, N. and R. Stalnaker (1999) Conceptual analysis, dualism, and the explanatory gap. *Philosophical Review* 108, 1–46.
Caston, V. (1997) Epiphenomenalism, ancient and modern. *Philosophical Review* 106, 309–63.
Dennett, D. C. (1991) *Consciousness Explained*. Boston, MA: Little, Brown.
Dretske, F. (1995) *Naturalizing the Mind*. Cambridge, MA: MIT Press.
Flanagan, O. (1992) *Consciousness Reconsidered*. Cambridge, MA: MIT Press.
Gendler, T. S. and Hawthorne, J. (eds.) (2002) *Conceivability and Possibility*. Oxford: Oxford University Press.
Hill, C. S. (1991) *Sensations: A Defense of Type Materialism*. Cambridge: Cambridge University Press.
Huxley, Thomas H. (1874) On the hypothesis that animals are automata, and its history. *Fortnightly Review* 16, 555–80. Excerpted in D. J. Chalmers (ed.), *Philosophy of Mind: Classical and Contemporary Readings*. Oxford: Oxford University Press, 2002. Page references are to this excerpted version.
Kim, J. (2005) *Physicalism, or Something Near Enough*. Princeton, NJ: Princeton University Press.
Marcel, A. J. (1988) Phenomenal experience and functionalism. In A. J. Marcel and E. Bisiach (eds.), *Consciousness in Contemporary Science*. Oxford: Clarendon Press.
Mele, A. R. (2005) Decisions, intentions, urges, and free will: why Libet has not shown what he says he has. In J. Campbell, M. O'Rourke, and D. Shier (eds.), *Explanation and Causation: Topics in Contemporary Philosophy*. Cambridge, MA: MIT Press.
Smart, J. C. C. (1959) Sensations and brain processes. *Philosophical Review* 68, 141–56.
Tye, M. (1995) *Ten Problems of Consciousness*. Cambridge, MA: MIT Press.
Velmans, M. (2002) How could conscious experience affect brains? *Journal of Consciousness Studies* 9, 3–29.
Watson, R. A. (1987) *The Breakdown of Cartesian Metaphysics*. Atlantic Highlands, NJ: Humanities Press International.
Wegner, D. M. (2002) *The Illusion of Conscious Will*. Cambridge, MA: MIT Press.

33

The Neurophilosophy of Consciousness

PETE MANDIK

The topic of phenomenal consciousness concerns what it means for mental states to be conscious states (as opposed to unconscious mental states) and what it means for such states to have phenomenal character, that is, to have properties in virtue of which there is "something it's like" for a subject to be in such a state. Traditional philosophical issues that phenomenal consciousness raises involve the relation of phenomenal consciousness to the rest of the world, especially as that world is conceived of by the natural sciences. Thus much philosophical discussion concerns whether the world as conceived of by physical theory can adequately accommodate phenomenal consciousness or if instead we are left with a dualism that cleaves reality into, for example, a nonphysical phenomenal consciousness and a physical everything else. Even among philosophers who agree that phenomenal consciousness is consistent with physicalism, there is much disagreement, for there are several proposals for how best to spell out the consistency of a physicalistic worldview that makes room for phenomenal consciousness. One way of portraying this cluster of issues is in terms of which natural science is best suited to study phenomenal consciousness and how to conceive of the relation between that science and the sciences involving the most basic aspects of reality (the physical sciences). One major view is that psychology is the proper science for understanding phenomenal consciousness and furthermore, that psychological investigation of phenomenal consciousness should be regarded as autonomous from sciences such as the neurosciences. In opposition is the view that the proper science is neuroscience and whatever contributions come from psychology are only valid insofar as psychological theories are reducible to neuroscientific theories. Increasingly, proponents of the latter view identify themselves as practitioners of neurophilosophy.

Neurophilosophy is a sub-genre of naturalized philosophy – philosophy that embraces Quine's (1969) vision of philosophy as continuous with the natural sciences – wherein the natural science in primary focus is neuroscience. It is perhaps worth addressing here in further detail what is distinctive of neurophilosophy as opposed to other kinds of naturalism. The role that neuroscience plays is, of course, key, but not just any mention of the brain in a philosophical theory will suffice to make it neurophilosophical. Neurophilosophical appeals to neuroscience involve explicit and detailed use of contemporary neuroscientific literature. Furthermore, neurophilosophy is not to be distinguished from other forms of naturalism by the philosophical *conclusions* that might be reached but by the role that contemporary neuroscience plays in the *premises* of the arguments for those conclusions. These points about different styles of naturalistic philosophizing may be illustrated in terms of some recent examples. For example, Jaegwon Kim is a kind of naturalist and even advocates a reduction of mental state types to physical state types. However, he is not thereby a neurophilosopher. His identification of the relevant physical state types makes no explicit reference to contemporary neuroscientific findings. The state types in question involve no familiarity with the typologies specific to either neurophysiology or neuroanatomy. In contrast, the research of neurophilosophers like Kathleen Akins makes explicit reference to contemporary neuroscientific findings in the arguments for various naturalistic conclusions. For example, she argues (1996) against traditional views of the role that sensory states play in grounding the contents of intentional states. Crucial to her arguments are detailed examinations of the neurophysiology of thermoreception (see Bickle & Mandik 1999 for a longer discussion of examples of neurophilosophical work such as Akins's).

Some authors draw a distinction between neurophilosophy and philosophy of neuroscience wherein the former involves the application of neuroscientific results to topics of philosophical concern, usually in the philosophy of mind, and the latter is a sub-discipline of the philosophy of science. Though often neurophilosophers are also philosophers of neuroscience, the current chapter focuses on the activities distinctive of the former group.

The term "neurophilosophy" entered philosophical parlance with the publication of Patricia Churchland's *Neurophilosophy* (1986), the aims of which were to introduce neuroscience to philosophers and philosophy to neuroscientists, with an emphasis on the former. Patricia Churchland and husband Paul Churchland are paradigmatic examples of neurophilosophers. Their professional training is primarily philosophical, their appointments are in philosophy departments, and they publish in philosophy journals. Because of this, neuroscience and philosophy do not have equal influence over neurophilosophy. Instead the primary forces that drive its development as an academic pursuit emanate from conventions of philosophical institutions. Thus neurophilosophical work on phenomenal consciousness proceeds largely by bringing neuroscientific theory and data to bear on philosophical questions concerning phenomenal consciousness.

Such questions are diverse. However, a useful way to focus the discussion – as well as to understand what has been of primary concern to neurophilosophical theories of phenomenal consciousness – will be to focus on just three questions: the question of state consciousness, the question of transitive consciousness, and the question of phenomenal character. (The terms "transitive consciousness" and "state consciousness" are due to David Rosenthal. For discussion, see Rosenthal 1993; Tye, chapter 2.) The question of state consciousness concerns in what consists the difference between mental states that are conscious and mental states that are unconscious. We have conscious mental states, such as my conscious perception of the words I type. Mental states vary with respect to whether they are conscious. Consider, for example, your memory of your mother's name. You may have had that memory for years but it obviously was not a *conscious* memory for the entire time between its initial acquisition and its current retrieval. In what does the difference between conscious and unconscious mental states consist? The question of transitive consciousness concerns what it is that we are conscious *of*. When one has a conscious state, typically, if not always, one is conscious *of* something, as when I am conscious of a buzzing insect. Things may vary with respect to whether I am conscious of them, as when I am only intermittently conscious of the conversation at a nearby table in a restaurant. What does it mean to be *conscious of* something? The question of phenomenal character concerns the so-called qualia of conscious states. Conscious states have certain properties – their phenomenal character – properties in virtue of which there is "something it's like" to be in that state. When I have a conscious perception of a cup of coffee there is, presumably, something it's like for me to have that perception and, for all I know, what it's like for you to have a conscious perception of a cup of coffee is quite different. What makes a conscious state have "something it's like" to be in that state? The phrase "phenomenal consciousness" does not denote a kind of consciousness distinct from state consciousness but is instead a term of art used by authors (e.g., Block 1995; Chalmers 1996) who are primarily interested in a certain aspect of conscious states, namely their phenomenal character (for a longer discussion see Mandik 2005).

Given the centrality of these questions, we will have several occasions to return to them throughout the present chapter. In brief summary they are:

The Question of State Consciousness:
In what consists the difference between mental states that are conscious and mental states that are unconscious?

The Question of Transitive Consciousness:
When one has a conscious mental state, what is one thereby conscious *of*?

The Question of Phenomenal Character:
When one has a conscious state, in what consists the properties in virtue of which there is something it's like for one to be in that state?

Neurophilosophical theories of consciousness bring neuroscience to bear on answering these three questions of consciousness. The question arises, of course, of what motivates the neurophilosophy of consciousness. The primary answer is that neurophilosophy has a certain appeal to those with an antecedent belief in physicalism, in that neurophilosophy seems especially well-suited to bridge the gap between the phenomenal and the physical. Attempting to bridge the gap by reducing the phenomenal all the way down to chemistry or microphysics may strike many as too far a distance to traverse. More plausible is to seek a higher-level physical set of phenomena, as offered in biology. Of the biological phenomena, the most plausible candidates are neural. The appeal of neurophilosophical approaches to phenomenal consciousness may become more evident upon examination of some sample theories.

Before examining the neurophilosophical theories, it will be useful to look at a small sample of some of the relevant neuroscience. Vision is one of the most important and best understood senses. Accordingly, most of the fruitful progress in combining philosophy and neuroscience has occurred in the domain of visual consciousness.

Neuroscience and Visual Consciousness

The processing of visual information in the brain can be understood as occurring in a processing hierarchy with the lowest levels in the retina and the highest levels in areas of the cerebral cortex. Processing begins after light is transduced by the rods and cones in the retina and electrochemical signals are passed to the retinal ganglia. From there, information flows through the optic nerve to the lateral geniculate nucleus (LGN) in the subcortex. From the LGN, information is passed to the first stage of cortical processing in the primary visual area of occipital cortex (area V1). From V1, the information is sent to other areas of occipital cortex and is then sent along a "ventral stream" from the occipital to the infero-temporal cortex as well as along a "dorsal stream" from the occipital to the posterior parietal cortex (Milner & Goodale 1995; Prinz, chapter 19; Crick & Koch, chapter 44; Goodale, chapter 48). Beyond that, information is sent to areas of the frontal cortex (Olson et al. 1999) as well as the hippocampus (Milner & Goodale 1995). As will be discussed further, information does not simply flow from lower levels to higher levels but there are many instances in which it flows from higher levels down to lower levels (Pascual-Leone & Walsh 2001). Furthermore, information is processed in various ways in different regions of the different levels and can be briefly characterized in the following ways. Information at the lowest levels is represented by neural activations that serve as detectors of features in specific locations defined relative to the retina (AKA retinocentric locations). Thus, at the lowest levels, neural activations in LGN and V1 constitute egocentric representations of visual features as in, for instance, the detection of an oriented line by a cell with a relatively small retinocentric receptive field. At progressively higher-level areas (such as visual areas V2 through V5), locally defined visual features are "grouped" or integrated as when local information about shading is grouped to give rise to representations of depth. Progressively higher levels of information processing increasingly abstract away from the egocentric information of the lower-level representations and give rise to progressively allocentric ("other-centered") representations as in view-point invariant representations in inferior temporal cortex that underwrite the recognition of objects from multiple angles and other viewing conditions. Thus, information represented at progressively higher levels of processing becomes progressively less egocentric and progressively more allocentric, the most allocentric representations being in the frontal areas and hippocampus (Mandik 2005).

The question arises of how best to apply the concepts of consciousness of interest to philosophers – state consciousness, transitive consciousness, and phenomenal character – in the context of a neuroscientific understanding of visual perception. We may make the most progress in this regard by focusing on breakdowns and anomalies of normal vision. We will briefly examine two such cases. The first is blindsight, a condition that results from a certain kind of brain damage (Weiscrantz, chapter 13). The second is motion-induced blindness, a condition that occurs in normal subjects under certain unusual conditions.

Blindsight is a condition in which lesions to V1 cause subjects to report a loss of consciousness in spite of the retention of visual ability. For so-called blind regions of their visual fields, blindsight subjects are nonetheless better than chance in their responses (such as directed eye movements or forced-choice identifications) to stimulus properties such as luminance onset (Pöppel, Held, & Frost 1973), wavelength (Stoerig & Cowey 1992), and motion (Weiskrantz 1995). Lack of consciousness is indicated in such studies by, for example, having the subject indicate by pressing one of two keys "whether he had any experience whatever, no matter how slight or effervescent" (Weiskrantz 1996).

Blindsight subjects' responses to stimuli in the blind portions of their visual fields give evidence that the stimuli are represented in portions of the brain. However, it is clear that these representational states are not conscious states. Thus, the kind of consciousness that seems most relevant in describing what blindsight patients lack is state consciousness. Furthermore, blindsight patients arguably also lack transitive consciousness with respect to the stimuli in the blind regions of their visual field. One consideration in favor of this view arises when we take the subject's own reports at face value. They claim not to be conscious of the stimuli in question. It would be difficult to affirm that blindsight subjects do have transitive consciousness of the relevant stimuli without affirming that all instances of representation are instances of transitive consciousness, and thus instances of unconscious consciousness.

Regarding the question of qualia, of whether there is anything it's like for blindsight subjects to have stimuli presented to the blind regions of their visual fields, I take it that it is quite natural to reason as follows. Since they are not conscious of the stimuli, and since the states that represent the stimuli are not conscious states, there must not be anything it's like to have stimuli presented to those regions. Of course, the reader may doubt this claim if the reader is not a blindsight subject. It will be useful in this regard to consider a case that readers will be more likely to have first-person access to. For precisely this reason it is instructive to look at the phenomenon of motion-induced blindness (Bonneh et al. 2001).

Motion-induced blindness may be elicited in normal subjects under conditions in which they look at a computer screen that has a triangular pattern of three bright yellow dots on a black background with a pattern of blue dots moving "behind" the yellow dots. As subjects fixate on the center of the screen, it appears to them that one or more of the yellow dots disappear (although in reality the yellow dots remain on the screen). The effect is quite salient and readers are encouraged to search the internet for "motion-induced blindness" and experience the effect for themselves. There are several lines of evidence that even during the "disappearance" the yellow dots continue to be represented in visual areas of the brain. The effect can be influenced by transcranial magnetic stimulation to the parietal cortex (a relatively late stage of visual processing in the brain). Additionally, the effect can be shown to involve nonlocal grouping of the stimulus elements. So, for example, if the yellow dots are replaced with a pair of partially overlapping circles, one yellow and one pink, sometimes an entire circle will disappear leaving the other behind even though some parts of the two different circles are very close in the visual field. As mentioned previously, the brain mechanisms thought to mediate such object groupings are relatively late in the visual processing hierarchy.

We may turn now to the applications of the concepts of transitive consciousness, state consciousness, and qualia to motion-induced blindness. First, motion-induced blindness looks to be a phenomenon involving transitive consciousness since in the one moment the subject is conscious of the yellow dot, in the next they are not conscious of the yellow dot, and along the way they are conscious of a yellow dot seeming to disappear. Second, we can see that motion-induced blindness allows for applications of the concept of state consciousness, since studies of motion-induced blindness provide evidence of conscious states that represent the presence of yellow dots as well as unconscious states that represent the presence of yellow dots.

Let us turn now to ask how the concept of phenomenal character applies in the context of motion-induced blindness. The best grip we can get on this question is simply by asking what it's like to see yellow dots disappear. When there is an unconscious state that represents the yellow dots or no transitive consciousness of yellow dot, there is, with respect to the yellow dot, nothing it's like to see it. Or, more accurately, what this instance of motion-induced blindness is like, is like *not* seeing a yellow dot. When the state representing the yellow dot is conscious, what it's like to be in that state is like seeing a yellow dot. One might suppose then, as will be discussed later, that what it's like to be in the conscious state is determined, at least in part, by the representational content of that state. In this case, it is the content of the representation of a yellow dot.

Neurophilosophical Theories of Consciousness

I will now turn to examine a sample of neurophilosophical theories of consciousness. In keeping with the definitions of neurophilosophy as well as the three questions, the discussion of this section will be centered on philosophical accounts of state consciousness, transitive consciousness, and phenomenal character that make heavy use of contemporary neuroscientific research in the premises of their arguments.

In keeping with the paradigmatic status of the work of the Churchlands in neurophilosophy, my primary focus will be on Paul Churchland's neurophilosophical work on consciousness. However, other philosophers have produced neurophilosophical accounts and I will discuss their work as well.

Paul Churchland articulates what he calls the "dynamical profile approach" to understanding consciousness (2002). According to the approach, a conscious state is any cognitive representation that is involved in:

1   a moveable attention that can focus on different aspects of perceptual inputs;
2   the application of various conceptual interpretations of those inputs;
3   holding the results of attended and conceptual interpreted inputs in a short-term memory that
4   allows for the representation of temporal sequences.

Note that these four conditions primarily answer the question of what makes a state a conscious one. Regarding the question of what we are conscious of, Churchland writes that "a conscious representation could have any content or subject matter at all" (p. 72) and he is especially critical of theories of consciousness that impose restrictions on the contents of conscious representations along the lines of requiring them to be self-representational or meta-representational (pp. 72–4).

Much of Churchland's discussion of the dynamical profile account of consciousness concerns how all of the four conditions may be implemented in recurrent neural networks. A recurrent neural network may be best understood in terms of contrast with feedforward neural networks, but we should first give a general characterization of neural networks. Neural networks are collections of interconnected neurons. These networks have one or more input neurons and one or more output neurons. They may additionally have neurons that are neither input nor output neurons and are called "interneurons" or "hidden-layer" neurons. Neurons have, at any given time, one of several states of activation. In the case of input neurons, the state of activation is a function of a stimulus. In the case of interneurons and output neurons, their state of activation is a function of the states of activation of other neurons that connect to them. The amount of influence the activation of one neuron can exert on another neuron is determined by the "weight" of the connection between them. Learning in neural networks is typically thought to involve changes to the weights of the connections between neurons (though it may also involve the addition of new connections and the "pruning" of old ones). In feedforward networks, the flow of information is strictly from input to output (via interneurons if any are present). In recurrent networks there are feedback (or "recurrent") connections as well as feedforward connections. (For further discussion of artificial neural networks, see Garson 2002.)

Let us turn now to Churchland's account of how the four elements of the dynamical profile of conscious states might be realized in recursive neural networks. It helps to begin with Churchland's notion of the conceptual interpretation of sensory inputs and we do well to begin with what Churchland thinks a concept is. Consider a connectionist network with one or more hidden layers that is trained to categorize input types. Suppose that its inputs are a retinal array to which we present grayscale images of human faces. Suppose that its outputs are two units, one indicating that the face is male and the other indicating that the face is female. After training, the configuration of weights will be such that diverse patterns of activation in the input layer provoke the correct response of "male" to the diversity of male faces and "female" for female faces. For each unit in the hidden layer, we can represent its state of activation along one of several dimensions that define activation space. A pattern of hidden layer activation will be represented as a single point in this space. This space will have two regions: one for males and one for females. Regions in the center of each of the two spaces will constitute "attractors" that define what, for the network, constitutes proto-typical female faces and prototypical male faces, respectively.

The addition of recurrent connections allows for information from higher layers to influ-ence the responses of lower layers. As Churchland puts the point:

> This information can and does serve to "prime" or "prejudice" that neuronal population's collective activity in the direction of one or other of its learned perceptual categories. The net-work's cognitive "attention" is now preferentially focused on one of its learned categories at the expense of the others. (Churchland 2002, p. 75)

Churchland is not explicit about what this might mean in terms of the example of a face cat-egorization network, but I suppose what this might mean is that if the previous face was a prototypical female, then the network might be more likely to classify an ambiguous stim-ulus as female. We can construe this as exogenous cueing of attention. Churchland goes on to further describe shifts of attention in recurrent networks that we might regard as endogenous. "Such a network has an ongoing *control* of its topical selections from, and its conceptual interpretations of, its unfolding perceptual inputs" (p. 76).

Recurrent connections allow for both a kind of short-term memory and the represen-tation of events spread out over time. In a feedforward network, a single stimulus event gives rise to a single hidden layer response, then a single output response. With recurrence however, even after the stimulus event has faded, activity in lower layers can be sustained by information coming back down from higher layers, and that activity can itself reactivate higher layers. Also, what response a given stimulus yields depends in part on what previous stimuli were. Thus, recurrent connections implement a memory. Decreasing connection weights shorten the time it takes for this memory to decay. The ability to hold on to infor-mation over time allows for the representation of events spread out over time, according to Churchland, and the representation in question will not be a single point in activation space but a trajectory through it.

Churchland (2002) does not go into much neuroanatomical or neurophysiological detail, but adverts, though tentatively, to the account in Churchland (1995) wherein he endorses Llinas's view whereby consciousness involves recurrent connections between the thalamus (a bilateral structure at the rostral tip of the brainstem) and cortex. Part of the appeal of localizing consciousness in these structures presumably involves the role hypoth-esized for recurrence as well as the ideas that consciousness involves systems responsible for wakefulness and arousal (thalamus), diverse "higher" functions (the various portions of the cortex), and a system that can act as a relay between the various "higher" functions (the thalamus again).

I will have more to say about this later, but for now we may briefly summarize Churchland's dynamic profile acount with respect to the three questions of consciousness as follows. With respect to the question of state consciousness, according to Churchland, conscious states are neural representations that have a particular dynamic profile. With respect to the question of transitive consciousness, Churchland's account imposes no limitations on what one can be conscious of; one could be conscious of just about anything according to Churchland. With repect to the question of phenomenal character, "what it's like" to have a conscious state is going to be determined by the representational content of that state. More will be said about these points after we have had the opportunity to examine some other neurophilosophical theories of consciousness.

The neurophilosophical account of consciousness by Prinz (2000, 2004) is relatively similar and fills in a lot of neuroanatomy and neurophysiology that Churchland leaves out. (For further detail see Prinz, chapter 19.) Prinz characterizes the processing hierarchy we discussed earlier and then notes that the contents of consciousness seem to match it with representations at the intermediate level of processing (areas V2–V5). This means that the contents of conscious states do not abstract entirely from points of view as does the highest level of the processing hierarchy, but neither are they the same as the representations at the lowest level. However, Prinz argues that intermediate representations are alone insufficient for consciousness. They must additionally be targeted by attention. Prinz thinks attention is required because of considerations having to do with the pathology of attention known as "neglect." Prinz cites Bisiach's (1992) study of neglect patients who were able to demonstrate certain kinds of unconscious recognition. Prinz infers from such results that not only did high-level areas in the visual hierarchy become activated (they are necessary for the kinds of recognition in question) but also that intermediate levels had to have been activated. Prinz seems to be assuming that information can only get to higher levels of cortical processing by way of the intermediate level, but one wonders if perhaps the intermediate level was bypassed via a subcortical route.

Given the large role that Prinz assigns to attention in his theory of consciousness, the question naturally arises as to what Prinz thinks attention is and what it does. Prinz endorses the account of attention by Olshausen, Anderson, and van Essen (1994), wherein attention involves the modulation of the flow of information between different parts of the brain. Furthermore, Prinz endorses the speculation that the attention crucial in making intermediate-level representations conscious, involves a mechanism whereby information flows from intermediate areas, through high-level visual areas (infero-temporal cortex) to working memory areas in the lateral prefrontal cortex. Pieces of information in working memory, "allow the brain to recreate an intermediate-level representation by sending information back from working memory areas into the intermediate areas" (2004, p. 210). Prinz (2000) summarizes, emphasizing attention's role, as follows:

> When we see a visual stimulus, it is propagated unconsciously through the levels of our visual system. When signals arrive at the high level, interpretation is attempted. If the high level arrives at an interpretation, it sends an efferent signal back into the intermediate level with the aid of attention. Aspects of the intermediate-level representation that are most relevant to interpretation are neurally marked in some way, while others are either unmarked or suppressed. When no interpretation is achieved (as with fragmented images or cases of agnosia), attentional mechanisms might be deployed somewhat differently. They might "search" or "scan"

the intermediate level, attempting to find groupings that will lead to an interpretation. Both the interpretation-driven enhancement process and the interpretation-seeking search process might bring the attended portions of the intermediate level into awareness. This proposal can be summarized by saying that visual awareness derives from Attended Intermediate-level Representations (AIRs). (p. 249)

Prinz's account of attention's role in consciousness seems a lot like Churchland's conceptual interpretation, short-term memory, and of course, attention requirements on consciousness. Tye raises objections to the sort of view advocated by Churchland and Prinz. Tye is critical of accounts of consciousness that build in constitutive roles for attention. Tye's claim is based on introspective grounds (1995, p. 6). The thought here is that one might have a pain for a length of time but not be attending to it the entire time. Tye insists that there is still something it's like to have an unattended pain. Tye infers from these sorts of considerations that the neural correlate of visual consciousness is lower in the processing hierarchy than an attention-based theory would locate it. Tye thus locates the neural correlates of conscious states in "the grouped array" located in the occipital lobe and, regarding the phenomenon of blindsight, rejects "the hypothesis that blindsight is due to an impairment in the linkage between the spatial-attention system and the grouped array" (Tye 1995, pp. 215–16) Tye accounts for the retained visual abilities of blindsight subjects (p. 217) in terms of a "tecto-pulvinar pathway" from retina to superior coliculus that continues through the pulvinar to various parts of the cortex, including both the parietal lobe and area V4. Thus, Tye seems to think consciousness is in V1. Prinz (2000) argues against this, citing evidence against locating consciousness in V1 (see Crick & Koch 1995 and Koch & Braun 1996 for reviews). Prinz writes:

As Crick and Koch emphasize, V1 also seems to lack information that is available to consciousness. First, our experience of colors can remain constant across dramatic changes in wavelengths (Land 1964). Zeki (1983) has shown that such color constancy is not registered in V1. Second, V1 does not seem responsive to illusory contours across gaps in a visual array (von der Heydt, Peterhans, & Baumgartner 1984). If V1 were the locale of consciousness, we would not experience the lines in a Kanizsa triangle. (pp. 245–6)

Turning from disagreements to agreements, we may note that Churchland, Prinz, and Tye all agree that conscious states are representational states. They also agree that what will differentiate a conscious representation from an unconscious representation will involve relations that the representation bears to representations higher in the processing hierarchy. For both Churchland and Prinz, this will involve actual interactions, and further, these interactions will constitute relations that involve representations in processes of attention, conceptual interpretation, and short-term memory. Tye disagrees on the necessity of actually interacting with concepts or attention. His account is "dispositional," meaning that the representations need only be poised for uptake by higher levels of the hierarchy.

Turning to the question of transitive consciousness, we see both agreements and disagreements between the three authors. Churchland, Tye, and Prinz all agree that what one is conscious of is the representational content of conscious states. In all cases, what the subject is conscious of is what the representational contents of the conscious states are. However, these theorists differ somewhat in what they think the contents can be. Churchland has the least restrictive view: any content can be the content of a conscious state. Prinz's is more restrictive: the contents are not going to include high-level invariant contents. Tye's is the most restrictive: the contents will only be first-order and non-conceptual. Tye thinks that they are non-conceptual since he thinks that creatures without concepts – perhaps non-human animals and human infants – can have states for which there is something it's like to have them even though they possess no concepts. Tye says little about what concepts are, and for this, among other reasons, it is difficult to evaluate his view. The reason Tye thinks the contents of consciousness are first-order is because he believes in the pre-theoretic obviousness of the transparency thesis whereby when one has a conscious experience, all that one is conscious of is what the experience is an experience of. Thus, if one has a conscious experience of a blue square, one is only aware of what the mental state represents – the blue square. One is not, Tye insists, able to be conscious of the state itself. So, for example, if the state itself is a pattern of activity in one's nervous system, one will not be able to be conscious of this pattern of activity, but only be able to be conscious of external world properties that the pattern represents. Mandik (2005, 2006) argues that Churchland's (1979) thesis of the direct introspection of brain states provides the resources to argue against the kinds of restrictions on content that Tye makes.

I will not spell out the full argument here, just indicate the gist of it. Conceptual content can influence what it's like to have a particular experience. What it is to look at a ladybug and conceive of it as an example of *Hippodamia convergens* is, intuitively, quite different from what it would be like to conceive of it as one's reincarnated great-great-grandmother. Thus, if a person had the conceptual knowledge that consciously perceiving motion involved activity in area MT, and acquired the skill of being able to automatically and without conscious inference apply that conceptual knowledge to experience, then that person would be able to be conscious of the vehicular properties of that experience.

I turn now to what neurophilosophical accounts have to say about phenomenal character. I focus, in particular, on the suggestion that phenomenal character is to be identified with the representational content of conscious states. I will discuss this in terms of Churchland's suggestion of how qualia should be understood in terms of neural state spaces.

Our experience of color provides the most often discussed example of phenomenal character by philosophers, and Churchland is no exception. When Churchland discusses color qualia, he articulates a reductive account of them in terms of Land's theory that human perceptual discrimination of reflectance is due to the sensory reception of three kinds of electromagnetic wavelengths by three different kinds of cones in the retina (Land 1964). In keeping with the kinds of state-space interpretations of neural activity that Churchland is fond of, he explicates color qualia in terms of points in three dimensional spaces, the three dimensions of which correspond to the three kinds of cells responsive to electromagnetic wavelengths. Each color sensation is identical to a neural representation of a color (a neural representation of a spectral reflectance). Each sensation can thus be construed as a point in this 3-D activation space and the perceived similarity between colors and the subjective similarities between corresponding color qualia are definable in terms of proximity between points within the 3-D activation space. "Evidently, we can reconceive [sic] the cube [depicting the three dimensions of coding frequencies for reflectance in color state space] as an internal 'qualia cube'" (1989, p. 105). Churchland thinks this approach generalizes to other sensory qualia, such as gustatory, olfactory, and auditory qualia (ibid., pp. 105–6). Bringing this view in line with the thesis of the direct introspection of brain states, Churchland writes:

The "ineffable" pink of one's current visual sensation may be richly and precisely expressible as a 95 Hz/80 Hz/80 Hz "chord" in the relevant triune cortical system. The "unconveyable" taste sensation produced by the fabled Australian health tonic Vegamite [sic.] might be quite poignantly conveyed as a 85/80/90/15 "chord" in one's four-channeled gustatory system (a dark corner of taste-space that is best avoided). And the "indescribable" olfactory sensation pro-duced by a newly-opened rose might be quite accurately described as a 95/35/10/80/60/55 "chord" in some six-dimensional system within one's olfactory bulb.

This more penetrating conceptual framework might even displace the common-sense framework as the vehicle of intersubjective description and spontaneous introspection. Just as a musician can learn to recognize the constitution of heard musical chords, after internalizing the general theory of their internal structure, so may we learn to recognize, introspectively, the *n*-dimensional constitution of our subjective sensory qualia, after having internalized the gen-eral theory of *their* internal structure. (Ibid., p. 106)

Three particular and related features of Churchland's view of qualia are of special note. The first is that qualia are construed in representational terms. The second follows from the first, namely, that qualia so construed are not intrinsic properties of sensations, and thus over-turns a relatively traditional view of qualia. The third is that it allows for intersubjective apprehensions of qualia. To see these points more clearly it will be useful to briefly examine the traditional account of qualia noting the role of supposedly intrinsic properties in the account.

It is difficult to say uncontroversial things about qualia; however, there are several points of agreement among many of those philosophers who believe that mental states have such properties. These philosophers describe qualia as (i) intrinsic proper-ties of conscious states that (ii) are directly and fully knowable only by that subject and (iii) account for "what it's like" for a subject to be in that state. More briefly, qualia are (i) intrinsic, (ii) subjective, and (iii) there is "something it's like" to have (states with) them. Less briefly, we can start with (iii) and work our way to (i) as follows. When I have a conscious perception of a cup of coffee there is, presumably, something it's like for me to have that perception and, for all I know, what it's like for you to have a conscious per-ception of a cup of coffee is quite different. Furthermore, for all that you can tell me about your experience, there is much that cannot be conveyed and thus is subjective, that is, directly and fully knowable only by you alone. The supposition that qualia are intrin-sic properties of conscious states serves as a possible, though questionable, explanation of their subjectivity. (See Mandik 2001 for a neurophilosophical account in which sub-jectivity is consistent with qualia being extrinsic.) The inference from subjectivity to the intrinsic nature of qualia may be articulated as follows. If something is defined by the relations that it enters into, then it is fully describable by the relations it enters into, and if it is not fully describable by the relations it enters into, it must not be defined by the rela-tions it enters into.

To construe qualia in terms of representational content, however, is to construe them as no longer intrinsic, since typical accounts will spell out representational content in terms of:

1 causal relations that sensory states bear to states of the external world;
2 causal relations that they bear to other inner states; or
3 some combination of the two sorts of relations.

In neural terms, a pattern of activation in a neural network is the bearer of representational content in virtue of:

1   the distal or proximal stimuli that elicit the activation;
2   other patterns of activation that influence it via, e.g., recurrent connections; or
3   some combination of the two.

While it is relatively clear how Churchland's view is supposed to rule out the view of qualia as being intrinsic, it is not so clear that it is equally able to rule out their being subjective. The above quoted passage contains Churchland's view that properties of neural states previously inexpressible could, if one acquired the relevant neuroscientific concepts and the skill to apply them introspectively, become expressible. However, this view seems to be in tension with the earlier-mentioned view that concepts influence phenomenal character. The phenomenal character of an experience prior to the acquisition and introspective application of a concept will not, then, be the same as the phenomenal character of an experience after the acquisition and introspective application of that concept. Thus, even within a general neurophilosophical view of consciousness, there may remain certain representational contents of neural states that are directly and fully knowable only by the subject who has them. Neurophilosophy, then, may be fully compatible with the subjectivity of phenomenal consciousness.

See also 2 Philosophical problems of consciousness; 13 The case of blindsight; 19 The intermediate level theory of consciousness; 44 A neurobiological framework for consciousness; 48 Duplex vision: separate cortical pathways for conscious perception and the control of action.

Further Readings

Churchland, P. S. (1986) Neurophilosophy. Cambridge, MA: MIT Press.
Churchland, P. M. (1989) A Neurocomputational Perspective. Cambridge, MA: MIT Press.
Churchland, P. M. (2002) Catching consciousness in a recurrent net. In A. Brook, and D. Ross (eds.), Daniel Dennett: Contemporary Philosophy in Focus, 64–80. Cambridge: Cambridge University Press.
Prinz, J. (2000) A neurofunctional theory of visual consciousness. Consciousness and Cognition 9, 243–59.

References

Akins, A. (1996) Of sensory systems and the "aboutness" of mental states. Journal of Philosophy 93, 337–72.
Bisiach, E. (1992) Understanding consciousness: clues from unilateral neglect and related disorders. In A. D. Milner and M. D. Rugg (eds.), The Neuropsychology of Consciousness, 113–39. London: Academic Press.
Block, N. (1995) On a confusion about a function of consciousness. Behavioral and Brain Sciences 18: 2, 227–88.
Bonneh, Y., Cooperman, A., and Sagi, D. (2001) Motion induced blindness in normal observers. Nature 411: 6839, 798–801.
Chalmers, D. (1996) The Conscious Mind. New York: Oxford University Press.
Churchland, P. M. (1979) Scientific Realism and the Plasticity of Mind. Cambridge: Cambridge University Press.

Churchland, P. M. (1989) *A Neurocomputational Perspective*. Cambridge, MA: MIT Press.

Churchland, P. M. (1995) *The Engine of Reason, The Seat of the Soul: A Philosophical Journey into the Brain*. Cambridge, MA: MIT Press.

Churchland, P. M. (2002) Catching consciousness in a recurrent net. In A. Brook, and D. Ross (eds.), *Daniel Dennett: Contemporary Philosophy in Focus*, 64–80. Cambridge: Cambridge University Press.

Churchland, P. S. (1986) *Neurophilosophy*. Cambridge, MA: MIT Press.

Crick, F. and Koch, C. (1995) Are we aware of activity in primary visual cortex? *Nature* 375, 121–3.

Garson, J. (2002) Connectionism. In Edward N. Zalta (ed.), *Stanford Encyclopedia of Philosophy* (Winter 2002 edn.), <http://plato.stanford.edu/archives/win2002/entries/connectionism/>.

Koch, C. and Braun, J. (1996) Towards a neuronal correlate of visual awareness. *Current Opinion in Neurobiology* 6, 158–64.

Land, E. H. (1964) The retinex. *Scientific American* 52, 247–64.

Mandik, P. (2001) Mental representation and the subjectivity of consciousness. *Philosophical Psychology* 14: 2, 179–202.

Mandik, P. (2005) Phenomenal consciousness and the allocentric–egocentric interface. In R. Buccheri, A. Elitzur, and M. Saniga (eds.), *Endophysics, Time, Quantum and the Subjective*. Singapore: World Scientific Publishing Co.

Mandik, P. (2006) The introspectability of brain states as such. In B. Keeley (ed.), *Paul M. Churchland: Contemporary Philosophy in Focus*. Cambridge: Cambridge University Press.

Milner, A. and Goodale, M. (1995) *The Visual Brain in Action*. New York: Oxford University Press.

Olshausen, B. A., Anderson, C. H., and van Essen, D. C. (1994) A neurobiological model of visual attention and invariant pattern recognition based task. *Journal of Neuroscience* 14, 6171–86.

Olson, C., Gettner, S., and Tremblay, L. (1999) Representation of allocentric space in the monkey frontal lobe. In N. Burgess, K. Jeffery, and J. O'Keefe (eds.), *The Hippocampal and Parietal Foundations of Spatial Cognition*, 359–80. New York: Oxford University Press.

Pascual-Leone, A. and Walsh, V. (2001) Fast backprojections from the motion to the primary visual area necessary for visual awareness. *Science* 292, 510–12.

Pöppel, E., Held, R., and Frost, D. (1973) Residual visual functions after brain wounds involving the central visual pathways in man. *Nature* 243, 295–6.

Prinz, J. (2000) A neurofunctional theory of visual consciousness. *Consciousness and Cognition* 9, 243–59.

Prinz, J. (2004) *Gut Reactions*. New York: Oxford University Press.

Quine, W. (1969) Epistemology naturalized. In *Ontological Relativity and Other Essays*, 69–90. New York: Columbia University Press.

Rosenthal, D. (1993) State consciousness and transitive consciousness. *Consciousness and Cognition*, 2: 4 (December), 355–63.

Stoerig, P. and Cowey, A. (1992) Wavelength discrimination in blindsight. *Brain* 115, 425–44.

Tye, M. (1995) *Ten Problems of Consciousness: A Representational Theory of the Phenomenal Mind*. Cambridge, MA: MIT Press.

von der Heydt, R., Peterhans, E., and Baumgartner, G. (1984) Illusory contours and cortical neuron responses. *Science* 224, 1260–2.

Weiskrantz, L. (1995) Blindsight: not an island unto itself. *Current Directions in Psychological Science* 4, 146–51.

Weiskrantz, L. (1996) Blindsight revisited. *Current Opinions in Neurobiology* 6: 2, 215–20.

Zeki, S. (1983) Colour coding in the cerebral cortex: the reaction of cells in monkey visual cortex to wavelengths and colour. *Neuroscience* 9, 741–56.

34

Type Materialism for Phenomenal Consciousness

BRIAN P. McLAUGHLIN

A state of phenomenal consciousness is a state such that it's like something for the subject of the state to be in it. Paradigm cases include bodily sensations such as, for instance, feeling pain, and sensory experiences such as visually experiencing red. The what-it-is-like aspect of a state is its phenomenal or qualitative character. (These qualitative characters are "qualia," in one of the many uses of that term.) Such characters are properties that are state types: their exemplifications are states of phenomenal consciousness. The problem of the place of such state types (or properties) in nature is perhaps the most difficult of the many-faceted problem known as the mind–body problem. Thus, it was with phenomenal consciousness in mind that Thomas Nagel (1979a, p. 64) once remarked: "consciousness is what makes the mind–body problem really intractable." Type materialism (or type physicalism) is a theory of the place of states of phenomenal consciousness in nature. It is the theory that qualitative mental states are type identical with certain neuroscientific states. Before examining the theory, some background is required.

We have long known that our states of phenomenal consciousness are somehow intimately related to what happens in our nervous systems. But it has also long been claimed that the precise nature of that relationship is mysterious. For example, Thomas Huxley famously remarked:

> How it is that anything so remarkable as a state of consciousness comes about as a result of irritating nervous tissue, is just as unaccountable as the appearance of the Djin, when Aladdin rubbed his lamp. (1866)

More recently, Colin McGinn has presented "the deep mystery" of phenomenal consciousness in this way:

> The specific problem I want to discuss concerns consciousness, the hard nut of the mind–body problem. How is it possible for conscious states to depend upon brain states? How can technicolour phenomenology arise from soggy grey matter? . . . How could the aggregation of millions of individually insentient neurons generate subjective awareness? We know that brains are the de facto causal basis of consciousness, but we have, it seems, no understanding whatever of how this can be so. It strikes us as miraculous, eerie, even faintly comic. Somehow, we feel, the water of the physical brain is turned into the wine of consciousness, but we draw a total blank on the

nature of this conversion . . . The mind–body problem is the problem of understanding how the miracle is wrought, thus removing the sense of deep mystery. (1989, pp. 394–5)

And David Chalmers tells us:

There is no question that experience is closely associated with physical processes in systems such as brains. It seems that physical processes give rise to experience, at least in the sense that producing a physical system (such as a brain) with the right physical properties inevitably yields corresponding states of experience. But how and why do physical processes give rise to experience? . . . This is the central mystery of consciousness. (2003, p. 248)

Chalmers (1995 and chapter 17) calls the problem of how and why physical processes in the brain give rise to experiences (i.e., states with qualitative characters), "the hard problem of consciousness."

There are currently a number of scientific projects that are aimed at finding the neural correlates of states of phenomenal consciousness. Whether any of these projects will succeed is of course an empirical issue. But it is generally acknowledged that for all we know, one of them will succeed. And some in the neuroscientific community believe that there is reason for optimism (Crick 1994 and chapter 44). Suppose, then, that some project for finding the neural correlates of states of phenomenal consciousness will in fact succeed. Indeed, suppose that we will someday find *strict* nomological neuroscientific correlates of types of states of phenomenal consciousness, and so will be able to confirm the following general thesis:

Correlation Thesis. For any type of state of phenomenal consciousness C there is a type of neuroscientific state N such that it is nomologically necessary that a being is in C if and only if the being is in N.

The first point to note is that this result would by no means settle the issue of the place of phenomenal consciousness in nature. The reason is that the correlation thesis is compatible with a variety of views of that matter, including such nonphysicalist views as Cartesian substance-dualism, emergent property dualism, neutral monism, and panpsychism. Indeed it is compatible with every major view of the place of phenomenal consciousness in nature. The second point to note is that Huxley, McGinn, Chalmers, and many other philosophers would maintain that the mystery of phenomenal consciousness – the hard problem of consciousness – would still remain even were such strict correlational laws found: How and why do the neuroscientific states in question give rise to states of phenomenal consciousness? How and why, for example, does neuroscientific state N (e.g., a certain state of a certain kind of neural network) give rise to C (e.g., a feeling of pain), rather than to some other kind of state of phenomenal consciousness distinct from C (e.g., a tickling feeling or a chill or a hot flash), or to no state of phenomenal consciousness at all? (See chapters 17 and 24.)

One epistemic possibility is that the correlational laws in question would be fundamental, irreducible laws of nature. This view was favored by the British Emergentist's Samuel Alexander (1920) and C. D. Broad (1925). It remains a position to which some philosophers are sympathetic. According to the British Emergentists, the mystery of consciousness cannot be removed or dispelled, for although neuroscientific states give rise to states of phenomenal consciousness, there is no explanation of how and why they do so. The fact that they do so is a brute, inexplicable fact that we must learn to accept with "natural piety."

One striking consequence of this emergent property dualism is that, on certain plausible assumptions, it entails that it is logically possible for there to be a world that is exactly like the actual world in every physical detail, but in which there are no states of phenomenal consciousness at all. In such a world, our physical duplicates would be *zombies* (Chalmers 1996). (A zombie is an individual that is an exact physical duplicate of a phenomenally conscious being, but is itself entirely devoid of phenomenal consciousness.)

Perhaps the leading concern about this emergent property dualism is that on certain plausible assumptions, it entails that states of phenomenal consciousness are epiphenomena. Some emergentists accept that result. But the claim that states of phenomenal consciousness are epiphenomena is deeply disturbing. Not only do we think that pains sometimes make us wince, itches sometimes make us scratch, and pleasant feelings sometimes make us smile, we also assume that we navigate through our environment in part on the basis of the way we phenomenally experience it as being. Moreover, it seems that we base our beliefs about the way the world is in part on how we phenomenally experience the world as being. And such basing relations seem to require causation. Indeed if states of phenomenal consciousness are epiphenomena, then one's belief that one is in pain would never be caused by one's feeling of pain; instead the pain and the belief would just accompany each other as dual effects of a common physical cause.

These causal concerns are among the central concerns that have led many philosophers to look for an alternative to emergent property dualism. And indeed the view that the psychophysical correlational laws in question would be fundamental laws of nature is by no means the only option. But if the law correlating a neuroscientific state N and a state of phenomenal consciousness C is explicable, one seems faced again with the hard problem: how and why does N give rise to C, rather than to some other type of conscious state, or to no state of consciousness at all?

Were analytical functionalism true, there would be no mystery. According to the role-functionalist version, it is analytically true that types of states of phenomenal consciousness are identical with types of role-states, that is, types of higher-order states of being in some state or other that occupies a certain causal (and/or counterfactual) role that is specifiable, in principle, in (broadly) physical terms. (There is also a "filler" version of analytical functionalism, but the differences between the filler version and the role version will be ignored for present purposes.) Such higher-order states are often called "functional states." The claim, then, is that it is analytically true that types of state of phenomenal consciousness are identical with types of functional states. The lower-order states that occupy the roles in question realize the functional states; and if more than one lower-order state occupies a given role, then the functional state is multiply realizable. According to role-functionalists, then, N would give rise to C by being a realization of C, that is, by its tokens playing the appropriate causal role. (Were we to confirm that C is nomologically correlated with N, it would follow that in nomologically possible worlds, only N realizes C. But the typical functionalist would claim that there are nevertheless other metaphysically possible ways of realizing it. We will return to the idea of multiple realization later.)

The main problem with analytical functionalism is that it seems to be false. It does not seem to be analytic that states of phenomenal consciousness are identical with functional states. There seem to be no analytical connections of the sort in question. For any functional state F and any state of phenomenal consciousness C, it seems coherently conceivable that an individual is in F yet not in C. It seems that our concepts of states of phenomenal consciousness (such as the concept of the feeling of pain) cannot be defined in physical terms.

Those who press the mystery of consciousness maintain that analytical functionalism is false. They claim, moreover, that if a type of state of phenomenal consciousness C turned out to be nomologically correlated with a type of functional state F, then the question would arise, how and why does F give rise to C? And they point out that one option would be that such a posteriori correlational laws are fundamental, and so must be accepted with natural piety.

Although our concepts of phenomenal consciousness seem to lack conceptual analyses in physical terms, if they nevertheless had contingent a priori physical reference-fixing conditions, then, again, there would be no mystery. Thus, suppose that it were a priori, despite being contingent, that the feeling of pain is the state that occupies causal role R, where R is specified in (broadly) physical terms. Then, if we could determine that neuroscientific state N is the occupant of R (or the occupant of R in normal beings of a certain kind K), we could deduce a priori from that fact that N is the feeling of the pain (or the feeling of pain in Ks). Unfortunately, however, our concepts of states of phenomenal consciousness seem to lack such a priori reference-fixing analyses. There seem to be no such a priori links between them and (even broadly) physical concepts. It seems that no physical condition is a priori sufficient for being in a state of phenomenal consciousness. To be sure, the idea that there are zombies is utterly absurd. But utter absurdity is one thing, a priori falsity another. It does not seem a priori false that there are zombies.

The absence of any a priori links between concepts of phenomenal consciousness and physical concepts that are adequate to enable us to answer the hard problem of consciousness has been called "the explanatory gap" between phenomenal consciousness and the physical (Levine 2001 and chapter 29). Indeed, given the absence of such a priori links, certain kinds of reductive explanations are impossible in the case in question. Type of states of phenomenal consciousness cannot be reductively explained via conceptual analyses stated in physical terms or via contingent a priori reference-fixing analyses stated in physical terms. In this sense, there is an unbridgeable explanatory gap.

Given the explanatory gap, it is hard to see how the hard problem of phenomenal consciousness – How and why do physical processes in the brain give rise to states of phenomenal consciousness? – can be answered. If one assumes that a neuroscientific state N gives rise to a state of phenomenal consciousness C, then the question will indeed arise as to *how* N gives rise to C. It seems that it will either be a brute, inexplicable fact that N gives rise to C (as the Emergentists claimed) or else there will be some mechanism by which N gives rise to C. But either way, it is indeed *hard* to see how the sense of mystery could be dispelled. If N gives rise to C directly, and so not via any mechanism, then it seems that the fact that N gives rise to C will be a brute a posteriori fact that we will have to accept with natural piety. But if instead N gives rise to C indirectly via some physical mechanism, then it is hard to see how knowledge of that mechanism could possibly remove the sense of mystery. For, given the absence of suitable a priori connections, the how-question would recur for the relevant physical factor(s) at work in the mechanism: if N gives rise to C by giving rise to P which, in turn, gives rise to C, then how does P give rise to C? The mystery of phenomenal consciousness can thus seem inescapable.

Notice, however, that a presupposition of the question "How does N give rise to C?" is that N *gives rise* to C. It is epistemically possible that this presupposition is false. Rather than N somehow giving rise to C, it might instead be the case that N *is* C. It may be that there is one type of state that is conceptualized in two different ways; two concepts – the concept of N and the concept of C – that in fact answer to the same state type; one state type that has, as it were, two names. States types are properties, and properties are one thing, concepts another. Properties are ways that things might be; concepts are ways of thinking of things as being. Two concepts that are not linked a priori may nevertheless answer to the same property. The concept of water is distinct from the concept of H_2O; and there is no direct a priori link between them. Nevertheless, the property of being water is identical with the property of being H_2O. Similarly, perhaps N is identical with C, despite the absence of any a priori link between the concept of N and the concept of C. There may be conceptual dualism (indeed conceptual pluralism), yet empirical property monism.

Type materialism for phenomenal consciousness is the view that types of states of phenomenal consciousness are identical with their *strict* neuroscientific correlates. According to type materialism, the explanation of why a neuroscientific state N is *strictly* nomologically correlated with a state of phenomenal consciousness C is that N = C. The logical symbol "=" here means "is identical with." Thus, the view entails:

> *The Identity Thesis.* For every type of state of phenomenal consciousness C, there is some type of neuroscientific state N such that C = N.

If type materialism is true, then states of phenomenal consciousness are causally efficacious; for they are neuroscientific states with causal effects. That would vindicate our common-sense belief in the causal efficacy of phenomenal consciousness.

The Identity Thesis entails the Correlation Thesis. As Saul Kripke (1980) has shown, for any A and B, if A = B, then necessarily B = A. He derived this principle from two enormously plausible assumptions. The first is Leibniz's principle, *the indiscernibility of identicals*: if A = B, then whatever is true of A is true of B. The second is that everything is such that it is necessarily identical with itself. The kind of necessity in question is metaphysical necessity: truth in every possible world. Thus, if N = C, then N and C are co-extensive in every possible world. It follows from that, that they are co-extensive in every nomologically possible world – in every possible world in which exactly our laws of nature hold. Thus, if the identity thesis is true, then the correlation thesis is true as well.

Notice that given that identities are necessary, if type materialism is true, then any possible exact physical duplicate of a phenomenally conscious being will itself be a phenomenally conscious being. Thus, if type materialism is true, zombies are impossible. Type materialists nevertheless acknowledge that it is not a priori false that there are zombies. They hold that Ψ can be impossible, even though it is not a priori false that Ψ. It is not a priori true that water = H_2O, and so not a priori false that water ≠ H_2O. It was an empirical discovery that water = H_2O. Nevertheless, given that water = H_2O, it is impossible that water ≠ H_2O. To take another example, it is only a posteriori knowable that Benjamin Franklin = the actual inventor of bifocals, for it is not a priori false that Benjamin Franklin ≠ the actual inventor of bifocals. But given that Benjamin Franklin = the actual inventor of bifocals, it is impossible that Benjamin Franklin ≠ the actual inventor of bifocals. Impossibility thus does not require a priori falsity. Of course, Benjamin Franklin might not have been the inventor of bifocals. The description "the inventor of bifocals" is non-rigid: what individual, if any, it picks out can vary from one possible world to another. In contrast, "the actual inventor of bifocals" is a rigid description: it picks out the same individual in any world in which it picks out anything.

According to type materialists, the specific psychophysical identity claims in question will be knowable only a posteriori, since there are no relevant a priori links between neuroscientific concepts and concepts of states of phenomenal consciousness. And thus the Identity Thesis itself will be knowable only a posteriori. Type materialists acknowledge that there is a kind of unbridgeable explanatory gap in this sense: types of states of phenomenal consciousness are not reducible to types of physical states via either conceptual analyses or contingent a priori reference-fixing analyses. But they deny that this explanatory gap entails an ontological gap. States of phenomenal consciousness, they maintain, are neuroscientific states.

As concerns any type of neuroscientific state N and any type of state of phenomenal consciousness C, if it is the case that N = C, then that would explain why N and C are nomologically correlated: they are co-extensive in every nomologically possible world because they are one and the same state. But we would not, of course, take the hypothesis that N = C to explain why N is correlated with C, unless we regarded it as epistemically justified. The justification for this identity hypothesis, however, need not be *epistemically prior* to the justification for belief in the nomological correlation. Type materialists hold that if N and C are nomologically correlated, then the justification for the hypothesis that N = C would be that it offers *the best explanation* of the correlation – best on holistic grounds of overall coherence and simplicity with respect to total theory. Indeed they typically offer a conditional defense of type materialism. They maintain that if the Correlational Thesis is true (an empirical issue), then the Identity Thesis would offer the best explanation of why it is true – indeed an explanation sufficiently good to warrant us in accepting the thesis. (See Hill 1991; Block & Stalnaker 1999; McLaughlin 2001; Papineau 2002.)

What, however, would explain the psychophysical identities? It is a frequently made point that identities are not themselves explainable (e.g., Causey 1977). There is no point to the question, "Why is N = C?" There is no point, that is, unless the intent of the question is to ask why we should believe that N = C. But that is a request for a justification (a reason for believing), not a request for an explanation. Explanations come to an end where identities are concerned. There can be no explanation of why something is identical with itself.

Nevertheless, although the question "Why is C = N?" has no point except as a request for a justification (rather than an explanation), the question "How is it possible for it to be the case that C = N?" is very much to the point. This is a request for a justification of the claim that it is possible that C = N (not a request for a mechanism). This how-question is to the point since there are "apparent excluders" of the possibility in question, that is, conditions that appear (or that can appear) required for it to be the case that C = N and that also appear (or can appear) to be such that they cannot obtain (Nozick 1981). Property dualists maintain that there are genuine excluders: conditions that are required for it to be the case that C = N and that cannot obtain. Indeed, most of the leading objections to type materialism purport to show, by appealing to one or another would-be excluder, that it is a priori impossible that C = N. An explanation of how it is possible that C = N would need to show why the apparent excluders of this possibility are not genuine excluders of it, but are instead merely apparent excluders of it. That would require either showing for each apparent excluder AE that AE is not required for it to be the case that N = C or else explaining how AE is possible (by explaining away AE's apparent excluders). Whether that can be done bears directly on the issue of whether the Identity Thesis would offer the best explanation of the Correlation Thesis; for if the Identity Thesis is a priori false, then of course it cannot explain anything. The claim that the Identity Thesis offers the best explanation of the Correlation Thesis requires explaining away the apparent excluders of the psychophysical identities in question; that is part of what is involved in showing that the identity hypotheses offer the best explanation of the correlations.

Let us consider some leading would-be objections to the possibility that N = C, and the leading type materialist responses to them.

Objection 1

Type materialists acknowledge that it is coherently conceivable that C ≠ N. Coherent conceivability, however, entails possibility. We cannot actually coherently conceive that water ≠ H_2O. We do sometimes take ourselves to be conceiving that water ≠ H_2O. But in such situations what we are really conceiving is that some epistemic counterpart of water fails to be H_2O. An epistemic counterpart of water is a kind of stuff that has the same observable macro-properties of water – stuff that looks, smells, tastes, and feels like water – what has been called in the literature "watery stuff." It is indeed coherently conceivable that an epistemic counterpart of water (a kind of watery stuff) is not H_2O. But it is also possible for an epistemic counterpart of water not to be H_2O. Similarly, we cannot actually coherently conceive that Benjamin Franklin ≠ the actual inventor of bifocals. When we take ourselves to be conceiving of that, what we are really conceiving is that someone other than Benjamin Franklin is the inventor of bifocals. And that is indeed possible. Although Benjamin Franklin is the inventor of bifocals, he might not have been; someone else might have been the inventor. It is, however, not open to the type materialist to maintain that when we take ourselves to conceive that C ≠ N, we are actually only conceiving that some epistemic counterpart of C ≠ N. The reason is that an epistemic counterpart of any type of state of phenomenal consciousness C will be C. The feeling of pain, for instance, is a certain kind of feeling. Any epistemic counterpart of the feeling of pain *is* the feeling of pain: what feels like pain *is* pain. Since coherent conceivability indeed entails possibility, and it is coherently conceivable that C ≠ N, it follows that it is possible that C ≠ N. And given the necessity of identity, it follows from that possibility that C ≠ N (see Kripke 1980 and Chalmers 1996).

Reply

The leading type materialist response is to reject the modal epistemology presupposed in the objection. Type materialists maintain that those of us untutored in that modal epistemology take ourselves to be able to conceive that water ≠ H_2O, and that Benjamin Franklin ≠ the actual inventor of bifocals. The modal epistemology presupposed in *Objection 1* accommodates a posteriori necessity, while retaining the idea that coherent conceivability entails possibility, by rejecting the idea that we have first-person authority about what it is we are conceiving. Thus, proponents of this modal epistemology maintain that although it seems to us that we are conceiving that water ≠ H_2O, that is not in fact what we are doing. An alternative to this modal epistemology, however, is to retain first-person authority about what we are conceiving and to reject instead the principle that coherent conceivability entails possibility. Type materialists maintain that there are in some cases reasons for being skeptical of our modal intuitions based on what we can coherently conceive. Consider a case that is independent of the one at issue. Platonic universals, unlike Aristotelian universals, are such that if they exist in any possible world, then they exist in every possible world. It seems coherently conceivable that there are Platonic universals. And it seems coherently conceivable that there are no Platonic universals. But if coherent conceivability entails possibility then, on uncontroversial modal assumptions, a contradiction will follow: there are Platonic universals and it is not the case that there are Platonic universals (cf. Yablo 1999). Of course, the claim that there are Platonic universals is of a special sort. It is such that if it is true, then it is necessarily true; and such that if it is false, then it is necessarily false. But that doesn't distinguish it from the identity claims in question: if it is true that C = N, then it is necessarily true that C = N; and if it is false that C = N, then it is necessarily false that C = N. Moreover, type materialists maintain that in the case of the psychphysical identity claims in question, there are specific reasons for being skeptical of our modal intuitions based on conceivability. Our neuroscientific concepts are theoretical concepts. Our concepts of states of phenomenal consciousness, in contrast, are one's that we can apply to ourselves directly on the basis of our awareness of our conscious states. Such concepts thus have very different roles in our cognitive architecture. And indeed, the roles are such that it would seem to us that we could be in N without being in C (and conversely), even if it were the case that N = C. We thus have grounds for skepticism about modal intuitions in these kinds of cases. Nevertheless, it may very well be the case that there is a conceptual tie between coherent conceivability and possibility. The fact that Ψ is coherently conceivable seems to be a prima facie reason to believe that it is possible that Ψ. That prima facie reason, however, can be defeated by considerations of overall coherence and theoretical simplicity. (See Hill 1997; Loar 1997; Hill & McLaughlin 1999; Yablo 1999; 2002; Balog 2000; and Papineau 2002.)

The above exchange by no means exhausts the discussions of modal epistemology in the relevant literature. There are further follow-up objections and further replies. The above exchange is intended only to give a sense of the debate. The points to note are that one of the leading lines of dualist objections to type materialism is that there is a sense of conceivability such that (i) it is conceivable that C ≠ N, and (ii) the fact it is conceivable that C ≠ N entails that it is possible that C ≠ N (e.g., Chalmers 2002); and that type materialists steadfastly maintain that there is no sense of conceivability such that (i) and (ii) are both true. Suffice it to note that this dispute remains unresolved.

Objection 2

States of phenomenal consciousness are subjective states: to fully understand what it is to be in them, we must know what it's like to be in them. Thus, for instance, one cannot fully understand what it is to be in pain without knowing what it's like to be in pain. In contrast, neuroscientific states are objective states. They can be fully understood in principle from an objective point of view. No state can be both subjective and objective. Hence, no type of state of phenomenal consciousness is a type of neuroscientific state (Nagel 1979b).

Reply

The distinction between the subjective and the objective is, in the first instance, an epistemic distinction. A state type is subjective or objective only under a conceptualization, that is, only under a concept. A state type S can be subjective under one concept (a phenomenal concept) and objective under another (a neuroscientific concept) (see Loar 1997; Sturgeon 2000; McLaughlin 2003a).

Objection 3

One can be directly aware of one's state of phenomenal consciousness C (e.g., one's feeling of pain). But no neuroscientific state is such that one can be directly aware of it. Hence, no state of phenomenal consciousness is a neuroscientific state.

Reply

The linguistic context "is directly aware of . . ." is extensional, and so subject to the rule of inference substitutivity of identicals. If one is directly aware of one's state of phenomenal consciousness C, and C = N, then one is directly aware of one's state N, whether one realizes that or not (indeed whether one even has the concept of N).

Follow up to Objection 3

But we can be *directly* aware of our states of phenomenal consciousness in the sense that we can be aware of them otherwise than via some contingent mode of presentation of them or some partial aspect of them. They are self-presenting. If they were neuroscientific states, our direct acquaintance with them would thus reveal them to be neuroscientific states. They would present themselves to us as neuroscientific states. But they do not present themselves to us as neuroscientific states. Hence, they are not neuroscientific states (Horgan & Tienson 2001).

Reply

We can indeed be directly aware of our states of phenomenal consciousness in the sense in question. We can be aware of them otherwise than via awareness of some contingent mode of presentation of them or some partial aspect of them. They are in that sense self-presenting. And it is indeed the case that they do not present themselves to us as neuroscientific states. But there is a distinction between their not presenting themselves as neuroscientific states and their presenting themselves as not being neuroscientific states. Such states do not present themselves to us as neuroscientific states, but it is not the case that they present themselves to us as not being neuroscientific states. The fact that a state does not present itself to us as X does not entail that it presents itself to us as not being X. Moreover, presentation-as is a conceptual matter. In the relevant sense, something is presented to us as X only if we exercise the concept of X. We can directly apply our concepts of phenomenal consciousness in introspection. Thus, we can directly introspect a state as, for example, a feeling of pain. In contrast, we cannot directly apply neuroscientific concepts in introspection; we cannot, for instance, directly introspect a state as N. That is why the states that we are directly aware of in introspection are not presented to us as neuroscientific states in introspection. But that fails to entail that the states presented to us in introspection are not neuroscientific states. Introspection-as is conceptual. The linguistic context "is introspectable as . . ." is hyper-intentional: necessarily co-extensive terms cannot be substituted within it *salva veritate* (McLaughlin 2001).

Now the type materialist can concede that we have a kind of knowledge by acquaintance of conscious states. But the type materialist will insist that such knowledge by acquaintance is different from knowledge by description. We can demonstrate such state types in introspection ("this type of feeling") and name them ("pain"). But introspective awareness and memories of such awareness yield no descriptive knowledge of the intrinsic nature of the types of states in question. They yield, rather, analogical descriptive knowledge such as that what it's like to have one experience E1 is more similar to what it's like to have another E2 than is what it's like to have a third E3 (e.g., what it's like to experience the hue blue is more similar to what it's like to experience the hue purple than it is to what it's like to experience the hue yellow). The type materialist claims that types of qualitative states that are so demonstrated, named, and analogically compared on the basis of introspective awareness and memory are neuroscientific states (McLaughlin 2003a).

Further counter-objections and replies can be found in the literature. But the above sketch serves to illustrate a common pattern in the debates. Dualists press an epistemological distinction and maintain that it supports an ontological distinction. Type materialists often concede the epistemological distinction, but deny that it supports the ontological distinction. They try to explain the epistemological distinction in terms of differences in the conceptual roles of phenomenal concepts and neuroscientific concepts, and maintain those differences do not entail that the concepts in question answer to different properties.

Thus far, the discussion has focused on objections to type materialism from the dualist camp. But type materialism is only one brand of physicalism for states of phenomenal consciousness. And some physicalists reject it in favor of other brands of physicalism. Psychofunctionalists maintain that types of states of phenomenal consciousness are identical with the types of functional states, higher-order states of being in some state or other that plays a certain causal role R, where the role R is specifiable in (broadly) physical terms. However, unlike analytical role functionalists, psychofunctionalists maintain that the type identities in question are only a posteriori knowable; and they deny as well that phenomenal concepts have contingent a priori reference fixing analyses in physical terms. Psychofunctional theories thus face essentially the same dualist objections as those discussed above. Suffice it to note, however, that the type materialist replies to these objections seem available, *mutatis mutandis*, to the psychofunctionalist. Some physicalists reject type materialism, and instead embrace psychofunctionalism.

What would decide between type materialism and psychofunctionalism? One of the advantages claimed for type materialism is that it has as a consequence that states of phenomenal consciousness themselves normally have (mostly) the causal role that folk psychology associates with them, rather than being states of being in some state or other that has that causal role. The main advantage claimed for psychofunctionalism over type materialism is that the former allows for the possibility that there are creatures very different from us in material constitution and composition that are nevertheless phenomenally conscious (Putnam 1975). It allows for that since functional states can be multiply physically realized.

In brief, responses by type materialists include the following. First, neuroscientific states can be abstract; so it is possible for two creatures that are different physically nevertheless to share certain neuroscientific states, and thus to share certain states of phenomenal consciousness (Polger 2004). Thus, for instance, we might very well share certain relevant neuroscientific states with bats.

Second, type materialism is in a way less restrictive than psychofunctionalism *if* psychofunctionalism requires that a state have the causal role that folk psychology associates with a conscious state in order to realize that state. Psychofunctionalists must, of course, tell us what the causal roles are that are a posteriori yet metaphysically necessary and sufficient for realizing a conscious state. Type materialism allows that there can be phenomenal consciousness in actual "absent folk role" cases. It allows, for instance, that a paralytic suffering from very severe Alzheimer's disease can feel pain. And it makes no demands on the causal roles that a creature's states must have to be states of phenomenal consciousness beyond those that are required for being the relevant neuroscientific states.

Third, states of phenomenal consciousness are states such that it's like something for the subject of the state to be in the state. Although many kinds of creatures occupy states that have causal roles that are to various extents similar to the causal roles that folk psychology associates with states of phenomenal consciousness in us, it is very much an open question how far phenomenal consciousness extends into the animal kingdom. Many kinds of creatures engage in pain-like behavior in response to bodily damage. But it by no means follows that all such creatures feel pain. Even though a lobster placed in boiling water will writhe, the lobster may not be feeling anything; it may not be like anything for the lobster. A chicken without a head racing around the yard may not be feeling anything at all. Dip the tip of a freshly detached insect leg in acid, and it will retract. But there may very well be no sensation at all. Of course, given the lack of a priori connections between our concepts of phenomenal consciousness and our physical concepts, we can imagine that even rocks have some sort of "phenomenal buzz." But the type materialist maintains that there is no reason whatsoever to believe that, and that indeed there is good reason to deny it. The fact, moreover, that a creature perceives the environment does not entail that the creature has phenomenal consciousness. Salmon track their way back to the streams in which they were spawned by detecting via a kind of olfaction (using organs on the salmon's cheeks) a trail of chemicals they released on the way to sea; they move in the direction of the cheek that detects the greatest abundance of such chemicals. But it may very well not be like anything for them to detect such chemicals. Indeed even the capacity to see does not require visual phenomenal consciousness. We know, for instance, that there are neural states involved when we see that are capable of guiding behaviors of considerable complexity and yet are not accompanied by states of phenomenal consciousness in us; think here of the neural states involved in the "action pathway" in visuo-motor processing (Milner & Goodale 1995 and Goodale, chapter 48). Although a bee, a chicken, and a lizard can all see, there may very well be nothing at all that it's like for them to see. Nagel (1979a) once asked what it's like to be a bat. There may be something that it's like to be a bat. But there may very well be nothing that it's like to be a bee, or a chicken, or a lobster.

Fourth, it is an open empirical question whether it is nomologically possible for there to be a silicon-based android that is disposed to behave overtly (both verbally and nonverbally) exactly like a normal human being. Nevertheless there seems no reason whatsoever to doubt that such a silicon-based android is metaphysically possible. Indeed there seems no reason whatsoever to doubt that it is metaphysically possible for a silicon-based android to occupy states that play the causal roles (*sans* those involving states of consciousness) that folk psychology associates with states of phenomenal consciousness (Block 2002). Type materialists emphasize that the relevant issue as concerns such silicon-based androids is whether they would have any of our states of phenomenal consciousness. The issue is not whether they would have beliefs, preferences, and intentions, or whether they would see or hear, or whether they would speak a language. Type materialism for phenomenal consciousness leaves those matters entirely open. Psychofunctionalists readily acknowledge that there is no behavior or functional organization or physical condition that a priori suffices for possessing phenomenal consciousness. They acknowledge that at best such conditions would provide prima facie reasons for attributing phenomenal consciousness. The type materialist agrees that such conditions can provide prima facie reasons. But the type materialist claims that we know in our own case that we are phenomenally conscious. And the type materialist holds that we tacitly rely on a kind of "same effect, same cause" assumption in attributing our types of states of phenomenal consciousness to other beings. Behavior and functional organization are evidence of any of the kinds of phenomenally conscious states that we can be in only insofar as they are evidence that a being is in the states that are invariably accompanied by those states of phenomenal consciousness in us. ("Accompany" is a neutral-term here. A state of phenomenal consciousness might accompany a brain state by being identical with it, or by being realized or somehow generated by it, or by being an immediate causal effect of it.) Certain behaviors and functional organizations provide reasons to attribute such states of phenomenal consciousness. But such reasons are defeasible. Were we to discover that an android lacks states that in us are invariably accompanied by the relevant states of phenomenal consciousness that would defeat (rebut) such reasons for thinking that the android is in those states of phenomenal consciousness.

Of course, if an android is disposed to behave outwardly exactly as a normal human being is, then we would find ourselves unable to effectively interact with it without treating it as if it were phenomenally conscious – indeed as if it had the sorts of states of phenomenal consciousness that we have. Effectively interacting with it might require taking what we might call "the sentient stance" toward the android (cf. Dennett's (1987) idea of "the intentional stance" (McLaughlin 2003b)). But in taking such a stance we would not thereby be committed to holding that the android literally has any of our states of phenomenal consciousness – or indeed is phenomenally conscious at all. Now if we were to interact with a community of such androids on a regular basis, terms such as "pain," "itch," "tickle," "experience of red," and the like, might acquire a purely functional use, one that is distinct from their phenomenal use (Hill 1991). Indeed, we could actually now stipulate such uses, if we liked (Chalmers 1996, ch. 1). If they did, then the terms would literally apply to the androids in their purely functional sense. But, the type materialist claims, the terms would not apply to the androids in their phenomenal sense. Androids would feel pain in the (new) purely functional sense, but they would not feel pain in the phenomenal sense; they would not have pain qualia. (For further discussion of the issue of whether androids could be phenomenally conscious, see Block 2002 and McLaughlin 2003b.)

There is another dispute between type materialism and a certain brand of psychofunctionalism. According to the brand in question, types of states of phenomenal consciousness are a posteriori identical with certain types of functional states with wide causal roles – causal roles involving factors outside of the brain. These factors external to the brain include bodily conditions in the case of bodily sensations, and environmental properties in the case of sensory experiences (visual experiences, auditory experiences, and the like); and, on some versions, they even invariably include facts about the evolutionary history of the being in question. Such wide psycho-functional theories go under the name "representational theories of phenomenal consciousness" (e.g., Dretske 1995; Lycan 1996; Tye 2000). Representational theories that purport to be *comprehensive* theories of phenomenal consciousness (theories that cover every type of state of phenomenal consciousness) have in common that (a) phenomenal characters are certain kinds of non-conceptual contents, and that (b) the psycho-semantics for what it is for a state to have any of the kinds of non-conceptual contents in question is externalist. (For more discussion see chapter 20.) Claim (a) is compatible with type materialism; it is open to a type materialist to maintain that phenomenal consciousness is thoroughly intentional. But the conjunction of (a) and (b) is incompatible with type materialism. The reason is that according to type materialism, phenomenal characters are neuroscientific state types (or properties) that are individuated independently of external (to the brain) factors.

One point of dispute between type materialism and representationalism, then, is this. According to type materialism, whether an individual is phenomenally conscious supervenes on the intrinsic physical states of the individual's brain; it is necessarily the case that if two individuals are exactly alike with respect to what intrinsic physical states their brains are in, then they are exactly alike with respect to what states of phenomenal consciousness they are in; for any state of phenomenal consciousness C, the one is in C if, and only if, the other is. Representationalists deny such supervenience. On their view, "qualia ain't in the head," and so neuroscientists who search for them there search in vain. The evolutionary versions of (comprehensive) representationalism have as a consequence that an individual who is an exact physical intrinsic duplicate of a normal phenomenally conscious human being would be a zombie (and so entirely devoid of phenomenal consciousness) if the individual failed to have a certain sort of evolutionary history. And on all versions of (comprehensive) representationalism, it is possible for there to be an object that is an exact intrinsic physical duplicate of the brain of a normal awake human being who is enjoying phenomenal consciousness but that nevertheless fails to instantiate any states of phenomenal consciousness at all; there could fail to be any phenomenal consciousness (any qualia) associated with the brain-duplicate. Type materialists deny that there could be such an object. (For further discussion of these issues, see Tye 2000; Levine 2003; and McLaughlin 2003a.)

These issues, like many others concerning the place of phenomenal consciousness in nature, remain matters of dispute in philosophy. Such is the present state of the philosophy of phenomenal consciousness.

Further Readings

Hill, C. (1991) *Sensations*. Cambridge: Cambridge University Press.

Hill, C. (1997) Imaginability, conceivability, possibility, and the mind–body problem. *Philosophical Studies* 87, 61–85.

Loar, B. (1997) Phenomenal states. In N. Block, O. Flanagan, and G. Guzeldere (eds.), *The Nature of Consciousness*, 597–617. Cambridge, MA: MIT Press.

Papineau, D. (2002) *Thinking about Consciousnesss*. Oxford: Clarendon Press.

Pologer, T. (2004) *Natural Minds*. Cambridge, MA: MIT Press.

Smart, J. J. C. (1959) Sensations and brain processes. *Philosophical Review* 68, 141–56.

References

Alexander, S. (1920) *Space, Time, and Deity*. 2 vols. London: Macmillan.

Balog, K. (2000) Conceivability, possibility, and the mind–body problem. *The Philosophical Review* 109, 497–528.

Block, N. (2002) The harder problem of consciousness. *The Journal of Philosophy* 99: 8, 391–425.

Block, N. and Stalnaker, R. (1999) Conceptual analysis, dualism, and the explanatory gap. *Philosophical Review* 108, 1–46.

Broad, C. D. (1925) *The Mind and Its Place in Nature*. London: Routledge and Kegan Paul.

Causey, R. L. (1977) *Unity of Science*. Dordrecht: Reidel.

Chalmers, D. J. (1995) Facing up to the problem of consciousness. *Journal of Consciousness Studies* 2: 3, 200–19.

Chalmers, D. J. (1996) *The Conscious Mind*. Oxford and New York: Oxford University Press.

Chalmers, D. J. (2002) Does conceivability entail possibility? In T. S. Gendler and J. Hawthorne (eds.), *Conceivability and Possibility*, 145–200. Oxford: Clarendon Press.

Chalmers, D. J. (2003) Consciousness and its place in nature. In S. Stich and F. Warfield (eds.), *Blackwell Guide to the Philosophy of Mind*. Oxford: Blackwell Publishing.

Crick, F. (1994) *The Astonishing Hypothesis*. New York: Scribner.

Dennett, D. C. (1987) *The Intentional Stance*. Cambridge, MA: MIT Press.

Dretske, F. (1995) *Naturalizing the Mind*. Cambridge, MA: MIT Press.

Hill, C. (1991) *Sensations*. Cambridge: Cambridge University Press.

Hill, C. (1997) Imaginability, conceivability, possibility, and the mind–body problem. *Philosophical Studies* 87, 61–85.

Hill, C. and McLaughlin, B. P. (1999) There are fewer things in reality than are dreamt of in Chalmers' philosophy. *Philosophy and Phenomenological Research* 59, 445–54.

Horgan, T. and Tienson, J. (2001) Deconstructing new wave materialism. In C. Gillet and B. Loewer (eds.), *Physicalism and Its Discontents*, 307–18. Cambridge: Cambridge University Press.

Huxley, T. H. (1866) *Lessons in Elementary Physiology*. London: Macmillan.

Kripke, S. (1980) *Naming and Necessity*. Cambridge, MA: Harvard University Press.

Levine, J. (2001) *Purple Haze*. Oxford: Oxford University Press.

Levine, J. (2003) Experience and representation. In Q. Smith and A. Jokic (eds.), *Consciousness: New Philosophical Perspectives*, 57–76. Oxford: Oxford University Press.

Loar, B. (1997) Phenomenal states. In N. Block, O. Flanagan, and G. Guzeldere (eds.), *The Nature of Consciousness*, 597–617. Cambridge, MA: MIT Press.

Lycan, W. (1996) *Consciousness and Experience*. Cambridge, MA: MIT Press/Bradford Book.

McLaughlin, C. (1989) Can we solve the mind–body problem? *Mind* 98, 249–66.

McLaughlin, B. P. (2001) In defense of new wave materialism: a response to Horgan and Tienson. In C. Gillet and B. Loewer (eds.), *Physicalism and Its Discontents*, 319–30. Cambridge: Cambridge University Press.

McLaughlin, B. P. (2003a) Colour, consciousness, and colour consciousness. In Q. Smith and A. Jokic (eds.), *Consciousness: New Philosophical Perspectives*, 97–156. Oxford: Oxford University Press.

McLaughlin, B. P. (2003b) A naturalist-phenomenal realist response to Block's harder problem. *Philosophical Issues* 13, 163–204.

Milner, A. D. and Goodale, M. A. (1995) *The Visual Brain*. Oxford: Oxford University Press.

Nagel, T. (1979a) What is it like to be a bat? In T. Nagel (ed.), *Mortal Questions*, 165–80. Cambridge: Cambridge University Press.

Nagel, T. (1979b) Subjective and objective. In T. Nagel (ed.), *Mortal Questions*, 196–214. Cambridge: Cambridge University Press.

Nozick, R. (1981) *Philosophical Explanations*. Cambridge, MA: Harvard University Press.

Papineau, D. (2002) *Thinking about Consciousnesss*. Oxford: Clarendon Press.

Pologer, T. (2004) *Natural Minds*. Cambridge, MA: MIT Press.

Putnam, H. (1975) *Mind, Language, and Reality: Philosophical Papers*, vol. 2. New York: Cambridge University Press.

Smart, J. J. C. (1959) Sensations and brain processes. *Philosophical Review* 68, 141–56.

Sturgeon, S. (2000) *Matters of Mind*. London: Routledge.

Tye, M. (2000) *Consciousness, Color, and Content*. Cambridge, MA: MIT Press.

Yablo, S. (1999) Concepts and consciousness. *Philosophy and Phenomenological Research* 59, 445–63.

Yablo, S. (2002) Coulda, woulda, shoulda. In T. S. Gendler and J. Hawthorne (eds.), *Conceivability and Possibility*, 443–92. Oxford: Clarendon Press.

35

Sensory and Perceptual Consciousness

AUSTEN CLARK

Asked on the Dick Cavett Show about her former Stalinist comrade Lillian Hellman, Mary McCarthy replied, "Every word she says is a lie, including 'and' and 'the.'" The language used to describe sensory and perceptual consciousness is worthy of about the same level of trust. One must adapt oneself to the fact that every ordinary word used to describe this domain is ambiguous; that different theoreticians use the same words in very different ways; and that every speaker naturally thinks that his or her usage is, of course, *the* correct one. Notice that we have already partially vindicated Mary McCarthy: even the word "the" cannot always be trusted.

The goal of this chapter is to describe – gingerly – some of the old and intricate familial relations between Sensation, Perception, and Consciousness. Like Hellman and McCarthy, they share a history, and sometimes the tensions in it flare up in vivid ways.

Sensation and Perception

The first contrast is one that is largely avoided by contemporary psychologists, but still found in the philosophical literature. The title suggests a difference between "sensory consciousness" and "perceptual consciousness." What might this difference be? As Ryle (1949) argued, in ordinary language "sensations" are mostly confined to proprioceptive events, such as pains, throbs, gnawings, tickles, cramps, qualms, aches, itches, and so on. But philosophers speak readily of the "sensation of red" or of "color sensations" and treat them as paradigmatic states of consciousness (Chalmers 1996, p. 6). This usage perhaps derives from older psychological models, in which every sensory modality was thought to be organized with some initial stages that are "sensory," followed at some point with stages of a more sophisticated kind called "perceptual." So even vision would start with "visual sensations" and proceed through various levels of processing until it arrives at "visual perceptions." Sensations were thought to be "raw," uninterpreted, pre-conceptual mental stuff, while perceptions were states organizing such inchoate elements into representations of determinate content that could underwrite judgments. Some theoretical traditions (such as the introspectionists) added the assumption that trained observers were, or could become, conscious of the elemental sensations, and could delineate their kinds (Herrnstein & Boring 1965).

This picture of a progression in which perceptions are constructed out of elemental sensations has been mostly abandoned in experimental psychology, and many psychologists now prefer to avoid the term "sensation" altogether, perhaps because of its introspectionist connotations. But the contrast lives on in philosophical discussion. Even there, the contrast can be divorced from many of the problematic claims of old psychological models (including constructionism, conceptual involvement, and consciousness), so that "sensory" comes to mean something close to "sensor": the registration of information from transducers (Dretske 1995). On this reading, sensory processes are just the states that come earliest in the series that culminates in perceptual judgments. So what a philosopher calls "visual sensation" a psychologist might call a state of "early vision" or "pre-attentive vision": visual processes that occur before any selections are made by selective attention. The only assumptions from earlier models that remain are that sensory processes are earlier than, and simpler than, perceptual processes. But other than that, there may be no essential difference in their kinds.

Sensation and Consciousness

The assumption that every sensation is a state of consciousness is much more problematic, but also deeply rooted in the etymology of the terms. To be "sensible of" something is, in one sense of the word, to be conscious of it; "insensible" can mean "unconscious." The comingled etymology makes the contrast problematic.

To start with the latter term, one useful way to disambiguate two major uses of the word "conscious" is to ask: When we use a sentence frame of the form "*x* is conscious," what are the values over which *x* can range? In one category, the *x*'s are creatures; in another they are particular mental states of creatures. In the first sense we are saying of an animal or a person, or of some animal- or person-like entity, that it is conscious, as opposed to unconscious or comatose. David Rosenthal (1997) calls this "creature consciousness"; David Armstrong (1997) called it "minimal" consciousness. It implies that the organism or system is sentient and awake: that it is at least somewhat mentally active, and responsive to its environment, as opposed to being insensible, unconscious, asleep, or comatose.

One connection between sensation and (creature) consciousness seems relatively robust. Creature consciousness is just the presence of some mental processes in a sentient creature. If *S* is a creature that is actually sensing something, then it is clearly sentient, and likewise, it has at least some minimal mental responsiveness. So if creature *S* senses something, *S* is (at that moment) a conscious creature. Sensing things entails creature consciousness.

The much more complicated case involves state consciousness. Is every sensation a conscious mental state? This is quite distinct from wondering whether the creature involved is conscious, since that is already established by its activity of sensing something, yet it does not settle this new question. Even though the creature is (clearly) conscious, only some of its mental states are conscious states, or states of which the creature is conscious. All the others are unconscious. So are sensations always in the first category, or sometimes in the second?

Implicit Perception

In many philosophical dialects, the word "sensation" is read so as to dictate an answer to this question: a creature cannot have a sensation of which it is unconscious. For these philosophers the sensation of red and the sensation of pain serve as paradigm examples of conscious mental states. In one sense, of course, they clearly are "states of consciousness": they are states that suffice to show their bearer is a conscious creature. It is fruitless to argue over the language; everyone has Humpty Dumpty's right to use a word however they like, even though unmitigated exercise of that right can make communication difficult.

If we think of sensory processes in the way that psychologists do, it is clear that there can be, and in fact are, sensory processes of whose occurrence the creature in question is not conscious. Psychologists call these episodes "perception without awareness" or "implicit perception"; they are episodes in which a person or other creature perceives something without being conscious of what it perceives. Various neuropsychological syndromes provide dramatic illustrations. For example, in "hemineglect" a patient who has suffered a lesion in a particular area of the right parietal cortex will find it difficult or impossible to shift attention to anything on the left side (of space, or of a given object) if there is also something on the right side (Driver & Vuilleumier 2001). These subjects will (often) ignore the food on the left side of their plate, will not groom the left side of their body, will not draw the numbers on the left side of a clock face, and in general will be unresponsive to stimuli on the left side if there is competition on the right. (The sides switch if the lesion is on the left side of the brain.) Yet this is not a sensory deficit – if there is no competition on the right side, such a patient can describe and respond to the stimulus on the left in a fairly normal way. The loss of sensitivity to stimuli on one side when competition is introduced on the other is called "extinction"; it suggests that the problem in hemineglect is not sensory, but rather an inability to shift attention when there are competing stimuli on both sides. The stimulus on the right side "grabs" attention, and thereafter, the patient cannot shift attention to anything on the left. Yet behaviorally the result is difficult to distinguish from simple loss of sensitivity; the inability to shift attention renders the patient "insensible" to events on the affected side. Even to be able to neglect the left side of the dinner plate (for example), these patients must sense its leftmost edge, so as to locate its centerline. Otherwise, how could their attentional systems know where the "left side" begins? They must therefore sense stimuli to which they cannot shift attention.

Other startling examples of perception without awareness are found in the large literature on the contrast between dorsal and ventral channels in vision (see chapter 48). Goodale and Milner (2003) describe a patient, called "DF," who became severely agnosic after an episode of carbon monoxide poisoning. She could not recognize objects visually, could not draw their shapes or indicate their orientation. But if the task shifted from one of description or identification to visual guidance of motion, she could respond well. For example, when asked to grasp an object whose shape she could not draw or describe, her anticipatory hand movements were appropriate for picking up the particular object. Even though she could not describe or indicate the direction of a slot in a wood frame in front of her, if asked to "post" a letter through the slot she could it do it without fumbling and with few errors. Goodale and Milner suggest that the dorsal channel is intact in DF, and that it is devoted to the visual guidance of movement. It does not contribute directly to a person's awareness of the objects around them. So DF's ability to post the letter shows that she has the sensory capacity to register the orientation of the slot, even though she is not aware of that orientation.

Perception without awareness can also be demonstrated in normal subjects using various experimental paradigms. One needs to show that the subject has picked up information that could only be registered perceptually, but that nevertheless the subject is not aware of what was perceived. The hard part is to show the latter. Paradigms that demonstrate that a stimulus has a "pre-attentive" effect show both that the stimulus has been sensed (because it has an effect) but that at the time of that effect the subject is not aware of it (because it is pre-attentive). The idea is that these effects are demonstrated to occur before any stimuli have been selected by selective attention.

A good example of a pre-attentive effect is "pop out," which is demonstrated in visual (or other kinds of) search tasks (Treisman 1998). A target is defined by some feature or combination of features, and varying numbers of distractors are displayed along with the target. The dependent variable is the speed with which the target is found among the distractors. "Pop out" occurs if the target can be found in more or less constant time, no matter how many distractors are present. A unique color cue (one red target among a bunch of green distractors, for example) will "pop out" no matter how many distractors are present; while if the color of the target is not unique, and it determines the target only in combination with some other feature that is also not unique, then finding the target is much harder. In such cases the speed of response is a linear function of the number of distractors, as if each one must be examined in turn.

Pop out shows that the contrast between the target feature and the distractor features is one that can be registered pre-attentively. One of its effects is precisely to guide selective attention, in constant time, to the target. So the pop out of red among many greens shows that the system can register the difference between red and all those greens and use it to guide attention to select the red target. In that brief interval before attention has been directed to the red target, the difference between red and green has been sensed, but the red target has yet to be attended to. It is plausible to think that the subject is not aware of that stimulus until he or she attends to it. So any example of pre-attentive exogenous direction of attention to novel targets is, at least briefly, an example in which something is perceived but the subject is, at the moment, unaware of it.

Phenomenal Properties

There are many sources of resistance to the suggestion that it is possible for subjects to perceive things, or sense things, of which they are unaware (or unconscious). One of the oldest and most deeply rooted points to a prominent feature of the sensory/perceptual domain: appearances therein do not always correspond to reality. Sometimes things are not as they appear: the shirt in the closet looks dark in this light (before dawn), but is really bright red; the water feels slimy, but is merely full of minerals; the voice seems to be coming from the dummy, but is really produced by the ventriloquist, and so on. The Greek word for "appearance" became "phenomenon," and these examples can all be described as presenting "phenomenal properties" or "properties of appearance" to the hapless percipient. The intuitive tie to consciousness is a simple one: how can the shirt "look dark" unless it looks dark *to* someone, who is furthermore conscious of it as looking dark? It takes some work to understand what these phenomenal properties are, and how they relate to consciousness.

A large part of the interest in phenomenal properties arises because in many cases they are not properties of anything that is perceived. The shirt merely *looks* dark, but in fact is bright red. This effect is called the "Purkinje shift." Under conditions of low illumination, red things will look much darker than blue things, but then, as the light increases, the red things will come to seem brighter. The apparent darkness of the shirt is not real. So what is it a property of? That is, in that situation what is the x if any such that x is dark? It certainly seems as if you see one! This has been a puzzle since ancient times, and there are many different lines of response. They bifurcate at the topmost level into two categories: those that agree that there is an entity x that has those properties, and those that do not. In the twentieth century the entities x alleged actually to have the properties that things merely appear to have were called "sense data." The other line denies that there are any such entities: if the shirt merely *looks* dark, there need not be an entity in the closet, or anywhere else, that actually *is* dark. Instead (says one crowd that hangs out in this group) one is merely representing there to be something dark in the closet, but that representation is a misrepresentation; it is inaccurate, or less than fully truthful ("non-veridical," as philosophers say). The dark appearance is an illusion; it is not real. The fact that one suffers such illusions is part of what has for millennia attracted philosophical interest to the topics of sensation and perception. It shows them to be characterized by "intentional inexistence": the capacity to represent something that is not so.

Ordinary language contains various locutions that invoke or characterize phenomenal properties, and one very useful step forward was to characterize them (semantically) as "verbs of appearance" (Chisholm 1957). These verbs are found in locutions with forms such as "x looks P," "x appears to be P," "x feels P," "x seems to be P," and so on, where what characterizes them all is that all such sentence frames can yield true sentences even though x in fact is not P. It merely looks P. We have many such "verbs of appearance," and in all those contexts, P is a predicate that characterizes the appearance, and so can be thought of as attributing a "phenomenal" property in that context. Chisholm used "being appeared-to" as a kind of generic verb of appearance, and turned the predicates into adverbs so as to emphasize the fact that they characterize a manner of being appeared-to. So, when one looks in the closet before dawn, one is being appeared-to darkly. It is a funny way of talking, but it makes the point that "dark" here characterizes *how* the shirt appears, its *manner* of appearance. Adverbs befit manners.

Since the red shirt is brighter than the blue shirt, how is it possible for it to appear to be darker when one looks at it before dawn? Another root assumption is that this feat demonstrates the presence of mentality: intentional inexistence is the hallmark of the mental. So to be appeared-to darkly is to be in a mental state representing there to be a dark thing thereabouts. The situation is in a certain way like those situations in which one sees a shirt that *is* dark: in both one represents there to be a dark shirt in the closet, but only in one of them is that representation veridical. How does one do this? The natural intuition is that darkness characterizes how the shirt seems at the time. But it only *seems* dark if (a) there is someone to whom it seems dark, and (b) that someone is aware of its seeming darkness. Phenomenal properties betoken mentality (because of their intentional character) and hence (on this line) consciousness.

This last step is one that relies on ancient presuppositions, reiterated in the early modern period by Descartes: that in order to be appeared-to, there must a subject to whom the appearance is presented; and that the appearance has a determinate content only if the subject is aware of it as having that content. One might be wrong about how things are, but (on this line) one cannot be wrong about how things seem. The reality of these properties is, then, constituted by the subject's awareness: how they seem to the one who apprehends them is the way they are. If something seems to be P, it is only because the subject is aware of it as seeming to be P. Were the subject aware of it seeming to be Q, then the phenomenal property would be Q, not P. Phenomenal properties were in this way creatures of consciousness: born of consciousness, and, like dust mites, surviving only under the protective mantle of consciousness. The sole arbiter of their content is the subject who is aware of them, and however they seem to be to that subject is the way they are (Searle 2004, pp. 111, 135). Descendants of these old premises underwrite the modern claims that "phenomenal consciousness" is a kind of consciousness (Block 1997); or that phenomenological properties are subjective phenomena that cannot be understood apart from the point of the view of the subject who is conscious of how things appear.

What It's Like vs. How It Appears

The formulation just mentioned alludes to Thomas Nagel's famous article "What is it like to be a bat?" which is a redolent contemporary source for the idea that phenomenal properties are somehow tied to consciousness. Nagel states explicitly that his target is consciousness: it is consciousness that makes the mind–body problem interesting, he says, but no available accounts are adequate even to characterize what it is. He offers two proposals. One: the fact that S "has conscious experiences at all" *means* that "There is something it's like to be" S – something it's like *for* S (Nagel 1979, p. 166). Two: that to say "M is a conscious state of S" is to say "There is something it's like for S to have M."

Nagel uses the "what it's like" formulation to point to what he calls the "subjective character" of experience. To understand "what it's like for the bat to echolocate" we have to understand something from the "point of view" of the bat. The question concerns what it's like *for* the bat; these phenomena are *pour-soi*, not *en-soi*, he says (Nagel 1979, p. 168). So the emphasis in "subjective" should be on the word "subject"; subjective features are those that require reference to the point of view of the *subject*, or to what it is *for* the subject. Lycan (1996) usefully dubs these "perspectival" features. Nagel goes on to argue that unless one can adopt, or at least understand, the point of view of the bat, one cannot understand "what it's like to be" a bat; and that the minds of different species might have structures that are sufficiently distinct to preclude this possibility. So, he suggests, there are facts that can only be understood from a particular point of view.

Much of this argument broaches other chapters in this volume (e.g., Tye, chapter 2; Chalmers, chapter 17; Levine, chapter 29). What concerns this chapter is the suggestion that the echolocatory perceptual experiences of a bat have a "subjective" or "perspectival" character; that facts about that experience are facts "for" the subject, requiring reference to the point of view of that subject. In two places Nagel notes that "phenomenological features" of experience are subjective in this sense (Nagel 1979, pp. 167 and 175, fn. 11). In another article he argues directly that appearances are "irreducibly subjective"; to acknowledge their subjectivity is, he says, to acknowledge "the fact that each is essentially an appearance *to* someone" (Nagel 1979, p. 207).

The idea is enormously useful, because it could explain why so many people think that phenomenal properties implicate consciousness. "How something seems" seems always to mean how something seems *for* a subject. "Being appeared-to" appears to require a subject to whom the appearances are presented. The appearances have a determinate content only if they have a determinate content for that subject. This is exactly Nagel's "subjective character." So we get from "being appeared-to" to subjective character; and the latter, according to Nagel, is equivalent to "having conscious experience."

The tug of the rhetoric is powerful, but before we are entirely swept away it is wise to stop and take stock. One seemingly minor problem is that "what it's like" and "how it appears" pick out distinct subject matters; the "it" for one cannot be the "it" for the other. Consider the echolocating bat: if we ask what it's like for the bat to have its echolocatory experiences, we confine the question to those experiences of which the bat is conscious. The question is how the bat apprehends certain of its own mental states: what it's like for it to have those mental states. This was Nagel's point: the locution picks out the conscious mental states. With this we can agree. But if we switch to "how it appears," and ask, for example, how a Luna moth appears to the bat, the "it" is no longer a mental state of the bat, but a moth that it perceives. Perhaps that moth presents a particular appearance to the bat ("it" appears a particular way) only if the bat is conscious of one of its own mental states, but the two locutions describe distinct existences, so it will take some argument to show a necessity in their connection.

The point is often obscured by the tendency to read "what it's like" to mean "what it resembles," so that "what it's like for the bat to echolocate a Luna moth" is read as "what the bat takes the Luna moth to resemble." This latter formulation *is* one way to characterize how the moth appears to the bat. But Nagel explicitly denies this interpretation of subjectivity: "what it's like" should *not* be read as "what it resembles" (Nagel 1979, p. 170, fn. 6).

How It Feels vs. How It Appears

We can add a third idiom to the already confusing mix. This one defines the phenomenal character of mental states as *how they feel*. States with phenomenal character have a "phenomenal feel." "On the phenomenal concept," says David Chalmers, "mind is characterized by the way it *feels*" (Chalmers 1996, p. 11). He proceeds to equate this with "what it's like":

> what it *means* for a state to be phenomenal is for it to feel a certain way . . . in general, a phenomenal feature of mind is characterized by what it's like for a subject to have that feature. (Chalmers 1996, p. 12)

Many more examples of this usage could be produced. For example, Tyler Burge: "To be phenomenally conscious, phenomenal states, or their phenomenal qualities, must be sensed or felt by the individual subject" (Burge 1997, p. 427). And John Searle:

> Every conscious state has a qualitative feel to it. Conscious states are in that sense always qualitative . . . If you think there is no qualitative feel to thinking two plus two equals four, try thinking it in French or German. To me it feels completely different to think *"zwei und zwei sind vier"* even though the intentional content is the same in German as it is in English. (Searle 2004, p. 134)

Instead of saying "all sensations are conscious," this line would say "all sensations have a feel." All sensations are felt by their bearer. You not only feel the pebble in your shoe, you also feel your sensation of the pebble. The latter feel makes you aware of the former one.

The English verb "to feel" is extraordinarily complex; it *does* have senses in which "S feels x" implies "S is conscious of x." And these days we all have our precious "feelings." Nevertheless, the usage under which every conscious mental state has a "phenomenal feel" does introduce a Humpty-Dumpty-like strain on the language. The "feel of a mental state" would be grammatically analogous to the feel of cotton: that which is felt when one feels the thing – the sensible qualities perceptible by touch; the texture, smoothness, and so on. For mental states to have a "feel" we must be using "feel" not in the sense of tactile perception, but rather in the sense in which we are aware (for example) of our precious feelings. So the phenomenal "feel" of a mental state would be that which is apprehended when one is aware of that mental state.

But if this is so, then "how it feels" applies to a mental state only if one is conscious of that mental state, and the difficulties noted above for "what it's like" apply here as well. "How it appears" allows "it" to range over any perceptible phenomena at all, while "how it feels" (in the intended sense) would apply only to the results of apprehending some of one's own mental states, the ones of which one is conscious. Unless whenever one perceives something one also apprehends one of one's own mental states, these two locutions will on occasion fly apart. Any episode of implicit perception will provide an example.

Qualia circa 1929

All this analysis is preparatory to Hamlet finally making his appearance on the stage. The troubled prince in this drama is called "Qualia." Strictly speaking, the word is plural, so in fact it names a gaggle of troubled princes. In one sense or another they are all qualities of perceptual experience, or the consciousness thereof; but there are at least three major families, three princely lines, that need to be distinguished.

The first is the oldest and simplest, and it is already familiar, since it is basically just a phenomenal property, a characteristic of how things appear. These are particularly interesting when found in episodes of what one might call *mere* appearance: episodes in which something merely looks elliptical, for example, but in fact is round. C. D. Broad made liberal use of the verbs of appearance to identify what he called the "facts of Sensible Appearance":

> we constantly make such judgments as "This *seems to me* elliptical, or red, or hot," as the case may be, and that about the truth of these judgments we do not feel the least doubt. We may, however, at the same time doubt or positively disbelieve that this *is* elliptical, or red, or hot. I may be perfectly certain at one and the same time that I have the peculiar experience expressed by the judgment: "This looks elliptical to me" and that in fact the object is not elliptical but is round. Appearance is *not* merely mistaken *judgment* about physical objects. (Broad 1927, pp. 236–7)

C. I. Lewis (1929) was one of the first philosophers to stipulate a use of the term "qualia": "There are recognizable qualitative characters of the given, which may be repeated in different experiences, and are thus a sort of universals; I call these 'qualia'" (Lewis 1929, p. 121). (The "given" is the raw unconceptualized input to the system, described in the first section.) An example of a quale is an elliptical appearance, understood as that which is common to experiences in which things are seen to be elliptical and to those in which some things merely *look* elliptical.

Within this family there are various distinct analyses (rivalrous siblings) for what qualia are, dependent on what one understands a property of sensible appearance to be. I mentioned sense data as one account of sensible appearance, and indeed one historically important notion of "qualia" treats them as properties of sense data (Moore 1953, pp. 30–4). But as noted above, there are other accounts of sensible appearance. Most contemporary accounts are representational: that something looks elliptical is a matter of it being visually represented *as* elliptical. If qualia are characteristics of sensible appearance, then on this account they would be characteristics of objects as represented perceptually. This is the view of William Lycan (1996). Vision represents what seem to be individuals (including such things as patches and spots), and qualia appear to be first-order properties of those individuals, such properties as "pointy" and "light green." Sometimes these representations are veridical, sometimes not. Lycan says:

> What are we to make of color qualia, the apparently first-order properties of apparent phenom-enal individuals? . . . Apparent singular reference to phenomenal individuals, such as pointy light-green spots in one's visual field, remains to be accounted for, and the obvious explanation is that the apparent singular reference is genuine. (Lycan 1996, pp. 70–1)

So qualia are properties that individuals are represented to have; they are properties of the "intentional object" of the perceptual representation. If the representation is veridical, then they are also properties of some real individual, and one can see that individual to have those properties.

Qualia Kicked Indoors

While it is fair to say that qualia are "properties of sensation" or "experiential properties," notice that both these formulations are ambiguous. They could mean either: (a) qualia are properties of the things sensed, or of that which one experiences; or (b) qualia are prop-erties of the sensings of things, or of the experiencing of things. While (a) allows for the possibility that qualia could be real properties of things in the real world – properties such as saltiness, being pointy, or even being light-green – option (b) kicks them indoors defini-tively, firmly ensconcing them as properties of mental states – properties not of things, but of the sensings or experiencings or representings of things. The latter became the dominant interpretation by the end of the twentieth century. It is common now to think of qualia as the "qualitative character" of perceptual or sensory states, properties of such states that help to explain why the things one perceives appear as they do. On this line, qualia no longer include properties such as greenness or pointiness, which one might actually see; instead they are those properties of one's visual states that can explain why the thing one sees appears to be green or pointy. Visual qualitative character is not something that is visible, but it helps to explain why visible things present the appearances they do.

We still need to characterize those appearances somehow; phenomenal property talk and the verbs of appearance will be with us still. This line changes our access to qualia: no longer are they properties one can observe, but instead they are theoretical, postulated so as to explain characteristics of perception or sensation. So our access to them is indirect and hypothetical. They are part of a model aiming to explain the facts of sensible appearance, and the properties of states and processes postulated in such models need not be introspectible.

Qualia Kicked Upstairs

The third of the family lines treats qualia not just as properties of mental states, but prop-erties exclusively of those mental states of which one is conscious. The same ambiguity between properties sensed vs. properties of sensings recurs here again, at a higher level. That is, one can treat qualia as characterizing the appearance of mental states to the subject who is conscious of them, or one can treat them as properties of the experiencings of those mental states, which help to explain their appearances.

If we treat qualia as characterizing "what it's like" to have a mental state, then they have been kicked both indoors and upstairs in just this way. Remember that there is something it's like to have a given mental state if and if only that mental state is a conscious mental state. If S is not conscious of having state M, then there is nothing it's like for S to have M. To characterize what it's like to have that mental state is therefore to characterize what it's like to be conscious of it. We have gone upstairs. These appearances now comprise how one's own mental states appear to oneself when one is conscious of them.

If something looks triangular to me, then the thing that looks triangular resembles a triangle. But "what it's like" to have a sensory state in virtue of which something looks triangular to me is a different subject matter altogether. In particular, what it's like to have that state does not in any sense resemble a triangle. Notice also that the reference of the pronoun "it" shifts in the two phrases.

It might sound odd to talk of how mental states appear to one who has them, but such talk is now common: "It is difficult to understand what could be meant by the objective character of an experience, apart from the particular point of view from which its subject apprehends it" (Nagel 1979, p. 173). Notice that here the subject is apprehending its own experience. Likewise: "Does it make sense, in other words, to ask what my experiences are *really* like, as opposed to how they appear to me?" (Nagel 1979, p. 178). The question presumes that one's own experiences appear somehow to oneself. The same implication follows from the idea that mental states are "felt" or have a "phenomenal feel." Recall that Chalmers says "what it means for a state to be phenomenal is for it to feel a certain way" (Chalmers 1996, pp. 11–12). "The way it feels" characterizes an appearance, and here the thing apprehended is one of one's own mental states. These appearances are "higher order" because they are not simply appearances of quotidian things such as the shape of the moth or the texture of cotton; instead they are appearances of one's *perception* of the shape of the moth, or of how the *sensation* of the texture of cotton feels. "Cottony" would not be an appropriate answer.

Conclusion

The language we use to describe sensory and perceptual consciousness is full of traps for the unwary. I have described some of the distinctions between sensing and perceiving; between conscious creatures and conscious mental states; between "how it appears," "what it's like," and "how it feels"; between various accounts of phenomenal properties, and between various accounts of the now infamous qualia. Armed with these distinctions, I hope the reader can avoid some of the traps. This would be all to the good, for it would allow future explorers to expend a greater portion of their efforts on the large, genuine puzzles that remain.

See also 2 Philosophical problems of consciousness; 17 The hard problem of consciousness; 21 Higher-order theories of consciousness; 29 Anti-materialist arguments and influential replies; 30 Functionalism and qualia.

Further Readings

Baars, B. J., Banks, W. P., and Newman, J. B. (eds.) (2003) *Essential Sources in the Scientific Study of Consciousness.* Cambridge, MA: MIT Press.

Block, N., Flanagan, O., and Güzeldere, G. (eds.) (1997) *The Nature of Consciousness: Philosophical Debates*. Cambridge, MA: MIT Press.

Goodale, M. and Milner, A. D. (2003) *Sight Unseen: An Exploration of Conscious and Unconscious Vision*. Oxford: Oxford University Press.

Weiskrantz, L. (1997) *Consciousness Lost and Found*. Oxford: Oxford University Press.

References

Armstrong, D. (1997) What is consciousness? In N. Block, O. Flanagan, and G. Güzeldere (eds.), *The Nature of Consciousness: Philosophical Debates*, 721–28. Cambridge, MA: MIT Press. Originally published in David Armstrong, *The Nature of Mind*, 55–67. Ithaca, NY: Cornell University Press, 1981.

Baars, B. J., Banks, W. P., and Newman, J. B. (eds.) (2003) *Essential Sources in the Scientific Study of Consciousness*. Cambridge, MA: MIT Press.

Block, N. (1997) On a confusion about a function of consciousness. In N. Block, O. Flanagan, and G. Güzeldere (eds.), *The Nature of Consciousness: Philosophical Debates*, 375–415. Cambridge, MA: MIT Press. Originally published in *Behavioral and Brain Sciences* 15 (1992), 183–247.

Broad, C. D. (1927) *Scientific Thought*. New York: Harcourt, Brace and Company.

Burge, Tyler (1997) Two kinds of consciousness. In N. Block, O. Flanagan, and G. Güzeldere (eds.), *The Nature of Consciousness: Philosophical Debates*, 427–33. Cambridge, MA: MIT Press.

Chalmers, David J. (1996) *The Conscious Mind*. New York: Oxford University Press.

Chisholm, Roderick (1957) *Perceiving: A Philosophical Study*. Ithaca, NY: Cornell University Press.

Dretske, Fred (1995) *Naturalizing the Mind*. Cambridge, MA: MIT Press.

Driver, Jon and Vuilleumier, Patrik (2001) Perceptual awareness and its loss in unilateral neglect and extinction. *Cognition* 79, 39–88.

Goodale, M. and Milner, A. D. (2003) *Sight Unseen: An Exploration of Conscious and Unconscious Vision*. Oxford: Oxford University Press.

Herrnstein, Richard J. and Boring, Edwin G. (eds.) (1965) *A Source Book in the History of Psychology*. Cambridge, MA: Harvard University Press.

Lewis, Clarence Irving (1929) *Mind and the World Order*. New York: Charles Scribner's Sons.

Lycan, William G. (1996) *Consciousness and Experience*. Cambridge, MA: MIT Press.

Moore, G. E. (1953) Sense-data. In his *Some Main Problems of Philosophy*, 28–40. London: George Allen and Unwin. Reprinted in Moore, 1993, 45–58.

Moore, G. E. (1993) *G. E. Moore: Selected Writings*, Thomas Baldwin (ed.). London: Routledge.

Nagel, Thomas (1979) *Mortal Questions*. Cambridge: Cambridge University Press.

Rosenthal, David (1997) A theory of consciousness. In N. Block, O. Flanagan, and G. Güzeldere (eds.), *The Nature of Consciousness: Philosophical Debates*, 729–53. Cambridge, MA: MIT Press.

Ryle, Gilbert (1949) *The Concept of Mind*. London: Hutchinson.

Searle, John R. (2004) *Mind: A Brief Introduction*. Oxford: Oxford University Press.

Treisman, Anne (1998) Feature binding, attention and object perception. *Philosophical Transactions of the Royal Society of London B* 353, 1295–306.

Weiskrantz, L. (1997) *Consciousness Lost and Found*. Oxford: Oxford University Press.

36

Self-Consciousness

JOSÉ LUIS BERMÚDEZ

The Problems of Self-Consciousness

Self-consciousness is primarily a cognitive, rather than an affective state. Although the term "self-consciousness" is often used in ordinary language to describe a particular state of hyper-sensitivity about certain features of one's character or appearance, in philosophy and cognitive science the expression is best reserved for a form of awareness of one's self. There is no single "problem of self-consciousness" associated with this type of self-awareness. Rather, self-consciousness is a topic located at the intersection of a range of different philosophical concerns. One set of concerns is *metaphysical* (having to do with how we explain what self-consciousness is). Another is *epistemological* (to do with the different types of knowledge obtained through self-consciousness). And a third has to do with the distinctive *role* that self-consciousness plays within the cognitive economy.

When discussing the phenomenon of consciousness in general philosophers generally think it possible to give an account of consciousness that is independent of how one understands the objects, properties, and events of which one is conscious. Self-consciousness is not like this. Almost all accounts of self-consciousness both are motivated by and have significant implications for particular ways of thinking about the self. There seems little prospect of understanding self-consciousness in complete independence of thinking about the metaphysics of the self.

A further important characteristic of the study of self-consciousness is that it has a prominent epistemological dimension. In thinking about self-consciousness we are, to an important extent, thinking about self-knowledge. One of the reasons that philosophers have found self-consciousness so fascinating over the years is that it seems to involve various forms of knowledge with a unique and privileged status. A complete account of self-consciousness will, ideally, not only accommodate but also explain the epistemological dimension of self-consciousness.

Finally, certain forms of action and ways of behaving are only made possible by self-consciousness. Without the capacity to be aware of our own thoughts, beliefs, and other mental states we would be unable to engage in many of the intellectual activities that are frequently thought to be characteristically human. Only self-conscious creatures are able to reflect upon their own mental lives or to develop strategies for the future, for example. Even more basic forms of action might be thought to depend upon self-consciousness. We cannot act upon the world without information about our own location and the disposition of our limbs, which requires at least a primitive form of self-awareness. These are all part of what philosophers sometimes describe as the *functional role* of self-consciousness.

Philosophical thinking about self-consciousness, therefore, has to do justice to the complex interconnections between the metaphysics of the self, the epistemology of self-knowledge, and the distinctive functional role of self-conscious thoughts. This article explores some of the principal claims and lines of argument that have been canvassed in this complex and fascinating area.

Self-Consciousness and the Metaphysics of the Self

Historically, philosophers have understood the nature of the self in many different ways. For present purposes we can distinguish two different (but related) questions that philosophers have addressed. The first is whether it is appropriate to describe selves as things (or substances, in the standard philosophical usage). Assuming that this is answered affirmatively, the second question asks what sort of a thing the self is. Is it a physical entity? Or a psychological entity? Or an entity that has both physical and psychological properties? This second question is standardly put as a question about the conditions of persistence, or survival, for selves. Philosophers approach the question of what a self is by asking what it is for a self at one time to be identical to a self at another time (which, it should be noted, is distinct from the epistemological question of what we count as good evidence for the survival or persistence of a self).

The first question is whether there are such things as selves at all. Should we include selves in a catalog of all the things that the world contains? Some philosophers have denied that there is a place for selves in our ontology. This view is standardly expressed as a form of *reductionism*, according to which what we think of as the self should really be analyzed as a complex set or "bundle" of suitably interrelated events, in such a way that a complete description of the world can be given without any sort of ineliminable references to selves. Most frequently, these suitably related events are taken to be psychological (as in Parfit 1984, the best known contemporary statement of reductionism about the self). But it is also open to the reductionist to include physical (i.e., bodily) events in the bundle.

The reductionist thesis does not, of course, rule out the possibility of self-consciousness. But it does rule out certain ways of understanding self-consciousness. If reductionism gives a correct account of the metaphysics of the self then we cannot adopt a perceptual model of self-consciousness. That is, we cannot think of self-consciousness as involving a direct awareness of the object that is the self, in the way that ordinary perception involves direct awareness of physical objects (including the body). This rules out both the dualist view that we have direct, introspective awareness of a nonphysical self, and the materialist view that we have (perhaps through somatic proprioception) direct but non-introspective awareness of a physical self.

In any event, reductionism is not widely accepted among philosophers, most of whom adopt some form of *substantivalism* about the self. According to the various versions of substance dualism, the self is a purely psychological entity that is connected to a particular body but that could exist without that body. It is open to dualists to hold that self-consciousness consists in direct awareness of that nonphysical entity – although Descartes himself rejected any such view, since he thought that it was impossible to have direct awareness of substance, whether physical or nonphysical. Most contemporary philosophers and cognitive scientists reject dualism, but there is no single account of the metaphysics of the self that is standardly accepted. Some philosophers (e.g., Olson 1997) take a *biological* approach to the self, holding the view that the self is identical to the embodied human animal and hence that the self persists exactly as long as the human animal persists. Others (e.g., Shoemaker 1984) adopt a *psychological* approach, taking the view that the persistence of a self requires certain forms of psychological continuity. A third group of philosophers (e.g., Unger 1990) put forward *hybrid* theories on which the persistence of the self requires certain forms of both biological and psychological continuity.

Debates about the criteria for persistence of selves have ramifications for theories of self-consciousness in a number of different ways. Most obviously, philosophers have objected to theories of self-consciousness on the grounds that they have undesirable metaphysical implications. Elizabeth Anscombe, for example, famously argued against accounts of self-consciousness that treat the first-person pronoun "I" as a referring expression on the grounds that the only sort of object to which "I" could refer would be a Cartesian ego (Anscombe 1975)

But theories of the metaphysics of the self can also contribute positively to how we understand self-consciousness. Adopting a biological or a hybrid approach to self-consciousness opens up the possibility of analyzing self-consciousness as a form of direct awareness of the self that is compatible with what many philosophers have taken to be a datum about introspective self-awareness. This datum is Hume's *elusiveness thesis* (see "Direct Awareness and Propositional Awareness" below) to the effect that one never encounters oneself as an object in introspective self-awareness. Philosophers who think of the self as an embodied animal can allow that we are directly (but non-introspectively) conscious of ourselves as objects through somatic proprioception.

Finally, if, as many philosophers have suggested, we think of self-consciousness in terms of the capacity to think thoughts that are about oneself in a distinctively self-conscious manner, then a metaphysical account of what the self is can help us to identify what properties are distinctively ascribed to oneself in this self-conscious way. So, for example, philosophers who hold that the survival of the self requires bodily continuity are likely to think that thoughts about one's bodily properties can count as self-conscious thoughts, while philosophers who privilege psychological continuity are likely to think that *canonical* self-conscious thoughts are thoughts about one's psychological properties.

Direct Awareness and Propositional Awareness

Although it is hard to dispute that self-consciousness is a form of awareness of one's self, the force of this characterization plainly depends upon how we understand "awareness" (as well as what we take the self to be).

We should start by distinguishing two different types of awareness – *direct awareness* and *propositional awareness* (Dretske 1995, 1999). One can be aware of something (as when I catch sight of someone walking up the garden path) or one can be aware that a particular state of affairs is the case (as when the sound of the doorbell alerts me to the fact that a visitor is at the door). In *direct awareness* the object of awareness is a particular thing. In *propositional awareness* the direct object of awareness is a proposition or state of affairs (a complex of particular things, properties and/or relations). A further difference between direct awareness and propositional awareness is that the former creates a *transparent* context while the latter creates an *opaque* context. If "JLB is directly aware of *x*" is a true report, then it will remain true whatever name referring to the same object is substituted for "*x*" in the report. Direct awareness is not sensitive to the mode of presentation of the object of which one is directly aware. All that is required for me to be directly aware of something is that I be able to discriminate it. I do not need to know what it is, or to conceptualize it in any way.

Propositional awareness, however, *is* sensitive to the mode of presentation of the state of affairs that is the object of awareness. I can be aware that a state of affairs holds when it is conceptualized in one way, but be unaware that it holds under a different conceptualization. If "JLB is propositionally aware that *x* is *F*" is a true report, it will not necessarily remain true if a co-referential name is substituted for "*x*" and/or a predicate true of the same objects for "*F*." My propositional awareness that a particular state of affairs holds is highly sensitive to how I think about that state of affairs. I might be propositionally aware that Bob Dylan is balding, in virtue of seeing that the person on the stage in front of me is losing their hair and knowing that that person is Bob Dylan, without being propositionally aware that Robert Zimmerman is balding, since I have no idea that Bob Dylan is Robert Zimmerman.

Self-consciousness, therefore, can be understood either in terms of direct awareness of the self or in terms of propositional awareness that the self has such-and-such a property, or stands in such-and-such relations. Some philosophers have maintained that there can be no such thing as self-consciousness at the level of *direct awareness*. David Hume maintained that the self could never be encountered in introspection:

> For my part, when I enter most intimately into what I call *myself*, I always stumble on some perception or other, of heat or cold, light or shade, love or hatred, pain or pleasure. I never catch *myself* at any time without a perception, and never can observe anything but the perception. (Hume 1739–40/1978, p. 252)

It is clear that this introspective report (the so-called *elusiveness thesis*) would be telling if the self were a purely psychological entity, since introspection would then be the only possible source of direct awareness of the self. But, as noted earlier, philosophers who think that the self is essentially embodied need not be troubled by Hume's point. They can simply point out that we do have direct awareness of the body through somatic proprioception. This direct awareness is either introspective or not. If it is then the elusiveness thesis seems false. But if, on the other hand, it is not, then the elusiveness thesis may not be all that important, since it is compatible with some forms of direct awareness of the self.

In any event, it is clear that propositional awareness *about* the self does not require direct awareness *of* the self. I can be aware that a particular state of affairs holds without being directly aware of one of the constituent objects in that state of affairs (as when the sound of the doorbell makes me aware that Georgina, whom I am expecting, is at the door, even though I have no direct awareness of Georgina), and so I can be aware that the self has certain properties without being directly aware of the self. Hence the truth or otherwise of the elusiveness thesis is not directly relevant to the possibility of propositional awareness of the self. Nor is it likely that propositional awareness concerning the self will be analyzable in terms of, or reducible to, direct awareness of the self. The intensional and cognitively mediated character of propositional awareness seems an insuperable obstacle to any such reductive or analytic project. This is not surprising. An exactly parallel situation holds for ordinary perceptual awareness, where there is no prospect of understanding what it is for me to see *that x is F* in terms of my direct perceptual awareness of *x*.

Propositional awareness of the self is in many ways more interesting than direct aware-ness of the self (if such there be). Self-consciousness is important because of the role it plays in the cognitive economy. Self-conscious subjects think about, and react to, the world in distinctive and characteristic ways that are not available to non-self-conscious subjects. Self-consciousness makes possible certain types of inference and reflection, and it does this because of the distinctive types of self-conscious thoughts that it makes available. As phil-osophers such as Castañeda (1969) and Perry (1979) have stressed, self-conscious thoughts have immediate implications for action. Whereas I may contemplate with equanimity the thought that the worst-performing philosopher in the department will shortly be ejected from the department, as soon as I realize that *I* am the person whose job is on the line I will be galvanized into action.

But what are these distinctive types of proposition? Self-consciousness makes available to the subject thoughts that are about the thinker of that thought, but not all thoughts about the person thinking them qualify as self-conscious. A thought might be about its thinker without the thinker being aware of that fact. So, for example, I might think that the last person to arrive at the party is ill-mannered without realizing that I am that person. A gen-uinely self-conscious thought is about the thinker of that thought in a way that does not leave any room for the thinker to fail to recognize that the thought concerns him. This is part and parcel of the distinctive functional role of self-consciousness. It is mirrored by the linguistic fact that any token of the first-person pronoun "I" always refers to its producer. Self-conscious thoughts would naturally be expressed with sentences involving the first-person pronoun.

Immunity to Error through Misidentification

Self-conscious thoughts can be based on a range of different sources of information. Some of these sources can provide information *either* about the self *or* about other people. Testi-mony is a case in point. I can learn facts about myself by being told them by others, in the same way as I might learn facts about anything else. But there are other sources of infor-mation about the self that provide information purely about the self. These sources of information are such that, if we know from them that somebody has a particular property, we *ipso facto* know that we ourselves have that property. Introspection is an example. If I know through introspection that someone is currently thinking about self-consciousness then I know that I myself am thinking about self-consciousness. Introspection cannot provide information about anybody other than me. This does not mean that introspection (and other comparable sources of information) cannot be mistaken. They certainly can be mis-taken, but there is a certain type of error that they do not permit. Judgments made on the basis of them cannot be mistaken about who it is who has the property in question. Such judgments are *immune to error through misidentification relative to the first-person pronoun* (Shoemaker 1968), an epistemological property that they inherit from the information sources on which they are based.

Self-conscious thoughts that are immune to error in this sense (such as the thought that I am in pain, where this is based on information from pain receptors) are clearly more fundamental than those that are not. They reflect ways of finding out about ourselves that are exclusively about the self and that do not require identifying an object *as* the self. Self-conscious thoughts that are not immune to error through misidentification must be analyzed in terms of those that are immune, because they will involve identifying an object as the self, and any such identification must be immune to error through misidentification on pain of an infinite regress. For this reason influential accounts of self-consciousness, such as those of Shoemaker (1963, 1968) and Evans (1982), have attributed a fundamental role to the phenomenon of immunity to error through misidentification.

The phenomenon of immunity to error through misidentification can shed important light on the epistemology of self-knowledge – in particular, on the phenomenon of privileged access. Privileged access is usually understood in terms of a certain class of beliefs about oneself being immune to a certain type of error, with the type of privileged access being a function of the type of immunity identified – immunity to correction (incorrigibility), immunity to doubt (indubitability), immunity to error (infallibility), immunity to ignorance (self-intimation) and so forth (see Alston 1971 for a comprehensive survey). These types of immunity are invariably discussed with reference to introspective beliefs about one's own psychological states. Immunity to error through misidentification arguably has a foundational role to play relative to the other types, in at least the following sense. A belief that has any of the other types of immunity is immune to error through misidentification, whereas the converse does not hold – a belief can be immune to error through misidentification without being incorrigible, indubitable, infallible, or self-intimating. Moreover, it may well be that there are in fact no other types of immunity – that incorrigibility, infallibility, self-intimation, etc. all turn out to be philosophers' fictions. In that case, immunity to error through misidentification would be foundational by default.

The Scope of Self-Consciousness

There are four different ways in which one can be aware of something (whether an object or a state of affairs):

1 by having information about it and acting accordingly
2 by perceiving it
3 by having beliefs about it
4 by having knowledge of it.

One can have information about something without perceiving it. There are many examples of this among neuropsychological disorders, including blindsight (Weiskrantz, chapter 13). The performance of blindsight patients on certain matching and other tasks shows that they are capable of performing certain perceptual discriminations in their blindfield, and hence that at some level they are picking up visual information about a portion of the distal environment that they are not perceiving (Weiskrantz, chapter 13 and 1986). Similarly, one can perceive something without having beliefs about it. Most simply, one might not believe the content of one's perception. Finally, one can have beliefs about something without having knowledge of it. The belief might be mistaken, or fail to be securely enough grounded to qualify as knowledge.

Each of these different ways of understanding "awareness" yields a different conception of self-consciousness. The strictest and narrowest conception identifies it with self-knowledge (the knowledge of propositions about the self whose natural linguistic expression would involve the first-person pronoun). Only slightly less strict is the view that self-consciousness involves believing the appropriate sort of propositions about the self. Both of these views have the consequence that self-consciousness is only available to creatures that can have beliefs, and on many conceptions of belief this significantly narrows the field of self-conscious subjects. This has struck some philosophers as undesirable.

Understanding awareness in terms of either information pick-up or perception significantly broadens the scope of self-consciousness in both ontogenetic and phylogenetic terms. There are important questions, however, about how these types of awareness of the self should be understood. It is easy to see how they can support a form of direct awareness of the self. But do they admit propositional awareness of the self? If so, what is the content of that awareness? It presumably differs from the content of beliefs and/or knowledge about the self. But in what ways? At this point appeal might be made to the notion of *nonconceptual content*. Whereas the content of beliefs, and propositional attitudes in general, is conceptual (in the sense that it can only be attributed to creatures possessing the concepts required to specify it), some authors have found it helpful to postulate the possibility of ways of representing the world in ways that are not constrained by the conceptual repertoire in this sense (Evans 1982; Cussins 1990; Peacocke 1992; Bermúdez 1998).

As a way of motivating a more inclusive conception of self-consciousness, consider again the distinctive functional role that self-conscious thoughts play in the cognitive economy. We have seen already that self-conscious thoughts have immediate implications for action (Castañeda 1969; Perry 1979), and it is natural to wonder whether all motivated action might not require some form of self-conscious thought. Let us call this the *thesis of essential self-consciousness*. If motivated action really does require some form of self-conscious thought, then *either* only creatures who are capable of knowledge and/or belief are capable of motivated action *or* the domain of self-consciousness must be extended until it is co-extensive with the domain of agents. The perceived need to accommodate the second of these options is a prime motivation for taking one of the broad readings of self-consciousness outlined above.

It is natural to point out that what is shown by the above example and the many others like it is that it is not possible for me to act on the basis of knowledge or belief that *a* is *F* where "*a*" is a term or expression that refers to me but when I do not know that it does. But it does not follow from this that all motivated action requires knowledge or belief that would be expressed in the (genuinely self-conscious) form "I am *F*." If I am hungry and see food then I will act accordingly. But it is hard to see where the self-conscious thought comes in. What I see is what I desire, namely, the food over there.

Defenders of the thesis of essential self-consciousness will suggest that this misrepresents the nature of perception, since perception of the external world has an irreducible first-person component (Gibson 1979; Bermúdez 1998, ch. 5). Perception is essentially perspectival and egocentric, most obviously in vision but also in the sense of touch. The world is not presented in perception as an abstract arrangement of objects, but rather as an array of objects that stand in certain spatial relations to the perceiver. The world is perceived from a point of view, where a perceiver's point of view is tied to his possibilities for acting upon the distal environment.

It is important for both the philosophy of self-consciousness and the philosophy of perception to provide an account of the content of visual perception that reflects its perspectival and egocentric nature. An account of this kind will stress the differences between the content of perception and the content of propositional attitudes such as belief, including: the unit-free way in which distances are presented in visual perception; the fact that the spatiality of the distal environment is perceived on an egocentric frame of reference; and the way in which the embodied self actually appears in the field of vision and the content of tactile perception. Nonetheless, although we should not expect the contents of visual perception to be propositions of the sort that serve as contents of propositional attitudes, the status of exteroceptive perception as a form of propositional awareness of the self emerges when one remembers that it essentially provides information about the relations between the embodied self and objects in the distal environment.

Can we broaden the scope of self-consciousness even further? Can the appropriate type of awareness be derived from non-perceptual information pick-up? Somatic proprioception seems the most plausible place to look. Many of the sources of proprioception, such as the information about limb position and movement provided by joint position sense, and the information about the body's orientation and state of balance derived from the vestibular system, have seemed to many to be better described at the level of information pick-up, rather than at the level of perceptual awareness – not least because there does not seem to be a sensory dimension to the information they provide. Yet they also seem to be providing information about properties of the embodied self – intrinsic properties in the case of joint position sense and relational properties in the case of the vestibular system. It may be, however, that these two information sources are best understood, not in isolation, but rather as embedded within somatic proprioception as a whole, and it has been argued that somatic proprioception does indeed provide a form of perceptual awareness of the body (see the essays in Bermúdez, Marcel, & Eilan 1995 for various perspectives on this issue).

Consciousness of the Self and Consciousness of the World

As has emerged above, the functional role of self-conscious thoughts is both distinctive and important. We have so far concentrated on just two aspects of that functional role – the role of information-sources that are immune to error through misidentification in generating first-person thoughts, and the immediate implications that such thoughts have for action. But the functional role of a given type of thought also includes its relations to other types of thought. They will be the subject of this section.

Self-consciousness is essentially a contrastive notion. Subjects are aware of themselves relative to, and as distinct from, other members of a contrast class of either other physical objects or other psychological subjects. In view of this it is natural to adopt what I shall term "The Interdependence Thesis," according to which a creature's capacity for self-consciousness is directly proportional to its capacity to represent the external world.

A classic expression of the Interdependence Thesis is Kant's claim, defended in the section of *The Critique of Pure Reason* entitled "The Transcendental Deduction of the Categories," that self-consciousness both depends upon and makes possible the perception of a spatio-temporal world composed of continuously-existing objects causally interacting in lawlike ways. The form of self-consciousness he is discussing (the unity of apperception that he describes in terms of the "I think" being able to accompany all my representations) is largely formal – essentially the awareness, with respect to each member of a series of thoughts and experiences, that it is one's own. The interdependence emerges from the two-way links between the unity of apperception and the possibility of applying the categorial concepts whose applicability Kant took to define the objectivity of the world. In this sense, Kant's version of the Interdependence Thesis is closely linked to his distrinctive version of transcendental idealism.

Philosophers such as P. F. Strawson (1966) and Gareth Evans (1982) have more recently attempted to defend a version of the Interdependence Thesis that is not committed to a Kantian transcendental idealism. Like Kant, however, they adopt what I earlier described as a narrow conception of self-consciousness – that is, the thesis that self-consciousness involves and requires conceptual awareness of the self. For Strawson and Evans the Interdependence Thesis holds because the capacity to have a suitably generalized understanding of the first-person pronoun (Evans) or to conceptualize the distinction between experience and what it is experience of (Strawson) requires the ability to formulate judgments reflecting a conception of the embodied self as located within an objective world possessing certain very general features. For Evans, possessing a mastery of the first-person concept that is integrated with thought about the rest of the world in a suitably productive and systematic way requires the ability to conceive of oneself "from the third-person point of view" as an objective particular in a unified spatio-temporal world. For Strawson, the ability to distinguish appearance from reality within the realm of experience requires the ability to ascribe experiences to oneself as a continuously existing particular.

Whether these arguments are sound or not, an important question emerges for those who have sought to defend a broader conception of self-consciousness. How, if at all, can a version of the Interdependence Thesis be motivated once we move below the level of self-knowledge and beliefs/knowledge about the world? Clearly, at the level of perceptual awareness and information pick-up it is not appropriate to construe the Interdependence Thesis in terms of connections between *judgments* about the self and *judgments* about the world. Yet unless some version of the Interdependence Thesis holds at these more primitive levels, it is unclear how they can support genuine forms of self-consciousness at all, given that the Interdependence Thesis reflects the essentially contrastive nature of self-consciousness.

Some materials for answering this challenge are offered in Bermúdez 1998, where it is shown how primitive nonconceptual and prelinguistic forms of self-consciousness can be appropriately contrastive. Analysing visual perception following the ecological approach of J. J. Gibson (1979) reveals the exterospecific and propriospecific dimensions of visual perception and how the dynamism of visual perception emerges from their interaction. Similarly, somatic proprioception provides a broadly perceptual awareness of the limits of the body as a physical object responsive to the will, and hence as clearly demarcated from all other physical objects. By the same token, it is possible for a creature to have a sense of itself as following a single path through space-time, and hence to possess a (nonconceptual) point of view on the world, as manifested in its memories and navigational understanding of space, rather than in high-level beliefs and judgments.

Self-Consciousness and the Cognitive Sciences

The foregoing sections of this chapter have focused on more or less traditional philosophical problems of self-consciousness. As this *Companion* attests, there is increasing interest in dialog and collaboration between philosophers, on the one hand, and cognitive scientists, psychologists, and neuroscientists, on the other. The exploration of self-consciousness is likely to prove a particularly fruitful area for such dialog and collaboration (see Gallagher 2000 for an overview). This final section points to some examples.

Many discussions of cognitive science make a distinction between central and peripheral processes (Fodor 1985). This is often tied to the distinction between modular and non-modular processes. Central processes are not encapsulated, domain-specific, mandatory and fast in the manner of peripheral processes such as those responsible for early vision and phonological analysis. On what I have been calling the narrow conception of self-consciousness, according to which self-consciousness is at root a matter of having certain distinctive types of thought about oneself, self-consciousness will have to be analyzed at the level of central processing. Those who follow Fodor (1985) in thinking that cognitive science can have little to say about central processes will draw appropriately pessimistic conclusions. More plausibly, it seems natural to think that the capacity to entertain self-conscious beliefs will depend upon some form of metarepresentational capacity, and hence should be analyzed as an element in what is often termed "theory of mind."

There exists a rich cognitive scientific literature in this area, which one might expect to be highly informative on the ontogenesis of higher-level self-consciousness, as well as on what happens when the mechanisms that subserve higher-level self-consciousness break down. With respect to the former of these, one might expect the capacity for higher-level self-consciousness to emerge as part of the overall "theory of mind" package at more or less the age of 4, but there are no doubt different stages and forms of self-awareness through which developing infants must pass (Rochat 2003). As far as pathology is concerned, Christopher Frith's influential analysis suggests that schizophrenia should be understood as a breakdown in the mechanisms that permit awareness of oneself as the author of one's thoughts and beliefs – and hence that it is, at least in part, a deficit of higher-order self-consciousness (Frith 1992; Campbell 1999). In both of these areas there is considerable scope for bringing philosophical analyses of self-consciousness into contact with empirical research.

The scope for dialog between philosophy and the cognitive sciences with respect to self-consciousness becomes much greater on what I have termed the broader conception of self-consciousness. The different areas of cognitive science can be expected to play a crucial role in exploring the more primitive dimensions of self-consciousness (Neisser 1993). We have already briefly seen how Gibson's ecological approach to visual perception can be of great help in understanding how visual perception incorporates an element of self-awareness. One would also expect the cognitive sciences to provide much-needed clarification of the different information systems and channels subserving somatic proprioception.

There is also scope for influence in the other direction. Accounts within cognitive science need to be sensitive to cognitive factors revealed by philosophical accounts of the nature of self-consciousness. A single example will make the point. I have already suggested that one way in which the Interdependence Thesis might be understood at the level of perceptual awareness and information pick-up is through a creature's possessing a (nonconceptual) point of view on the world in virtue of having certain navigational abilities. It seems plausible to stress the role of the following capacities in underwriting a creature's grasp of the spatial organization of its environment and its location within that environment:

- the capacity to think about different routes to the same place;
- the capacity to keep track of changes in spatial relations between objects caused by its own movements relative to those objects;

- the capacity to think about places independently of the objects or features located at those places.

Recognizing the centrality of these cognitive capacities influences how we interpret some important recent work on animal representations of space and their neurophysiological coding. Chapters 5 and 6 of Gallistel (1980) defend the thesis that all animals from insects upward deploy cognitive maps with the same formal characteristics in navigating around the environment. Gallistel argues that the cognitive maps that control movement in animals all preserve the same set of geometric relations within a system of Earth-centered (*geocentric*) coordinates. These relations are metric relations. The distinctive feature of a metric geometry is that it preserves all the geometric relations between the points in the coordinate system. Gallistel's thesis is that, although the cognitive maps of lower animals have far fewer places on them, they record the same geometrical relations between those points as humans and other higher animals.

Without challenging Gallistel's central thesis that all animal cognitive maps from insects up preserve geometric relations, it nonetheless seems wrong to draw the conclusion that all animals represent space in the same way. Just as important as how animals represent spatial relations between objects is how they represent their own position within the object-space thus defined. And it is here, in what we should think of as not just their awareness of space but also their self-conscious awareness of themselves as spatially located entities, that we see the major variations and the scale of gradations that the theorists whom Gallistel is criticizing have previously located at the level of the cognitive map.*

See also 4 Animal consciousness; 13 The case of blindsight; 14 Split-brain cases; 15 Philosophical psychopathology and self-consciousness; 16 Coming together: the unity of conscious experience; 35 Sensory and perceptual consciousness; 53 Phenomenological approaches to consciousness.

Note

* This article contains some material from my entry on self-consciousness in the *Macmillan Encyclopedia of Cognitive Science*.

Further Readings

Bermúdez, J. L. (1998) *The Paradox of Self-Consciousness*. Cambridge, MA: MIT Press.
Cassam, Q. (ed.) (1994) *Self-Knowledge*. Oxford: Oxford University Press.
Perry, J. (1979) The problem of the essential indexical. In *The Problem of the Essential Indexical and Other Essays*. Oxford. Oxford University Press.
Shoemaker, S. (1968) Self-reference and self-awareness. *Journal of Philosophy* 65, 555–67.

References

Alston, W. (1971) Varieties of privileged access. *American Philosophical Quarterly* 8, 223–41.
Anscombe, E. (1975/1994). The first person. Reprinted in Q. Cassam (ed.), *Self-Knowledge*, 140–59. Oxford: Oxford University Press.

Bermúdez, J. L. (1998) *The Paradox of Self-Consciousness*. Cambridge, MA: MIT Press.

Bermúdez, J. L., Marcel, A. J., and Eilan, N. (eds.) (1995) *The Body and the Self*. Cambridge, MA: MIT Press.

Campbell, J. (1999) Schizophrenia, the space of reasons and thinking as a motor process. *The Monist* 82, 609–25.

Cassam, Q. (ed.) (1994) *Self-Knowledge*. Oxford: Oxford University Press.

Castañeda, H.-N. (1969) The phenomeno-logic of the I. Reprinted in Q. Cassam (ed.), *Self-Knowledge*, 160–6. Oxford: Oxford University Press.

Cussins, A. (1990) The connectionist construction of concepts. In M. Boden (ed.), *The Philosophy of Artificial Intelligence*, 368–440. Oxford: Oxford University Press.

Dretske, F. (1995) *Naturalizing the Mind*. Cambridge, MA: MIT Press.

Dretske, F. (1999) The mind's awareness of itself. In *Perception, Knowledge and Belief*, 158–77. Cambridge: Cambridge University Press.

Evans, G. (1982) *The Varieties of Reference*. Oxford: Oxford University Press.

Fodor, J. (1985) *The Modularity of Mind*. Cambridge, MA: MIT Press.

Frith, C. (1992) *The Cognitive Neuropsychology of Schizophrenia*. Brighton: Laurence Erlbaum.

Gallagher, S. (2000) Philosophical conceptions of the self: implications for cognitive science. *Trends in Cognitive Science* 4, 14–21.

Gallistel, C. R. (1990) *The Organization of Learning*. Cambridge, MA: MIT Press.

Gibson, J. J. (1979) *The Ecological Approach to Visual Perception*. Boston, MA: Houghton-Mifflin.

Hume, D. (1739–40/1978) *A Treatise of Human Nature*. Edited by L. A. Selby-Bigge and revised by P. H. Nidditch. Oxford: Clarendon Press.

Neisser, U. (ed.) (1993) *The Perceived Self*. Cambridge: Cambridge University Press.

Olson, E. (1997) *The Human Animal*. Oxford: Oxford University Press.

Parfit, D. (1984) *Reasons and Persons*. Oxford: Oxford University Press.

Peacocke, C. (1992) *A Study of Concepts*. Cambridge, MA: MIT Press.

Rochat, P. (2003) Five levels of self-awareness as they unfold early in life. *Consciousness and Cognition* 12, 717–31.

Shoemaker, S. (1963) *Self-Knowledge and Self-Identity*. Ithaca, NY: Cornell University Press.

Shoemaker, S. (1968) Self-reference and self-awareness. *Journal of Philosophy*, 65, 555–67.

Shoemaker, S. (1984) Personal identity: a materialist's account. In S. Shoemaker and R. Swinburne (eds.), *Personal Identity*. Oxford: Blackwell.

Strawson, P. F. (1966) *The Bounds of Sense*. London: Methuen.

Unger, P. (1990) *Identity, Consciousness, and Value*. Oxford: Oxford University Press.

Weiskrantz, L. (1986) *Blindsight*. Oxford: Oxford University Press.

37

Consciousness and Intentionality

GEORGE GRAHAM, TERENCE HORGAN,
AND JOHN TIENSON

Introduction

The mental begins and ends with consciousness and intentionality. Consciousness and intentionality help to define the mental *qua* mental.

Consciousness, as we refer to this phenomenon in the current chapter, is the property of a mental state in virtue of which there is something it's like for a subject or person to be in that state. There is something it's like, for example, to see a certain shade of red or to feel a certain sharp pain. Intentionality is the property of a mental state in virtue of which the state is directed at, is about, or represents something other than itself. Intentionality is instantiated when a perceptual belief is about a crooked picture on the wall, a desire is for ice cream, a fear is of flying, and a memory is of things past.

What is the relationship between these two features of mentality? What, if any, is the connection between consciousness and intentionality?

Consciousness and intentionality, insist some philosophers, although perhaps often co-occurring, are mutually independent or separable. They take place in two separable dimensions of our mental lives. One dimension consists of our subjective experiences in which there is something it's like to be us. The other consists of our lives as intentional beings in which we represent what is going on in the external world as well as, on occasion, in ourselves.

Consciousness and intentionality, insist others, are interdependent or inseparable. According to a strong and unqualified form of inseparatism (a term defined just below), the fact that a mental state is conscious means or entails that it is intentional. The fact that a mental state is intentional means or entails that it is conscious. Our conscious mental states are intentional states: they inform us about the world and ourselves. Our intentional mental states are conscious states: there is something it's like to represent the world and ourselves.

We like to use two neologisms to speak of the above two conceptions of the relationship between consciousness and intentionality. *Separatism* says that consciousness and intentionality are two mutually independent or separable aspects of our mental lives. *Inseparatism* says that consciousness and intentionality are interdependent or inseparable.

In the work of philosophers from Descartes (1596–1650) and Locke (1632–1704) to Brentano (1838–1917) and Husserl (1859–1938), consciousness and intentionality were typically treated as inseparable aspects of our mental lives (as noted by Chalmers 2004). In 1690 Locke wrote: "'tis altogether as intelligible to say, that a body is extended without parts, as that any thing *thinks without being conscious of it*, or perceiving, that it does so" (*Essay*, Book 2, ch. 1, section 19, p. 115). By contrast, in the tradition of late twentieth-century Anglo-American philosophy, the separatist position has been the dominant view. Jaegwon Kim (1998) writes: "It has been customary to distinguish between two broad categories of mental phenomena, the intentional and the phenomenal" (p. 101). (The word "phenomenal" is sometimes used to identify the feature of a conscious mental state that makes it conscious, viz., its what-is-likeness or phenomenology. We shall observe this practice in what follows.) Endorsing categorical separability Kim adds: "If someone should ask us to create a device with consciousness . . . I don't think we would know how to begin" (p. 102). However, if asked to design a structure with intentionality, he remarks, "it seems to me that we can go about designing" such a thing (p. 103).

If Kim is right, then Locke, Descartes, and many others are wrong. Intentionality is independent of consciousness. To produce the first is not to produce the second. In addition, numerous theorists maintain that independence runs in the opposite direction. A subject's mental state can be conscious without instantiating any intentional structure. There are conscious mental states that don't represent anything whatsoever. John Searle (1983) gives as examples of such states, forms of elation, depression, or anxiety in which one is not "elated, depressed, or anxious about anything" (p. 2). "Many conscious states," he says, "are not intentional" (ibid.).

In this chapter, our strategy is not merely expository of possible links between consciousness and intentionality, although it is in part that. Our aim is committal or positional. We argue that there is a good case to be made for the sort of inseparatist position that we favor. Aspects of the same inseparatist position outlined here are examined and defended by us in a series of earlier papers. It was first introduced in synoptic terms in Horgan and Tienson (2002), extended in Horgan, Tienson, and Graham (2003), and refined in Horgan, Tienson, and Graham (2005), Horgan, Tienson, and Graham (forthcoming), as well as Graham, Horgan, and Tienson (forthcoming). It was distinguished from representationalism in Graham and Horgan (2000) (among other places). It has drawn criticism in one or another respect from Dennett (2005), Georgalis (2003), Raffman (2005), and Wilson (2003), with a reply to Raffman in Graham and Horgan (2005) and a reply by Graham and Horgan to Dennett currently under composition.

The present chapter, although complementary to our earlier papers, is self-contained. It constructs the position in ways different from what is said by us elsewhere, by further exploring and arguing against some separatist criticisms of inseparatism. We restrict our attention in this chapter to one particularly important aspect of inseparatism: the relation between phenomenal character and intentional content (see also Graham, Horgan, & Tienson forthcoming).

Other contemporary philosophers and theorists have developed inseparatist or nearly inseparatist theses similar to ours in various ways. We shall mention some of this work, and the philosophers responsible for it, but our primary aim is to introduce and try to make plausible the specific version of inseparatism that we favor. Useful survey and discussion of various issues connected with the relation between consciousness and intentionality, complete with bibliographies, may be found in Siewert (2003) and Chalmers (2004). Among philosophers who have contributed importantly to the topics of consciousness and intentionality with one or more inseparatist sympathies or sensitivities are Barry Dainton, Owen Flanagan, Alvin Goldman, Uriah Kriegel, Brian Loar, Colin McGinn, Nicholas Geogalis, David Pitt, and Galen Strawson, as well as Siewert and Chalmers.

After spelling out inseparatism more carefully, we shall say something about why one might believe, as we do, that the position is true. Finally, we will briefly sketch two questions about or challenges to inseparatism and say something, again briefly, about how the inseparatist might reply to each.

Inseparatism Described and Refined

Inseparatism is a thesis implying that the mental is a unified rather than a bifurcated phenomenon; the features of consciousness and intentionally are interdependent or inseparable. We have claimed elsewhere that there are different components to the inseparatist position. These include different sub-theses as well as descriptions of different dimensions of connectivity between consciousness and intentionality (Horgan & Tienson 2002 and Horgan, Tienson, & Graham 2006). Some of the dimensions of connectivity include the phenomenology of perceptual experience, the phenomenology of first-person agency, the phenomenology of attitude type, and of intentional content. Here we shall restrict our attention to the relation between phenomenal and intentional content, but keeping in mind that the total inseparatist outlook is more rangy and complex.

Although we will eventually need a qualification or two, we can put this restricted inseparatism thus (where "C" stands for content and "Ins" for inseparatism):

(C-Ins): Every paradigmatic mental state is **phenomenally intentional** in content.

A mental state is phenomenally intentional in content just in case the intentional content of the state (viz. what it's about or represents or is directed at) is determined or constituted by its conscious or phenomenal character or what-it's-likeness alone. Nothing non-phenomenal is a proper part of a mental state's intentional content.

Two comments on C-Ins. In the first place, this thesis is restricted to paradigmatic or incontestable mental states (e.g., perceptual beliefs). To clarify: at the present time, debates about the nature of the mental are ongoing in philosophy and cognitive science. It is contestable whether certain states of certain sorts deserve to be classified as mental. Much depends upon how the concept of the mental is regimented or understood and with the manner or extent to which certain candidate mental states depart from exemplary or paradigm instances of mentality. Consider, for example, states of a subject or agent that are said to be *subdoxastic* (Stich 1978). Subdoxastic states are states that are distinguished from paradigmatic mental states by their so-called inferential isolation and inaccessibility to consciousness. One class of such states includes those allegedly identified by E. H. Hess (1975) as information states which subconsciously compare the diameters of pupils in other people's eyes. Such states are highly specialized computational mechanisms (cf. Fodor 1983). Are they mental? Approximately mental? Proto-mental? Quasi-mental? Well, certainly, they are not paradigmatically mental. (Nor are states of so-called *extended cognition*, states which contain parts that do not fall within the skin and scalp boundaries of a human or animal body – such as the arrangement of the parts of a disassembled bicycle indicating the order in which the parts are to be reassembled – Clark 1997; compare with Rupert 2004.) Paradigmatic mental states are states that every competent speaker would classify as mental. Perceptual beliefs, for example, are paradigmatic mental states; no one would deny that they are mental. Perceptual beliefs, such as the perceptual belief that a beach ball in front of one is red, are inferentially connected with other beliefs and attitudes and occur in consciousness. C-Ins is best understood as not applying to subdoxastic states over which theoretical controversy about their mentality looms.

Second, we shall think of *phenomenal intentional* content as follows. Intentional content is conscious or phenomenal just when (i) it presents itself immediately or directly to the subject or person who is in the state, and (ii) such content is fully constituted by the what-it's-likeness of this immediate or direct presentation. As a result the subject can *just tell* what he or she is thinking of; this capacity to just tell what is going on in one's phenomenology is the by-product of the distinctively self-presentational character of phenomenal conscious-ness. So, for example, suppose one is now in a mental state with the distinctive conscious or phenomenal character of a-picture-is-hanging-on-the-wall-in-front-of oneself. According to C-Ins, undergoing this conscious experience constitutively determines that the phe-nomenal intentional content of the state is that a picture is hanging on the wall in front of oneself.

This does not mean, of course, that it is *true* that a picture is hanging on the wall in front of oneself. For that to be true the world must satisfy the content. The content, contrariwise, may be part of a dream, hallucination, or otherwise misrepresenting thought. Furthermore, since this what-it's-like feature is entirely constituted phenomenologically, the content itself might present itself to one in a direct or immediate way even if the subject had never been in suitable causal-perceptual contact with any picture, any wall, or indeed any concrete object whatever. The picture-on-the-wall content might be part of a lifelong dream or hal-lucination, or might be induced by an enormously clever set of sensory transducers hooked up to my brain which is permanently envatted in a pictureless room.

Suppose you wonder whether Clinton would have made a better presidential candidate than Kerry. This same content could be instantiated by a conscious creature's mental state even if the thought-constituents expressed by the singular terms "Clinton" and "Kerry" were used by the creature to refer to the different individuals (e.g., in a Twin Earthly envi-ronment) than these thought-constituents refer to when employed by ourselves – or even if these thought-constituents were used in such a way that they fail to refer to any individuals at all (e.g., in an envatted-brain environment).

Elsewhere we have used the term "phenomenal intentionality" for what we are here calling phenomenal intentional content. On our view, phenomenal intentionality is to be distinguished from what we call *externalistic* intentionality. Some thoughts – specifically, ones that deploy thought-constituents that purport to refer to individuals or to natural kinds – have both phenomenal intentionality and externalistic intentionality. The latter arises as a joint product of (i) phenomenal intentionality and (ii) certain specific relations (e.g., causal relations) between a cognitive agent and actual reference-eligible individuals or natural kinds in the agent's surrounding environment. Reference eligibility for a thought-constituent – what sort of entity the thought-constituent *could* refer to – is determined by the phenomenal intentionality of that thought constituent. The conscious character of the thought alone determines what the thought is about in the sense of phenomenal intention-ality. See the discussion of phenomenal intentionality vs. mental reference in Horgan and Tienson (2002), and the related discussion of phenomenal intentionality vs. externalistic intentionality in Horgan, Tienson, and Graham (2005).

Suppose, for another instance, you are in the mental state of appearing to yourself to raise your hand at a meeting of the local neighborhood association to vote for its presi-dent. We would classify such a state as an instance of "the phenomenology of first-person agency," which, for us, is one sort of inseparatist connection between consciousness and intentionality (Horgan, Tienson, & Graham 2003). According to C-Ins, undergoing this conscious experience constitutively determines that your mental state is about your raising your hand at a meeting.

Instead of talking of the presentational immediacy of conscious or phenomenal content, some theorists prefer to deploy what may seem to be a quite different description of content that is conscious. Some say that the only way to identify the conscious content of a mental state (intentional or otherwise) is to speak of its so-called "phenomenal quality." Typically cited examples include the way things look, taste, or smell, or the way an itch feels. When you taste bitter chocolate, for instance, there is an immediate way the chocolate appears to you: it tastes bitter or has a bitter quality. Phenomenal qualities are often spoken of as the *qualia* of conscious experience (cf. Flanagan 1992, p. 65) (singular *quale*). Qualia are said to be definitive of conscious content.

We certainly have no objection to speaking of the "qualitative character" of experience as being definitive of consciousness or of conscious content. We have sometimes engaged in such talk ourselves (Graham & Horgan 2000). But we have done so only provided that the pertinent concept of quality is not restricted to qualia in the narrow denotation of sensations (say, the feel of an itch) or concrete sensory images (say, the bitterness of the chocolate's taste). When philosophers restrict the notion of qualia to a narrow band of qualities, usually this is as a preface to embracing separatism. One separatist argument goes something like this: Distinctively conscious content is constituted by sensations or concrete sensory images; states with intentional structure are not constituted by sensations or such images; so, intentional content is separable from conscious content and more generally intentionality is separable from consciousness. No sensation needs to be part of thinking of a crooked picture; no sensory image needs to be part of wondering whether Bill Clinton would have been a more successful Democratic candidate for president than John Kerry or whether justice, as John Rawls said, is fairness.

What happens to the content of conscious intentional states, according to some separatists, if "conscious content" is understood as applying only to narrow qualia and conscious intentional states lack such qualia as proper to and distinctive of them? Proponents of separatism typically admit a distinction between intentional mental states that are conscious in content and those that are not, but they typically claim that the relevant notion of consciousness is not phenomenal or qualitative but rather what Ned Block (1995) dubs *access consciousness*. A state is access conscious, says such a separatist, when (roughly) it is introspectively accessible. From the perspective of the variety of inseparatism that we ourselves favor, however, the introspective accessibility of conscious intentional mental states is not a different kind of consciousness from phenomenal consciousness. Rather, intentional states are accessible *by virtue* of being phenomenally conscious. Introspective accessibility is a feature of states that are phenomenally conscious rather than a defining feature of a second and distinct type of consciousness. Such accessibility is a by-product of the fact that phenomenally conscious states are *self-presentational* in a way that non-phenomenal states are not.

Returning to the example of wondering whether Clinton would have been a more successful candidate than Kerry, we claim that such a thought-content has a quality – but with "quality" understood broadly rather than narrowly. The "quale" of such a thought, on the broad-band or ecumenical conception that we favor rather than the narrow conception of qualia, consists of (what might be called) its cognitive quality – rather than a sensory quality or a concrete sensory-imagistic quality. No concrete image. No particular sensation;

just the what-it's-like of undergoing an occurrent psychological state with the content *that Clinton would have been a more successful candidate than Kerry*. Barry Dainton (2000, p. 13) notes: "Thoughts often occur without any distinctive sensory garb." "Yet [their] content could not be clearer." (There is also the specific what-it's-like of a state's being a specific *attitude* toward its content – in the present example, the what-it's-like of *wondering* whether p, as opposed to believing that p, doubting that p, hoping that p, etc.)

It might be objected that we have construed phenomenal qualities so ecumenically that inseparatism just becomes true by definition. "Phenomenal" is defined so broadly that nothing incontestably conscious counts as non-phenomenal. Our reply is that there is a what-it's-like to any incontestably conscious state, and, following one current trend, we are using "phenomenal" for what-it-is like. Don't you find, in your own case, that (for example) there is a difference in what it's like to think that rabbits have tails and what it's like to think that collections of undetached rabbit parts have tail-subsets, a phenomenal difference that goes beyond any auditory or visual-syntactic imagery (since the sign-design "rabbit" might have meant "collection of undetached rabbit parts" and the sign-design "has a tail" might have meant "has a tail-subset")? The phenomenal *is* broad enough to include occurrent thoughts. Neither ordinary folk nor philosophers (Descartes included) are gripped by radical skepticism about what their current thoughts are; the only adequate explanation for the non-grippingness of "internal-world skepticism" is that occurrent thoughts are phenomenally self-presenting (Horgan, Tienson, & Graham 2006).

For another example of what we have in mind by "quality," compare what it's like to listen to a conversation in your mother tongue (English, let us suppose) with what it's like to listen to a conversation in a language you utterly fail to comprehend (perhaps Urdu). The conversation in your mother tongue directly appears or presents itself as meaningful to you, whereas the conversation in the alien language does not. You might infer that the alien conversation is meaningful, but it does not directly present itself that way to you. Meaning, notes Dainton (2000), can be just "as much a phenomenal feature of what [you] hear as the timbre or pitch of [a] voice" (p. 12). (See also Galen Strawson 1994, p. 4. Other philosophers who take a broad-band approach to qualia include Flanagan 1992 and Goldman 1993.)

Two Implications of Thesis C-Ins

Thesis C-Ins has two important implications. *First implication*: Since phenomenally conscious states are mental (and we assume incontestably so), every phenomenally conscious state also is intentional. This implication is, of course, part of what makes inseparatism inseparatist: the fact that a state is conscious means also that it is intentional.

Second implication: Since phenomenally intentional content is determined by phenomenal character *alone*, such content is entirely constituted by features internal or intrinsic to phenomenology. This fact, in conjunction with the fact that phenomenology is self-presenting to the experiencing subject, explains why (as noted above) subjects can "just tell" what the content of their mental state is. Conscious contents immediately present themselves to their subjects. Moreover, as we have recently remarked, being able to just tell what a mental state is about is resistant to the sorts of radical doubts about the external world that Descartes famously described in the *First Meditation*. Radical skepticism achieves no hold on phenomenal intentional content because self-presentational phenomenology forecloses the possibility of an epistemic gap between how phenomenal states seem to the subject and how they really are – although arguably, such skepticism should take hold for intentional mental states if or insofar as their intentionality is not phenomenally constituted (see Horgan, Tienson, & Graham 2006 for detailed discussion).

Radical Cartesian doubts certainly can arise about whether my current mental states possess *externalistic* intentionality at all (cf. section above) – which they do not if I'm in a lifelong Evil Deceiver or brain-in-vat situation – and about what their specific external-istic content is. Such doubts can also arise about the content of past, now non-occurrent mental states. Much of our conscious mental life occurs in moments of retrospection. It can immediately seem to me that I remember my toothache of yesterday, although in fact I had no ache yesterday. The remembering (seeming to remember) is self-presented, not the remembered (ache). The kind of content that we would claim is not susceptible to the grip of radical skepticism, on the other hand, is the *phenomenal* intentionality of one's *current* conscious cognitive states.

The first implication of C-Ins mentioned above is also embraced by advocates of so-called "representational theories" of phenomenal consciousness (Dretske 1995 and Tye 1995, 2003, among others). According to representationalism, everything paradigmati-cally conscious or phenomenal is intentional or directed at something (see chapter 20). On the sort of representationalist view expressed by Dretske and Tye (see above), our sensory experiences (e.g., pains) inform us of our body; our perceptual experiences (e.g., visual experiences) represent the local environment. Emotions have intentional objects (as when we fear flying). Even what Searle classifies as simple elation, depression, or anxiety, which Searle says fail to possess intentional structure, possess intentionality. So-called "objectless anxiety," for example, is a kind of representation of everything, and not of any one particu-lar thing or situation, as fearful or as a source of anxiety.

Advocates of representationalism typically reject the second implication of C-Ins. They argue that phenomenal intentional content is nonintrinsic and is constituted by certain kinds of objective relations (e.g., causal or co-variational relations) between the occurrence of phe-nomenal states and certain external properties or relations. They sometimes put their view by saying that phenomenal intentional content is external or "not in the head." For insepara-tists such as ourselves, however, although the external world most surely is causally relevant to some matters central to a subject's conscious intentional embedding in the world, we do not believe that the main or fundamental kind of intentionality is such an external relation and that such intentionality is partially constituted "outside the head." (On our view, *exter-nalistic* intentionality is indeed an external relation. It is not, however, the fundamental kind of mental content since it is determined jointly by phenomenal intentionality and certain externalistic relations between the experiencing agent and the wider environment – see the section below entitled "An epistemic gap counter-argument against C-Ins.")

Suppose I believe that a picture on the wall in front of me is crooked. Although the occurrence or immediate presentation of the content *a-picture-on-the-wall-in-front-of-me-is-crooked* might be caused by something in my environment (such as an actual crooked picture on the wall), and therein might also be made true by the world, the content itself might present itself to me in a direct or immediate way even if I have never been in suitable causal-perceptual contact with any picture, any wall, or indeed any concrete object what-ever. As mentioned above, the crooked-picture content might be part of a lifelong dream or hallucination, or might be induced by an enormously clever set of sensory transducers hooked up to my brain.

Why Endorse Thesis C-Ins?

There are no proofs for C-Ins. Like many other theses presented in this book, it cannot be established decisively. It is, however, a plausible position to take given the plausibility of certain other sets of propositions about the mental. We shall now specify two of those sets of propositions and say a few words about each of them. No full-scale defense of either can be mounted in the present context.

Set One. Consider your own case

We begin with a set that is also of the sort that helps to make representationalism about consciousness plausible, although it is consistent with our inseparatist non-representationalist conviction that phenomenal content is intrinsic and not, as in typical versions of representationalism, something extrinsic. We call it the "consider your own case" set.

If you consider the case of your own conscious experience you will note, we claim, that it is representational or intentional, in the sense that what you are aware of, fundamentally, is what the experience is *of*, not the experience as such. For example, right now you are consciously representing things as being a certain way in the world. Your visual or perceptual phenomenology, for instance, might involve the representation of a book on a desk in front of you, with various books and papers distributed on the desk and perhaps a mug of coffee or glass of juice off to the left.

Consider, in particular, your current color experiences. Contrary to what separatists typically claim, these experiences are not nonintentional "add-ons" to one's intentional perceptual mental states; for example, they are not what Block (2003) calls nonintentional "mental paint." On the contrary, you are experiencing colors as properties instantiated on the surfaces of various apparent objects – properties apparently instantiated by the books, the papers, the cup or glass, and the other objects. Color experiences are no less intentional than the other aspects of perceptual awareness.

Right now, too, perhaps, your sensory-body phenomenology might include that your left elbow, which is resting on the table, feels discomforted. The discomfort is experienced or represented as in the elbow, while the elbow itself is experienced as on the table top. In addition, you might have an attitude-type phenomenology; you might experience yourself as feeling, emotionally, a certain way. It might be the case that you feel sad or depressed (although, of course, we hope not). If asked, you might describe yourself as depressed but not about anything specific. Your experience of being depressed is an affectation of your consciousness of things in general. As a depressed character in an Ingmar Bergman movie puts it: "Everything's getting meaner and grayer, with no dignity" (quoted in Church 2003, p. 175). No one concrete thing is so represented; everything is so represented.

Set Two. Identity of content

This second set concerns the question of what constitutes similarity and difference in intentional content. When two intentional contents are the same, what makes them the same? When different, what makes them different? Here is an answer.

Each and every type of intentional content has its own identity. An intentional content's identity distinguishes it from distinct (nonidentical) contents. (This may be put by saying that an intentional content's identity or distinctness consists in its determinacy.) So, for example, if Lois Lane is having a thought that she would express by saying "I am kissing Clark Kent," this is not the same as having a thought that she would express by saying "I am kissing Superman," although Clark is Superman. The content I-am-kissing-Clark-Kent is not one and the same as the content I-am-kissing-Superman. Now, in theory, content-identity may be fixed or made determinate either by something physical (or "physical/functional") that is not phenomenological (such as an organism's physical causal relationship to its environment) or by something phenomenological (such as its phenomenal content or character). Physically and apart from phenomenology, however, there is, we would argue, no "one, determinate, right answer" to the question of what is the content of an intentional state (Dennett 1987, p. 319 and see also Quine 1960, ch. 2 and pp. 216–21; compare with Keeley 1999). For, even if content differences always correspond to physical differences – even if, for example, there is no difference in what two mental states are about unless there is a corresponding difference in the physical or brain states of the subject – the content of each mental state is not determinately fixed once those physical facts (including perhaps physical facts about internal–environmental linkages) are fixed. Fortunately, however, for the identity or determinate character of intentional content, content identity or determinacy is fixed phenomenally. For example, the what-it's-like of thinking "Lo, a rabbit" is different from the what-it's-like of thinking "Lo, a collection of undetached rabbit parts." The difference in content is a *phenomenal* intentional difference.

Remember, a subject can "just tell" what she is thinking, fearing, wishing, etc., when she is in a conscious mental state of thinking, fearing, or wishing. Conscious content is immediately or directly presented to the subject in the form of what-it-is-like to be in the mental state with that content. She knows that her thoughts have such-and-such a content.

A lot needs to be said about Set Two if it is to be defended (Graham, Horgan, & Tienson forthcoming). One key proposition in the set is that identity of intentional content is not determined by physical facts. This proposition is hotly contested in the literature. Many philosophers, including typical representationalists, argue that it is false. So, in order to defend the proposition one has to show that, in effect, Daniel Dennett is right when he says that when physical facts fall short of intentional content determination, "as they always must, there will always be uninterpretable gaps . . . so that no further [physical fact] could settle what the [thinker] in question really [thinks]" (Dennett 1987, p. 140). Combine the defense of this proposition with defense of the additional proposition that intentional content is fixed phenomenally (a proposition that Dennett robustly rejects), and defense of Set Two is a full-scale philosophical project.

The project of defense may be cast as a dialectical dilemma. Let us assume that there are only two ways, theoretically, in which intentional content might be determinate: it might be determinate physically or phenomenologically. (We are presupposing that if other modes of determination suggest themselves – such as by a subject's instantiating plausible mentalistic or intentionalistic interpretations of their behavior – then such prima facie alternative modes ultimately rely upon either physical or phenomenological determination. In the section below entitled "Nonconscious intentional mental states as suitably causally integrated," we discuss a manner in which intentional content determination might rely upon phenomenological determination even when the intentional content of a certain state is not itself phenomenal.)

Now consider the following propositions:

i   Intentional content is determinate.

ii Determinacy of intentional content is not physical.

iii Determinacy of intentional content is not phenomenological.

Here is the dilemma. All three propositions cannot be true. Propositions (ii) and (iii) entail that intentional content is not determinate or real or genuine – which would make proposition (i) false. Proposition (i) entails that something must constitute the determinacy of content – which would make either or both of (ii) or (iii) false.

Denial of (i) evidently amounts to denial of *realism* about mental states with intentionality; strictly speaking, there are no such states. Dennett (1987) adopts this strategy, in consequence using the absence of determinate intentional content in defense of a sort of quasi-realist or instrumentalist picture of intentional-state attributions (which he calls Intentional Systems Theory). Denial of (ii) is taken by typical representationalists and various others. Denial of (iii) is taken by Searle (1990), who in effect argues for phenomenal content-individuation as the basis of intentional content determinacy – more specifically that a mental state has a determinate intentional content only if it is conscious at some time or another, at least potentially. Phenomenology and not physicality is the ground for all determinate (or what Searle calls "aspectual") intentional content.

Our sympathies, of course, lie with the denial of (iii), and with the idea that phenomenal intentionality grounds the determinacy of intentional content. This idea provides powerful motivation for thesis C-Ins, given the bleak prospects for grounding determinate intentionality any other way.

Nonconscious Mental States: Three Alternative Positions

Now we turn to two questions about inseparatism or C-Ins in particular. Here is the first.

If indeed the determinacy or identity of intentional content depends essentially upon phenomenology, then an obvious question arises about whether there can be nonconscious mental states with determinate intentional content. Common sense as well as much theoretical psychology posits various kinds of nonconscious mental states with determinate intentional content. But such putative states, being nonconscious, have no phenomenology – no what-it's-like-ness for the subject.

Consider, for example, Shakespeare's writing of *Hamlet*. Many critics offer interpretations of Shakespeare's intentions in writing the play that presuppose that at least some of his intentions were not consciously available to him. In doing so some critics appeal to the theory of the dynamic unconscious of Freud, and others may appeal to the information-processing unconscious of cognitive psychology. Some use the convictions of common sense or belief-desire folk psychology. It is a virtual axiom of folk psychology that some cases of belief and desire are nonconscious. No matter the theoretical vehicle, however, if Shakespeare's nonconscious intentions (or beliefs or desires) really existed and explain features of *Hamlet*, then although the concept of mental states with intentional structure may include as a subset states with phenomenal or conscious intentional content, the very idea of an intentional state is not tethered to or exhausted by states with phenomenal intentionality. Nonconscious intentional content may have lurked behind writing: "To be, or not to be – that is the question."

So here is the question about C-Ins: Does Thesis C-Ins leave room for the possibility of nonconscious mental states with genuine, determinate, intentional content? We will sketch three alternative positions on the matter that might be taken by an advocate of C-Ins. We will remain neutral among them here, because this is a matter on which we have not achieved a settled mutual opinion.

Before proceeding, let us clarify one point. The question or issue at hand does not concern so-called "dispositional" mental states – viz., non-occurrent mental states consisting of nothing more than the subject's disposition to instantiate the corresponding occurrent mental states. Rather, it concerns whether – and if so, how – thesis C-Ins can allow for the possibility of *occurrent* mental states that have determinate intentional content and yet are nonconscious.

If the dispositional/occurrent distinction is non-exhaustive, then the issue at hand may also extend to mental states or structures that are neither occurrent and episodic nor merely dispositional either. Horgan and Tienson (1995, 1996) argue that certain standing-structural features of the human cognitive system – as opposed to occurrent, episodic, states or events – both (i) sometimes figure importantly in the psychological etiology of an occurrent mental state, and (ii) are appropriately assigned intentional content; they call this *morphological* content, since it is assigned to aspects of the cognitive system's morphology or structure. They also argue that morphological content often figures in psychological processing without becoming occurrent itself, and hence, without becoming conscious – a theme further developed in Henderson and Horgan (2000). The issue now at hand, concerning putatively determinate intentional content that is nonconscious, extends to morphological content.

Nonconscious intentional mental states as impossible

This position simply denies the possibility of nonconscious mental states with determinate intentional content. It claims that genuine, determinate, intentional content is possessed only by states that are phenomenally conscious: the only genuinely mental intentionality is phenomenal intentionality, which is always conscious.

In order to embrace this first position, advocates of C-Ins would not necessarily need to dispute the practical utility of attributing nonconscious intentional mental states to oneself or to others. They could contend that such states are not *prototypically* mental (not paradigm beliefs, say), *because* they lack determinate content. They could be neutral on just what sort of states these are. One possibility is to regard them as information bearing states but just not mental (i.e., just not possessed of determinate intentionality). Perhaps such information bearing states function similarly to paradigmatic mental states, behaviorally speaking. This may not mean that they are precisely the same dispositionally speaking, where precision is measured in part by how acting on them consciously appears to their subjects. However, it may mean that from a third-person point of view there are no readily discernible differences between the behaviors associated with the two states.

In order for proponents of C-Ins to make this first sort of rejoinder work, they would need to do at least three things. First, they would need to argue that attribution of nonconscious but "intentional" mental states *as if* possessing determinate content may have predictive or explanatory utility even if the subject of the attribution fails to be in such states. Second, proponents would need to argue that if the subject really does have intentional states with determinate content and such states are attributed to them, the relevant content cannot be specified independently of the assumption of its having (for the subject) a phenomenal mode of individuation or determinacy. Finally, proponents would need to argue that although the phenomenal or immediately self-presented content of the subject's intentional states is available only to the subject, nevertheless people often can make evidentially warranted third-person attributions of mental states with such phenomenal intentional content. We are not in the dark about the phenomenal lights, so to speak, that occur in other people's minds.

Nonconscious intentional mental states as potentially conscious

This second position allows for the possibility of occurrent mental states that are nonconscious and yet have determinate intentional content, but insists that any such states must be *potentially* conscious, for the agent. Searle is the best known advocate of this view (e.g., Searle 1983, 1990, 1992). One major challenge for such a view is to spell out just what the relevant potentialities are supposed to consist in, given that there are several very different sorts of dimensions along which potentiality may be described. Then even if this identification or spelling out of relevant potentiality can be successfully accomplished, a further serious challenge is to plausibly motivate the claim that the specified form of potential consciousness – and *only* this form – transmits determinate intentional content onto such merely-potentially-conscious occurrent states.

The position has the advantage of accommodating *some* of the putatively nonconscious mental states that are posited by common-sense psychology and by certain branches of theoretical psychology. But apparently it cannot accommodate all of them – for instance, unconscious occurrent states whose content is so deeply repressed and so abhorrent that these states cannot be brought to consciousness (e.g., desires constituting Freud's Oedipus complex), or unconscious occurrent information-processing states that are prevented by the structure of human cognitive architecture from ever occurring consciously (e.g., the information-processing sub-doxastic states of early visual processing posited by computational theories of vision like that of Marr 1982).

Nonconscious intentional mental states as suitably causally integrated

This position allows for the possibility of two kinds of determinately intentional nonconscious mental states: not only ones that are potentially conscious, but also ones that cannot occur consciously. The thought is that determinate intentional content attaches to nonconscious states by virtue of the overall pattern of causal-dispositional interconnections that these states, together with phenomenally conscious states, bear to one another. The phenomenally conscious states serve as "anchor points" of determinate intentionality. The states that are not phenomenally conscious get their determinate intentionality from these anchor points together with the overall causal-dispositional profile P of the whole system S of (actual and potential) occurrent states of which the phenomenally conscious ones are a proper subset. The determinate content of nonconscious states in this system arises from the following putative fact: there is a unique overall content-assignment I, to the actual and potential occurrent states in the system S, that meets these two constraints:

i I assigns to each phenomenally conscious state in S its phenomenal intentional content;
ii under I, intentional-state transitions conforming to the overall causal-dispositional pattern P are systematically content-appropriate.

The key idea is that although causal-dispositional interconnections *alone* cannot confer determinate intentional content on the states of the system (not even if one factors in causal-dispositional connections to states of the subject's environment and to behavioral states), nevertheless these interconnections, *in combination with the already-determinate intentional content of those states in S with phenomenal intentionality*, can and do confer determinate intentional content upon the remaining states in S – the nonconscious ones. Given the overall pattern of interactions among the states in S, and given the intentional contents of the conscious states in S, there is only one way to assign intentional contents to the nonconscious states in S under which the state-transitions are systematically content-appropriate; and the actual, determinate, intentional contents of the nonconscious states in S are those that conform to this uniquely "rationality-preserving" content-assignment. (The expression "rationality-preserving" here needs to be understood, of course, broadly enough to encompass cognitive state-transitions that are irrational in certain ways despite being, in some sense, content-appropriate. Cognitive processes that generate paranoid delusions, for example, are content-appropriate in the intended sense, and hence are rationality-preserving in the broad sense, despite being patently irrational by more demanding standards of rationality than those needed to sustain the attribution of psychological states.)

Perhaps the principal challenge that would need to be addressed by advocates of this position is this: arguing persuasively, with respect to a system S that includes a broad range of putatively content-determinate unconscious mental states (in addition to the subject's conscious intentional states), that there really is only one overall content-assignment that is suitably content-appropriate, suitably rationality-preserving. Or, at any rate, one would need to argue that there is a unique such overall content-assignment *near enough*; moderate degrees of local content-indeterminacy presumably are tolerable, in an overall system of internal states most of which have determinate intentional content. Although it is not obvious that this challenge can be met, it certainly is not obvious that it *cannot* be. When phenomenal-intentionality preservation and rationality preservation are *combined* as constraints on a correct overall assignment of contents to both conscious and unconscious states, their joint constraining power is very powerful indeed. Perhaps it is powerful enough to fend off indeterminacy arguments of the Dennett/Quine kind – arguments that look so very powerful when phenomenal intentionality is left out of account.

An Epistemic Gap Counter-Argument against C-Ins

A second question may be posed for C-Ins. A critic might ask whether divergence should be allowed between the apparent content of a conscious intentional state and its actual or objective content. She might claim that we have no reason to accept that conscious intentional content actually is the content of an intentional state.

With this question in mind, the following line of objection is likely to arise against C-Ins. It may be charged that there is an epistemic gap between the subjectively apparent intentional content of a mental state and its actual objective content. Just because I seem to myself to believe that a picture on the wall in front of me is crooked does not mean that (in believing something) this proposition is *what* I believe. I might be thinking of a mirror on the wall in front of me, believing falsely of my mental state that I am thinking of a picture. So, phenomenal intentional content is not determinate of (actual objective) intentional content.

Our rejoinder to the charge should be clear (cf. Horgan & Tienson 2002; Horgan, Tienson,

& Graham 2005). C-Ins denies that there is an epistemic gap between the apparent or immediately self-presenting intentional content of a mental state and the actual objective *phenomenal* content. Remember there are (we assume) but two candidate ways to fix content. Hypothetically, content may be fixed either physically or phenomenally. But (we assume) it cannot be fixed physically. So unless (contrary to our view) content can be fixed or determined physically, there is no conceptual space for a distinction between phenomenal or subjectively apparent content and actual objective content. There is no non-phenomenal determination of content identity. The apparent content is actual content. That said, however, there is a distinction to be made within the theory supporting C-Ins between the intentional content (which is phenomenal) and the objective *satisfiers* (if any) of that content. If it immediately seems to me that I am thinking of a picture on the wall in front of me, then that is what I am thinking. However, if there is no picture on the wall in front of me but, say, a mirror, then my thought is inaccurate or not veridical; the content fails to be satisfied by the world. Content-satisfaction is not itself content but it is objective and not apparent.

There is a related distinction (to the one just mentioned) to be made within the theory supporting C-Ins between the constituents of the content and the particulars or properties to which the constituents purport to refer. For instance, suppose you think that Clinton would have made a more successful US presidential candidate than Kerry. In expressing this thought suppose you use certain proper names such as "Clinton" and "Kerry." Your thought's actually referring to the specific individuals to whom it purports to refer (viz. Clinton and Kerry) depends upon there being certain suitable external relations connecting you to the unique eligible referents (viz. Clinton and Kerry).

A brain-in-a-vat physical/phenomenal duplicate of you would have (we maintain) matching thought constituents that fail to refer at all, because the brain-in-a-vat duplicate would not bear suitable causal connections to any suitably reference-eligible individual in its own external world.

Actual or successful reference (as in the Clinton/Kerry example) certainly may depend upon there being certain suitable external relations between thinker and world. But *putatively* referring to the world does not require such connections; a thinker can putatively refer without actually referring. So, to sum up, there is an epistemic space between putative and actual reference as well as between intentional content and objective content-satisfaction. However, since phenomenal intentional content is entirely constituted phenomenologically and is intrinsic rather than extrinsic, there is no epistemic space between apparent and real phenomenal intentional content.

The objections or questions discussed thus far in this chapter are not the only challenges that have been or might be posed to C-Ins. One might worry whether C-Ins's commitment to phenomenal individuation of intentional content, combined with rejection of physical individuation, is tantamount to dualism. If so, and if dualism is a bad thing, then C-Ins is an unappealing view of the interface between consciousness and intentionality. One might also raise doubts about subjects' abilities to "just tell" the content of their own thoughts or to do so in a manner that is immediate or direct. Still another worry is whether there might be types of intentional contents (such as the referents of demonstratives like "this" or "that" perhaps) for which phenomenal individuation is inadequate and some sort of physical relation of thinker to environment must be identified if content is to be understood as determinate. Nor do these worries or challenges exhaust the list. Not surprisingly, then, different writers approach the problem of the relationship between consciousness and intentionality with different background convictions and concerns. To some the problem of externalistic content is uppermost. To others the issue of attribution of unconscious states with intentional structure is paramount. For still others the anti-dualist materialist metaphysics of mind is dominant.

Inseparatism and the Impulse to Unity

Substantive theories in the philosophy of mind often attempt to discover or impose a unity on the diverse and scattered concepts that make up our mental concepts both in ordinary life and psychological science. Some philosophers attempt to account for a full range of our mental concepts in terms of a small number of basic or elementary concepts. Often the impulse to unity is expressed by trying to make a case for materialistic monism. This is the view that any and all mental phenomena are, at bottom, physical phenomena. Materialism has certain salient features that make it attractive to many philosophers. And it provides a metaphysical research program that is widely promoted. But, on our view, an important prelude to the metaphysics of mind, materialist or otherwise, bids us to properly conceive what makes the mental "mental" or at least paradigmatically "mental" in the first place. For us it is the interdependent presence of consciousness and intentionality. The mental is mental because it is conscious and possessed of intentional structure. It is not that one separable kind of mentality is conscious and another is intentional and that the two often run in tandem. It is that the two are, in some sense, inseparable. This chapter has attempted to make a running start at a case for inseparability. Still many more issues concerning the relation between consciousness and intentionality await detailed exploration.

Note

We thank two anonymous referees for valuable comments and suggestions on the penultimate version of this chapter.

Further Readings

Chalmers, D. (2004) The representational character of experience. In B. Leiter (ed.), *The Future for Philosophy*, 153–80. Oxford: Oxford University Press.

Horgan, T. and Tienson, J. (2002) The phenomenology of intentionality and the intentionality of phenomenology. In D. Chalmers (ed.), *Philosophy of Mind: Classical and Contemporary Readings*, 520–33. Oxford: Oxford University Press.

Siewert, C. (2003) Consiousness and intentionality. In E. Zalta (ed.), *Stanford Encyclopedia of Philosophy*. http://plato.stanford.edu/archives/fall2003/entries/consciousness-intentionality/

References

Block, N. J. (1995) On a confusion about the function of consciousness. *Behavioral and Brain Sciences* 18, 227–47.

Block, N. J. (2003) Mental paint. In M. Hahn and B. Ramberg (eds.), *Reflections and Replies: Essays on the Philosophy of Tyler Burge*, 165–200. Cambridge, MA: MIT Press.

Chalmers, D. (2004) The representational character of experience. In B. Leiter (ed.), *The Future for Philosophy*, 153–80. Oxford: Oxford University Press.

Church, J. (2003) Depression, depth, and the imagination. In J. Phillips and J. Morley (eds.), *Imagination and Its Pathologies*, 175–86. Cambridge, MA: MIT Press.

Clark, A. (1997) *Being There: Putting Brain, Body, and World Together Again*. Cambridge: MA: MIT Press.

Dainton, B. (2000) *Stream of Consciousness: Unity and Continuity in Conscious Experience*. London: Routledge.

Dennett, D. C. (1987) *The Intentional Stance*. Cambridge, MA: MIT Press.

Dennett, D. C. (2005) What Robo Mary knows. In *Sweet Dreams: Philosophical Obstacles to a Science of Consciousness*, 103–29. Cambridge, MA: MIT Press.

Dretske, F. (1995) *Naturalizing the Mind*. Cambridge, MA: MIT Press.

Flanagan, O. (1992) *Consciousness Reconsidered*. Cambridge, MA: MIT Press.

Fodor, J. (1983) *Modularity of Mind*. Cambridge, MA: MIT Press.

Georgalis, N. (2003) The fiction of phenomenal intentionality. *Consciousness and Emotion* 4, 243–56.

Goldman, A. (1993) The psychology of folk psychology. In A. Goldman (ed.), *Readings in Philosophy and Cognitive Science*, 347–80. Cambridge, MA: MIT Press.

Graham, G. and Horgan, T. (2000) Mary Mary, quite contrary. *Philosophical Studies* 99, 59–87.

Graham, G. and Horgan, T. (2005) Mary Mary au contraire: a reply to Raffman. *Philosophical Studies* 122, 203–12.

Graham, G., Horgan, T., and Tienson, J. (forthcoming) Phenomenology, intentionality and the unity of mind. In A. Beckerman and B. McLaughlin (eds.), *The Oxford Handbook in the Philosophy of Mind*. New York: Oxford University Press.

Henderson, D. and Horgan, T. (2000) Iceberg epistemology. *Philosophy and Phenomenological Research* 61, 497–535.

Hess, E. H. (1975) The role of pupil size in communication. In Rita Atkinson and Richard Atkinson (eds.), *Mind and Behavior*. San Francisco, CA: Freeman.

Horgan, T. and Tienson, J. (1995) Connectionism and the commitments of folk psychology. *Philosophical Perspectives* 9, 127–52.

Horgan, T. and Tienson, J. (1996) *Connectionism and the Philosophy of Psychology*. Cambridge, MA: MIT Press.

Horgan, T. and Tienson, J. (2002) The phenomenology of intentionality and the intentionality of phenomenology. In D. Chalmers (ed.), *Philosophy of Mind: Classical and Contemporary Readings*, 520–33. Oxford: Oxford University Press.

Horgan, T., Tienson, J., and Graham, G. (2003) The phenomenology of first person agency. In S. Walter and H.-D. Heckmann (eds.), *Physicalism and Mental Causation: The Metaphysics of Mind and Action*, 323–40. Exeter: Imprint Academic.

Horgan, T., Tienson, J., and Graham, G. (2005) Phenomenal intentionality and the brain in a vat. In R. Schantz (ed.), *The Externalist Challenge: New Studies in Cognition and Intentionality*, 297–317. Berlin, New York: de Gruyter.

Horgan, T., Tienson, J., and Graham, G. (2006) Internal-world skepticism and the self-presentational nature of phenomenology. In U. Kriegel and K. Williford (eds.), *Consciousness and Self-Representation*, 41–61. Cambridge, MA: MIT Press. [Also in (2005) M. Reicher and J. Marek (eds.), *Experience and Analysis: Proceedings of the 27th International Wittgenstein Symposium*, 191–207. Vienna: Varlagsgellschaft.]

Keeley, B. (1999) Fixing content and function in neurobiological systems: the neuroethology of electroreception. *Biology and Philosophy* 14, 395–430.

Kim, J. (1998) *Mind in a Physical World: An Essay on the Mind–Body Problem and Mental Causation*. Cambridge, MA: MIT Press.

Locke, J. (1690/1975) *An Essay Concerning Human Understanding*. Ed. with intro. by P. H. Nidditch. Oxford: Clarendon Press.

Marr, D. (1982) *Vision: A Computational Investigation into the Human Representation and Processing of Visual Information*. San Francisco, CA: Freeman.

Quine, W. V. O. (1960) *Word and Object.* Cambridge, MA: MIT Press.

Raffman, D. (2005) Even zombies can be surprised: a reply to Graham and Horgan. *Philosophical Studies* 122, 189–202.

Rupert, R. (2004) Challenges to the hypothesis of extended cognition. *Journal of Philosophy* 101, 389–428.

Searle, J. (1983) *Intentionality.* Cambridge: Cambridge University Press.

Searle, J. (1990) Consciousness, explanatory inversion, and cognitive science. *Behavioral and Brain Sciences* 13, 585–96.

Searle, J. (1992) *The Rediscovery of the Mind.* Cambridge, MA: MIT Press.

Siewert, C. (2003) Consiousness and intentionality. In E. Zalta (ed.), *Stanford Encyclopedia of Philosophy.* http://plato.stanford.edu/archives/fall2003/entries/consciousness-intentionality/

Stich, S. (1978) Belief and subdoxastic states. *Philosophy of Science* 45, 499–518.

Strawson, G. (1994) *Mental Reality.* Cambridge, MA: MIT Press.

Tye, M. (1995) *Ten Problems of Consciousness: A Representational Theory of the Phenomenal Mind.* Cambridge, MA: MIT Press.

Tye, M. (2003) *Consciousness and Persons: Unity and Identity.* Cambridge, MA: MIT Press.

Wilson, R. (2003) Phenomenology and intentionality. *Pacific Philosophical Quarterly* 84, 413–31.

Part V

MAJOR TOPICS IN THE SCIENCE OF CONSCIOUSNESS

TOPICS IN THE COGNITIVE PSYCHOLOGY OF CONSCIOUSNESS

38

Attention and Consciousness

NILLI LAVIE

Attention and Consciousness

Philosophical discussions of attention and conscious awareness have often questioned not only how attention and conscious awareness relate to each other but also whether the two are separate entities or may in fact be one and the same. Empirical research however has tended to assume that attention and consciousness are two separate functions and has mainly focused on whether attention is necessary for conscious awareness. This chapter reviews the empirical research of the role of attention in conscious awareness (see Velmans (2000) for review of the philosophical discussions regarding their relationship and ontological status).

Personal experience often suggests that whether one is conscious or not of what is happening in the environment depends on attention. For instance, while driving in a busy motorway one might fail to notice the exit junction if not paying particular attention to the road signs. Or while engaging in an interesting phone conversation one might fail to notice a change in the background noise indicating that the water in the kettle has boiled or that the printer has stopped printing, etc.

Laboratory research, however, has produced inconsistent findings regarding the role of attention in conscious perception. In many experiments, people reported being unaware of any information that they were instructed to ignore and have remained oblivious to unattended events (even when these were quite peculiar!) suggesting that the ignored events were simply unnoticed. These types of results led to an "early selection" view of attention in which attention has an early effect on information processing, excluding unattended information from early perceptual processes straight after the rudimentary perceptual analysis of simple visual or auditory features (e.g., color or pitch), on which the selection of information to pay attention to is based.

However, numerous cases of failures to ignore irrelevant information have been documented as well and these provided support for a "late selection" view of attention in which paying attention to the task can only affect later post-perceptual processes such as memory or response selection (so that these are based just on the attended information). Perception is an automatic process in this view in the sense that identification and extraction of semantic meaning for all stimuli (e.g., visual objects, words, etc.) are capacity-free and proceed involuntarily independent of attention. The debate between the early and late selection views fueled many experiments over the past decades of research. However, as this research only appeared to shift the pendulum temporarily toward either the early selection view or the late selection view and back again, it seems to have led to a theoretical impasse and has led some to doubt that the early and late selection debate can ever be resolved.

However, recent research suggests that a resolution to this debate can be gained by considering the role of attentional load in determining the effects of attention on awareness. Only when attention is fully loaded with task-relevant processing will other task-irrelevant information fail to reach awareness. By contrast, when processing task-relevant information only poses a low load on attention, task-irrelevant information will reach awareness though subjects are not deliberately paying attention to this irrelevant information, or even though subjects deliberately attempt to ignore irrelevant potentially distracting information.

In this chapter, I describe the debate on the role of attention in conscious perception as well as its resolution. Since most of the modern research has focused on the effects of attention on visual awareness the earlier studies that examined the role of attention in the perception of information received through hearing will not be reviewed in detail.

The debate on whether perception depends on attention has typically discussed the role of attention in perception in general, often not making a distinction between conscious and unconscious perception. However, as the focus of this chapter is specifically on the effects of attention on awareness, the results of this debate will be discussed with a view to examining how they bear on the issue of the role of attention in conscious awareness.

Assessment of the Role of Attention in Conscious Perception: Direct vs. Indirect Measures

An important consideration in assessing how each study bears on the role of attention in conscious perception is the measures of perception used in the study, specifically, whether direct measures or indirect measures were used. Direct measures of awareness involve either overt verbal report (in which subjects simply verbally report about their perception) or manual report (in which subjects make manual responses, e.g., press a designated button to indicate their awareness). These measures are direct in the sense that assessment of awareness and its content requires no inference: the subjects simply report what they are aware of.

There are two main limitations to the assessment of attentional effects on awareness with such direct measures:(i) If subjects' reports are collected retrospectively, following the presentation of the unattended information (e.g., at the end of the experiment), they may reflect the content of memory rather than the content of unattended perception. (ii) If subjects are told in advance that they should indicate their awareness of the unattended information upon its presentation, one cannot assume that the reported information is truly unattended: presumably subjects will pay attention to the information they are asked to report about. For these reasons, much research has used indirect measures of awareness. These are typically assessed on-line upon presentation of the unattended information. The extent and even the content of unattended information can be inferred from the effects the unattended information has on the responses to the attended information (e.g., effects on reaction times). Such indirect measures reflect perception of unattended information online, as and when it is presented, and are thus immune to alternative accounts in terms of memory. However, as they are based on measures of the effects on attended processing such as reaction times they cannot lead to any direct conclusions regarding the subjective conscious experience of the unattended information. Ideally, the same question is addressed in studies using both types of measures. Fortunately, the resolution of the early and late selection debate within load theory has used both types of measures.

The Early and Late Selection Debate: Direct Measures

Attention research began with the invention of the *dichotic listening technique* (Cherry 1953) that was designed to assess the effects of attention on perception of verbal information presented auditorily (typically using headphones). In these experiments, participants selectively attended to one channel of information (e.g., repeating aloud, i.e., shadowing, a stream of words presented to one ear, or presented by a female speaker), while ignoring another channel of information (e.g., words presented to the other ear, or presented by a male speaker). At the end of the experiment subjects were asked to report about the information presented in the unattended channel. The results showed that people could recall very little content from the irrelevant ear, failing to detect changes in the language or even that bits of speech were played backward in the unattended message (Cherry 1953), and failing to recognize words that were repeated as often as 35 times in the unattended ear (Moray 1959).

The subject's own name was somewhat of an exception: 33 percent of the subjects noticed the mention of their name in the unattended channel in Moray's (1959) study.

The better detection of the subject's own name even when presented in the ignored ear was initially taken to support the late selection view as it appeared to show that people are aware of some semantic content in the unattended channel. However, it could merely reflect reduced threshold for recognition of highly familiar pertinent content.

On the whole, the dichotic listening studies clearly show that the majority of subjects fail to report the majority of content in the unattended ear. These results provided support for the early selection view of attention (e.g., Broadbent 1958) as they suggest that the unattended information was not perceived.

However, because the reports were made retrospectively at the end of the experiment, the failures to report unattended words could have been due to a greater tendency to forget unattended material rather than to no perception of this material. The conclusions are also restricted to perception of verbal material through hearing. Similar criticisms apply to the study of the effects of attention on visual perception with a visual analog of the *dichotic listening paradigm*: the *selective reading paradigm* devised by Neisser (1969, cited in Neisser & Becklen 1975). In this paradigm, subjects were asked to read aloud lines of text printed in red, while ignoring alternating lines of text printed in black. When asked to report at the end of the reading task about the content of text in the ignored lines, subjects reported very little knowledge of the ignored text and even failed to recall words that were presented repeatedly, across three pages of text, in every one of the ignored lines. These results therefore provided support for an early selection effect of attention on the perception of visual information. However, as in the dichotic listening paradigm, it is not clear to what extent the failures to report reflect failures of perception or of memory.

In addition, in studies of visual perception it is important to ensure that the effects of attention can be clearly dissociated from the effects of eye fixation. People naturally tend to fixate their eyes on the visual information to which they attend, and away from information

Figure 38.1 A frame with the gorilla-man from the video clip used in the Simons and Chabris (1999) experiment.

they wish to ignore. They do so in order to bring the fovea, the retinal area of greatest visual acuity, to the attended information. It is therefore important to establish that effects on perceptual awareness are not simply due to the greater retinal acuity of the fixated information accompanied by reduced visual acuity of the ignored information.

The subjects in Neisser's study would have doubtless fixated on the lines they read. The failures to report text in the ignored lines cannot therefore be clearly attributed to attention as it may have been due to reduced visual acuity of the non-fixated text instead. Finally, the effects of attention on verbal comprehension cannot speak to the role of attention in perception in general. One might claim, for example, that attention may only be needed for higher-level understanding of verbal material but not for more basic visual perception of the environment involving recognition of familiar objects. It was therefore important to examine the effects of attention on the perception of nonverbal stimuli.

Neisser and Becklen (1975) designed the *selective looking paradigm* for precisely this reason. They asked subjects to monitor one of two superimposed video episodes: hand game and ball game, for certain target events (an attacking stroke in the hand game, or a ball pass from one player to another in the ball game) and press a key whenever a target event occurred. The results showed that most subjects failed to notice odd events in the unattended episode. For example, only 4 of 24 subjects attending to the ball game noticed that the hand game players temporarily stopped playing and shook hands instead, and only 5 of the 24 subjects attending to the hand game noticed the replacement of the original male ball-players with female players! These results provide further support for the early selection view that attention determines visual perception in general (i.e., not just verbal comprehension, c.f. the selective reading paradigm).

This method has been recently revived in research by Daniel Simons. For example, Simons and Chabris (1998) reported similar failures to report the presence of a man dressed up in a gorilla suit passing by the ball-game players that subjects were instructed to attend to in their adaptation of Neisser and Becklen's (1975) selective looking paradigm (see Figure 38.1). These results demonstrate striking failures to notice unattended events. Moreover although subjects made their reports retrospectively in these selective looking studies, the failures to report the peculiar events are unlikely to be due to a failure of memory: it is unlikely that subjects had noticed the gorilla-man but simply forgot about it at the end of the experiment.

Simons and Chabris (1999) attempted to further relate these failures to attention by varying the difficulty of the attended task. They asked participants either to count the number of ball-passes made between one of two teams of basketball players in a video-clip ("easy task" condition), or to maintain two separate counts for the number of bounce passes and aerial passes ("hard task" condition). Awareness for an unexpected gorilla-man walking through the playing space was reported more often by participants in the easy task condition than participants in the hard task condition. Since subjects should pay attention more closely to the more difficult task, the finding of a greater rate of failures to report the unattended gorilla-man with the more difficult task suggests the level of awareness for unattended events depends directly on the extent to which attention was fully focused on the relevant task. (This idea receives more detailed discussion in the section on load theory of attention.)

However, like the selective reading paradigm many of the results obtained in the selective looking paradigm could be subject to an alternative interpretation in terms of eye movements rather than attention. The task of monitoring the ball game is likely to have involved eye movements pursuing the ball trajectories and such eye movements may have led to actual blurring of the unattended events on the retina. In other words, subjects may have failed to report the ignored events because they were in fact less visible due to a blurred image on the retina not due to inattention.

Even the difficulty manipulation used in Simons and Chabris's (1999) study could be criticized on that basis. It is possible, indeed likely, that the hard task involved a greater tendency for eye movements than the easy task, as the discrimination between aerial and bounce passes would benefit from looking up (for aerial throws) and down (for bounce passes) whereas monitoring all ball passes can be made without this discrimination. Thus the unattended gorilla-man may have simply been less visible during performance of the hard task due to a greater rate of eye movements (and hence retinal blurring) in the hard (vs. easy) task.

Fortunately, the same pattern of results was found when observers monitored similar selective looking videos to those used in Neisser and Becklen's study while ensuring that their eyes remained fixating on a central location with eye movement monitoring (Littman & Becklen 1976). These results rule out the general alternative account for the results obtained in the selective looking task in terms of eye movements, and hence make a stronger case for an early selection effect of attention on conscious perception rather than mere effects of eye movements on the retinal signal. Further research on the role of attentional load in determining the rate of "inattentional blindness" (reviewed later under the subheading "the role of perceptual load in inattentional blindness") also suggests that it is the specific increase in demand on attention involved in harder vs. easier tasks (not a greater rate of eye movements) that determines the rate of awareness or conversely "inattentional blindness."

A recent line of study made a further attempt to relate the failures of awareness within the selective looking paradigm to attention. Most et al. (2001) presented subjects with several shapes (e.g., black or white triangles or circles) moving randomly around the screen, "bouncing" off the edges. Attention was paid to one set of colored shapes (counting the number of bounces), while the other set was ignored. Awareness of an unexpected cross-shape crossing the screen was assessed by asking the subjects to recall whether there was anything unusual immediately following their completion of the dynamic task. Subjects were more likely to report the unexpected cross when it was closer in color to the attended set, suggesting that what people notice depends on what they pay attention to.

The selective looking experiments discussed so far all involved monitoring dynamic events. However, a static task has been developed as well. Rock and Gutman (1981) presented subjects with a stream of two superimposed figures at fixation (one red, the other black) and asked them to pay attention to one set of the figures (e.g., make esthetic judgments of the figures in red). They found that recognition level for the unattended figures in a surprise recognition test at the end of the stream was only slightly better than chance. As the attended and unattended figures were superimposed at fixation the effects of attention were clearly not due to eye movements.

These results, however, could be attributed to failures of recognition memory as the subjects were asked at the end of a stream about all unattended objects in the stream. Mack and Rock (1998) developed this paradigm further devising an "inattentional blindness" task in which subjects are simply asked just about one object on the final display straight after it was presented thus minimizing demands on memory. In this task, subjects typically perform a task for a few trials and are then presented with an additional unexpected task-irrelevant stimulus on the final critical trial. Immediately after the task-response, participants are asked to report on whether they detected this extra stimulus. On a subsequent control trial, the participants are requested not to perform the task, just detect instead whether there is any extra stimulus on the display. A failure to detect the critical stimulus when it is unattended in the critical trial (appearing unexpectedly during performance of a task), but successful detection when it is attended (in the fully attended control trial), is taken to reflect blindness due to lack of attention toward the stimulus, hence the term "inattentional blindness" (Mack & Rock 1998).

It is important to note nevertheless that the fully-attended control trial differs from the critical trial in several aspects that entail processes other than attention. First, the critical stimulus is expected on the control trials, and participants are likely to look for it intentionally (either due to explicit instruction to look for something extra in some studies, or due to the preceding awareness probe raising their expectations of something unusual). Thus, the comparison of control and critical trials confounds effects of attention with effects of expectation and intention. Second, awareness reports are made after a task response and a surprise awareness question in critical trials, but can be made immediately following display presentation in control trials. Reduced rates of awareness in critical (vs. control) trials may therefore reflect greater rates of forgetting during the longer delay from display presentation until the awareness question in the critical trials (vs. control trials.) Some recent research that has overcome these criticisms is reviewed later (see "the role of perceptual load in inattentional blindness"). In summary, the research using direct measures of unattended perception reviewed so far has invariably supported the early selection view: subjects appeared to have no conscious recollection of the unattended information. The results however are open to alternative accounts in terms of reflecting memory rather than perception and effects of expectation rather than attention.

The Early and Late Selection Debate: Indirect Measures

Most of the research using on-line measures of perception of the unattended information as and when it is presented has used indirect measures assessing perception of the unattended information via the effects it has on reaction times (RTs) to concurrent targets. Interestingly, many of the initial studies using such indirect reaction time measures lent support to the late selection view, showing that subjects have in fact perceived the unattended information. For example, in the case of the dichotic listening paradigm, Lewis (1970) reported that the speed of shadowing of words in the attended channel was affected by the presentation of synonyms and semantic associates (e.g., bread and butter) in the unattended channel, whereas unattended synonyms slowed down shadowing RTs, unattended associates sped up shadowing RTs (see Pashler (1998) for other dichotic listening experiments that have used indirect measures to assess unattended processing on-line). However, it is important to note that priming effects on RTs need not indicate full awareness of the semantic content in the unattended channel. Partial recognition of the semantic information in the unattended channel may be sufficient to speed up shadowing of the information in the attended channel but may not necessarily be sufficient for full awareness of that information as assessed in direct measures of detection of the unattended information. Indeed, when Treisman and Geffen (1967) asked subjects to indicate detection of target words overtly (by tapping on the table when these targets are presented, whether in the attended ear or in the unattended ear), while they shadow words presented to one ear, 87 percent of the attended words were detected, whereas only 8 percent of unattended targets were detected. Treisman and Geffen's study was somewhat of a milestone in that it allowed an apparent consensus on an early selection view of attention in the case of the dichotic listening paradigm, in which attention acts to attenuate perception of irrelevant information.

However that consensus was restricted to the dichotic listening paradigm, and research of the effects of attention on visual processing on-line, using indirect measures, has evolved into a controversy as it produced results that were conflicting with those obtained with the direct measures of attention effects described in the previous section.

The most popular indirect measure for the extent to which ignored visual information is nevertheless perceived is some form of Stroop-like task. The original Stroop demonstration, showing that color naming responses are slower when the color stimulus is a word naming another color, cannot lead to any clear conclusion about the extent of unattended processing, simply because it is highly likely that subjects cannot withhold attention from one aspect of an object (the word identity) while paying attention to another aspect of the very same object (its color). The findings that interference to color naming remains even when the color and word are presented in separate stimuli (e.g., a color patch at fixation with a color word in the periphery) in some cases even presented far apart (separated by 5 degrees of visual angle (Gatti & Egeth 1978)) provided support for the late selection view that ignored stimuli are perceived. Here again, as in the case of the selective reading paradigm discussed earlier, one might claim that reading may be a special case as it is so highly learned that it is automatized and hence the fact that reading does not depend on attention need not mean that visual perception in general is independent of attention as stipulated by the late selection view.

The response competition paradigm (Eriksen & Eriksen 1974) is a variation of the Stroop task that can allow more general conclusions about unattended perception and has indeed become a popular index of unattended processing. In a typical response competition task subjects are to make speeded manual responses to indicate which of a specified set of target stimuli was presented (e.g., press one key for a target letter X and another for a target letter N), while ignoring any other irrelevant stimuli. The target letter is typically presented in the center and distractor stimuli in the periphery. The extent to which distractors are perceived is assessed through measuring target reaction times in the presence of distractors that are either incompatible with the correct target response (e.g., distractor "X" with target "N"), compatible with the correct response (e.g., distractor "X" with target "X"), or neutral with respect to the correct response (e.g., distractor "S" with target "X"). If target responses are slower in the presence of an incompatible distractor compared to a compatible or a neutral distractor, then this indicates that the identity of the distractor was perceived. Many studies using this response competition task have demonstrated distractor compatibility effects on target reaction time suggesting the distractors were perceived despite the clear spatial separation between target and distractors (see Lavie & Tsal (1994) for review), in support of the late selection view that irrelevant distractors that are presumably unattended are perceived.

In addition, ignored distractors have also been shown to produce effects of negative priming, namely, slowing down of subsequent target responses when the ignored distractor on one trial has become the target of the next trial. These negative priming effects led to a late selection theory of attention in which ignored distractors are perceived, but attention serves to inhibit the distractor responses (Tipper 1985).

A Resolution of the Debate in Terms of the Distinction between Direct and Indirect Measures?

On the whole, then, the majority of direct measures of unattended processing provided support for the early selection view, whereas the majority of studies using indirect measures assessing unattended processing via effects on target reaction time provided support for the late selection view. It may therefore be tempting to conclude that methodological differences between direct and indirect measures are responsible for the difference in results. For example, a late selection theorist could perhaps claim that the indirect measures (that supported late selection, for example in Stroop-like tasks) are simply a more sensitive way to reveal unattended perception than the explicit reports that supported early selection in the dichotic listening and selective looking experiments. Alternatively, an early selection theorist might claim that the indirect measures of distractor interference effects on reaction times may not indicate full perception. Unconscious registration of the distractor identity may be sufficient for producing reaction time effects but not for full conscious perception.

However, the picture has become more complex with the accumulation of evidence for early selection in studies using indirect measures for distractor processing, resulting in no apparent effects of irrelevant distractors on target reaction times in cases when the target is cued in cluttered displays (Yantis & Johnston 1990). In addition, negative priming effects were found to depend on various factors that did not appear to bear on the extent to which distractors are ignored (e.g., the similarity of the displays across trial, see Fox (1995) for review). These results cast doubt on the extent to which negative priming indeed reflects inhibition of responses to perceived distractors. The existence of discrepant evidence even within the same task has led some to doubt that the early and late selection debate can ever be resolved (e.g., Allport 1993).

Resolution of the Early and Late Selection Debate within Perceptual Load Theory

Lavie and Tsal (Lavie 1995; Lavie & Tsal 1994) suggested that the early and late selection debate can be resolved within a hybrid load model of selective attention that combines aspects from both the early and late selection views while applying a capacity theory previously used to explain performance in divided (rather than selective) attention tasks (Kahneman 1973). According to this model, task-irrelevant distractors can be excluded from perception when the level of perceptual load in processing of task-relevant stimuli is sufficiently high to exhaust perceptual capacity, leaving no capacity available for distractor processing. However, in situations of low perceptual load, any spare capacity left over from the less demanding relevant processing will "spill over" to the processing of irrelevant distractors. Thus, in this model early selection is predicted for situations of high perceptual load, while late selection is predicted for situations of low perceptual load. A review of the previous selective attention studies provided support for this model (Lavie & Tsal 1994). The experimental situations in the studies that provided support for late selection clearly involved a low level of perceptual load (often with just one target and one distractor identity present), whereas the experimental situations in the studies that provided support for early selection could be generally characterized as carrying a higher level of load (e.g., the selective looking paradigm typically involved many people presented and various dynamic events occurring). The response competition studies showing early selection (e.g., Yantis & Johnston 1990) had a greater number of stimuli presented then those showing late selection (e.g., Gatti & Egeth 1978). In a series of behavioral studies, Lavie and her colleagues directly manipulated the level of perceptual load in target processing, and measured the effects on irrelevant distractor processing. The concept of perceptual load implies either that more items are added, for the same task, or that for the same number of items, a more demanding perceptual task is carried out under higher perceptual load. It is these items or operations that consume attentional capacity in the relevant processing and thereby block irrelevant processing. In line with this claim, Lavie (1995) demonstrated that increasing the number of items that were relevant for target perception or increasing the perceptual processing requirements for the same items (e.g., comparing simple presence detection vs. complex discrimination of feature conjunctions), led to reduced response competition effects as well as reduced negative priming effects from irrelevant distractors (Lavie & Fox 2000).

These studies clearly demonstrate that interference effects from distractors on target reaction times are reduced in tasks of high (compared to low) perceptual load, however they cannot provide information about the effects of perceptual load on conscious perception of such distractors. Although the perceptual load model interprets the elimination of distractor effects on reaction times by higher loads as reflecting an overall reduction in distractor perception (i.e., implying no conscious perception of distractors with high perceptual load), the reaction time effects are equally consistent with alternative interpretations proposing no role for perceptual load in determining conscious perception. For example, one could claim that perceptual load influences unconscious perceptual processes but has no effects on conscious perception. On such an interpretation, task-irrelevant distractors never enter awareness under either condition of load: distractor interference effects on reaction times seen in conditions of low load merely reflect unconscious recognition of distractor/target response associations. Alternatively, one could also claim that distractors always enter awareness, regardless of load. With this interpretation, the reduction of distractor effects on reaction times by higher perceptual loads reflects an influence of load on post-perceptual processes such as response selection. Although there is some counter evidence ruling out two specific alternative accounts (a) that reduced distractor reaction-time interference effects with high load are due to dissipation of distractor effects during longer reaction times for high load (Lavie & DeFockert 2003) and (b) that perceptual load increases active suppression of the distractor responses under high load (Lavie & Fox 2000), the reaction-time load studies leave open the general possibility that perceptual load effects are on responses rather than on conscious awareness.

Converging results from neuroimaging tests of perceptual load theory clearly show that load effects on distractor processing are not confined to reaction time measures. These studies demonstrated that high load eliminates visual cortex activity related to task-irrelevant distractors. For example, Rees, Frith, and Lavie (1997) found that neural activity related to motion (vs. stationary) distractors in visual cortex (e.g., MT) was found in conditions of low load in a relevant task on words at fixation (detection of the letter case) but was eliminated by high load in the relevant task (involving more complex word discrimination). Other studies found that visual cortex activity related to a task-irrelevant checkerboard depended on the level of load in a relevant task, decreasing as load was increased (e.g., Schwartz et al. 2005). Yi et al. (2004) similarly showed that when subjects attempt to ignore pictures of places presented in the background, while monitoring for face repetitions at fixation, parahippocampal activity related to the place backgrounds is substantially reduced by increasing the load in the face identification task.

These results convincingly show that visual cortex activity related to distractor perception is determined by the level of load in the task-relevant processing. However, apart from Rees, Frith, and Lavie's (1997) study, this research typically has not assessed the effects of distractors on conscious subjective experience. Rees, Frith, and Lavie did accompany their neuroimaging experiment with assessment of the subjective duration of motion after-effects from the motion distractors presented during either low load or high load tasks. They found that the subjective duration of the motion after-effect was significantly reduced by high load for each subject. This result is encouraging for the suggestion that perceptual load determines conscious awareness at least in the case of visual motion.

To establish the role of perceptual load in visual awareness it is important to examine whether perceptual load effects on awareness can generalize across various measures of visual awareness. Two recent studies examined the effects of perceptual load on explicit overt reports about subjective awareness in the inattentional blindness and in the change blindness paradigms.

The Role of Perceptual Load in "Inattentional Blindness"

Cartwright-Finch and Lavie (2006) manipulated perceptual load within Mack and Rock's inattentional blindness paradigm. In some experiments they asked subjects to perform a visual search task of either low or high load (Figure 38.2); in other experiments they asked subjects to make a difficult line length discrimination judgment in the high load condition compared with an easy length discrimination (cross arms with very different lengths) or with a simple color discrimination for the very same stimulus used in the high load condition. They found that the level of perceptual load in the task determined the rates of inattentional blindness: whereas subjects were often aware of the irrelevant stimulus in situ-

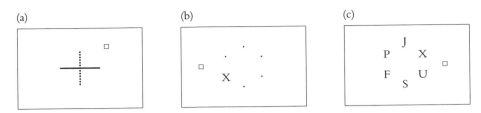

Figure 38.2 Load procedure in the inattentional blindness study of Cartwright-Finch and Lavie (reported in Lavie 2006).

An example of a stimulus display on a critical trial is shown for (*a*) the cross task under both conditions of perceptual load. One line was green (solid line in the picture) and one was blue (dotted line in the picture). In the low-load condition, subjects were asked to indicate which arm was green. In the high-load condition, they were asked to indicate which arm was longer. (*b*) the letter search task in the low-load condition and (*c*) the letter search task in the high-load condition.

ations of low load, they typically failed to notice the irrelevant stimulus in situations of high load. Cartwright-Finch and Lavie's tasks used short exposure durations that preclude the possibility of eye movements during display presentation. Their results thus concur with the suggestion from Simons and Chabris's studies that the level of demand on attention (rather than the likelihood of eye movements as discussed earlier) is critical in determining "inattentional blindness." Importantly, as Cartwright-Finch and Lavie did not compare the rates of inattentional blindness between the critical trial and the control trial but instead between critical trials of different levels of load, the effects of perceptual load on the level of inattentional blindness cannot be due to variation of intentions or expectations across conditions. The critical stimulus was equally task-irrelevant and equally unexpected across the varying levels of perceptual load. These results therefore offer compelling evidence that the availability of attention for the processing of a task-irrelevant stimulus, as varied by perceptual load, determines whether that stimulus reaches conscious perception.

Inattentional blindness measures, however ask about awareness for an unexpected object. Although the effects of load on inattentional blindness cannot be due to varying levels of expectation, as the irrelevant stimulus was equally unexpected under all conditions of load, the conclusion from these inattentional blindness experiments remains restricted to cases of awareness for an unexpected object. Moreover, the retrospective measure of awareness with a surprise question following task responses involves a memory component. The effects of load may therefore be attributed to weaker encoding of the unexpected stimulus into memory with high load than low load. It is therefore important to ask whether perceptual load can determine awareness in other paradigms, that do not rely on a retrospective surprise question about an unexpected stimulus in their measure of awareness. The "change blindness" paradigm provides such a measure, as I describe next.

The Role of Attention in Determining Awareness of Change or "Change Blindness"

Rensink (1997) developed a change detection flicker task, which appears to suggest a major role for attention in conscious detection of changes (see also Noë, chapter 39).

Figure 38.3 An example of a typical display used in Rensink, O'Regan, and Clark's (1997) change blindness experiments.

Under normal circumstances awareness reports will show very little failure to detect any change between the images. However, when the sensory transient that a change involves is interrupted by an intervening blank interval between the two successive images that produces a "flicker," observers will often fail to detect the change, exhibiting "change blindness."

With respect to the memory and expectation criticisms of the inattentional blindness paradigm, in the change blindness paradigm subjects are instructed in advance that their task is to detect whether a change occurred between two successive images and report about it immediately following the images. Thus, unlike inattentional blindness, the event for which awareness is reported is expected and awareness reports are given immediately following the images.

Load on attention appears to play a critical role in change blindness. The images of natural scenes used to demonstrate change blindness should load attention as they are typically rich in detail and often fairly cluttered in this flicker task (see Figure 38.3 for a typical display). Indeed cuing the object that changes removes any difficulty in detecting change (see Rensink 1997) suggesting that allocation of focused attention to the object of change is needed to detect a change in this paradigm, and that the failure to detect changes when uncued is due to attention being loaded with the processing of other objects in the cluttered scene.

In line with this suggestion it has also been found that objects that capture attention,

(a)

(b)

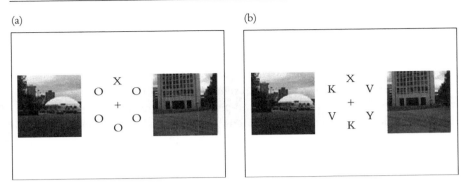

Figure 38.4 Load procedure in the Beck and Lavie change blindness study (reported in Lavie 2006).

An example of one stimulus display is shown for (*a*) the low-load condition and (*b*) the high-load condition.

either by virtue of containing a singleton feature, or by virtue of their significant socio-biological meaning (e.g., human faces; Ro, Russell, & Lavie 2001), do not suffer from change blindness as much as other objects that do not capture attention.

All of the experiments reviewed thus far, however, used a flicker task in which observers were free to move their eyes and the displays cycle until the change is detected. It is therefore unclear whether the improved performance for the faces, singletons, or for any cued item, was due to the allocation of attention to them or to eye movements toward these items. Recent research by Beck and Lavie, reported in Lavie (2006), tested whether the rate of change detection and conversely the rate of change blindness reports in the flicker task depend on the degree to which attention is available to focus on the changing object or is loaded by processing objects in another task while monitoring eye fixation. They combined the change detection task with a concurrent letter search task (Figure 38.4). The degree to which attentional resources were engaged in the letter search task (and thus more or less available for the change detection task) was manipulated by varying the level of perceptual load in the search task (Figure 38.4). Their results showed that the rate of change detection critically depended on the level of load in the search task: subjects failed to detect the change far more often in the conditions of high (vs. low) load in the letter search task. Analysis of the eye position data confirmed that the results were due to availability of attention for change detection rather than a greater rate of eye movements to the changing objects in conditions of low load.

Finally, the evidence for the role of attention in determining conscious awareness is consistent with several neuroimaging experiments that found that activity in the frontoparietal attentional network is associated with awareness reports. For example, Beck et al. (2001) found that successful change detection (as opposed to change blindness) was associated not only with visual cortex activity related to the specific changing object (e.g., greater activity in the fusiform face area when the change concerned a face) but also with activity in regions of the frontoparietal cortex commonly associated with directed attention. Furthermore, disrupting these areas with transcranial magnetic stimulation resulted in greater change blindness (Turatto, Sandrini, & Miniussi 2004; Beck et al. 2005) suggesting that these areas play a causal role in detecting change.

Conclusion

Although the question of whether attention determines conscious awareness has been debated for many years, understanding of the apparently discrepant data within the framework of load theory suggests a promising resolution. Attention and its related neural activity in the frontoparietal network appear to play a critical role in determining awareness. This role can be clearly revealed in situations that present a load on attention. In such situations, people are unaware of the information to which they do not attend. In situations of low load, however, due to a "spill-over" of attention, people will be aware of other sources of information to which they do not intend to pay attention. Findings that people are aware of information that they were instructed not to attend to therefore do not undermine the role of attention in determining awareness, but instead question people's ability to exert voluntary control over their allocation of attention, being unable to simply stop allocating attention at will.

See also 19 The intermediate level theory of consciousness; 39 Inattentional blindness, change blindness, and consciousness; 40 Preconscious processing

Further Readings

Shiffrin, R. (1997) Attention, automatism, and consciousness. In J. D. Cohen and J. W. Schooler (eds.), *Scientific Approaches to Consciousness*, Hillsdale, NJ: Lawrence Erlbaum Associates.

Velmans, M. (2000) *Understanding Consciousness*. London: Routledge/Psychology Press/Taylor & Francis, ch. 4, 57–69.

References

Allport, A. (1993) Attention and control: have we been asking the wrong questions? A critical review of twenty-five years. In D. E. Meyer and S. Kornblum (eds.), *Attention and Performance* XIV, 183–218. Cambridge, MA: MIT Press.

Beck, D., Muggleton, N., Walsh, V., and Lavie, N. (2005) Right parietal lobe plays a critical role in change blindness. *Cerebral Cortex* 16, 712–17.

Beck, D. M., Rees, G., Frith, C. D., and Lavie, N. (2001) Neural correlates of change awareness and change blindness. *Nature Neuroscience* 4: 6, 645–50.

Broadbent, D. E. (1958) *Perception and Communication*. London: Pergamon Press.

Cartwright-Finch, U. and Lavie, N. (2006) The role of perceptual load in inattentional blindness. *Cognition* February 13.

Cherry, C. (1953) Some experiments on the reception of speech with one and with two ears. *Journal of the Acoustical Society of America* 25, 975–9.

Eriksen, B. A. and Eriksen, C. W. (1974) Effects of noise letters upon the identification of a target letter in a non-search task. *Perception and Psychophysics* 16, 143–9.

Fox, E. (1995) Negative priming from ignored distractors in visual selection: a review. *Psychonomic Bulletin and Review* 2, 145–73.

Gatti, S. V. and Egeth, H. E. (1978) Failure of spatial selectivity in vision. *Bulletin of the Psychonomic Society* 11, 181–4.

Kahneman, D. (1973) *Attention and Effort*. Englewood Cliffs, NJ: Prentice Hall.

Lavie, N. (1995) Perceptual load as a necessary condition for selective attention. *Journal of Experimental Psychology: Human Perception and Performance* 21, 451–68.

Lavie, N. (2005) Distracted and confused? Selective attention under load. *Trends in Cognitive Sciences* 9, 75–82.

Lavie, N. (2006) The role of perceptual load in visual awareness. *Brain Research* 1080: 1, 91–100.

Lavie, N. and DeFockert, J. W. (2003) Contrasting effects of sensory limits and capacity limits in visual selective attention. *Perception and Psychophysics* 65, 202–12.

Lavie, N., and Fox, E. (2000) The role of perceptual load in negative priming. *Journal of Experimental Psychology: Human Perception and Performance* 26, 1038–52.

Lavie, N. and Tsal, Y. (1994) Perceptual load as a major determinant of the locus of selection in visual attention. *Perception and Psychophysics* 56, 183–97.

Lewis, J. L. (1970) Semantic processing of unattended messages using dichotic listening. *Journal of Experimental Psychology* 85, 225–8.

Littman, D. and Becklen, R. (1976) Selective looking with minimal eye movements. *Perception and Psychophysics* 20, 77–9.

Mack, A. and Rock, I. (1998) *Inattentional Blindness*. Cambridge, MA: MIT Press.

Moray, N. (1959) Attention and dichotic listening: affective cues and the influence of instructions. *Quarterly Journal of Experimental Psychology* 11, 56–60.

Most, S. B., Simons, D. J., Scholl, B. J., Jimenez, R., Clifford, E., and Chabris, C. F. (2001) How not to be seen: the contribution of similarity and selective ignoring to sustained inattentional blindness. *Psychological Science* 12, 9–17.

Neisser, U. and Becklen, R. (1975) Selective looking: attending to visually specified events. *Cognitive Psychology* 7, 480–94.

Pashler, H. (1998) *The Psychology of Attention*. London: MIT Press.

Rees, G., Frith, C. D., and Lavie, N. (1997) Modulating irrelevant motion perception by varying attentional load in an unrelated task. *Science* 278, 1616–19.

Rensink, R. A., O'Regan, J. K., and Clark, J. J. (1997) To see or not to see: the need for attention to perceive changes in scenes. *Psychological Science* 8, 368–73.

Ro, T., Russell, C., and Lavie, N. (2001) Changing faces: a detection advantage in the flicker paradigm. *Psychological Science* 12, 94–9.

Rock, I. and Gutman, D. (1981) The effect of inattention on form perception. *Journal of Experimental Psychology: Human Perception and Performance* 7, 275–85.

Schwartz, S., Vuilleumier, P., Hutton, C., Maravita, A., Dolan, R. J., and Driver, J. (2005) Attentional load and sensory competition in human vision: modulation of fMRI responses by load at fixation during task-irrelevant stimulation in the peripheral visual field. *Cerebral Cortex* 15, 770–86.

Simons, D. J. and Chabris, C. F. (1999) Gorillas in our midst: sustained inattentional blindness for dynamic events. *Perception* 28, 1059–74.

Tipper, S. P. (1985) The negative priming effect: inhibitory effects of ignored primes. *Quarterly Journal of Experimental Psychology* 37A, 571–90.

Treisman, A. M. and Geffen, G. (1967) Selective attention: perception or response? *Quarterly Journal of Experimental Psychology* 19, 1–18.

Turatto, M., Sandrini, M., and Miniussi, C. (2004) The role of the right dorsolateral prefrontal cortex in visual change awareness. *NeuroReport* 15, 2549–52.

Velmans, M. (2000) *Understanding Consciousness*, London: Routledge/Psychology Press/Taylor & Francis, ch. 4, 57–69.

Yantis, S. and Johnston, J. C. (1990) On the locus of visual selection: evidence from focused attention tasks. *Journal of Experimental Psychology: Human Perception and Performance* 16, 135–49.

Yi, D. J., Woodman, G.F., Widders, D., Marois, R., and Chun, M. M. (2004) Neural fate of ignored stimuli: Dissociable effects of perceptual and working memory load. *Nature Neuroscience* 7, 992–6.

39

Inattentional Blindness, Change Blindness, and Consciousness

ALVA NOË

Recent work on the psychology of scene perception demonstrates that perceivers may fail to notice substantial events or changes taking place in full view. Perceivers are normally sensitive to change-related flickers of movement ("transients"). "Change blindness" occurs when these transients fail to grab attention, either because they are masked (as when the entire picture is refreshed), or because there are no transients (as when the change occurs gradually) (see O'Regan forthcoming and Simons & Ambinder 2005 for recent reviews). A related phenomenon is "inattentional blindness" (Mack & Rock 1998). In inattentional blindness, perceivers fail to notice features, events, or changes in full view because their attention is focused elsewhere. In a now famous demonstration, Simons and Chabris (1999) ask perceivers to pay attention to the manner in which a ball is passed among a group of players. Perceivers who are engaged in this task frequently fail to notice that a person in a gorilla suit is walking among the players! Other phenomena have been described recently that lend further support to the idea that our ability to perceive detail is vulnerable to disruption, such as repetition blindness (Kanwisher 1987; Chun 1997) and the attentional blink (Chun & Potter 1995). In this article I use the term "detail blindness" to refer to this class of phenomena. The question I want to consider is: What does detail blindness teach us about consciousness? I review two different lines of response and I propose a third.

A First Approach: There Are No Representations

According to an influential line of argument, detail blindness (DB) shows ordinary perceivers are conscious of much less than they may think. Indeed, it is sometimes claimed that DB shows that our sense that we visually experience a detailed scene is an illusion. In this spirit, Blackmore et al. 1995 write:

> we believe that we see a complete, dynamic picture of a stable, uniformly detailed, and colourful world, [but] [o]ur stable visual world may be constructed out of a brief retinal image and a very sketchy, higher-level representation along with a pop-out mechanism to redirect attention. The richness of our visual world is, to this extent, an illusion.

And O'Regan (1992), who has since change his mind about this, wrote:

despite the poor quality of the visual apparatus, we have the subjective impression of great richness and "presence" of the visual world. But this richness and presence are actually an illusion.

What justifies this "grand illusion" hypothesis (as it has been called by Noë, Pessoa, & Thompson 2000; see also Noë 2002a, 2002b)? The basic reasoning is as follows: First, DB shows, it is claimed, that when we see a scene, the brain does not construct a detailed internal representation of it. If there were such a detailed internal representation, then, so the reasoning goes, we would be able to detect changes by comparing the current scene with our stored representation. Rensink (2000, p. 18) articulated the implicit reasoning: Change blindness

> suggests that little detailed information is being accumulated – otherwise, change detection would be easy, either by comparing immediate visual input with the contents of the buffer, or by detecting the anomalous structures formed by superimposing the original and the changed images.

The claim that DB shows that we see less than we think we do by showing that there are no detailed internal representations, is theoretically suggestive. To appreciate this, consider that traditional visual theory starts from the idea that we enjoy rich, picture-like experiences. The main problem for traditional theory has been to explain how it is that we can enjoy such experiences when the "input" to vision, in the form of light striking the eyes, is impoverished. We experience a stable scene in sharp focus and uniform detail, from the center out to the periphery, even though (i) the resolving power of the eye is nonhomogenous (owing to the variable distribution of photoreceptors outside the high-resolution central fovea), (ii) there is a blind spot in each eye (where there are no photoreceptors), and (iii) the eye is in nearly constant motion (causing a jittery and unstable retinal image). How do we manage to experience the world the way we experience it? How do distorted, jittery, upside-down, gappy images in two eyes yield a single impression of a stable, gap-free visual field? Enter the representationalist hypothesis: The brain integrates information available in successive fixations and builds up a single, stable, detailed representation. The content of this representation is the content of what is experienced, of what is seen. Vision, on this view, is the process whereby the brain generates such a detailed internal representation (Marr 1982).

DB shows, at least according to the line of reasoning we are considering, that the brain lacks the detailed internal representations whose existence would be necessary for us to enjoy detailed visual impressions. If we lack the necessary representational substrates, then we also lack the experiences we (theorists) mistakenly think we have. Moreover, if this line of argument is right, traditional vision science must be overthrown. It has been barking up the wrong tree in trying to discover the processes whereby the brain produces representations. DB in this way calls the very foundations of visual theory into question.

Problems with the "No Representations" Approach

The "no representation" argument is flawed and does not show what it tries to show. The largest problem is that the existence of DB does not entail that we lack detailed internal representations (Noë, Pessoa, & Thompson 2000; Simons & Rensink 2005); and so it does not show that we lack the experience we would need those representations to have. True, the nonexistence of detailed representations would explain DB, for the sort of reasons Rensink (2000) mentioned (quoted above). But this is not the only hypothesis that would explain DB. An alternative (first) would be to suppose that there are stable, detailed internal representations in the brain of what is seen, but that there are limits on our ability to compare the current scene with those stored representations. Such a view would account for DB without denying that there are representations, and so it would account for DB without claiming that visual experience is a grand illusion. A second way to account for DB is available: perhaps there is a detailed representation of what is seen, but the representation fades quickly. If this were the case, then it might be impossible to perform a comparison of the current representation with the just faded one, because only the first representation had faded. If this is right, DB would be a kind of failure of short-term memory, not a failure of perceptual experience. There are other possibilities as well. To mention a third: perhaps certain changes are hard to detect, not because they aren't experienced, but because they lack attention-grabbing salience.

In fact, recent work supplies some evidence in favor of each of these alternatives. Simons et al. 2002 show that perceivers may sometimes fail to notice changes to detail, even though the detail is represented. Subjects in their study did not notice that a person with whom they had been talking no longer held an unusually colored basketball after some people passed by momentarily blocking their view. When asked whether they'd noticed anything unusual, subjects replied that they had not; they evinced evidence of having been blind to the change. But when the subjects were asked point blank whether they noticed that the interlocutor had been holding a basketball, a high proportion of subjects acknowledged that they had and were in fact able to describe the ball's unusual pattern. Not only did they see the ball and its pattern, but information about the ball was represented; the existence of the representation of this information only comes out when the right probe is used. Simons et al. argue that this study shows that DB results from a failure to perform the right comparison, rather than from a failure to represent the information (Mitroff & Simons 2005).

Work by Lamme (2003, 2004) suggests that DB may be a memory problem. Using a Sperling-like task (Sperling 1960), they show that an appropriate cue, after the completion of the looking task, will enable subjects to report any detail to which they otherwise exhibit change blindness. Lamme, and also Block (in draft), argue that this is strong evidence not only of representation of the detail, but that the detail was experienced. Change blindness would seem to reflect that the experienced detail is unavailable for report, as if forgotten.

Finally, Zelinsky (2003) argues that variability in change detection performance depends on similarity of features that change; changes in features that lack similarity are easier to detect than changes in very similar features. The significance of this analysis is that change detection results not from a failure to represent items, but from some similarity-based constraints on the comparison of represented items.

Each of these groups of studies supports the conclusion that DB leaves completely unsettled whether there are detailed internal representations. It also leaves open the question of whether or not the relevant detail is experienced.

This is not the only problem with the "no representations" approach. There are also problems of a more conceptual nature. The argument relies on a confused account of the relation between *what is represented* and *what is seen*. We might accept that it is impossible to experience unrepresented detail without accepting that all represented detail is experienced. The fact that something is represented, then, wouldn't show that it was seen, if by "seen" we mean "visually experienced." This objection weighs not only against "no represen-tation" theorists, but also against those, like Lamme (2003, 2004) and Block (in draft), who treat the existence of informational representation as prima facie evidence that what is thus represented is experienced. It is possible that cues, in Lamme's study, causally enable us to experience detail that was, until then, not experienced but represented. Block and Lamme presumably take it that subjects naively have the impression that they saw all the detail and reason that that fact, together with independent evidence of the existence of representations of the relevant detail (perhaps also with further neural facts), makes it plausible that there was experience. But there is a problem with this line of reasoning that will receive more attention in the next section when we turn to what I call the New Skepticism. The problem is that it is not in fact the case that we take ourselves to see everything in front of us in sharp focus and uniform detail. First-person reflection does not support this claim. This is not to say that perceivers lack a sense of the presence of the detailed scene. It is one thing to say that a scene is experienced *as highly detailed*, and another to say that one experiences *all the detail*. There is nothing that we can point to in the phenomenology that makes it plausible to say that "we really saw it all." It is this kind of indeterminacy that gives weight to Den-nett's argument to the effect that it is a mistake to think of phenomenal consciousness as the sort of thing that could be present/absent just like that.

A second further problem with the "no representation" view is that after decades of research in cognitive science, talk of "representations" remains vague and theoretically problematic (Searle 1992). Just what is a mental (or neural) representation anyway? This problem affects discussions on both sides of the representation issue.

A Second Approach: The New Skepticism

A second influential line of argument, championed by Daniel Dennett (1991), also argues that visual consciousness is a grand illusion, but does so without relying on the problematic "DB entails there are no detailed internal representations" reasoning.

Traditional skepticism, in philosophy, questions whether we can ever know, on the basis of experience, that things are as they seem. The skeptic says no. But traditional skepticism never called into question whether we know how things seem. This is precisely the target of the new skepticism. According to the new skepticism, perceptual consciousness is a kind of false consciousness. Visual consciousness is a confabulation, a grand illusion. We think we experience the visual field in sharp focus and uniform detail, from the center out to the periphery. But we do not. We are the victims of an illusion – an illusion not concerning how things are, but about how things seem to us to be.

DB confirms the grand illusion hypothesis, by providing direct evidence that our pre-theoretical ideas about perceptual consciousness are misguided. How do we think about our perceptual experience, pretheoretically? It is widely stated that we believe that when we open our eyes the entire scene is represented in our experience, in sharp focus and high res-olution, from the center of the visual field out to the periphery. As Blackmore et al. (1995) had written (cited earlier): "we believe that we see a complete, dynamic picture of a stable, uniformly detailed, and colourful world." In a similar vein, Rensink (2000) had asked: "Why do we feel that somewhere in our brain is a complete, coherent representation of the entire scene?" The answer, Rensink seems to assume, is provided by a consideration of our phe-nomenology. Experience presents itself to us as picture-like.

What DB shows, it is then claimed, is that our experience isn't really like this. We think we see a whole, stable, detailed scene, whereas in fact we only really experience one or two features, together perhaps with a few sketchy, indeterminate background elements.

What clinches the "new skepticism" argument is the astonishment that perceivers evince when they are confronted with DB demonstrations. They laugh aloud and express shock and disbelief that they could really have failed to see what are, they now can tell, large, obvious, salient changes. As Dennett has argued, what better evidence could there be that ordinary perceivers are committed to an "experience as pictures in the head" conception of their own phenomenology than this surprise and disbelief in the favor of proof that visual experience is *not* detailed and pictorial in this way?

Problems with the New Skepticism

Surprise is indeed the correlate of epistemic commitment, as Dennett has stressed (2001, 2002). The question we must ask is, to what does our surprise in the face of DB indicate that we are committed? We have been considering one possibility: that we are committed to the idea that when we see, we suppose that we experience the scene in sharp focus and uniform detail from the center out to the periphery. But there is a simpler possibility: that we simply overestimate how good we are at noticing changes.

This simpler possibility finds support from attention to ordinary perceptual experience. Nothing could be more familiar to each of us than the fact that, very frequently, in order to see what is happening around us, or in order to get a better look at something, it is necessary to move our eyes, head, and body. Perceivers are continuously and effortlessly engaged in visual explorations. If we take ourselves to have the whole scene in consciousness all at once, then why should we be such visual busy-bodies? Moreover, why is it not the case that our need continuously to look and readjust our vantage point to secure our visual targets is not the source of surprise? If we were committed to the problematic "we see it all" conception of our perceptual consciousness, then we ought to be surprised by our need for active exploration. Upshot: we are not committed to such a (mis)conception; and so we are not the victims of a grand illusion.

Far from it being the case that we take ourselves to have all detail in consciousness all at once, in sharp focus and uniform detail, nothing could in our everyday experience be more settled than that when we see, some things are in focus, while other things are present vaguely or indeterminately, perhaps as mere background. To be told that not everything in the visual field is in sharp focus all at once is not to be told something surprising. The point is not that we do not take ourselves to have perceptual access to a detailed and determinate world. We do. But to say this – that we take ourselves, when we see, to be confronted with a detailed world – is not to say that, when we see, we take ourselves to internalize all that detail and represent it all at once (as it might be represented in a picture).

Lay perceivers are *not* committed to the "visual experiences are like pictures in the head" conception of their own seeing. For this reason, the demonstration that visual experiences are *not* like pictures in the head is no skin off the back of ordinary perception. And so it certainly does not show that they are victims of a kind of grand illusion.

The new skepticism assumes that perceivers occupy something like the standpoint of traditional vision scientists who assume, as their starting point, that the brain builds up detailed internal pictures. But the standpoint of ordinary perception is much closer, I would suggest, to a different kind of expert: the magician or stage set designer. They know perfectly well that perception is vulnerable to deception, and that perceivers are not photographers who then carry about and refer to their mental snapshots.

There is a puzzle about how we *can* have the idea that, when we see, we see a detailed, determinate visual world if in fact it is not the case that, when we see, we actually take ourselves to see *all* the detail. We have already touched on the solution to this (for more extended discussion, see Noë 2004): the world, when we see it, presents itself to us as *available* or as *accessible*, not as represented. DB does nothing to undermine our perceptual sense of the availability of the world.

Toward a New Approach

Suppose that one day we discover that there is a detailed, three-dimensional, analog model of the perceived world in the brain (in the pineal gland, say); that what we experience, at a moment in time is represented in this mental model. This would be a startling and important discovery. On reflection, however, it should be clear that this discovery would not bring us any closer to understanding how or why it is that we manage to *experience* the world in visual perception. What is it about the 3-D internal model thanks to which we are *phenomenally conscious* of the world around us? After all, we don't *see* the model. What is it about the neural activity underlying this imagined representation thanks to which we have the sense of it all? Representations in the head, however detailed, do not (would not) explain visual consciousness.

This *explanatory gap* for visual consciousness is the starting point for a new approach to the question of DB's significance for the theory of consciousness. Traditional visual theory has always assumed that vision is a process whereby the brain produces a representation corresponding to what is seen. But traditional approaches have failed to bridge the explanatory gap. This impasse motivates a more radical break with the traditional approach. Let us take seriously the possibility that vision is *not* a process of representation-building. That is, let us rethink the characterization of what vision is at what Marr called "the computational level" (1982). To do this is not to assume that there are no representations in visual processing; to establish that would require empirical evidence. The point is precisely that whether and to what degree there are representations is an empirical question, not something to be built into our very analysis of what vision is (Noë, Pessoa, & Thompson 2000).

Accounts that demote representations from theoretical pride of place have obvious attractions. If the brain isn't in the business of building representations of the scene, then visual science can liberate itself of the burden of explaining how the brain performs this difficult engineering task. Such a proposal makes evolutionary sense: the senses are important, from an evolutionary standpoint, because they enable us to do what we need to do, for example, to flee our predators, find our mates, etc. What matters is *action*, not representation. The largest obstacle to the "no detailed internal representations strategy" had seemed to be consciousness: whether or not we need consciousness, we've got consciousness. We experience the detailed environment, so we must represent the detailed environment. But it is just this last move that we've already seen fit to reject. There's nothing in our phenomenology that would suggest that we take ourselves, when we see, to experience all the environmental detail. We take the detail to be *out there*, not in our heads; to be in the world, not in our consciousness.

What we need – according to this line of thought – is an account of perceptual consciousness that gives pride of place not to *representation*, but rather, to engaged action on and interaction with the world. This is not the place to outline the features of such an approach. There exist a range of attempts in this direction. To mention only two, Gibson's (1979) project can be located in this vicinity; more recently, O'Regan and I have tried to develop an action-oriented, non-representationist account of perception (O'Regan & Noë 2001a, 2001b; Noë 2004).

How does DB bear on all this? We have seen that DB doesn't entail "no central representations." It does, however, sit comfortably with such a proposal. Indeed, from the standpoint of such a non-representational perspective, DB is what one would expect. If we do not represent what we experience in consciousness, and if perceptual consciousness relies on our situated *access* to the perceptual world, then it is not at all surprising that we should fail to experience what takes place outside of attention. The real significance of DB, I would argue, is that it lends support to approaches to perceptual consciousness that are broadly non-representationist in the way I have outlined.

See also 38 Attention and consciousness; 50 Neural dominance, neural deference, and sensorimotor dynamics.

Further Readings

Mack, A. and Rock, I. (1998) *Inattentional Blindness*. Cambridge, MA: MIT Press.
Noë, A. (2002b) Is the visual world a grand illusion? In *Is the Visual World a Grand Illusion?* Thorverton, UK: Imprint Academic. (This is a special issue of the *Journal of Consciousness Studies*.)
Noë, A. (2004) *Action in Perception*. Cambridge, MA: MIT Press.
Simons, D. J. and Rensink, R. A. (2005) Change blindness: past, present, future. *Trends in Cognitive Sciences* 9: 1, 16–20.

References

Blackmore, S. J., Brelstaff, G., Nelson, K., and Troscianko, T. (1995) Is the richness of our visual world an illusion? Transsaccadic memory for complex scenes. *Perception* 24, 1075–81.
Block, N. (in draft) The mind–body problem in a neuroscientific context.
Chun, M. M. (1997) Types and tokens in visual processing: a double dissociation between the attentional blink and repetition blindness. *Journal of Experimental Psychology: Human Perception and Performance* 23, 738–55.
Chun, M. M. and Potter, M. C. (1995) A two-stage model for multiple target detection in rapid serial visual presentation. *Journal of Experimental Psychology: Human Perception and Performance* 21, 109–27.
Dennett, D. C. (1991) *Consciousness Explained*. London: The Penguin Press.
Dennett, D. C. (2001) Surprise, surprise. *Behavioral and Brain Sciences* 24, 982.
Dennett, D. C. (2002) How wrong could I be? How could I be so wrong? In A. Noë (ed.), *Is the Visual World a Grand Illusion?* Thorverton: Imprint Academic.
Gibson, J. J. (1979) *The Ecological Approach to Visual Perception*. Hillsdale, NJ: Lawrence Erlbaum.
Kanwisher, N. G. (1987) Repetition blindness: type recognition without token individuation. *Cognition* 27, 117–43.
Lamme, V. A. F. (2003) Why visual awareness and attention are different. *Trends in Cognitive Sciences* 7, 12–18.

Lamme, V. A. F. (2004) Separate neural definitions of visual consciousness and visual attention; a case for phenomenal awareness. *Neural Networks* 17, 861–72.

Mack, A. and Rock, I. (1998) *Inattentional Blindness*. Cambridge, MA: MIT Press.

Marr, D. (1982) *Vision*. New York: W. H. Freeman and Sons.

Mitroff, S. R. and Simons, D. J. (2005) Nothing compares two views: Change blindness results from failures to compare retained information. *Perceptual Psychophysics* 66, 1268–81.

Noë, A. (2002a) *Is the Visual World a Grand Illusion?* Thorverton, UK: Imprint Academic. (This is a special issue of the *Journal of Consciousness Studies*.)

Noë, A. (2002b) Is the visual world a grand illusion? In *Is the Visual World a Grand Illusion?* Thorverton, UK: Imprint Academic. (This is a special issue of the *Journal of Consciousness Studies*.)

Noë, A. (2004) *Action in Perception*. Cambridge, MA: MIT Press.

Noë, A., Pessoa, L., and Thompson, E. (2000) Beyond the grand illusion: what change blindness really teaches us about vision. *Visual Cognition* 7, 93–106.

O'Regan, J. K. (1992) Solving the "real" problems of visual perception: the world as an outside memory. *Canadian Journal of Psychology* 46: 3, 461–88.

O'Regan, J. K. and Noë, A. (2001a) A sensorimotor approach to vision and visual consciousness. *Behavioral and Brain Sciences* 24, 5.

O'Regan, J. K. and Noë, A. (2001b) Authors reply: acting out our sensory experience. *Behavioral and Brain Sciences* 24, 5.

O'Regan, J. K. (forthcoming) Change blindness. *Macmillan Encyclopedia of Cognitive Science*.

Rensink, R. A. (2000) The dynamic representation of scences. *Visual Cognition* 7, 17–42.

Searle, J. (1992) *The Rediscovery of Mind*. Cambridge, MA: MIT Press.

Simons, D. J. and Ambinder, M. (2005) Change blindness: theory and consequences. *Current Directions in Psychological Science* 14, 44–8.

Simons, D. J. and Chabris, C. F. (1999) Gorillas in our midst: sustained inattentional blindness for dynamic events. *Perception* 28, 1059–74.

Simons, D. J. and Rensink, R. A. (2005) Change blindness: past, present, future. *Trends in Cognitive Sciences* 9: 1, 16–20.

Simons, D. J., Chabris, C. F., Schnur, T. T., and Levin, D. T. (2002) Evidence for preserved representations in change blindness. *Consciousness and Cognition* 11, 78–97.

Sperling, G. (1960) The information available in brief visual presentations. *Psychological Monographs* 74: 11, 1–29.

Zelinsky, G. J. (2003) Detecting changes between real-world objects using spatichromatic filters. *Psychonomic Bulletin and Review* 10: 3, 533–55.

40

Preconscious Processing

PHIL MERIKLE

An important characteristic of mental life is that we are aware or conscious of the results of many of our cognitive processes. Whether we are thinking, or perceiving, or listening, or remembering, our cognitive processes, as we know them, lead to outcomes that are accompanied by phenomenal awareness. In contrast to the processes leading to phenomenal awareness, an issue which has fascinated psychologists, philosophers, and more recently, neuroscientists, is whether cognitive processes which can be described as being unconscious, preconscious, or subconscious also lead to outcomes which have an impact on mental life.

The distinction between conscious and unconscious cognitive processes has a long history. As noted by Whyte (1960) in his review of the history of the unconscious, the genesis of the distinction between conscious and unconscious mental processes can be traced to Descartes. Following Descartes, the concept of unconscious mental processes was further developed in the writings of philosophers such as Leibniz, Kant, and Herbart. In psychology, some of the first empirical psychological studies conducted in the latter part of the nineteenth and early part of the twentieth centuries were directed at assessing whether it is possible to perceive sufficient information without awareness to influence perceptual judgments (see Miller 1942).

Despite the long history of the distinction between conscious and unconscious cognitive processes, there is still no agreement as to the role of unconscious or preconscious cognitive processes. A primary reason for this slow progress in understanding the role of unconscious processes revolves around issues regarding how to measure awareness or, in other words, how to distinguish conscious from unconscious cognitive processes. These issues have been addressed most extensively in the context of research studies investigating perception without awareness, and the vast majority of these studies have involved visual perception. For this reason, in the following discussion of preconscious processing, references and examples will be primarily to studies of perception without awareness in vision.

Measuring Awareness

The predominant experimental approach for studying preconscious processing is to establish a dissociation between perception and awareness. For example, in his classic studies,

Marcel (1983) found that visually presented words were perceived independent of whether observers were aware or unaware of the words. Marcel distinguished aware from unaware perception by assessing stimulus detection. Observers were required to discriminate between the presence and absence of a briefly presented visual word. Marcel assumed that successful detection indicated awareness and that unsuccessful detection indicated an absence of awareness. Perception independent of awareness was measured by assessing the impact of a word that named a color (e.g., the word *yellow*) on the speed with which the observers named a subsequently presented color patch (e.g., a red square). The finding that surprised many investigators at that time was that the words influenced how quickly the observers were able to name the color patches independent of whether the words were perceived with or without awareness. Even more surprising was the fact that the impact of the words on the speed with which the colors were named was the same whether the words were perceived with awareness or perceived without awareness. Many investigators considered Marcel's findings as providing strong evidence for perception without awareness and for the general importance of preconscious processes.

The logic underlying Marcel's experiment and in fact any experiment based on a dissociation between awareness and perception is straightforward. However, despite the straightforward logic, it has proven difficult to find completely convincing evidence of preconscious processing based on demonstrations of dissociations between awareness and perception. This difficulty is related to the fact that before any dissociation between awareness and perception provides convincing evidence for preconscious processes, it is necessary to have a measure of awareness which is potentially sensitive to *all* relevant conscious experiences and to show convincingly that this measure does not to exhibit any sensitivity when observers are assumed to be unaware. For example, in Marcel's experiment, it must be assumed that stimulus detection is an *exhaustive* measure of all relevant conscious experience (see Reingold & Merikle 1990), and there must be some assurance that there was absolutely no stimulus detection in the unaware condition of the experiment. The difficulties in satisfying the exhaustiveness assumption have made it possible for skeptics to question whether in fact there is any evidence whatsoever for preconscious processing (e.g., Holender 1986). However, despite the strong assumption required and the extreme empirical demands, establishing dissociations between awareness and perception has remained the dominant approach for studying preconscious processing.

Validating Measures of Awareness

Ever since Eriksen's (1960) classic critique of the perception without awareness literature, it has been widely assumed that because of the limitations of verbal responses in conveying an individual's perceptual experiences, it is best to assess awareness using objective behavioral measures such as stimulus detection or stimulus discrimination. For this reason, over the years since 1960, there has been an ongoing attempt to find behavioral measures that successfully distinguish conscious from nonconscious perception. Many different behavioral measures have been tried. Perhaps the most widely used behavioral measure is *stimulus detection* whereby observers are required to distinguish between the presence and absence of a stimulus. It is generally assumed that an inability to distinguish between the presence and absence of stimulus indicates an absence of awareness whereas an ability to distinguish between the presence and absence of a stimulus indicates awareness.

Many other behavioral measures have also been used to distinguish conscious from non-conscious perception. These measures include (a) *position discrimination* which requires observers to discriminate whether a visual stimulus is presented to the left or right of fixation, (b) *word discrimination* which requires observers to discriminate whether a visually presented letter string forms a proper word (e.g., yellow) or forms a nonword (yollew), and (c) *n-alternative forced-choice* whereby following the presentation of a target stimulus, it is presented in the context of one or more distractor stimuli and observers are asked to select the target stimulus. The common assumption underlying all of these behavioral measures is that failure to perform the discrimination of interest indicates an absence of awareness and success in making the discrimination of interest indicates the presence of awareness.

One issue that is rarely if ever addressed concerns how a behavioral measure of awareness is validated. Generally, investigators simply assume that the behavioral measures of awareness used in their studies are valid. The basis for assuming that any particular behavioral measure distinguishes conscious from unconscious perception is rarely if ever stated. Usually, it is thought that measures such as stimulus detection and n-alternative forced-choice are *intuitively obvious* measures of awareness. The supporting argument is that if insufficient information is perceived to guide either stimulus detection or forced-choice responses, then it is reasonable to assume that no critical information was consciously perceived.

But there is a much more fundamental way in which all behavioral measures of awareness are validated and which is generally unrecognized by investigators. Namely, behavioral measures of awareness are validated by the subjective experiences of the observers and the investigators. When performance as indexed by an assumed behavioral measure of awareness approximates a chance level *and* both the observers and the investigator have no subjective awareness of perceiving the critical stimuli, then the investigator is likely to assume that the measure provides a satisfactory assessment of conscious perception, or more precisely, the absence of conscious perception. In contrast, if performance approximates a chance level *and* either the observers or the investigator experience phenomenal awareness of the stimuli, then it is highly unlikely that the investigator will assume that the measure provides a satisfactory assessment of the absence of conscious perception.

Validating behavioral measures of awareness in terms of subjective experience is not an unreasonable approach. In fact, there is really no other way to bridge the gap between subjective experience and behavior. One reason a measure such as stimulus detection is so intuitively appealing as a measure of the absence of awareness, is that it is rare to find anyone who exhibits a level of detection performance which approximates chance *and* who reports the subjective experience of seeing the critical stimuli. Thus, subjective experience typically coincides with behavior; in other words, when there is no stimulus detection, there is no subjective experience of perceiving the critical stimuli. Once it is recognized that behavioral measures of awareness can only be considered valid if they accurately reflect subjective experience, then it is possible to question whether behavioral measures are really necessary to distinguish conscious from unconscious states. Why not simply assess subjective experience?

Subjective vs. Behavioral Measures of Awareness

Studies of preconscious processing based on assessments of subjective experience date from the late 1800s. A classic study by Sidis (1898) provides a good example of the general approach. Sidis showed observers cards, each containing a single digit or letter. The observers were seated at a distance from the cards on which they claimed they could not see anything but dimmed blurred spots "which often disappeared from their field of view" (p. 171). Despite not having any conscious awareness of the specific letter or digit printed on each card, Sidis found that when he asked the observers to guess the identity of the letters and digits, their guesses were considerably more accurate than would be expected on the basis of chance responding. Based on this dissociation between the observers' assessments of their subjective awareness of the letters and digits and their guesses about the identity of the letters and digits, Sidis concluded that the observers perceived the letters and digits without awareness.

When awareness is assessed in terms of observers' statements about their subjective experiences, it is relatively easy to demonstrate that such perception occurs even though observers do not believe that they have perceived adequate information to guide their responses (see Merikle, Smilek, & Eastwood 2001 for overview). In fact, this phenomenon is so robust that it can be used as a classroom demonstration (cf., Adams 1957). However, despite the robustness of the findings, there is a tremendous reluctance, particularly among psychologists, to distinguish aware from unaware perception solely on the basis of observers' reports regarding their subjective experiences. This reluctance can be traced to the continuing influence of behaviorism and its edicts regarding the unreliability of reports of conscious experiences and the general irrelevance of consciousness for understanding behavior. It is widely thought that observers' reports of their subjective experiences when viewing stimuli are influenced by many factors other than their phenomenal awareness or lack of phenomenal awareness of the stimuli. Likewise, it is generally thought that observers' statements regarding the presence or absence of an awareness may be more indicative of their preconceived ideas concerning perception than of a "true" description of their phenomenal awareness. For these reasons, there is a strong bias among psychologists to use objective rather than subjective measures to assess awareness, even though, as noted above, objective measures can only be validated in terms of subjective experience.

An important consequence of relying on objective rather than subjective measures to assess awareness is that the transition from preconscious processing to conscious processing with increased stimulus duration or increased stimulus intensity is defined incorrectly. The assumption that an absence of awareness is indicated by a failure to discriminate between the presence and absence of a stimulus or to discriminate between alternative stimulus states is relatively non-controversial. When observers cannot make such discriminations, the stimulus conditions are such that there is rarely if ever any subjective awareness of the stimuli. Thus objective performance and subjective experience lead to the same conclusion. However, it is often assumed by those who use objective measures that success in discriminating between alternative stimulus states indicates awareness of the perceptual characteristics that distinguish the alternative stimulus states. This second assumption is difficult if not impossible to validate because it is inconsistent with subjective experience. It is well known that it is possible to make correct forced-choice decisions regarding stimuli even when there is no phenomenal awareness of the stimuli as assessed by observers' descriptions of their subjective experiences. In fact, this is precisely what the experiments conducted by Sidis (1898) and so many other investigators have demonstrated time and time again (see Miller 1942; Adams 1957). Thus, in many instances, objective measures of performance will suggest that there is conscious perception, whereas subjective measures of phenomenal experience will suggest that there is no conscious perception.

This discrepancy between objective and subjective measures in estimating the transition between preconscious processing and conscious processing has important consequences for understanding preconscious processing. Typically, objective measures lead to more conservative estimates than subjective measures of the minimal stimulus conditions associated with the transition between preconscious and conscious perception. For this reason, if objective measures are used to identify the transition between preconscious and conscious perception, the impact of preconscious processes will in all likelihood be underestimated. The consequence of this underestimation is that incorrect conclusions will be made regarding both conscious and preconscious processes. The role of conscious processes will be overestimated and the role of preconscious processes will appear much more minimal and much more limited than is actually the true state of affairs. Given these considerations and the fact that objective measures are always validated by subjective experience, it appears that when all things are considered, subjective measures of awareness provide both more direct and more accurate indications of the presence or absence of awareness than is provided by objective measures.

Empirical Approaches

Empirical approaches to the study of preconscious processes can for the most part be classified as falling into one of three general categories. First, there are studies in which observers are shown displays containing a single target stimulus and the presentation conditions are degraded to such an extent that the observers are generally unaware of the stimuli. Second, there are studies in which observers focus their attention at one location in a visual display and are then shown displays containing multiple stimulus objects, each located at a different spatial location. Finally, there are studies involving neurological patients with syndromes that lead them to claim not to see stimuli that nevertheless influence their decisions, and studies involving surgical patients undergoing general anesthesia who claim not to have any explicit memories for events during anesthesia but who nevertheless seem to have implicit memories for these events.

Variations in Stimulus Conditions

The studies most often associated with the concept of preconscious perceptual processing are those studies in which the stimulus conditions are so degraded that observers are generally unaware of the target stimuli. These studies typically involve establishing awareness thresholds. The general assumption underlying these studies is that the awareness threshold identifies the set of stimulus conditions which marks the boundary between perception with and without awareness. Although this assumption is rarely if ever completely justified, with a few notable exceptions (e.g., Holender 1986), it is generally believed that properly established awareness thresholds are adequate for distinguishing conscious perception with awareness from preconscious or unconscious perception without awareness.

Ever since the first published studies in the late nineteenth century, there have been countless studies demonstrating perception without awareness in which awareness thresholds have been based on direct assessments of subjective experience (i.e., subjective measures). More recently, particularly since the publication of Marcel's (1983) classic studies, there have been innumerable studies of perception without awareness in which objective measures have been used to provide indirect assessments of subjective experience. The results from studies involving both subjective and objective measures of awareness provide overwhelming evidence that many types of stimulus information are perceived without awareness. Many of the earlier studies have been reviewed by Adams (1957) and Miller (1942). These studies established clearly that relatively simple stimuli such as lines (horizontal, vertical, or diagonal), shapes (circles, triangles, or squares) and graphemes (letters or digits) are perceived even when there is no awareness of perceiving the stimuli. In more recent studies (for reviews and summaries see Merikle & Daneman 1998; Merikle et al. 2001), it has been shown that the lexical status of letter strings (i.e., word vs. nonword), the meanings of words, and even the emotions expressed in faces are perceived without awareness.

Given the solid foundation for preconscious processing without awareness based on behavioral studies, in recent years investigators have begun to explore the neural correlates underlying preconscious processing. The predominant approach has been to use behavioral data to establish awareness thresholds and then to explore the neural correlates of preconscious processing using functional magnetic resonance imaging (fMRI) or event-related potentials (ERPs). In many studies, words have been used as the critical stimuli. It has been found that semantic analysis of words perceived without awareness activates not only the brain areas associated with sensory analysis but also the brain areas associated with the motor programming of the responses to the words. In addition, words perceived without awareness activate areas of the visual cortex involved in reading and this activation is independent of the physical characteristics of the words (see Dehaene et al. 2001). There are also a number of recent studies in which the critical stimuli have been pictures of human faces with positive (e.g., happy) or negative (e.g., fearful) facial expressions. These studies have focused on exploring whether faces perceived without awareness activate the amygdala, a group of nuclei located in the temporal lobe, which receives information from all modalities and which plays a critical role in processing emotional responses. The evidence from these studies is clear. Both positive and negative faces can lead to significant changes in activation in the amygdala even when the faces are presented under stimulus conditions that are below the threshold for awareness (e.g., Williams et al. 2004).

Variations in the Distribution of Attention

An alternative to controlling awareness by varying the stimulus conditions is to control awareness by varying how observers distribute their attention. For example, observers can be shown visual displays containing stimuli at more than one spatial location and can be instructed to focus their attention at just one location. Under these conditions, observers are generally aware of the stimulus at the attended location, in that they can report this stimulus, but they are generally unaware of the stimuli at the unattended locations, in that they are generally unable to report these stimuli (see also chapter 38).

Some of the most compelling evidence to date that unattended and unnoticed stimuli are perceived without awareness comes from the studies by Mack and Rock (1998) on inattentional blindness. Mack and Rock controlled awareness by instructing observers where to focus their attention. The visual displays used by Mack and Rock had a small centrally located fixation cross which observers viewed for 1500 ms before a large cross was presented briefly (i.e., 200 ms) in one of the four quadrants of the displays. The lengths of the vertical and horizontal arms of the large crosses were not matched and for any given cross, either the vertical or the horizontal arm was longer. The participants were instructed simply to report on each trial which arm of the large cross was longer.

In a typical experiment, each participant was presented with a series of three trials. All three trials consisted of the fixation display followed by a display with a large cross in one quadrant. Importantly, on the third trial in a series, in addition to the large cross, there was also a single word presented in the center of the display at the location of the fixation cross. Following presentation of the third display, the participants first reported whether the horizontal or vertical arm of the large cross was longer. They were then asked whether they had seen anything other than the cross. Surprisingly, approximately 60 percent of the participants claimed that they had not noticed anything other than the cross. Thus, these participants were "blind" to the presentation of the word. However, despite this "blindness" for seeing the word, when the participants who claimed not to see anything other than the cross were presented with five words and asked to select the word that had been presented, many more participants than would be expected on the basis of chance responding actually chose the correct word. Thus, the findings reported by Mack and Rock provide clear evidence that words which observers do not notice because their attention is directed elsewhere are nevertheless perceived without awareness.

In many respects, studies of the perception of unattended and unnoticed stimuli provide a better experimental analog of how stimuli are perceived without awareness in the natural environment than is provided by studies in which awareness is controlled by degrading the stimulus or viewing conditions. Rarely are people confronted by situations where the viewing conditions are so poor that it is impossible to become aware of an object even when attention is focused at the spatial location of the object. In contrast, it is very common in the natural environment for people to be in situations where there are many unattended stimuli outside their immediate focus of attention that are not consciously experienced.

Neurological and Surgical Patients

Studies of neurological patients and surgical patients undergoing general anesthesia provide an alternative approach for exploring preconscious processing. A striking characteristic of a number of neurological syndromes is that even though patients claim at times not to be consciously aware of particular stimuli, their responses can be shown to be influenced by the very stimuli that they claim not be aware of. Likewise, surgical patients undergoing general anesthesia typically claim not to be aware of any information presented during surgery. Nevertheless, these patients may show memory for this information presented during surgery when tested following surgery. Studies of neurological patients and surgical patients undergoing general anesthesia provide information regarding preconscious processing which complements the information obtained in studies in which either the stimulus conditions or the distribution of attention are varied.

Researchers first claimed to have found evidence of memory for events during anesthesia during the early 1960s. These claims were made regarding patients who had been administered what was considered to be adequate general anesthesia and who were thus not supposed to have any memory for events during surgery. Following these claims, there were a number of studies over the next 35 years, based on a variety of experimental procedures (see also Kihlstrom & Cork, chapter 49). The results of these studies showed a confusing pattern of positive and negative findings. For this reason, Merikle and Daneman (1996) conducted a meta-analysis of all relevant studies. The results of the meta-analysis indicated that there is memory for events during anesthesia as long as memory is tested within 24 to 36 hours of surgery. Thus, the results of the meta-analysis support the claim that there is perception without awareness during general anesthesia. However, given that there was no direct measurement of the depth of anesthesia during surgery in any of the studies included in the meta-analysis, it is always possible that there may have been brief episodes of consciousness or awareness during surgery that were undetected by the attending anesthesiologists and were not recalled by the patients following surgery.

Fortunately, there are now at least two studies in which the depth of anesthesia was monitored during surgery, particularly during the time when the critical to-be-remembered stimuli were presented to the patients (Deeprose et al. 2004; Lubke et al. 1999). In both studies, the depth of anesthesia was monitored by the bispectral index (BIS), which is based on real-time analysis of the EEG. The results of both studies lead to the same conclusion. Namely, there is memory for events during anesthesia, at least for some patients, even when there is adequate general anesthesia, as indicated by the BIS. It is still unclear exactly what types of information are perceived without awareness during anesthesia, although it has been suggested that memory for events during anesthesia is primarily perceptual and not conceptual. In any case, it can now be concluded that the results of the studies investigating memory for events during anesthesia provide evidence of preconscious processing even when there is no awareness whatsoever of the external environment.

A defining characteristic of a number of neurological syndromes is that there is a dissociation between the patients' self-reports of their phenomenal awareness and their objective performance. Perhaps the best known example is blindsight, which is found in patients who have damage to their primary visual cortex (see also Weiskrantz, chapter 13). These patients report having no phenomenal awareness of objects viewed in the "blind" area of their visual field. Nevertheless, they can correctly "guess" the shape, orientation, or size of objects at a better than chance level when presented with forced-choice tasks (Weiskrantz 1986). More recently, it has been shown that patients with blindsight can even discriminate between faces with different emotional expressions (de Gelder, Vroomen, & Pourtois 2001). In many ways, the findings from studies of patients with blindsight are reminiscent of the findings reported by researchers in the late nineteenth century showing that observers who experience no phenomenal awareness of stimuli can nevertheless make accurate judgments about those stimuli (e.g., Sidis 1898). Blindsight illustrates that although the primary visual cortex is necessary for visual perception with awareness, there are other pathways in the brain not involving the primary visual cortex that support perception without awareness.

Visual neglect is another neurological syndrome defined by a loss of phenomenal awareness. In contrast to patients with blindsight, the primary visual cortex of patients with visual neglect is typically intact. The most common causes of visual neglect are lesions to the inferior parietal lobe in the right hemisphere. Such lesions lead to deficits in phenomenal awareness for stimuli that appear toward the contralesional (i.e., left) side of space. Patients with visual neglect may be completely unaware of contralesional sights or sounds such that they may only eat food from the right side of a plate and they may omit details from the left side of a picture they are attempting to copy. One way in which visual neglect manifests itself is in situations in which stimuli are presented simultaneously to the left and right visual fields. For example, if patients with lesions in the right parietal lobe are shown a picture of an apple to the left of fixation and a picture of a comb to the right of fixation, most patients will be able to name the comb but few if any of the patients will name the apple.

In contrast to the limited information perceived without awareness by patients with blindsight, patients with visual neglect seem to perceive considerable information regarding stimuli presented toward the contralesional side of space (see Driver & Mattingley 1998). For example, patients can judge whether neglected words or pictures are the same as or different from words or pictures perceived with awareness, and neglected stimuli can influence patients' reactions to stimuli perceived with awareness in the opposite visual field. Even more striking are findings showing that the meanings of neglected stimuli are perceived and can lead to semantic priming. One way to view the differences in preconscious processing revealed by blindsight and neglect patients is to think of blindsight patients as having deficits akin to losses of sensory information, whereas the deficits exhibited by neglect patients are more akin to attentional deficits (see Driver & Vuilleumier 2001). Viewed in this way, it is perhaps not surprising that there is more extensive preconscious processing in patients with visual neglect, who typically have lesions in the right parietal lobe, than in blindsight patients, who typically have damage to the primary visual cortex.

Current Issues

By and large much of the research investigating preconscious processing has been directed at establishing the conditions that lead to preconscious processing. For this reason, there has been considerable emphasis on finding the best way to distinguish preconscious processing from conscious processing. What have been generally absent are discussions of both the characteristics of preconscious processes and the impact of preconscious processes. Now that preconscious processes are firmly established, attention is beginning to be directed toward a number of issues related to the general nature of these processes. Three issues currently attracting attention are (1) the types of information subject to preconscious processing, (2) individual differences in sensitivity to preconscious processes, and (3) the influence of preconscious processes on conscious experience.

An important issue concerns the types of information that are analyzed by preconscious processes, particularly those preconscious processes which do not necessarily lead to conscious experience. If these preconscious processes are only sensitive to relatively low-level stimulus characteristics, then they may play a limited role in human cognition. On the other hand, if these preconscious processes are sensitive to high-level stimulus characteristics such as meaning or semantics, then they may have a considerable impact on the way people experience the world. By and large, there is fairly general agreement that preconscious processes are sensitive to stimulus characteristics such as orientation, color, motion, and even co-variations between objects and events in the environment. In addition, with regard to words, the stimuli favored in so many psychological experiments, there is also generally good agreement that preconscious processes are sensitive to orthographic, phonological, and even lexical information. However, where there is disagreement is in regard to the issue of whether preconscious processes are sensitive to semantic information. The experimental data show both positive and negative findings.

Many of the research studies directed at establishing whether preconscious processes are sensitive to semantic information even when such processing does not lead to conscious awareness have involved assessments of the effects of masked primes on the reactions of participants to target stimuli. In these studies, an initial stimulus (i.e., the prime) is presented and followed by a second stimulus (i.e., the mask) which degrades the prime. The stimulus parameters are set in such a way as to ensure that there is no awareness of the prime. Once the parameters have been set, the effects of primes on the participants' reactions to target stimuli are assessed to establish what types of information in the primes are perceived without awareness.

Both words and numbers have been used as the primes and targets to establish whether preconscious processes are sensitive to semantics or meaning. In the experiments that involve words as the primes and the targets, no evidence has been found that the meanings of words are perceived when there is no awareness of the primes (e.g., Abrams & Greenwald 2000; Kouider & Dupoux 2004). Rather the findings suggest that what appears to be a semantic influence of the primes can actually be attributed to the preconscious analysis of subword fragments of the primes. In contrast, the consistent finding in studies in which numbers have been used as primes and targets is that the abstract concept of magnitude is perceived without awareness (e.g., Naccache & Dehaene 2001; Greenwald et al. 2003). Thus, studies involving numbers, in contrast to studies involving words, have shown consistently that preconscious processes are sensitive to semantic information even when the preconscious processes do not lead to subsequent conscious experiences. It is highly improbable that the perceptual system functions so that preconscious processes are sensitive to the semantic information in numbers but are insensitive to the semantic information in words. Rather, a more probable explanation of the discrepancy between the studies involving words as stimuli and the studies involving numbers as stimuli is that the somewhat different procedures used in the two types of studies led to differences in the experimental contexts which in turn influenced how the participants approached the tasks presented to them.

Differences in the way that participants approach experimental tasks can have important consequences on their sensitivity to preconscious processes. In Marcel's (1983) classic experiments involving masked stimuli, he found that the participants were either "passive" and simply chose the response that "felt right" on each trial, or were "active" and adopted a conscious strategy to guide response selection on each trial. Importantly, Marcel's results indicated that it was only the "passive" participants who showed evidence of being sensitive to graphemic and semantic information in the stimuli. Thus, under conditions where there was no subjective awareness of the stimuli, the "passive" participants showed considerably more sensitivity to preconscious processes than the "active" participants. In addition, preconscious processes provided sufficient information for the "passive" participants to make semantic judgments regarding the masked stimuli.

The basic implications of Marcel's findings have been confirmed by other researchers. In one study, Snodgrass, Shevrin, and Kopka (1993) presented participants with one of four different words (pleasure, fighting, rose, or pain) under conditions of masking. The task for the participants was simply to indicate which word had been presented on each trial. The stimulus conditions were such that a group of participants who were instructed to adopt an *active strategy* and to look carefully for any possible cues as to which word was presented did not show any evidence of perceptual sensitivity to the words. In contrast, another group of participants who were instructed to adopt a *passive strategy* and to say whatever word "popped" into their minds showed some ability to discriminate among the four words. Thus, as with the findings reported by Marcel (1983), Snodgrass and his colleagues found that the participants who adopted a passive strategy exhibited greater perceptual sensitivity to the masked words than the participants who adopted an active strategy.

Recent studies involving visual search also show that strategic factors can be important in determining the effects of preconscious perceptual processes (Smilek, Dixon, & Merikle, forthcoming). Smilek and colleagues asked participants to search for targets embedded among distractors from either the same category or different category. The participants were instructed to search for targets either by *actively* directing their attention to the targets or by *passively* letting the targets just "pop into their minds." The results showed that the passive participants searched more efficiently than the active participants, and it was only the passive participants who were sensitive to the categorical relationship between the targets and distractors. Overall, these findings are completely consistent with the findings reported by Marcel (1983) and Snodgrass, Shevrin, and Kopka (1993). Taken together, they indicate that preconscious perceptual processes are sensitive to many types of stimulus information, including conceptual/semantic information, but that participants may only be influenced by preconscious processes when they are passive and rely on automatic processes.

An important consequence of preconscious perceptual processes is that they can influence how stimuli perceived with awareness are consciously experienced. This function of preconscious processes has been demonstrated in several experiments based on the Müller-Lyer illusion. The Müller-Lyer illusion occurs when horizontal lines of equal length are made to appear unequal in length by the addition of angular lines at each end of the horizontal lines which point either inward to make a horizontal line appear shorter or outward to make a horizontal line appear longer. Moore and Egeth (1997) conducted an experiment based on the Müller-Lyer illusion in which observers judged for three consecutive trials the length of two horizontal lines embedded in a background of randomly placed black and white dots. On the critical fourth trial, the background dots were organized so that they formed inward angular lines on one horizontal line and outward angular lines on the other horizontal line. Not surprisingly, the observers judged the horizontal line with the outward angular lines as being longer. Surprisingly, however, when the observers were asked whether they noticed any pattern in the dots, no observer reported noticing a pattern. Thus, this instance of inattentional blindness (Mack & Rock 1998) shows that how the horizontal lines were consciously experienced was influenced by the background dots even though the observers had no awareness that the dots formed angular lines at the ends of the horizontal lines.

Studies of patients with visual neglect have also shown that preconscious perceptual processes can influence conscious experiences. In one study (Mattingley, Bradshaw, & Bradshaw 1995), patients with left visuospatial neglect were asked to bisect horizontal lines. The patients bisected the lines with a bias toward the right. These findings indicate that the patients were generally unaware of at least a portion of the horizontal lines in the left visual field. However, when Mattingley and colleagues added either outward and inward pointing lines to the *left* end of the lines, the Müller-Lyer illusion was induced in that the lines with the outward pointing lines were bisected more to the right, and the lines with the inward pointing lines were bisected more to the left. Thus, as found by Moore and Egeth (1997) for normal individuals, how the horizontal lines were consciously experienced by patients with visual neglect was influenced by information in the left visual field that they were unaware of perceiving. These findings provide further evidence that preconscious perceptual processes can influence how stimuli are consciously experienced.

Research investigating preconscious processes has expanded considerably in recent years. For this reason, there is every reason to believe that knowledge concerning the characteristics of preconscious processes will increase significantly in the future. In this way, a greater understanding will develop regarding the ways in which preconscious processes have an impact on the way that the world is perceived.

See also 13 The case of blindsight; 38 Consciousness and attention; 41 Implicit and explicit memory and learning; 42 Consciousness of action; 48 Duplex vision: separate cortical pathways for conscious perception and the control of action; 49 Consciousness and anesthesia.

Further Readings

de Gelder, B., de Haan, E., and Heywood, C. (eds.) (2001) *Out of Mind: Varieties of Unconscious Processes*. New York: Oxford University Press.
Dehaene, S. (ed.) (2001) *The Cognitive Neuroscience of Consciousness*. Cambridge, MA: MIT/Elsevier.
Goodale, M. A. and Milner, A. D. (2004) *Sight Unseen: An Exploration of Conscious and Unconscious Vision*. New York: Oxford University Press.
Wilson, T. D. (2002) *Strangers to Ourselves: Discovering the Adaptive Unconscious*. Cambridge, MA: Harvard University Press.

References

Abrams, R. L. and Greenwald, A. G. (2000) Parts outweigh the whole (word) in unconscious analysis of meaning. *Psychological Science* 11, 118–24.
Adams, J. K. (1957) Laboratory studies of behavior without awareness. *Psychological Bulletin* 54, 383–405.
de Gelder, B., Vroomen, J., and Pourtois, G. (2001) Covert affective cognition and affective blindsight. In B. de Gelder, E. H. F. de Haan, and C. A. Heywood (eds.), *Out of Mind: Varieties of Unconscious Processes*, 205–21. New York: Oxford University Press.
Deeprose, C., Andrade, J., Varma, S., Edwards, N. (2004) Unconscious learning during surgery with propofol anaesthesia. *British Journal of Anaesthesia* 79, 171–7.
Dehaene, S., Naccache, L., Cohen, L., Le Bihan, D., Mangin, J.-F., Poline, J.-B., et al. (2001) Cerebral mechanisms of word masking and unconscious repetition priming. *Nature Neuroscience* 4, 752–8.
Driver, J. and Mattingley, J. B. (1998) Parietal neglect and visual awareness. *Nature Neuroscience* 1, 17–22.
Driver, J. and Vuilleumier, P. (2001) Perceptual awareness and its loss in unilateral neglect and extinction. *Cognition* 79, 39–88.
Eriksen, C. W. (1960) Discrimination and learning without awareness: a methodological survey and evaluation. *Psychological Review* 67, 279–300.
Greenwald, A. G., Abrams, R. L., Naccache, L., and Dehaene, S. (2003) Long-term semantic memory versus contextual memory in unconscious number processing. *Journal of Experimental Psychology: Learning, Memory, and Cognition* 29, 235–47.
Holender, D. (1986) Semantic activation without conscious identification in dichotic listening, parafoveal vision, and visual masking: a survey and appraisal. *Behavioral and Brain Sciences* 9, 1–23.
Kouider, S. and Dupoux, E. (2004) Partial awareness creates the "illusion" of subliminal semantic priming. *Psychological Science* 15, 75–81.

Lubke, G. H., Kerssens, C., Phaf, H., and Sebel, P. S. (1999) Dependence of explicit and implicit memory on hypnotic state in trauma patients. *Anesthesiology* 90, 670–80.

Mack, A. and Rock, I. (1998) *Inattentional Blindness*. Cambridge, MA: MIT Press.

Marcel, A. J. (1983) Conscious and unconscious perception: experiments in visual masking and word recognition. *Cognitive Psychology* 15, 197–237.

Mattingley, J. B., Bradshaw, J. L., and Bradshaw, J. A. (1995) The effects of unilateral visuospatial neglect on perception of Müller-Lyer figures. *Perception* 24, 415–33.

Merikle, P. M. and Daneman, M. (1996) Memory for unconsciously perceived events: evidence from anesthetized patients. *Consciousness and Cognition* 5, 525–41.

Merikle, P. M. and Daneman, M. (1998) Psychological investigations of unconscious perception. *Journal of Consciousness Studies* 5, 5–18.

Merikle, P. M., Smilek, D., and Eastwood, J. D. (2001) Perception without awareness: perspectives from cognitive psychology. *Cognition* 79, 115–34.

Miller, J. G. (1942) *Unconsciousness*. New York: Wiley.

Moore, C. M. and Egeth, H. (1997) Perception without attention: evidence of grouping under conditions of inattention. *Journal of Experimental Psychology: Human Perception and Performance* 23, 339–52.

Naccache, L. and Dehaene, S. (2001) Unconscious semantic priming extends to novel unseen stimuli. *Cognition* 80, 215–29.

Reingold, E. M. and Merikle, P. M. (1990) On the inter-relatedness of theory and measurement in the study of unconscious processes. *Mind and Language* 5, 9–28.

Sidis, B. (1898) *The Psychology of Suggestion*. New York: Appleton.

Smilek, D., Dixon, M. J., and Merikle, P. M. (2006) *Brain Research* 1080, 73–90.

Snodgrass, M., Shevrin, H., and Kopka, M. (1993) The mediation of intentional judgments by unconscious perceptions: the influences of task strategy, task preference, word meaning, and motivation. *Consciousness and Cognition* 2, 169–93.

Weiskrantz, L. (1986) *Blindsight: A Case Study and Implications*. New York: Oxford University Press.

Whyte, L. L. (1960) *The Unconscious before Freud*. New York: Basic Books.

Williams, M. A., Morris, A. P., McGlone, F., Abbott, D. F., and Mattingley, J. B. (2004) Amygdala responses in fearful and happy facial expressions under conditions of binocular suppression. *Journal of Neuroscience* 24, 2898–904.

41

Implicit and Explicit Memory and Learning

JOHN F. KIHLSTROM, JENNIFER DORFMAN,
AND LILLIAN PARK

Learning and memory are inextricably intertwined. The capacity for learning presupposes an ability to retain the knowledge acquired through experience, while memory stores the background knowledge against which new learning takes place. During the dark years of radical behaviorism, when the concept of memory was deemed too mentalistic to be a proper subject of scientific study, research on human memory took the form of research on verbal learning (Schwartz & Reisberg 1991; Anderson 2000).

Explicit and Implicit Memory

In the earliest years of scientific psychology, research focused on immediate conscious experience, in the form of sensations and percepts analyzed first by psychophysicists such as Weber and Fechner and then by structuralists such as Wundt and Titchener. Wundt believed that "higher" mental processes were not amenable to experimental study. But Hermann von Ebbinghaus proved him wrong in 1885: by counting repetitions and calculating savings in relearning, Ebbinghaus invented the verbal-learning paradigm that has dominated the scientific study of memory ever since (Tulving & Craik 2000).

Principles of Conscious Recollection

For most of the century following Ebbinghaus, the psychology of memory was concerned with conscious recollection – with the ability to recall or recognize events that had occurred in the past. From this research has emerged a small set of principles that largely govern how human memory operates (Kihlstrom 1996).

- *stage analysis*: memories are analogous to books in a library, or the information contained within them: mental representations of events are encoded as memory traces, which are retained in memory storage and retrieved in the course of ongoing experience, thought, and action.
- *elaboration*: memory for an event is a function of the degree to which that event is related to pre-existing knowledge at the time of encoding.

- *organization*: memory is also a function of the degree to which events are related to each other.
- *time-dependency*: memory fades with time, mostly by virtue of interference among competing memory traces.
- *availability vs. accessibility*: Encoded memories, available in memory storage, may not be accessible when retrieval is attempted.
- *cue-dependency*: the probability of retrieving an event is a function of the informational value of cues provided at the time of retrieval.
- *encoding specificity*: retrieval is most effective when cues present at the time of retrieval match those processed at the time of encoding.
- *schematic processing*: events that are relevant to currently active beliefs, expectations, and attitudes are remembered better than those that are irrelevant; events that are incongruent with these mental schemata are remembered better than those that are congruent.
- *reconstruction*: memory reflects a mix of information contained in the memory trace and knowledge derived from other sources; in the final analysis, memories are beliefs, and remembering an event is more like writing a story from fragmentary notes than reading it from a book.
- *interpersonal*: remembering is an act of interpersonal communication as well as of information retrieval, and so memories are shaped by the social context in which remembering occurs.

Taxonomy of Memory and Knowledge

These principles apply to so-called "long-term" memory (William James called it *secondary memory*). But the domain of memory also includes modality-specific *sensory registers* (e.g., *iconic* and *echoic* memory), and *primary memory* (also known as *short-term or working* memory), which may operate on somewhat different principles. For example, the time-dependency characteristic of forgetting from the sensory registers is produced by decay and displacement rather than interference. Primary memory is sometimes viewed as a separate memory system from secondary memory; in other theories, primary memory is identified with representations stored in long-term memory that are currently in a state of activation. Primary or working memory is closely identified with consciousness.

The knowledge stored in long-term memory comes in two broad forms. *Declarative knowledge* constitutes our fund of factual knowledge, and can be represented by sentence-like propositions. *Procedural knowledge* consists of our cognitive repertoire of rules and skills, and can be represented by "if-then" structures known as productions. Within the domain of declarative knowledge, we can distinguish *episodic* memory, or autobiographical memory for events that have occurred in our personal past, and *semantic* memory, a sort of impersonal mental dictionary. Procedural knowledge can be further classified into motoric and perceptual-cognitive skills. The declarative–procedural distinction has its immediate origins in computer science and artificial intelligence, but can be traced back to Ryle's distinction (in *The Concept of Mind*, 1949) between "knowing that" and "knowing how," and Bergson's assertion (in *Matter and Memory*, 1911) that "the past survives in two forms" – as recollections and as habits. Episodic memory is what most people mean by "memory," as opposed to "knowledge."

Priming Effects in Amnesia and Normal Memory

For most of its history, the scientific study of episodic memory was concerned mostly with conscious recollection, to the extent that it was concerned with consciousness at all, and the notion of unconscious memory was relegated mostly to the Freudian fantasyland. But beginning in the 1960s, research began to suggest that the notion of unconscious memories was valid after all – if not in the Freudian form. Of particular interest were studies of patients with the *amnesic syndrome* associated with bilateral damage to the hippocampus and related structures in the medial temporal lobe, or to the mammillary bodies and related structures in the diencephalon. In 1968, Warrington and Weiskrantz reported an experiment in which amnesic patients were asked to study a list of familiar words. Compared with control subjects, the patients performed very poorly on standard tests of recall and recognition. However, when they were presented with three-letter stems or fragments, and asked simply to complete the cues with the first word that came to mind, amnesics and controls were equally likely to complete the cues with items from the studied list.

This is a *priming effect*, in which the processing of one item influences the processing of another item. In positive priming, the prime facilitates processing of the target; in negative priming, the prime inhibits processing of the target. In this instance, the priming effect indicates that the studied items were encoded in memory, retained in storage, and influenced performance on the completion test. The fact that equivalent levels of priming occurred in neurologically intact subjects, who remembered the priming episode normally, and amnesic patients, who had very poor memory, indicates that priming can be dissociated from conscious recollection. On the basis of such evidence as this, Schacter distinguished between two expressions of episodic memory: explicit and implicit (Schacter 1987). Explicit memory refers to conscious recollection of a past event, as exemplified by performance on recall and recognition tests. By contrast, implicit memory refers to any effect of an event on subsequent experience, thought, or action. Priming is, of course, just such an effect. The dissociation between priming and recall in amnesic patients indicates implicit memory can persist in the absence of explicit memory.

Spared priming in amnesic patients has now been confirmed in a host of studies, and has been extended to a wide variety of other forms of amnesia:

- anterograde and retrograde amnesia occurring as a consequence of electroconvulsive therapy (ECT) for depression;
- anterograde amnesia produced by general anesthesia administered to surgical patients (see also Kihlstrom & Cork, chapter 49);
- anterograde amnesia associated with conscious sedation in outpatient surgery (see also Kihlstrom & Cork, chapter 49);
- memory disorders observed in dementia, including Alzheimer's disease, as well as those encountered in normal aging;
- hypnotic and posthypnotic amnesia following appropriate suggestions to hypnotizable subjects;
- "functional" or "psychogenic" amnesias encountered in genuine cases of dissociative disorder, including dissociative amnesia, dissociative fugue, and the interpersonality amnesia of dissociative identity disorder (also known as multiple personality disorder).

In each of these cases, the memory disorder primarily impairs explicit memory and spares implicit, which is either wholly or relatively intact. It is in this sense that implicit memory persists in the absence of explicit memory. However, implicit memory can be observed in individuals with normal memory functions as well. For example, normal subjects show significant savings in relearning for items that they can neither recall nor recognize. And while elaboration is an important determinant of explicit memory, "depth of processing" has relatively little impact on many priming effects. In nonamnesic individuals implicit memory may be said to be independent of explicit memory, in that priming does not depend on whether the prime is consciously remembered.

The Vocabulary of Implicit Memory

In general, dissociations between explicit and implicit memory come in several forms (Richardson-Klavehn, Gardiner, & Java 1996). In *population dissociations*, a condition like amnesia or aging affects explicit memory, but not implicit memory. In *functional dissociations*, an experimental variable (like depth of processing) affects explicit memory but not implicit memory. Of course, the dissociations can also go the other way: shifting from auditory presentation at time of study to visual presentation at time of test can have a big effect on implicit memory, but relatively little effect on explicit memory. In *single dissociations*, a single variable effects one expression of memory, explicit or implicit, but not the other. In *double dissociations*, a single variable has opposite effects on explicit and implicit memory. Double dissociations are the "Holy Grail" of cognitive neuropsychology, because they provide compelling evidence that two functions, such as explicit and implicit memory, are mediated by separate cognitive modules or brain systems. But they are also exceedingly rare. Many ostensible double dissociations are more like *twin dissociations*, in which one variable affects explicit but not implicit memory, while another variable affects implicit but not explicit memory.

Implicit memory is usually tested with a priming task, but priming comes in a number of different forms. Most research has focused on *repetition priming*, in which the target of the priming test is a recapitulation, in whole or in part, of the prime itself. For example, subjects might study a word like *doctor* and then be asked to complete the stem *doc-* or the fragment *d-c-o-* with the first word that comes to mind, to identify the word *doctor* when presented against a noisy background, or to decide whether the letter string *doctor* is a legal word. But *semantic priming* effects can also be observed when subjects who have studied a word like *doctor* are asked to give free associations to cues like *nurse*, or to generate instances of categories like *occupations*. Repetition priming can be mediated by a *perception-based representation* that is limited to the physical attributes of the prime and its configuration in space and time, but semantic priming requires a *meaning-based* representation that includes information about the semantic and conceptual features of the prime. Semantic priming can be studied with the same tasks normally used to measure repetition priming, such as perceptual identification and lexical decision, provided that the target does not recapitulate the prime.

Explicit and implicit memory are sometimes referred to as "declarative" and "procedural" memory, or "declarative" and "nondeclarative" memory (Squire, Knowlton, & Musen 1993), respectively. The declarative–procedural distinction was initially based on the view that preserved learning in amnesia was limited to procedural knowledge such as cognitive and motor skills, and an interpretation of priming as procedural (*if-then*) in nature. But amnesic patients can acquire new declarative knowledge as well, provided that they do not have to remember the circumstances in which they learned it; and semantic priming is arguably mediated by semantic memory, which is a component of declarative knowledge. While some implicit expressions of memory may be mediated by procedural or nondeclarative knowledge, the declarative–nondeclarative distinction risks confusing the interpretation of explicit memories as representations that can be consciously "declared" with the propositional format in which declarative knowledge is represented.

Similarly, tests of explicit and implicit memory are sometimes referred to as "direct" and "indirect." That is to say, recall tests memory directly, while savings or priming test memory indirectly. It should be understood, though, that the direct–indirect distinction applies to memory tests and not to expressions of memory. In principle, priming could be used to assess consciously accessible memories that the subject declines to report, much as psycho-physiological measures are used in forensic lie-detection. Along the same lines, explicit and implicit memory are sometimes referred to as "intentional" and "incidental" respectively. That is to say, in recall tests subjects are instructed to intentionally remember some past event, while priming occurs incidentally when the subject is performing some non-memory task. The intentional–incidental distinction reminds us that there are two aspects of consciousness relevant to memory: conscious awareness and conscious control (Butler & Berry 2001). A conscious memory might well emerge, unintentionally and inadvertently, in the course of a priming test – a situation that is sometimes referred to as "involuntary explicit memory." Involuntary conscious recollection has been a topic of literary discussion at least since the time of Proust (Salaman 1970), and of scientific investigation since the time of Galton (Crovitz 1970), but it should be distinguished from implicit memories that are inaccessible to conscious recollection in the first place.

In the final analysis, both the "direct–indirect" and "intentional–incidental" dichoto-mies fail to capture the essence of the explicit–implicit distinction – which is that explicit memory is conscious recollection, and implicit memory is unconscious memory, of the past. But if implicit memory is unconscious memory, why not simply call it that? The answer is more likely to be found in sociology than psychology, as those who would make a science of unconscious mental life have sought to avoid the taint of Freudian psychoanalysis. Even without the specter of Freud looming over their shoulders, the topic of consciousness still makes some psychologists nervous (Flanagan 1992). Still, what makes implicit memory interesting is not that implicit tests provide indirect, possibly surreptitious, assessments of what a person remembers; nor that implicit expressions of memory occur involuntar-ily. What makes implicit memory interesting is that it represents the dynamic influence of memory in the absence of conscious recollection.

Theories of Implicit Memory

Based on the "modularity" view popular in cognitive neuroscience, a number of theor-ists have suggested that explicit and implicit memory reflect the performance of separate memory systems in the brain (Schacter & Tulving 1994). For example, Squire has identified explicit memory with a medial temporal-lobe memory system including the hippocampus and related structures (Squire & Zola-Morgan 1991). Damage to this system will impair explicit memory but spare implicit memory, which is mediated by other brain systems, presumably cortical in nature. At the other end, Tulving and Schacter have proposed that repetition priming is mediated by a set of *perceptual representation systems* that store representations of the physical structure of the prime, but not its meaning (Tulving & Schacter 1990). For example, a *visual word form system* associated with the extrastriate cortex mediates visual stem-completion, while an *auditory word-form system* mediates auditory perceptual identification. Semantic priming, in turn, is held to be mediated by a separate semantic memory system.

Another take on the multiple-systems view is provided by Bowers and Marsolek (Bowers & Marsolek 2003). Instead of invoking multiple memory systems, they propose that implicit memory is a byproduct of brain systems that are devoted to perceptual pattern recognition, conceptual processing, and motor behavior, rather than memory per se. On their view, implicit memory is a byproduct of the learning capability of these systems. These systems have memory, in that they are capable of encoding and recognizing information, but they are not memory systems. Although Bowers and Marsolek's approach is based on contemporary theories of object recognition, psycholinguistics, and concept formation, it has its deeper roots in a proposal by Ewald Hering, the nineteenth-century sensory physiologist, that memory is "a universal function of all organized matter" (Hering 1870/1880, p. 63). Hering's ideas, in turn, were promoted by Samuel Butler, author of *Erewhon* (1872) and *The Way of All Flesh* (1903), in a ground-breaking book on *Unconscious Memory* (1880) that actually predated Ebbinghaus. Unconscious memory, on Hering's and Butler's view, may be likened to the "memory" of a paper clip – which, when once bent, is easier to bend again in the same direction. Paper clips do not have memory systems, but they do have a physical structure that allows them to retain traces of stimulation. Bowers and Marsolek do not have much to say about explicit memory, which presumably *is* mediated by a dedicated brain system.

By contrast with the multiple-systems view, other theories hold that explicit and implicit expressions of memory are the products of a single memory system. For example, Mandler's *activation view* argues that priming in all of its forms is mediated by the automatic activation and integration, at the time of encoding, of pre-existing knowledge structures corresponding to the prime; explicit memory, by contrast, requires effortful elaboration to establish new relations among activated structures (Mandler 1980). But activation, integration, and elaboration all take place within a single memory system. Roediger's *transfer-appropriate processing* view (Roediger & McDermott 1993) holds that most implicit memory tasks, such as repetition priming, are "perceptually driven," in that they require access only to surface features of an object; by contrast, explicit memory tasks are "conceptually driven," in that they require access to semantic or contextual information associated with the studied item. In this view, dissociations occur because explicit memory depends on "top-down" or "symbolic" processing, while implicit memory depends on "bottom-up" or "data-driven" processing.

Yet a third single-systems view invokes Jacoby's *process dissociation framework* to explain dissociations between explicit and implicit memory (Jacoby 1991). In this view, explicit memory is largely a product of conscious, controlled, effortful, deliberate processing, while implicit memory is largely a product of unconscious, automatic, effortless, involuntary processing. Jacoby has also introduced a method, the *process dissociation procedure* (PDP), which measures the relative contributions of automatic and controlled processing to any task by pitting them against each other in the "method of opposition" (MOP). A typical result of the PDP is to confirm that the performance of normal subjects on a memory task is mediated by a mix of controlled and automatic processes, while the performance of amnesic patients is largely supported by automatic processes.

Testing the Theories

Each of these views has its strengths and weaknesses, not least because they evolved in different research contexts. Multiple-systems theories are based largely on work with neurological patients, while single-system theories emerged mostly from work on neurologically intact subjects. The multiple-systems views bask in the reflected glory of cognitive neuroscience, but are bedeviled by the temptation to invoke a new memory system to explain every new dissociation revealed by research. The activation view gives a plausible account of priming results, but finds it difficult to explain how activation could persist for days or months – as it is sometimes observed to do. The transfer-appropriate processing view can explain not only dissociations between explicit and implicit memory, but also those that occur between two explicit or two implicit memory tasks (one perceptual, the other conceptual in nature), but has some difficulty explaining dissociations between semantic priming and explicit memory, both of which are, in its terms, conceptually driven. A further question is whether it is appropriate to term explicit memory as conceptually driven in the first place.

The PDP view, for its part, offers a way to reconcile single-system and multiple-system views, on the assumption that automatic and controlled processes are based on separate processing modules that operate on a single memory store. At the very least, it has provided an increasingly popular technique for measuring the contributions of automatic and controlled processes to task performance, and offers a way to reconcile single-system and multiple-system views. However, the mathematics of the PDP requires the troubling assumption that these processes are independent of each other. An alternative view, also consistent with a single-system view of memory, describes automatic processes as embedded in, and thus redundant with, controlled ones. For example, Mandler has proposed that the automatic activation and integration of stored information, which is the basis for implicit memory, precedes the effortful elaboration of these knowledge structures, which is the basis for explicit memory. In such a system, explicit memory entails implicit memory, even if the reverse is not the case.

One area where the various theories make competing predictions is with respect to implicit memory for novel, unfamiliar information. Activation theories would seem to suggest that this is not possible, because there is – by definition – no pre-existing knowledge structure stored in memory to be activated, or modified, by perceptual input. By contrast, the other theories are, at least in principle, open to the acquisition of new information. In fact, there is considerable evidence for priming of novel nonverbal items such as dot patterns and novel objects – though not, apparently, for line drawings of "impossible" objects that cannot exist in three-dimensional space (much like the drawings of the Swiss artist M. C. Escher). Although interpretation of these findings remains somewhat controversial, priming for novel stimuli would seem to be inconsistent with activation/modification views of implicit memory. Instead, they appear to support the multiple-systems view that repetition priming, at least, is the product of perceptual representation systems that encode and preserve structural descriptions of stimulus events. Priming does not occur for impossible objects because the perceptual representation system cannot form a structural description of objects that cannot exist in three-dimensional space.

The situation with respect to priming for verbal materials is more complicated. Early results, which showed priming for words such as *candy* and *number* (which have pre-existing representations in semantic memory) but not for pseudowords like *canber* and *numdy* (which do not), are consistent with the activation view of implicit memory. Bowers found priming for words (e.g., *kite*), nonwords that followed the rules of English orthography (e.g., *kers*) and for illegal nonwords (e.g., *xyks*), again contradicting the activation view. However, as Bowers himself noted, the priming he obtained for illegal nonwords may have been contaminated by explicit memory, which softens the blow somewhat. On the other hand, Dorfman found priming for pseudowords made up of familiar morphemes (e.g., *genvive*) and familiar syllables (e.g., *fasney*), but not for pseudosyllabic pseudowords (e.g., *erktofe*) made up of elements that are neither morphemes nor syllables in English. These results are consistent with the view that priming of novel (and familiar) words results from the activation and integration of pre-existing sublexical components stored in memory. Priming cannot occur where there are no such components to be activated.

The theoretical debate continues back and forth, but theoretical development is hampered by the fact that experimental research on implicit memory is narrowly focused on a single experimental paradigm – namely, repetition priming. It has been estimated that some 80 percent of implicit memory tests are perceptual in nature, involving variants on repetition priming. Viewed in this light, it is not surprising to find theorists proposing that implicit memory is the product of a perceptual representation system, or of perceptually based processing. But if implicit memory includes semantic priming, as well as repetition priming, such theories are too limited to account for the entire phenomenon. Repetition priming may be independent of depth of processing – although a more accurate statement would be that it is only *relatively* independent; but this is unlikely to be the case for semantic priming. Repetition priming may be modality specific – though not *hyperspecific*; but again, this is unlikely to be the case for semantic priming. Research on implicit memory must move beyond repetition priming if we are ever to determine its true nature.

Interactions Between Explicit and Implicit Memory

Owing largely to the hegemony of cognitive neuroscience, the most popular theory of implicit memory remains some version of the multiple-systems view. For example, Schacter and Tulving have proposed that while repetition priming is mediated by a perceptual representation system, semantic priming is mediated by a semantic memory system and spared procedural learning (see "Explicit and Implicit Learning," below) by a procedural memory system (Schacter & Tulving 1994). Even so, claims for a strict separation of these memory systems should not be made too strongly. If these various memory modules were truly independent of each other, we would expect to see neurological cases where explicit memory is spared and implicit memory impaired. The reverse, of course, is what is commonly observed in amnesia. In fact, only one case has been reported in which implicit memory is impaired and explicit memory intact – and that one is uncertain. The patient, known as M. S., who has an extensive scotoma secondary to brain surgery, performed poorly on a visual test of repetition priming, but normally on test of recognition – a reversal of the usual finding in amnesic patients. However, M. S. also showed normal performance on a test of conceptual priming, so it can hardly be said that he lacks implicit memory.

Whatever their underlying basis, the interaction between explicit and implicit memory can also be observed in other ways. Subjects who consciously recognize that the items on a perceptual-identification test come from a previously studied wordlist may develop a mental set that actually enhances their priming performance – which is why researchers in this area take care to assess "test awareness" in their subjects, and why Jacoby's "process dissociation" procedure has become so popular. Amnesic patients are not able to take advantage of explicit memory, of course, but that does not mean that conscious recollection cannot influence priming in other circumstances.

Moreover, there is considerable evidence that subjects can take strategic advantage of implicit memory to enhance their performance on tests of explicit memory. Although free recall epitomizes conscious recollection, both Mandler and Jacoby have argued that recognition judgments can be mediated by either conscious recollection of the test item, or by a feeling of familiarity that might be based on priming. If so, then when implicit memory is spared, subjects can strategically capitalize on the priming-based feeling of familiarity to enhance their performance on recognition tests. We know that, as a rule, recognition is superior to recall in normal subjects and this is also true for neurological patients with the amnesic syndrome, depressed patients receiving ECT, demented patients suffering from Alzheimer's disease, and normal subjects with posthypnotic amnesia. In addition, studies of recollective experience indicate that amnesic recognition is typically accompanied by intuitive feelings of familiarity, rather than full-fledged remembering.

Accordingly, it seems reasonable to suggest that successful recognition in amnesia can be mediated by spared implicit memory. This claim has been vigorously debated by Squire and his colleagues, who insist that priming is inaccessible to conscious awareness, and so cannot serve as a basis for recognition. Despite methodological issues cutting this way and that, studies employing the process-dissociation procedure clearly indicate that amnesic recognition is mediated by a priming-based feeling of familiarity – as theory suggests they might be, and as the subjects themselves say they are. It may be that recollection and familiarity are governed by separate memory systems; but against a further proliferation of memory systems, it may be more parsimonious to conclude that explicit and implicit memory interact after all.

Explicit and Implicit Learning

Traditionally, learning has been defined as a relatively permanent change in behavior that occurs as a result of experience. Early investigators – Pavlov and Thorndike, Watson and Skinner – construed learning as conditioning – the formation of associations between environmental stimuli and an organism's responses to them (Bower & Hilgard 1981; Schwartz & Reisberg 1991). However, the cognitive revolution in psychology has led to a reconstrual of learning as a relatively permanent change in *knowledge* that occurs as a result of experience – declarative and procedural knowledge that the organism will subsequently use for its own purposes in predicting and controlling environmental events. Thus, in classical conditioning the organism forms expectations concerning the likely consequences of events, and in instrumental conditioning the organism forms expectations concerning the likely consequences of its own behaviors. How this knowledge translates into behavior is another matter.

In addition to classical and instrumental conditioning, researchers have studied *perceptual learning*, involving long-lasting changes in perception or perceptual-motor coordination, as in the case of prism adaptation to inverted or distorted images; and *conceptual learning*, by which individuals induce abstract concepts from encounters with specific instances – not to mention language learning, and especially the learning of a second language. Although these forms of learning seem to be mediated by direct experience, Bandura has described *social learning*, also known as vicarious or observational learning, in which the individual gains knowledge by observing other people. Social learning comes in two broad forms: by example, through imitation and modeling; and by precept, through sponsored teaching.

At least in the case of humans (and certainly other primates, probably other mammals, perhaps other vertebrates, and maybe some invertebrates), this cognitive emphasis on individuals acquiring knowledge to help them predict and control events in the world implied that learning was a conscious activity. This is also true of perceptual learning, which occurs more rapidly with active than passive movements of the observer. And its emphasis on the role of observing, modeling, and teaching – not to mention the fact that civilization has created institutions to support these activities – marks social learning, too, as a conscious act of mind. Nevertheless, it is also true that some organisms, such as the sea mollusk *aplysia*, can learn even though they probably do not have enough neurons, much less a cerebral cortex, to support consciousness. Even in humans, who have a capacity for consciousness, it has long been evident that some learning can take place unconsciously (Adams 1957; Razran 1961).

Implicit Learning

The concept of *implicit learning* was introduced into the psychological literature well before that of implicit memory. In a pioneering series of experiments published in 1967, Reber asked subjects to memorize lists of letter strings, each of which had been generated by a Markov-process artificial grammar – a set of rules that specified what letters could appear in the string, and in what order. Over trials, the subjects found it easier to memorize grammatical strings, compared to random strings, indicating that their learning was exploiting the grammatical structure. Moreover, when presented with new strings, subjects were able to distinguish between grammatical and nongrammatical strings at levels significantly better than chance, indicating that they had acquired some knowledge of the grammar. Yet when queried, the subjects were unable to specify the grammatical rule itself. They had learned the grammar, and this knowledge had guided their behavior, but they were not aware that they had learned anything, and they were not aware of what they had learned (Reber 1993).

At roughly the same time, neuropsychologists noticed that, over trials, amnesic patients improved their performance on such tasks as maze learning, pursuit-rotor learning, and mirror-reversed learning. Clearly, then, amnesic patients had the capacity to acquire new skills, but they did not recognize the tasks, nor did they remember the learning experiences; moreover, they seemed to have no conscious awareness of their newly acquired knowledge. Later studies showed that amnesic patients could learn artificial grammars, just as neurologically intact individuals do.

By analogy with memory, we can define explicit learning as a relatively permanent change in knowledge or behavior that is accompanied by conscious awareness of what has been learned. Implicit learning, then, refers to a relatively permanent change in knowledge or behavior in the absence of conscious awareness of what has been learned. Sometimes evidence for implicit learning is taken as evidence for implicit memory, but implicit memory is more narrowly restricted to the learning *episode* itself, while implicit learning covers the knowledge acquired in that episode. In a famous case published in 1911, Claparede described an amnesic patient who forgot an episode in which he pricked her hand with a pin while greeting her, but who was consciously aware that "Sometimes people hide pins in their hands" (Kihlstrom 1995). This patient was conscious of what she had learned, but displayed *source amnesia* (also known as cryptomnesia, or unconscious plagiarism), a concept more closely related to implicit memory. Implicit learning goes beyond the formation of simple associations, as in classical or instrumental conditioning, and involves the acquisition of knowledge of some complexity, at some level of abstraction.

Varieties of Implicit Learning

Implicit learning has been studied in a wide variety of experimental paradigms, in addition to artificial grammars and motor learning (for comprehensive reviews, see Berry & Dienes 1993; Seger 1994; Stadler & Frensch 1998; Frensch & Runger 2003):

- Concepts: In a paradigm somewhat similar to artificial grammar learning, subjects learn to identify instances of novel concepts, such as patterns of dots that vary around a prototype, without being able to describe the defining or characteristic features of the concepts themselves.
- Covariation detection: subjects learn the association between two features, such as hair length and personality, but cannot identify the basis for their predictions.
- Sequence learning: subjects learn the sequence in which certain stimuli will occur – for example, the appearance of a target in a particular location on a computer screen – without being able to specify the sequence itself.
- Dynamic systems: subjects learn to control the output of a complex system by manipulating an input variable, without being able to specify the relationship between the two.

In each of these cases, subjects demonstrate, by performance measures such as accuracy or response latency in judgment, or prediction or control of behavior, that they have acquired knowledge from experience; yet they are unable to provide an accurate account of the methods by which they achieve these results. They have learned something new, but they do not know what they know.

What is Learned in Implicit Learning?

Observations of preserved learning capacity in amnesic patients led Cohen and Squire to propose that amnesia impaired declarative memory ("knowing *that*"), but spared procedural memory ("knowing how"; Cohen & Squire 1980). Perceptual and motor skills, such as covariation detection, sequence learning, and motor learning, can certainly be represented as systems of *if-then* productions, but it is not at all clear that all forms of implicit learning are procedural in nature. For example, there is evidence that amnesic patients can acquire new conceptual knowledge in amnesia – knowledge that, ordinarily, would be represented in the propositional format characteristic of declarative memory.

In this respect, artificial grammar learning is an interesting case. The structure of a Markov-process finite-state grammar lends itself easily to translation into a production system: *If* the first letter is a P, *then* the next letter must be a T or a V; *If* the first letter is a T, *then* the next letter must be an S or an X; and so on. However, subjects memorizing grammatical strings might simply abstract what a "prototypical" grammatical string looks like. When making grammaticality judgments, subjects could then compare test items to this stored prototype – or, perhaps, to the specific instances stored in memory during the memorization phase of the experiment. In either case, the unconscious knowledge acquired through implicit learning would more closely resemble declarative than procedural knowledge – yet another reason not to use "declarative" instead of "explicit" to label conscious memory.

In principle, both prototypes and rule systems are abstract knowledge representations that go beyond the specific instances encountered in the study set. Accordingly, an important question concerns the degree to which implicit learning is generalizable beyond the specific. That is, can subjects apply a grammar learned from strings of Ps, Vs, and Ts to test strings composed of Ls, Bs, and Ys? Reber reported that this was the case, although subsequent research has often found that transfer is substantially degraded. Studies of transfer in other domains have also yielded mixed results. Of course, the degree of transfer will depend on the degree of initial learning. In the artificial grammar experiments, classification performance typically ranges between 60 and 80 percent correct, with the more frequent outcomes at the lower end of this range. Viewed against a base rate of 50 percent correct, a performance at 65 percent may be statistically significant, but may not leave a lot of room to show incomplete transfer.

Is Implicit Learning Really Unconscious?

Implicit learning is distinct from mere *incidental learning*, where knowledge is acquired in the absence of instructions or intention to learn, but the person is conscious of what he or she has learned (Eysenck 1982). The critical feature of implicit learning is that it is unconscious, in the sense that the subjects are unaware of what they have learned. Documenting dissociations between explicit and implicit learning, then, is a somewhat tricky business. Many studies do not give a great deal of detail about the methods by which subjects' conscious knowledge was assessed, but it is probably not enough merely to ask subjects in the artificial-grammar experiments to describe the rule that governs the letter strings, and count them as "unconscious" when they fail to do so. In the first place, unless the test stimuli are very carefully constructed, even partial awareness of the rule – that the first letter must be either a *P* or a *T*, for example, may be enough to permit subjects to discriminate between grammatical and ungrammatical strings at better than chance levels. Although investigators of explicit and implicit memory have developed rigorous standards for matching explicit and implicit tasks, similar standards are generally lacking in studies of implicit learning.

The argument that implicit learning is really unconscious is sometimes bolstered by the fact that amnesic patients show preserved implicit learning. Of course, amnesics also forget the learning *episode* as well, confusing implicit learning with implicit memory. In this regard, it is somewhat disconcerting to note that subjects can show significant implicit "learning" even in the absence of any learning experience! That is to say, in some experimental procedures involving classification performance, it is possible for subjects to intuit the structure of the target category from test instances, even when they were denied an opportunity to learn the category during a prior study phase.

However, implicit learning is not always, or entirely, spared in amnesic patients. For example, amnesics show normal levels of perceptual learning in a visual search task, but impaired learning when contextual cues are added to the procedure. Even intact implicit learning by amnesic patients does not mean that explicit and implicit learning must be mediated by different brain systems. Dissociations between recognition and concept learning can be simulated in a computational model of exemplar memory that has only one system for storing memory, with different thresholds for recognition and classification.

It is sometimes claimed that implicit learning, precisely because it is automatic and unconscious, is a very powerful (as well as more primitive) form of learning – more powerful than conscious forms of learning that emerged more recently in evolutionary history (Reber 1993). While it does seem amazing that subjects can pick up knowledge of something as complex as an artificial grammar or a dynamic system automatically, and apply it unconsciously, claims for the superiority of unconscious processing sometimes seem to reflect a Romantic notion of the unconscious that goes back to von Hartmann (Hartmann 1868/1931, p. 40), who wrote that the unconscious "can really outdo all the performances of conscious reason." Unfortunately, enthusiasts of implicit learning have not always compared implicit learning to conscious, deliberate knowledge acquisition. How well would subjects perform if we actually showed them the finite-state grammar, or if we gave them feedback about their classification performance? What if we simply told subjects the sequence of quadrants in which the target would appear?

The Implicit and the Unconscious

Together with the concept of automaticity, research on implicit learning and memory constituted psychology's first steps toward a revival of interest in unconscious mental life (Kihlstrom 1987). Although the psychological unconscious suffered much in the twentieth century from taint by Freudian psychoanalysis the concepts and methods employed to study implicit learning and memory have now been extended to other domains, such as perception and even thinking – and beyond cognition to emotion and motivation (Kihlstrom 1999). In this way, the study of implicit learning and memory offers a new, non-Freudian perspective on unconscious mental life – and, in turn, on consciousness itself.

See also 38 Attention and consciousness; 40 Preconscious processing; 49 Consciousness and anesthesia.

Further Readings

Anderson, J. R. (2000) *Learning and Memory: An Integrated Approach*, 2nd edn. New York: Wiley.

Bower, G. H. and Hilgard, E. R. (1981) *Theories of Learning*, 5th edn. Englewood Cliffs, NJ: Prentice Hall.

McConkey, J. (ed.) (1996) *The Anatomy of Memory: An Anthology*. Oxford: Oxford University Press.

Tulving, E. and Craik, F. I. M. (eds.) (2000) *Oxford Handbook of Memory*. Oxford: Oxford University Press.

References

Adams, J. K. (1957) Laboratory studies of behavior without awareness. *Psychological Bulletin* 54, 383–405.

Anderson, J. R. (2000) *Learning and Memory: An Integrated Approach*, 2nd edn. New York: John Wiley and Sons.

Berry, D. C. and Dienes, Z. (1993) *Implicit Learning: Theoretical and Empirical Issues*. Hove: Erlbaum.

Bower, G. H. and Hilgard, E. R. (1981) *Theories of Learning*, 5th edn. Englewood Cliffs, NJ: Prentice Hall.

Bowers, J. S. and Marsolek, C. J. (eds.). (2003) *Rethinking Implicit Memory*. Oxford: Oxford University Press.

Butler, L. T. and Berry, D. C. (2001) Implicit memory: intention and awareness revisited. *Trends in Cognitive Sciences* 5, 192–7.

Cohen, N. J. and Squire, L. R. (1980) Preserved learning and retention of pattern analyzing skill in amnesia: dissociation of knowing how and knowing that. *Science* 210, 207–10.

Crovitz, H. F. (1970) *Galton's Walk: Methods for the Analysis of Thinking, Intelligence and Creativity*. New York: Harper and Row.

Eysenck, M. W. (1982) Incidental learning and orienting tasks. In C. R. Puff (ed.), *Handbook of Research Methods in Human Memory and Cognition*, 197–238. New York: Academic.

Flanagan, O. (1992) *Consciousness Reconsidered*. Cambridge, MA: MIT Press.

Frensch, P. A. and Runger, D. (2003) Implicit learning. *Current Directions in Psychological Science* 12: 1, 13–17.

Hartmann, E. V. (1868/1931) *Philosophy of the Unconscious: Speculative Results according to the Inductive Method of Physical Science*. London: Routledge and Kegan Paul.

Hering, E. (1870/1880) On memory. In S. Butler (ed.), *Unconscious Memory* (new edn., 1910), 63–86. London: Fifield.

Jacoby, L. L. (1991) A process dissociaton framework: separating automatic from intentional uses of memory. *Journal of Memory and Language* 30, 513–41.

Kihlstrom, J. F. (1987) The cognitive unconscious. *Science* 237: 4821, 1445–52.

Kihlstrom, J. F. (1995) Memory and consciousness: an appreciation of Claparede and *Recognition et Moïeté. Consciousness and Cognition: An International Journal* 4: 4, 379–86.

Kihlstrom, J. F. (1996) Memory research: the convergence of theory and practice. In D. Hermann, C. McEvoy, C. Hertzog, P. Hertel, and M. K. Johnson (eds.), *Basic and Applied Memory Research: Theory in* Context, vol. 1, 5–25. Mahwah, NJ: Erlbaum.

Kihlstrom, J. F. (1999) Conscious and unconscious cognition. In R. J. Sternberg (ed.), *The Nature of Cognition*, 173–204. Cambridge, MA: MIT Press.

Mandler, G. (1980) Recognizing: the judgment of previous occurrence. *Psychological Review* 87: 3, 252–71.

Razran, G. (1961) The observable unconscious and the inferable conscious in current Soviet psychophysiology: interoceptive conditioning, semantic conditioning, and the orienting reflex. *Psychological Review* 68, 81–147.

Reber, A. S. (1993) *Implicit Learning and Tacit Knowledge: An Essay on the Cognitive Unconscious*. Oxford: Oxford University Press.

Richardson-Klavehn, A., Gardiner, J. M., and Java, R. I. (1996) Memory: task dissociations, process dissociations, and dissociations of consciousness. In G. Underwood (ed.), *Implicit Cognition*, 85–158. Oxford: Oxford University Press.

Roediger, H. L. and McDermott, K. B. (1993) Implicit memory in normal human subjects. In F. Boller and J. Grafman (eds.), *Handbook of Neuropsychology*, 63–131. Amsterdam: Elsevier Science Publishers.

Salaman, E. (1970) *A Collection of Moments: A Study of Involuntary Memories*. London: Longman.

Schacter, D. L. (1987) Implicit memory: history and current status. *Journal of Experimental Psychology: Learning, Memory, and Cognition* 13, 501–18.

Schacter, D. L. and Tulving, E. (eds.) (1994) *Memory Systems*. Cambridge, MA: MIT Press.

Schwartz, B. and Reisberg, D. (1991) *Learning and Memory*, 1st edn. New York: Norton.

Seger, C. A. (1994) Implicit learning. *Psychological Bulletin* 115, 163–96.

Squire, L. R. and Zola-Morgan, S. (1991) The medial temporal lobe memory system. *Science* 253, 1380–6.

Squire, L. R., Knowlton, B., and Musen, G. (1993) The structure and organization of memory. *Annual Review of Psychology* 44, 453–95.

Stadler, M. A. and Frensch, P. A. (eds.) (1998) *Handbook of Implicit Learning*. Thousand Oaks, CA: Sage.

Tulving, E. and Craik, F. I. M. (eds.) (2000) *The Oxford Handbook of Memory*. New York: Oxford University Press.

Tulving, E. and Schacter, D. L. (1990) Priming and human memory systems. *Science* 247: 4940, 301–6.

42

Consciousness of Action

MARC JEANNEROD

Introduction

The most commonly studied aspects of consciousness relate to awareness of external reality: they deal with perceptual questions such as "What is it?" and "Where is it?" that the self has to resolve about objects in its environment. At variance with these studies, this chapter deals with a rather poorly explored aspect, consciousness of action. Yet, this is a critical aspect because action, as an internally generated event, relates to the productions of the self and, for this reason, is closely connected to self-consciousness.

The definition of an action is a problem in itself. At the physiological level, an action is defined as a set of muscular contractions and joint rotations executed in fulfillment of a specific goal. Actions, however, often involve several steps: the "simple" action of reaching for a glass, for instance, can be part of the more "complex" action of drinking, itself part of the still more complex action of attending a dinner. Philosophers tend to draw a distinction between such complex actions, characterized by long-term goals and which unfold over time, and their elementary constituents (the physiologist's simple actions), characterized by short-term goals and which are primarily oriented toward objects. According to Searle (1983) a complex action would rely on what he calls a "prior intention," whereas simple actions would rely on more limited motor intentions, what Searle calls "intentions in action": thus, given the prior intention to drink, one forms the motor intention to grasp the glass.

In this chapter, we will mostly concentrate on the simple type of actions. One reason for this choice is that such simple goal-directed actions are currently used in the behavioral experiments where the issue of consciousness of action has been tested. In fact, these experiments will reveal that simple actions such as reaching for a target or moving a lever, far from being incomplete or simplified forms of action, can provide considerable insight into the most complex processes of action generation. The second, and probably more important, reason for concentrating on simple actions is that, better than complex actions, they can easily be imagined or mentally simulated. This striking ability for a subject to mentally simulate performing an action prompts us to complete our above definition. This definition should not be limited to the overt, executed, aspects of the action: it should now include its covert aspects, those which correspond to the internal state that precedes any behavioral manifestation. By this definition, the two aspects, covert and overt, of an action bear a close relationship with each other, such that they are parts of a single continuum.

Although an overt action necessarily involves a covert counterpart, a covert action does not necessarily involve an overt counterpart, for example if the represented action is not executed (Jeannerod 1994).

Given this definition of an action, consciousness of action can be examined at several different levels. One level is that of action recognition. It can be studied by examining to what extent a subject is aware of his/her own action, and is able to make conscious judgments about the content of that action. Another level is that of action attribution, which can be studied by examining how an action can be attributed to its proper agent or, in other words, how a subject can make a conscious judgment about who is the agent of that action (an agency judgment). The first of these levels raises the issue of the duality of the modes of generation of action, whether it is executed automatically or consciously controlled. The second level raises the issue of the differentiation between the self and other selves and its relation to self-consciousness.

Cues for Action Recognition

Automatic vs. controlled actions

Most of our actions directed at external objects are prepared and executed automatically. Once started, they are performed accurately and rapidly (within less than one second). The brevity of execution time leaves little room for top-down control of execution itself. Rather, it suggests that these object-oriented actions are organized, or represented, prior to execution. During the action of grasping an object, for example, the changes in finger position appropriate for making a stable grasp of the object occur during the reaching component that transports the hand at the object location, that is, far ahead of contact with the object. The representation that accounts for such anticipatory adjustments must therefore encode those properties of the object that are relevant to potential interactions with the agent, according to his intentions or needs: object's shape and size are relevant to grip formation (maximum grip size, number of fingers involved), its texture and estimated weight are relevant to anticipatory computation of grip and load forces, etc.

The term *pragmatic representation* has been proposed (see Jeannerod 1997) for qualifying this mode of representing objects as goals for action. The most striking characteristic of a pragmatic representation is its implicit functioning and, correlatively, its nonconscious nature. It opposes another type of representation, not directly related to action (*the semantic representation*) whereby the same objects can be processed for identification, naming, etc. This distinction stresses the fact that objects are multiply represented, according to the task in which they are involved. For the purpose of this chapter, which is to discuss the degree of consciousness attached to different forms of action, we have to examine the reasons why pragmatic processing of object related actions turns out to be nonconscious.

One possible hypothesis for explaining the automaticity of object-oriented actions is that these actions are nonconscious because this is a prerequisite for their accuracy. The hypothesis can be decomposed in the following way. First, one must assume that the representation coding for a goal directed movement has a short life span. In fact, it should not exceed the duration of the movement itself, so that the representation of that goal can be erased before another segment of the action starts. Second, one must also assume that consciousness is a slow process, and that the above temporal constraint does not leave enough time for consciousness to appear. Experimental data support this view: if a target briskly changes its location immediately prior to a pointing movement toward that target (e.g., during the saccadic eye movement that precedes the pointing movement), subjects usually remain unaware of the target displacement (they see only one, stationary, target); yet, they correctly point at the final target location (e.g., Bridgeman, Kirch, & Sperling 1981). Goodale, Pélisson, and Prablanc (1986) reported a pointing experiment where the target occasionally made jumps of several degrees, unnoticed by the subjects. They found that the subjects were nonetheless able to adjust the trajectory of their moving hand to the target position. Interestingly, no additional time was needed for producing the correction, and no secondary movement was observed, suggesting that the visual signals related to the target shift were used without delay for adjusting the trajectory.

According to this view, generating a motor response to a stimulus and building a perceptual experience of that same stimulus would activate different mechanisms with different time constants. This point was specifically addressed by Castiello, Paulignan, and Jeannerod (1991) in an experiment where an object was briskly displaced at the onset of the reach and grasp movement toward that object. They measured both the time to re-orient the movement in the direction of the new object location, and the time at which the subject perceived the change in object location. They found that the change in movement direction occurred very shortly (ca. 100 ms) after the object displacement. In contrast, the subject's report of that displacement was delayed by up to 350 ms. This result indicates that the change in movement direction was generated automatically and was not based on a consciously generated correction.

Indeed, it is common experience that goal-directed movements executed under conscious control are usually slow and inaccurate, for example during the first attempts at learning a new skill. This effect can be shown experimentally by delaying the onset of a goal-directed movement by only a few seconds after the presentation of the stimulus: this delay results in a severe degradation of the accuracy of the movement (Jakobson & Goodale 1991). In this condition, according to the above hypothesis, it's likely that the representation of the movement rapidly deteriorates and the fast automatic mechanism cannot operate.

Lack of awareness of automatic actions

The next question is: to what extent do automatically generated actions remain outside the conscious experience of the agent? This question can be addressed experimentally by placing a subject in a situation where what he/she sees or feels from his/her action does not correspond to what he/she actually does. Such a dissociation of an action and its sensory consequences produces a conflict between the normally congruent signals (e.g., visual, proprioceptive, central motor commands) which are generated during execution of that action. Since its initial version (Nielsen 1963), this dissociation paradigm has greatly contributed to our knowledge of the mechanisms of action recognition.

In one of the versions of this paradigm, Fourneret and Jeannerod (1998) instructed subjects to draw straight lines between a starting position and a target, using a stylus on a digital tablet. The output of the stylus and the target were displayed on a computer screen. The subjects saw the computer screen in a mirror placed so as to hide their hand. On some trials, the line seen in the mirror was made by an electronic device to deviate from the line actually drawn by the subject. Thus, in order to reach the target, the subject had to deviate his/her movement in the direction opposite to that of the line seen in the mirror.

At the end of each trial, the subject was asked to indicate verbally in which direction he thought his hand had actually moved. The results were twofold: first, the subjects were consistently able to trace lines that reached the target, that is, they accurately corrected for the deviation. Second, they gave verbal responses indicating that they thought their hand had moved in the direction of the target, hence ignoring the actual movements they had performed. This latter result shows that normal subjects were unable to consciously monitor the discordance between the different signals generated by their own movements and that the mechanism correcting for the deviation was entirely automatic. When asked to make a judgment about their motor performance, subjects falsely attributed the movement of the line to their hand. In other words, they tended to adhere to the visible aspect of their performance, and to ignore the way it has been achieved. In the Fourneret and Jeannerod experiment, the deviation of the line was limited to 10°, a deviation that remained compatible with the mechanism for automatic correction. What would happen if a larger deviation were introduced, such that the target could not be reached? Slachevsky et al. (2001), using the same apparatus, introduced deviations of increasing amplitude up to more than 40°. They found that, as movement accuracy progressively deteriorated, subjects became aware of the deviation at an average value of 14°. Beyond this point, they were able to report that the movement of their hand erred in a direction different from that seen on the screen.

The fact that the degree of awareness of a dissociation between an action and its sensory consequences increases with the magnitude of the dissociation was recently confirmed by Knoblich and Kircher (2004). In their experiment, the subjects had to draw circles on a writing pad at a certain rate. As in the previous experiments, subjects saw on a computer screen an image of their movement, represented by a moving dot. The velocity of the moving dot could be either the same as that of the subject's movement, or it could be unexpectedly accelerated by a variable factor of up to 80 percent. In order to compensate for the change in velocity and to keep the dot moving in a circle, as requested by the instruction, subjects had to decrease the velocity of their hand movement by a corresponding amount. Subjects were instructed to indicate any perceived change in velocity of the moving dot by lifting their pen. The results showed that the subjects failed to detect the smaller changes in velocity; for example, they could detect only half the changes when the velocity was increased by 40 percent, whereas the detection rate increased for faster velocity changes. Yet, subjects were found to be able to compensate for all changes in velocity, including those that they did not consciously detect. Knoblich and Kircher (2004) make the interesting remark that the signal for conscious detection is processed in the same way as any sensory signal, that is, it follows the classical psychophysical function relating sensory magnitude to stimulus magnitude. Yet, in their experiment, as well as in the Fourneret and Jeannerod (1998) experiment, the signal was not sensory in nature: instead, it was generated by a system that integrates visual and motor information and is sensitive to the discrepancy between these internal cues.

A neurophysiological model for action recognition

The system for action recognition has been described using a simple feedforward model. Roughly speaking, such a model includes a representation of the goal of the forthcoming movement (the desired state), which can be used as a reference for completion of the movement, and which generates output signals for executing it. During execution, the reafferent signals (i.e., the signals arising as a consequence of the movement itself) are checked against the desired state. The goal of the desired action must be kept in memory for a sufficient duration to allow the comparison to operate. If the comparison reveals a mismatch with respect to the desired state, an immediate correction may be generated. If, on the other hand, no mismatch occurs and the desired state is reached, the memory can be erased. The model offers the possibility that the comparison process could also take place ahead of execution itself: a representation of the anticipated desired state as it would occur if it were executed and of the reafferences that it would generate is built and matched with the initial internal model. If this comparison does not anticipate any mismatch, then the system would proceed to the next step. This type of model (e.g., von Holst 1954; Jeannerod 1995; Wolpert, Ghahramani, & Jordan 1995) may account for the distinction between self-produced and externally produced changes in the external world. According to these authors, if perceived changes were correlated with self-generated output signals, they were registered as consequences of one's own action. If not, by contrast, they were registered as originating from an external source. The correlation between efferent signals and the resultant incoming signals is thus an unambiguous feature of self-generated changes.

This model of the control of action can be directly applied to the problem of self-recognition. If one assumes that the recognition of a self-produced action is based on the concordance between a desired (or intended) action and its sensory consequences, then this hypothesis can be tested experimentally. Haggard, Clark, and Kalogeras (2002), using a paradigm initiated by Libet et al. (1983), instructed subjects to make a simple voluntary movement (a key press) at a time of their choice. The action of pressing the key caused an auditory signal to appear after a fixed delay of 250 ms. In separate sessions, the subjects were asked, either to report the position of a clock hand at the time they thought they had pressed the key, or at the time where they heard the auditory signal. Haggard, Clark, and Kalogeras found that the time interval between the two estimated events was shorter than what it should be, that is, 250 ms. Subjects tended to perceive their key press occurring later, and the auditory signal occurring earlier, than was actually the case. This shrinkage of perceived time between the two events did not happen in a control situation where the finger movement was not voluntary, but was produced by a magnetically induced stimulation of motor cortex. The authors conclude that intentional action binds together the conscious representation of the action and its sensory consequences. This binding effect might contribute to self-attributing one's own actions.

A further step in identifying the mechanism of action recognition is to compare brain activity during the processing of externally produced stimuli and stimuli resulting from self-produced movements. Blakemore, Frith and Wolpert (1999), using PET, found that the presentation of externally produced tones resulted in an activity in the right temporal lobe greater than when the tones were the consequence of self-produced movements. This result suggests that, in the self-produced condition, the sensory signals reaching the recipient cortical area in the temporal lobe are modulated by the central command signals originating from the volitional system. Another PET experiment (Fink et al. 1999) explored the effect of a conflict between finger movements executed by a subject and the visual feedback given to the subject about his movements. When the executed finger movements no longer correlated with the seen ones, an increased activity was observed in the posterior parietal cortex (areas 40 and 7) bilaterally. Activation of dorsolateral prefrontal cortex on both sides was also found.

A new experiment using a similar paradigm was undertaken by Farrer et al. (2003). In this study, it was conjectured that processes underlying the sense of agency or the consciousness of action should not be all or none states, but should rather be based on continuous monitoring of the different action-related signals, from sensory (kinesthetic, visual) and central (motor command) origin. To test this hypothesis, Farrer et al. devised an experimental situation where the visual feedback provided to the subjects about their own movements could be either congruent with these movements or distorted to a variable degree. The subjects were instructed to continuously move a joystick with their right hand. The hand and the joystick were hidden from subjects' view. Instead, the subjects saw the electronically reconstructed image of a hand holding a joystick appearing at the precise location of their own hand. When the subject moved, the electronic hand also moved by the same amount and in the same direction: subjects rapidly became acquainted with this situation and felt the movements of the electronic hand as their own. Distortions were introduced in this system, such that the movements seen by the subjects could be rotated with respect to those they actually performed. A gradual rotation was produced by using a 25° rotation, a 50° rotation and finally a situation where the movements appearing on the screen had no relation to those of the subjects (they were actually produced by an experimenter). Thus, in the condition with no distortion, the subjects were likely to feel in full control of their own movements, whereas in the maximally distorted condition, they were likely to feel that they were not in control, but rather being overridden by the movements of another agent. Subjects were instructed to concentrate on their own feelings of whether they felt in control of the movements they saw.

The most interesting result, however, was an activation at the level of the inferior parietal lobule Introducing a discordance between executed movements and the visual reafference from these movements produced an activation in several brain areas: the rostral part of the dorsal premotor cortex, the pre-SMA, and the right anterior cingulate gyrus were involved. The most interesting result, however, was an activation at the level of the inferior parietal lobule on the right side. A decreasing feeling of control of one's own action due to larger and larger degrees of distortion was associated with a proportional increase in activity of this area. The most likely interpretation of this result is that the mismatch between normally congruent sets of movement related signals required an increased level of processing of these signals, which was reflected in an increase in metabolic activity.

The role of the right inferior parietal lobule, which is demonstrated by the above experiments (Fink et al. 1999; Farrer et al. 2003) is consistent with the effects of lesions in this area. Patients suffering from such lesions frequently deny ownership of the left side of their body. They may even report delusions about their left body half by contending that it belongs to another person despite contradictory evidence from touch or sight (e.g., Daprati et al. 2000). Conversely, a transient hyperactivity of a similar area of the parietal lobe (during epileptic fits for example) may produce impressions of an alien phantom limb (see Spence et al. 1997). Taken together, these observations stress the role of the parietal lobe in integrating available signals for building representations that are essential for self-recognition. Indeed, parietal lesioned patients, when faced with ambiguous situations such as those described above, fail to discriminate their own actions from actions performed by an experimenter (Sirigu et al. 1999).

The problem raised by these results is to determine how the modulation of activity for different degrees of discordance between an intended and an executed action, mainly in the posterior parietal cortex and in the dorsolateral prefrontal cortex, can be at the origin of the feelings of being in control of an action and attributing it to oneself. The action monitoring model, although it does not provides a direct answer to this question, suggests that the sense of agency and self-attribution arise from the comparison of the peripheral signals produced by the subject's motor activity with the internal model (or the representation) of the action.

What Is Consciously Represented in Actions?

We now have to consider the difference between the neural content of motor representations, as it is revealed by analyzing the action itself, and its conceptual content, which can be consciously monitored and manipulated. Indeed, the content of the conscious level of an action should not include the complete set of details of what has been actually performed and how it has been performed. Introspectively, an agent seems to only have access to the general context of the action, its ultimate goal, its consequences and the possible alternatives to it, and its author. In this section, we will analyze the main aspects of the representation of an action in an attempt to determine those that can be consciously accessed. For the sake of clarity, we will make a distinction between the movements that compose the action, the goal toward which it is directed, and the agent who performs it.

Reaching nonconsciously for conscious goals

The movements that compose an action do not simply reflect the interaction of the self with the external world. They pertain to central mechanisms that constitute the action representation. This assumption, which is supported by the above experimental evidence, appears in contradiction with other influential theories of action generation, notably Gibson's ecological theory (Gibson 1979). Here, we report further evidence using a paradigm that has been extensively tested over the past 10 or 15 years, that of motor imagery. This paradigm, uncontaminated by the execution of an action and its consequences on the external world, can be regarded as giving privileged access to the content of the representational stages of actions. Yet, we will provide evidence that action representations, as studied through motor imagery, follow the same optimization rules and obey the same biomechanical constraints as actual actions

In order to do this, we have to concentrate for a moment on mental chronometry, which is still widely used in the study of mental images. Mental chronometry is based on subjects' responses in situations designed to probe their processing of external or internal events. Thus, the time to give a response is thought to reflect the existence and the duration of the covert mental processes which contribute to the response generation. In the case of mental visual imagery, response time has been shown to reveal the implicit, nonconscious, processing used to reach a conscious response. In the classical example of comparing two visual 3-D shapes presented at different orientations, the time to give the conscious response to the question of whether the two shapes are same or different, is a function of the degree of rotation, hence revealing a likely nonconscious process of mental "rotation" used by the subject to match the two shapes upon one another (Shepard & Metzler 1971). A similar separation between conscious and nonconscious processing is found in mental motor imagery. Consider, for example, the task of mentally simulating the action of alternatively hitting two targets. The rate of hitting is paced by a metronome, beating at an increasing frequency. The subject is instructed to warn the experimenter whenever he or she feels unable to keep mentally hitting the targets as the metronome frequency increases. Sirigu et al. (1996) found that the critical frequency at which subjects failed to hit the imaginary targets was determined by the difficulty of the task; that is, the subjects could not follow high metronome rates when instructed to mentally hit small targets or targets placed far away from each other. This is exactly what happens when subjects execute the action of hitting real targets, as predicted by Fitts's law (Fitts 1954). In the mental task, all that the subjects (consciously)

knew is that, when metronome frequency increased, they experienced an increasing difficulty to imagine themselves hitting the targets. But they were unaware of the fact that their
responses followed the same regularity as if they were actually hitting real targets.

Another illustrative example of the existence, in motor imagery, of an implicit content
distinct from the explicit content is provided by experiments involving the recognition of
body parts, like the hand. In one of these experiments, subjects had to judge whether two
drawings of a hand represented hands of the same side (right or left) or not. One hand was
presented in its canonical orientation, the other was presented with a variable degree of
rotation with respect to the first. Just as in the above comparison of two neutral 3-D shapes,
the time to give the response reflected the degree of mental rotation needed to bring the
two hands on top of each other. Unlike the comparison of the neutral 3-D shapes, however,
response times were influenced not only by the angle, but also by the direction of the rotation of the two hands. Obviously, neutral 3-D shapes can be rotated at the same rate in
any direction, whereas the rotation of a hand is limited by the biomechanics of the arm.
According to Parsons (1994), hand rotation response times thus reflect biomechanically
compatible trajectories, to the same extent as for executed movements. Similar effects on
response times have been observed for making judgments on how to use hand held objects
or tools (Frak, Paulignan, & Jeannerod 2001). The implicit processing involved in the representation of actions influences the way we consciously process the visual world.

The mental chronometry data about the dual nature (conscious and nonconscious) of
motor representations are strengthened by data from neuroimaging experiments. Studying the pattern of brain activity during the process of generating an action, either limited
to its covert part, as in intending or mentally simulating, or also including overt motor
performance, reveals that activated areas partly overlap during different modalities of representation. During mental simulation of a movement, activity increases in several areas
directly concerned with motor behavior. At the cortical level, the primary motor area, as
well as area 6 in the anterior part of the frontal gyrus and area 40 in the inferior parietal
lobule are activated. Subcortically, the caudate nucleus and the cerebellum are also activated (Jeannerod & Frak 1999).

The picture that emerges from the behavioral results described earlier in this chapter, and
the above anatomical results is twofold. The mechanisms which pertain to the motor plant,
and are responsible for action execution proper, operate automatically and nonconsciously,
whereas those that determine the goal of the action can be consciously represented. In other
words, a subject may, at the same time, be aware of what to obtain and remain unaware
of the detailed mechanisms necessary to obtain it. This distinction between the goal of an
action and the means to achieve it is a problem in itself, however. The problem arises with
the definition of the goal of the action. As already stressed in the Introduction, motor representations are recursive structures, in the sense that sub-goals that account for automatic
execution of the individual movements are embedded into a broader goal, which accounts
for the unfolding of the whole action. The system in which this ultimate goal is stored must
have different characteristics from those of the short-term storage system required for performance of individual movements.

Could it be that simple actions are those, which, by definition, escape consciousness,
whereas the sequence of simple actions leading to the final goal has to be maintained in a
conscious working memory until completion? This may be an oversimplification. As we
saw above, there are limitations to the capacity of the automatic system. Consider the case
where the subject is automatically executing the simple action of grasping the pot with

the conscious intention of preparing tea: if the pot handle is too hot, the action will be interrupted and re-initiated in a different way. In this case, the subject uses a conscious correction strategy and becomes aware of what was the normally nonconscious sub-goal of a simple action. This result confirms the introspective observation that any action segment, simple as it may be, can become conscious when it fails to reach its goal (e.g., Pacherie 1997; Jeannerod 2003).

The illusion of being a conscious agent

At this point, the problem of action consciousness and action recognition clearly merges with that of self-consciousness and action attribution. Being the conscious agent of an action is one modality of being self-conscious. The ability to recognize oneself as the agent of a behavior or a thought – the sense of agency – is the way by which the self builds as an entity independent from the external world. By way of consequence, self-recognition is a prerequisite for attributing a behavior to its proper agent, be it oneself or another person. Yet, there are several modalities involved in the question of a self. One modality is that of the *narrative self*, which mainly considers the personal, or conscious attributes of the self; the other one is that of the *embodied self*, which refers to subpersonal attributes of the self and its relation to the behaving body.

As a narrator, we obviously know who we are, where we are, what we are presently doing, and what we were doing before. Unless we become demented, we have a strong feeling of continuity in our conscious experience. We rely on declarative memory systems where souvenirs (albeit distorted) can be retrieved, and can be used as a material for describing our prior actions. The concept of self-consciousness as understood here requires the ability for consciously experiencing oneself as an acting being, which enables one to attribute to oneself one's own actions. As an embodied self, we identify ourselves as the owner of a body and the author of actions with definite consequences in the surrounding world. At variance with the narrative self, the type of self-consciousness that is linked to the experience of the embodied self is discontinuous: it operates on a moment-to-moment basis, as it is bound to particular bodily events. The embodied self mostly carries an implicit mode of action-consciousness, where consciousness becomes manifest only when required by the situation. The related information has a short life span and usually does not survive the bodily event for very long.

The narrative self and the embodied self are two distinct entities. The conscious sense of will that we may experience when we execute an action, which is at the origin of our narrative continuity, arises from the belief that our thoughts can have a causal influence on our behavior. While we tend to perceive ourselves as causal, we actually ignore the cause from which our actions originate. The same could be said about the experience of freedom that arises when we express a preference and which is at the origin of the conscious sense of volition. Conscious free choice, like conscious will, is not a direct perception of a causal relation between a thought and an action, but rather a feeling based on the causal inference one makes about the data that do become available to consciousness – the thought and the observed action. This dissociation between the two levels of the self has been considered by some as the origin of an illusion (e.g., Wegner 2002). Because the conscious thought and the observed action are consistently associated, even though they may not be causally related, the narrative self tends to build a cause-and-effect story. The embodied self, in contrast, by avoiding conscious introspection, reaches simpler (and perhaps more secure) conclusions about who is the agent of an action by monitoring on-line the degree of congruence between central and peripheral signals generated by the action.

See also 40 Preconscious processing; 48 Duplex vision: separate cortical pathways for conscious perception and the control of action; 51 Benjamin Libet's work on the neuroscience of free will.

Further Readings

Jeannerod, M. (2006) *Motor Cognition: What Actions Tell the Self*. Oxford: Oxford University Press.
Roessler, J. and Eilan, N. (eds.) (2003) *Agency and Self-Awareness: Issues in Philosophy and Psychology*. Oxford: Oxford University Press.
Wegner, D. (2002) *The Illusion of Conscious Will*. Cambridge, MA: MIT Press.

References

Blakemore, S. J., Frith, C., and Wolpert, D. (1999) Spatio-temporal prediction modulates the perception of self-produced stimuli. *Journal of Cognitive Neuroscience* 11, 551–9.
Bridgeman, B., Kirch, M., and Sperling, A. (1981) Segregation of cognitive and motor aspect of visual function using induced motion. *Perception and Psychophysics* 29, 336–42.
Castiello, U., Paulignan, Y. and Jeannerod, M. (1991) Temporal dissociation of motor responses and subjective awareness: a study in normal subjects. *Brain* 114: 2639–55.
Daprati, E., Sirigu, A., Pradat-Diehl, P., Franck, N., and Jeannerod, M. (2000) Recognition of self produced movement in a case of severe neglect. *Neurocase* 6, 477–86.
Farrer, C., Franck, N., Georgieff, N., Frith, C. D., Decety, J., and Jeannerod, M. (2003) Modulating the experience of agency: a PET study. *Neuroimage* 18, 324–33.
Fink, G. R., Marshall, J. C., Halligan, P. W., Frith, C. D., Driver, J., Frackowiack, R. S. J., et al. (1999) The neural consequences of conflict between intention and the senses. *Brain* 122, 497–512.
Fitts, P. M. (1954) The information capacity of the human motor system in controlling the amplitude of movement. *Journal of Experimental Psychology* 47: 381–91.
Fourneret, P. and Jeannerod, M. (1998) Limited conscious monitoring of motor performance in normal subjects. *Neuropsychologia* 36: 11, 1133–40.
Frak, V. G., Paulignan, Y., and Jeannerod, M. (2001) Orientation of the opposition axis in mentally simulated grasping. *Experimental Brain Research* 136: 1, 120–7.
Gibson, J. J. (1979) *The Ecological Approach to Visual Perception*, Boston, MA: Houghton Mifflin.
Goodale, M. A., Pélisson, D., and Prablanc, C. (1986) Large adjustments in visually guided reaching do not depend on vision of the hand or perception of target displacement. *Nature* 320, 748–50.
Haggard, P., Clark, S., and Kalogeras, J. (2002) Voluntary action and conscious awareness. *Nature Neuroscience* 5: 4, 282–5.
Holst, E. von (1954) Relations between the central nervous system and the peripheral organs. *British Journal of Animal Behaviour* 2, 89–94.
Jakobson, L. S. and Goodale, M. A. (1991) Factors affecting higher order movement planning: a kinematic analyis of human prehension. *Experimental Brain Research* 86, 199–208.
Jeannerod, M. (1994) The representing brain: neural correlates of motor intention and imagery. *Behavioral and Brain Sciences* 17, 187–245.
Jeannerod, M. (1995) Mental imagery in the motor context. *Neuropsychologia* 33, 1419–32.
Jeannerod, M. (1997) *The Cognitive Neuroscience of Action*. Oxford: Blackwell.

Jeannerod, M. (2003) Consciousness of action and self-consciousness: a cognitive neuroscience approach. In J. Roessler and N. Eilan (eds.), *Agency and Self-Awareness: Issues in Philosophy and Psychology*, 128–49. New York: Oxford University Press.

Jeannerod, M. and Frak, V. G. (1999) Mental simulation of action in human subjects. *Current Opinion in Neurobiology* 9: 6, 735–9.

Knoblich, G. and Kircher, T. T. J. (2004) Deceiving oneself about being in control: conscious detection of changes in visuomotor coupling. *Journal of Experimental Psychology. Human Perception and Performance* 30, 657–66.

Libet, B., Gleason, C. A., Wright, E. W., and Perl, D. K. (1983) Time of conscious intention to act in relation to cerebral activities (readiness potential). The unconscious initiation of a freely voluntary act. *Brain* 102: 193–224.

Nielsen, T. I. (1963) Volition: a new experimental approach. *Scandinavian Journal of Psychology* 4, 225–30.

Pacherie, E. (1997) Motor images, self-consciousness and autism. In J. Russell (ed.), *Autism as an Executive Disorder*, 215–55. Oxford: Oxford University Press.

Parsons, L. M. (1994) Temporal and kinematic properties of motor behavior reflected in mentally simulated action. *Journal of Experimental Psychology. Human Perception and Performance* 20, 709–30.

Searle, J. (1983) *Intentionality: An Essay in the Philosophy of Mind.* Cambridge: Cambridge University Press.

Shepard, R. N. and Metzler, J. (1971) Mental rotation of three dimensional objects. *Science* 171: 701–3.

Sirigu, A., Duhamel, J.-R., Cohen, L., Pillon, B., Dubois, B., and Agid, Y. (1996) The mental representation of hand movements after parietal cortex damage. *Science* 273, 1564–8.

Sirigu, A., Daprati, E., Pradat-Diehl, P., Franck, N., and Jeannerod, M. (1999) Perception of self-generated movement following left parietal lesion. *Brain* 122 (Part 10), 1867–74.

Slachevsky, A., Pillon, B., Fourneret, P., Pradat-Diehl, P., Jeannerod, M., and Dubois, B. (2001) Preserved adjustment but impaired awareness in a sensory-motor conflict following prefrontal lesions. *Journal of Cognitive Neuroscience* 13, 332–40.

Spence, S. A., Brooks, D. J., Hirsch, S. R., Liddle, P. F., Meehan, J., and Grasby, P. M. (1997) A PET study of voluntary movement in schizophrenic patients experiencing passivity phenomena (delusions of alien control). *Brain* 120, 1997–2011.

Wegner, D. (2002) *The Illusion of Conscious Will.* Cambridge, MA: MIT Press.

Wolpert, D. M., Ghahramani, Z., and Jordan, M. I. (1995) An internal model for sensorimotor integration. *Science* 269, 1880–2.

TOPICS IN THE NEUROSCIENCE OF CONSCIOUSNESS

43

Methodologies for Identifying the Neural Correlates of Consciousness

GERAINT REES AND CHRIS FRITH

Preliminaries

In this chapter we describe attempts to identify experimentally the neural correlates of the contents of conscious experience in humans. The principal methodological approach of the work reviewed here is to contrast the neural activity evoked by conscious vs. unconscious information processing. This contrast permits these studies to enquire about what is special concerning the neural activity specifically associated with the contents of conscious experience. Such an approach first requires the demonstration of the occurrence of unconscious information processing.

Behavioral Correlates of Unconscious Processing

There is now substantial evidence that processing outside awareness can influence behavior (though see Holender 1986 for a skeptical critique). For example, words presented rapidly and then masked so that they are not seen can nevertheless subsequently elicit priming of behavioral responses related to the meaning of those words (Marcel 1983). This suggests that the words have been processed unconsciously to the level of identifying their meaning. Although whether this is mediated directly by unconscious activation of semantic representations has been questioned, further evidence for unconscious priming from masked number primes has also been provided (e.g., Naccache & Dehaene 2001).

Behavioral evidence for unconscious processing does not only arise from priming paradigms. For example, during binocular rivalry incompatible monocular images compete for dominance. Despite complete perceptual dominance of one monocular image, sensitivity to input from the suppressed eye is only moderately (and not fully) reduced (for a review of this area, see Blake & Logothetis 2004). Indeed, selective adaptation by suppressed images can be of equal magnitude as for dominant images, suggesting that information about suppressed visual stimulation may reach early visual areas largely unattenuated. Similarly, after-effects due to adaptation to stimuli that cannot be consciously perceived suggest that visual processing of basic stimulus features can occur outside awareness (e.g., He, Cavanagh, & Intriligator 1996).

Finally, evidence for unconscious processing is not exclusively related to sensation and perception. Fast corrective arm movements during visually guided reaching are automatically driven by target movements, of which the subject may be unaware (Pisella et al. 2000). Moreover, accurate reaching movements can be made to targets presented in the blind hemifield of patients with posterior cerebral lesions and hemianopia (Danckert et al. 2002). Indeed, even the ability of neurologically normal individuals to consciously monitor motor performance is quite limited (Fourneret & Jeannerod 1998).

Neural Correlates of Unconscious Processing

Measurements of brain activity using functional MRI, positron emission tomography, or electrophysiological techniques such as EEG and MEG can reveal unconscious information processing in the absence of any behavioral signs (although see Hannula, Simons, & Cohen 2005 for a critical review of the behavioral methodology used to establish such findings). Modest but reliable unconscious activation of the human ventral visual pathway has been consistently observed both for simple visual stimuli and for more complex words, faces, and objects. Different types of masking can be used to render stimuli invisible, but activation is nevertheless identifiable in early retinotopic visual cortex (e.g., Haynes & Rees 2005), word-selective areas (Dehaene et al. 2001), and face and object-selective areas (Moutoussis & Zeki 2002) of the ventral visual pathway. Such observations are not restricted to masking paradigms, as unconscious activation of the ventral visual pathway during the attentional blink can reflect both object identity (Marois, Chun, & Gore 2000) and semantic processing of visual stimuli (Luck, Vogel, & Shapiro 1996).

Unconscious activation of visual cortex can also be identified following parietal damage causing visual extinction. Patients with visual extinction show deficient awareness for contralesional visual stimuli, particularly when a competing stimulus is also present ipsilesionally. When visual stimuli are presented to patients with visual extinction, areas of both primary and extrastriate visual cortex that are activated by a seen left visual field stimulus are also activated by an unseen and extinguished left visual field stimulus (see Driver et al. 2001 for a review). Indeed, unconscious processing of an extinguished face stimulus extends even to face selective cortex (the fusiform face area or FFA).

Brain activation associated with unconscious perception is not confined to the cortex. Subcortical structures associated with emotional perception such as the amygdala can be activated by fearful face stimuli that are rendered invisible through masking (Morris, Ohman, & Dolan 1999), during suppression in binocular rivalry (Pasley, Mayes, & Schultz 2004), or in response to the emotional content of invisible words (Naccache et al. 2005).

Taken together, both behavior and measurements of brain activity show that substantial sensory and motor processing can occur outside awareness. While much of this reflects neural processes in primary sensory and sensory association cortices, it is by no means confined to those structures and has been noted in most brain structures. The neuroscientific challenge is therefore to understand how the neural correlates of conscious processing differ from these neural correlates of unconscious processing.

Neural Correlates of Conscious Processing

Having established the occurrence of unconscious information processing in the human brain, we now turn to studies that have sought to identify the neural correlates of conscious information processing. Specifically, these studies contrast quantitative and qualitative differences in brain activity between conscious and unconscious processing of the same stimulus.

Spontaneous changes in consciousness

In many situations, the contents of consciousness can change spontaneously in the absence of any changes in the sensory input. Paradigms in which such spontaneous changes occur are extremely attractive for identifying neural correlates of consciousness, for any changes in brain activity in such situations cannot reflect changes in the sensory input, which remains constant.

Stimuli close to threshold

For any type of sensory stimulus a perceptual threshold can be defined, at which it becomes difficult or impossible to detect or discriminate that stimulus. By presenting stimuli close to threshold, a proportion of stimuli reach awareness on some trials while others do not. Several studies have attempted to determine whether any extra neural activity is associated with stimuli that reach awareness. For very simple detection of a low-contrast stimulus, trials on which the stimulus reaches consciousness evoke significantly greater activity in primary visual cortex compared to identical trials that do not reach consciousness (Ress & Heeger 2003). Electrical activity associated with conscious perception of threshold-level stimuli occurs at occipital sensors after approximately 100 ms, prior to the emergence of differences in activity over parietal and prefrontal cortex (Pins & ffytche 2003). These data suggest an important role for primary visual cortex in conscious representation of simple visual features such as luminance contrast.

Conscious identification of objects has been investigated by using degraded pictures to investigate neural correlates of successful identification at perceptual threshold. The magnitude of occipitotemporal activity evoked by visually presented objects correlates strongly with recognition performance (Grill-Spector et al. 2000) and successful detection of a face stimulus presented during the attentional blink evokes activity in the "fusiform face area," plus prefrontal cortex (Marois, Yi, & Chun 2004). For visual verbal stimuli, parietal cortical activation is associated with conscious recognition (Kjaer et al. 2001). Successful identification evokes an event-related negativity (Ojanen, Revonsuo, & Sams 2003) and is associated with both occipital MEG responses (Vanni et al. 1996) and modulation of the parieto-occipital alpha rhythm (Vanni, Revonsuo, & Hari 1997). This electrophysiological evidence is consistent with interactions between visual and parietal cortex mediating successful identification.

An object that can easily be identified when presented to one eye alone will be invisible under binocular presentation if complementary colors are used for presentation to each eye (e.g., left eye: red face on green background, right eye: green face on red background). Even in the absence of conscious perception, presentation of such stimuli elicits activity in ventral visual areas specialized for the object presented. When the object is consciously perceived activity in these areas increases (Moutoussis & Zeki 2002).

The ability of observers to detect changes in a visually presented object can also be rendered particularly difficult to detect by introducing a flicker between changes. Changes that are not consciously perceived nevertheless evoke some activity in the ventral visual pathway (e.g., Beck et al. 2001), and that activity may precede conscious change detection

(Niedeggen, Wichmann, & Stoerig 2001). When the change is consciously perceived, there is further enhancement of activity in ventral visual cortical areas that represent the type of change, plus activation of parietal and prefrontal cortices (e.g., Beck et al. 2001). This pattern of activity may reflect the deployment of attention (Pessoa & Ungerleider 2004).

Ambiguous stimuli

Bi-stable perception arises when a physical stimulus readily allows two different perceptual interpretations. For example, when dissimilar images are presented to the two eyes, they compete for perceptual dominance causing binocular rivalry. Each monocular image is visible in turn for a few seconds while the other is suppressed. Because perceptual transitions occur spontaneously without any change in the physical stimulus, neural correlates of this change in the contents of consciousness may be distinguished from neural correlates attributable to stimulus characteristics. Brain activity time-locked to these perceptual transitions can be identified in prefrontal and parietal cortices (e.g., Lumer, Friston, & Rees 1998), while fluctuations in brain activity specifically related to the content of perceptual experience can be identified in ventral visual cortex. Response fluctuations during rivalry that are further along the ventral visual pathway, such as in the "fusiform face area" (Tong et al. 1998) are generally larger than those observed in V1 (Lee, Blake, & Heeger 2005; Polonsky et al. 2000) and equal in magnitude to responses evoked by physical (rather than perceptual) alternation of stimuli. This suggests that early visual cortex may represent both the seen and the suppressed monocular images, but competition between the two is increasingly resolved as signals progress down the ventral visual pathway, consistent with similar ERP measurements (Kaernbach et al. 1999) and the behavioral data reviewed above. But competition can also occur at very early stages of visual processing, including the lateral geniculate nucleus (Haynes, Deichmann, & Rees 2005) and monocular representations of the retinal blind spot in primary visual cortex (Tong & Engel 2001). Thus, neural correlates of changes in perceptual content during rivalry can be identified throughout the ventral visual pathway, consistent with competition occurring at multiple levels simultaneously. In contrast, activity associated with transitions between states is time-locked to frontal and parietal activity. Consistent with the involvement of such a distributed network, large-scale changes in intra- and inter-hemispheric synchronization can be observed during rivalrous fluctuations (Tononi et al. 1998).

Other forms of bi-stable perception that do not involve binocular rivalry also evoke activity in ventral visual structures appropriate to whichever competing percept is currently perceived (e.g., Kleinschmidt et al. 1998). Fluctuations in conscious perception are associated with large-scale changes in synchronous electrical oscillations (e.g., Rodriguez et al. 1999) and also elicit frontal and parietal activity at the time of perceptual transitions (Kleinschmidt et al. 1998). Strikingly, such frontal and parietal activity is also associated with spontaneous changes in the contents of consciousness in very different paradigms, such as the emergence of a figure in spontaneous stereo pop out (Portas, Strange, et al. 2000), or during perception of fragmented figures (Eriksson et al. 2004).

Taken together, these data suggest a model whereby distributed object representations in the ventral visual pathway compete for perceptual dominance, perhaps biased by top-down signals from frontal and parietal cortex. Successful stabilization of a unitary conscious percept is associated both with an activated representation in ventral visual cortex of the perceptual content, plus activity in frontal and parietal cortex.

Hallucinations

A hallucination is a false sensory perception in the absence of an external stimulus, often associated with drug use, sleep deprivation, and neurological or psychiatric disease. During visual hallucinations, brain activation can be observed in object-selective regions of the ventral visual pathway whose selectivity corresponds to the content of the hallucination (ffytche et al. 1998). During auditory hallucinations in schizophrenia, activation of subcortical nuclei and limbic structures (Silbersweig et al. 1995) plus primary auditory cortex (Dierks et al. 1999) is observed. Finally, hallucination of a supernumerary limb following stroke is associated with activation of medial prefrontal cortex in the supplementary motor area (McGonigle et al. 2002). Hallucinations are therefore associated with activation of either sensory or motor cortices in which modality and neuronal specificities correspond closely to that of the hallucinatory perceptual content.

The problem of report

The studies discussed so far seek to identify neural activity related to conscious mental representations. It is necessary to show that these relationships are not simply the concomitant consequence of changes in stimulation or changes in behavior. The most common way to do this is to keep these unwanted effects constant. Hence the emphasis on paradigms in which, for example, subjective experience changes while stimulation remains constant. However, in all the studies discussed so far, participants reported whether or not they were aware of the stimulus. This raises the possibility that the different behaviors associated with different reports of awareness might confound interpretation of such studies. For example, in one study participants were presented with masked words and were asked to attempt to name them. When the words were consciously identified, naming was associated with activity in frontoparietal cortex (Dehaene et al. 2001); but this activity may simply reflect the neural correlates of naming rather than consciousness per se. This is an extreme example, and any such potential behavioral confounds are typically much more subtle, such as using slightly different responses to indicate awareness vs. unawareness of stimulation. Nevertheless, these differences may represent potentially important confounds. One approach to circumvent this problem is not to require behavioral report at all. For example, brain activity during binocular rivalry in the absence of behavioral reports shows a coordination of activity among multiple brain regions in frontal and parietal cortex similar to that demonstrated in previous studies that required subjective reports. This suggests that frontoparietal activity associated with rivalry is independent of the requirement to make behavioral reports.

Modifying the contents of consciousness

Changes in the contents of consciousness are not only driven by spontaneous fluctuations but can also be systematically altered by either top-down signals (e.g., directing the subject's attention toward or away from some aspect of a stimulus) or by altering the context in which a stimulus is presented.

Directed attention

When subjects are engaged in a demanding task, irrelevant but highly salient stimuli outside the immediate focus of attention can go entirely unnoticed. This phenomenon is known as inattentional blindness, and suggests that consciousness may depend on attention. Brain activity evoked by irrelevant sensory stimulation in ventral occipital and temporal cortex is reduced when attention is withdrawn (e.g., Rees, Frith, & Lavie 1997). Moreover, when inattentional blindness results for unattended words, then brain activity no longer differentiates between such meaningful words and random letters (Rees et al. 1999). This suggests that attention is required both for brain activity associated with the higher processing of sensory stimuli, and for their subsequent representation as the contents of consciousness.

Attention can also modify activity associated with awareness of action. We pay little attention to the sensory consequences of action when that action is self-generated. This is accompanied by reduced activity in somatosensory cortex (Blakemore, Rees, & Frith 1998; Weiller et al. 1996). Even neural responses to the indirect sensory consequences of action, such as a tone caused by a button press, are reduced (Shafer & Markus 1973). When, through hypnosis, subjects falsely believe that the actions they are performing are not self-generated, then activity in somatosensory cortex increases (Blakemore, Oakley, & Frith 2003).

When attention is focused on the intention that precedes an action activity increases in the preSMA (Lau et al. 2004). Awareness of action errors is also associated with medial frontal activity (Luu, Flaisch, & Tucker 2000).

Illusions

An illusion occurs when real external stimuli are misperceived and represented in consciousness in an incorrect fashion. The content of the illusory perception typically depends on the spatial and temporal context in which it occurs. For example, sensory after-effects are illusory sensory perceptions in the absence of sensory stimulation that typically occur following an extended period of adaptation to a sensory stimulus. After-effects that are contingent on prior adaptation to color or motion activate either V4 (e.g., Sakai et al. 1995) or V5/MT (e.g., Tootell et al. 1995) respectively, and the time course of such activation reflects phenomenal experience (Tootell et al. 1995). Perception of illusory or implied motion in a static visual stimulus results in activation of V5/MT (e.g., Zeki, Watson, & Frackowiak 1993), while perception of illusory contours activates areas of early retinotopic extrastriate cortex (e.g., Hirsch et al. 1995). Common to these experimental paradigms are changes in phenomenal experience without corresponding physical stimulus changes. Perceptual illusions can also be used to manipulate feelings of ownership of a rubber hand. When participants feel that the hand is theirs, then activity in the premotor cortex reflects this conscious perception of ownership (Ehrsson, Spence, & Passingham 2004). Thus both perceptual and motor illusions lead to specific modification of brain activity. Altered brain activity is observed in areas of the brain known to contain neurons whose stimulus specificities encompass the attribute represented in consciousness.

Imagination

A conscious percept can be created by the act of imagination. In patients with implanted electrodes for pre-surgical epilepsy mapping, single neurons in the human medial temporal lobe that fire selectively when particular visual stimuli are presented (Kreiman, Koch, & Fried 2000a) are also activated when the individual imagines the same stimuli (Kreiman, Koch, & Fried 2000b). Similarly, neuronal populations elsewhere in the ventral visual pathway with stimulus specificity for faces or places are activated during imagery of these categories of object (O'Craven & Kanwisher 2000). Imagery is not restricted to perceptual experiences alone. When an intention is generated but the corresponding action not executed, the resulting motor imagery activates brain areas typically associated with the generation of action (Jeannerod 2003). This involvement of motor areas in motor imagery extends to the observation and recognition of actions performed or intended by other agents. For example, imagining other people simulating actions activates right parietal, precuneus, and frontopolar cortex (Ruby & Decety 2001).

Modulation by state

Altering the overall level of consciousness can lead to corresponding modifications in the contents of consciousness. While primary sensory cortical activity can still be elicited when sensory stimuli are presented to subjects rendered unconscious through sleep (Portas, Krakow, et al. 2000) or coma (Laureys et al. 2002), activation of extrastriate and higher structures in coma appears to be absent and any thalamocortical coupling is decreased relative to the conscious state (Laureys et al. 2000). Less dramatic modifications of state associated with meditation also modify activity in posterior sensory cortices, with the notable exception of primary sensory cortex (Lou et al. 1999). Thus, it seems that primary sensory cortices continue to process stimuli when the conscious state is perturbed, but activity in secondary sensory and higher cortical areas is strikingly reduced, consistent with a role for these areas in representing the contents of consciousness.

Parametric tracking of variations in consciousness

The psychophysical relationship between changes in physical features of a stimulus and consciousness need not be a simple linear one. For example, while the interval between mask and stimulus increases linearly, the awareness of the stimulus can show a variety of nonlinear functions, depending on the type of masking (Haynes, Driver, & Rees 2005). Such dissociations between physical stimulus parameters and awareness provide an opportunity to identify whether there are some brain areas where activity tracks the stimulus parameters, while in other areas activity tracks the perceptual pattern.

Awareness for words or visually presented objects that are presented rapidly and followed by a physically overlapping mask is typically reduced. Maximal effectiveness of this backward masking occurs when the interval between target and mask is shortest, with a monotonic decrease in masking as the interval is lengthened. When masking is effective in erasing visually presented words from awareness, areas of ventral occipitotemporal visual cortex continue to respond to the physical presence of the stimuli (Dehaene et al. 2001). Such activity is therefore not sufficient for consciousness. In structures such as the medial temporal cortex, thought to be later in the processing pathway, single neuron responses to visually presented objects are entirely abolished by masking sufficient to abolish awareness (Kreiman, Fried, & Koch 2002). However, awareness of masked words leads to enhancement of activity in ventral visual cortex (Dehaene et al. 2001), and recognition performance for masked objects is strongly correlated to occipitotemporal activity (Grill-Spector et al.

2000). Masked but consciously perceived words are specifically associated with spontaneous electrical oscillations at a frequency near 40 Hz (Summerfield, Jack, & Burgess 2002), and such "gamma band" activity can also be identified when observers consciously individuate masked auditory stimuli (Joliot, Ribary, & Llinas 1994).

Necessary and Sufficient Neural Processes?

All of the studies discussed in the preceding sections have attempted to correlate changes in brain activity with changes in the contents of consciousness. Such correlational studies cannot determine whether such neural activity plays a causal role in determining the contents of consciousness. In particular, they cannot show whether the areas that have been identified in association with particular contents of consciousness are either necessary or sufficient for such conscious experiences to occur. Identification of necessary and sufficient brain activity requires explicit experimental manipulation of that activity. If manipulation of brain activity changes consciousness, then a causal role for that brain activity can be inferred. Manipulations of brain activity can be performed with direct electrical stimulation, using transcranial magnetic stimulation and as a consequence of brain lesions (although in humans, the latter is clearly not under direct experimental control).

Effects of direct electrical stimulation

Electrical stimulation applied directly to human occipito-temporal cortex can evoke a striking variety of visual experiences, ranging from the conscious perception of simple form when stimulation is applied to the occipital lobe, to more complex experiences of form or color as more anterior structures are stimulated (Lee et al. 2000). This demonstrates that visual input from the retina and subcortical structures is not necessary for conscious visual experience. Different conscious visual experiences are elicited by stimulation of different areas of visual cortex, consistent not only with the functional organization of visual cortex but also with the notion that the presence of a particular feature or visual attribute in consciousness requires activation of the corresponding functionally specialized region of visual cortex.

Is V1 necessary?

Phosphenes can be elicited by transcranial magnetic stimulation of visual cortex in subjects rendered blind through retinal disease, but not when blindness results from damage to primary visual cortex (Cowey & Walsh 2000). This suggests that while the retina is not necessary, primary visual cortex may be necessary for this type of conscious visual experience. Such a notion is supported by observations of strong activation of extrastriate visual cortex when the blind field is visually stimulated in patients with V1 damage and hemianopia (Goebel et al. 2001). But visual stimulation of the blind field in patients with V1 damage can lead to awareness without any corresponding perilesional V1 activation (Kleiser et al. 2001) so V1 activity cannot be necessary for consciousness in all cases. One possibility is that the precise timing of V1 activity plays an important role. If feedback signals from V5/MT to V1 are disrupted by transcranial magnetic stimulation (TMS), then awareness of motion is impaired (Pascual-Leone & Walsh 2001). Similarly, using TMS to disrupt processing of a backward mask presented after a target can lead to unmasking and corresponding visibility of the original target (Ro et al. 2003). These data suggest that signals in V1 representing feedback from other ventral visual (or higher cortical) areas may be required for awareness.

Are parietal/frontal cortex necessary?

For perception

When parietal cortex is damaged, then visual cortex activity alone is not sufficient to result in awareness (see Driver et al. 2001 for a review). Nor does activity in somatosensory cortex necessarily lead to tactile awareness following parietal damage (Valenza et al. 2004). Similarly, amygdala and orbitofrontal cortex can be activated by emotional stimuli without awareness after parietal damage (Vuilleumier et al. 2002). These examples show that stimuli presented to a patient suffering from parietal damage causing visual neglect and extinction can undergo substantial cortical processing despite not reaching awareness, consistent with the idea that signals in parietal (and possibly frontal) cortex are required for normal conscious perception. Moreover, in visual extinction after parietal damage, awareness of contralateral stimulation is associated with enhanced covariation of activity in undamaged parietal, prefrontal, and visual areas. Disruption of parietal or prefrontal cortex in normal volunteers with transcranial magnetic stimulation impairs change detection (e.g., Beck et al. 2006). These results suggest that an interaction between frontal, parietal, and stimulus-specific representations in sensory cortices may be necessary for awareness.

For awareness of action

Parietal cortex has a critical role in the awareness of one's own movements. Patients with parietal lesions have difficulty imagining making movements. They can no longer reproduce in their imagination the time needed to make a real movement (Sirigu et al. 1996). They are also unaware of the details of their own real movements so that they can no longer distinguish visual feedback of their movements from similar movements made by other people (Sirigu et al. 1999). Patients with parietal lesions can report the time at which they initiate a movement, but can no longer report the time at which they had the intention to move (Sirigu et al. 2004).

Prefrontal cortex also has a role in awareness of action. Patients with prefrontal lesions can make normal adjustments to their movements when performing tasks in which there is sensory-motor conflict, while at the same time being unaware of the conflict (Slachevsky et al. 2001).

Conclusions

The concept of an essential node

A consistent finding throughout the literature is that specific regions of the brain are essential for particular contents of consciousness (e.g., V5/MT for motion). If V5/MT is damaged or removed, then motion will not be experienced. This shows that such functionally specialized areas are necessary for consciousness of the attribute that is represented in the neural specificities of that area. Direct or indirect cortical stimulation of such a functionally specialized visual area also generally seems to be able to invoke a corresponding perceptual experience, suggesting that inputs from earlier visual areas are not necessary for a particular type of experience. The level or type of activity is important. For most functionally specialized brain areas, activation has been observed or inferred in the absence of any awareness of the specific attribute represented. This unconscious activation is typically either weaker or has a different character (e.g., not synchronized) than for conscious perception. Taken together, these data are consistent with the notion that particular contents of consciousness are associated with specific types of neural activity in particular functionally specialized areas. Activity in such an "essential node" (Zeki & Bartels 1999) is necessary for conscious experience. But is activation of an essential node sufficient for conscious awareness? It is difficult to understand in what sense an isolated bit of brain tissue could be said to be conscious. Empirical evidence that shows specific associations of parietal and frontal activity with awareness, plus long-range coupling of these structures with appropriate sensory representations during awareness, suggests that activity in individual functionally specialized areas is not sufficient. Such activated sensory representations may have to interact with higher areas to be represented in the contents of consciousness.

Selective attention and consciousness

There is a close relationship between selective attention and consciousness. The pattern of activity associated with stimuli that enter consciousness is very similar to the pattern of activity that is associated with stimuli at the focus of attention. This suggests that the neural mechanisms of attention and awareness may be linked. Two key processes may therefore be involved in bringing sensory stimulation to awareness. First, competition between stimuli occurs in primary sensory and association cortices. Such competition is probably resolved in regions of parietal cortex that receive inputs from multiple modalities, reflecting the fact that in the natural environment most stimuli are multimodal. Second, top-down biasing signals, probably controlled by prefrontal and/or parietal cortex, can influence the outcome of this competition. To become part of an integrated conscious representation a stimulus must win the competition with other stimuli, both within and between modalities. It must be salient (i.e., unexpected in relation to the recent history of stimulation) and/or must have value for the subject (through instruction or experience). In the brain this will depend upon interactions between frontal cortex, parietal cortex, and the essential node for the particular content. These interactions in turn require a neural substrate, most likely involving cortico-subcortical loops.

What next?

Many paradigms are now available for linking neural activity with the contents of conscious experience. None of these paradigms is entirely satisfactory. For example, in most cases some form of report must indicate the presence of consciousness. In these cases should some of the neural activity observed be attributed to the report rather than the conscious experience? Or is reportability an intrinsic feature of conscious experience?

Although none may be entirely satisfactory, it is striking that the results from the various different paradigms are so consistent. The contents of conscious experience are determined by the location of the neural activity, by which essential node is active. But activity in an essential node does not seem to be enough. Interaction with other areas, particularly parietal and frontal cortex seems to be necessary. This pattern is identical to results from studies of selective attention. So should we equate the contents of conscious with the focus of attention? Or is this result a consequence of our theoretical limitations? The biased competition model of selective attention is currently one of the few models available where there is a good fit between descriptions at the cognitive and at the physiological level.

Recent methodological advances have made it relatively easy to study the neural correlates of consciousness. What we need now are equivalent theoretical and conceptual advances on the side of the relationship concerned with consciousness as such.

Further Readings

Koch, C. (2004) *The Quest for Consciousness: A Neurobiological Approach*. Englewood, CO: Roberts.

References

Beck, D. M., Muggleton, N., Walsh, V., and Lavie, N. (2006) Right parietal cortex plays a critical role in change blindness. *Cerebral Cortex* May 16: 5, 712–17.

Beck, D. M., Rees, G., Frith, C. D., and Lavie, N. (2001) Neural correlates of change detection and change blindness. *Nature Neuroscience* 4: 6, 645–50.

Blake, R. and Logothetis, N. K. (2002) Visual competition. *Nature Review: Neuroscience* 3: 1, 13–21.

Blakemore, S. J., Oakley, D. A., and Frith, C. D. (2003) Delusions of alien control in the normal brain. *Neuropsychologia* 41: 8, 1058–67.

Blakemore, S. J., Rees, G., and Frith, C. D. (1998) How do we predict the consequences of our actions? A functional imaging study. *Neuropsychologia* 36: 6, 521–29.

Cowey, A. and Walsh, V. (2000) Magnetically induced phosphenes in sighted, blind and blindsighted observers. *NeuroReport* 11: 14, 3269–73.

Danckert, J., Ferber, S., Doherty, T., Steinmetz, H., Nicolle, D., and Goodale, M. A. (2002) Selective, non-lateralized impairment of motor imagery following right parietal damage. *Neurocase* 8: 3, 194–204.

Dehaene, S., Naccache, L., Cohen, L., Bihan, D. L., Mangin, J. F., Poline, J. B. et al. (2001) Cerebral mechanisms of word masking and unconscious repetition priming. *Nature Neuroscience* 4: 7, 752–8.

Dierks, T., Linden, D. E., Jandl, M., Formisano, E., Goebel, R., Lanfermann, H. et al. (1999) Activation of Heschl's gyrus during auditory hallucinations. *Neuron* 22: 3, 615–21.

Driver, J., Vuilleumier, P., Eimer, M., and Rees, G. (2001) Functional magnetic resonance imaging and evoked potential correlates of conscious and unconscious vision in parietal extinction patients. *Neuroimage* 14, S68–75.

Ehrsson, H. H., Spence, C., and Passingham, R. E. (2004) That's my hand! Activity in premotor cortex reflects feeling of ownership of a limb. *Science* 305: 5685, 875–7.

Eriksson, J., Larsson, A., Riklund Ahlstrom, K., and Nyberg, L. (2004) Visual consciousness: dissociating the neural correlates of perceptual transitions from sustained perception with fMRI. *Consciousness and Cognition* 13: 1, 61–72.

ffytche, D. H., Howard, R. J., Brammer, M. J., David, A., Woodruff, P., and Williams, S. (1998) The anatomy of conscious vision: an fMRI study of visual hallucinations. *Nature Neuroscience* 1: 8, 738–42.

Fourneret, P. and Jeannerod, M. (1998) Limited conscious monitoring of motor performance in normal subjects. *Neuropsychologia* 36: 11, 1133–40.

Goebel, R., Muckli, L., Zanella, F. E., Singer, W., and Stoerig, P. (2001) Sustained extrastriate cortical activation without visual awareness revealed by fMRI studies of hemianopic patients. *Vision Research* 41: 10–11, 1459–74.

Grill-Spector, K., Kushnir, T., Hendler, T., and Malach, R. (2000) The dynamics of object-selective activation correlate with recognition performance in humans. *Nature Neuroscience* 3: 8, 837–43.

Hannula, D. E., Simons, D. J., and Cohen, N. J. (2005) Imaging implicit perception: promise and pitfalls. *Nature Review: Neuroscience* 6: 3, 247–55.

Haynes, J. D. and Rees, G. (2005) Predicting the orientation of invisible stimuli from activity in human primary visual cortex. *Nature Neuroscience* 8: 5, 686–91.

Haynes, J. D., Deichmann, R., and Rees, G. (2005) Eye-specific suppression in human LGN reflects perceptual dominance during binocular rivalry. *Nature* 438, 496–9.

Haynes, J. D., Driver, J., and Rees, G. (2005) Visibility reflects dynamic changes of effective connectivity between V1 and fusiform cortex. *Neuron* 46: 5, 811–21.

He, S., Cavanagh, P., and Intriligator, J. (1996) Attentional resolution and the locus of visual awareness. *Nature* 383: 6598, 334–7.

Hirsch, J., DeLaPaz, R. L., Relkin, N. R., Victor, J., Kim, K., Li, T. et al. (1995) Illusory contours activate specific regions in human visual cortex: evidence from functional magnetic resonance imaging. *Proceedings of the National Academy of Sciences* 92: 14, 6469–73.

Holender, D. (1986) Semantic activation without conscious identification in dichotic listening, parafoveal vision, and visual masking: a survey and appraisal. *Behavioral and Brain Sciences* 9, 1–66.

Jeannerod, M. (2003) The mechanism of self-recognition in humans. *Behavioural Brain Research* 142: 1–2, 1–15.

Joliot, M., Ribary, U., and Llinas, R. (1994) Human oscillatory brain activity near 40 Hz coexists with cognitive temporal binding. *Proceedings of the National Academy of Sciences* 91: 24, 11,748–51.

Kaernbach, C., Schroger, E., Jacobsen, T., and Roeber, U. (1999) Effects of consciousness on human brain waves following binocular rivalry. *NeuroReport* 10: 4, 713–16.

Kjaer, T. W., Nowak, M., Kjaer, K. W., Lou, A. R., and Lou, H. C. (2001) Precuneus-prefrontal activity during awareness of visual verbal stimuli. *Consciousness and Cognition* 10: 3, 356–65.

Kleinschmidt, A., Buchel, C., Zeki, S., and Frackowiak, R. S. (1998) Human brain activity during spontaneously reversing perception of ambiguous figures. *Proceedings of the Royal Society B: Biological Sciences* 265: 1413, 2427–33.

Kleiser, R., Wittsack, J., Niedeggen, M., Goebel, R., and Stoerig, P. (2001) Is V1 necessary for conscious vision in areas of relative cortical blindness? *Neuroimage* 13: 4, 654–61.

Kreiman, G., Fried, I., and Koch, C. (2002) Single-neuron correlates of subjective vision in the human medial temporal lobe. *Proceedings of the National Academy of Sciences* 99: 12, 8378–83.

Kreiman, G., Koch, C., and Fried, I. (2000a) Category-specific visual responses of single neurons in the human medial temporal lobe. *Nature Neuroscience* 3: 9, 946–53.

Kreiman, G., Koch, C., and Fried, I. (2000b) Imagery neurons in the human brain. *Nature* 408: 6810, 357–61.

Lau, H. C., Rogers, R. D., Haggard, P., and Passingham, R. E. (2004) Attention to intention. *Science* 303: 5661, 1208–10.

Laureys, S., Faymonville, M. E., Luxen, A., Lamy, M., Franck, G., and Maquet, P. (2000) Restoration of thalamocortical connectivity after recovery from persistent vegetative state. *Lancet* 355: 9217, 1790–1.

Laureys, S., Faymonville, M. E., Peigneux, P., Damas, P., Lambermont, B., Del Fiore, G. et al. (2002) Cortical processing of noxious somatosensory stimuli in the persistent vegetative state. *Neuroimage* 17: 2, 732–41.

Lee, H. W., Hong, S. B., Seo, D. W., Tae, W. S., and Hong, S. C. (2000) Mapping of functional organization in human visual cortex: electrical cortical stimulation. *Neurology* 54: 4, 849–54.

Lee, S. H., Blake, R., and Heeger, D. J. (2005) Traveling waves of activity in primary visual cortex during binocular rivalry. *Nature Neuroscience* 8: 1, 22–3.

Lou, H. C., Kjaer, T. W., Friberg, L., Wildschiodtz, G., Holm, S., and Nowak, M. (1999) A 15O-H2O PET study of meditation and the resting state of normal consciousness. *Human Brain Mapping* 7: 2, 98–105.

Luck, S. J., Vogel, E. K., and Shapiro, K. L. (1996) Word meanings can be accessed but not reported during the attentional blink. *Nature* 383: 6601, 616–18.

Lumer, E. D., Friston, K. J., and Rees, G. (1998) Neural correlates of perceptual rivalry in the human brain. *Science* 280: 5371, 1930–4.

Luu, P., Flaisch, T., and Tucker, D. M. (2000) Medial frontal cortex in action monitoring. *Journal of Neuroscience* 20: 1, 464–69.

McGonigle, D. J., Hanninen, R., Salenius, S., Hari, R., Frackowiak, R. S., and Frith, C. D. (2002) Whose arm is it anyway? An fMRI case study of supernumerary phantom limb. *Brain*, 125 (Pt 6), 1265–74.

Marcel, A. J. (1983) Conscious and unconscious perception: experiments on visual masking and word recognition. *Cognitive Psychology* 15: 2, 197–237.

Marois, R., Chun, M. M., and Gore, J. C. (2000) Neural correlates of the attentional blink. *Neuron* 28: 1, 299–308.

Marois, R., Yi, D. J., and Chun, M. M. (2004) The neural fate of consciously perceived and missed events in the attentional blink. *Neuron* 41: 3, 465–72.

Morris, J. S., Ohman, A., and Dolan, R. J. (1999) A subcortical pathway to the right amygdala mediating "unseen" fear. *Proceedings of the National Academy of Sciences* 96: 4, 1680–5.

Moutoussis, K. and Zeki, S. (2002) The relationship between cortical activation and perception investigated with invisible stimuli. *Proceedings of the National Academy of Sciences* 99: 14, 9527–32.

Naccache, L. and Dehaene, S. (2001) The priming method: imaging unconscious repetition priming reveals an abstract representation of number in the parietal lobes. *Cerebral Cortex* 11: 10, 966–74.

Naccache, L., Gaillard, R., Adam, C., Hasboun, D., Clemenceau, S., Baulac, M. et al. (2005) A direct intracranial record of emotions evoked by subliminal words. *Proceedings of the National Academy of Sciences* 102: 21, 7713–17.

Niedeggen, M., Wichmann, P., and Stoerig, P. (2001) Change blindness and time to consciousness. *European Journal of Neuroscience* 14: 10, 1719–26.

O'Craven, K. M. and Kanwisher, N. (2000) Mental imagery of faces and places activates corresponding stimulus-specific brain regions. *Journal of Cognitive Neuroscience* 12: 6, 1013–23.

Ojanen, V., Revonsuo, A., and Sams, M. (2003) Visual awareness of low-contrast stimuli is reflected in event-related brain potentials. *Psychophysiology* 40: 2, 192–7.

Pascual-Leone, A. and Walsh, V. (2001) Fast backprojections from the motion to the primary visual area necessary for visual awareness. *Science* 292: 5516, 510–12.

Pasley, B. N., Mayes, L. C., and Schultz, R. T. (2004) Subcortical discrimination of unperceived objects during binocular rivalry. *Neuron* 42: 1, 163–72.

Pessoa, L. and Ungerleider, L. G. (2004) Neural correlates of change detection and change blindness in a working memory task. *Cerebral Cortex* 14: 5, 511–20.

Pins, D. and ffytche, D. (2003) The neural correlates of conscious vision. *Cerebral Cortex* 13: 5, 461–74.

Pisella, L., Grea, H., Tilikete, C., Vighetto, A., Desmurget, M., Rode, G. et al. (2000) An "automatic pilot" for the hand in human posterior parietal cortex: toward reinterpreting optic ataxia. *Nature Neuroscience* 3: 7, 729–36.

Polonsky, A., Blake, R., Braun, J., and Heeger, D. J. (2000) Neuronal activity in human primary visual cortex correlates with perception during binocular rivalry. *Nature Neuroscience* 3: 11, 1153–9.

Portas, C. M., Krakow, K., Allen, P., Josephs, O., Armony, J. L., and Frith, C. D. (2000) Auditory processing across the sleep–wake cycle: simultaneous EEG and fMRI monitoring in humans. *Neuron* 28: 3, 991–9.

Portas, C. M., Strange, B. A., Friston, K. J., Dolan, R. J., and Frith, C. D. (2000) How does the brain sustain a visual percept? *Proceedings of the Royal Society B: Biological Sciences* 267: 1446, 845–50.

Rees, G., Frith, C. D., and Lavie, N. (1997) Modulating irrelevant motion perception by varying attentional load in an unrelated task. *Science* 278: 5343, 1616–19.

Rees, G., Russell, C., Frith, C. D., and Driver, J. (1999) Inattentional blindness versus inattentional amnesia for fixated but ignored words. *Science* 286: 5449, 2504–7.

Ress, D., and Heeger, D. J. (2003) Neuronal correlates of perception in early visual cortex. *Nature Neuroscience* 6: 4, 414–20.

Ro, T., Breitmeyer, B., Burton, P., Singhal, N. S., and Lane, D. (2003) Feedback contributions to visual awareness in human occipital cortex. *Current Biology* 13: 12, 1038–41.

Rodriguez, E., George, N., Lachaux, J. P., Martinerie, J., Renault, B., and Varela, F. J. (1999) Perception's shadow: long-distance synchronization of human brain activity. *Nature* 397: 6718, 430–3.

Ruby, P. and Decety, J. (2001) Effect of subjective perspective taking during simulation of action: a PET investigation of agency. *Nature Neuroscience* 4: 5, 546–50.

Sakai, K., Watanabe, E., Onodera, Y., Uchida, I., Kato, H., Yamamoto, E. et al. (1995) Functional mapping of the human colour centre with echo-planar magnetic resonance imaging. *Proceedings of the Royal Society B: Biological Sciences* 261: 1360, 89–98.

Shafer, W. P. and Marcus, M. M. (1973) Self-stimulation alters human sensory brain responses *Science* 181, 175–7.

Silbersweig, D. A., Stern, E., Frith, C., Cahill, C., Holmes, A., Grootoonk, S. et al. (1995) A functional neuroanatomy of hallucinations in schizophrenia. *Nature* 378: 6553, 176–9.

Sirigu, A., Duhamel, J. R., Cohen, L., Pillon, B., Dubois, B., and Agid, Y. (1996) The mental representation of hand movements after parietal cortex damage. *Science* 273: 5281, 1564–8.

Sirigu, A., Daprati, E., Pradat-Diehl, P., Franck, N., and Jeannerod, M. (1999) Perception of self-generated movement following left parietal lesion. *Brain* 122 (Pt 10), 1867–74.

Sirigu, A., Daprati, E., Ciancia, S., Giraux, P., Nighoghossian, N., Posada, A. et al. (2004) Altered awareness of voluntary action after damage to the parietal cortex. *Nature Neuroscience* 7: 1, 80–4.

Slachevsky, A., Pillon, B., Fourneret, P., Pradat-Diehl, P., Jeannerod, M., and Dubois, B. (2001) Preserved adjustment but impaired awareness in a sensory-motor conflict following prefrontal lesions. *Journal of Cognitive Neuroscience* 13: 3, 332–40.

Summerfield, C., Jack, A. I., and Burgess, A. P. (2002) Induced gamma activity is associated with conscious awareness of pattern masked nouns. *International Journal of Psychophysiology* 44: 2, 93–100.

Tong, F. and Engel, S. A. (2001) Interocular rivalry revealed in the human cortical blind-spot representation. *Nature* 411: 6834, 195–9.

Tong, F., Nakayama, K., Vaughan, J. T., and Kanwisher, N. (1998) Binocular rivalry and visual awareness in human extrastriate cortex. *Neuron* 21: 4, 753–9.

Tononi, G., Srinivasan, R., Russell, D. P., and Edelman, G. M. (1998) Investigating neural correlates of conscious perception by frequency-tagged neuromagnetic responses. *Proceedings of the National Academy of Sciences* 95: 6, 3198–203.

Tootell, R. B., Reppas, J. B., Dale, A. M., Look, R. B., Sereno, M. I., Malach, R. et al. (1995) Visual motion aftereffect in human cortical area MT revealed by functional magnetic resonance imaging. *Nature* 375: 6527, 139–41.

Valenza, N., Seghier, M. L., Schwartz, S., Lazeyras, F., and Vuilleumier, P. (2004) Tactile awareness and limb position in neglect: functional magnetic resonance imaging. *Annals of Neurology* 55: 1, 139–43.

Vanni, S., Revonsuo, A., and Hari, R. (1997) Modulation of the parieto-occipital alpha rhythm during object detection. *Journal of Neuroscience* 17: 18, 7141–7.

Vanni, S., Revonsuo, A., Saarinen, J., and Hari, R. (1996) Visual awareness of objects correlates with activity of right occipital cortex. *NeuroReport* 8: 1, 183–6.

Vuilleumier, P., Armony, J. L., Clarke, K., Husain, M., Driver, J., and Dolan, R. J. (2002) Neural response to emotional faces with and without awareness: event-related fMRI in a parietal patient with visual extinction and spatial neglect. *Neuropsychologia* 40: 12, 2156–66.

Weiller, C., Juptner, M., Fellows, S., Rijntjes, M., Leonhardt, G., Kiebel, S. et al. (1996) Brain representation of active and passive movements. *Neuroimage* 4: 2, 105–10.

Zeki, S. and Bartels, A. (1999) Toward a theory of visual consciousness. *Consciousness and Cognition* 8: 2, 225–59.

Zeki, S., Watson, J. D., and Frackowiak, R. S. (1993) Going beyond the information given: the relation of illusory visual motion to brain activity. *Proceedings of the Royal Society B: Biological Sciences* 252: 1335, 215–22.

A Neurobiological Framework for Consciousness

FRANCIS CRICK AND CHRISTOF KOCH

The problem of consciousness is largely empirical. Its most difficult aspect is the problem of qualia – the elements that make up consciousness. No one has produced any plausible explanation as to how the painfulness of pain or the redness of red arises from, or is identical to, the actions of the brain. The history of the past three millennia has shown that it is fruitless to approach this problem head-on. Instead, we are attempting to find the neural correlates of consciousness (NCC), in the hope that when we can explain the NCC in causal terms, this will make the problem of qualia clearer (Crick & Koch 1998). In round terms, the NCC are the minimal sets of neuronal events jointly sufficient for any one specific aspect of a conscious percept.

Our main interest is not the enabling factors needed for all forms of consciousness, such as the activity of the ascending reticular system in the brainstem, but the general nature of the neuronal activities that produce each particular aspect of consciousness, such as an object with a specific color, shape, or movement.

As a matter of tactics, we have concentrated on visual perception, putting to one side some of the more difficult aspects of consciousness, such as emotion and self-consciousness. One of the key advantages of the visual domain is the existence of illusions that systematically vary the relationship between the retinal stimulus and the conscious percept (such as binocular rivalry, motion-induced blindness, masking, bi-stable illusions and so on). We have been especially interested in the alert macaque monkey, because to find the NCC, it is necessary to investigate not only widespread neural activities but also the detailed behavior of single neurons (or small groups of neurons) on very fast timescales. It is difficult to conduct such investigations systematically in people. Methods such as functional magnetic resonance imaging (fMRI) are quite coarse in both space (the smallest volume of *bold* activity that is typically recorded encompasses about one million cells) and time (with a timescale of seconds) and therefore provide only a limited view of the relevant microvariables. However, experiments on visual psychology are much easier to do with humans than with monkeys. Moreover, humans can report what they are conscious of. For these reasons, experiments with monkeys and humans should be pursued in parallel. In this chapter – based on an earlier paper by us (Crick & Koch 2003) – we summarize our neurobiological framework for approaching these problems, while the relevant empirical data are summarized in Koch (2004).

Before we start, a preamble on the cerebral cortex. One general characteristic of the operations of the cortex is the astonishing variety and specificity of the actions performed by the cortical system. The visual system of the higher mammals handles an almost infinite variety of visual inputs and reacts to them in detail with remarkable accuracy. Clearly, the system is highly evolved, is likely to be specified epigenetically in considerable detail, and can learn a large amount from experience.

The main function of the sensory cortex is to construct and use highly specific feature detectors, such as those for orientation, motion, or faces. The features to which any cortical neuron responds are usually highly specific but multidimensional. That is, a single neuron does not respond to a single feature but to a family of related features. Such features are sometimes called the receptive field of that neuron. The visual fields of neurons higher in the visual hierarchy are larger and respond to more complex features than those lower down. The non-classical receptive field (Allman, Miezin, & McGuinness 1985) expresses the relevant context of the classical receptive field.

An important but neglected aspect of the firing of a neuron (or a small group of associated neurons) is its projective field (Lehky & Sejnowski 1988). This term describes the perceptual and behavioral consequences of stimulating such a neuron in an appropriate manner (Graziano, Taylor, & Moore 2002). Both the receptive field and the projective field are dynamic, not merely static, and both can be modified by experience.

Many of the pretty pictures produced by brain imaging with their restricted blobs of hemodynamic activity suggest that cortical action is highly local. Nothing could be farther from the truth. In the cortex, there is continual and extensive interaction, both in the near neighborhood and also very widely, thanks to the many long cortico-cortical and cortico-thalamo-cortical routes. This is much less true of the thalamus itself. Thus, almost any visual input will activate most of the gray matter in the occipital lobe.

The visual cortex is arranged in a semi-hierarchical manner (Felleman & Van Essen 1988). That is, most cortical areas do not detect simple correlations in the visual input but detect correlations between correlations being expressed by other cortical areas. This remarkable feature of the cortex is seldom emphasized.

If two brief stimuli are similar, the brain blends them together. If they are different but in contradiction, such as a face and a house, the brain does not blend them but instead selects one of them, as in binocular rivalry.

The incoming visual information is usually not enough to lead to an unambiguous interpretation (Poggio, Torre, & Koch 1985). In such cases the cortical networks "fill in" – that is, they make their best guess, given the incomplete information. Such filling-in is likely to happen in many places in the brain. This general principle is an important guide to much of human behavior (as in "jumping to conclusions").

Let us consider the NCC and their attendant properties. We are mainly interested in time periods of the order of a few hundred milliseconds, or at the most several seconds, so that we can put to one side processes that take more time, such as the permanent establishment of a new memory. A framework is not a detailed hypothesis; rather it is a suggested point of view for an attach on a scientific problem, often suggesting testable hypothesis. Biological frameworks differ from frameworks in physics and chemistry because of the nature of evolution. Biological systems do not have rigid laws, as physics has. Evolution produces mechanisms, and often sub-mechanisms, so that there are a few "rules" in biology which do not have occasional exceptions.

A good framework is one that sounds reasonably plausible relative to available scientific data and that turns out to be largely correct. It is unlikely to be correct in all the details. A framework often contains unstated (often unrecognized) assumptions, but this is unavoidable. Our framework is divided into ten headings.

The Unconscious Homunculus

A good way to look at the overall behavior of the cerebral cortex is that the front of the brain is "looking at" the sensory systems, most of which are at the back of the brain. This division of labor does not lead to an infinite regress (Attneave 1961). This idea at this stage is necessarily rather vague. By "looking" we mean in neuroanatomical terms that the long-distance projections from sensory cortices in the back into premotor and frontal cortex in the front are strong connections, able to drive their postsynaptic targets (largely) in layer 4 (see "Driving and Modulating Connections" below).

We discussed in Crick and Koch (2000) the extent to which the neural activity in the frontal regions of cortex is largely inaccessible to consciousness. Jackendoff (1987), for example, has proposed that humans are not directly conscious of their thoughts, but only of sensory representations of them in their imagination (see chapter 19 by Prinz on the work of Jackendoff).

The hypothesis of the homunculus – a conscious entity, residing inside the skull, between the eyes and looking out at the world – is, in broad terms, how everyone thinks of him- or herself. It would be surprising if this overwhelming illusion did not in some way reflect the general organization of the brain. Much of the complex machinery underpinning everyday decisions resides in the frontal lobes. We argue that only the results of these decisions, not the processes underlying them, are accessible to consciousness. If one situates these computations that underly multidimensional choices such as "Should I marry him or not?" at the apex of the information processing pyramid with its internal representations of beliefs, desires, and thoughts, then the representations that are sufficient for conscious sensation reside at intemediate levels, above the nonconscious representations of the external world in sensory cortices.

Zombie Modes and Consciousness

Many actions in response to sensory inputs are rapid, transient, stereotyped, and *uncon-scious* (Milner & Goodale 1995; Rossetti 1998; see also Goodale, chapter 48). They could be thought of as cortical reflexes. We support the suggestion by Milner and Goodale that the brain has many sensory-motor actions – we call these zombie agents or actions (Koch & Crick 2001) – characterized by rapid and somewhat stereotyped responses, in addition to a slower, all-purpose conscious mode. The conscious mode deals more slowly with broader, less stereotyped aspects of the sensory inputs (or a reflection of these, as in imagery) and takes time to decide on appropriate thoughts and responses. It is needed because otherwise a vast number of different zombie modes would be required to react to unusual events. The conscious system may interfere somewhat with the concurrent zombie system. It would be a great evolutionary advantage to have both zombie modes that respond rapidly in a stereotyped manner, and a slightly slower system that allows time for thinking and planning more complex behavior. This latter aspect would be one of the functions of this conscious mode.

It seems likely that visual zombie modes in the cortex mainly use the dorsal stream in the parietal region (Milner & Goodale 1995). However, some parietal activity also affects consciousness by producing attentional effects on the ventral stream, at least under some circumstances. The conscious mode for vision depends largely on the early visual areas (beyond V1) and especially on the ventral stream. There are no recorded cases of purely parietal damage that led to a complete loss of conscious vision.

In a zombie mode, the main flow of information is largely forward. It could be considered a forward traveling net-wave. A net-wave is a propagating wave of neural activity, but it is not the same as a wave in a continuous medium. Neural networks in a cortex have both short and long connections, so a net-wave may, in some cases, jump over intervening regions. In the conscious mode it seems likely that the flow is in both directions, so that it resembles more a standing net-wave.

Coalitions of Neurons

The cortex is a very highly and specifically interconnected neural network. It has many types of both excitatory and inhibitory interneurons and acts by forming transient *coalitions* of neurons, the members of which support each other in some way. Coalitions imply assemblies – an idea that goes back at least to Hebb (1949) – and competition between them (see also Edelman & Tononi 2000). Desimone and Duncan (1995) suggested, as a result of experiments on the macaque, that selective attention biases the competition between rivalrous cell assemblies, but they did not explicitly relate this idea to consciousness.

The various neurons in a coalition in some sense support each other, either directly or indirectly, by increasing the activity of their fellow members. The dynamics of coalitions are not simple. In general, at any moment the winning coalition is somewhat sustained, and embodies what we are conscious of.

Coalitions can vary in size and in character. For example, a coalition produced by visual imagination (with one's eyes closed) may be less widespread than a coalition produced by a vivid and sustained visual input. In particular, the former may fail to reach down to the lower echelons of the visual hierarchy. Coalitions in dreams may be somewhat different from waking ones. Under some conditions of binocular rivalry, the dominant image changes into the previously suppressed one at a sufficiently slow speed that a wave, traveling a few degrees per second, can be observed to cross the field of view (Wilson, Blake, & Lee 2001); this is a manifestation of the two coalitions, spread out over visual cortex, competing for perceptual dominance.

If there are coalitions in the front of the cortex, they may have a somewhat different character from those formed at the back of the cortex. Frontal coalitions may reflect feelings such as moods (e.g., happiness) and, perhaps, the feeling of "authorship" related to perceived volition (Wegner 2002). Such feelings may be more diffuse and may persist for a longer time than coalitions in the back of cortex. Jackendoff (1987) uses the terms affect or valuations for what we have called feelings. Our first working assumption (the homunculus) implies that it is better not to regard the back plus the front as one single coalition, but rather as two or more rather separate coalitions that interact massively, but not in an exactly reciprocal manner.

Explicit Representations and Essential Nodes

An explicit representation of a particular aspect of the visual scene implies that a small set of neurons exists that responds as a detector for that feature, without further complex neural processing. A possible probe – an operational test – for an explicit representation might be whether a single layer of linear, thresholded "units" could deliver the correct answer. For example, if such a layer was fed the activity of retinal neurons, it would not be able to recognize a face. However, if fed from the relevant parts of inferior temporal cortex, it could reliably signal "face" or "no face." There is much evidence from both humans and monkeys that if there are no such neurons, or if they are all lost from brain damage, then the subject is unable to consciously perceive that aspect directly (see chapter 45 by Zeki). Well-known clinical examples are achromatopsia (loss of color perception), prosopagnosia (loss of face recognition), and akinetopsia (loss of motion perception). In all cases, one or a few attributes of conscious experience have been lost, while most other aspects remain intact. In the macaque, a small, irreversible lesion of the motion area MT/V5 leads to a deficit in motion perception that recovers within days. Larger lesions cause a more permanent loss.

It should be noted that an explicit representation is a necessary but not a sufficient condition for the NCC to occur.

The cortical system can be described in terms of essential nodes, a term introduced by Zeki (see chapter 45). The cortical neural networks (at least for perception) can be thought of as having nodes. Each node is needed to express one aspect of one percept or another. An aspect cannot become conscious unless there is an essential node for it. This is a necessary but not a sufficient condition. For consciousness there may be other necessary conditions, such as projecting to the front of the brain (Crick & Koch 1995). A node by itself cannot produce consciousness. Even if the neurons in that node were firing appropriately, such firing would produce little effect if their output synapses were inactivated. A node is a node, not a network. Thus, a particular coalition is an active network, consisting of the relevant set of interacting nodes, that temporarily sustains itself.

Much useful information can be obtained from lesions. In humans, the damaged area is usually fairly large. It is not clear what effects a very small, possibly bilateral, reversible lesion would have in the macaque, because it is difficult to discover exactly what a monkey is conscious of. The smallest useful node may be a cortical column (Mountcastle 1998) or perhaps a portion of one. The feature which that node represents is (broadly) its columnar property. This is because although a single type of pyramidal cell usually sends its information to only one or two cortical areas, the pyramidal cells in a column project the columnar property collectively to many cortical and subcortical areas, and thus can lend greater support to any coalition that is forming.

The Higher Levels First

For a new visual input, the neural activity first travels rapidly and unconsciously up the visual hierarchy to a high level, possibly in the front of the brain (this might instantiate a zombie mode). Signals then start to move backward down the hierarchy, so that the first stages to reach consciousness are at the higher levels (showing the gist of the scene; Biederman 1972), which send these "conscious" signals again to prefrontal cortex, followed by corresponding activity at successive lower levels (to provide the visual details; see also Hochstein & Ahissar 2002). This is an oversimplified description. There are also many side connections in the hierarchy.

How far up the hierarchy the initial net-wave travels may depend upon whether attention is diffused or focused at some particular level.

Driving and Modulating Connections

In considering the physiology of coalitions, it is especially important to understand the nature of neural connections (the net is not an undirected one). The classification of neuronal inputs is still in a primitive state. It is a mistake to think of all excitatory neural connections as being of the same type. Connections to a cortical neuron fall roughly into several different broad classes. An initial classification would divide them into driving and modulating inputs (Crick & Koch 1998). For cortical pyramidal cells, driving inputs may largely contact the basal dendrites, whereas modulatory inputs include back-projections (largely to the apical dendrites) or diffuse projections, especially those from the intralaminar nuclei of the thalamus.

This classification may be too simple. In some cases, a single type of input to a neuron may be driving, as in the input from the lateral geniculate nucleus to primary visual cortex. In other cases several types of driving inputs may be needed to make that neuron fire at a significant rate. It is possible that the connections from the back of the brain to the front are largely driving, while the reverse pathways are largely modulatory, but this is not experimentally established. This general pattern would not hold for cross-modal connections. It's likely that cortical layer V cells which project to the thalamus are driving while those from layer VI are modulating (Sherman & Guillery 2001).

This tentative classification is largely for excitatory cells. Based on the available neuroanatomical evidence, we proposed that strong loops of driving connections are unlikely to occur under normal conditions (Crick & Koch 1998).

Snapshots

Has a successful coalition any special characteristics? We propose that conscious awareness (for vision) is a series of static snapshots, with motion "painted" on them. By this we mean that perception occurs in discrete epochs. For the relevant psychophysical evidence, see Van Rullen & Koch (2003). All the other conscious attributes of the percept at that moment are part of the snapshot. It is unlikely that different aspects of perception (e.g., color and motion, or form and sound) are necessarily synchronized to each other. Indeed, substantial lags between the perception of different attributes have been reported (Moutoussis & Zeki 1997; Zeki 1998).

Sacks (2004) has described in arresting detail patients with certain migraine attacks (including himself) and others who suffer from cinematographic vision, a temporary condition in which visual perception appears like a slowed movie, running at a few frames per second. The subject experiences the world as consisting of a succession of "stills," without any movement between the images. It is important that this clinical condition be studied under more controlled conditions in the laboratory.

The durations of successive snapshots are unlikely to be constant (they are difficult to measure directly). Moreover, the time of a snapshot for shape, say, may not exactly coincide with that for, say, color. It is possible that these durations may be related to the alpha rhythm or even the theta rhythm.

To reach consciousness, some (unspecified) neural activity for that particular feature has to reach above a threshold. It is unlikely to do so unless it is, or is becoming, the member of a successful coalition. It is held above threshold, possibly as a constant value of the activity, for a certain time (the time of that snapshot). Since specific attributes of conscious perception are all-or-none, so should the underlying NCC (for instance, either firing at a low or at a high level). Sergent and Dehaene (2004) have provided direct psychophysical evidence for a threshold process operating during the attentional blink.

What could be special about this form of activity? It might be some particular way of firing, such as a sustained high rate, some sort of synchronized firing, or firing in bursts. Or it might be the firing of special types of neurons, such as those pyramidal cells that project to the front of the brain (de Lima, Voigt, & Morrison 1990). Dedicated neurons may seem unlikely, but if true, it would greatly simplify the problem, both experimentally and theoretically.

What is required to maintain this special activity above threshold? Positive feedback loops are critical here. At least three broad and distinct systems of such pathways can be distinguished: (i) reciprocal, cortico-cortical connections that involve interactions between the back and the front of cortex as well as local feedback among cortical regions (Edelman (1989) calls these reentrant circuits), (ii) loops that involve the thalamus and, in particular, the intralaminar nuclei of the thalamus (Bogen 1997), and (iii) those that involve the claustrum (Crick & Koch 2005). Positive feedback can, by iteratively exciting a coalition, push its activity increasingly upward so that the activity not only reaches above some critical threshold but is maintained there for some time (these are partial descriptions of conscious coalitions forming, growing, or disappearing). This is not to rule out something peculiar about the internal dynamics of the neuron or its closely associated local partners that makes it maintain its activity above a threshold for a while.

There is no evidence for a regular clock in the brain on the second or fraction of a second timescale. The duration of the snapshot for any one perceived attribute is likely to vary somewhat, depending on factors such as sudden on and off signals, habituation, and competition.

Attention and Binding

Attention can usefully be divided into rapid, saliency-driven, bottom-up forms and slower, volitionally controlled, top-down forms. Either form of attention can also be diffused or more focused. Attention probably acts by biasing the competition between rival coalitions, especially in their formation (Desimone & Duncan 1995). Bottom-up attention may often start from certain layer V neurons that project to parts of the thalamus and the superior colliculus. Top-down attention from the front of the brain may go by somewhat diffuse back-projections to apical dendrites in layers I, II, and III, and perhaps also via the intralaminar nuclei of the thalamus (since these have inputs from the front of the brain). Even though such projections are widespread, it does not follow that they are not specific. To attend to red involves specific connections to many places in cortex. An attractive hypothesis is that the thalamus is largely the organ of attention. The reticular nucleus of the thalamus may help select among attentional signals on a broad scale. Whereas attention can produce consciousness of a particular object or event by biasing competition among coalitions, activities associated with non-attended objects are quite transient, giving rise to fleeting consciousness (Rensink 2000).

Thus, attention and consciousness are separate processes (Tsuchiya & Koch 2007). Some sort of attentional bias is probably necessary to give rise to a dominant coalition whose associated representational content the subject is aware of. However, attention by itself may not be sufficient for consciousness (Dehaene & Naccache 2001; Dehaene & Changeux 2004).

What is binding? This is the term used for the process that brings together rather different aspects of an object/event, such as its shape, color, movement, and so on. Binding can be of several types (Crick & Koch 1990). It is important to realize that if binding has been laid down epigenetically, or learned by experience, it is already embodied in one or more essential nodes, so no special binding mechanism is needed. An example of this would be an oriented simple cell in V1 that combines form information (spatial orientation) with positional information. If the binding required is (relatively) novel, then in some way the activities of separate essential nodes must be made to act together (see Singer, chapter 47).

Work in psychophysics (Van Rullen, Reddy, & Koch 2004) suggests that "parallel vs. serial" search and "pre-attentive vs. attentive" processing describe two independent dimensions rather than variations along a single dimension. These results can all be expressed in terms of the relevant neural networks. Several objects/events can be handled simultaneously, that is, more than one object/event can be attended to at the same time, if there is no significant overlap in any cortical neural network. In other words, if two or more objects/events have no very active essential nodes in common, they can be consciously perceived. Under such conditions, several largely separate coalitions may exist. If there is necessarily such an overlap, then (top-down) attention is needed to select one of them by biasing the competition between them.

This approach largely solves the classical binding problem, which was mainly concerned with how two different objects or events could be bound simultaneously. On this view, the binding of the features of single object/event is simply the membership of a particular coalition. There is no single cortical area where it all comes together. The effects of that coalition are widely distributed over both the back and the front of the brain. Thus, effectively, they bind by interacting in a diffuse manner.

Styles of Firing

Synchronized firing (including various oscillations) may be used for several purposes to increase the effectiveness of a group of neurons while not necessarily altering their average firing rate (Singer & Gray 1995). The extent and significance of synchronized firing in primate cortex remains controversial (Shadlen & Movshon 1999). Computations show (Salinas & Sejnowski 2001) that this effectiveness is likely to depend on how the correlated input influences the excitatory and inhibitory neurons in the recipient region to which the synchronized neurons project.

We no longer think (Crick & Koch 1990) that synchronized firing, such as the so-called 40 Hz oscillations, is a sufficient condition for the NCC.

One likely purpose of synchronized firing is to assist a nascent coalition in its competition with other (nascent) coalitions. If the visual input is simple, such as a single bar in an otherwise empty field, there might be no significant competition and synchronized firing may not occur. Such firing may not be needed once a successful coalition has reached consciousness, when it may be able to maintain itself without the assistance of synchrony, at least for a time.

At any essential node, the earliest spike to arrive may sometimes have the advantage over spikes arriving shortly thereafter (Van Rullen & Thorpe 2001). In other words, the exact timing of a spike may influence the competition.

Penumbra and Meaning

Let us consider a small set of neurons that fires to, say, some aspect of a face. The experimenter can discover what visual features interest such a set of neurons, that is, get it to fire strongly, but how does the brain know what that firing represents? This is the problem of "meaning" in its broadest sense.

The NCC at any one time will only directly involve a fraction of the total pyramidal cells, but this firing will influence many neurons that are *not* part of the NCC. These we call the *penumbra*. The penumbra consists of both synaptic effects and firing rates. The penumbra is not the result of just the sum of the effects of each essential node separately, but the effects of that NCC as a whole. This penumbra includes past associations of NCC neurons, the expected consequences of the NCC, movements (or at least possible plans for movement) associated with NCC neurons, and so on. For example, a hammer represented in the NCC is likely to influence plans for hammering.

The penumbra, by definition, is not itself conscious, though part of it may become part of the NCC as the NCC shift. Some of the penumbra neurons may project back to parts of the NCC and thus help to support the NCC. The penumbra neurons may be the site of unconscious priming (see Merikle, chapter 40).

Related Ideas

As this book attests, in the past 20 years there has been a flood of publications about consciousness. For many years Baars (see chapter 18) has argued that consciousness must be widely distributed. He and other authors have proposed that consciousness is "global" or has a "unity," but have provided few details about what exactly they mean by this. We think that unity is a problematic concept. For instance, in binocular rivalry during transitions, the percept may consist of a patchwork of the two input images (yet at any one location, only a fragment from one image – and not from the two – is perceived). To what extent is this a unified percept? Indeed, what would a non-unified percept even look like?

There are several accounts expressing ideas that overlap considerably with ours (see also Bachmann 2000). The first of these is by Edelman and Tononi (2000) (see also Tononi, chapter 22). Their "dynamic core" is very similar to our coalitions. They also divide consciousness into "primary consciousness" (which is what we are mainly concerned with) and "higher-order consciousness" (which we have for the moment put to one side). In their book, Edelman and Tononi state strongly that they do not think there is a special subset of neurons that alone expresses the NCC.

A framework somewhat similar to ours has been described by Changeux and Dehaene (Dehaene & Naccache 2001; Dehaene & Changeux 2004). They emphasize the all-or-none nature of conscious percepts, the accessibility of their associated content to many systems (working memory, planning, language, and so on), in accordance with global workspace models (Baars 1997). Its neuronal basis are the pyramidal neurons in layers 2 and 3 that are spread throughout the cerebral cortex and that have long axons. Dehaene and Changeux (2005) have shown in computer simulations how the underlying neuronal networks could act to give rise to quasi-threshold, meta-stable coalitions. Changeux's (2004) book outlines the relevant experimental evidence for their theory and also deals with neural activity in the front of cortex which we have, for the time being, left on one side.

General Remarks

Almost all of the ideas discussed here have already been suggested, either by us or by others. The framework we have proposed, however, knits all these ideas together, establishing a coherent scheme accounting for the NCC in philosophical, psychological, and neural terms. What ties these various suggestions together is the idea of competing coalitions. The illusion of a homunculus inside the head, looking at the sensory activities of the brain, suggests that the coalitions at the back are in some way distinct from the coalition(s) at the front. The two types of coalitions interact extensively but not exactly reciprocally.

Zombie modes show that not all motor outputs from the cortex are carried out consciously. Consciousness depends on certain coalitions that rest on the properties of very elaborate neural networks. We consider attention to consist of mechanisms that bias the competition between these nascent coalitions.

The idea of snapshots is a guess at the dynamic properties of the parts of a successful coalition, since coalitions are not static but constantly changing. The penumbra, on the other hand, consists of all the neural activity produced by the current NCC that is not strictly part of the NCC.

We also speculate that the actual NCC may be expressed by only a small set of neurons, in particular those that project from the back of cortex to those parts of the front of cortex that are not purely motor. However, there is much neural activity leading up to and supporting the NCC, so it is important to study this activity as well as the NCC proper. Moreover, discovering the temporal sequence of such activities (e.g., A precedes B) will help us to move from correlation to causation.

Our framework is a guide to constructing more detailed hypotheses, so that they can be tested against already existing experimental evidence, and, above all, to suggest new experiments. The aim is to couch all such explanations in terms of the behavior of identified neurons and of the dynamics of very large neural assemblies. For instance, we speculated in Crick and Koch (1995) that due to a lack of direct projections from V1 (in the macaque monkey) into the frontal regions of cortex involved in planning, the NCC are not to be found in V1; primary visual cortex is necessary for normal seeing (with open eyes) but higher cortical regions are needed for conscious, visual perception. Although controversial at first, much current evidence from the monkey (Logothetis 1998) and, more recently from human brain imaging (Lee, Haynes, & Rees 2005) is in agreement with this hypothesis. That is, a retinal input that gives rise to vigorous firing activity in V1 remains perceptually invisible if no coalition in the upper regions of the cortical hierarchy represent it.

Recently, we have once again (Crick 1994) focused on the claustrum; this is a thin but continuous sheet of forebrain neurons, embedded in white matter, above the basal ganglia but below the insula cortex (Sherk 1986; Tanné-Gariépy, Boussaoud, & Rouiller 2002). Like the thalamus, the majority of its cells are principal neurons that receive input from cortex and project back there. In the monkey, most cortical areas project to different sectors of the claustrum; V1 appears to be an exception to this rule. However, V1 does receive, like most other cortical regions, a direct excitatory input from the claustrum. The claustrum projection to cortex is neither local, nor global but is somewhere in between, patch-wise. An analogy that comes to mind is that of a conductor (the claustrum) coordinating a group of players in the orchestra (the various cortical regions). It is possible that this loop, from a cortical area X to its claustrum target region and back to X, may be involved in selective attention or even in the maintenance of the NCC itself. The claustrum has to be considered in relation to the other large systems of loops referred to earlier. It may be involved in binding information across modalities (see Crick & Koch 2005).

What Now?

Understanding consciousness will be immeasurably aided by characterizing the NCC sufficiently well in mature adults, in developing infants, in animals, and in humans, in health and in disease. Indeed, it is quite likely that most – but maybe not all – of the puzzling aspects of consciousness will resolve themselves. One of us has outlined in a book (Koch 2004) a detailed program of neurobiological exploration of the mammalian cortex that will be necessary to achieve these aims. This program will need to be supported by a systematic program to elucidate and catalog the neuroanatomy of cerebral cortex and its satellites at the molecular, synaptic, and cellular level. Key will be experiments that track down the footprints of consciousness in behaving animals while recording the spiking activity of hundreds and more neurons. It is particularly important to move from correlation to causation, by interfering selectively, deliberately, transiently, and reversibly with specific neural subpopulations in experimental animals and during neurosurgery in patients (Crick et al. 2004). In this manner, we are likely to once and for all untangle the Gordian knot at the heart of the ancient mind–body problem.

See also 22 The information integration theory of consciousness; 43 Methodologies for identifying the neural correlates of consciousness; 47 Large-scale temporal coordination of cortical activity as a prerequisite for conscious experience; 48 Duplex vision: separate cortical pathways for conscious perception and the control of action.

Acknowledgments

We thank the J. W. Kieckhefer Foundation, the W. M. Keck Foundation Fund for Discovery in Basic Medical Research at Caltech, NIH, NIMH, NSF, and the Mind Science Foundation for financial support.

Further Readings

Dawkins, M. S. (1993) *Through Our Eyes Only? The Search for Animal Consciousness*. Oxford: Oxford University Press.

Edelman, G. M. and Tononi, G. (2000) *A Universe of Consciousness: How Matter Becomes Imagination*. New York: Basic Books.

Goodale, M. A. and Milner, A. D. (2004) *Sight Unseen*. Oxford: Oxford University Press.

Koch, C. (2004) *The Quest for Consciousness: A Neurobiological Approach*. Englewood, CO: Roberts.

References

Allman, J., Miezin, F., and McGuinness, E. (1985) Stimulus specific responses from beyond the classical receptive field: neurophysiological mechanisms for local–global comparisons in visual neurons. *Annual Review of Neuroscience* 8, 407–30.

Attneave, F. (1961) In defense of homunculi. In W. A. Rosenblith (ed.), *Sensory Communication*, 777–82. New York: MIT Press and John Wiley.

Baars, B. J. (1997) *In the Theater of Consciousness: The Workspace of the Mind*. New York: Oxford University Press.

Bachmann, T. (2000) *Microgenetic Approach to the Conscious Mind*. Amsterdam: John Benjamins.

Biederman, I. (1972) Perceiving real-world scenes. *Science* 177: 7, 77–80.

Bogen, J. E. (1997) Some neurophysiologic aspects of consciousness. *Seminars Neurobiology* 17, 95–103.

Changeux, J.-P. (2004) *The Physiology of Truth: Neuroscience and Human Knowledge*. Cambridge, MA: Harvard University Press.

Crick, F. C. (1994) *The Astonishing Hypothesis*. New York: Scribner.

Crick, F. C. and Koch, C. (1990) Towards a neurobiological theory of consciousness. *Seminars in the Neurosciences* 2, 263–75.

Crick, F. C. and Koch, C. (1995) Are we aware of neural activity in primary visual cortex? *Nature* 375: 121–3.

Crick, F. C. and Koch, C. (1998) Constraints on cortical and thalamic projections: the no-strong-loops hypothesis. *Nature* 391, 245–50.

Crick, F. C. and Koch, C. (1998) Consciousness and neuroscience. *Cerebral Cortex* 8, 97–107.

Crick, F. C. and Koch, C. (2000) The unconscious homunculus. *Neuro-Psychoanalysis* 2, 3–11.

Crick, F. C. and Koch, C. (2003) A framework for consciousness. *Nature Neuroscience* 6, 119–27.

Crick, F. C. and Koch, C. (2005) What is the function of the claustrum? *Philosophical Transactions of the Royal Society London B* 360, 1271–9.

Crick, F. C., Koch, C., Kreiman, G., and Fried, I. (2004) Consciousness and neurosurgery. *Neurosurgery* 55: 2, 273–82.

de Lima, A. D., Voigt, T., and Morrison, J. H. (1990) Morphology of the cells within the inferior temporal gyrus that project to the prefrontal cortex in the macaque monkey. *Journal of Comparative Neurology* 296, 159–72.

Dehaene, S. and Changeux, J.-P. (2005) Ongoing spontaneous activity controls access to consciousness: a neuronal model for inattentional blindness. *PLoS Biology* 3, e141.

Dehaene, S. and Naccache, L. (2001) Towards a cognitive neuroscience of consciousness: Basic evidence and a workspace framework. *Cognition* 79, 1–37.

Desimone, R. and Duncan, J. (1995) Neural mechanisms of selective visual attention. *Annual Review of Neuroscience* 18, 193–222.

Edelman, G. M. (1989) *The Remembered Present: A Biological Theory of Consciousness*. New York: Basic Books.

Edelman, G. M. and Tononi, G. A. (2000) *Universe of Consciousness*. New York: Basic Books.

Felleman, D. J. and Van Essen, D. C. (1991) Distributed hierarchical processing in the primate cerebral cortex. *Cerebral Cortex* 1, 1–47.

Graziano, M. S., Taylor, C. S., and Moore, T. (2002) Complex movements evoked by microstimulation of precentral cortex. *Neuron* 34, 841–51.

Haynes, J. D. and Rees, G. (2005) Predicting the orientation of invisible stimuli from activity in human primary visual cortex. *Nature Neuroscience* 8, 686–91.

Hebb, D. (1949) *The Organization of Behavior: A Neuropsychological Theory*. New York: John Wiley.

Hochstein, S. and Ahissar, M. (2002) View from the top: hierarchies and reverse hierarchies in the visual system. *Neuron* 36, 791–804.

Jackendoff, R. (1987) *Consciousness and the Computational Mind*. Cambridge, MA: MIT Press.

Koch, C. (2004) *The Quest of Consciousness: A Scientific Approach*. Denver, CO: Roberts.

Koch, C. and Crick, F. C. (2001) On the zombie within. *Nature* 411, 893.

Lehky, S. R. and Sejnowski, T. J. (1988) Network model of shape-from-shading: neural function arises from both receptive and projective fields. *Nature* 333, 452–54.

Logothetis N. K. (1998) Single units and conscious vision. *Philosophical Transactions of the Royal Society London B* 353, 1801–18.

Milner, D. A. and Goodale, M. A. (1995) *The Visual Brain in Action*. Oxford: Oxford University Press.

Mountcastle, V. B. (1998) *Perceptual Neuroscience*. Cambridge, MA: Harvard University Press.

Moutoussis, K. and Zeki, S. (1997) A direct demonstration of perceptual asynchrony in vision. *Proceedings of the Royal Society of London B: Biological Sciences* 264, 393–9.

Poggio, T., Torre, V., and Koch, C. (1985) Computational vision and regularization theory. *Nature* 317, 314–19.

Rensink, R. A. (2000) Seeing, sensing, and scrutinizing. *Vision Research* 40, 1469–87.

Rossetti, Y. (1998) Implicit short-lived motor representations of space in brain damaged and healthy subjects. *Consciousness and Cognition* 7, 520–58.

Sacks, O. (2004) In the river of consciousness. *New York Review of Books* 51: 1, 41–4.

Salinas, E. and Sejnowski, T. J. (2001) Correlated neuronal activity and the flow of neural information. *Nature Review: Neuroscience* 2, 539–50.

Sergent, C. and Dehaene, S. (2004) Is consciousness a gradual phenomenon? Evidence for an all-or-none bifurcation during the attentional blink. *Psychological Science* 15, 720–8.

Shadlen, M. N. and Movshon, J. A. (1999) Synchrony unbound: a critical evaluation of the temporal binding hypothesis. *Neuron* 24, 67–77, 111–25.

Sherman, S. M. and Guillery, R. (2001) *Exploring the Thalamus*. San Diego, CA: Academic Press.

Sherk, H. (1986) The claustrum and the cerebral cortex. In E. G. Jones and A. Peters (eds.), *Cerebral Cortex*, vol. 5, 467–99. New York: Plenum Press.

Singer, W. and Gray, C. M. (1995) Visual feature integration and the temporal correlation hypothesis. *Annual Review of Neuroscience* 18, 555–86.

Tanné-Gariépy J., Boussaoud D., and Rouiller E. M. (2002) Projections of the claustrum to the primary motor, premotor, and prefrontal cortices in the macaque monkey. *Journal of Comparative Neurology* 454, 140–57.

Tsuchiya, N. and Koch, C. (2007) Attention and consciousness: two distinct brain processes. *Trends in Cognitive Sciences*, in press.

Van Rullen, R. and Koch, C. (2003) Is perception discrete or continuous? *Trends in Cognitive Sciences* 7, 207–13.

Van Rullen, R. and Thorpe, S. J. (2001) The time course of visual processing: from early perception to decision-making. *Journal of Cognitive Neuroscience* 13: 4, 454–61.

Van Rullen, R., Reddy, L., and Koch, C. (2004) Visual search and dual-tasks reveal two distinct attentional resources. *Journal of Cognitive Neuroscience* 16: 1, 4–14.

Wegner, D. (2002) *The Illusion of Conscious Will*. Cambridge, MA: MIT Press.

Wilson, H. R., Blake, R., and Lee, S. H. (2001) Dynamics of travelling waves in visual perception. *Nature* 412, 907–10.

Zeki, S. M. (1998) Parallel processing, asynchronous perception, and a distributed system of consciousness in vision. *Neuroscientist* 4, 365–72.

45

A Theory of Micro-consciousness

SEMIR ZEKI

Consciousness is often regarded as the most complex problem in the Universe, a belief that I find it difficult to agree with, since we do not know what else exists in the Universe. It is often spoken of as the last frontier in science, implying that we have crossed all the other frontiers, which is not at all evident to me. Neurobiologists also suppose that they are edging ever closer to understanding the NCC or the neural correlate of consciousness (in the singular), which implies that consciousness is a single, unified entity, a belief further reinforced by the commonly used term "unity of consciousness." It is this last belief that I question in this chapter. I put forward the view that consciousness consists instead of many micro-consciousnesses that are distributed in space and in time and that the unified consciousness that we commonly speak of is only possible through the use of language and communication.

The Functional Specialization of the Visual Brain

The *theory of micro-consciousness* has its roots in a fundamental fact about the visual brain, namely that it consists of many visual areas, and that these are specialized to process different attributes of the visual scene. The two together lead to a general theory of functional specialization in the visual brain, which supposes that different attributes of the visual scene are processed in geographically distinct areas of the brain (Zeki 1978). While there has been debate about the extent of functional specialization in the visual brain, there is now near unanimous agreement that color and motion have specialized cortical centers and neural pathways leading to them. These two specializations are sufficient to argue the case for multiple consciousnesses.

In the human brain, the cortical center for processing visual motion corresponds to area V5 and its satellites (the V5 complex) while that for processing color signals corresponds to areas V4 and V4α. That the two specialized centers are geographically distinct from one another (Figure 45.1) has advantages; it allows us to study the consequences of lesions in one without contamination by lesions in the other area. Clinical evidence shows that damage to the cortex of the V5 complex leads to the syndrome of *cerebral akinetopsia* (an inability to perceive visual motion) while damage to the V4 complex leads to the syndrome of *achromatopsia*, or an inability to see the world in color (Zeki 1990, 1991). As

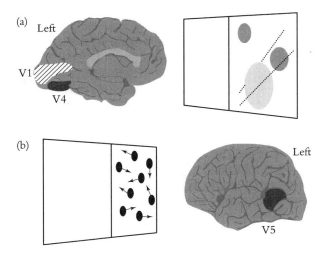

Figure 45.1 Visual areas V4 (*a*) and V5 (*b*) of the human brain, specialized for color and motion, respectively.

Each receives inputs from the primary visual cortex (V1) and registers the relevant activity in the contralateral hemifield. Lesions in V4 produce achromatopsia – the inability to see colors; motion vision remains intact. Lesions in V5 produce akinetopsia, the inability to see motion; color vision is unaffected.

interesting as this selective positive evidence is the negative evidence, for clinical studies are in unanimous agreement that motion vision, along with other kinds of vision, remains unaffected by damage restricted to the V4 complex. Conversely, color vision, along with other kinds of vision, remains unaffected by damage restricted to the V5 complex. This evidence therefore constitutes a powerful double dissociation between the motion and color processing systems of the brain. Clinical evidence thus gives powerful support to the notion of a specialization of function in the visual brain, derived from anatomical and physiological studies. From the viewpoint of the argument here, one could say with accuracy that there is a functional specialization in the visual brain even if these are the only two specializations (which of course they are not).

Processing Sites in the Visual Brain Are also Perceptual Sites

The next step in the argument leading to the theory of micro-consciousness is the demonstration that the areas of the visual brain, acknowledged to be processing sites for different attributes, are also perceptual centers. In addition to the clinical evidence reviewed above, there is direct evidence from clinical studies (Zeki & ffytche 1998) and from combined psychophysical/imaging experiments in humans (Moutoussis & Zeki 2002). Patients blinded by lesions of V1 can sometimes experience the motion of high contrast, rapidly moving, stimuli consciously (the Riddoch syndrome). The most likely pathway mediating the visual input in these patients, and thus enabling the visual experience, is the one that reaches V5 (the cortical visual motion center) directly through subcortical centers, either the lateral geniculate nucleus or the superior colliculus and the pulvinar, or both (Sincich et al. 2004) (Figure 45.2). Whichever pathway is used, it is significant that the signals arrive in V5 without passing through V1, and hence apparently do not necessarily need to be "pre-processed" there, whatever that may mean. Imaging evidence shows that the conscious experience of visual motion in such patients (who are otherwise blind) correlates with activity of a certain minimum strength in V5 (Zeki & ffytche 1998). The dependence of a conscious visual experience upon strength of activation within specialized areas receives strong support from psychophysical and imaging experiments (Moutoussis & Zeki 2002). Using dichoptic stimulation, where identical visual stimuli are presented for brief periods to the two eyes separately, thus leading to binocular fusion, one finds that when the two stimuli are identical in every respect (for example, an outline red house, or face, against a green background), subjects are able to identify (i.e., perceive) the stimulus correctly. But when the stimuli presented to the two eyes are of reverse color contrast (for example, outline red house against a green background to the right eye and outline green house against a red background to the left eye), subjects report seeing only yellow. Under these conditions, imaging experiments show that the same specific areas of the brain, specialized for the processing and seeing of houses or faces respectively, are active, regardless of whether the subjects saw the stimulus (were conscious of it) or not. The difference between the two states is that, in the former, the activity is higher than in the latter. Other experiments have largely confirmed this positive correlation between strength of activity in an area and the generation of a conscious correlate for it (Rees et al. 2000; Dehaene et al. 2001). We do not know yet whether this higher activity is due to the recruitment of previously inactive cells, to an increased discharge of already active cells, or to an increase in synaptic input without an increase in firing rate. This positive correlation obviates the need to postulate separate cortical area(s) necessary for perception and nonconscious processing. We refer to processing sites at which activity can acquire a conscious correlate and does not require further processing as *essential nodes* (Zeki & Bartels 1999). It is an interesting question whether each visual area can potentially function as an essential node or whether some should be excluded. In particular it has been supposed that area V1 should be excluded from such a role (Crick & Koch 1990). But all the clinical (Zeki et al. 1999) and experimental (Ress & Heeger 2003; Lamme 2004) evidence indicates that V1 is an essential node and/or it becomes one in some pathological conditions. Of course, processing–perceptual sites (essential nodes) are not sufficient on their own in generating a conscious correlate; they depend upon enabling systems in the brain stem (Zeki & ffytche 1998) and possibly additional uncharted cortical systems (see below).

That processing areas are also perceptual areas has important implications. Traditionally, even the perception of elementary visual attributes such as color were thought to be dependent upon higher cognitive faculties and thus upon a "top-down" influence brought to bear on the activities of the processing centers. Both Hermann von Helmholtz and Ewald Hering invoked higher cognitive factors such as learning, judgment, and memory to account for the remarkable perceptual capacity of the brain to discount the wavelength composition of the light reflected from a surface and assign a constant color to it. Yet all human color imaging experiments have been unanimous in not showing any particular activation of the frontal lobes, traditionally regarded as one of the higher cognitive centers. Instead the activation seems to be limited to the color center, the V4 complex, and the areas that feed it, namely V1 and V2. This seems to imply that assigning a constant color to a surface is more of a straightforward computational process (Land 1977) that engages the

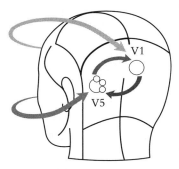

Figure 45.2 The flow of visual information from the retina to V1 and V5.

Notice that V5 receives a dual input from the retina, one through V1 and another that bypasses.

color center and the areas feeding it. As well, the result seems to suggest that processing in an area may have a conscious correlate (i.e., become perceptually explicit and not require further processing) (Zeki & Bartels 1999), without necessarily depending upon some kind of "top-down" influence from higher areas. The same is true for other visual stimuli such as the Kanizsa triangle, the interpretation of which has been supposed to be due to top-down influences (Gregory 1972). Once again, imaging experiments are unanimous in not showing involvement or engagement of areas in the frontal cortex during the perception of such stimuli (Hirsch et al. 1995; ffytche & Zeki 1996). Thus involvement of higher centers is not essential, which is not to say that it is not important or that there never is any involvement of "higher" centers in visual perception and consciousness.

Perceptual Asynchrony and Temporal Hierarchies in Visual Perception

The multiple visual areas of the brain and their specializations impose a new problem, not considered necessary to address in the mid-twentieth century when it was thought that there was a single visual area in the brain, or later when it was hypothesized that the visual areas are hierarchically organized, with each area undertaking the same processing as its antecedents, but at a more complex level (see Zeki 1993). The problem that functional specialization of the visual areas raises is how these areas interact to provide the unified image in the brain, in which all the different visual attributes are apparently seen in precise spatial and temporal registration. In fact, psychophysical experiments show that, over brief time windows, we do not see all attributes at the same precise time, a powerful pointer to how the visual brain is organized (Moutoussis & Zeki 1997). In particular, it has been shown that color is perceived before motion by ~80 ms. and that locations are perceived before colors (Pisella et al. 1998), which are perceived before orientations (Moutoussis & Zeki 1997). The latter demonstration effectively rules out alternate explanations (Nishida & Johnston 2002) couched in terms of the difference being due to a difference in first and second order attribute processing. The supposition (Moutoussis & Zeki 1997) that this asynchrony is rather due to differences in processing time for different visual attributes has been supported by recent experiments (Arnold & Clifford 2002).

The Distribution of Micro-consciousnesses in Space and Time

Because a (micro-)consciousness for color is the correlate of activity in V4 and that for motion a correlate of activity in the geographically separate V5, it follows that *micro-conciousnesses are distributed in space*. Because we become conscious of the two attributes at different times, it follows that *micro-consciousnesses are distributed in time*. The psycho-physical results also show that there is a temporal hierarchy of micro-consciousnesses, that for color preceding that for orientation which, in turn precedes that for motion. Of course, it is also true that over longer periods of time, in excess of 500 ms, we do see different attributes in perfect temporal and spatial registration, which itself demands an explana-tion. The value of the experiments detailed above is in the insights that they give us into brain mechanisms of consciousness and binding even if they do not account for how and why, in the longer term, the brain is capable of registering the different attributes as if they are perceived at the same precise time. One of the insights these psychophysical experi-ments give is related directly to the consequences of the demonstrated temporal hierarchy of conscious perception on the problem of binding. Because of differences in time taken to perceive color and motion, subjects consistently mis-bind the color perceived at time t to the motion perceived at time $t-1$ (Moutoussis & Zeki 1997). Put more simply, they bind the (veridically) correct color perceived at time t with the (veridically) incorrect direction of motion, the direction that had been registered 100 ms before. It follows that, over very brief time windows, the brain does not wait for each area to complete its processings; rather it simply binds what has been processed and reached a perceptual level. This in turn suggests strongly that *binding is a post-conscious phenomenon* (Zeki & Bartels 1999), and does not itself generate the conscious experience, as some have supposed (Crick & Koch 1990).

A further indication that binding may be post-conscious comes from psychophysical experiments which demonstrate that associating color to motion occurs after associating color to color or motion to motion (Bartels & Zeki 2006). In these experiments, subjects fixate a cross and a stimulus appears on each side of the screen. The one on the left can be either of two colors and the one on the right of two other colors. The task of the subjects is to determine which of the two pairs appear simultaneously on the left and the right. With an identical paradigm, one can also ask subjects to pair the direction of motion in one half of the screen with the direction of motion in the other half, or the color in one half with the direc-tion of motion in the other half. One can then extend the rate of alternation in the attribute of the stimulus on each side of the fixation point to fast rates. At high rates of oscillations, the stimuli on either side can be perceived correctly but cannot be associated or bound.

I refer to consciousness of a stimulus or of a percept that is compound, in the sense that it consists of more than one attribute, as a *macro-consciousness*, to distinguish it from micro-consciousness of a single attribute alone (e.g., color). Consistent with the theory of micro-consciousnesses, it is interesting to note that a macro-consciousness may be the result of false binding, as when the veridically "correct" color is bound to the veridically "wrong" motion or form (Moutoussis & Zeki 1997). We have argued that this results from the brain binding what it has already processed (Moutoussis & Zeki 1997). It should be noted that once a macro-consciousness is formed from two or more micro-consciousnesses, the constitu-ent micro-consciousnesses cease to exist in that we become aware at any given moment t of the composite and not of the constituents, which is not to say that we cannot become micro-conscious of the constituents if we pay attention to the constituents rather than the composite.

Three Levels of Hierarchy in Consciousness

A macro-consciousness need not, of course, be limited to a bound visual percept. It could equally signify consciousness of a percept that includes a visual and an auditory component, or of several visual components that, together, constitute a distinct new entity, for example a moving red bus. It thus becomes possible to distinguish three hierarchical levels of consciousness: the levels of micro-consciousness, of macro-consciousness, and of the unified consciousness. Of necessity, one level depends upon the presence of the previous one but one level need not trigger the next one. Within each level, one can postulate a temporal hierarchy. This has been demonstrated for the level of micro-consciousness, because color and motion are perceived at different times. It has also been demonstrated for the level of the macro-consciousnesses, because binding between attributes (e.g., color and motion) takes longer than binding within attributes (e.g., color and color). These temporal differences in turn lead one to postulate a set of temporal hierarchies, in which the binding of one set of attributes leading to a given macro-consciousness would take longer than the binding of another set of attributes leading to another macro-consciousness, and the binding of several attributes would take longer still. Although the necessary experiments in this domain have yet to be done, such a result would be predicted.

Micro- and macro-consciousnesses with their individual temporal hierarchies really refer to what has been coined as phenomenal consciousness, as opposed to access consciousness (Block 1996). Only with the additional involvement of language and communicative capabilities could the micro- and macro-consciousnesses lead to the final, unified consciousness, that of myself as the perceiving person. This and this alone qualifies as the unified consciousness, and this alone can be described in the singular. Kant probably saw, hesitatingly, the relation between the micro-consciousness (his "empirical consciousness") and the unified consciousness. He wrote:

> All presentations have a necessary reference to a *possible* empirical consciousness. For if they did not have this reference, and becoming conscious of them were entirely impossible, then this would be tantamount to saying that they do not exist at all. But all empirical consciousness has a necessary reference to a transcendental consciousness (a consciousness that precedes all particular experience), viz., the consciousness of myself as original apperception. (Kant 1781; original emphasis)

Here, I disagree only with the suggestion that the "empirical" (micro-) consciousness has a *necessary* reference to the unified, transcendental consciousness. It will only do so when reportability is involved and that necessitates the use of language and communicative action. Kant also suspected that the various attributes must themselves be synthesized first, before being synthesized into the "pure consciousness," although he could not have been aware of the principles of functional specialization. He continues: "But because every appearance contains a manifold, so that different perceptions are in themselves encountered in the mind sporadically and individually, these perceptions need to be given a combination that in sense itself they cannot have. Hence there is in us an active power to synthesize this manifold" (which he calls "imagination") (Kant 1781).

Kant supposed that the "transcendental" consciousness is present a priori, before any experience is acquired, from which we would conclude that there is an ontological hierarchy in consciousness. It is hard to be conclusive in this regard, but it is worth pointing out that consciousness of oneself as the perceiving person amounts to being aware of being aware, and I believe that this requires communication with others and, especially although not exclusively, the use of language. The cortical programs to construct visual attributes must also be present before any experience is acquired and all experience must therefore be read into them. It seems more likely that, ontogenetically, the micro-consciousnesses precede the unified consciousness and that the programs for them are also present at birth. Hence, even though in adult life the unified consciousness sits at the apex of the hierarchy of consciousnesses, ontogenetically it is the micro-consciousnesses that occupy this position.

The Autonomy of the Processing-Perceptual Systems

In the argument leading to the theory of micro-consciousness, the individual visual areas have been endowed with substantial autonomy. It is interesting to address the question of the extent of this autonomy. It is unlikely that individual areas will be totally autonomous of the rest of the brain or of the cerebral cortex. Indeed, imaging experiments and clinical evidence show that there are enabling systems in the midbrain and pontine reticular formation on which conscious experience is critically dependent (Zeki & ffytche 1998). The extent to which a specialized visual area is dependent upon other cortical areas, visual or non-visual, can today best be addressed by asking which areas can be excluded as being essential to conscious experience, rather than being merely important for it. One suggestion that has strong adherents is that a feedback to V1 is critical since experiments have shown that a return input from specialized areas to V1 is important for the richness and sophistication of conscious experience (Finkel & Edelman 1989; Lamme 2004). But the fact that patients blinded by lesions in V1 can experience high contrast rapid visual motion consciously (Zeki & ffytche 1998; Stoerig & Barth 2001) shows as conclusively as is now possible that a *feedback* input to V1 is not necessary for visual consciousness. This is not the same thing as saying that feedback in general is not necessary for conscious experience, as it is perfectly possible that the patient whose V5 activity results in motion perception does so because V5 receives feedback from other higher areas. Nor does this statement imply that feedback to V1 is not important and enriching of the conscious experience.

If an area such as V5, though crippled by being disconnected from V1, can nevertheless function sufficiently for activity within it to result in a conscious correlate, it is worth extending the search to enquire what other areas may be necessary for activity in visual areas to acquire a (phenomenal) conscious correlate, either through a direct feedforward input or through a *feedback* or through both. A set of areas, vaguely defined as the "fronto-parietal network of areas," and believed to constitute a neurologically equally vague "work-space," has been considered critical for conscious experience (Rees et al. 2000; Dehaene & Naccache 2001). This may well be so for the unified or access (reportable) consciousness, but it is far from clear that it is critical for what has been called phenomenal visual experience. The evidence for the involvement of such a hypothetical work-space would currently be critically dependent upon techniques that sample the entire population of neurons which constitute such a network and therefore for the moment at least is critically dependent on brain imaging studies. One difficulty with such studies is that, in the contrasts made, an area that may be active but only at a low level may not show up in the brain contrasts; excluding it from involvement would nevertheless be unjustifiable. Within these constraints, the mandatory involvement in all consciousness of this "network of areas" that constitute the "work space" is not so far very promising. Human imaging experiments which have compared brain activity in eyes open vs eyes closed condition, when one would expect that a sudden conscious experience of the visual world would engage the frontal cortex, have not detected activity in the frontal-parietal network (Zeki et al. 1991; Marx et al. 2004). Moreover, in dichoptic viewing experiments that are so arranged that subjects sometimes consciously see the stimulus and sometimes not, imaging experiments show that it is only when subjects do not see the stimulus (though it is processed) that the frontal cortex is active; when they see it and can report it correctly, the frontal cortex is not active (Moutoussis & Zeki 2002). Similar results have been obtained by Pins et al. (ffytche and Pins 2003). It is therefore entirely possible that, in generating a phenomenal awareness, the specialized visual areas of the brain are not dependent upon the frontal or the parietal cortex. Other experiments show that the frontal cortex is engaged only when reportability is part of the conscious experience (Marois, Yi, & Chun 2004), thus serving further to highlight the difference between phenomenal and reportable conscious experiences, and therefore strengthen the theory of micro-consciousness.

See also 43 Methodologies for identifying the neural correlates of consciousness; 44 A neurobiological framework for consciousness; 47 Large-scale temporal coordination of cortical activity as a prerequisite for conscious experience; 48 Duplex vision: separate cortical pathways for conscious perception and the control of action.

Further Readings

Zeki, S. (1995) Behind the seen: the functional specialization of the brain in space and time. The Ferrier Lecture. *Philosophical Transactions of the Royal Society of London B: Biological Sciences* 360: 1458, 1145–83.

Zeki, S. and ffytche, D. H. (1998) The Riddoch syndrome: insights into the neurobiology of conscious vision. *Brain* 121 (Pt 1), 25–45.

References

Arnold, D. H. and Clifford, C. W. (2002) Determinants of asynchronous processing in vision. *Philosophical Transactions of the Royal Society of London B: Biological Sciences* 269, 579–83.

Bartels, A. and Zeki, S. (2006) The temporal order of binding visual attributes. *Vision Research* 46: 14, 2280–6

Block, N. (1996) How can we find the neural correlate of consciousness? *Trends in Neurosciences* 19, 456–9.

Crick, F. C. and Koch, C. (1990) Towards a neurobiological theory of consciousness. *Seminars in Neuroscience* 2, 263–75.

Dehaene, S. and Naccache, L. (2001) Towards a cognitive neuroscience of consciousness: basic evidence and a workspace framework. *Cognition* 79, 1–37.

Dehaene, S., Naccache, L., Cohen, L., Bihan, D. L., Mangin, J. F. et al. (2001) Cerebral mechanisms of word masking and unconscious repetition priming. *Nature Neuroscience* 4, 752–8.

ffytche, D. H. and Pins, D. (2003) Are neural correlates of visual consciousness retinotopic? *NeuroReport* 14: 16, 2011–4.

ffytche, D. H. and Zeki, S. (1996) Brain activity related to the perception of illusory contours. *Neuro-image* 3, 104–8.

Finkel, L. H. and Edelman, G. M. (1989) Integration of distributed cortical systems by reentry: a computer simulation of interactive functionally segregated visual areas. *Journal of Neuroscience* 9, 3188–208.

Gregory, R. L. (1972) Cognitive contours. *Nature* 238, 51–2.

Hirsch, J., DeLaPaz, R. L., Relkin, N. R., Victor, J., Kim K. et al. (1995) Illusory contours activate specific regions in human visual cortex: evidence from functional magnetic resonance imaging. *Proceedings of the National Academy of Sciences* 92, 6469–73.

Kant, I. (1781) *Kritik der reinen Vernunft*, trans. W. S. Pluhar (1996) as *Critique of Pure Reason*. Indianapolis: Hackett.

Lamme, V. A. (2004) Separate neural definitions of visual consciousness and visual attention; a case for phenomenal awareness. *Neural Networks* 17, 861–72.

Land, E. H. (1977) The retinex theory of color vision. *Scientific American* 237, 108–28.

Marois, R., Yi, D. J., Chun, M. M. (2004) The neural fate of consciously perceived and missed events in the attentional blink. *Neuron* 41, 465–72.

Marx, E., Deutschlander, A., Stephan, T., Dieterich, M., Wiesmann, M., and Brandt, T. (2004) Eyes open and eyes closed as rest conditions: impact on brain activation patterns. *Neuroimage* 21, 1818–24.

Moutoussis, K. and Zeki, S. (1997) Functional segregation and temporal hierarchy of the visual perceptive systems. *Proceedings of the Royal Society of London B: Biological Sciences* 264, 1407–14.

Moutoussis, K. and Zeki, S. (2002) The relationship between cortical activation and perception investigated with invisible stimuli. *Proceedings of the National Academy of Sciences* 99, 9527–32.

Nishida, S. and Johnston, A. (2002) Marker correspondence, not processing latency, determines temporal binding of visual attributes. *Current Biology* 12, 359–68.

Pisella, L., Arzi, M., and Rossetti, Y. (1998) The timing of color and location processing in the motor context. *Experimental Brain Research* 121, 270–6.

Rees, G., Wojciulik, E., Clarke, K., Husain, M., Frith, C., and Driver, J. (2000) Unconscious activation of visual cortex in the damaged right hemisphere of a parietal patient with extinction. *Brain* 123 (Pt 8), 1624–33.

Ress, D. and Heeger, D. J. (2003) Neuronal correlates of perception in early visual cortex. *Nature Neuroscience* 6, 414–20.

Sincich, L. C., Park, K. F., Wohlgemuth, M. J., and Horton, J. C. (2004) Bypassing V1: a direct geniculate input to area MT. *Nature Neuroscience* 7, 1123–8.

Stoerig, P. and Barth, E. (2001) Low-level phenomenal vision despite unilateral destruction of primary visual cortex. *Consciousness and Cognition* 10, 574–87.

Zeki, S. M. (1978) Functional specialisation in the visual cortex of the rhesus monkey. *Nature* 274, 423–8.

Zeki, S. (1990) A century of cerebral achromatopsia. *Brain* 113, 1721–77.

Zeki, S. (1991) Cerebral akinetopsia (visual motion blindness): a review. *Brain* 114, 811–24.

Zeki, S. (1993) *A Vision of the Brain*. Oxford: Blackwell Scientific.

Zeki, S. and Bartels, A. (1999) Toward a theory of visual consciousness. *Consciousness and Cognition* 8, 225–59.

Zeki, S. and ffytche, D. H. (1998) The Riddoch syndrome: insights into the neurobiology of conscious vision. *Brain* 121 (Pt 1), 25–45.

Zeki, S., Watson, J. D., Lueck, C. J., Friston, K. J., Kennard, C., and Frackowiak, R. S. (1991) A direct demonstration of functional specialization in human visual cortex. *Journal of Neuroscience* 11, 641–9.

Zeki, S., Aglioti, S., McKeefry, D., and Berlucchi, G. (1999) The neurological basis of conscious color perception in a blind patient. *Proceedings of the National Academy of Sciences* 96, 14,124–9.

46

Global Disorders of Consciousness

NICHOLAS D. SCHIFF

Overview

This chapter proposes a conceptual framework for neurophysiological mechanisms underlying human consciousness. The conceptual framework is derived from consideration of global disorders of human consciousness and integrates clinical observational data, experimental studies in animals, and measurements of brain function in the setting of severe injuries. The normal wakeful state of consciousness is characterized by alert appearance, responsiveness to external stimuli, goal-directed behavior, and the capacity to communicate. Several neurological disorders dissociate an appearance of wakefulness from these other accompanying behavioral features. Although neurological observations alone cannot provide a model of the necessary neuronal substrates of the conscious state, correlations of localized injury patterns producing global disorders of consciousness provide important clues to the contributions of several cerebral structures. These correlations can be compared with detailed experimental studies of the anatomical connections and functional properties of specific neuronal populations to infer mechanisms supporting the normal conscious state. Perhaps the most important future application of a mature model of the neuronal basis of consciousness will be to draw inferences about the likelihood of recovery of consciousness and cognition in brain-injured patients. Some of the limitations of existing methods and models to achieve this goal are discussed below.

At present, studies of the neural correlates of consciousness in normal subjects focus on identification of patterns of distributed brain activations under varying experimental conditions (see Singer chapter 47, and Rees & Frith, chapter 43). Applying the insights gained from such studies to determine awareness in brain-injured subjects is a challenging problem and exposes the limitations of inferences based on these existing results. This chapter makes contact with several other topics discussed elsewhere in this compilation. The neurological conditions reviewed below can be compared with the discussions by Hobson, in chapter 7, of normal states of consciousness and their physiological correlates. The conceptual analysis of neurological disorders of consciousness and the possible neurophysiological mechanisms proposed here complement discussions of the dynamic architecture required for on-line conscious processing by Tononi in chapter 22, models of the neuronal correlates of consciousness developed by Crick and Koch in chapter 44, and the relationship of consciousness to goal-directed behavior considered by Jeannerod in chapter 42.

Patterns of Cerebral Injuries Underlying Global
Disorders of Consciousness

Profound alteration or total loss of consciousness accompanies many different neurological injuries (see Plum & Posner 1982 for review). Specific nosological features, the localization of injuries, and the functional level of behavior associated with a syndrome, index different global disorders of consciousness. Separate functional classifications include unresponsive states, states preserving minimal evidence of sensorimotor integration, and global behavioral disruptions that nonetheless preserve a capacity for communication and goal-directed behavior. Later in this chapter measurements of cerebral activity from patients exhibiting total unresponsiveness or minimal evidence of awareness and interaction are compared and interpreted in light of proposed underlying brain mechanisms. In this section emphasis is placed on observational data that associates syndromes of global disruption of the conscious state with localized damage of specific cerebral structures. This review highlights the importance of injuries to subcortical structures in producing global impairment of the conscious state as a result of their presumed role in the organization of ongoing brain dynamics. The selection of syndromes briefly reviewed here includes two conditions associated with unresponsive states, *coma* and the *vegetative state*, and others that exhibit a range of behavioral responses, from minimal evidence of sensorimotor integration to more fully expressed behaviors (for a more comprehensive review, see Schiff & Plum 2000).

Coma is characterized by unresponsiveness to internal or external stimuli and an unvarying eyes-closed motionless state. The comatose patient shows no evidence of awareness of self or environment. Cyclical state changes (e.g., marked by alternating periods of eye opening or closure) are not observed. Coma as a rule reflects one of two broad mechanisms of brain dysfunction. Diffuse injuries that functionally impair both cerebral hemispheres produce coma and typically involve both the cerebral cortex and subcortical systems. These injuries are most often the result of severe brain trauma or oxygen deprivation (see discussion below). Alternatively, relatively discrete bilateral injuries to subcortical structures may produce coma (see Figure 46.1).

Parvizi and Damasio (2003) described a series of patients with circumscribed injuries to the brainstem that produced acute coma. The damage was in the rostral pons and dorsal midbrain in the majority of patients, regions containing cholinergic and other afferents that project strongly to thalamus or cortex. Another focal injury pattern producing acute coma consists of brainstem lesions that begin more rostrally in the midbrain (at the mesencephalic reticular formation) and typically extend into the thalamus. Castaigne et al. (1981) reviewed this pattern of midbrain and thalamic lesions from human autopsies and found that the anterior and posterior thalamic intralaminar nuclei were damaged in most of their cases. Both types of isolated bilateral upper brainstem and paramedian thalamic injuries (with or without midbrain involvement) can produce initial coma with a variable duration that is typically short, lasting only hours or 1–2 days at most. Restricted bilateral brainstem lesions typically give way to faster and more complete recoveries than bilateral thalamic injuries, particularly if the midbrain is involved on one or both sides. None of the brainstem coma cases studied by Parvizi and Damasio remained unconscious for greater than one week. In contrast, some patients with isolated paramedian thalamic lesions never recover from enduring global disorders of consciousness or recover over very long intervals. Given

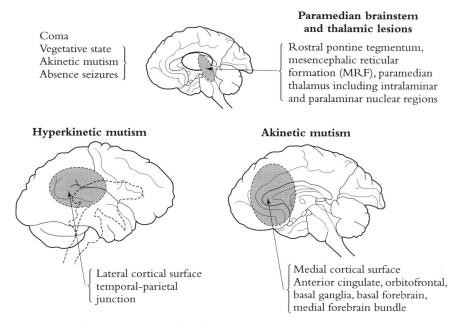

Coma
Vegetative state
Akinetic mutism
Absence seizures

**Paramedian brainstem
and thalamic lesions**

Rostral pontine tegmentum,
mesencephalic reticular
formation (MRF), paramedian
thalamus including intralaminar
and paralaminar nuclear regions

Hyperkinetic mutism

Akinetic mutism

Lateral cortical surface
temporal-parietal
junction

Medial cortical surface
Anterior cingulate, orbitofrontal,
basal ganglia, basal forebrain,
medial forebrain bundle

Figure 46.1 Schematic diagram of localized lesions producing global disorders of human consciousness.

this important difference, direct injuries to the paramedian thalamus per se must contribute significantly to the clinical outcome even if fibers of passage from the brainstem play a role; most of the brainstem pathways have other direct routes to cortex (see below).

Behaviorally the *vegetative state* (VS) differs from coma only in the recovery of irregular cyclic arousal patterns that are absent in the comatose patient. Like patients in a coma, VS patients show no behavioral evidence of awareness of self or the environment. When VS lasts more than 30 days it is arbitrarily labeled as *persistent vegetative state* (PVS); beyond specific time points, based on mechanism of injury, PVS is considered *permanent* (Jennett 2002). The structural anatomical damage that can precipitate a persistent vegetative state overlaps with the injuries producing coma. Patients remaining in a permanent vegetative state show specific patterns of diffuse brain injury following both trauma and oxygen deprivation leading to widespread disconnection of the corticothalamic system. Interestingly, subcortical damage is profound in both types of injuries producing permanent VS. Patients with non-traumatic VS invariably suffer severe bilateral thalamic damage often also associated with diffuse cortical damage and VS following traumatic injuries correlates with overwhelming damage to cerebral white matter producing severe thalamic degeneration in the majority of patients (Adams, Graham, & Jennett 2000). The cerebral cortex is generally spared following severe trauma resulting in VS, again emphasizing the role of subcortical structures. As discussed earlier, however, localized pontine injuries producing acute coma do not lead to enduring VS.

VS is importantly differentiated from the *minimally conscious state* (MCS) by the demonstration of unequivocal but inconsistent evidence of awareness of self or the environment (Giacino et al. 2002). This functional classification is associated with a variety of pathologies that include variations on syndromes discussed below that preserve minimal evidence of sensorimotor integration. Physiological correlates of MCS are discussed in the last section of this chapter.

MCS patients may exhibit the syndrome of *akinetic mutism*, a term used in the literature to describe different behavioral abnormalities that can be organized as subtypes (see Schiff & Plum 2000 for review). The classical phenotype of akinetic mutism resembles a state of hypervigilance. Patients may appear attentive and vigilant but remain motionless while visually tracking examiners moving around the room. Here, the term akinetic mutism indicates a recovery of a crude wakeful attentiveness without evidence of any other functional behavior to distinguish the condition from VS. The classic injury pattern associated with this syndrome is a bilateral injury to the anterior medial regions of the cerebral cortex (as schematically diagrammed in Figure 46.1). Most often this injury arises through the rupture of an arterial aneurysm located at the connection of the anterior cerebral arteries that supply blood to this part of the brain. In addition to the cortical injuries, damage to the basal ganglia and basal forebrain arise in this setting.

Another behavioral syndrome sometimes referred to as akinetic mutism is characterized by severe memory loss, markedly slowed behavioral responses, and apathetic appearance. This form of akinetic mutism often arises from injuries that combine damage to the medial caudal thalamus and medial dorsal mesencephalon (encompassing the mesencephalic reticular formation). A persistent dementia characterizes the recovery phase of this later disorder that is often described as "slow syndrome." Patients with slow syndrome show severe apathy and excessive sleepiness, yet they may speak with understandable words and respond accurately. In addition to damage to the mesencephalon and thalamus, this form of akinetic mutism may be seen following injuries to the caudate nuclei, bilateral injuries to the globus pallidus interna (see Mega & Cohenour 1997), or selective interruption of the medial forebrain bundle that supplies dopaminergic fibers to the medial cortical regions often affected in the hypervigilant form of the disorder (see Schiff & Plum 2000 for review). Both forms of akinetic mutism can be related to disruption of the parallel subsystems of segregated cortico-striatopallidal-thalamocortical loops that link the frontal lobes, basal ganglia, and thalamus (Mega & Cohenour 1997).

Hyperkinetic mutism is a recently described disorder in which patients exhibit unrestrained but coordinated motor activity in the absence of any external evidence of awareness of self or the environment. Hyperkinetic mutism has been described following bilateral destruction of temporal parietal occipital junctions and wider lesions encompassing occipital-parietal regions. This behavioral pattern overlaps the Kluver and Bucy (1939) syndrome (psychic blindness, hypermetamorphosis, hyperorality, emotional dyscontrol, and severe amnesia) described first in nonhuman primates following large, bilateral resections of the temporal lobe. Hyperkinetic mutism can be seen as the opposite of akinetic mutism, with preserved unconscious expression of frontal intentional mechanisms unmodulated by a decoding of the meaning of integrated polysensory signals processed in the inferior parietal lobe or posterior temporal lobes. The condition appears to represent a state of behavioral unawareness despite a frenzy of motor activity.

Epilepsies producing alteration of consciousness may selectively impair awareness and goal-directed behaviors producing VS, akinetic mutism, and hyperkinetic mutism. Absence seizures and complex partial seizures both reflect such global alterations of consciousness and share the features of attentional and intentional failure, loss of working memory and loss of perception during the events. Patients experiencing long-lasting absence seizures and complex partial seizures can exhibit automatic behaviors similar to those seen in hyperkinetic mutism. Blumenfeld and co-workers proposed an anatomical overlap in the origins of absence and temporal seizures based on neuroimaging studies (Blumenfeld & Taylor 2003). In their studies, common recruitment of central thalamic and upper brainstem structures was associated with both seizures types; absence seizures produced increased metabolic activity across the cortex whereas temporal lobe seizures showed reductions of metabolism widely across fronto-parietal cortical regions. The differences in impact on cortical metabolism suggest separate mechanisms of functional disruption that likely depend on variations in recruitment of inhibitory and excitatory neuronal populations.

The cellular basis of the absence seizure is the subject of a long-standing debate (Blumenfeld & Taylor 2003). Generation within corticothalamic networks is indicated by both clinical and experimental studies of absence seizures. Cortico-thalamic projections that support large-scale coherent EEG patterns seen with absence seizures and normal sleep rhythms involve the nucleus reticularis of the thalamus (NRT) in conjunction with thalamo-cortical relay cells as the essential substrate beyond a cortical initiation of the seizure (Contreras & Steriade 1995). The intralaminar thalamic nuclei appear to play a specific role in the spread and generalization of these seizures (Seidenbecher & Pape 2001). Complex partial seizures of the temporal lobe vary in the quality and degree of their alteration of consciousness. Clinical features may, however, be indistinguishable from absence seizures and quantitative EEG analyses support the inference that common circuits are recruited in both seizure types (Schiff, Labar, & Victor 1999).

Taken together, an overlap exists between the anatomical substructures recruited in absence and temporal lobe seizures and those that, when injured, induce coma, vegetative states, and akinetic mutism. Unlike other conditions that may produce brief unconsciousness without any evidence of lasting structural injury such as concussions, syncope, or anesthesia, arousal is preserved during the absence seizure demonstrating a unique and selective loss of integration of forebrain activity. The syndromes reviewed above provide vague hints about how such large-scale patterns of dynamic activity in the human forebrain may organize the corticothalamic system during normal conscious wakeful states. In the following section the specific neuronal cell types impacted by these injuries, their micro-circuitry, and known physiological properties are considered to further develop intuitions about the underlying mechanisms producing global disorders of consciousness.

Contribution of Brainstem Arousal Systems and Meso-diencephalic "Gating" Systems to Conscious State and Goal-Directed Behaviors

The preceding discussion of neurological lesions producing global disorders of consciousness indicates the important role of specific brainstem and other subcortical gray matter structures in supporting the normal wakeful state. A common functional mechanism linking these neuronal populations is proposed below. Normal consciousness integrates actions with cognitive functions of attention, short-term memory, motor preparation, and learning. This pluripotentiality is partially reflected in the concept of arousal (Garey et al. 2003). Arousal is a state function of the brain that reflects global modulations of the thalamocortical system producing well-ordered transitions from wakefulness though stages of sleep (Steriade & Llinas 1988). With the exception of coma, all the disorders reviewed above preserve some form of patterned arousal. Within the normal arousal state of wakefulness, cerebral activity is dynamically organized around goal-directed behaviors. It is likely that ongoing interactions among the brainstem arousal systems and the subcortical structures highlighted in Figure 46.1 provide the essential support for the formation of distributed cerebral activations necessary for moment-to-moment behavior.

The "arousal systems" consist of brainstem neuronal populations that control the state changes associated with the sleep–wake cycle. Cholinergic, serotoninergic, noradrenergic, and histaminergic nuclei located predominantly in the brainstem, basal forebrain, and posterior hypothalamus, are considered core components of the arousal systems (Parvizi & Damasio 2003). Another system, the hypocretin-orexin neurons of the hypothalamus provide an on-switch for sleep–wake behaviors (Sutcliffe & de Lecea 2002).

Cholinergic pathways that originate in the laterodorsal tegmental and pedunculopontine nuclei project rostrally to the thalamus where they exert opposing effects on thalamic reticular neurons (NRT) and thalamocortical relay neurons (TCR), see Figure 46.2. Acting on nicotinic receptors on TCR neurons, the brainstem cholinergic afferents depolarize membrane potentials and thereby lower firing thresholds. Synapses from the same cholinergic neurons onto NRT cells activate muscarinic receptors producing hyperpolarization and inhibition of these inhibitory neurons with the net effect of further excitation of TCR output (see Steriade, Jones, & McCormick 1997). Cholinergic nuclei located more rostrally in the basal forebrain project widely to the cerebral cortex. Noradrenergic and cholinergic afferents innervate layer I (and other layers) of the cortex parallel to afferents from the paramedian thalamus (as discussed below). Collectively these arousal inputs to layer I act to depolarize apical dendrites of neurons in layers II, III, and V (cortical output layer) increasing overall cortical activity across layers by lower firing thresholds. Both systems project to the thalamus as well, where they preferentially innervate the paramedian regions (Erro, Lanciego, & Gimenez-Amaya 1999). Anatomical studies demonstrate high degrees of interconnection among these brainstem neuronal populations comprising the arousal systems providing a basis for complex interactions across the sleep–wake cycle (Smiley et al. 1999). Behavioral-specific effects of noradrenergic, dopaminergic, and cholinergic neuromodulators have been described (Clayton et al. 2004). Thus, phasic activations of these brainstem populations likely play some role in organizing behaviors, although a more selective role in shaping the formation of behavioral states can be identified for closely related systems in the midbrain and thalamus, as argued below.

As reviewed above, bilateral injuries that can produce absence seizures, akinetic mutism, vegetative states, and coma often involve neurons of the mesencephalic reticular formation (MRF, primarily the nucleus cuneiformis) and the thalamic intralaminar nuclei (ILN). Historically the ILN were originally considered to form the core of forebrain arousal systems, together with the NRT and MRF (Moruzzi & Magoun 1949) and experimental studies indicate that these neurons play an important role in supporting the state changes of corticothalamic systems that underlie sleep–wake cycles but do not necessarily drive these state changes (Steriade, Jones, & McCormick 1997). Their functional role in the wakeful forebrain appears to be to organize interregional corticocortical and thalamocortical networks that are engaged in the performance of many behavioral tasks (reviewed in Schiff & Purpura 2002).

Several anatomical specializations of the intralaminar nuclei and paralaminar regions allow for such a role. The ILN project widely, but with regional selectivity, across the cere-

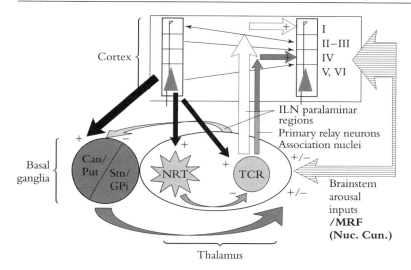

Figure 46.2 The functional connectivity of the neuronal populations.

In this cartoon sketch the main feedback loops of the cerebrum are characterized. The cerebral cortex is represented by two isolated columns (one showing feedforward connections to Layer I and the other "higher-order" area showing feedback connections to Layer IV and outputs from the column). As diagrammed, the ILN, in conjunction with the arousal system inputs, acts to modulate activity in the cortical columns through depolarization of apical dendrites arising in Layer I from neurons in deeper layers. In addition, broad activation of the thalamus through disinhibition of the ILN and other relay neurons is produced by arousal inputs. The other main excitatory and inhibitory influence on corticothalamic dynamics originates in the excitation or inhibition produced by the confluence of cortical and thalamic (primarily ILN) inputs to the basal ganglia that can only feed back to the cortex through the thalamus. See text for further details.

brum to layer I paralleling the pattern of arousal system innervation. Thalamic synaptic inputs arriving in layer I of the cerebral cortex are considered modulatory whereas synapses onto layer IV (the granular layer) reflect input from primary sensory relay nuclei (primary sensory cortices) or association nuclei (association cortices, see Guillery & Sherman 2002). These thalamic intralaminar nuclei have extensive reciprocal connections with the frontal and prefrontal cortices (van der Werf, Witter, & Groenewegen 2002) and are also all heavily innervated by cholinergic, noradrenergic, and hypothalamic orexin system (Parvizi & Damasio 2003). Additionally, the mesencephalic reticular formation projects directly to the ILN and drives these thalamic neurons during periods of wakefulness (Steriade & Glenn 1982). Projections from the ILN are unique in providing the largest thalamic efference to the basal ganglia as indicated in Figure 46.2. The rostral components of the intralaminar nuclei tend to project to prefrontal, posterior parietal, and primary sensory areas and provide more diffuse innervation of the basal ganglia, whereas the more caudal components project to pre-motor and anterior parietal cortices and form topographically organized connections with the basal ganglia (Groenewegen & Berendse 1994). Van der Werf, Witter, and Groenewegen (2002) comprehensively evaluated the efferent and afferent connections of the ILN within the rat brain. Their studies demonstrate that ILN collectively provide access to several parallel cerebral networks roughly corresponding to the cortico-striatopallidal-thalamocortical "loop" systems described in nonhuman primates by Alexander, Delong, and Strick (1986). Groenewegen and Berendse (1994) had earlier proposed that the ILN provide an anatomical substrate for interactions among these relatively segregated loop pathways under the control of the prefrontal cortex. As shown in Figure 46.2, ILN projections to the basal ganglia may serve as a parallel pathway of either activation or suppression of thalamocortical output (see Schiff & Purpura 2002 for review of physiological studies supporting this inference).

Jones (2001) has recently redefined the primate intralaminar and other thalamic subdivisions into two classes of neurons on the basis of correlation with differential calcium-binding protein expression. One class of thalamic neurons, the "matrix" neurons, projects to layer I across relatively wide cortical territories. The other class of thalamic neurons, the "core" neurons, have more area-specific cortical projections and form synapses in granular layers of the cortex. Most ILN subdivisions are strongly enriched with matrix neurons. Jones proposes that the matrix neurons act collectively as a functional system to organize global corticothalamic synchrony. These neurons are dispersed within the thalamus and may explain both the vulnerability of the brain to paramedian thalamic injuries and the redundancies suggested by the potential to recover from some injuries to these regions (Schiff 2004).

Intralaminar nuclei neurons also form synapses on cell bodies within output layers V and VI of the cortex (Macchi 1993). The dual projections of ILN neurons (top and bottom) within a cortical column are proposed to underpin a coincidence detection mechanism that facilitates responses to specific thalamic inputs received in the granular layers (Llinas, Leznik, & Urbino 2002). Larkum, Zhu, and Sakmann (1999) demonstrated a biophysical mechanism consistent with this model. Co-activation of the apical dendrites (in layer I) and soma of layer V pyramidal neurons induced a back-propagating action potential leading to the generation of burst firing that could produce synaptic modification around coincident firing patterns. Llinas et al. (2002) recently demonstrated that combined stimulation of the ILN and the ventrobasal nucleus (a specific thalamic relay nucleus projecting into cortical layer IV) in a mouse slice model of the corticothalamic system generated a supralinear summation of locally evoked potentials consistent with this mechanism. Depolarization of apical dendrites of neurons in layers II–III and V by ILN afferents may also promote sustained (or "persistent") cortical activity and activate mechanisms of long-term potentiation dependent on NMDA receptors (Mair 1994) or other mechanisms (McCormick et al. 2003). Thus, the anatomical specializations of the "matrix" neuron rich ILN and paralaminar regions of surrounding thalamic nuclei provide a unique substrate for support of distributed cerebral persistent activity through effects on both cortical and basal ganglia activity (Purpura & Schiff 1997).

Human neuroimaging studies and animal neurophysiological studies also support such a key role for the ILN in establishing distributed persistent activity associated with working memory, sustained attention, and motor intention (reviewed in Schiff & Purpura 2002). Kinomura et al. (1996) studied subcortical contributions to the short-term focusing of attention using functional PET studies in normal human subjects performing a reaction-time task utilizing either visual or somatosensory cues. Activation of both the rostral and caudal ILN components accompanied the sustained attention period of the task. Paus et al. (1997) demonstrated a complementary finding that vigilance decrements across a long-term monitoring task (~60 minutes) correlated with decreased blood flow in a network linking the medial thalamus, tegmental brainstem, and the anterior cingulate cortex. The anterior cingulate cortex is reciprocally connected with the anterior intralaminar nuclei and provides wide layer I projections to the prefrontal cortex suggesting it may act as an extension of the ILN within the prefrontal cortex (cf. Paus 2001).

Cortical recordings from primates in wakeful states correlate cortical persistent activity with attentional control (Fries et al. 2001), motor preparation and exploration (Murthy & Fetz 1996), and working memory (Pesaran et al. 2002). In an awake-behaving primate model of the Kinomura et al. experiment central thalamic neurons demonstrated sustained activity during the attentional delay period (Schiff et al. 2001). In a series of studies in rats, Mair and colleagues have demonstrated that lesions in the rostral intralaminar region produce broad deficits in holding behaviorally relevant information obtained across sensory modalities (Burk & Mair 1998). In addition, similar lesions of the rat rostral ILN produce deficits in initiating motor behavior (Burk & Mair 2001). Recent primate studies have shown that rostral intralaminar and paralaminar neurons exhibit delay period activity during working memory tasks in awake-behaving monkeys (Wyder et al. 2004).

Thus, in conjunction with the MRF and NRT, the ILN appear to link arousal states to the control of moment-to-moment intention and "attentional gating." The experimental studies and clinical observations reviewed above suggest a specific physiological basis for this "gating" function: the ILN may facilitate the formation, distribution, maintenance, and dissolution of sustained cerebral activity representing elementary cognitive building blocks for organized behavior during wakefulness. Taken together, the existing literature suggests that distributed cerebral persistent activity underpins the elementary cognitive functions of sustained attention, working memory, and motor intentions. As diagrammed in Figure 46.2, the dual ILN projections to the basal ganglia and frontal and prefrontal cortices likely provide an essential substrate for frontal lobe influences on the formation of distributed cerebral persistent activity. Wide disabling of the dynamical fine structure of this ongoing activity during wakefulness may be the mechanism linking bilateral structural lesions of the MRF, ILN, and anterior medial cortical regions (cingulate, supplementary motor, and orbitofrontal regions) and functional disturbances (absence and related seizure types) to global disorders of consciousness.

Neurophysiological Characterization of Brain Function in Disorders of Consciousness

The conceptual framework developed above can now be used to interpret quantitative measurements of brain function in VS and MCS. Patients with very severe brain injuries producing these conditions present significant challenges for identifying their potential to recover consciousness. At present, there are no physiological measurements that reliably correlate with a potential for recovery of consciousness (however, reliable measures that indicate failure to recover consciousness in certain circumstances do exist). The relatively circumscribed lesions that are associated with specific syndromes as discussed above are not typically encountered. The more common situation is a complex brain injury with a mixed pattern of features and a functional level of recovery that may or may not reflect residual cognitive capacities. The principal challenge of further neurophysiological characterization of brain function following severe injuries is to organize an approach to this problem based on brain mechanisms.

Brain-imaging techniques have been widely applied to the study of consciousness in normal human subjects (see chapters 43 and 44). Functional MRI (fMRI) and functional positron emission tomography (^{15}O-PET) studies have identified areas of brain activation in response to selective stimulation by correlating changes in either blood oxygen level or regional cerebral blood flow with neuronal activation. Only a small number of studies have employed these techniques to examine the neuronal activation patterns that characterize global disorders of consciousness. Studies of resting brain metabolism quantified by fluorodeoxyglucose positron emission tomography (FDG-PET) imaging have been more consistently applied to the evaluation of neurological patients. FDG-PET studies in VS patients demonstrate that overall cerebral metabolism is often reduced to 40–50 percent of normal levels providing a physiological correlate of unconsciousness in these patients found in clinical examinations (reviewed in Schiff et al. 2002). Regional glucose metabolic rates can be directly correlated with the level of neuronal activity (firing rates) in cerebral structures; measurements of cerebral metabolism and neuronal activity suggest an equivalence of metabolic rate and the mean firing rate of local neuronal populations (Smith et al. 2002). Although in the normal brain, fMRI signal activations are correlated with local neuronal activity, alterations of the mechanisms of cerebral autoregulation may change these relationships in patients with brain injuries.

Laureys et al. (2000, 2002) have carried out studies in VS patients using ^{15}O-PET paradigms to assess cerebral network responses to elementary sensory stimuli. In their studies, VS patients recruit only primary sensory cortical regions in response to stimulus sets that generate widespread network activations in normal subjects. When covariance measures are applied to the signal activations, the VS brains show disconnection of these primary cortical regions from higher-order processing areas. These patients failed to establish correlated patterns of activity across regions of the frontal and parietal lobes that arise in normal subjects when they perceive sensory stimuli (see Rees & Frith, chapter 43). Based on these findings Laureys et al. concluded that the residual cortical activations do not reflect cortical processing associated with awareness in VS patients. The ^{15}O-PET findings are also consistent with evoked potential studies done in other VS patients that typically show loss of longer latency ("late") components reflecting ongoing cerebral integrative activity (Rothstein, Thomas, & Sumi 1991). These neuroimaging and clinical electrophysiological studies support the view that in VS, the brain lacks distributed network activity and organized dynamics of the corticothalamic system; this dynamical alteration is correlated with marked reduction of overall neuronal activity reflected in very suppressed cerebral metabolic rates.

Modularity in the Vegetative State

The conclusion that VS can be modeled as a widespread functional disconnection of the corticothalamic systems must be considered separately in the context of patients with transient functional impairments of cerebral function vs. overwhelming structural brain injuries due to trauma or oxygen deprivation. In some patients with less uniform patterns of injury, who otherwise meet the criteria for permanent VS, occasional fragments of activity may be identified that nonetheless do not indicate awareness. In a study of a series of PVS patients, three such rare patients with unusual fragments of behavior were identified. The behaviors correlated with isolated cerebral activity measured using FDG-PET, structural MRI, and magnetoencephalography (MEG) (Schiff et al. 2002).

Within this group one patient occasionally expressed single words in the absence of environmental stimulation despite a 20-year period of VS. The patient had suffered over-

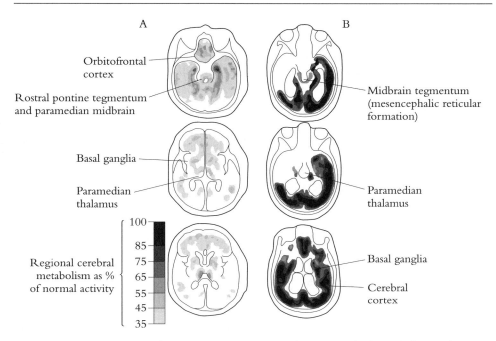

Figure 46.3 Co-registration of FDG-PET measurements of resting cerebral metabolism and structural MRI images (adapted from Schiff et al. 2002).

whelming injuries to subcortical structures with complete destruction of the right basal ganglia and thalamus and extensive injury to the left thalamus along with less extensive cortical injuries. FDG-PET measurements of resting metabolism demonstrated a marked reduction in global cerebral metabolism of <50 percent of normal across most brain regions. A collection of regions in the left hemisphere expressed higher levels of metabolism that included left sided thalamo-cortical-basal ganglia networks that support human language function, including Heschl's gyrus, Broca's area and Wernicke's area. MEG activation patterns following bilateral auditory stimulation were restricted to the left hemisphere in primary auditory areas, providing evidence that some thalamocortical relay fibers remained spared and functionally active. The combined anatomic, metabolic, and physiological data support the inference that a residual modular circuit remained active in this overwhelmingly damaged brain sporadically generating isolated spoken words as motor fixed action patterns (Schiff et al. 1999).

Figure 46.3 shows FDG-PET measurements of resting metabolism for two other VS patients studied. The grayscales indicate the level of regional metabolic rate compared to normal metabolic rate for the cerebral substructures (see Schiff et al. 2002 for details). Patient A suffered a diffuse injury to the brain as the result of oxygen deprivation. This injury produced more severe damage in the posterior regions of the brain. The patient remained in VS but unusually demonstrated continuous fragmentary motor behaviors that were not directed and could not be modulated by environmental stimulation. As seen in Figure 46.3a overall brain metabolism was less than 40 percent of normal with small areas demonstrating increased metabolic rates. The islands of activity seen in this patient's brain reflecting preserved metabolic activity correlated with the set of subcortical structures producing *akinetic mutism* when severely injured. As indicated by arrows, the MRF, the paramedian thalamus, basal ganglia, orbitofrontal, and prefrontal cortices remain relatively more active. This finding suggests that this patient represents a vegetative variation of hyperkinetic mutism in which the unconscious motor activity remains unregulated and unresponsive to sensory stimulation due to the loss of posterior cerebral function.

Patient B shows a unique pattern of metabolic activity for VS with relative sparing of cortical and basal ganglia metabolic rates. Average cerebral metabolism in this patient's brain was ~65 percent of normal. The patient had suffered a diffuse traumatic injury that included swelling of the brain and severe compression of the thalamus and midbrain producing extensive structural injuries to the paramedian regions of both structures. As noted above, permanent VS can be correlated with such injuries. Remarkably high metabolic rates found in the patient's brain are however a surprise and require further interpretation. In this patient the combination of overwhelming bilateral mesencephalic and paramedian thalamic injuries and grossly preserved cortical glucose metabolism can be interpreted to reflect lack of integration of presumably damaged yet partially preserved, isolated cerebral networks as observed in other VS patients (see discussion in Schiff et al. 2002). The finding supports the view that the tegmental mesencephalon and paramedian thalamus act as crucial gating systems that provide selective, integrative inputs to organize cerebral dynamics in the cortex, thalamus, and basal ganglia essential for consciousness. As proposed above, a loss of distributed patterns of activation through these connections may result in the failure of the formation of cerebral persistent activity.

Brain Function in the Minimally Conscious State

The demonstrated modularity of brain function in VS patients indicates that connected substructures may retain some physiological activity even in the absence of overall cerebral integration and organized behavior. The findings raise the question of at what point cerebral network connections and central integrative processes recover sufficiently to support awareness, goal-directed behavior, and the capacity to communicate necessary for unequivocal behavioral evidence of consciousness. This question invites consideration of brain mechanisms underlying MCS.

At present only a few studies have examined brain function in the MCS population. Boly et al. (2004) studied five patients meeting the criteria for MCS using the same elementary auditory stimuli tested in the ^{15}O-PET paradigm tested in VS patients (cf. Laureys et al. 2000). In their study, both MCS patients and healthy controls showed activation of auditory association regions in the superior temporal gyrus that did not activate in the VS patients. MCS patients and control subjects showed stronger correlation of the auditory cortical responses with frontal cortical regions than VS patients. These findings indicate that neuronal signals propagate more widely in the MCS brain suggesting a correlate of greater sensorimotor integration observed in MCS patients.

In a study combining fMRI, FDG-PET and quantitative EEG studies in two MCS patients who had suffered severe brain injuries, fMRI identified preserved large-scale network activations despite very low resting metabolic rates measured by FDG-PET (Schiff et al. 2005). Brain activations measured using fMRI paradigms comparing response to somatosensory and linguistic stimuli against unstimulated baselines demonstrated widely connected networks across both hemispheres in the two MCS patients. Language networks activated by spoken narratives, however, failed to produce a similar response when a time-reversed version of the signal was presented. This finding dissociated the MCS patients and normal controls. For both patients studied, global resting metabolic rates remained near VS levels. The dissociation of network activations in response to the two stimulus types in this context suggests an interpretation of the limited behavioral responses seen in these MCS patients. The low resting metabolic activity likely reflects a broad reduction of neuronal activity typically characterizing the normal resting brain state. In normal subjects this activity may index the anticipatory nature of consciousness either in the preparation of goal-directed activity or intentionally driven perceptual processing (cf. Gusnard & Raichle 2001). The low resting activity may explain the failure of similar stimuli to activate large-scale networks in the MCS patients – their ongoing brain activity may be insufficient to recruit these potentially viable systems, suggesting a failure of environmental awareness in absence of superthreshold stimulation.

Another point is that the network activations produced by the language stimuli in these subjects include regional activation of higher-order polysensory areas in the frontal and parietal cortices correlated in normal subjects with conscious awareness (cf. Rees & Frith, chapter 43). Without the benefit of a communicated report from the patients it is impossible to gauge their level of awareness, if any, of the content of the spoken narratives. These observations point out the important limitation that functional imaging techniques alone cannot identify awareness in patients with disorders of consciousness. The findings do suggest that functional imaging may provide useful correlates of the differences in MCS and PVS patients evident at the bedside.

Conclusions

Human consciousness is a dynamic process organized by the corticothalamic systems and their subcortical connections. Patterns of injuries producing global disorders of consciousness emphasize the important contribution of the paramedian thalami and their interconnections with the basal ganglia and brainstem to organizing brain dynamics underlying normal conscious behavior. Although functional imaging techniques make it possible to measure brain activity in patients with severe brain injuries, it is not possible to unequivocally assign a correlation of brain activations and awareness per se or to assign a particular cognitive level to such measurements. This limitation is well illustrated in MCS patients where evidence of interaction at the bedside and widespread activation of distributed cerebral networks can be demonstrated despite a failure to communicate with the patient. Recovery following impaired consciousness is a core concern for physicians and patients and clinical neurology will likely continue to provide important insight into the basic mechanisms of human consciousness. An explanation in terms of the functional integrity of specific brain networks and physiological processes will ultimately be crucial to frame a general model of the causes and correlates of consciousness.

See also 7 Normal and abnormal states of consciousness; 9 Clinical pathologies and unusual experiences; 10 Altered states of consciousness: drug-induced states; 49 Consciousness and anesthesia.

Further Readings

Boly, M., Faymonville, M. E., Peigneux, P., Lambermont, B., Damas, P., Del Fiore, G. et al. (2004) Auditory processing in severely brain injured patients: differences between the minimally conscious state and the persistent vegetative state. *Archives of Neurology* 61: 2, 233–8.

Laureys, S. L., Owen, A. M., and Schiff, N. D. (2004) Brain function in coma, vegetative state and related disorders. *Lancet Neurology* 3: 9, 537–46.

Schiff, N. D. (2005) Modeling the minimally conscious state: measurements of brain function and therapeutic possibilities. *Progress in Brain Research* 150: 477–97.

Schiff, N. D., Rodriguez-Moreno, D., Kamal, A., Kim, K. H., Giacino, J., Plum, F., et al. (2005) fMRI reveals intact large-scale networks in two minimally conscious patients. *Neurology* 64, 514–23.

References

Adams, J. H., Graham, D. I., and Jennett, B. (2000) The neuropathology of the vegetative state after acute insult. *Brain* 123, 1327–38.

Alexander, G. E., DeLong, M. R., and Strick, P. L. (1986) Parallel organization of functionally segregated circuits linking basal ganglia and cortex. *Annual Review of Neuroscience* 9, 357–81.

Blumenfeld, H. and Taylor, J. (2003) Why do seizures cause loss of consciousness? *Neuroscientist* 9: 5, 301–10.

Boly, M., Faymonville, M. E., Peigneux, P., Lambermont, B., Damas, P., Del Fiore, G. et al. (2004) Auditory processing in severely brain injured patients: differences between the minimally conscious state and the persistent vegetative state. *Archives of Neurology* 61: 2, 233–8.

Burk, J. A. and Mair, R. G. (1998) Thalamic amnesia reconsidered: excitotoxic lesions of the intralaminar nuclei, but not the mediodorsal nucleus, disrupt place delayed matching-to-sample performance in rats (*Rattus norvegicus*). *Behavioral Neuroscience* 112, 54–67.

Burk, J.A and Mair, R. G. (2001) Effects of intralaminar thalamic lesions on sensory attention and motor intention in the rat: a comparison with lesions involving frontal cortex and hippocampus. *Behavioural Brain Research* 123, 49–63.

Castaigne, P., Lhermitte, F., Buge, A., Escourolle, R., Hauw, J. J., and Lyon-Caen, O. (1981) Paramedian thalamic and midbrain infarcts: clinical and neuropathological study. *Annals of Neurology* 10: 2, 127–48.

Clayton, E. C., Rajkowski, J., Cohen, J. D., and Aston-Jones, G. (2004) Phasic activation of monkey locus ceruleus neurons by simple decisions in a forced-choice task. *Journal of Neuroscience* 24: 44, 9914–20.

Contreras, D. and Steriade, M. (1995) Cellular basis of EEG slow rhythms: a study of dynamic corticothalamic relationships. *Journal of Neuroscience* 15, 604–22.

Erro, E., Lanciego, J. L., and Gimenez-Amaya, J. M. (1999) Relationships between thalamostriatal neurons and pedunculopontine projections to the thalamus: a neuroanatomical tract-tracing study in the rat. *Experimental Brain Research* July 127: 2, 162–70.

Fries, P., Reynolds, J. H., Rorie, A. E., and Desimone, R. (2001) Modulation of oscillatory neuronal synchronization by selective visual attention. *Science* 291, 1560–3.

Garey, J., Goodwillie, A., Frohlich, J., Morgan, M., Gustafsson, J. A., Smithies, O. et al. (2003) Genetic contributions to generalized arousal of brain and behavior. *Proceedings of the National Academy of Sciences* 100: 19, 11,019–22.

Giacino, J. T., Ashwal, S., Childs, N., Cranford, R., Jennett, B., Katz, D. I. et al. (2002) The minimally conscious state: definition and diagnostic criteria. *Neurology* 58, 349–53.

Gronewegen, H. and Berendse, H. (1994) The specificity of the "nonspecific" midline and intralaminar thalamic nuclei. *Trends in Neuroscience* 17: 52–66.

Guillery, R. W. and Sherman, S. M. (2002) Thalamic relay functions and their role in corticocortical communication: generalizations from the visual system. *Neuron* 33: 2, 163–75.

Gusnard, D. A. and Raichle, M. E. (2001) Searching for a baseline: functional imaging and the resting human brain. *Nature Review: Neuroscience* 2: 10, 685–94.

Jennett, B. (2002) *The Vegetative State.* Cambridge: Cambridge University Press.

Jones, E. G. (2001) The thalamic matrix and thalamocortical synchrony. *Trends in Neurosciences* 24, 595–601.

Kinomura, S., Larssen, J., Gulyas, B., and Roland, P. E. (1996) Activation by attention of the human reticular formation and thalamic intralaminar nuclei. *Science* 271, 512–15.

Kluver, H. and Bucy, P. C. (1939) Preliminary analysis of functions of the temporal lobe in monkeys. *Archives of Neurology and Psychiatry* 42: 979–1000.

Larkum, M. E., Zhu, J. J., and Sakmann, B. (1999) A new cellular mechanism for coupling inputs arriving at different cortical layers. *Nature* 398, 338–41.

Laureys, S., Faymonville, M. E., Degueldre, C., Fiore, G. D., Damas, P., Lambermont, B. et al. (2000) Auditory processing in the vegetative state. *Brain* 123, 1589–601.

Laureys, S., Faymonville, M. E., Peigneux, P., Damas, P., Lambermont, B., Del Fiore, G. et al. (2002) Cortical processing of noxious somatosensory stimuli in the persistent vegetative state. *Neuroimage* 17: 2, 732–41.

Llinas, R. R., Leznik, E., and Urbano, F. J. (2002) Temporal binding via cortical coincidence detection of specific and nonspecific thalamocortical inputs: a voltage-dependent dye-imaging study in mouse brain slices. *Proceedings of the National Academy of Sciences* 99, 449–54.

Macchi, G. (1993) The intralaminar system revised. In D. Minciacchi, M. Macchi, A. Molinari, and T. Jones (eds.), *Thalamic Networks for Relay and Modulation*, 175–84. Oxford: Pergamon Press.

McCormick, D. A., Shu, Y., Hasenstaub, A., Sanchez-Vives, M., Badoual, M., and Bal, T. (2003) Persistent cortical activity: mechanisms of generation and effects on neuronal excitability. *Cerebral Cortex* 13: 11, 1219–31.

Mair, R. G. (1994) On the role of thalamic pathology in diencephalic amnesia. *Reviews: Neuroscience* 5: 2, 105–40.

Mega, M. S. and Cohenour, R. C. (1997) Akinetic mutism: disconnection of frontal-subcortical circuits. *Neuropsychiatry, Neuropsychology, and Behavioral Neurology* 10: 4, 254–9.

Moruzzi, G. and Magoun, H. W. (1949) Brainstem reticular formation and activation of the EEG. *Electroencephalography and Clinical Neurophysiology* 1, 455–73.

Murthy, V. N. and Fetz, E. E. (1996) Synchronization of neurons during local field potential oscillations in sensorimotor cortex of awake monkeys. *Journal of Neurophysiology* 76, 3968–82.

Parvizi, J. and Damasio, A. R. (2003) Neuroanatomical correlates of brainstem coma. *Brain* 126, 1524–36.

Paus, T. (2001) Primate anterior cingulate cortex: where motor control, drive and cognition interface. *Nature Review: Neuroscience* 2: 6, 417–24.

Paus, T., Zatorre, R., Hofle, N., Caramanos, Z., Gotman, J., Petrides, M., and Evans, A. (1997) Time-related changes in neural systems underlying attention and arousal during the performance of an auditory vigilance task. *Journal of Cognitive Neuroscience* 9, 392–408.

Pesaran, B., Pezaris, J. S., Sahani, M., Mitra, P. P., and Andersen, R. A. (2002) Temporal structure in neuronal activity during working memory in macaque parietal cortex. *Nature Neuroscience* 5, 805–11.

Plum, F. and Posner, J. (1982) *Diagnosis of Stupor and Coma.* New York: F. A. Davis.

Purpura, K. and Schiff, N. D. (1997) The thalamic intralaminar nuclei: a role in visual awareness. *The Neuroscientist* 3, 8–15.

Rothstein, T. L., Thomas, E. M., and Sumi, S. M. (1991) Predicting outcome in hypoxic-ischemic coma. A prospective clinical and electrophysiologic study. *Electroencephalography and Clinical Neurophysiology* 79: 2, 101–7.

Schiff, N. D. (2004) The neurology of impaired consciousness: challenges for cognitive neuroscience. In Michael S. Gazzaniga (ed.), *The Cognitive Neurosciences*, 3rd edn. Cambridge. MA: MIT Press.

Schiff, N. D. and Plum, F. (2000) The role of arousal and "gating" systems in the neurology of impaired consciousness. *Journal of Clinical Neurophysiology* 17, 438–52.

Schiff, N. D. and Purpura, K. P. (2002) Towards a neurophysiological basis for cognitive neuromodulation through deep brain stimulation. *Thalamus and Related Systems* 2: 1, 51–69.

Schiff, N. D., Kalik, S. F., and Purpura, K. P. (2001) Sustained activity in the central thalamus and extrastriate areas during attentive visuomotor behavior: correlation of single unit activity and local field potentials. *Society for Neuroscience 31st Annual Meeting* (722.12).

Schiff, N. D., Labar, D. L., and Victor, J. D. (1999) Common dynamics in temporal lobe and absence seizures. *Neuroscience* 91: 2, 417–28.

Schiff, N. D., Ribary, U., Plum, F., and Llinas, R. (1999) Words without mind. *Journal of Cognitive Neuroscience* 11: 6, 650–6.

Schiff, N., Ribary, U., Moreno, D., Beattie, B., Kronberg, E., Blasberg, R. et al. (2002) Residual cerebral activity and behavioral fragments in the persistent vegetative state. *Brain* 125, 1210–34.

Schiff, N. D., Rodriguez-Moreno, D., Kamal, A., Kim, K. H., Giacino, J., Plum, F. et al. (2005) fMRI reveals intact large-scale networks in two minimally conscious patients. *Neurology* 64: 3, 514–23.

Seidenbecher, T. and Pape, H. C. (2001) Contribution of intralaminar thalamic nuclei to spike-and-wave-discharges during spontaneous seizures in a genetic rat model of absence epilepsy. *European Journal of Neuroscience* 13, 1537–46.

Smiley, J. F., Subramanian, M., and Mesulam, M. M. (1999) Monoaminergic-cholinergic interactions in the primate basal forebrain. *Neuroscience* 93: 3, 817–29.

Smith, A. J., Blumenfeld, H., Behar, K. L., Rothman, D. L., Shulman, R. G., and Hyder, F. (2002) Cerebral energetics and spiking frequency: the neurophysiological basis of fMRI. *Proceedings of the National Academy of Sciences USA* 99: 16, 10,765–70.

Steriade, M. and Glenn, L. L. (1982) Neocortical and caudate projections of intralaminar thalamic neurons and their synaptic excitation from midbrain reticular core. *Journal of Neurophysiology* 48, 352–71.

Steriade, M. and Llinas, R. R. (1988) The functional states of the thalamus and the associated neuronal interplay. *Physiological Reviews* 68: 3, 649–742.

Steriade, M., Jones, E., and McCormick, D. (eds.) (1997) *Thalamus*. Amsterdam: Elsevier Publishers.

Sutcliffe, J. G. and de Lecea, L. (2002) The hypocretins: setting the arousal threshold. *Nature Review: Neuroscience* 3: 5, 339–49.

van der Werf, Y. D., Witter, M. P., and Groenewegen, H. J. (2002) The intralaminar and midline nuclei of the thalamus. Anatomical and functional evidence for participation in processes of arousal and awareness. *Brain Research Reviews* 39: 2–3, 107–40.

Wyder, M. T., Massoglia, D. P., and Stanford, T. R. (2004) Contextual modulation of central thalamic delay-period activity: representation of visual and saccadic goals. *Journal of Neurophysiology* 91: 6, 2628–48.

47

Large-Scale Temporal Coordination of Cortical Activity as a Prerequisite for Conscious Experience

WOLF SINGER

The term "consciousness" has several different connotations ranging from awareness of one's perceptions and sensations to self-awareness, the perception of oneself as an agent that is endowed with intentionality and free will. Here, the position will be defended that these various manifestations of consciousness should be tractable within neurobiological description systems, provided that it is possible to reduce the problem to the question of how brains perceive and represent the contents of perception. If one is conscious, one is always conscious of something. The respective contents of conscious experience can be perceptual objects of the outer world or states of one's own organism, in which case information is provided to the brain by extero- and enteroceptive senses. However, the contents of consciousness can also be processes initiated within the brain itself and in the absence of any external stimuli. Thus, conscious experience appears to involve a cognitive process that monitors neuronal activation patterns irrespective of whether these result from sensory input or are internally generated. This suggests two conclusions: First, since sensory signals can be readily processed and influence motor responses without being consciously perceived, the cognitive operations leading to conscious experience must differ from straightforward sensory-motor processing either because they involve additional structures such as higher-order cortical areas or because they are organized differently leading to more complex dynamical states of the involved networks. Second, because the primary sensory processes and the internally generated states can both be subject to conscious processing and then can coexist and be bound together, they must have the same format. In other words, the neuronal activation patterns representing the contents of conscious experience must have certain signatures in common, irrespective of whether they are due to sensory input or result from self-generated activity. These signatures should be identifiable by analyzing the differences in the spatio-temporal activation patterns associated with conscious and nonconscious processing, respectively.

Two non-exclusive possibilities may be considered. Conscious and nonconscious processes could involve the same anatomical substrate but differ with respect to certain state variables such as temporal coherence or synchrony or they could require recruitment of additional structures, conscious processing necessitating the engagement of particular cortical areas or a minimum number of cooperating cortical areas. In any case a mechanism is required that is capable of monitoring both the results of primary sensory processes and the results of computations based exclusively on information stored within the system. The most likely substrate for such cognitive processes of higher order are cortical areas that have been added in the course of evolution and that treat the results of lower order processes in the same way as these treat input from the sensory periphery. Part of the inner eye function of consciousness could thus be realized by an iteration of selfsimilar cortical functions. This interpretation is compatible with the neuroanatomical evidence that the phylogenetically more recent cortical areas are remote from primary sensory input and communicate mainly with one another and areas of lower order (Krubitzer 1998). This scenario is also compatible with the graded emergence of the ability for conscious processing that is correlated with the graded expansion of the cerebral cortex during evolution and with the graded maturation of cortical areas during ontogeny. The evolutionary changes of the mammalian brain consist essentially of an apposition of new cortical areas and comparative behavioral studies suggest that this increasing corticalization goes hand in hand with the increasing ability to represent and combine information at a conscious level. During ontogenetic development the increasing differentiation of conscious processing from rudimentary awareness of sensations to the fully expressed self-consciousness of the adult goes in parallel with the gradual maturation of the phylogenetically more recent cortical areas.

Several arguments let it appear likely that the computational operations performed by cortical modules always obey the same basic principles irrespective of the type of input that is processed. These arguments are derived from the evidence that the microcircuitry of different cortical areas is strikingly similar and that auditory cortex, if supplied with visual input, develops functional properties that closely resemble those of visual cortex. Thus, it can be assumed that the phylogenetically more recent cortical areas which are receiving their input mainly from the older areas treat this input in very much the same way as the latter treat the input that is provided to them by the sense organs. If so, the ability of brains to become aware of their own operations and states would have to be attributed to an iteration of the same cognitive operations that support primary sensory processing. The explanatory gap in the study of the neuronal correlates of consciousness would then be reducible to the general question of how the cerebral cortex processes signals and generates representations. If this question is answered with respect to primary sensory functions, the discovered strategies should be generalizable to the formation of the meta-representations, the coherent, global representations that are believed to be the basis of conscious experience.

Two Representational Strategies

If the argument is valid that the internal monitoring functions that lead to consciousness rest on the same cognitive operations as the sensory processes which deal with signals conveyed by the sense organs, the search for the neuronal substrate of phenomenal awareness converges with the search for the nature of the neuronal codes used by the cerebral cortex to represent and store perceptual objects. In the following paragraphs I shall expose hypotheses on the putative nature of neuronal representations.

The hypothesis proposed here is that evolved brains use two complementary strategies in order to represent contents (see also Singer 1995, 1999). The first strategy is thought to rely on individual neurons that are tuned to particular constellations of input activity. Through their selective responses, these neurons establish explicit representations of particular constellations of features. It is commonly held that the specificity of these neurons is brought about by selective convergence of input connections in hierarchically structured feedforward architectures. This representational strategy allows for rapid processing and is ideally suited for the representation of frequently occurring stereotyped combinations of features; but this strategy is expensive in terms of the number of required neurons and not suited to cope with the virtually infinite diversity of possible feature constellations encountered in real world objects. The second strategy, according to the proposal, consists of the temporary association of large numbers of widely distributed neurons into functionally coherent assemblies which as a whole represent a particular content whereby each of the participating neurons is tuned to one of the elementary features of composite perceptual objects. This representational strategy is more economical with respect to neuron numbers because, as already proposed by Hebb (1949), a particular neuron can, at different times, participate in different assemblies just as a particular features can be part of many different perceptual objects. Moreover, this representational strategy is more flexible. It allows for the rapid de novo representation of constellations that have never been experienced before because there are virtually no limits to the dynamic association of neurons in ever-changing constellations. Thus, for the representation of highly complex and permanently changing contents this second strategy of distributed coding appears to be better suited than the first explicit strategy.

The meta-representations postulated as substrate for conscious experience have to accommodate contents that are particularly unpredictable and rich in combinatorial complexity. In order to support the unity of consciousness, the computational results of a large number of subsystems have to be bound together in ever-changing constellations and at the same rapid pace as the contents of awareness change. It appears then as if the second representational strategy that is based on the formation of dynamic assemblies would be more suitable for the implementation of the meta-representations that support consciousness than the explicit strategy. Further support for this view comes from considerations on the state dependency and the non-locality: that is, the distributed nature of mechanisms supporting conscious experience. If conscious experience depends on the ability to dynamically bind the results of subsystem computations into a unified meta-representation, conditions required for the formation of meta-representations ought to be the same as those required for awareness to occur. Neuronal codes that are readily observable in deep anesthesia, or during slow wave sleep, or in the absence of attention should not be accepted as sufficient correlates of awareness or consciousness although they are likely to be necessary components of the more global states required for the manifestation of consciousness. In this sense, the local codes would be a subset but not the full set of correlates of consciousness. At low processing levels, the response properties of individual neurons tend to differ only little in awake and anesthetized brains. Therefore, it is unlikely that the explicit representations encoded by these neurons are the substrate of the meta-representations that support consciousness. However, neurons in higher cortical areas that are part of attention controlling networks or participate in executive functions undergo drastic changes of their response properties during states in which consciousness is absent. This suggests that the activity of these neurons depends on cooperative interactions that only come into play when the brain is awake and attentive. As discussed later, such cooperativity could be the result of the coordinating mechanisms that are required for the dynamic binding of distributed neuronal responses into coherent representations. One candidate mechanism for dynamic binding is the synchronization of neuronal responses with high temporal precision. Such synchronization raises the impact that the activity of distributed neurons has on common target structures and thereby enhances responses to distributed inputs. Just as synchronization is abolished in the same brain states that are incompatible with conscious experience, it appears that the organizing mechanisms that bind distributed responses and thereby enhance responses of cells at higher processing stages play an important role in the maintenance of consciousness.

If the meta-representations postulated as substrate of conscious experience were indeed based on widely distributed codes rather than on responses of local groups of neurons then consciousness should be rather resistant to local lesions. While lesions in subsystems are expected to prevent conscious experience of the contents provided by the respective subsystems, consciousness per se should not be jeopardized. It should break down only if lesions interfere with the coordinating mechanisms that permit establishment of globally coherent cell assemblies. This prediction is by and large in agreement with the known consequences of circumscribed cortical lesions. They eliminate from conscious experience the specific contents processed by the lesioned areas but there is no distinct site of the neocortex whose destruction would lead to a loss of consciousness. It is only after lesions affect the global coordination of cortical functions that consciousness is abolished.

These considerations suggest that the contents of conscious experience are represented by distributed codes. The following sections will, therefore, focus on the evidence for such coding strategies.

The Signature of Distributed Codes

In distributed coding, an important constraint needs to be met. A mechanism is required that permits dynamic association of selected neurons into distinct, functionally coherent assemblies and labels grouped responses in a way that assures their joint processing. Numerous theoretical studies have addressed the question how assemblies can self-organize through cooperative interactions among distributed but interconnected neurons (Braitenberg 1978; Edelman 1987; Palm 1990; Gerstein & Gochin 1992). Here the focus will be on the question how responses of cells that have been grouped into an assembly can be tagged as related. Such tagging is equivalent with assuring that responses are processed together, and this is best achieved by jointly raising their saliency. In principle there are at least three non-exclusive options. First, non-grouped responses can be inhibited, second, the amplitude of the selected responses can be enhanced, and third, the selected cells can be made to discharge in precise temporal synchrony. All three mechanisms enhance the relative impact of the grouped responses. The first two strategies, which rely on the modulation of discharge rates, have been thoroughly investigated and appear to be common at all levels of processing. However, they have certain disadvantages when used for the labeling of assemblies because they may introduce ambiguities (von der Malsburg 1985) and reduce processing speed (Singer et al. 1997). Ambiguities could arise because discharge rates of cells vary over a wide range as a function of the match between stimulus and receptive field properties and these modulations would not be distinguishable from those signaling the relatedness of responses. Processing speed would be reduced because rate-coded assemblies can only be identified after a sufficient number of spikes have been integrated to distinguish high from low rates. Therefore, they need to be maintained for some time in order to be distinguishable, which reduces substantially the rate with which different assemblies can follow one another.

Both restrictions, the ambiguity and the slow processing speed, can be overcome if the selection and labeling of responses is achieved through synchronization of individual discharges (von der Malsburg 1985; Gray et al. 1989; Singer & Gray 1995). Expressing the relatedness of responses by synchronization resolves the ambiguities resulting from stimulus-dependent rate fluctuations because synchronization can be modulated independently of rates. Synchronization also accelerates the rate at which different assemblies can follow one another because the selected event is the individual spike or a brief burst of spikes and saliency is enhanced only for those discharges that are precisely synchronized. The rate at which different assemblies can follow one another without getting confounded is then limited only by the duration of the interval over which synaptic potentials summate effectively (for a detailed discussion, see Singer 2000).

Experimental Evidence for Grouping by Synchrony

Following the discovery of stimulus related response synchronization among neurons in the cat visual cortex (Gray & Singer 1987, 1989), numerous experiments have been performed in the search for a correlation between the occurrence of response synchronization and cognitive processes. One of the predictions to be tested was that synchronization probability should reflect some of the Gestalt-criteria according to which the visual system groups related features during scene segmentation. Among the grouping criteria examined so far are continuity, vicinity, similarity, and colinearity in the orientation domain, and common fate in the motion domain (Gray et al. 1989; Engel, König, & Singer 1991; Engel et al. 1991b; Freiwald, Kreiter, & Singer 1995; Kreiter & Singer 1996 for the monkey; Castelo-Branco et al. 2000 for the cat). So far, the results of these investigations are compatible with the hypothesis that the probability of response synchronization reflects the Gestalt criteria applied for perceptual grouping. Stimulus-specific response synchronization has been found within and across different areas, and even between hemispheres (for review, see Singer 1999). Most importantly, none of these synchronization phenomena were detectable by correlating successively recorded responses to the same stimuli. This indicates that synchronization was not due to stimulus locking but to internal dynamic coordination of spike timing. The observed temporal coherence among responses was much greater than expected from mere covariation of event related rate changes.

Studies involving lesions (Engel et al. 1991a; Nowak et al. 1995) and developmental manipulations (Löwel & Singer 1992; König et al. 1993) indicate that the interactions responsible for these dynamic synchronization phenomena are mediated to a substantial extent by cortico-cortical connections. The criteria for perceptual grouping should then be reflected in the architecture of these connections and this postulate agrees with the evidence that cortico-cortical connections preferentially link neurons with related feature preferences (for review, see Schmidt et al. 1997).

Response Synchronization and Behavioral States

Evidence indicates that highly precise, internally generated synchrony is considerably more pronounced in the awake than in the anesthetized brain (for review, see Singer 1999). Of particular interest in this context is the finding that response synchronization is especially pronounced when the global EEG desynchronizes and when subjects are attentive. Stimulating the mesencephalic reticular formation in anesthetized animals leads to a transient desynchronization of the EEG, resembling the transition from slow wave sleep to rapid eye movement sleep. Munk et al. (1996) and Herculano-Houzel et al. (1999) have shown that stimulus-specific synchronization of neuronal responses is drastically facilitated when the EEG is in a desynchronized rather than in a synchronized state.

Direct evidence for an attention related facilitation of synchronization has been obtained from cats that had been trained to perform a visually triggered motor response (Roelfsema et al. 1997). Simultaneous recordings from visual, association, somatosensory, and motor areas revealed that the cortical areas involved in the execution of the task synchronized their activity, predominantly with zero phase-lag, as soon as the animals prepared themselves for the task and focused their attention on the relevant stimulus. Immediately after the appearance of the visual stimulus, synchronization increased further over the recorded areas, and these coordinated activation patterns were maintained until the task was completed. However, once the reward was available and the animals engaged in consummatory behavior, these coherent patterns collapsed and gave way to low frequency oscillatory activity that did not exhibit any consistent phase relations. This close correspondence between the execution of an attention demanding visuo-motor performance and the occurrence of zero phase-lag synchrony suggests a functional role of the temporal patterning in the large-scale coordination of cortical activity. It appears as if attentional mechanisms imposed a coherent subthreshold modulation on neurons in cortical areas that need to participate in the execution of the anticipated task and thereby permit rapid synchronization of selected responses. According to this scenario, the attentional mechanisms would induce what one might call a state of expectancy in the respective cortical areas by imposing on them a specific, task-related dynamic activation pattern. Once stimulus-driven input becomes available, this patterned activity would act like a dynamic filter that causes rapid synchronization of selected responses, thereby accomplishing the required grouping and binding of responses and in addition assuring rapid transmission of the synchronized activity (for more details, see Fries et al. 2001).

Conscious Perception

A close correlation between response synchronization and conscious perception and a remarkable dissociation between responses of individual neurons and perception has been found in experiments on binocular rivalry. When the two eyes are presented with patterns that cannot be fused into a single coherent percept, the two patterns are perceived in alternation rather than as a superposition of their components. This implies that there is a central gating mechanism which selects in alternation the signals arriving from the two eyes for further processing. Interocular rivalry is thus a suitable paradigm for investigating the neuronal correlates of conscious perception.

Multiunit and field potential responses were recorded with chronically implanted electrodes from up to 30 sites in cat primary visual cortex while the animals were exposed to rivalrous stimulation conditions (Fries et al. 1997, 2001). In order to assure that the animals exhibited interocular rather than just figural rivalry they had been made strabismic shortly after birth as this is a condition that favors alternating use of the two eyes. Because the animal performs tracking eye movements only for the pattern that is actually perceived, patterns moving in opposite directions were presented dichoptically in order to determine from the tracking movements which signals were actually perceived by the animal. The outcome of these experiments was surprising as it turned out that the discharge rate of neurons in primary visual cortex failed to reflect the suppression of the non-selected signals. A close and highly significant correlation existed, however, between changes in the strength of response synchronization and the outcome of rivalry. Cells mediating responses of the eye that won in interocular competition and were perceived consciously increased the synchronicity of their responses upon introduction of the rivalrous stimulus while the reverse was true for cells driven by the eye that became suppressed. Thus, in this particular case of competition, selection of responses for further processing appears to be achieved by raising the saliency of responses through synchronization rather than enhancing discharge frequency. Likewise, suppression is not achieved by inhibiting responses but by desynchronization.

Thus, at least in primary visual areas, there is a remarkable dissociation between perception and the discharge rate of individual neurons. Cells whose responses are not perceived and are excluded from controlling behavior respond as vigorously as cells whose responses are perceived and support behavior. Another puzzling result of the rivalry study is that responses that win the competition increase their synchronicity upon presentation of the rivalrous stimulus. This suggests the action of a mechanism that enhances the saliency of the selected responses by improving their synchronicity in order to protect them against the interference caused by the rivalrous stimulus.

In conclusion, evaluation of internally generated correlation patterns permits the extraction of information about stimulus configurations, behavioral states, and perception that cannot be obtained by analyzing the responses of individual neurons sequentially. The relevant variable containing this additional information is the rather precise synchronization of a fraction of the discharges constituting the respective responses. The data indicate further that responses containing synchronized epochs have a higher probability of being processed further and, eventually, of being perceived consciously.

The Generality of Synchronicity

Studies in non-visual sensory modalities and in the motor system indicate that synchrony and oscillatory activity are ubiquitous phenomena in the nervous system. Synchronization occurs in a variety of distinct frequency bands and has been found in all sensory modalities. Synchronization in the high frequency range (beta and gamma oscillations) has been observed in the olfactory system, the auditory cortex, the somatosensory system, the prefrontal cortex, the motor cortex and the hippocampus (for review, see Singer 2004).

Synchronization also seems to play a role in the linkage between cortical assemblies and subcortical target structures such as the superior colliculus. This possibility is suggested by the existence of precise temporal relationships between the discharges of neurons in areas of the visual cortex and the superior colliculus (Brecht, Singer, & Engel 1998). In these experiments, it could be shown that corticotectal interactions are strongly dependent on the temporal coherence of cortical activity. If cortical neurons engage in synchronous oscillatory activity either with partners within the same cortical area or with cells in other cortical areas, their impact on tectal cells is enhanced, indicating that tectal cells are driven more effectively by synchronous than by asynchronous cortical activity. This finding is consistent with the idea that the temporal organization of activity patterns plays an important role in defining the output of the cortex.

Taken together, the available evidence suggests that comparable synchronization phenomena are found in a large number of different functional systems. Thus, it seems justified to generalize the results obtained in the visual cortex and to suggest that temporal coordination of discharges may be of general relevance for neural information processing. Importantly, there is now abundant evidence that precise synchronization such as that associated with oscillations in the beta and gamma band occurs also in the human brain. EEG and MEG studies have provided evidence that these synchronous high frequency oscillations are related to cognitive functions such as feature binding, visual search, focused attention, short- and long term memory, and conscious perception (for review, see Tononi et al. 1998; Engel et al. 1999a, 1999b; Tallon-Baudry & Bertand 1999; Varela et al. 2001).

Conclusion

The hypothesis proposed here is based on the following assumptions: (i) phenomenal awareness emerges from the formation of meta-representations, (ii) these are realized by the evolutionary addition of higher-order cortical areas that process the output of lower-order areas in the same way as these process their respective input, (iii) in order to account for the required combinatorial flexibility these meta-representations are likely to consist of the coordinated responses of dynamically bound assemblies of distributed neurons rather than of the responses of individual specialized cells, (iv) the selection and binding mechanism that groups neurons into assemblies and labels their responses as related is the transient synchronization of discharges with a precision in the millisecond range, (v) the formation of such dynamically associated, synchronized cell assemblies requires activated brain states characterized by "desynchronized" EEG and is facilitated by attentional mechanisms. The data reviewed above support these premises and define conditions that need to be fulfilled in order to allow for conscious experience.

Obviously, for a content to be perceived consciously it is a prerequisite that neurons coding for this content are active. However, by measuring responses of individual neurons it is impossible to decide whether a recorded response is just a necessary or whether it is a sufficient condition for conscious experience. If neurons in a particular transmission chain stop responding, the content conveyed by that group of neurons cannot be perceived. Hence, correlations between perceptual awareness and cellular responses indicate only that the discharges of cells at a particular processing stage are necessary for a particular content to reach the level of awareness. In order to find out whether additional prerequisites, such as the binding of these responses into widely distributed assemblies, have to be fulfilled, variables need to be determined permitting assessment of order parameters beyond the level of single units. This can only be achieved with recording techniques that disclose the spatio-temporal activation profile of large numbers of neurons. In this context it is note-worthy that methods such as EEG and MEG recordings which assess global activation patterns and monitor only activity that is sufficiently synchronous to add up to a measura-ble signal, differentiate best between brain states where consciousness is or is not possible. This favors the hypothesis that the generation of the meta-representations that support conscious experience requires temporal coordination of activity well beyond the level of single cell firing. Consciousness manifests itself only during brain states characterized by "desynchronized" EEG. These states, in turn, favor the occurrence of high frequency oscil-lations and long-distance synchronization of neuronal responses with a precision in the millisecond range. It seems not unreasonable, therefore, to pursue the hypothesis that the meta-representations required for consciousness to manifest itself consist of large assem-blies of distributed neurons whose signature of relatedness is the internally generated synchronicity of discharges. Thus, consciousness, rather than being associated with the activation of a particular group of neurons in a particular region of the brain, appears to be an emergent property of a particular dynamical state of the distributed cortical network – a state that is characterized by a critical level of precise temporal coherence across a suffi-ciently large population of distributed neurons.

See also 18 The global workspace theory of consciousness; 22 The information integration theory of consciousness; 45 A theory of micro-consciousness.

Further Readings

Engel, A. K. and Singer, W. (2001) Temporal binding and the neural correlates of sensory awareness. *Trends in Cognitive Sciences* 5: 1, 16–25.

Engel, A. K., Fries, P., and Singer, W. (2001) Dynamic predictions: oscillations and synchrony in top-down processing. *Nature Reviews: Neuroscience* 2: 704–16.

Fries, P., Neuenschwander, S., Engel, A. K., Goebel, R., and Singer, W. (2001) Rapid feature selective neuronal synchronization through correlated latency shifting. *Nature Neuroscience* 4: 2, 194–200.

Singer, W. (1999) Neuronal synchrony: a versatile code for the definition of relations? *Neuron* 24: 49–65.

References

Braitenberg, V. (1978) Cell assemblies in the cerebral cortex. In R. Heim and G. Palm (eds.), *Archi-tectonics of the Cerebral Cortex. Lecture Notes in Biomathematics 21, Theoretical Approaches in Complex Systems*, 171–88. Berlin: Springer-Verlag.

Brecht, M., Singer, W., and Engel, A. K. (1998) Correlation analysis of corticotectal interactions in the cat visual system. *Journal of Neurophysiology* 79, 2394–407.

Castelo-Branco, M., Goebel, R., Neuenschwander, S., and Singer, W. (2000) Neural synchrony corre-lates with surface segregation rules. *Nature* 405, 685–9.

Edelman, G. M. (1987) *Neural Darwinism: The Theory of Neuronal Group Selection*. New York: Basic Books.

Engel, A. K., König, P., and Singer, W. (1991) Direct physiological evidence for scene segmentation by temporal coding. *Proceedings of the National Academy of Sciences* 88, 9136–40.

Engel, A. K., König, P., Kreiter, A. K., and Singer, W. (1991a) Interhemispheric synchronization of oscillatory neuronal responses in cat visual cortex. *Science* 252, 1177–9.

Engel, A. K., Kreiter, A. K., König, P., and Singer, W. (1991b) Synchronization of oscillatory neuronal responses between striate and extrastriate visual cortical areas of the cat. *Proceedings of the National Academy of Sciences* 88, 6048–52.

Engel, A. K., Fries, P., König, P., Brecht, M., and Singer, W. (1999a) Temporal binding, binocular rivalry, and consciousness. *Consciousness and Cognition* 8: 2, 128–51.

Engel, A. K., Fries, P., König, P., Brecht, M., and Singer, W. (1999b) Does time help to understand consciousness? *Consciousness and Cognition* 8: 2, 260–8.

Freiwald, W. A., Kreiter, A. K., and Singer, W. (1995) Stimulus dependent intercolumnar synchronization of single unit responses in cat area 17. *NeuroReport* 6, 2348–52.

Fries, P., Roelfsema, P. R., Engel, A. K., König, P., and Singer, W. (1997) Synchronization of oscillatory responses in visual cortex correlates with perception in interocular rivalry. *Proceedings of the National Academy of Sciences* 94, 12,699–704.

Fries, P., Neuenschwander, S., Engel, A. K., Goebel, R., and Singer, W. (2001) Rapid feature selective neuronal synchronization through correlated latency shifting. *Nature Neuroscience.* 4: 2, 194–200.

Gerstein, G. L. and Gochin, P. M. (1992) Neuronal population coding and the elephant. In A. Aertsen and V. Braitenberg (eds.), *Information Processing in the Cortex, Experiments and Theory*, 139–73. Berlin: Springer-Verlag.

Gray, C. M. and Singer, W. (1987) Stimulus-specific neuronal oscillations in the cat visual cortex: a cortical functional unit. *Society for Neuroscience Abstracts* 13, 1449.

Gray, C. M. and Singer, W. (1989) Stimulus-specific neuronal oscillations in orientation columns of cat visual cortex. *Proceedings of the National Academy of Sciences USA* 86, 1698–702.

Gray, C. M., König, P., Engel, A. K., and Singer, W. (1989) Oscillatory responses in cat visual cortex exhibit inter-columnar synchronization which reflects global stimulus properties. *Nature* 338, 334–7.

Hebb, D. O. (1949) *The Organization of Behavior*. New York: John Wiley and Sons.

Herculano-Houzel, S., Munk, M. H. J., Neuenschwander, S., and Singer, W. (1999) Precisely synchronized oscillatory firing patterns require electroencephalographic activation. *Journal of Neuroscience* 19: 10, 3992–4010.

König, P., Engel, A. K., Löwel, S., and Singer, W. (1993) Squint affects synchronization of oscillatory responses in cat visual cortex. *European Journal of Neuroscience* 5, 501–8.

Kreiter, A. K. and Singer, W. (1996) Stimulus-dependent synchronization of neuronal responses in the visual cortex of awake macaque monkey. *Journal of Neuroscience* 16, 2381–96.

Krubitzer, L. (1998) Constructing the neocortex: influence on the pattern of organization in mammals. In M. S. Gazzaniga and J. S. Altman (eds.), *Brain and Mind: Evolutionary Perspectives*, 19–34. Strasbourg: HFSP.

Löwel, S. and Singer, W. (1992) Selection of intrinsic horizontal connections in the visual cortex by correlated neuronal activity. *Science* 255, 209–12.

Munk, M. H. J., Roelfsema, P. R., König, P., Engel, A. K., and Singer, W. (1996) Role of reticular activation in the modulation of intracortical synchronization. *Science* 272, 271–4.

Nowak, L. G., Munk, M. H. J., Nelson, J. I., and Bullier, J. A. C. (1995) Structural basis of cortical synchronization. I. Three types of interhemispheric coupling. *Journal of Neurophysiology* 74, 2379–400.

Palm, G. (1990) Cell assemblies as a guideline for brain research. *Concepts in Neuroscience* 1, 133–47.

Roelfsema, P. R., Engel, A. K., König, P., and Singer, W. (1997) Visuomotor integration is associated with zero time-lag synchronization among cortical areas. *Nature* 385, 157–61.

Schmidt, K. E., Goebel, R., Löwel, S., and Singer, W. (1997) The perceptual grouping criterion of colinearity is reflected by anisotropies of connections in the primary visual cortex. *European Journal of Neuroscience* 9, 1083–9.

Singer, W. (1995) Development and plasticity of cortical processing architectures. *Science* 270, 758–64.

Singer, W. (1999) Neuronal synchrony: a versatile code for the definition of relations? *Neuron* 24, 49–65.

Singer, W. (2000) Response synchronization: a universal coding strategy for the definition of relations. In M. S. Gazzaniga (ed.), *The New Cognitive Neurosciences*, 2nd edn., 325–38. Cambridge, MA: MIT Press.

Singer, W. (2004) Synchrony, oscillations, and relational codes. In L. M. Chalupa and J. S. Werner (eds.), *The Visual Neurosciences*, 1665–81. Cambridge, MA: MIT Press, A Bradford Book.

Singer, W. and Gray, C. M. (1995) Visual feature integration and the temporal correlation hypothesis. *Annual Review of Neuroscience* 18, 555–86.

Singer, W., Engel, A. K., Kreiter, A. K., Munk, M. H. J., Neuenschwander, S., and Roelfsema, P. R. (1997) Neuronal assemblies: necessity, signature and detectability. *Trends in Cognitive Sciences* 1: 7, 252–61.

Tallon-Baudry, C. and Bertrand, O. (1999) Oscillatory gamma activity in humans and its role in object representation. *Trends in Cognitive Sciences* 3: 4, 151–62.

Tononi, G., Srinivasan, R., Russell, D. P., and Edelman, G. M. (1998) Investigating neural correlates of conscious perception by frequency-tagged neuromagnetic responses. *Proceedings of the National Academy of Sciences* 95, 3198–203.

Varela, F., Lachaux, J.-P., Rodriguez, E., and Martinerie, J. (2001) The brainweb: phase synchronization and large-scale integration. *Nature Review: Neuroscience* 2, 229–39.

von der Malsburg, C. (1985) Nervous structures with dynamical links. *Berichte der Bunsen-Gesellschaft – Physical Chemistry, Chemical Physics* 89, 703–10.

Duplex Vision: Separate Cortical Pathways for Conscious Perception and the Control of Action

MELVYN A. GOODALE

Introduction

Almost all of our direct knowledge of the world beyond our bodies comes from vision. The important role that vision plays in our lives is reflected not only in the fact that we have large and mobile eyes, but also in the large amount of brain tissue that is devoted to visual processing. It has been estimated, for example, that more than half of the cerebral cortex in the macaque monkey, another highly visual animal, is devoted to the processing of visual signals. But vision does not simply provide information about objects and events in the world; in humans, at least, it provides a conscious percept of that world that is so compelling that it is sometimes difficult to comprehend that this experience arises entirely from the activity of ensembles of neurons in the central nervous system.

It seems self-evident that the actions we perform on visible objects make use of the same visual representation that allows us to perceive those objects. This idea, which is commonly accepted by many philosophers and scientists, is sometimes referred to as the "assumption of experience-based control" (Clark 2002). According to this view, the visual system creates a single "general-purpose" representation of the external world that provides a platform for both cognitive operations as well as the real time control of goal-directed actions. There are good reasons to believe, however, that such a monolithic account is incorrect. Indeed, it will be argued in this chapter that incoming visual signals are sent to separate, and to some extent, independent visual systems, in which the processing has been shaped by the particular output mechanisms that each system serves. The construction of a conscious percept is certainly an important function of vision but the visual control of actions – from saccadic eye movements to skilled grasping movements of the hand and limb – depends on visual mechanisms that are functionally and neurally separate from those mediating our conscious perception of the world.

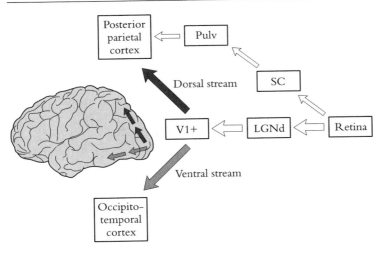

Figure 48.1 Retinal input to the dorsal and ventral streams.

The diagram of the human brain (left hemisphere) on the left shows the approximate routes of the cortico-cortical projections from early visual cortex to the posterior parietal and the occipito-temporal cortex, respectively. LGNd: lateral geniculate nucleus, pars dorsalis; Pulv: pulvinar; SC: superior colliculus; V1+: primary visual cortex and other early visual cortical areas (adapted with permission from Milner and Goodale 1995).

Two Visual Pathways in the Cerebral Cortex

Although the eyes send direct projections to more than a dozen separate sites in the human brain, one of the most prominent pathways runs from the eye to the dorsal part of the lateral geniculate nucleus in the thalamus and from there to an area in the occipital lobe known variously as striate cortex, area 17, primary visual cortex, or V1. Beyond area V1, visual information is conveyed to a complex network of areas extending from the occipital lobe into the parietal and temporal lobes. Despite the complexity of the interconnections between these different areas, two broad "streams" of visual projections from area V1 have been identified: a ventral stream projecting eventually to the inferior part of the temporal lobe and a dorsal stream projecting to the posterior part of the parietal lobe (Ungerleider & Mishkin 1982). A schematic diagram of these pathways can be found in Figure 48.1. Of course, not only are the two streams are intimately interconnected but the different areas within them send prominent projections back to area V1. Moreover, both streams also receive inputs from a number of other subcortical visual structures, such as the superior colliculus in the midbrain, which projects to areas in the dorsal stream (via the thalamus). Although most of what we know about the organization of these pathways in the primate brain is derived from neurophysiological and neuroanatomical studies in the monkey, the advent of neuroimaging, particularly functional magnetic resonance imaging (fMRI), has revealed that the projections from area V1 to extra-striate regions in the human brain can be separated into ventral and dorsal streams similar to those seen in the monkey (Tootell, Tsao, & Vanduffel 2003).

The natural question that arises is what the difference is between the visual processing carried out by the two streams. To put it another way, why is it that two separate visual streams evolved in the cerebral cortex? In a theoretical paper published more than ten years ago, Goodale and Milner (1992) proposed that the ventral stream plays the major role in constructing the perceptual representation of the visual world and the objects within it, while the dorsal stream mediates the visual control of actions directed at those objects. Note that this is *not* the distinction between "what" and "where" (object vision and spatial vision) that was originally put forward by Ungerleider and Mishkin (1982), who first described the two streams in the monkey. In the Goodale and Milner scheme, the structural and spatial attributes of an object are processed by both streams, but for different purposes. In the ventral stream, they argued, the transformations deliver the enduring characteristics of objects and their relations, permitting the formation of long-term perceptual representations that constitute the contents of our visual consciousness. Such representations play an essential role in the identification of objects and enable us to classify objects and events, attach meaning and significance to them, and establish their causal relations. Such operations are essential for accumulating a knowledge base about the world, communicating with others, and planning future courses of action. In contrast, the transformations carried out by the dorsal stream deal with the moment-to-moment information about the size, geometrical structure, location, and disposition of a goal object – and thereby mediate the visual control of skilled actions, such as reaching out and grasping that object. As such, the dorsal stream can be regarded as a cortical extension of the dedicated visuomotor modules in the midbrain and brainstem that mediate visually guided movements in all vertebrates. The two streams of visual processing work together in the production of adaptive behavior. The perceptual representations constructed by the ventral stream interact with various high-level cognitive mechanisms and enable an organism to select a particular course of action with respect to objects in the world while the visuomotor networks in the dorsal stream (and associated cortical and subcortical pathways) are responsible for the programming and on-line control of the particular movements that action entails.

An integral part of the two-visual systems proposal is the idea that *vision-for-action* requires fundamentally different computations from those used by perception – computations that reflect the real metrics of the world within viewer-centered (egocentric) frames of reference. To be able to grasp an object successfully, for example, it is essential that the brain compute the real size of the object. In addition, spatial information about the object must be computed in frames of reference that take into account the orientation and position of the object with respect to the effector that is to be used to perform the action (i.e., in eye-centered, head-centered, torso-centered, shoulder-centered coordinates, or even hand- or finger-centered frames of reference). In addition, because observers and goal objects often do not stay in a static relationship with one another, the required coordinates for action are most effectively computed immediately before the movements are initiated; that is, in *real time*. A corollary of real-time visuomotor transformation is that neither the coordinates for a particular action nor the resulting motor program needs to be stored in memory – indeed such storage could create interference between competing action plans for multiple objects in the visual array, or between action plans to the same object following a change in the spatial relationship between target and actor. In line with this argument, there is evidence that grasping movements initiated *after* the goal object has been removed from view are qualitatively different from the actions that are programmed while the object is visible (even if, in both cases, the goal is not visible during the execution of the movement). These findings suggest that the control of actions directed to remembered objects may depend heavily on processing in the ventral stream – processing that does not typically intrude on the control of visually guided actions.

In contrast to the vision-for-action system, *vision-for-perception* computes the size, location, shape, and orientation of an object primarily in relation to other objects and surfaces in the scene. Thus, the metrics of perception are inherently relative and the frames of reference are largely scene-based, which explains why we are so sensitive to size-contrast illusions and other visual illusions that depend on comparisons between different objects in the visual array. Encoding an object in a scene-based frame of reference (sometimes called an allocentric frame of reference) permits a representation of the object that preserves the relations between the object parts and its surroundings without requiring precise information about absolute size of the object or its exact position with respect to the observer. Indeed, if perceptual representations were to attempt to deliver the real metrics of all objects in the visual array, the computational load would be astronomical.

Vision-for-perception also operates over a much longer timescale than that used in the vision-for-action. In fact, object recognition would not be possible unless perceptual information about previously encountered objects were stored in memory – and an allocentric representation system is ideal for storing this information. But to generate long-term representations of objects and their relations, perceptual mechanisms must be "object-based"; that is, constancies of size, shape, color, lightness, and relative location need to be maintained across different viewing conditions. Some of these mechanisms might use a network of viewer-centered representations of the same object; others might use an array of canonical representations; still others might be truly "object-centered." But whatever the particular coding might be, it is the identity of the object, not its disposition with respect to the observer that is of primary concern to the perceptual system. In summary, according to the two-visual-systems hypothesis, it is the nature of the functional requirements of perception and action that lies at the root of the division of labor in the ventral and dorsal visual projection systems of the primate cerebral cortex (for a detailed review, see Goodale, Westwood, & Milner 2004).

Neurological Evidence

Some of the most compelling evidence for the Goodale and Milner (1992) account of dual visual processing has come from work with neurological patients. It has been known for a long time, for example, that patients with damage to the posterior parietal cortex, the main terminus of the dorsal stream, have difficulty reaching in the correct direction to objects placed in different positions in the visual field contralateral to their lesion, even though they have no difficulty reaching out and grasping different parts of their body indicated by the experimenter (Bálint 1909). In addition, patients with damage to this region of the cerebral cortex often show an inability to rotate their hand or open their fingers properly to grasp an object placed in front of them, even when the object is always placed in the same location (Perenin & Vighetto 1988). As soon as their fingers make contact with the object, of course, these patients are able to use haptic information to adjust their hand to the correct posture. But despite showing a clear deficit in the visual control of reaching and grasping (known clinically as "optic ataxia"), these same patients are able to describe the orientation, size, shape, and even the relative spatial location of the very objects they are unable to grasp correctly (see Figure 48.2). In short, even though these patients can perceive objects, they cannot use

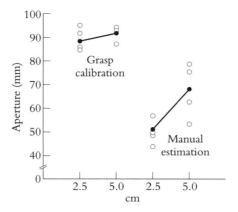

Figure 48.2 Maximum grip aperture and manual estimation of object width by a patient (R. V.) with optic ataxia from bilateral lesions of the posterior parietal cortex.

R. V.'s manual estimates of object width are reasonably correlated with the actual width. Nevertheless, when she reaches out to pick up the object, she opens her hand extremely wide and her maximum grip aperture in flight shows no relationship with the real size of the goal object.

vision to control real-time actions directed at those objects. Paradoxically, if patients with optic ataxia are encouraged to slow down and initiate their grasp after the object has been removed from view, they can sometimes improve their performance dramatically – presumably because they are now using a stored representation of the target laid down by mechanisms in the ventral stream, rather than real-time computations of the object's features, which would normally engage the visuomotor mechanisms in the (damaged) dorsal stream.

Other patients, with damage to ventral rather than dorsal stream structures, show the complementary pattern of deficits and spared visual abilities. Consider, for example, patient D. F., a young woman who suffered damage to part of her ventral stream as a result of anoxia from carbon monoxide poisoning. D. F. has "visual form agnosia" (Milner et al. 1991). Even though her "low-level" visual abilities are reasonably intact, she can no longer recognize everyday objects or the faces of her friends and relatives; nor can she identify even the simplest of geometric shapes. At the same time, however, she is able to perceive the color and surface properties of objects. Her deficit appears to be largely restricted to the form and shape of objects. If a familiar object is placed in her hand, of course, she has no trouble identifying it by touch.

Remarkably, however, D. F. shows strikingly accurate visual guidance of her hand movements when she attempts to pick up the very objects she cannot identify visually (Goodale, Milner, Jakobson, & Carey 1991). Thus, when she reaches out to grasp objects of different sizes, her hand opens wider, mid-flight, for larger objects than it does for smaller ones, just as it does in people with normal vision (see Figure 48.3). Similarly, she rotates her hand and wrist quite normally when she reaches out to grasp objects in different orientations, and she places her fingers correctly on the surface of objects with different shapes when she attempts to pick them up. At the same time, she is quite unable to distinguish between any of these objects when they are presented to her in simple discrimination tests. She even fails in manual "matching" tasks in which she is asked to show how wide an object is by opening her index finger and thumb a corresponding amount (Figure 48.3). D. F.'s spared

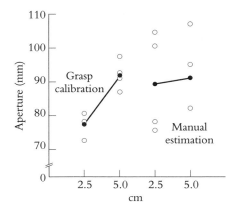

Figure 48.3 Maximum grip aperture and manual estimation of object width by a patient (D. F.) with visual form agnosia from bilateral lesions of the ventrolateral occipital cortex.

D. F. shows excellent grip scaling, opening her hand wider in flight for the wider object. Despite her normal grip scaling, she is unable to estimate the width of the same objects in an explicit perceptual judgment, showing considerable trial-to-trial variability.

visuomotor skills are not limited to grasping. She can step over objects and walk around furniture in a cluttered room, even though her perceptual judgments about these obstacles are far from normal. In short, even though D. F. cannot perceive the size, shape, and orientation of objects, she can use these same object features to control her object-directed actions.

Neuroimaging has revealed that an area in the ventral stream implicated in object recognition (the lateral occipital area) is severely damaged in D. F.'s brain. When she is shown line drawings of common objects while her brain is being scanned with an fMRI machine, she shows none of the normal activity that is typically seen in healthy observers (James et al. 2003). It is interesting to note, however, that D. F. does show robust ventral-stream activity when shown colored photographs of objects, reflecting the fact that it is her perception of form that is compromised rather than her perception of color or other surface properties of objects. When D. F. is asked to reach out and grasp objects while in the brain scanner, she displays a normal pattern of activity in an area of the dorsal stream that has been shown to play a critical role in the visual control of grasping in both humans and monkeys (Culham & Kanwisher 2001).

Although D. F. shows relatively normal real-time control of object-directed actions such as grasping, that control deteriorates rapidly when a delay is introduced between viewing the goal object and initiating the movement. Unlike healthy individuals, D. F. is unable to use visual memory of the size, shape, and orientation of the goal object to drive delayed grasping, presumably because she did not perceive those features of the object in the first place. It is not that her facility to remember things is damaged, but rather that she had no perceptual information to store in her memory. When she reaches out and grasps an object in real time, of course, her intact dorsal stream is still capable of transforming visual information about the size, shape, and location of the object – but this transformation occurs only when a movement is about to executed and cannot be stored in anticipation of a delayed movement.

In summary, the demonstration of opposite patterns of lost and spared abilities in

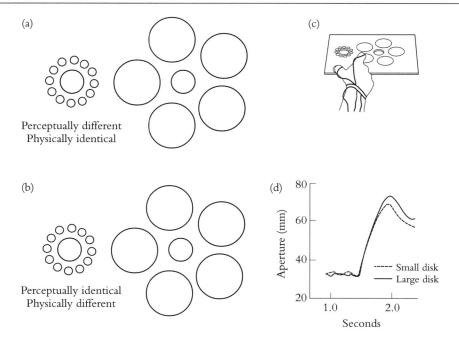

Figure 48.4 Grasping the Ebbinghaus illusion.

Panel a shows the classic Ebbinghaus illusion, in which the target circle within the annulus of large circles appears to be smaller than the target circle within the annulus of small circles. The two target circles are actually the same size. Panel b shows how the actual size of the target circles can be adjusted to make them appear equal in size. Panel c shows a target display in which people are required to pick up one of two target disks within the Ebbinghaus illusion. Their grip aperture in flight is recorded using small light emitting diodes attached to the finger, thumb, and wrist. Panel d shows that people open their hand by different amounts in flight for the two targets when the targets differ in size (see Panel b), even though they believe that the two targets are identical in size (adapted with permission from Aglioti et al. 1995).

neurological patients discussed above (referred to as a "double dissociation" in the neuro-psychological literature) strongly suggests that the two streams of visual processing serve quite different purposes: the ventral stream, it seems, enables us to experience the world in all its richness and detail, while the dorsal stream provides the moment-to-moment visual control of specific goal-directed actions (for review, see Milner & Goodale 1995). This duplex account of visual processing is also supported by a wealth of anatomical, electro-physiological, and behavioral studies in the monkey. In addition, the last ten years have witnessed an exponential increase in the number of functional neuroimaging studies of the human visual system; the evidence emerging from these studies not only reinforces the idea that there are two relatively independent streams of visual processing in human cerebral cortex, but also that the division of labor between the two streams is best characterized as a distinction between vision-for-perception and vision-for-action. (For recent reviews of the monkey and neuroimaging literature, see Cohen & Andersen 2002; Culham & Kanwisher 2001; Grill-Spector 2003; Tanaka 2003).

Evidence from Visual Illusions

Indirect evidence for the two visual systems proposal also comes from experiments with visual illusions in normal observers. Classical visual illusions never fail to impress. Even when the trick is explained to us, we continue to perceive apparent differences in size, orientation, movement, and distance that we know are not there. As Richard Gregory (1997) has pointed out, illusions provide a useful tool for investigating how the visual system constructs our percepts of the world. One important class of illusions depends on pictorial cues – the kinds of cues that are commonly exploited by painters to create a realistic three-dimensional world on a two-dimensional canvas. Systematic manipulation of these cues can create powerful illusions by taking advantage of the way in which the perceptual machinery in ventral stream carries out an obligatory analysis of the visual array. But does this mean that all of our visually driven behavior must fall victim to these kinds of pictorial illusions? As it turns out, there is a body of work suggesting that the visual control of action can remain largely unaffected by illusions that at the same time are perceptually compelling. For example, it has been shown in a number of laboratories that the opening of the grasping hand in flight is unaffected by the Ebbinghaus illusion, a robust pictorial illusion in which a target disk surrounded by smaller circles appears to be larger than the same disk surrounded by larger circles (see Figure 48.4) – although grip opening is exquisitely sensitive to real changes in the size of the target disk (Aglioti, De Souza, & Goodale 1995).

What is going on here? When we reach out to pick up an object, particularly one we have not seen before, our visuomotor system has to compute its size accurately if we are to pick it up efficiently – that is, without fumbling or re-adjusting our grip. As we saw earlier in the chapter, it is not enough to know that the target object is larger or smaller than neighboring objects; the visuomotor systems controlling hand aperture must compute the target object's real size. For this reason, one might expect the mechanisms mediating the visual control of grip scaling to focus entirely on the target itself and to ignore surrounding objects. As a consequence, the computations will be immune to size-contrast illusions, and indeed to other size illusions that depend on comparing the relative sizes or positions of objects in the visual array.

Of course, the visuomotor mechanisms controlling grasping and other actions do not always escape visual illusions. Although many illusions originate chiefly within the depths of the ventral stream, others are thought to arise in primary visual cortex or in one of the other retinotopic areas, which feed not only into the ventral stream but also into the dorsal stream. Thus, illusions such as the simultaneous tilt illusion (see Figure 48.5a), which appear to be generated in early visual areas, affect both perceptual judgments and visuomotor responses, whereas the rod and frame illusion (see Figure 48.5b), which like the Ebbinghaus illusion probably originates in higher-order ventral stream areas, affects only perceptual judgments (Milner & Dyde 2003). Moreover, if delays are introduced between viewing the display and initiating the action, even higher-order illusions will affect grip aperture, presumably because the visual memories driving the motor response were laid down by perceptual processing in the ventral stream.

According to the two visual systems proposal put forward by Goodale and Milner, visual perception of the world depends upon activity in the ventral stream. But even though the generation of a visual percept involves quite different computations from those mediating the immediate control of action (which is presumed to be carried out by the dorsal stream),

(a) Simultaneous tilt illusion

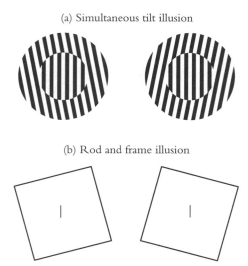

(b) Rod and frame illusion

Figure 48.5 The "simultaneous tilt illusion" (Panel a) and the "rod and frame illusion" (Panel b).

In both illusions, the central line or stripes appear to be tilted in opposite directions according the tilt of the striped background (Panel a) or the frame (Panel b). The simultaneous tilt illusion is the result of local effects within the primary visual cortex and/or other early visual cortical areas – and as a consequence is passed on to both the ventral and the dorsal stream, affecting both perception and the control of action. The rod and frame illusion depends on the same kinds of perceptual mechanisms as other pictorial illusions, presumably arising in higher ventral-stream areas. Thus, this illusion affects perceptual judgments but not the control of action (adapted with permission from Milner and Dyde 2003).

that percept must ultimately serve the production of a goal-directed act. Perception is not an end in itself, in biological terms, but rather a means to an end. In other words, unless percepts are translated into action, they will have no consequences for the individuals possessing them. Indeed, without behavioral consequences, the brain mechanisms generating percepts could never have evolved. To put it another way: both visual streams exist to serve action – the difference between them is that the dorsal stream provides direct, moment-to-moment, control of our movements, whereas the ventral stream exerts its control in a much more indirect fashion. For a recent review of the evidence for the two streams of visual processing, see Goodale and Milner (2004).

Biological Tele-assistance

But how do the two streams work together in the production of adaptive behavior? A useful metaphor can be found in robotic engineering. That metaphor is *tele-assistance* or supervised control. In tele-assistance, an experienced human operater identifies a potential goal object in a dangerous or distant workspace (the bottom of a deep mine or even the surface of another planet) by means of a video camera or some other device mounted on a semi-autonomous robot that is actually located in that workspace. The human operator can then instruct the robot to perform a desired action on that goal object. The robot uses its on-board range finders and other sensors to calibrate and control the goal-directed action (picking up a geological specimen, for example). Tele-assistance is much more flexible than completely autonomous robotic control, which by necessity is limited to the specific working environment for which the robot has been programmed and cannot cope easily with novel or unexpected events. Tele-assistance is also more efficient than tele-operation, in which a human operator has direct control of the movement of a distant robot. Although tele-operation has the advantage that the operator can recognize and can deal (theoretic-ally at least) with unexpected events in the workplace, the direct cognitive-motor control afforded by tele-operation is extremely sensitive to temporal delay and changes in spatial scale. Tele-assistance, however, combines the cognitive control of tele-operation with the sensorimotor flexibility of an autonomous robot, which can program and control its own movements.

The interaction between the ventral and dorsal streams is an excellent example of where the principle of tele-assistance has been instantiated in biology. The ventral stream (together with associated cognitive networks) is like the human operator in conventional tele-assistance; it uses a representation of the world that is rich and detailed but not met-rically precise. When a particular goal object has been flagged, dedicated visuomotor networks in the dorsal stream (in conjunction with other sensorimotor control systems) are then activated to perform the desired motor act. Thus, the dorsal stream, which com-putes the real metrics of the goal object within egocentric frames of reference, resembles the semi-autonomous robot in tele-assistance.

Consciousness and the Two Streams

The notion that the ventral stream (in association with other cognitive systems) is like the human operator in tele-assistance also resonates with the idea that it is visual processing in this stream that constructs the contents of our visual consciousness, the neural correlates of what Block refers to as "phenomenal consciousness" (Block 2005). In other words, with respect to vision, the ventral stream is connected with our thinking, conscious, human side, not our automatic, unconscious, robotic side. But this does not mean that the construction of a conscious visual percept is somehow an end in itself. Presumably, visual phenome-nology must confer some kind of advantage on the organisms that possess it, otherwise it would never have evolved in the first place. But although there has been much specu-lation about the evolution of consciousness (e.g., Rolls 1997; Searle 1998; Velmans 2002; Churchland 2003; Merker 2005), there is no general agreement about what the nature of this advantage might be. Setting aside the issue of qualia, however, there is some consensus that consciousness has a special relationship with working memory, with the idea that we can hold the contents of our conscious experience in "our mind's eye." Indeed, it has been argued that only conscious representations of the visual world can enter working memory (e.g., Courtney et al. 2003) – and as a consequence can become part of our long-term visual knowledge of the world. In other words, by helping to construct a conscious representation of the world, the ventral stream enables us to use visual information "off-line" – allowing us to escape the present and giving us enormous flexibility over the control of our behavior. But in the end, it is still the visuomotor networks in the dorsal stream that are responsible for the visual control of the final goal-directed act.

It is worth emphasizing once more that even though we are typically aware of the actions we perform, the visual information that the dorsal stream uses to control those actions remain quite inaccessible to consciousness. At the same time, because the ventral stream provides a conscious representation of the world, it is difficult to resist the assumption of experience-based control (Clark 2002), the intuition that it is one's perception of the goal object that is guiding the action we direct toward it rather than quite separate visuomotor transformations carried out in the dorsal stream at the moment an action is generated.

See also 13 The case of blindsight; 40 Preconscious processing; 42 Consciousness of action; 43 Methodologies for identifying the neural correlates of consciousness; 44 A neurobiological framework for consciousness.

Further Readings

Goodale, M. A. and Milner, A. D. (2004) *Sight Unseen: An Exploration of Consciousness and Unconscious Vision*. Oxford: Oxford University Press.

Jeannerod, M. (1997) *The Cognitive Neuroscience of Action*. Oxford: Blackwell.

Koch, C. (2004) *The Quest for Consciousness: A Neurobiological Approach*. Englewood, CO: Roberts and Company.

Milner, A. D. and Goodale, M. A. (1995) *The Visual Brain in Action*. Oxford: Oxford University Press. A short précis of *The Visual Brain in Action* can be found at the following website: http://psyche.cs.monash.edu.au/v4/psyche-4-12-milner.html

References

Aglioti, S., DeSouza J. F., and Goodale, M. A. (1995) Size-contrast illusions deceive the eye but not the hand. *Current Biology* 5, 679–85.

Baars, B. J. and Franklin, S. (2003) How conscious experience and working memory interact. *Trends in Cognitive Sciences* 7, 166–72.

Bálint, R. (1909) Seelenlämung des "Schauens," optische Ataxie, räumliche Störung der Aufmerksamkeit. *Monatschrift für Psychiatrie und Neurologie* 25, 51–81.

Block, N. (2005) Two neural correlates of consciousness. *Trends in Cognitive Sciences* 9: 2, 46–52.

Churchland, P. S. (2003) Self-representation in nervous systems. *Science* 296, 308–10.

Clark, A. (2002) Is seeing all it seems? Action, reason and the grand illusion. *Journal of Consciousness Studies* 9, 181–202.

Cohen, Y. E. and Andersen, R. A. (2002) A common reference frame for movement plans in the posterior parietal cortex. *Nature Reviews: Neuroscience* 3, 553–62.

Courtney, S. M., Petit, L., Haxby, J. V., and Ungerleider, L. G. (1998) The role of prefrontal cortex in working memory: examining the contents of consciousness. *Philosophical Transactions of the Royal Society of London B: Biological Sciences* 353, 1819–28.

Culham, J. C. and Kanwisher, N. G. (2001) Neuroimaging of cognitive functions in human parietal cortex. *Current Opinion in Neurobiology* 11, 157–63.

Goodale, M. A. and Milner, A. D. (1992) Separate visual pathways for perception and action. *Trends in Neurosciences* 15: 1, 20–5.

Goodale, M. A. and Milner, A. D. (2004) *Sight Unseen: An Exploration of Consciousness and Unconscious Vision*. Oxford: Oxford University Press.

Goodale, M. A., Milner, A. D., Jakobson, L. S., and Carey, D. P. (1991) A neurological dissociation between perceiving objects and grasping them. *Nature* 349, 154–6.

Goodale, M. A., Westwood, D. A., and Milner, A. D. (2004) Two distinct modes of control for object-directed action. In C. A. Heywood, A. D. Milner, and C. Blakemore (eds.), *The Roots of Visual Awareness. Progress in Brain Research*, vol. 144, 131–44. Amsterdam: Elsevier.

Gregory, R. (1997) *Eye and Brain: The Psychology of Seeing*, 5th edn. Oxford: Oxford University Press.

Grill-Spector, K. (2003) The neural basis of object perception. *Current Opinion in Neurobiology* 13: 2, 159–66.

James, T. W., Culham, J., Humphrey, G. K., Milner, A. D., and Goodale, M. A. (2003) Ventral occipital lesions impair object recognition but not object-directed grasping: an fMRI study. *Brain* 126, 2463–75.

Merker, B. (2005) The liabilities of mobility: a selection pressure for the transition to consciousness in animal evolution. *Consciousness and Cognition* 14: 89–114.

Milner, A. D. and Dyde, R. (2003) Why do some perceptual illusions affect visually guided action, when others don't? *Trends in Cognitive Sciences* 7, 10–11.

Milner, A. D. and Goodale, M. A. (1995) *The Visual Brain in Action*. Oxford: Oxford University Press.

Milner, A. D. and Goodale, M. A. (2006) *The Visual Brain in Action*, 2nd edn. Oxford: Oxford University Press. A short precis may be found at http://psyche.cs.monash.edu.au/v4/psyche-4-12-milner.html

Milner, A. D., Perrett, D. I., Johnston, R. S., Benson, P. J., Jordan, T. R., Heeley, D. W. et al. (1991) Perception and action in visual form agnosia. *Brain* 114, 405–28.

Perenin, M.-T. and Vighetto, A. (1988) Optic ataxia: a specific disruption in visuomotor mechanisms. I. Different aspects of the deficit in reaching for objects. *Brain* 111, 643–74.

Rolls, E. T. (1997) Consciousness in neural networks? *Neural Networks* 10, 1227–40.

Searle, J. R. (1998) How to study consciousness scientifically. *Philosophical Transactions of the Royal Society of London B: Biological Sciences* 353, 1935–42.

Tanaka, K. (2003) Columns for complex visual object features in the inferotemporal cortex: clustering of cells with similar but slightly different stimulus selectivities. *Cerebral Cortex* 13: 90–9.

Tootell, R. B., Tsao, D. Y., and Vanduffel, W. (2003) Neuroimaging weighs in: humans meet macaques in "primate" visual cortex. *Journal of Neuroscience* 23, 3981–9.

Ungerleider, L. G. and Mishkin, M. (1982) Two cortical visual systems. In D. J. Ingle, M. A. Goodale, and R. Mansfield (eds.). *Analysis of Visual Behavior*, 549–86. Cambridge, MA: MIT Press.

Velmans, M. (2002) How could conscious experiences affect brains? *Journal of Consciousness Studies* 9: 3–29.

49

Consciousness and Anesthesia

JOHN F. KIHLSTROM AND RANDALL C. CORK

The purpose of general anesthesia is to render surgical patients unconscious, and thus insensitive to pain and oblivious to events occurring during the procedure. For this reason, anesthesia – like sleep and coma – often enters into philosophical and scientific discussions of consciousness. How do we know that the patient is unconscious? Appearances to the contrary notwithstanding, are there reasons to think that anesthetized patients are actually conscious after all? Assuming that they are actually unconscious, is it possible for them to acquire and retain unconscious memories of pain and surgical events? What can the biological mechanisms of general anesthesia tell us about the neural correlates of consciousness?

The Evolution of General Anesthesia

Up until the middle of the nineteenth century, anesthesia was not a feature of surgery. Instead, patients were simply required to withstand the pain of the procedure, perhaps with the aid of alcohol, opiates (such as laudanum), a bite-board, and physical restraints. Humphrey Davy (1778–1829), the pioneering electrochemist, discovered the effects of nitrous oxide on headache and dental pain during his research on respiratory physiology; but his report went unnoticed in the medical community and the substance was quickly consigned to use at "laughing gas" parties. In 1845, Horace Wells, an American dentist, attempted to use nitrous oxide for anesthesia during a dental extraction, but the demonstration failed. But on October 16, 1846, William Morton, another dentist, employed ether in the surgical removal of a tumor with no signs or reports of pain in the patient. That event is now celebrated in hospitals and medical schools throughout the world as "Ether Day" (Fenster 2001). Morton died in 1868, and his tombstone in Cambridge's Mount Auburn Cemetery carries the following epitaph, composed by Bigelow:

> Inventor and Revealer of Inhalation Anesthesia:
> Before Whom, in All Time, Surgery was Agony;
> By Whom, Pain in Surgery was Averted and Annulled;
> Since Whom, Science has Control of Pain.

Soon thereafter, chloroform was introduced as an alternative to ether, which had an unpleasant odor and other side effects. Anesthesia was also extended from surgery to obstetrics, although some physicians had qualms about dangers to the neonate, Queen Victoria essentially ended the debate when she received chloroform for the birth of her eighth child, Prince Leopold. Nevertheless, some professionals and others continued to debate a "calculus of suffering" by which some individuals, and some conditions, were deemed more worthy of anesthesia than others (Pernick 1985).

Debates aside, progress in anesthesia continued. In 1868, nitrous oxide, mixed with oxygen to circumvent drug-induced asphyxia, was introduced to medicine – after having served for half a century as entertainment at "laughing gas" parties. Also that year, following the development of the hypodermic needle, morphine was added to the procedure to reduce the amount of inhalant required to produce anesthesia, and to prevent shock, nausea, and other negative sequelae. In 1876, the sequential use of nitrous oxide and oxygen to induce anesthesia, and ether or chloroform to maintain it, was introduced. In the mid-1880s, cocaine and its derivatives, such as novocaine, joined morphine as adjuncts to analgesic practice.

Throughout the twentieth century, the techniques for delivering and maintaining anesthesia were improved (Stoelting & Miller 2000). Beginning in the 1930s, a succession of drugs was introduced for the rapid induction of anesthesia: barbiturates such as thiopental (sodium pentothal), then benzodiazepines such as diazepam and midazolam began to substitute for barbiturates; and most recently propofol, a synthetic drug which also permits rapid recovery from anesthesia, with fewer lingering after-effects. Although inhaled anesthetics suppress voluntary responses to what are euphemistically called "surgical stimuli," curare was introduced in the 1940s to suppress involuntary, reflexive responses as well. It has since been replaced by drugs such as de-tubocurarine, vecuronium, and succinylcholine. A new generation of inhalational agents including halothane, enflurane, and isoflurane, which were less volatile than ether and less toxic than chloroform, came into use after World War II. More recently, intravenous opioid anesthetics such as fentanyl and sufentanyl, as well as new drugs to induce anesthesia, such as propofol, have emerged as alternatives to inhalational agents.

In current practice, general anesthesia begins with a pre-operative visit by the anesthetist. Immediately before the operation, the patient typically receives a benzodiazepine sedative, followed by an infusion of oxygen to displace nitrogen in the lungs. In *rapid sequence induction*, a short-acting drug such as thiopental or propofol is employed to induce initial unconsciousness before administering neuromuscular blockade to produce muscle relaxation (the anesthetic euphemism for total paralysis of the skeletal musculature). In an alternative procedure, called *inhalation* or *mask induction*, the patient may receive nitrous oxide and oxygen plus a volatile anesthetic; in this case, however, anesthesia develops more slowly. Subsequently, inhalants such as isoflurane, desflurane, or sevoflurane may be used to maintain anesthesia induced by other drugs. In *intravenous anesthesia*, the inhalants are replaced by drugs such as sufentanyl and propofol. In any event, because of the use of muscle relaxants, the patient must be respirated through intubation of the trachea. At the end of the operation, the patient may receive a drug such as neostygmine to reverse the neuromuscular blockade and permit the resumption of normal breathing, as well as morphine to help alleviate postoperative pain. Any residual inhaled anesthetic is removed by the patient's normal respiration.

The technique just described, known as *balanced anesthesia*, achieves the tripartite goals of general anesthesia: sedation, loss of consciousness (sometimes referred to as "narcosis" or "hypnosis"), and muscle relaxation. By contrast, various forms of *local* or *regional anesthesia* can be achieved by injection of local anesthetics such as lidocaine into the subarachnoid (*spinal anesthesia*) or epidural (*epidural anesthesia*) spaces of the spinal cord, or the peripheral nerves supplying some body part (*nerve block*). In such procedures, adequate anesthesia is defined more narrowly as a loss of tactile sensation, and there is no loss of consciousness. In *conscious sedation*, local or regional anesthetics are combined with benzodiazepine sedatives: again, there is no general loss of consciousness, though the use of benzodiazepines will likely render the patient amnesic for the procedure. In *hypesthesia*, subclinical doses of general anesthetics are administered to nonpatient volunteers for studies of learning and memory (Andrade 1996).

Mechanisms of Anesthesia

Although modern scientific medicine generally disdains "empirical" treatments that are known to be efficacious, even though their scientific bases are not known, the mechanisms underlying general anesthesia remain a matter of considerable mystery. As a first pass, it seems plausible that general anesthetics reversibly disrupt neural activity by inhibiting either neural excitability or synaptic activity. Beyond that, things get murky.

To complicate things further, the various classes of anesthetic agents appear to have somewhat different mechanisms of action (Stoelting & Miller 2000). For example, many intravenous "hypnotic" drugs – including propofol, barbiturates such as thiopental, and benzodiazepines such as diazepam – appear to interact with gamma-aminobutyric acid (GABA), an inhibitory neurotransmitter, to increase the time that chloride ion channels are open, resulting in a hyperpolarization of cell membranes. However, ketamine, another intravenous anesthetic, interacts with excitatory N-methyl-D-aspartate (NMDA) receptors instead. Natural and synthetic opioid anesthetics such as fentanyl, of course, act on opioid receptors, inhibiting presynaptic release of neurotransmitters such as acetylcholine and substance P. However, even in high doses these drugs do not, by themselves, induce loss of consciousness. For this purpose, they are often combined with nitrous oxide and oxygen. Nitrous oxide, for its part, has effects on NMDA receptors similar to those of ketamine. Current evidence is broadly consistent with anesthetic action on both synaptic excitation and inhibition, with the contribution of each process varying from agent to agent.

The molecular and cellular mechanisms by which inhaled anesthetics such as isoflurane achieve their effects have been the subject of intense investigation and debate (Franks & Lieb 1994). According to the Myer-Overton rule known since the late nineteenth century, there is a strong correlation between the potency of an anesthetic gas and its solubility in lipids, suggesting that the expansion of nerve cell membranes effectively might close the ion channels by which sodium enters the cell to induce an action potential. It is now believed that the inhalants bind directly to specific pockets of relevant proteins rather than altering the lipid bilayer itself. In this way, they create a dynamic block of channels involved in synaptic excitation; some anesthetics also intensify synaptic inhibition. Although the general view is that anesthetics act on the postsynaptic side, there are some indications that they inhibit presynaptic neurotransmitter release as well.

The concept of balanced anesthesia implies that there are likely to be a number of separate mechanisms working together to produce analgesia (lack of pain), a sleep-like loss of consciousness (sometimes referred to as "hypnosis"), immobility (voluntary responses to surgical stimuli, as opposed to the spinal reflexes suppressed by muscle relaxants such as vecuronium), and amnesia (lack of memory for surgical events). According to one proposal, inhalants such as isoflurane, which induce both immobility and amnesia, achieve these effects by different routes: immobility by acting on GABA receptors in the spinal cord, and amnesia by suppressing activity in the hippocampus.

As it happens, the specific proteins affected by inhaled anesthetics are receptors for GABA, among other neurotransmitters. Thus, the inhaled anesthetics may share a mechanism with the intravenous anesthetics after all. Along the same lines, the inhaled anesthetics share some pharmacological properties, such as tolerance, withdrawal, and cross-tolerance, with alcohol and sedative hypnotics such as barbiturates. However, there are now several anesthetic agents that violate the Meyer-Overton rule, and it is known that some gases can bind to the proteins implicated in anesthesia yet not cause anesthesia. Although much attention has focused on GABA, Hans Flohr has implicated NMDA instead (Flohr 2000). Both nitrous oxide and ketamine act as antagonists on NMDA receptors, blocking glutamate, an excitatory neurotransmitter – as does xenon, a newly developed anesthetic. Even if the intravenous anesthetics share a final common pathway with some inhaled anesthetics, other inhalants may achieve the same effects by rather different means.

Some theorists have sought to solve the mystery of anesthesia by invoking another mystery, namely quantum theory. Roger Penrose, a British mathematical physicist, and Stuart Hameroff, an American anesthesiologist, have famously speculated that consciousness is a product of certain processes described by quantum theory (Penrose 1994; Hameroff 1998). Briefly, quantum coherence (by which individual particles are unified into a wave function) produces a unified conscious self; non-local entanglement (which connects separate particles) is responsible for associative memory; quantum superposition (by which particles simultaneously exist in two or more states) produces alternative unconscious mental representations; and the collapse of the wave function (by which particles attain a definite state) brings one of these alternative mental states into conscious awareness. Within the context of this theory, Hameroff has further proposed that these processes take place in microtubules – proteins found in the walls of neurons that are shaped like hollow tubes.

Although the conventional view is that microtubules serve a structural function, supporting the structure of the cell, it is also true that they are built out of proteins – and certain proteins are known to be the site of anesthetic activity. Penrose and Hameroff contend that consciousness is actually a product of processes occurring in this microtubular cytoskeleton, which are in turn magnified by the neuron itself. In this view, anesthetics exert their effects on the specific proteins that make up these microtubules, disrupting the "quantum coherence" and thus the conscious awareness that it generates. As opposed to conventional theories of anesthesia, which focus on processes operating at the synapse, the Hameroff–Penrose theory shifts attention to processes operating inside the neural cell itself. The Penrose–Hameroff theory of both consciousness and anesthesia has attracted a great deal of interest, but at this stage it remains highly speculative, and has been criticized on both logical and empirical grounds (Grush & Churchland 1995).

Anesthesia and Awareness

Clinically, the success of general anesthesia is marked by three criteria:

- the patient's lack of response to intraoperative stimulation during the surgical procedure itself;

- upon awakening, the patient reports no awareness of pain during the procedure;
- nor does the patient report any memories of other surgical events.

Information relevant to these issues is typically gleaned from a brief post-operative interview in which the patient is asked such questions as "What was the last thing you remember before you went to sleep? What is the first thing you remember after you woke up? Can you remember anything in between these two periods? Did you dream during your operation?" Evaluated in these terms, anesthesia is almost always successful. Nevertheless, the use of muscle relaxants in balanced anesthesia makes it possible to perform surgery under lighter doses of anesthetic agents – increasing the risk of intraoperative awareness and postoperative recall at the same time as they decrease the risk of anesthetic morbidity. It was also recognized early on that the use of muscle relaxants increased the risks further, by preventing inadequately anesthetized patients from communicating their intraoperative awareness to the surgical team – a situation reminiscent of Harlan Ellison's science-fiction classic, *I Have No Mouth and I Must Scream* (1967).

Nevertheless, the incidence of anesthetic awareness is extremely low, with recent estimates of surgical awareness hovering around 0.2 percent of general surgical cases (Jones & Aggarwal 2001). A "closed case" analysis of 5,480 malpractice claims against anesthesiologists from 1970 to 1999 found only 22 cases of alleged intraoperative awareness and another 78 cases of postoperative recall. Occasionally, the incident is so serious as to result in post-traumatic stress disorder; but more commonly, the patient is left with only vague – and nondistressing – memories of intraoperative events. In general surgery, intraoperative awareness and postoperative recall are usually attributable to light anesthesia, machine malfunction, errors of anesthetic technique, and increased anesthetic requirements – for example, on the part of patients who are obese or abuse alcohol or drugs. The incidence of surgical recall arises in special circumstances, such as trauma, cardiac, or obstetrical surgery, where cardiovascular circumstances dictate lighter planes of anesthesia. Even then, the incidence of surgical recall is remarkably low – in part because even in the absence of anesthesia, the benzodiazepines often used for sedation are themselves amnesic agents (Polster 1993). In fact, modern anesthetic practice may underestimate the incidence of *intraoperative awareness* by interfering with *postoperative memory*. That is to say, an inadequately anesthetized patient may be aware of surgical events at the time they occur, but be unable to remember them later because of sedative-induced anterograde amnesia.

However low, the possibility of surgical awareness means that, in addition to monitoring various aspects of vital function during the operation, the anesthetist must also monitor the patient's state of consciousness, or *anesthetic depth* (Ghoneim 2001a). This task would be made easier if psychology and cognitive science could reach consensus on the neural or behavioral correlates of consciousness. In the absence of such criteria, anesthesiologists have often been forced to improvise. One set of standards simply relies on measures of anesthetic potency. Research has determined the *minimum alveolar concentration* (MAC) of inhalant which prevents movement in response to surgical stimulation in 50 percent of patients; *MAC-aware* is the concentration required to eliminate awareness of the stimulation. As a rule, MAC-aware is roughly half of MAC, suggesting that some of the movement in response to surgical stimulation is mediated by subcortical structures, and does not necessarily reflect conscious awareness. Similar standards for adequate anesthesia, based on blood plasma levels, have been worked out for intravenous drugs such as propofol.

It should be noted that the operational definition of MAC-aware means that 50 percent of patients will be aware of surgical events despite the presence of anesthetic – although a dose amounting to about 1.3 MAC does seem to do the trick. Nevertheless, it is important to supplement knowledge of dose-response levels with more direct evaluations of the patient's conscious awareness. Unfortunately, many obvious clinical signs of consciousness – such as talking or muscle movement in response to surgical stimulation are obviated by the use of muscle relaxants. Accordingly, some anesthesiologists rely on presumed autonomic signs of consciousness, such as the *PRST score* based on the patient's blood pressure, heart rate, sweating, and secretion of tears.

In modern practice, most methods for monitoring the depth of anesthesia involve the central nervous system. Analyses of the EEG power spectrum (derived by a fast Fourier transform of the raw EEG signal) show that anesthetized patients typically have a median EEG frequency of 2–3 Hz or less, with "spectral edge frequencies," at the very high end of the distribution, within or below the range of alpha activity (8–12 Hz). Another derivative of the raw EEG is provided by bispectral analysis, which employs a complicated set of transformations to yield a *bispectral index* (BIS) that ranges from close to 100 in subjects who are normally awake, to values well under 60 in patients who are adequately anesthetized. Another common monitoring technique employs event-related potentials (ERPs, also known as evoked potentials, or EPs) elicited in the EEG by weak somatosensory, auditory, or even visual stimulation. Adequate anesthesia reduces the amplitude of the various peaks and troughs in the ERP, as well as the latency of various components representing brainstem response and early and late cortical responses. Of course, the late "cognitive" components of the ERP would be expected to disappear entirely during adequate anesthesia. An *AEP index* of consciousness reflects the degree to which three "midlatency" components of the auditory ERP are delayed with respect to their normal occurrence between 20 and 45 milliseconds after the stimulus.

Although most physiological indices of anesthetic depth have been validated against such criteria as movement in response to painful surgical stimulation, they have also been compared to various aspects of memory performance (Kerssens & Sebel 2001). In one study, a 0.2 percent end-tidal concentration (a measure related to MAC) of isoflurane produced a substantial impairment of performance on a continuous recognition test even over retention intervals as short as 8 seconds, while a 0.4 percent end-tidal concentration reduced recognition after 32 seconds to zero. Another study showed similar effects for low and high doses of propofol. In a study comparing midazolam, isoflurane, alfentanyl, and propofol, a 50 percent reduction in recall was associated with an average BIS score of 86, while an average BIS of 64 yielded reductions of 95 percent.

Of course, the simple fact that anesthesia impairs recall does not mean that anesthetized patients lack on-line awareness of what is going on around them. In principle, at least, they could experience an anterograde amnesia for surgical events similar to that which occurs in conscious sedation. In the absence of a reliable and valid physiological index of conscious awareness – something that is not likely to be available any time soon – what is needed is some kind of direct behavioral measure of awareness, such as the patient's self-report. In balanced anesthesia, of course, such reports are precluded by the use of muscle relaxants. But a variant on balanced anesthesia known as the *isolated forearm technique* (IFT) actually permits surgical patients to directly report their level of awareness in response to commands and queries (Russell 1989). Because muscle relaxants tend to bind relatively quickly to receptors in the skeletal musculature, if the flow of blood is temporarily restricted to one forearm by means of a tourniquet, the muscles in that part of the body will not be paralyzed.

And therefore, the patient can respond to the anesthetist's instruction to squeeze his or her hand, or raise their fingers – that is, if they are aware of the command in the first place.

Interestingly, response to the IFT is not highly correlated with ostensible clinical signs of consciousness. Nor does it predict postoperative recollection of intraoperative events. In one study, more than 40 percent of patients receiving general anesthesia for caesarian section responded positively to commands; yet only about 2 percent had even fragmentary recollections of the procedure. On the assumption that a patient who responds discriminatively to verbal commands is clearly conscious to some extent, the IFT indicates that intraoperative awareness is somewhat greater than has previously been believed. However, discriminative behavior also occurs in the absence of perceptual awareness, as in cases of "subliminal" perception, masked priming, and blindsight (see Merikle, chapter 40; Weiskrantz, chapter 13). Estimates of intraoperative awareness may indeed be suppressed by an anterograde amnesia, which effectively prevents patients from remembering, and thus reporting, any awareness that they experienced during surgery.

Unconscious Processing during Anesthesia

While adequate general anesthesia abolishes conscious recollection of surgical events by definition, it is possible that unconscious (or, for that matter, conscious) intraoperative perception may lead to unconscious postoperative memory that influences the patient's subsequent experience, thought, and action outside of phenomenal awareness. Although clinical lore within anesthesiology includes the "fat lady syndrome," in which an overweight patient's postoperative dislike of her surgeon is traced to unkind remarks he made about her body while she was anesthetized, documented cases are hard to find. In the late 1950s and early 1960s David Cheek, a Los Angeles physician and hypnotherapist, described a number of patients who, when hypnotized, remembered meaningful sounds that occurred in the operating room – particularly negative remarks. Cheek claimed to have corroborated these reports, and attributed unexpectedly poor postoperative outcomes to unconscious memories of untoward surgical events. Unfortunately, the interview method he employed, hypnotic "ideomotor signaling," is highly susceptible to experimenter bias, and information that would corroborate such memories is not always available. Accordingly, the possibility cannot be excluded that patients' postoperative "memories," recovered through this technique, are confabulations.

Despite these methodological problems, Cheek's suggestion was subsequently supported by Bernard Levinson, who as an experiment staged a bogus crisis during surgery. After the anesthesia had been established (with ether), the anesthesiologist, following a script, asked the surgeon to stop because the patient's lips were turning blue. After announcing that he was going to give oxygen, and making appropriate sounds around the respirator, he informed the surgeon that he could carry on as before. One month later, Levinson hypnotized each of the patients – all of whom had been selected for high hypnotizability and ability to experience hypnotic age regression – and took them back to the time of their operation. Levinson reported that four of the ten patients had verbatim memory for the incident, while another four became agitated and anxious; the remaining two patients seemed reluctant to relive the experience. Levinson's provocative experiment suggested that surgical events could be perceived by at least some anesthetized patients, and preserved in memory – even if the memories were ordinarily unconscious, and accessible only under hypnosis.

Despite Levinson's report, unconscious perception during general anesthesia remained largely unexplored territory until the matter was revived by Henry Bennett. Inspired by the apparent success of Cheek's "ideomotor signaling" technique for revealing unconscious memories, Bennett gave anesthetized surgical patients a tape-recorded suggestion that, when interviewed postoperatively, they would perform a specific behavioral response, such as lifting their index finger or pulling on their ears. Although no patient reported any conscious recollection of the suggestion, approximately 80 percent of the patients responded appropriately to the experimenter's cue. Bennett, following Cheek, suggested that unconscious memories were more likely to be revealed with nonverbal than with verbal responses.

At about the same time, Evans and Richardson reported that intraoperative suggestions, delivered during general anesthesia, led to improved patient outcome on a number of variables, including a significantly shorter postoperative hospital stay. Again, the patients had no conscious recollection of receiving these suggestions. Although this study was not concerned with memory per se, the apparent effects of suggestions on post-surgical recovery certainly implied that the suggestions themselves had been processed, if unconsciously, at the time they occurred.

As it happens, subsequent studies have failed to confirm the findings of either Bennett et al. or Evans and Richardson. And more recently, a double-blind study inspired by Levinson's report, in which nonpatient volunteers received subanesthetic concentrations of either desflurane or propofol, failed to obtain any evidence of memory for a staged crisis. Nevertheless, these pioneering studies, combined with an increasing interest in consciousness and unconscious processing within the wider field of psychology and cognitive science, stimulated a revival of interest in questions of awareness, perception, and memory during and after surgical anesthesia, which have been carried out with progressively improved paradigms.

Of particular importance to this revival was the articulation, in the 1980s, of the distinction between two different expressions of episodic memory – explicit and implicit (Schacter 1987). Explicit memory is conscious recollection, as exemplified by the individual's ability to recall or recognize some past event. Implicit memory, by contrast, refers to any change in experience, thought, or action that is attributable to a past event – for example, savings in relearning or priming effects. From the 1960s through the 1980s, a growing body of evidence indicated that explicit and implicit memory were dissociable. For example, amnesic patients show priming effects even though they cannot remember the priming events themselves; and they can learn new cognitive and motor skills, even though they do not remember the learning experience. Similarly, normal subjects show savings in relearning material that they can neither recall nor recognize as having been learned before. And, again in normal subjects, priming is relatively unaffected by many experimental manipulations that have profound effects on recall and recognition. In a very real sense, then, implicit memory is unconscious memory, occurring in the absence of, or at least independent of, the individual's conscious recollection of the past (see also Kihlstrom, Dorfman, & Park, chapter 41). Accordingly, the experimental paradigms developed for studying implicit memory in amnesic patients and normal subjects were soon adapted to the question of unconscious processing of intraoperative events in anesthesia (Kihlstrom 1993; Kihlstrom & Schacter 1990).

In our first study, patients receiving isoflurane anesthesia for elective surgery were played, through earphones, an auditory list of 15 paired associates consisting of a familiar word as the cue and its closest semantic associate as the target – for example, *ocean–water*

(Kihlstrom et al. 1990). The stimulus tape was presented continuously from the first incision to the last stitch, for an average of 67 repetitions over an average of 50 minutes. In the recovery room, the patients were read the cue terms from the stimulus list, as well as a closely matched set of cues from a control list of paired associates, and asked to recall the word with which each cue had been paired on the list read during surgery: this constituted the test of explicit memory. For the test of implicit memory, they were read the same cues again, and asked simply to respond with the first word that came to mind. The subjects recalled no more target words from the presented list than from a control list, thus showing that they had very poor explicit memory for the experience. On the free-association test, however, they were more likely to produce the targeted response from the presented list, compared to control targets, thus displaying a priming effect. Compared to explicit memory, which was grossly impaired (as would be expected with adequate anesthesia), implicit memory was relatively spared.

Despite this early success, subsequent studies employing similar paradigms produced a mix of positive and negative results. For example, we precisely replicated the procedure described above with another group of patients receiving sufentanyl, and found that explicit and implicit memory were equally impaired (Cork, Kihlstrom, & Schacter 1992). Although the two studies, taken together, suggested the interesting hypothesis that different anesthetic agents might have different effects on implicit memory, a more parsimonious conclusion might have been that the isoflurane effects were spurious. In a debate at the Second International Symposium on Memory and Awareness in Anesthesia, held in 1992, experimental psychologists and anesthesiologists agreed that memory for events during anesthesia had not yet been convincingly demonstrated. Over the next few years, however, the literature began to settle, so that a comprehensive quantitative review of 44 studies could conclude that adequately anesthetized patients can, indeed, show postoperative memory for unconsciously processed intraoperative events (see also Bonebakker et al. 1996; Merikle & Daneman 1996; Cork, Couture, & Kihlstrom 1997).

The Limits of Implicit Memory in Anesthesia

Although the more recent literature continues to contain a mix of positive and negative results, there are simply too many positive findings to be ignored (Ghoneim 2001b). At the same time, the literature contains enough negative studies, and other anomalous results, to warrant further investigation. For example, Merikle and Daneman concluded that the evidence for unconscious processing during general anesthesia was not limited to "indirect" measures of implicit memory, and extended to "direct" measures of explicit memory as well (Merikle & Daneman 1996). This is a surprising statement, given that adequately anesthetized patients lack conscious recollection by definition. However, these authors included in their survey only the few tests of explicit memory that encouraged guessing, and excluded the many studies that discouraged guessing. While guessing yields a more exhaustive measure of conscious recollection, it is also true that guessing can be biased, unconsciously, by priming itself. Therefore, it is likely that some of the "explicit" memory identified by Merikle and Daneman is, in fact, contaminated by implicit memory. In support of this idea, a study employing the "process dissociation" procedure confirmed that postoperative memory was confined to automatic priming effects, and did not involve conscious recollection (Lubke et al. 1999).

A persisting issue is whether postoperative implicit memory might be an artifact of fluctuations in anesthetic depth which occur naturally during surgery. In the study just described, even implicit memory varied as a function of the patient's level of anesthesia. Patients showed more priming for words presented at BIS levels above 60, and no priming for items presented at BIS levels below 40. A subsequent study from the same group, which confined stimulus presentation to BIS levels ranging from 40 to 60, yielded no evidence of implicit memory (Kerssens, Ouchi, & Sebel 2005). Although implicit memory may be spared at a depth of anesthesia sufficient to abolish explicit memory, implicit memory itself may be abolished at deeper levels. Still, it is not clear that the abolition of implicit memory is a benefit worth the risks of maintaining very deep levels of anesthesia throughout surgery.

Explicit and implicit memory are also dissociated in *conscious sedation*, an anesthetic technique that is increasingly popular in outpatient surgery. In conscious sedation, the patient receives medication for analgesia and sedation, and perhaps regional anesthesia, but remains conscious throughout the procedure. It is well known that high doses of sedative drugs have amnesic effects on their own, such that patients often have poor memory for events that occurred during the procedure. As it happens, sedative amnesia produced by drugs such as diazepam or propofol also dissociates explicit and implicit memory (Polster 1993; Cork, Heaton, & Kihlstrom 1996). As with general anesthesia, studies employing the process-dissociation procedure confirm that sedative amnesia impairs conscious recollection, but spares automatic priming effects.

Most work on implicit memory employs tests of *repetition priming*, such as stem- or fragment-completion, in which the target item recapitulates, in whole or in part, the prime itself – for example, when the word *ashtray* primes completion of the stem *ash-*. Repetition priming can be mediated by a perception-based representation of the prime, which holds information about the physical properties of the item, but not about its meaning. But there are other forms of priming, such as semantic priming, where the relationship between prime and target is based on "deeper" processing of the prime – for example, when the prime *cigarette* primes completion of the stem *ash-* with *-tray* as opposed to *-can*. Semantic priming requires more than physical similarity between prime and target, and must be mediated by a meaning-based representation of the prime. The distinction between repetition and semantic priming is sometimes subtle. For example, in the isoflurane study described earlier, the paired associates presented as primes were linked by meaning, but because both elements of the pair were presented at the time of study, the priming effect observed could have been mediated by a perception-based representation, rather than a meaning-based one. The point is that implicit memory following surgical anesthesia is fairly well established when it comes to repetition priming, but conclusions about semantic priming are much less secure. Fewer studies have employed semantic priming paradigms, and relatively few of these studies have yielded unambiguously positive results (Ghoneim 2001b). If semantic priming occurs at all following general anesthesia, it is most likely to occur for items presented at relatively light levels of anesthesia, as indicated by indices such as BIS. At deeper planes of anesthesia, implicit memory – if it occurs at all – is likely to be limited to repetition priming.

The distinction between perception-based and meaning-based priming may have implications for the use of intraoperative suggestions to improve post-surgical outcome. If implicit memory following anesthesia is limited to repetition priming, implying that the anesthetized patient's state of consciousness does not permit semantic analysis of the intraoperative message, it is hard to see how such suggestions could have any effects at all. In fact, a comparative study found that intraoperative suggestions had no more effect on post-operative pain than did *pre*-operative suggestions of the same sort – or, for that matter, the pre- and intraoperative reading of short stories. Intraoperative suggestions will do no harm, and patients may derive some "placebo" benefit from the simple knowledge that they are receiving them during surgery. To the extent that intraoperative suggestions do some good, the limitations on information processing during anesthesia may mean that any positive effects are more likely to be mediated by their prosody, and other physical features, than by their meaning: a soothing voice may be more important that what the voice says. If anesthesiologists want patients to respond to the specific semantic content of therapeutic messages, such messages are probably better delivered while patients are awake, during the pre-operative visit that is already established as the standard of care.

Implicit Memory or Implicit Perception?

Priming effects are evidence of implicit memory, but they can also serve as evidence of implicit perception – a term coined to refer to the effect of an event on experience, thought, and action, that is attributable to a stimulus event, in the absence of (or independent of) conscious perception of that event (Kihlstrom, Barnhardt, & Tataryn 1992). Implicit perception is exemplified by "subliminal" perception of degraded stimuli, as well as neurological syndromes such as "blindsight" and neglect (see Merikle, chapter 40; Weiskrantz, chapter 13). In general anesthesia, the patients are presumably unaware of the priming events at the time they occurred. For that reason, evidence of implicit memory following general anesthesia is also evidence of implicit perception.

See also 7 Normal and abnormal states of consciousness; 41 Implicit and explicit memory and learning; 46 Global disorders of consciousness.

Further Readings

Fenster, J. M. (2001) *Ether Day: The Strange Tale of America's Greatest Medical Discovery and the Haunted Men Who Made It.* New York: HarperCollins.
Ghoneim, M. M. (2001) *Awareness during Anesthesia.* Oxford: Butterworth-Heinemann.
Jordan, C., Vaughan, D. J. A., and Newton, D. E. F. (eds.) (2000) *Memory and Awareness in Anaesthesia* IV. London: Imperial College Press.

References

Andrade, J. (1996) Investigations of hypesthesia: using anesthetics to explore relationships between consciousness, learning, and memory. *Consciousness and Cognition* 5, 562–80.
Bonebakker, A. E., Jelicic, M., Passchier, J., and Bonke, B. (1996) Memory during general anesthesia: practical and methodological aspects. *Consciousness and Cognition* 5, 542–61.
Cork, R. C., Couture, L. J., and Kihlstrom, J. F. (1997) Memory and recall. In T. L. Yaksh, C. Lynch, W. M. Zapol, M. Maze, J. F. Biebuyck, and L. J. Saidman (eds.), *Anesthesia: Biologic Foundations*, 451–67. New York: Lippincott-Raven.
Cork, R. C., Heaton, J. F., and Kihlstrom, J. F. (1996) Is there implicit memory after propofol sedation? *British Journal of Anaesthesia* 76, 492–8.

Cork, R. C., Kihlstrom, J. F., and Schacter, D. L. (1992) Absence of explicit or implicit memory in patients anesthetized with sufentanil/nitrous oxide. *Anesthesiology* 76, 892–8.

Fenster, J. M. (2001) *Ether Day: The Strange Tale of America's Greatest Medical Discovery and the Haunted Men who Made It.* New York: HarperCollins.

Flohr, H. (2000) NMDA receptor-mediated computational processes and phenomenal consciousness. In T. Metzinger (ed.), *Neural Correlates of Consciousness*, 245–58. Cambridge, MA: MIT Press.

Franks, N. P., and Lieb, W. R. (1994) Molecular and cellular mechanisms of general anaesthesia. *Nature* 367, 607–14.

Ghoneim, M. M. (2001a) Awareness during anesthesia. In M. M. Ghoneim (ed.), *Awareness during Anesthesia*, 1–22. Oxford: Butterworth-Heinemann.

Ghoneim, M. M. (2001b) Implicit memory for events during anesthesia. In M. M. Ghoneim (ed.), *Awareness During Anesthesia*, 23–68. Oxford: Butterworth-Heinemann.

Grush, R., and Churchland, P. S. (1995) Gaps in Penrose's toilings. *Journal of Consciousness Studies* 2, 10–29.

Hameroff, S. R. (1998) "Funda-mentality": Is the conscious mind subtly linked to a basic level of the universe? *Trends in Cognitive Sciences* 2, 119–27.

Jones, J. G. and Aggarwal, S. (2001) Monitoring the depth of anesthesia. In M. M. Ghoneim (ed.), *Awareness During Anesthesia*, 69–91. Oxford: Butterworth-Heinemann.

Kerssens, C. and Sebel, P. S. (2001) BIS and memory during anesthesia. In M. M. Ghoneim (ed.), *Awareness During Anesthesia*, 103–16. Oxford: Butterworth-Heinemann.

Kerssens, C., Ouchi, T., and Sebel, P. S. (2005) No evidence of memory function during anesthesia with propofol or isoflurane with close control of hypnotic state. *Anesthesiology* 102, 57–62.

Kihlstrom, J. F. (1993) Implicit memory function during anesthesia. In P. S. Sebel, B. Bonke, and E. Winograd (eds.), *Memory and Awareness in Anesthesia*, 10–30. Englewood Cliffs, NJ: Prentice-Hall.

Kihlstrom, J. F. and Schacter, D. L. (1990) Anaesthesia, amnesia, and the cognitive unconscious. In B. Bonke, W. Fitch, and K. Millar (eds.), *Awareness and Memory in Anaesthesia*, 21–44. Amsterdam: Swets & Zeitlinger.

Kihlstrom, J. F., Barnhardt, T. M., and Tataryn, D. J. (1992) Implicit perception. In R. F. Bornstein and T. S. Pittman (eds.), *Perception Without Awareness: Cognitive, Clinical, and Social Perspectives*, 17–54. New York: Guilford Press.

Kihlstrom, J. F., Schacter, D. L., Cork, R. C., and Hurt, C. A. (1990) Implicit and explicit memory following surgical anesthesia. *Psychological Science* 1: 5, 303–6.

Lubke, G. H., Kerssens, C., Phaf, H., and Sebel, P. S. (1999) Dependence of explicit and implicit memory on hypnotic state in trauma patients. *Anesthesiology* 90, 670–80.

Merikle, P. M. and Daneman, M. (1996) Memory for unconsciously perceived events: evidence from anesthetized patients. *Consciousness and Cognition* 5, 525–41.

Penrose, R. (1994) *Shadows of the Mind.* Oxford: Oxford University Press.

Pernick, M. S. (1985) *A Calculus of Suffering: Pain, Professionalism, and Anesthesia in 19th-Century America.* New York: Columbia University Press.

Polster, M. R. (1993) Drug-induced amnesia: implications for cognitive neuropsychological investigations of memory. *Psychological Bulletin* 114, 477–93.

Russell, I. F. (1989) Conscious awareness during general anaesthesia: relevance of autonomic signs and isolated arm movements as guides to depth of anaesthesia. In J. G. Jones (ed.), . *Depth of Anaesthesia: Ballière's Clinical Anaesthesiology*, vol. 3, 511–32. London: Ballière Tindall.

Schacter, D. L. (1987) Implicit memory: history and current status. *Journal of Experimental Psychology: Learning, Memory, and Cognition* 13, 501–18.

Stoelting, R. K. and Miller, R. D. (2000) *Basics of Anesthesia*, 4th edn. New York: Churchill Livingstone.

50

Neural Dominance, Neural Deference, and Sensorimotor Dynamics[1]

SUSAN HURLEY

Neural Dominance vs. Neural Deference

Why is neural activity in a particular area expressed as experience of red rather than green, or as visual experience rather than auditory experience? Indeed, why does it have any conscious expression at all? These familiar questions indicate the explanatory gap between neural activity and "what it's like" qualities of conscious experience. (See Levine, chapter 29.) The comparative explanatory gaps, intermodal and intramodal, can be separated from the absolute explanatory gap and associated zombie issues. Here I focus on comparative gaps: Why is neural activity in a given area expressed as *this* type of experience rather than *that* type of experience?

Light is shed on comparative gaps by the distinction between neural dominance and neural deference, which applies to various examples of neural plasticity and perceptual adaptation (cf. von Melcher et al. 2000; Merzenich 2000; Pallas 2001). I here illustrate and explain the distinction – thereby addressing the comparative explanatory gaps – in dynamic sensorimotor terms.

What happens to qualities of experience when input from a given source is rerouted to nonstandard neural targets? Suppose, schematically, that input A normally activates neural target area 1, associated with the A-feeling, and input B normally activates neural target area 2, associated with the B-feeling. Suppose input A is somehow rerouted to project instead to neural area 2. Such rerouting could result from surgical intervention, abnormal neural projections, or external mechanisms, such as distorting goggles; it could cross between sensory modalities or stay within one. (These modulations of rerouting are spelled out and examined in Hurley & Noë 2003.) When input from A activates area 2, will the B-feeling or the A-feeling arise (see Figure 50.1)?

It can go either way. In some cases of rerouting, activity in area 2 from source A is associated with the A-feeling: neural activity in the target area "defers" to the nonstandard sources of input and takes on the qualitative expression typical of the new source. In cases of deference, neural activity in a given area changes not just its function but also its qualitative expression. In other cases, activity in area 2 from source A retains the B-feeling: neural activity "dominates" its nonstandard source, and retains the qualitative expression it would have if it were activated normally, from its normal input source. Note that since the input source has changed, qualitative expression in cases of dominance will be illusory; the source of input will be experienced as something it is not.

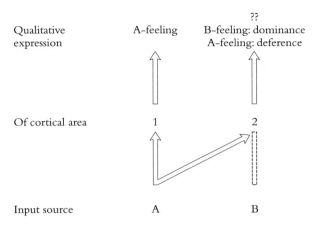

Figure 50.1 *Neural dominance:* the activation of 2 by A feels like the activation of 2 by B normally would, i.e. the B-feeling. The normal qualitative expression of 2 is unchanged.

Neural deference: the activation of 2 by A feels like the activation of 1 by A, i.e. the A-feeling. The qualitative expression of 2 is changed to reflect the new source of input.

Examples

Dominance: phantom limbs and colored-hearing synesthesia

Neural dominance is illustrated by phantom limb cases, where the normal qualitative expression of neural activity in a given area appears not to change, despite change in the input source. Normally, tactile inputs from face (source A) and arm (source B) map onto adjacent areas of somatosensory cortex, for face (neural target area 1) and for arm (neural target area 2). After amputation of part of an arm, tactile inputs from the face (source A) appear to invade the deafferented cortex (target area 2), whose normal qualitative expression is a feeling of an arm being touched (the B-feeling). When this neural area is activated from its new source, the face, it retains its normal qualitative expression, the touch-to-arm feeling (the A-feeling). Touches to the face now activate both somatosensory cortex for face (area 1) and what would normally be somatosensory cortex for arm (area 2). So, when the experimenter blindfolds the amputee patient, strokes the patient's face, and asks him what he feels, the patient responds that he feels his phantom arm as well as his face being stroked (Ramachandran & Blakeslee 1998, pp. 28, 38; Ramachandran & Hirstein 1998).

Another example of dominance is colored-hearing synesthesia, in which a specific sound, usually the sound of a specific word or the initial letter of a word, induces experience of a specific color (for details see Cytowic 1997; Frith & Paulesu 1997; Hurley & Noë 2006). This appears to result from nonstandard neural projections, either additional to normal projections or which weren't pruned in the normal way during development (Grossenbacher 1997; Harrison & Baron-Cohen 1997b; Maurer 1997; Ramachandran & Hubbard 2003, p. 51). Recent imaging work (Nunn et al. 2002) has found clear activation in V4, an area of visual cortex believed to support experience of color (Hadjikhani et al. 1998; cf. Tootell & Hadjikhani 1998; Zeki et al. 1998), when synesthetes with colored-hearing listen

	Normal subjects	Non-ACE synesthetes	ACE synesthetes
Normal color experience	Left V4 and right V4; left V4 more active	Right V4 more active	Left V4 and right V4; left V4 more active
Synesthetic color experience	XXX	Left V4	Left V4 Hippocampus SMA

Figure 50.2 Synesthesia and the alien color effect.

to spoken words. Activation of this area under the same conditions is not found in normal subjects. This suggests that language inputs get routed in synesthetes not just to their normal destinations but also to this area of visual cortex, where they elicit color experiences. So again here, cortical activation dominates over the source of stimulation.

Alien Color Effect (ACE) is an intriguing form of colored-hearing synesthesia discovered by Jeffrey Gray and co-workers (Gray et al. 2002). In ACE, color words induce experience of incongruent colors. For example, when an ACE child correctly answers "red" in response to being asked what color a bus is, she may experience synesthetic green. This results in distinctive interference effects in color-naming tasks: subjects with higher levels of ACE are slower to name the normal colors of objects.

Interestingly, when synesthetes experience color, neural activity in V4 shows lateralization, which differs between non-ACE and ACE colored hearing (Figure 50.2; see Gray et al. 2002; Gray et al. 2006). When nonsynesthetic subjects and ACE subjects perceive normal colors, both left and right V4 are (differentially) active, though left V4 more so than right V4. ("Differentially," in that V4 activity remains when activation produced by looking at black and white Mondrians is subtracted by brain imaging techniques from activation produced by looking at colored Mondrians. In comparisons of activity levels between groups or brain areas, we are thus looking at differences between differences.) Left V4 is active when ACE synesthetes hear colored words. By contrast, when non-ACE synesthetes perceive normal colors, right V4 is more active than left V4; but when they hear colored words, left V4 is active. Language areas are of course also lateralized to the left. Moreover, there is additional hippocampal and supplementary motor area activation in ACE synesthetes when they perceive synesthetic colors (see Gray et al. 2006). (Gray and McNaughton (2000) attribute to the hippocampal system a general role in conflict resolution, which might explain its additional activation where synesthetically induced colors are incongruent with their inducers. Gray et al. (2006) also suggest that additional motor activation reflects the need for ACE subjects to inhibit a prepotent response, namely, utterance of the name of the synesthetically induced color when asked to name the inducing color.)

Consider an ACE example of neural dominance. Suppose that A is stimulation of auditory channels generated by the spoken word "white" and B is a pattern of light entering the eye from a yellow visual stimulus. Input from A activates area 1, whose normal qualitative expression is experience of hearing the word "white". Input from B activates area 2, whose normal qualitative expression is experience of yellow. Area 2 is not disconnected from input B, but there are additional nonstandard neural projections: input from A also activates area 2 (left V4), perhaps via area 1, again eliciting area 2's normal qualitative expression, experi-

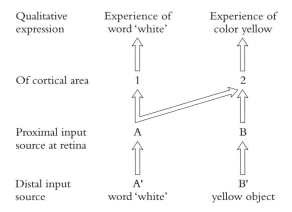

Variant of alien color effect (ACE) in synesthetes. Qualitative expression of area 2 unchanged for non-standard input source: dominance for color

Figure 50.3 *Neural dominance:* the activation of 2 by A feels like the activation of 2 by B normally would, i.e. the B-feeling. The normal qualitative expression of 2 is unchanged.

ence of yellow. Area 2 thus retains its normal qualitative expression even when activated by an input from a different modality (see Figure 50.3).

Work on neural correlates of consciousness may lead us to expect neural dominance, as in the interpretations of phantom limbs and synesthesia just given. However, it is important to note that neural deference also occurs.

Examples of deference: Braille reading, TVSS, and color adaptation

Neural deference is illustrated when congenitally blind persons read Braille. Brain imaging work on congenitally and early blind subjects reveals activation in visual cortex during tactile tasks, including Braille reading, whereas normal controls show deactivation (measured by PET scans) of visual cortex during tactile tasks (Sadato et al. 1996, 1998; see also Buchel 1998; Buchel et al. 1998; other imaging work has shown that visual cortex of blind subjects is activated by sound changes, when the task is to detect these changes (Kujala et al. 2000)). In Braille reading by these subjects, visual cortex (target area 2) receives tactile inputs (source A) that would normally project to somatosensory cortex (target area 1). How do these blind persons experience such activation of visual cortex: as visual or as tactile? This question is directly addressed by work that uses transcranial magnetic stimulation (TMS) to produce transient interference with visual cortex activity during Braille reading. In early blind subjects, TMS applied to visual cortex produced both errors in Braille reading and reports of tactile illusions ("missing dots," "extra dots," and "dots don't make sense") (Cohen et al. 1997a, b, 1999). Speech was unaffected by TMS, and blind subjects given a chance to correct their reports after TMS had ended did not do so, suggesting that errors were not due to interference with speech output. In normal subjects, by contrast, TMS to visual cortex had no effect on tactile tasks or sensations, whereas similar stimulation is known to disrupt the visual performance of normal subjects. In these blind subjects, visual cortex seems not only to perform a tactile perceptual function, but also

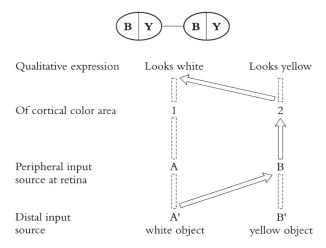

Adaptation to Kohler's color-divided goggles. Qualitative expression of area changes for non-standard input source: deference for color

Subject's view: right half of each lens yellow, left half blue

Qualitative expression	Looks white	Looks yellow
Of cortical color area	1	2
Peripheral input source at retina	A	B
Distal input source	A' white object	B' yellow object

Figure 50.4 *Neural deference:* the activation of area 2 by light from white object A' passing through yellow lens looks, after adaptation, like the activation of area 1 by light from white object A', i.e. looks white. Prior to adaptation, the activation of 2 by light from white object A' passing through yellow lens looked like the activation of 2 by light from yellow object B'. The qualitative expression of two changes, reflecting the new source of input.

to have tactile qualitative expression. Visual cortex defers qualitatively to its nonstandard tactile inputs.

Deference is also found in congenitally blind subjects who have adapted to Tactile Visual Substitution Systems (TVSS; see work by Bach-y-Rita 1972, 1984, 1996), in which stimulation is applied by mechanical or electronic "fingers" on a pad placed over the skin or tongue, corresponding to input from a camera or computer screen. Learning to use such a system produces activation of visual cortex in congenitally blind but not in sighted subjects. When TMS was applied to the visual cortex of TVSS trained subjects, it "induced clear tactile sensations" in the blind but not the sighted subjects (Kupers & Ptito 2004, though in this case there was no interference with task performance). Again, visual cortex defers qualitatively to nonstandard tactile inputs.

A third example of deference is provided by the color adaptation Ivo Kohler (1964; see also Peppman and Wieland 1966) reports as a consequence of wearing color-divided goggles. Each lens of these goggles is blue to the left and yellow to the right (from the wearer's perspective). When the subject first puts on the goggles, a white object viewed through the yellow half of the lenses would look yellowish. But over time the subject adapts and regains color constancy, so that a white object looks white as he tracks it, whether viewed through the yellow or the blue half-lenses. Prior to adaptation, light from a yellow object B' with a certain ratio of wavelengths generates input that activates neural target area 2 and the object looks yellow. After adaptation, light from white object A' passing through the yellow half-lenses has the same ratio of wavelengths and activates the same target area, but the object now looks white (see Figure 50.4). Thus, the qualitative expression of activity in that target area appears to defer, with adaptation, to the changed source of input.

Other examples of neural deference include the recruitment of auditory cortex to visual functions in rewired ferrets and perceptual adaptation to long-term wearing of left–right reversing goggles (Hurley & Noë 2003).

On reflection, we should not be surprised that neural deference is found as well as neural dominance. After all, neural activity at a given location in the brain can have quite different properties; the character of experience can correlate with neural properties other than location of neural activity. (For example, when visual input is surgically rerouted to neural targets in auditory areas of the brain of newborn ferrets, cells in those areas develop non-standard visual properties. As a result of this rerouting two-dimensional retinotopic maps, similar to those normally found in visual area V1, form in the auditory cortex (Roe et al. 1990, 1992). Some single cells in the auditory cortex develop orientation and direction selectivity normally found in cells in visual cortex. Groups of cells in the auditory cortex form orientation modules and acquire some visual field properties (Roe et al. 1990, 1992; Pallas & Sur 1993; Sur et al. 1999; Sharma et al. 2000).) As a result, neural deference is compatible with the supervenience of qualities of experience on neural properties – just as the existence of explanatory gaps is! Nevertheless, correlation is not explanation, and the distinction between deference and dominance cries out for explanation.

The general puzzle raised by the distinction between neural dominance and neural deference is: Why does experience defer to nonstandard inputs in some cases of rerouting but not others? Deference may be mediated by induced changes in neural properties in a given area of the brain, but this does not explain why rerouting induces deference in some cases but not others. If we can explain the difference between dominance and deference, we'll have gone some way to address the comparative explanatory gaps and to understanding why activity in a given neural area is expressed in this type of experience rather than that.

Comparing the color-related illustrations of dominance and deference underscores the general puzzle: Why does experience defer to nonstandard inputs in some cases of rerouting but not others? What account could explain both why we find dominance in synesthesia but deference in Kohler's adapted goggle-wearer? When input is rerouted in the ACE subject from the word "white" to a neural target area whose normal qualitative expression is experience of yellow, that illusory qualitative expression – experience of yellow – persists and does not adapt away, despite the presence of interference effects with color naming (see Gray 2003 on why a functionalist should thus expect ACE to adapt away). But when input is rerouted from a white object through the yellow lenses to a neural target area whose normal qualitative expression is experience of yellow, qualitative expression adapts to reflect the objective whiteness of the object perceived: the white object looks white to the adapted subject, not yellow. Why does the illusory ACE experience not adapt, while the illusory goggle-induced color experience does adapt?

Explaining Dominance vs. Deference

Consider first what does not explain qualities of experience. As cases of deference underscore, qualities of experience are not explained simply by the occurrence of correlated neural activity in certain areas of the brain – though this point holds independently, given the widely remarked qualitative inscrutability of "neural correlates of consciousness."

Correlation is not explanation. For example, suppose we found that experience of white correlates with the firing of certain "constancy cells," both before and after Kohler adaptation. Nevertheless, these fire in the presence of different wavelength ratios before and after adaptation input from a population of "wavelength cells." Taking the wavelength and constancy cell activations together, we still have deference rather than dominance. What drives such deference still needs explanation; it is not explained simply by correlation, for example, of experience of white with the firing of certain cells.

Nor are qualities of experience explained simply in terms of peripheral input source. In some cases of deference, such as the Braille reading example, the rerouting of inputs that yields deference is internal; in other cases, such as adaptation to goggles, the rerouting of inputs is external. Deference induced by external rerouting involves no rerouting from peripheral inputs to neural target areas, so cannot be explained in terms of changed sources of peripheral inputs. For example, the neural paths available to inputs from yellow light that enters the eye from the yellow lenses of the goggles are the same as the neural paths available to inputs from yellow light that enters the eye from yellow objects. Nor would it be plausible to suggest that an external rerouting itself can explain deference.

Hurley and Noë (2003) put forward a dynamic sensorimotor hypothesis as a general account of the difference between dominance and deference. On this view, what rerouting does do, whether it is internal or external, is to change the characteristic dynamic sensorimotor patterns in which given neural areas participate as the agent interacts with her environment. Rerouting effects a remapping from sources of input, whether peripheral or external, to neural target areas; it also induces higher-order changes, in the relations between mappings from various different sources of input to different neural areas and from those areas back out to effects on those sources of input, which are in turn fed back to various neural areas. The hypothesis is that the difference between dominance and deference is a resulting difference in dynamic sensorimotor integration.

According to the dynamic sensorimotor view, different modalities, such as vision or audition or touch, are governed by different characteristic global patterns of dynamic interdependence between sensory stimulation and active movement (Hurley 1998a, especially ch. 9; O'Regan & Noë 2001a, 2001b, 2001c; Noë & O'Regan 2002; Hurley & Noë 2003). Dynamic structures characteristic of specific modalities or qualities underly surface sensorimotor patterns. For example, to see something is to interact with it in a way governed by the underlying sensorimotor dynamic characteristic of vision, while to hear something is to interact with it in a different way, governed by the different underlying sensorimotor dynamic characteristic of audition (for details of distinctive sensorimotor patterns charcteristic of different modalities see O'Regan & Noë 2001a, 2001c). Your visual impressions are affected by eye movements and blinks in specific, lawlike ways, while eye movements and blinks are irrelevant to the character of your auditory impressions. Again, as you approach an object, visual field flow expands, while as you withdraw, visual field flow contracts. By contrast, as you approach the source of a sound slowly, the amplitude of the auditory stimulus increases, while as you withdraw the amplitude decreases; there are also Doppler effects. Specific qualities within a modality are likewise governed by more specific underlying patterns of dynamic sensorimotor contingency. Different colors have characteristically different sensorimotor profiles (see Noë 2004, ch. 4, and work in progress by Philipona et al.).

Perceivers are familiar with these distinctively different underlying dynamic sensorimotor patterns. Note that these are complex dynamic patterns, environmentally embedded as well as embodied; they are not captured by simple motions such as pointing or grasping (cf. Jacob & Jeannerod 2003, p. 172; see discussion in Hurley & Noë 2006 on the relations between dynamic sensorimotor views and the two visual system theories). Such characteristic patterns govern and are exploited by agents' skillful perceptual activities in their environments, their perceptual know-how. Action enables perception as much as vice versa; neither is more naturally regarded as an effect of the other. Moreover, the relevant dynamic sensorimotor patterns are neither strictly internal to the brain nor strictly external and behavioral; they pass back and forth promiscuously between brain, behavior, and environment as the agent interacts in time with his environment. They may remain internal to the brain, or extend to the bodily periphery or into the environment; dynamic interactionist externalism admits all of these possibilities. No particular boundary should be assumed a priori to contain the sensorimotor dynamics that explain experience.

The dynamic sensorimotor account explains both deference and dominance in terms of characteristic dynamic sensorimotor patterns that can be distributed across brain, body, and environment. The neural aspects of such characteristic patterns can be implemented in variable brain areas. Such neural variability is illustrated across normal development, as a child's brain passes from early exuberant synaptogenesis (at about 6 months, the primary visual cortex is producing about 100,000 new synapses a second!) through a period of pruning extending over many years that results in greater localization of function, all while the child enjoys experiences and interactions of familiar kinds (Huttenlocher 2002, pp. 41, 47; Hurley, forthcoming). Neural variability is also illustrated in cases of neural plasticity and adaptation. When rerouting of inputs is imposed on an active agent, the dynamic sensorimotor patterns in which given neural areas participate can alter. Patterns characteristic of a modality or of a specific quality within a modality can be newly established, or relocated to new neural pathways; a given area of cortex may find itself newly integrated into a certain dynamic sensorimotor pattern. Changes in the neural paths of such characteristic sensorimotor patterns after rerouting can disrupt agents' perceptual know-how and with it the qualitative character of experience, but with practice such know-how can be reacquired. Deference reflects agents' know-how in relation to underlying sensorimotor dynamics that are characteristic of specific modalities or qualities, but which use nonstandard neural paths that include areas of cortex that would normally participate in different sensorimotor patterns. For example, practice by the congenitally blind with tactile visual substitution systems enables what would normally be the visual cortex to participate in a dynamic sensorimotor pattern with characteristically tactile aspects, so that new skills and experiences become available to the subject (Kupers & Ptito 2004).

Hurley and Noë (2003) propose that the difference between dominance and deference can be explained in terms of such skill-governing sensorimotor dynamics. This account predicts deference where two general conditions are met:

1 *Relocated implementation of underlying sensorimotor dynamic*: Perceptual experiences of the A kind and the B kind normally arise out of distinct underlying patterns of sensorimotor dynamics; without rerouting, neural area 1 participates in the A-pattern, and area 2 in the B-pattern. Rerouting relocates the A-pattern so that area 2 participates in it, although no critical information or structure has been lost (see J. J. Gibson's account of Kohler adaptation, in the introduction to Kohler 1964). In effect, the underlying A-pattern is preserved, though aspects of its neural implementation are systematically transformed by the rerouting. The critical dynamic sensorimotor pattern can be neurally implemented in different ways.

2   *Practical knowledge*: active acquisition of skill relying on reimplementation. The agent is able actively to explore and reacquire practical skills, relying on the new implementation of the characteristic A-pattern that now involves neural area 2.

These are not two entirely separate conditions, but in effect two ways of describing dynamic sensorimotor integration of the rerouted input, first at a subpersonal level and then at a personal level. Neural plasticity can be viewed, on this account, as reflecting the capacity of neural activity to acquire functions flexibly, to some degree. Evolution plus normal developmental interactions tend to generate certain standard or default sensorimotor dynamics for neural activity in a given area, but these can change when rerouting and subsequent practice reintegrate neural activity in that area into a new sensorimotor dynamic with a different function. Dynamic sensorimotor reintegration of rerouted input predicts deference.

Accommodating dominance is especially important for interactionist forms of externalism that explain qualities of experience in terms that include patterns of embodied interaction with environments. Dominance is associated with illusions. It is tempting to think that such interactionist externalism cannot explain illusions; but this challenge can be disarmed. It is generated by a false assumption: that the relevant patterns of interaction must in all cases be located on one or the other side of some boundary between world and behavior, on the one hand, and neural processes on the other. But such boundary assumptions, on this view, are symptoms of an insufficiently dynamic and active conception of what experience is and how it can be explained.

In particular, the dynamic sensorimotor approach predicts dominance when the subpersonal reimplementation condition above is not met because rerouted input from A does not result in the relocation of dynamic sensorimotor pattern A so that area 2 participates in it. Reimplementation could fail despite rerouting, for various reasons:

- *Neural constraints*. Perhaps the neural structures in the new target area are simply not up to the new task, chemically or computationally, so simply do not accommodate the underlying dynamic. When visual inputs are rerouted to auditory cortex in newborn ferrets, changes are induced in auditory cells so that they come to have some properties of visual cells (Roe et al. 1990, 1992; Pallas & Sur 1993; Sur et al. 1999; Sharma et al. 2000). However, such changes may not always be possible; neural plasticity is not unlimited.
- *Already engaged*. Perhaps the new target area is already integrated into a different, competing dynamic sensorimotor pattern, involving different inputs – from area B, say – which is still active and has not itself been relocated or discontinued in some way.

Dominance is also predicted from a personal-level perspective when the practical knowledge condition above is not met, because the agent is relatively passive and so fails to acquire skillful practical familiarity with the relocated pattern A.

- *Passivity*. The agent may not be active in ways that would provide practical familiarity and skill with the reimplemented sensorimotor dynamics, such as intermodal and motor feedback patterns.

When dynamic sensorimotor reintegration of the rerouted input fails in these ways, the rerouted input can be said to dangle. Dangling of rerouted input predicts dominance. Again, failures of these conditions for reintegration and deference are different aspects of a lack of sensorimotor integration: inactivity by the agent may leave a new input dangling, until her activity ties it into a relevant dynamic sensorimotor pattern through co-stimulation and feedback.

This account predicts deference in the Braille and Kohler goggle cases, since the conditions for deference are met in these cases. Concerning the Braille cases: tactile input rerouted to the visual cortex in the early and congenitally blind relocates characteristically tactile dynamic sensorimotor patterns so that the visual cortex participates in them; since the agent is blind, patterns subserving visual experience do not compete. Moreover, the Braille readers are active and have practical familiarity with these nonstandardly implemented but characteristically tactile patterns. Concerning Kohler's goggle-adaptation cases: the higher-order dynamic sensorimotor pattern associated with a specific color constancy is reimplemented neurally without loss of information, in the way Gibson suggests. The pattern doesn't compete with existing patterns in its new implementation, since all specific patterns for color constancy have been reimplemented by the goggles, in complementary ways. Moreover, Kohler's subjects acquire practical familiarity with this reimplementation through activity while wearing the goggles over a long period.

By contrast, dominance is predicted in the phantom referral case, since the active skill condition for integration is not met: the rerouted input from face-stroking to the area of cortex that once signalled touch to arm is now dangling as a result of inactivity. Why? Because the experimenter, not the subject himself, does the face stroking while the subject is blindfolded and passive, so no feedback or co-stimulation is set up. If instead the subject strokes his or her own face (input source A), while also watching in a mirror, our account predicts, correctly, that the stroking would come to be felt as stroking to the face only (the A-feeling); tactile experience would then defer (Ramachandran & Hirstein 1998, p. 1615). Such self-stroking would relocate the face-stroking pattern (the A-pattern) to the disused arm area of the cortex (area 2), and allow the subject to reacquire practical familiarity with it. Moreover, no arm-stroking pattern (B-pattern) would actively compete with the relocated face-stroking pattern (A-pattern) to retain the participation of the disused arm area of the cortex (area 2), since there is no longer an arm to participate with this area in producing such a pattern.

Dominance in Synesthesia

Explaining dominance in synesthesia is a challenge for the dynamic sensorimotor account. As Gray (2003) asks, why doesn't synesthetic color experience adapt away? After all, synesthetes don't expect the same movement-related sensorimotor dependencies to hold for synesthetic colors as for normally perceived colors, and they don't confuse synesthetic and normal colors. Why should two different patterns of interaction continue to be associated with the same color qualities? For example, in the example of ACE above, why should hearing "white" continue to induce any synesthetic color experience at all, let alone an incongruent one?

In fact, it isn't hard for the dynamic sensorimotor approach to explain dominance in ACE synesthesia, owing to the evidence cited above that V4 neural activity in ACE appears to be lateralized differently from that in non-ACE synesthesia. (What explains the difference in lateralization is another issue!) Recall that both ACE synesthesia and normal color perception by ACE synesethetes activate primarily left V4. This means that dominance is predicted by the sensorimotor account on "already engaged" grounds: the nonstandard projection is from heard color words to left V4, which is integrated into dynamic sensorimotor patterns in active use in normal color perception and which have not been relocated or interrupted. The activation produced by the nonstandard projection from heard color words to left V4 thus merely "dangles," producing incongruent synesthetic color experiences and creating some interference effects with color naming in so doing.

Gray (2003; Gray et al. 2002) urges that dysfunctional interference effects with color naming associated with ACE would, on a functionalist view, produce pressure for ACE to adapt away. Perhaps such adaptation has occurred in some cases; if so, it would be hard to detect. But neural constraints may not always permit such a solution. The reimplementation needed to avoid the characteristic incongruence of ACE simply may not be neurally available in certain cases. Such implementational limitations are important to recognize; the dynamic sensorimotor explanation is not committed to the equipotentiality of neural tissue or the lack of specifically neural constraints on experience.

The "already engaged" explanation of dominance doesn't work so well, however, for non-ACE synesthetes, in whom neural activity for synesthetic color experience is lateralized to left V4 while that for normal color perception is lateralized to right V4 (see Figure 50.2; Gray et al. 2006). To the extent colored hearing and normal color perception do not share neural resources the way they do in ACE, the "already engaged" basis for predicting dominance does not apply. Another explanation of dominance is needed here.

This might be found by comparing synesthesia with other examples of dominance, in sensations referred to as "phantom limbs" following amputation (see Ramachandran & Hubbard 2001a, pp. 981–2, comparing synesthesia and phantom limbs). Recall that the area of cortex that is disused by its normal inputs after amputation appears to be colonized by inputs from other sources. However, it can retain its original qualitative expression rather than deferring to the new source of input, such that stroking the face is felt as stroking the phantom limb. This example was explained in terms of failure of the conditions for deference, since the subject was blindfolded and passive as the experimenter stroked his face.

But phantoms also provide examples of neural deference. For example, as predicted, when the subject strokes his own face the referred sensation does adapt away. And not just specific referred sensations but whole phantom limbs have a tendency to adapt away over time. Phantom limbs can be congenital as well as acquired as a result of losing a limb. Almost everyone who loses a limb will acquire a phantom, but only about 17 percent of those born without limbs have phantoms (Gallagher et al. 1998; Ramachandran & Hirstein 1998). However, unlike phantoms acquired by losing a limb, congenital phantoms do not seem to adapt away. Congenital phantoms appear to be cases of dominance.

As indicated, deference for synesthesia analogous to adaptation of phantom limb experience would be hard to detect. Since synesthesia is almost always congenital rather than acquired (rarely, tumors or drugs may induce it transiently), if it adapts away it presumably does so before it is detected. It has been suggested that we are all synesthetes in infancy, but that the projections that produce synesthesia are normally pruned (Maurer 1997). Perhaps synesthesia should be regarded as a congenital color phantom, resulting from the activation of an area of cortex that is not being used for its normal functions, whether because of lateralization of normal color perception (in synesthesia) or lack of a limb to provide normal inputs (in phantom limbs). In neither case does the congenital anomalous experience adapt away. Can dominance in these cases be explained in similar ways?

To answer this question, we must first try to understand why congenital phantoms do not adapt away even though acquired phantoms often do show adaptation. If we can understand this, it may help to explain dominance in synesthesia. What explains the difference between dominance in congenital phantoms and deference in acquired phantoms?

Ramachandran addresses this issue. He compares the adaptation of phantom limb experience induced by his mirror box with the lack of adaptation in congenital phantoms. Ramachandran's patient had an immobilized phantom hand, paralyzed in a painful clenched position for ten years since he had lost his limb (Lord Nelson had a similar phantom pain). Ramachandran used a box in which mirrors had been positioned to create an illusion of the patient's intact clenched hand in the felt clenched position of his phantom hand. The patient was asked to try to unclench both his hands simultaneously. When he opened his intact hand and saw it open in the mirrors, in the felt position of his phantom hand, he felt his phantom hand unclench as well. Moreover, the movement in his phantom relieved the pain in his phantom.

Ramachandran's explanation of the change in experience induced by the mirror box is similar to the explanation of deference in terms of sensorimotor reintegration (Hurley & Noë 2003). He suggests that when the brain sends out motor commands for movement, and copies of these commands, but gets no corresponding feedback of actual arm movement because the arm is missing, it learns that the arm does not move but is paralyzed in a position that would be painful in a real arm. The illusory feedback created by the mirror box allows it temporarily to unlearn paralysis by reference to normal expectations of sensory feedback from arm movement (Ramachandran et al. 1995; Ramachandran & Rogers-Ramachandran 1996, 2000; Ramachandran & Blakeslee 1998, pp. 47ff; Ramachandran & Hirstein 1998). In effect, the illusory visual feedback of phantom movement created by the mirrors instantiates patterns of sensorimotor contingency familiar to the subject from before the loss of the limb. Experience of the phantom changed accordingly, from paralyzed and painful to neither.

However, this explanation faces a puzzle similar to that encountered in comparing color adaption to synesthesia. The question arose: If experience of color adapts to Kohler's goggles, why doesn't synesthetic color experience also adapt? Similarly, we may wonder, if experience of acquired phantoms adapts in the way Ramachandran explains, why does experience of phantom limb movements in congenital phantoms persist? Why doesn't experience of congenital phantoms adapt also?

Ramachandran explains the difference between adaptation in phantoms resulting from amputation (freezing, telescoping, or disappearance of the phantom) and lack of adaptation in congenital phantoms. A normal adult has a lifetime of practical familiarity with the sensorimotor dynamics of arm movement. These are missing after amputation; since neural "expectations" of normal sensorimotor feedback are "disappointed," experience of arm movement adapts to bring it into line with the absence of normal sensorimotor dynamics. As a result of such "learned paralysis," the phantom may freeze, shrink, or even disappear over time. In effect, this is to explain deference as a limiting case of reintegration: a normal pattern of sensorimotor contingencies is not relocated and reimplemented, but missing altogether. Practical familiarity with this absence is acquired and experience comes to reflect it, for example, in the freezing of a phantom.

By contrast, Ramachandran continues, movement in a congenital phantom may persist indefinitely because the congenital absence of a limb to provide co-stimulation and feedback relationships between various modalities and motor activity means that there are no neural "expectations" of normal sensorimotor feedback from such a limb to be "disappointed." So no adaptation is called for. In effect, the phantom corresponds to part of an innate body image or schema that has never been integrated into a normal dynamic sensorimotor pattern – that has always dangled (Ramachandran & Blakeslee 1998, p. 57; Ramachandran & Hirstein 1998, pp. 1624–5; see also and compare Gallagher et al. 1998). Neural dominance here reflects a biological default setting in the somatosensory cortex for limb experience that cannot be overwritten by familiarity with absence of the normal sensorimotor dynamics of arm movement: you cannot adaptively acquire familiarity with the *lack* of something that has never been present to begin with. In effect, the practical knowledge condition for deference is not satisfied.

Can some synesthetic colors be explained in a similar way, in terms of lack of a conflicting reference point for adaptation? The parallel here to Ramachandran's suggestion about congenital phantom limbs would again appeal to a biological default setting in V4, this time for color experience. While the normal sensorimotor dynamics of color perception are absent for synesthetic colors, they would not be "expected," since synesthesia is congenital. Normal and synesthetic colors have always had different sensorimotor dynamics in synesthetes, so no adaptation is called for; this duality is experienced as normal, and there is no conflicting reference point. Synesthetic colors have always dangled and have never been integrated into the sensorimotor dynamics for normal colors, apart from minor interference effects.

This "lack of conflicting reference point" explanation of dominance may be part of the story, but isn't fully satisfactory, for several reasons. First, its appeal to a biological default setting, while certainly not ruled out by the dynamic sensormotor account, has an aspect of brute force. Second, the two cases are somewhat different. A person born without a limb has no familiarity with the normal sensorimotor dynamics of the missing limb as a reference point for adaptation, but a synesthete is familiar with both the sensorimotor dynamics of normal colors and their absence for synesthetic colors. A closer analogy would be to a congenitally color-blind synesthete (cf. the color-anomalous synesthete S. S.; see Ramachandran & Hubbard 2003, p. 53). Third, the duality of sensorimotor profiles for normal and synesthetic colors provides no account of the quality that experience of synesthetic red has in common with normal perception of red by synesthetes.

For these reasons a fresh look at the problem is needed. Perhaps we should reconsider the characterization of what needs to be explained about congenital phantoms and synesthesia as non-adaptation of anomalous congenital experience. That characterization is what leads to the "no conflicting reference point" account suggested by Ramachandran. But perhaps there *is* early adaptation in many cases of congenital phantoms and synesthesia, so that these are not all cases of dominance after all. Perhaps congenital phantoms do normally adapt away and only the rare cases of nonadaptation come to light and make up the 17 percent figure. Similarly, perhaps early synesthesia does indeed adapt away in the vast majority of cases, and only the rare cases of nonadaptation remain to be recognized as cases of synesthesia (Maurer 1997). We have no reason to assume otherwise, since such adaptation would presumably occur early and be virtually invisible. On this view, the problem becomes one of getting evidence about whether early synesthesia often does adapt away before it comes to light.

The dynamic sensorimotor approach thus suggests that adaptation of congenital anomalous experience may be more common than we tend to suppose, and prompts us to devise better ways to detect it. If this prediction is correct, then what will need to be explained is not lack of adaptation in such congenital cases, but why a few residual congenital cases of phantom limbs and color phantoms persist, even though many other such cases adapt away. Some of the residual cases may be handled by the neural constraint, already engaged, or by no-conflicting-reference-point explanations sketched above. Lack of adaptation in known cases of congenital phantom limbs and synesthesia would still need to be explained, but how it can or should be explained will depend critically on how those cases can be contrasted, which we are not yet in a position to say.

Concluding Remarks and Context

Neural plasticity and perceptual adaptation phenomena provide a rich set of materials with which to work in explaining why neural activity in certain areas is associated with *this* quality of experience rather than *that* and thus attempting to bridge the comparative explanatory gaps. These phenomena prompt interactive externalists to return to the brain, although without giving up their externalism. The key to the dynamic sensorimotor strategy in explaining qualities of experience is its rejection of the inner/outer boundary that too often defines the options. Rather, experience should be explained in terms of interactions that cross back and forth between embodied brain and environment with dynamic promiscuity.

See also 30 Functionalism and qualia; 39 Inattentional blindness, change blindness, and consciousness; 44 A neurobiological framework for consciousness.

Note

1 This chapter draws heavily on and elaborates Hurley and Noë (2003), which introduced the distinction between dominance and deference and explained it in dynamic sensorimotor terms. Thanks especially to Alva Noë; this chapter strongly reflects our ongoing collaboration. Thanks also for helpful input to Dominic ffytche, Jeffrey Gray, Ron Kupers, and Erik Myin.

Further Readings

Cohen, L. G., Celnik, P., Pascual-Leone, A., Corwell, B., Faiz, L., Dambrosia, J. et al. (1997a) Functional relevance of cross-modal plasticity in blind humans. *Nature* 389, 180–3.

Gray, J. A. (2003) How are qualia coupled to functions? *Trends in Cognitive Sciences* 7: 5, 192–4.

Gray, J. A., Parslow, D. M., Brammer, M. J., Chopping, S., Vythelingum, G., and ffychte, D. (2006) Evidence against functionalism from neuroimages of the alien colour effect in synaesthesia. *Cortex* 42, 309–18.

Hurley, S. and Noë, A. (2003) Neural plasticity and consciousness. *Biology and Philosophy* 18, 131–68.

Hurley, S. and Noë, A. (2006) Can hunter-gatherers hear colour? In G. Brennan, R. Goodin, F. Jackson, and M. Smith (eds.), *Common Minds: Essays for Philip Pettit*. Oxford: Oxford University Press.

Ramachandran, V. S. and Hirstein, W. (1998), The perception of phantom limbs *Brain* 121: 9, 1603–30.

References

Aglioti, S., Goodale, M. A., and DeSousa, J. F. X. (1995) Size-contrast illusions deceive the eye but not the hand. *Current Biology* 5, 679–85.

Bach-y-Rita, Paul (1972), *Brain Mechanisms in Sensory Substitution*. New York: Academic Press.

Bach-y-Rita, Paul (1984) The relationship between motor processes and cognition in tactile visual substitution. In W. Prinz and A. F. Sanders (eds.), *Cognition and Motor Processes*, 149–60. Berlin: Springer-Verlag.

Bach-y-Rita, Paul (1996) Substitution sensorielle et qualia. In J. Proust (ed.), *Perception et Intermodalité*, ed. J. Proust. Paris: Presses Universitaires de France. Reprinted in English translation in A. Noë and E. Thompson (2002) *Vision and Mind: Selected Readings in the Philosophy of Perception*. Cambridge, MA: MIT Press.

Baron-Cohen, Simon and Harrison, John E. (eds.) (1997) *Synaesthesia: Classic and Contemporary Readings*. Oxford: Blackwell.

Buchel, C. (1998), Functional neuroimaging studies of Braille reading: cross-modal reorganization and its implications. *Brain* 121, 1193–4.

Buchel, C., Price, C., Frackowiak, R. S. J., and Friston, K. (1998) Different activation patterns in the visual cortex of late and congenitally blind subjects. *Brain* 121, 409–19.

Cohen, L. G., Celnik, P., Pascual-Leone, A., Corwell, B., Faiz, L., Dambrosia, J. et al. (1997a) Functional relevance of cross-modal plasticity in blind humans, *Nature* 389, 180–3.

Cohen, L. G., Weeks, R., Celnik, P., and Hallett, M. (1997b) Role of the occipital cortex during Braille reading (cross-modal plasticity) in subjects with blindness acquired late in life. *Society for Neuroscience Abstracts* (92.1).

Cohen, L. G., Weeks, R. A., Sadato, N., Celnik, P., Ishii, K., and Hallett, M. (1999), Period of susceptibility of cross-modal plasticity in the blind. *Annals of Neurology* 45: 4, 451–60.

Cytowic, Richard E. (1997) Synaesthesia: phenomenology and neuropsychology. In S. Baron-Cohen and J. Harrison (eds.), *Synaesthesia: Classic and Contemporary Readings*, 17–39. Oxford: Blackwell.

Frith, Christopher D. and Paulesu, Eraldo (1997) The physiological basis of synaesthesia. In S. Baron-Cohen and J. Harrison (eds.), *Synaesthesia: Classic and Contemporary Readings*, 123–47. Oxford: Blackwell.

Gallagher, S., Butterworth, G. E., Lew, A., and Cole, J. (1998) Hand–mouth coordination, congenital absence of limb, and evidence for innate body-schemas. *Brain and Cognition* 38, 53–65.

Gray, J. A. (2003) How are qualia coupled to functions? *Trends in Cognitive Sciences* 7: 5, 192–4.

Gray, J. A. and McNaughton, N. (2000). *The Neuropsychology of Anxiety: An Enquiry into the Functions of the Septo-hippocampal System* (2nd edn.). Oxford: Oxford University Press.

Gray, J. A., Chopping, S., Nunn, J., Parslow, D., Gregory, L., Williams, S. et al. (2002) Implications of synaesthesia for functionalism: theory and experiments. *Journal of Consciousness Studies* 9: 12, 5–31.

Gray, J. A., Parslow, D. M., Brammer, M. J., Chopping, S., Vythelingum, G., and ffytche, D. (2006) Evidence against functionalism from neuroimages of the alien colour effect in synaesthesia. *Cortex* 42, 309–18.

Grossenbacher, Peter G. (1997), Perception and sensory information in synaesthetic experience. In S. Baron-Cohen and J. Harrison (eds.), *Synaesthesia: Classic and Contemporary Readings*, 148–72. Oxford: Blackwell.

Hadjikhani, M., Liu, A. K., Dale, A., Cavanagh, P., and Tootell, R. B. H. (1998) Retinotopy and color sensitivity in human visual cortical area V8. *Nature Neuroscience* 1, 235–41.

Harrington, T. (1965) Adaptation of humans to colored split-field glasses. *Psychonomic Science* 3, 71–2.

Harrison, John E. and Baron-Cohen, Simon (1997a) Synaesthesia: an introduction. In S. Baron-Cohen and J. Harrison (eds.), *Synaesthesia: Classic and Contemporary Readings*, 3–16. Oxford: Blackwell.

Harrison, John E. and Baron-Cohen, Simon (1997b) Synaesthesia: a review of psychological theories. In S. Baron-Cohen and J. Harrison (eds.), *Synaesthesia: Classic and Contemporary Readings*, 109–22. Oxford: Blackwell.

Hurley, S. L. (1998) *Consciousness in Action*. Cambridge, MA: Harvard University Press.

Hurley, S. (forthcoming) Varieties of externalism. In R. Menary (ed.), *The Extended Mind*. Aldershot: Ashgate.

Hurley, S. and Noë, A. (2003) Neural plasticity and consciousness. *Biology and Philosophy* 18, 131–68.

Hurley, S. and Noë, A. (2006) Can hunter-gatherers hear colour? In G. Brennan, R. Goodin, F. Jackson, and M. Smith (eds.), *Common Minds: Essays for Philip Pettit*. Oxford: Oxford University Press.

Huttenlocher, P. (2002) *Neural Plasticity*. Cambridge, MA: Harvard University Press.

Jacob, P. and Jeannerod, M. (2003) *Ways of Seeing*. Oxford: Oxford University Press.

Kohler, I. (1951) Über Aufbau und Wandlungen der Wahrnehmungswelt. *Österreichische Akademie der Wissenschaften. Sitzungsberichte, philosophish-historische Klasse* 227, 1–118.

Kohler, I. (1964) *The Formation and Transformation of the Perceptual World*. Published as a monograph in *Psychological Issues* vol. 3 (monograph 12). New York International University Press. [This is a translation of Kohler 1951.]

Kujala, T., Alho, K., and Naatenen, R. (2000) Cross-modal reorganization of human cortical functions. *Trends in Neuroscience* 23: 3, 115–20.

Kupers, Ron and Ptito, Maurice (2004) "Seeing" through the tongue: cross-modal plasticity in the congenitally blind. *International Congress Series* (*Frontiers in Human Brain Topology*. Proceedings of ISBET 2004, the 15th World Congress of the International Society of Brain Electromagnetic Topography) 1270, 79–84.

Maurer, Daphne (1997) Neonatal synaesthesia: implications for the processing of speech and faces. In S. Baron-Cohen and J. Harrison (eds.), *Synaesthesia: Classic and Contemporary Readings*, 224–42. Oxford: Blackwell.

Merzenich, Michael (2000) Seeing in the sound zone. *Nature* 404, 820–1.

Noë, A. (2004) *Action in Perception*. Cambridge, MA: MIT Press.

Noë, A. and O'Regan, K. (2002) On the brain-basis of visual consciousness: a sensorimotor account. In A. Noë and E. Thompson (eds.), *Vision and Mind: Selected Readings in the Philosophy of Perception*, 567–598. Cambridge, MA: MIT Press.

Nunn, J. A., Gregory, L. J., Brammer, M., Williams, S. C. R., Parslow, D. M., Morgan, M. J. et al. (2002) Functional magnetic resonance imaging of synesthesia: activation of color vision area V4/V8 by spoken words. *Nature Neuroscience* 5: 4, 371–4.

O'Regan, K. and Noë, A. (2001a) A sensorimotor account of vision and visual consciousness. *Behavioral and Brain Sciences* 24: 5, 883–917.

O'Regan, K. and Noë, A. (2001b) Acting out our sensory experience. *Behavioral and Brain Sciences* 24: 5, 955–75.

O'Regan, K. and Noë, A. (2001c) What it's like to see: a sensorimotor theory of perceptual experience. *Synthese* 129, 1: 79–103.

Pallas, S. L. (2001) Intrinsic and extrinsic factors that shape neocorticial specification. *Trends in Neuroscience* 24: 7, 411–23.

Pallas, S. L. and Sur, M. (1993) Visual projections induced into the auditory pathway of ferrets: II. Corticocortical connections of primary auditory cortex. *Journal of Comparative Neurology* 337: 2, 317–33.

Peppman, P. and Wieland, B. (1966) Visual distortion with two-colored spectacles. *Perceptual and Motor Skills* 23, 1043–8.

Philipona, D., O'Regan, J. K., and Coenen, O. (work in progress) On the intrinsic sensorimotor structure of colors. Abstract at http://webhost/ua.ac.be/assc8/089Phil.html.

Ramachandran, V. S. and Blakeslee, Sandra (1998) *Phantoms in the Brain*. London: Fourth Estate.

Ramachandran, V. S. and Hirstein, W. (1998) The perception of phantom limbs. *Brain* 121: 9, 1603–30.

Ramachandran, V. S. and Hubbard, E. M. (2001a) Psychophysical investigations into the neural basis of synaesthesia. *Proceedings of the Royal Academy of London* 268, 979–83.

Ramachandran, V. S. and Hubbard, E. M. (2001b) Synaesthesia – a window into perception, thought and language. *Journal of Consciousness Studies* 8: 12, 3–34.

Ramachandran, V. S. and Hubbard, E. M. (2003) The phenomenology of synaesthesia. *Journal of Consciousness Studies* 10: 8, 49–57.

Ramachandran, V. S. and Rogers-Ramachandran, D. (1996) Synaesthesia in phantom limbs induced with mirrors. *Proceedings of the Royal Society* 263, 377–86.

Ramachandran, V. S. and Rogers-Ramachandran, D. (2000) Phantom limbs and neural plasticity. *Archives of Neurology* 57, 317–20.

Ramachandran, V. S., Rogers-Ramachandran, D., and Cobb, S. (1995) Touching the phantom limb. *Nature* 377, 490–1.

Roe, A. W., Pallas, S. L., Hahm, J., and Sur, M. (1990) A map of visual space induced in primary auditory cortex. *Science* 250: 4982, 818–20.

Roe, A. W., Pallas, S. L., Kwon, Y. H., and Sur., M. (1992) Visual projections routed to the auditory pathway in ferrets. *Journal of Neuroscience* 12: 9, 3651–64.

Sadato, N., Pascual-Leone, A., Grafman, J., Ibanez, V., Deiber, M. P., Dold, G., and Hallett, M. (1996) Activation of the primary visual cortex by Braille reading in blind subjects. *Nature* 380: 6574, 526–8.

Sadato, N., Pascual-Leone, A., Grafman, J., Deiber, M. P., Ibanez, V., and Hallett, M. (1998) Neural networks for Braille reading by the blind. *Brain* 121: 7, 1213–29.

Sharma, J., Angelucci, A., and Sur, M. (2000) Induction of visual orientation modules in auditory cortex. *Nature* 404: 6780, 841–7.

Sur, M., Angelucci, A., and Sharma, J. (1999) Rewiring cortex: the role of patterned activity in development and plasticity of neocortical circuits. *Journal of Neurobiology* 41: 1, 33–43.

Thompson, E. (1995) *Colour Vision*. London: Routledge.

Tootell, R. B. H. and Hadjikhani, N. (1998) Has a new color area been discovered? Reply to Zeki. *Nature Neuroscience* 1: 5, 335–6.

von Melcher, L., Pallas, S. L., and Sur, M. (2000) Visual behaviour mediated by retinal projections directed to the auditory pathway. *Nature* 404: 6780, 871–6.

Zeki, S., McKeefry, D. J., Bartels, A., and Frackowiak, R. S. J. (1998) Has a new color area been discovered? *Nature Neuroscience* 1, 5: 335–6.

51

Benjamin Libet's Work on the Neuroscience of Free Will

WILLIAM P. BANKS AND SUSAN POCKETT

Introduction

Approximately 40 years ago, Kornhuber and Deecke (1965) back-averaged EEG epochs from a series of movements made by their experimental subjects and found that voluntary movements are always preceded by a large, slow, event-related potential, which they named in German the *Bereitschaftspotential*. The English translation, now used interchangeably with the original term, is readiness potential (RP). Two decades later, Benjamin Libet (Libet et al. 1983) asked another set of participants to report exactly when they decided to initiate a particular voluntary movement, and then correlated this reported time of deciding to move (time W) with the objectively observed time of onset of the readiness potential in the same subjects. Libet's now-famous finding was that the RP began at least 350 ms before time W (see Figure 51.1). This single experimental result immediately ignited a heated debate, which has lasted another two decades so far and shows every sign of heating up still further.

The issue is this. Libet's clear-cut finding was that his subjects consciously and freely "decided" to initiate an action only after the neurological preparation to act was well under way. This implies that the conscious decision was not the cause of the action. As a conclusion this may seem to be relatively innocuous, but it is not. If conscious decisions are not the cause of actions, it follows that we do not have conscious free will. Even worse, because the ability consciously to initiate actions is an essential property of self, the denial of conscious, personal origination of action is a challenge to our sense of selfhood. The implication is that we, our conscious selves, are not free actors with control over our choices in life. We are only conduits for unconsciously made decisions. Libet's one simple experiment has slipped our entire self-concept from its moorings.

On the basis of the evidence, the conclusions outlined above seem compelling, but they are so counter-intuitive that Libet himself refused to draw them. His conclusion was that although consciousness clearly could not have *initiated* the movement his subjects made, it was still capable of stepping in and *vetoing* it before it was performed (Libet 1985; Libet 1999). Free will is thus rescued, though consigned to a seriously restricted role in vetoing action. We discuss this possibility at greater length later.

However, despite Libet's attempt to salvage free will in the veto response, the more radical conclusion that free will is simply illusory has refused to go away. Indeed, with the

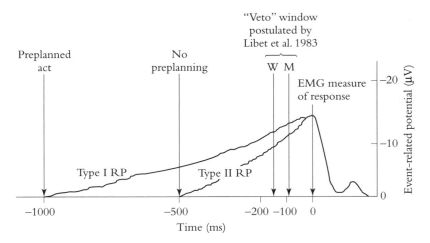

Figure 51.1 Schematic diagram of a readiness potential (RP) showing decision time (W) and reported time of movement (M) relative to the time of the EMG for movement at 0 ms.

Two kinds of readiness potential are shown (Libet et al. 1983). The Type II potential is obtained when participants reported no pre-planning of the movement. The Type I RP is recorded when participants said they planned the movement. W and M in both cases lead the response by about the same interval. The diagram shows the RP using the standard EEG convention of –ve up, and as recorded from C_z, which is the electrode placed on the vertex. The RP in some studies begins well before –1000 ms, and the shape can vary with electrode placement and experimental conditions.

publication of a series of results from experiments of a different sort (Wegner & Wheatley 1999; Wegner 2002) it has actually gained ground. The idea that perceived freedom of action is an illusion fits into a long tradition of philosophic and psychological thinking (Freud 1954; Festinger 1957; Skinner 1971; Ross & Nisbett 1991; Gazzaniga 1997, 1998; Velmans 2000; Ferguson & Bargh 2004). Libet's findings are the first direct neurophysiological evidence in support of this thesis. It is no surprise that his work has been the subject of a great deal of interest and further research.

Much of this research has examined the possibility that Libet's results are flawed in some way. If the results are invalid, the conclusions about volition may not be necessary. Three sources that encapsulate this research and analysis are the Open Peer Commentary to Libet in *Behavioral and Brain Sciences* (1985), a special issue of *The Journal of Consciousness Studies* (1999) on the volitional brain, and most recently a special issue of the journal *Consciousness and Cognition* (2002). Below we consider the major questions about the paradigm.

Controversial Issues about Libet's Experiments

The questions about Libet's findings can be put into three categories: (A) does the basic finding hold up from a technical point of view – are there any methodological problems? (B) Can the movements studied legitimately be considered as examples of free will? and (C) what exactly are the subjects reporting on when they say they decided at a particular instant to make the movement?

A Does Libet's finding that RPs begin before consciousness of the decision to make the movement stand up methodologically?

Several sub-questions inhere in this question:

1   Has the work been repeated in independent laboratories?
2   How variable are the numbers? Could the effect be attributed to noise?
3   Are there any random or systematic errors built in to the methods of determining either
    (a) the time at which the readiness potential starts, or
    (b) the time at which subjects become conscious of deciding to act?
    If so, could these have affected the overall result?

The answers, insofar as we can determine them, are as follows.

1   The work has been repeated in three independent laboratories so far. Keller and Heck-hausen (1990), Haggard and Eimer (1999), and Trevena and Miller (2002) have all (among other things) repeated the basic experiment. They all obtained roughly the same result.
2   The numbers are very variable. The original, scrupulously reported results in Table 1 of Libet et al. (1983) show a variation in time of initiation of the RP from −25 ms to −1200 ms in relation to movement onset, depending on whether or not the subject admitted to having preplanned some of the movements in that particular block of 40 trials. (Blocks of 40 trials were the smallest unit of analysis because averaging over trials is needed to get a reasonable signal to noise ratio.) Preplanning was seen to correlate with earlier RP initiation, as illustrated in Figure 51.1.

    The difference between RP onset and decision time ranged from 35 ms to 1052 ms. Thus, while the RP did start *on average* about 350 ms before the reported decision to move, the variability was such that in three out of the five subjects studied, some of the reported decision times were earlier than the RP onset, and a few reported decision times were actually later than the movement. These reports were presumably from the same people who reported sometimes being surprised to find that they performed actions before they decided to move (Libet et al. 1982).

    Given this variability, the natural question is whether the observed delay of W after the beginning of the RP can be attributed to chance. Libet et al. (1983) report standard errors that are small relative to the effect. That and the fact that all five participants showed the effect, plus the replications by subsequent investigators, puts the likelihood that it was all by chance at a vanishingly low level.

3a There is one source of random and one source of systematic error built in to the method of determining RP onset time.

    The source of random error is simply the difficulty of telling when the RP begins (Trevena & Miller 2002, p. 167). This particular event-related potential starts quite gradually, and even after averaging the ongoing EEG is quite noisy, so it is hard to determine precisely where to put the onset of the RP. However, even under the most conservative estimate, it is clear that in the available plots the RP begins well before W. In addition, Trevena and Miller (2002, p. 175) estimated the beginning of their RPs statistically and found that the earliest significant negative potential was actually about 300 ms earlier than it is by less rigorous estimates.

The source of systematic error, also pointed out by Trevena and Miller (2002), is that the latency of evoked potentials depends on whether latencies are measured from individual trials and then averaged, or whether the latency is measured from the averaged wave-form (Callaway et al. 1984). In the latter case, the measured latency is close to the latency for those trials with the earliest onset. Libet et al. (1983) used the latter method, so Trevena and Miller suggest that the time between the RPs and W may have been much shorter than Libet et al. found. Unfortunately, it is not possible to test directly how significant this effect might be in Libet's experiments, because RPs cannot be visualized in single trials. Trevena and Miller conclude that the effect would not be large enough to negate Libet's main finding.

3b There are several errors built in to the method of determining decision time. We will address first the random and then the potentially more significant systematic sources of error.

Random variability is, as we noted, fairly high. One source of variability is the resolution of the measurement of decision time. To measure W subjects were asked to watch a spot of light revolving in a circle at 2.56 seconds per revolution and remember where the spot was at the instant they decided to make the movement. Libet et al. (1983) used two different modes for subjects to recall clock positions of the moving spot at instant of decision – either they reported the "clock-time" of the spot in seconds (each "clock-second" corresponding to an actual time of 42.7 ms), or they reported whether the clock position at the time of decision was before or after a position on the clock face that varied pseudorandomly for each trial. These two modes of response gave essentially the same results. Assuming that the subjects reported their decision time in terms of discrete "clock-seconds," it can be seen that for the first mode of reporting, the resolution of the method *for each trial* is about + 21.5 ms. In the second mode of responding, because the clock had discrete stopping places every 15 ms, this error is + 7.5 ms. However, what we are interested in is not the error associated with each individual trial, but the error associated with the mean of a large number of estimates of time W by each subject. The effect of the measurement error on the standard error of the overall mean declines as the number of trials increases. With 40 trials in each block, the effect of these already small errors would be negligible.

In addition to random variability, there could be systematic errors of perception or estimation of the location of the moving spot of light. Unlike random errors, which would average to zero over many trials, systematic sources of error could lead to an artifactual over- or under-estimation of the time between the onset of the RP and the decision to act. Possible sources of systematic error include the following.

i   Klein (2002a) and van de Grind (2002) suggest the flash-lag effect as a possible systematic source of error. The flash-lag effect (Nijhawan 1994) causes misperception of the position of moving spots of light with respect to stationary flashed spots of light. The effect originally found was consistent with a forward extrapolation of the moving object, but variations in relative brightness can cause moving lights to lag flashed lights as well as lead them as if their motion was extrapolated (Purushothaman et al. 1998; Krekelberg & Lappe 2000). Pockett (2002b) provides a brief review of work on this phenomenon, as does van de Grind (2002). Given the intrinsic difference between comparing two lights and comparing a reported decision and a moving spot of light, it is difficult to determine whether the flash-lag effect might bias Libet's effect, and if it does, in which direction the error would be. However if the flash-lag effect is a factor, the largest flash-lag effects in the literature indicate that the bias would be no more than 100 ms either way (see Trevena & Miller 2002).

ii Another class of systematic errors would result from a sensory delay in perception of the spot of light. The clock-position method of determining decision time assumes that there is effectively no time lag involved in the perception by the subject of the revolving spot of light. But this is likely not to be the case. It does, after all, take about 100 ms for a visual event to cause an evoked potential in the cortex. Since the spot moves about two clock intervals in this time, when it was actually at, say, 6 o'clock at the instant of decision, the representation of the 4 o'clock position of the spot would only just have formed in the participant's cortex. The participant would thus report the spot as being at about 4 o'clock, closer in time by 100 ms to the beginning of the RP than it really was.

This issue was brought up by several contributors to the original Open Peer Commentary in the *Behavioral and Brain Sciences* article (Libet 1985). Libet's reply was that his own previous work showed that it takes not just a few ms but a full 500 ms (half a second) for a stimulus to enter consciousness; but then a process he calls "subjective back-referral" cancels out this lag. This response ignores that fact that the previous work referred to is very much more controversial than the work under discussion here and that the existence of subjective backward referral is a matter of serious dispute (e.g., Churchland 1981a, 1981b; Glynn 1990; Gomes 1998, 2002; Pockett 2002a, 2002b).

However, the main point with regard to this potential source of error is probably that correcting it would serve to make the difference between RP onset and decision time *greater*, not smaller. This can easily be seen by looking at Figure 51.1 and mentally shifting time W 100 ms to the right. This potentially serious source of error would not operate to generate Libet's main result – rather the reverse.

iii Libet showed that his participants misreport not only the times of their own movements (see time M in Figure 51.1) but also, to a lesser extent, the times of external experimenter-delivered stimuli. He incorporated a correction for this latter bias into his estimates of the time difference between RP onset and decision time, showing that the biases (which varied from day to day) do not change the main finding. The assumptions in this correction could be questioned, but the effect holds up with or without them.

iv Joordens, van Duijn, and Spalek (2002) show that when subjects are asked to use the clock method to report the time they perceived the clock face to change color, they remember the color change as occurring 70 ms later than it actually did. The authors speculate that this effect could be due to either a memory bias or a decision bias. The important point for this discussion is that *if* subjective perception of an externally generated event like a color change can legitimately be compared with perception of an internally generated event like a decision to move (which is not clear), this finding suggests that Libet's subjects may have reported their decision times as being later than they actually were. This kind of error *would* work to generate Libet's main finding, but it is clearly not sufficient for full explanation of it.

v Libet et al. (1983) observed that when there are two simultaneous events to report (clock position and decision), one could have systematic reporting priority over the other and thus be artifactually reported at a time shifted from the mean. The law of prior entry (Titchener 1908) is often cited in these cases. Simply put, an attended object comes to awareness more quickly than unattended objects. The truth of the prior entry effect is not universally accepted (Spence, Shore, & Klein 2001). Even if it were, it is not known whether the spot of light or the decision "entered" first. More solidly established than prior entry (and a larger effect) is the widely researched finding that processing is speeded for attended or expected locations (Eriksen & Collins 1969; Posner, Snyder, & Davidson 1980; Eriksen & Yeh 1985: but see Johnson & Haggard 2003). How attentional facilitation might influence the basic effect is unknown because we do not know whether the decision or the spot of light is the focus of attention.

vi Haggard and colleagues (see for example Haggard & Clark 2003) have investigated what they call the intentional binding effect. The time of intended actions (Libet's M) is perceived as closer to their effects than they are in actuality, and unintended actions are perceived as more separated from the effects than they are. If the same distortion applies to W, the bias would move W closer to the response and thus increase the measured time after the beginning of the RP and make the lag of W after RP onset seem larger than it is. The size of the binding effect is, however, much too small to account for the effect. Because there is no W in the production of unintended actions, there is no way to determine if W shifts as M does.

In summary, there are several possible systematic errors inherent in the method of measuring decision time, but some of these act to reduce the Libet effect rather than to generate it, and others have an unknown or indeterminate direction. The rest would need to add their maximum biases all in the same direction to generate the 350 ms effect – and if Trevena and Miller's statistical estimate is correct, the measured effect should be approximately 650 ms rather than 350 ms. On average, we conclude that readiness potentials do start before the subject consciously "decides" to move.

B Are the movements studied legitimate examples of "free will"?

The act being studied in this research is a simple finger movement. It has no consequences and carries no credit or blame or risk, unlike many of the decisions we make in our daily lives. It seems to be about as free an action as one could make. However, it is also about the most trivial action one could perform. Can it stand as a representative of willed action?

One approach would be to view Libet's apparatus as being like Galileo's inclined planes or Foucault's pendulum and other set-ups that abstract a feature from nature to study (see Libet 1999, pp. 53–4; Eccles & Zeier 1980, cited in Deecke & Kornhuber 2003). Under this view, Libet's procedure is a useful analytical tool to use in the study of the neuroscience of decision.

A differing opinion would be that the action being studied is an extreme of volition so trifling that it has properties unlike most members of the vast category of willed decisions. Only at this extreme does the RP come before the conscious decision. This is a position that could be tested empirically, and indeed there are apparently some differences in brain activity between consequential and inconsequential decisions (Greene et al. 2001; Heekeren et al. 2003). One study has addressed the question of whether the requirement to choose which of two movements to perform makes a difference in Libet-style experiments. Haggard and Eimer (1999) found that neither time W nor time M was affected when the subject was required to choose between moving their right or their left hand. However, the question of what relation a more complex or personally involving decision has to the RP does not seem to have been studied, as Libet (2003) notes.

In sum, the question of whether the decision in Libet's paradigm is representative of freely willed acts in general is still open. This is an issue that is experimentally approachable.

C What are the subjects reporting when they say they decided to move and how does this relate to neural events?

The original decision to make a series of movements for the purpose of this experiment was made before the experimental session began. All decisions about *what* movements to make and *how* to make them were determined before any measurements were made. The only decisions that were under study in these experiments were decisions about *when* to make each particular movement, Timing of volition is the thus the only aspect open to study in Libet et al. (1983). Haggard and Eimer (1999) and Trevena and Miller (2002) had their participants choose which hand to use as well as when to respond, with little change in the basic effect.

Because the decision is an unobservable event whose meaning is defined by the participant, the instructions given to the participants by the experimenter are important. In Libet et al. (1983) participants were asked to wait until the timing spot had revolved once and then to "let the urge to act appear on its own at any time without any preplanning or concentration on when to act" and report the earliest appearance of a conscious "wanting" or "urge" to make particular movements. This suggests that W is more a passive registration of the onset of a feeling than an act of will (Marks (1985) makes the same point in terms of signal detection theory; see also van de Grind 2002, pp. 258–60). If so, one could argue that this experiment is a measure of the participant's self-defined criterion about where in the RP to report an "urge," not a measure of the timing of volition. If some manipulations of criteria greatly influence the effect, we would need to reconsider the whole matter.

Dennett (2003) suggested an "ink drying" metaphor to explain the delay of W after the onset of the RP. A contract could be signed at time t_1, but it cannot be passed on to the attorneys until the ink is dried. That would take place later, at time t_2. Likewise, the decision to act could be made at time t_1 (possibly at the beginning of the RP, or before) and only a bit later, at time t_2, would the neural record of the act be consolidated and sent to a conscious recognition center. While this metaphor gives room for wide latitude in the beginning of the action, the real act of decision is unconscious, by definition, and the problem of conscious volition remains.

An entirely different possibility is that the metaphor by which a mental event is counted as having a beginning and end and an identifiable time of occurrence is just wrong (see Merikle & Cheeseman 1985; Durgin & Sternberg 2002). The assumption that brain events have a time-course that exactly mirrors our experience is excessively strong, especially since most of our brain's activity is unconscious. The metaphor of a mental event as a "thing" with a definite beginning and end is directly imported from folk psychology (see Churchland 1981) and must be considered at best as prescientific. The meaning of the report that we thought *this* or decided *that* at a specific moment is not as clear as it appears to our folk-theoretic-informed intuitions (see Clark 1999). In this critical light it is difficult to see what the temporal judgments mean. Research or, better, a scientific account of the relations between brain and action is needed. This is a tall order.

Dennett (1991, 2003; Dennett & Kinsbourne 1992) has addressed a similar concern in the multiple drafts conception of the phenomenal present. His resolution could be described in terms of the massive parallelism of processes in the brain. With such an abundance of activity within a narrow time frame, how are the events put into the linear order that is the usual conscious experience? Whatever the processes are, they could introduce shifts in the perceived time or order of events. Time shifts are easily shown in apparent motion phenomena and versions of the "cutaneous rabbit" effect (Geldard & Sherrick 1972). These time shifts are small, mostly less than 100 ms, and would not eliminate the 350 ms effect. However, the prospect of new and possibly dramatic effects remains a concern as long as we do not understand the brain mechanisms for these shifts in the perceived time of events.

Haggard and Clark (2003, pp. 696–8) proposed a synthesis of the components of voluntary action that gives a plausible account of the relations between goals, intentions, actions, and the sense of personal agency (see Spence & Frith (1999), for a similar approach). Their explanation of the "decision" seems reasonable physiologically and is not subject to the conceptual problems we have discussed. They assume a judgmental process that could be related to a stream of ordered neural events rather than a specific, discrete neural event corresponding to the perception. They characterize the moment of reported action (Libet's M) as the "perceptual center" of the process in their experiment. The point of decision (W) would be a center under different instructions. Rather intricate neurological processes determine the center, as would be the case, for example, in their account of intentional binding. They attribute this to the feedback and feedforward that results in a sense of personal agency in an action. This is quite far from the concept of an intention as a metaphorical "object," and it is open to scientific investigation.

RP vs. LRP as Precursor of the Conscious Decision

Trevena and Miller (2002) studied both the RP and the LRP (lateralized readiness potential). The LRP typically develops in motor area in the hemisphere contralateral to the movement in the last 300–500 ms of the overall RP. They propose that it is the LRP that should be compared to W, not the RP, because the LRP indicates specific motor preparation while the RP results from general preparation. The LRP is closer in time than the RP to W, but W still comes after the LRP in their data. Nevertheless, Trevena and Miller argue that their finding that 20 percent of W responses precede the LRP is consistent with a conscious effect on the choice of response. Klein (2002b) notes that a small temporal bias could wipe out this 20 percent. While the LRP may well be the appropriate neural response to measure in this paradigm, their evidence that W comes before it seems too weak to support a conclusion.

Haggard and Eimer (1999) had earlier made the same proposal, with more convincing evidence. They sorted blocks into two categories, those with W judgments earlier than the median (i.e., coming further in advance of the response than the median) and those with W later than the median. They averaged the onset of the RPs and the LRPs in both categories. RP onset was little different for early and late Ws. However, there was a positive relationship between W and LRP. For the cases when W was early, the mean LRP onset was also early. Late Ws had late LRP onsets. The mean LRPs overall began an average of 455 ms before W (a much wider margin than Trevena and Miller found), leaving stand the conclusion that W comes after unconscious preparation. However, the data imply that the LRP is the significant correlate with the decision, not the RP.

In a jointly authored article (Haggard & Libet 2001) that is really a sort of dialog, Libet notes some large differences in measured times between his results (Libet et al. 1983) and Haggard and Eimer's. He argues that these differences are large enough to raise questions about the meaning of the results. Further, he makes a strong case for the Haggard and Eimer RPs being dominated by Type I (preplanned) decisions. If this is the case, their findings would at least need to be hedged as applying only to Type I RPs. This issue needs to be resolved experimentally.

The Veto Response

Libet (2002, 2003a) concludes that W follows a prior unconscious intention generated by lawful neurophysiological events, but he proposes that the veto, which aborts the response presumably between W and M (see Figure 51.1), is entirely free and is the outcome of a nondeterministic brain process. This is a potential refuge for free will and an issue of some importance. It is critical for this hypothesis that the veto not have its own unconscious antecedent. Libet et al. (1983) had prearranged times for their participants to veto some motions, and these show the RP rising up to about 150 to 250 ms before the time the response would have been made and then flattening or falling. This result is consistent with Libet's hypothesis but does not settle the matter because these were not truly spontaneous vetoes. There is no point from which to back-average to image the precursor of an uncued non-response (Libet 1985, p. 538), and the question of whether an RP precedes a truly free veto is still open. However, several experiments have investigated the veto under conditions that allow back-averaging (see, e.g., Chisholm, Karrer, & Cone 1984; Konttinen, Lyytinen, & Era 1999). Velmans (2003) reviewed their results and concluded that there is evidence for preconscious generation of the veto response. Libet (2003b) maintained that these paradigms do not measure a free veto response and thus do not address the question. The issue remains unresolved.

How Do Libet's Findings Affect Philosophical Positions on Freedom of the Will?

The question of the freedom of the will is as old as philosophy and vast in its implications. As Clark (1999) put it, the question of free will forces us to take positions "on a host of other fundamental and necessarily interlocking issues: what we ultimately consist of as selves, the relation of mind to body, the role of consciousness in behaviour" and more, including scientific method, ethics, and the "possibility of the supernatural" (p. 279).

There are several definitions of free will. At one extreme is *libertarian* free will, according to which free actions are unconstrained and uncaused by any physical process. It is therefore incompatible with the concept of the physical world as a closed, deterministic causal system. This obvious contradiction is a deep problem. One solution goes back to Descartes, who formulated what is termed substance dualism. Material substance has one set of principles, and mental or spiritual substance has another. Mind and matter are two entirely different things. This formulation is notorious for insoluble problems and is commonly rejected as a scientific theory. However, the basic problem is solved: in the spiritual world there are no physical events whatever, no determinism, and the absolute freedom of will does not contradict determinism in the physical world. If this is the only possible resolution, libertarian free will requires dualism.

How do Libet's findings bear on dualism? His position (Libet 2003a) is that his main finding does not support libertarian free will and has no need for dualism. He claims, on the other hand, that the veto is a case of libertarian free will executed by a nondeterministic agent (Libet 1994, 1999, 2003a). It is difficult not to call this dualistic, but just classifying it as nondeterministic is enough to make it tough to reconcile with normal science. If the veto could be shown to have its own RP, then this argument loses much ground. Meanwhile, the only argument for this theory is based on the counter-intuitive rejection of free will. This is the weakest sort of argument (see Churchland 1997; Gomes 1998; Clark 1999). Until empirical evidence is obtained, the jury is out. The burden of proof is on the exceptional hypothesis of a non-physical field.

The main alternatives to dualism are various forms of monism, which assume only one kind of substance. These can range from the idealism of Bishop Berkeley, which asserts that everything is mental substance (see also Hut & Shepard 1997), to the more common materialism that assumes that the one substance is physical matter. A specific version of materialism is physicalism, which postulates that the nexus of causal relations in the physical world is sufficient to explain any current state of affairs, including our actions and mental lives. At this point, given the available evidence, we are left with the default option of physicalism, which excludes libertarian free will.

Compatibilist accounts reject libertarian free will. A central assumption for compatibilists is that free will is not absolute freedom but the unfettered ability to act. It does not matter if the intention to act is determined by a neural mechanism that operates outside of consciousness. The point is that we are free when there are no external constraints, such as a gun to the head, that compel action. When we see compatibilist definitions at work in the legal system, such inner constraints as "insanity" are often counted as being as pertinent as external constraints.

Compatibilists may have the best account of freedom in the Libet paradigm. Because the compatibilist concept of freedom relies on a lack of external constraints rather than an absolute isolation from a causal chain, the fact that the RP precedes W is not a problem. The preconscious processes that lead up to a decision, whether conceived as brain processes or unconscious ideas, do not deny freedom in compatibilist terms. On the contrary, some might consider this as the first neurophysiological evidence for a compatibilist account of action.

In Libet et al. (1983), Type I (preplanned) RPs begin some 500 ms before Type II (spontaneous) RPs. In both types of trials the time between W and the response was about the same size. The interval between the onset of the RP and W was consequently greater when the response was preplanned. If the difference between the beginning of the RP and W measures the length of the unconscious preparation, then it would seem that the more we plan an action, the longer we are unconscious of the final preparation to act. By extension really important decisions might have the longest period of unconscious incubation. Important decisions certainly require more "preplanning" than trivial decisions. Problem-solving and artistic creation have long been associated with unconscious thinking (Krippner 1981). Mental activity that is not conscious may have far more importance in everyday life than in the Libet paradigm. Further, the veto that Libet claims as the refuge of libertarian free will takes place in such a narrow slice of time that it seems more an impulsive action than a conscious deliberation leading to a decision. Its speed is at the opposite extreme from the long incubation that is associated with consequential, personally involving actions.

Velmans (2000, 2002, 2003) offers a comprehensive compatibilist account. The unconscious antecedents of conscious motivations are included as part of the self, and thus the identity and individuality of an acting person is reflected in his or her consequent actions and conscious experience. This position discounts the criterion that a person needs to be conscious of the decision at the time that it is made for it to be free. Libet (1999, pp. 52–3) finds this to be an unacceptable definition of free will. For Libet (and many others) free will means conscious free choice.

Conclusions

A range of conclusions have been drawn from Libet's findings. Libet himself has sought a place for free will in the "veto" response, which he insists has no neural antecedent and thus is free in the libertarian sense. He recognizes that this position requires a non-physical, nondeterministic agent, but it offers a way for libertarian free will to exist. We need vastly more empirical evidence to accept a nondeterministic process.

The conclusion that seems most compatible with Libet's result is that the decision to act in his experiment is prepared preconsciously, some 350 ms or more before the conscious report of a decision. The unwelcome consequence is that the conscious will is not the original determinant of action. Our sense of conscious agency would be illusory in this case, and our sense of ownership of this action is misplaced. The resolution by Velmans, that the preconscious activity is indeed part of the self, posits that the signature of our internal unconscious processes accounts for our gut feeling that these acts are ours and done by us, even though we are not conscious of the origins.

This compatibilist conclusion leaves as a question the role of consciousness in behavior. Causal efficacy of mental events seems untenable in a purely physicalist world unless they are somehow physical, and then their relation to conscious experience is a philosophical problem. Here we face the volitional equivalent of the problem of perceptual qualia, which is also unresolved. An empirical approach like that outlined by Haggard and Clark (2003) or Spence and Frith (1999) holds the best promise for progress.

Benjamin Libet's work is the first neurophysiological study of volition. Nothing in the time since his early publications has surpassed his work in significance. The results are grist for the mill in discussions of every aspect of volition and will figure importantly in thinking about volition for some time to come. The results seem consistent with a compatibilist account, but fundamental questions such as the role of consciousness in behavior remain open. Research in the neurophysiology of volition is the best way to approach such questions. Perhaps the strongest contribution of Libet's work is to move the issue from logical and philosophical debate to the empirical realm of cognitive neuroscience.

See also 32 The causal efficacy of consciousness; 40 Preconscious processing; 42 Consciousness of action.

Further Readings

Haggard, P. and Clark, S. (2003) Intentional action: conscious experience and neural prediction. *Consciousness and Cognition* 12: 4, 695–707.

Libet, B. (2002) The timing of mental events: Libet's experimental findings and their implications. *Consciousness and Cognition* 11: 2, 291–9.

Libet, B. (2003) Timing of conscious experience. Reply to the 2002 commentaries on Libet's findings. *Consciousness and Cognition* 12: 3, 321–31.

Libet, B. (2003) Can conscious experience affect brain activity? *Journal of Consciousness Studies* 10: 12, 24–8.

Pockett, S., Banks, W. P., and Gallagher, S. (2005) *Does Consciousness Cause Behavior? An Investigation of the Nature of Volition.* Cambridge, MA: MIT Press.

Velmans, M. (2002) How could conscious experiences affect brains? *Journal of Consciousness Studies* 9: 11, 3–29.

Velmans, M. (2003) Preconscious free will. *Journal of Consciousness Studies* 10: 12, 42–61.

References

Callaway, E., Halliday, R., Naylor, H., and Thouvenin, D. (1984) The latency of the average is not the average of the latencies. *Psychophysiology* 21, 571.

Chisholm, Ronald, Karrer, Rathe, and Cone, Randall (1984) Movement-related ERPs during right vs. left hand squeeze: effects of age, motor control, and independence of components. *Annals of the New York Academy of Sciences* 425, 445–9.

Churchland, P. M. (1981) Eliminative materialism and the propositional attitudes. *Journal of Philosophy* 78, 67–90.

Churchland, P. S. (1981a) On the alleged backwards referral of experiences and its relevance to the mind–body problem. *Philosophy of Science* 48, 165–81.

Churchland, P. S. (1981b) The timing of sensations: reply to Libet. *Philosophy of Science* 48, 492–97.

Churchland, P. S. (1997) The Hornswoggle problem. In J. Shear (ed.), *Explaining Consciousness: The Hard Problem.* Cambridge, MA: MIT Press.

Clark, Thomas W. (1999) Fear of mechanism: a compatibilist critique of "The Volitional Brain." *Journal of Consciousness Studies* 6: 8–9, 279–93.

Consciousness and Cognition (2002) 11: 2.

Deecke, L. and Kornhuber, H. H. (2003) Human freedom, reasoned will, and the brain: the *Bereitschaftspotential* story. In M. Jahanshi and M. Hallett (eds.), *The Bereitschaftspotential*, 283–315. New York: Kluwer.

Dennett, D. (1991) *Consciousness Explained.* Boston, MA: Little, Brown.

Dennett, D. C. (2003) *Freedom Evolves.* New York: Penguin.

Dennett, D. and Kinsbourne, M. (1992) Time and the observer: the where and when of consciousness in the brain. *Behavioral and Brain Sciences* 15, 183–247.

Durgin, Frank H. and Sternberg, Saul (2002) The time of consciousness and vice versa. *Consciousness and Cognition* 11: 2, 284–90.

Eccles, J. C. and Zeier, H. (1980) *Gehirn und Geist.* Zürich: Kindler.

Eriksen, C. W. and Collins, J. F. (1969) Temporal course of selective attention. *Journal of Experimental Psychology* 80, 254–61.

Eriksen, C. W. and Yeh, Y. (1985) Allocation of attention in the visual field. *Journal of Experimental Psychology: Human Perception and Performance* 11, 583–97.

Ferguson, M. J. and Bargh, J. A. (2004) How social perception can automatically influence behavior. *Trends in Cognitive Sciences* 8: 1, 33–9.

Festinger, Leon (1957) *Theory of Cognitive Dissonance.* Stanford, CA: Stanford University Press.

Freud, S. (1954) *Psychopathology of Everyday Life.* London: E. Benn.

Gazzaniga, M. S. (1997) Why can't I control my brain? Aspects of conscious experience. In Masao Ito, Yasushi Miyashita et al. (eds.), *Cognition, Computation, and Consciousness*, 69–79. Washington, DC: American Psychological Association.

Gazzaniga, M. S. (1998) *The Mind's Past*. Berkeley: University of California Press.

Geldard, F. A. and Sherrick, C. E. (1972) The cutaneous "rabbit": a perceptual illusion. *Science* 178: 4057, 178–9.

Glynn, I. M. (1990) Consciousness and time. *Nature* 348, 477–9.

Gomes, G. (1998) The timing of conscious experience: a critical review and reinterpretation of Libet's research. *Consciousness and Cognition* 7, 559–95.

Gomes, G. (2002) Problems in the timing of conscious experience. *Consciousness and Cognition* 11, 191–7.

Greene, J. D., Sommerville, B. R., Nystrom, L. E., Darley, J. M., and Cohen, J. D. (2001) An fMRI investigation of emotional engagement in moral judgment. *Science* 293: 5537, 2105–8.

Haggard, P. and Clark, S. (2003) Intentional action: conscious experience and neural prediction. *Consciousness and Cognition* 12: 4, 695–707.

Haggard, P. and Eimer, M. (1999) On the relation between brain potentials and awareness of voluntary movements. *Experimental Brain Research* 126, 128–33.

Haggard, P. and Libet, B. (2001) Conscious intention and brain activity. *Journal of Consciousness Studies* 8: 11, 47–63.

Heekeren, H. R., Wartenburger, I., Schmidt, H., Schwintowski, H.-P., and Villringer, A. (2003) An fMRI study of simple ethical decision-making. *NeuroReport* 14: 9, 1215–19.

Hut, P. and Shepard, R. N. (1997) Turning the hard problem upside down and sideways. In J. Shear (ed.). *Explaining Consciousness: The Hard Problem*. Cambridge, MA: MIT Press.

Johnson, H. and Haggard, P. (2003) The effect of attentional cueing on conscious awareness of stimulus and response. *Experimental Brain Research* 150, 490–6.

Joordens, S., Van Duijn, M., and Spalek, T. M. (2002) When timing the mind one should also mind the timing: bias in the measurement of voluntary actions. *Consciousness and Cognition* 11, 231–40.

Journal of Consciousness Studies (1999) 6: 8–9.

Keller, I. and Heckhausen, H. (1990) Readiness potentials preceding spontaneous motor acts: voluntary vs. involuntary control. *Electroencephalography and Clinical Neurophysiology* 76, 351–61.

Klein, S. A. (2002a) Libet's temporal anomalies: a reassessment of the data. *Consciousness and Cognition* 11, 198–214.

Klein, S. A. (2002b) Libet's research on the timing of conscious intention to act: a commentary. *Consciousness and Cognition* 11, 273–9.

Konttinen, N., Lyytinen, H., and Era, P. (1999) Brain slow potentials and postural sway behavior during sharpshooting performance. *Journal of Motor Behavior* 31: 1, 11–20.

Kornhuber, H. H. and Deecke, L. (1965) Hirnpotentialänderungen bei Willkürbewegungen und passiven Bewegungen des Menschen: Bereitschaftspotential und reafferente Potentiale. *Pflugers Archiv für Gesamte Physiologie* 284, 1–17.

Krekelberg, B. and Lappe, M. (2000) A model of the perceived relative positions of moving objects based upon a slow averaging process. *Vision Research* 40: 2, 201–15.

Krippner, S. (1981) Access to hidden reserves of the unconscious through dreams in creative problem-solving. *Journal of Creative Behavior* 15: 1, 11–22.

Libet, B. (1985) Unconscious cerebral initiative and the role of conscious will in voluntary action. *Behavioral and Brain Sciences* 8, 529–66.

Libet, B. (1994) A testable field theory of mind–brain interaction. *Journal of Consciousness Studies* 1: 1, 119–26.

Libet, B. (1999) Do we have free will? *Journal of Consciousness Studies* 6, 47–57.

Libet, B. (2002) The timing of mental events: Libet's experimental findings and their implications. *Consciousness and Cognition* 11: 2, 291–99.

Libet, B. (2003a) Can conscious experience affect brain activity? *Journal of Consciousness Studies* 10: 12, 24–8.

Libet, B. (2003b) Timing of conscious experience. Reply to the 2002 commentaries on Libet's findings. *Consciousness and Cognition* 12: 3, 321–31.

Libet, B., Wright, E. W. Jr, Feinstein, B., and Pearl, D. K. (1982) Readiness potentials preceding unrestricted "spontaneous" vs pre-planned voluntary acts. *Electroencephalography and Clinical Neurophysiology* 54, 322–35.

Marks, L. E. (1985) Toward a psychophysics of intention. *Behavioral and Brain Sciences* 8, 547.

Merikle, P. M. and Cheeseman, J. (1985) Conscious and unconscious processes: same or different? *Behavioral and Brain Sciences* 8, 547–8.

Nijhawan, R. (1994) Motion extrapolation in catching. *Nature* 370, 256–7.

Pockett, S. (2002a) On subjective back-referral and how long it takes to become conscious of a stimulus: a reinterpretation of Libet's data. *Consciousness and Cognition* 11, 144–61.

Pockett, S. (2002b) Backward referral, flash-lags and quantum free will: a response to commentaries on articles by Pockett, Klein, Gomes and Trevena and Miller. *Consciousness and Cognition* 11, 314–25.

Posner, M. I., Snyder, R. R., and Davidson, D. J. (1980) Attention and the detection of signals. *Journal of Experimental Psychology: General* 109, 160–74.

Purushothaman, G., Patel, S. S., Bedell, H. E., and Ogmen, H. (1998) Moving ahead through differential visual latency. *Nature* 396, 424.

Ross, L. and Nisbett, R. E. (1991) *The Person and the Situation: Perspectives of Social Psychology*. New York: McGraw-Hill.

Skinner, B. F. (1971) *Beyond Freedom and Dignity*. New York: Knopf.

Spence, C., Shore, D. I., and Klein, R. M. (2001) Multisensory prior entry. *Journal of Experimental Psychology: General* 130, 799–832.

Spence, S. A. and Frith, C. D. (1999) Towards a functional anatomy of volition. *Journal of Consciousness Studies* 6: 8–9, 11–29.

Titchener, E. B. (1908) *Lectures on the Elementary Psychology of Feeling and Attention*. New York: Macmillan.

Trevena, J. A. and Miller, J. (2002) Cortical movement preparation before and after a conscious decision to move. *Consciousness and Cognition* 11, 162–90.

van de Grind, W. (2002) Physical, neural, and mental timing. *Consciousness and Cognition* 11, 241–64.

Velmans, Max (2000) *Understanding Consciousness*. Florence, KY: Taylor and Francis/Routledge.

Velmans, Max (2002) How could conscious experiences affect brains? *Journal of Consciousness Studies* 9: 11, 3–29.

Velmans, Max (2003) Preconscious free will. *Journal of Consciousness Studies* 10: 12, 42–61.

Wegner, D. M. (2002) *The Illusion of Conscious Will*. Cambridge, MA: MIT Press.

Wegner, D. M. and Wheatley, T. (1999) Apparent mental causation: sources of the experience of will. *American Psychologist* 54: 7, 480–92.

FIRST-PERSON CONTRIBUTIONS TO THE SCIENCE OF CONSCIOUSNESS

52

Cognition, Fringe Consciousness, and the Legacy of William James

BRUCE MANGAN

In the West, from the time of the Greeks until the mid-seventeenth century, virtually all human cognitive activity was presumed to be conscious. This view shifted during the Enlightenment as various philosopher-scientists began to see that cognition rested on non-conscious processes. Kant gave the most influential, but highly abstract, expression of this insight, and it was soon reinterpreted in biological terms by Schopenhauer. By the 1870s, Helmholtz had achieved a fully modern view of human cognition: It is a product of the nervous system; only a small part of neural activity is involved with consciousness, and nonconscious neural processes alone are capable of executing what in today's terms we would call complex information processing.

This new understanding of cognition – as an interplay of conscious and nonconscious domains – spawned a massive research program. From the mid-nineteenth to the early twentieth centuries, some of the most acute scientific minds in history examined our phenomenology for clues about its neural substrate. We know in retrospect that this method worked quite well; its most sustained success was probably in the investigation of the physiology of vision. Mach discovered lateral inhibition by noting the purely subjective experience of intensity variations in the objectively homogeneous stripes now called Mach Bands in his honor. Helmholtz based his theory of tri-chromatic receptors on phenomenological evidence. Working back from even more subjective, introspective facts about color experience (e.g., most colors seem to be mixtures but a few, such as yellow and red, do not), Hering discovered opponent process cells.

William James's treatment of consciousness grew directly from this tradition. James, too, held that consciousness was infused by neural activity which careful introspection could detect. However, James's chief interest was in examining the character of conscious experience per se, and understanding the brain was for James a means to this end. And we know that the late nineteenth-century view of the brain he adopted *is* broadly correct. At the neural level it is wildly dynamic, with many localized processes of changing intensities interacting with one another in a flux of relationships.

This dynamic view of the brain helped guide James's phenomenology. James saw that on close inspection consciousness did not contain a series of discrete or recurring objects (as, say, Locke and Hume assumed), but rather a continuous process of shifting events, sometimes more concentrated, sometimes more diffuse. And just as brain activity is pervaded by a spray of changing relationships, so consciousness is pervaded by a spray of changing relational experiences. This is the most radical aspect of James's phenomenology, and it is still often overlooked. Relational experiences, or what he also called the "fringe" of consciousness, are as basic and variegated as are sensory experiences. On James's account, most of the cognitive content in consciousness is constituted by feelings of relation – from our sense of a specific meaning to our general recognition of rationality and of temporal integration.

James's work, especially his *Principles of Psychology* (1890), attracted immediate attention. Thinkers otherwise as different as Edmund Husserl (whose notion of the "horizon" came directly from James) and Bertrand Russell were much in his debt. But within a few years of James's death, behaviorism seized power in the English-speaking world. For more than half a century, introspection was proscribed as "unscientific." James's star rose again with the cognitive revolution as the explicit study of consciousness gradually returned, and today James is probably the single most cited person in the cognitive literature on consciousness. But decades of unopposed behaviorist propaganda have had their effect. Even now most researchers take introspection to be a dubious research technique.

The strongest argument for introspection "in principle" is that it has worked in fact. Without question introspective evidence is *sometimes* solid and scientifically fruitful. We need look no further than to Helmholtz, Mach, and Hering to establish this point, or to the completely subjective Gestalt principles of perceptual organization, or to the James-inspired work on the feeling-of-knowing and metacognition to be considered later.

So the standard behaviorist objection to introspection rests on a non-sequitur. While agreement about a given introspective claim may not always be possible, it hardly follows that agreement is never possible. Certainly we cannot assume that introspection will decisively answer every question put to it. The trick in using introspection is to investigate experiences that *do* yield reliable and useful findings, even though in most cases this can only be decided after the fact. But limitations of this sort are hardly unique to introspection. They apply to most research techniques in science. Experiments often fail, pilot experiments especially. And even when an experiment is successful in the narrow sense, it can lead nowhere. But does anyone think this means that the experimental *method* is dubious?

James's legacy is rich, in part because his phenomenology is so solid and, as it turns out, so useful, for example in forming a foundation for later cognitive research on attention, and the relation of consciousness to memory. Unfortunately the lingering prejudice against introspection has kept most of James's heirs from taking full advantage of their inheritance. In this chapter we will look at just one topic raised by James's work, namely, feelings of relation or fringe consciousness, by considering (1) James's own account of fringe phenomenology and its cognitive functions, (2) various lines of subsequent research which support James's analysis and are unified by it, and (3) implications of the fringe not considered by James.

The third point touches on some of the most perplexing questions in consciousness research. In science the description of a phenomenon ideally leads to its explanation. But many doubt this paradigm can be applied to our phenomenology. How can we explain, say, why a given pattern of nerve firings is experienced as red and not green? As we will see, fringe experience has no distinct sensory content and actively eludes our attentive grasp, and yet these and other aspects of its phenomenology *do* seem accessible to scientific modes of explanation, chiefly functional analysis and a conservation principle. Another and longer-standing puzzle concerns the causal efficacy of consciousness. At least from the time of Thomas Huxley, a school of thinking has held that consciousness in fact does nothing at all. Here, too, fringe experience may shed new light on a classic problem, since the functional analysis of the fringe strongly (but not conclusively) implies that consciousness does indeed play an active role in human cognition. In any case the fringe helps clarify mechanisms of conscious/nonconscious interpenetration if not their interaction.

The fringe, then, appears to be involved with a wide range of cognitive activity in consciousness. Its analysis may yield a unifying theory of considerable power.

James's Cognitive Phenomenology

James's usefulness stems not only from the general agreement his introspective findings command and the degree to which they mesh with later research, but also from the literary skill with which they are evoked, and their relative lack of theoretical preconceptions. The one commitment James brought to his phenomenology was a special interest in its dynamics, reflecting his view of brain activity.

The fringe: elusive, but at the heart of consciousness and cognition

The contents of consciousness fall into two broad categories on James's account: experiences that can be held and inspected in attention, and experiences that cannot. The former have distinct sensory content. But the latter do not; they are "feelings of relation" and they generally resist our attentive grasp. For if we try to attend to feelings of relation directly, this "is really annihilating them." They are immediately overlaid by a sensory experience of some sort, and the sensory component has such "vigor and stability" that it "eclipses and swallows up [feelings of relation] in its glare" (James 1890, p. 243).

James insists that feelings of relation perform absolutely fundamental cognitive functions. They make up the connective tissue which binds the relatively clear contents of consciousness together into larger wholes, and thereby constitute, among other things, our sense of temporality, continuity, meaning, and context:

> The definite images of traditional psychology form but the very smallest part of our minds as they actually live. The traditional psychologist talks like one who should say a river . . . consists of molded forms of water. Even were . . . pails and pots all standing in the stream, still between them the free water would continue to flow. Every definite image in the mind is steeped and dyed in the free water that flows around it. With it goes the sense of its relations, near and remote, the dying echo of whence it came to us, the drawing sense of whither it is to lead. The significance, the value, of the image is all in this halo or penumbra that surrounds and escorts it, – or rather that is fused into one with it and has become bone of its bone and flesh of its flesh. (ibid., p. 255)

James's use of converging metaphors here is typical. They all aim to evoke the enveloping and penetrating character of feelings of relation in quasi-poetic terms. Feelings of relation are likened to water flowing around and into rigid containers, to dye impregnating cloth, to a peripheral diaphanous glow, and, more obliquely, to sexual union via the language of a wedding ceremony. James also used a number of less poetic terms to suggest the phenomenological character of these feelings, including "vague," "transitive," "indefinite," and "fringe" experiences. James gave the relatively stable aspect of consciousness many names too, among them "definite sensorial images," "substantive experience," and "the nucleus." For better or worse, subsequent scholarship has tended to settle on the "fringe" as the covering term for feelings of relation, and since Mangan (1993a), "nucleus" has been used increasingly to refer to the definite, sensory-dominated aspect of experience on which we *can* focus attention.

The nucleus/fringe formulation helps us cut through some of the thicket of terms in James's cognitive phenomenology, but it is crucial not to take the peripheral implication of the term "fringe" too strictly. Again, feelings of relation infuse nuclei as well as surround them. The nucleus is a relatively stable "sensorial" experience, able to "be held by the mind for an indefinite time, and contemplated without changing" (ibid., p. 243). On occasion, feelings of relation can become the dominant component of consciousness, but this is usually just for brief moments during the transition from one nucleus to the next.

Broadly speaking, the most inclusive function of the fringe is to represent a mass of germane relational information – i.e., context information – about a given nucleus. And this is the basis of cognition in consciousness, albeit obscurely: "Knowledge about a thing is knowledge of its relations . . . Of most of its relations we are only aware in the penumbral nascent way of a 'fringe' of inarticulate affinities" (ibid., p. 259).

How, then, is James able to establish the existence of these fringe feelings when they are so easily overpowered by the sensory component of the nucleus? James's technique is often indirect, relying on memory. His genius is evident in his examples; they are rich with implications and at the same time are so commonplace that they command virtually universal assent. For example, James may ask us to recall the moment of transition between one nucleus and the next, when the power of nuclei to obscure the fringe is relatively weak. We discover "psychic transitions, always on the wing, so to speak, and not to be glimpsed except in flight. Their function is to lead from one set of images to another" (ibid., p. 253). Consider the first glimmer of forming an intention:

> Has the reader never asked himself what kind of mental fact is his intention of saying a thing before he has said it? It is an . . . absolutely distinct state of consciousness . . . and yet how much of it consists of definite sensorial images, either of words or of things? Hardly anything! Linger, and the words and things come into the mind; the anticipatory intention, the divination is no more. But as the words that replace it arrive, it welcomes them successively and calls them right if they agree with it, and wrong if they do not. It has therefore a nature of its own of the most positive sort, and yet what can we say about it without using words that belong to the latter mental facts that replace it? (ibid., p. 253)

A great deal is packed into this passage. It illustrates James's general contention that the fringe, per se, lacks sensory content, and also that consciousness involves a series of pulses during which the fringe is briefly dominant before the nucleus regains its full force. This can be likened to a series of Gestalt figure/ground shifts, with fringe and nucleus oscillating in relative salience. When the "definite sensorial images" of the nucleus do arrive, fringe experiences still envelop them – in this case James notes the feelings of "right" and "wrong," the experiential polarity on which all conscious evaluation is based. James also notes a further reason the fringe is so easy to overlook. Almost of necessity we designate fringe experiences in terms of the nuclei to which they lead.

Imminence, continuity and the stream of consciousness

This brings us to what is arguably the most remarkable feature of the fringe – its power to imply or suggest, at a given moment, the presence of detailed information that is not, at that moment, in consciousness.

> Suppose we try to recall a forgotten name. The state of our consciousness is peculiar. There is a gap therein; but no mere gap. It is a gap that is intensely active. A sort of a wraith of the name is in it, beckoning us in a given direction, making us at moments tingle with the sense of closeness, and then letting us sink back without the longed-for term. If the wrong names are proposed to us, this singularly definite gap acts immediately to negate them. They do not fit into its mold. (James 1890, p. 251)

In the tip-of-the-tongue (TOT) phenomenon, we probably come as close as we can get, in normal cognition, to experiencing a fringe state in relative isolation for any length of time. Here the fringe is the "anticipatory intention" we have all felt when a particular word seems about to enter consciousness, but in fact does not. This feeling of imminence is then something completely distinct from the word itself. The feeling contains contextual or relational information *about* the word, presented in a radically different phenomenological mode. This includes sketchy intimations about the word's "function, tendency and particular meaning in the sentence" (ibid., p. 244). These anticipatory fringe contents are definite in the functional sense that they defiantly distinguish right from wrong contents. But James never tires of emphasizing that phenomenology, fringe experiences are peculiarly "indefinite," "vague," "nascent," "dimly perceived," "shadowy," "inarticulate."

The fringe, then, has the power to evoke the dim sense of *future* contents of consciousness in a *present* content of consciousness. To feel a word on the tip of one's tongue is just one especially striking case of this capacity. In general "all of us have this permanent consciousness of whither our thought is going. It is a feeling like any other, a feeling of what thoughts are next to arise before they have arisen" (ibid., p. 255). Sometimes this vista of the imminent future feels vast. "When very fresh, our minds carry an immense horizon with them. The present image shoots its perspective far before it, irradiating in advance the regions in which lie the thoughts unborn" (ibid., p. 256). In this way, too, we are able to experience in a summary, generalized way, the lingering spirit of huge masses of information that, strictly speaking, have long since passed: "the shadowy scheme of the 'form' of an opera, play, or book, which remains in our minds and on which we pass judgment when the actual thing is gone" (ibid., p. 255).

The fringe function of imminence gives consciousness its sense of flow and continuity. Our sense of time rests on the ability of the fringe to evoke, dimly, past and future in the present. The fringe, as the conscious locus of "memory and expectation, the retrospective and prospective sense of time . . . give[s] that continuity to consciousness without which it could not be called a stream" (ibid., p. 606). Discussions of James in particular and consciousness in general often make much of continuity. But from a cognitive standpoint, the continuity of consciousness is a derivative consequence of fringe operation. *Our sense of continuity has, in itself, no evident cognitive function.* The misplaced emphasis on continuity is probably one reason discussions of James so often miss the fringe and feelings of relation – in this case the relation of past and future to the present.

Related Cognitive Theory and Research

The fringe lets us integrate a wide range of empirically based findings, some of which are considered here. For a more comprehensive and web-accessible summary, see Mangan (2001).

Figure/ground and change blindness

The figure/ground relation as treated by Gestalt psychology resonates with the nucleus/fringe distinction in four ways. The ground and the fringe (1) are both phenomenologically vague, fuzzy, unobtrusive; (2) both surround a far more delineated core; (3) both extend into the core, for on the classic Gestalt account the ground seems to run under or behind the figure. Finally, (4) both the fringe and the ground mediate retrieval. James did not recognize this point, nor did the Gestalt tradition seem to either, until Irving Rock's research on "inattentive" experience, which also elaborated point (3): "In daily life . . . [when] we are not attending to a pattern at which we are looking, there is the distinct impression, nevertheless, that something is there and has certain phenomenal characteristics . . . By virtue of the iconic representation, we as observers recognize that the *potential* to transmute this impression is there" (Rock & Gutman 1981; their emphasis).

Change blindness is one offshoot of this research. Slow changes in stimuli can pass unnoticed, and then shock us when we discover the change. Why the sense of surprise? Because most of the context information we experience about a visual situation is *not, paradoxically, encoded visually, but as a non-sensory feeling* that certain visual stimuli are imminent. In change blindness, changes in the objective stimuli become increasingly dissociated from their conscious (but non-sensory) representation which is not felt to change. Finally our cognitive system rectifies this shortfall, and we are startled by how far the dissociation was able to go.

Implicit and meta-cognition, feeling-of-knowing, intuition

Running through these various technical terms is a common element. All refer to cases in which subjects are unable to identify an explicit reason for their judgments, even though they can make them with consistency, and often with conviction. To indicate this capacity people typically use terms that seem to refer to fringe experience: "gut feelings," "just knowing," "feelings-of-knowing," "hunches," "intuitions," and so on. These cases suggest a fringe/nucleus dissociation. The subject has a fringe experience that signals a relational evaluation (e.g., something is right or wrong relative to a given context), but the nucleus which in normal cognition would specify this information is absent.

The seminal study in this line of research is Hart's (1965) "Memory and the feeling-of-knowing experience," based explicitly on James's treatment of the tip-of-the-tongue phenomenon. Hart elicited TOTs by using such questions as "Who was the Union general at the battle of Gettysburg?" When a subject had a TOT, he or she was asked to rate their degree of "feeling-of-knowing." The greater the rating, the more likely the subject was able to correctly identify the missing word.

In artificial grammar experiments, subjects distinguish strings of letters generated by various arrangement rules, but are virtually never able to state the rule in question explicitly. They rely instead on "gut feelings." Arthur Reber links this phenomenological capacity to traditional notions of intuition and evaluation.

[T]he individual has a sense of what is right or wrong, a sense of what is the appropriate or inappropriate response to make in a given set of circumstances, but is largely ignorant of the reasons for that mental state . . . To have a vague feeling of the goal of an extended process of thought, to "get the point" without really being able to verbalize it . . . is to have gone through an implicit learning experience. (Reber 2003, p. 625)

Edelman's "remembered present"

Gerald Edelman's attempt to integrate phenomenology and neurophysiology was substantially influenced by James. Probably the chief point of linkage is in Edelman's account of our sense of "now" – James's "saddle-back" of duration or "specious present." He sees clearly that while our subjective sense of the passing moment is unified, the neural mechanisms which carry out this feat are extremely diverse, complex, massively parallel, and occupy many interacting loci in the brain, especially the thalamus and cortex.

Dynamic reentrant interactions in the thalamocortical system must be thought of as successive in time – new perceptual categorizations are reentrantly connected to memory systems before they themselves become part of an altered memory system. This bootstrapping between memory and perception is . . . the so-called specious present of William James. I have called this . . . "the remembered present" to point up the dynamic interaction . . . that gives rise to consciousness. (Edelman 2004)

Cognitive linguistics

To ground semantics, Leonard Talmy (2000) proposed a set of experiential gradients running from "concrete perception to abstract conception" which independently capture many aspects of fringe experience. Toward the more abstract end of the palpability gradient, for example, "an entity is experienced as being abstract, unmanifest, intangible, and impalpable." In the abstract region of the clarity gradient "an entity is experienced as being vague, indistinct, indefinite, or murky." Talmy recognizes that many feelings fundamental to our use of language have virtually no sensory component. For example, the linguistic "category of 'modality' with such member notions as . . . *can*, *must* and *should*, has little concrete or sensed counterpart."

But it does not take a professor of linguistics to recognize that our feeling of meaningfulness (or what James called "dynamic meaning"; see below) is something quite distinct from a sensory experience. Many, perhaps most, children discover this before the sixth grade when they repeat a word to the point that they (and we) naturally say it has lost its meaning. Only the naked sound remains. Technically called "semantic satiation," this phenomenon has been studied experimentally since the early years of the last century (Severance & Washburn 1907).

Modern Extensions of James's Fringe

Science tries to move from describing phenomena to explaining them. At the descriptive level James's treatment of consciousness is remarkably rich, but beyond linking it to the dynamics of neural activity, James has very little to say about why consciousness would have the particular phenomenological character he observed. Why is the nucleus/fringe arrangement such a basic feature of the structure of consciousness? Why can't we make a fringe experience *itself* a stable nucleus? Why does the attempt to do this instead bring a new nucleus into consciousness? Why is the fringe the chief repository of relational information in consciousness? Why is this information non-sensory? Why is the fringe experience of "right direction" or "rightness" so ubiquitous?

Probably the most sustained attempt to explain fringe phenomenology from a cognitive standpoint is found in my own work (Mangan 1991, 1993a, 1993b, 2001, 2003). It aims to bring a standard mode of biological explanation – functional adaptation – to the study of consciousness. Just as we can explain, say, the shape of our teeth via their ingestive functions (e.g., biting, tearing, grinding) *so we can explain some characteristics of our phenomenology via their cognitive functions.*

Why is the fringe elusive?

James constantly notes the elusive character of fringe experiences: they cannot be turned into nuclei by an act of attention. If we do try to focus on the fringe, we almost instantly find ourselves inspecting a new, sensory-dominated nucleus instead – something very different from the fringe aspect of experience we tried to isolate and attend to a moment before. "As a snowflake crystal caught in the warm hand is no longer a crystal but a drop, so, instead of catching the feeling of relation moving to its term, we find we have caught some substantive thing . . . The attempt at introspective analysis in these cases is in fact like seizing a spinning top to catch its motion" (James 1890, p. 244). In functional terms, I would argue that this points to a mechanism for voluntary retrieval in consciousness. And if so, the elusive quality of the fringe is an adaptation to facilitate retrieval.

Fringe mediated retrieval is usually so trouble-free and rapid that it passes unnoticed. But during a TOT the system malfunctions; it is frozen in mid-cycle and we have introspective access to the most obscure part of the process. We find ourselves grasping at fringe experience in relatively pure form – at a beckoning, diffuse, structured vacancy, shorn of its normal overlay of sensory experience. Our aim is not to make the fringe *itself* a stable object of attention, and in general the design of fringe phenomenology disinclines us from doing so. Our frustration during a TOT shows how deeply we presume that grasping at the fringe *is* the way to bring a substantive nucleus quickly into consciousness.

Put more abstractly, we "call" information into consciousness by attending to the fringe feelings which imply that information. The fringe is designed to deflect direct acts of attention because this allows the transformation of imminent to explicit information in consciousness. So when someone points, we do not focus on the finger but on the object it indicates. If attention did stay fixed at the finger, the finger's pointing function would cease.

Another way to see this is to consider a partial analogy with the icons that hug the periphery of a typical computer screen. To call new information to the screen, we first identify the relevant icon, move the cursor to it, and click the mouse. The center of the screen then immediately fills with the information that a moment before was implied by the icon, but was itself off-screen. What, then, would happen if clicking on an icon enlarged and clarified the icon itself and moved *it* to the center of the screen? Of course the icon's call function would to that extent short-circuit. The purpose of clicking on, "attending to," an icon is not to make the icon clearer or more central, but to bring the detailed information the icon implies to the center of the screen and make that information a "nucleus." In both cases there is every reason to design the retrieval system so that the target itself does not become an object of detailed inspection or otherwise interfere with the information it helps us retrieve.

Of course analogies are not identities. And yet one apparent dis-analogy in the fringe/icon comparison (we can focus indefinitely on an icon) suggests a deeper parallel. Relatively few pixels are allocated for the display of any given icon. Most pixels go to the central workspace. Here allocation is limited by a trade-off relationship.

Conservation trade-offs

The key constraint on consciousness is its limited capacity. This long-standing point can be reformulated phenomenologically in a way that may look like a truism, but has great explanatory power. *There is a maximum resolution or articulation capacity that consciousness does not exceed.* In other words, the amount of detail we can experience about anything at a given moment is limited. This mandates various trade-offs: When more articulation capacity is concentrated in one region of the field of consciousness, less is available elsewhere.

The figure/ground structure of perception is a straightforward example of this principle. The figure enjoys detailed articulation, while its ground is blurry and ill-defined. In reversible figures like the classic face/vase image, we experience high articulation in only one figure at a time, and low in the other, even though both figures are objectively able to bear highly articulated experience. Here the exception proves the rule. With a bit of effort people can briefly attend to both the face and vase figures at the same time. But when they do, they report that *neither* figure is as highly articulated (e.g., is as detailed, vivid, dimensional) as *either* was when experienced sequentially. Similar trade-offs occur with auditory stimuli when, say, we try to listen to two simultaneous conversations. Sensory and non-sensory experience also appear to be bound by a trade-off relationship. Without realizing its implication, James occasionally suggests that as the sensory nucleus becomes less prominent, the fringe becomes more prominent, and visa versa.

From this perspective fringe experiences – vague, indefinite, fuzzy, without sensory content – appear to use little articulation capacity. And yet most context information in consciousness is represented by the fringe. Why is so little articulation capacity devoted to context information? Paradoxically, this is probably because the context information relevant to a given nucleus is so vast. Even a very slight increase in articulation devoted to presenting all the relevant context information would require a very large decrease in focal capacity.

We can then explain the nucleus/fringe structure of consciousness as the result of a basic tension between two conflicting functional demands: presenting specific information and presenting its context. The articulation limit mandates trade-offs. The diminished clarity of peripheral sensory experience is an adaptation which works to minimize the load on consciousness's limited articulation capacity. The non-sensory quality of fringe experience carries this load-reduction strategy one step further.

To return to the computer screen analogy. For similar design reasons – a limited number of pixels – a standard screen must trade-off between the level of detail allocated to the central workspace and pixels allocated to peripheral displays. More pixels devoted to the focal task mean fewer for the display of peripheral information.

Finessing articulation limits

In the early years of the cognitive revolution, Mandler, following Lashly and Miller, emphasized that consciousness receives the results of very complex nonconscious processing.

Detailed cognitive work is nonconscious, some of its fruits are conscious. And probably the most difficult cognitive task of all is to correctly assemble and apply context information.

The overall function of the fringe is to finesse the limited articulation capacity of consciousness and thereby serve as an interface mechanism. Though completely conscious, the fringe stands between nonconscious and focal conscious processing, using a few wisps of experience to radically *condense* or *summarize* nonconscious information of extreme complexity. The fringe both implies the existence of this information and gives us selective access to it, binding conscious and nonconscious processes into an integrated cognitive system.

Two fringe experiences are absolutely essential to accomplish this finesse. For want of better covering terms, I call them "rightness" and "wrongness." They do not themselves "compute" anything, but signal consciousness the degree to which nonconscious processing has determined that a given nucleus does or does not fit its appropriate context. James only discussed the phenomenology of these experiences in passing. He did see their crucial role in conscious cognition, but did not consider their summarizing or interface functions.

The rightness/wrongness polarity captures the ultimate evaluative relationship in conscious cognition. At the same time it inclines us to act.

> Relation . . . to our topic of interest is constantly felt in the fringe, and particularly the relation of harmony and discord, of furtherance and hindrance of the topic. When the sense of furtherance is there, we are "all right"; with the sense of hindrance we are dissatisfied and cast about for other thoughts. (James 1890, p. 259)

The cognitive application of these experiences is very wide. They constitute, for example, what James calls "dynamic meaning," our sense that something is, or is not, meaningful. "Dynamic meaning is usually reduced to the base fringe we have described of felt suitability or unfitness to the context and conclusion" (ibid., p. 265). It "pertains to the 'fringe' of the subjective state . . . [It] is an absolutely positive sort of feeling, transforming what would otherwise be a mere noise or vision into something *understood* . . . The image per se, the nucleus, is functionally the least important part of the thought" (ibid., p. 472). Here we encounter the phenomenological bottom line of cognition. Rightness signals that whatever it infuses is correct, understood, appropriate, meaningful, coherent, to be accepted; wrongness that whatever it infuses is incorrect, misunderstood, inappropriate, meaningless, incoherent, to be rejected.

In the most inclusive functional terms, the role of consciousness is to deal with novel or unexpected information. However, consciousness withdraws, and habituation and automatization set in, when something becomes well-known, expected, mastered. In this sense the aim of conscious cognition is to deal with the *unfamiliar* – problem-solving in its broadest sense. And in general what we mean by solving a problem is finding or assembling what, for us, is missing context information. The thrust of conscious activity is to find in a new situation the *right* response, the *right* interpretation. To do this, consciousness must somehow transcend its limitations, and access information it cannot itself contain in detailed form. It is the summary fringe experience indicating right (or wrong) context fit that finesses this bottleneck, and is the datum on which all conscious evaluation rests.

It is then crucial not to confuse rightness with familiarity. Determining familiarity is a far less demanding cognitive problem, and from the standpoint of consciousness it is a far less important cognitive datum. Probably the lingering prejudice against phenomenological analysis has led to this confusion. Many experimental paradigms which officially measure "familiarity" in reality measure "rightness." In a target search experiment, we are not looking for the most familiar target but the right target, the target specified at the beginning of the experiment. In a feeling-of-knowing paradigm, we are not trying to retrieve the most familiar name but the right name, the name that fits the context specified by the antecedent question.

Missing the familiarity/rightness distinction seriously obscures our understanding of consciousness. Familiarity means finding a passive match, while rightness takes us to the active center of conscious processing – the evaluation and use of novel information.

Causal Efficacy of Consciousness?

So far my analysis has assumed that conscious processing and feelings of volition do just what they seem to do. But this view is not without its problems. The psychologist and philosopher Max Velmans has developed what is probably the most wide-ranging case against the presumption that consciousness is causally efficacious (in the sense that it directly causes brain activity viewed from a third person perspective) drawing on experimental findings, abstract arguments, and phenomenological analysis influenced by James.

Here we touch on what is arguably the most far reaching question we can ask about consciousness in a cognitive/biological context: Does it do anything? Depending on one's point of view, it is either ironic or telling that Huxley, "Darwin's Bulldog," was so emphatic about consciousness's supposed lack of function. For Darwin's great gift to science was his mode of functional analysis. If consciousness has no function in the standard sense, then it is incommensurate with the most powerful method of biological explanation we currently possess. Yet if consciousness does have an adaptive function (or functions), then the high road to biological understanding is open before us, and the study of consciousness can pursue Darwin's "top-down" method of biological analysis, complementing such "bottom-up" methods as neurophysiological research.

Velmans's critique

In a recent series of papers, Velmans (2002, 2003) considers three of these difficulties. First, consciousness occupies no discernible place in third-person science. If the brain is examined from an external perspective, all neural processing, from input to output, can be accounted for by known biophysical principles without reference to consciousness. There are no "gaps" in processing for consciousness to fill. Second, our conscious experiences typically occur "too late to causally affect the processes to which they most obviously relate" (2003). This is based on experimental findings such as Libet's work which shows that a feeling of volition and its associated act can both be caused by the same antecedent neural event. Rather than the conscious wish causing the act, Velmans takes a feeling of volition to be an accurate representation of a *preconscious* voluntary decision. As noted by Lashley, Miller, and Mandler, this conforms to the general finding that consciousness often contains the results of cognitive processing, but not the processing details.

Velmans's third point centers on the phenomenology of conscious control or, rather, its supposed absence. "One is not conscious of one's own brain/body processing. So how could there be conscious control of such processing?" (Velmans 2002, p. 8). He asks us to consider "hesitation pauses" in speech. If the causal efficacy hypothesis were right, we would expect these pauses to contain experiences "associated with the formation of ideas . . . [and] conscious planning of what to say . . . But nothing is revealed of the processes that formulate ideas, translate these into a form suitable for expression in language, search for and retrieve words from memory, or assess which words are most appropriate" (ibid., p. 9).

But we can certainly be ignorant of the details of a complex process and still have the power to initiate, influence, or control it, especially in conjunction with a little feedback, for example, driving a car, using a computer, making a baby. Higher levels of neural organization control, but do not themselves contain, the information used to execute lower level functions. And the fringe component of a hesitation pause does represent *some* information about the underlying cognitive process – as Velmans himself, on reconsideration, would seem to grant:

> I agree that, *viewed from a first-person perspective*, fringe conscious experiences seem to function in the ways that Mangan describes. We have a feeling of what we want to say before we say it and in this sense the feeling provides an implicit target. We also have a sense of whether our words fit our meaning, indicating whether they are "on target" and so on . . . In sum, I agree with Mangan that the fringe of consciousness contains feelings and judgments about material at the focus of attention thereby providing context in a highly compressed form. But this does not resolve the issue of how such feelings arise or how first-person experiences could have third-person causal effects on the brain. (Velmans 2003, p. 57 – Velmans's emphasis)

On one far-reaching point I completely agree with Velmans. If there is not enough information *in* consciousness – that is, relevant phenomenological contents – to support making volitional decisions, then consciousness cannot be a locus of volition. But the converse also applies: *If the requisite information is present in some form, then we have suggestive evidence that consciousness does indeed do what commonsense assumes.* The fringe's radical capacity to condense context information, its apparent call function, and the feedback capacity offered by the experiences of rightness and wrongness, all seem elegantly designed to support the exercise of volition in consciousness, and so provide a new argument for it (Mangan 1991, 2001, 2003).

See also 32 The causal efficacy of consciousness; 40 Preconscious processing; 53 Phenomenological approaches to consciousness; 55 An epistemology for the study of consciousness.

Further Readings

James, W. (1890/1950) *The Principles of Psychology*, vol. 1. New York: Dover Publications.
Mangan, B. B. (2001) Sensation's ghost: the non-sensory "fringe" of consciousness. *Psyche* 7: 18, http://psyche.cs.monash.edu.au/v7/psyche-7-18-mangan.html
Mangan, B. B. (2003) The conscious "fringe": bringing William James up to date. In B. J. Baars, W. P. Banks, and J. B. Newman (eds.), *Essential Sources in the Scientific Study of Consciousness*, 741–59. Cambridge, MA: MIT Press.

References

Edelman, G. M. (2004) *Wider than the Sky: The Phenomenal Gift of Consciousness*. New Haven, CT: Yale University Press.

Hart, J. T. (1965) Memory and the feeling-of-knowing experience. *Journal of Educational Psychology* 56: 4, 208–16.

James, W. (1890/1950) *The Principles of Psychology*, vol. 1. New York: Dover Publications.

Mangan, B. B. (1991) "Meaning and the structure of consciousness: an essay in psychoaesthetics." University of California, Berkeley, doctoral dissertation.

Mangan, B. B. (1993a) Taking phenomenology seriously: the fringe and its implications for cognitive research. *Consciousness and Cognition* 2: 2, 89–108.

Mangan, B. B. (1993b) Some philosophical and empirical implications of the fringe. *Consciousness and Cognition* 2: 2, 142–54.

Mangan, B. B. (2001) Sensation's ghost: the non-sensory fringe of consciousness. *Psyche: An Interdisciplinary Journal of Research on Consciousness* 7: 18, http://psyche.cs.monash.edu.au/v7/psyche-7-18-mangan.html

Mangan, B. B. (2003) The conscious "fringe": bringing William James up to date. In B. J. Baars, W. P. Banks, and J. B. Newman (eds.), *Essential Sources in the Scientific Study of Consciousness*, 741–59. Cambridge, MA: MIT Press.

Reber, A. S. (2003) Implicit learning and tacit knowledge. In B. J. Baars, W. P. Banks, and J. B. Newman (eds.), *Essential Sources in the Scientific Study of Consciousness*, 603–30. Cambridge, MA: MIT Press.

Rock, I. and Gutman, D. (1981) The effects of inattention on form perception. *Journal of Experimental Psychology: Human Perception and Performance* 7: 2, 275–85.

Severance, E. and Washburn, M. F. (1907) The loss of associative power in words after long fixation. *Americal Journal of Psychology* 18: 182–6.

Talmy, L. (2000) *Toward a Cognitive Semantics*. Cambridge, MA: MIT Press.

Velmans, M. (2002) How could conscious experience affect brains? *Journal of Consciousness Studies* 9: 12, 3–29.

Velmans, M. (2003) Preconscious free will. *Journal of Consciousness Studies* 10: 12, 42–61.

53

Phenomenological Approaches to Consciousness

SHAUN GALLAGHER

In contrast to naturalistic approaches to consciousness which investigate how consciousness is grounded in physical states, classic phenomenological approaches of the sort explicated by Husserl (1913/1982) take consciousness itself to be the necessary (a priori or transcendental) ground that enables us to conceive of physical states in the first place. That is, transcendental phenomenology emphasizes the fact that any knowledge we have of the world, including the knowledge of physical states in natural science, can be had only on the basis of consciousness itself. We do science only when we are conscious; and consciousness provides the *sine qua non* access we have to studying the physical world. A third-person statement to the effect that consciousness depends on physical or functional states presupposes the first-person consciousness of the subject making the statement. On this transcendental approach, then, the first investigation (in the order of knowledge rather than time) ought to be about the nature of the first-person experience that gives us the access and the wherewithal to understand the world and its physical states. Phenomenologists thus begin by pushing aside precisely the kinds of questions that naturalistic approaches are most interested in; for example, questions about how the brain causally relates to consciousness. Indeed, this is the first step into phenomenology and the first step of the phenomenological method. It is referred to as the phenomenological *epoché*.

The *epoché*, as the first part of the method called "phenomenological reduction," consists in the "bracketing" of our folk or scientific opinions, beliefs, and theories about consciousness. The phenomenologist suspends judgment about whether and how the brain generates consciousness, about whether a dualist or materialist ontology is correct, about whether the consciousness–brain relation is best characterized as an identity claim, or a functional or emergent relation, and so on. These are simply not the phenomenological questions. This is not to say, however, that phenomenologists believe the brain has nothing to do with consciousness, or that naturalistic investigations of brain function are wrong-headed or useless. Phenomenology is not opposed to science, although it is opposed to scientism, the claim that science is the only way to explain everything that is. This first step simply sets aside natural scientific questions about consciousness for the purpose of gaining insight into what conscious experience is like. A phenomenology of consciousness in this sense is nonetheless relevant to a naturalistic investigation insofar as we need to have a good description of consciousness, to know what consciousness is, if, as psychologists or neuroscientists, we intend to explain how consciousness works or how it is generated.

The Intentionality of Consciousness

The method of phenomenological reduction involves further steps of turning toward experience itself and providing systematic and precise descriptions of that experience. These phenomenological descriptions attempt to capture a number of different things. How do things appear in various states of consciousness – that is, how do I experience them? What are the invariable (or variable) structures of experience? How is perceptual consciousness different from memory, or imaginative consciousness? To organize these descriptions the phenomenologist is helped by the realization that consciousness is intentional. This is the first thing that we come to understand through the phenomenological reduction. As we examine our experience, we immediately realize that our consciousness is always *of* something, is always directed *at* something (Husserl 1900–1/2001). Turning our reflective attention to experience itself does not result in closing a door to the world or locking ourselves up in a solipsistic subjectivity. Rather, we find that we are open to the world precisely by the intentional structure of consciousness – the fact that when I am conscious I am always conscious of something. The "something" appears straightforwardly as an (intentional) object of our conscious experience; it is the something of which we are aware. Intentional experience is the inevitable and the exclusive way in which we come to understand the world, perceptually, conceptually, esthetically, emotively, mathematically, scientifically, and so forth.

The task for the phenomenologist is to describe intentional experience in all its details, although still within the attitude imposed by the *epoché*. That is, the phenomenologist is not concerned about the metaphysical status of the intentional object, or about theories about its place in a causal chain of being. Rather, the phenomenologist is strictly concerned about how things appear in conscious experience. Husserl (1913/1982) comes to refer to this aspect of phenomenal appearance as the "noematic" aspect of experience. If I see an apple tree in front of me, the phenomenological question is not whether the tree exists, or how it got there, but simply how it appears in my experience of it. It appears, in a complex perspective, to have a certain shape, a certain color, to be presented on a certain background; and all of these things can change if I start to move around the tree. Any further judgments that I make about the tree seemingly go back to the original experience of it. The thematic focus of the phenomenologist, however, is not the tree, or the truth or falsity of judgments that I may be able to make about the tree; it is rather the experiential encounter I have with it, the tree as noematic correlate of my experience.

The noema, for example the tree-as-experienced, is correlated to the spatial perspectives and limitations that are defined by my consciousness as it is embodied in the world. My consciousness is like a window that opens on to the world. What appears through that window is some piece of the world, the apple tree in this case. The apple tree itself may be more than what appears in my consciousness (if, for example, it is more than a figment of my imagination), but the noema is simply that appearance, and is therefore an aspect of consciousness rather than an aspect of the objective world. The tree itself may have an irregular shape or may be changing its shape as the wind blows, but the appearance (noema) of the tree is not irregularly shaped or blowing in the wind; if [physical conditions in the environment, and processes in my sensory organs and brain are such that] the tree appears to be green, the appearance (noema) of the tree is not green. The thing that appears needs to be distinguished from the appearance of the thing. The noema, then, is not the intentional object (the apple tree) but an aspect of consciousness which gives us access to the intentional object. In this sense, the noematic aspect of consciousness is simply a way to describe the intentionality of consciousness; it is, as Husserl suggests, part of the structure of intentionality.

The noematic content may vary for a number of different reasons. Some variation may be due to precisely the kinds of causes that phenomenologists have methodically ignored (the wind is blowing, information is being processed differently in my brain, etc.); other changes may be correlated to my own bodily movements, and these are things that I can be aware of and can describe phenomenologically. It is also possible that the noematic content, or some core features of it, may remain relatively stable, but other changes may be introduced by consciousness itself. I can, for example, change my mode of experience from a perceptual one to one accomplished in a different cognitive operation. So, for example, I can close my eyes and remember the tree as I previously perceived it. I can make aesthetic or economic judgments about the tree. Throughout these changes I can be affected emotionally by my experience of the tree. Again, in phenomenological reflection I can provide a description of these different modes of consciousness and how they are structured. In this case I am not attending to the noematic aspects of consciousness, but to the *noetic* aspects that define my experience as consisting in states or acts of perception, or memory, or imagination, or judgment, or in affective states. The differences between the experiential attitudes of seeing, vs. desiring, vs. believing, vs. remembering something to be the case, are differences that we live through in our experience and as such can be captured by a phenomenological description. This kind of noetic analysis generally leads phenomenologists to acknowledge the primacy of perception. In most cases, perception constitutes a starting point for other cognitive operations. Thus, for example, Husserl describes episodic memory as involving a reenactment of perceptual aspects of consciousness (Marbach 1993).

To ask whether intentionality is an objectively causal relation or a purely subjective phenomenon is to enter into an old debate that extends back to medieval times and that comes into the phenomenological tradition by way of Brentano. Husserl and the phenomenologists do address this question, and it will be helpful to consider it because it can help to clarify an important distinction between doing phenomenology in the strict sense (developing descriptions under the rule of the phenomenological reduction) and engaging in phenomenological philosophy. In proposing an answer to this question, the phenomenologist is required to step outside of the strict descriptive method and present philosophical arguments. For the phenomenologist, however, these arguments should be supported by phenomenological evidence. Thus, for example, we can argue that the intentional relation is not a causal one in the sense that one object (the perceived object) causes a reaction in something else (consciousness), since perceptual (real worldly) objects are not the only sorts of objects that we can experience. As Dan Zahavi (2003, p. 14) puts it:

> When I am sitting at my desk, I cannot only think about the backside of the moon, I can also think about square circles, unicorns, next Christmas or the principle of noncontradiction. When I am thinking about *absent* objects, *impossible* objects, *nonexisting* objects, *future* objects, or *ideal* objects, my directedness toward these objects is obviously not brought about because I am causally influenced by the objects in question.

In this sense the intentional relation is not a "real" one, that is, a relation that would involve something like a causal relation between two objectively existing relata. On the other hand, the intentional relation cannot be a purely subjective or intra-mental one since there is a clear differentiation between consciousness and the intentional object (Husserl 1984, p. 385). The intentional content can remain the same even as the noetic or cognitive act changes from perception to memory, to judgment, to belief, to desire, and so forth. Unless we were to contend that with every cognitive act we were conscious of a new object, or that different people were unable to see the same tree, then the object must have some independence from the consciousness we have of it.

Can we offer a phenomenological description of how a particular noetic-noematic experience comes to appearance in consciousness? There is a debate in the phenomenological literature on Husserl's proposal that intentional consciousness can be further analyzed into a schematic structure that involves an apprehension of sensory material, for which he uses the Greek term *hyle* (material) or "hyletic data" – a level of non-intentional sense content: sensations of pain, color, sound, etc. This "apprehension–hyletic content" schema is a process that we may become aware of only in unusual limit cases, or in a precise phenomenological reflection. For example, I may in some instances become aware of certain auditory properties of sound as I listen to a familiar melody. These properties, which are purely acoustical aspects stripped of any meaning, are not something I am aware of in my ordinary mode of listening to music. Husserl would say that in this case we are experiencing the hyletic data that make up the raw sensory content of consciousness, prior to an interpreting apprehension that draws meaning to what I hear and constitutes it as a musical melody. Similarly, when I suddenly notice the aroma of some wonderful food that is being prepared, in reflection I may come to realize that for some time I had been affected by that aroma but without being aware of it, or without it consciously registering as that specific aroma (McKenna 1982). Prior to my explicit awareness, then, the olfactory effect constituted a hyletic experience that I came to apprehend or interpret as the aroma. Husserl claims that we live through these hyletic experiences but that we do not attend to or perceive them as such. In contrast, other phenomenologists, such as Sartre (1943/1956, pp. lix, 314), Merleau-Ponty (1945/1962, p. 405), and Gurwitsch (1966, pp. 175–286), argue that what Husserl calls hyletic data are simply abstract aspects of the objective world – the sound of the instruments, the odor of the food, the color of the object, etc. – not as they are experienced, but as they are reified and misread into our experience by reflection. Pre-reflectively, what I experience is simply the world; by an involuted reflection, however, I take certain aspects of what I experience and regard them as actual elements of consciousness. Hyletic data are not part of the structure of consciousness in any real sense; they are aspects of what we experience. There is no need, within consciousness, for a schema that involves an animating apprehension of hyletic data to account for how the world comes to be presented in a meaningfully organized fashion. Husserl, according to the critics, over-intellectualized the perceptual process, giving responsibility for the rational organization of meaningless sense-data to an interpretive apprehension, when in fact the experience of the world is delivered already organized by processes that take place at the level of embodiment (see Merleau-Ponty 1945/1962; Gallagher 1986).

Temporal Structure of Consciousness

Not only can we distinguish between the noematic content of consciousness and the noetic performances such as perception, but it is also the case that consciousness has a changing yet continuous character, sometimes expressed in William James's (1892) phrase, the "stream of consciousness." Consider what experience would be like if different moments of consciousness were discrete in such a way that what we experienced in each moment was not temporally connected with what we experienced just before. Even if the world consisted in a set of stable objects, there would be no coherence to our experience; we would experience a flash of existence at a time, and this flash would not be integrated with the previous moment or the next one. One might think that this discontinuous strobe-like existence would require that we remember from one moment to the next what we have experienced, and make judgments that would somehow summarize or collate the succession of moments into a coherent object. But if consciousness were genuinely discontinuous, so would be our memory and our judgment. Our experience would be, in another of James's famous phrases, "a blooming, buzzing confusion." For example, we would not be able to experience a movement or a melody as it develops. We would not even be able to remember an earlier moment and attempt to synthesize it with a later moment in order to infer something like a movement or melody. What must consciousness be like, then, if this is not our experience?

Husserl (1928/1991) worked out a description of how it is possible to actually hear a melody, see a movement, or perceive identity over time. One moment of consciousness is not disconnected from the previous one or the next one. If things appear in a continuous or continually developing way, which they do in normal waking consciousness, then previous phases of experience must be in some way tied together with subsequent ones. Some of the things that we experience, of course, may themselves be disjointed events but the experience of them appears to involve an integrated successive flow rather than a disjointed, start and stop progression. And if experience were not this way, then *all* events would appear disjointed. The question is precisely how one moment of consciousness is interconnected with the previous and subsequent ones. Husserl's answer is a detailed explication of the structure of what he calls internal time-consciousness. As one moment of consciousness fades into the past, we do not call upon memory, as a new cognitive act of consciousness, to somehow capture that moment (a position that Husserl attributed to Brentano). Indeed, even in remembering something our experience is structured as a connected streaming process, and it would start an infinite regress to say that memory is responsible for retaining the past phases of memory. Rather, there is, implicit in the very nature of consciousness (no matter if it is perception, memory, imagination, a train of conceptual thought, etc.), a binding of one moment to the next. This binding process is what Husserl calls "retention" in regard to past moments of consciousness, and "protention" in regard to the future. Husserl's model explains not only how the perception of a temporal object, such as a melody, is possible, given a changing stream of consciousness, it also explains how consciousness unifies *itself* across time.

If we imagine a momentary phase of consciousness, abstracting it from the flowing continuum of consciousness, it appears to be structured by three functions:

1 *primal impression*, which allows for the consciousness of an object (a musical note, for example) that is simultaneous with the current phase of consciousness;
2 *retention*, which retains the previous phase of consciousness and its intentional content (the just past note of the melody); and
3 *protention*, which anticipates experience that is just about to happen.

Since retention retains the entire just-past phase, which also includes retention of the previous phase, then there is a retentional continuum that stretches back over prior experience, maintaining the sense of the past moments in the present.

On this model of the basic flow of consciousness, the continuity involved in retention has two aspects. First, since the prior phases of consciousness include their respective primal impressions of the previously sounded notes, retention establishes a continuity of the experienced object. Husserl calls this the "transverse intentionality" (*Querintentionalität*) of retention (1928/1991, p. 85). This feature accounts for the temporal coherence of what we experience. Second, retention provides for the intentional unification of consciousness itself since retention maintains within the present phase of consciousness the sense of the previous phases of consciousness as being immediately past and fading further into the past. Husserl characterizes this as the longitudinal intentionality (*Längsintentionalität*) of retention.

One can explicate the phenomenology here by considering the example of speaking a sentence, such as "The cat is on the mat." When in saying this sentence I reach the word "on," I am no longer saying the previous words, but I, and anyone who is listening to me, still retain a sense of the beginning of the sentence, otherwise the sentence would not be meaningful. Retention keeps the intentional sense of the words available even after the words are no longer sounded. Importantly, as I am uttering the sentence, I not only have a sense of the sentence as it develops, but I also have a sense that *I* am the one who has just said the words, and who is uttering the sentence. This sense of self is built into experience at the very basic level of the retentional function, and indeed, it is the retentional structure of consciousness that makes it possible.

In addition, at the moment that I am uttering the word "on," I have some anticipatory sense, a "protention," of where the sentence is going, or at the very least, that the sentence is heading to some kind of ending. This sense of knowing where the sentence (the thought, my experience) is heading, even if not completely definite, seems essential to the experience I have of speaking in a meaningful way. It helps to provide a sense that I am speaking in a sentential fashion, rather than a meaningless set of phrases. More generally, this is a feature of all normal experience. We do not go blindly into the future; we have an experiential heading.

Self-Awareness

This retentional–protentional flow structure of consciousness is important for understanding the phenomenological view on self-consciousness. Consciousness is not simply a straightforward consciousness of an object, it is at the same time a consciousness of itself. My experience of the passage of a melody is at the same time a non-observational, non-reflective awareness of my own flowing experience, since retention holds a sense of the past phases of consciousness in the present. At the very least, and basic to any more developed self-consciousness at the conceptual or narrative level, I am immediately aware of the surrounding seconds (the specious present) of experience in the continuity of my own subjectivity. This self-awareness, which is non-reflective or "pre-reflective" in the sense that it does not require a reflective act of consciousness, delivers a sense of ipseity, a sense that this thinking process is mine – that *I* am the one who is listening to the melody or uttering the sentence. And my anticipatory sense of the next note of the melody, or of where the sentence is heading, or that I will continue to think, is also, implicitly, an anticipatory sense that these will be experiences *for me*, or that *I* will be the one listening, speaking, or thinking.

This notion of a non-reflective self-awareness does a large amount of work. Not only does it allow for the basic sense of self implicit in consciousness, it can also help to account for the possibility of reflection, to explain why there is a subjective or qualitative "feel" to consciousness, and to give an account of why mental states are conscious, an account which differs from those given by higher-order representational theories (Seager and Bourget, chapter 20; Carruthers, chapter 21).

Non-reflective self-awareness is distinguished from a more explicitly reflective self-consciousness. While engaged in a world-directed action, for example, I attend to the object or event that is the focus of my concern; I do not attend to myself, but I do have an implicit awareness of what I am doing. I am there for myself, even when I do not expressly direct my attention back to myself. As Sartre puts it,

> every positional consciousness of an object is at the same time a non-positional consciousness of itself. If I count the cigarettes which are in that case . . . [it] is very possible that I have no positional consciousness of counting them. Then I do not [explicitly] know myself as counting. Yet . . . I have a non-thetic [non-reflective] consciousness of my adding activity. If anyone questioned me, indeed, if anyone should ask, "What are you doing there?" I should reply at once, "I am counting." (Sartre 1943, pp. 19–20 [1956, p. liii]; also see, e.g., Heidegger 1989, p. 226 [1982, p. 159])

This contrasts with Brentano's position, according to which, as I count the cigarettes, or to use his example, as I listen to music, I am equally aware of two objects: the music and myself.

> In the same mental phenomenon in which the sound is present to our minds we simultaneously apprehend the mental phenomenon itself. What is more, we apprehend it in accordance with its dual nature insofar as it has the sound as content within it, and insofar as it has itself as content at the same time. We can say that the sound is the *primary object* of the *act* of hearing, and that the act of hearing itself is the *secondary object*. (Brentano 1874, pp. 179–80 [1973, pp. 127–8])

Husserl and phenomenologists such as Sartre and Heidegger disagree: my awareness of my experience is not an awareness of it *as an object*. My awareness is non-objectifying in the sense that I am not a spectator; I am not introspecting or attending to this experience in a thematic way. Of course, this is exactly what I can do in an act of reflection. Indeed, in order for reflection to be possible, my conscious experience has to become my intentional object, and for that to happen, it has to be already available as something that I can attend to. Retention is precisely the process that keeps my own consciousness available for my reflective regard. If that were not the case, then reflection, in the sense of an introspective reflection, could not be distinguished from memory.

On the phenomenological view, to have a self-experience does not entail the apprehension of an object called "the self"; it does not entail the existence of a distinctive experience of a self alongside other experiences (Sartre 1936). When Hume (1739) famously declared that he could find only perceptions or feelings, but could not find a self when he searched his experiences, it seems clear that he overlooked the specific ipseity of his own experiences. Indeed, he was not looking just anywhere for the self; he was looking only among his *own* experiences, and he seemingly recognized them as his own. His ability to reflectively introspect on his own experience is based on the immediate self-awareness that he failed to recognize as an awareness of self.

Phenomenologists are in agreement with philosophers like Nagel (1974) and Searle (1992), that to have an experience necessarily means that there is *something it's like* for the subject to have that experience. Indeed, this applies not only to the obvious cases of pain, pleasure, emotion, and other bodily sensations, it extends to all kinds of experiences, including perception, desire, and thought. What it's like to taste a lemon is different from what it's like to remember tasting a lemon, or from what it's like to see a lemon, or to count the lemons on the table, or to think about photographing a lemon. These experiential qualitative differences are not anonymous; they are given in a first-person perspective. That is, they are given not only as differential qualities, but with the common element that they are *my* experiences. The taste, the memory, the visual experience, the thinking are all experiences that *I* am undergoing or living through. But this is an essential part of what it means to say that there is something it's like to experience these things. Unless a mental process is characterized by this implicit self-awareness there would be no one there undergoing the experience, and there would be nothing it's like to undergo the process.

This first-order, non-reflective self-awareness is also what allows me to say that when I listen to music, or count cigarettes, I am doing so consciously. If I were not aware that I was doing so, then I would be doing so unconsciously. This contrasts with higher-order (e.g., higher-order thought/perception or HOT/HOP) accounts of what makes a mental state conscious (e.g., Armstrong 1968; Carruthers, chapter 21 and 1996, 2000; Rosenthal 1997). Higher-order theories propose that a higher-order level of cognition is what makes the first-order level of phenomenal experience conscious. Without the higher-order cognition, the mental state, for example of hearing music or counting cigarettes, would be unconscious. On this view, the intransitive qualitative feel of experience presupposes a capacity for higher-order awareness: "such self-awareness is a conceptually necessary condition for an organism to be a subject of phenomenal feelings, or for there to be anything that its experiences are like" (Carruthers 1996, p. 152). For Carruthers, what is required is a reflective self-awareness. In contrast to this idea, the phenomenologists contend that the fact that at the first-order, pre-reflective level, something is experienced, "and is in this sense conscious, does not and cannot mean that this is the object of an act of consciousness, in the sense that a perception, a presentation, or a judgment is directed upon it" (Husserl 1900–1/2001, I, p. 273). The self-consciousness that makes experience conscious in the very moment of that experience is not a higher-order monitoring or an additional mental state. Rather, it is an intrinsic feature of the first-order experience.

Phenomenologists thus reject the view that a mental state is conscious because it is a state we are conscious *of* – that is, they reject the view that a mental state becomes conscious only because another mental state takes it as an object. If that were the case, we would find ourselves involved in an infinite regress, assuming that the higher-order state is conscious. Higher-order theorists, however, may maintain that the higher-order state is not conscious. As Rosenthal suggests (1997, p. 745), the second-order state could become conscious only if accompanied by a (nonconscious) third-order thought. Even if it is possible to avoid the regress in this way, however, an appeal to nonconscious states in order to explain what makes a first-order state conscious doesn't explain anything. That is, it is not clear why the relation between two otherwise nonconscious processes should make one of them conscious (see Zahavi 1999).

The phenomenological alternative of non-reflective self-consciousness involves neither infinite regress nor magical emergence. "[T]here is no infinite regress here, since a consciousness has no need at all of a reflecting [higher-order] consciousness in order to be conscious of itself. It simply does not posit itself as an object" (Sartre 1936, p. 29 [1957, p. 45]). Rather, to be non-reflectively self-aware is, as Sartre puts it, the mode of existence of consciousness itself. This is not a mystery, however, since one can give a reasoned account of how non-reflective self-awareness is possible due to the temporal structure of experience.

Embodied Consciousness

If the account so far seems overly mentalistic, it is important to note that for such phenomenologists as Husserl, Heidegger, and Merleau-Ponty, consciousness is both embodied and situated in the world. The first-person point of view on the world is always defined by the situation of the perceiver's body, which concerns not simply location and posture, but action in pragmatic contexts and interaction with other people. The subject, as perceiver/actor, is embodied, not simply in an objective sense, but in an enactive way that is tacitly self-given in the perception or action. The phenomenologists follow Husserl's terminological distinction between *Leib* and *Körper*, that is, between the lived body, i.e., the body as it is non-reflectively living, and the body as it is perceived or thought of as an intentional object (Husserl 1952).

My conscious perception of an object in the environment involves complex proprioceptive and kinesthetic information about my bodily situation that allows me to be able to reach for something or use it without first having to look for my hand. Every sensory appearance is correlated to a kinesthetic experience (Husserl 1907/1997) and this produces within experience an implicit and pervasive reference to one's lived body. To what extent these embodied processes reach the level of explicit consciousness, or whether most of it remains at a recessive level may differ from one subject to the next, or from one situation to the next. The important point is that these proprioceptive and kinesthetic processes have an effect on consciousness and on our capacities for attention and action. To the extent that I am conscious of these lived bodily processes in some situations, this consciousness is quite different from the perception that I have of an object. To find where an object is located I may have to look or feel around, but I never have to do that in regard to my body. I am non-reflectively aware, not only of where my hands and feet are, but also of what I can do with them. Husserl thus suggests that this body awareness registers as an "I can." My lived body, when it perceives something, uses something, or moves through the world, enactively experiences; it is itself non-reflectively in that experience, in terms of affectivity or action, capability or disposition to action.

The body is also the anchor for the egocentric spatial framework that characterizes perceptual consciousness and one's orientation toward the world. In this regard, phenomenologists call attention to the importance of bodily movements (the movements of the eye, manipulations by the hand, the locomotion of the body, etc.) for consciousness of space and spatial objects (see Husserl 1907/1997; Merleau-Ponty 1945/1962). In those movements that are taken up in intentional action, however, the body tends to efface itself. When I run after the bus, to use one of Sartre's examples, I certainly have a sense of what I am doing and what I *can* do, but I am not aware of my precise movements or postures. I am not aware, for example, of how my arms may be moving in coordination with my legs. While my bodily activity is fully integrated with the intentional action that I am performing, I am not explicitly conscious of those movements, although I am implicitly (non-reflectively) conscious that I am running. In this sense, the effects of embodiment permeate my experience.

There is something it's like to jump to catch a ball, and part of what it's like is that I am in fact jumping. There is something different to what it's like to sit and imagine (or remember) myself jumping to catch the ball, and at least part of that difference has to do with the fact and the experience that I am sitting rather than jumping, although none of this may be explicit in my experience. (Gallagher & Zahavi 2005)

For some phenomenologists, it is this juncture of embodiment and consciousness which holds promise for bridging phenomenology and natural scientific approaches to consciousness, even acknowledging the difference in disciplinary attitudes. Merleau-Ponty (1942/1963) once indicated that there is a truth in naturalism that is important for phenomenology. What natural science has to say about the body is necessarily correlated with the first-person accounts of phenomenology since the lived body and the scientifically studied, biological body are one and the same body. Despite the different approaches taken by phenomenology and neuropsychology or the cognitive neuroscience of consciousness, there should be no inconsistencies. The issue for continuing investigation is whether phenomenology can say things about consciousness that natural science cannot say, and vice versa.

See also 20 Representationalism about consciousness; 21 Higher-order theories of consciousness; 35 Sensory and perceptual consciousness.

Further Readings

Bernet, R., Kern, I., and Marbach, E. (1993) *An Introduction to Husserlian Phenomenology.* Evanston, IL: Northwestern University Press.

Madison, G. (1981) *The Phenomenology of Merleau-Ponty: A Search for the Limits of Consciousness.* Athens: Ohio University Press.

Sokolowski, R. (2000) *Introduction to Phenomenology.* Cambridge: Cambridge University Press.

Wider, K. (1997) *The Bodily Nature of Consciousness: Sartre and Contemporary Philosophy of Mind.* Ithaca, NY: Cornell University Press.

Zahavi, D. (2003) *Husserl's Phenomenology.* Stanford, CA: Stanford University Press.

References

Armstrong, D. M. (1968) *A Materialist Theory of the Mind.* London: Routledge and Kegan Paul.

Brentano, F. (1874/1973) *Psychologie vom empirischen Standpunkt / Psychology from an Empirical Standpoint.* L. L. McAlister, trans. Hamburg/London: Felix Meiner/Routledge.

Carruthers, P. (1996) *Language, Thoughts and Consciousness. An Essay in Philosophical Psychology.* Cambridge: Cambridge University Press.

Carruthers, P. (2000) *Phenomenal Consciousness.* Cambridge: Cambridge University Press.

Gallagher, S. (1986) Hyletic experience and the lived body. *Husserl Studies* 3, 131–66.

Gallagher, S. and Zahavi, D. (2005) Phenomenological approaches to self-consciousness. *Stanford Encyclopedia of Philosophy.* http://www.plato.stanford.edu/entries/self-consciousness-phenomenological/>

Gurwitsch, A. (1966) *Studies in Phenomenology and Psychology.* Evanston, IL: Northwestern University Press.

Heidegger, M. (1982) *The Basic Problems of Phenomenology.* A. Hofstadter, trans. Bloomington: Indiana University Press.

Hume, D. (1739/1975) *A Treatise of Human Nature*. L. A. S. Bigge (ed.). Oxford: Clarendon Press.

Husserl, E. (1900–1/2001) *Logical Investigations*. J. N. Findlay, trans. London: Routledge.

Husserl, E. (1901/1984) *Logische Untersuchungen. Zweiter Teil: Untersuchungen zur Phänomenologie und Theorie der Erkenntnis [Logical Investigations. Second Part: Investigations Concerning Phenomenology and the Theory of Knowledge]*. Ursula Panzer (ed.). The Hague: Martinus Nijhoff.

Husserl, E. (1907/1997) *Thing and Space: Lectures of 1907*. R. Rojcewicz, trans. Dordrecht: Kluwer.

Husserl, E. (1913/1982) *Ideas Pertaining to a Pure Phenomenology and to a Phenomenological Philosophy, First Book: General Introduction to a Pure Phenomenology*. F. Kersten, trans. The Hague: Martinus Nijhoff.

Husserl, E. (1928/1991) *On the Phenomenology of the Consciousness of Internal Time (1893–1917)*. J. B. Brough, trans. The Hague: Kluwer.

Husserl, E. (1952/1989) *Ideas Pertaining to a Pure Phenomenology and to a Phenomenological Philosophy, Second Book. Studies in the Phenomenology of Constitution*. M. Biemel (ed.), R. Rojcewicz and A. Schuwer, trans. Dordrecht: Kluwer.

James, W. (1892) *Psychology: The Briefer Course*. London: Macmillan.

McKenna, W. (1982) *Husserl's "Introductions to Phenomenology": Interpretation and Critique*. Dordrecht: Kluwer.

Marbach, E. (1993) *Mental Representation and Consciousness: Towards a Phenomenological Theory of Representation and Reference*. Dordrecht: Kluwer.

Merleau-Ponty, M. (1942/1963) *La Structure du comportement*. Paris: Presses Universitaires de France. Translated as *The Structure of Behaviour*. Boston: Beacon Press.

Merleau-Ponty, M. (1945/1962) *Phenomenology of Perception*. C. Smith, trans. London: Routledge and Kegan Paul.

Nagel, T. (1974) What is it like to be a bat? *Philosophical Review* 83, 435–50.

Rosenthal, D. M. (1997) A theory of consciousness. In N. Block, O. Flanagan, and G. Güzeldere (eds.), *The Nature of Consciousness*, 729–53. Cambridge, MA: MIT Press.

Sartre, J.-P. (1936/1957) *The Transcendence of the Ego*. F. Williams and R. Kirkpatrick, trans. New York: The Noonday Press.

Sartre, J.-P. (1943/1956) *Being and Nothingness*. H. E. Barnes, trans. New York: Philosophical Library.

Searle, J. R. (1992) *The Rediscovery of the Mind*. Cambridge, MA: MIT Press.

Zahavi, D. (1999) *Self-Awareness and Alterity: A Phenomenological Investigation*. Evanston, IL: Northwestern University Press.

Zahavi, D. (2003) Inner time-consciousness and pre-reflective self-awareness. In D. Welton (ed.), *The New Husserl: A Critical Reader*, 157–80. Bloomington: Indiana University Press.

54

Eastern Methods for Investigating Mind and Consciousness

JONATHAN SHEAR

The Need for Systematic First-Person Methodologies

The study of human consciousness poses unique difficulties for science. Consciousness and its contents are intrinsically private, "first-person" phenomena and scientific method relies on public, "third-person" data for establishing objective facts. This might seem to imply that consciousness is *in principle* beyond the range of scientific investigation. Scientific method, however, is quite capable of studying things purely indirectly when they are not observable. The quantum fluctuations of empty space underlying all chemical transformations are a clear example, known with exquisite accuracy from their effects, despite the fact that (according to standard quantum theory) it is impossible *in principle* to observe them directly. And for over a century psychologists and other researchers have routinely evaluated scientific theories and claims about consciousness in terms of public, objectively observable correlates and effects (experiential reports, physiological states, behavioral dispositions, etc.). But such objective phenomena have to be correlated with internal, subjective experiences to be taken to be about consciousness at all. And this presents researchers with some major problems.

One of the major factors in the enormous progress scientific knowledge has made in recent centuries is the development of highly sophisticated objective means for exploring the world around us, from proton-scattering microscopes, X-ray crystallography and computer-assisted gene-splicing to continent-wide radio telescope arrays and satellite gravitational-mapping. However, for various historical reasons, modern science has not paid comparable attention to developing sophisticated means for exploring the inner world of consciousness. As a result, while contemporary research on consciousness often uses very sophisticated objective methodologies (electroencephalography (EEG), functional magnetic resonance imagery (fMRI), molecular biochemistry, etc.) for investigating the *correlates* of subjective states, the methods used to locate and identify *the subjective states themselves* are generally rather simple and commonsensical by contrast (remembering a string of numbers, visualizing a scene, feeling an emotion, focusing on a computer generated pattern, etc.). In short, there is a great asymmetry between the sophistication of the means used to explore the objective and the subjective sides of the correlations essential to the scientific study of consciousness. And relying on what amounts to merely commonsensical, "Aristotelian" methodologies to explore the subjective domain can only be expected to limit our progress, no matter how sophisticated our objective methodologies are.

Eastern Meditation Traditions

The task of developing sophisticated scientifically useful first-person methodologies does not have to begin *de novo*, however. Meditation traditions in Eastern cultures have devoted a great deal of attention to developing systematic procedures for exploring the inner domain of consciousness for many centuries. The main purpose of these traditions has generally been to produce such things as inner "bliss," psychological "freedom," "higher" states of consciousness, contact with the "divine," and even simple worldly success, rather than the exploration of consciousness per se. Nevertheless, in the service of such ends Yoga, Vedanta, Therevada, Mahayana Buddhism, Taoism, Sufism, and other major meditation traditions have developed a wide variety of procedures using different modalities (sensory, affective, cognitive, non-cognitive, etc.) and objects (body, breath, feelings, thoughts, mental images) to explore and develop the full range of human consciousness. The results of these explorations are not always consistent, and the theories they have given rise to often differ, especially at their more metaphysical levels. Nevertheless, some common features emerge. These include widespread claims that it is possible to refine consciousness (and underlying physiology) to display the ground, structures, and dynamics of consciousness underlying all human experience, generate unusual higher states of consciousness, and enhance ordinary mental and physical functioning in the process (Shear 2006).

Research on Meditation

These claims, if true, would clearly be of great significance for the scientific study of consciousness. Thus it is not surprising that as researchers in the West have begun to be familiar with them these claims have become the subject of ongoing scientific scrutiny, and thousands of studies have now been conducted, with over a thousand published in recent decades. The results of these studies often appear to be inconsistent, however. Some studies using standard scientific protocols, for example, show significant reduction of metabolic activity during and after the practice, as often predicted in the traditional literature. But other studies show no significant change, or even increased metabolic activity. The same lack of consistency appears in studies of other physiological variables such as blood chemistry, EEG coherence, respiration, autonomic stability, and overall physical health. Similarly, while some studies show significant positive effects on psychological variables such as anxiety, creativity, and self-actualization, as predicted in the traditional literature, other studies do not. The same thing has to be said about studies of sociological variables such as grade point averages, job performance, substance abuse, and prisoner rehabilitation (Wallace, Orme-Johnson, & Dillbeck 1990; Murphy & Donovan 1999).

Interpreting the Research – Two Common Mistakes

Given the differences between different meditation procedures, however, different outcomes are just what we ought to expect. It should not be at all surprising, for example, that procedures that emphasize regulating the breath and procedures that ignore the breath should produce distinctly different respiratory effects both in and out of meditation, as research has shown (Austin 1998, pp. 93–9). Nor should it be surprising, as research has also shown, that procedures emphasizing concentration and those emphasizing effortless-ness should have different effects on psychological and physiological measures of anxiety (Eppley, Abrams, & Shear 1989). And the same thing can be said about other variables studied. But interest in meditation is something on the whole new in the West, and this has made it easy to overlook the differences between procedures and regard them all as more or less the same, and expect them all to produce similar effects. This in turn has led to two common, but opposing, misinterpretations of the actual research results.

The first mistake, sometimes made by critics of the notion of meditation in general, has been to note the conflicting outcomes, and conclude that "meditation" (considered gener-ically) has no scientifically significant effects. Methodologically, however, lumping all meditations together in this way is just as inappropriate as lumping all medicines together, and concluding from conflicting outcomes that no medicines produced significant effects either. A second, opposite mistake arising from lumping meditation procedures together, sometimes made by supporters of the notion of meditation in general, is to assume that when a particular procedure produces significant results on some variable, comparable results can be expected from other procedures as well. No knowledgeable person, of course, would make such a mistake with regard to medicines, even those differing only as different isomers of the same chemical.

Such errors, found in a wide variety of publications (including introductory psychology texts), highlight the importance of attending to proper scientific methodology in interpret-ing research. This is especially important in the field of meditation research. For meditation has often been associated with all sorts of claims, from the commonsensical to the fantas-tic, and it is all too easy to use solid research to give an inappropriate halo of credibility to extreme claims, and, conversely, associations of meditation with extreme claims to dis-count solid research. While the traditional meditation-related literature can provide natural beginning points for scientific research, care has to be taken to evaluate each claim and procedure on its own individual merits, rather than lumping them together and drawing inappropriate conclusions, whether positive or negative.

Levels of Awareness

Eastern meditation traditions on the whole are generally more concerned with the *develop-ment* of consciousness than investigation of it as an end in itself. Nevertheless, investigation of consciousness is usually held to be a crucial part of this development, and important similarities are readily locatable in most traditions' accounts. A common feature of these accounts is the claim that our ordinary awareness is the product of the conscious and unconscious influence of a number of levels of awareness. These, following the typology of Yoga and Vedanta, include from the "surface" inward, (i) the externally oriented *senses*, (ii) the discursive thinking *mind*, (iii) the *intellect* capable of discriminating between the mind's diverse contents, (iv) the *ego* that experiences these contents and takes them to be its own, (v) *pure positive affect* (happiness, bliss, etc.), the desire for which underlies the ego's responses to different experiences, and finally (vi) *pure consciousness itself*, without which experience could not exist in the first place.

We are all familiar with the first two of these levels, senses and thinking mind, intro-spectively. The third and fourth levels, intellect and ego, are mainstays of commonsense psychology, despite the fact that they are at best very hard to specify introspectively, as the disputes between Descartes, Hume, and Kant make clear. The last two levels, pure positive affect and pure consciousness, however, are not only outside the grasp of ordinary intro-spection but unknown to, and even ungraspable by, common sense. Thus it is not surprising that Western psychology and philosophy have traditionally paid a great deal of attention to the first four levels, and very little, in the absence of the relevant experiences, to the last two. Eastern meditative traditions, however, maintain that it is possible to gain clear experiential knowledge of all of these levels, including the deepest, and that this knowledge is necessary for full understanding of human nature.

Pure Consciousness

Experience of the deepest level, that of pure consciousness awake to its own nature in and by itself, is generally held to be especially important. The defining characteristic of this experience is the *complete absence* of all sounds, tastes, thoughts, feelings, images, and any-thing else that one can ever imagine. Techniques for achieving this experience differ. (They can be effortless or intensively concentrative, involve the meanings of thoughts or ignore it, attend to bodily awareness or be purely mental, etc.) But they have in common the idea that it is possible for all empirical content to disappear, while one nevertheless remains awake. The ancient Indian *Upanishads* offer the analogy of the *space* that remains when all objects are removed (the space that was necessary for their existence in the first place). But this is just an analogy, for as the *Upanishads* also make clear, the experience itself is devoid even of any subjective "space" in which phenomenal objects could appear.

What then is the experience like? By all accounts, it is not *like* anything. One can have it and remember it – one knows that one was not asleep. But one does not remember it *as* anything at all. It is just *itself* – unimaginable and indescribable.

Such an empty experience might at first glance seem completely uninteresting, even if it could in fact be had. Nevertheless, almost every major meditation tradition holds that it is necessary for full knowledge of human consciousness, and essential for its full development. In particular, it is widely held both to facilitate growth of higher states of consciousness and to provide an optimum platform for exploration of the fine structure and dynamics of awareness in general.

The experience itself is extraordinarily abstract. Indeed it is the logical ultimate of abstrac-tion, since by all accounts it is what remains after everything that can possibly be removed from experience has been removed, while one nevertheless remains awake. Given this extreme abstractness, it is not surprising that different traditions interpret it differently according to their own metaphysical perspectives, and it has been referred to by terms as different as "pure consciousness," "being," "nothingness" and "self." Many traditions use various combinations of such terms, despite their seemingly contradictory nature, or even (as in Zen) *because of* their contradictory nature, to emphasize the experience itself, as con-trasted with mere concepts *about* it. In short, the experience is one thing, and metaphysical interpretations of it are quite another. Eastern traditions, to be sure, sometimes argue about whether there can be more than one kind of completely contentless experience. We will return to such questions later. For our present purposes, however, it is enough to note that tradition after tradition emphasizes that all thinking and concepts, including the most cher-ished doctrines, have to be left behind before the experience of pure consciousness, *as it is in and by itself*, can emerge with clarity.

This experience of pure consciousness (or pure "emptiness," "suchness," "being," etc.) by itself, at the deepest level of inner awareness, is widely held to provide the optimum ground for first-person investigation of the subtle components and dynamics of consciousness held to underlie all ordinary experience. It is also generally held to be the first stage of an extended developmental process. For there is widespread agreement that in addition to being experienceable by itself, pure consciousness can in time also come to be recognized along with all the other, more familiar contents of experience, as further "higher" states of consciousness develop. Different traditions describe various stages and sub-stages, but three major, widely reported higher states can readily be identified: pure consciousness (1) *by itself*, (2) *along with* one's other experiences, and (3) as *the ground* of all experience. Nevertheless, the idea of pure consciousness is on the whole something new to Western investigators, and important objections to its very possibility have been raised.

Philosophical Objections to the Idea of "Pure Consciousness"

Some thirty years ago, the philosopher Steven Katz raised an *in principle* objection to the notion of a pure consciousness experience. Katz argued that all human experiences arise in cultural contexts and are "shaped" by culture-dependent elements such as one's language, images, beliefs, and symbols. Thus there cannot be any experiences that are the same across different cultures. As a result, there cannot be any single (type of) experience across different cultures for the phrase "pure consciousness" to refer to in the first place (Katz 1978). There is a simple logical response to this objection however. The defining characteristic of the experience in question is the *complete absence* of any empirical content. So any experience correctly identified as of pure consciousness has no content at all to be "shaped" by such things as language and expectations, or mark it as culturally determined in any other way. Indeed, meditation traditions regularly emphasize that all such factors have to be left behind before the experience can occur. Another way of putting this is to note that if two experiences differ, at least one of them has to have some content, and could not properly qualify as a pure consciousness experience in the first place.

A second objection, often associated with the tradition of philosophical phenomenology, is that consciousness always has to be *of* something. As a result, the notion of contentless consciousness is simply contradictory. This argument reflects the obvious fact that consciousness *ordinarily* has objective content that it is *of*. However this fact obviously does not by itself imply that, as a matter of empirical fact, consciousness always *has to* (in contrast to *usually does*) have such content. And there is no a priori reason why one should restrict the term "consciousness" in this way, in the face of the relevant historical usages. This seeming *in principle* objection has often been traced to Kant, who raised the idea of "pure original unchanging consciousness" having no empirical content or distinguishing feature of its own, but rejected it as outside the grasp of all human awareness. Kant's rejection, however, was quite careful. For he held that there was no *logical* problem with the notion of pure consciousness, and even raised the possibility that conscious beings other than people might experience it themselves. It is just that as a matter of empirical fact, such experiences are, as he argued, outside our grasp (Kant 1964, pp. 157, 250, etc.). If Eastern (and a few Western monastic) meditation traditions are correct, however, Kant's rejection is simply a result of the fact that his knowledge of the range of possible experience was limited here.

Research on Pure Consciousness

Even if such objections to the bare *possibility* of experiences of pure consciousness do not hold up, the question of whether a given experience is ever *in fact* properly identifiable as being of pure consciousness still remains. Here some actual research results turn out to be relevant. This research arose in response to unique claims about physiological correlates of this particular experience found in texts of major meditation traditions. These traditions claim that as awareness settles down in meditation, the body gains a deeply restful state in which metabolic activity decreases markedly. (It should be noted that not every technique either has, or even intends to have, this effect.) That metabolic activity might decrease during meditation is not so surprising, for one is sitting quietly with eyes closed. But many traditions (Yoga, Vedanta, Zen, etc.) go much further and claim that when the deep level of pure, contentless consciousness is reached in meditation, metabolic activity decreases so much that respiration spontaneously becomes *suspended entirely*. Indeed, this correlation is so widely recognized that traditional Zen texts, for example, sometimes use the expression "*chi shi*" (i.e., "breath stops") to refer to the experience itself. This further physiological claim has now been corroborated in laboratory settings where, using subjects practicing the basic transcendental meditation (TM) technique, researchers have found episodes of what appear to be the experience in question (marked by subjects' button presses) to be highly correlated with periods of complete respiratory suspension (indicated by completely flat segments lasting a half-minute or so on otherwise regularly rising and falling pneumotachygraph tracings). In addition there was no compensatory hyperventilation after these periods, as there would be if the breath had been held, and, even more strikingly, the oxygen and carbon dioxide pressures in the blood remain constant, precisely the opposite of what happens when breath is held. These periods were also differentiated from sleep apnea (where respiration also stops briefly) and onset of drowsy-state sleep by various physiological parameters (Farrow & Hebert 1982; Travis & Wallace 1997).

The above results indicate that a very unusual, specific physiology is in fact associated with reports of the pure consciousness experience, as the texts of so many meditation traditions have claimed for centuries. (The experience has also been associated with high levels of EEG coherence and other parameters unknown to ancient observers.) The most natural explanation of the conjunction of reports of contentless awareness and this unusual physiology, in culture after culture throughout history, is that the reports reflect the experience people naturally have when in this particular physiological state (rather than being, as Katz's argument would have it, unexplained coincidental products of the many, often very different cultural contexts in which they occur).

These observations have another, more practical implication as well. For they suggest that the above physiological measures can serve as an objective, third-person measure to help evaluate the reliability of people's first-person reports of the experience. And this is precisely the kind of correlation that first-person methodologies need in order to become properly integrated into the body of scientific methodologies in general.

Absolutely Contentless?

It should be noted, however, that even if the natural response to this experience is to describe it as "contentless," it is still appropriate to raise the question of whether it is in fact actually *completely* contentless. For while experiences associated with the above phys-iological state might be so subtle and abstract that they naturally *seem* to be completely contentless, they might nevertheless actually have *some*, albeit very abstract, content. Indeed, one might, for example, have an experience that one at first took to be contentless, only to conclude after having another even more abstract one later that it did in fact have some content now recognizable by the fact that it is absent from the newer experience.

This is not an entirely fanciful possibility. Texts of Eastern traditions list various extremely abstract experiences, and major traditions have debated related questions for centuries. Some traditions (e.g., Therevada) argue (against Yoga, Vedanta, and Zen) that all states properly called "conscious" have to have *some* content, even if nothing but "voidness" itself. Others (e.g., Tibetan Buddhism) are sometimes thought to hold that several apparently contentless experiences exist. Others (e.g., Yoga) hold that experiences can differ by having different physiological substrates, even when, as completely objectless, they are indistin-guishable phenomenologically. Moreover, within each system the experiences differentiated are usually held to have importantly different psychological and behavioral effects.

These distinctions, however, have little or no bearing on the topic of meditation as a tool for empirical investigation of consciousness. Thus, for simplicity, the phrase "pure consciousness" will continue to be used here to refer to the experience of empirically con-tentless awareness, without concern, in the absence of relevant research, for whether the experience is absolutely contentless or only seems to be so, or whether the phrase as used here ultimately turns out to refer to a single experience or a family of closely related ones.

Two Applications in the Field of Adult Development

In the middle of the last century, Abraham Maslow and other psychologists observed that highly creative, successful people in diverse fields often display a cluster of psychological traits, now often referred to in terms of "self-actualization." These include, among other things, acceptance of self and others, autonomy, creativity, democratic interpersonal values, spontaneity, field-independence, and efficient perception of reality. They also found that the most highly "self-actualized" individuals often report what are now called "peak experi-ences," including experiences of pure consciousness and other related states described in the traditional meditation literature. The same literature also maintains that psychological traits characteristic of "self-actualization" are common results of successful meditation practice in general, and these advanced experiences in particular. These reports led psych-ologists to investigate whether meditation techniques could in fact produce growth of self-actualization as well as experiences of "higher" states.

Studies have now found growth on standard measures of self-actualization follow-ing (in varying degrees) the practice of different procedures, and correlations between meditation-induced experiences of pure consciousness and growth of traits characteristic of self-actualization (Alexander, Rainforth, & Gelderloos 1991; Murphy & Donovan 1999; Wallace et al. 1990). These results reinforce the correlations between these experiences and high levels of self-actualization observed previously by self-actualization researchers. They also suggest that, to the extent that meditation techniques prove capable of producing experiences of pure consciousness reliably, researchers may for the first time be able to deter-mine whether these experiences play an active role in the growth of self-actualization, as traditional texts would suggest, or are merely peculiar artifacts, as has often been thought.

An application in the study of what Maslow and others call the "further reaches" of adult development can also be noted. Since the work of Walter Stace in the last century, two experiences have been widely held to be the most important, culture-invariant experiences in the literature of mysticism. These experiences, referred to since Stace as the "introvertive" and "extrovertive" mystical experiences, respectively, turn out to be the first and third of the three "higher" states described earlier, namely pure consciousness (i) by itself and (iii) permeating all other awareness. If meditation techniques prove capable of producing both of them reliably – the second, more advanced of the two is naturally much more rare – researchers would have a way to begin to investigate their development, phenomenology, and effects in a scientific way.

The above examples suggest something of how meditation, as a tool to produce experiences of higher states of consciousness, can facilitate research on "higher" levels of adult development. It may also be expected to contribute in a very different, more general way as well.

Investigating Consciousness from Within

While they may approach the investigation of the nature of consciousness somewhat differently, different meditation traditions generally agree that the non-fluctuating nature of the deepest level of consciousness can become a permanent aspect of one's awareness along with ordinary experience. Furthermore, since this level is free of distorting content of its own, it provides an optimum platform for investigating the other contents of mind. By analogy, a waveless body of water provides the optimal platform for studying the fine structure and dynamics of ripples and waves as they emerge in response to specific inputs. In other words, the less internal "noise" a system generates, the more accurate its reception can be expected to be.

Thus in its first three chapters, the *Yoga Sutras*, for example, (i) defines "yoga" as reducing the fluctuations of the mind until pure consciousness is experienced and (ii) describes methods intended to stabilize consciousness along with the experience of objects until it "can shine with the light of the object alone," devoid of all distracting fluctuations, and (iii) describes methods to introduce inputs into this non-fluctuating awareness as a way (among other things) to investigate all the layers of phenomenal experience, subtle to gross. Therevada and Tibetan Buddhism are also particularly well known for emphasizing the development of awareness so steady that it can attend to a single mental or physical object for very long periods of time without being disturbed by a single thought, and using this awareness to observe the fine fabrics of awareness dispassionately. Centuries of such observations have enabled these and other traditions to produce extensive, detailed maps of subtle structures and mechanisms said to underlie experience in general.

These traditional maps however cannot simply be accepted as scientific. Indeed, they are not even always consistent. Some of these differences may perhaps be more philosophical than empirical, but others are straightforwardly empirical (for example, the orders-of-magnitude differences of duration of supposed "minimal elements" of consciousness reported in different texts of Therevada). Nevertheless, the results of centuries of exploration and mapping would still seem to offer natural beginning points for modern meditation-related research into consciousness, especially where the results of different traditions appear to agree.

Important objections to the very notion of using meditation as a tool for scientific research have been raised, however.

Changing the Observer

In science, useful refinement of observation often arises from refining external instruments of observation. But in meditation, as Bertrand Russell argued a century ago, it is the observer who is changed. And unusual perceptions produced by nervous systems in altered states are likely to be misleading, if not simply false, as perceptions generated by nervous systems altered by alcohol show. Thus, Russell concluded, the very fact that nervous systems are significantly changed by meditation practices makes any unusual experiences they produce inherently suspect (Russell 1961).

There is however a straightforward response to this objection. Change, even of the nervous system, can be for the better as well as for the worse, as surgical interventions fortunately sometimes demonstrate. Thus determining whether a particular type of change is for the better or the worse is an empirical matter. And relevant evidence exists. Anecdotally, throughout history meditation has typically been associated with enhanced, rather than impaired, mental and perceptual acuity. Indeed, this is one of the reasons widely given for its long-standing association with martial arts, where accuracy of perception and response is crucial, and criteria are clear and demanding. Research now indicates that central nervous system and psychological functioning associated with particular meditation procedures are often enhanced in a variety of ways (autonomic stability, EEG coherence, intelligence, creativity, self-actualization, reduced anxiety, etc.). Moreover, some of this research is specifically perception-related (re decreased susceptibility to perceptual illusions, quicker reaction time, better mind–body coordination, etc.) (Wallace, Orme-Johnson, & Dillbeck 1990; Murphy & Donovan 1999). Thus Russell's presumption of detrimental alterations of nervous system functioning, the basis of his *in principle* rejection of the usefulness of meditation-related experiences, does not appear to be supported by the evidence.

The question of meditation-induced changes nevertheless remains quite important, since such changes can easily skew results quite apart from questions of perceptual accuracy. For to the extent that meditation changes a person's physiology and consciousness, it is precisely this *changed* consciousness that will be displayed. In addition the very *act* of looking at mental content introspectively can easily alter this content, since the mind producing the content is the same one that is being altered by the process of looking. The analogy of looking at one's face in a mirror is often cited in related discussions of first-person methodology: If one looks at oneself in a mirror, one can only see what one looks like *as looking at oneself*, rather than what one may have looked like just a moment before, independently of this self-reflective posture. Furthermore, the longer one looks, the more the interactive process of looking at oneself is likely to affect what one sees, whether in a mirror or introspectively. Meditation traditions may attempt to circumvent this problem by training one to observe the contents of consciousness dispassionately, from deeper non-fluctuating levels of awareness. Success here is an empirical, rather than merely conceptual matter, however. Thus what is needed here (as elsewhere in science) are methods to identify the elements of an observation that reflect the nature of what is to be investigated, as distinct from artifacts of the observing process.

This is a well-known, general problem in scientific methodology, and the issues in the case of first-person methodologies are often especially complex (Varela & Shear 1997; Velmans 2000). Nevertheless, for meditation research, a simple approach may prove particularly helpful.

Integrating First- and Third-Person Methodologies

Consider, for example, the following simple schema for integrating aspects of Eastern meditative and modern scientific theories and methods.

- Identify a potentially significant presumed component (and/or state, structure, dynamic, etc.) of consciousness described in Eastern texts, but not yet identified and/or studied scientifically.
- Locate and recruit expert meditators supposedly capable of sustaining attention on the component in question.
- Examine central nervous system correlates (by means of EEG, fMRI, biochemical markers, etc.) of purported episodes of the component to identify, if possible, a physiological "signature" of the presence of this component.
- Determine if experts trained in other meditation procedures display the same signature for attention to the component.
- Determine if "naïve" subjects display this signature during experiences where the component is supposed to play a significant (even if typically unnoticed) role.

Success with these steps would then provide evidence both (a) that the component in question was not a mere meditation-induced artifact, and (b) that it played a role in the mental processes of people in general. Physiological markers identified by the procedure could in turn also help identify relevantly adept meditators to serve as investigators. This schema is only the barest of outlines, and each step raises further methodological questions. Such subtler considerations aside, however, a few examples should illustrate, in a rough and ready way, how it might work.

Sample Applications

Eastern traditions, as noted earlier, often postulate the existence of a number of more or less discrete levels of awareness, including, from surface to depths, (i) *senses*, (ii) *thinking mind*, (iii) *intellect*, (iv) *ego*, (v) *bliss*, and (vi) *pure consciousness*. These traditions also generally hold that ordinary thought develops in stages from the deepest level up to the surface, as displayed in meditation. Such claims, if true, would have wide-ranging significance. One could begin to test them by studying expert meditators reportedly capable of sustaining awareness at each of these levels, to see if consistent physiological signatures could be located. In principle this may not be too difficult. As noted earlier, research relevant to level (vi) has been conducted already on experts from different traditions, and fMRI research relative to levels (i) and (ii) is standard.

One could then study non-meditating highly creative thinkers who report engaging in pre-verbal mental work that later develops into normal verbal thought, to see if at such times they display signatures comparable to those of the expert meditators at level (iii) above. Positive results would indicate that these signatures are not merely meditation-induced artifacts. It would also provide experimental support for the claims that the abilities of highly creative, self-actualized individuals were related to their being able to tap "deeper" levels of inner awareness, and that in some cases at least, these levels were the same as those meditation produces.

Since highly creative thinkers also often report peak experiences comparable to levels (iv) through (vi), one could in principle look for parallel signatures here, too. This research would be much more difficult to conduct, inasmuch as peak experiences often (but not necessarily) appear to come "on their own," rather than being producible at will. Nevertheless, positive results, if obtained, would extend the above conclusions to levels (iv) to (vi) as well.

For a different, somewhat more complex application of the above schema, consider a well-known problem about ordinary introspection. As common sense would have it, when one experiences something such as a patch of blue color, one knows by experience that one is experiencing it oneself. This would in turn seem to imply that the *experiencing* and the *self* must both somehow be *in* the experience. Locating these extra components introspectively, however, has proven notoriously difficult, as Hume noted so forcefully. For when we look at an experience and try to locate the experiencing and/or the self, this "being experienced by oneself" aspect typically seems, somehow, both unlocatable and (necessarily) "there."

Buddhist psychology generally responds to this problem in the following way. It maintains, much like Hume, that ordinary experience is composed of a vast number of momentary experiences succeeding each other with great rapidity. As a result, any ordinary introspective act is actually composed of a large number of these fleeting momentary experiences. This allows analysis of the above problem of introspection in terms of three distinct types of experience: (i) a momentary experience of the blue color one is looking at, (ii) another kind of momentary experience in which one *remembers* the first one *as experienced*, and (iii) a complex, longer kind of experience in which both of the first two types repeatedly appear and disappear (cf. Wallace 1999, pp. 178–80). This suggests a simple application of the above research schema, namely, to locate putative adepts in the relevant (e.g., *vipassana*) meditation procedures, and look for central nervous system correlates (fMRI, EEG, etc.) of putting sustained attention on (what seemed to them to be) each of the first two types of experience above. If the Buddhist theory is correct, one would expect very different correlates, since one experience is supposed to be memory dominated while the other is not. If appropriately different physiological signatures were found, one could then examine naïve subjects to see whether, as the theory would predict, both signatures were found intermixed during the introspective act of looking for the "being experienced by oneself" aspect of a present experience of a blue field.

Positive results would have significant implications for theories about the sense of self, the mechanics of self-introspection, and the meaning of "self" in Western psychology, phenomenology, and analytic philosophy, respectively. Negative results re the naïve subjects would have implications for Buddhist psychology. And results might simply be inconclusive, for a variety of technical reasons. What is most important here, however, is that such experiments are, in principle at least, readily devisable.

Possible research is one thing, however, and actual research quite another. In particular, whether meditators with the necessary level of proficiency actually exist will remain an open question, ancient texts and contemporary claims notwithstanding, unless or until appropriate candidates come forth and are studied. Nevertheless, it should by now be apparent that, given the many detailed Eastern accounts of components and developmental stages of all sorts of mental objects (perceptions, memories, thoughts, feelings, sense of self, etc.), the scope and potential significance of such research are enormous.

Implications for Philosophy as a Whole

Philosophical theories often reflect introspective observations that seem apparent, if not simply self-evident, to their proponents. For example, according to Descartes knowledge of one's self as a conscious being is not arrived at by reasoning. It is given self-evidently "in a simple mental intuition" that "your mind sees, feels, [and] handles" (Descartes 1987, pp. 299–301). Hume responded that when *he* introspected he encountered only discrete perceptions such as "heat or cold, light or shade, love or hatred, pain or pleasure," and he was certain that there was nothing in him at all corresponding to Descartes's "self." As a result he concluded that he and Descartes were "essentially different in this particular" and that he "could no longer reason with him" here (Hume 1980, p. 252). It might thus seem that conflicting introspective assertions basic to competing, influential philosophical theories must simply be accepted or not – to the detriment of reasoned philosophical discussion.

In the context of Eastern approaches, however, the above accounts are easily recognized as descriptions of introspection at two *different levels* of consciousness, those of (i) the senses and (iv) the ego, respectively. This would suggest that the real problem here is not one of incompatible introspective results, since both are parts of a single larger picture. It is, instead, one of drawing inferences from such experiences without the benefit of the appropriate, empirically derived schema.

Whether meditation procedures can allow us to experience the full range of the many structures, states, and levels of consciousness described in Eastern texts remains to be seen. If they can, they may enable us to generate maps of consciousness that have a completeness never before seen in the West, and that are corroborated, to the extent that this is possible, by the best Western investigative methods.

The work already done in relation to the level of (vi) pure consciousness is a beginning example. As we have already seen, the existence of the experience of pure consciousness appears to falsify the common philosophical claim that consciousness always has to have a phenomenal object. It can be argued moreover that this experience, unavailable to Descartes, Hume, and Kant, provides a unique perspective for reevaluating fundamental "paradoxes" about self arising from their analyses (Shear 1998), as Kant himself suggested it would. And it appears to have significant implications for ethics as well (Shear 2002).

Conclusion

Meditation-related research, carefully interpreted on a procedure-by-procedure and outcome-by-outcome basis, has significant implications for psychology and philosophy. It indicates that meditation can promote the growth of a variety of positive psychological traits. It also appears capable both of enhancing growth of self-actualization in general, and of generating experiences of "higher" states associated with high levels of self-actualization. Research on the most basic of these states, pure contentless consciousness, indicates that it occurs as the natural correlate of a specific physiological state. The experience of this state, basic to many Eastern traditions, has implications for a number of philosophical topics. It appears to falsify the claim, widely accepted among Western thinkers, that consciousness always has to have a phenomenal object. And it suggests a simple, empirically significant definition of "consciousness" as "that which remains when all phenomenal content is removed and one remains awake." The above results, coupled with long-standing Eastern maps of consciousness, suggest the potential value of further, related research on states and structures of consciousness, and the possibility of generating maps of internal awareness uniquely useful for psychology, philosophy, and consciousness studies in general. These examples suggest the importance of taking advantage of the long history of Eastern explorations of consciousness, and integrating the results into our own modern scientific approaches.

See also 11 Meditation; 12 Mystical experience; 53 Phenomenological approaches to consciousness; 55 An epistemology for the study of consciousness.

Further Readings

Shear, Jonathan (ed.) (2006) *The Experience of Meditation: Experts Introduce the Major Traditions.* St Paul, MN: Paragon House.

Shear, J. and Jevning, R. (1999) Pure consciousness: scientific exploration of meditation techniques. In F. Varela and J. Shear (eds.), *The View from Within: First-Person Approaches to the Study of Consciousness.* Thorverton, UK: Imprint Academic.

Wallace, B. A. (1999) The Buddhist tradition of Samatha: methods for refining and examining consciousness. In F. Varela and J. Shear (eds.), *The View from Within: First-Person Approaches to the Study of Consciousness.* Thorverton, UK: Imprint Academic.

References

Alexander, C. N., Rainforth, M. V., and Gelderloos, P. (1991) Transcendental meditation, self actualization, and psychological health: a conceptual overview and meta-analysis. *Journal of Social Behavior and Personality* 6: 5, 189–247.

Austin, James H. (1998) *Zen and the Brain.* Cambridge, MA: MIT Press.

Descartes, René (1987) *Descartes' Philosophical Writings.* E. Anscombe and P. T. Geach, trans. New York: Macmillan/Library of Liberal Arts.

Eppley, K., Abrams, A, and Shear, J. (1989) Differential effects of relaxation techniques on trait anxiety: A meta-analysis. *Journal of Clinical Psychology* 45: 6, 957–74.

Farrow, J. T. and Hebert, R. (1982) Breath suspension during the transcendental meditation technique. *Psychosomatic Medicine* 44: 2, 133–53.

Hume, David (1980) *A Treatise of Human Nature*, 2nd edn., L. A. Selby-Bigge (ed.). Oxford: Oxford University Press.

Kant, Immanuel (1964) *Critique of Pure Reason.* Norman Kemp Smith, trans. New York: Macmillan.

Katz, Stephen T. (1978) Language epistemology, and mysticism. In S. Katz (ed.), *Mysticism and Philosophical Analysis.* New York: Oxford University Press.

Murphy, Michael and Donovan, Steven (1999) *The Physical and Psychological Effects of Meditation: A Review of Contemporary Research with a Comprehensive Bibliography, 1931–1996.* Sausalito, CA: IONS. http://www. noetic.org/research/medbiblio/index.htm

Russell, Bertrand (1961) Critique of mysticism. In B. Russell, *Religion and Science.* New York: Oxford University Press.

Shear, J. (1998) Experiential clarification of the problem of self. *Journal of Consciousness Studies* 4: 5/6, 673–86.

Shear, J. (2002) Ethics and the experience of happiness. In G. William Barnard and Jeffrey J. Kripal (eds.), *Crossing Boundaries: Essays on the Ethical Status of Mysticism.* New York: Seven Bridges Press.

Shear, Jonathan (ed.) (2006) *The Experience of Meditation: Experts Introduce the Major Traditions.* St Paul, MN: Paragon House.

Travis, F. and Wallace, R. (1997) Autonomic markers during respiratory suspensions; possible markers of transcendental consciousness. *Psychophysiology* 34, 39–46.

Varela, Francisco and Shear, Jonathan (eds) (1997) *The View from Within: First-Person Approaches to the Study of Consciousness.* Thorverton, UK: Imprint Academic.

Velmans, Max (ed.) (2000) *Investigating Phenomenal Consciousness: New Methodologies and Maps.* Amsterdam: John Benjamins.

Wallace, B. A. (1999) The Buddhist tradition of Samatha: methods for refining and examining consciousness. In F. Varela and J. Shear (eds.), *The View from Within: First-Person Approaches to the Study of Consciousness.* Thorverton, UK: Imprint Academic.

55

An Epistemology for the Study of Consciousness

MAX VELMANS

The nature of consciousness is commonly thought to present a deep problem for science. Psychology and its sister disciplines have nevertheless developed many different methodologies for investigating its phenomenology, in studies of sensation, perception, emotion, thinking, and many other areas that deal directly or indirectly with how phenomena are experienced. Many examples can be found in the chapters of this book. Over the last 20 years or so, there has also been a renewed interest in the development of first-person research methods that focus on "what it's like for subjects to be" in various situations of interest to investigators, for example with the expanded use of phenomenologically inspired *qualitative methods* that are used both in isolation and in conjunction with triangulating third-person quantitative methods in psychological research (see, for example, Denzin & Lincoln 2000 for a review). Complementary first- and third-person methods are also routinely used (without embarrassment or apology) in much of neuropsychology, for example in the search for the neural correlates of consciousness using neuroimaging techniques (see Rees and Frith, chapter 43). There have also been in depth re-evaluations of how the use of such combined first- and third-person methods can be refined, for example in the field of neurophenomenology and more generally in cognitive neuroscience (see, e.g., readings in Varela & Shear 1999; Velmans 2000a; Jack & Roepstorff 2003, 2004).

The Investigation of Conscious Experiences

However, these advances in consciousness studies do not fit easily into the ways that we normally think about science. Given their first-person nature, how is it possible to investigate conscious experiences? Most people assume that the physical objects we see around us are *public*, *objective*, and *observer-independent* (they exist independently of the mind of the observer) making them suitable for investigation by traditional third-person methods. By contrast, percepts of objects and other contents of consciousness are generally thought to be *private*, *subjective*, and *observer-dependent* (their existence depends on the mind of the observer) which is thought to impede their investigation. If physical science relies on public, objective data, how can one establish a "science of consciousness" which relies, at least in part, on subjective experiences? During much of the twentieth century this problem was thought to be so acute that behaviorist psychology tried to exclude the study of consciousness from science, redefining psychology as the "study of behavior." In the words of John Watson (1913), "Psychology as a behaviorist views it is a purely objective experimental branch of natural science. Its theoretical goal is the prediction and control of behavior. Introspection forms no essential part of its method nor is the scientific value of its data dependent upon the readiness with which they lend themselves to interpretation in terms of consciousness" (p. 158). Indeed, "The time has come when psychology must discard all reference to consciousness; when it need no longer delude itself into thinking that it is making mental states the object of observation" (ibid, p. 163).

The problem of forming a science of consciousness is made more difficult by the way that consciousness and its contents are usually conceived. Substance dualists such as Descartes believed consciousness to be a state of the mind, and the mind to be an immaterial substance (*res cogitans*), placing it beyond the remit of materialist science; the nature of consciousness, on this view, is a matter for philosophers and theologians. In reaction to this, physicalists of various persuasions have tried to deal with "the problem of consciousness" by denying that consciousness exists or attempting to reduce it to something "objective" such as overt behavior or a state or function of the brain (see, for example, Baars, chapter 18, Searle, chapter 25, or the discussion of Dennett by Schneider, chapter 24).

In what follows, I suggest that these ways of conceptualising both the problems faced by a science of consciousness and how to resolve them are mistaken. While methodologies for the study of phenomenal consciousness continue to develop and various difficulties still need to be faced and overcome, it will be clear from the chapters in this book that many productive research programmes already exist. I also argue that the seemingly irresolvable dualist vs. physicalist debate about the nature of consciousness has its roots in widespread, but nevertheless false assumptions about its phenomenology that they *share*. Insofar as they misdescribe the experienced features of conscious experience, they misconstrue the problems of investigating it, giving a misleading impression of how scientific investigations of consciousness can and do proceed.

Common Assumptions about How Physical Phenomena Relate to Psychological Phenomena

A brief account of dualist and reductionist assumptions about conscious phenomenology is given in Velmans, chapter 27 of this book (see also Velmans 2000b, chs 2 to 6 for a more detailed discussion). What assumptions do they share? Substance dualists *split* the world in two ways: for example, dualist models of perception (a) separate the perceiving subject from the perceived object, and (b) separate the experience *of* the object (its conscious phenomenology) in the mind of the subject from the subject's brain (see Figure 27.1). Reductionists accept split (a) – that the perceiving subject is distinct from the perceived object – but they question split (b). While they often accept that experiences *seem* to be immaterial phenomena "in the mind," they argue that science will eventually show these to be nothing more than physical states or functions of the brain (see Figure 27.2).

In short, while dualists and reductionists disagree about the ontology of conscious experiences (about what they really *are*), by and large they agree about how they *appear* (about their phenomenology). They also agree that "physical phenomena" in the world are completely *distinct* from "conscious percepts of those phenomena" in the subject's mind or brain – underpinning the view that "physical phenomena" are public and objective while

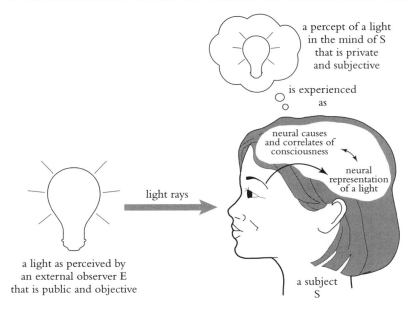

a percept of a light
in the mind of S
that is private
and subjective

is experienced
as

neural causes
and correlates of
consciousness

neural
representation
of a light

light rays

a light as perceived by
an external observer E
that is public and objective

a subject
S

Figure 55.1 A dualist way of viewing the relation of observations to experiences (adapted from figures drawn by John Wood for Velmans 2000).

"conscious phenomena" are private and subjective. This separation of physical from conscious phenomena is illustrated by the way these are conventionally thought to relate to each other in studies of visual perception, as shown in Figure 55.1.

In this basic experimental arrangement, the subject (S) is asked to focus on the light (the stimulus) and report on or respond to what she experiences, while the experimenter (E) controls the stimulus and observes S's behavior and what is going on in her brain. E has observational access to the stimulus and to S's brain states and behavior, but has no access to what S experiences. In principle, other experimenters can also observe the stimulus and S's brain states and behavior. Consequently, what E has access to is said to be "public" and "objective." As E does not have access to S's experiences, these are said to be "private" and "subjective" and a problem for science, in the ways noted above. This apparently radical difference in the *epistemic status* of the data accessible to E and S is enshrined in the words commonly used to describe what they perceive. That is, E makes *observations*, whereas S merely has *subjective experiences*.

This way of looking at things forms an adequate working model for many studies. It also fits in with our common (naïve realist) assumption that what we see out in space is the *object itself* and that we have an additional, veridical experience *of* that object in our mind or brain. However, it is easy to show that something about this way of looking at things must be wrong.

First, science tells us that the perceived color, shape, location in phenomenal space, and other visual features of an object such as the light in Figure 55.1 are just surface *representations* of what that object is like, constructed by our visual systems. This is neatly demonstrated by neurological syndromes in which specific features of the visual system are damaged. For example, without color vision (achromatopsia) the visual world appears

entirely colored in black, white, and shades of gray; with other syndromes there is an inability to see form, or movement, or depth in space, and so on (see Zeki, chapter 45). Nor
are the surface representations constructed by a normally functioning (but unaided) visual
system complete representations of those surfaces – as a microscope will easily show. Such
surface appearances are also very different to the descriptions of the deeper structure of
the objects and the space in which they are embedded given by physics, for example by
relativity theory and quantum mechanics. So, although we normally treat the perceived
object (the phenomenal object) as if it truly is the "physical object," what we experience is
nevertheless how that object *looks to us*, and not (in any complete sense) how it is *in itself*.
Similarly, although we normally think of the 3-D phenomenal space in which the perceived
object is embedded as "physical space," it too is how space looks to us (phenomenal space)
rather than space itself (I give a deeper analysis of how phenomenal objects and the phenomenal space in which they appear to be embedded relate to objects and space themselves
in chapter 27; a more detailed analysis is also given in Velmans 2000b, ch. 7).

Note that it follows from this that, while perceived objects are in one sense "physical"
(there really are objects there that have appearances), they are in another sense "psychological" (the way that they appear depends not just on the objects themselves but on the
way that those appearances are constructed by our visual systems).

Second, we *do not* have any experience of an object "in our mind" or "in our brain" *in
addition* to the object as perceived out in the world. Rather, such phenomenal objects *constitute* what we experience – and in terms of their *phenomenology*, an object as perceived and
our experience *of* the object are one and the same. When looking at this print, for example,
the print that one sees out here on the page is the only "print experience" that one has. So
the naïve realist view that what we see out in space is the *object itself* and that we have an
additional, veridical experience *of* that object in our mind or brain is wrong in two ways – it
is neither consistent with third-person science, nor with first-person experience.

If so, we need to rethink the experimental arrangement shown in Figure 55.1 in the
reflexive way shown in Figure 55.2. This makes it clear that when S attends to the light stimulus she does *not* have an experience *of* a light that is subjectively located "in her mind"
or "in her brain," with its attendant problems for science. She just experiences a light in a
room. Indeed, what the subject experiences is very similar to what the experimenter experiences when he gazes at the light (she just sees the light stimulus from a different angle), in
spite of the different terms they might use to describe what they experience (a "physical
light stimulus" vs. a "subjective experience of light"). If so, there can be no actual difference
in the subjective vs. objective status of the *phenomenology* of the light "experienced" by S
and "observed" by E.

When an Experimenter Is also a Subject

Another way to grasp the same point is to note that *the roles of S and E are interchangeable*.
What makes one human being a "subject" and another an "experimenter"? As I have noted in
Velmans 2000b, ch. 8, their different roles are defined largely by *differences in their interests* in
the experiment, reflected in differences in what they are required to do. The subject is required
to focus only on her *own* experiences (of the light), which she needs to respond to or report
on in an appropriate way. The experimenter is interested primarily in the *subject's* experiences,
and in how these depend on the light stimulus or brain states that he can "observe."

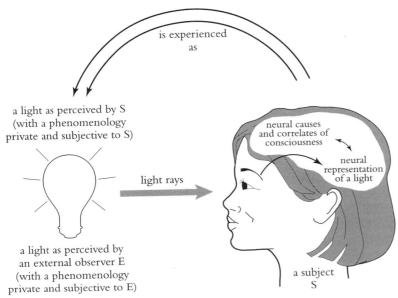

is experienced
as

a light as perceived by S
(with a phenomenology
private and subjective to S)

neural causes
and correlates of
consciousness

neural
representation
of a light

light rays

a light as perceived by
an external observer E
(with a phenomenology
private and subjective to E)

a subject
S

Figure 55.2 A reflexive way of viewing the relation of observations to experiences (adapted from figures drawn by John Wood for Velmans 2000).

To exchange roles, S and E merely have to turn their heads, so that E focuses exclusively on the light and describes what he experiences, while S focuses her attention not just on the light (which she now thinks of as a "stimulus") but also on events she can observe in E's brain, and on E's reports of what he experiences. In this situation, E becomes the "subject" and S becomes the "experimenter." Following current conventions, S would now be entitled to think of her observations (of the light and E's brain) as "public and objective" and to regard E's experiences of the light as "private and subjective."

However, this outcome is absurd, as the phenomenology of the light remains the same, viewed from the perspective of either S or E, whether it is *thought of* as an "observed stimulus" or an "experience." Nothing has changed in the character of the light that E and S can observe other than the focus of their interest. That is, in terms of *phenomenology* there is no difference between "observed phenomena" and "experiences."

But which is it? If the phenomenology of the light remains the same whether it is thought of a "stimulus" or an "experience," is the phenomenon *private and subjective* or is it *public and objective*? This is a subtle matter that we need to examine with care.

The Sense in which All Experienced Phenomena Are Private and Subjective

In dualism, "experiences" are private and subjective, while "physical phenomena" are public and objective as noted above. However, according to the reflexive model there is no *phenomenal* difference between the physical phenomena that we "observe" and the physical phenomena that we "experience." When we turn our attention to the external world, physical phenomena just *are* what we experience. If so, there is a sense in which physical phenomena are "private and subjective" just like the other things we experience. For example, I cannot experience your phenomenal mountain or your phenomenal tree. I only have access to my own phenomenal mountain and tree. Similarly, I only have access to my own phenomenal light stimulus and my own observations of its physical properties (in terms of meter readings of its intensity, frequency, and so on). That is, we *each live in our own private, phenomenal world.*

If we each live in our own private, phenomenal world then each "observation" is, in a sense, private. This was evident to the father of operationalism, the physicist P. W. Bridgman (1936), who concluded that, in the final analysis, "science is only my private science." However, this is clearly not the whole story. When an entity or event is placed beyond the body surface (as the entities and events studied by physics usually are) it can be perceived by any member of the public suitably located in space and time. Under these circumstances such entities or events are "public" in the sense that there is *public access* to the observed entity or event *itself.*

Public Access to the Stimulus Itself

While we normally think of the phenomena that we perceive as being "physical," this distinction between the phenomena perceived by any given observer and the stimulus entity or event *itself* is important. Being appearances, perceived phenomena *represent* things themselves, but are not identical to them (see above). The light perceived by E and S, for example, can be described in terms of its perceived brightness and color. But, in terms of physics, the stimulus is better described as electromagnetism with a given mix of energies and frequencies. As with all visually observed phenomena, the phenomenal light only *becomes* a phenomenal light once the stimulus interacts with an appropriately structured visual system – and the result of this observed–observer interaction is an *experienced* light which is private to the observer in the way described above. However, if the stimulus itself is beyond the body surface and has an independent existence, it remains there *to be* observed whether it is observed (at a given moment) or not. That is why the stimulus itself is *publicly accessible* in spite of the fact that each observation/experience of it is private to a given observer.

Public in the Sense of Similar Private Experiences

To the extent that observed entities and events are subject to similar perceptual and cognitive processing in different human beings, it is also reasonable to assume a degree of *commonality* in the way such things are experienced. Although each experience remains private, it may be a private experience that others share. For example, unless observers are suffering from red/green color blindness, we normally take it for granted that they perceive electromagnetic stimuli with wavelength 700 nm as red and those of 500 nm as green. Given the privacy of light phenomenology there is no way to be certain that others experience "red" and "green" as we do ourselves (the classical problem of "other minds"). But in normal life, and in the practice of science, we adopt the working assumption that the same stimulus, observed by similar observers under similar conditions, will produce similar observations or experiences. Thus, while *experienced* entities and events (phenomena) remain private to each observer, if their perceptual, cognitive, and other observing apparatus is similar, we assume that their experiences (of a given stimulus) are similar. Consequently, experienced phenomena may be "public" in the special sense that other observers have similar or shared experiences.

In sum:

1   There is only *private* access to individual observed or experienced *phenomena*.
2   There can be *public* access to the entities and events that serve as the stimuli for such phenomena (the entities and events which the phenomena represent). This applies, for example, to the entities and events studied by physics.
3   If the perceptual, cognitive, and other observing apparatus of different observers is similar, we assume that their experiences (of a given stimulus) are similar. In this special sense, experienced phenomena may be *public* insofar as they are *similar or shared private experiences*.

From Subjectivity to Inter-subjectivity

This reanalysis of private vs. public phenomena also provides a natural way to think about the relation between *subjectivity* and *inter-subjectivity*. Each (private) observation or experience is necessarily *subjective*, in that it is always the observation or experience of a *given* observer, viewed and described from his or her individual perspective. However, once that experience is shared with another observer it can become *inter*-subjective. That is, through the sharing of a similar experience, subjective views and descriptions of that experience potentially converge, enabling inter-subjective agreement about what has been experienced.

How different observers establish inter-subjectivity through negotiating agreed descriptions of shared experiences is a complex process that we do not need to examine here. Suffice it to say that it involves far more than shared experience. One also needs a shared language, shared cognitive structures, a shared world-view or scientific paradigm, shared training and expertise, and so on. To the extent that an experience or observation can be *generally* shared (by a community of observers), it can form part of the database of a communal science.

The Quest for Objectivity

The terms "objectivity" and "inter-subjectivity" are often used interchangeably in philosophy of science, for example in the writings of Karl Popper. However, in his book *Objective Knowledge*, Popper makes the added claim that the logical content of books, and the world of scientific problems, theories, and arguments form a kind of "third world" of objective knowledge, and "knowledge in this objective sense is totally independent of anybody's claim to know; it is also independent of anybody's belief, or disposition to assert, or assert, or to act. Knowledge in the objective sense is knowledge without a knower; it is knowledge without a knowing subject" (Popper 1972, p. 109).

But note that, so far, the above analysis of inter-subjectivity avoids any reference to "objectivity" in spite of the fact that it deals with a standard *physical* phenomenon (an observed light). Intersubjectivity of the kind described above requires the *presence* of subjectivity rather than its *absence*.

Popper is right, of course, to note that knowledge that is codified into books and other artifacts has an existence that is, in one sense, observer-free. That is, the *books* exist in our libraries after their writers are long dead and their readers absent, and they form a repository of knowledge that can influence future social and technological development in ways which extend well beyond that envisaged by their original authors. However the *knowledge itself* is not observer-free. Rather, it is valuable precisely because it encodes individual or collective experience. Nor, strictly speaking, is the print in books "knowledge." As Searle (1997) points out, words and other symbolic forms are intrinsically just ink marks on a page. They only become *symbols*, let alone convey meaning, to creatures that know how to interpret and understand them. But then the knowledge is in the knowing agent, not in the book. If so, the autonomous existence of books (and other media) provides no basis for "objective knowledge" of the kind that Popper describes, namely knowledge "that is totally independent of anybody's claim to know," "knowledge without a knower," and "knowledge without a knowing subject." On the contrary, without knowing subjects, there is no knowledge *of any kind* (whether objective or not).

Four Kinds of Objectivity

Given the above, I would argue for a more nuanced understanding of scientific "objectivity." I would agree that:

1 Science can be "objective" in the sense of "inter-subjective" (see above).
2 Descriptions of observations or experiences (observation statements) can be "objective" in the sense of being dispassionate, accurate, truthful, and so on.
3 Scientific method can also be "objective" in the sense that it follows well-specified, repeatable procedures (perhaps using standard measuring instruments).

However, one cannot make observations without engaging the experiences and cognitions of a conscious subject (unobserved meter readings are not "observations"). If so

4 Science *cannot* be "objective" in the sense of being *observer-free*.

Intra-subjective and Inter-subjective Repeatability

According to the reflexive model of perception in Figure 55.2 and the analysis above, there is no phenomenal difference between *observations* and *experiences*. Each observation results from an interaction of an observer with an observed. Consequently, each observation is observer-dependent and unique. This applies even to observations made by the same observer, of the same entity or event, under the same observation conditions, *at different times* – although under these circumstances the observer may have no doubt that he/she is making *repeated* observations of the same entity or event.

If the conditions of observation are sufficiently standardized (e.g., using meter readings, computer printouts, and so on) the observation may be repeatable within a community of

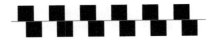

Figure 55.3 In what way does the central line tilt?

(suitably trained) observers, in which case inter-subjectivity can be established by *collective agreement*. Once again, however, it is important to note that different observers cannot have a numerically *identical* experience. Even if they observe the same event, at the same location, at the same time, they each have their own, unique experience. *Inter*-subjective repeatability resembles *intra*-subjective repeatability in that it merely requires observations to be sufficiently similar to be taken for "tokens" of the same "type." This applies particularly to observations in science, where repeatability typically requires inter-subjective agreement among scientists observing similar events at *different* times and in *different* geographical locations.

Consequences of the Above Analysis for a Science of Consciousness

The analysis has, so far, focused on physical events. But the same analysis can be applied to the investigation of events that are usually thought of as "mental" or "psychological" (thoughts, images, dreams, feelings, etc.). Although the *methodologies* appropriate to the study of physical and mental phenomena may be very different, the same *epistemic* criteria apply to their scientific investigation. Physical phenomena and mental (psychological) phenomena are just different kinds of phenomena that observers experience (whether they are experimenters or subjects).

This convergence of psychological with physical phenomena is self-evident in situations where the same phenomenon can be thought of as either "physical" or "psychological" depending on one's interest in it. At first glance, for example, a visual illusion of the kind shown in Figure 55.3, might seem to present difficulties, for the reason that physical and psychological descriptions of this phenomenon conflict.

Physically, the figure consists entirely of squares, separated by a horizontal line. But subjectively, the line seems to tilt down to the left, and the squares do not seem to be entirely square. However, these physical and psychological descriptions result from two different observation procedures. To obtain the physical description, an experimenter E can place a straight edge against each line, thereby obscuring the cues responsible for the illusion and providing a fixed reference against which the curvature and orientation of the line can be judged. To confirm that the line is actually straight, other experimenters ($E_{1 \text{ to } n}$) can repeat this procedure. Insofar as they each observe the line to be straight under these conditions, their observations are public, inter-subjective, and repeatable.

But, the fact that the line *appears* to be bent and to tilt to the left (once the straight edge is removed) is similarly public, inter-subjective, and repeatable (among subjects $S_{1 \text{ to } n}$). Consequently, the illusion can be investigated using relatively conventional scientific procedures, even though the *illusion* is unambiguously *mental*. One can, for example, simply move the straight edge outside the figure making it seem parallel to the central line – thereby obtaining a measure of the angle of the illusion. Similar criteria apply to the study of other mental events. $S_{1 \text{ to } n}$ might, for example, all report that a given increase in light intensity produces a just noticeable difference in brightness, an experience/observation that is inter-subjective and repeatable. Alternatively, $S_{1 \text{ to } n}$ might all report that a given anesthetic removes pain or, if they stare at a red light spot, that a green after-image appears, making such phenomena similarly public, inter-subjective, and repeatable.

The Empirical Method

In sum, it is possible to give a non-dualist account of the empirical method, that is, a non-dualist account of what scientists actually do when they test their theories, establish inter-subjectivity, repeatability, and so on which accepts that, in terms of *phenomenology*, the phenomena that scientists "observe" and the phenomena that scientists "experience" are one and the same. While this forces one to re-examine the sense in which observed phenomena are "public and objective" rather than "private and subjective," the crucial *role* of observations in theory testing and development remains unchanged.

The above analysis also retains a number of senses in which observations can be made "objective." That is, observations can be "objective" in the sense of *inter-subjective*, and the observers can "be objective" in the sense of being dispassionate, accurate, and truthful. Procedures can also "be objectified" in the sense of being standardized and explicit. No observations, however, can be objective in the sense of being *observer-free*. Looked at in this way, there is no unbridgeable, epistemic gap that separates physical phenomena from psychological phenomena.

In short, once the *empirical method* is stripped of the dualist splitting of "public, objective" from "private, subjective" phenomena, it applies as much to the science of consciousness as it does to the science of physics in that it adheres to the following principle:

If observers $E_{1 \text{ to } n}$ (or subjects $S_{1 \text{ to } n}$) carry out procedures $P_{1 \text{ to } n}$ under observation conditions $O_{1 \text{ to } n}$ they should observe (or experience) result R.

(Assuming that $E_{1 \text{ to } n}$ and $S_{1 \text{ to } n}$ have similar perceptual and cognitive systems, that $P_{1 \text{ to } n}$ are the procedures which constitute the experiment or investigation, and that $O_{1 \text{ to } n}$ include *all* relevant background conditions, including those internal to the observer, such as their attentiveness, the paradigm within which they are trained to make observations, and so on – where the values of subscript n can differ for E, S, P, and O respectively.)

Or, to put it more simply:

If you carry out these procedures you will observe or experience these results.

How Methods Used to Study Consciousness Differ from Methods Used in Physics

It goes without saying that the empirical method, formulated in this way, provides only basic, *epistemic* conditions for the study of consciousness. One also requires *methodologies* appropriate to the subject matter – and the methodologies required to study conscious appearances are generally very different from those used in physics. There are many ways in which the phenomena we usually think of as physical or psychological differ from each other and among themselves (in terms of their relative permanence, stability, measurability, controllability, describability, complexity, variability, dependence on the observational arrangements, and so on). Even where the *same* phenomenon is the subject of both psychological and physical investigation (as might be the case with the light in Figure 55.2 or the visual illusion in Figure 55.3 above) the *interests* of psychologist and physicist differ, requiring different investigative techniques. These differences in interests or in the phenomena themselves can greatly complicate systematic study and it is not my intention to minimize these difficulties. Unlike entities and events *themselves*, one cannot hook measuring instruments up to conscious appearances. For example, an instrument that measures the intensity of the light in Figure 55.2 (in lumens) cannot measure its experienced brightness. Given this, one needs some method of systematizing subjective judgments and consequent reports, for example, by recording minimal discriminable differences in brightness, in the ways typically used in psychophysical experiments.

Symmetries and Asymmetries of Access

Physical and psychological investigations also have systematic differences in the typical *relation* of the observer to that which is observed. For experimental purposes, the entities and events studied by physics are located *external* to the observers. Placed this way, such entities and events afford *public access* (see above) and different observers establish intersubjectivity, repeatability, and so on by using similar exteroceptive systems and equipment to observe them. E and S in Figure 55.2, for example, might observe the light via their visual systems, supplemented by similar instruments that measure its intensity, frequency, and other physical properties. When S and E (and any other observer suitably placed in space and time) use similar means to access information about a given entity or event we may say that they have *symmetrical access* to the observed (in this case, to the stimulus light itself). If the event of interest is located on the surface of or within S's body, or within S's brain, as would be the case in the study of physiology or neurophysiology, it remains external to E. Thus placed, it can still afford public, symmetrical access to a community of other, suitably placed external observers ($E_{1 \text{ to } n}$). Consequently, such events can be investigated by the same "external" means employed in other areas of natural science.

However, E and S (and any other observers) have *asymmetrical access* to each other's *experiences* of an observed (asymmetrical access to *each other's* observed phenomena). That is, they know what it's like to have their own experiences, but they can only access the experiences of others indirectly via their verbal descriptions or non-verbal behavior. This applies to *all* observed phenomena; for example, it applies even if the observed is a simple physical stimulus, such as the light in Figure 55.2. As E does not have direct access to S's experience of the light and vice versa, there is no way for E and S to be *certain* that they have a similar experience (whatever they might claim). E might nevertheless *infer* that S's experience is similar to his own on the assumption that S has similar perceptual apparatus, operating under similar observation arrangements, and on the basis of S's similar observation reports. S normally makes similar assumptions about E. It is important to note that this has not impeded the development of physics and other natural sciences, which simply ignore the problem of "other minds" (uncertainty about what other observers actually experience). They just take it for granted that if *observation reports* are the same, then the corresponding *observations* are the same, and consequently that the observed entities and events are the same. The success of natural science testifies to the pragmatic value of this approach.

Given this, it seems justifiable to apply the same pragmatic criteria to the observations of subjects in studies of consciousness (i.e., to their "subjective reports"). If, given a standard stimulus and standardized observation conditions, different subjects give similar reports of what they experience, then (barring any evidence to the contrary) it is reasonable to assume that they have similar experiences. Ironically, psychologists have often agonized over the merits of observation reports *when produced by subjects*, although like other scientists, they take them for granted *when produced by experimenters*, on the grounds that the observations of subjects are "private and subjective," while those of experimenters are "public and objective." As experimenters do not have direct access to each other's experiences any more than they have access to the experiences of subjects, this is a fallacy, as we have seen. Provided that the observation conditions are sufficiently standardized, the observations reported by subjects can be made public, inter-subjective, and repeatable among a community of subjects in much the same way that observations can be made public, inter-subjective, and repeatable among a community of experimenters. This provides an epistemic basis for a science of consciousness that includes its phenomenology.

In sum, asymmetries of access complicate, but do not prevent the investigation of experience. In Figure 55.2, E has access, in principle, to the events and processes in S's visual system, but not to S's experience. While S focuses exclusively on the light, she has access to her experience, but not to the antecedent processing in her visual system. Under these circumstances, the information available to S *complements* the information available to E. To obtain a complete account of visual perception one needs to utilize *both* sources of information. In Velmans 1991a, 1991b, and 2000b I have argued that a similar analysis can be applied to all situations where both first- and third-person information about the operation of a mental process is available. First- and third-person accounts of the mind are complementary and mutually irreducible. A complete account of mind requires both.

There is, of course, much more to be said about suitable methods for the investigation of consciousness. And it has to be admitted that the methodological problems are sometimes complex and the solutions sometimes controversial, particularly in the use of those introspective and phenomenological methods where subjects become the primary investigators of themselves (see Gallagher, chapter 53, and Shear, chapter 54). But this does not alter the fact that the *phenomena* of consciousness observed under these conditions are potentially public (in the sense of being private experiences that are shared), inter-subjective and repeatable. Consequently, the need to use and develop methodologies appropriate to the study of such phenomena does not place them beyond science. Rather, it is part of science – although in this case, a form of first-person science.

Critical Realism

The grounding of science in inter-subjectivity rather than some observer-free objectivity places scientific knowledge back where it belongs, in individual researchers and scientific communities. Individuals, interacting with their communities, establish inter-subjectively shared, consensus realities. Different social and scientific communities may, of course, hold very different views about the nature of the world, and investigate it in ways determined by very different paradigms. Grounding science in inter-subjectivity therefore introduces a measure of social relativism. But it does not, in my view, open the way to an unfettered social relativism.

Knowledge may exist only in the knower (or a community of knowers), but *it is constrained by the nature of that which is known.* Consequently, the epistemology developed here (and in Velmans 1990, 1993, 1999, 2000b) adopts a form of *critical realism* that is entirely standard in mainstream science. It assumes that experiences are experiences *of* entities and events (in the external world, body, brain, or mind itself) and that these experiences are representations of those entities and events. This allows that there may be many different ways of experiencing a given entity or event (from different perspectives, distances, with attention directed to different properties, and so on), but it also accepts that, for given purposes, representations can differ in their accuracy or utility. In the visual system, for example, there are clear differences between "veridical" percepts, illusions, and hallucinations that can be tested by physical interaction with the world. In a similar way, there are many ways of construing or theorizing about the nature of observed entities and events appropriate to the purposes of different social and intellectual communities. But this does not prevent an assessment of the relative merits of different theories, for example in terms of their ability to explain, predict, or control observed events, that is, in terms of their ability to *fulfill* the purposes for which they are to be used.

Critical Phenomenology

The analysis above also supports a form of *critical phenomenology* (CP) – a commonsense, natural, but nonreductive approach to the study of mind. This adopts the conventional view that human experiences have causes and correlates in the external world, body, and brain that can be investigated by a range of *third-person methods* commonly used in cognitive science, neuroscience, and related sciences. However, CP recognizes that third-person methods do *not* provide direct access to subjects' experiences, and that the causes and correlates of conscious experiences are not the experiences themselves (see Velmans 1998, 2000b, chs. 3, 4 and 5 for an extensive discussion). Subjects do, however, have access to their own experiences, on which they can report. Consequently, third-person methods have to be supplemented by *first-person methods* that guide subjects to attend to aspects of their conscious experience that are of interest to experimenters (or to the subjects themselves).

It will be apparent to those familiar with the issues that this even-handed, nonreductive approach to first- and third-person methods distinguishes CP from more behaviorally oriented approaches such as Dennett's *heterophenomenology*, which tries to restrict the science of consciousness to third-person methods. I do not have space to do a fuller comparison here, but see the on-line dialog with Dennett in Velmans 2001, Dennett 2003, and Velmans 2006 for a more detailed analysis.

Why call this approach "*critical* phenomenology" rather than just "phenomenology"? First, to dissociate it from the classical, philosophical versions of phenomenology discussed by Gallagher in chapter 53, in which third-person methods and third-person science have a minor (and sometimes suspect) role. Instead, critical phenomenology adopts a form of "psychological complementarity principle" in which first-person descriptions of experience and third-person descriptions of correlated brain states are accounts of what is going on in the mind that are complementary and mutually irreducible. A complete account of mind requires both (see above). Second, while CP takes subjective experiences to be real, it remains cautious about the veridical nature of phenomenal reports in that it assumes neither first- nor third-person reports of phenomena to be incorrigible, complete, or unrevisable – and it remains open about how such reports should be interpreted within some body of theory.

Critical phenomenology is also open to the possibility that first-person investigations can be improved by the development of more refined first-person investigative methods, just as third-person investigations can be improved by the development of more refined third-person methods. It also takes it as read that first- and third-person investigations of the mind can be used conjointly, either providing triangulating evidence for each other, or, in other instances, informing each other. Third-person observations of brain and behavior for example can sometimes inform and perhaps alter interpretations of first-person experiences (very subtle differences in first-person experience for example can sometimes be shown to have quite distinct, correlated differences in accompanying neural activity in the brain). Likewise, first-person accounts of subjective experience can inform third-person accounts of what is going on in the brain – indeed, without such first-person accounts, it would be impossible to discover the neural correlates of given conscious experiences. In adopting the view that subjective conscious experiences are real, but our descriptions and understanding of them revisable, CP exemplifies the *critical realism* outlined above.

Finally, CP is *reflexive*, taking it for granted that *experimenters* have first-person experiences and can describe those experiences much as their subjects do. And crucially, experimenter's *third-person reports of others* are based, in the first instance, on their *own first-person experiences* in the ways shown above.

In what way can the phenomena that we experience form part of science? If this analysis is correct, the "phenomena" observed by experimenters are as much a part of the world that they experience as are the "subjective experiences" of subjects. If so, the *whole* of science may be thought of as an attempt to make sense of the phenomena that we observe or experience.

See also 1 A brief history of the scientific approach to the study of consciousness; 2 Philosophical problems of consciousness; 53 Phenomenological approaches to consciousness; 54 Eastern methods for investigating mind and consciousness.

Further Readings

Velmans, M. (1993) A reflexive science of consciousness. In *Experimental and Theoretical Studies of Consciousness. CIBA Foundation Symposium* 174, 81–99. Chichester: Wiley.
Velmans, M. (2000) *Understanding Consciousness*. London: Routledge/Psychology Press.

References

Bridgman, P. W. (1936) *The Nature of Physical Theory*. Princeton, NJ: Princeton University Press.
Dennett, D. (2003) Who's on first? Heterophenomenology explained. *Journal of Consciousness Studies* 10: 9/10, 10–30.
Denzin, N. K. and Lincoln, Y. S. (eds.) (2000) *Handbook of Qualitative Research*, 2nd edn. Thousand Oaks, CA: Sage.

Jack, A. and Roepstorff, A. (eds.) (2003) *Trusting the Subject? Vol. 1: The Use of Introspective Evidence in Cognitive Science*. Exeter: Imprint Academic.

Jack, A. and Roepstorff, A. (eds.) (2004) *Trusting the Subject? Vol. 2: The Use of Introspective Evidence in Cognitive Science*. Exeter: Imprint Academic.

Popper, K. R. (1972) *Objective Knowledge: An Evolutionary Approach*. Oxford: Clarendon Press.

Searle, J. (1997) *The Mystery of Consciousness*. London: Granta Books.

Varela, F. and Shear, J. (1999) *First-Person Approaches to the Study of Consciousness*. Exeter: Imprint Academic.

Velmans, M. (1990) Consciousness, brain, and the physical world. *Philosophical Psychology* 3, 77–99.

Velmans, M. (1991a) Is human information processing conscious? *Behavioral and Brain Sciences* 14: 4, 651–69.

Velmans, M. (1991b) Consciousness from a first-person perspective. *Behavioral and Brain Sciences* 14: 4, 702–26.

Velmans, M. (1993) A reflexive science of consciousness. In *Experimental and Theoretical Studies of Consciousness, CIBA Foundation Symposium* 174, 81–99. Chichester: Wiley.

Velmans, M. (1998) Goodbye to reductionism. In S. Hameroff, A. Kaszniak, and A. Scott (eds.), *Towards a Science of Consciousness II: The Second Tucson Discussions and Debates*, 45–52. Cambridge, MA: MIT Press.

Velmans, M. (1999) Intersubjective science. *Journal of Consciousness Studies* 6: 2/3, 299–306.

Velmans, M. (ed.) (2000a) *Investigating Phenomenal Consciousness: New Methodologies and Maps*. Amsterdam: John Benjamins.

Velmans, M. (2000b) *Understanding Consciousness*. London: Routledge/Psychology Press.

Velmans, M. (2001) Heterophenomenology versus critical phenomenology: a dialogue with Dan Dennett. On-line debate at http://cogprints.soton.ac.uk/documents/disk0/00/00/17/95/index.html.

Velmans, M. (2006) Heterophenomenology versus critical phenomenology. *Phenomenology and the Cognitive Sciences* 5: 3/4 (in press) (E-print at http://cogprints.org/4741/).

Watson, J. B. (1913) Psychology as the behaviorist views it. *The Psychological Review* 20, 158–77.

List of Useful Web Resources in Consciousness Studies

Association for the Scientific Study of Consciousness (ASSC)

Website of an important association of scientists who work on consciousness. Contains listings of books that they publish and upcoming conference information.
http://assc.caltech.edu/index.htm

Center for Consciousness Studies, The University of Arizona

Contains conference announcements and an archive of web courses.
http://www.consciousness.arizona.edu/

Cogprints Archive

An archive of around 2,500 on-line papers in psychology, neuroscience, linguistics, philosophy, and biology, with around 450 of the papers being relevant to consciousness.
http://cogprints.org/

Journal of Consciousness Studies at Imprint Academic

The website of the main interdisciplinary journal devoted to the study of consciousness. Includes sample papers, links, and conference announcements.
http://www.imprint.co.uk/

On-line Papers on Consciousness

A directory of over 2,500 on-line papers, compiled by David Chalmers, mainly on the topic of consciousness, largely written by academic philosophers or scientists.
http://consc.net/online.html

People with On-line Papers on Consciousness

List of links to those who have on-line papers on consciousness, compiled by David Chalmers.
http://consc.net/people.html#consc

Phenomenology and Cognitive Science

Site listing papers and other links to resources investigating the links between phenomenology and its relation to cognitive science and neuroscience. Nonreductionist in orientation. Maintained by Eugenio Borrelli.
http://www.swif.uniba.it/lei/mind/topics/00000032.htm

Phenomenology and the Cognitive Sciences

Site listing resources for the investigation of phenomenology and its relation to cognitive science and neuroscience. Maintained by Shaun Gallagher.
http://www.philosophy.ucf.edu/pcs.html

PSYCHE: An Interdisciplinary Journal of Research on Consciousness

Website of a major on-line consciousness studies journal which mainly focuses on publishing book reviews and symposia.
http://psyche.cs.monash.edu.au/

Science and Consciousness Review

Contains articles and information about events and new scientific findings in consciousness studies. Maintained by psychologist Bernie Baars.
www.sci-con.org/

Stanford Encyclopedia of Philosophy

On-line encyclopedia of philosophy created and maintained by Stanford University. Contains numerous entries on philosophical topics concerning consciousness.
plato.stanford.edu/

Name Index

Subject Index

40 Hz hypothesis, 32, 245, 296, 344, 364, 574

ability hypothesis, 399
absence seizure, 593
access consciousness, 24, 59, 65, 472, 585–6
accessibility, 230
action, 540–8, 694
  attribution, 541, 548
  automatic, 541–3
  complex, 540
  covert, 540–1
  guidance, 253–4
  overt, 540–1
  recognition, 541–5, 548
  representation in, 546–8
  as separate from perception, 616–26
  simple, 540, 547–8
activation, 101, 112, 423–4
  -synthesis theory, 101, 108–10
  theories, 530–1
Activation-Input Source-Neuromodulation
  Model, 101, 108–12
adaptation, 73–5, 79–81, 83–4, 651
affective consciousness, 114–28
  emotional-affects, 115
  homeostatic-affects, 115
  sensory-affects, 115
agency, 204–6, 412, 541, 545, 548, 664
agnosia, 251–3, 357, 620
akinetic mutism, 592–4, 600
alcohol, 147–8
allocentric planning, 253
ambiguous stimuli, 556
aminergic demodulation, 108
amnesia, 527–8, 532–3, 534–7
  dense, 16
  source, 535

analogy, 342–3
anesthesia, 141–2, 150, 310, 518–20, 610,
    628–38
  awareness and, 631–4
  balanced, 629–30
  conscious sedation, 630, 637
  depth of, 632–3, 637
  evolution of, 628–30
  implicit memory in, 635–8
  mechanisms of, 630–1
  Myer-Overton rule, 630–1
  unconscious processing during, 634–6
animals
  dissimilarity arguments against
      consciousness, 64–5
  methodological arguments against
      consciousness, 65
  nonhuman, 9–10, 17, 58–68, 121–6, 175–6,
      178, 272, 441, 466, 577, 610–11
  similarity arguments for and against
      consciousness, 64–6
  welfare, 68
anxiety, 130–2, 147
appearance–reality distinction, 67, 327, 355–6,
    448–9, 452, 454, 464
architecture models, 93–4, 244, 589
arousal systems, 593–7
artificial intelligence (AI), 87–90
associationism, 10
assumption of experience-based control, 616
asynchronies, 583
ataxia
  optic, 620–1
attention, 13, 31, 94, 108, 133, 257–8, 307, 425–6,
    489–502, 573–4, 610, 612
  covert, 13, 15
  directed, 558